UNIVERSITY CASEBOOK SERIES®

EMPLOYMENT LAW

CASES AND MATERIALS

NINTH EDITION

MARK A. ROTHSTEIN
Herbert F. Boehl Chair of Law and Medicine
University of Louisville

LANCE LIEBMAN
William S. Beinecke Professor Emeritus of Law
Columbia University

KIMBERLY A. YURACKO
Dean and Judd and Mary Morris Leighton Professor of Law
Northwestern Pritzker School of Law

CHARLOTTE GARDEN
Professor of Law
Seattle University School of Law

FOUNDATION
PRESS

University Casebook Series is a trademark registered in the U.S. Patent and Trademark Office.

© 1987, 1991, 1994, 1998, 2003, 2007 FOUNDATION PRESS
© 2011 By THOMSON REUTERS/FOUNDATION PRESS
© 2015 LEG, Inc. d/b/a West Academic
© 2020 LEG, Inc. d/b/a West Academic
    444 Cedar Street, Suite 700
    St. Paul, MN 55101
    1-877-888-1330

Printed in the United States of America

ISBN: 978-1-68328-732-2

PREFACE TO THE NINTH EDITION

Employment Law, a vibrant and dynamic subject, presents a difficult challenge to casebook editors. As in prior editions, we have attempted to balance the presentation of foundational doctrine with emerging issues, to stimulate student interest in a fascinating legal field, and to offer material that works well in courses of different lengths and emphases. The Ninth Edition, although retaining the general format and key elements of prior editions, is substantially new, with some reorganized chapters, many new cases and readings, and several new areas of inquiry. We appreciate the excellent contribution of Professor Paul Secunda in revising Chapters 6, 12, and 13.

Professor Rothstein would like to acknowledge production coordinator Robert Klein. Professor Liebman thanks faculty assistants, Tatyana Gourov and Michael Roig. Professor Yuracko would like to thank faculty assistant Jane Brock. Professor Garden would like to thank Edward Hones for outstanding research assistance.

As with the eight previous editions, we are indebted to colleagues in the Employment Law field who gave us helpful suggestions and to our students, whose insights and questions continue to make teaching Employment Law challenging and enjoyable.

M.A.R.

L.L.

K.A.Y.

C.G.

March 2020

SUMMARY OF CONTENTS

TABLE OF CONTENTS

PART III. TERMS AND CONDITIONS OF EMPLOYMENT

TABLE OF CASES

The principal cases are in bold type.

UNIVERSITY CASEBOOK SERIES®

EMPLOYMENT LAW

CASES AND MATERIALS

NINTH EDITION

PART I

BACKGROUND

CHAPTER 1

WORK AND LAW

A. WORK AND SOCIETY

Students in professional school are undoubtedly aware of the growing role of their chosen occupation in how they view themselves and how they are viewed by others. At least in early twenty-first century America, to a great extent, we are what we do. Thoreau said that "[w]hat exercise is to the body, employment is to the mind and morals." Individuals who enjoy their work and derive satisfaction and financial security from their careers are indeed fortunate. Those with less rewarding vocations may consider work a necessary drudgery or even a source of indignity or unfair treatment. For society's most vulnerable members, full-time, safe, and reasonably compensated employment may be an elusive quest.

In 2018, approximately 63% of the U.S. population of working age—155 million individuals—was employed; another 5.1 million unemployed would have worked if they could have found jobs. Most of those who work do so for someone else: we are a nation of employees. The amount of time we spend at work generally constitutes the largest single activity of our waking hours, and for many individuals, work provides an identity and extended family that are otherwise missing. But conflict in the employment relationship seems destined to occur. Owners, managers, and administrators of business and government are responsible for the operation of their respective enterprises, which requires them to make decisions that affect the workforce. Looking at the production of goods and services strictly in economic terms, efficiency and profitability of the firm are the hallmarks of a successful operation. Yet, what is efficient, expedient, or profitable for a business is not necessarily also beneficial to its employees, and may even be harmful. A textile company's decision to relocate its manufacturing plant overseas because of cheaper production costs may make economic sense for its stockholders but spell economic disaster for the workers. The employee drug test that might enable an employer to reduce the production costs associated with substance abuse in the workforce invades employee privacy.

How should the law handle the inevitable tensions that arise in the employment relationship? Traditionally, the law considered employment to be a matter of private contract between the employer and employee. The law of master and servant developed originally as an offshoot of the law of domestic relations, and master and servant alike were bound by obligations to each other. Just as a man (in those days) was master of his home, so too was he master of his business. He could impose whatever working conditions he wished on employees. If he were an unduly harsh master, however, then he might be unable to hire competent help, but he was not otherwise subject to sanction. With the advent of the industrial revolution in the nineteenth century and the laissez-faire attitude of the era, the freedom of contract approach expanded. In the United States, the rule was quickly established that the employment relationship was one between equals: the employee was free to quit and seek alternate employment whenever he or she wanted, and the employer was free to fire the employee at any time.

The first serious efforts to regulate the law of the employment relationship appeared at the end of the nineteenth century. Growing awareness of the hazards associated with certain occupations and industries and the inherent inequality of bargaining power between employer and employee led to the passage of the first protective statutes, many of which were initially struck down as unconstitutional infringements on the freedom of contract. Gradually, and in a piecemeal fashion, legislative and judicial activism at both the state and federal levels began to curtail the employers' freedom of action. In 1935, the National Labor Relations Act gave employees the right to organize into unions and bargain collectively with their employers. Unionization and collective bargaining are often seen as the way for employees to obtain better working conditions, but as of 2018, unionized employees accounted for only 6.5% of the private sector workforce. Also in 1935, Congress enacted the Social Security Act to establish a federally administered employee retirement system, with benefits extended to permanently disabled workers in 1956.

In 1938, Congress enacted the Fair Labor Standards Act, which prohibited child labor and established a federal minimum wage and premium pay for overtime. In 1963, the Equal Pay Act made it unlawful for employers to discriminate between men and women with respect to wages. Title VII of the Civil Rights Act of 1964 prohibited all discrimination in employment on the basis of race, color, religion, sex, or national origin. In 1967, the Age Discrimination in Employment Act prohibited discrimination on the basis of age. The Occupational Safety and Health Act of 1970, along with the Mine Safety and Health Act, established minimum health and safety standards for the workplace. Employment rights for individuals with disabilities were initially enacted with the Rehabilitation Act of 1973. The Employee Retirement Income Security Act was enacted in 1974 to protect pension and other benefit entitlements. Since the mid-1980s Congress has enacted, among other employment legislation, the Worker Adjustment Retraining and Notification Act, the Employee Polygraph Protection Act, the Americans with Disabilities Act, the Civil Rights Act of 1991, the Family and Medical Leave Act, and the Genetic Information Nondiscrimination Act. In 2010, Congress enacted the Patient Protection and Affordable Care Act, which, among other things, provides for more comprehensive federal regulation of employment-based health coverage. Many state legislatures also have enacted their own versions of federal legislation, in some cases providing greater protection than federal law.

Despite the explosion of legislation, however, significant aspects of employment, such as a right to be fired only for cause, are not addressed by virtually any legislation, and large segments of the workforce, such as managers, executives, and agricultural workers, are exempted from many laws. The statutory scheme is a patchwork of protection. Each of the various statutes has its own coverage, procedures, and substantive content. There is no comprehensive scheme at the federal or state level to regulate the employment relationship. Nor is one likely to be enacted in the foreseeable future. As a result, recent developments in the law have included a revival of the common law as a means of regulating aspects of the employment relationship not already subject to statutory rules and regulations.

This text follows the individual employee through the employment relationship, starting with applying for a job and ending with separation from employment, which may occur through quitting, being fired, being laid off, or retiring. In between are employer selection procedures, wages and hours, benefits, employee liberty, safety and health, and disabling injury and illness. The focus is on individual rights in employment rather than collective bargaining, which is the topic of a separate course. The dominant query is: How should the law regulate the employment relationship? A number of secondary themes recur. How can employee demands for self-determination in the workplace be reconciled with the employer's right to control the means and methods of production? What social or economic goals can or should be accomplished through the employment relationship? How should conflicts between individual rights and collective rights be resolved? What is the proper accommodation of parallel or conflicting state and federal law?

As you study the remaining materials in this chapter, consider the significance of the attitudes toward work presented in the introductory readings. What position should the law take toward work, employer "rights," and employee "rights"? Can you construct a theory of employment law? The *Bammert* case (p. 10) provides a context in which to begin considering possible theories.

Alain De Botton, Workers of the World, Relax*
N.Y. Times, Sept. 6, 2004, at A19.

The most remarkable feature of the modern workplace has nothing to do with computers, automation or globalization. Rather, it lies in the Western world's widely held belief that our work should make us happy.

All societies throughout history have had work right at their center; but ours—particularly America's—is the first to suggest that it could be

---

* © Copyright 2004 by the New York Times. Reprinted by permission.

something other than a punishment or penance. Ours is the first to imply that a sane human being would want to work even if he wasn't under financial pressure to do so. We are unique too, in allowing our choice of work to define who we are, so that the central question we ask of new acquaintances is not where they come from or who their parents are but, rather, what it is they do—as though only this could effectively reveal what gives a human life its distinctive timbre.

It wasn't always like this. Greco-Roman civilization tended to view work as a chore best left to slaves. For both Plato and Aristotle, fulfillment could be reached only when one had the command of a private income and could escape day-to-day obligations and freely devote oneself to the contemplation of ethical and moral questions. The entrepreneur and merchant may have had a nice villa and a heaping larder, but they played no role in the antique vision of the good life.

Early Christianity took a similarly bleak view of labor, adding the even darker thought that man was condemned to toil in order to make up for the sin of Adam. Working conditions, however abusive, could not be improved. Work wasn't accidentally miserable—it was one of the planks upon which earthly suffering was irrevocably founded. St. Augustine reminded slaves to obey their masters and accept their pain as part of what he termed in "The City of God," the "wretchedness of man's condition."

The first signs of the modern, more cheerful attitude toward work can be detected in the city-states of Italy during the Renaissance, and in particular, in the biographies of the artists of the time. In descriptions of the lives of men like Michelangelo and Leonardo, we find some now familiar-sounding ideas about what our labors could ideally mean for us: a path to authenticity and glory. Rather than a burden and punishment, artistic work could allow us to rise above our ordinary limitations. We could express our talents on a page or on a canvas in a way we never could in our everyday lives. Of course, this new vision applied only to a creative elite (no one yet thought to tell a servant that work could develop his true self: that was a claim waiting for modern management theory), but it proved to be the model for all successive definitions of happiness earned through work.

It was not until the late 18th century that the model was extended beyond the artistic realm. In the writings of bourgeois thinkers like Benjamin Franklin, Diderot and Rousseau, we see work recategorized not only as a means to earn money, but also as a way to become more fully ourselves. It is worth noting that this reconciliation of necessity and happiness exactly mirrored the contemporary re-evaluation of marriage: just as marriage was rethought as an institution that could deliver both practical benefits and sexual and emotional fulfillment (a handy conjunction once thought impossible by aristocrats, who saw a need for a mistress and a wife), so too work was now alleged to be capable of delivering both the money necessary for survival and the stimulation and self-expression that had once been seen as the exclusive preserve of the leisured.

Simultaneously, people began to experience a new kind of pride in their work, in large part because the way that jobs were handed out took on a semblance of justice. In his autobiography, Thomas Jefferson explained that his proudest achievement had been to create a meritocratic United States where "a new aristocracy of virtue and talent" replaced the old aristocracy of unfair privilege and in many cases, brute stupidity. Meritocracy endowed jobs with a new quasi-moral quality. Now that prestigious and well paid posts seemed to be available on the basis of actual intelligence and ability, your job title could perhaps say something directly meaningful about you.

Over the 19th century, many Christian thinkers, especially in the United States, changed their views of money accordingly. American Protestant denominations suggested that God required his followers to lead a life that was successful both temporally and spiritually. Fortunes in this world were evidence that one deserved a good place in the next— an attitude reflected in the Rev. Thomas P. Hunt's 1836 bestseller "The Book of Wealth: In Which It Is Proved From the Bible That It Is the Duty of Every Man to Become Rich." John D. Rockefeller was not shy to say that it was the Lord who had made him rich, while William Lawrence, the Episcopal bishop of Massachusetts, writing in 1892, argued, "We like the Psalmist, occasionally see the wicked prosper, but only occasionally," adding, "Godliness is in league with riches."

As meritocracy came of age, demeaning jobs came to seem not merely regrettable, but just like their more exciting counterparts, also deserved. No wonder people started asking each other what they did—and listening very carefully to the answers.

NOTES AND QUESTIONS

1.   As de Botton points out, the workplace is a source of increasing importance in promoting individual self-esteem and developing a sense of community. See also Vicki Schultz, Life's Work, 100 Colum. L. Rev. 1881 (2000). How does or should this broader role of work be reflected in modern employment law?

2.   The workplace also is increasingly used to implement public policies. Thus, perhaps as a result of an inability or unwillingness to deal with large social problems in other settings, employers have been assigned substantial responsibility for financing health care; conducting health risk assessments, and providing substance abuse, mental health, and wellness programs; providing group life, disability, and long-term care insurance; providing day-care and elder care; providing remedial education and job retraining; and enforcing laws dealing with illicit drugs and illegal immigration. Are employers well suited to assume these responsibilities? What are the costs and benefits of allocating these roles to employers?

Nicholas Kristof, It's Now the Canadian Dream[*]

New York Times, May 15, 2014, A25.

It was in 1931 that the historian James Truslow Adams coined the phrase "the American dream."

The American dream is not just a yearning for affluence, Adams said, but also for the chance to overcome barriers and social class, to become the best that we can be. Adams acknowledged that the United States didn't fully live up to that ideal, but he argued that America came closer than anywhere else.

Adams was right at the time, and for decades. When my father, an eastern European refugee, reached France after World War II, he was determined to continue to the United States because it was less class bound, more meritocratic and offered more opportunity.

Yet today the American dream has derailed, partly because of growing inequality. Or maybe the American dream has just swapped citizenship, for now it is more likely to be found in Canada or Europe— and a central issue in this year's political campaigns should be how to repatriate it.

A report last month in The Times by David Leonhardt and Kevin Quealy noted that the American middle class is no longer the richest in the world, with Canada apparently pulling ahead in median after-tax income. Other countries in Europe are poised to overtake us as well.

In fact, the discrepancy is arguably even greater. Canadians receive essentially free health care, while Americans pay for part of their health care costs with after-tax dollars. Meanwhile, the American worker toils, on average, 4.6 percent more hours than a Canadian worker, 21 percent more hours than a French worker and an astonishing 28 percent more hours than a German worker, according to data from the Organization for Economic Cooperation and Development.

Canadians and Europeans also live longer, on average, than Americans do. Their children are less likely to die than ours. American women are twice as likely to die as a result of pregnancy or childbirth as Canadian women. And, while our universities are still the best in the world, children in other industrialized countries, on average, get a better education than ours. Most sobering of all: A recent O.E.C.D. report found that for people aged 16 to 24, Americans ranked last among rich countries in numeracy and technological proficiency.

Economic mobility is tricky to measure, but several studies show that a child born in the bottom 20 percent economically is less likely to rise to the top in America than in Europe. A Danish child is twice as likely to rise as an American child.

When our futures are determined to a significant extent at birth, we've reverted to the feudalism that our ancestors fled.

"Equality of opportunity—the 'American dream'—has always been a cherished American ideal," Joseph Stiglitz, the Nobel-winning economist at Columbia University, noted in a recent speech. "But data now show that this is a myth: America has become the advanced country not only with the highest level of inequality, but one of those with the least equality of opportunity."

Consider that the American economy has, over all, grown more quickly than France's. But so much of the growth has gone to the top 1 percent that the bottom 99 percent of French people have done better than the bottom 99 percent of Americans.

Three data points:

- The top 1 percent in America now own assets worth more than those held by the entire bottom 90 percent.

- The six Walmart heirs are worth as much as the bottom 41 percent of American households put together.

- The top six hedge fund managers and traders averaged more than $2 billion each in earnings last year, partly because of the egregious "carried interest" tax break. President Obama has been unable to get financing for universal prekindergarten; this year's proposed federal budget for pre-K for all, so important to our nation's future, would be a bit more than a single month's earnings for those six tycoons.

* * *

It's time to bring the American dream home from exile.

NOTES AND QUESTIONS

1.   The current level of income and wealth inequality in the United States is comparable to the period at the beginning of the twentieth century, before enactment of the federal income tax, the Fair Labor Standards Act and state minimum wage laws, Social Security and income support for the elderly, unionization and collective bargaining, the G.I. Bill and widespread access to higher education, and other laws and policies that fostered development of the middle class. One of the rationalizations for American laissez-faire capitalism and its "rugged individualism" social policy has been that, even though there are wide gaps between the "haves" and "have nots," there is vertical social mobility. In other words, through talent and hard work, in a few years or a few generations (especially for immigrants), an individual or his or her children can go from the bottom to the top of the income ladder. What effect does the new "locked in" nature of socioeconomic position have on America's social narrative?

2.   One way of quantifying the American Dream is to calculate the percentage of children age 30 who earned more than their parents at the

same age. Using deidentified tax records, researchers made the following calculation. For children born in 1940, 92% earned more than their parents. That figure has declined steadily for children born after 1950 (79%), 1960 (72%), 1970 (71%), and 1980 (50%). David Leonhardt, The American Dream Quantified at Last, N.Y. Times, Dec. 11, 2016, at SR2.

3. Among the recent scholarship on the issue of economic inequality are Thomas Piketty, Capital in the Twenty-first Century (2014); Howard J. Sherman & Paul D. Sherman, Inequality, Boom, and Bust: From Billionaire Capitalism to Equality and Full Employment (2018); Ganesh Sitaraman, The Crisis of the Middle-Class Constitution: Why Economic Inequality Threatens Our Republic (2017); Joseph E. Stigletz, The Price of Inequality: How Today's Divided Society Endangers Our Future (2013).

4. For the purposes of this course, there are two related questions. First, how, if at all, have labor and employment laws contributed to the rising inequality? Second, how, if at all, have labor and employment laws been affected by the rising inequality?

B. LEGAL INTERVENTION

Bammert v. Don's Super Valu, Inc.
646 N.W.2d 365 (Wis. 2002).

■ DIANE S. SYKES, J.:

Karen Bammert was employed at Don's Super Valu, Inc. in Menomonie for approximately 26 years. Her husband is a Menomonie police sergeant. Don's is owned by Don Williams, whose wife, Nona, was arrested for drunk driving on June 7, 1997. Bammert's husband participated in the drunk driving field investigation by administering a portable breathalyzer test to Nona Williams, which she failed.

On August 28, 1997, Bammert was fired by Don's in retaliation for her husband's participation in Nona Williams' drunk driving arrest. At the time of her termination, she was an assistant manager at the supermarket.

Bammert sued for wrongful discharge. Don's moved to dismiss, and the Dunn County Circuit Court, the Honorable Eric J. Wahl, dismissed the complaint for failure to state a claim, concluding that the employment-at-will doctrine's public policy exception, announced by this court in Brockmeyer v. Dun & Bradstreet (Wis. 1983), did not apply. The court of appeals affirmed. We accepted review and now affirm.

* * *

Bammert was an at-will employee. In general, at-will employees are terminable at will, for any reason, without cause and with no judicial remedy. Whether Bammert has an actionable claim for wrongful discharge turns on the question of whether the public policy exception to the employment-at-will doctrine can be extended to a retaliatory discharge based upon the conduct of a non-employee spouse.

The starting point for any wrongful discharge case is *Brockmeyer*. There, we adopted a public policy exception to the long-standing employment-at-will doctrine which allows an at-will employee to sue for wrongful discharge "when the discharge is contrary to a fundamental and well-defined public policy as evidenced by existing law." *Brockmeyer* noted that ordinarily, an employer may discharge an at-will employee " 'for good cause, for no cause, or even for cause morally wrong, without being thereby guilty of legal wrong.' "

The court in *Brockmeyer* specifically declined to engraft a broad implied duty of good faith onto the at-will employment relationship. "Imposing a good faith duty to terminate would unduly restrict an employer's discretion in managing the work force" and " 'subject each discharge to judicial incursions into the amorphous concept of bad faith.' " Instead, the court concluded that "in the interests of employees, employers and the public, a narrow public policy exception" was justified, applicable only where the discharge "clearly contravenes the public welfare and gravely violates paramount requirements of public interest."[2]

In adopting the exception, the court recognized that "public policy" is too broad a concept to be sufficient as a legal standard for evaluating discharge claims, and therefore articulated several guidelines:

> The public policy must be evidenced by a constitutional or statutory provision. An employee cannot be fired for refusing to violate the constitution or a statute. Employers will be held liable for those terminations that effectuate an unlawful end.

> We intend to recognize an existing limited public policy exception. An employer may not require an employee to violate a constitutional or statutory provision with impunity. If an employee refuses to act in an unlawful manner, the employer would be violating public policy by terminating the employee for such behavior. To say that the employer could be prosecuted for criminal involvement as a result of the activities would be little solace for the discharged employee.

> Courts should proceed cautiously when making public policy determinations. No employer should be subject to suit merely because a discharged employee's conduct was praiseworthy or because the public may have derived some benefit from it.

Accordingly, to state a claim for wrongful discharge under *Brockmeyer*, a plaintiff must identify a constitutional, statutory, or

---

[2] *Brockmeyer* also held that the cause of action for wrongful discharge pursuant to the public policy exception sounds in contract, not tort: "The contract action is essentially predicated on the breach of an implied provision that an employer will not discharge an employee for refusing to perform an act that violates a clear mandate of public policy."

administrative provision that clearly articulates a fundamental and well-defined public policy. Not every statutory, constitutional, or administrative provision invariably sets forth a clear public policy mandate. The determination of whether a public policy is sufficiently fundamental and well-defined is made by reference to the content of the provision. If a plaintiff identifies a public policy sufficient to trigger the exception, and further demonstrates that the termination violated that public policy, the burden shifts to the employer to show just cause for the termination.

* * *

Bammert's claim must be evaluated against this backdrop. She has identified two public policies as being implicated here: Wis. Stat. § 346.63, which prohibits the operation of a motor vehicle while under the influence of an intoxicant; and Wis. Stat. § 765.001(2), which describes the intent of the Family Code as including the promotion of the institution of marriage, for the preservation of the family, society, the state, morality, and indeed, all civilization.

We would be hard-pressed to say that these are not fundamental, well-established public policies. Clearly, both statutes reflect compelling public interests—one requiring the diligent pursuit and punishment of drunk drivers and the other requiring the vigorous promotion of the institution of marriage. But on the assumed facts of this case, that conclusion doesn't get us very far.

Bammert was not fired for *her* participation in the enforcement of the laws against drunk driving; she was fired for *her husband's* participation in the enforcement of those laws. Discharges for conduct outside of the employment relationship by someone other than the discharged employee are not actionable under present law. The public policy generally favoring the stability of marriage, while unquestionably strong, provides an insufficient basis upon which to enlarge what was meant to be, and has always been, an extremely narrow exception to employment-at-will.

Bammert advocates an expansion of the public policy exception far beyond that contemplated by our case law, and she cites no authority for it. Up to now, where the exception has been applied, the public policy at issue has always been vindicated by the employee himself or herself, within the context of the employment relationship.

In contrast, Bammert's claim identifies a public policy completely unrelated to her employment, being enforced by someone else, who is employed elsewhere. That the "someone else" is her husband makes her discharge obviously retaliatory, and reminds us of the sometimes harsh reality of employment-at-will, but it does not provide acceptable grounds for expansion of the public policy exception beyond its present boundaries.

* * *

Line-drawing would be required but almost impossible to do in any principled way. For now, the rule would apply to police officers' spouses fired in retaliation for the officers' conduct in the line of duty—but what about the spouses of prosecutors, or judges, or DNR investigators, or IRS agents? What about discharges in retaliation for the conduct of the employee's parents, children, or siblings? The Family Code's strong endorsement of the stability of marriage is accompanied by an equally strong endorsement of the family as a central and fundamentally important societal institution. If the statute is sufficient to justify application of the public policy exception to discharges in retaliation for the conduct of non-employee spouses, it is certainly sufficient to justify extension of the exception to discharges in retaliation for the conduct of non-employee parents, children, and siblings.

Public policy comes in many variations, is implicated in many contexts, and is carried out by many people, both publicly and privately. Once expanded in the manner argued here, the public policy exception would no longer be subject to any discernable limiting principles. It would arguably apply to retaliatory discharges based upon the conduct of *any* non-employee relative, for the fulfillment of or refusal to violate public policy in a wide variety of ways and in a manner completely unconnected to the employment relationship.

The public policy exception cannot be stretched that far and still be recognizable under *Brockmeyer's* limited formulation. Accordingly, we decline to recognize a cause of action for wrongful discharge under the public policy exception to the at-will employment doctrine for terminations in retaliation for the conduct of a non-employee spouse.

The decision of the court of appeals is affirmed.

■ WILLIAM A. BABLITCH, J. (dissenting):

* * *

Retaliation for Bammert's husband's actions as a police officer was the reason Bammert was fired. In my view, this is unacceptable. There is a strong public policy in vigorous enforcement of the law. Society is not served by police officers being influenced in how they do their job because of the potential consequences of a retaliatory firing. Furthermore, extending the employment at-will doctrine to protect police officers is consistent with past precedent. Unfortunately, the majority opinion does not agree. The result is that an individual will be able to influence a police officer in the form of a retaliatory firing. For these reasons, I respectfully dissent.

* * *

There is no legitimate reason to protect the conduct of this employer. In a normal circumstance, this employer could not reach the person that the employer wishes to retaliate against. In this circumstance, the employee is married to one of the officers participating in the arrest, which allows the employer to therefore reach this officer. Normally, the officer would be protected from the disgruntled arrestee, but in this case, the arrestee can reach the officer. As stated previously, we do not allow retaliation against a police officer for performing his or her duty, but in this circumstance the employer has a way around the protection of the officer. In my opinion, this loophole that allows an employer to retaliate against a police officer must be put in line with the rest of our laws, and the loophole that provides a retaliatory tool for the employer must be closed, thereby protecting police officers.

Furthermore, society owes its police officers a duty not to put them in the no-win position that Bammert's husband was placed in. On the one hand, he was sworn to uphold the laws of Wisconsin. On the other hand, if he keeps his oath and upholds the laws of our state, he is put in the position that the person that he assists in arresting could retaliate against him. The majority gives Bammert's husband a choice: either do your job and assist in the arrest of the drunk driver or protect your family by looking the other way. I want to eliminate this no-win situation by giving police officers the tools to do their job without the fear of retaliation. We owe such officers, like Bammert's husband, that much.

NOTES AND QUESTIONS

1.   What rule should the legal system apply to Karen Bammert's lawsuit? At common law, at least since the late nineteenth century, Bammert was an employee at will; she could be dismissed for any reason or for no reason. See, e.g., Horace G. Wood, Law of Master and Servant § 134, at 273 (1877):

> With us the rule is inflexible, that a general or indefinite hiring is prima facie a hiring at will, and if the servant seeks to make it out a yearly hiring, the burden is upon him to establish it by proof. * * * [I]t is an indefinite hiring and is determinable at the will of either party.

Should this be the law in the twenty-first century? If not, should there be a right not to be unjustly fired for:

(a) Every worker?

(b) Permanent or long-term workers? Defined how?

(c) Only those workers who exercise their statutory right to form a union and bargain for a contract?

(d) Only those workers who obtain a written contract when they take a job?

If some dismissals should be unlawful, which ones? Bammert's? Why? Would the result be that courts sit in judgment about the facts of and the justification for the millions of dismissals that occur every year in the U.S.? Can the courts handle this role?

2.   The majority opinion in *Bammert* noted that the court's prior holdings had limited the public policy exception to cases where the public policy directly involved the employee. The majority was concerned about the "line

drawing" or "slippery slope" problem of deciding how to limit application of the doctrine when children, parents, or siblings are involved, instead of a spouse of the employee. Is the problem of line-drawing sufficient to deny relief to Bammert?

3. The plaintiff was employed in the defendant's dental office. When the dentist learned that the employee's adult daughter was contemplating bringing a dental malpractice action against him, he discharged her mother. The plaintiff brought an action for wrongful discharge in which she claimed, among other things, that her discharge violated the state's public policies of freedom of association and open access to the courts. Has the plaintiff asserted a legally cognizable claim? See Fortunato v. Office of Stephen M. Silston, D.D.S., 856 A.2d 530 (Conn. Super. Ct. 2004) (held: yes). Can you distinguish *Bammert*? See also Thompson v. North American Stainless, LP, 562 U.S. 170 (2011) (discharging fiancé of woman who filed sex discrimination claim violated anti-retaliation section of Title VII of the Civil Rights Act of 1964).

4. The dissent in *Bammert* focused on the public policy of vigorous enforcement of the law. "[S]ociety owes its police officers a duty not to put them in the no-win position that Bammert's husband was placed in." Neither the majority nor the dissent emphasized the plight of Karen Bammert. She was a loyal and productive employee of the supermarket for 26 years. The high court of a progressive state like Wisconsin was unprepared to say that, independent of the events surrounding her husband, she had a right to be free from arbitrary discharge.

5. What, if any, "rights" do employees have in their jobs? Are they property rights, contract rights, statutory rights, constitutional rights, or some other rights? Should these rights depend on whether the employer is private or public, whether the employees are represented by a union, or the basis of the employer's action? If Bammert should be given legal protection, what mechanism should be used? Should establishing employee rights be the province of a court, legislature, administrative agency, or some other entity? Who should enforce these rights?

6. Should the law also attempt to regulate the hiring of employees? If so, should the law on hiring be the same as the law on firing? What system should be used to regulate employment? The courts? An administrative agency? Arbitration? What are the economic and social costs of legal intervention? What are the economic and social costs of not intervening?

7. Why is a job so important in our society? How should this influence the desirability of legal regulation of the employment relationship?

———

This book considers all these questions and many other similar issues about the law of employment relationships in the U.S. Throughout, you should keep in mind some general questions: What is the proper role of law in establishing and enforcing employer and employee behavior? Can courts supervise the American workplace? Is law a good substitute for union representation of workers? If ideas and norms are changing, how should courts find the values that they express and apply? Can we use law to establish the kinds of workplaces where we would like to be an employee? What are the problems and the costs of doing so?

CHAPTER 2

THE DEVELOPMENT OF EMPLOYMENT LAW

Chapter 1 explored the social and cultural significance of work. What are the legal consequences of employment? What does it mean to be an employee or an employer? Working for someone (or having someone work for you) establishes a relationship with legal rights and obligations. The employer-employee relationship is not monolithic. Indeed, the desire to be characterized as employer and employee may vary according to the legal consequences. In order to avoid the minimum wage standards of the Fair Labor Standards Act, a company may argue that an individual is an independent contractor rather than an employee. But if that same individual is injured in the course of providing services to the business, the company may argue that the individual is an employee, who may not sue in tort and whose only recourse is to file a workers' compensation claim. Should the definition of employer and employee be different for different purposes? What establishes the existence of an employment relationship?

The materials in Chapter 2 trace the development of employment law in the modern workplace. The focus is varied and includes discussions of why the law has developed as it has and whether the law has fostered efficiency and equity. More specifically, how *should* the law regulate employment? Private contract (individual or collective) permits the parties to engage in free bargaining over the terms and conditions of work. Government regulation, by forcing the parties to behave in certain ways, accomplishes social ends that the marketplace does not achieve. Is there an optimal mix of private bargain and government regulation? Is efficient production in conflict with the political and social goals of the various regulatory statutes? Finally, should legal regulation change to take account of the changing demographics, economics, and technology of the workplace? How will the employment policies and relationships of the future affect employment law?

A. THE FOUNDATIONS OF EMPLOYMENT LAW

1. EMPLOYER—EMPLOYEE

Marc Linder, What Is an Employee? Why It Does, But Should Not, Matter*
7 Law & Ineq. 155, 156–158 (1989).

Although wage labor in fourteenth and fifteenth-century England connoted freedom when contrasted to the prior condition of serfdom, it also signaled a loss of independence. The expropriation of the land or "capital" which accompanied the change undermined this anti-feudal emancipatory meaning.

This two-fold sense of "freedom" comprising wage labor still survives. Wage laborers are both formally free to work when, where and for whom they please, *and* substantively free from the direct access to the means of production and subsistence that once undergirded the independence of small producers. While the wage-earners in capitalist societies have at times displayed the militancy and autonomy befitting the liberating component of the first meaning, they have also succumbed to their role as the dependent creatures of capital contained in the second meaning. Workers promote an ideological view of the state as an agency that can be manipulated to create the modicum of social security and work-related protection that, at least for certain sectors of the working class, cannot be gained directly from their capitalist employers. Fostering this view, workers have come to believe in an image of themselves as passive beneficiaries of forces that operate outside of the employer-employee relationship.

Paradoxically, entitlements to those benefits are almost universally contingent on being an employee, rather than being self-employed. The variety of benefits and protections in the United States conditioned on the existence of an employment relationship is impressive: unemployment compensation, workers compensation, collective bargaining rights, minimum wages and maximum hours, social security, pensions, occupational safety and health, and anti-discrimination protection. What an employee *is*, however, has often been left vague, has varied from benefit program to benefit program and from jurisdiction to jurisdiction, and has changed over time. No sound theoretical or empirical ground justifies this lack of uniformity. Indeed, the very existence of this hodgepodge is largely unknown not only to the affected workers, but also to the legislators, administrators and judges who are responsible for articulating policies, formulating definitions and drawing lines.

---

*   Reprinted by permission.

NOTES AND QUESTIONS

1.　The employer-employee relationship is based on contract. Yet there is an unmistakable influence of property law in the employment setting. The employer's ability to impose a wide range of conditions on employment often is justified because the work is performed on the employer's property, with the employer's materials and equipment, and even utilizing the employer's intangible property such as its good will and intellectual property. Does the employee have any such "property" interests in employment? How might greater property rights affect the employment rights of workers?

2.　Section 1.01 of the Restatement (Third) of Employment Law provides that an individual renders services as an employee of an employer if "(a) the individual acts, at least in part, to serve the interests of the employer, (2) the employer consents to receive the individual's services, and (3) the employer controls the manner and means by which the individual renders his or her services or otherwise effectively prevents the individual from rendering services as an independent businessperson." Importantly, the Restatement distinguishes an employee from an independent contract and a volunteer. As to independent contractors, the Restatement § 1.01(2) provides: "An individual renders services as an independent businessperson when the individual in his or her own interest exercises entrepreneurial control over important business decisions, including whether to hire and where to assign assistants, whether to purchase and where to deploy equipment, and whether and when to provide service to other customers." As to volunteers, the Restatement § 1.02 provides: "An individual is a volunteer and not an employee if the individual renders uncoerced services without being offered a material inducement." Can you think of situations when these definitions would be important?

3.　For an argument for reciprocal fiduciary duties of employers and employees, see Matthew T. Bodie, Employment as Fiduciary Responsibility, 105 Geo. L.J. 819 (2017).

Lemmerman v. A. T. Williams Oil Co.

350 S.E.2d 83 (N.C. 1986).

■ FRYE, JUSTICE.

The sole issue on this appeal is whether the Court of Appeals correctly affirmed the trial court's conclusion that plaintiff Shane Tucker was an employee of the defendant, A.T. Williams Oil Company. For the reasons set forth in this opinion, we conclude that the Court of Appeals was correct in so affirming.

On 1 December 1982, plaintiff Shane Tucker, then aged eight, slipped on a sidewalk on defendant's property and fell, cutting his hand. He and his mother, plaintiff Sylvia Tucker, filed this action against defendant on 26 June 1984. In their complaint, plaintiffs alleged in essence that Shane Tucker's injuries were proximately caused by defendant's negligence. They sought damages for medical expenses, lost wages, and pain and suffering. R. Douglas Lemmerman was appointed guardian ad litem for the minor plaintiff Shane.

Defendant filed an answer and raised as one of its defenses lack of subject matter jurisdiction. It asserted that the child Shane was its employee as defined by the Workers' Compensation Act and that the Industrial Commission accordingly had exclusive jurisdiction over plaintiffs' claim. Following preliminary discovery, defendant moved to dismiss for lack of subject matter jurisdiction. Upon the parties' stipulation that the trial judge find jurisdictional facts, Judge DeRamus made findings and concluded that Shane was an employee injured within the course and scope of his employment with defendant as defined in the Workers' Compensation Act. The judge therefore dismissed plaintiffs' action for lack of subject matter jurisdiction. Plaintiffs appealed to the Court of Appeals, which affirmed with a dissent by Webb, J., on the question of whether the evidence supported the conclusion that plaintiff Shane was an employee of defendant.

"By statute the Superior Court is divested of original jurisdiction of all actions which come within the provisions of the Workmen's Compensation Act." The Act provides that its remedies shall be an employee's only remedies against his or her employer for claims covered by the Act. N.C.G.S. § 97–10.1 (1985). Remedies available at common law are specifically excluded. Therefore, the question of whether plaintiff Shane Tucker was defendant's employee as defined by the Act is clearly jurisdictional. This issue is not affected by the fact that the minor may have been illegally employed because the Act specifically includes within its provisions illegally employed minors.[1] N.C.G.S. § 97–2(2) (1985).

* * *

Plaintiff Shane testified at his deposition that he routinely accompanied his mother to her job as part-time cashier at defendant's store and service station, a Wilco. According to his description, he ordinarily did his homework, ate a snack, and performed odd jobs about the station. These jobs consisted of picking up trash in the store, taking out the garbage, and stocking cigarettes and drinks. He had been doing these jobs for almost a month at the time of the accident. The child said that the jobs generally took him between half an hour and one hour to complete. In return, the store manager, Ken Schneiderman, would pay him a dollar, occasionally more depending on the amount of work he had done. A fair reading of the child's testimony discloses that he clearly expected to be paid for his efforts.

---

[1] The argument has been made that since the minor plaintiff may have been illegally employed, see N.C.G.S. § 95–25.5, defendant should not be allowed to prevail upon this defense. However, "[a] universal principle as old as the law is that the proceedings of a court without jurisdiction of the subject matter are a nullity." Burgess v. Gibbs, 262 N.C. 462, 465, 137 S.E.2d 806, 808 (1964). "If a court finds at any stage of the proceedings it is without jurisdiction, it is its duty to take notice of the defect and * * * dismiss the suit." Id. Therefore, if the Industrial Commission has jurisdiction over the claim of an illegally employed minor and the superior court does not, the superior court would have the duty to raise this issue *ex mero motu*.

The child also testified that on the day of the accident he had nearly finished his tasks and was on his way to ask Schneiderman if there was anything else Schneiderman wanted him to do when he slipped and fell. He said at one point that he believed that Schneiderman did later give him his dollar, although he was not clear on this point.

The child's mother, Sylvia Tucker, corroborated Shane's account. She testified that at the time of the accident, she was working from 4 p.m. to 7 p.m. as a part-time cashier at Wilco. Schneiderman had Shane "put up stock, straighten the shelves up and pick up trash inside the building" and occasionally outside as well. Mrs. Tucker testified that her understanding was that the child was going to be paid for what he did. Although she told Schneiderman originally that Shane would work without being paid, he rejected this offer and told both her and the child that he would pay Shane for his work. She believed that Schneiderman paid Shane a dollar a day.

* * *

We believe that this evidence amply supports the trial judge's findings that Schneiderman, who had the authority to hire and fire employees, hired the minor plaintiff to do odd jobs as needed in defendant's service station/convenience store business. Specifically, these tasks included stocking cigarettes and drinks, and picking up trash. At the time of the accident, Shane was engaged in doing these tasks.

* * *

[P]laintiffs argue that Shane could not have been an employee because Schneiderman did not comply with certain procedural formalities. He did not take an application from Shane or report him on the list of employees he turned into his supervisor for withholding purposes. His normal practice was to pay employees from the cash register; he paid Shane from his pocket.

We do not believe that any of these factors is dispositive. Our Court of Appeals has held that failure to follow technical procedures such as withholding F.I.C.A. and income taxes is not controlling on the issue of whether an employer-employee relationship exists. We also do not think that Schneiderman's method of paying Shane was as significant under the facts of this case as it might otherwise be, because all wages came out of Schneiderman's commission. He therefore paid all of the employees at Wilco out of his own money.

[P]laintiffs contend that Shane was not an employee but instead performed gratuitous services. In addition to Schneiderman's testimony denying that he hired Shane, rejected by the trial judge, plaintiffs cite Mrs. Tucker's original statement to Schneiderman that he did not have to pay the child. However, this evidence in fact supports the opposite conclusion, that Shane was an employee. Schneiderman was offered the chance to avail himself of Shane's gratuitous services, but he specifically rejected it and said that he wanted to pay the child for his work. The evidence shows, and the judge found, that he did so.

Finally, plaintiffs contend that if Shane was an employee, he was Schneiderman's personal employee. We disagree. Schneiderman had the authority to hire employees for defendant, and the evidence shows and the trial judge found that the tasks the child performed were in the course of defendant's business, not Schneiderman's personal affairs.

* * *

For all of the foregoing reasons, the decision of the Court of Appeals is affirmed.

AFFIRMED.

■ MARTIN, JUSTICE, dissenting.

I must respectfully dissent. First, the majority opinion allows the defendant corporation to profit from its own illegal act. Here, defendant corporation claims that it hired plaintiff Shane, an eight-year-old child, as an employee. Defendant's act would be a direct violation of N.C.G.S. § 95–25.5(d), punishable by imposition of civil penalties. This statute establishes the public policy of this state that it is unlawful for employers to employ children thirteen years of age or less.

The public policy of North Carolina also will not permit a wrongdoer to take advantage of or enrich itself as a result of its own wrong. "It is a basic principle of law and equity that no man shall be permitted to take advantage of his own wrong. * * * " Further citation of authority is not necessary for this basic principle of law. The principle is especially applicable where, as here, the power of the parties is so disparate—an eight-year-old child versus a large corporation! The inequity of defendant's plea in bar is thus magnified by the relationship of the parties.

* * *

Even if this Court allows defendant to rely upon an inequitable defense, the evidence fails, in at least one respect, to support a finding that plaintiff child was defendant's employee. We must not overlook that defendant has the burden of proof to sustain its plea in bar. As the majority states, the right to demand payment from the *employer,* A.T. Williams Oil Company, is an essential element of the employment status. Defendant has failed to carry its burden as to this element.

The evidence in many respects is in conflict. However, defendant has failed to produce a shred of evidence that the eight-year-old child had a right to demand payment for his services from A.T. Williams Oil Company. Also, there is no evidence that plaintiff child could have made such a demand from Schneiderman, albeit defendant argues that plaintiff was its employee and not Schneiderman's. All of the testimony showed that the infrequent payment of amounts ranging from twenty-five cents to a dollar came out of Schneiderman's own money, out of his own pocket. The payments were not made from the cash register, as were payments to defendant's employees. Thus, the record is simply devoid of any evidence that the child could have demanded payment from the corporate defendant for services he rendered to Schneiderman.

On the other hand, the record is replete with evidence that plaintiff child was *not* an employee of defendant's. Shane was not a listed employee for workers' compensation purposes; his name was not reported to the defendant corporation for tax withholding purposes; Schneiderman testified explicitly that Shane was not an employee.

* * *

Likewise, here defendant desired to employ Sylvia Tucker, plaintiff child's mother, to work in the convenience store. She could not do so unless defendant agreed to let her eight-year-old son come to the store after school and remain until she completed her work. Defendant agreed to this plan. While on the premises the child from time to time performed menial tasks for Schneiderman, who sometimes would give the boy payments ranging from twenty-five cents to a dollar for his work. This is entirely consistent with the problem of a working mother who needs employment but must also supervise her young child. Shane was on the premises not as an employee of the corporate defendant, but because it was necessary in order for his mother to work. Such are the demands of our modern society.

NOTES AND QUESTIONS

1. Was Shane Tucker an "employee" in the ordinary sense of the word? Before his injury, did Shane, Mrs. Tucker, Mr. Schneiderman, or the A. T. Williams Oil Company consider him an employee?

2. The court suggests that Shane would be entitled to workers' compensation. Is there something wrong with an eight year-old, who is too young to be a legal employee, receiving workers' compensation? Does the court's decision further the public policy of prohibiting child labor?

Some courts have held that illegally employed minors, injured or killed on the job, should be limited to workers' compensation. See Roberts v. George W. Hill & Co., 23 S.W.3d 635 (Ky.2000) (injured minor employee limited to workers' compensation remedy); Fanion v. McNeal, 577 A.2d 2 (Me.1990) (minor, even though employed in violation of child labor laws, was limited to remedies provided by workers' compensation act and was precluded from wrongful death action). Other courts have found this outcome to be unjust and contrary to public policy. See Blancato v. Feldspar Corp., 522 A.2d 1235 (Conn.1987) (child may void an illegal contract and thus may pursue workers' compensation claim or tort action). See generally Richard R. Carlson, Why the Law Still Can't Tell an Employee When it Sees One and How it Ought to Stop Trying, 22 Berkeley J. Emp. & Lab. L. 295 (2001).

3. Because workers' compensation precludes most tort awards, injured individuals sometimes argue that they are independent contractors who can sue in tort rather than employees limited to workers' compensation relief. Eckis v. Sea World, infra p. 808, held that plaintiff, who was bitten by Shamu the killer whale while riding Shamu at Seaworld, was an employee and so could not sue in tort.

4. In Nationwide Mut. Ins. Co. v. Darden, 503 U.S. 318 (1992), the Supreme Court said "traditional agency law criteria" should guide the question of who is an employee for the purpose of applying federal pension law. The pension statute, the Employee Retirement Income Security Act of 1974 (ERISA), is considered at length in Chapter 13. Justice Souter said, correctly, that the statute's definition of employee ("any individual employed by an employer") is "completely circular and explains nothing." He said the law's reach should be measured by the "general common law of agency rather than * * * the law of any particular State." Interestingly, similar "circular" definitions of employee and employer are contained in numerous federal and state statutes. For example, § 3(6) of the Occupational Safety and Health Act (discussed in detail in Chapter 8) defines an employee as "an employee of an employer who is employed in a business of his employer which affects commerce." It remains to be seen whether the *Nationwide* approach will be applied to these other federal and state statutes.

In Clackamas Gastroenterology Assocs. v. Wells, 538 U.S. 440 (2003), the Supreme Court held that in determining who is a business partner, and therefore not counted as an employee for purposes of the Americans with Disabilities Act, the trial court should examine whether the partner operates independently and manages the business or is subject to the firm's control. See generally Ann C. McGinley, Functionality or Formalism? Partners and Shareholders as "Employees" under the Anti-Discrimination Laws, 57 SMU L. Rev. 3 (2004).

You will see some of these issues in further detail in the consideration of particular programs later in the book. There is no single test of "employee"; the relationship is categorized differently for different regulatory purposes.

5. Despite the plethora of employment legislation enacted in the United States, discussed in the later chapters of this book, many workers are largely excluded from the regulatory protections. Among those excluded from coverage are the following; workers for small employers below the statutory minimum number of employees for coverage; workers classified as independent contractors; workers not meeting the definition of employee (e.g., prison labor, participants in welfare-to-work programs, trainees, and students); employees specifically excluded from coverage (e.g., domestic household employees, agricultural workers); and undocumented alien workers. For a further discussion, see Emily A. Spieler, (Re)assessing the Grand Bargain: Compensation for Work Injuries in the United States, 1900–1917, 69 Rutgers L. Rev. 891 (2017); Noah Zatz, Nonprofit Oversight Under Siege: Does Work Law Have a Future if the Labor Market Does Not? 91 Chi. Kent. L. Rev. 181 (2016).

2. INDEPENDENT CONTRACTORS

Keith Cunningham-Parmeter, From Amazon to Uber: Defining Employment in the Modern Economy[*]

97 B.U.L. Rev. 1673, 1676–77, 1680–86 (2016).

Since the end of the Great Recession, U.S. businesses have aggressively engaged in a series of organizational changes from classifying workers as independent contractors to hiring subcontractors, to utilizing staffing agencies to delegate employment-related responsibilities to outsiders. Although the strategic use of contactors existed long before the most recent economic downturn, the Great Recession dramatically increased this trend. Regrettably for workers caught in these settings, employment law violations represent a common practice. In addition to avoiding employment liabilities, firms that hire contractors fail to contribute to essential components of America's social safety net such as Social Security and unemployment benefits. And the scope of the problem is growing. By 2020, up to forty percent of workers are projected to become contingent "pseudo-employees," many of whom will lack the ability to enforce basic workplace protections.

Given the potential cost-savings they offer, these organizational changes represent the "future of work" for which the law must account. Unfortunately, current judicial pronouncements on these issues often embrace a cabined vision of employment that shields firms from liability. This constrained understanding of employer-employee configurations ultimately limits the reach of protective statutes, thereby resulting in a misalignment between modern workplace structures and employment rights.

* * *

1. The Rise of the Contractor Defense

    A. *Working but not employed*

The uniforms that many workers wear today do not necessarily reflect the identities of their actual employers. For example, the satellite television installer who drives a DirecTV-branded truck may not actually report to DirecTV. Likewise, the Westin housekeeper who cleans hotel rooms may not receive a paycheck from the hotel chain where she works. The process of "vertical integration," wherein firms generate goods and services internally, has drastically declined over the last several decades. Given the choice between producing a service in-house or buying it from outside sources, companies increasingly turn to third parties for essential services. This growing commodification of work-related tasks has birthed

---

[*]   Reprinted by permission.

an entire industry of labor intermediaries who sell discrete services in individualized packages to business.

Given the low price and availability of vendor-supplied labor, many formerly self contained companies now rely on vast networks of contractors to maintain operations. For example, some hospitals and hotels assign nearly all of their operations housekeeping, maintenance, recordkeeping, etc. to third parties. Similarly, when Amazon recently opened a distribution center in Tennessee, it announced that 3500 of the 4500 new employees would actually work for an outside agency that contracted with Amazon. But even though Amazon may not share an official employment relationship with workers in situations like this, the company can still exert significant influence over workers' pay and working conditions by controlling the firms that formally employ them.

Unsurprisingly, these movements have caused the number of people employed by labor-only agencies to explode in recent years. Since 2010, the staffing industry has added more jobs to the U.S. economy than any other sector. While total employment in the labor market has grown by six percent since 2009, the staffing industry has grown by forty-one percent. Many of the workers involved in these arrangements are not temporary laborers at all, but rather assume the identity of "permatemps" who receive their paychecks from supplying firms while providing labor to companies that never formally employ them. Once a niche field in the 1970s that offered only short-term work in areas such as secretarial assistance, nursing help, and day labor, the temporary staffing sector now supplies labor to numerous industries. Given this expansion, many end-user companies today see "temporary" staffing agencies as permanent extensions of their human resources departments.

* * *

B.   The Gig Economy and Independent Contractors

No industry better exemplifies the vast expansion of independent contracting than the on-demand or "gig" economy. Rooted in an economic model in which individuals sell services to one another, online platforms help facilitate varied forms of peer-to-peer work. Although on-demand workers represent a relatively small segment of the labor force, the number of jobs in this area is increasing rapidly. Take Uber: Valued at $50 billion, Uber is the fastest-growing startup in the world. In fact, the ride-broker's growth has been so explosive that its private market value now equals that of mainstay public companies like Target and Kraft Foods. Uber claims that it "owns no vehicles" and "employs no drivers." But even as the rideshare firm denies its employer status, it adds hundreds of thousands of driver-partners to its platform each month.

Uber's ascension has devastated taxi companies in many regions. In New York City, for example, the number of rides provided by Uber jumped in two years from 300,000 to 3.5 million, while traditional cabs lost 2.1 million rides during the same period. In 2015, San Francisco's largest taxi company, Yellow Cab, filed for bankruptcy. And Uber's long-term business plan extends well beyond ridesharing. The company now delivers, or plans to deliver food (UberEats), retail goods (UberRush), and flu shots (UberHealth), offering all of these services with nonemployee labor.

Because it categorizes its "partners" as independent contractors, Uber does not extend any employment rights including unemployment benefits, workers' compensation, or overtime to its drivers. The rideshare firm gains immediate economic advantages from this strategy. Uber can save up to thirty percent in payroll taxes simply by classifying its drivers as nonemployees. And Uber is not the only platform taking advantage of this exempt category of workers. Indeed, the gig economy is chock-full of firms that hire independent contractors to gain similar bottom-line benefits. From Lyft drivers to TaskRabbit gardeners, many peer marketplaces categorize their workers as nonemployees.

As first glance, the classification of on-demand workers as independent contractors might seem perfectly appropriate given that workers in the industry can accept gigs whenever they choose. But the significant influence that on-demand firms have over working conditions from setting non-negotiable wage rates, to implementing behavior codes, to "deactivating" (i.e. firing) individuals who perform poorly reflects a more traditional employer-employee dynamic.

O'Connor v. Uber Technologies, Inc.
904 F.3d 1087 (9th Cir. 2018).

■ CLIFTON, CIRCUIT JUDGE:

Current and former Uber drivers filed several putative class actions alleging on behalf of themselves and other drivers that Uber Technologies, Inc. and related defendants (collectively referred to as "Uber"), violated various federal and state statutes by, among other things, misclassifying drivers as independent contractors rather than employees. Multiple cases were consolidated for appeal to this court. Uber appeals the district court's orders denying Uber's motions to compel arbitration, orders granting class certification in *O'Connor*, and orders controlling class communications pursuant to Federal Rule of Civil Procedure 23(d).

We previously considered and reversed the district court's orders denying Uber's motions to compel arbitration in Mohamed v. Uber Technologies, Inc., 848 F.3d 1201, 1206 (9th Cir. 2016). Plaintiffs offer additional arguments in the current appeal why the arbitration agreements are unenforceable, but those arguments are unpersuasive. As the class certification by the district court was premised on the district court's determination that the arbitration agreements were unenforceable, the class certification must also be reversed. The Rule

23(d) orders were based on the district court's denial of the motions to compel arbitration and its granting of class certification. As both of those decisions must be reversed, there is no longer a basis for the district court's restrictions on Uber's communication with class and putative class members, so these orders are moot and must be reversed as well.

I. Background

Two Uber drivers filed a putative class action complaint against Uber on August 16, 2013, initiating the *O'Connor* action. It alleged claims for failure to remit the entire gratuity paid by customers to drivers in violation of California Labor Code § 351 ("Tips Claim"), and for misclassifying the drivers as independent contractors and failing to pay their business expenses (including vehicles, gas, and maintenance) in violation of California Labor Code § 2802 ("Expense Reimbursement Claim").

Within a week of filing suit, the *O'Connor* Plaintiffs filed a motion under Rule 23(d) requesting that the district court declare the 2013 arbitration agreement unconscionable, or, in the alternative, requiring Uber to provide enhanced notice and opportunities for the drivers to opt out of arbitration. On December 6, 2013, the district court granted the *O'Connor* Plaintiffs' alternative request, enjoined Uber from enforcing its arbitration agreement against those drivers who entered into the agreement but did not opt out, required Uber to revise the agreement to include enhanced notice provisions, and directed Uber to extend the opt out period for an additional thirty days once the revised agreements were distributed. Uber's updated licensing agreement was issued on June 21, 2014. Uber also sent licensing agreements in November 2014 and April 2015 that were materially identical to the June 2014 agreement (collectively "2014 arbitration agreement").

Plaintiff Mohamed filed a putative class action complaint against Uber and Hirease, LLC, an independent company that conducts background checks, on November 24, 2014, asserting various federal and California state law claims. We have already provided background on that case in our decision in *Mohamed*. Here it is sufficient to note that the district court denied Uber's motion to compel arbitration pursuant to its 2013 and 2014 arbitration agreements, holding, among other things, that the arbitration provisions were unenforceable because they were unconscionable. Based on the same reasoning, the district court also denied Uber's motions to compel arbitration in [this and companion cases].

In April 2015, the *O'Connor* Plaintiffs moved for certification of a class of approximately 160,000 individuals who had driven for Uber in the state of California at any time since August 16, 2009. The district court granted class certification in part in an order filed on September 1, 2015, certifying the following class for the Plaintiffs' Tips Claim:

All UberBlack, UberX, and UberSUV drivers who have driven for Uber in the state of California at any time since August 16, 2009, and who (1) signed up to drive directly with Uber or an Uber subsidiary under their individual name, and (2) are/were paid by Uber or an Uber subsidiary directly and in their individual name, and (3) did not electronically accept any contract with Uber or one of Uber's subsidiaries which contain the notice and opt-out provisions previously ordered by this Court (including those contracts listed in the Appendix to this Order), *unless* the driver timely opted-out of that contract's arbitration agreement.

The district court excluded drivers who worked for a distinct third-party transportation company, or who contracted or were paid under corporate or fictitious names, out of concern that individualized issues would predominate if they were included. The district court, in addition, excluded any drivers who signed the Uber contracts that included enhanced notice and opt-out provisions previously ordered by the district court, unless the driver timely opted-out of the arbitration agreement. The district court declined to certify the *O'Connor* Plaintiffs' Expense Reimbursement Claim at that time because it was uncertain whether the *O'Connor* Plaintiffs could determine whether a particular expense was "necessary" on a classwide basis.

In response to a supplemental motion for class certification by the *O'Connor* Plaintiffs, the district court, on December 9, 2015, certified an additional subclass of Uber drivers including those who accepted arbitration agreements in 2014 and 2015:

All UberBlack, UberX, and UberSUV drivers who have driven for Uber in the state of California at any time since August 16, 2009, and meet all the following requirements: (1) who signed up to drive directly with Uber or an Uber subsidiary under their individual name, and (2) are/were paid by Uber or an Uber subsidiary directly and in their individual name, and (3) electronically accepted any contract with Uber or one of Uber's subsidiaries which contain the notice and opt-out provisions previously ordered by this Court, and did not timely opt out of that contract's arbitration agreement.

In the same order the district court also certified the original class and subclass to pursue the Expense Reimbursement Claim based on the *O'Connor* Plaintiffs' proposal to rely on the Internal Revenue Service's mileage reimbursement rate, which approximates a driver's necessary business expenses.

Uber issued a new arbitration agreement to all of its drivers on December 11, 2015. Plaintiffs filed separate motions to enjoin Uber from distributing and enforcing this new agreement and to enjoin any further communications by Uber to class and putative class members. The district court granted the motion in part on December 23, 2015, citing its authority under Federal Rule of Civil Procedure 23(d) to control communications by Uber to the class members and putative class members. Although the district court did not prohibit Uber from sending out arbitration agreements in the future (except to members of the *O'Connor* certified class), it ruled that: (1) the December 11, 2015 agreement shall have no effect on the rights of certified class members to pursue the claims certified in *O'Connor*; (2) its arbitration provision was not enforceable against non-class member drivers who had already agreed to it; (3) Uber had to issue a new version of the agreement with enhanced notice and opt out provisions and provide drivers with 30-days to decide to opt out or not; and (4) during the pendency of the Uber cases, all cover letters, notices and arbitration provisions given to new or prospective drivers had to be approved by the district court.

In *Mohamed*, we reversed the district court's denial of Uber's motion to compel arbitration. We held that the relevant provisions in the respective agreements delegated the threshold question of arbitrability to the arbitrator, that the delegation provisions were not adhesive pursuant to California law and were therefore not procedurally unconscionable, and that the provisions permitting drivers to opt-out of arbitration were not illusory but provided the drivers with a meaningful opportunity to opt out.

In response to *Mohamed*, the district court terminated its December 23, 2015 Rule 23(d) order, and stated that "Uber is permitted to issue the December 2015 Agreement to new drivers without satisfying the enhanced notice provisions required by the Court" and current drivers as well. The district court refused to vacate the order retroactively, however, explaining that "it will not deem the December 2015 Agreement effective as to drivers who did not timely opt out of the arbitration agreement during the pendency of the Rule 23(d) orders," from December 10, 2015 to August 18, 2016.

Approximately a dozen appeals arising from these cases were filed with this court. They were consolidated for appeal, and supplemental consolidated briefing was ordered and received.

II. Motions to Compel Arbitration

An order denying a motion to compel arbitration is reviewed de novo. Underlying factual findings are reviewed for clear error. "[Q]uestions of arbitrability must be addressed with a healthy regard for the federal policy favoring arbitration." Moses H. Cone Mem'l Hosp. v. Mercury Constr. Corp. , 460 U.S. 1 (1983).

Based on our decision in *Mohamed*, the district court's orders denying Uber's motions to compel arbitration must be reversed. Plaintiffs do not dispute the application of *Mohamed* regarding the issues our previous decision discussed to the other cases consolidated in the current appeal, but they argue that the arbitration agreements are unenforceable for two other reasons.

The first reason is that even if the arbitration agreements would otherwise be enforceable, Plaintiffs argue they are irrelevant here because the lead plaintiffs in *O'Connor* constructively opted out of arbitration on behalf of the entire class. The sole authority offered by Plaintiffs for this proposition is a Georgia Supreme Court decision, Bickerstaff v. Suntrust Bank, 299 Ga. 459, 788 S.E.2d 787 (2016). The argument is unpersuasive for multiple reasons. Nothing gave the *O'Connor* lead plaintiffs the authority to take that action on behalf of and binding other drivers. Nor did *Bickerstaff* hold that individuals in the lead plaintiffs' position had the authority to make such an election for others. Perhaps more importantly, Plaintiffs provide no federal case law that has relied on *Bickerstaff*, nor could they. That decision rested exclusively on state law grounds and did not discuss the Federal Arbitration Act ("FAA"), 9 U.S.C. § 2.

Section 2 of the FAA "requires courts to enforce agreements to arbitrate according to their terms," in order "to place an arbitration agreement upon the same footing as other contracts . . . and to overrule the judiciary's longstanding refusal to enforce agreements to arbitrate," (internal quotation marks and citation omitted). To that end, section 2 declares that "a contract evidencing a transaction involving commerce to settle by arbitration a controversy thereafter arising out of such contract or transaction . . . shall be valid, irrevocable, and enforceable, save upon such grounds as exist at law or in equity for the revocation of any contract." 9 U.S.C. § 2. An arbitration-specific rule, such as the one set forth in *Bickerstaff*, would be preempted by the FAA. Plaintiffs' new argument provides no support for the district court's orders denying the motions to compel arbitration.

The second alternative argument offered by Plaintiffs is that the arbitration agreements are unenforceable because they contain class action waivers that violate the National Labor Relations Act of 1935 ("NLRA"), 29 U.S.C. §§ 151–169. After oral argument, we withdrew submission of this consolidated appeal pending resolution by the Supreme Court of another case that posed a similar question. The Court answered that question and rejected Plaintiffs' argument in Epic Systems Corp. v. Lewis, ___ U.S. ___, 138 S.Ct. 1612 (2018) [infra p. 65].

In sum, the district court's orders denying Uber's motions to compel arbitration in *O'Connor*, *Yucesoy*, and *Del Rio* must be reversed.

* * *

Reversed and remanded.

NOTES AND QUESTIONS

1.   The district court in O'Connor v. Uber Technologies, Inc., 82 F. Supp.3d 1133 (N.D. Cal. 2015), reversed, 904 F.3d 1087 (2018), rejected Uber's argument that it was not subject to California's employment laws because it was not the employer of its drivers. Uber claimed it was a "technology company" that facilitated independent contractors to provide transportation services. The court, however, noted that Uber derived its revenue from the

rides provided by its drivers and exercised a significant amount of control over the drivers. "Uber is no more a 'technology company' than Yellow Cab is a 'technology company' because it uses CB radios to dispatch taxi cabs, John Deere is a 'technology company' because it uses computers and robots to manufacture lawn mowers, or Domino Sugar is a 'technology company' because it uses modern irrigation techniques to grow its sugar cane." 82 F.Supp.3d at 1141.

2. In McGillis v. Department of Economic Opportunity, 210 So.3d 220 (Fla. Dist. Ct. App. 2017), an Uber driver was "deactivated" based on alleged violations of Uber's privacy policy. When the driver filed for "reemployment assistance" under Florida law his claim was rejected on the ground that he was not an employee. In affirming the denial of his claim, the Florida appellate court stated: "Due in large part to the transformative nature of the internet and smartphones, Uber drivers like McGillis decide whether, when, where, with whom, and how to provide rides using Uber's computer programs. This level of free agency is incompatible with the control to which a traditional employee is subject."

Assuming that the court in *McGillis* is correct, that Uber drivers are not employees under traditional common law criteria, should they be excluded from unemployment insurance, workers' compensation, minimum wage and maximum hour provisions, and all of the other laws designed to protect the interests of workers? Do we need a new conceptualization of employment laws to replace the New Deal era foundations of many labor and employment laws?

3. On June 7, 2017, Secretary of Labor Alexander Acosta announced the immediate withdrawal of Labor Department interpretations from 2015 and 2016 involving independent contractors and joint employment. Of particular relevance is the guidance dealing with misclassification of employees as independent contractors, which contains a presumption that "most workers are employees." The Obama Administration had aggressively enforced the FLSA to obtain wages for workers, mostly low income, who were deemed independent contractors and therefore not subject to overtime provisions and other protections.

4. On September 18, 2019, California Governor Gavin Newsom signed into law Assembly Bill 5, to be codified at Cal. Lab. Code § 2750.3, which revamps the state's test for classifying workers as independent contractors. Essentially adopting the so-called ABC test of Dynamex Operations West, Inc. v. Superior Court, 416 P.3d 1 (Cal. 2018), the law presumes that a worker is an employee unless the business can demonstrate all of the following factors: (1) the business is not able to control or direct what the worker does, either by contract or in actual practice; (2) the worker performs tasks outside of the entity's usual business; and (3) the worker is engaged in an independently established trade, occupation, or business. The law contains a number of exceptions, including exclusions from the ABC test for health care professionals, lawyers, architects, engineers, accountants, and insurance agents. If a category of worker is exempted, the test of S.G. Borello & Sons v. Department of Industrial Relations, 769 P.2d 399 (Cal. 1989), will apply. Under *Borello*, the principal factor is whether "the person to whom service is rendered has the right to control the manner and means of accomplishing the result desired." The Massachusetts Independent Contractor Statute, Mass. Gen. Laws Ch. 149, § 148B(a), also presumes that a worker is an employee unless the three prongs of the ABC test are established.

5. For a further discussion, see Miriam A. Cherry, Are Uber and Transportation Network Companies the Future of Transportation (Law) and Employment (Law)?, 4 Tex. A & M L. Rev. 173 (2017); Orly Lobel, The Law of the Platform, 101 Minn. L. Rev. 87 (2016); Benjamin Means & Joseph A. Seiner, Navigating the Uber Economy, 49 U.C. Davis L. Rev. 1511 (2016); Paul M. Secunda, Uber Retirement, 2017 U. Chi. L. Forum 435 (2017).

3. EMPLOYMENT AT WILL

Jay M. Feinman, The Development of the Employment at Will Rule*

20 Am.J. Legal Hist. 118, 118–123, 125–126 (1976).

American law originally adopted the rules of English law on duration of service contracts. Toward the end of the nineteenth century, however, English and American law diverged. While the English used presumptions of long-term hiring and required reasonable notice of termination, American lawyers and courts developed the rule of termination at will.

* * *

English courts at an early point developed a relatively sophisticated approach to the termination of master-servant relationships. They identified two questions: What is the duration of the relation presumed to be when none is specifically stated? What length of notice must be given before the relation can be terminated? The English, unlike the Americans, saw that the questions were not the same and eventually developed a response to the second that mitigated somewhat the strictness of the early response to the first.

The duration of service relationships was a concern in early stages of English law, but the law was best formulated and made prominent only with the statement of a rule and policy by Blackstone:

> If the hiring be general, without any particular time limited, the law construes it to be a hiring for a year; upon a principle of natural equity, that the servant shall serve, and the master maintain him, throughout all the revolutions of the respective seasons, as well when there is work to be done as when there is not.

The rule thus stated expressed a sound principle: injustice would result if, for example, masters could have the benefit of servants' labor during

---
*   Reprinted by permission.

planting and harvest seasons but discharge them to avoid supporting them during the unproductive winter, or if servants who were supported during the hard season could leave their masters' service when their labor was most needed. But the source of the yearly hiring rule was not solely, as might be supposed from Blackstone's statement, in the judges' concern for fairness between master and servant. The rule was also shaped by the requirements of the Statutes of Labourers, which prescribed a duty to work and prohibited leaving an employment or discharging a servant before the end of a term, and by the Poor Laws, which used a test of residence and employment to determine which community was responsible for the support of a person. Thus, despite a concern with the "revolution of the seasons," the rule articulated by Blackstone was not restricted to agricultural and domestic workers. The presumption that an indefinite hiring was a hiring for a year extended to all classes of servants. Because the rule was designed for domestic servants broadly construed, however, those who were clearly not in that group were sometimes excluded. The types of employment now considered usual—where the hours or days of work were limited, or the employment only for a certain job—would sometimes be held not to import a yearly hiring, indicating some sophistication by the law in not extending a concept designed for one purpose beyond its reasonable reach.

* * *

As the law was faced with an increasing variety of employment situations, mostly far removed from the domestic relations which had shaped the earlier law, the importance of the duration of contract question diminished and the second issue, the notice required to terminate the contract, moved to the fore. Even when they recognized hirings as yearly ones, the courts refused to consider the contracts as entire and instead developed the rule that, unless specified otherwise, service contracts could be terminated on reasonable notice.

What constituted reasonable notice was a question of fact to be decided anew in each case, but certain conventions grew up. Domestic servants, who presumably no longer needed the benefit of the seasons, could be given a month's notice. Other types of employees could also be given a month's notice; three months was another common term, although some special cases required six or even twelve months' notice. Although notice was a separate question in each case, the custom of the trade was often determinative.

* * *

While English law followed a relatively clear path, American law at the same time exhibited a confusion of principles and rules. Through the middle of the nineteenth century, American courts and lawyers relied heavily on English precedents but often came to different results.

In colonial times some hirings, such as of day laborers, were conventionally terminable at will. Agricultural and domestic service relations often followed the English rule of yearly hirings. In the nineteenth century, however, whatever consensus existed about the state of the law dissolved. For example, Tapping Reeve's pioneering domestic relations treatise at mid-century stated the English presumption of yearly hiring but noted that no such rule existed in Connecticut. But, in the same year that Reeve's second edition was published, the New York Court of Appeals held that the English rule of yearly hiring was still in effect in New York, even giving Blackstone's "benefit of the seasons" rationale. Shortly thereafter Charles Manly Smith's treatise on master and servant, the first devoted solely to the subject in the United States, was published in Philadelphia. Covering English law with reference to American cases, Smith's treatise was noted for its exhaustive discussion of the intricacies of the law and it had significant impact for that reason. Smith stated a presumption that a general hiring was a yearly hiring for all servants, the presumption was rebuttable by custom or other evidence, and, in spite of a yearly hiring, the relation was terminable on notice where that was customary.

The confusion over the nature of the field of master and servant law contributed to the confusion over the duration of service contracts issue. Master and servant law was originally classed as a domestic relation. The master-servant relation was personal, often familial; servants were described as "menial" not derogatorily but because they resided intra moenia, within the walls of the master's house. As the nineteenth century progressed, however, the true master-servant relation became overshadowed by the number of employees whose relationship to their employers was essentially commercial and therefore did not fit the pattern. The resulting tension influenced the direction of the law, with the earlier perception acting as a force delaying accommodations to new economic conditions.

* * *

By the 1870's the dissolution of the earlier law was apparent. Although the presumption of yearly hiring was recognized as anachronistic, the concept of reasonable notice had not caught on. Attempts were made to provide new, more fitting rules. * * *

* * *

Thus the time was ripe for a sure resolution of the problem; it was achieved by an Albany lawyer and prolific treatise writer named Horace Gay Wood. Wood sliced through the confusion and stated the employment at will doctrine in absolutely certain terms:

> With us the rule is inflexible, that a general or indefinite hiring is prima facie a hiring at will, and if the servant seeks to make it out a yearly hiring, the burden is upon him to establish it by proof. * * * [I]t is an indefinite hiring and is determinable at the

will of either party, and in this respect there is no distinction between domestic and other servants.

The puzzling question is what impelled Wood to state the rule that has since become identified with his name. Wood's master and servant treatise, like his other works, won him acclaim for his painstaking scholarship, but that comprehensiveness and concern for detail were absent in his treatment of the duration of service contracts. First, the four American cases he cited in direct support of the rule were in fact far off the mark. Second, his scholarly disingenuity was extraordinary; he stated incorrectly that no American courts in recent years had approved the English rule, that the employment at will rule was inflexibly applied in the United States, and that the English rule was only for a yearly hiring, making no mention of notice. Third, in the absence of valid legal support, Wood offered no policy grounds for the rule he proclaimed.

Whatever its origin and the inadequacies of its explanation, Wood's rule spread across the nation until it was generally adopted.

* * *

NOTES

1.   Regardless of Wood's motivation for advancing the employment at will rule, it rapidly became standard doctrine, endorsed even by the Supreme Court. In Adair v. United States, 208 U.S. 161 (1908), the Court struck down as unconstitutional a federal statute making it a crime for an employer engaged in interstate commerce to discharge an employee solely because of membership in a labor organization. Such a restriction on the right of contract was perceived by the Court to be an impermissible invasion of personal liberty. It was inappropriate for government "to compel any person in the course of his business and against his will to accept or retain the personal services of another, or to compel any person, against his will, to perform personal services for another." The Court viewed the right of the employer to "dispense with the services" of any employee as correlative with the employee's right to quit for whatever reason. In Coppage v. Kansas, 236 U.S. 1 (1915), the Court applied the same reasoning to state efforts to regulate the employer's right to discharge employees and struck down a Kansas statute that made it unlawful for any firm or individual to require nonmembership in a union as a condition of employment. The case would be different, the Court reasoned, only if coercion or duress were involved; otherwise, the individual's decision to enter into a contract of employment was seen as one freely entered into, and one that the judiciary would not second-guess. According to the Court, the individual employee had two options: he could be hired (or remain employed) and withdraw from union activities, or if he preferred, he could remain in the union and forego employment. See also Andrew P. Morriss, Exploding Myths: An Empirical and Economic Reassessment of the Rise of Employment At-Will, 59 Mo.L.Rev. 679 (1994).

2. In Payne v. Western & Atl. R.R., 81 Tenn. 507 (1884), the railroad ordered its employees to stop trading at a store owned by the plaintiff. The Supreme Court of Tennessee upheld the railroad's prerogative to discharge its employees, if it so chose, for any reason—for good cause, no cause, or bad cause. Compare Richard A. Epstein, In Defense of the Contract at Will, 51 U.Chi.L.Rev. 947 (1984) (approving result in *Payne*), with Matthew W. Finkin, "In Defense of the Contract at Will"—Some Discussion Comments and Questions, 50 J.Air L. & Comm. 727 (1985) (criticizing *Payne* and Epstein).

3. In Henry v. Pittsburgh & L.E.R. Co., 21 A. 157 (Pa.1891), a railroad ticket agent was discharged because there were financial irregularities in his department, even though there was no evidence that the agent was personally responsible. The railroad then told the local newspaper that the agent was terminated for dishonesty. The court held that no action would lie against the railroad.

4. Taken together, *Payne* and *Henry* illustrate three aspects of the common law "at will" rule: the employer was free to impose any conditions of employment, to discharge an employee at any time for any reason, and to effect the discharge in virtually any manner.

5. For an analysis of Wood's rule reaching a conclusion contrary to Feinman's, that Wood was correct in his reading of prior cases, see Mayer G. Freed & Daniel D. Polsby, The Doubtful Provenance of "Wood's Rule" Revisited, 22 Ariz.St.L.J. 551 (1990).

B. SOURCES OF MODERN EMPLOYMENT LAW

This section explores major themes in the development of contemporary employment law. In the late nineteenth century, patronage politics began to give way to a more professional, career-oriented public sector bureaucracy. Although state and federal governments have devised detailed procedures for regulating basic elements of hiring, firing, compensation, and conditions of employment, civil service laws still have not resolved the question of the permissible scope of political activities of public employees.

The rise of collective bargaining in the late nineteenth and early twentieth centuries culminated in the National Labor Relations Act or Wagner Act of 1935. Although this book addresses individual rather than collective rights, the impact of collective bargaining remains important. The union movement's political agenda often has dictated the legislative regulation of all employment and the recent decline in union density has had consequences for the rights of nonunion employees.

A third theme of this section is the increased governmental role in regulating private sector employment. Originally begun in response to the Great Depression, new waves of regulatory initiatives have centered on occupational safety and health, employee pensions, and health benefits. Is workplace regulation effective and efficient? Are we inevitably committed to increased regulation?

Beginning in the 1960s, civil rights laws were enacted at the federal and state levels to prohibit discrimination in employment on the basis of race, color, religion, sex, national origin, age, and disability. This section reviews the historical and conceptual foundations of this legislation. Subsequent chapters (especially Chapter 4) provide detailed analyses of antidiscrimination law.

The 1970s and 1980s saw the courts undertake a major reassessment of the vitality of the at-will doctrine. Recognizing that strict adherence to the doctrine would often cause harsh results, the courts in many jurisdictions carved out a series of tort and contract exceptions. This trend is summarized in this section and explored in depth in Chapter 10.

It is important to remember that, unlike tax law, commercial law, or even labor law, there is no single source of employment law. What has come to be called "employment law" is an amalgam of numerous state and federal constitutional, statutory, regulatory, and common law rights and remedies. Different assumptions and different objectives may underlie each of these attempts to interpose the law into the employment relationship. Because there is no coherent, contemporaneously adopted body of law, there are numerous gaps and overlaps. Thus, preemption and election of remedies are two recurring themes. An important and as yet unresolved issue is the legality and effect of employer-imposed arbitration procedures as a substitute for statutory protections and common law actions.

1.   CIVIL SERVICE/PUBLIC EMPLOYMENT

During the nineteenth century, the number of government employees at the federal, state, and local levels increased significantly to reflect the nation's growing and increasingly complex government. One of the many untested legal issues was whether constitutional protections, especially the First Amendment, applied to public sector employees. In the well-known case of McAuliffe v. Mayor & City of New Bedford, 29 N.E. 517 (Mass. 1892), a police officer was discharged for engaging in political activity in contravention of city police regulations. In upholding the discharge against a First Amendment challenge, Justice Oliver Wendell Holmes, Jr., famously stated: "The petitioner may have a constitutional right to talk politics, but he has no constitutional right to be a policeman." Ever since this case, legal scholars and the courts have debated the relationship between the rights of citizens and the rights of public employees. This same issue is further explored in Chapters 7 and 10.

The attempt to regularize and fairly regulate public employment gave rise to civil service laws, which have been amended by statute and clarified by regulations on a frequent basis.

Louis Lawrence Boyle, Reforming Civil Service Reform: Should the Federal Government Continue to Regulate State and Local Government Employees?*

7 J.L. & Politics 243, 268–80 (1991).

After President Garfield was assassinated in 1881 by a disgruntled office-seeker, the Pendleton Act was passed in 1883. The Supreme Court has since stated that the Pendleton Act was passed as a result of the "strong discontent with the corruption and inefficiency of the patronage system of public employment." Not only did the Pendleton Act weaken the spoils system by creating a class of federal employees who had to obtain their offices through a merit system of competitive examinations, but it also prohibited political solicitations of federal employees. This prohibition on political solicitation was continued in 1925 when Congress passed the Federal Corrupt Practices Act in response to such scandals in the Harding Administration as the Teapot Dome Scandal.

Although machine politicians like Plunkitt of Tammany Hall railed against these civil service reforms, the political party in power managed to continue receiving financial support from government employees, despite laws to the contrary. Furthermore, the patronage system, while damaged by the Pendleton Act, was not eliminated. By the turn of the century, the majority of government jobs were not subject to the Civil Service competitive examinations. Even a 1907 executive order issued by President Theodore Roosevelt, a former Civil Service Commissioner, restricting the political activity of civil service employees, did not affect a majority of the federal, state and local government employees.

Although the initial reform of the Pendleton Act was in need of additional reform, a political crisis was necessary for its implementation. Despite the brief surge for reform in response to the scandals in the Harding administration, that significant crisis came in 1939, after the political parties had again shifted in their positions of power. This time with the New Deal Democrats in control, a coalition of Republicans and anti-New Deal Democrats joined forces to pass the Hatch Act, sponsored by Senator Carl Hatch, a New Mexico Democrat. The driving force behind the Hatch Act was a series of charges that President Roosevelt had exploited Works Progress Administration relief workers and its officers, including his failed attempts to purge disloyal Democrats from the ballot in the 1938 primaries.

The 1939 Hatch Act tightened the prohibitions on the political activity of federal employees. Congress acted so quickly in considering the Hatch Act, however, that it had to be amended prior to final passage to exempt the President, the Vice President and members of Congress

---

*   Reprinted by permission.

from its restrictions, which would have prevented these federal employees from seeking re-election.

* * *

III. The Continuing Reform of the Hatch Act

When Congress passed the Hatch Act in 1939 and then extended its application to state and local government employees in 1940, protests from the states characterized the Hatch Act as "probably the most unpopular legislation ever imposed on our State and local governments." No doubt some of that protest may have been due to the intrusion of the federal government into the regulation of the political activity of state employees. An annoyance for some states is that there is no statute of limitations applicable to Hatch Act cases, so that states may be forced to terminate employment for an individual who long ago may have inadvertently violated the Hatch Act. The most egregious problem which the Hatch Act created for the states appeared in the manner in which Congress chose to have the Hatch Act enforced. Once the federal Civil Service Commission determined that an individual had violated the Hatch Act, the state or local government had two options. The state or local agency could terminate the individual's employment and not rehire that individual for at least eighteen months. Alternatively, the state or local agency where the individual had been employed would lose federal loans or grants equivalent to two years of pay at the rate the employee was receiving when he or she violated the Hatch Act. Due to their opposition to the Hatch Act, however, not all states summarily dismissed their employees for the exercise of their first amendment freedoms. The Supreme Court, in *Oklahoma v. United States Civil Service Commission*,[2] upheld the right of Congress to force state and local governments to choose between federal funds and a potentially valuable employee. To this day, Congress continues to influence state and local government policy by linking compliance with federal funds.

In an effort to appease the opposition of the state governments, Congress in 1950 amended the Hatch Act to allow the Civil Service Commission to determine whether a violation of the Hatch Act warranted removal. Although removal had previously been mandatory, it became one of two options in 1950. The second option consisted of a minimum suspension for 90 days without pay, which in 1960 was reduced to 30 days suspension without pay.

* * *

Due to the continuing protests from the states, it is not surprising that, when Congress again became zealous about reform after the Watergate incident in 1972, it turned its attention once again to reforms in the Hatch Act and even included two reforms in the same measure. In 1974, Congress amended the Hatch Act to resolve some of the states'

---

[2]   330 U.S. 127 (1946).

concerns by loosening somewhat the restrictions on the political activity of state and local government employees. When Congress passed the Hatch Act in 1939 and then extended its application to state and local employees in 1940, the state and local government employees were initially subject to the same restrictions as were federal employees. One of the changes Congress made in 1974 was to allow state and local government employees to be candidates in completely nonpartisan elections. Federal courts and administrative agencies have interpreted nonpartisan as allowing participation "only if none of the candidates could be considered partisan." Individuals seeking election as an independent or as a bipartisan candidate do not qualify for this exemption.

Another 1974 amendment was the replacement of the prohibition on taking "an active part in political management or political campaigns" with the prohibition only on being "a candidate for elective office." Federal courts have interpreted this change as allowing state and local employees to participate in political campaigns as long as they do not run for office themselves.

* * *

In 1978, in still another series of reforms, Congress replaced the Civil Service Commission with the Merit Systems Protection Board (MSPB) and potentially brought more federal employees within the coverage of the Hatch Act and the MSPB.

The MSPB now lists five permissible political activities for state and local government employees. Where appropriate, reference is made to cases illustrating these permissible activities. State and local government employees:

— May be a candidate for public office in a nonpartisan election[;]

— May campaign for and hold elective office in political clubs and organizations[;]

— May actively campaign for candidates for public office in partisan and nonpartisan elections[;]

— May contribute money to political organizations or attend political fundraising functions[; and]

— May participate in any activity not specifically prohibited by law or regulation[.]

Likewise, MSPB lists three general prohibitions on the political activity of state and local employees. Where appropriate, reference is made to cases illustrating these prohibitions. A state or local government employee may *not*:

— Use his official authority or influence for the purpose of interfering with or affecting the result of an election or a nomination for office; or

— Directly or indirectly coerce, attempt to coerce, command, or advise a [s]tate or local officer or employee to pay, lend, or contribute anything of value to a political party, committee, organization, agency, or person for a political purpose.

— Be a candidate for elective public office in a partisan election.

* * *

NOTES

1. The Hatch Act Reform Amendments of 1993, Pub.L. 103–94, conferred greater rights on public employees to engage in partisan political activity. In contrast to prior laws, an employee "may take an active part in political management or in political campaigns." There are exceptions, however, including that an individual may not: (1) solicit campaign contributions from subordinates or persons having business pending before the agency; (2) engage in political activity while on duty; (3) use government facilities or property for a political purpose; and (4) run for a partisan political office.

2. Along with the prohibition of political activity, the Hatch Act and its amendments embrace the "merit principle" in the selection and promotion of government employees. The law also contains a broad range of "prohibited personnel practices." These include discrimination based on race, color, religion, national origin, age, sex, disability, marital status, or political affiliation. Nepotism, retaliation, and other treatment violating merit principles also are prohibited.

3. As of 2019, about 22 million American workers were employed by federal, state, and local governments. For most of these workers, civil service laws control selection procedures through the use of competitive examinations and merit systems. Civil service laws also prohibit discrimination based on race, color, sex, religion, national origin, age, disability, and other classifications. Federal employees are covered by Title VII under § 717; state and local government employees were brought under the general coverage of Title VII with the 1972 Amendments.

Rutan v. Republican Party
497 U.S. 62 (1990).

■ JUSTICE BRENNAN delivered the opinion of the Court:

To the victor belong only those spoils that may be constitutionally obtained. Elrod v. Burns, 427 U.S. 347 (1976), and Branti v. Finkel, 445 U.S. 507 (1980), decided that the First Amendment forbids government officials to discharge or threaten to discharge public employees solely for not being supporters of the political party in power, unless party affiliation is an appropriate requirement for the position involved. Today we are asked to decide the constitutionality of several related political patronage practices—whether promotion, transfer, recall, and hiring decisions involving low-level public employees may be constitutionally based on party affiliation and support. We hold that they may not.

I.

The petition and cross-petition before us arise from a lawsuit protesting certain employment policies and practices instituted by Governor James Thompson of Illinois.[1] On November 12, 1980, the Governor issued an executive order proclaiming a hiring freeze for every agency, bureau, board, or commission subject to his control. The order prohibits state officials from hiring any employee, filling any vacancy, creating any new position, or taking any similar action. It affects approximately 60,000 state positions. More than 5,000 of these become available each year as a result of resignations, retirements, deaths, expansion, and reorganizations. The order proclaims that "no exceptions" are permitted without the Governor's "express permission after submission of appropriate requests to [his] office." * * *

Requests for the Governor's "express permission" have allegedly become routine. Permission has been granted or withheld through an agency expressly created for this purpose, the Governor's Office of Personnel (Governor's Office). Agencies have been screening applicants under Illinois' civil service system, making their personnel choices, and submitting them as requests to be approved or disapproved by the Governor's Office. Among the employment decisions for which approvals have been required are new hires, promotions, transfers, and recalls after layoffs.

By means of the freeze, according to petitioners, the Governor has been using the Governor's Office to operate a political patronage system to limit state employment and beneficial employment-related decisions to those who are supported by the Republican Party. In reviewing an agency's request that a particular applicant be approved for a particular position, the Governor's Office has looked at whether the applicant voted in Republican primaries in past election years, whether the applicant has provided financial or other support to the Republican Party and its candidates, whether the applicant has promised to join and work for the Republican Party in the future, and whether the applicant has the support of Republican Party officials at state or local levels. * * *

II.

In *Elrod*, we decided that a newly elected Democratic sheriff could not constitutionally engage in the patronage practice of replacing certain office staff with members of his own party "when the existing employees lack or fail to obtain requisite support from, or fail to affiliate with, that party." The plurality explained that conditioning public employment on the provision of support for the favored political party "unquestionably inhibits protected belief and association." It reasoned that conditioning

---

[1]   The cases come to us in a preliminary posture and the question is limited to whether the allegations of petitioners Rutan et al., state a cognizable First Amendment claim, sufficient to withstand respondents' motion to dismiss under Federal Rule of Civil Procedure 12(b)(6). Therefore, for purposes of our review we must assume that petitioners' well-pleaded allegations are true. * * *

employment on political activity pressures employees to pledge political allegiance to a party with which they prefer not to associate, to work for the election of political candidates they do not support, and to contribute money to be used to further policies with which they do not agree. The latter, the plurality noted, had been recognized by this Court as "tantamount to coerced belief." At the same time, employees are constrained from joining, working for or contributing to the political party and candidates of their own choice. "[P]olitical belief and association constitute the core of those activities protected by the First Amendment," the plurality emphasized. * * *

The Court then decided that the government interests generally asserted in support of patronage fail to justify this burden on First Amendment rights because patronage dismissals are not the least restrictive means for fostering those interests. The plurality acknowledged that a government has a significant interest in ensuring that it has effective and efficient employees. It expressed doubt, however, that "mere difference of political persuasion motivates poor performance" and concluded that, in any case, the government can ensure employee effectiveness and efficiency through the less drastic means of discharging staff members whose work is inadequate. The plurality also found that a government can meet its need for politically loyal employees to implement its policies by the less intrusive measure of dismissing, on political grounds, only those employees in policymaking positions. Finally, although the plurality recognized that preservation of the democratic process "may in some instances justify limitations on First Amendment freedoms," it concluded that the "process functions as well without the practice, perhaps even better." Patronage, it explained, "can result in the entrenchment of one or a few parties to the exclusion of others" and "is a very effective impediment to the associational and speech freedoms which are essential to a meaningful system of democratic government." * * *

We first address the claims of the four current or former employees. Respondents urge us to view *Elrod* and *Branti* as inapplicable because the patronage dismissals at issue in those cases are different in kind from failure to promote, failure to transfer, and failure to recall after layoff. Respondents initially contend that the employee petitioners' First Amendment rights have not been infringed because they have no entitlement to promotion, transfer, or rehire. We rejected just such an argument in *Elrod* and *Branti,* as both cases involved state workers who were employees at will with no legal entitlement to continued employment. * * *

Likewise, we find the assertion here that the employee petitioners had no legal entitlement to promotion, transfer, or recall beside the point.

Respondents next argue that the employment decisions at issue here do not violate the First Amendment because the decisions are not punitive, do not in any way adversely affect the terms of employment, and therefore do not chill the exercise of protected belief and association by public employees. This is not credible. Employees who find themselves in dead-end positions due to their political backgrounds are adversely affected. They will feel a significant obligation to support political positions held by their superiors, and to refrain from acting on the political views they actually hold, in order to progress up the career ladder. Employees denied transfers to workplaces reasonably close to their homes until they join and work for the Republican Party will feel a daily pressure from their long commutes to do so. And employees who have been laid off may well feel compelled to engage in whatever political activity is necessary to regain regular paychecks and positions corresponding to their skill and experience.

The same First Amendment concerns that underlay our decisions in *Elrod* and *Branti* are implicated here. Employees who do not compromise their beliefs stand to lose the considerable increases in pay and job satisfaction attendant to promotions, the hours and maintenance expenses that are consumed by long daily commutes, and even their jobs if they are not rehired after a "temporary" layoff. These are significant penalties and are imposed for the exercise of rights guaranteed by the First Amendment. Unless these patronage practices are narrowly tailored to further vital government interests, we must conclude that they impermissibly encroach on First Amendment freedoms.

We find, however, that our conclusions in *Elrod* and *Branti* are equally applicable to the patronage practices at issue here. A government's interest in securing effective employees can be met by discharging, demoting or transferring staffmembers whose work is deficient. A government's interest in securing employees who will loyally implement its policies can be adequately served by choosing or dismissing certain high-level employees on the basis of their political views. Likewise, the "preservation of the democratic process" is no more furthered by the patronage promotions, transfers, and rehires at issue here than it is by patronage dismissals. * * *

Petitioner James W. Moore presents the closely related question whether patronage hiring violates the First Amendment. Patronage hiring places burdens on free speech and association similar to those imposed by the patronage practices discussed above. A state job is valuable. Like most employment, it provides regular paychecks, health insurance, and other benefits. In addition, there may be openings with the State when business in the private sector is slow. There are also occupations for which the government is a major (or the only) source of employment, such as social workers, elementary school teachers, and prison guards. Thus, denial of a state job is a serious privation. * * *

Almost half a century ago, this Court made clear that the government "may not enact a regulation providing that no Republican * * * shall be appointed to federal office." Public Workers v. Mitchell, 330 U.S. 75, 100 (1947). What the First Amendment precludes the

government from commanding directly, it also precludes the government
from accomplishing indirectly. Under our sustained precedent,
conditioning hiring decisions on political belief and association plainly
constitutes an unconstitutional condition, unless the government has a
vital interest in doing so. We find no such government interest here, for
the same reasons that we found the government lacks justification for
patronage promotions, transfers or recalls. * * *

If Moore's employment application was set aside because he chose
not to support the Republican Party, as he asserts, then Moore's First
Amendment rights have been violated. Therefore, we find that Moore's
complaint was improperly dismissed.

III.

We hold that the rule of *Elrod* and *Branti* extends to promotion,
transfer, recall, and hiring decisions based on party affiliation and
support and that all of the petitioners and cross-respondents have stated
claims upon which relief may be granted. We affirm the Seventh Circuit
insofar as it remanded Rutan's, Taylor's, Standefer's, and O'Brien's
claims. However, we reverse the Circuit Court's decision to uphold the
dismissal of Moore's claim. All five claims are remanded for proceedings
consistent with this opinion. It is so ordered.

■ JUSTICE STEVENS, concurring:

To avoid the force of * * * authority * * * Justice Scalia would weigh
the supposed general state interest in patronage hiring against the
aggregated interests of the many employees affected by the practice. This
defense of patronage obfuscates the critical distinction between partisan
interest and the public interest. It assumes that governmental power and
public resources—in this case employment opportunities—may
appropriately be used to subsidize partisan activities even when the
political affiliation of the employee or the job applicant is entirely
unrelated to his or her public service. The premise on which this position
rests would justify the use of public funds to compensate party members
for their campaign work, or conversely, a legislative enactment denying
public employment to nonmembers of the majority party. If such
legislation is unconstitutional—as it clearly would be—an equally
pernicious rule promulgated by the Executive must also be invalid. * * *

The tradition that is relevant in this case is the American
commitment to examine and reexamine past and present practices
against the basic principles embodied in the Constitution. The
inspirational command by our President in 1961 is entirely consistent
with that tradition: "Ask not what your country can do for you—ask what
you can do for your country." This case involves a contrary command:
"Ask not what job applicants can do for the State—ask what they can do
for our party." Whatever traditional support may remain for a command
of that ilk, it is plainly an illegitimate excuse for the practices rejected by
the Court today.

■ JUSTICE SCALIA, with whom THE CHIEF JUSTICE and JUSTICE KENNEDY join, and with whom JUSTICE O'CONNOR joins as to Parts II and III, dissenting.

Today the Court establishes the constitutional principle that party membership is not a permissible factor in the dispensation of government jobs, except those jobs for the performance of which party affiliation is an "appropriate requirement." It is hard to say precisely (or even generally) what that exception means, but if there is any category of jobs for whose performance party affiliation is not an appropriate requirement, it is the job of being a judge, where partisanship is not only unneeded but positively undesirable. It is, however, rare that a federal administration of one party will appoint a judge from another party. And it has always been rare. See Marbury v. Madison, 1 Cranch 137 (1803). Thus, the new principle that the Court today announces will be enforced by a corps of judges (the Members of this Court included) who overwhelmingly owe their office to its violation. Something must be wrong here, and I suggest it is the Court.

* * *

The choice between patronage and the merit principle—or, to be more realistic about it, the choice between the desirable mix of merit and patronage principles in widely varying federal, state, and local political contexts—is not so clear that I would be prepared, as an original matter, to chisel a single, inflexible prescription into the Constitution. Fourteen years ago, in Elrod v. Burns, the Court did that. *Elrod* was limited however, as was the later decision of Branti v. Finkel, to patronage firings, leaving it to state and federal legislatures to determine when and where political affiliation could be taken into account in hirings and promotions. Today the Court makes its constitutional civil-service reform absolute, extending to all decisions regarding government employment. Because the First Amendment has never been thought to require this disposition, which may well have disastrous consequences for our political system, I dissent.

NOTES AND QUESTIONS

1. Patronage is as old as American government and much older in the England from which our traditions derived. Why should the Supreme Court now declare that this system is unconstitutional?

2. Justice Scalia asserts that this decision will weaken the political parties and that the result may be bad for American democracy? Do you agree?

3. Can a court-mandated civil service system be effective? How can judges create the detailed supervisory rules that nonpatronage systems require?

4. Earlier cases had barred political discrimination in discharge. Should the Constitution be held to protect the political beliefs of current employees but to allow politics to govern new hiring? How would you defend such a distinction?

5. In Borzilleri v. Mosby, 874 F.3d 187 (4th Cir. 2017), the plaintiff, an Assistant State's Attorney with nine years' service, was discharged without cause four days after the newly-elected State's Attorney took office. The plaintiff alleged she was discharged because she had supported a rival candidate in the primary. Among other things, the plaintiff argued that because assistant prosecutors are officers of the court with distinct ethical obligations in prosecuting cases, the position does not involve policymaking. The Fourth Circuit rejected this argument and agreed with all the courts of appeals to consider the issue that assistant prosecutors have broad discretionary powers and therefore occupy policymaking positions. The Baltimore City State's Attorney's office at issue in the case employed over 100 prosecutors. Does this mean that upon election the new State's Attorney could discharge and replace all of them?

6. Besides First Amendment claims involving freedom of expression and association, two other constitutional arguments are often raised by public sector employees. First, the Fourth Amendment has been used to challenge allegedly unconstitutional searches and seizures in the workplace involving property (e.g., searches of desks, lockers, and cars) and the person (e.g., urine drug testing). Second, the Fifth and Fourteenth Amendments have been the bases of due process and equal protection claims.

2. COLLECTIVE BARGAINING

From the earliest days of the American trade union movement, business sought help from the judiciary in its struggle against unionization. During the 1880s, equity courts began issuing sweeping injunctions against strike activities by the growing number of labor unions. Although the English rule initially followed by American courts did not ordinarily permit the issuance of injunctions, many railroads were in receivership and therefore under the control of equity courts, which enjoined strikes by railroad employees. In In re Debs, 158 U.S. 564 (1895), the Supreme Court upheld the contempt conviction of Eugene V. Debs of the American Railway Union for his part in the Pullman strike of 1894.

After the Pullman strike, President Cleveland appointed the United States Strike Commission to investigate the national labor scene. The Commission's report recommended that employees be permitted to organize into unions and to bargain collectively. Congress responded by passing the Erdman Act in 1898. The law was limited to employees engaged in the operation of interstate trains. It imposed criminal penalties for the discharge or threatened discharge of employees for union membership and provided for conciliation and mediation of railway labor disputes. The Act was declared unconstitutional by the Supreme Court in Adair v. United States, 208 U.S. 161 (1908).

In 1914, Congress passed the Clayton Act, §§ 6 and 20 of which provided that the antitrust laws, especially the Sherman Act, did not apply to labor unions. The Railway Labor Act, passed in 1926, provided that "collective action, without interference, influence, or coercion exercised by either party over the self-organization or designation of representatives by the other" was to be the manner of selection for representatives. The Act was upheld in Texas & New Orleans R.R. Co. v. Brotherhood of Ry. & Steamship Clerks, 281 U.S. 548 (1930).

The Norris-LaGuardia Act was enacted in 1932. The Act outlawed "yellow dog" contracts (in which workers promised not to join a union) and prohibited the federal courts from issuing injunctions in labor disputes. The following year Congress passed the National Industrial Recovery Act (NIRA). Section 7(a) of NIRA granted employees the right to organize and bargain collectively, but it was declared unconstitutional in A.L.A. Schechter Poultry Corp. v. United States, 295 U.S. 495 (1935).

Less than two months later, Congress enacted the National Labor Relations Act (NLRA or Wagner Act). The NLRA declared it to be the policy of the United States to encourage collective bargaining; established the National Labor Relations Board (NLRB) to regulate union organizing, representation elections, and unfair labor practices; gave employees the rights of self-organization and collective bargaining; and prohibited certain employer unfair labor practices.

The NLRA was held to be constitutional by the Supreme Court by a five-to-four vote, in NLRB v. Jones & Laughlin Steel Corp., 301 U.S. 1 (1937). According to Chief Justice Hughes, the NLRA "purports to reach only what may be deemed to burden or obstruct * * * commerce, and thus qualified, it must be construed as contemplating the exercise of control within constitutional bounds."

In 1938, Congress passed the Fair Labor Standards Act, which set minimum wage rates, required higher pay for overtime, and prohibited the use of child labor in goods or services involved in interstate commerce.

After World War II unions were much more powerful and largely unchecked by law. Asserting a need to return a "balance" to labor-management relations, Congress passed the Labor Management Relations Act (LMRA or Taft-Hartley Act) in 1947 over President Truman's veto. Taft-Hartley amended the NLRA to give employees the right to refrain from (as well as participate in) union activities; expanded the NLRB from three to five members; and added a series of prohibited unfair labor practices by unions.

To control internal union affairs, in 1959 Congress passed the Labor-Management Reporting and Disclosure Act (LMRDA or Landrum-Griffin). This "bill of rights" for union members requires periodic financial and other reports from unions, regulates union elections and union funds, and prohibits Communists and certain ex-felons from holding union office. The LMRDA also makes some minor changes in the NLRA.

The NLRA is based on the commerce clause and covers businesses "affecting commerce." This is determined by the dollar volume of the enterprise. The NLRA specifically excludes federal, state, and local government employees, agricultural employees, supervisory employees, and railway and airline employees (who are covered under the Railway Labor Act).

The vast majority of the NLRB's actions are concerned with: (1) conducting and certifying the results of union representation elections, which if won by the union will require the union and company to bargain in good faith over wages, hours, and terms and conditions of employment; and (2) investigating and prosecuting unfair labor practice charges brought by employees, unions, and employers.

A vast body of substantive law has developed under the NLRA during its nearly 80 years of existence. It is beyond the scope of this book to explore these developments in any detail. Nevertheless, some brief mention of NLRA law is essential for understanding the framework in which collective bargaining is regulated.

Section 8(a)(1) of the NLRA makes it an unfair labor practice for an employer "to interfere with, restrain, or coerce employees" in the exercise of their rights to self-organization and collective bargaining. An employer may not discharge or otherwise discriminate against employees for discussing unionization (especially during nonwork time and in nonwork areas), wearing union buttons and insignia, or signing union authorization cards. Republic Aviation Corp. v. NLRB, 324 U.S. 793 (1945).

Collective bargaining takes place in bargaining units comprised of employees at a single plant with similar wage scales, hours, job responsibilities, and working conditions. If 30 percent of the employees in a bargaining unit sign cards authorizing a particular union to represent them, the NLRB will order and conduct a representation election. If more than 50 percent sign cards the employer may voluntarily recognize and bargain with the union, although it need not do so. Linden Lumber Div., Summer & Co. v. NLRB, 419 U.S. 301 (1974). During the election campaign, a period of about two or three weeks, neither side may threaten or coerce voters nor promise benefits based on the outcome of the election. NLRB v. Gissel Packing Co., 395 U.S. 575 (1969). If the union loses (fails to obtain a majority), another election may not be held for at least one year. If the union wins, it is the collective bargaining representative of all the employees in the unit, regardless of whether they supported the union.

Sections 8(a)(5), 8(b)(3), and 8(d) require that the union and employer bargain in good faith over wages, hours, and other terms and conditions of employment. The NLRA does not require that both sides reach an agreement, only that they meet and confer, and bargain in good faith. If an agreement is reached, it will set out the wages, hours, and terms of employment. Most collective bargaining agreements set out disciplinary procedures and prohibit the discharge of employees unless there is "just cause." Grievances and disputes between labor and management are usually subject to arbitration in accordance with the collective bargaining agreement.

Unions sometimes strike to pressure an employer into making concessions in collective bargaining. The primary strike is legal under the NLRA, but secondary strikes (against customers and suppliers) usually are not and may be enjoined by the courts. Although the employer may not discharge employees engaged in protected, concerted activity (including the primary strike), the Supreme Court has held that the employer may hire permanent replacements. NLRB v. Mackay Radio & Tel. Co., 304 U.S. 333 (1938). In effect, strikers may lose their jobs and need only be placed on a preferential hiring list for the next available opening. If the employees strike simply to protest employer unfair labor practices the employer may hire only temporary replacements.

Charges of unfair labor practices must be filed with the NLRB within six months of their alleged occurrence. The General Counsel of the NLRB has unreviewable discretion in deciding whether to proceed with an unfair labor practice charge. Initial adjudications are made by an administrative law judge and are then subject to review by the five-member NLRB. Appeals and petitions for enforcement then may be filed in the United States Courts of Appeal. NLRB remedies are usually limited to back pay, reinstatement, orders to bargain, and cease and desist orders.

NOTE ON UNION SECURITY

An important aspect of an individual's employment relationship concerns whether the individual can be required to or prohibited from joining a union or paying dues or other fees to a union. Section 3 of the Norris-LaGuardia Act, enacted in 1932, proscribes "*yellow dog contracts*," in which the employee promises not to join a union. In 1935, when the Wagner Act (NLRA) was passed, section 7 declared that employees have the right "to form, join, or assist labor organizations." Thus, although employees could not be prohibited from joining a union, there was no provision that prohibited requiring an employee to join a union as a condition of obtaining or retaining employment.

A union security clause is a provision in a collective bargaining agreement that describes the obligations of employees to support the union. The most demanding provision is one providing for a *closed shop*. A closed shop provision obligates the employer to hire only union members and to discharge employees who drop or lose their membership. Under the NLRA the closed shop was legal. Congress was concerned that the closed shop had caused disruptive union activity and had been used to oust dissenters from their jobs by expelling them from union membership. In 1947, the Taft-Hartley Act amended section 7 to add that employees also have the right to refrain from union activity, except "to the extent that such right may be affected by an agreement requiring membership in a labor organization as a condition of employment as authorized in section 8(a)(3)." Section 8(a)(3) outlawed the closed shop by adding a grace period of at least 30 days before an employee can be required to pay union dues or fees. It also banned union fees and dues unless membership is made available to the employee on the same terms as to other members and prohibited an employer from discharging an employee for nonmembership in a union if the employer "has reasonable grounds for believing that membership was denied or terminated for reasons other than the failure of the employee to tender the periodic dues and the initiation fees uniformly required as a condition of acquiring or retaining membership."

Section 8(a)(3) therefore legalizes the *union shop,* whereby an employee may be required to become a union member in order to retain a job, although the employee need not be a member at the time of hiring and has a grace period of at least 30 days to join the union. In NLRB v. General Motors Corp., 373 U.S. 734 (1963), the Supreme Court construed quite narrowly § 8(a)(3)'s use of the word "membership."

> It is permissible to condition employment upon membership, but membership, insofar as it has significance to employment rights, may in turn be conditioned only upon payment of fees and dues. "Membership" as a condition of employment is whittled down to its financial core.

Id. at 742.

Although the union shop is legal, in reality, the most demanding provision enforceable is one that mandates an *agency shop,* in which employees need not join the union but are required to pay the union an amount equal to the union's initiation fees and dues. There is one important difference between a union shop and an agency shop. Pursuant to many union constitutions, union discipline (e.g., honoring strikes) may be maintained through the assessment of fines enforceable in state court. Thus, while the agency shop eliminates the problem of "free riders" benefitting from union services without paying, union control is weakened. In 1980, Congress amended section 19 of the NLRA to permit employees with bona fide religious objections to joining or financially supporting labor organizations to contribute an equivalent amount of money to an approved charity. (The permissible reach of union security arrangements for government employees is even narrower. In Davenport v. Washington Educ. Ass'n, 551 U.S. 177 (2007), the Supreme Court held that the First Amendment's guarantee of freedom of association prohibits a public sector union from collecting agency fees for political activities to which nonunion members object. According to the Court, agency fees could only be *required* for reasonable costs of contract negotiation and administration.)

In Janus v. AFSCME, 138 S.Ct. 2448 (2018), an Illinois public sector employer, whose employees were represented by AFSCME, charged all employees an agency (or "fair share") fee equal to about 78% of union dues for contract administration and other union expenses. The fee excluded union costs for lobbying and political activity. Nevertheless, the Supreme

Court, five-to-four, in an opinion by Justice Alito, held that charging agency fees against unwilling employees amounted to a violation of the First Amendment. In so ruling, the Court overruled Abood v. Detroit Board of Education, 431 U.S. 209 (1977). In dissent, Justice Kagan wrote that there was no justification for overruling established precedent that was workable and on which numerous public employers and employees relied.

Another important change in union security made by the Taft-Hartley amendments is the enactment of section 14(b), which prohibits an agreement requiring membership in a labor organization as a condition of employment in any state or territory with a contrary state law. ("Membership" includes financial contribution under an agency shop. Retail Clerks Local 1625 v. Schermerhorn, 373 U.S. 746 (1963).) Pursuant to section 14(b), nearly half the states, almost all in the south and west, have enacted *right to work laws* proscribing union membership as a condition of employment. For unions, this means that they have both the discipline and free-rider problems. Union density in right to work states is much lower than in states without such laws.

The conservative shift in state legislatures has resulted in the enactment of more state right to work laws. As of 2020, there were right to work laws in 28 states, including the mid-western states of Indiana, Iowa, Michigan, Missouri, Nebraska, and Wisconsin. For a further discussion, see Raymond L. Hogler, The End of American Labor Unions: The Right-to-Work Movement and the Erosion of Collective Bargaining (2015).

Paul C. Weiler, Governing the Workplace*
7–13 (1990).

The Rise and Decline of Collective Bargaining

Unquestionably, thirty years ago one would not have dreamed of settling such a contentious issue as drug testing through the use of legal authority in the civil jury process. The favored instrument, instead, would have been direct voluntary negotiation between the employer and a union which the employees had selected for purposes of collective bargaining. Sometimes such problems were explicitly addressed by the parties, which would negotiate detailed programs to deal with them. Alternatively, the matters might first have arisen under the umbrella of the general contract protection against unjust discipline and discharge, and been taken through the grievance arbitration procedure for resolution. Even that process was ultimately subject to the control of the immediate parties, who could select and remove their arbitrators as well as revise arbitration rulings for future cases.

In the eyes of its proponents the institution of collective bargaining had several important virtues. First, while a solitary employee—a Barbara Luck, for example—would probably have little realistic chance

     *   Reprinted by permission of the publishers from GOVERNING THE WORKPLACE by Paul C. Weiler, Cambridge, Mass.: Harvard University Press, Copyright © 1990 by the President and Fellows of Harvard College.

of avoiding either invasion of privacy by a drug test or loss of her job if she refused to provide a urine sample, her prospects would be much better if she were to band together with all her fellow employees in pursuit of that goal. At a minimum, such an association would provide a forum in which the employees could discuss and formulate their concerns, then use a skilled representative to voice their position to a management team representing the employer, and in all likelihood exert considerable influence on the design, if not the existence, of any drug testing program.

At the same time, any restraints on management prerogatives would be those that had been mutually accepted by the parties themselves, given their respective needs and priorities. In other employment relationships in which the participants had different views about what was important, they were free to go their own way on this and other issues. Indeed, the initial judgments made in the original setting were equally open to renegotiation as experience seemed to dictate. Nor is this just an imaginary scenario with respect to the drug issue itself. Inveterate readers of the sports pages will have observed essentially that scenario unfolding as collective bargaining in the several professional sports has grappled in a variety of ways with the common problem of drugs and testing throughout the eighties.

In sum, collective bargaining was and is a governance mechanism which offers employees a blend of *protection* and *participation* through private, local, and voluntary settlement of workplace problems. However, the existence and shape of the institution itself is assumed to be a matter of public concern and is thus the object of substantial legal support and influence. A half century ago the National Labor Relations Act (NLRA) was enacted to encourage the organization of employees for purposes of collective bargaining whenever employees in a work unit favored that option; to protect the employees in question from coercion and restraint in making their choice; and to require the employer to recognize and deal with any union that might be selected by a majority of the employees. Since the mid-thirties, then, our federal labor policy has been to facilitate the *reconstruction* of the unfettered individualistic labor market so as to give employees greater group leverage in dealing with what were often large, powerful corporate employers. But the actual terms and conditions of employment which flowed from the bargaining process were, with rare exceptions, determined by the mutual agreement of the parties. The content of their agreement would reflect the parties' respective needs and resources, shaped both by the state of the labor market and by the external product and capital markets in which the firm and its employees had to operate.

For the first twenty years of its life, this New Deal labor policy was highly successful in its own terms. The scope of union representation in collective bargaining, which had been roughly 15 percent of the private sector labor force just before enactment of the NLRA, soared to nearly 40 percent by the mid-fifties; all indications were that this figure would rise to 45 or even 50 percent some time thereafter. Indeed, the influence of the union movement was actually much broader than the direct measures of "union density" might indicate. The core of union membership was male, blue-collar production workers in manufacturing industries, many of whom were employed by the larger, more successful firms—such as General Motors, U.S. Steel, and General Electric—which were pacesetters in sophisticated management techniques. Thus the human resource innovations developed in collective bargaining between these firms and their unions soon set a pattern which was imitated by unionized firms for their nonunion white-collar workers, and by nonunion firms for both their blue-collar and white-collar labor force.

In the mid-fifties there began a remarkable turnaround in the fortunes of collective bargaining, and the institution started on a long and inexorable downhill slide. Associated with the decline was an equally marked change in the composition of the work force. The pendulum swung from manufacturing to service industries, from blue-collar to white-collar jobs, from an almost exclusively male work force to a high percentage of female workers, and from the northern to the southern regions of the country. The established unions found that they could not put down substantial roots among the new and growing segments of the labor force (at least in the private if not the public sector); therefore, even if these unions had been able to maintain their existing positions in their traditional constituencies, their proportionate statistical share of the overall labor force would decrease.

But starting in the early seventies, union coverage began to fall even in its traditional bastions. Union representation typically suffers significant attrition when already organized plants are closed and firms go out of business. That trend was even more pronounced in the early eighties, when the "rust belt" reeled under the pressures of intensified foreign competition and a deep recession. Just to stay even, unions annually had to organize their proportionate share of the workers in the new plants and firms which opened to supply new markets. But the dominant industrial unions such as the United Auto Workers, the Steel Workers, the Electrical Workers, the Teamsters, and the construction building trades were not able to secure bargaining rights in many of the new units, either in the fast-growing "sun belt" or even in the north. By the mid-eighties, then, private sector union coverage had fallen from its 40 percent share in the mid-fifties to just over 15 percent only three decades later. Recall that the latter was roughly the same percentage as had obtained a half-century earlier, when the Wagner Act was enacted in order to expand the prospects for collective employee action. [By 2019, union membership in the private sector had fallen to 6.4%—eds.].

* * *

With respect to the apparent decline in employee demand, two factors seem to be operating side by side. One is that human resource management by many American employers has become more professional, more sophisticated, and more attuned to the needs and interests of the employees. Increasingly sustained efforts are being made to provide decent wages and benefits, to eliminate unfair treatment of individual employees, and to produce a secure and congenial workplace environment. Part of the reason for the improvement in personnel practice is the expectation that it will attract and retain a high-quality, well-motivated work force. Needless to say, another powerful factor is the employer's hope that such measures will head off any felt need among the employees to explore an alternative instrument—unionization—to secure favorable conditions on the job.

At the same time there has been a gradual alteration in the character of unionism itself. From one perspective, unionization has been and can be viewed as an *activity* of the employees themselves, whereby they participate as a group in the improvement of their own working conditions. In its current image, though, the union is usually perceived as an *entity* external to the employees: as a large, bureaucratic organization whose full-term officials periodically negotiate a long-term contract behind closed doors with the employer, and then represent a fairly small number of employees who are aggrieved by the way management administers the contract during its lifetime.

NOTES AND QUESTIONS

1.   In the U.S., widespread opposition to unions among employers has spurred the growth of numerous "management consultants" who advise companies how to thwart union organizing activity, defeat unions in NLRB elections, and frustrate unions in collective bargaining. Indeed, many corporate personnel policies are designed to preempt unions. Why are American employers so anti-union? Why are American employees less willing to commit themselves to the union movement?

2.   During the last 50 years, despite problems in organizing workers and at the bargaining table, unions have had a fair degree of success in the political arena. Due in no small part to union support laws have been enacted on employment discrimination, safety and health, and pensions. From a union perspective, sweeping national reform may be more efficient and effective than individual collective bargaining. Also, by establishing minimum standards for all employers, unionized employers (and their employees) are not at a competitive disadvantage with regard to nonunion employers. Is it also possible, however, that unions are contributing to their own demise? With the government mandating nondiscrimination, safety and health, and other matters perhaps workers have less need for unions. Would a statutory prohibition against unjust dismissal be the death knell for unions? In Western Europe there are both comprehensive social legislation and union density. Why not here?

3.   For a further discussion of these issues, see Kate Adrias, The New Labor Law, 126 Yale L. J. 2 (2016); Rick Bales, Resurrecting Labor, 77 Md. L. Rev.

1 (2017); Cynthia L. Estlund, The Ossification of American Labor Law, 102 Colum. L. Rev. 1527 (2002).

3.   GOVERNMENT REGULATION OF EMPLOYMENT

Katherine V.W. Stone, From Widgets to Digits: Employment Regulation for the Changing Workplace*
122–123 (2004).

While the New Deal employment system provided job security and relative prosperity to many, it also created an invidious division between insiders and outsiders, a division that often fell along racial and gender lines. The primary sector—the unionized workforce within large firms—was the privileged core, made up primarily of white men. As a core, it generated a periphery in which women, minorities, migrant workers, and rural Americans were clustered. The labor laws and the employment practices of large firms reinforced a sharp divide between those inside and those outside the corporate family. Insiders benefited from the collective bargaining laws and the implicit job security of the internal labor market; outsiders had neither. However, in the New Deal system, outsiders were covered by two other types of labor laws—minimal employment standards and, from the 1960s, employment discrimination laws.

Federal and state employment laws provided a safety net and set a floor of benefits for those workers who remained outside the bilateral collective bargaining system. The minimum wage and unemployment compensation laws were originally conceived as a safety net to set a floor for labor conditions for those not protected by the collective bargaining system. Over the past thirty years, the employment laws have expanded in number and scope as the extent of the collective bargaining system has contracted. In the 1970s, individual employment protections were expanded by national legislation to provide occupational safety and health protection and pension insurance, expanded protection against discrimination for government employees and pregnant women, and, in the Civil Service Reform Act of 1978, protection for federal employee whistleblowers who reported employer wrong-doing. In the 1980s, the federal government enacted the Worker Adjustment and Retraining Notification Act (WARN) requiring that employers give their employees advance notice of plant closings and mass layoffs, and the Employee Polygraph [Protection] Act to provide protection for worker privacy interests. In the same period, numerous states enacted legislation to protect the job security, privacy, dignity, and other concerns of

---

employees. Thus, as union density declined in the private sector, statutory protections became the main source of worker rights.

4. NONDISCRIMINATION

One great achievement of the civil rights movement of the 1960s was enactment of the Civil Rights Act of 1964, Title VII of which prohibits discrimination in employment on the basis of race, color, religion, sex, or national origin. The law is notable for numerous reasons, including the theoretical bases and premises underlying its provisions.

Title VII was enacted to redress the wide disparity in unemployment rates and income levels between whites and minorities, primarily African Americans. Although Title VII was the first major, modern, federal employment discrimination statute, it must be considered as part of the overall effort to protect and promote civil rights. For example, Titles II and VI of the Civil Rights Act of 1964 prohibit discrimination in public accommodations and government services. Other legislation enacted at this time included the Voting Rights Act of 1965 and Title VIII of the Civil Rights Act of 1968, which prohibits discrimination in housing.

Because of its civil rights focus, Title VII was not intended to contain a comprehensive prohibition of all irrational or unfair practices of employers. Attacks on the employment at will doctrine, at least with regard to wrongful discharge, would begin in earnest over the next two decades. Title VII was intended to address invidious discrimination in discrete categories: race, color, religion, sex, and national origin. Two other bases of discrimination, age and disability, were addressed by separate legislation enacted in 1967 (the Age Discrimination in Employment Act) and 1990 (the Americans with Disabilities Act).

When Title VII was first proposed, it did not include protection against gender-based discrimination. Representative Howard W. Smith (D.Va.) was seeking to kill Title VII, and he thought that including the ban on sex discrimination would make the law unsupportable by many of his colleagues. To his surprise and chagrin, the amendment adding sex to the bill was overwhelmingly passed. Newer scholarship has emphasized the efforts of such groups as the National Woman's Party to lay the groundwork for laws prohibiting discrimination in employment on the basis of gender. See, e.g., Jo Freeman, How "Sex" Got into Title VII: Persistent Opportunism as a Maker of Public Policy, 9 L. & Inequality 163 (1991).

Even though Title VII was designed to address the economic consequences of discrimination, it is clear that protection against psychic and dignitary harms is an important part of the Title VII scheme. "The psychological injury inflicted by generalizations based on race is compounded by the frustrating and cumulative nature of their material injuries. Racial generalizations are pervasive and have traditionally operated in the same direction—to the disadvantage of members of the minority group. . . . As door after door is shut in one's face, the individual acts of discrimination combine into a systematic and grossly inequitable frustration of opportunity." Paul Brest, Foreword: In Defense of the Antidiscrimination Principle, 90 Harv. L. Rev. 1, 10 (1976). See also Larry Alexander, What Makes Wrongful Discrimination Wrongful? Biases, Preferences, Stereotypes, and Proxies, 141 U. Pa. L. Rev. 149 (1992).

Title VII prohibits five categories of discrimination (race, color, religion, sex, national origin). Some judges, lawyers, and commentators imprecisely say that to bring a case alleging discrimination under Title VII the plaintiff must be "a member of a protected class." Generally, this statement is intended to mean that the plaintiff must be in a disfavored group along the dimensions subject to Title VII, such as nonwhites, women, or members of a minority religion. In fact, Title VII does *not* speak of protected classes; it proscribes discrimination based on five criteria. Thus, all people (members of majority as well as minority groups) are covered by Title VII if they are subject to employment discrimination for the unlawful reason of race, color, religion, sex, or national origin.

An important, unresolved issue is whether the purpose of Title VII is to achieve equal opportunity or equal results. If equal treatment prospectively does not lead to equal results (e.g., because of a long history of unequal treatment and unequal opportunity), then what steps, if any, are permissible for an employer to undertake voluntarily or for a court to order to lead to equal results? See Owen M. Fiss, A Theory of Fair Employment Laws, 38 U. Chi. L. Rev. 235 (1971).

5. MODIFICATION OF THE AT-WILL RULE

Daniel J. Libenson, Leasing Human Capital: Toward a New Foundation for Employment Termination Law*

27 Berkley J. Emp. & Lab. L. 111, 127–129 (2006).

* * *

Whatever the scholarly view of employment at will and what should replace it, legislatures and courts have done something that no scholar supports. They have created piecemeal exceptions to the at-will rule in a hodgepodge of statutes and common law rulings. Although one scholar has predicted the at-will rule's "impending death" based on the increasing number of exceptions, a powerful ghost still looms. The law governing employment termination lies somewhere along a continuum between at-will and good cause, but no one can say precisely where. And

---

to the extent that we can say where the law is, it is hard to say why, and it would be foolhardy to rest assured that it will stay there.

* * *

Motivated perhaps by the concerns raised by academics, state courts have used common law contract and tort principles to chip away at the employment-at-will rule. Many courts, for example, have recognized a tort of "wrongful discharge" when the discharge is contrary to public policy, such as when employees are fired for refusing to commit perjury, serving on juries, whistleblowing, or engaging in political speech. The breadth of this wrongful discharge tort varies tremendously. In one scholar's view, a few states "have, for all intents and purposes, adopted the position that a cause of action arises anytime a termination is based on . . . anything that undermines the broad notion of public good as defined by the courts," something close to Blades's abusive discharge tort. But most states require that the violated public policy is "clearly established" in a statute, constitution, or other specific source of law.

Courts have also stretched contract principles to limit the right to fire. Although early decisions held that an employers' right to fire could be limited only if they had contractually agreed to a specific durational term, courts have been willing to interpret less than definitive statements as establishing such a contractual agreement. Many courts have also been willing to find evidence in employee handbooks and policy manuals that the employer has contractually bound itself not to fire at will, but in a legal-evolutionary arms race, employers have learned to evade such a finding by putting disclaimers of contractual intent in handbooks. Terminated employees have also urged courts with occasional success to hold that the covenant of good faith and fair dealing, which is implied by law in every contract, means that termination may be for good cause only.

It is difficult to say what has motivated legislatures and courts to move away from the at-will rule in this limited fashion. To be sure, many exceptions to the rule vindicate important social policies such as protection of racial minorities and whistleblowers, and others purport simply to apply tort and contract principles to the employment relationship. But the haphazard nature of the exceptions and courts' applications of them also suggests that the exception doctrines are embraced and stretched by courts eager to correct what they see as unjust firings. In this view, the exceptions are resisted and narrowed by courts more sympathetic to employers. The result of this doctrinal tug of war is that employers and employees find it difficult to predict whether a given termination will stand up to judicial scrutiny.

* * *

The common law and statutory exceptions have gone far beyond what the defenders of employment at will view as justified by market failure and not nearly far enough for the scholars who believe that employees have a right to keep their jobs as long as they have not given good cause to be fired. Employers find the current landscape of employment termination law difficult to navigate and have reacted with extreme defensive measures to minimize the risk of lawsuits. These defensive measures include criminal background checks, credit searches, personality testing, involving human resources professionals and lawyers to document disciplinary matters in great detail, failing to fire poor performing employees who deserve to be fired and who are creating extra work for other employees, and enacting inflexible rules and policies that damage the human relationships in the workplace. These defensive measures are extremely expensive and demoralizing to employers and employees alike. Most employees, on the other hand, probably feel no more or less secure than they would without these protections; Pauline Kim's data [see infra at 995] suggest that most employees think they have more protection than they actually do, and the ones who know the law probably realize that they would have a hard time finding a lawyer and winning a case even if they were fired under questionable circumstances.

NOTES

1. The Restatement (Third) of Employment Law follows the traditional employment at will rule, subject to several judicially developed and legislatively imposed exceptions. Section 2.01 describes the "default rule" as follows: "Either party may terminate an employment relationship with or without cause unless the right to do so is limited by statute, other law or public policy, or an [express or implied] agreement, binding employer promise, or binding employer statement."

2. For a complete discussion of wrongful discharge litigation, see Chapter 10.

Yardley v. Hospital Housekeeping Systems, LLC

470 S.W.3d 800 (Tenn. 2015).

■ SHARON G. LEE, CHIEF JUSTICE.

We accepted a question of law certified by the United States District Court for the Middle District of Tennessee to determine whether a job applicant has a cause of action under the Tennessee Workers' Compensation Act against a prospective employer for failure to hire if the prospective employer failed to hire the job applicant because that applicant had filed, or is likely to file, a workers' compensation claim against a previous employer, and if such a cause of action exists, what standard should apply. We hold that there is no cause of action for failure to hire under the Tennessee Workers' Compensation Act.

Factual and Procedural Background

Beginning in 1998, Kighwaunda M. Yardley worked as a housekeeping aide at the University Medical Center ("the Hospital") in

Lebanon. In 2010, Ms. Yardley was hurt on the job and began receiving workers' compensation benefits. Between June 2010 and September 2012, she received medical treatment for her injury. As of July 1, 2012, she was performing light duty work for the Hospital's materials management group with the expectation that when released to full duty, she would return to her job as a housekeeping aide.

On January 1, 2012, the Hospital entered into a contract with Hospital Housekeeping Systems ("the Company"), whereby the Company agreed to provide housekeeping services for the Hospital beginning July 1, 2012. As part of its contract, the Company agreed to interview the Hospital's current housekeeping employees and, at the Company's discretion, hire the employees to continue in their positions. The Company hired most of the Hospital's housekeeping staff. As of July 1, 2012, Ms. Yardley had neither been interviewed nor hired because she was still on light duty. When Ms. Yardley was released to full duty, she sought to return to work in the housekeeping department. The Hospital referred her to the Company for employment. In August 2012, she spoke with the Company's Division Vice President, Michael Cox, who, according to Ms. Yardley, told her that the Company would not hire anyone receiving workers' compensation benefits. In an email to the Company, Mr. Cox said that Ms. Yardley had "been out on Workers['] Comp with the hospital long before [the Company's] arrival," that her shoulder was hurting her again, and that "[b]ringing her on board with [the Company] would seem to be a Workers['] Comp claim waiting to happen." Mr. Cox said he "would advise against [hiring Ms. Yardley] IF we have that option." After she was not hired, Ms. Yardley sued the Company in the United States District Court for the Middle District of Tennessee.

We accepted the following certified question of law from the federal district court: If a prospective employer refuses to hire a job applicant because that applicant had filed, or is likely to file, a workers' compensation claim incurred while working for a previous employer, can that applicant maintain a cause of action under the Workers' Compensation Act ("the Act") against the prospective employer for failure to hire, and if such a claim exists, should courts apply the motivating factor standard of causation, as they do with retaliatory discharge claims?

Analysis

* * *

This is a case of first impression. In Tennessee, there is no statutory or common law cause of action for retaliatory failure to hire. Ms. Yardley asks this Court to create this cause of action. Relying on public policy grounds and retaliatory discharge cases from this and other jurisdictions, Ms. Yardley argues that if employers can lawfully refuse to hire job applicants because applicants have filed, or are likely to file, workers' compensation claims, this action by employers will have a chilling effect on workers' decisions to file claims and obtain their rightful remedies under the Act. She also asserts that if employers are allowed to refuse to hire applicants on such a basis, it would frustrate the purpose of the Second Injury Fund, see Tenn. Code Ann. § 50–6–208 (2014), which the Legislature established to encourage the hiring of workers who have suffered previous injuries. Amicus curiae Tennessee Employment Lawyers Association argues that an employer's failure to hire a job applicant because the applicant asserted a claim for compensation against a previous employer constitutes a device that would relieve an employer of an obligation under the Act; such devices are prohibited by Tennessee Code Annotated section 50–6–114 (2014).

The Company and amicus curiae Tennessee Defense Lawyers Association oppose the creation of a cause of action for retaliatory failure to hire. They argue that there was no employer-employee relationship between Ms. Yardley and the Company and, therefore, the retaliatory discharge cases cited by Ms. Yardley are distinguishable. They contend that Tennessee's employment-at-will doctrine should be protected, that employers should be free to hire and fire as they choose, and that an exception to the employment-at-will doctrine should not be made in this case.

* * *

One exception to the employment-at-will doctrine is that an at-will employee may not be fired for taking an action encouraged by public policy. Filing a workers' compensation claim is an action encouraged by public policy. Therefore, an employer may not lawfully discharge an employee for filing a workers' compensation claim. An employee who believes that she has been fired for filing a workers' compensation claim may bring a claim for retaliatory discharge. This cause of action was recognized "to enforce the duty of the employer, to secure the rights of the employee[,] and to carry out the intention of the [L]egislature."

To decide whether a job applicant may bring a retaliatory failure to hire action against a prospective employer, we start by examining Tennessee Code Annotated section 50–6–114(a). When interpreting statutes, our primary function is to carry out the Legislature's intent without broadening the statute beyond its intended scope. To carry out this function, we presume that every word in a statute has meaning and purpose and should be given full effect, as long as the result does not violate the Legislature's obvious intent. When the statutory language is clear and unambiguous, we simply apply its plain meaning.

Tennessee Code Annotated section 50–6–114 provides, in part, "No contract or agreement, written or implied, or rule, regulation or other device, shall in any manner operate to relieve any employer . . . of any obligation created by this chapter. . . ." Although an employer's decision to fire an employee for filing a worker's compensation claim has been held to be an unlawful device, this holding does not apply to Ms. Yardley because she was not an employee of the Company. The Act applies to employers and employees. An employer is defined as "any individual, firm, association or corporation . . . using the services of not less than five (5) persons for pay." An employee is defined as a "person . . . in the service of an employer . . . under any contract of hire or apprenticeship, written or implied." Under this definition, Ms. Yardley was not an employee, but merely a job applicant. As such, the Company had no obligation to her under the Act.

Ms. Yardley argues that retaliatory discharge cases are analogous. The elements of a common law prima facie case for a workers' compensation retaliatory discharge claim are: (1) the plaintiff was an employee of the defendant at the time of the injury; (2) the plaintiff made a claim against the defendant for workers' compensation benefits; (3) the defendant terminated the plaintiff's employment; and (4) the claim for workers' compensation benefits was a substantial factor in the employer's motivation to terminate the employee's employment.

Ms. Yardley cites a number of retaliatory discharge cases to support her position and argues that the Tennessee and out-of-state cases cited form the basis for a retaliatory failure-to-hire cause of action. But these cases are distinguishable, as they all involve parties who had been in an employer-employee relationship with each other at the time the tort allegedly occurred. Ms. Yardley was not an employee of the Company, and thus, there was never a relationship. This is an important distinction. The employer-employee relationship involves mutual acquiescence, and certain levels of trust and dependence are created upon its formation. Both parties have rights and responsibilities that naturally flow from that relationship and which are not present before the relationship is formed. For this reason, failure to hire cannot be equated with termination of employment, as employees and job applicants are on different footing.

A few states have statutory provisions expressly allowing claims for retaliatory failure to hire. See, e.g., Fla. Stat. § 440.105(2)(a) 2 (2015); 775 Ill. Comp. Stat. Ann. 5/6–101 (2015); La. Rev. Stat. Ann. 23:1361 (2014); Me. Rev. Stat. tit. 5, § 4572 (2014); Mass. Gen. Laws Ann. ch. 152, § 75B (2015). Tennessee does not. We have found no judicial decision recognizing a claim for retaliatory failure to hire under state common law or public policy, and a number of courts have expressly refused to recognize such claims. See, e.g., Baker v. Campbell Cnty. Bd. of Educ., 180 S.W.3d 479, 484 (Ky. Ct. App. 2005) (holding that no cause of action exists under Kentucky public policy for retaliatory failure to hire); see also Peck v. Elyria Foundry Co., 347 Fed. Appx. 139, 148 (6th Cir. 2009) (declining to recognize failure-to-hire claims as a public policy exception to the employment-at-will doctrine under Ohio law); Sanchez v. Philip Morris, Inc., 992 F.2d 244, 249 (10th Cir. 1993) (declining to recognize common law failure-to-hire claims under Oklahoma law); Wordekemper v. W. Iowa Homes & Equip., Inc., 262 F. Supp.2d 973, 988 (N.D. Iowa

2003) (noting that "Iowa has never recognized a cause of action for retaliatory failure to hire or rehire a prospective employee based on that employee's past workers' compensation claims"); cf. Warnek v. ABB Combustion Eng'g Servs., Inc., P.2d 453, 455–57 (Wash. 1999) (declining to recognize a common law claim for failure to rehire an employee on the basis of filing a workers' compensation claim, as "[t]here is a distinction between discharge . . . during the course of employment and not being rehired for new employment").

Ms. Yardley argues that if employers may legally refuse to hire job applicants because they have current or prospective workers' compensation claims, then employees will be discouraged from filing such claims. We find the alleged harm to be too speculative to justify an exception to the employment-at-will doctrine. This State has an interest in ensuring that its citizens have access to employment and the ability to earn a livelihood, but at the same time, employers should have freedom to choose their employees.

* * *

Conclusion

We respectfully decline to create an exception to the employment-at-will doctrine, and we therefore hold that a job applicant does not have a cause of action under the Tennessee Workers' Compensation Act against a prospective employer for failure to hire if the prospective employer refused to hire the job applicant because that applicant had filed, or is likely to file, a workers' compensation claim against a previous employer.

NOTE

At common law an employer could hire or fire any employee at will. Judicial limitations on the at will rule have been concerned exclusively with wrongful discharge. Why have the courts been unwilling to create a cause of action in tort or contract for wrongful refusal to hire? See generally Mark A. Rothstein, Wrongful Refusal to Hire: Attacking the Other Half of the Employment-At-Will Rule, 24 Conn.L.Rev. 97 (1991).

6. ARBITRATION

Epic Systems Corp. v. Lewis
138 S.Ct. 1612 (2018).

■ JUSTICE GORSUCH delivered the opinion of the Court.

* * *

I.

The three cases before us differ in detail but not in substance. Take *Ernst & Young LLP v. Morris*. There Ernst & Young and one of its junior accountants, Stephen Morris, entered into an agreement providing that they would arbitrate any disputes that might arise between them. The agreement stated that the employee could choose the arbitration provider and that the arbitrator could "grant any relief that could be granted by . . . a court" in the relevant jurisdiction. The agreement also specified individualized arbitration, with claims "pertaining to different [e]mployees [to] be heard in separate proceedings."

After his employment ended, and despite having agreed to arbitrate claims against the firm, Mr. Morris sued Ernst & Young in federal court. He alleged that the firm had misclassified its junior accountants as professional employees and violated the federal Fair Labor Standards Act (FLSA) and California law by paying them salaries without overtime pay. Although the arbitration agreement provided for individualized proceedings, Mr. Morris sought to litigate the federal claim on behalf of a nationwide class under the FLSA's collective action provision, 29 U.S.C. § 216(b). He sought to pursue the state law claim as a class action under Federal Rule of Civil Procedure 23.

Ernst & Young replied with a motion to compel arbitration. The district court granted the request, but the Ninth Circuit reversed this judgment. The Ninth Circuit recognized that the Arbitration Act generally requires courts to enforce arbitration agreements as written. But the court reasoned that the statute's "saving clause," removes this obligation if an arbitration agreement violates some other federal law. And the court concluded that an agreement requiring individualized arbitration proceedings violates the NLRA by barring employees from engaging in the "concerted activit[y]," of pursuing claims as a class or collective action.

Judge Ikuta dissented. In her view, the Arbitration Act protected the arbitration agreement from judicial interference and nothing in the Act's saving clause suggested otherwise. Neither, she concluded, did the NLRA demand a different result. Rather, that statute focuses on protecting unionization and collective bargaining in the workplace, not on guaranteeing class or collective action procedures in disputes before judges or arbitrators.

Although the Arbitration Act and the NLRA have long coexisted— they date from 1925 and 1935, respectively—the suggestion they might conflict is something quite new. Until a couple of years ago, courts more or less agreed that arbitration agreements like those before us must be enforced according to their terms.

The National Labor Relations Board's general counsel expressed much the same view in 2010. Remarking that employees and employers "can benefit from the relative simplicity and informality of resolving claims before arbitrators," the general counsel opined that the validity of such agreements "does not involve consideration of the policies of the National Labor Relations Act."

But recently things have shifted. In 2012, the Board—for the first time in the 77 years since the NLRA's adoption—asserted that the NLRA effectively nullifies the Arbitration Act in cases like ours. D.R. Horton, Inc., 357 N.L.R.B. 2277. Initially, this agency decision received a cool reception in court. In the last two years, though, some circuits have either agreed with the Board's conclusion or thought themselves obliged to defer to it under Chevron U.S.A. Inc. v. Natural Resources Defense Council, Inc., 467 U.S. 837 (1984). More recently still, the disagreement has grown as the Executive has disavowed the Board's (most recent) position, and the Solicitor General and the Board have offered us battling briefs about the law's meaning. We granted certiorari to clear the confusion.

II.

We begin with the Arbitration Act and the question of its saving clause.

Congress adopted the Arbitration Act in 1925 in response to a perception that courts were unduly hostile to arbitration. No doubt there was much to that perception. Before 1925, English and American common law courts routinely refused to enforce agreements to arbitrate disputes. Scherk v. Alberto-Culver Co., 417 U.S. 506, 510, n. 4 (1974). But in Congress's judgment arbitration had more to offer than courts recognized—not least the promise of quicker, more informal, and often cheaper resolutions for everyone involved. So Congress directed courts to abandon their hostility and instead treat arbitration agreements as "valid, irrevocable, and enforceable." 9 U.S.C. § 2. The Act, this Court has said, establishes "a liberal federal policy favoring arbitration agreements." Moses H. Cone Memorial Hospital v. Mercury Constr. Corp., 460 U.S. 1, 24 (1983).

Not only did Congress require courts to respect and enforce agreements to arbitrate; it also specifically directed them to respect and enforce the parties' chosen arbitration procedures. Indeed, we have often observed that the Arbitration Act requires courts "rigorously" to "enforce arbitration agreements according to their terms, including terms that specify *with whom* the parties choose to arbitrate their disputes and *the rules* under which that arbitration will be conducted." American Express Co. v. Italian Colors Restaurant, 570 U.S. 228, 233 (2013).

On first blush, these emphatic directions would seem to resolve any argument under the Arbitration Act. The parties before us contracted for arbitration. They proceeded to specify the rules that would govern their arbitrations, indicating their intention to use individualized rather than class or collective action procedures. And this much the Arbitration Act seems to protect pretty absolutely. You might wonder if the balance Congress struck in 1925 between arbitration and litigation should be revisited in light of more contemporary developments. You might even ask if the Act was good policy when enacted. But all the same you might find it difficult to see how to avoid the statute's application.

Still, the employees suggest the Arbitration Act's saving clause creates an exception for cases like theirs. By its terms, the saving clause allows courts to refuse to enforce arbitration agreements "upon such grounds as exist at law or in equity for the revocation of any contract." § 2. That provision applies here, the employees tell us, because the NLRA renders their particular class and collective action waivers illegal. In their view, illegality under the NLRA is a "ground" that "exists at law . . . for the revocation" of their arbitration agreements, at least to the extent those agreements prohibit class or collective action proceedings.

The problem with this line of argument is fundamental. Put to the side the question whether the saving clause was designed to save not only state law defenses but also defenses allegedly arising from federal statutes. Put to the side the question of what it takes to qualify as a ground for "revocation" of a contract. Put to the side for the moment, too, even the question whether the NLRA actually renders class and collective action waivers illegal. Assuming (but not granting) the employees could satisfactorily answer all those questions, the saving clause still can't save their cause.

It can't because the saving clause recognizes only defenses that apply to "any" contract. In this way the clause establishes a sort of "equal-treatment" rule for arbitration contracts. The clause "permits agreements to arbitrate to be invalidated by 'generally applicable contract defenses, such as fraud, duress, or unconscionability.'" At the same time, the clause offers no refuge for "defenses that apply only to arbitration or that derive their meaning from the fact that an agreement to arbitrate is at issue." Under our precedent, this means the saving clause does not save defenses that target arbitration either by name or by more subtle methods, such as by "interfer[ing] with fundamental attributes of arbitration."

This is where the employees' argument stumbles. They don't suggest that their arbitration agreements were extracted, say, by an act of fraud or duress or in some other unconscionable way that would render any contract unenforceable. Instead, they object to their agreements precisely because they require individualized arbitration proceedings instead of class or collective ones. And by attacking (only) the individualized nature of the arbitration proceedings, the employees' argument seeks to interfere with one of arbitration's fundamental attributes.

* * *

III.

But that's not the end of it. Even if the Arbitration Act normally requires us to enforce arbitration agreements like theirs, the employees reply that the NLRA overrides that guidance in these cases and commands us to hold their agreements unlawful yet.

This argument faces a stout uphill climb. When confronted with two Acts of Congress allegedly touching on the same topic, this Court is not at "liberty to pick and choose among congressional enactments" and must instead strive " 'to give effect to both.' " A party seeking to suggest that two statutes cannot be harmonized, and that one displaces the other, bears the heavy burden of showing " 'a clearly expressed congressional intention' " that such a result should follow. The intention must be " 'clear and manifest.' " And in approaching a claimed conflict, we come armed with the "stron[g] presum[ption]" that repeals by implication are "disfavored" and that "Congress will specifically address" preexisting law when it wishes to suspend its normal operations in a later statute.

These rules exist for good reasons. Respect for Congress as drafter counsels against too easily finding irreconcilable conflicts in its work. More than that, respect for the separation of powers counsels restraint. Allowing judges to pick and choose between statutes risks transforming them from expounders of what the law is into policymakers choosing what the law should be. Our rules aiming for harmony over conflict in statutory interpretation grow from an appreciation that it's the job of Congress by legislation, not this Court by supposition, both to write the laws and to repeal them.

Seeking to demonstrate an irreconcilable statutory conflict even in light of these demanding standards, the employees point to Section 7 of the NLRA. That provision guarantees workers

"the right to self-organization, to form, join, or assist labor organizations, to bargain collectively through representatives of their own choosing, and to engage in other concerted activities for the purpose of collective bargaining or other mutual aid or protection."

From this language, the employees ask us to infer a clear and manifest congressional command to displace the Arbitration Act and outlaw agreements like theirs.

But that much inference is more than this Court may make. Section 7 focuses on the right to organize unions and bargain collectively. It may permit unions to bargain to prohibit arbitration. But it does not express approval or disapproval of arbitration. It does not mention class or collective action procedures. It does not even hint at a wish to displace the Arbitration Act—let alone accomplish that much clearly and manifestly, as our precedents demand.

Neither should any of this come as a surprise. The notion that Section 7 confers a right to class or collective actions seems pretty unlikely when you recall that procedures like that were hardly known when the NLRA was adopted in 1935. Federal Rule of Civil Procedure 23 didn't create the modern class action until 1966; class arbitration didn't emerge until later still; and even the Fair Labor Standards Act's collective action provision postdated Section 7 by years. And while some forms of group litigation existed even in 1935, Section 7's failure to mention them only reinforces that the statute doesn't speak to such procedures.

A close look at the employees' best evidence of a potential conflict turns out to reveal no conflict at all. The employees direct our attention to the term "other concerted activities for the purpose of . . . other mutual aid or protection." This catchall term, they say, can be read to include class and collective legal actions. But the term appears at the end of a detailed list of activities speaking of "self-organization," "form[ing], join[ing], or assist [ing] labor organizations," and "bargain[ing] collectively." And where, as here, a more general term follows more specific terms in a list, the general term is usually understood to " 'embrace only objects similar in nature to those objects enumerated by the preceding specific words.' " All of which suggests that the term "other concerted activities" should, like the terms that precede it, serve to protect things employees "just do" for themselves in the course of exercising their right to free association in the workplace, rather than "the highly regulated, courtroom-bound 'activities' of class and joint litigation." None of the preceding and more specific terms speaks to the procedures judges or arbitrators must apply in disputes that leave the workplace and enter the courtroom or arbitral forum, and there is no textually sound reason to suppose the final catchall term should bear such a radically different object than all its predecessors.

The NLRA's broader structure underscores the point. After speaking of various "concerted activities" in Section 7, Congress proceeded to establish a regulatory regime applicable to each of them. The NLRA provides rules for the recognition of exclusive bargaining representatives, explains employees' and employers' obligation to bargain collectively, § 158(d), and conscribes certain labor organization practices. The NLRA also touches on other concerted activities closely related to organization and collective bargaining, such as picketing. It even sets rules for adjudicatory proceedings under the NLRA itself. Many of these provisions were part of the original NLRA in 1935, while others were added later. But missing entirely from this careful regime is any hint about what rules should govern the adjudication of class or collective actions in court or arbitration. Without some comparably specific guidance, it's not at all obvious what procedures Section 7 might protect. Would opt-out class action procedures suffice? Or would opt-in procedures be necessary? What notice might be owed to absent class members? What standards would govern class certification? Should the same rules always apply or should they vary based on the nature of the suit? Nothing in the NLRA even whispers to us on any of these essential questions. And it is hard to fathom why Congress would take such care to regulate all the other matters mentioned in Section 7 yet remain mute about this matter alone—unless, of course, Section 7 doesn't speak to class and collective action procedures in the first place.

* * *

IV.

* * *

The policy may be debatable but the law is clear: Congress has instructed that arbitration agreements like those before us must be enforced as written. While Congress is of course always free to amend this judgment, we see nothing suggesting it did so in the NLRA—much less that it manifested a clear intention to displace the Arbitration Act. Because we can easily read Congress's statutes to work in harmony, that is where our duty lies.

So ordered.

■ JUSTICE THOMAS, concurring.

* * *

■ JUSTICE GINSBURG, with whom JUSTICE BREYER, JUSTICE SOTOMAYOr, and JUSTICE KAGAN join, dissenting.

The employees in these cases complain that their employers have underpaid them in violation of the wage and hours prescriptions of the Fair Labor Standards Act of 1938 (FLSA), 29 U.S.C. § 201 et seq., and analogous state laws. Individually, their claims are small, scarcely of a size warranting the expense of seeking redress alone. But by joining together with others similarly circumstanced, employees can gain effective redress for wage underpayment commonly experienced. To block such concerted action, their employers required them to sign, as a condition of employment, arbitration agreements banning collective judicial and arbitral proceedings of any kind. The question presented: Does the Federal Arbitration Act (Arbitration Act or FAA), 9 U.S.C. § 1 et seq., permit employers to insist that their employees, whenever seeking redress for commonly experienced wage loss, go it alone, never mind the right secured to employees by the National Labor Relations Act (NLRA), 29 U.S.C. § 151 et seq., "to engage in . . . concerted activities" for their "mutual aid or protection"? The answer should be a resounding "No."

In the NLRA and its forerunner, the Norris-LaGuardia Act (NLGA), 29 U.S.C. § 101 *et seq.*, Congress acted on an acute awareness: For workers striving to gain from their employers decent terms and conditions of employment, there is strength in numbers. A single employee, Congress understood, is disarmed in dealing with an employer. The Court today subordinates employee-protective labor legislation to the Arbitration Act. In so doing, the Court forgets the labor market imbalance that gave rise to the NLGA and the NLRA, and ignores the destructive consequences of diminishing the right of employees "to band together in confronting an employer." Congressional correction of the Court's elevation of the FAA over workers' rights to act in concert is urgently in order.

To explain why the Court's decision is egregiously wrong, I first refer to the extreme imbalance once prevalent in our Nation's workplaces, and Congress' aim in the NLGA and the NLRA to place employers and employees on a more equal footing. I then explain why the Arbitration Act, sensibly read, does not shrink the NLRA's protective sphere.

* * *

Despite the NLRA's prohibitions, the employers in the cases now before the Court required their employees to sign contracts stipulating to submission of wage and hours claims to binding arbitration, and to do so only one-by-one. When employees subsequently filed wage and hours claims in federal court and sought to invoke the collective-litigation procedures provided for in the FLSA and Federal Rules of Civil Procedure, the employers moved to compel individual arbitration. The Arbitration Act, in their view, requires courts to enforce their take-it-or-leave-it arbitration agreements as written, including the collective-litigation abstinence demanded therein.

In resisting enforcement of the group-action foreclosures, the employees involved in this litigation do not urge that they must have access to a judicial forum. They argue only that the NLRA prohibits their employers from denying them the right to pursue work-related claims in concert in any forum. If they may be stopped by employer-dictated terms from pursuing collective procedures in court, they maintain, they must at least have access to similar procedures in an arbitral forum.

* * *

Recognizing employees' right to engage in collective employment litigation and shielding that right from employer blockage are firmly rooted in the NLRA's design. Congress expressed its intent, when it enacted the NLRA, to "protec[t] the exercise by workers of full freedom of association," thereby remedying "[t]he inequality of bargaining power" workers faced. There can be no serious doubt that collective litigation is one way workers may associate with one another to improve their lot.

Since the Act's earliest days, the Board and federal courts have understood § 7's "concerted activities" clause to protect myriad ways in which employees may join together to advance their shared interests. For example, the Board and federal courts have affirmed that the Act shields employees from employer interference when they participate in concerted appeals to the media, legislative bodies, and government agencies. "The 74th Congress," this Court has noted, "knew well enough that labor's cause often is advanced on fronts other than collective bargaining and grievance settlement within the immediate employment context."

Crucially important here, for over 75 years, the Board has held that the NLRA safeguards employees from employer interference when they pursue joint, collective, and class suits related to the terms and conditions of their employment. For decades, federal courts have endorsed the Board's view, comprehending that "the filing of a labor related civil action by a group of employees is ordinarily a concerted activity protected by § 7." The Court pays scant heed to this longstanding line of decisions.

In face of the NLRA's text, history, purposes, and longstanding construction, the Court nevertheless concludes that collective proceedings do not fall within the scope of § 7. None of the Court's reasons for diminishing § 7 should carry the day.

* * *

Further attempting to sow doubt about § 7's scope, the Court asserts that class and collective procedures were "hardly known when the NLRA was adopted in 1935." In particular, the Court notes, the FLSA's collective-litigation procedure postdated § 7 "by years" and Rule 23 "didn't create the modern class action until 1966."

First, one may ask, is there any reason to suppose that Congress intended to protect employees' right to act in concert using only those procedures and forums available in 1935? Congress framed § 7 in broad terms, "entrust[ing]" the Board with "responsibility to adapt the Act to changing patterns of industrial life." With fidelity to Congress' aim, the Board and federal courts have recognized that the NLRA shields employees from employer interference when they, e.g., join together to file complaints with administrative agencies, even if those agencies did not exist in 1935.

Moreover, the Court paints an ahistorical picture. As Judge Wood, writing for the Seventh Circuit, cogently explained, the FLSA's collective-litigation procedure and the modern class action were "not written on a clean slate." By 1935, permissive joinder was scarcely uncommon in courts of equity. Nor were representative and class suits novelties. Indeed, their origins trace back to medieval times And beyond question, "[c]lass suits long have been a part of American jurisprudence." Early instances of joint proceedings include cases in which employees allied to sue an employer. It takes no imagination, then, to comprehend that Congress, when it enacted the NLRA, likely meant to protect employees' joining together to engage in collective litigation.

Because I would hold that employees' § 7 rights include the right to pursue collective litigation regarding their wages and hours, I would further hold that the employer-dictated collective-litigation stoppers, i.e., "waivers," are unlawful. As earlier recounted, § 8(a)(1) makes it an "unfair labor practice" for an employer to "interfere with, restrain, or coerce" employees in the exercise of their § 7 rights. Beyond genuine dispute, an employer "interfere[s] with" and "restrain[s]" employees in the exercise of their § 7 rights by mandating that they prospectively renounce those rights in individual employment agreements. The law could hardly be otherwise: Employees' rights to band together to meet their employers' superior strength would be worth precious little if employers could condition employment on workers signing away those rights. Properly assessed, then, the "waivers" rank as unfair labor practices outlawed by the NLRA, and therefore unenforceable in court.

II.

* * *

The FAA's legislative history also shows that Congress did not intend the statute to apply to arbitration provisions in employment contracts. In brief, when the legislation was introduced, organized labor voiced concern. Herbert Hoover, then Secretary of Commerce, suggested that if there were "objection[s]" to including "workers' contracts in the law's scheme," Congress could amend the legislation to say: "but nothing herein contained shall apply to contracts of employment of seamen, railroad employees, or any other class of workers engaged in interstate or foreign commerce." Congress adopted Secretary Hoover's suggestion virtually verbatim in § 1 of the Act, and labor expressed no further opposition.

Congress, it bears repetition, envisioned application of the Arbitration Act to voluntary, negotiated agreements. Congress never endorsed a policy favoring arbitration where one party sets the terms of an agreement while the other is left to "take it or leave it."

In recent decades, this Court has veered away from Congress' intent simply to afford merchants a speedy and economical means of resolving commercial disputes. In 1983, the Court declared, for the first time in the FAA's then 58-year history, that the FAA evinces a "liberal federal policy favoring arbitration." Soon thereafter, the Court ruled, in a series of cases, that the FAA requires enforcement of agreements to arbitrate not only contract claims, but statutory claims as well. Further, in 1991, the Court concluded in Gilmer v. Interstate/Johnson Lane Corp., 500 U.S. 20, 23 (1991), that the FAA requires enforcement of agreements to arbitrate claims arising under the Age Discrimination in Employment Act of 1967, a workplace antidiscrimination statute. Then, in 2001, the Court ruled in Circuit City Stores, Inc. v. Adams, 532 U.S. 105, 109 (2001), that the Arbitration Act's exemption for employment contracts should be construed narrowly, to exclude from the Act's scope only transportation workers' contracts.

Employers have availed themselves of the opportunity opened by court decisions expansively interpreting the Arbitration Act. Few employers imposed arbitration agreements on their employees in the early 1990's. After Gilmer and Circuit City, however, employers' exaction of arbitration clauses in employment contracts grew steadily. Moreover, in response to subsequent decisions addressing class arbitration, employers have increasingly included in their arbitration agreements express group-action waivers. It is, therefore, this Court's exorbitant application of the FAA—stretching it far beyond contractual disputes between merchants—that led the NLRB to confront, for the first time in

2012, the precise question whether employers can use arbitration agreements to insulate themselves from collective employment litigation.

* * *

III.

The inevitable result of today's decision will be the underenforcement of federal and state statutes designed to advance the well-being of vulnerable workers.

The probable impact on wage and hours claims of the kind asserted in the cases now before the Court is all too evident. Violations of minimum-wage and overtime laws are widespread. One study estimated that in Chicago, Los Angeles, and New York City alone, low-wage workers lose nearly $3 billion in legally owed wages each year. The U.S. Department of Labor, state labor departments, and state attorneys general can uncover and obtain recoveries for some violations. Because of their limited resources, however, government agencies must rely on private parties to take a lead role in enforcing wage and hours laws.

If employers can stave off collective employment litigation aimed at obtaining redress for wage and hours infractions, the enforcement gap is almost certain to widen. Expenses entailed in mounting individual claims will often far outweigh potential recoveries.

NOTES AND QUESTIONS

1.   The majority and dissent disagree on the "agreement" to arbitrate all disputes in individual proceedings. The majority views this as a contractual term agreed to by both the employer and the employee. The dissent, however, considers it coerced, a product of a "take it or leave it" offer of employment. To what degree should the outcome of the case depend on how the agreement is viewed?

2.   In Circuit City Stores, Inc. v. Adams, 532 U.S. 105 (2001), Saint Clair Adams applied for a job with Circuit City and signed an application form stating that all disputes under statutory or common law would be settled by arbitration. Circuit City employees were not covered by a collective bargaining agreement. Two years later, Adams brought an action in state court alleging discrimination under California law, and Circuit City then brought an action in federal district court to enjoin the state court action and compel arbitration pursuant to the Federal Arbitration Act (FAA), 9 U.S.C. §§ 1–9. The Ninth Circuit reversed the district court and held that the FAA did not apply to contracts of employment. The Supreme Court reversed. Justice Kennedy, writing for a five-justice majority, said that section 1 of the FAA controlled. It provides that the FAA does not apply to "contracts of employment of seamen, railroad employees, or any other class of workers engaged in foreign or interstate commerce." According to the majority, Adams was not within the narrow class of employees exempted from the FAA. Justice Stevens, writing for the four-justice dissent, used the legislative history of the FAA to assert that the purpose of the FAA was to enforce commercial and admiralty contracts. When unions objected that the law

might be used to compel arbitration in employment disputes, the language of section 1 was added to clarify that the FAA did not apply to *any* employment contracts, and the reference to seamen and railroad employees was just an example of the types of employees exempted.

3. In Stolt-Nielsen S.A. v. AnimalFeeds International Corp., 559 U.S. 662 (2010), the Supreme Court held that a court may not compel arbitration on a class-wide basis when an agreement is "silent" on the availability of such arbitration. In Lamps Plus, Inc. v. Varela, 139 S.Ct. 1407 (2019), the Court held that the *Stolt-Nielsen* rule also applies when an agreement is "ambiguous" rather than silent on class-wide arbitration. Both cases were 5–4 decisions.

4. In Armendariz v. Foundation Health Psychcare Services, Inc., 6 P.3d 669 (Cal.2000), the California Supreme Court held that a contract requiring employees to waive their rights to bring actions for sexual harassment under state law was contrary to public policy and unlawful. Subsequently, the Ninth Circuit relied on *Armendariz* to hold that a compulsory arbitration agreement was unconscionable under California law. Circuit City Stores v. Mantor, 335 F.3d 1101 (9th Cir. 2003), cert. denied, 540 U.S. 1160 (2004). The court said it was procedurally unconscionable because it was a contract of adhesion; it was substantively unconscionable because it limited the remedies available to the employee to injunctive relief, up to one year of back pay, and up to two years of front pay, compensatory damages, and punitive damages up to the greater of the amount of back pay and front pay awarded or $5,000. The employee also was required to pay Circuit City a $75 filing fee, which the court said "was not the type of expense that the employee would be required to bear in federal court." Finally, the arbitration agreement contained a strict one-year statute of limitations that could not be extended by the continuing violation doctrine available in actions brought under California discrimination law.

5. Mandatory arbitration provisions have been criticized on a variety of grounds, such as being presented to employees on a take-it-or-leave-it basis, and limiting employees' likelihood and magnitude of recovery. Arbitration proceedings also frequently contain nondisclosure agreements, which may conceal patterns of serious misconduct, especially sexual harassment. Recently, some large employers in the technology sector have indicated that they will not apply their arbitration provisions to claims of sexual harassment.

6. In October 2019, California Governor Gavin Newsom signed into law AB 51, which prohibits employers from imposing mandatory employee arbitration agreements as a condition of employment. The law was immediately challenged in federal court by various employer groups. The ultimate holding in the case is of considerable importance because other states often follow the lead of California.

PART II

Establishing the Employment Relationship

CHAPTER 3

THE HIRING PROCESS

How do people find jobs? There are numerous ways, such as referrals by relatives and friends, word-of-mouth, employment agencies, newspaper and other advertising, union hiring halls, and the Internet. Although the process used often varies with the job sought and the parties involved, it is frequently unstructured and informal. Until recently, it also has been largely free of legal regulation. This chapter considers the role of law in regulating the job search and hiring process, including eligibility for employment, methods of information gathering used by employers, and the application of certain criteria in making hiring decisions.

A. THE LABOR POOL

1. NEPOTISM

Kotch v. Board of River Port Pilot Commissioners
330 U.S. 552 (1947).

■ MR. JUSTICE BLACK delivered the opinion of the Court.

Louisiana statutes provide in general that all seagoing vessels moving between New Orleans and foreign ports must be navigated through the Mississippi River approaches to the port of New Orleans and within it, exclusively by pilots who are State Officers. New State pilots are appointed by the governor only upon certification of a State Board of River Pilot Commissioners, themselves pilots. Only those who have served a six month apprenticeship under incumbent pilots and who possess other specific qualifications may be certified to the governor by the board. Appellants here have had at least fifteen years experience in the river, the port, and elsewhere, as pilots of vessels whose pilotage was not governed by the State law in question. Although they possess all the statutory qualifications except that they have not served the requisite six months apprenticeship under Louisiana officer pilots, they have been denied appointment as State pilots. Seeking relief in a Louisiana state court, they alleged that the incumbent pilots, having unfettered discretion under the law in the selection of apprentices, had selected with occasional exception, only the relatives and friends of incumbents; that the selections were made by electing prospective apprentices into the pilots' association, which the pilots have formed by authority of State law; that since "membership * * * is closed to all except those having the favor of the pilots" the result is that only their relatives and friends have and can become State pilots. The Supreme Court of Louisiana has held that the pilotage law so administered does not violate the equal protection clause of the Fourteenth Amendment, 209 La. 737, 25 So.2d 527.

* * *

Studies of the long history of pilotage reveal that it is a unique institution and must be judged as such. In order to avoid invisible hazards, vessels approaching and leaving ports must be conducted from and to open waters by persons intimately familiar with the local waters. The pilot's job generally requires that he go outside the harbor's entrance in a small boat to meet incoming ships, board them and direct their course from open waters to the port. The same service is performed for vessels leaving the port. Pilots are thus indispensable cogs in the transportation system of every maritime economy. Their work prevents traffic congestion and accidents which would impair navigation in and to the ports. It affects the safety of lives and cargo, the cost and time expended in port calls, and in some measure, the competitive attractiveness of particular ports. Thus, for the same reasons that governments of most maritime communities have subsidized, regulated, or have themselves operated docks and other harbor facilities and sought to improve the approaches to their ports, they have closely regulated and often operated their ports' pilotage system.

The history and practice of pilotage demonstrate that, although inextricably geared to a complex commercial economy, it is also a highly personalized calling. A pilot does not require a formalized technical education so much as a detailed and extremely intimate, almost intuitive, knowledge of the weather, waterways and conformation of the harbor or river which he serves. This seems to be particularly true of the approaches to New Orleans through the treacherous and shifting channel of the Mississippi River. Moreover, harbor entrances where pilots can most conveniently make their homes and still be close to places where they board incoming and leave outgoing ships are usually some distance from the port cities they serve. These "pilot towns" have begun, and generally exist today, as small communities of pilots perhaps near, but usually distinct from the port cities. In these communities young men have an opportunity to acquire special knowledge of the weather and water hazards of the locality and seem to grow up with ambitions to become pilots in the traditions of their fathers, relatives, and neighbors. We are asked, in effect, to say that Louisiana is without constitutional authority to conclude that apprenticeship under persons specially interested in a pilot's future is the best way to fit him for duty as a pilot officer in the service of the State.

The States have had full power to regulate pilotage of certain kinds of vessels since 1789 when the first Congress decided that then existing state pilot laws were satisfactory and made federal regulation unnecessary. Louisiana legislation has controlled the activities and appointment of pilots since 1805—even before the Territory was admitted as a State. The State pilotage system, as it has evolved since

1805, is typical of that which grew up in most seaboard states and in foreign countries. Since 1805 Louisiana pilots have been State officers whose work has been controlled by the State.

* * *

It is within the framework of this longstanding pilotage regulation system that the practice has apparently existed of permitting pilots, if they choose, to select their relatives and friends as the only ones ultimately eligible for appointment as pilots by the governor.

* * *

The practice of nepotism in appointing public servants has been a subject of controversy in this country throughout our history. Some states have adopted constitutional amendments or statutes, to prohibit it. These have reflected state policies to wipe out the practice. But Louisiana and most other states have adopted no such general policy. We can only assume that the Louisiana legislature weighed the obvious possibility of evil against whatever useful function a closely knit pilotage system may serve. Thus the advantages of early experience under friendly supervision in the locality of the pilot's training, the benefits to morale and esprit de corps which family and neighborly tradition might contribute, the close association in which pilots must work and live in their pilot communities and on the water, and the discipline and regulation which is imposed to assure the State competent pilot service after appointment, might have prompted the legislature to permit Louisiana pilot officers to select those with whom they would serve.

The number of people, as a practical matter, who can be pilots is very limited. No matter what system of selection is adopted, all but the few occasionally selected must of necessity be excluded.

* * *

The object of the entire pilotage law, as we have pointed out, is to secure for the State and others interested the safest and most efficiently operated pilotage system practicable.

* * *

[W]e cannot say that the practice appellants attack is the kind of discrimination which violates the equal protection clause of the Fourteenth Amendment.

Affirmed.

■ MR. JUSTICE RUTLEDGE, dissenting.

The unique history and conditions surrounding the activities of river port pilots, shortly recounted in the Court's opinion, justify a high degree of public regulation. But I do not think they can sustain a system of entailment for the occupation. If Louisiana were to provide by statute in haec verba that only members of John Smith's family would be eligible for the public calling of pilot, I have no doubt that the statute on its face would infringe the Fourteenth Amendment. And this would be true, even though John Smith and the members of his family had been pilots for generations. It would be true also if the right were expanded to include a number of designated families.

In final analysis this is, I think, the situation presented on this record. While the statutes applicable do not purport on their face to restrict the right to become a licensed pilot to members of the families of licensed pilots, the charge is that they have been so administered. And this charge not only is borne out by the record but is accepted by the Court as having been sustained.

The result of the decision therefore is to approve as constitutional state regulation which makes admission to the ranks of pilots turn finally on consanguinity. Blood is, in effect, made the crux of selection. That, in my opinion, is forbidden by the Fourteenth Amendment's guaranty against denial of the equal protection of the laws.

* * *

Conceivably the familial system would be the most effective possible scheme for training many kinds of artisans or public servants, sheerly from the viewpoint of securing the highest degree of skill and competence. Indeed, something very worth while largely disappeared from our national life when the once prevalent familial system of conducting manufacturing and mercantile enterprises went out and was replaced by the highly impersonal corporate system for doing business.

But that loss is not one to be repaired under our scheme by legislation framed or administered to perpetuate family monopolies of either private occupations or branches of the public service. It is precisely because the Amendment forbids enclosing those areas by legislative lines drawn on the basis of race, color, creed, and the like, that, in cases like this, the possibly most efficient method of securing the highest development of skills cannot be established by law. Absent any such bar, the presence of such a tendency or direct relationship would be effective for sustaining the legislation. It cannot be effective to overcome the bar itself. The discrimination here is not shown to be consciously racial in character. But I am unable to differentiate in effects one founded on blood relationship.

* * *

■ MR. JUSTICE REED, MR. JUSTICE DOUGLAS and MR. JUSTICE MURPHY join in this dissent.

NOTES AND QUESTIONS

1.   How might some open competitive system for appointment adversely affect the public interest in pilotage?

2. To what extent should an individual's ability to work closely with current employees be taken into account? Are there dangers in a widespread application of the concept of coworker preference?

3. The Louisiana law at issue in *Kotch* had the effect of excluding the vast majority of citizens, rather than a discrete minority, from working as pilots. Does this fact affect the Court's analysis?

4. One of the consequences of the Louisiana pilotage system may have been to institutionalize and perpetuate racial discrimination. If true, does this make the law unconstitutional? Is intent to discriminate required? See Washington v. Davis, 426 U.S. 229 (1976) (intent to discriminate required in constitutionally-based actions). For more information about harbor pilots, see Michael Totty, Harbor Pilot: Great Job, But Good Luck Getting It, Wall St.J., Nov. 29, 1995, at T1.

5. Does "family" belong on a list with "race, color, creed and the like," as Justice Rutledge thinks? If Justice Rutledge is right, should a parent be able to turn over to a child the parent's proprietary business? Is there a difference in the "property" involved?

6. In Backlund v. Hessen, 104 F.3d 1031 (8th Cir. 1997), an applicant for a city firefighter position with the highest test score was passed over in favor of three lower ranking candidates who were related to fire department employees. The plaintiff claimed that the nepotism violated equal protection. In reversing the district court's dismissal of the claim, the Eighth Circuit distinguished *Kotch* and observed that in *Kotch* the state justified its policy in light of "the unique character of river piloting." It held that "*Kotch* makes it abundantly clear that nepotism in governmental hiring requires some measure of justification before it can pass constitutional muster."

7. Nepotism, per se, does not violate the nondiscrimination provisions of Title VII of the Civil Rights Act of 1964, but if the effect of nepotism is discrimination on the basis of race, sex, or some other proscribed classification, then it likely violates anti-discrimination law. In Asbestos Workers, Local 53 v. Vogler, 407 F.2d 1047 (5th Cir. 1969), the union had a policy restricting membership to sons or close relatives of current members. The effect of the policy was to perpetuate the exclusion of minorities from the all-white union. The court invalidated the policy. See Adamson v. Multi Cmty. Diversified Servs., Inc., 514 F.3d 1136 (10th Cir. 2008) (anti-nepotism policy did not violate Title VII).

8. Does an employer's anti-nepotism rule violate a state prohibition on marital status discrimination? Compare Manhattan Pizza Hut, Inc. v. State Human Rights Appeal Board, 415 N.E.2d 950 (N.Y.1980) (no), with Kraft, Inc. v. State, 284 N.W.2d 386 (Minn.1979) (yes). Does a city's anti-nepotism policy violate the constitutional right to marry? See Parks v. City of Warner Robins, 43 F.3d 609 (11th Cir. 1995) (held: no). See also Vaughn v. Lawrenceburg Power System, 269 F.3d 703 (6th Cir. 2001) (public employer's anti-nepotism rule did not violate First Amendment freedom of association).

9. These issues about prohibited discrimination are considered in depth in Chapter 4. As you study that chapter, consider whether *Kotch* is good law today.

2. WORD-OF-MOUTH

EEOC v. Consolidated Service Systems

989 F.2d 233 (7th Cir. 1993).

■ POSNER, CIRCUIT JUDGE.

The Equal Employment Opportunity Commission brought this suit in 1985 against a small company which provides janitorial and cleaning services at a number of buildings in the Chicago area. The owner of the company is a Korean immigrant, as are most of its employees. The suit charges that the company discriminated in favor of persons of Korean origin, in violation of Title VII of the Civil Rights Act of 1964, 42 U.S.C. § 2000e et seq., by relying mainly on word of mouth to obtain new employees. After a bench trial, the district judge dismissed the suit on the ground that the Commission had failed to prove discrimination. * * *

Between 1983, when Mr. Hwang, the company's owner, bought the company from its previous owner, also a Korean, and the first quarter of 1987, 73 percent of the applicants for jobs with Consolidated, and 81 percent of the hires, were Korean. Less than 1 percent of the work force in Cook County is Korean and at most 3 percent of the janitorial and cleaner work force. It doesn't take a statistician to tell you that the difference between the percentage of Koreans in Consolidated's work force and the percentage of Koreans in the relevant labor market, however exactly that market is defined, is not due to chance. But is it due to discrimination? The district judge found it was not, and we do not think his finding was clearly erroneous.

There is no direct evidence of discrimination. The question is whether the circumstantial evidence compels an inference of discrimination—*intentional* discrimination ("disparate treatment," in the jargon of Title VII cases), for the EEOC has not appealed from the district court's rejection of its disparate-impact theory of liability.

We said that Consolidated is a small company. The EEOC's lawyer told us at argument that the company's annual sales are only $400,000. We mention this fact not to remind the reader of David and Goliath, or to suggest that Consolidated is exempt from Title VII (it is not), or to express wonderment that a firm of this size could litigate in federal court for seven years (and counting) with a federal agency, but to explain why Mr. Hwang relies on word of mouth to obtain employees rather than reaching out to a broader community less heavily Korean. It is the cheapest method of recruitment. Indeed, it is practically costless. Persons approach Hwang or his employees—most of whom are Korean too—at work or at social events, and once or twice Hwang has asked employees whether they know anyone who wants a job. At argument the EEOC's lawyer conceded, perhaps improvidently but if so only slightly so, that Hwang's recruitment posture could be described as totally passive. Hwang did buy newspaper advertisements on three occasions—once in a

Korean-language newspaper and twice in the *Chicago Tribune*—but as these ads resulted in zero hires, the experience doubtless only confirmed him in the passive posture. The EEOC argues that the single Korean newspaper ad, which ran for only three days and yielded not a single hire, is evidence of discrimination. If so, it is very weak evidence. The Commission points to the fact that Hwang could have obtained job applicants at no expense from the Illinois Job Service as further evidence of discrimination. But he testified that he had never heard of the Illinois Job Service and the district judge believed him.

If an employer can obtain all the competent workers he wants, at wages no higher than the minimum that he expects to have to pay, without beating the bushes for workers—without in fact spending a cent on recruitment—he can reduce his costs of doing business by adopting just the stance of Mr. Hwang. And this is no mean consideration to a firm whose annual revenues in a highly competitive business are those of a mom and pop grocery store. Of course if the employer is a member of an ethnic community, especially an immigrant one, this stance is likely to result in the perpetuation of an ethnically imbalanced work force. Members of these communities tend to work and to socialize with each other rather than with people in the larger community. The social and business network of an immigrant community racially and culturally distinct from the majority of Americans is bound to be largely confined to that community, making it inevitable that when the network is used for job recruitment the recruits will be drawn disproportionately from the community.

No inference of intentional discrimination can be drawn from the pattern we have described, even if the employer would prefer to employ people drawn predominantly or even entirely from his own ethnic or, here, national-origin community. Discrimination is not preference or aversion; it is acting on the preference or aversion. If the most efficient method of hiring, adopted because it is the most efficient (not defended because it is efficient—the statute does not reference to efficiency, 42 U.S.C. § 2000e–2(k)(2)), just happens to produce a work force whose racial or religious or ethnic or national-origin or gender composition pleases the employer, this is not intentional discrimination. EEOC v. Chicago Miniature Lamp Works, 947 F.2d 292, 299 (7th Cir. 1991). The motive is not a discriminatory one. "Knowledge of a disparity is not the same thing as an intent to cause or maintain it." Or if, though the motives behind adoption of the method were a mixture of discrimination and efficiency, Mr. Hwang would have adopted the identical method of recruitment even if he had no interest in the national origin of his employees, the fact that he had such an interest would not be a "but for" cause of the discriminatory outcome and again there would be no liability. There is no evidence that Hwang is biased in favor of Koreans or prejudiced against any group underrepresented in his work force, except what the Commission asks us to infer from the imbalance in that force and Hwang's passive stance.

We said the passive stance is the cheapest method of recruitment. It may also be highly effective in producing a good work force. There are two reasons. The first is that an applicant referred by an existing employee is likely to get a franker, more accurate, more relevant picture of working conditions than if he learns about the job from an employment agency, a newspaper ad, or a hiring supervisor. The employee can give him the real low-down about the job. The result is a higher probability of a good match, and a lower probability that the new hire will be disappointed or disgruntled, perform badly, and quit. Second, an employee who refers someone for employment may get in trouble with his employer if the person he refers is a dud; so word of mouth recruitment in effect enlists existing employees to help screen new applicants conscientiously.

If this were a disparate-impact case (as it was once, but the Commission has abandoned its claim of disparate impact), and, if, contrary to EEOC v. Chicago Miniature Lamp Works, word of mouth recruitment were deemed an employment practice and hence was subject to review for disparate impact, as assumed in Clark v. Chrysler Corp., 673 F.2d 921, 927 (7th Cir. 1982), and held in Thomas v. Washington County School Board, 915 F.2d 922, 924–26 (4th Cir. 1990), then the advantages of word of mouth recruitment would have to be balanced against its possibly discriminatory effect when the employer's current work force is already skewed along racial or other disfavored lines. But in a case of disparate treatment, the question is different. It is whether word of mouth recruitment gives rise to an inference of intentional discrimination. Unlike an explicit racial or ethnic criterion or, what we may assume without deciding amounts to the same thing, a rule confining hiring to relatives of existing employees in a racially or ethnically skewed work force, as in *Thomas,* word of mouth recruiting does not compel an inference of intentional discrimination. At least it does not do so where, as in the case of Consolidated Services Systems, it is clearly, as we have been at pains to emphasize, the cheapest and most efficient method of recruitment, notwithstanding its discriminatory impact. Of course, Consolidated had some non-Korean applicants for employment, and if it had never hired any this would support, perhaps decisively, an inference of discrimination. Although the respective percentages of Korean and of non-Korean applicants hired were clearly favorable to Koreans (33 percent to 20 percent), the EEOC was unable, as explained more fully below, to find a single person out of the 99 rejected non-Koreans who could show that he or she was interested in a job that Mr. Hwang ever hired for. Many, perhaps most, of these were persons who responded to the ad he placed in the *Chicago Tribune* for a contract that he never got, hence never hired for.

The Commission cites the statement of Consolidated's lawyer that his client took advantage of the fact that the Korean immigrant community offered a ready market of cheap labor as an admission of "active" discrimination on the basis of national origin. It is not discrimination, and it is certainly not active discrimination, for an employer to sit back and wait for people willing to work for low wages to apply to him. The fact that they are ethnically or racially uniform does not impose upon him a duty to spend money advertising in the help-wanted columns of the *Chicago Tribune*. The Commission deemed Consolidated's "admission" corroborated by the testimony of the sociologist William Liu, Consolidated's own expert witness, who explained that it was natural for a recent Korean immigrant such as Hwang to hire other recent Korean immigrants, with whom he shared a common culture, and that the consequence would be a work force disproportionately Korean. Well, of course. People who share a common culture tend to work together as well as marry together and socialize together. That is not evidence of illegal discrimination.

Although the Commission's witness list contained the names of 99 persons whom Hwang had refused to hire allegedly because they were not Korean, at trial it presented only four of these persons as witnesses. One was a woman whose national origin the record does not disclose, but we shall assume that she is not Korean. She applied for a job with Consolidated in response to one of the ads he had placed in the *Tribune*. She was not hired. Hwang testified that he hired no one who responded to the ad because he failed to receive the contract which he had placed the ad in expectation of receiving. The district judge believed him. The judge also thought it odd that this witness had been a receptionist both before she applied for the job with Consolidated and after she failed to get it. He doubted that she had really wanted a job cleaning buildings.

The next witness had responded to the same ad. His national origin, too, is not of record but we may assume from his name and from the fact that the EEOC offered him as a witness that he is not Korean. Apart from believing Hwang's testimony that the ad had been placed to obtain workers for a job that never materialized, the judge found this witness's testimony "incredible," in part because he gave contradictory evidence. The judge disbelieved the third witness as well, sensing that he had not really wanted a job with Consolidated because he had just quit a higher-paying job. The last witness was adamant that he had learned about the job opening at Consolidated from the *Chicago Sun-Times*, in which Consolidated had never advertised. In addition, he had been fired from his previous job because he had been caught stealing from his employer. He also testified that he was seeking a job that paid almost twice what Consolidated was offering.

This was a sorry parade of witnesses, especially when we recall that the Commission culled it from a list of 99. We can hardly fault the district judge for concluding from all the evidence that the Commission had failed to prove that Consolidated was deliberately discriminating in favor of Koreans.

In a nation of immigrants, this must be reckoned an ominous case despite its outcome. The United States has many recent immigrants, and today as historically they tend to cluster in their own communities, united by ties of language, culture, and background. Often they form small businesses composed largely of relatives, friends, and other members of their community, and they obtain new employees by word of mouth. These small businesses—grocery stores, furniture stores, clothing stores, cleaning services, restaurants, gas stations—have been for many immigrant groups, and continue to be, the first rung on the ladder of American success. Derided as clannish, resented for their ambition and hard work, hated or despised for their otherness, recent immigrants are frequent targets of discrimination, some of it violent. It would be a bitter irony if the federal agency dedicated to enforcing the antidiscrimination laws succeeded in using those laws to kick these people off the ladder by compelling them to institute costly systems of hiring. There is equal danger to small black-run businesses in our central cities. Must such businesses undertake in the name of nondiscrimination costly measures to recruit non-black employees?

* * *

AFFIRMED.

NOTES AND QUESTIONS

1. To what extent is the court concerned about a small, minority-owned business? Suppose the business were neither small nor minority-owned. Would word-of-mouth recruitment be more objectionable? Suppose the result of word-of-mouth recruitment were the *exclusion* of minorities. Would (or should) the court be as willing to sanction the use of this technique?

2. Judge Posner focuses on the asserted efficiency of word-of-mouth recruitment for this small employer. Is this the proper province of the court, or are matters of weighing efficiency against nondiscrimination and other societal values the proper role of the legislature?

3. Should Title VII be concerned about fairness in process or fairness in outcomes? What costs are reasonable to impose on employers to engage in "unnecessary" efforts to recruit a more diverse work force?

4. Between 1979 and 1987, a Chicago wire press shop hired 87 people for low-skilled press jobs, none of whom were black. There was no other specific evidence of discrimination. The employer's defense was that black workers were unwilling to work in the jobs because they were held mostly by Polish- and Spanish-speaking workers. Has the employer violated Title VII? See EEOC v. O & G Spring & Wire Forms Specialty Co., 38 F.3d 872 (7th Cir. 1994), cert. denied, 513 U.S. 1198 (1995) (held: yes, because the employer failed to show that black workers were less likely than other English speakers to want to work alongside Polish-speaking workers).

A NOTE ON INFORMATION AND REFERRAL SOURCES

A.   Want Ads

Discriminatory want ads are expressly prohibited by Title VII of the Civil Rights Act of 1964 and the Age Discrimination in Employment Act (ADEA). Section 704(b) of Title VII provides:

> It shall be an unlawful employment practice for an employer, labor organization, [or] employment agency * * * to print or publish or cause to be printed or published any notice or advertisement relating to employment by such an employer or membership in or any classification or referral for employment by such labor organization, or relating to any classification or referral for employment by such an employment agency, * * * indicating any preference, limitation, specification, or discrimination, based on race, color, religion, sex, or national origin, except that such a notice or advertisement may indicate a preference, limitation, specification, or discrimination based on religion, sex, or national origin when religion, sex, or national origin is a bona fide occupational qualification for employment.

Most of the litigation under section 704(b) has involved alleged sex discrimination, where ads for "boys," "girls," "men," and "women" have been struck down. What about an ad for a salesman, bus boy, waitress, or longshoreman? In Hailes v. United Air Lines, 464 F.2d 1006 (5th Cir. 1972), it was held to violate Title VII for United to advertise for "stewardesses."

Although the content of want ads has been regulated, the ads themselves may be run in publications with a limited readership. For example, a want ad run in a general circulation newspaper could not indicate that the Chung Fu Restaurant had openings for Chinese waiters. But, it would not be unlawful for Chung Fu to place a want ad only in a Chinese newspaper. Similarly, Way Out Fashions could not run a want ad seeking college-age students to work as sales clerks. But, Way Out could announce sales openings in a want ad run only in a campus newspaper. Is the current state of the law realistic? Is more or less regulation appropriate? Is *Consolidated Service Systems* the appropriate judicial response?

In Pittsburgh Press Co. v. Pittsburgh Comm'n on Human Relations, 413 U.S. 376 (1973), the Supreme Court held that a newspaper's First Amendment rights were not abridged by finding that it violated a city fair employment ordinance by having a gender-segregated want ad column. Since that time, virtually all newspapers have abandoned gender-segregated want ads and also refuse to publish any discriminatory help wanted ads. The same is not true for internet websites, such as Craigslist.org, which impose no restrictions on want ads. Consequently, some ads contain legally impermissible criteria; this issue is discussed in greater detail below.

B.   Employment Agencies

Most states began licensing and regulating employment agencies during the Great Depression, when high unemployment led to some unscrupulous and exploitative agency practices. These laws typically required employment agency licensing and bonding, prohibited advance charging, and set maximum fees. The laws were challenged as being unconstitutional, but they were upheld as being necessary and reasonable regulations. See, e.g., National Employment Exch. v. Geraghty, 60 F.2d 918 (2d Cir. 1932); Abbye Employment Agency, Inc. v. Robinson, 2 N.Y.S.2d 947 (N.Y.Sup. Ct. 1938).

Today, in addition to the regulation of fees, discrimination in referrals is prohibited. Section 703(b) of Title VII provides: "It shall be an unlawful employment practice for an employment agency to fail or refuse to refer for employment, or otherwise to discriminate against, any individual because of his race, color, religion, sex, or national origin, or to classify or refer for employment on the basis of his race, color, religion, sex, or national origin." Section 701(c) of Title VII provides: "The term 'employment agency' means any person regularly undertaking with or without compensation to procure for employees opportunities to work for an employer and includes an agent of such person."

In Kaplowitz v. University of Chicago, 387 F.Supp. 42 (N.D.Ill.1974), the court held that a law school placement office was an employment agency for purposes of Title VII. But see Bonomo v. National Duckpin Bowling Congress, Inc., 469 F.Supp. 467 (D.Md.1979) (criticizing *Kaplowitz*). In Rumsfeld v. Forum for Academic & Institutional Rights, Inc., 547 U.S. 47 (2006), the Supreme Court held that the Solomon Amendment, 10 U.S.C. § 983, which ties federal funding for institutions of higher education with giving military recruiters access equal to that of other recruiters, does not violate law schools' First Amendment rights. The law schools sought to bar recruiters because of their opposition to discrimination on the basis of sexual orientation.

Every state has its own state employment service, which attempts to find appropriate jobs for the unemployed. These state agencies, mandated by a provision of the Federal Unemployment Tax Act, 26 U.S.C. § 3301, also are responsible for the distribution of insurance benefits. For further discussion of unemployment insurance, see Chapter 12.

In addition to statutory duties, employment agencies owe a common law duty of reasonable care to their clients. For example, in one case an employment agency received a phone call from a man who asked them to send over someone to do routine office work at a motorcycle repair shop. The agency dispatched a woman to the caller's "office," which was an empty room. The man then repeatedly sexually assaulted her and kidnapped her. Another employment agency had refused to refer anyone to the purported employer because he sounded "fishy." The employment agency's failure to make further inquiries of the caller made it liable for negligence. Keck v. American Employment Agency, 652 S.W.2d 2 (Ark. 1983).

C.   Hiring Halls

In some industries, such as construction and longshoring, unions serve as a job referral service. An employer needing workers would merely contact the union. In theory, the use of a hiring hall benefits both employers and workers. For employers, it facilitates recruitment and allows flexibility in hiring a workforce only as needed. For workers, it simplifies the job search process.

The problem with hiring halls has centered around the union's role in administering them. Section 8(b)(2) of the National Labor Relations Act (NLRA) makes it an unfair labor practice for a union "to cause or attempt to cause an employer to discriminate against an employee" in violation of section 8(a)(3). Section 8(a)(3) makes it an unfair labor practice for an employer "by discrimination in regard to hire or tenure of employment or any term or condition of employment to encourage or discourage membership in any labor organization."

In International Bhd. of Teamsters, Local 357 v. NLRB, 365 U.S. 667 (1961), the Supreme Court held that union hiring halls are not illegal per se. According to the Court, section 8(a)(3) only prohibits encouragement or discouragement of union membership accomplished by discrimination. Therefore, even if a hiring hall encourages union membership, it is not illegal if the hiring hall is run in a nondiscriminatory manner. In another words, union members may not be given preference over nonunion workers in job referrals. Discrimination by a union in hiring hall referrals is actionable under section 301 of the Labor Management Relations Act, in addition to being an unfair labor practice under the NLRA. Breininger v. Sheet Metal Workers Local Union No. 6, 493 U.S. 67 (1989). Hiring halls also have been held not to violate a state right to work law. Stricker v. Swift Bros. Constr. Co., 260 N.W.2d 500 (S.D. 1977).

A union hiring hall is permitted to use other reasonable criteria in making referrals. Thus, referrals may be made on the basis of seniority in the industry, *Teamsters;* residence in a particular area, Local Union 8, Electrical Workers, 221 N.L.R.B. 1131 (1975); or passing a union-administered examination, Electrical Workers, Local 592, 223 N.L.R.B. 899 (1976).

Another area in which unions control job opportunities is through apprenticeships and training programs. Race or gender discrimination in admission to such programs may violate Title VII. Some of the practices found to be discriminatory include the use of tests and admissions criteria which are not job related, Hameed v. International Ass'n of Bridge, Structural, & Ornamental Iron Workers, 637 F.2d 506 (8th Cir. 1980); recruitment efforts aimed only at whites, United States v. Sheet Metal Workers, Local Union 36, 416 F.2d 123 (8th Cir. 1969); and discriminatory application of admissions requirements, Sims v. Sheet Metal Workers, Local Union 65, 489 F.2d 1023 (6th Cir. 1973).

D.   Internet

The use of the Internet in linking prospective employers and employees extends well beyond placing job announcements and resumes on-line. The expanded use of social networking sites in employee recruitment may become commonplace.

> Recruiting for the vast majority of professional jobs will start in one of the highly trafficked social networking sites, such as Facebook, LinkedIn, YouTube, Twitter, and Second Life. Though [some

organizations] are already doing this, an overwhelming number of companies—we predict at least 80 percent—will begin to tap online social networks as the first stop to recruiting global talent. Prospective employees may potentially have their first interview via their avatar, followed by several video chats and reference checks on social networks. This is social recruiting, where companies leverage a range of social media and professional networks, online and offline, to acquire talent.

Jeanne C. Meister & Karie Willyerd, The 2020 Workplace: How Innovative Companies Attract, Develop, and Keep Tomorrow's Employees Today 217 (2010). What challenges are raised for individuals and employers in using these technologies?

An important, but as yet unresolved issue, is whether current employment laws are adequate to regulate the use of the Internet and social networks in recruiting employees. For example, does Title VII apply to Internet websites used to recruit employees? For example, the Attorney General of Illinois recently opened an investigation into potential age discrimination by job search sites. One news report concerning the investigation reported that some job search sites have categories such as "Senior Citizen Jobs," or "Careers at 50+." Others have applicants enter their qualifications using drop-down menus for categories such as "years attended college" that do not go back far enough to be useful to older workers. Bob Sullivan, Online Job Sites May Block Older Workers, CNBC March 12, 2017 https://www.cnbc.com/2017/03/10/online-job-sites-may-block-older-workers. html. Should different legal rules apply to craigslist, which merely serves as a bulletin board for postings by individuals and entities (including employers), than to monster.com or careerbuilder.com, which are designed to be electronic job search sites? Courts have drawn this distinction in the context of fair housing law. Compare Chicago Lawyers' Committee for Civil Rights Under Law, Inc. v. Craigslist, Inc., 518 F.3d 666 (7th Cir. 2008) with Fair Housing Counsel of San Fernando Valley v. Roommates.com, 521 F.3d 1157 (9th Cir. 2008).

Other issues arise when employers use Facebook to advertise jobs. Facebook allows job posters to select a target audience to whom the ad will be visible. Journalists found that dozens of companies used this capability to exclude older workers from seeing their job ads. Julia Angwin, Noam Scheiber, and Ariana Tobin, Facebook Job Ads Raise Concerns About Age Discrimination, New York Times Dec. 20, 2017 https://www.nytimes.com/2017/12/20/business/facebook-job-ads.html. The EEOC has recently concluded that an employer's decisions to limit the audience able to view Facebook job ads based on age or race provides reasonable cause to believe the employer has violated Title VII or the ADEA. Further, Facebook recently settled a lawsuit over its own role in these advertisements, agreeing to eliminate users' abilities to target job ads by age or gender, among other changes.

Another important issue concerns employers' use of social media sites such as Facebook to screen job applicants. Do prospective employees have any legal remedy when an employer learns information it could not legally seek directly (such as race or religion)? Does this pre-screening violate any privacy rights of prospective employees? Does an employer have a right to learn the information or any obligation to third parties to obtain it? Are there First Amendment considerations? See Nancy Leong, The Race-Neutral Workplace of the Future, 51 U.C. Davis L. Rev. 719 (2017); Pauline Kim, Data-Driven Discrimination at Work, 58 Wm. & Mary L. Rev. 857 (2017); Michelle Poore, A Call for Uncle Sam to Get Big Brother Out of Our Knickers: Protecting Privacy and Freedom of Speech Interests in Social Media Accounts, 40 N. Ky. L. Rev. 507 (2013); Michelle Scheinman, Cyberfrontier: New Guidelines for Employers Regarding Employee Social Media, 44 McGeorge L. Rev. 731 (2013); Nancy B. Schess, Then and Now: How Technology Has Changed the Workplace, 30 Hofstra Lab. & Empl. L.J. 435 (2013).

NOTE

In 2004, the EEOC and other agencies jointly proposed a definition of an Internet "applicant." Under the proposal, a person would be an applicant if three conditions are met: (1) the employer has acted to fill a particular position; (2) the individual has followed the employer's standard procedures for submitting applications; and (3) the individual has expressed an interest in the particular position. 69 Fed. Reg. 10,152 (2004). What, if any, unique practical or legal issues are raised by applications over the Internet?

3.   INDIVIDUALS UNAUTHORIZED TO WORK IN THE U.S.

According to the Department of Homeland Security, in 2015 there were approximately 12 million undocumented people in the United States. Most enter the United States to work. In theory, if people without work authorization could not find jobs because of their immigration status, then they would be less inclined to risk entering the country. Thus, the Immigration Reform and Control Act of 1986 (IRCA), 8 U.S.C. §§ 1324a, 1324b, seeks to decrease unauthorized immigration by prohibiting, as the statute puts it, "unlawful employment of aliens." The number of people in the U.S. without authorization in 2017, 11 million, was roughly the same as it was in 2011. Jens Manuel Krogstad, Jeffrey S. Passel and D'Vera Cohn, Five Facts About Illegal Immigration in the US, Pew Research Center, April 27, 2017, available at http://www. pewresearch.org/fact-tank/2017/04/27/5-facts-about-illegal-immigration-in-the-u-s/.

IRCA applies to all employers, regardless of size or industry. It prohibits employers from hiring undocumented workers and provides civil penalties of $250 to $2,000 for each undocumented worker hired. For subsequent offenses, penalties of up to $10,000 may be assessed and for a "pattern or practice" of violations, the employer is subject to a $3,000 criminal fine and six months imprisonment.

Employers are required to ask all job applicants for documents, such as a passport, a birth certificate, or a driver's license, to confirm that they are either citizens or otherwise authorized to work in the United States. The employer is not required to check the authenticity of documents.

The Act also offers legal status to those who entered the United States illegally before January 1, 1982, and have resided continuously since then. Making false statements in an application for legal status is subject to a $2,000 fine and up to five years imprisonment.

From 1986 to 2003, IRCA was enforced by the Immigration and Naturalization Service (INS). In March 2003, as part of a reorganization of federal law enforcement after 9/11, the INS and Customs Service were combined into a single new agency, Immigration and Customs Enforcement (ICE), part of the Department of Homeland Security.

Comprehensive immigration reform has been stalled in Congress for several years. The lack of federal legislation and continued problems with preventing illegal immigration have led several states to enact their own immigration laws. The laws generally bar employers that hire undocumented aliens from entering into contracts with the state. See, e.g., La. Rev. Stat. tit. 23, § 996; Pa. Cons. Stat. Ann. Tit. 43, § 166.2; Tenn. Code Ann. Tit. 12, ch. 4. The most aggressive of the state laws is the Legal Arizona Workers Act of 2007, Ariz. Rev. Stat. §§ 23–211 to 23–216. Under the Act, an Arizona employer that knowingly or intentionally hires unauthorized aliens is subject to sanctions in addition to those posed under IRCA, up to and including the permanent revocation or the employer's business license, making the employer effectively unable to do business legally in Arizona. See infra at p. 102.

Immigration laws continue to be highly contentious and politically charged. Various solutions have been proposed, including amnesty, more enforcement actions against employers, increased border security, and guest worker programs. Besides being a political issue, illegal immigration is an important employment issue. Unauthorized workers constitute five percent of the work force; they are engaged in various occupations, including agriculture, construction, manufacturing, and various services. As the population ages, there is likely to be an increasing shortage of nursing home workers and other health care aides, another common job filled by undocumented workers.

As you read the following cases on undocumented workers, consider how well the current legal regime is working to achieve public policy, whether the proper balance is being struck between immigration regulation and other objectives, and in what ways the law could become more responsive to this area of concern and debate.

Aramark Facility Services v. Service Employees International Union

530 F.3d 817 (9th Cir. 2008).

■ HALL, CIRCUIT JUDGE:

I. INTRODUCTION

This case arose from the response by Aramark Facility Services ("Aramark") to a "no-match letter" from the Social Security Administration ("SSA"), which indicated that Aramark had reported information for 48 of its employees at the Staples Center in downtown Los Angeles that did not match the SSA's database. Suspecting immigration violations, Aramark told the listed employees they had three days to correct the mismatches by proving they had begun the process of applying for a new social security card. Seven to ten days later, Aramark fired the 33 employees who did not timely comply.

Staples Center, Los Angeles

Local 1877 of the Service Employees International Union ("SEIU") filed a grievance on behalf of the fired workers, contending the terminations were without just cause and thus in breach of the collective bargaining agreement ("CBA") between Aramark and SEIU. An arbitrator ruled for SEIU and awarded the fired workers back-pay and reinstatement, finding there was no convincing information that any of the fired workers were undocumented. The district court vacated the award on the ground that it violated public policy. SEIU timely appealed.

This case boils down to a single issue: whether the SSA's no-match letter—and the fired employees' responses—put Aramark on constructive notice that it was employing undocumented workers. If so, the arbitrator's award would force Aramark to violate federal immigration law, and therefore was properly vacated as against public policy. If not, the award must stand.

As we explain below, Aramark has not established constructive knowledge of any immigration violations. Constructive knowledge is to be narrowly construed in the immigration context and requires positive information of a worker's undocumented status. Moreover, we are required to defer to the arbitrator's factual findings even when evaluating an award for violation of public policy. Accordingly, given the extremely short time that Aramark gave its employees to return with further documents and the arbitrator's finding that Aramark had no "convincing information" of immigration violations, the employees' failure to meet the deadline simply is not probative enough of their immigration status to indicate that public policy would be violated if they were reinstated and given backpay. Therefore, the district court erred and the award must be confirmed.

II. FACTUAL AND PROCEDURAL BACKGROUND

A. The Letter Sent to Aramark and Aramark's Response

Aramark is a corporation that employs approximately 170,000 people in the United States, and its facilities management division provides labor for the Staples Center, a 19,000-seat sports and entertainment venue in downtown Los Angeles. In early 2003, Aramark received letters from the SSA notifying it that the social security numbers of some 3,300 of its employees nationwide did not match those in the SSA's database. Aramark reacted to these "no-match" letters by asking its regional managers to confirm that the information it provided SSA matched the information provided by employees and, if so, to require corrective steps from the employees they supervised. On April 15 and 16, 2003, instructions were relayed to 48 Aramark employees working at the Staples Center, who were represented by SEIU and employed pursuant to a CBA between SEIU and Aramark. Aramark's instructions to the Staples Center employees read as follows:

1. Please return to the [SSA] office to correct [the] discrepancy

2. Return to Aramark Facility Services at Staples Center with one of two items.

    a) A new social security card, [sic] photo copies will not be accepted

    b) Verification form that shows a new card is being processed.

3. You have three working days from the post-marked date of this letter to bring either.

[ ]You have 90 days from the date of re-application on your receipt to bring in your new card.

4.   A new card or verification of renewal must be in the office no later then [sic] close of business 4pm on Wednesday April 23rd, 2003.

If you fail to comply with this letter and you do not bring in the proper documents then unfortunately your employment with Aramark will be terminated. (emphasis added).

No employee was aware of the policy before receiving the mismatch letter. Believing the three-day turnaround time was too onerous, SEIU requested an extension, but Aramark denied this request.

Fifteen of the Staples Center employees obtained the requested documentation in time and continued to work. However, 33 employees did not timely comply and were fired. The last day of work for virtually all of them was either April 16, 2003, or April 18, 2003. Most were officially fired effective April 23, while a few were fired April 28, 2003. Although the instruction letters from Aramark stated that employees were expected to visit an SSA office and provide the initial documentation within three days, the employees were actually given seven to ten days to provide the required paperwork, though nothing in the record indicates that they knew they had this much time. The fired workers were told that they would be rehired if they supplied the required documentation; nothing indicates *when* they received this information.

Though it suspected immigration violations, Aramark did not know for sure why the terminated employees did not provide additional documents and even argued to the arbitrator that they could have had "valid" work eligibility. Each of the fired employees had, at the time they were hired, properly completed the federal Employee Eligibility Verification Form ("Form I-9") and provided Aramark with facially valid documents establishing their identity and eligibility to work in the United States. Moreover, Aramark was not notified by any federal agency that its workers were suspected of being undocumented.

B. Arbitration

After the terminations, SEIU filed a grievance on behalf of the Staples Center employees, contending that Aramark had violated the CBA by firing them without just cause. Pursuant to the CBA, the matter was submitted to binding arbitration. Over two days of hearings, the parties presented testimony concerning the no-match letters, Aramark's obligation to comply with applicable tax and immigration laws, and the procedures by which the Staples Center employees were fired.

Ultimately, the arbitrator concluded that there was no "convincing information" that any of the terminated workers were undocumented. He thus found that the firings were without just cause, ruled in favor of SEIU, and awarded the workers back-pay and reinstatement.

C. District Court Proceedings

After the arbitrator's ruling, Aramark filed a complaint in U.S. District Court to vacate the arbitration award, and SEIU counter-claimed to confirm it. The parties filed cross-motions for summary judgment, and at a hearing held September 29, 2006, the district court ruled in favor of Aramark. The court reasoned that because the fired employees failed to indicate that they were beginning the process of correcting the SSN mismatch, Aramark had constructive notice that they were ineligible to work in the United States. Therefore, the court held that the arbitrator's award of reinstatement and back-pay violated public policy because it would require Aramark to violate the immigration laws. SEIU timely appealed.

III. STANDARD OF REVIEW

We review vacation of arbitration awards like "any other district court decision * * * accepting findings of fact that are not 'clearly erroneous' but deciding questions of law de novo." Here, the district court resolved the matter on the parties' cross-motions for summary judgment, which necessarily present questions of law. We must therefore decide de novo whether there are any genuine issues of material fact and whether the district court correctly applied the relevant substantive law.

IV. DISCUSSION

A. The Legal Standard for Review of the Arbitrator's Award

"The scope of review of an arbitrator's decision in a labor dispute is extremely narrow." Arbitration awards are ordinarily upheld so long as they represent a "plausible interpretation of the contract." However, one narrow exception to this generally deferential review is the "now-settled rule that a court need not, in fact cannot, enforce an award which violates public policy." "[T]he question of public policy is ultimately one for resolution by the courts." The public policy exception is Aramark's sole basis for attacking the arbitration award in this case.

"To vacate an arbitration award on public policy grounds, we must (1) find that an explicit, well defined and dominant policy exists here and (2) that the policy is one that specifically militates against the relief ordered by the arbitrator." In evaluating a public policy argument, we "must focus on the award itself, not the behavior or conduct of the party in question." We have stressed that "courts should be reluctant to vacate arbitral awards on public policy grounds," because "[t]he finality of arbitral awards must be preserved if arbitration is to remain a desirable alternative to courtroom litigation." Moreover, before the award will be vacated as against public policy, the policy violation must be "clearly shown."

* * *

B. Analysis

* * *

1. The Asserted Public Policy

The main public policy to which Aramark points is expressed in the Immigration Reform and Control Act of 1986 ("IRCA"), Pub.L. No. 99–603, 100 Stat. 3359 (1986). Specifically, Aramark cites the laws that (1) employers are subject to civil and criminal liability if they employ undocumented workers "knowing" of their undocumented status, and (2) the term "knowing" includes constructive knowledge. We agree that these policies are germane to the arbitrator's reinstatement award because they would necessarily be violated if Aramark knowingly reinstated undocumented workers. They are also germane to the back-pay award because the Supreme Court has held that immigration policy precludes such awards to undocumented workers. These policies are "explicit," "well-defined," and "dominant," expressed not by "general considerations" but by the IRCA, its implementing regulations, and Supreme Court case law interpreting it. They are therefore an adequate basis for Aramark's public policy attack.

2. Whether the Policy Specifically Militates Against the Award

The more difficult question is whether these policies "specifically militate" against the arbitrator's award here—that is, whether the arbitrator's award would have forced Aramark to reinstate and provide back-pay to undocumented workers where Aramark had "constructive knowledge" that they were undocumented.

As defined in the relevant regulation, "[c]onstructive knowledge is knowledge that may fairly be inferred through notice of certain facts and circumstances that would lead a person, through the exercise of reasonable care, to know about a certain condition." 8 C.F.R. § 274a.1(*l*). We have stressed that, for purposes of the IRCA, "constructive knowledge" is to be narrowly construed. Collins Foods Int'l, Inc. v. INS, 948 F.2d 549, 554–55 (9th Cir. 1991). In *Collins,* we reversed an ALJ's holding that the employer had constructive knowledge of an immigration violation because it had extended an offer of employment over the telephone and overlooked that the employee's social security card was fraudulent. We distinguished other cases finding constructive knowledge on the grounds that the employer there did not have "positive information" that the employee was undocumented. In those distinguishable cases, on which Aramark relies heavily here, the INS specifically visited the employer and notified it that its employees were suspected unlawful aliens and should be terminated if inspection of their documents did not allay the concerns.

Here, Aramark essentially argues that two facts gave it constructive notice of immigration violations: (1) the no-match letters themselves and (2) the employees' responses (or lack thereof). We address each contention in turn.

a.   The Letters Themselves

Given the narrow scope of the constructive knowledge doctrine, the "no-match" letters themselves could not have put Aramark on constructive notice that any particular employee mentioned was undocumented. To understand why, some background on the purpose of the no-match letters is helpful. The SSA routinely sends the letters when an employer's W-2 records differ from the SSA's database regarding an employee's social security number ("SSN"). When there is a discrepancy, the SSA cannot post an employee's social security earnings to his or her account, and instead must deposit the funds into a national "earnings suspense fund," which is a very large fund containing more than 250 million mismatched records and totaling more than $500 billion. The Inspector General of the SSA believes that "the chief cause of wage items being posted to the [earnings suspense fund] instead of an individual's earnings record is unauthorized work by noncitizens." However, the main purpose of the no-match letters is not immigration-related, but rather is simply to indicate to workers that their earnings are not being properly credited.

In addition to misuse by undocumented workers, SSN mismatches could generate a no-match letter for many reasons, including typographical errors, name changes, compound last names prevalent in immigrant communities, and inaccurate or incomplete employer records. By SSA's own estimates, approximately 17.8 million of the 430 million entries in its database (called "NUMIDENT") contain errors, including about 3.3 million entries that mis-classify foreign-born U.S. citizens as aliens.

As a result, an SSN discrepancy does not *automatically* mean that an employee is undocumented or lacks proper work authorization. In fact, the SSA tells employers that the information it provides them "does not make any statement about . . . immigration status" and "is not a basis, in and of itself, to take any adverse action against the employee." This information is included in the no-match letters, and was added at the urging of advocacy groups such as amicus National Immigration Law Center to combat abuses by employers who assumed that the workers mentioned in the letters were undocumented.

Moreover, employers do not face any penalty from SSA, which lacks an enforcement arm, for ignoring a no-match letter. The IRS also imposes no sanctions stemming from the no-match letters. It requires no additional solicitations of an employee's SSN unless it sends a "penalty notice" to the employer indicating that the SSN is incorrect—a notice Aramark does not contend it received. The IRS also does not require any reverification of a worker's documents following receipt of a mismatch notice from the SSA.

* * *

In sum, the letters Aramark received are not intended by the SSA to contain "positive information" of immigration status, and could be triggered by numerous reasons other than fraudulent documents, including various errors in the SSA's NUMIDENT database. Indeed, the letters do not indicate that the government suspects the workers of using fraudulent documents. Rather, they merely indicate that the worker's earnings were not being properly credited, *one explanation of which* is fraudulent SSNs. This falls short of the "positive information" from the government that was held to provide constructive notice. * * * Without more, the letters did not provide constructive notice of any immigration violations.

b. Employees' Reactions

Aramark also maintains that constructive notice resulted from the fired workers' *reactions* to the no-match letters and Aramark's directive to return quickly with documents from the SSA. It argues that it provided the employees a reasonable time in which to correct their SSN discrepancies, and that their failure to do so is sufficiently probative of their immigration status to rise to the level of "constructive notice" that they were undocumented.

We disagree. Though the question is a close one, two considerations weigh against a finding of constructive notice here: (1) the arbitrator's findings, and (2) the short turnaround time. Moreover, contrary to the district court's conclusion, the analysis is unaffected by Aramark's offer to rehire any terminated employees who later came forward with proper documentation.

* * *

V. CONCLUSION

This case turns on the deference owed to the arbitrator's factual findings, as well as the narrowness of both the public policy exception and the doctrine of constructive knowledge in the immigration context. Though it seems reasonable to suspect that some of the fired workers were undocumented, the law did not permit the district court to rely on this suspicion in vacating the arbitration award.

NOTES AND QUESTIONS

1. Employees must complete and employers must execute and maintain an Employment Eligibility Verification Form, known as Form I-9. Employers are required to ask all job applicants for a passport, birth certificate, or driver's license, to confirm that they are either citizens or aliens authorized to work in the United States. The employer is not required to check the authenticity of the documents.

2. The effect of the collective bargaining agreement is to assign to Aramark the burden of proving that the terminated employees were unauthorized to work in the US. Does this make sense? If the employees were not unionized, what result?

3. *Aramark* illustrates the dilemma faced by employers. Too little effort to follow up on suspected undocumented workers could subject the company to civil and criminal liability under IRCA. See, e.g., Collins Foods, Int'l, Inc. v. INS, 948 F.2d 549 (9th Cir. 1991). Overzealous efforts to discharge employees with unclear immigration status, as in this case, could result in employers being liable for back pay to the workers they discharge. According to the court, in what way did Aramark err in its verification efforts?

4. Under IRCA, ICE can levy either civil or criminal penalties against employers found guilty of paperwork or illegal hiring violations. Civil penalties of $250 to $10,000 may be assessed against an employer who knowingly hires or continues to hire an unauthorized worker. An employer who engages in a "pattern or practice" of hiring undocumented workers is subject to criminal fines of up to $3,000 for each undocumented employee and up to six months in jail.

5. Under IRCA, fines for repeated violations of the illegal hiring provisions of the Act are more severe than "first level" fines. In Furr's/Bishop's Cafeterias, L.P. v. INS, 976 F.2d 1366 (10th Cir. 1992), the Attorney General asserted that enhanced fines against a company for a subsequent IRCA violation at a different establishment of the company were appropriate because the company retained the power to terminate unauthorized employees, discipline managers, and conduct company wide education programs. The company argued that each establishment should be considered separately. The Tenth Circuit upheld the increased fines.

6. Employer sanctions present a special problem for employers who cannot find qualified U.S. workers to fill certain skilled or professional positions. U.S. law permits employers to "sponsor" immigrant workers for permanent residence by proving through a Department of Labor procedure known as "labor certification" that no U.S. workers are qualified or available for the job offered. Even after approval, however, immigrant workers often face a long wait under the visa quota system before they can actually apply for permanent resident status. The ICE position is that an employer is subject to sanctions upon learning through the labor certification process that an immigrant worker is not authorized to work in the United States. This policy will certainly deter employers from assisting immigrants with the labor certification process and may have a negative impact on sectors where U.S. workers are typically in short supply.

Chamber of Commerce v. Whiting
563 U.S. 582 (2011).

■ CHIEF JUSTICE ROBERTS delivered the opinion of the Court, except as to Parts II-B and III-B.

Federal immigration law expressly preempts "any State or local law imposing civil or criminal sanctions (other than through licensing and similar laws) upon those who employ . . . unauthorized aliens." 8 U.S.C. § 1324a(h)(2). A recently enacted Arizona statute—the Legal Arizona Workers Act—provides that the licenses of state employers that knowingly or intentionally employ unauthorized aliens may be, and in certain circumstances must be, suspended or revoked. The law also requires that all Arizona employers use a federal electronic verification system to confirm that the workers they employ are legally authorized workers. The question presented is whether federal immigration law preempts those provisions of Arizona law. Because we conclude that the State's licensing provisions fall squarely within the federal statute's savings clause and that the Arizona regulation does not otherwise conflict with federal law, we hold that the Arizona law is not preempted.

I.

A.

In 1952, Congress enacted the Immigration and Nationality Act (INA). That statute established a "comprehensive federal statutory scheme for regulation of immigration and naturalization" and set "the terms and conditions of admission to the country and the subsequent treatment of aliens lawfully in the country." De Canas v. Bica, 424 U.S. 351, 353, 359 (1976).

In the years following the enactment of the INA, several States took action to prohibit the employment of individuals living within state borders who were not lawful residents of the United States.

* * *

We first addressed the interaction of federal immigration law and state laws dealing with the employment of unauthorized aliens in *De Canas*. In that case, we recognized that the "[p]ower to regulate immigration is unquestionably . . . a federal power." At the same time, however, we noted that the "States possess broad authority under their police powers to regulate the employment relationship to protect workers within the State," that "prohibit[ing] the knowing employment . . . of persons not entitled to lawful residence in the United States, let alone to work here, is certainly within the mainstream of [the State's] police power," and that the Federal Government had "at best" expressed a peripheral concern with [the] employment of illegal entrants at that point in time. As a result, we declined to hold that a state law assessing civil fines for the employment of unauthorized aliens was preempted by federal immigration law.

Ten years after *De Canas*, Congress enacted the Immigration Reform and Control Act (IRCA). IRCA makes it "unlawful for a person or other entity . . . to hire, or to recruit or refer for a fee, for employment in the United States an alien knowing the alien is an unauthorized alien." 8 U.S.C. § 1324a(a)(1)(A). IRCA defines an "unauthorized alien" as an alien who is not "lawfully admitted for permanent residence" or not otherwise authorized by the Attorney General to be employed in the United States.

* * *

IRCA also restricts the ability of States to combat employment of unauthorized workers. The Act expressly preempts "any State or local law imposing civil or criminal sanctions (other than through licensing and similar laws) upon those who employ, or recruit or refer for a fee for employment, unauthorized aliens." Under that provision, state laws imposing civil fines for the employment of unauthorized workers like the one we upheld in *De Canas* are now expressly preempted.

* * *

B.

Acting against this statutory and historical background, several States have recently enacted laws attempting to impose sanctions for the employment of unauthorized aliens through, among other things, "licensing and similar laws." Arizona is one of them. The Legal Arizona Workers Act of 2007 allows Arizona courts to suspend or revoke the licenses necessary to do business in the State if an employer knowingly or intentionally employs an unauthorized alien.

Under the Arizona law, if an individual files a complaint alleging that an employer has hired an unauthorized alien, the attorney general or the county attorney first verifies the employee's work authorization with the Federal Government pursuant to 8 U.S.C. § 1373(c). Section 1373(c) provides that the Federal Government "shall respond to an inquiry by a" State "seeking to verify or ascertain the citizenship or immigration status of any individual . . . by providing the requested verification or status information." The Arizona law expressly prohibits state, county, or local officials from attempting "to independently make a final determination on whether an alien is authorized to work in the United States." If the § 1373(c) inquiry reveals that a worker is an unauthorized alien, the attorney general or the county attorney must notify United States Immigration and Customs Enforcement officials, notify local law enforcement, and bring an action against the employer.

When a complaint is brought against an employer under Arizona law, "the court shall consider only the federal government's determination pursuant to" 8 U.S.C. § 1373(c) in "determining whether an employee is an unauthorized alien." Good-faith compliance with the federal I-9 process provides employers prosecuted by the State with an affirmative defense.

A first instance of "knowingly employ[ing] an unauthorized alien" requires that the court order the employer to terminate the employment of all unauthorized aliens and file quarterly reports on all new hires for a probationary period of three years. The court may also "order the appropriate agencies to suspend all licenses . . . that are held by the employer for [a period] not to exceed ten business days." A second knowing violation requires that the adjudicating court "permanently revoke all licenses that are held by the employer specific to the business location where the unauthorized alien performed work."

With respect to both knowing and intentional violations, a violation qualifies as a "second violation" only if it occurs at the same business location as the first violation, during the time that the employer is already on probation for a violation at that location.

The Arizona law also requires that "every employer, after hiring an employee, shall verify the employment eligibility of the employee" by using E-Verify. "[P]roof of verifying the employment authorization of an employee through the e-verify program creates a rebuttable presumption that an employer did not knowingly employ an unauthorized alien."

C.

* * *

The Court of Appeals affirmed the District Court in all respects, holding that Arizona's law was a " 'licensing and similar law[ ]' " falling within IRCA's savings clause and that none of the state law's challenged provisions was "expressly or impliedly preempted by federal policy."

II.

The Chamber of Commerce argues that Arizona's law is expressly preempted by IRCA's text and impliedly preempted because it conflicts with federal law. We address each of the Chamber's arguments in turn.

A.

* * *

IRCA expressly preempts States from imposing "civil or criminal sanctions" on those who employ unauthorized aliens, "other than through licensing and similar laws." The Arizona law, on its face, purports to impose sanctions through licensing laws. The state law authorizes state courts to suspend or revoke an employer's business licenses if that employer knowingly or intentionally employs an unauthorized alien. The Arizona law defines "license" as "any agency permit, certificate, approval, registration, charter or similar form of authorization that is required by law and that is issued by any agency for the purposes of operating a business in" the State. That definition largely parrots the definition of "license" that Congress codified in the Administrative Procedure Act.

Apart from that general definition, the Arizona law specifically includes within its definition of license documents such as articles of incorporation, certificates of partnership, and grants of authority to foreign companies to transact business in the State. These examples have clear counterparts in the APA definition just quoted.

A license is "a right or permission granted in accordance with law . . . to engage in some business or occupation, to do some act, or to engage in some transaction which but for such license would be unlawful." Webster's Third New International Dictionary 1304 (2002). Articles of incorporation and certificates of partnership allow the formation of legal entities and permit them as such to engage in business and transactions "which but for such" authorization "would be unlawful." As for state-issued authorizations for foreign businesses to operate within a State, we have repeatedly referred to those as "licenses." Moreover, even if a law regulating articles of incorporation, partnership certificates, and the like is not itself a "licensing law," it is at the very least "similar" to a licensing law, and therefore comfortably within the savings clause.

The Chamber and the United States as amicus argue that the Arizona law is not a "licensing" law because it operates only to suspend and revoke licenses rather than to grant them. Again, this construction of the term runs contrary to the definition that Congress itself has codified. It is also contrary to common sense. There is no basis in law, fact, or logic for deeming a law that grants licenses a licensing law, but a law that suspends or revokes those very licenses something else altogether.

* * *

B.

As an alternative to its express preemption argument, the Chamber contends that Arizona's law is impliedly preempted because it conflicts with federal law. At its broadest level, the Chamber's argument is that Congress "intended the federal system to be exclusive," and that any state system therefore necessarily conflicts with federal law. But Arizona's procedures simply implement the sanctions that Congress expressly allowed Arizona to pursue through licensing laws. Given that Congress specifically preserved such authority for the States, it stands to reason that Congress did not intend to prevent the States from using appropriate tools to exercise that authority.

And here Arizona went the extra mile in ensuring that its law closely tracks IRCA's provisions in all material respects. The Arizona law begins by adopting the federal definition of who qualifies as an "unauthorized alien."

Not only that, the Arizona law expressly provides that state investigators must verify the work authorization of an allegedly unauthorized alien with the Federal Government, and "shall not attempt to independently make a final determination on whether an alien is authorized to work in the United States." What is more, a state court "shall consider only the federal government's determination" when deciding "whether an employee is an unauthorized alien." As a result, there can by definition be no conflict between state and federal law as to worker authorization, either at the investigatory or adjudicatory stage.

* * *

The Chamber and JUSTICE BREYER assert that employers will err on the side of discrimination rather than risk the " 'business death penalty' " by "hiring unauthorized workers." That is not the choice. License termination is not an available sanction simply for "hiring unauthorized workers." Only far more egregious violations of the law trigger that consequence. The Arizona law covers only knowing or intentional violations. The law's permanent licensing sanctions do not come into play until a second knowing or intentional violation at the same business location, and only if the second violation occurs while the employer is still on probation for the first. These limits ensure that licensing sanctions are imposed only when an employer's conduct fully justifies them. An employer acting in good faith need have no fear of the sanctions.

As the Chamber points out, IRCA has its own anti-discrimination provisions, Arizona law certainly does nothing to displace those. Other federal laws, and Arizona anti-discrimination laws, provide further protection against employment discrimination—and strong incentive for employers not to discriminate.

All that is required to avoid sanctions under the Legal Arizona Workers Act is to refrain from knowingly or intentionally violating the employment law. Employers enjoy safe harbors from liability when they use the I-9 system and E-Verify—as Arizona law requires them to do. The most rational path for employers is to obey the law—both the law barring the employment of unauthorized aliens and the law prohibiting discrimination—and there is no reason to suppose that Arizona employers will choose not to do so.

As with any piece of legislation, Congress did indeed seek to strike a balance among a variety of interests when it enacted IRCA. Part of that balance, however, involved allocating authority between the Federal Government and the States. The principle that Congress adopted in doing so was not that the Federal Government can impose large sanctions, and the States only small ones. IRCA instead preserved state authority over a particular category of sanctions—those imposed "through licensing and similar laws."

* * *

III.

* * *

Because Arizona's unauthorized alien employment law fits within the confines of IRCA's savings clause and does not conflict with federal immigration law, the judgment of the United States Court of Appeals for the Ninth Circuit is affirmed.

It is so ordered.

■ JUSTICE KAGAN took no part in the consideration or decision of this case.

■ JUSTICE BREYER, with whom JUSTICE GINSBURG joins, dissenting.

* * *

Arizona calls its state statute a "licensing law," and the statute uses the word "licensing." But the statute strays beyond the bounds of the federal licensing exception, for it defines "license" to include articles of incorporation and partnership certificates, indeed virtually every state-law authorization for any firm, corporation, or partnership to do business in the State. Congress did not intend its "licensing" language to create so broad an exemption, for doing so would permit States to eviscerate the federal Act's pre-emption provision, indeed to subvert the Act itself, by undermining Congress' efforts (1) to protect lawful workers from national-origin-based discrimination and (2) to protect lawful employers against erroneous prosecution or punishment.

* * *

First, the state statute seriously threatens the federal Act's antidiscriminatory objectives by radically skewing the relevant penalties. For example, in the absence of the Arizona statute, an Arizona employer who intentionally hires an unauthorized alien for the second time would risk a maximum penalty of $6,500. But the Arizona statute subjects that same employer (in respect to the same two incidents) to mandatory, permanent loss of the right to do business in Arizona—a penalty that Arizona's Governor has called the "business death penalty." At the same time, the state law leaves the other side of the punishment balance—the antidiscrimination side—unchanged.

This is no idle concern. Despite the federal Act's efforts to prevent discriminatory practices, there is evidence that four years after it had become law, discrimination was a serious problem. In 1990, the General Accounting Office identified "widespread discrimination . . . as a result of" the Act. Sixteen percent of employers in Los Angeles admitted that they applied the I-9 requirement "only to foreign-looking or foreign-sounding persons," and 22 percent of Texas employers reported that they "began a practice to (1) hire only persons born in the United States or (2) not hire persons with temporary work eligibility documents" because of the Act. If even the federal Act (with its carefully balanced penalties) can result in some employers discriminating, how will employers behave when erring on the side of discrimination leads only to relatively small fines, while erring on the side of hiring unauthorized workers leads to the "business death penalty"?

Second, Arizona's law subjects lawful employers to increased burdens and risks of erroneous prosecution. In addition to the Arizona law's severely burdensome sanctions, the law's procedures create enforcement risks not present in the federal system. The federal Act creates one centralized enforcement scheme, run by officials versed in immigration law and with access to the relevant federal documents. The upshot is an increased likelihood that federal officials (or the employer) will discover whether adverse information flows from an error-prone source and that they will proceed accordingly, thereby diminishing the likelihood that burdensome proceedings and liability reflect documentary mistakes.

Contrast the enforcement system that Arizona's statute creates. Any citizen of the State can complain (anonymously or otherwise) to the state attorney general (or any county attorney), who then "shall investigate," and, upon a determination that that the "complaint is not false and frivolous . . . shall notify the appropriate county attorney to bring an action." This mandatory language, the lower standard ("not frivolous" instead of "substantial"), and the removal of immigration officials from the state screening process (substituting numerous, elected county attorneys) increase the likelihood that suspicious circumstances will lead to prosecutions and liability of employers—even where more careful investigation would have revealed that there was no violation.

Why would Congress, after deliberately limiting ordinary penalties to the range of a few thousand dollars per illegal worker, want to permit far more drastic state penalties that would directly and mandatorily destroy entire businesses? Why would Congress, after carefully balancing sanctions to avoid encouraging discrimination, want to allow States to destroy that balance? Why would Congress, after creating detailed procedural protections for employers, want to allow States to undermine them? Why would Congress want to write into an express pre-emption provision—a provision designed to prevent States from undercutting federal statutory objectives—an exception that could so easily destabilize its efforts? The answer to these questions is that Congress would not have wanted to do any of these things. And that fact indicates that the majority's reading of the licensing exception—a reading that would allow what Congress sought to forbid—is wrong.

■ JUSTICE SOTOMAYOR, dissenting.

* * *

Congress made explicit its intent that IRCA be enforced uniformly. IRCA declares that "[i]t is the sense of the Congress that . . . the immigration laws of the United States should be enforced vigorously and uniformly." Congress structured IRCA's provisions in a number of ways to accomplish this goal of uniform enforcement.

First, and most obviously, Congress expressly displaced the myriad state laws that imposed civil and criminal sanctions on employers who hired unauthorized aliens. Congress could not have made its intent to preempt state and local laws imposing civil or criminal sanctions any more " 'clear [or] manifest.' "

Second, Congress centralized in the Federal Government enforcement of IRCA's prohibition on the knowing employment of unauthorized aliens. IRCA instructs the Attorney General to designate a specialized federal agency unit whose "primary duty" will be to prosecute violations of IRCA. IRCA also instructs the Attorney General to establish procedures for receiving complaints, investigating complaints having "a substantial probability of validity," and investigating other violations.

* * *

Third, Congress provided persons "adversely affected" by an agency order with a right of review in the federal courts of appeals. In this way, Congress ensured that administrative orders finding violations of IRCA would be reviewed by federal judges with experience adjudicating immigration-related matters.

Fourth, Congress created a uniquely federal system by which employers must verify the work authorization status of new hires. Under this system, an employer must attest under penalty of perjury on a form designated by the Attorney General (the I-9 form) that it has examined enumerated identification documents to verify that a new hire is not an unauthorized alien. Good-faith compliance with this verification requirement entitles an employer to an affirmative defense if charged with violating IRCA. Notably, however, IRCA prohibits use of the I-9 form for any purpose other than enforcement of IRCA and various provisions of federal criminal law. Use of the I-9 form is thus limited to federal proceedings, as the majority acknowledges.

Finally, Congress created no mechanism for States to access information regarding an alien's work authorization status for purposes of enforcing state prohibitions on the employment of unauthorized aliens. The relevant sections of IRCA make no provision for the sharing of work authorization information between federal and state authorities even though access to that information would be critical to a State's ability to determine whether an employer has employed an unauthorized alien. In stark contrast, a separate provision in the same title of IRCA creates a verification system by which States can ascertain the immigration status of aliens applying for benefits under programs such as Medicaid and the food stamp program.

* * *

NOTES AND QUESTIONS

1.   In a related case, Arizona v. United States, 567 U.S. 387 (2012), the Supreme Court declared unconstitutional three provisions of another Arizona immigration law, the Support Our Law Enforcement and Safe Neighborhoods Act. The Court held that federal law preempted the following provisions: (1) making it a state misdemeanor to fail to comply with federal alien-registration requirements; (2) making it a state misdemeanor for an unauthorized alien to seek or engage in work in the state; and (3) authorizing state and local officers to arrest without a warrant a person the office has probable cause to believe has committed an act that makes the person "removable" from the United States. The Court reversed an injunction prohibiting enforcement of a provision requiring officers making a stop, detention, or arrest to verify the person's immigration status.

2.   Not surprisingly, the *Whiting* decision has been subject to scholarly criticism. See, e.g., Keith Cunningham-Parmeter, Forced Federalism: States as Laboratories of Immigration Reform, 62 Hastings L.J. 1673 (2011); Kevin

R. Johnson, Immigration and Civil Rights: State and Local Efforts to Regulate Immigration, 46 Ga. L. Rev. 609 (2012).

3. In Hoffman Plastic Compounds, Inc. v. NLRB, 535 U.S. 137 (2002), Joe Castro and three coworkers were selected for layoff to rid the company of union supporters. The NLRB found that this conduct by the employer violated section 8(a)(3) of the NLRA and it ordered the employees to be reinstated with back pay. At the back pay hearing, Castro admitted he was a Mexican citizen and had obtained employment with fraudulent documents. The NLRB and the court of appeals held that he was not barred from recovering back pay under either the NLRA or IRCA. The Supreme Court, five-to-four, reversed. Chief Justice Rehnquist's majority opinion said that awarding back pay in a case like this "not only trivializes the immigration laws, it also condones and encourages future violations." In dissent, Justice Breyer wrote that employers would benefit from their wrongdoing and therefore have an incentive to find and hire unauthorized immigrant workers because they can be fired without having any meaningful legal recourse.

4. Several cases consider whether undocumented workers are protected under various labor and employment laws. For example, in Patel v. Quality Inn South, 846 F.2d 700 (11th Cir. 1988), cert. denied, 489 U.S. 1011 (1989), the court held that undocumented aliens are "employees" under the FLSA and therefore subject to the statute's wage and hour protections. The Eleventh Circuit said there was no indication in the legislative history of IRCA that the law was intended to limit rights granted to workers under the FLSA. In addition, according to the court, interpreting the FLSA to cover undocumented aliens furthered the purpose of IRCA in discouraging unauthorized migration. If unscrupulous employers are not able to get away with paying sub-minimum wages to undocumented workers, they will have fewer incentives to hire them. This need for "comparability" in legal protections for workers regardless of their immigration status has been argued in cases dealing with various federal and state laws, but the results have been inconsistent.

5. Are undocumented immigrants protected under Title VII? The courts are not in agreement. Compare Egbuna v. Time-Life Libraries, Inc., 153 F.3d 184 (4th Cir. 1998) (en banc) (not covered) with Rivera v. NIBCO, Inc., 364 F.3d 1057 (9th Cir. 2004) (covered). In EEOC v. Phase 2 Investments, Inc., 310 F.Supp.3d 550 (2018), the district court read *Egbuna* narrowly as precluding unauthorized workers from bringing Title VII claims based on failure to hire, but not other types of Title VII claims. The court observed that in failure to hire claims, plaintiffs must show that they were qualified for the position, and that they necessarily cannot meet this requirement when they are not authorized to work. However, other types of Title VII claims, such as hostile work environment claims, do not require plaintiffs to show they were qualified for the position as part of their prima facie case.

6. In Bollinger Shipyards, Inc. v. Director, Office of Workers' Comp. Programs, 604 F.3d 864 (5th Cir. 2010), an undocumented worker who had falsely stated he was a U.S. citizen and provided a false Social Security number to his employer, was injured while working as a pipefitter. The Fifth

Circuit held that the Longshore and Harbor Workers' Compensation Act (LHWCA) provides that aliens are entitled to compensation and does not differentiate between documented and undocumented aliens.

7. In 2006, Congress enacted legislation specifically prohibiting undocumented aliens from receiving unemployment insurance. 26 U.S.C. §§ 3304(a)(14)(A), (c) (2006).

8. States vary as to whether they give specific protections to undocumented workers when such protections are not preempted or prohibited under federal law. The two most common situations involve state wage payment laws (requiring that employers pay wages owed) and workers' compensation (medical expenses and lost wages) for injuries and illnesses sustained on the job.

9. In Reyes v. Van Elk, 56 Cal.Rptr.3d 68 (Cal. Ct. App. 2007), the plaintiff employee sued his employer for wages allegedly due under California wage law. The trial court granted summary judgment in favor of the employer based on *Hoffman*. The Court of Appeals reversed, noting that Cal. Lab. Code § 1171.5 expressly provides that immigration status is irrelevant to claims under California's labor, employment, civil rights, and employee housing laws. The court said that allowing employers to hire undocumented workers and pay them less than the wage mandated by the state would create a strong incentive for employers to do so. It also would drive down the wages and working conditions of documented workers. Accord, Coma Corp. v. Kansas Dep't of Labor, 154 P.3d 1080 (Kan. 2007).

10. Some states statutorily prohibit workers' compensation awards to undocumented workers. See, e.g., Wyo. Stat. Ann. § 27–14–102(a)(vii). But see In re Arellano, 344 P.3d 249 (Wyo. 2015) (upholding workers' compensation benefits; amendment to workers' compensation statute was interpreted to cover undocumented workers whom employers reasonably believed were authorized to work in the U.S. because the purpose of the amendment was to preclude common law actions for damages filed by undocumented workers who sustained injuries on the job). In states without such a prohibition, most courts have upheld the awards using reasoning similar to *Patel*, note 4 supra. See, e.g., Farmers Bros. Coffee v. Workers' Comp. Appeals Bd., 35 Cal.Rptr.3d 23 (Cal. Ct. App. 2005); Dowling v. Slotnik, 712 A.2d 396 (Conn. 1998). See Hernandez v. U.S.D. 233, 390 P.3d 875 (Kan. 2017) (workers' compensation award upheld for claimant who was not legally authorized to work in the United States and who used false name and documents to apply for job). But cf. Ramroop v. Flexo-Craft Printing, Inc., 896 N.E.2d 69 (N.Y. 2008) (claimant denied vocational rehabilitation services because, as an undocumented alien, he could not be lawfully employed in the United States). See also Torres v. Precision Indus., Inc., 2014 WL 3827820 (Tenn. Ct. App. 2014) (upholding retaliatory discharge claim based on public policy brought by unauthorized alien). See generally Robert I. Correales, Workers' Compensation and Vocational Rehabilitation Benefits for Undocumented Workers: Reconciling the Purported Conflicts Between State Law, Federal Immigration Law, and Equal Protection to Prevent the Creation of a Disposable Workforce, 81 U. Denver L. Rev. 347

(2003); Keith Cunningham-Parmeter, Redefining the Rights of Undocumented Workers, 58 Am. U.L. Rev. 1361 (2009).

11. Seasonal worker Vicente Salas sued Sierra Chemical Company under California law for failing to reasonably accommodate his back injury and refusing to rehire him in retaliation for filing a workers' compensation claim. During litigation it was discovered that Salas fraudulently used someone else's Social Security number to obtain employment. The California Supreme Court held that federal immigration law does not preempt California laws that apply to all workers "regardless of immigration status." Although the doctrines of after-acquired evidence and unclean hands may limit the remedies available, they do not bar the claims. See Salas v. Sierra Chemical Co., 327 P.3d 797 (Cal. 2014).

12. In 2013, California enacted a law that makes it illegal for employers to report or threaten to report a worker's immigration status, or the status of family members, in retaliation for a worker exercising such employment rights as complaining about unsafe working conditions or sexual harassment. Employers that violate the law are subject to revocation of their business licenses and civil penalties of up to $10,000 per violation. Cal. Bus. & Prof. Code § 494.6; Cal. Lab. Code §§ 98.6, 244.

13. In California, and to varying degrees in other states, the law seems to be that employers are prohibited from hiring unauthorized workers, but once they are hired, they have the same state statutory rights as citizens. Is this good policy? Should unauthorized aliens be permitted to bring actions for common law wrongful discharge?

14. More aggressive enforcement of immigration laws under the Trump Administration has resulted in a significant drop in workers' compensation claims filed in California by undocumented workers. What are the likely consequences for these workers, their employers, and workers authorized to work in the United States?

4. EMPLOYMENT OF VETERANS

Since the Civil War, many federal and state civil service laws have contained provisions giving honorably discharged veterans a preference in appointment, promotion, and retention. In Personnel Adm'r v. Feeney, 442 U.S. 256 (1979), the Supreme Court held that veterans preference statutes which accord an absolute employment preference to veterans are legitimate rewards for military service and do not violate the Equal Protection Clause even though the preference disproportionately excludes women.

The Uniformed Services Employment and Reemployment Rights Act of 1994 (USERRA), 38 U.S.C. § 4311, prohibits hiring discrimination against current, past, and potential future service members when military service is a motivating factor in the adverse action. USERRA also requires employers to reinstate individuals who have left their employment to fulfill military obligations. The individual must be reinstated to a position and with seniority equivalent to what he or she would have had if the service had not occurred. The employer need not offer reemployment if it would be unreasonable because of a change in circumstances, it would cause the employer undue hardship, the individual had no reasonable expectation of reemployment, or there was a legally justified reason to discharge the employee before departure for military service. Veterans also are entitled to hiring preferences under several federal and state laws. The Veterans Preference Act of 1944, 5 U.S.C. §§ 851–869, which gives veterans a preference for federal civil service jobs, has been amended several times and is now codified in various laws regulating the federal civil service, including the Veterans Opportunities Act of 1998, 5 U.S.C. § 3330a. A variety of state laws also provide for veterans preferences in state employment. See V.I. Brown, Veterans Preference Employment Statutes: A State-by-State and Federal Government Handbook (2001).

5. HIRING THE UNEMPLOYED

According to the Bureau of Labor Statistics, as of November 2019, the mean duration of unemployment in the United States was 20.2 weeks, and the percentage of individuals unemployed for 27 or more weeks was 20.8%. www.bls.gov/news.release/pdf/empsit.pdf. The figures vary according to several demographic factors, including gender, race, and age. For example, workers age 55–64 have a much higher duration of unemployment.

Long-term unemployed workers (those out of work 27 or more weeks) have a more difficult time obtaining interviews or job offers for various reasons. Individuals who have been out of the work force for an extended period of time may lose some of their skills, lose touch with their network of contacts, or may not interview well because of numerous prior rejections. There are also some employers that simply refuse to consider any long-term unemployed individuals. According to one review of job vacancy postings on Monster.com, CareerBuilder, and Craigslist, hundreds of employers said they would only consider or "strongly prefer" currently employed or recently unemployed individuals. Catherine Rampell, The Help-Wanted Sign Comes With a Frustrating Asterisk, N.Y. Times July 26, 2011, at B1. Apparently, these employers believe that individuals out of work for extended periods of time are less capable, productive, or desirable.

Under current law, the most likely legal challenges to such employer practices would be "disparate impact" claims for age or race discrimination, under the ADEA and Title VII, but these types of cases are difficult to prove. See Chapter 4. At the state level, New Jersey was the first state to prohibit employment notices that bar unemployed workers from applying; Oregon and the District of Columbia have also enacted similar legislation. At the city level, the New York City Council enacted legislation in 2013, over the veto of Mayor Bloomberg, that permits unemployed individuals who believe they were subject to discrimination because they were out of work to sue prospective employers for compensatory and punitive damages, and to obtain attorney fees.

At the federal level, the Obama Administration's "jobs bill" would have prohibited employers with 15 or more employees from discriminating against job applicants because they are unemployed. No action was taken on the bill. In California, Governor Brown vetoed similar legislation because he said it might interfere with the state's efforts to link unemployed job-seekers with prospective employers.

In New Jersey Dep't of Labor & Workforce Dev. v. Craig Ultrasonics, 82 A.3d 258 (N.J. Super. Ct. App. Div. 2014), an employer challenged the constitutionality of the New Jersey law that imposed a $1000 fine on employers that publish an advertisement stating that a job applicant must be currently employed in order to be considered. The court rejected the employer's argument that the law violated the First Amendment. "Because the statute only prohibits an employer from stating in its ads that current employment is a prerequisite to the acceptance of an applicant's materials, . . . [it] is no more extensive than necessary to serve the government's asserted interest." 82 A.3d at 272.

B. APPLICATIONS, INTERVIEWS, AND REFERENCES

1. APPLICATIONS

Starbucks Corp. v. Superior Court

86 Cal.Rptr.3d 482 (Cal. Ct. App. 2008).

■ IKOLA, J.—Petitioner Starbucks Corporation (Starbucks) petitions for a writ of mandate directing the trial court to vacate its order denying Starbucks' motion for summary judgment, and to enter a new order granting the motion.

Real parties in interest Eric Lords, Hon Yeung, and Donald Brown (collectively plaintiffs) represent a class of some 135,000 unsuccessful job applicants at Starbucks. They allege that the Starbucks employment application contains an "illegal question" about prior marijuana convictions that are more than two years old. They seek statutory damages of $200 per applicant—a remedy which, by Starbucks' estimation, could total a whopping $26 million.

Starbucks in San Francisco

Plaintiffs' lawsuit suffers from two fundamental flaws, either of which provides ample grounds for writ relief. First, Starbucks attempted to disclaim an interest in such prohibited information, and two of the plaintiffs understood Starbucks not to be seeking it. Second, no plaintiff had any marijuana-related convictions to reveal.

Nothing in the statutes in question authorizes job applicants to automatically recover $200 per person without proof they were aggrieved persons with an injury the statute was designed to remedy.

FACTUAL AND PROCEDURAL BACKGROUND

Starbucks uses the same two-page job application form nationwide for store level employees. The application's first page includes a question (the "convictions question"), which asks: "Have you been convicted of a crime in the last seven (7) years?" It further explains: "If Yes, list convictions that are a matter of public record (arrests are not convictions). A conviction will not necessarily disqualify you for employment."

The reverse side of the Starbucks application contains various disclaimers for United States applicants, as well as three different states: Maryland, Massachusetts, and California. These disclaimers are located in a 346-word paragraph directly above the signature line. The California portion of the disclaimer provides: "CALIFORNIA APPLICANTS ONLY: Applicant may omit any convictions for the possession of marijuana (except for convictions for the possessions of marijuana on school grounds or possession of concentrated cannabis) that are more than two (2) years old, and any information concerning a referral to, and participation in, any pretrial or post trial diversion program."[1]

In June 2005 plaintiffs filed their class action lawsuit on behalf of an estimated 135,000 Starbucks job applicants who sought jobs at some 1,500 Starbucks locations throughout California. Plaintiffs contended that the convictions question on the Starbucks application is illegal under California law, which prohibits employers from asking about marijuana-related convictions that are more than two years old. Plaintiffs sought to recover actual damages or $200 each, whichever is greater. (Lab.Code, §§ 432.7, subd. (c), 432.8.)

Plaintiffs contended that the California disclaimer was "buried within a block of type," did not specifically refer to the convictions question, and was placed near the end of the document. They feared that applicants either would overlook the disclaimer, or would not want to go back and cross out their previous responses, or ask for a clean copy.

Plaintiffs each applied for a job at Starbucks in early 2005 by filling out a job application. None had a marijuana arrest or conviction. None was hired.

Lords read the entire Starbucks application, including the California disclaimer. He understood the clause to mean that he did not need to report a marijuana conviction more than two years old. He truthfully answered "No" to the convictions question. He had no prior marijuana convictions: "I've never smoked it in my life." Lords explained that he was bringing the lawsuit "for other people." Lords said he did not have a

---

[1] The pertinent paragraph on the Starbucks application provides, in full: "I hereby authorize Starbucks to thoroughly investigate my background, references, employment record and other matters related to my suitability for employment. I authorize persons, schools, my current employer (if applicable), and previous employers and organizations contacted by Starbucks to provide any relevant information regarding my current and/or previous employment and I release all persons, schools, employers of any and all claims for providing such information. I understand that misrepresentation or omission of facts may result in rejection of this application, or if hired, discipline up to and including dismissal. I understand that I may be required to sign a confidentiality and/or non-compete agreement, should I become an employee of Starbucks Coffee Company. I understand that nothing contained in this application, or conveyed during any, interview which may be granted, is intended to create an employment contract. I understand that filling out this form does not indicate there is a position open and does not obligate Starbucks to hire me. (U.S. APPLICANTS ONLY: I understand and agree that my employment is at will, which means that it is for no specified period and may be terminated by me or Starbucks at any time without prior notice for any reason. MARYLAND APPLICANTS ONLY: Under Maryland law, an employer may not require or demand, as a condition of employment, prospective employment, or continued employment, that an individual submit to or take, a lie detector or similar test. An employer who violates this law is guilty of misdemeanor and subject to a fine not exceeding $100. MASSACHUSETTS APPLICANTS ONLY: It is unlawful in Massachusetts to require or administer a lie detector test as a condition of employment or continued employment. An employer who violates this law shall be subject to criminal penalties and civil liability.) CALIFORNIA APPLICANTS ONLY: Applicant may omit any convictions for the possession of marijuana (except for convictions for the possessions of marijuana on school grounds or possession of concentrated cannabis) that are more than two (2) years old, and any information concerning a referral to, and participation in, any pretrial or post trial diversion program."

The disclaimer for "U.S. applicants" leads us to surmise that the Starbucks application may be used for Starbucks international locations as well.

personal stake in the matter, and did not believe that he was not hired because of his truthful answer to the convictions question.

Yeung read the entire application, including the California disclaimer, and understood it to mean that he was not required to disclose any information regarding marijuana convictions more than two years old. Yeung had no such arrests or convictions. Despite this, he wrote the following response to the question regarding convictions: "I refuse to answer."

Brown made a similar response to the convictions question on his Starbucks application. Although he never had been arrested for a crime, and has never used marijuana, Brown responded to the convictions questions, "Refuse to answer!" As he explained, "[I]t's no one's business."

The court certified a class of all California applicants who submitted an employment application to Starbucks with the convictions question since June 23, 2004, and who each seeks no more than $200 in damages. The court determined that "[t]he mere offering of the application containing the impermissible question is a violation of the Labor Code. Damages may be calculated simply by multiplying the probable number of applicants during the class period times $200.00."

The court denied Starbucks' motion for summary judgment. The court determined that the convictions question on its face violated sections 432.7, subdivision (c) and 432.8, and doubted the legal sufficiency of the California disclaimer. "A triable issue of material fact remains whether the location of the limiting language on the application, the size of the font in which the limitation is printed, and the location of the limitation within the block paragraph is sufficient to alert a reasonable job applicant that the question concerning criminal convictions does not apply to marijuana related convictions more than two years old." The court questioned whether an average applicant would see the California disclaimer because the location and font size (which the court guessed to be eight point) was "not effective to draw the attention of the job applicant."

The court concluded that plaintiffs had standing to assert the statutory violation "based on the fact they were given the job application containing the offending question when applying for employment with the defendant. . . . The plain language of those sections establishes a strict liability standard of conduct where a job applicant seeks to recover only the minimum statutory damage amount of $200." The court determined that proof of damages was not a necessary element to the plaintiffs' ability to recover the statutory minimum of $200 per applicant.

* * *

Starbucks filed a petition for writ of mandate from the order denying summary judgment. Starbucks declared that, given the size of the class, "this litigation poses such great monetary risks to Starbucks (at least $26 million) that it may be forced to settle rather than risk an adverse judgment." We issued an order to show cause why a summary judgment should not be granted and stayed the proceedings below.

LEGAL SUFFICIENCY OF THE STARBUCKS APPLICATION

Section 432.8 was enacted during the 1970's as part of comprehensive reform legislation which was designed to distinguish minor marijuana offenses from more serious felony drug offenses and to "minimize or eliminate the lingering social stigma flowing from what is now perceived to be a relatively minor form of criminal activity."

(1) California law already had prohibited employers from asking job applicants about arrests that did not result in a conviction. The statute prohibits employers from soliciting such disclosure "through any written form or verbally. . . ." The marijuana reform legislation extended this prohibition to marijuana convictions that are more than two years old.

* * *

Starbucks says that its employment application, as a matter of law, complies with the California statutory scheme, and cannot be construed to ask applicants to disclose information about marijuana convictions "it expressly tells them not to disclose."

(2) We disagree. We see no problem with the language of the California disclaimer, but we see significant problems with its placement. Had Starbucks included the California disclaimer immediately following the convictions question, Starbucks would have been entitled to a summary judgment in its favor on the reasonableness of the employment application.

But we cannot accept Starbucks' assurances that this "clear and conspicuous" test is satisfied by its placement of the California disclaimer at the very end of a 346-word paragraph, with a U.S. disclaimer, followed by a host of irrelevant provisions from states like Maryland and Massachusetts.[5] Starbucks emphasizes that its California disclaimer is placed in boldface type, but so are the U.S., Maryland, and Massachusetts disclaimers. Any value to be gained by emphasis is submerged in a veritable sea of boldface type.

* * *

The unintended consequence of Starbucks' one-size-fits-all style for its employment applications is a lack of clarity for which California law strives. We cannot say, as a matter of law, that the Starbucks application unambiguously directs applicants not to disclose prohibited marijuana-related convictions.

---

[5] The disclaimers are not even listed in alphabetical order; California inexplicably follows Maryland and Massachusetts.

PLAINTIFFS' ENTITLEMENT TO RECOVERY

Our determination that the Starbucks application may present an ambiguity to the average California job seeker is only the start, not the end, of our inquiry. While a potential violation of the marijuana reform legislation may be "in the air" because of potential ambiguities in the California disclaimer, the question remains, on summary judgment, whether there are triable issues of fact to bring it "down to earth," and to specifically bring plaintiffs, and the tens of thousands of class members they purport to represent, within the class of persons intended to be benefitted by the statutory cause of action in section 432.7, subdivision (c).

(3) Starbucks raises two obstacles to plaintiffs' attempts to recover $200 for themselves and the other class members. First, Starbucks argues that the California disclaimer, even if ambiguous, was not ambiguous as to plaintiffs, two of whom testified at their depositions to sharing the same understanding of the application as did Starbucks. Second, Starbucks argues that none of the plaintiffs are entitled to an automatic $200 recovery because none had any marijuana convictions to disclose. The points are well-taken.

A.   Lack of Ambiguity as to Plaintiffs Lords and Yeung

While the wording of the Starbucks application may establish a potential ambiguity in the abstract, there is no evidence that it made any difference in how Lords and Yeung filled out their job applications. There is no evidence that either of them believed that he was being asked to disclose marijuana-related convictions that were more than two years old.

Both Lords and Yeung admitted during their respective deposition testimony that they read the Starbucks application, including the California disclaimer, and understood the application did not ask for information about marijuana-related convictions more than two years old. Each testified he knew he did not have to disclose information regarding marijuana convictions more than two years old.

* * *

There are practical reasons why Lords's and Young's actual understanding is critical. Without it, there would be nothing to stop them from freely roaming throughout the state "as knights errant *amici* searching for deficiencies . . . where no harm has been caused them or anyone else as a result. . . ." This could create a whole new category of employment-professional job seekers, whose quest is to voluntarily find (and fill out) job applications which they know to be defective solely for the purpose of pursuing litigation. This is not the law in California.

Starbucks having carried its initial burden of production on summary judgment to show that Lords and Yeung were not confused by the Starbucks application, these plaintiffs have failed to show the existence of a triable issue of material fact on ambiguity.

NOTES AND QUESTIONS

1. Starbucks attempted to use jurisdiction-specific disclaimers while retaining a single application form for multiple jurisdictions. Was this a tall, *grande*, or *venti* mistake?

2. Title VII of the Civil Rights Act of 1964 does not specifically prohibit employers from asking any questions about an applicant's race, color, religion, sex, or national origin. Nevertheless, "inquiries which either directly or indirectly disclose such information, unless otherwise explained, may constitute evidence of discrimination prohibited by Title VII." EEOC, Pre-Employment Inquiries (Office of Pub. Affairs 1981). Thus, by declining to ask such questions employers avoid obtaining information that might be used in an effort to prove discrimination.

3. The equal employment laws of many states go beyond the Title VII prohibitions, especially in the area of preemployment inquiries. The following are nonexclusive examples of fair and unfair preemployment inquiries under Washington state law. Besides inquiries in the following table, all preemployment inquiries that "unnecessarily elicit the protected status of a job applicant are prohibited by these statutes irrespective of whether or not the particular inquiry is covered in this regulation."

Preemployment Inquiries
Wash. Admin. Code § 162–12–140
[edited version]

SUBJECT	FAIR PREEMPLOYMENT INQUIRIES	UNFAIR PREEMPLOYMENT INQUIRIES
Age	Inquiries as to birth date and proof of true age are permitted.	Any inquiry that implies a preference for persons under 40 years of age.
Arrests and Convictions	Inquiries concerning arrests must include whether charges are still pending, have been dismissed, or led to a conviction of a crime involving behavior that would adversely affect job performance, and the arrest occurred within the last ten years. Exempt from this rule are law enforcement agencies and state agencies, school districts, businesses and other organizations that have a direct responsibility for the supervision, care, or treatment	Any inquiry that does not meet the requirements for fair preemployment inquiries.

of children, mentally ill persons, developmentally disabled persons, or other vulnerable adults.

Citizenship	Whether applicant is prevented from lawfully becoming employed in this country because of visa or immigration status. Whether applicant can provide proof of a legal right to work in the United States after hire.	Whether applicant is citizen. Requirement before job offer that applicant present birth certificate, naturalization or baptismal certificate that divulges applicant's national origin, descent, or birth place.
Family	Whether applicant can meet specified work schedules or has activities, commitments or responsibilities that may prevent him or her from meeting work attendance requirements.	Specific inquiries concerning spouse, spouse's employment or salary, children, child care arrangements, or dependents.
Disability	Whether applicant is able to perform the essential functions of the job for which the applicant is applying, with or without reasonable accommodation.	Inquiries about the nature, severity or extent of a disability or whether the applicant requires reasonable accommodation prior to a conditional job offer. Whether applicant has applied for or received worker's compensation.
Height and Weight	Being of a certain height or weight will not be considered to be a job requirement unless the employer can show that all or substantially all employees who fail to meet the requirement would be unable to perform the job in question with reasonable safety and efficiency.	Any inquiry which is not based on actual job requirements and not consistent with business necessity.
Marital Status	None.	( ) Mr. ( ) Mrs. ( ) Miss ( ) Ms. Whether the applicant is married, single, divorced,

		separated, engaged, widowed, etc.
Military	Inquiries concerning education, training, or work experience in the armed forces of the United States.	Type or condition of military discharge. Applicant's experience in military other than U.S. armed forces. Request for discharge papers.
Name	Whether applicant has worked for this company or another employer under a different name and, if so, what name. Name under which applicant is known to references if different from present name.	Inquiry into original name where it has been changed by court order or marriage. Inquiries about a name that would divulge marital status, lineage, ancestry, national origin, or descent.
National Origin	Inquiries into applicant's ability to read, write and speak foreign languages, when such inquiries are based on job requirements.	Inquiries into applicant's lineage, ancestry, national origin, descent, birthplace, or mother tongue.
Organizations	Inquiry into organization memberships, excluding any organization the name or character of which indicates the race, color, creed, sex, marital status, religion, or national origin or ancestry of its members.	Requirement that applicant list all organizations, clubs, societies, and lodges to which he or she belongs.
Photographs	May be requested *after* hiring for identification purposes.	Request that applicant submit a photograph, mandatorily or optionally, at any time before hiring.
Pregnancy (see also Disability)	Inquiries as to a duration of stay on job or anticipated absences which are made to males and females alike.	All questions as to pregnancy, and medical history concerning pregnancy and related matters.
Race or color	None.	Any inquiry concerning race or color of skin, hair, eyes, etc.
Relatives	Name of applicant's relatives already employed by this company or by any competitor.	Any other inquiry regarding marital status, identity of one's spouse, or spouse's occupation.

Religion or Creed	None.	Inquiries concerning applicant's religious preference, denomination, religious affiliations, church, parish, pastor, or religious holidays observed.
Residence	Inquiries about address to the extent needed to facilitate contacting the applicant.	Names or relationship of persons with whom applicant resides. Whether applicant owns or rents own home.
Sex	None.	Any inquiry concerning gender.

4. The Washington regulation goes beyond the categories of discrimination prohibited under federal law: race, color, religion, sex, national origin, age, and disability. Other states do not specifically prohibit soliciting the information, although a discriminatory inference may be drawn if the employer solicits such information. See, e.g., Neb.Rev.Stat. § 48–1104.

5. As of 2019, 35 states have enacted "ban the box" laws, which prohibit broad inquiries into an applicant's past criminal convictions. Some employers do not ask the applicant to supply information about convictions, but they obtain that information from other sources. See generally Jonathan J. Smith, Banning the Box but Keeping the Discrimination? Disparate Impact and Employers' Overreliance on Criminal Background Checks, 49 Harv. C.R.-C.L. L. Rev. 197 (2014). There is some debate about the effectiveness of "ban the box" laws, including whether they might be linked with an increase in employer discrimination against racial minorities. See Amanda Agan & Sonja Starr, Ban the Box, Criminal Records, and Racial Discrimination: A Field Experiment, 133 Quarterly J. of Econ. 191 (2017) (discussing experiment suggesting that banning the box increased racial disparity in callback rates); but see Dallan Flake, Do Ban-the-Box Laws Really Work? 104 Iowa L. Rev. 1079 (2019) (discussing experiment suggesting that "ban the box" laws increase the likelihood that ex-offenders will be hired without increasing discrimination against racial minorities).

6. Application forms usually provide much information that may be used in a discriminatory fashion, beginning with the applicant's name. According to one study, applicants with "black-sounding" names, such as Tamika, Aisha, Rasheed, and Tremayne, were much less likely to get an interview than identically qualified applicants with "white-sounding" names, such as Carrie, Kristen, Jay, and Brad. Applicants who lived in "better" neighborhoods also received more interviews than those who did not. All occupations and industries had differential "call back" rates, although they varied in degree of difference between presumed white and black applicants.

See Kendra Hamilton, What's in a Name?, Black Issues in Higher Education, June 19, 2003 at 28.

7. Applicants who misstate their background, qualifications, work history, or other matters need not be hired when the misstatements are discovered. If the misstatements are not discovered until after the individual begins work, the misstatements will establish cause for discharge. If the misstatement is not discovered until after an allegedly unlawful discharge, the courts will determine the applicability of the "after-acquired evidence," which will decide what effect, if any, the post-discharge evidence of wrongdoing (which may include preemployment and employment related matters) should have. See McKennon v. Nashville Banner Publishing Co., 513 U.S. 352 (1995) (after-acquired evidence may limit remedies, but it does not bar an action for employment discrimination).

8. Many job applications ask whether the applicant will permit the prospective employer to contact his or her current employer. Suppose that after an applicant indicates that she does not wish the prospective employer to contact her current employer, the prospective employer nonetheless contacts the current employer? Does the applicant have a cause of action against the prospective employer? See Sullivan v. United States Postal Serv., 944 F.Supp. 191 (W.D.N.Y. 1996) (held: plaintiff could proceed with a claim under the Privacy Act where he was fired after defendants disclosed to plaintiff's then-employer that plaintiff has submitted an application to the Postal Service).

NASA v. Nelson
562 U.S. 154 (2011).

■ JUSTICE ALITO delivered the opinion of the Court.

In two cases decided more than 30 years ago, this Court referred broadly to a constitutional privacy "interest in avoiding disclosure of personal matters." Whalen v. Roe, 429 U.S. 589, 599–600 (1977); Nixon v. Administrator of General Services, 433 U.S. 425, 457 (1977). Respondents in this case, federal contract employees at a Government laboratory, claim that two parts of a standard employment background investigation violate their rights under Whalen and Nixon. Respondents challenge a section of a form questionnaire that asks employees about treatment or counseling for recent illegal-drug use. They also object to certain open-ended questions on a form sent to employees' designated references.

We assume, without deciding, that the Constitution protects a privacy right of the sort mentioned in Whalen and Nixon. We hold, however, that the challenged portions of the Government's background check do not violate this right in the present case. The Government's interests as employer and proprietor in managing its internal operations, combined with the protections against public dissemination provided by the Privacy Act of 1974, 5 U.S.C. § 552a, satisfy any "interest in avoiding disclosure" that may "arguably ha[ve] its roots in the Constitution."

The National Aeronautics and Space Administration (NASA) is an independent federal agency charged with planning and conducting the Government's "space activities." NASA's workforce numbers in the tens of thousands of employees. While many of these workers are federal civil servants, a substantial majority are employed directly by Government contractors. Contract employees play an important role in NASA's mission, and their duties are functionally equivalent to those performed by civil servants.

One NASA facility, the Jet Propulsion Laboratory (JPL) in Pasadena, California, is staffed exclusively by contract employees. NASA owns JPL, but the California Institute of Technology (Cal Tech) operates the facility under a Government contract. JPL is the lead NASA center for deep-space robotics and communications. Most of this country's unmanned space missions—from the Explorer 1 satellite in 1958 to the Mars Rovers of today—have been developed and run by JPL. JPL scientists contribute to NASA earth-observation and technology-development projects. Many JPL employees also engage in pure scientific research on topics like "the star formation history of the universe" and "the fundamental properties of quantum fluids."

Twenty-eight JPL employees are respondents here. Many of them have worked at the lab for decades, and none has ever been the subject of a Government background investigation. At the time when respondents were hired, background checks were standard only for federal civil servants. In some instances, individual contracts required background checks for the employees of federal contractors, but no blanket policy was in place.

The Government has recently taken steps to eliminate this two-track approach to background investigations. In 2004, a recommendation by the 9/11 Commission prompted the President to order new, uniform identification standards for "[f]ederal employees," including "contractor employees." The Department of Commerce implemented this directive by mandating that contract employees with long-term access to federal facilities complete a standard background check, typically the National Agency Check with Inquiries (NACI).

An October 2007 deadline was set for completion of these investigations. In January 2007, NASA modified its contract with Cal Tech to reflect the new background-check requirement. JPL management informed employees that anyone failing to complete the NACI process by October 2007 would be denied access to JPL and would face termination by Cal Tech.

The NACI process has long been the standard background investigation for prospective civil servants. The process begins when the applicant or employee fills out a form questionnaire. Employees who work in "non-sensitive" positions (as all respondents here do) complete Standard Form 85 (SF-85).

Most of the questions on SF-85 seek basic biographical information: name, address, prior residences, education, employment history, and personal and professional references. The form also asks about citizenship, selective-service registration, and military service. The last question asks whether the employee has "used, possessed, supplied, or manufactured illegal drugs" in the last year. If the answer is yes, the employee must provide details, including information about "any treatment or counseling received." A "truthful response," the form notes, cannot be used as evidence against the employee in a criminal proceeding. The employee must certify that all responses on the form are true and must sign a release authorizing the Government to obtain personal information from schools, employers, and others during its investigation.

Once a completed SF-85 is on file, the "agency check" and "inquiries" begin. The Government runs the information provided by the employee through FBI and other federal-agency databases. It also sends out form questionnaires to the former employers, schools, landlords, and references listed on SF-85. The particular form at issue in this case—the Investigative Request for Personal Information, Form 42—goes to the employee's former landlords and references.

Form 42 is a two-page document that takes about five minutes to complete. It explains to the reference that "[y]our name has been provided by" a particular employee or applicant to help the Government determine that person's "suitability for employment or a security clearance." After several preliminary questions about the extent of the reference's associations with the employee, the form asks if the reference has "any reason to question" the employee's "honesty or trustworthiness." It also asks if the reference knows of any "adverse information" concerning the employee's "violations of the law," "financial integrity," "abuse of alcohol and/or drugs," "mental or emotional stability," "general behavior or conduct," or "other matters." If "yes" is checked for any of these categories, the form calls for an explanation in the space below. That space is also available for providing "additional information" ("derogatory" or "favorable") that may bear on "suitability for government employment or a security clearance."

All responses to SF-85 and Form 42 are subject to the protections of the Privacy Act. The Act authorizes the Government to keep records pertaining to an individual only when they are "relevant and necessary" to an end "required to be accomplished" by law. Individuals are permitted to access their records and request amendments to them. Subject to certain exceptions, the Government may not disclose records pertaining to an individual without that individual's written consent.

About two months before the October 2007 deadline for completing the NACI, respondents brought this suit, claiming, as relevant here, that the background-check process violates a constitutional right to informational privacy. The District Court denied respondents' motion for a preliminary injunction, but the Ninth Circuit granted an injunction pending appeal, and later reversed the District Court's order. The court held that portions of both SF-85 and Form 42 are likely unconstitutional and should be preliminarily enjoined.

* * *

As noted, respondents contend that portions of SF-85 and Form 42 violate their "right to informational privacy." This Court considered a similar claim in *Whalen*, which concerned New York's practice of collecting "the names and addresses of all persons" prescribed dangerous drugs with both "legitimate and illegitimate uses." In discussing that claim, the Court said that "[t]he cases sometimes characterized as protecting 'privacy'" actually involved "at least two different kinds of interests": one, an "interest in avoiding disclosure of personal matters"; the other, an interest in "making certain kinds of important decisions" free from government interference. The patients who brought suit in *Whalen* argued that New York's statute "threaten[ed] to impair" both their "nondisclosure" interests and their interests in making healthcare decisions independently. The Court, however, upheld the statute as a reasonable exercise of New York's broad police powers.

Whalen acknowledged that the disclosure of "private information" to the State was an "unpleasant invasion of privacy," but the Court pointed out that the New York statute contained "security provisions" that protected against "public disclosure" of patients' information. This sort of "statutory or regulatory duty to avoid unwarranted disclosures" of "accumulated private data" was sufficient, in the Court's view, to protect a privacy interest that "arguably ha[d] its roots in the Constitution." The Court thus concluded that the statute did not violate any right or liberty protected by the Fourteenth Amendment.

Four months later, the Court referred again to a constitutional "interest in avoiding disclosure." Former President Nixon brought a challenge to the Presidential Recordings and Materials Preservation Act, a statute that required him to turn over his presidential papers and tape recordings for archival review and screening. In a section of the opinion entitled "Privacy," the Court addressed a combination of claims that the review required by this Act violated the former President's "Fourth and Fifth Amendmen[t]" rights. The Court rejected those challenges after concluding that the Act at issue, like the statute in *Whalen*, contained protections against "undue dissemination of private materials." Indeed, the Court observed that the former President's claim was "weaker" than the one "found wanting . . . in *Whalen*," as the Government was required to return immediately all "purely private papers and recordings" identified by the archivists. Citing Fourth Amendment precedent, the Court also stated that the public interest in preserving presidential papers outweighed any "legitimate expectation of privacy" that the former President may have enjoyed.

The Court announced the decision in *Nixon* in the waning days of October Term 1976. Since then, the Court has said little else on the subject of an "individual interest in avoiding disclosure of personal matters." A few opinions have mentioned the concept in passing and in other contexts. But no other decision has squarely addressed a constitutional right to informational privacy.

As was our approach in *Whalen*, we will assume for present purposes that the Government's challenged inquiries implicate a privacy interest of constitutional significance. We hold, however, that, whatever the scope of this interest, it does not prevent the Government from asking reasonable questions of the sort included on SF-85 and Form 42 in an employment background investigation that is subject to the Privacy Act's safeguards against public disclosure.

As an initial matter, judicial review of the Government's challenged inquiries must take into account the context in which they arise. When the Government asks respondents and their references to fill out SF-85 and Form 42, it does not exercise its sovereign power "to regulate or license." Rather, the Government conducts the challenged background checks in its capacity "as proprietor" and manager of its "internal operation." Time and again our cases have recognized that the Government has a much freer hand in dealing "with citizen employees than it does when it brings its sovereign power to bear on citizens at large." This distinction is grounded on the "common-sense realization" that if every "employment decision became a constitutional matter," the Government could not function.

* * *

Respondents argue that, because they are contract employees and not civil servants, the Government's broad authority in managing its affairs should apply with diminished force. But the Government's interest as "proprietor" in managing its operations, the fact that respondents' direct employment relationship is with Cal Tech—which operates JPL under a Government contract—says very little about the interests at stake in this case. The record shows that, as a "practical matter," there are no "[r]elevant distinctions" between the duties performed by NASA's civil-service workforce and its contractor workforce. The two classes of employees perform "functionally equivalent duties," and the extent of employees' "access to NASA . . . facilities" turns not on formal status but on the nature of "the jobs they perform."

At JPL, in particular, the work that contract employees perform is critical to NASA's mission. Respondents in this case include "the lead trouble-shooter for . . . th[e] $568 [million]" Kepler space observatory, the leader of the program that "tests . . . all new technology that NASA will use in space," and one of the lead "trajectory designers for . . . the Galileo Project and the Apollo Moon landings." This is important work, and all of it is funded with a multibillion dollar investment from the American taxpayer. The Government has a strong interest in conducting basic background checks into the contract employees minding the store at JPL.

With these interests in view, we conclude that the challenged portions of both SF-85 and Form 42 consist of reasonable, employment-related inquiries that further the Government's interests in managing its internal operations. As to SF-85, the only part of the form challenged here is its request for information about "any treatment or counseling received" for illegal-drug use within the previous year. The "treatment or counseling" question, however, must be considered in context. It is a follow-up to SF-85's inquiry into whether the employee has "used, possessed, supplied, or manufactured illegal drugs" during the past year. The Government has good reason to ask employees about their recent illegal-drug use. Like any employer, the Government is entitled to have its projects staffed by reliable, law-abiding persons who will " 'efficiently and effectively' " discharge their duties. Questions about illegal-drug use are a useful way of figuring out which persons have these characteristics.

In context, the follow-up question on "treatment or counseling" for recent illegal-drug use is also a reasonable, employment-related inquiry. The Government, recognizing that illegal-drug use is both a criminal and a medical issue, seeks to separate out those illegal-drug users who are taking steps to address and overcome their problems. The Government thus uses responses to the "treatment or counseling" question as a mitigating factor in determining whether to grant contract employees long-term access to federal facilities.

This is a reasonable, and indeed a humane, approach, and respondents do not dispute the legitimacy of the Government's decision to use drug treatment as a mitigating factor in its contractor credentialing decisions. Respondents' argument is that, if drug treatment is only used to mitigate, then the Government should change the mandatory phrasing of SF-85—"Include [in your answer] any treatment or counseling received"—so as to make a response optional. As it stands, the mandatory "treatment or counseling" question is unconstitutional, in respondents' view, because it is "more intrusive than necessary to satisfy the government's objective."

We reject the argument that the Government, when it requests job-related personal information in an employment background check, has a constitutional burden to demonstrate that its questions are "necessary" or the least restrictive means of furthering its interests. So exacting a standard runs directly contrary to *Whalen*. The patients in *Whalen*, much like respondents here, argued that New York's statute was unconstitutional because the State could not "demonstrate the necessity" of its program. The Court quickly rejected that argument, concluding that New York's collection of patients' prescription information could "not be held unconstitutional simply because" a court viewed it as "unnecessary, in whole or in part."

That analysis applies with even greater force where the Government acts, not as a regulator, but as the manager of its internal affairs. SF-85's "treatment or counseling" question reasonably seeks to identify a subset of acknowledged drug users who are attempting to overcome their problems. The Government's considered position is that phrasing the question in more permissive terms would result in a lower response rate, and the question's effectiveness in identifying illegal-drug users who are suitable for employment would be "materially reduced." That is a reasonable position, falling within the "'wide latitude'" granted the Government in its dealings with employees.

* * *

In light of the protection provided by the Privacy Act's nondisclosure requirement, and because the challenged portions of the forms consist of reasonable inquiries in an employment background check, we conclude that the Government's inquiries do not violate a constitutional right to informational privacy.

* * *

For these reasons, the judgment of the Court of Appeals is reversed, and the case is remanded for further proceedings consistent with this opinion.

It is so ordered.

■ JUSTICE KAGAN took no part in the consideration or decision of this case.

■ JUSTICE SCALIA, with whom JUSTICE THOMAS joins, concurring in the judgment.

* * *

In sum, I would simply hold that there is no constitutional right to "informational privacy." Besides being consistent with constitutional text and tradition, this view has the attractive benefit of resolving this case without resort to the Court's exegesis on the Government's legitimate interest in identifying contractor drug abusers and the comfortingly narrow scope of NASA's "routine use" regulations. I shall not fill the U.S. Reports with further explanation of the incoherence of the Court's "substantive due process" doctrine in its many manifestations, since the Court does not play the substantive-due-process card. Instead, it states that it will "assume, without deciding" that there exists a right to informational privacy.

The Court's sole justification for its decision to "assume, without deciding" is that the Court made the same mistake before—in two 33-year-old cases, Whalen v. Roe, 429 U.S. 589 (1977) and Nixon v. Administrator of General Services, 433 U.S. 425 (1977). But stare decisis is simply irrelevant when the pertinent precedent assumed, without deciding, the existence of a constitutional right.

NOTES AND QUESTIONS

1. Although the background investigation in this case involved current employees, most background investigations take place before hiring. For a discussion of other privacy issues involving current employees, see Chapter 7.

2. Should the same privacy standards apply to private employers, private employers at government facilities, government employers, and government in its non-employer role? What does Justice Alito say?

3. In three cases, *Whalen, Nixon,* and *Nelson,* the Supreme Court assumed without deciding that there is a constitutional right to informational privacy, and then upheld the challenged government action. Similarly, virtually all of the lower courts have upheld information disclosure requirements. Therefore, merely recognizing a constitutional right may be insufficient to provide meaningful protection. See Mark A. Rothstein, Constitutional Right to Informational Health Privacy in Critical Condition, 39 J.L. Med. & Ethics 280 (2011).

4. In another privacy case, FAA v. Cooper, 566 U.S. 284 (2012), a licensed pilot failed to disclose his HIV status to the Federal Aviation Administration (FAA) to maintain his flight medical certificate. At the same time, he applied for and received Social Security Disability Income (SSDI) benefits due to his HIV status. When the Department of Transportation (the FAA's parent agency) and the Social Security Administration (SSA) launched an investigation into FAA certification of medically unfit individuals, Cooper's name appeared on a list of pilots receiving SSDI. His license was revoked and he was fined and sentenced to probation for making false statements to a government agency. He then sued alleging a violation of the Privacy Act, claiming that the disclosure of confidential medical information by the SSA to DOT caused him mental and emotional distress. The Supreme Court, five-to-three, in an opinion by Justice Alito, held that "actual damages" recoverable under the Privacy Act are limited to pecuniary loss and therefore damages for mental and emotional distress are not recoverable. Justice Sotomayor's dissenting opinion asserted that the majority opinion "allows a swath of government violations to go unremedied."

2. INTERVIEWS

Lysak v. Seiler Corp.

614 N.E.2d 991 (Mass. 1993).

■ O'CONNOR, JUSTICE.

The plaintiff, Patricia Lysak, states in her complaint that her employer, the defendant, The Seiler Corporation, terminated her employment because she was pregnant, and that therefore the termination violated the prohibition found in G.L. c. 151B, § 3, against discrimination in employment because of sex. [T]his court [has] held that pregnancy is a sex-linked classification. After a jury trial, the jury found for the defendant and a judgment was entered accordingly. The plaintiff appealed and we transferred the case here on our own initiative. On appeal, the plaintiff argues that the trial judge erred by not directing a verdict in her favor pursuant to her request. She also argues that the judge erred by not giving a jury instruction that she had requested and by excluding testimony concerning her emotional distress. We affirm the judgment.

We summarize the evidence relevant to the first two issues, beginning with the plaintiff's testimony. The plaintiff testified that, after being interviewed on February 20, 1987, by William Zammer, the defendant's president, she was employed by the defendant as its marketing director beginning March 23, 1987. On April 24, 1987, she told Zammer that she was pregnant. Zammer was extremely upset by that revelation. He told her that the situation was "untenable" and that she could not continue in the position for which she had been employed. He said that he felt "personally betrayed." Zammer told her that she had lied to him about being career oriented. She denied that she had lied. On the Monday following April 24, the plaintiff proposed to Zammer that her employee status be terminated and that, instead, she be considered an independent contractor. The plaintiff and defendant then entered into such a relationship which lasted until the middle of July, 1987.

According to the plaintiff's testimony, when Zammer interviewed her for employment on February 20, 1987, Zammer and she did not discuss any plans she might have had with regard to either having or not having more children. The plaintiff was pregnant at the time of her interview with Zammer and, because of positive laboratory tests and her doctor's confirmation, she knew at that time that she was pregnant.

Zammer's testimony in substance was that, when he and the plaintiff first met on February 20, 1987, she told him, without any solicitation by him, that her husband stayed home and took care of their two children with the help of an au pair and that "she was not planning on having any more kids." Zammer's testimony was that he would have hired the plaintiff if he had known she was pregnant, but, because she told him, without being asked, that she had no intention of having more children and that was a lie, he felt betrayed. Zammer testified that on the Monday following the April 24 disclosure of her pregnancy, the plaintiff told him that she had made a mistake, that she had lied to him and wanted to make it up to him. According to his testimony, Zammer told the plaintiff that she had lied to him and he would not be able to trust her anymore. Nevertheless, he accepted her proposal that she and the defendant would enter into an independent contractor relationship because the defendant had some unfinished projects that needed prompt completion and she could complete them.

On appeal, the plaintiff's first contention is that she was denied a directed verdict to which she was entitled. It is very seldom that a verdict dependent on oral evidence can be directed in favor of the party with the burden of proof. Nevertheless, the plaintiff says she was entitled to a directed verdict in this case because of the principle articulated in Kraft v. Police Comm'r of Boston, 410 Mass. 155, 571 N.E.2d 380 (1991). In that case, the plaintiff was required to complete two forms under oath in connection with his application for appointment as a police officer. The forms unlawfully required him to give information about his mental health history. He gave false information and several years later the defendant commissioner terminated his employment because he "had failed to disclose his Veteran[s'] Administration Hospital admissions on his answers to application questions." The defendant commissioner argued to this court that the relevant statute, G.L. c. 151B, § 4(9A) (1988 ed.), did not bar him from inquiring into the mental health hospitalization history of an applicant for a position that would require the carrying of a gun. We held that the inquiries were prohibited by the statute, and that "[t]he commissioner had no authority to discharge [the plaintiff] for giving false answers to questions that the commissioner under law had no right to ask." Based on *Kraft,* the plaintiff argues that, "accepting the defendant's version of the facts," that is, that Zammer discharged the plaintiff for giving unsolicited false information about whether she was pregnant, Zammer, and therefore the defendant, violated the law by discharging the plaintiff, at least constructively, on April 24, 1987. Therefore, the plaintiff argues, the discharge cannot stand.

Kraft does not help the plaintiff. A rule that bars an employer from discharging an employee because of the employee's false responses to the employer's unlawful inquiries, does not bar a discharge due to unsolicited, volunteered, false statements made by the employee. Any result other than the one reached in *Kraft* at best would have ignored the employer's unlawful inquiries, and at worst would have rewarded the employer for them. In either event, employers in the future would have been encouraged to violate the law. Here, however, there was no evidence, binding on the defendant, that unlawful inquiries had been made. Therefore, the evidence warranted the jury's verdict that the defendant's discharge of the plaintiff was lawful, and the plaintiff was not entitled to a directed verdict.

Next, the plaintiff contends that it was error for the trial judge not to give proposed jury instruction number 17. The first of that proposed instruction's two sentences states: "Because the Defendants [could] not legally make any employment decisions based solely on the fact that Mrs. Lysak was pregnant, and because they also could not legally inquire whether she was pregnant, you are instructed that, as a matter of law, they could not base any employment decision on any alleged misrepresentation by Mrs. Lysak concerning her pregnancy." That instruction could not properly have been given for the same reason, stated above, that the plaintiff was not entitled to a directed verdict. Contrary to the requested instruction, the defendant could properly have based an employment decision on an unsolicited misrepresentation by the plaintiff concerning pregnancy if the jury found those to be the facts.

The second and final sentence of the proposed instruction at issue on appeal states: "Therefore, if you find that the Defendants did in fact base an employment decision in whole or in part on the alleged misrepresentation by Mrs. Lysak about the pregnancy, the Defendants must prove that the same decision would have been made absent a consideration of any information about the pregnancy." The second sentence would have been an incorrect instruction, too, because, although it is less than clear, it appears to be based on the same incorrect legal premise that underlies the first sentence. Furthermore, the plaintiff did not preserve for review the judge's failure to give the requested second sentence as required by Mass.R.Civ.P. 51(b), 365 Mass. 816 (1974). At the conclusion of the jury instructions, plaintiff's counsel protested to the judge his failure to give the requested "instruction that a lie about a protected category of information is not a defense towards sex discrimination." The proposed second sentence of requested instruction number 17 focused on a different issue regarding shifting of the burden of proof as to causation once unlawful discrimination has been shown to be a factor motivating discharge. Plaintiff's counsel did not discuss that issue with the judge.

* * *

Judgment affirmed.

NOTES AND QUESTIONS

1.   Does the holding in *Kraft,* that an employee may not be discharged for giving a false response to a question that the employer had no lawful right to ask, constitute adequate protection for employees who are asked unlawful questions? Is there a better solution?

2.   A county veterans service agency was interviewing candidates for the position of director of the agency. When Maureen Barbano interviewed for the position, one of the members of the interviewing committee told her that he would not consider "some woman" for the position; he also asked what her plans were for having a family and whether her husband would object to her transporting male veterans. The Second Circuit held that the county violated Title VII by rejecting her application. Barbano v. Madison County, 922 F.2d 139 (2d Cir. 1990). Suppose that, despite the discriminatory interview, the applicant is found to be unqualified for the position. Has the employer violated Title VII? See Mitchell v. Jones Truck Lines, Inc., 754 F.Supp. 584 (W.D.Tenn. 1990) (held: no).

3.   A frequent criticism of the interview technique is that interviewers tend to prefer individuals who are most like themselves. If valid, what legal problems might follow from this observation? As counsel for an employer, what would you advise the employer to do to make the interview process fairer in both appearance and reality?

4.   Although the purpose of most interviews is to evaluate the applicant, they also may be used as a recruitment device, giving the interviewer an opportunity to extoll the virtues of the company. During this process, however, the interviewer may make representations which will bind the employer. For example, in Weiner v. McGraw-Hill, Inc., 443 N.E.2d 441 (N.Y.1982), Mr. Weiner was assured in the initial employment interview that McGraw-Hill terminated employees only for just cause. His employment application specified that employment would be subject to the provisions of McGraw-Hill's "Handbook on Personnel Policies and Procedures," which stated that "the company will resort to dismissal for just and sufficient cause only * * *." The New York Court of Appeals held that an action for breach of contract would lie based on Mr. Weiner's dismissal.

5.   Many employers have begun performing job interviews in which a computer prompts candidates to answer a series of predetermined questions. Although the use of a computer saves time and permits interviews from remote locations, there may be some problems with the range of questions asked. For example, some computer programs are designed to produce psychological profiles and to ask questions about drug use, honesty, and other sensitive matters. See Matt Richtel, Online Revolution's Latest Twist: Job Interviews With a Computer, N.Y. Times, Feb. 6, 2000, at 1.

6.   A "salt" is an individual who obtains employment at a non-union facility for the purpose of organizing the employees to join a union. The practice is often protected under the National Labor Relations Act. In applying for the job, is it permissible for the "salt" to lie to get the job? See Hartman Bros. Heating & Air Conditioning, Inc. v. NLRB, 280 F.3d 1110 (7th Cir. 2002) (held: lawful to lie about status as salt, union organizer, or union supporter, but not about qualifications for the job).

7.   Cities including Philadelphia and New York City have adopted laws banning employers from asking about applicants' salary histories. The purpose of these laws is to prevent an employee's new employer from replicating past pay discrimination, and instead determine salary based on qualifications. The Philadelphia Chamber of Commerce filed a lawsuit challenging the Philadelphia law as a violation of its members' First Amendment rights. A district court then enjoined the law, but the Third Circuit reversed. The appeals court applied the First Amendment test that applies to commercial speech, holding that the city had adequately proven that the law directly advanced its interest in pay equity. Greater Philadelphia Chamber of Commerce v. Philadelphia, 949 F.3d 116 (2020). As of the date this book went to print, the case was ongoing.

3. REFERENCES

Kadlec Medical Center v. Lakeview Anesthesia Associates

527 F.3d 412 (5th Cir. 2008).

■ REAVLEY, CIRCUIT JUDGE:

Kadlec Medical Center and its insurer, Western Professional Insurance Company, filed this diversity action in Louisiana district court against Louisiana Anesthesia Associates (LAA), its shareholders, and Lakeview Regional Medical Center (Lakeview Medical). The LAA shareholders worked with Dr. Robert Berry—an anesthesiologist and former LAA shareholder—at Lakeview Medical, where the defendants discovered his on-duty use of narcotics. In referral letters written by the defendants and relied on by Kadlec, his future employer, the defendants did not disclose Dr. Berry's drug use.

While under the influence of Demerol at Kadlec, Dr. Berry's negligent performance led to the near-death of a patient, resulting in a lawsuit against Kadlec. Plaintiffs claim here that the defendants' misleading referral letters were a legal cause of plaintiffs' financial injury, i.e., having to pay over $8 million to defend and settle the lawsuit. The jury found in favor of the plaintiffs and judgment followed. We reverse the judgment against Lakeview Medical, vacate the remainder of the judgment, and remand.

I. Factual Background

Dr. Berry was a licensed anesthesiologist in Louisiana and practiced with Drs. William Preau, Mark Dennis, David Baldone, and Allan Parr at LAA. From November 2000 until his termination on March 13, 2001, Dr. Berry was a shareholder of LAA, the exclusive provider of anesthesia services to Lakeview Medical (a Louisiana hospital).

In November 2000, a small management team at Lakeview Medical investigated Dr. Berry after nurses expressed concern about his undocumented and suspicious withdrawals of Demerol. The investigative team found excessive Demerol withdrawals by Dr. Berry and a lack of documentation for the withdrawals.

Lakeview Medical CEO Max Lauderdale discussed the team's findings with Dr. Berry and Dr. Dennis. Dr. Dennis then discussed Dr. Berry's situation with his partners. They all agreed that Dr. Berry's use of Demerol had to be controlled and monitored. But Dr. Berry did not follow the agreement or account for his continued Demerol withdrawals. Three months later, Dr. Berry failed to answer a page while on-duty at Lakeview Medical. He was discovered in the call-room, asleep, groggy, and unfit to work. Personnel immediately called Dr. Dennis, who found Dr. Berry not communicating well and unable to work. Dr. Dennis had

Dr. Berry taken away after Dr. Berry said that he had taken prescription medications.

Lauderdale, Lakeview Medical's CEO, decided that it was in the best interest of patient safety that Dr. Berry not practice at the hospital. Dr. Dennis and his three partners at LAA fired Dr. Berry and signed his termination letter on March 27, 2001, which explained that he was fired "for cause":

> [You have been fired for cause because] you have reported to work in an impaired physical, mental, and emotional state. Your impaired condition has prevented you from properly performing your duties and puts our patients at significant risk. * * * [P]lease consider your termination effective March 13, 2001.

At Lakeview Medical, Lauderdale ordered the Chief Nursing Officer to notify the administration if Dr. Berry returned.

Despite recognizing Dr. Berry's drug problem and the danger he posed to patients, neither Dr. Dennis nor Lauderdale reported Dr. Berry's impairment to the hospital's Medical Executive Committee, eventually noting only that Dr. Berry was "no longer employed by LAA." Neither one reported Dr. Berry's impairment to Lakeview Medical's Board of Trustees, and no one on behalf of Lakeview Medical reported Dr. Berry's impairment or discipline to the Louisiana Board of Medical Examiners or to the National Practitioner's Data Bank. In fact, at some point Lauderdale took the unusual step of locking away in his office all files, audits, plans, and notes concerning Dr. Berry and the investigation.

After leaving LAA and Lakeview Medical, Dr. Berry briefly obtained work as a *locum tenens* (traveling physician) at a hospital in Shreveport, Louisiana. In October 2001, he applied through Staff Care, a leading *locum tenens* staffing firm, for *locum tenens* privileges at Kadlec Medical Center in Washington State. After receiving his application, Kadlec began its credentialing process. Kadlec examined a variety of materials, including referral letters from LAA and Lakeview Medical.

LAA's Dr. Preau and Dr. Dennis, two months after firing Dr. Berry for his on-the-job drug use, submitted referral letters for Dr. Berry to Staff Care, with the intention that they be provided to future employers. The letter from Dr. Dennis stated that he had worked with Dr. Berry for four years, that he was an excellent clinician, and that he would be an asset to any anesthesia service. Dr. Preau's letter said that he worked with Berry at Lakeview Medical and that he recommended him highly as an anesthesiologist. Dr. Preau's and Dr. Dennis's letters were submitted on June 3, 2001, only sixty-eight days after they fired him for using narcotics while on-duty and stating in his termination letter that Dr. Berry's behavior put "patients at significant risk."

On October 17, 2001, Kadlec sent Lakeview Medical a request for credentialing information about Berry. The request included a detailed confidential questionnaire, a delineation of privileges, and a signed consent for release of information. The interrogatories on the questionnaire asked whether "[Dr. Berry] has been subject to any disciplinary action," if "[Dr. Berry has] the ability (health status) to perform the privileges requested," whether "[Dr. Berry has] shown any signs of behavior/personality problems or impairments," and whether Dr. Berry has satisfactory "judgment."

Nine days later, Lakeview Medical responded to the requests for credentialing information about fourteen different physicians. In thirteen cases, it responded fully and completely to the request, filling out forms with all the information asked for by the requesting health care provider. The fourteenth request, from Kadlec concerning Berry, was handled differently. Instead of completing the multi-part forms, Lakeview Medical staff drafted a short letter. In its entirety, it read:

> This letter is written in response to your inquiry regarding [Dr. Berry]. Due to the large volume of inquiries received in this office, the following information is provided.

> Our records indicate that Dr. Robert L. Berry was on the Active Medical Staff of Lakeview Regional Medical Center in the field of Anesthesiology from March 04, 1997 through September 04, 2001. If I can be of further assistance, you may contact me at (504) 867–4076.

* * *

Kadlec then credentialed Dr. Berry, and he began working there. After working at Kadlec without incident for a number of months, he moved temporarily to Montana where he worked at Benefis Hospital. During his stay in Montana, he was in a car accident and suffered a back injury. Kadlec's head of anesthesiology and the credentialing department all knew of Dr. Berry's accident and back injury, but they did not investigate whether it would impair his work.

After Dr. Berry returned to Kadlec, some nurses thought that he appeared sick and exhibited mood swings. One nurse thought that Dr. Berry's entire demeanor had changed and that he should be watched closely. In mid-September 2002, Dr. Berry gave a patient too much morphine during surgery, and she had to be revived using Narcan. The neurosurgeon was irate about the incident.

On November 12, 2002, Dr. Berry was assigned to the operating room beginning at 6:30 a.m. He worked with three different surgeons and multiple nurses well into the afternoon. According to one nurse, Dr. Berry was "screwing up all day" and several of his patients suffered adverse affects from not being properly anesthetized. He had a hacking cough and multiple nurses thought he looked sick. During one procedure, he apparently almost passed out.

Kimberley Jones was Dr. Berry's fifth patient that morning. She was in for what should have been a routine, fifteen minute tubal ligation.

When they moved her into the recovery room, one nurse noticed that her fingernails were blue, and she was not breathing. Dr. Berry failed to resuscitate her, and she is now in a permanent vegetative state.

Dr. Berry's nurse went directly to her supervisor the next morning and expressed concern that Dr. Berry had a narcotics problem. Dr. Berry later admitted to Kadlec staff that he had been diverting and using Demerol since his June car accident in Montana and that he had become addicted to Demerol. Dr. Berry wrote a confession, and he immediately admitted himself into a drug rehabilitation program.

Jones's family sued Dr. Berry and Kadlec in Washington. Dr. Berry's insurer settled the claim against him. After the Washington court ruled that Kadlec would be responsible for Dr. Berry's conduct under respondeat superior, Western, Kadlec's insurer, settled the claim against Kadlec.

II. Procedural History

* * *

Plaintiffs' surviving claims for intentional and negligent misrepresentation arise out of the alleged misrepresentations in, and omissions from, the defendants' referral letters for Dr. Berry. These claims were tried to a jury, which returned a verdict in favor of the plaintiffs on both claims. The jury awarded plaintiffs $8.24 million, which is approximately equivalent to the amount Western spent settling the Jones lawsuit ($7.5 million) plus the amount it spent on attorneys fees, costs, and expenses (approximately $744,000) associated with the Jones lawsuit.

* * *

III. Discussion

A.   The Intentional and Negligent Misrepresentation Claims

The plaintiffs allege that the defendants committed two torts: intentional misrepresentation and negligent misrepresentation. The elements of a claim for *intentional* misrepresentation in Louisiana are: (1) a misrepresentation of a material fact; (2) made with intent to deceive; and (3) causing justifiable reliance with resultant injury. To establish a claim for intentional misrepresentation when it is by silence or inaction, plaintiffs also must show that the defendant owed a duty to the plaintiff to disclose the information. To make out a *negligent* misrepresentation claim in Louisiana: (1) there must be a legal duty on the part of the defendant to supply correct information; (2) there must be a breach of that duty, which can occur by omission as well as by affirmative misrepresentation; and (3) the breach must have caused damages to the plaintiff based on the plaintiff's reasonable reliance on the misrepresentation.

* * *

1. *The Affirmative Misrepresentations*

The defendants owed a duty to Kadlec to avoid affirmative misrepresentations in the referral letters. In Louisiana, "[a]lthough a party may keep absolute silence and violate no rule of law or equity, * * * if he volunteers to speak and to convey information which may influence the conduct of the other party, he is bound to [disclose] the whole truth." In negligent misrepresentation cases, Louisiana courts have held that even when there is no initial duty to disclose information, "once [a party] volunteer[s] information, it assume[s] a duty to insure that the information volunteered [is] correct."

Consistent with these cases, the defendants had a legal duty not to make affirmative misrepresentations in their referral letters. A party does not incur liability every time it casually makes an incorrect statement. But if an employer makes a misleading statement in a referral letter about the performance of its former employee, the former employer may be liable for its statements if the facts and circumstances warrant. Here, defendants were recommending an anesthesiologist, who held the lives of patients in his hands every day. Policy considerations dictate that the defendants had a duty to avoid misrepresentations in their referral letters if they misled plaintiffs into thinking that Dr. Berry was an "excellent" anesthesiologist, when they had information that he was a drug addict. Indeed, if defendants' statements created a misapprehension about Dr. Berry's suitability to work as an anesthesiologist, then by "volunteer[ing] to speak and to convey information which * * * influence[d] the conduct of [Kadlec], [they were] bound to [disclose] the whole truth." In other words, if they created a misapprehension about Dr. Berry due to their own statements, they incurred a duty to disclose information about his drug use and for-cause firing to complete the whole picture.

We now review whether there is evidence that the defendants' letters were misleading. We start with the LAA defendants. The letter from Dr. Preau stated that Dr. Berry was an "excellent anesthesiologist" and that he "recommend[ed] him highly." Dr. Dennis's letter said that Dr. Berry was "an excellent physician" who "he is sure will be an asset to [his future employer's] anesthesia service." These letters are false on their face and materially misleading. Notably, these letters came only sixty-eight days after Drs. Dennis and Preau, on behalf of LAA, signed a letter terminating Dr. Berry for using narcotics while on-duty and stating that Dr. Berry's behavior put "patients at significant risk." Furthermore, because of the misleading statements in the letters, Dr. Dennis and Dr. Preau incurred a duty to cure these misleading statements by disclosing to Kadlec that Dr. Berry had been fired for on-the-job drug use.

The question as to whether Lakeview Medical's letter was misleading is more difficult. The letter does not comment on Dr. Berry's proficiency as an anesthesiologist, and it does not recommend him to Kadlec. Kadlec says that the letter is misleading because Lakeview

Medical stated that it could not reply to Kadlec's detailed inquiry in full "[d]ue to the large volume of inquiries received." But whatever the real reason that Lakeview Medical did not respond in full to Kadlec's inquiry, Kadlec did not present evidence that this could have affirmatively misled it into thinking that Dr. Berry had an uncheckered history at Lakeview Medical.

* * *

In sum, we hold that the letters from the LAA defendants were affirmatively misleading, but the letter from Lakeview Medical was not. Therefore, Lakeview Medical cannot be held liable based on its alleged affirmative misrepresentations. It can only be liable if it had an affirmative duty to disclose information about Dr. Berry. We now examine the theory that, even assuming that there were no misleading statements in the referral letters, the defendants had an affirmative duty to disclose. We discuss this theory with regard to both defendants for reasons that will be clear by the end of the opinion.

2.   *The Duty to Disclose*

In Louisiana, a duty to disclose does not exist absent special circumstances, such as a fiduciary or confidential relationship between the parties, which, under the circumstances, justifies the imposition of the duty. Louisiana cases suggest that before a duty to disclose is imposed the defendant must have had a pecuniary interest in the transaction. In Louisiana, the existence of a duty is a question of law, and we review the duty issue here *de novo*.

* * *

Plaintiffs argue that policy considerations weigh in favor of recognizing a duty to disclose. They contend that imposing a duty on health care employers to disclose that a physician's drug dependence could pose a serious threat to patient safety promotes important policy goals recognized by Louisiana courts. The Louisiana legislature recently adopted legislation that requires health care entities to "report [to the appropriate professional licensing board] each instance in which the health care entity * * * [t]akes an adverse action against a health care professional due to impairment or possible impairment." This shows that the legislature has recognized the importance of reporting possible impairments that could affect patient safety.

Despite these compelling policy arguments, we do not predict that courts in Louisiana—absent misleading statements such as those made by the LAA defendants—would impose an affirmative duty to disclose. The defendants did not have a fiduciary or contractual duty to disclose what it knew to Kadlec. And although the defendants might have had an ethical obligation to disclose their knowledge of Dr. Berry's drug problems, they were also rightly concerned about a possible defamation claim if they communicated negative information about Dr. Berry. As a general policy matter, even if an employer believes that its disclosure is protected because of the truth of the matter communicated, it would be burdensome to impose a duty on employers, upon receipt of a employment referral request, to investigate whether the negative information it has about an employee fits within the courts' description of *which* negative information must be disclosed to the future employer. Finally, concerns about protecting employee privacy weigh in favor of not mandating a potentially broad duty to disclose.

NOTES AND QUESTIONS

1. From the perspective of Kimberly Jones and her family, is there a moral difference between the deliberate omission of Lakeview Medical Center and the deliberate commissions of the physicians of Louisiana Anesthesia Associates? Should the law recognize a distinction?

2. Why do you think the defendants were unwilling to write a truthful letter of recommendation or file a report of Dr. Berry's drug problem?

3. The American Medical Association's Code of Medical Ethics provides in part: "A physician shall uphold the standards of professionalism, be honest in all professional interactions, and strive to report physicians deficient in character or competence, or engaging in fraud or deception, to appropriate entities." American Medical Association, Code of Medical Ethics 2012–2013 ed., Preamble § II (2012). Section 9.031 also requires the reporting of impaired, incompetent, or unethical colleagues. Do you think the anesthesiologists should be sanctioned for writing the letters of recommendation or failing to report Dr. Berry to the state medical licensing board?

4. In general, communications to prospective employers, as well as internal communications, are all subject to a qualified or conditional privilege. Miron v. University of New Haven Police Dep't, 931 A.2d 847 (Conn. 2007). The privilege will be lost, however, if there is malice or excessive publication. Chambers v. American Trans Air, Inc., 577 N.E.2d 612 (Ind. Ct. App. 1991); Setliff v. Akins, 616 N.W.2d 878 (S.D. 2000).

5. Communications to government agencies may be subject to an absolute privilege. In Circus Circus Hotels, Inc. v. Witherspoon, 657 P.2d 101 (Nev. 1983), Witherspoon was discharged because an agent of the Nevada Gaming Control Board allegedly saw him "past posting" a toke bet, which constitutes the crime of swindling in Nevada. Witherspoon sued the casino over a letter it sent to the Nevada Employment Security Department about his eligibility for unemployment compensation and a statement it made to a prospective employer that Witherspoon "was a good kid, and he went sour." The Nevada Supreme Court held that statements to the state Employment Security Department were "absolutely privileged" as long as the communication has "some bearing on the subject matter of the proceeding." Regarding the casino's statement to a prospective employer, the court stated, "A qualified or conditional privilege exists where a defamatory statement is made in good faith on any subject matter in which the person communicating has an interest, or in reference to which he has a right or a duty, if it is made to a person with a corresponding interest or duty." Specifically, the court held, "A former employer has a qualified or conditional privilege to make otherwise defamatory communications about the character or conduct of former employees to present or prospective employers, as they have a common interest in the subject matter of the statements."

6. According to a 2018 survey by the National Association of Professional Background Screeners and HR.com, 95% of respondents indicated their organization conducts some type of background or reference checks. https:// pubs.thepbsa.org/pub.cfm?id=9E5ED85F-C257-C289-9E8E-A7C7A8C58 D00. However, many organizations have a policy not to provide any references about current or former employees for fear of legal liability. In fact, there is little to fear. Few defamation actions are brought as a result of negative references and, because of the conditional privilege, even fewer actions are successful.

7. In the age of the Internet, references are being replaced by on-line searches. According to a 2010 survey by Microsoft, 75 percent of U.S. recruiters and human resources professionals indicated that their companies require them to do on-line research about job applicants, including search engines, social networking sites, and personal websites and blogs. In addition, 70 percent of recruiters report that they have rejected candidates because of information found on-line. Should employers have to disclose that they perform on-line searches of all applicants?

8. The Fair Credit Reporting Act, 15 U.S.C. §§ 1681–1681u, enacted in 1980, is the most sweeping congressional attempt to limit private sector information abuse. The Act requires consumers to be informed if they are the subject of a consumer credit report and, if an adverse decision is reached, they may obtain disclosure of information in their file. Consumers may request deletion of erroneous material in their file and may submit their own statement disputing file contents. The Act also prohibits dissemination of information more than seven years old and requires reasonable recordkeeping and reporting procedures. Violators of the Act are subject to criminal penalties and civil liability.

The Fair and Accurate Credit Transactions Act (FACT Act) of 2003, Pub. L. 108–159, 117 Stat. 1998 (2003), substantially amended the FCRA. Although the main purpose of the amendments was to deal with identity theft and fraud, there are several provisions applicable to employment. As amended, for an employer to obtain a consumer report, it must make "clear and conspicuous" disclosure in writing to the consumer before the report is procured that a report will be obtained for employment purposes and the consumer has authorized the report in writing. Special rules apply when there is an application by mail, telephone, computer, or similar means. Before taking an adverse action based on a consumer report, the employer must provide to the consumer a copy of the report and a written description of the rights of consumers under the FCRA. In Syed v. M-I, the Ninth Circuit held that an employer failed to comply with the FRCA's disclosure requirement, which mandates a document that "consists solely of the disclosure," when it printed a liability waiver on the same page. 853 F.3d 492 (9th Cir. 2017).

9. Should a rejected applicant have the right to learn the reason for not being hired? Statutes give this right to rejected credit applicants; why not to applicants for employment? In Lewis v. Equitable Life Assurance Society, 389 N.W.2d 876 (Minn. 1986), four employees were discharged for "gross insubordination" for refusing to change their expense accounts following a business trip. Only one of the four was able to get another job. When they applied for jobs with other companies and said they were fired for gross insubordination, they were not hired. They then sued their former employer for defamation, asserting that they were compelled to republish the defamatory statement of the reason for their discharge. Although it was true that they were fired for gross insubordination, the Minnesota Supreme Court held that truth goes to the underlying implication of the statement. Thus, the court held that the jury could well have concluded that the statement was false and that it was published with malice, which was necessary to negate the employer's conditional privilege. An award of $75,000 to each of the women was affirmed. The court, however, reversed the $150,000 punitive damages awarded to each plaintiff.

In 1987, the Minnesota legislature responded to *Lewis* by enacting a statute providing that an employee who has been discharged may, within 15 working days following the discharge, request in writing that the employer inform the employee of the reason for the discharge. The employer then has 10 working days to inform the employee in writing of the "truthful reason" for the discharge. The statement furnished to the employee may not be used as the basis of an action for defamation. Minn.Stat.Ann. § 181.933. What effect, if any, do you think this statute will have on claims for defamation?

10. *Lewis* represents the minority rule. See, e.g., Sullivan v. Baptist Mem. Hosp., 995 S.W.2d 569 (Tenn. 1999). The Colorado legislature has prohibited all defamation claims based on compelled self-publication. Colo.Rev.Stat. Ann. § 13–25–125.5. See generally Markita D. Cooper, Beyond Name, Rank and Serial Number: "No Comment" Job Reference Policies, Violent Employees and the Need for Disclosure-Shield Legislation, 5 Va. J. Soc. Pol'y & L. 287 (1998); Markita D. Cooper, Between a Rock and a Hard Case: Time for a New Doctrine of Compelled Self-Publication, 72 Notre Dame L.Rev. 373 (1997). The most recent jurisdiction to reject compelled self-publication is Texas. Exxon Mobil Corp. v. Rincones, 520 S.W.3d 572 (2017).

11. When Larry Buck was fired without reason by Frank B. Hall & Co., Buck hired a private investigator, Lloyd Barber, to discover Hall's true reasons for firing him. Barber contacted three managers of the Hall company. He told them he was an investigator, but claimed that he was seeking information about Buck because Buck was under consideration for a position of trust and responsibility with another company. Barber taped the interviews in which Buck was described as untrustworthy, untruthful, disruptive, paranoid, hostile, guilty of padding his expense account, irrational, ruthless, disliked by office personnel, a "classical sociopath," "a zero," and a Jekyll and Hyde personality who lacked scruples. Otherwise, they said he was a nice guy. Do these statements constitute actionable defamation? See Frank B. Hall & Co. v. Buck, 678 S.W.2d 612 (Tex.Ct.App. 1984), cert. denied, 472 U.S. 1009 (1985) (held: statements were published even though publishers were mistaken as to the identity of the person to whom the publication was made).

Pauline T. Kim & Erika Hanson, People Analytics and the Regulation of Information under the Fair Credit Reporting Act

61 St. Louis U.L.J. 17, 17–20 (2016).

People analytics—the use of big data and computer algorithms to make personnel decisions—has been drawing increasing public and scholarly scrutiny. Software is now available for screening applicants to identify the most promising candidates, or searching online profiles to find top prospects for recruitment. Algorithms claim to predict which workers will be most productive or which employees are most likely to leave their jobs. These tools are built by collecting and analyzing vast amounts of data about individual characteristics and behaviors that go far beyond traditional factors like education and training. The datasets are subject to data mining, a process by which computers examine the data to uncover statistical patterns. Those patterns are then used to make predictions about future cases and to inform decision-making.

As workplace use of data analytic tools expands, commenters are raising alarms about the potential unfairness of relying on them to make consequential employment decisions. Some concerns focus on the potential intrusiveness of the data gathering required to develop and use these tools. People analytics depend on the collection of large amounts of information, some of it highly personal. Efforts to harvest health-related data, or information about off-duty behavior and activities on social media potentially threaten employees' personal privacy. Even relatively trivial bits of information—when aggregated with other data about an individual—can reveal highly sensitive personal information. For example, information recorded by electronic activity trackers and collected as part of employee wellness programs can be analyzed to reveal when an employee is pregnant or trying to conceive.

Other commenters charge that people analytic tools can be unfair if the data contains errors or mischaracterizations. Inaccurate information in individuals' consumer records may cause them to unjustifiably lose out on employment opportunities. Employees have alleged that inaccuracies in reports about their criminal records or credit histories caused employers to deny them jobs. Similarly, when algorithms rely on error-ridden personal data, they may make inaccurate predictions that arbitrarily reduce individuals' employment opportunities. Even when personal information is technically accurate, it can be presented in ways that are misleading. And algorithms may draw inferences or make predictions that are unjustified, resulting in the arbitrary denial of employment opportunities.

In addition, big data tools may produce discriminatory effects. Although workforce analytics may sometimes help to counter biased human judgments, data is not always objective or neutral. Scholars have documented numerous ways that reliance on algorithms can result in discrimination. Relatively trivial information, such as zip code or Facebook "likes," may correlate closely with protected characteristics like race or gender, or reveal a person's political or religious views. These types of data may operate as proxies, allowing a biased employer to hide its discriminatory intent behind a seemingly neutral data model. Even when no discrimination is intended, algorithms can produce discriminatory outcomes. If, for example, the underlying data reflects biased judgments about workers' performance, an algorithm built using that data may simply reproduce that bias. In other cases, the data used to create the algorithm may not be representative of the workforce, resulting in a skewed model that systematically disadvantages groups of workers along the lines of race or other protected classification.

* * *

The FCRA establishes certain procedural requirements, and these can sometimes help individual workers challenge inaccurate information about them. However, although employers face significant liability risks if they disregard the statute's requirements, the FCRA in fact does little to curb invasive data collection practices or to address the risks of discriminatory algorithms. Examining how the FCRA does and does not apply to people analytics reveals the limitations of a purely procedural approach. Given these limits, protecting employee privacy and preventing workplace discrimination will require looking to other models of regulation.

C. TRUTH DETECTING DEVICES AND PSYCHOLOGICAL AND PERSONALITY TESTING

1. THE POLYGRAPH

National Research Council, The Polygraph and Lie Detection

12, 13, 212, 216 (2003).

THE INSTRUMENT, THE TEST, AND THE EXAMINATION

Polygraph testing combines interrogation with physiological measurements obtained using the polygraph, or polygraph instrument, a piece of equipment that records physiological phenomena—typically, respiration, heart rate, blood pressure, and electrodermal response (electrode conductance at the skin surface). A polygraph examination includes a series of yes/no questions to which the examinee responds while connected to the sensors that transmit data on these physiological phenomena by wire to the instrument, which uses analog or digital technology to record the data. Because the original analog instruments recorded data with several pens writing lines on a moving sheet of paper, the record of physiological responses during the polygraph test is known as the polygraph chart.

A variety of other technologies have been developed that purport to use physiological responses to make inferences about deceptiveness. These range from brain scans to analysis of voice tremors; some evidence relevant to these techniques is discussed in this report.

PHYSIOLOGICAL PHENOMENA

The physiological phenomena that the instrument measures and that the chart preserves are believed by polygraph practitioners to reveal deception. Practitioners do not claim that the instrument measures deception directly. Rather, it is said to measure physiological responses that are believed to be stronger during acts of deception than at other times. According to some polygraph theories, a deceptive response to a question causes a reaction—such as fear of detection or psychological arousal—that changes respiration rate, heart rate, blood pressure, or skin conductance relative to what they were before the question was asked and relative to what they are after comparison questions are asked. A pattern of physiological responses to questions relevant to the issue being investigated that are stronger than those responses to comparison questions indicate that the examinee may be deceptive.

* * *

SCIENTIFIC KNOWLEDGE

Basic Science

Polygraph accuracy *Almost a century of research in scientific psychology and physiology provides little basis for the expectation that a polygraph test could have extremely high accuracy.* The physiological responses measured by the polygraph are not uniquely related to deception. That is, the responses measured by the polygraph do not all reflect a single underlying process: a variety of psychological and physiological processes, including some that can be consciously controlled, can affect measures and test results. Moreover, most polygraph testing procedures allow for uncontrolled variation in test administration (e.g., creation of the emotional climate, selecting questions) that can be expected to result in variations in accuracy and that limit the level of accuracy that can be consistently achieved.

Theoretical Basis *The theoretical rationale for the polygraph is quite weak, especially in terms of differential fear, arousal, or other emotional states that are triggered in response to relevant or comparison questions. We have not found any serious effort at construct validation of polygraph testing.*

Research Progress *Research on the polygraph has not progressed over time in the manner of a typical scientific field.* It has not accumulated knowledge or strengthened its scientific underpinnings in any significant manner. Polygraph research has proceeded in relative isolation from related fields of basic science and has benefited little from conceptual, theoretical, and technological advances in those fields that are relevant to the psychophysiological detection of deception.

Future Potential *The inherent ambiguity of the physiological measures used in the polygraph suggest that further investments in improving polygraph technique and interpretation will bring only modest improvements in accuracy.*

* * *

Preemployment Screening *The relevance of available research to preemployment polygraph screening is highly questionable because such screening involves inferences about future behavior on the basis of polygraph evidence about past behaviors that are probably quite different in kind.* The validity for such inferences depends on specifying and testing a plausible theory that links evidence of past behavior, such as illegal drug use, to future behavior of a different kind, such as revealing classified information. We have not found any explicit statement of a plausible theory, let alone evidence appropriate for judging either construct or criterion validity for this application. Conclusions about polygraph accuracy for these applications must be drawn by educated extrapolation from research that addresses situations that differ systematically from the intended applications.

The polygraph actually is most accurate in the law enforcement setting because, through traditional detective work, the pool of suspects given examinations is likely to have a relatively high percentage of guilty persons. By contrast, when polygraphs are used where there is a lower percentage of guilty persons, such as in mass preemployment screening, the accuracy of the test goes down sharply. Yet, polygraph results are inadmissible in criminal cases they have been responsible for thousands of employment decisions.

Despite scientific evidence of the inaccuracy of polygraphs, numerous employers assert that they are highly effective in screening out workers who steal and engage in other forms of misconduct. In fact, often the reason for the "effectiveness" of the polygraph is that many people who take polygraphs think the test is accurate and that it will detect lies. Therefore, they admit to various kinds of wrongdoing and are not hired or are fired as a result. The polygraph is credited with ferreting out these people. Is influencing people to divulge wrongdoing a justification for using polygraphs?

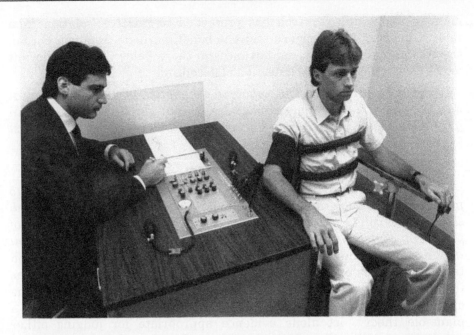

Photo courtesy of John E. Reid and Associates, Inc. The examiner is Michael Adamec and the subject is portrayed by Michael Masokas, both of John E. Reid and Associates, Inc. Note: Pneumograph tubes are placed around the subject's chest and abdomen to measure abdominal and thoracic respiration; the blood pressure cuff around the right arm measures blood pressure and pulse; electrodes attached to two fingers of the left hand measure galvanic skin response; the back of the chair and the chair seat have inflatable rubber bladders to record muscular contractions and pressures. The subject is placed in a position so that he or she looks straight ahead, with the instrument and examiner to the right side and rear.

EMPLOYEE POLYGRAPH PROTECTION ACT

The federal Employee Polygraph Protection Act, 29 U.S.C. §§ 2001–2009, went into effect in 1988. The Act, applicable to most private employers, prohibits most uses of polygraphs in employment. The Act does not prohibit the use of paper and pencil honesty questionnaires or tests. Employers who violate the Act are subject to a civil penalty of $10,000, injunctive actions by the Secretary of Labor, and private civil actions.

The Act contains the following exemptions: (1) it does not apply to federal, state, or local government employers; (2) it does not prohibit the testing by the federal government of experts, consultants, or employees of federal contractors engaged in national security intelligence or counterintelligence; (3) it permits the testing of employees who are reasonably suspected of involvement in a workplace incident that results in economic loss or injury to the employer's business; (4) it permits the testing of some prospective employees of private armored car, security alarm, and security guard firms; and (5) it permits the testing of some current and prospective employees in firms authorized to manufacture, distribute, or dispense controlled substances.

In polygraph examinations under the last three exemptions, some specific additional provisions apply. Among other things, the examinee may not be asked any questions about religious beliefs, racial beliefs, political beliefs, sexual behavior, or union affiliation. See Mennen v. Easter Stores, 951 F.Supp. 838 (N.D.Iowa 1997) (employer violated Employee Polygraph Protection Act where it failed to comply with procedural guidelines for use of polygraph to investigate theft). See also Watson v. Drummond, 436 F.3d 1310 (11th Cir. 2006) (employer did not violate EPPA where polygraph was offered to discharged employee at request of employee's union); Polkey v. Transtecs Corp., 404 F.3d 1264 (11th Cir. 2005) (employer violated EPPA because, among other reasons, it failed to satisfy burden of establishing reasonable suspicion of employee's involvement in a workplace incident resulting in economic loss).

The Act is enforced by the Secretary of Labor, who has promulgated implementing regulations at 29 C.F.R. Part 801.

NOTES AND QUESTIONS

1. As many as two million polygraphs were performed each year in the private sector prior to the passage of the Employee Polygraph Protection Act. Roughly 85 percent of these polygraphs are now prohibited.

2. Before enactment of the federal law in 1988, 18 states and the District of Columbia had laws regulating or prohibiting the use of polygraphs, 25 states had licensing requirements for polygraph examiners, and only 14 states neither prohibited polygraphs nor licensed examiners.

3. The Employee Polygraph Protection Act prohibits the use of polygraphs by "employers." Is an employer liable for the EPPA violations of private investigators working for the employer? See Laney v. Getty, 19 F.Supp. 3d 737 (E.D. Ky. 2014) (held: yes).

4. Is it possible for the victim of an allegedly erroneous polygraph examination to bring a negligence action against the polygraph examiner? See Zampatori v. UPS, 479 N.Y.S.2d 470 (Sup.Ct.1984) (held: yes). But see Calbillo v. Cavender Oldsmobile, Inc., 288 F.3d 721 (5th Cir. 2002) (independent polygraph examiner did not owe a duty of reasonable care to employees tested).

5. In Theisen v. Covenant Med. Ctr., Inc., 636 N.W.2d 74 (Iowa 2001), an employee suspected of making an obscene phone call to another employee was fired when he refused to submit a voice print for analysis. In an action based on wrongful discharge, the Iowa Supreme Court held that the state polygraph statute did not apply to a voice print analysis.

6. New advances in neuroscience imagining can, for the first time, reliably measure changes in brain activity associated with thoughts, feelings, and behaviors. In principle, these technologies, including functional magnetic resonance imaging and electroencephalography, allow researchers to link brain activity patterns directly to the cognitive or affective processes or states they produce. See Paul Root Wolpe et al., Emerging Neurotechnologies for Lie Detection: Promises and Perils, 5 Am. J. Bioethics No. 2, at 39 (2005). What are the implications for truth detection in the workplace?

PROBLEM FOR DISCUSSION: SHOULD POLYGRAPHS BE USED IN THE PREEMPLOYMENT SETTING?

Joe Smith applies for the job of security guard with Ace Security Company. Ace has the contract to supply security guards at a day care center. At a preemployment polygraph examination he is asked the following question: "Have you ever molested a child?" Joe says "no." The polygraph examiner claims he is lying.

Assume that 1% of applicants *have* molested children (a high estimate). Further assume that the polygraph is 80% "accurate" (a high estimate). Note: 80% accurate means that the polygraph can correctly identify as positive 80% of all individuals tested who have the tested-for trait (sensitivity) and can correctly identify as negative 80% of all individuals who do not have the tested-for trait (specificity).

If 1,000 applicants were given a polygraph the results would be as follows:

Subjects	No. with Positive Test	No. with Negative Test
10 child molesters	8 (true positives)	2 (false negatives)
990 Not child molesters	198 (false positives)	792 (true negatives)

Of the 206 individuals with a positive test result only 8 would actually be child molesters. The predictive value of any positive result is $8/206$, or 3.88%. Therefore, even if Joe has a "positive" test result the odds of him actually being a child molester are only 1 in 25.

1.   You are an attorney who has been called by Joe. He really needs the job and feels terribly that people think that he might be a child molester. He knows that the administrator of the day care center (who approves all security guards) is considering whether to accept the polygraph findings. You schedule a meeting with the administrator to argue that the polygraph is unreliable. What arguments would you make?

2.   Suppose you were counsel to Ace or the day care center. Using the polygraph is 4 times more accurate than not using anything. In addition, if you find another applicant who "passes" the polygraph, the predictive value (negative) is $792/794$ or 99.7%. Thus, you would be 99.7% sure that the person you hired would not be a child molester. What responsibility does the day care center owe to the children and their parents? What do you recommend?

2. OTHER TRUTH DETECTING DEVICES AND PSYCHOLOGICAL AND PERSONALITY TESTS

David T. Lykken, A Tremor in the Blood*
195–96, 199–201 (1981).

In the fall of 1976, the Minnesota Legislature was considering a bill to ban polygraph testing of employees. An unexpected witness at the first committee hearing was Sister Terressa, a member of a teaching order, whose forthright and determined manner carried no suggestion of the cloister. She told the committee that some months earlier she had applied for a part-time job with B. Dalton Bookstores in Minneapolis. The application procedure included a disconcerting questionnaire called the Reid Report. Inquiry revealed that B. Dalton used the results on this test, scored by John E. Reid Associates in Chicago, as their basis for assessing the trustworthiness of potential employees. After weeks had passed without further word, Sister Terressa called the bookstore to learn the fate of her application. She was told that she had been rejected because of her performance on the Reid Report. "They said I had the lowest score on the 'honesty test' that they had ever seen!" Partly because of Sister Terressa's indignant and effective testimony, the present Minnesota statute forbids the use in employment applications of polygraph tests, voice stress analysis, or "any test purporting to test the honesty of any employee or prospective employee."

The misclassification of one outraged nun is not a sufficient reason for the statutory prohibition of a test. B. Dalton, like every other retailer, suffers losses from employee theft. If the Reid Report is generally accurate as a predictor of trustworthiness, then its use will diminish these losses. No test, no predictor, is perfect; if an employer uses any selection criterion whatsoever, then there will be a few persons rejected, like Sister Terressa, who would have been entirely satisfactory employees.

* * *

The new honesty questionnaires like the Reid Report, the Stanton Survey, the Personnel Security Inventory, were constructed by polygraphers for use by business clients unwilling or unable to pay the higher cost of polygraph screening. The provenance of these questionnaires is readily apparent when one studies the test items. One group of questions invites the respondent to admit to various crimes misdemeanors ranging from homicide, to forgery, to stealing from the company, to lying to the boss. These yes-no items are supplemented by rating scales such as:

---

*   Reprinted by permission of McGraw-Hill Book Company, New York, N.Y.

What total value in merchandise and property have you taken without permission from employers? (Circle nearest value.)

$5,000 $2,500 $1,000 $750 $500 $250 $100 $50 $0

Or:

How honest are you? Be objective and do not exaggerate.

High Above Average	Above Average	About Average	Slightly Below Average	Below Average

Dr. Philip Ash, research director for the Reid organization, explains: "Incredible as it may seem, applicants in significant numbers do admit to practically every crime in the books."

Supplementing these "admissions" items are sets of questions intended to measure the respondent's "punitiveness" and his "attitudes toward theft." Typical "punitiveness" items are:

An employer discovers that a long-service, trusted employee has been taking a few dollars out of the cash register every week. Should the employer have him arrested?

Or:

What should be done if an employee occasionally smokes marijuana on the job? (Circle one)

Ignore   Warn   Suspend   Fire   Arrest

Some "theft attitude" items:

How many people that you know are really honest?

95%   80%   60%   40%   20%   5%

How many employees take small things from their employers from time to time?

95%   80%   60%   40%   20%   5%

How many people cheat on their income tax?

95%   80%   60%   40%   20%   5%

If you would like to see how you might fare on an honesty test, decide how you would answer these sample questions. Did you recommend jailing that old, trusted employee who's been taking a few dollars from the till each week? And also the young man caught smoking marijuana? Then you are doing well so far. Did you say that nearly all the people you know are really honest? And did you think that almost no one steals from his employer or cheats on his income taxes? Then, unless you have confessed to something serious on the "admissions" questions, you will probably get the job.

The rationale for such scoring is that a thief will be unlikely to recommend harsh punishment for acts he might himself commit and he will probably contend that most people are as dishonest as he. The trouble with this rationale is that the logic does not work in both directions. It is not likely that most people who recommend leniency are thieves. It is not true that all those who see the world as a sinful place are great sinners themselves. Ironically, polygraphers insist that most employees are occasionally dishonest and they are so sure that most people cheat on their income taxes that this situation is often used as a "known lie" control question in polygraph tests. Yet, when a job applicant reveals a similar degree of cynicism on the honesty questionnaire, the report to the employer will be "Not recommended for employment."

We can now begin to understand why it was that Sister Terressa got such a bad score on the Reid Report. We may doubt that she had anything sinister to reveal on the "admissions" questions (although no doubt she honestly confessed whatever youthful misdeeds she could remember). But Sister Terressa was handicapped by Christian charity, which ensured that she would do badly on the "punitiveness" items. And she was an intelligent, educated woman, with some experience of the world, and these qualities prevented her from expressing the naive assessment of humankind required to do well on the "attitude toward theft" items. A clever thief might achieve a good score on the honesty questionnaire—by answering deceptively. But, if the questions are to be answered honestly, then what is required is a punitive, authoritarian personality combined with a worldview like that of the three monkeys who hear-no-evil, see-no-evil, speak-no-evil. Oh, brave new world of work, that has such creatures in it!

NOTES AND QUESTIONS

1.   In part because polygraphs have been outlawed, millions of paper and pencil honesty tests are given each year to applicants and employees. These tests are only prohibited in Massachusetts, Mass.Gen.Laws Ann. ch. 149, § 19B(1). In Rhode Island they may be used so long as they are not the "primary basis for an employment decision." R.I.Gen.Laws §§ 28–6.1–1 to 28–6.1–4. In all other states they may be used without qualification.

2.   Plaintiffs in states without legislation specifically prohibiting written honesty tests have been unsuccessful in using their anti-polygraph laws against these tests. For example, in State v. Century Camera, Inc., 309 N.W.2d 735 (Minn.1981), the Supreme Court of Minnesota construed the state anti-polygraph law's language prohibiting the use of "any test purporting to test honesty." It held that the prohibition is limited to tests which "purport to measure physiological changes in the subject tested * * *."

Therefore, the prohibition does not apply to written honesty questionnaires. The court was concerned that without such a construction the statute would be unconstitutionally vague. See also Pluskota v. Roadrunner Freight Sys., Inc., 524 N.W.2d 904 (Wis.App.1994) review denied, 531 N.W.2d 325 (Wis.1995) (Wisconsin law barring employer's use of polygraphs, voice stress analysis, or psychological stress evaluators does not extend to paper and pencil honesty tests). See generally David C. Yamada, The Regulation of Pre-Employment Honesty Testing: Striking a Temporary(?) Balance Between Self-Regulation and Prohibition, 39 Wayne L.Rev. 1549 (1993); Katrin U. Byford, Comment, The Quest for the Honest Worker: A Proposal for Regulation of Integrity Testing, 49 SMU L.Rev. 329 (1996).

3. One part of the Reid Report includes 100 questions about theft and honesty. A second part includes 93 questions about gambling, drinking, drug habits, outstanding loans, alimony, spouse's salary, and other matters. The honesty section is scored by Reid Associates, which reports to the employer that the applicant is recommended for employment, qualifiedly recommended, not recommended, or gives no opinion. The 93-item factual questionnaire with the personal data is returned to the employer to be placed in the employee's personnel file.

4. The Reid Report is most commonly used by banks, discount stores, insurance companies, drug stores, brokerage houses, trucking firms, and fast food restaurants.

5. Would a claim for wrongful discharge lie based on the refusal to take the Reid Report or based on its results?

6. What legal actions could have been brought by Sister Terressa?

7. Another test used by employers is the Psychological Stress Evaluator (PSE). This and other voice analyzers seek to detect the tension in the voice of someone who is lying. Some employers use the PSE to analyze tape recordings of telephone conversations with applicants, who are asked questions on the phone. Presumably, this is less expensive than a personal interview.

PROBLEM FOR DISCUSSION: PREVENTING EMPLOYEE THEFT

Estimates of the amount of employee theft in the United States each year range from $10 to $50 billion. If polygraphs and honesty questionnaires cannot be used, what is an employer to do? Would shifting the focus from the hiring stage to the working stage be better or would employers be encouraged to use surveillance cameras, locker searches, frisking of workers, and other techniques that are actually more invasive than an honesty questionnaire or polygraph?

Dr. Lykken, an outspoken critic of polygraphs, recommended checking references more closely, instituting better security procedures, boosting employee morale such as through profit-sharing plans, and nonintrusive surveillance and sanctions. Are these measures likely to be effective? Do they raise other legal or economic concerns?

If you represented a retailer, what would you recommend?

Susan J. Stabile, The Use of Personality Tests as a Hiring Tool: Is the Benefit Worth the Cost?*

4 U. Pa. J. Lab. & Emp. L. 279, 279, 280 (2002).

The costs of making bad hiring decisions and the difficulties of getting meaningful information from reference checks of prospective employees have led many employers to use personality tests as part of their hiring process. Employers choose from a wide variety of tests in an effort to both weed out job candidates with undesirable traits, such as dishonesty, or tendencies toward violence or tardiness, and to judge the "fit" between the prospective employee and the job by seeking to identify prospective employees possessing personality traits likely to predict success in the job in question. Since the development of the first modern personality tests in the early part of this century, personality assessment has grown to a $400 million-a-year industry. While some employers are convinced that personality tests are akin to astrology and tell no more than an interviewer could learn during a standard interview, other employers swear by them and are convinced that they are hiring better workers as a result of their use.

The widespread use of personality tests as a means of determining which employees to hire raises a number of issues, ranging from the validity and reliability of the tests to concerns about invasion of privacy and discrimination against minorities. These issues raise the question whether the benefits of personality tests outweigh the costs of employing them.

William D. Hooker, Psychological Testing in the Workplace**

11 Occup.Med.: State of the Art Revs. 699 (1996).

Psychological testing has played a significant role in the workplace for more than 50 years. This involvement continues to grow as the number of disability and accommodation claims increase and as ongoing psychology research in personnel selection and productivity assists employers to pick the right person for the job. At least 3,000 different tests are sold commercially by at least 450 vendors targeted at the workplace. In the testing situation, the behavior or test response is measured in correctness, speed, accuracy, or quality.

Psychological tests are used extensively in preemployment screening and personnel selection. Selecting the right person for the job is the goal of using achievement, aptitude, and personality tests at the preemployment stage. Achievement tests measure proficiency in a specific area. Achievement tests are used in personnel selection if the specific knowledge, skill, or ability (KSAs) relevant to that job can be

---

*   Reprinted by permission.
** Reprinted by permission.

identified. It is assumed that the knowledge, skill, or ability being measured on the test is transferable to the task demands of the job itself. Achievement tests can take the form of paper-and-pencil tests, hands-on demonstrations, or work samples. Examples of achievement tests are a multiple-choice test of drug knowledge for a pharmacy technician applicant, a hand-on demonstration of a word processing program by a transcriptionist applicant, or a medical board examination for a physician.

Aptitude testing is commonly used instead of achievement testing because most jobs are too multifaceted for achievement testing to be practical. Aptitude tests are used as a general measure of a person's potential to learn a specific body of knowledge. Aptitude tests are extensively used in the military and civilian workplace as personnel selection tools because they generally do a good job of predicting overall job performance. Types of aptitude tests include measures of manual dexterity, psychomotor speed, verbal reasoning, numerical ability, spatial perception and reasoning, ability to learn and remember, and other cognitive abilities. They are sometimes referred to as cognitive ability tests. Cognitive ability tests that have predictive validity for subsequent job performance are used for personnel selection. Other specialized tests of cognitive ability, such as intelligence and neuropsychological measures, are used in evaluations of disability, fitness for duty, and vocational rehabilitation.

The last type of psychological testing is personality and psychological functioning assessment. These tests measure personality traits, temperament, personal preferences, interests and attitudes, ways of thinking about oneself, styles of relating to others, and psychological symptoms and problems. In the personnel selection phase, these types of tests have special applications as well as limitations. A limited version of personality testing termed "honesty" or "integrity" tests are increasingly used to select employees who will more likely display productive workplace behavior. More extensive personality testing is frequently used in personnel selection for high-risk jobs in which public safety is at stake. Personality and psychological functioning tests are extensively used in disability, fitness for duty, and vocational rehabilitation evaluations.

The development and use of psychological tests in a scientifically valid manner is one of the major attributes that defines the field of psychology and distinguishes it from psychiatry or social work. Psychological tests are different from the pop questionnaires found in self-help magazines. They must meet technical standards for construction and validation based on research, and users would possess the test knowledge and professional training to use them correctly. Not all psychological tests that are marketed to the employer meet scientific standards. Information about the reliability and validity of tests targeted for the workplace is not uniformly made available by the publishers. The employer using these tests for personnel selection is legally bound to demonstrate that the test is valid and necessary to fill a specific job. Employers must rely on publishers' claims that these tests are valid for their intended use. However, the literature from some of the smaller or single-test publishers are often full of exaggerated claims and the potential for misuse is high. Not all test users will understand the test and recognize its applications and its limitations.

NOTE

A more critical view of psychological and personality testing in the workplace is presented in Annie Murphy Paul, The Cult of Personality: How Personality Tests Are Leading Us to Miseducate Our Children, Mismanage Our Companies, and Misunderstand Ourselves (2004). Reportedly, tens of millions of people take personality tests each year, helping to make up a $400 million industry. The most popular test, the Myers-Briggs Type Indicator, is used by 89 of the Fortune 100 companies. Designed in the 1940s by a Pennsylvania housewife in her living room, the test is designed to reveal personality traits for matching individuals with certain jobs. There is little evidence of the test's reliability or validity. Other tests commonly used in the workplace setting were designed to diagnose and classify mental illness and have never been validated for use in a population of individuals without psychiatric problems.

Employers considering using psychological or personality testing should also consider whether those tests might violate the Americans with Disabilities Act, which limits employers' abilities to require employees to undergo "medical examinations." See Karraker v. Rent-A-Center, Inc., 411 F.3d 831 (7th Cir. 2005) (Minnesota Multiphasic Personality Inventory test was a "medical examination" under the ADA). See also Alan M. Goldstein & Shoshanah D. Epstein, Personality Testing in Employment: Useful Business Tool. Or Civil Rights Violation? 24 The Labor Lawyer 243 (2008). This topic is discussed further below.

Greenawalt v. Indiana Department of Corrections

397 F.3d 587 (7th Cir. 2005).

■ POSNER, CIRCUIT JUDGE.

Two years after Kristin Greenawalt was hired by the Indiana Department of Corrections as a research analyst, she was told that to keep her job she would have to submit to a psychological examination. The record, limited as it is to the complaint, is silent on the reason for so belated a demand. But she complied and later brought this suit under 42 U.S.C. § 1983 against the Department and two of its officials (whom she sued in their individual capacity)—her immediate supervisor and the official who had ordered her to take the test. She claimed that the test, which lasted two hours and inquired into details of her personal life, constituted an unreasonable search in violation of her Fourth Amendment right to be free from unreasonable searches and seizures.

Also, invoking the supplemental jurisdiction of the district court, 28 U.S.C. § 1367, she claimed that whether or not the test was a search, requiring her to take it if she wanted to keep her job both invaded her privacy and deliberately inflicted emotional distress on her, and so violated Indiana's common law of torts. She asked for damages plus an injunction that would require the defendants to expunge the results of the test from her personnel file.

The district judge dismissed the suit on the pleadings. He ruled that the Department of Corrections could not be sued under section 1983 because it is not a "person" within the meaning of that statute, and that the suit against the individual defendants was barred by the doctrine of official immunity because the right that the plaintiff was seeking to enforce had not been clearly established in the case law when she brought the suit. Having thus dismissed the plaintiff's federal claims, the judge relinquished jurisdiction over her state-law claims.

The judge was mistaken about the defendants' immunity concerning the injunctive relief sought, because the defense of official immunity is applicable only to liability for damages. But the error is of no consequence because section 1983 does not permit injunctive relief against state officials sued in their individual as distinct from their official capacity. So the suit was properly dismissed against the individual defendants insofar as it sought injunctive relief, as well as against the Department. All that is left is the damages claims against the two individual defendants.

* * *

So let us consider whether subjecting a public employee to a probing psychological examination is a search. If it is, then it may well have been an unreasonable one in this case, and thus violate the Fourth Amendment, because Greenawalt is merely a researcher. She has no contact with prisoners, is not armed or privy to state secrets, and has no other powers or opportunities, so far as we can tell, that would warrant imposing such a condition of employment. But we need not decide this, as we do not think a psychological test is a search.

Almost any quest for information that involves a physical touching, which a test does not, is nowadays deemed a "search" within the meaning of the Fourth Amendment, which the Fourteenth Amendment has been interpreted as making fully applicable to state action. Drawing a tiny amount of blood from an unconscious person to determine the level of alcohol in his blood is a search, and so even is administering a breathalyzer test, where physical contact is at its minimum—the subject's lips merely touch the breathalyzer. And so finally is a urine test, in which the subject is required merely to provide a urine sample, so that the test instrument does not touch the subject's body at all. The invasion of privacy caused by submitting to the kind of psychological test given to the plaintiff in this case may well have been more profound than the invasion caused by a blood test, a breathalyzer test, or a urine test, though we cannot say for sure; the test is not in the record—all we know is that, according to the complaint, "the battery of psychological tests examined Ms. Greenawalt's personality traits, psychological adjustments and health-related issues." It is true that she consented to take the test, but had she not done so she would have lost her job, which, if she had a constitutional right not to take the test, would place a heavy burden on the exercise of her constitutional rights.

Many cases say that the Fourth Amendment is intended to protect privacy. Although this is historically inaccurate, it is not uncommon for constitutional provisions to be supplied with rationales that the framers and ratifiers of the provisions would not have recognized. Nor is the term "a searching inquiry" an oxymoron; wiretapping is deemed a search even when there is no trespass (the tap will usually be on a section of the phone line that is outside the premises on which the phone being tapped resides), though all that is taken is thoughts, often concerning private matters, expressed in conversation. Cases involving the rifling of an employee's desk, such as O'Connor v. Ortega, 480 U.S. 709 (1987), are similar in this regard: the employee has no property or possessory interest in his desk, yet the invasion of his interest in privacy makes the rifling a search.

Nevertheless we do not think that the Fourth Amendment should be interpreted to reach the putting of questions to a person, even when the questions are skillfully designed to elicit what most people would regard as highly personal private information. The cases we have cited show, it is true, that a Fourth Amendment claim does not depend on the claimant's being able to establish an invasion of such interests that tort law traditionally protects as the interest in bodily integrity (protected by the tort of battery), in freedom of movement (protected by the tort of false imprisonment), and in property (protected by the torts of trespass and of conversion). But that is all they show, so far as bears on the issue in this case. The implications of extending the doctrine of those cases to one involving mere questioning would be strange. In a case involving sex or some other private matter, a government trial lawyer might be required to obtain a search warrant before being allowed to conduct a cross-examination—or the judge before being allowed to ask a question of the witness. Police might have to obtain search warrants or waivers before conducting routine inquiries, even of the complaining witness in a rape case, since they would be inquiring about the witness's sexual behavior. Questioning in a police inquiry or a background investigation or even a credit check would be in peril of being deemed a search of the person about whom the questions were asked. Psychological tests, widely used in a variety of sensitive employments, would be deemed forbidden by the Constitution if a judge thought them "unreasonable."

It was practical considerations such as these that moved us in United States v. Childs, 277 F.3d 947, 950 (7th Cir. 2002) (en banc), to hold that asking a question of a person already in custody is not a "seizure" of the person within the meaning of the Fourth Amendment. "By asking one question about marijuana, officer Chiola did not make the custody of Childs an 'unreasonable' seizure. What happened here must occur thousands of times daily across the nation: Officers ask persons stopped for traffic offenses whether they are committing any other crimes. That is not an unreasonable law-enforcement strategy, either in a given case or in gross; persons who do not like the question can decline to answer." Of course, Greenawalt's situation is different. Theoretically, a person subject to routine police questions can simply decline to answer without suffering any adverse consequences. Had Greenawalt refused to agree to the psychological examination, she would have lost her job.

Even though administering a lie-detector test involves placing sensors on the skin of the person being interrogated, the Supreme Court has suggested that because the objective is to obtain testimonial rather than physical evidence, the relevant constitutional amendment is not the Fourth but the Fifth. The observation is even more apropos with respect to interrogations that do not involve a physical touching. The Fourth Amendment was not drafted, and has not been interpreted, with interrogations in mind. We are not surprised to have found no appellate case that supports the plaintiff's position—which by the way shows that the district judge was absolutely correct in ruling that the individual defendants had a good defense of immunity.

Our conclusion that the plaintiff has not stated a Fourth Amendment claim does not leave people in her position remediless—or indeed leave her remediless. States are free to protect privacy more comprehensively than the Fourth Amendment commands; and Greenawalt is free to continue to press her state-law claims in state court, where they belong. In most states if prison officials were to publicize highly personal information obtained from someone in Greenawalt's position by the kind of test of which she complains, she would have a state-law claim for invasion of her tort right of privacy. Indiana, it is true, has thus far refused to recognize this branch of the tort law of privacy. But the Fourth Amendment does not expand accordion-like to fill what may be a gap in the privacy law of a particular state. And there are other strings to the plaintiff's state-law bow; it is possible, though perhaps unlikely in light of Cullison v. Medley, 570 N.E.2d 27, 31 (Ind. 1991), that Indiana recognizes "intrusion into a person's emotional solace" as an actionable invasion of privacy. Greenawalt may also be able to obtain mileage from cases, none however in Indiana, that hold that requiring a public employee to take a lie-detector test without good cause is an invasion of privacy. She may also be able to prove intentional infliction of emotional distress.

Perhaps it could even be argued that the administration by public officers of a particularly intrusive, and gratuitously humiliating, psychological test is a deprivation, without due process of law, of an interest in privacy that is an aspect of the liberty protected by the due process clauses of the Fifth and Fourteenth Amendments. There is a hint in Whalen v. Roe, 429 U.S. 589 (1977), that the "interest in nondisclosure of private information" might indeed constitute a part of that liberty. And *Whalen* does not stand completely alone. We need not wrestle the issue to the ground. There is no due process claim in this case. It is enough to decide this case that the Fourth Amendment does not provide a remedy for the unpleasantness of being subjected to a psychological test, and that if we are wrong still there is no doubt that the existence of such a remedy was not clearly established when this suit was filed.

AFFIRMED.

NOTES AND QUESTIONS

1. The court held that requiring a psychological test was not a search under the Fourth Amendment. In analogous common law invasion of privacy cases some courts have held that if the applicant or employee refuses to take the test (or agrees to the intrusive condition), then there has been no invasion of privacy; if the individual does agree, then he or she is considered to have waived his or her rights. See Chapter 7.

2. How do you rate Greenawalt's chances of success under the other theories discussed by the court, including invasion of privacy and intentional infliction of emotional distress? Would a statutory remedy be better? If so, what should the statute provide?

3. The Minnesota Multiphasic Personality Inventory (MMPI) remains one of the most widely used psychological tests. This test was originally devised in 1943 to identify and classify individuals who were mentally ill and there is no evidence of its utility as a preemployment test. Moreover, its 567 questions touch on a variety of sensitive and personal matters; the answers presumably would become a part of the employee's personnel file. The MMPI-2 was released in 1989, and the MMPI-2RF, a 338-question instrument, was released in 2008, although the MMPI-2 is still widely used. The following is a sample of questions from the MMPI-2:

True or False

12.   My sex life is satisfactory.

20.   I am very seldom troubled by constipation.

121.   I have never indulged in any unusual sex practices.

142.   I have never had a fit or convulsion.

189.   I like to flirt.

209.   I like to talk about sex.

246.   I believe my sins are unpardonable.

270.   It does not bother me particularly to see animals suffer.

287.   Many of my dreams are about sex.

336. Someone has control over my mind.

371. I have often wished I were a member of the opposite sex.

379. I got many beatings when I was a child.

416. I have strong political opinions.

429. Except by doctor's orders I never take drugs or sleeping pills.

489. I have a drug or alcohol problem.

556. I worry a great deal over money.

4. In Karraker v. Rent-A-Center, Inc., 411 F.3d 831 (7th Cir. 2005), the employer required employees seeking promotions to take the MMPI and other tests. The Seventh Circuit held that the MMPI was a medical examination because, even though it was not interpreted by a psychologist (as experts note it should be), the test was designed to reveal mental illness. Therefore, the use of the MMPI violated section 102(d)(4) of the ADA because medical examinations and inquiries of current employees must be job-related and consistent with business necessity.

5. Another surprisingly popular personality assessment technique is handwriting analysis ("graphology" or "graphoanalysis"). An estimated 6,000 U.S. employers use handwriting analysis to predict the personalities of individuals. It is cheaper ($25 to $350) and simpler (12 to 14 lines of handwriting on unlined paper) than traditional psychological tests, but its scientific validity is far from established. Many of the "handwriting consultants" to industry have no formal training or learned handwriting analysis through a correspondence course. See Julie A. Spoh, The Legal Implications of Graphology, 75 Wash. U.L.Q. 1307 (1997). The following figure gives some samples of handwriting analysis.

Handwriting Analysis Techniques

Source: Handwriting Analysis, 37 BNA Bull. to Management No. 19 (May 8, 1986), p. 152.

6. Are there legal and policy questions surrounding the use of personality and psychological tests? If you question the use of these tests is it because (a) they have not been proven to be accurate as a preemployment test; (b) they are irrelevant to legitimate job-related concerns; (c) they are overly intrusive and ask personal and sensitive questions; (d) they generate personnel files with information of an extremely personal nature; (e) they result in hiring a homogeneous and passive work force; or (f) they incorrectly seek a "hi-tech" shortcut to eliminate interviews, references, and traditional employee selection measures?

PROBLEM FOR DISCUSSION: LIMITING PSYCHOLOGICAL AND PERSONALITY TESTING IN EMPLOYMENT

There are many occupations, such as police officer, airline pilot, and physician, in which an individual's mental state is extremely relevant to ability to perform the job. Similarly, in numerous job placement situations an individual's personality is an extremely important factor. For example, it may be very important to know whether an individual likes working alone, traveling, or large crowds or whether the individual is outgoing or reserved or patient or short-tempered. Should an employer be permitted to inquire into these matters? If so, how?

If you were to draft a state statute seeking to prohibit some of the abuses of psychological and personality testing yet permit limited employer inquiries, what would you include in your law?

D. MEDICAL SCREENING

1. PURPOSE

Mark A. Rothstein, Jessica Roberts, and Tee L. Guidotti, Limiting Occupational Medical Evaluations under the Americans with Disabilities Act and the Genetic Information Nondiscrimination Act

45 Am. J.L. & Med. 523, 525, 560–561, 565–566 (2015).

In the United States, occupational medical evaluations of applicants and employees began I the mid-nineteenth century. The use of medical criteria for selection and retention of employees was largely unregulated for over a century; employers and their physicians (either employees or consultants) had largely unfettered discretion in deciding what criteria to apply in making recommendations about individuals' fitness for various types of employment. The first regulation of occupational medical evaluations was incidental to legislation intended primarily to prevent discrimination in employment on the basis of disability (originally referred to as "handicap"). At the same time that workplace medical evaluations became subject to legal scrutiny, evolving professional norms of occupational medicine began limiting the scope of medical inquiry for fitness-for-duty and other evaluations.

* * *

Fitness-for-duty remains a central concern in occupational medicine and the most common area in which issues of the ADA—and less commonly, GINA—arise. Rather than assessing future risk of illness or disability, fitness-for-duty involves assessing present capacity to do the job as well as potential risk to self and others when performing work functions. Some employers attempted to control healthcare costs or reduce employee turnover by trying to identify future risk through medical screening. In the twentieth century, especially in the early decades, there had been a history of applying novel testing protocols to predict future disability, and tests were performed without proper scientific validation or with susceptibility to harm by chemical exposure. Sometimes the was the result of new test being adopted before it was properly evaluated, and sometimes it resulted from the enthusiasm of management champions who seized on something they had heard about, but did not understand, as a way to reduce workers' compensation costs by excluding workers at risk. The result was that many workers who were entirely fit to do the work were unfairly disqualified from employment on the basis of tests of no value. Some of these tests, such as low-back X-rays (used to predict risk of low back pain but actually worthless), even carried some risk of harm, and few of them had any value or predictive accuracy. This is one reason that most test currently used in routine occupational medical practice are simple and very old, such as the chest X-ray; another is that the limitations of the test are well known and results can be readily interpreted on the basis of vast experience, unlike a more sophisticated but novel test with which there is little experience.

* * *

In recent years, the conduct of occupational medical evaluations has been influenced by two independent but related factors: (1) the composition and practice standards of the occupational medicine workforce * * * and (2) increased legal regulation. * * * To begin with, it is clear that the practice of occupational medicine has evolved. Although the actual number of physicians practicing occupational medicine full or part-time has remained relatively stable for the last thirty years (at sub-optimal levels), the practice arrangements and conduct of medical evaluations have changed, There is little evidence on whether the actual practice patterns of physicians differ based on their employment arrangements, but occupational medical evaluations in all settings have change in recent years to embrace more evidence-based medicine and more limited and targeted medical evaluations. Thus, controversial past practices, such as comprehensive medical questionnaires, single-sex "fetal protection" policies, and low-back X-ray practices, are no longer used. These modifications of occupational medicine practices may have taken place in any event, but they were certainly hastened by new developments in the law—both statutory and case law.

2. MEDICAL EXAMINATIONS AND INQUIRIES

Medical Evaluations Under the Americans with Disabilities Act

The Americans with Disabilities Act of 1990 (ADA) regulates the way companies conduct medical examinations and inquiries of applicants and employees. The employment provisions of the ADA apply to employers with 15 or more employees.

Section 102(d)(2) of the ADA prohibits "traditional" preemployment medical examinations and questionnaires. An employer may not "conduct a medical examination or make inquiries of a job applicant as to whether such applicant is an individual with a disability or as to the nature or severity of such disability." The only permissible inquiries are about the ability of the applicant to perform job-related functions.

After a conditional offer of employment an employer may require an "employment entrance examination" (preplacement examination) pursuant to section 102(d)(3). These examinations need not be job-related, but they must be given to all employees in a job category regardless of disability. The information obtained must be stored in separate files and treated as confidential. Supervisors and managers may be told only about an employee's work restrictions and necessary accommodations.

Similar provisions apply to periodic medical examinations of employees. Under section 102(d)(4), all medical examinations and inquiries must be "job-related and consistent with business necessity." Employers may offer medical examinations of a non-job-related nature, such as comprehensive medical examinations and wellness programs, but employee participation must be voluntary.

Harrison v. Benchmark Electronics Huntsville, Inc.
593 F.3d 1206 (11th Cir. 2010).

■ SILER, CIRCUIT JUDGE:

INTRODUCTION

John Harrison sued Benchmark Electronics Huntsville, Inc. ("BEHI"), alleging, inter alia, that BEHI engaged in an improper medical inquiry, in violation of the Americans with Disabilities Act of 1990 ("ADA"), 42 U.S.C. § 12112(d)(2). The district court granted summary judgment in favor BEHI on all claims. We reverse.

In November 2005, Aerotek, a company that places temporary workers at BEHI, assigned Harrison to work at BEHI. Harrison worked as a "debug tech," and his responsibilities included identifying problems with, repairing, and testing electronic boards. Although he suffers from epilepsy and takes barbiturates to control his condition, the Equal

Employment Opportunity Commission ("EEOC") determined that he did not have a disability as defined under the ADA.

At the time Harrison commenced his temporary position at BEHI, the company had a practice of screening temporary employees for potential permanent employment. If a supervisor believed that a temporary employee would meet BEHI's needs, he would invite that employee to submit an application for employment and complete the necessary drug testing and background check. Usually, after a candidate had cleared both a background and drug test,[1] human resources would extend him an offer, unless the hiring manager instructed otherwise.

On May 19, 2006, Harrison submitted an application for permanent employment, at the request of his supervisor, Don Anthony. Along with his application, he consented to a drug test. In July 2006, Anthony called Faye Robinson, the director of BEHI's human services department, to get the requisitions for three permanent positions, including the position for which Harrison had applied. He identified Harrison as the only person he was interested in employing. After corporate had approved his requisitions, Anthony told Harrison to take the drug test, and he complied. Harrison was at no time informed that his performance was deficient or that he had an attitude problem.

In July 2006, Lena Williams, employed in BEHI's human resources department, was notified that Harrison's test had come back positive and was awaiting review by a Medical Review Officer ("MRO"). She called Anthony and asked him to "send [Harrison] her way." She stated that she did not tell Anthony about the positive drug screen at any time, because she had a duty to keep such information confidential. Robinson also testified that as a matter of policy her department never discloses the results—positive or negative—of an employee's drug test.

Regardless of how he found out about the drug test results, Anthony informed Harrison that he had tested positive for barbiturates. Harrison responded by claiming to have a prescription, which Anthony instructed him to retrieve. Anthony then called the MRO and passed the phone to Harrison, who answered a series of questions about the medication. The MRO asked him how long he had been disabled, what medication he took, and how long he had taken it. He replied that he had epilepsy since he was two years old, he took barbiturates to control it, and he stated the amount of his dosage. Anthony did not ask any questions, but he remained in the room during this colloquy and heard Harrison's responses to the MRO's questions.

On July 19, 2006, the MRO reported to Williams that Harrison's drug test had been cleared. By this time, Williams had also received clearance to hire Harrison, information she passed on to Anthony.

---

[1]   Although Harrison was technically a contract employee of Aerotek, both parties have treated the drug test, administered in conjunction with his application for permanent employment with BEHI, as a pre-employment inquiry subject to 42 U.S.C. § 12112(d).

However, Anthony told human resources not to prepare an offer letter for Harrison. Anthony then asked Aerotek not to return Harrison to BEHI. On August 18, 2006, Aerotek informed Harrison that he would not be returning to BEHI, because he had a performance and attitude problem, and because he had been accused of threatening Anthony. He was fired from Aerotek that same day.

Through the course of the litigation, Anthony has asserted three reasons to support his decision not to hire Harrison: (1) he was too busy preparing for a company-wide audit to extend the offer; (2) Harrison had made threats against him; and (3) several employees had expressed concern to him about Harrison's competence. Anthony maintains that, in light of these concerns, he simply needed more time to evaluate Harrison. BEHI has also asserted that Anthony lacked the authority to hire Harrison, because corporate had closed all open positions and revoked all previously approved requisitions for employees, including the position for which Harrison applied, on August 10, 2006. Harrison argues that the revocation cannot support Anthony's decision not to hire him, because it came weeks after Anthony told human resources not to prepare the offer letter.

On May 3, 2007, Harrison sued BEHI in the United States District Court for the Northern District of Alabama. He alleged various violations of the ADA: namely, that (1) BEHI engaged in an improper medical inquiry, (2) he was not hired due to a perceived disability, and (3) he was terminated due to a perceived disability. BEHI denied these claims and moved for summary judgment, focusing solely on the perceived disability claim. In his response, Harrison maintained that he had made out a prima facie case for an improper medical inquiry and a perceived disability. BEHI replied, arguing that (1) the Eleventh Circuit has not yet recognized a private right of action for the making of an improper medical inquiry; (2) even if it had, Harrison failed to plead it; and (3) regardless, the undisputed material facts established that BEHI was entitled to judgment as a matter of law.

The district court granted BEHI's motion, as to both the pre-employment medical inquiry and perceived disability claims. With regard to the medical inquiry claim, the court "agree[d]" with BEHI that Harrison had failed to plead it. Despite this statement, the court went on to examine the merits of the pre-employment medical inquiry claim. The court first acknowledged that we have never held that a private right of action exists for such claims. Even assuming a private right of action, however, the court held that Harrison could not make out a prima facie case for an improper medical inquiry. Because Harrison "tested positive for barbiturates," the court held that BEHI was then authorized to ask Harrison whether he "had a legitimate use for such medication."

* * *

Before addressing the merits of Harrison's appeal, we must first examine whether he, a non-disabled individual, can state a private cause of action for a prohibited medical inquiry in violation of § 12112(d). We have not yet decided "whether a plaintiff has a private right of action under 42 U.S.C. § 12112(d)(2)." Harrison urges us to join our sister circuits who are unanimous in recognizing a private cause of action irrespective of the plaintiff's disability status under § 12112(d)(2).

* * *

In the pre-offer stage, which is at issue in this case, "a covered entity shall not conduct a medical examination or make inquiries of a job applicant as to whether such applicant is an individual with a disability or as to the nature or severity of such disability." § 12112(d)(2)(A). An employer may only inquire into the "ability of an applicant to perform job-related functions." § 12112(d)(2)(B) (emphasis added); see 29 C.F.R. § 1630.14(a) (providing that an employer may make "pre-employment inquiries into the ability of an applicant to perform job-related functions, and/or may ask an applicant to describe or to demonstrate how, with or without reasonable accommodation, the applicant will be able to perform job-related functions"). Section 12112(d)(2)'s prohibition is premised on Congress's belief that "[h]istorically, employment application forms and employment interviews requested information concerning an applicant's physical or mental condition." Congress believed that employers were using this information "to exclude applicants with disabilities— particularly those with so-called hidden disabilities such as epilepsy, diabetes, emotional illness, heart disease and cancer—before their ability to perform the job was even evaluated." Thus, subsection (d)(2) "assure[s] that misconceptions do not bias the employment selection process."

* * *

Turning first to the statutory language at issue in this case, the plain language of § 12112(d)(2) does not predicate suit under the statute on an applicant's disability status. In contrast to the ADA's general prohibition of disability discrimination in § 12112(a), which refers only to "qualified individuals with disabilities," § 12112(d)(2) refers broadly to "applicants." An "applicant" is "[a] person who submits a formal application to do something or for a position, especially as part of recruitment or selection process; a candidate." The Oxford English Dictionary (11th ed.2008). We assume that Congress used this term as it is commonly and ordinarily understood, and in the absence of any limiting language, we do not infer otherwise.

* * *

Giving effect to the full statute, § 12112(d)(2) does not limit coverage to applicants who are also "qualified individuals with disabilities," and we do not infer such a restriction. In addition, we note that a contrary reading would go against "clear evidence of contrary legislative intent." In enacting § 12112(d), Congress sought to prevent employers from using pre-employment medical inquiries "to exclude applicants with disabilities—particularly those with so-called hidden disabilities such as epilepsy, diabetes, emotional illness, heart disease, and cancer—before their ability to perform the job was even evaluated." The legislative history of § 12112(d)(2) indicates that "Congress wished to curtail all questioning that would serve to identify and exclude persons with disabilities from consideration for employment by drafting [§ 12112(d)]." Allowing non-disabled applicants to sue will enhance and enforce Congress's prohibition. Moreover, a contrary reading would vitiate § 12112(d)(2)'s effectiveness: "It makes little sense to require an [applicant] to demonstrate that he has a disability to prevent his [potential] employer from inquiring as to whether or not he has [one]." When viewed in its full statutory context, and consistent with our sister circuits' holdings, subsection (d)(2) does not require a showing of disability.

Finally, Harrison objects to the district court's holding that he failed to make out a prima facie case for a prohibited medical inquiry under § 12112(d)(2)(A). The district court reasoned that because the questions posed to Harrison were permissible questions following a test for illegal drug use, he failed to state a claim under the statute.

Section 12112(d)(2) prohibits medical examinations and certain medical inquiries at the pre-offer stage. Consistent with Congress's intent, the regulations adopted under the ADA by the EEOC provide that an employer may make "pre-employment inquiries into the ability of an applicant to perform job-related functions, and/or may ask an applicant to describe or to demonstrate how, with or without reasonable accommodation, the applicant will be able to perform the job related functions." 29 C.F.R. § 1630.14(a); see also 56 Fed.Reg. 35725, 35732 (1991). The regulations clarify that while it is appropriate for an employer to inquire into an applicant's ability to perform job-related functions, it is illegal for him to make targeted disability-related inquiries. The EEOC has defined "disability-related" questions as those "likely to elicit information about a disability." On the other hand, "if there are many possible answers to a question and only some of those answers would contain disability-related information, the question is not 'disability-related.' "

In addition to allowing inquiries directed at an applicant's ability to perform job-related functions, the ADA recognizes an exemption for drug tests. See § 12114 ("For purposes of this subchapter, a test to determine the illegal use of drugs shall not be considered a medical examination."). Employers may also ask follow-up questions in response to a positive drug test, see 29 C.F.R. § 1630.3(a), as correctly noted by the district court. However, the regulations, coupled with the EEOC's guidelines, make clear that disability-related questions are still prohibited. As the legislative history of § 12112(d)(2) makes clear, the drug-test exemption "should not conflict with the right of individuals who take drugs under medical supervision not to disclose their medical condition before a conditional offer of employment has been given."

While the district court correctly concluded that employers may conduct follow-up questioning in response to a positive drug test, it failed to acknowledge any limits on this type of questioning. Since the district court did not recognize that § 12112(d)(2) prohibits disability-related inquiries, it found that the facts supported summary judgment. Harrison testified that Anthony told him his drug test was positive, that he disclosed his prescription, that he was then taken to Anthony's office where he answered questions about his medication, and that Anthony remained in the room during this interview. Anthony denied ever knowing that Harrison suffered from epilepsy, and he acknowledged that it would be improper for him to be present during the MRO interview. Although BEHI was permitted to ask follow-up questions to ensure that Harrison's positive drug test was due to a lawful prescription, a jury may find that these questions exceeded the scope of the likely-to-elicit standard, and that Anthony's presence in the room violated the ADA, especially considering the conflict between Harrison's testimony—that to answer the MRO's questions he was forced to disclose the fact and extent of his epilepsy—and Anthony's—that he never knew Harrison suffered from the condition. A reasonable jury could infer that Anthony's presence in the room was an intentional attempt likely to elicit information about a disability in violation of the ADA's prohibition against pre-employment medical inquiries. On summary judgment we must give Harrison the benefit of that inference.

REVERSED AND REMANDED.

NOTES AND QUESTIONS

1.   As *Harrison* illustrates, under the ADA there are important differences in the legality of an employer's medical inquiries at different times in the employment process. Before a conditional offer of employment, employers are severely constrained in their ability to obtain medical information, but the constraint ends after a conditional offer of employment. In *Harrison,* the drug test occurred before a conditional offer of employment and therefore the inquiry into why Harrison tested positive for barbiturates had to be carefully limited. Why not require the drug test *after* a conditional offer of employment?

2.   After a conditional offer of employment, employers are permitted to require the individual to sign an authorization for disclosure of all of his or her health records. There are no limits on the scope of the information, and the nationwide adoption of comprehensive, longitudinal electronic health records means that employers will have access to substantially all of the health records of conditional offerees, irrespective of the jobs for which they are being considered. Should individuals have a right to limit disclosures or otherwise refuse to divulge the information? For current employees, employers are only permitted to make medical inquiries of a job-related

nature. In addition, the Genetic Information Nondiscrimination Act (GINA), discussed infra, prohibits employers from obtaining genetic information about applicants and employees.

3. In Cossette v. Minnesota Power & Light, 188 F.3d 964 (8th Cir. 1999), the Eighth Circuit held that the ADA protects even nondisabled employees from the unlawful disclosure of medical information.

4. In Garrison v. Baker Hughes Oilfield Operations, Inc., 287 F.3d 955 (10th Cir. 2002), after a conditional offer of employment, the employer required a medical examination including completion of a medical history form. The plaintiff untruthfully answered that he had never suffered hearing loss or injuries to his neck, shoulder, elbow, hand, back, abdomen, lungs, knee, and feet. After learning of his prior injuries, the employer withdrew the offer of employment, even though the individual was capable of performing the job. The plaintiff claimed it was unlawful discrimination; the employer claimed that it was based on his giving untruthful answers. Based on a "mixed motive" instruction (see Price Waterhouse v. Hopkins, infra p. 227), the jury found for the plaintiff and awarded the plaintiff $3,580.36 in damages. The Tenth Circuit affirmed.

5. The traditional view is that there is no physician-patient relationship between an applicant or employee and a physician retained by an employer to assess the health of the applicant or employee. See, e.g., Lotspeich v. Chance Vought Aircraft, 369 S.W.2d 705 (Tex.Civ.App. 1963). This is because the examination is not performed for the benefit of the examinee nor is there any contemplation of treatment. As a result, there may be no duty on the part of the physician to notify the individual of test results or diagnoses or to refer the individual for treatment. The courts so holding apply the "benefit" or "treatment" rule. If the examination is to benefit the employer, not the employee, then there is no physician-patient relationship. Similarly, if no treatment is contemplated, then there is no physician-patient relationship. In the absence of such a relationship, there is generally no duty on the part of the physician to exercise reasonable care.

The majority rule, no duty, is illustrated by Medical Center of Central Georgia, Inc. v. Landers, 616 S.E.2d 808 (Ga. Ct. App. 2005). An employee was given a chest x-ray as part of an OSHA-mandated medical examination for employees exposed to asbestos. Although the x-ray indicated a spot on the employee's lung, he was not informed of the results until a year later when he had another x-ray. The employee brought a medical malpractice action against the physician and his independent practice group, which conducted the medical examinations under contract with the employee's employer. (Note: If the physician were a salaried employee of the company, the lawsuit would be barred by workers' compensation, see Ch. 9 infra.) The Georgia Court of Appeals held that OSHA's medical examination requirement did not create a legal duty running from the physician to the employee, and there was no common law physician-patient relationship from which a duty could be established. A small, but growing, number of courts rejects this reasoning and finds at least some duty is owed to the employee. See, e.g., Green v. Walker, 910 F.2d 291 (5th Cir. 1990).

6. Employee medical records often contain sensitive personal information on topics such as psychiatric problems, drug and alcohol abuse, and reproductive matters. They also contain the medical data upon which personnel decisions frequently are made. Despite the crucial nature of these records, employees usually have no legal right to see them; and despite their often sensitive nature, there are few restrictions on the intra-company and extra-company disclosure of such records.

Some states have laws giving all employees a right to see their personnel files or medical records. See, e.g., Conn.Gen.Stat.Ann. § 31–128c; Wis.Stat. Ann. § 103.13. In addition, OSHA's Access to Employee Exposure and Medical Records Standard, 29 C.F.R. § 1910.20, requires that the employer provide access to both exposure records and medical records. The standard, however, does not apply to applicants and only covers employees who are exposed to toxic substances.

Regarding disclosure of information, California's Confidentiality of Medical Information Act, Cal.Civ.Code Ann. §§ 56 to 56.37, is the most extensive state law. It provides in part:

> Each employer who receives medical information shall establish appropriate procedures to ensure the confidentiality and protection from unauthorized use and disclosure of that information. These procedures may include, but are not limited to, instruction regarding confidentiality of employees and agents handling files containing medical information, and security systems restricting access to files containing medical information.

> * * *

> No employer shall use, disclose, or knowingly permit its employees or agents to use or disclose medical information which the employer possesses pertaining to its employees without the patient having first signed an authorization * * * permitting such use or disclosure [except if the disclosure of the records is compelled by legal process, the records are an issue in a pending legal action, the information is used in administering an employee benefits plan, or the information is used in diagnosis or treatment].

Under the law, an individual whose records have been disclosed may recover compensatory damages, punitive damages up to $3,000, attorney fees up to $1,000, and costs of litigation. Violations are also punishable as misdemeanors. This statute is, by far, the most sweeping protection for employee privacy.

7. A truck driven by an employee of Wharton Transport Corporation struck the rear of a car parked on the side of a road and occupied by a family. The collision resulted in the death of one child, severe injuries to three other children, and minor injuries to the father. The truck driver was not hurt. Wharton paid $426,314.25 to settle the case brought by the occupants of the car and then brought an indemnity action against Dr. Bridges, the physician it had retained to determine whether the truck driver was physically fit to drive a truck in interstate commerce (as required by ICC regulations). Wharton alleged that Dr. Bridges was negligent in certifying the driver as physically fit when a subsequent examination indicated that the driver had a variety of severe impairments, as follows: (1) only 5 percent vision in his left eye and blurred vision in his right eye caused by chorioretinitis; (2) severe osteoarthritis in both legs causing a loss of flexion and range of motion; (3) chronic degenerative disc disease in his neck and lower back which impaired his ability to move his neck and head; and (4) chronic fatigue, depression, and emotional exhaustion. Can Wharton recover from Dr. Bridges? See Wharton Transp. Corp. v. Bridges, 606 S.W.2d 521 (Tenn.1980) (held: yes). Could the injured family members recover from Dr. Bridges?

PROBLEM FOR DISCUSSION: REFUSING TO HIRE SMOKERS

According to the Centers for Disease Control and Prevention, cigarette smoking causes over 480,000 deaths a year in the United States, including 42,000 deaths from second-hand smoke. A substantial portion of the economic consequences of these deaths (and illnesses) is borne by employers in lost productivity, health care costs, and increased insurance.

Traditionally, employers attempting to dissuade employees from smoking have prohibited smoking on the job and have instituted or supported smoking cessation programs. A relatively new approach is to refuse to hire individuals who smoke. These policies stem from three separate premises. First, cigarette smoke has a synergistic relationship with some workplace exposures (such as asbestos) that greatly magnifies the toxic effect of the substance. These policies aim to decrease occupational illness and related claims. Second, in some states "heart and lung" laws establish a legal presumption that any heart or lung illness suffered by a police officer or firefighter is work related. Hiring only nonsmokers saves money by eliminating compensable cigarette-related illnesses. Third, because morbidity and mortality rates for smokers greatly exceed those for nonsmokers, hiring only nonsmokers saves money on health care and other benefits.

Those who support policies of refusing to hire smokers argue that it is a controllable behavioral problem, that employers have a legitimate right to limit health care expenditures, and that these policies will reduce smoking and save lives. Those who oppose these policies argue that many smokers are unable to quit, that if all employers adopted such policies there would be a large class of unemployable individuals, and that smoking should be discouraged by other means. They also assert that to verify whether employees were not smoking at home, employers would be tempted to use surveillance, polygraphs, urine screens, and other intrusive measures.

What are your views? If you believe that employers should not be able to refuse to hire smokers, what legal approaches would you recommend to protect these individuals?

NOTES

1.   About half the states have enacted laws prohibiting employers from conditioning employment on an employee's refraining from using "lawful

tobacco products" or engaging in "lawful activities" during nonworking hours.

2. In Grusendorf v. City of Okla. City, 816 F.2d 539 (10th Cir. 1987), the court upheld the dismissal of a fire fighter trainee who violated a no smoking rule of the fire department by taking three puffs of a cigarette during a lunch break. Similarly, in City of N. Miami v. Kurtz, 653 So.2d 1025 (Fla.1995), cert. denied, 516 U.S. 1043 (1996), the Florida Supreme Court upheld a city policy requiring all applicants to sign an affidavit stating that they have not smoked within the last year. Rejecting the argument that this violated state or federal constitutional privacy, the court held that the regulation was justified by the city's interest in reducing the costs from smoking-related illnesses. For a further discussion, see Jessica L. Roberts, Healthism and the Law of Employment Discrimination, 99 Iowa L. Rev. 571 (2014); Mark A. Rothstein, Refusing to Employ Smokers: Good Public Health or Bad Public Policy?, 62 Notre Dame L.Rev. 940 (1987).

3. Charles Wood, an assistant kiln operator in a cement plant was given a medical examination as part of his application to change his status from part-time to full-time. A chest x-ray indicated a mass in his lung, which required medical attention. At the recommendation of the examining physician, Wood's employment offer was conditioned on his stopping smoking. Wood agreed. He was subsequently discharged when a required urine test was positive for cotinine, the metabolite of nicotine. Wood sued, asserting that his discharge violated a state law prohibiting the discharge of an employee for using tobacco products off the premises during nonworking hours. The Supreme Court of South Dakota held that, under the circumstances, the no-smoking restriction placed on the employee was a reasonable bona fide occupational requirement within the meaning of the statute. Wood v. South Dakota Cement Plant, 588 N.W.2d 227 (S.D. 1999). See generally Leslie Zellers, Meliah A. Thomas, & Marice Ashe, Legal Risks to Employers Who Allow Smoking in the Workplace, 97 Am. J. Pub. Health 1376 (2007). As of July 2014, 39 states had laws requiring that private sector workplaces be smoke free. Some states have special provisions applicable to bars and restaurants.

E. DRUG TESTING AND OTHER LABORATORY PROCEDURES

1. DRUG TESTING

Stacy Hickox, It's Time to Rein in Employer Drug Testing*
11 Harv. L. & Pol'y Rev. 419 (2017).

INTRODUCTION

Drug testing by employers has become so common that few question its effect on privacy. Even fewer question its effectiveness in identifying unqualified applicants or making retention decisions. At the same time, use of at least some drugs has become more common and is sometimes legal. Even "illegal" use sometimes occurs as an extension of prescription drugs or avoids criminal prosecution under the growing number of state statutes allowing the use of marijuana for medical or even recreational purposes. This raises the important question of whether a positive drug test, without other evidence of negative effects of drug usage, should be the basis for important employment decisions.

Despite widespread legalization, all drug users continue to be at risk of losing employment or never getting hired based on their legal use of marijuana, because most legalization statutes fail to address employment rights. Some states regulate the process of drug testing, but very few place any limits on employers' decisions based on those test results. With little regulation, employers continue to drug test both applicants and employees on a regular basis.

That patchwork remains today. Some states have adopted limited guidelines for or restrictions on drug testing of employees without regulating employers' decisions based on test results. At the same time, courts have imposed very few constraints on drug testing by private sector employers, deferring to the notion of employment at will. In the public sector, the Fourth Amendment generally limits drug testing to those suspected of being under the influence or working in a safety-sensitive position, but does little to limit employers' decisions based on those tests.

I. PREVALENCE OF DRUG TESTING BY EMPLOYERS

Employers in both the public and private sectors regularly test employees and applicants for illegal drug use for a variety of reasons. In 2011, 57% of surveyed employers drug tested all job applicants, and an additional 10% tested applicants for selected jobs, while 36% tested current employees. Most recently, employers have expanded the testing of employees on a random basis, and often test all applicants. This

---

* Reprinted by permission.

widespread use of drug testing means that approximately 43% of all applicants and almost 30% of current employees are drug tested.

II. EFFECTIVENESS OF DRUG TESTING

A. *Accuracy*

Drug tests are frequently inaccurate, with accuracy inversely related to the frequency of their usage. Employers most often opt for urine testing, either at the workplace or a laboratory. In addition, almost a quarter of employers report using breath-alcohol testing, while only eight percent report using hair or blood testing. The "instant" urine test, often performed at the workplace, is the least reliable. This test results in false positive rates as high as sixty-five percent because the test often cannot distinguish one type of drug from another. Saliva can also be used to detect prior use of drugs in the previous twenty-four to forty-eight hours. Despite this high rate of false positives, positivity rates for urine tests of U.S. employees average only four percent.

Hair testing will identify drug use for as long as three previous months, but false positive results are common in part because hair can test positive without ingestion of the drug. Hair testing also can have a disparate impact on African Americans, because dark-haired people with higher concentrations of melanin are far more likely to test positive. None of these tests indicate impairment or the amount of drug that has been detected.

Because of the unreliability of urine testing, both experts and the Department of Health and Human Services (HHS) agree that the results of a urine test must be confirmed by an alternative testing technique. Some employers have followed this advice. Follow-up tests may cost more, but are much more accurate in identifying the level of a drug in someone's system.

Use of a medical review officer (MRO) is another important piece of the drug testing process to ensure the reliability of test results, as recommended by federal regulations. MROs ensure that a drug test is not reported as positive if resulting from a prescribed medication and sometimes report a negative result for medical marijuana users. Despite the importance of using MROs, the majority of employers relying on urinalysis do not use a MRO to analyze results. The absence of MRO review has been described as a "source of legal liability and problems for companies and laboratories."

B. *Measuring Impairment*

Even with reliable drug testing processes, positive test results do not indicate impairment at work, because a drug test only establishes some prior use. Consequently, a positive drug test will not predict performance issues or any threat to safety. Urine, drug, and metabolite concentrations do not correlate with behavior, because they "cannot ascertain the quantity of a drug consumed, the time of consumption, or its effect on the user." For this reason, even the manufacturer of the widely-used EMIT urine test has warned that the test "does not indicate intoxication." Conversely, recent ingestion that can cause impairment may not result in a positive drug test because the drug has not metabolized.

National Treasury Employees Union v. Von Raab
489 U.S. 656 (1989).

■ JUSTICE KENNEDY delivered the opinion of the Court.

We granted certiorari to decide whether it violates the Fourth Amendment for the United States Customs Service to require a urinalysis test from employees who seek transfer or promotion to certain positions.

The United States Customs Service, a bureau of the Department of the Treasury, is the federal agency responsible for processing persons, carriers, cargo, and mail into the United States, collecting revenue from imports, and enforcing customs and related laws. An important responsibility of the Service is the interdiction and seizure of contraband, including illegal drugs. In 1987 alone, Customs agents seized drugs with a retail value of nearly 9 billion dollars. In the routine discharge of their duties, many Customs employees have direct contact with those who traffic in drugs for profit. Drug import operations, often directed by sophisticated criminal syndicates, may be effected by violence or its threat. As a necessary response, many Customs operatives carry and use firearms in connection with their official duties.

In December 1985, respondent, the Commissioner of Customs, established a Drug Screening Task Force to explore the possibility of implementing a drug screening program within the Service. After extensive research and consultation with experts in the field, the Task Force concluded "that drug screening through urinalysis is technologically reliable, valid and accurate." Citing this conclusion, the Commissioner announced his intention to require drug tests of employees who applied for, or occupied, certain positions within the Service. The Commissioner stated his belief that "Customs is largely drug-free," but noted also that "unfortunately no segment of society is immune from the threat of illegal drug use." Drug interdiction has become the agency's primary enforcement mission, and the Commissioner stressed that "there is no room in the Customs Service for those who break the laws prohibiting the possession and use of illegal drugs."

In May 1986, the Commissioner announced implementation of the drug-testing program. Drug tests were made a condition of placement or employment for positions that meet one or more of three criteria. The first is direct involvement in drug interdiction or enforcement of related laws, an activity the Commissioner deemed fraught with obvious dangers to the mission of the agency and the lives of customs agents. The second criterion is a requirement that the incumbent carry firearms, as the Commissioner concluded that "[p]ublic safety demands that employees who carry deadly arms and are prepared to make instant life or death decisions be drug free." The third criterion is a requirement for the incumbent to handle "classified" material, which the Commissioner determined might fall into the hands of smugglers if accessible to employees who, by reason of their own illegal drug use, are susceptible to bribery or blackmail.

After an employee qualifies for a position covered by the Customs testing program, the Service advises him by letter that his final selection is contingent upon successful completion of drug screening. An independent contractor contacts the employee to fix the time and place for collecting the sample. On reporting for the test, the employee must produce photographic identification and remove any outer garments, such as a coat or a jacket, and personal belongings. The employee may produce the sample behind a partition, or in the privacy of a bathroom stall if he so chooses. To ensure against adulteration of the specimen, or substitution of a sample from another person, a monitor of the same sex as the employee remains close at hand to listen for the normal sounds of urination. Dye is added to the toilet water to prevent the employee from using the water to adulterate the sample.

Upon receiving the specimen, the monitor inspects it to ensure its proper temperature and color, places a tamper-proof custody seal over the container, and affixes an identification label indicating the date and the individual's specimen number. The employee signs a chain-of-custody form, which is initialed by the monitor, and the urine sample is placed in a plastic bag, sealed, and submitted to a laboratory.

The laboratory tests the sample for the presence of marijuana, cocaine, opiates, amphetamines, and phencyclidine. Two tests are used. An initial screening test uses the enzyme-multiplied-immunoassay technique (EMIT). Any specimen that is identified as positive on this initial test must then be confirmed using gas chromatography/mass spectrometry (GC/MS). Confirmed positive results are reported to a "Medical Review Officer," "[a] licensed physician * * * who has knowledge of substance abused disorders and has appropriate medical training to interpret and evaluate the individual's positive test result together with his or her medical history and any other relevant biomedical information." After verifying the positive result, the Medical Review Officer transmits it to the agency.

Customs employees who test positive for drugs and who can offer no satisfactory explanation are subject to dismissal from the Service. Test results may not, however, be turned over to any other agency, including criminal prosecutors, without the employee's written consent.

* * *

In Skinner v. Railway Labor Executives Assn., [489 U.S. 602 (1989)] decided today, we hold that federal regulations requiring employees of private railroads to produce urine samples for chemical testing implicate the Fourth Amendment, as those tests invade reasonable expectations of privacy. Our earlier cases have settled that the Fourth Amendment protects individuals from unreasonable searches conducted by the Government, even when the Government acts as an employer, and, in view of our holding in *Railway Labor Executives* that urine tests are searches, it follows that the Customs Service's drug testing program must meet the reasonableness requirement of the Fourth Amendment.

While we have often emphasized, and reiterate today, that a search must be supported, as a general matter, by a warrant issued upon probable cause, our decision in *Railway Labor Executives* reaffirms the longstanding principle that neither a warrant nor probable cause, nor, indeed, any measure of individualized suspicion, is an indispensable component of reasonableness in every circumstance. As we note in *Railway Labor Executives,* our cases establish that where a Fourth Amendment intrusion serves special governmental needs, beyond the normal need for law enforcement, it is necessary to balance the individual's privacy expectations against the Government's interests to determine whether it is impractical to require a warrant or some level of individualized suspicion in the particular context.

It is clear that the Customs Service's drug testing program is not designed to serve the ordinary needs of law enforcement. Test results may not be used in a criminal prosecution of the employee without the employee's consent. The purposes of the program are to deter drug use among those eligible for promotion to sensitive positions within the Service and to prevent the promotion of drug users to those positions. These substantial interests, no less than the Government's concern for safe rail transportation at issue in *Railway Labor Executives,* present a special need that may justify departure from the ordinary warrant and probable cause requirements.

Petitioners do not contend that a warrant is required by the balance of privacy and governmental interests in this context, nor could any such contention withstand scrutiny. We have recognized before that requiring the Government to procure a warrant for every work-related intrusion "would conflict with 'the common-sense realization that government offices could not function if every employment decision became a constitutional matter.'" Even if Customs Service employees are more likely to be familiar with the procedures required to obtain a warrant than most other Government workers, requiring a warrant in this context would serve only to divert valuable agency resources from the Service's primary mission. The Customs Service has been entrusted with pressing responsibilities, and its mission would be compromised if it were required to seek search warrants in connection with routine, yet sensitive, employment decisions.

Furthermore, a warrant would provide little or nothing in the way of additional protection of personal privacy. A warrant serves primarily to advise the citizen that an intrusion is authorized by law and limited in its permissible scope and to interpose a neutral magistrate between the citizen and the law enforcement officer "engaged in the often competitive enterprise of ferreting out crime." But in the present context, "the circumstances justifying toxicological testing and the permissible limits of such intrusions are defined narrowly and specifically * * *, and doubtless are well known to covered employees." Under the Customs program, every employee who seeks a transfer to a covered position knows that he must take a drug test, and is likewise aware of the procedures the Service must follow in administering the test. A covered employee is simply not subject "to the discretion of the official in the field." The process becomes automatic when the employee elects to apply for, and thereafter pursue, a covered position. Because the Service does not make a discretionary determination to search based on a judgment that certain conditions are present, there are simply "no special facts for a neutral magistrate to evaluate."

Even where it is reasonable to dispense with the warrant requirement in the particular circumstances, a search ordinarily must be based on probable cause. Our cases teach, however, that the probable-cause standard "is peculiarly related to criminal investigations." In particular, the traditional probable-cause standard may be unhelpful in analyzing the reasonableness of routine administrative functions, especially where the Government seeks to *prevent* the development of hazardous conditions or to detect violations that rarely generate articulable grounds for searching any particular place or person. Our precedents have settled that, in certain limited circumstances, the Government's need to discover such latent or hidden conditions, or to prevent their development, is sufficiently compelling to justify the intrusion on privacy entailed by conducting such searches without any measure of individualized suspicion. We think the Government's need to conduct the suspicionless searches required by the Customs program outweighs the privacy interests of employees engaged directly in drug interdiction, and of those who otherwise are required to carry firearms.

The Customs Service is our Nation's first line of defense against one of the greatest problems affecting the health and welfare of our population. We have adverted before to "the veritable national crisis in law enforcement caused by smuggling of illicit narcotics." Our cases also reflect the traffickers' seemingly inexhaustible repertoire of deceptive practices and elaborate schemes for importing narcotics. The record in this case confirms that, through the adroit selection of source locations, smuggling routes, and increasingly elaborate methods of concealment, drug traffickers have managed to bring into this country increasingly large quantities of illegal drugs. The record also indicates, and it is well known, that drug smugglers do not hesitate to use violence to protect their lucrative trade and avoid apprehension.

Many of the Service's employees are often exposed to this criminal element and to the controlled substances they seek to smuggle into the country. The physical safety of these employees may be threatened, and many may be tempted not only by bribes from the traffickers with whom they deal, but also by their own access to vast sources of valuable contraband seized and controlled by the Service. The Commissioner indicated below that "Customs [o]fficers have been shot, stabbed, run over, dragged by automobiles, and assaulted with blunt objects while performing their duties." At least nine officers have died in the line of duty since 1974. He also noted that Customs officers have been the targets of bribery by drug smugglers on numerous occasions, and several have been removed from the Service for accepting bribes and other integrity violations.

It is readily apparent that the Government has a compelling interest in ensuring that front-line interdiction personnel are physically fit, and have unimpeachable integrity and judgment. * * * This national interest in self protection could be irreparably damaged if those charged with safeguarding it were, because of their own drug use, unsympathetic to their mission of interdicting narcotics. A drug user's indifference to the Service's basic mission or, even worse, his active complicity with the malefactors, can facilitate importation of sizable drug shipments or block apprehension of dangerous criminals. The public interest demands effective measures to bar drug users from positions directly involving the interdiction of illegal drugs.

The public interest likewise demands effective measures to prevent the promotion of drug users to positions that require the incumbent to carry a firearm, even if the incumbent is not engaged directly in the interdiction of drugs. Customs employees who may use deadly force plainly "discharge duties fraught with such risks of injury to others that even a momentary lapse of attention can have disastrous consequences." We agree with the Government that the public should not bear the risk that employees who may suffer from impaired perception and judgment will be promoted to positions where they may need to employ deadly force. Indeed, ensuring against the creation of this dangerous risk will itself further Fourth Amendment values, as the use of deadly force may violate the Fourth Amendment in certain circumstances.

Against these valid public interests we must weigh the interference with individual liberty that results from requiring these classes of employees to undergo a urine test. The interference with individual privacy that results from the collection of a urine sample for subsequent chemical analysis could be substantial in some circumstances. We have recognized, however, that the "operational realities of the workplace" may render entirely reasonable certain work-related intrusions by supervisors and co-workers that might be viewed as unreasonable in other contexts. While these operational realities will rarely affect an employee's expectations of privacy with respect to searches of his person, or of personal effects that the employee may bring to the workplace, it is plain that certain forms of public employment may diminish privacy expectations even with respect to such personal searches. Employees of the United States Mint, for example, should expect to be subject to certain routine personal searches when they leave the workplace every day. Similarly, those who join our military or intelligence services may not only be required to give what in other contexts might be viewed as extraordinary assurances of trustworthiness and probity, but also may expect intrusive inquiries into their physical fitness for those special positions.

We think Customs employees who are directly involved in the interdiction of illegal drugs or who are required to carry firearms in the line of duty likewise have a diminished expectation of privacy in respect to the intrusions occasioned by a urine test. Unlike most private citizens or government employees in general, employees involved in drug interdiction reasonably should expect effective inquiry into their fitness and probity. Much the same is true of employees who are required to carry firearms. Because successful performance of their duties depends uniquely on their judgment and dexterity, these employees cannot reasonably expect to keep from the Service personal information that bears directly on their fitness. While reasonable tests designed to elicit this information doubtless infringe some privacy expectations, we do not believe these expectations outweigh the Government's compelling interests in safety and in the integrity of our borders.

Without disparaging the importance of the governmental interests that support the suspicionless searches of these employees, petitioners nevertheless contend that the Service's drug testing program is unreasonable in two particulars. First, petitioners argue that the program is unjustified because it is not based on a belief that testing will reveal any drug use by covered employees. In pressing this argument, petitioners point out that the Service's testing scheme was not implemented in response to any perceived drug problem among Customs employees, and that the program actually has not led to the discovery of a significant number of drug users. Counsel for petitioners informed us at oral argument that no more than 5 employees out of 3,600 have tested positive for drugs. Second, petitioners contend that the Service's scheme is not a "sufficiently productive mechanism to justify [its] intrusion upon Fourth Amendment interests," because illegal drug users can avoid detection with ease by temporary abstinence or by surreptitious adulteration of their urine specimens. These contentions are unpersuasive.

Petitioners' first contention evinces an unduly narrow view of the context in which the Service's testing program was implemented. Petitioners do not dispute, nor can there be doubt, that drug abuse is one of the most serious problems confronting our society today. There is little reason to believe that American workplaces are immune from this pervasive social problem, as is amply illustrated by our decision in *Railway Labor Executives.* * * *

The mere circumstance that all but a few of the employees tested are entirely innocent of wrongdoing does not impugn the program's validity. * * * The Service's program is designed to prevent the promotion of drug users to sensitive positions as much as it is designed to detect those employees who use drugs. Where, as here, the possible harm against which the Government seeks to guard is substantial, the need to prevent its occurrence furnishes an ample justification for reasonable searches calculated to advance the Government's goal.

We think petitioners' second argument—that the Service's testing program is ineffective because employees may attempt to deceive the test by a brief abstention before the test date, or by adulterating their urine specimens—overstates the case. As the Court of Appeals noted, addicts may be unable to abstain even for a limited period of time, or may be unaware of the "fade-away effect" of certain drugs. More importantly, the avoidance techniques suggested by petitioners are fraught with uncertainty and risks for those employees who venture to attempt them. A particular employee's pattern of elimination for a given drug cannot be predicted with perfect accuracy, and, in any event, this information is not likely to be known or available to the employee. * * * Thus, contrary to petitioners' suggestion, no employee reasonably can expect to deceive the test by the simple expedient of abstaining after the test date is assigned. Nor can he expect attempts at adulteration to succeed, in view of the precautions taken by the sample collector to ensure the integrity of the sample. In all the circumstances, we are persuaded that the program bears a close and substantial relation to the Service's goal of deterring drug users from seeking promotion to sensitive positions.

In sum, we believe the Government has demonstrated that its compelling interests in safeguarding our borders and the public safety outweigh the privacy expectations of employees who seek to be promoted to positions that directly involve the interdiction of illegal drugs or that require the incumbent to carry a firearm. We hold that the testing of these employees is reasonable under the Fourth Amendment.

We are unable, on the present record, to assess the reasonableness of the Government's testing program insofar as it covers employees who are required "to handle classified material." We readily agree that the Government has a compelling interest in protecting truly sensitive information from those who, "under compulsion of circumstances or for other reasons, * * * might compromise [such] information." We also agree that employees who seek promotions to positions where they would handle sensitive information can be required to submit to a urine test under the Service's screening program, especially if the positions covered under this category require background investigations, medical examinations, or other intrusions that may be expected to diminish their expectations of privacy in respect of a urinalysis test.

It is not clear, however, whether the category defined by the Service's testing directive encompasses only those Customs employees likely to gain access to sensitive information. Employees who are tested under the Service's scheme include those holding such diverse positions as "Accountant," "Accounting Technician," "Animal Caretaker," "Attorney (All)," "Baggage Clerk," "Co-op Student (All)," "Electric Equipment Repairer," "Mail Clerk/Assistant," and "Messenger." We assume these positions were selected for coverage under the Service's testing program by reason of the incumbent's access to "classified" information, as it is not clear that they would fall under either of the two categories we have already considered. Yet it is not evident that those occupying these positions are likely to gain access to sensitive information, and this apparent discrepancy raises in our minds the question whether the Service has defined this category of employees more broadly than necessary to meet the purposes of the Commissioner's directive.

We cannot resolve this ambiguity on the basis of the record before us, and we think it is appropriate to remand the case to the court of appeals for such proceedings as may be necessary to clarify the scope of this category of employees subject to testing. Upon remand the court of appeals should examine the criteria used by the Service in determining what materials are classified and in deciding whom to test under this rubric. In assessing the reasonableness of requiring tests of these employees, the court should also consider pertinent information bearing upon the employees' privacy expectations, as well as the supervision to which these employees are already subject.

* * *

The judgment of the Court of Appeals for the Fifth Circuit is affirmed in part and vacated in part, and the case is remanded for further proceedings consistent with this opinion.

It is so ordered.

■ JUSTICE MARSHALL, with whom JUSTICE BRENNAN joins, dissenting.

For the reasons stated in my dissenting opinion in Skinner v. Railway Labor Executives' Association, I also dissent from the Court's decision in this case. Here, as in *Skinner,* the Court's abandonment of the Fourth Amendment's express requirement that searches of the person rest on probable cause is unprincipled and unjustifiable. But even if I believed that balancing analysis was appropriate under the Fourth Amendment, I would still dissent from today's judgment, for the reasons stated by Justice Scalia in his dissenting opinion and for the reasons noted by the dissenting judge below relating to the inadequate tailoring of the Customs Service's drug-testing plan.

■ JUSTICE SCALIA, with whom JUSTICE STEVENS joins, dissenting.

* * *

What is absent in the Government's justifications—notably absent, revealingly absent, and as far as I am concerned dispositively absent—is the recitation of *even a single instance* in which any of the speculated horribles actually occurred: an instance, that is, in which the cause of bribe-taking, or of poor aim, or of unsympathetic law enforcement, or of compromise of classified information, was drug use. Although the Court points out that several employees have in the past been removed from the Service for accepting bribes and other integrity violations, and that at least nine officers have died in the line of duty since 1974, there is no indication whatever that these incidents were related to drug use by Service employees. Perhaps concrete evidence of the severity of a problem is unnecessary when it is so well known that courts can almost take judicial notice of it; but that is surely not the case here. The Commissioner of Customs himself has stated that he "believe[s] that Customs is largely drug-free," that "[t]he extent of illegal drug use by Customs employees was not the reason for establishing this program," and that he "hope[s] and expect[s] to receive reports of very few positive findings through drug screening." The test results have fulfilled those hopes and expectations. According to the Service's counsel, out of 3,600 employees tested, no more than 5 tested positive for drugs.

* * *

Today's decision would be wrong, but at least of more limited effect, if its approval of drug testing were confined to that category of employees assigned specifically to drug interdiction duties. Relatively few public employees fit that description. But in extending approval of drug testing to that category consisting of employees who carry firearms, the Court exposes vast numbers of public employees to this needless indignity. Logically, of course, if those who carry guns can be treated in this fashion, so can all others whose work, if performed under the influence of drugs, may endanger others—automobile drivers, operators of other potentially dangerous equipment, construction workers, school crossing guards. A similarly broad scope attaches to the Court's approval of drug testing for those with access to "sensitive information." Since this category is not limited to Service employees with drug interdiction duties, nor to "sensitive information" specifically relating to drug traffic, today's holding apparently approves drug testing for all federal employees with security clearances—or, indeed, for all federal employees with valuable confidential information to impart. Since drug use is not a particular problem in the Customs Service, employees throughout the government are no less likely to violate the public trust by taking bribes to feed their drug habit, or by yielding to blackmail. Moreover, there is no reason why this super-protection against harms arising from drug use must be limited to public employees; a law requiring similar testing of private citizens who use dangerous instruments such as guns or cars, or who have access to classified information would also be constitutional.

There is only one apparent basis that sets the testing at issue here apart from all these other situations—but it is not a basis upon which the Court is willing to rely. I do not believe for a minute that the driving force behind these drug-testing rules was any of the feeble justifications put forward by counsel here and accepted by the Court. The only plausible explanation, in my view, is what the Commissioner himself offered in the concluding sentence of his memorandum to Customs Service employees announcing the program: "Implementation of the drug screening program would set an important example in our country's struggle with this most serious threat to our national health and security." Or as respondent's brief to this Court asserted: "if a law enforcement agency and its employees do not take the law seriously, neither will the public on which the agency's effectiveness depends." What better way to show that the Government is serious about its "war on drugs" than to subject its employees on the front line of that war to this invasion of their privacy and affront to their dignity? To be sure, there is only a slight chance that it will prevent some serious public harm resulting from Service employee drug use, but it will show to the world that the Service is "clean," and—most important of all—will demonstrate the determination of the Government to eliminate this scourge of our society! I think it obvious that this justification is unacceptable; that the impairment of individual liberties cannot be the means of making a point; that symbolism, even symbolism for so worthy a cause as the abolition of unlawful drugs, cannot validate an otherwise unreasonable search.

There is irony in the Government's citation, in support of its position, of Justice Brandeis's statement in Olmstead v. United States, 277 U.S. 438, 485 (1928) that "[f]or good or for ill, [our Government] teaches the whole people by its example." Brandeis was there *dissenting* from the Court's admission of evidence obtained through an unlawful Government wiretap. He was not praising the Government's example of vigor and enthusiasm in combatting crime, but condemning its example that "the end justifies the means." An even more apt quotation from that famous Brandeis dissent would have been the following:

"[I]t is * * * immaterial that the intrusion was in aid of law enforcement. Experience should teach us to be most on our guard to protect liberty when the Government's purposes are beneficent. Men born to freedom are naturally alert to repel invasion of their liberty by evil-minded rulers. The greatest dangers to liberty lurk in insidious encroachment by men of zeal, well-meaning but without understanding."

Those who lose because of the lack of understanding that begot the present exercise in symbolism are not just the Customs Service employees, whose dignity is thus offended, but all of us—who suffer a coarsening of our national manners that ultimately give the Fourth Amendment its content, and who become subject to the administration of federal officials whose respect for our privacy can hardly be greater than the small respect they have been taught to have for their own.

NOTES AND QUESTIONS

1.   In Skinner v. Railway Labor Execs.' Ass'n, 489 U.S. 602 (1989), the Supreme Court, 7–2, upheld Federal Railroad Administration regulations requiring railroads to conduct post-accident drug tests of railroad crews. Justices Marshall and Brennan dissented. Part of the dissent is as follows:

> The issue in this case is not whether declaring a war on illegal drugs is good public policy. The importance of ridding our society of such drugs is, by now, apparent to all. Rather, the issue here is whether the Government's deployment in that war of a particularly draconian weapon—the compulsory collection and chemical testing of railroad workers' blood and urine—comports with the Fourth Amendment. Precisely because the need for action against the drug scourge is manifest, the need for vigilance against unconstitutional excess is great. History teaches that grave threats to liberty often come in times of urgency, when constitutional rights seem too extravagant to endure. The World War II relocation-camp cases, Hirabayashi v. United States, 320 U.S. 81 (1943); Korematsu v. United States, 323 U.S. 214 (1944), and the Red Scare and McCarthy-Era internal subversion cases, Schenck v. United States, 249 U.S. 47 (1919); Dennis v. United States, 341 U.S. 494 (1951), are only the most extreme reminders that when we allow fundamental freedoms to be sacrificed in the name of real or perceived exigency, we invariably come to regret it.

* * *

> In his first dissenting opinion as a Member of this Court, Oliver Wendell Holmes observed:

> "Great cases, like hard cases, make bad law. For great cases are called great, not by reason of their real importance in shaping the law of the future, but because of some accident of immediate overwhelming interest which appeals to the feelings and distorts the judgment. These immediate interests exercise a kind of hydraulic pressure which makes what previously was clear seem doubtful, and before which even well settled principles of law will bend." Northern Securities Co. v. United States, 193 U.S. 197, 400–401 (1904).

> A majority of this Court, swept away by society's obsession with stopping the scourge of illegal drugs, today succumbs to the popular pressures described by Justice Holmes. In upholding the FRA's plan for blood and urine testing, the majority bends time-honored and textually-based principles of the Fourth Amendment—principles the Framers of the Bill of Rights designed to ensure that the Government has a strong and individualized justification when it seeks to invade an individual's privacy. I believe the Framers would be appalled by the vision of mass governmental intrusions upon the integrity of the human body that the majority allows to become reality. The immediate victims of the majority's constitutional timorousness will be those railroad workers whose

bodily fluids the Government may now forcibly collect and analyze. But ultimately, today's decision will reduce the privacy all citizens may enjoy, for, as Justice Holmes understood, principles of law, once bent, do not snap back easily. I dissent.

2. As with Justice Scalia's dissent in *Von Raab,* Justice Marshall's dissent in *Skinner* suggests that the facts of the case led the majority to reach an unsound legal conclusion. Do you agree? What facts are most compelling for each side?

3. Justice Scalia charged that the drug testing program was "symbolic," i.e., politically motivated. Does Justice Kennedy reject this argument or does he say, in effect, that regardless of the motivation the drug testing program is reasonable?

4. Constitutional challenges to government-mandated drug testing after *Von Raab* have focused on the government's need to test. This determination often is based on the nature of the employees' duties. See, e.g., American Fed'n of Gov't Employees Local 2391 v. Martin, 969 F.2d 788 (9th Cir. 1992) (upholding testing of Labor Department employees in safety-sensitive or security-sensitive positions); American Fed'n of Gov't Employees Local 1533 v. Cheney, 944 F.2d 503 (9th Cir. 1991) (upholding Navy's testing of civilian employees required to hold top secret security clearances).

5. The Drug-Free Workplace Act of 1988, 41 U.S.C. §§ 701 et seq., as amended, applies to employers with federal contracts in excess of $100,000. Under the Act, each covered employer must publish and distribute a policy prohibiting the unlawful manufacture, distribution, dispensing, possession, or use of controlled substances in the workplace; provide for penalties for employees convicted of drug related violations on the job; and establish an employee awareness program on the dangers and penalties of workplace drug abuse, and the availability of resources for drug rehabilitation and counseling. Drug testing is not required. Employers failing to meet these requirements may have their federal contracts terminated and may be debarred from future contracts for up to five years.

6. The Omnibus Transportation Employee Testing Act, 49 U.S.C. §§ 45101–45106, codified earlier Department of Transportation regulations requiring the drug testing of employees in the transportation industry. It also adds the requirement of random alcohol testing for six million employees. See 49 C.F.R. Part 40.

7. A Department of Transportation (DOT) regulation applies to the drug tests of employees in aviation, rail, motor carrier, and other industries regulated by DOT who are returning to work after successfully completing drug treatment or who failed or refused to take an earlier drug test. As to these individuals, the urine drug tests must be taken using "direct observation" of the specimen production. Does the regulation constitute an unreasonable search and seizure under the Fourth Amendment? See BNSF Ry. Co. v. U.S. Dep't of Transp., 566 F.3d 200 (D.C.Cir. 2009) (held: no violation; safety-sensitive duties of employees in pervasively regulated industry justified the regulation).

8. Several states have enacted laws limiting drug testing. Most of the laws are similar in the following respects: (1) all of the laws seek to limit drug testing, but do not prohibit testing completely; (2) all of the laws permit the preemployment testing of applicants and some permit the periodic testing of employees if advance notice is given; (3) exceptions are often made for public safety officers and employees in safety-sensitive jobs; (4) "for cause" testing is generally allowed if there is "probable cause," "reasonable cause," or "reasonable suspicion" that an employee is impaired; (5) most of the laws require that the sample collection be performed in private; (6) all of the laws require confirmatory testing; and (7) most of the laws specifically require that drug testing records be kept confidential.

Other states regulate various procedures used in private or public sector drug testing. For example, they specify that notices must be posted to advise employees of the testing, require the use of certified laboratories, or grant employees the right to have the sample retested.

Utah's Drug and Alcohol Testing Act, Utah Code Ann. §§ 34–38–1 to 34–38–15, differs significantly from the other laws. The Utah law permits drug testing as a condition of hiring or continued employment so long as employers and managers also submit to testing periodically. In encouraging drug testing, the statute requires that employers performing drug testing have a written testing policy and that confirmatory tests be used. If an employer satisfies these requirements, the law immunizes the employer from liability for defamation or other torts based on the drug testing. It also prohibits any action based on the failure to conduct a drug test.

In Chandler v. Miller, 520 U.S. 305 (1997), the Supreme Court struck down a Georgia statute that required candidates for designated state offices to present a certificate from a state-approved laboratory that they have taken and have had a negative result on a urinalysis drug test within 30 days prior to qualifying for nomination or election. The Court held that the purely "symbolic" function of the law was insufficient to pass scrutiny under the Fourth Amendment.

9. In Lanier v. City of Woodburn, 518 F.3d 1147 (9th Cir. 2008), an applicant challenged a city's policy requiring that all applicants pass a preemployment drug test. The city's main justification was that drug abuse is a serious societal problem. The Ninth Circuit struck down the policy, holding, based on Chandler v. Miller, that a suspicionless drug test not involving a safety-sensitive position or drug interdiction must be based on special needs and may not be merely symbolic.

10. Challenges to private sector drug testing have relied on various theories, including the claim that the testing violates a state constitution's right to privacy. These challenges generally have been unsuccessful. Compare Luedtke v. Nabors Alas. Drilling, Inc., 768 P.2d 1123 (Alaska 1989) (rejecting theory) with Semore v. Pool, 266 Cal.Rptr. 280 (Cal. Ct. App.1990) (adopting theory). See also Alverado v. Washington Pub. Power Supply Sys., 759 P.2d 427 (Wash.1988), cert. denied, 490 U.S. 1004 (1989) (state law claim preempted by federal regulation of nuclear power plant). In Ross v. RagingWire Telecomms., Inc., 174 P.3d 200 (Cal. 2008), the California

Supreme Court held that firing an employee for failing a drug test for marijuana did not violate the state Compassionate Use Act. The court held that there was no evidence that the statute was intended to apply in the workplace.

11. As of 2018, 33 states and the District of Columbia had laws permitting individuals with certain medical conditions, such as cancer, glaucoma, and chronic pain, to use medical cannabis without fear of prosecution. (Some of these states also authorize recreational use of cannabis.) Is it or should it be lawful for an employer to discharge an employee who tests positive for marijuana even if the employee has a state-issued medical marijuana card? Should it depend on the nature of the job? In Coats v. Dish Network, L.L.C., 303 P.3d 147 (Colo. Ct. App. 2013) cert. granted (Colo. 2014), the plaintiff, who is quadriplegic, was discharged after he tested positive for cannabis. The plaintiff claimed that his off-duty use of cannabis was a "lawful" activity under Colorado law. The court affirmed dismissal of the plaintiff's complaint because, even though cannabis use is legal under Colorado law, it is unlawful under federal law. The dissent argued that lawfulness should be based on Colorado law. The Supreme Court of Colorado unanimously affirmed. Coats v. Dish Network, L.L.C., 350 P.3d 849 (Colo. 2015). The plaintiff challenged his firing under a Colorado law that prohibits discharge of an employee for engaging in "lawful activity" off the job (primarily designed to protect cigarette smokers). Would the plaintiff have had a better chance by alleging that permitting him to smoke cannabis at home for pain relief was a reasonable accommodation for his disability and therefore was required by the Americans with Disabilities Act or state disability nondiscrimination law? See Barbuto v. Advantage Sales and Marketing, 477 Mass. 456 (2017) (employee who used medical cannabis to manage Crohn's disease stated a claim of handicap discrimination under state law because off-site use of cannabis could be a permissible employment accommodation).

12. Despite its widespread use by public and private employers there is very little evidence that drug testing is effective in improving productivity or preventing accidents. If this is true, why do you think drug testing has remained so popular among employers? See generally National Research Council/Institute of Medicine, Under the Influence? Drugs and the American Workforce (1994); Mark A. Rothstein, Workplace Drug Testing: A Case Study in the Misapplication of Technology, 5 Harv.J.L. & Tech. 65 (1991).

2.   GENETIC DISCRIMINATION

a.   THE PROBLEM

The Human Genome Project was an international, scientific research project to map and sequence all of the genetic material of humans. Begun in 1990, it was expected to last 15 years, but advances in technology and the competition from a public-private race to complete the work resulted in completion of the draft sequence in 2003 (the 50th anniversary of the discovery of the DNA double helix by Watson and Crick). From the outset, there was great concern among members of the public that an increase in genetic information might lead to "genetic discrimination" in employment, health insurance, and other areas. In fact, in numerous public opinion surveys since 1990 an overwhelming percentage of people surveyed express great concern about this issue. As discussed in the following article, however, the term "genetic discrimination" can be variously defined.

Mark A. Rothstein & Mary R. Anderlik, What Is Genetic Discrimination and When and How Can It Be Prevented?[*]

3 Genetics in Med. 354, 354–355 (2001).

The two most common uses of the term discrimination differ dramatically in the degree of disapproval they connote. On the one hand, the term discrimination may be used to indicate a type of distinction that invariably is or should be socially unacceptable. We refer to this as the civil rights definition. For example, the Council for Responsible Genetics position paper on genetic discrimination does not define the term discrimination, but the negative connotation is clear from its use. Discrimination is linked to evaluating people based on "questionable stereotypes" rather than their individual merits and abilities, invading people's privacy, the morally and publicly unacceptable stratification of the community into "haves" and "have-nots," and the punishment of people for characteristics over which they have no control in violation of cherished beliefs in justice and equality. The proper response to discrimination is legal prohibition.

On the other hand, the term discrimination may be used as an all-purpose descriptor for the practice of making distinctions. Further, some individuals and entities link social unacceptability with irrationality, that is, they believe that only irrational distinctions should be socially unacceptable. We refer to this as the actuarial definition. For example, in the insurance industry, the term discrimination is considered neutral and simply refers to classification for purposes of underwriting. On the industry view, discrimination only becomes problematic where there is no sound actuarial basis for the manner in which risks are classified, or individuals with equivalent risks are treated differently. Often, in the business context, "irrational" means that the distinction cannot be defended in economic terms or, in the case of insurance, by reference to sound actuarial principles.

For both definitions, the term genetic discrimination also conveys that adverse treatment is based solely on the genotype of asymptomatic individuals. Differential treatment on the basis of phenotype is frequently rational and accepted as a social necessity, such as where an employer bases a hiring decision on a job-related need for visual acuity. Cases of adverse treatment based on the phenotypic expression of a

---

[*]   Reprinted by permission.

genetic characteristic fit well within the analytical framework of laws dealing with disability-based or health status-based discrimination generally. The most important of these laws is the Americans with Disabilities Act. To the contrary, cases of adverse treatment of phenotypically "normal" individuals fit poorly within the disability discrimination framework. A large majority of the public considers discrimination against these individuals as unfair because current opportunities are being denied to seemingly unaffected individuals merely because a genetic test or assessment indicates an increased risk of future incapacity.

We define discrimination as drawing a distinction among individuals or groups plus an element of either irrationality or social unacceptability or both. Our definition draws upon elements of both the civil rights and actuarial definitions. When discrimination is defined in this way, the term clearly has a negative connotation, but it does not necessarily equate with a legal proscription of the classification. The appropriate legal and policy response to social unacceptability—a widely shared sense within a polity that some activity or state of affairs is "wrong"— will depend on the circumstances. In addition to or in lieu of legal prohibitions backed by criminal, civil, or administrative penalties are withdrawals of public funding, public condemnation, professional standards, and direct citizen action against the offending parties, for example, in the form of an economic boycott. Our definition recognizes that some forms of irrational discrimination are accepted, or at least tolerated, by society and some forms of discrimination are socially unacceptable despite the fact that they are rational.

Table 1 illustrates the application of our definition of discrimination by indicating how a sample of selection criteria for employment would be arrayed along dimensions of social acceptability and rationality. Note that standards for judging social acceptability will vary according to the context. While employers are generally not prohibited from basing hiring decisions on Zodiac signs, even though this is clearly irrational, an insurer would have to offer some actuarial basis for the distinction in order to meet the requirements of state insurance laws. One justification for differences in the law of employment and insurance is that, in our society, there is no history of systematic mistreatment of Virgos relative to Capricorns in employment, and the costs of policing idiosyncratic factors in isolated hiring decisions would be very high. On the other hand, risk classification in insurance involves assigning individuals to risk pools and hence insurance practices have the potential to *create* systematic mistreatment. Insurance underwriting policies also are more amenable to regulation than hiring decisions.

Table 1.   Categories of Discrimination in Employment

	Rational	Irrational
Acceptable	• Choosing based on relative skill or other job-related criteria	• Choosing based on Zodiac sign
	• Choosing based on medical assessment of ability to perform the job	• Choosing based on a coin toss
Unacceptable	• Excluding persons with cancer based on concerns about health care costs	• Excluding based on religion (in a secular enterprise)
	• Excluding pregnant women because they may shortly go on maternity leave	• Excluding based on national origin

NOTES AND QUESTIONS

1. Where do you think the issue of genetic discrimination should be placed on the preceding table?

2. How would you compare the stigma of genetic discrimination relative to the stigma associated with other forms of employment discrimination? Is this a relevant consideration? For a discussion of the appropriateness of the antidiscrimination model of preventing genetic discrimination, see Pauline T. Kim, Genetic Discrimination, Genetic Privacy: Rethinking Employee Protections for a Brave New Workplace, 96 Nw. U.L. Rev. 1497 (2002). For the counter-argument, that genetic discrimination should not be regulated, see Colin S. Diver & Jane Maslow Cohen, Genophobia: What is Wrong with Genetic Discrimination?, 149 U.Pa. L. Rev. 1439 (2001); Richard A. Epstein, The Legal Regulation of Genetic Discrimination: Old Responses to New Technology, 79 B.U.L. Rev. 1 (1994).

3. In 1995, the EEOC issued its first official interpretation of the coverage of genetic predisposition under the ADA.

> This part of the definition of "disability" applies to individuals who are subjected to discrimination on the basis of genetic information related to illness, disease, or other disorders. Covered entities that discriminate against individuals on the basis of such genetic information are regarding the individuals as having impairments that substantially limit a major life activity. Those individuals, therefore, are covered by the third part of the definition of "disability."

EEOC Compliance Manual, Volume 2, EEOC Order 915.002, Definition of the Term "Disability," reprinted in Daily Lab.Rep., Mar. 16, 1995, at E-1, E-23. This interpretation has never been tested in court.

4.   In Norman-Bloodsaw v. Lawrence Berkeley Lab., 135 F.3d 1260 (9th Cir. 1998), the Ninth Circuit reversed the district court and held that employees who alleged that their blood was tested for, among other things, sickle cell trait, without their consent had stated a valid claim under the federal and state constitutions and Title VII. See generally Elizabeth Pendo, Race, Sex, and Genes at Work: Uncovering the Lessons of *Norman-Bloodsaw*, 10 Hous. J. Health L. & Pol'y 227 (2010).

5.   Burlington Northern Santa Fe Railroad (BNSF) is the nation's second largest railroad company. In March 2000, BNSF began a pilot program that included genetic testing for employees who claimed work-related carpal tunnel disease. Rail industry safety rules and negotiated union contracts allow BNSF to require employees to undergo medical examinations to evaluate work-related injury claims. Since the initiation of the new policy, approximately 125 of its 40,000 active employees filed claims for carpal tunnel-related injuries. Of those 125, genetic testing was performed on 23 employees. None of the employees was told that the blood sample they were giving was being sent to a research laboratory for genetic analysis.

BNSF's practice of requiring genetic tests came to the attention of the Equal Employment Opportunity Commission (EEOC) when Janice Avary, a registered nurse and wife of a BNSF employee, began looking into the reason why BNSF was requiring her husband to submit seven vials of blood after he filed a claim for a carpal tunnel injury. When the company's medical liaison mentioned possible genetic tests, Avary became alarmed. She called the railroad's headquarters to inform them that they could not subject her husband to a genetic test without his permission (under Iowa state law). According to Avary, BNSF told her that if her husband refused the exam, he could face an investigation for insubordination.

As a result of this experience, Gary Avary filed a complaint with the EEOC. Soon after, five more workers told the EEOC that they had given blood during the medical exams but were unaware of its ultimate use. While the union and the EEOC were investigating the claims against BNSF, Gary Avary received a disciplinary letter from BNSF as a result of his failure to comply with the examination. In response to this letter and to BNSF's practice of requiring genetic testing, on February 9, 2001, EEOC filed its first court action challenging genetic testing. EEOC v. Burlington Northern Santa Fe R.R. Co., No. C01–4013 (N.D. Iowa 2001). In its petition, the EEOC asked for a preliminary injunction against BNSF requiring the company to end genetic testing of employees who have filed claims for work-related injuries based on carpal tunnel syndrome.

The EEOC claimed that the genetic testing violated the ADA because it is not job-related or consistent with business necessity. Section 102(d)(4) of the ADA provides that any medical examinations or inquiries of current employees must be either voluntary or job-related and consistent with business necessity, meaning that they measure the ability to perform the job safely and efficiently. EEOC's position was that the unproven test was not job-related. On February 12, 2001, BNSF announced that it would suspend its practice of requiring genetic testing, and a settlement agreement was approved by the court on May 6, 2002. A total of $2.2 million was paid to 36 employees who were subjected to genetic testing or who the employer attempted to test.

b.   LEGISLATIVE RESPONSES

(i)   State Laws

State laws prohibiting genetic discrimination in employment date back to the 1970s. At that time, widespread and ill-advised carrier testing for sickle cell trait caused confusion, resulting in discrimination against unaffected carriers. Florida, Louisiana, and North Carolina enacted laws prohibiting discrimination based on sickle cell trait. Wisconsin enacted the first comprehensive genetic nondiscrimination law in 1991. In the next two decades, two-thirds of the states enacted laws prohibiting genetic discrimination in employment. A continually updated list of state genetic nondiscrimination laws is available from the National Conference of State Legislatures, www.ncsl.org/default.aspx?tabid= 14280.

The state laws generally prohibit employers from requiring genetic testing as a condition of employment and prohibit discrimination based on genetic information. In most states, the definition of genetic information includes family health history, but in some states it is limited to the results of a DNA-based genetic test. With the exception of California and Minnesota, the laws do not prohibit employers from requiring that individuals sign a blanket authorization for the disclosure of their health records after a conditional offer of employment.

As discussed below, federal legislation was enacted in 2008. Nevertheless, state laws may still be important, because in many states they apply to small employers below the federal statutory minimum of 15 employees. See Chapter 4 infra.

(ii)   Genetic Information Nondiscrimination Act (GINA)

The Genetic Information Nondiscrimination Act of 2008 (GINA) was signed into law by President Bush on May 21, 2008, after a 13-year struggle in Congress. Previously, in 2000, President Clinton issued Executive Order 13145, which prohibited genetic discrimination in federal government employment. The executive order was designed to pave the way for legislation covering the private sector, but GINA was not enacted for another eight years because some members of Congress considered it unnecessary or intrusive.

GINA has two main titles. Title I prohibits genetic discrimination in individual and group health insurance. This provision has been largely rendered moot by the enactment in 2010 of the Patient Protection and

Affordable Care Act, P.L. 111–148 (2010), which prohibits the exclusion of health insurance coverage based on any health condition. For a further discussion, see Chapter 6 infra.

Title II of GINA prohibits genetic discrimination in employment. It bars employers from requesting, requiring, or purchasing genetic information about employees, applicants, or their family members (section 202(b)). There are several exceptions to the ban on acquiring genetic information, including inadvertent acquisition, requests for FMLA documentation, and optional genetic monitoring for the effects of occupational exposures (section 202(b)).

Genetic information is defined as information about the individual's genetic tests, the genetic tests of family members, or the manifestation of a disease or disorder in a family member (section 201(4)). GINA does not apply to manifested diseases or disorders of the individual. Although the ADA prohibits discrimination based on a manifested condition, there is a gap in coverage between discrimination based on an unexpressed genotype (covered by GINA) and discrimination based on the manifestation of an impairment that constitutes a substantial limitation of a major life activity (covered by the ADA). See Mark A. Rothstein, GINA, the ADA, and Genetic Discrimination in Employment, 36 J.L. Med. & Ethics 837 (2008). Employers are prohibited from engaging in various unlawful employment practices, including refusing to hire, discharging, or discriminating in terms or conditions of employment, based on genetic information (section 202(a)).

For private sector employers, GINA has the same coverage and remedies as Title VII (section 207), except that disparate impact claims may not be brought (section 208). GINA is enforced by the EEOC, with implementing regulations appearing at 29 C.F.R. Part 1635. Both the ADA and GINA permit employers to collect private health information as part of a "voluntary" wellness program, but neither statute defines voluntary. The EEOC has issued amended regulations and interpretive guidance on employer sponsored wellness programs under GINA and the ADA. 81 Fed. Reg. 31126 (2016). However, a district court vacated the EEOC's rule allowing employers to offer financial incentives to encourage employees to participate in employer-sponsored wellness plans, including by disclosing confidential medical information. AARP v. EEOC, 292 F.Supp. 3d 238 (D.D.C. 2017).

Lowe v. Atlas Logistics
102 F.Supp.3d 1360 (N.D. Ga. 2015).

■ AMY TOTENBERG, DISTRICT JUDGE.

Atlas Logistics Group Retail Services (Atlanta), LLC ("Atlas") operates warehouses for the storage of products sold at a variety of grocery stores. So one could imagine Atlas's frustration when a mystery employee began habitually defecating in one of its warehouses. To solve the mystery of the devious defecator, Atlas requested some of its employees, including Jack Lowe and Dennis Reynolds, to submit to a cheek swab. The cheek cell samples were then sent to a lab where a technician compared the cheek cell DNA to DNA from the offending fecal matter. Lowe and Dennis were not a match. With the culprit apparently still on the loose, Lowe and Dennis filed suit under the Genetic Information Nondiscrimination Act ("GINA"), 42 U.S.C. § 2000ff et seq., which generally prohibits employers from requesting genetic information from its employees.

The matter is before the Court on the parties' Cross-Motions for Summary Judgment. The legal question before the Court is whether the information requested and obtained by Atlas was "genetic information" covered by GINA. For the reasons that follow, the Court concludes that it is. Thus, the Court GRANTS Plaintiffs' Motion for Partial Summary Judgment and DENIES Defendant's Motion for Summary Judgment.

* * *

III. Analysis

According to Plaintiffs Jack Lowe and Dennis Reynolds, the undisputed facts show that Atlas requested information about Speckin Labs's comparison of Lowe's and Reynolds's DNA to the fecal sample. These facts, Plaintiffs argue, demonstrate that Atlas violated 42 U.S.C. § 2000ff–1(b), which makes it "an unlawful employment practice for an employer to request, require, or purchase genetic information with respect to an employee." Plaintiffs therefore move for Partial Summary Judgment as to Atlas's liability under this section of GINA.

Atlas responds and argues in its Motion for Summary Judgment that the information the company requested concerning Lowe's and Reynolds's DNA analysis does not constitute "genetic information" as defined in GINA. According to Defendant's interpretation of GINA, "genetic information" refers only to information related to an individual's propensity for disease. For this reason, Defendant moves for summary judgment as to all of Plaintiffs' claims. The issue before the Court, therefore, is whether the term "genetic information" as used in GINA encompasses the information Atlas requested in this case.

* * *

A. The Unambiguous Statutory Language of GINA

The Court begins its analysis with the language of GINA. GINA makes it "an unlawful employment practice for an employer to request, require, or purchase genetic information with respect to an employee. Section 2000ff–1(b) lists six exceptions to this general prohibition, but Atlas admits that none of the statutory exceptions apply here. The parties' disagreement centers on a single phrase in Section 2000ff–1(b): "genetic information."

GINA defines genetic information as "with respect to any individual, information about (i) such individual's genetic tests, (ii) the genetic tests of family members of such individual, and (iii) the manifestation of a disease or disorder in family members of such individual." 42 U.S.C. § 2000ff(4). Parts (ii) and (iii) do not apply to Lowe and Reynolds's claims, as the PowerPlex 21 analysis was not performed on DNA of their family members. Therefore, the DNA analysis would only qualify as "genetic information" under GINA if the analysis qualifies as a "genetic test."

"Genetic test" is also defined in GINA. The statute defines "genetic test" as "an analysis of human DNA, RNA, chromosomes, proteins, or metabolites, that detects genotypes, mutations, or chromosomal changes." 42 U.S.C. § 2000ff(7). The extent of GINA's guidance ends with its definition of "genetic test:" none of the words included in 42 U.S.C. § 2000ff(7) are further defined in GINA.

If all the Court considers is the language of GINA, the undisputed evidence in the record establishes that the DNA analysis at issue here clearly falls within the definition of "genetic test." The parties agree that Dr. Howenstine [of the testing laboratory] conducted an "analysis" of Lowe's and Reynolds's DNA. And the undisputed evidence in the record shows that this analysis at a minimum detects genotypes and mutations. Because the parties agree that Atlas requested a comparison of Lowe's and Reynolds's DNA to the fecal DNA found in the warehouse, Atlas's request and course of action appear to constitute a violation of 42 U.S.C. § 2000ff–1(b)'s prohibition against requesting genetic information from employees.

Defendant argues that this straightforward but broad interpretation of GINA is erroneous. Defendant urges the Court to interpret the "genetic test" language of GINA to exclude analyses of DNA, RNA, chromosomes, proteins, or metabolites if such analyses do not reveal an individual's propensity for disease. This proposed definition of "genetic tests"—a definition which limits genetic tests to those related to one's propensity for disease—renders other language in GINA superfluous, and should thus be rejected.

Section 2000ff–1(b) makes it unlawful to request, require, or purchase genetic information, except in six contexts. Section 1(b)(6), in turn, expressly allows employers to request, require, or purchase some genetic information which has nothing to do with the propensity for disease. Specifically, an employer is not liable under GINA where it conducts a "DNA analysis ... for purposes of human remains identification, and requests or requires genetic information of such employer's employees, but only to the extent that such genetic information is used for analysis of DNA identification markers for quality control to detect sample contamination." 42 U.S.C. § 2000ff–1(b)(6). This exception would be unnecessary if Atlas's construction of GINA were correct, because under Atlas's construction, the term "genetic information" already excludes DNA analyses for purposes of human remains identification—a type of analysis unrelated to testing for disease propensity. Thus, the exception in § 2000ff–1(b)(6) weighs against Atlas's interpretation.

Atlas's reliance on GINA's legislative history to argue otherwise is unpersuasive. According to Atlas, this human remains identification exception was created to address a concern raised by the Bureau of Alcohol, Tobacco, and Firearms ("ATF"). drafting of GINA, ATF expressed its concern that its DNA profile index, developed for forensic purposes, seemed to violate GINA as drafted. And Congress apparently carved out the narrow exception for law enforcement agencies in response to ATF's concerns. But Atlas does not explain why such an exception would be necessary if, as Atlas would have it, the definition of "genetic information" already excludes the type of information in ATF's index— genetic information unrelated to one's propensity for disease. The Court therefore rejects Atlas's interpretation, which is inconsistent with the plain terms of the statute.

* * *

IV. Conclusion

For the reasons discussed above, the Court finds Atlas liable under 42 U.S.C. § 2000ff and GRANTS Plaintiffs Jack Lowe and Dennis Reynolds Partial Motion for Summary Judgment as to liability. The Court DENIES Defendant Atlas Logistics Group Retail Services (Atlanta), LLC Motion for Summary Judgment as to all claims.

NOTES AND QUESTIONS

1.   Unlike all of the other discrimination laws enforced by the EEOC, since the effective date of GINA in 2010 until 2015 there were only 24 non-frivolous charges filed with the EEOC alleging violations of GINA, and 21 of them involved employer efforts to obtain or use family health histories. Only three cases alleged improper activity with regard to an employee's genetic information. Mark A. Rothstein, Jessica Roberts, & Tee L. Guidotti, Limiting Medical Evaluations under the Americans with Disabilities Act and the Genetic Information Nondiscrimination Act, 41 Am. J.L. & Med. 523, 554 (2015). See also Bradley A. Areheart & Jessica L. Roberts, GINA, Big Data, and the Future of Employee Privacy, 128 Yale L.J. 710 (2019).

2.   Section 202(b)(1) of GINA provides that, subject to certain exceptions, employers are not permitted "to request, require, or purchase genetic information with respect to an employee or a family member of an employee." Section 201(a)(4) defines "genetic information" as information about an "individual's genetic tests, the genetic tests of family members of such individual, and the manifestation of a disease or disorder in family members of such individual." Neither provision requires that the information is sought or obtained by the employer with the intent of making a predictive assessment of the health risks of the individual (i.e., the applicant or employee). Neither provision requires that the information involves conditions of a heritable nature so that a predictive assessment is possible.

And neither definition requires the employer to use the information in a way that adversely affects the interests of the individual.

3.   In Allen v. Verizon Wireless, 2013 U.S. Dist. Lexis 80228 (D. Conn. 2012), the plaintiff requested leave to take care of her mother. When her employer denied the request for short-term disability leave, the employee claimed that the use of her mother's medical history information was a violation of GINA. The court cited with approval to the analysis in *Poore*, including the heritability argument. Again, the question is more easily resolved by reference to the regulations, which provide that it is not unlawful for an employer to request family medical information when there is a request for FMLA leave or an employer policy "that permits the use of leave to take care of a sick family member and that requires all employees to provide information about the health condition of the family member to substantiate the need for leave." 29 C.F.R. § 1635.8(b)(3).

4.   Each year there are at least 12.3 million employment entrance examinations (see p. 167 supra). Mark A. Rothstein & Meghan K. Talbott, Compelled Disclosures of Health Records: Updated Estimates, 45 J.L. Med. & Ethics 149 (2017). As part of this process, employers may lawfully require conditional offerees to sign an authorization for the disclosure of their entire health records, except for genetic information. Given current health information technology and law, is it realistic to expect that sensitive health information, including genetic information, can be protected from disclosure to employers? Is it worth the effort and expense to protect this information from disclosure? Do younger generations of workers attach the same importance to privacy as prior generations?

To address the possibility that custodians of health care records will provide employers with family medical history information or other genetic information in health records sought by the employer, the EEOC's GINA regulations contain a "safe harbor" provision.

> If a covered entity uses language such as the following, any receipt of genetic information will be deemed inadvertent: "The Genetic Information Nondiscrimination Act of 2008 (GINA) prohibits employers and other entities covered by GINA Title II from requesting or requiring genetic information of an individual or family member of the individual, except as specifically allowed by this law. To comply with this law, we are asking that you not provide any genetic information when responding to this request for medical information." . . .

29 C.F.R. § 1635.8(b)(1)(i)(B).

Mark A. Rothstein, GINA's Beauty Is Only Skin Deep

22 Gene Watch No. 2, at 9 (April–May 2009).

GINA was *not* enacted in response to a wave of genetic discrimination, defined as the adverse treatment of an individual based on genotype. There have been very few documented cases of such discrimination. To some degree, GINA was enacted to prevent discrimination in the future when health records will routinely contain genetic information and genetic testing will be so inexpensive that it's cost-effective to perform it on a widespread basis. The real reason for enacting GINA was to assure people that they could undergo genetic testing without fear of genetic discrimination. As any clinical geneticist or genetic counselor will tell you, these fears are real.

According to section 2(5) of GINA, federal legislation "is necessary to fully protect the public from discrimination and allay their concerns about the potential for discrimination, thereby allowing individuals to take advantage of genetic testing, technologies, research, and new therapies."

* * *

GINA makes it unlawful for an employer to request, require, or purchase genetic information regarding an applicant or employee. This is an important issue, because individuals are concerned with employers merely having access to their genetic information. The problem is that the provision is infeasible and therefore is not being followed.

Under the ADA, after a conditional offer of employment, it is lawful for an employer to require individuals to undergo a preplacement medical examination and to sign an authorization releasing all of their medical records to the employer. In effect, GINA now qualifies this by saying that employers can require the release of all medical information except genetic information. GINA defines genetic information as the genetic tests of the individual, genetic tests of the individual's family members, and family health histories. Because this information is commonly interspersed in medical records there is no practical way for the custodians of the health records (e.g., physicians, hospitals) to send only non-genetic information. In practice, when presented with a limited or unlimited request, the custodians usually send the entire records.

The development and adoption of electronic health records (EHRs) and networks hold the possibility of using health information technology to limit the scope of health information disclosed for any particular purpose. Unfortunately, there have been no efforts undertaken to design health records with the capacity to segment or sequester sensitive health information (including but not limited to genetic information) to facilitate more targeted access or disclosures. Without such efforts, health privacy will decline precipitously with the shift to EHRs because records increasingly will be comprehensive (i.e., containing information generated by substantially all health care providers) and longitudinal (i.e., containing information over an extended period of time). Thus, when employers and other third parties require access to an individual's health records the amount of information they receive will be much more extensive than they receive today.

GINA represents an incremental approach to problems that do not lend themselves to incremental approaches. Numerous entities have economic interests in learning about an individual's current or likely future health. GINA consists of halfway measures limited to health insurance and employment that do not provide adequate assurances to the public that genetic information will not be used to their detriment in other ways.

* * *

GINA prohibits employers from requesting or requiring the release of genetic information in comprehensive health records at a time when it is infeasible to separate genetic information from other health records.

If GINA serves to declare the unacceptability of genetic-based discrimination and begins a process of careful consideration of a wide range of health related issues, then it will be valuable. But it is far from clear that GINA will have such an effect. It is not clear that GINA, by singling out genetic information for special treatment, will not increase the stigma associated with genetics and encourage other condition-specific, rather than comprehensive, legislation. It is not clear whether GINA will be the first step to meaningful legislation or cause legislative fatigue based on the erroneous assumption that the issues already had been resolved. It is not clear whether consumers will understand GINA's limitations or mistakenly rely on its presumed protections. In the short term, the worst thing that could happen is for advocates of genetic rights and fairness in health care to be satisfied with GINA or exult in its enactment.

NOTES AND QUESTIONS

1.   For a further discussion of GINA, see Jessica Roberts, The Genetic Information Nondiscrimination Act as an Antidiscrimination Law, 86 Notre Dame L. Rev. 597 (2011); Jessica Roberts, Preempting Discrimination: Lessons from the Genetic Information Nondiscrimination Act, 63 Vand. L. Rev. 439 (2010).

2.   GINA and comparable state laws prohibiting genetic discrimination in employment and other domains are based on a two-part strategy: (1) enact separate laws to deal with genetic privacy and discrimination; and (2) promote the vision of a "genome-blind" society in which genetic variation is suppressed or ignored. Is this approach, regarding genetic discrimination as another form of civil rights violation, the most appropriate strategy for the twenty-first century?

> At least in the context of employment discrimination, the legislative approach has been to embrace the notion that information about genetic variation should be suppressed or ignored. In numerous contexts, however, both within and beyond the workplace, it may not be beneficial to ignore individual genetic variation or to pretend that individual differences have no meaning.

* * *

The civil rights model of "sameness" and the fiction that "all difference is irrelevant" are inappropriate legal models for genetic diversity. Moreover, ignoring differences is not the only way to protect privacy and prevent invidious discrimination based on genetic variation.

Mark A. Rothstein, Legal Conceptions of Equality in the Genomic Age, 25 Law & Inequality 429, 455–56 (2007).

F. NEGLIGENT HIRING

The preceding sections of this chapter explored the ineffectiveness, inaccuracy, intrusiveness, and undesirability of many of the commonly used employee selection criteria. What are the alternatives? Is it appropriate for employers to use only minimal hiring criteria, with little or no inquiry into an employee's prior employment record? Consider the following case.

Malorney v. B & L Motor Freight, Inc.
496 N.E.2d 1086 (Ill. Ct. App. 1986).

■ JUSTICE MURRAY delivered the opinion of the court:

This is an interlocutory appeal pursuant to Supreme Court Rule 308 by defendant B & L Motor Freight, Inc. (B & L) from a trial court order denying its motion for summary judgment. This court granted defendant's motion for leave to appeal upon certification of the issue by the trial court. The issue certified is whether defendant had a duty under the circumstances of this case to investigate Edward Harbour's non-vehicular criminal record and to verify his negative response regarding criminal offenses which he furnished on his employment application prior to employing him and furnishing him an over-the-road truck with sleeping facilities.

The circumstances of this case are as follows. Edward Harbour applied for a position of over-the-road driver with defendant B & L. On the employment application, Harbour was questioned as to whether he had any vehicular offenses or other criminal convictions. His response to the vehicular question was verified by B & L; however, his negative answer regarding criminal convictions was not verified by B & L. In fact, Harbour had a history of convictions for violent sex-related crimes and had been arrested the year prior to his employment with B & L for aggravated sodomy of two teenage hitchhikers while driving an over-the-road truck for another employer. Upon being hired by B & L, Harbour was given written instructions and regulations, including a prohibition against picking up hitchhikers in a B & L truck.

Subsequently, on January 24, 1978, at an Indiana toll road plaza, Harbour picked up plaintiff Karen Malorney, a 17-year-old hitchhiker. In the sleeping compartment of his truck, he repeatedly raped and sexually assaulted plaintiff, threatened to kill her, and viciously beat her. After being released, plaintiff notified police. Harbour was arrested, convicted, and sentenced to 50 years with no parole. Plaintiff's complaint charges defendant B & L with recklessness and wilful and wanton misconduct in negligently hiring Harbour as an over-the-road driver without adequately checking his background and providing him a vehicle with a sleeping compartment. Plaintiff seeks compensatory and punitive damages from B & L.

Defendant B & L filed a motion for summary judgment contending that it had no duty to verify Harbour's negative response to the question regarding criminal convictions. In denying defendant's motion, the trial court found that (1) Harbour was hired as an over-the-road driver and furnished with a truck equipped with sleeping quarters; (2) B & L instructed Harbour not to pick up hitchhikers; and (3) it is common knowledge that hitchhikers frequent toll plazas which would show that B & L knew drivers are prone to give rides to hitchhikers. The court concluded that these facts show that B & L had a duty to check Harbour's criminal background and certified the issue for interlocutory appeal.

Defendant argues that it had no duty to investigate Harbour's non-vehicular criminal background nor to verify his denial thereof because of a lack of foreseeability that he would use the truck to pick up and sexually assault a hitchhiker. To impose such a duty would be against public policy by placing too great a burden on employers. On the other hand, plaintiff posits the argument that factual issues exist which preclude summary judgment and require a jury determination. We agree and must affirm the trial court for the following reasons.

Defendant correctly argues that the existence of a duty is a question of law to be determined by the court, rather than by the factfinder. However, once a duty has been found, the question of whether the duty was properly performed is a fact question to be decided by the trier of fact, whether court or jury.

The existence of a legal duty is not dependent on foreseeability alone, but includes considerations of public policy and social requirements. In Illinois, two duties, among others not pertinent here, are imposed by law on owners of vehicles who permit or hire other persons to drive on our highways. The first duty requires that the degree of care which an owner should exercise in selecting a driver is that which a reasonable person would exercise under the circumstances. An owner or employer also owes a duty in connection with the entrustment of vehicles to others. In other words, a vehicle owner has a duty to deny the entrustment of a vehicle to a driver it knows, or by the exercise of reasonable diligence could have known, is incompetent. In addition to these duties, it is well settled in Illinois that a cause of action exists against an employer for negligently hiring a person the employer knew, or should have known, was unfit for the job.

B & L contends that a reasonable and prudent motor carrier could not foresee that one of its drivers would rape and assault a hitchhiker. The court in Neering v. Illinois Central R.R. Co. (1943), 383 Ill. 366, 50 N.E.2d 497, in discussing foreseeability stated that the ultimate injury must be the natural and probable result of the negligent act or omission such that an ordinary and prudent person ought to have foreseen as likely its occurrence as a result of the negligence. It is not essential that one should have foreseen the precise injury which resulted from the act or omission. This interpretation thus requires an employer to exercise that degree of care reasonably commensurate with the perils and hazards likely to be encountered in the performance of an employee's duty, i.e., such care as a reasonably prudent person would exercise in view of the consequences that might reasonably be expected to result if an incompetent, careless, or reckless agent was employed for a particular duty.

Applying these principles to the present case, it is clear that B & L had a duty to entrust its truck to a competent employee fit to drive an over-the-road truck equipped with a sleeping compartment. Lack of forethought may exist where one remains in voluntary ignorance of facts concerning the danger in a particular act or instrumentality, where a reasonably prudent person would become advised, on the theory that such ignorance is the equivalent of negligence. Bearing in mind the facts that B & L gave Harbour an over-the-road vehicle with a sleeping compartment and that B & L probably knew, or should have known, that truckers are prone to give rides to hitchhikers despite rules against such actions, the question now becomes one of fact—whether B & L breached its duty to hire a competent driver who was to be entrusted with a B & L over-the-road truck.

Regarding defendant's public policy argument, there is no evidence in the record to justify the contention that the cost of checking on the criminal history of all truck driver applicants is too expensive and burdensome when measured against the potential utility of doing so.

Finally, we note that a question of foreseeability is at times a question for the court and at times, if varying inferences are possible, a question for the jury. In the present case, B & L did have a duty to check into Harbour's background so as to ascertain whether he would be a fit employee. Based on the circumstances of this case, it is apparent that reasonable persons could arrive at different conclusions as to whether B & L used due care in the performance of this duty when it employed Harbour. Questions which are composed of such qualities sufficient to cause reasonable persons to arrive at different results should never be determined as matters of law. Questions of negligence, due care, and proximate cause are questions of fact to be determined by the factfinder.

In affirming the trial court's denial of summary judgment, we are not expressing any opinion as to the resolution of the facts in this case. Plaintiff has the heavy burden of proving that defendant B & L negligently performed a duty it owed her in entrusting Harbour with an over-the-road truck, and if negligence is found, that it proximately caused her injury. These questions, including the issue of whether defendant negligently hired Harbour by not checking his criminal background, are questions for the trier of fact and become a question of law only when the ultimate facts have been determined by the factfinder.

For these reasons, the order denying summary judgment for defendant is affirmed and the cause is remanded for further proceedings.

Affirmed and remanded.

■ LORENZ and PINCHAM, JJ., concur.

NOTES AND QUESTIONS

1.   If B & L had checked with Harbour's prior employer, do you think the prior employer would have been forthcoming with the information of his arrest for aggravated sodomy? Is there a reluctance to divulge this type of information for fear of liability for defamation? For a decision contrary to *Malorney* based on similar facts, see C.C. v. Roadrunner Trucking, Inc., 823 F.Supp. 913 (D.Utah 1993). Would B & L be liable if Harbour sexually assaulted a hotel clerk rather than a hitchhiker? See Connes v. Molalla Transp. Sys. Inc., 831 P.2d 1316 (Colo.1992) (held: no liability under theory of negligent entrustment).

2.   Suppose B & L hired Harbour based on reliance on a non-negative recommendation. Could Malorney sue Harbour's prior employer? See Moore v. St. Joseph Nursing Home, Inc., 459 N.W.2d 100 (Mich.Ct. App.1990) (former employer had no duty to disclose former employee's dangerous proclivities to inquiring prospective employer).

3.   If the former employer knows of the former employee's dangerous proclivities, should there be a difference between giving no recommendation, giving a non-negative recommendation, and giving a positive recommendation? When Robert Gadams applied for the position of vice principal in the Livingston Union School District, his former employers wrote letters of recommendation for him in which they described him as dependable and reliable, as having a pleasant personality, as setting high standards, and as an "administrator who relates well to his students." They neglected to disclose that he had resigned under pressure due to charges of sexual misconduct involving several incidents of touching or molesting female students. Are these former employers liable when the individual is hired and then engages in additional acts of sexual misconduct? See Randi W. v. Muroc Joint Unified Sch. Dist., 929 P.2d 582 (Cal.1997) (former employer writing a letter of recommendation owed to prospective employer and third persons a duty not to misrepresent the facts surrounding the qualifications and character of former employee).

Many employers believe they have been placed in a dilemma. If they fail to check out their employees, they may be liable for negligent hiring or some other tort. If they check out their employees too aggressively, they may be liable for invasion of privacy, discrimination, or some other cause of action.

Is there a way to reconcile the employers' conflicting obligations? See generally Stephen F. Befort, Pre-Employment Screening and Investigation: Navigating Between a Rock and a Hard Place, 14 Hofstra Lab.L.J. 365 (1997).

4. In many states information about criminal convictions (or other contacts with the criminal justice system) is restricted, and not easily available to prospective or current employers. See, e.g., Massachusetts Criminal Offender Record Information System Act, Mass.Gen.Laws Ch. 6 §§ 167–178; Massachusetts Fair Information Practices Act, Mass.Gen.Laws Ch. 66A §§ 1–3. Some state laws allow persons to apply for jobs without revealing their criminal records. See, e.g., Mass.Gen.Laws Ch. 276 § 100C. Hawaii law prohibits employers from discriminating on the basis of an "arrest and court record," except if a conviction is less than 10 years old and "bears a rational relationship to the duties and responsibilities of the position." Haw.Rev.Stat. § 378–2 et seq. In Wright v. Home Depot, 142 P.3d 265 (Hawai'i 2006), the court held that the statute applies to current and prospective employees. Recent cases to uphold the potential liability of employers for negligent retention and supervision include Anicich v. Home Depot U.S.A., Inc., 852 F.3d 643 (7th Cir. 2017) (applying Illinois law, the court held that the employer's duty to monitor its employees extended to a supervisor's known harassing conduct that culminated in the employee's murder); Delorenzo v. HP Enterprise Services LLC, 207 F. Supp.3d 26 (D.D.C. 2016) (in cases based on fatal shooting of 7 employees at Washington Navy Yard by contractor's employee, all negligence actions were dismissed except for negligent retention and supervision).

5. Suppose B & L refused to hire any person who had an arrest record. Would this be permissible? Suppose blacks were shown to be arrested at a rate much greater than whites (especially arrests for "suspicion"). Would this policy violate Title VII? See Gregory v. Litton Sys. Inc., 316 F.Supp. 401 (C.D.Cal. 1970), modified on other grounds, 472 F.2d 631 (9th Cir. 1972) (held: yes). Suppose the policy were limited to convictions? See Green v. Missouri Pac. R.R., 549 F.2d 1158 (8th Cir. 1977) (held: to be lawful, policy must consider the nature and gravity of the offense, the time elapsed since conviction, and the nature of the job involved). See also El v. SEPTA, 479 F.3d 232 (3d Cir. 2007) (upholding employer's business necessity defense for refusal to hire on the basis of a criminal conviction).

6. There are two types of negligent hiring cases. First, the employee injures some third party. E.g., Malorney; Cramer v. Housing Opportunities Comm'n, 501 A.2d 35 (Md.1985). Second, the employee injures a co-employee. In the second type of case the issue is often raised whether the injured worker's exclusive remedy is workers' compensation. See Sheerin v. Holin Co., 380 N.W.2d 415 (Iowa 1986) (injured workers permitted to sue employer in tort). For a further discussion of actions brought against employers for workplace injuries and illnesses, see Chapter 9.

7. Does the tort of negligent hiring require proof that the misconduct was within the wrongdoer's scope of employment? See J. v. Victory Tabernacle Baptist Church, 372 S.E.2d 391 (Va.1988) (held: no; negligent hiring is independent tort and is not dependent on respondeat superior).

8. Federal laws require background checks on certain classes of employees. For example, the U.S.A. Patriot Act, Pub. L. No. 107–56, 115 Stat. 272 (Oct. 26, 2001), requires background checks for drivers of motor vehicles transporting hazardous substances. See 49 U.S.C. § 5103a. The National Child Protection Act of 1993, 42 U.S.C. § 5119, establishes procedures for national criminal background checks for child care workers. In each state, an authorized criminal justice agency reports child abuse crime information to the national criminal history background check system. The states may then require certain "entities"—public, private, for-profit, not-for-profit, or voluntary providers of child care or child care placement services—to contact the authorized state agency to request a national background check on the individual to determine if the individual "has been convicted of a crime that bears upon an individual's fitness to have responsibility for the safety and well-being of children."

9. Many states require the fingerprinting of workers in a variety of job classifications, such as alcoholic beverage workers, farm labor contractors, jockeys, pawnbrokers, private detectives, professional boxers, school bus drivers, stockbrokers, and taxi drivers. Do such requirements constitute an unlawful invasion of privacy? Is it legal for a city to require employees of establishments serving liquor by the drink to register with the police department, be fingerprinted and photographed, and procure an identification card? See Iacobucci v. City of Newport, 785 F.2d 1354 (6th Cir. 1986), rev'd on other grounds, 479 U.S. 92 (1986) (held: yes). New York (N.Y.Lab. Code § 201–a) and California (Cal.Lab. Code § 1051) limit employer use of fingerprints. What employee interests are furthered by these laws? New York's law was passed to prevent private employers from using fingerprinting as a way of blacklisting union leaders and members. Friedman v. Valentine, 30 N.Y.S.2d 891 (N.Y. Sup.Ct.1941), aff'd, 42 N.Y.S.2d 593 (N.Y. App.Div.1943).

10. Closely related to negligent hiring cases are actions for alleged negligent supervision, in which the plaintiff asserts that the defendant knew (perhaps from information learned after an employee's hiring) that the employee posed a risk of harm to the plaintiff and that the harm was reasonably foreseeable. In Keller v. Koca, 111 P.3d 445 (Colo. 2005), a twelve year-old girl was sexually assaulted by an employee of the defendant's dry cleaning business. As general manager of the facility, the employee had keys to the business, but he did not have the authority to bring third parties to the premises during non-working hours. The assault occurred when the employee took the girl, the daughter of an acquaintance, to the store on a Sunday morning, ostensibly to open the business so that the carpets could be professionally cleaned. On three occasions prior to the assault, young women employees quit after they were allegedly sexually harassed and fondled by the general manager, but the owner refused to take any action. The Colorado Supreme Court reversed an award for the plaintiff and held that the defendant owed her no duty. "While [the defendant] may have had a duty to take reasonable steps to protect women employees and customers from the known risk of harm that [the general manager] posed to these women during working hours, this known risk does not extend to the sexual assault suffered by [the plaintiff]." Can you distinguish Malorney? Is there an analogy between the sleeping compartment of the truck and the keys to the store?

11. Should there be any limits placed on an employer's ability to refuse to hire an individual for any job because of the individual's prior criminal record? If, upon completing their sentences for any crime, all ex-convicts were unemployable, then they would be much more likely to engage in future criminal conduct. Is there a way for public policy to balance both the public interests at stake? See Obabueki v. IBM, 145 F.Supp.2d 371 (S.D.N.Y.2001) (employer did not violate New York State law making it unlawful to refuse to hire an individual based on a prior criminal conviction unless there is a "direct relationship" between the conviction and the employment sought). Cf. Selix v. Boeing Co., 919 P.2d 620 (Wash.Ct.App.1996), review denied, 930 P.2d 1230 (Wash.1997) (discharge of employee based on prior assault conviction did not violate public policy of rehabilitation of felons). Hawaii, Kansas, New York, Pennsylvania, and Wisconsin have laws prohibiting discrimination in employment on the basis of a criminal conviction. All of the laws have exceptions if the conviction relates to the job. Fourteen states prohibit discrimination in public employment based on a prior conviction. See generally Jonathan J. Darrow, Adverse Employment Consequences Triggered by Criminal Convictions: Recent Cases Interpret State Statutes Prohibiting Discrimination, 42 Wake Forest L. Rev. 991 (2007).

CHAPTER 4

DISCRIMINATION

After gathering information about interested applicants, an employer must select one individual to fill a particular job opening. Generally, employers and human resource directors speak in terms of "hiring the best person for the job" from the available applicant pool. But how does an employer determine who is the "best" from a number of candidates? Whether the position available is skilled or unskilled, that task is not easy, nor would different employers necessarily reach the same conclusion about a single applicant.

Traditionally, employers have had the right to hire whomever they pleased, and selection methods still reflect considerable diversity. Employers with large numbers of relatively unskilled jobs to fill can hire applicants on a "first come, first served" basis once a minimal threshold of competence is established. Frequently, however, the employer needs to be more critical in its selection procedures. When the employer has too many applicants to consider each one individually, the typical response is to narrow the original applicant pool by imposing initial qualifications which the employer believes will improve the overall quality of the workforce and which an applicant must meet before his or her application will be considered. Examples of this are requirements that applicants have a high school diploma or achieve a certain score on a standardized test.

Once the applicant pool is narrowed in size, the employer will consider individual qualifications, education, experience, references, test and interview results, and other characteristics—the information garnered through procedures discussed in Chapter 3—in an effort to determine the best qualified candidate. Some skills are objectively quantifiable, such as the ability to type or to operate a drill press. Intangible traits or characteristics—reliability, interpersonal skills, analytical ability, leadership, or creativity—may be equally important to successful job performance, however. As a result, an employer usually seeks a mix of qualities rather than a single measurable trait or skill. Because many desirable traits are not quantifiable, much of the employer's final decision-making is ultimately subjective. Different applicants have different mixes of characteristics, and it is often difficult to single out one who stands head and shoulders above the others. Faced with several candidates who have relatively equal qualifications, the employer will nonetheless find some criterion on which to base the final selection: more education, higher test scores, more years of experience, family connections, an amorphous "gut feeling" arising from the interview process. Nepotism and the "old boy" network of personal and professional contacts are classic ways for small employers especially to fill infrequent job openings, or for larger employers to fill top-level managerial and executive positions.

Historically, these selection methods, left unregulated, resulted in identifiable groups, such as women, blacks, and other minorities, being underrepresented in the more desirable sectors of the workforce relative to their availability and ability to work. Title VII of the Civil Rights Act of 1964, 42 U.S.C. § 2000e et seq., was enacted to eliminate discrimination in employment on the basis of "race, color, religion, sex, or national origin." Later, the non-discrimination principle was extended to other classifications. See, e.g., the Age Discrimination in Employment Act of 1967 and the Americans with Disabilities Act of 1990, both discussed in this chapter. State laws provide parallel or extended coverage. This chapter shows the continuing struggle to alter employment practices through legal regulation and the continuing controversy over the dividing line between appropriate bases for employer decision making and illegal use of prejudicial criteria.

The concept of nondiscrimination is not easy to define and apply. Employers seek the authority to choose the best individual for a job, and legislators and judges are reluctant to infringe on the employer's managerial prerogatives. Reasonable persons differ over interpretation of both the employer's obligations under the law and the consequences of the employer's actions; these differences of opinion have required the courts to develop a jurisprudence that balances the employer's right to manage its business free from unnecessary governmental intrusion and the statutory rights of different individuals competing for the same position. Essentially, the law plays a negative role in employee selection. Although it proscribes certain practices, the law does not prohibit irrationality per se (such as hiring only individuals whose Social Security numbers end with an even digit); it only prohibits employer action—rational or irrational in terms of economic efficiency—that is improperly motivated or has unacceptable consequences.

As you read the materials in this chapter, consider the following questions: Should the law prohibit discrimination only when it involves certain impermissible criteria? Why have we chosen the current list of proscribed criteria? Is the law interfering unduly with employer prerogatives? What are the societal consequences of legal intervention or nonintervention? And how extensively throughout the employer-employee relationship does the law monitor and intervene?

Although this chapter includes the major treatment of discrimination, the topic is covered elsewhere in the book, including Chapter 3 (medical and psychological evaluations), Chapter 6 (discrimination in health benefits), Chapter 10 (discharge), and Chapter 13 (mandatory retirement).

A. DISCRIMINATION ON THE BASIS OF RACE OR SEX

1. SOURCES OF PROTECTION

a. TITLE VII OF THE CIVIL RIGHTS ACT OF 1964

Title VII is one of the eleven titles of the landmark Civil Rights Act of 1964, 42 U.S.C. § 2000. It outlaws discrimination in employment based on race, color, religion, sex, or national origin. Signed by President Lyndon Johnson in 1964, the Civil Rights Act of 1964 barred discrimination in voting rights (Title I), public accommodations (Title II), education (Title III), use of federal funds (Title VI), and employment (Title VII).

The Supreme Court held that the Commerce Clause and the Fourteenth Amendment authorized Congress to enact the statute. Heart of Atlanta Motel, Inc. v. United States, 379 U.S. 241 (1964); Katzenbach v. McClung, 379 U.S. 294 (1964).

Title VII, dealing with employment, prohibits discrimination based on race, color, religion, sex, and national origin. The legislative history of Title VII shows that the primary focus of the law was racial discrimination. It also shows that Congress was concerned with eliminating not only specific instances of employment discrimination but its broader economic and social effects as well.

Title VII's proscription against discrimination applies broadly to all aspects of employment. The most important section of Title VII is § 703:

> Sec. 703(a) It shall be an unlawful employment practice for an employer—(1) to fail or refuse to hire or to discharge any individual, or otherwise to discriminate against any individual with respect to his compensation, terms, conditions, or privileges of employment, because of such individual's race, color, religion, sex, or national origin; or

> (2) to limit, segregate, or classify his employees or applicants for employment in any way which would deprive or tend to deprive any individual of employment opportunities or otherwise adversely affect his status as an employee, because of such individual's race, color, religion, sex, or national origin.

Section 703(b) prohibits discrimination by employment agencies on similar grounds (see Chapter 3, supra), and § 703(c) prohibits such discrimination by labor unions.

When Title VII was first proposed, it did not include protection against discrimination based on gender. Representative Howard W. Smith (D.Va.), an opponent of Title VII, thought that including a ban on sex discrimination would encourage other representatives to oppose the legislation. (At the same time, Rep. Smith was a staunch advocate of women's rights.) Scholars have noted the efforts of groups such as the

National Woman's Party in laying the groundwork for laws prohibiting employment discrimination on the basis of gender. See, e.g., Jo Freeman, How "Sex" Got into Title VII: Persistent Opportunism as a Maker of Public Policy, 9 L. & Inequality 163 (1991).

Section 703 also contains important exceptions to the nondiscrimination obligation. Discrimination is permitted where:

(1) religion, sex, or national origin (but not race) is a bona fide occupational qualification (BFOQ) reasonably necessary to the normal operation of the business;

(2) the employer acts pursuant to a bona fide seniority or merit system, or measures earnings by quantity or quality of production;

(3) the employer acts on the results of a professionally developed ability test that "is not designed, intended, or used to discriminate because of race, color, religion, sex, or national origin";

(4) differences in pay based among sexes are authorized by the Equal Pay Act of 1963 (discussed in Chapter 5).

The Act applies to private employers with 15 or more employees. It also applies to federal, state, and local government employers. All employees of a covered employer are protected, regardless of their status (i.e., management personnel, professionals). Exclusions from the Act's coverage include:

(1) educational institutions owned or supported by a religious organization and employing members of that religion;

(2) businesses operating on or near an Indian reservation and giving preferential treatment to Indians; and

(3) members of the Communist Party.

The Act also established the Equal Employment Opportunity Commission (EEOC) and charged it with investigating charges of discrimination and enforcing federal antidiscrimination laws. As part of its mandate, the EEOC was required to engage in conciliation efforts with an employer in instances in which the EEOC determined that there was reasonable cause to believe that the charge was true. The adequacy of such pre-suit conciliation efforts has become its own source of litigation in EEOC initiated lawsuits. In Mach Mining, LLC v. EEOC, 135 S.Ct. 1645 (2015), the Supreme Court vacated a Seventh Circuit decision that shielded pre-suit conciliation efforts from judicial review. In *Mach*, the Supreme Court held that a court could review whether the EEOC had satisfied its conciliation obligation as a prerequisite to a Title VII action, but the scope of judicial review was narrow and the remedy for failing to conciliate was not dismissal, but a stay of the action and an order to the EEOC to conciliate. The Court then set forth the EEOC's pre-suit conciliation obligations in a two-part test. First, the EEOC "must inform the employer about the specific allegation." Second, the EEOC must try to engage the employer in an informal method of "conference, conciliation, and persuasion." Id. at 1652, 1656. On remand, the district court held that the EEOC had satisfied its conciliation obligations. EEOC v. Mach Mining, LLC, 161 F.Supp.3d 632 (S.D. Ill. 2016).

b.   AMENDMENTS TO TITLE VII

Title VII has been amended four times. The Equal Employment Opportunity Act of 1972 expanded the Act's coverage and increased the EEOC's enforcement power. The Pregnancy Discrimination Act of 1978 added § 701(k), which expanded the definition of sex discrimination to include discrimination on the basis of "pregnancy, childbirth, and related medical conditions." (The issue of pregnancy-based discrimination in benefits is discussed in Chapter 6.) The Civil Rights Act of 1991 overruled Supreme Court cases related to burden of proof and other issues, granted the right to a jury trial, and added compensatory and punitive damages to the available relief. The Lilly Ledbetter Fair Pay Act of 2009 expanded the ability of plaintiffs to recover for pay discrimination.

c.   STATE FAIR EMPLOYMENT PRACTICE LAWS

Section 708 of Title VII specifically permits parallel state regulation of employment discrimination so long as the state law does not conflict with Title VII. Every state has a law that prohibits discrimination in employment. Although most of the laws are patterned after Title VII, there are two important distinctions. First, most state fair employment practice (FEP) laws have narrower exemptions for small employers than Title VII does, so that state law may be the only source of protection against discrimination for some applicants and employees. Second, some state legislatures have gone beyond the federal proscriptions against discrimination on the basis of race, color, religion, sex, and national origin (Title VII), age (ADEA), and disability (ADA) to ban discrimination based on other criteria. Marital status and sexual orientation discrimination are prohibited by some state laws. There are also other state prohibitions. See, e.g., Minnesota's prohibition of discrimination against recipients of public assistance, Minn.Stat.Ann. § 363A.09.

d.   THE FOURTEENTH AMENDMENT AND RECONSTRUCTION ERA CIVIL RIGHTS STATUTES

During Reconstruction, Congress enacted the Civil Rights Act of 1866 over the veto of President Andrew Johnson. The Act was a response to "black codes," which had been enacted in several southern states to impose severe legal restrictions on blacks. At the time of passage, some doubted the constitutionality of this law. In 1868, however, the Fourteenth Amendment was ratified at least in part to validate the 1866 statute.

AMENDMENT XIV (1868)

§ 1. All persons born or naturalized in the United States, and subject to jurisdiction thereof, are citizens of the United States and of the State wherein they reside. No State shall make or enforce any law which shall abridge the privileges or immunities of citizens of the United States; nor shall any State deprive any person of life, liberty, or property, without due process of law; nor deny to any person within its jurisdiction the equal protection of the laws.

* * *

§ 5. The Congress shall have power to enforce, by appropriate legislation, the provisions of this article.

In 1870, the Civil Rights Act of 1866 was reenacted in the Enforcement Act of 1870, in order to remove any doubt about the 1866 law's constitutionality.

The main provision of the Civil Rights Act of 1866, reenacted in 1870, is currently codified at 42 U.S.C. § 1981.

§ 1981. Equal rights under the law

(a) All persons within the jurisdiction of the United States shall have the same right in every State and Territory to make and enforce contracts, to sue, be parties, give evidence, and to the full and equal benefit of all laws and proceedings for the security of persons and property as is enjoyed by white citizens, and shall be subject to like punishment, pains, penalties, taxes, licenses, and exactions of every kind, and to no other.

(b) For purposes of this section, the term "make and enforce contracts" includes the making, performance, modification, and termination of contracts, and the enjoyment of all benefits, privileges, terms, and conditions of the contractual relationship.

(c) The rights protected by this section are protected against impairment by nongovernmental discrimination and impairment under color of State law.

In 1975, in Johnson v. Railway Express Agency, Inc., 421 U.S. 454 (1975), the Supreme Court held that section 1981 prohibits purely private discrimination in contracts, including employment. Until 1976, it was not clear whether the "as is enjoyed by white citizens" language of section 1981 authorized whites to sue for discrimination under section 1981. In McDonald v. Santa Fe Trail Trans. Co., 427 U.S. 273 (1976), the Supreme Court held that section 1981 was intended "to proscribe discrimination in the making or enforcement of contracts against, or in favor of, any race."

In Saint Francis College v. Al Khazraji, 481 U.S. 604 (1987), the Supreme Court permitted a section 1981 action by a U.S. citizen born in Iraq who alleged that as an Arab he had been discriminated against when denied tenure. Justice White wrote: "Plainly all those who might be deemed Caucasian today were not thought to be of the same race at the time § 1981 became law." He showed references in the 1866 congressional debate to the Chinese, Spanish, Anglo-Saxon, Jewish, Mexican, Mongolian, German, and Gypsy races. The law thus applied to "identifiable classes of persons who are subjected to intentional discrimination solely because of their ancestry or ethnic characteristics."

Procedurally, section 1981 actions may be brought in state or federal court. An employer is covered regardless of the number of employees. State statutes of limitations apply and there is no administrative exhaustion requirement. Compensatory and punitive damages are available.

The other relevant Reconstruction Era Civil Rights Act is the Civil Rights Act of 1871, also known as the Ku Klux Klan Act. The Act contains both civil and criminal sections. The two most important civil sections are now codified at 42 U.S.C. §§ 1983 and 1985.

§ 1983. Civil action for deprivation of rights

> Every person who, under color of any statute, ordinance, regulation, custom, or usage, of any State or Territory or the District of Columbia, subjects, or causes to be subjected, any citizen of the United States or other person within the jurisdiction thereof to the deprivation of any rights, privileges, or immunities secured by the Constitution and laws, shall be liable to the party injured in an action at law, suit in equity, or other proper proceeding for redress.

§ 1985. Conspiracy to interfere with civil rights preventing officer from performing duties

> Depriving persons of rights or privileges

> (3) If two or more persons in any State or Territory conspire or go in disguise on the highway or on the premises of another, for the purpose of depriving, either directly or indirectly, any person or class of persons of the equal protection of the laws, or of equal privileges and immunities under the laws; in any case of conspiracy set forth in this section, if one or more persons engaged therein do, or cause to be done, any act in furtherance of the object of such conspiracy, whereby another is injured in his person or property, or deprived of having and exercising any right or privilege of a citizen of the United States, the party so injured or deprived may have an action for the recovery of damages, occasioned by such injury or deprivation, against any one or more of the conspirators.

Under section 1983 the plaintiff may be any citizen whose civil rights have been violated. Protected civil rights include due process, equal protection, privileges and immunities of citizenship, and statutory rights. Employment discrimination based on race, color, religion, sex, national origin, and other classifications not rationally related to a legitimate state interest may be redressed under section 1983.

Under the Fourteenth Amendment and the "under color of" language in section 1983, "state action" is required to establish a violation of section 1983. Therefore, section 1983 may not be used in actions against federal officials or in cases of private discrimination. In Monell v. Department of Social Services, 436 U.S. 658 (1978), the Supreme Court held that municipalities may be sued under section 1983 for both damages and injunctive relief. In Alabama v. Pugh, 438 U.S. 781 (1978), however, the Court held that the Eleventh Amendment precludes section 1983 actions against states per se, although state officials may be sued in their individual and official capacities. Actions under section 1983 may be brought in state or federal court.

When Title VII was originally enacted in 1964, government employers were not covered by the statute and the Fourteenth Amendment and the civil rights acts were the only means by which government employees could redress discrimination in employment. The 1972 amendments to Title VII brought government employers under its coverage. Although sections 1981, 1983, and 1985 offer possible alternatives to Title VII, Title VII remains the workhorse of employment discrimination law because of its extensive coverage and the availability of the Equal Employment Opportunity Commission to assist individuals in pressing and resolving charges of discrimination. The civil rights acts are most useful for individuals not covered by Title VII and for those who have missed the relatively short statute of limitations for filing a Title VII charge.

Does the Equal Protection Clause provide a cause of action to a government employee who says that his or her dismissal was for arbitrary, vindictive, or malicious reasons? The plaintiff would not be asserting that the mistreatment was because of membership in a group such as race, gender, or age. These claims are therefore denominated "class-of-one"—that the employee was intentionally treated differently from others similarly situated and thus there was no rational basis for the action. Some circuits allowed these actions. The Supreme Court said no—that government, like private employers, can live in an employment-at-will world and discharge for reasons that may appear arbitrary. Chief Justice Roberts said that government as regulator must satisfy a constitutional standard of rationality but that government as employer has greater discretion unless, as with civil service, collective bargaining, or individual contracts, it chooses to grant greater security of employment. Engquist v. Oregon Dep't of Agriculture, 553 U.S. 591 (2008) (6–3).

e.   EXECUTIVE ORDER 11246

On September 24, 1965, President Johnson issued Executive Order 11246. The key provision of the Executive Order is section 202, which prohibits employment discrimination by government contractors.

> The Contractor will not discriminate against any employee or applicant for employment because of race, creed, color, or national origin. The Contractor will take affirmative action to ensure that applicants are employed, and that employees are treated during employment, without regard to their race, creed, color, or national origin. Such action shall include, but not be limited to, the following: employment, upgrading, demotion, or transfer; recruitment or recruitment advertising; layoff or termination; rates of pay or other forms of compensation; and selection for training, including apprenticeship.

On October 13, 1967, the President issued Executive Order 11375, adding sex to the categories for which nondiscrimination and affirmative action by government contractors are mandated. The Executive Orders, which cover about one-third of all workers, are important because they force many employers to go beyond Title VII nondiscrimination to implement affirmative action programs.

The contractor's nondiscrimination and affirmative action obligations also apply to subcontractors and vendors with which it trades. Failure to comply with the Orders may subject the contractor to cancellation, termination, or suspension of the contract and, in the most egregious cases, ineligibility for new government contracts.

The Executive Orders' dual requirements of nondiscrimination and affirmative action are enforced by the Office of Federal Contract Compliance Programs (OFCCP) within the Department of Labor and monitored through reporting requirements contained in the Executive Order. The Secretary of Labor has issued detailed regulations implementing the Executive Order, 41 C.F.R. Chapter 60. All government contracts in excess of $10,000 are subject to the Order. Contractors with 50 or more employees and contracts for more than $50,000 are required to have a written affirmative action plan. If a contract is in excess of $10,000,000, the contract cannot be awarded until a pre-award compliance review of the affirmative action program has been completed and approved. Contractors in violation of the Order are subject to administrative enforcement proceedings by the OFCCP. These administrative remedies are exclusive and individuals may not sue the contractor directly. Individuals may file complaints with OFCCP and may sue the Secretary of Labor to compel performance of obligations under the Executive Order.

2. WHAT IS UNLAWFUL DISCRIMINATION?

a. DISPARATE TREATMENT

The Supreme Court interpreted Title VII to prohibit two major types of unlawful discrimination by employers: practices that constitute deliberate differential, or disparate, treatment; and practices such as high school diploma requirements that, while neutral on their face, nonetheless have the consequence of discriminating on the basis of a classification proscribed by Title VII. Cases in this second category are labeled adverse impact or disparate impact. Adverse impact cases declare that the discriminatory consequence of an employer's facially neutral practice is unlawful discrimination. Disparate treatment, on the other hand, focuses on intent rather than effects, such as when an employer refuses to hire women or people with a particular disability or of a particular age.

McDonnell Douglas Corp. v. Green
411 U.S. 792 (1973).

■ MR. JUSTICE POWELL delivered the opinion of the Court.

Petitioner, McDonnell Douglas Corp., is an aerospace and aircraft manufacturer headquartered in St. Louis, Missouri, where it employs over 30,000 people. Respondent, a black citizen of St. Louis, worked for petitioner as a mechanic and laboratory technician from 1956 until August 28, 1964 when he was laid off in the course of a general reduction in petitioner's work force.

Respondent, a long-time activist in the civil rights movement, protested vigorously that his discharge and the general hiring practices of petitioner were racially motivated. As part of this protest, respondent and other members of the Congress on Racial Equality illegally stalled their cars on the main roads leading to petitioner's plant for the purpose of blocking access to it at the time of the morning shift change. The District Judge described the plan for, and respondent's participation in, the "stall-in" as follows:

> [F]ive teams, each consisting of four cars would "tie up" five main access roads into McDonnell at the time of the morning rush hour. The drivers of the cars were instructed to line up next to each other completely blocking the intersections or roads. The drivers were also instructed to stop their cars, turn off the engines, pull the emergency brake, raise all windows, lock the doors, and remain in their cars until the police arrived. The plan was to have the cars remain in position for one hour.

> Acting under the "stall in" plan, plaintiff (respondent in the present action) drove his car onto Brown Road, a McDonnell access road, at approximately 7:00 a.m., at the start of the

morning rush hour. Plaintiff was aware of the traffic problems that would result. He stopped his car with the intent to block traffic. The police arrived shortly and requested plaintiff to move his car. He refused to move his car voluntarily. Plaintiff's car was towed away by the police, and he was arrested for obstructing traffic. Plaintiff pleaded guilty to the charge of obstructing traffic and was fined. . . .

[O]n July 25, 1965, petitioner publicly advertised for qualified mechanics, respondent's trade, and respondent promptly applied for re-employment. Petitioner turned down respondent, basing its rejection on respondent's participation in the "stall-in" . . . Shortly thereafter, respondent filed a formal complaint with the Equal Employment Opportunity Commission, claiming that petitioner had refused to rehire him because of his race and persistent involvement in the civil rights movement, in violation of §§ 703(a)(1) and 704(a) of the Civil Rights Act of 1964, 42 U.S.C. §§ 2000e–2(a)(1) and 2000e–3(a). The former section generally prohibits racial discrimination in any employment decision while the latter forbids discrimination against applicants or employees for attempting to protest or correct allegedly discriminatory conditions of employment.

* * *

The District Court also found that petitioner's refusal to rehire respondent was based solely on his participation in the illegal demonstrations and not on his legitimate civil rights activities. The court concluded that nothing in Title VII or s 704 protected "such activity as employed by the plaintiff in the 'stall in' and 'lock in' demonstrations."

On appeal, the Eighth Circuit affirmed that unlawful protests were not protected activities under s 704(a)[6], but reversed the dismissal of respondent's § 703(a)(1) claim relating to racially discriminatory hiring practices.

* * *

The critical issue before us concerns the order and allocation of proof in a private, non-class action challenging employment discrimination. The language of Title VII makes plain the purpose of Congress to assure equality of employment opportunities and to eliminate those discriminatory practices and devices which have fostered racially stratified job environments to the disadvantage of minority citizens.

The broad, overriding interest, shared by employer, employee, and consumer, is efficient and trustworthy workmanship assured through fair and racially neutral employment and personnel decisions. In the implementation of such decisions, it is abundantly clear that Title VII tolerates no racial discrimination, subtle or otherwise.

---

[6]   Respondent has not sought review of this issue.

In this case respondent, the complainant below, charges that he was denied employment "because of his involvement in civil rights activities" and "because of his race and color." Petitioner denied discrimination of any kind, asserting that its failure to re-employ respondent was based upon and justified by his participation in the unlawful conduct against it. Thus, the issue at the trial on remand is framed by those opposing factual contentions.

* * *

The complainant in a Title VII trial must carry the initial burden under the statute of establishing a prima facie case of racial discrimination. This may be done by showing (i) that he belongs to a racial minority; (ii) that he applied and was qualified for a job for which the employer was seeking applicants; (iii) that, despite his qualifications, he was rejected; and (iv) that, after his rejection, the position remained open and the employer continued to seek applicants from persons of complainant's qualifications. In the instant case, we agree with the Court of Appeals that respondent proved a prima facie case. Petitioner sought mechanics, respondent's trade, and continued to do so after respondent's rejection. Petitioner, moreover, does not dispute respondent's qualifications and acknowledges that his past work performance in petitioner's employ was "satisfactory."

The burden then must shift to the employer to articulate some legitimate, nondiscriminatory reason for the employee's rejection. We need not attempt in the instant case to detail every matter which fairly could be recognized as a reasonable basis for a refusal to hire. Here petitioner has assigned respondent's participation in unlawful conduct against it as the cause for his rejection. We think that this suffices to discharge petitioner's burden of proof at this stage and to meet respondent's prima facie case of discrimination.

The Court of Appeals intimated, however, that petitioner's stated reason for refusing to rehire respondent was a "subjective" rather than objective criterion which "carr[ies] little weight in rebutting charges of discrimination." This was among the statements which caused the dissenting judge to read the opinion as taking "the position that such unlawful acts as Green committed against McDonnell would not legally entitle McDonnell to refuse to hire him, even though no racial motivation was involved. . . ." Regardless of whether this was the intended import of the opinion, we think the court below seriously underestimated the rebuttal weight to which petitioner's reasons were entitled. Respondent admittedly had taken part in a carefully planned "stall-in," designed to tie up access to and egress from petitioner's plant at a peak traffic hour. Nothing in Title VII compels an employer to absolve and rehire one who has engaged in such deliberate, unlawful activity against it.

* * *

Petitioner's reason for rejection thus suffices to meet the prima facie case, but the inquiry must not end here. While Title VII does not, without more, compel rehiring of respondent, neither does it permit petitioner to use respondent's conduct as a pretext for the sort of discrimination prohibited by § 703(a)(1). On remand, respondent must, as the Court of Appeals recognized, be afforded a fair opportunity to show that petitioner's stated reason for respondent's rejection was in fact pretext. Especially relevant to such a showing would be evidence that white employees involved in acts against petitioner of comparable seriousness to the "stall-in" were nevertheless retained or rehired. Petitioner may justifiably refuse to rehire one who was engaged in unlawful, disruptive acts against it, but only if this criterion is applied alike to members of all races.

Other evidence that may be relevant to any showing of pretext includes facts as to the petitioner's treatment of respondent during his prior term of employment; petitioner's reaction, if any, to respondent's legitimate civil rights activities; and petitioner's general policy and practice with respect to minority employment. In short, on the retrial respondent must be given a full and fair opportunity to demonstrate by competent evidence that the presumptively valid reasons for his rejection were in fact a coverup for a racially discriminatory decision.

Respondent had engaged in a seriously disruptive act against the very one from whom he now seeks employment. And petitioner does not seek his exclusion on the basis of a testing device which overstates what is necessary for competent performance, or through some sweeping disqualification of all those with any past record of unlawful behavior, however remote, insubstantial, or unrelated to applicant's personal qualifications as an employee. Petitioner assertedly rejected respondent for unlawful conduct against it and, in the absence of proof of pretext or discriminatory application of such a reason, this cannot be thought the kind of "artificial, arbitrary, and unnecessary barriers to employment" which the Court found to be the intention of Congress to remove.

In sum, respondent should have been allowed to pursue his claim under § 703(a) (1). If the evidence on retrial is substantially in accord with that before us in this case, we think that respondent carried his burden of establishing a prima facie case of racial discrimination and that petitioner successfully rebutted that case. But this does not end the matter. On retrial, respondent must be afforded a fair opportunity to demonstrate that petitioner's assigned reason for refusing to re-employ was a pretext or discriminatory in its application.

NOTES AND QUESTIONS

1.   In *McDonnell Douglas*, the Supreme Court established a burden shifting framework for disparate treatment discrimination claims. The structure allowed the plaintiff to raise an initial presumption of discrimination by establishing a fairly basic prima facie case. After that, a

burden of production, not proof, switched to the employer to state a legitimate, nondiscriminatory reason for its employment decision. Once the employer did so, the burden then shifted back to the plaintiff to satisfy her ultimate burden of proving that discrimination was the but for cause of the employment discrimination.

In Texas Dept. of Community Affairs v. Burdine, the Supreme Court indicated that the plaintiff could satisfy her ultimate burden of proof either by showing that the employer's stated reason for its hiring decision was false or by showing that the true motive was discrimination. As the Court explained: "The plaintiff retains the burden of persuasion. She now must have the opportunity to demonstrate that the proffered reason was not the true reason for the employment decision. This burden now merges with the ultimate burden of persuading the court that she has been the victim of intentional discrimination. She may succeed in this either directly by persuading the court that a discriminatory reason more likely motivated the employer or indirectly by showing that the employer's proffered explanation is unworthy of credence." 450 U.S. 248, 256 (1981).

In St. Mary's Honor Center v. Hicks, 509 U.S. 502 (1993), however, the Supreme Court clarified its burden shifting framework from *McDonnell Douglas* and held that a plaintiff did not necessarily satisfy her ultimate burden of proof simply by showing that the employer's stated reason for its employment action was false. The Court explained that once the employer satisfied its burden of production, it eliminated any presumption of discrimination established by the prima facie case. The plaintiff then retained the ultimate burden of showing that discrimination was the but for cause of the employer's decision. While proving that the employer's stated reasons for its decision were false could constitute evidence of discriminatory intent, such proof did not guarantee the plaintiff victory. The plaintiff needed to convince the court that the decision was made because of a prohibited classification. What purpose does the *McDonnell Douglas* framework serve after *Hicks*? Do the first two stages of the framework narrow the scope of the court's analysis in any way?

2.   What does it mean for an employee to be "similarly situated" to other employees for the purposes of the *McDonnell Douglas* standard? The Eighth Circuit used a "low threshold" to define this term in Wimbley v. Cashion, 588 F.3d 959 (8th Cir. 2009). Wimbley, a female prison guard, was disciplined for discharging pepper spray under questionable circumstances. Evidence showed that a male guard who used pepper spray in a comparable situation was disciplined less severely. The court held that differential punishment for similar conduct was sufficient to establish "similar situation" for the purposes of the *McDonnell Douglas* standard. In Coleman v. Donohue, 667 F.3d 835 (7th Cir. 2012), the Seventh Circuit made clear that evidence of a similarly situated comparator may serve not only as an element of the plaintiff's prima facie case under *McDonnell Douglas* but also as evidence that the employer's legitimate nondiscriminatory reason was pretextual.

3.   Discharge of a white employee because his child was biracial would violate Title VII. Tetro v. Elliott Popham Pontiac, Oldsmobile, Buick, & GMC Trucks, Inc., 173 F.3d 988 (6th Cir. 1999).

4. Tyson Foods' plant manager had referred to each of the petitioners as "boy." The court of appeals said that "[w]hile the use of 'boy' when modified by a racial classification like 'black' or 'white' is evidence of discriminatory intent, the use of 'boy' alone is not evidence of discrimination." The Supreme Court disagreed: "Although it is true the disputed word will not always be evidence of racial animus, it does not follow that the term, standing alone, is always benign. The speaker's meaning may depend on various factors including context, inflection, tone of voice, local custom, and historical usage." Ash v. Tyson Foods, Inc., 546 U.S. 454 (2006) (per curiam). On remand, the Eleventh Circuit resolved the implications of the term "boy" in favor of Tyson Foods. The court found that "even if [the term were] somehow construed as racial, we conclude that the comments were ambiguous stray remarks not uttered in the context of the [employment] decisions at issue." Ash v. Tyson Foods, Inc., 190 F.App'x 924, 926 (11th Cir. 2006). In a later proceeding, the court reversed the district court's judgment against Tyson Foods, holding the evidence was insufficient to support the jury's verdict that Tyson had committed intentional discrimination based on race. Ash v. Tyson Foods, Inc., 392 Fed.Appx. 817 (11th Cir. 2010).

5. A plaintiff can establish a prima facie case of gender discrimination simply by showing she was replaced by a man, regardless of their comparative qualifications; she need not show that they were similarly situated. See Vincent v. Brewer, 514 F.3d 489 (6th Cir. 2007).

6. A white assistant basketball coach at Iona College was terminated after coaching the team to a losing record three years in a row. The coach sued the college under Title VII claiming that he was fired because of his marriage to an African American woman. The relevant clause in Title VII states that it is an "unlawful employment practice for an employer * * * to discharge any individual * * * because of such individual's race." 42 U.S.C. § 2000e–2(a)(1). Does this language prohibit an employer from discriminating against an employee on the basis of an interracial marriage? See Holcomb v. Iona College, 521 F.3d 130 (2d Cir. 2008) (held: yes).

Price Waterhouse v. Hopkins
490 U.S. 228 (1989).

■ JUSTICE BRENNAN announced the judgment of the Court and delivered an opinion, in which JUSTICE MARSHALL, JUSTICE BLACKMUN and JUSTICE STEVENS join.

Ann Hopkins was a senior manager in an office of Price Waterhouse when she was proposed for partnership in 1982. She was neither offered nor denied admission to the partnership; instead, her candidacy was held for reconsideration the following year. When the partners in her office later refused to repropose her for partnership, she sued Price Waterhouse under Title VII of the Civil Rights Act of 1964, charging that the firm had discriminated against her on the basis of sex in its decisions regarding partnership. * * *

Ann Hopkins in front of the Supreme Court.
Source: Bruce Young/New York Times

At Price Waterhouse, a nationwide professional accounting partnership, a senior manager becomes a candidate for partnership when the partners in her local office submit her name as a candidate. All of the other partners in the firm are then invited to submit written comments on each candidate—either on a "long" or a "short" form, depending on the partner's degree of exposure to the candidate. Not every partner in the firm submits comments on every candidate. After reviewing the comments and interviewing the partners who submitted them, the firm's Admissions Committee makes a recommendation to the Policy Board. This recommendation will be either that the firm accept the candidate for partnership, put her application on "hold," or deny her the promotion outright. The Policy Board then decides whether to submit the candidate's name to the entire partnership for a vote, to "hold" her candidacy, or to reject her. The recommendation of the Admissions Committee, and the decision of the Policy Board, are not controlled by fixed guidelines: a certain number of positive comments from partners will not guarantee a candidate's admission to the partnership, nor will a specific quantity of negative comments necessarily defeat her application. Price Waterhouse places no limit on the number of persons whom it will admit to the partnership in any given year.

Ann Hopkins had worked at Price Waterhouse's Office of Government Services in Washington, D.C., for five years when the partners in that office proposed her as a candidate for partnership. Of the 662 partners at the firm at that time, 7 were women. Of the 88 persons proposed for partnership that year, only 1—Hopkins—was a woman. Forty-seven of these candidates were admitted to the partnership, 21 were rejected, and 20—including Hopkins—were "held" for reconsideration the following year.[1] Thirteen of the 32 partners who had submitted comments on Hopkins supported her bid for partnership. Three partners recommended that her candidacy be placed on hold, eight stated that they did not have an informed opinion about her, and eight recommended that she be denied partnership.

In a jointly prepared statement supporting her candidacy, the partners in Hopkins' office showcased her successful 2-year effort to secure a $25 million contract with the Department of State, labeling it "an outstanding performance" and one that Hopkins carried out "virtually at the partner level." Despite Price Waterhouse's attempt at trial to minimize her contribution to this project, Judge Gesell specifically found that Hopkins had "played a key role in Price Waterhouse's successful effort to win a multi-million dollar contract with the Department of State." Indeed, he went on, "[n]one of the other partnership candidates at Price Waterhouse that year had a comparable record in terms of successfully securing major contracts for the partnership."

The partners in Hopkins' office praised her character as well as her accomplishments, describing her in their joint statement as "an outstanding professional" who had a "deft touch," a "strong character, independence and integrity." Clients appear to have agreed with these assessments. At trial, one official from the State Department described her as "extremely competent, intelligent," "strong and forthright, very productive, energetic and creative." Another high-ranking official praised Hopkins' decisiveness, broadmindedness, and "intellectual clarity"; she was, in his words, "a stimulating conversationalist." Evaluations such as these led Judge Gesell to conclude that Hopkins "had no difficulty dealing with clients and her clients appear to have been very pleased with her work" and that she "was generally viewed as a highly competent project leader who worked long hours, pushed vigorously to meet deadlines and demanded much from the multidisciplinary staffs with which she worked."

On too many occasions, however, Hopkins' aggressiveness apparently spilled over into abrasiveness. Staff members seem to have borne the brunt of Hopkins' brusqueness. Long before her bid for partnership, partners evaluating her work had counseled her to improve her relations with staff members. Although later evaluations indicate an

---

[1] Before the time for reconsideration came, two of the partners in Hopkins' office withdrew their support for her, and the office informed her that she would not be reconsidered for partnership. Hopkins then resigned. Price Waterhouse does not challenge the Court of Appeals' conclusion that the refusal to repropose her for partnership amounted to a constructive discharge. That court remanded the case to the District Court for further proceedings to determine appropriate relief, and those proceedings have been stayed pending our decision. We are concerned today only with Price Waterhouse's decision to place Hopkins' candidacy on hold. Decisions pertaining to advancement to partnership are, of course, subject to challenge under Title VII. Hishon v. King & Spalding, 467 U.S. 69 (1984).

improvement, Hopkins' perceived shortcomings in this important area eventually doomed her bid for partnership. Virtually all of the partners' negative remarks about Hopkins—even those of partners supporting her—had to do with her "interpersonal skills." Both "[s]upporters and opponents of her candidacy," stressed Judge Gesell, "indicated that she was sometimes overly aggressive, unduly harsh, difficult to work with and impatient with staff."

There were clear signs, though, that some of the partners reacted negatively to Hopkins' personality because she was a woman. One partner described her as "macho"; another suggested that she "overcompensated for being a woman"; a third advised her to take "a course at charm school." Several partners criticized her use of profanity; in response, one partner suggested that those partners objected to her swearing only "because it[']s a lady using foul language." Another supporter explained that Hopkins "ha[d] matured from a tough-talking somewhat masculine hard-nosed mgr to an authoritative, formidable, but much more appealing lady ptr candidate." But it was the man who, as Judge Gesell found, bore responsibility for explaining to Hopkins the reasons for the Policy Board's decision to place her candidacy on hold who delivered the *coup de grace:* in order to improve her chances for partnership, Thomas Beyer advised, Hopkins should "walk more femininely, talk more femininely, dress more femininely, wear make-up, have her hair styled, and wear jewelry."

Dr. Susan Fiske, a social psychologist and Associate Professor of Psychology at Carnegie-Mellon University, testified at trial that the partnership selection process at Price Waterhouse was likely influenced by sex stereotyping. * * *

In previous years, other female candidates for partnership also had been evaluated in sex-based terms. * * *

Judge Gesell found that Price Waterhouse legitimately emphasized interpersonal skills in its partnership decisions, and also found that the firm had not fabricated its complaints about Hopkins' interpersonal skills as a pretext for discrimination. Moreover, he concluded, the firm did not give decisive emphasis to such traits only because Hopkins was a woman; although there were male candidates who lacked these skills but who were admitted to partnership, the judge found that these candidates possessed other, positive traits that Hopkins lacked.

The judge went on to decide, however, that some of the partners' remarks about Hopkins stemmed from an impermissibly cabined view of the proper behavior of women, and that Price Waterhouse had done nothing to disavow reliance on such comments. He held that Price Waterhouse had unlawfully discriminated against Hopkins on the basis of sex by consciously giving credence and effect to partners' comments that resulted from sex stereotyping. Noting that Price Waterhouse could avoid equitable relief by proving by clear and convincing evidence that it would have placed Hopkins' candidacy on hold even absent this discrimination, the judge decided that the firm had not carried this heavy burden. * * *

In passing Title VII, Congress made the simple but momentous announcement that sex, race, religion, and national origin are not relevant to the selection, evaluation, or compensation of employees. Yet, the statute does not purport to limit the other qualities and characteristics that employers *may* take into account in making employment decisions. The converse, therefore, of "for cause" legislation, Title VII eliminates certain bases for distinguishing among employees while otherwise preserving employers' freedom of choice. This balance between employee rights and employer prerogatives turns out to be decisive in the case before us.

Congress' intent to forbid employers to take gender into account in making employment decisions appears on the face of the statute. In now-familiar language, the statute forbids an employer to "fail or refuse to hire or to discharge any individual, or otherwise to discriminate with respect to his compensation, terms, conditions, or privileges of employment," or to "limit, segregate, or classify his employees or applicants for employment in any way which would deprive or tend to deprive any individual of employment opportunities or otherwise adversely affect his status as an employee, *because of* such individual's * * * sex." We take these words to mean that gender must be irrelevant to employment decisions. To construe the words "because of" as colloquial shorthand for "but-for causation," as does Price Waterhouse, is to misunderstand them.

But-for causation is a hypothetical construct. In determining whether a particular factor was a but-for cause of a given event, we begin by assuming that that factor was present at the time of the event, and then ask whether, even if that factor had been absent, the event nevertheless would have transpired in the same way. The present, active tense of the operative verbs of § 703(a)(1) ("to fail or refuse"), in contrast, turns our attention to the actual moment of the event in question, the adverse employment decision. The critical inquiry, the one commanded by the words of § 703(a)(1), is whether gender was a factor in the employment decision *at the moment it was made.* Moreover, since we know that the words "because of" do not mean "*solely* because of," we also know that Title VII meant to condemn even those decisions based on a mixture of legitimate and illegitimate considerations. When, therefore, an employer considers both gender and legitimate factors at the time of making a decision, that decision was "because of" sex and the other, legitimate considerations—even if we may say later, in the context of litigation, that the decision would have been the same if gender had not been taken into the account.

To attribute this meaning to the words "because of" does not, as the dissent asserts, divest them of causal significance. A simple example illustrates the point. Suppose two physical forces act upon and move an object, and suppose that either force acting alone would have moved the object. As the dissent would have it, *neither* physical force was a "cause" of the motion unless we can show that but for one or both of them, the object would not have moved; to use the dissent's terminology, both forces were simply "in the air" unless we can identify at least one of them as a but-for cause of the object's movement. Events that are causally overdetermined, in other words, may not have any "cause" at all. This cannot be so.

We need not leave our common-sense at the doorstep when we interpret a statute. It is difficult for us to imagine that, in the simple words "because of," Congress meant to obligate a plaintiff to identify the precise causal role played by legitimate and illegitimate motivations in the employment decision she challenges. We conclude, instead, that Congress meant to obligate her to prove that the employer relied upon sex-based considerations in coming to its decision.

* * *

To say that an employer may not take gender into account is not, however, the end of the matter, for that describes only one aspect of Title VII. The other important aspect of the statute is its preservation of an employer's remaining freedom of choice. We conclude that the preservation of this freedom means that an employer shall not be liable if it can prove that, even if it had not taken gender into account, it would have come to the same decision regarding a particular person. . . .

* * *

The central point is this: while an employer may not take gender into account in making an employment decision (except in those very narrow circumstances in which gender is a BFOQ), it is free to decide against a woman for other reasons. We think these principles require that, once a plaintiff in a Title VII case shows that gender played a motivating part in an employment decision, the defendant may avoid a finding of liability only by proving that it would have made the same decision even if it had not allowed gender to play such a role. This balance of burdens is the direct result of Title VII's balance of rights.

* * *

In saying that gender played a motivating part in an employment decision, we mean that, if we asked the employer at the moment of the decision what its reasons were and if we received a truthful response, one of those reasons would be that the applicant or employee was a woman. In the specific context of sex stereotyping, an employer who acts on the basis of a belief that a woman cannot be aggressive, or that she must not be, has acted on the basis of gender.

Although the parties do not overtly dispute this last proposition, the placement by Price Waterhouse of "sex stereotyping" in quotation marks throughout its brief seems to us an insinuation either that such stereotyping was not present in this case or that it lacks legal relevance. We reject both possibilities. As to the existence of sex stereotyping in this case, we are not inclined to quarrel with the District Court's conclusion that a number of the partners' comments showed sex stereotyping at work. As for the legal relevance of sex stereotyping, we are beyond the day when an employer could evaluate employees by assuming or insisting that they matched the stereotype associated with their group, for " '[i]n forbidding employers to discriminate against individuals because of their sex, Congress intended to strike at the entire spectrum of disparate treatment of men and women resulting from sex stereotypes.' " An employer who objects to aggressiveness in women but whose positions require this trait places women in an intolerable and impermissible Catch-22: out of a job if they behave aggressively and out of a job if they don't. Title VII lifts women out of this bind.

Remarks at work that are based on sex stereotypes do not inevitably prove that gender played a part in a particular employment decision. The plaintiff must show that the employer actually relied on her gender in making its decision. In making this showing, stereotyped remarks can certainly be *evidence* that gender played a part.

The courts below held that an employer who has allowed a discriminatory impulse to play a motivating part in an employment decision must prove by clear and convincing evidence that it would have made the same decision in the absence of discrimination. We are persuaded that the better rule is that the employer must make this showing by a preponderance of the evidence.

* * *

Price Waterhouse appears to think that we cannot affirm the factual findings of the trial court without deciding that, instead of being overbearing and aggressive and curt, Hopkins is in fact kind and considerate and patient. If this is indeed its impression, petitioner misunderstands the theory on which Hopkins prevailed. The District Judge acknowledged that Hopkins' conduct justified complaints about her behavior as a senior manager. But he also concluded that the reactions of at least some of the partners were reactions to her as a *woman* manager. Where an evaluation is based on a subjective assessment of a person's strengths and weaknesses, it is simply not true that each evaluator will focus on, or even mention, the same weaknesses. Thus, even if we knew that Hopkins had "personality problems," this would not tell us that the partners who cast their evaluations of Hopkins in sex-based terms would have criticized her as sharply (or criticized her at all) if she had been a man. It is not our job to review the evidence and decide that the negative reactions to Hopkins were based on reality; our perception of Hopkins' character is irrelevant. We sit not to determine whether Ms. Hopkins is nice, but to decide whether the partners reacted negatively to her personality because she is a woman.

We hold that when a plaintiff in a Title VII case proves that her gender played a motivating part in an employment decision, the defendant may avoid a finding of liability only by proving by a preponderance of the evidence that it would have made the same decision even if it had not taken the plaintiff's gender into account. Because the courts below erred by deciding that the defendant must make this proof by clear and convincing evidence, we reverse the Court of Appeals' judgment against Price Waterhouse on liability and remand the case to that court for further proceedings.

It is so ordered.

■ JUSTICE O'CONNOR, concurring in the judgment.

* * *

Where an individual disparate treatment plaintiff has shown by a preponderance of the evidence that an illegitimate criterion was a *substantial* factor in an adverse employment decision, the deterrent purpose of the statute has clearly been triggered. More importantly, as an evidentiary matter, a reasonable factfinder could conclude that absent further explanation, the employer's discriminatory motivation "caused" the employment decision. The employer has not yet been shown to be a violator, but neither is it entitled to the same presumption of good faith concerning its employment decisions which is accorded employers facing only circumstantial evidence of discrimination. Both the policies behind the statute, and the evidentiary principles developed in the analogous area of causation in the law of torts, suggest that at this point the employer may be required to convince the factfinder that, despite the smoke, there is no fire.

* * *

In this case, the District Court found that a number of the evaluations of Ann Hopkins submitted by partners in the firm overtly referred to her failure to conform to certain gender stereotypes as a factor militating against her election to the partnership. The District Court further found that these evaluations were given "great weight" by the decisionmakers at Price Waterhouse. In addition, the District Court found that the partner responsible for informing Hopkins of the factors which caused her candidacy to be placed on hold, indicated that her "professional" problems would be solved if she would "walk more femininely, talk more femininely, wear make-up, have her hair styled, and wear jewelry." As the Court of Appeals characterized it, Ann Hopkins proved that Price Waterhouse "permitt[ed] stereotypical attitudes towards women to play a significant, though unquantifiable, role in its decision not to invite her to become a partner."

At this point Ann Hopkins had taken her proof as far as it could go. She had proved discriminatory input into the decisional process, and had proved that participants in the process considered her failure to conform to the stereotypes credited by a number of the decisionmakers had been a substantial factor in the decision. It is as if Ann Hopkins were sitting in the hall outside the room where partnership decisions were being made. As the partners filed in to consider her candidacy, she heard several of them make sexist remarks in discussing her suitability for partnership. As the decisionmakers exited the room, she was *told* by one of those privy to the decisionmaking process that her gender was a major reason for the rejection of her partnership bid. * * * [O]ne would be hard pressed to think of a situation where it would be more appropriate to require the defendant to show that its decision would have been justified by wholly legitimate concerns.

* * *

In my view, in order to justify shifting the burden on the issue of causation to the defendant, a disparate treatment plaintiff must show by direct evidence that an illegitimate criterion was a substantial factor in the decision. . . .

Thus, stray remarks in the workplace, while perhaps probative of sexual harassment, cannot justify requiring the employer to prove that its hiring or promotion decisions were based on legitimate criteria. Nor can statements by nondecisionmakers, or statements by decisionmakers unrelated to the decisional process itself suffice to satisfy the plaintiff's burden in this regard. * * * Race and gender always "play a role" in an employment decision in the benign sense that these are human characteristics of which decisionmakers are aware and may comment on in a perfectly neutral and nondiscriminatory fashion. For example, in the context of this case, a mere reference to "a lady candidate" might show that gender "played a role" in the decision, but by no means could support a rational factfinder's inference that the decision was made "because of" sex. What is required is what Ann Hopkins showed here: direct evidence that decisionmakers placed substantial negative reliance on an illegitimate criterion in reaching their decision.

* * *

In this case, I agree with the plurality that petitioner should be called upon to show that the outcome would have been the same if respondent's professional merit had been its only concern. On remand, the District Court should determine whether Price Waterhouse has shown by a preponderance of the evidence that if gender had not been part of the process, its employment decision concerning Ann Hopkins would nonetheless have been the same.

■ JUSTICE KENNEDY, with whom THE CHIEF JUSTICE and JUSTICE SCALIA join, dissenting.

* * *

We established the order of proof for individual Title VII disparate treatment cases in McDonnell Douglas Corp. v. Green, and reaffirmed this allocation in Texas Dept. of Community Affairs v. Burdine. Under

Burdine, once the plaintiff presents a prima facie case, an inference of discrimination arises. The employer must rebut the inference by articulating a legitimate nondiscriminatory reason for its action. The final burden of persuasion, however, belongs to the plaintiff. *Burdine* makes clear that the "ultimate burden of persuading the trier of fact that the defendant intentionally discriminated against the plaintiff remains at all times with the plaintiff." I would adhere to this established evidentiary framework, which provides the appropriate standard for this and other individual disparate treatment cases. Today's creation of a new set of rules for "mixed-motive" cases is not mandated by the statute itself. The Court's attempt at refinement provides limited practical benefits at the cost of confusion and complexity, with the attendant risk that the trier of fact will misapprehend the controlling legal principles and reach an incorrect decision.

* * *

Although the District Court's version of Title VII liability is improper under any of today's opinions, I think it important to stress that Title VII creates no independent cause of action for sex stereotyping. Evidence of use by decisionmakers of sex stereotypes is, of course, quite relevant to the question of discriminatory intent. The ultimate question, however, is whether discrimination caused the plaintiff's harm. Our cases do not support the suggestion that failure to "disclaim reliance" on stereotypical comments itself violates Title VII. Neither do they support creation of a "duty to sensitize." As the dissenting judge in the Court of Appeals observed, acceptance of such theories would turn Title VII "from a prohibition of discriminatory conduct into an engine for rooting out sexist thoughts."

Employment discrimination claims require factfinders to make difficult and sensitive decisions. Sometimes this may mean that no finding of discrimination is justified even though a qualified employee is passed over by a less than admirable employer. In other cases, Title VII's protections properly extend to plaintiffs who are by no means model employees. As Justice Brennan notes, courts do not sit to determine whether litigants are nice. In this case, Hopkins plainly presented a strong case both of her own professional qualifications and of the presence of discrimination in Price Waterhouse's partnership process. Had the District Court found on this record that sex discrimination caused the adverse decision, I doubt it would have been reversible error. That decision was for the finder of fact, however, and the District Court made plain that sex discrimination was not a but-for cause of the decision to place Hopkins' partnership candidacy on hold. Attempts to evade tough decisions by erecting novel theories of liability or multi-tiered systems of shifting burdens are misguided.

The language of Title VII and our well-considered precedents require this plaintiff to establish that the decision to place her candidacy on hold was made "because of" sex. Here the District Court found that the "comments of the individual partners and the expert evidence of Dr. Fiske do not prove an intentional discriminatory motive or purpose," and that "[b]ecause plaintiff has considerable problems dealing with staff and peers, the Court cannot say that she would have been elected to partnership if the Policy Board's decision had not been tainted by sexually based evaluations." Hopkins thus failed to meet the requisite standard of proof after a full trial. I would remand the case for entry of judgment in favor of Price Waterhouse.

NOTES AND QUESTIONS

1. On remand, the district court found that Price Waterhouse had not established by a preponderance of the evidence that it would have refused a partnership to Hopkins notwithstanding the gender stereotyping that infected its consideration of her. As to remedy, the court ordered that she be offered a partnership effective July 1, 1990, with compensation and benefits as if she had been admitted to the partnership on July 1, 1983. Because she had not tried hard enough for equivalent work in the intervening years, she was awarded back pay (including interest) of only $371,175. Hopkins v. Price Waterhouse, 737 F.Supp. 1202 (D.D.C.1990), affirmed, 920 F.2d 967 (D.C.Cir. 1990). For the plaintiff's view of the case, see Ann Hopkins, Price Waterhouse v. Hopkins: A Personal Account of a Sexual Discrimination Plaintiff, 22 Hofstra Lab. & Emp. L.J. 357 (2005). Ann Hopkins died in 2018 at age 74.

2. In 1996, Price Waterhouse named Frances C. Engoron the firm's first female senior partner. Ms. Engoron assumed a unique title in a Big Six accounting firm: Senior Partner, Intellectual Capital. Her duties were to oversee recruiting, human resources, career development, and training. Lee Berton, First Female Senior Partner is Named By Price Waterhouse For Recruiting, Wall St.J., February 2, 1996, at B13.

3. Until Hishon v. King & Spalding, 467 U.S. 69 (1984), courts had regarded partnership decisions as exempt from Title VII review. *Hishon* unanimously rejected that argument. Cf. Kirleis v. Dickie, McCamey & Chilcote, P.C., 2010 WL 2780927 (3d Cir. 2010) (Class A shareholder/director of law firm was an employer, not an employee, for Title VII purposes and therefore precluded from bringing an action alleging sex discrimination).

4. Can a collective decision-making process about a position (partner in accounting firm) for which different decision-makers apply different criteria ever be cleansed of considerations of race and gender? If not, then the burden of persuasion—the issue that divided the Court in *Price Waterhouse*—will be of great significance. Can the answer to this issue be found in the statutory language? How do you evaluate the social costs of putting the burden on the plaintiff versus the costs of placing it on the employer?

5. Ms. Hopkins brought a disparate treatment action. She (and the many other women who did not become partners at Price Waterhouse) might have brought a disparate impact challenge. After reading the next section, consider the *Price Waterhouse* facts against the standard for establishing disparate impact liability.

6. What would you tell Price Waterhouse to do to ensure that its promotion procedures satisfy anti-discrimination law?

7. The Civil Rights Act of 1991 responded to *Price Waterhouse* by allowing an unlawful employment practice to be established "when the complaining party demonstrates that race, color, religion, sex, or national origin was a motivating factor for any employment practice, even though other factors also motivated the practice." 42 U.S.C. § 2000e–2(m). If, however, the employer demonstrates that it would have taken the same action absent the impermissible motivating factor, the court may grant the plaintiff declaratory relief, certain types of injunctive relief, and partial attorney's fees, but it may not award damages. 42 U.S.C. § 2000–B5(g)(2)(B). For a recent lucid account of the burdens and remedies under mixed motive law, see Harris v. City of Santa Monica, 56 Cal. 4th 203 (2013). Is this standard different from that proposed in earlier, unsuccessful legislation which would have established liability if the plaintiff could show that impermissible factors *contributed* to the employment practice?

Also, the Act made changes in Title VII procedures and remedies. For the first time, both compensatory and punitive damages are available, but only for intentional discrimination and subject to caps based on the size of the workforce (up to a cap of $300,000 for employers with more than 500 employees). Punitive damages are available only if the employer acted "with malice or with reckless indifference" to the plaintiff's statutory rights. In many Title VII cases, jury trial is now available.

Direct evidence of discrimination is no longer required for a plaintiff to prevail in a mixed-motive Title VII case. The plaintiff can succeed by proving his or her case by a preponderance of the evidence using direct or circumstantial evidence. Desert Palace, Inc. v. Costa, 539 U.S. 90 (2003).

8. McKennon v. Nashville Banner Publishing Co., 513 U.S. 352 (1995), which held that a valid claim of discrimination is not defeated by after-acquired evidence of wrongdoing by the employee, is discussed in Chapter 10, infra.

9. Consider the experiment, "Nonverbal Affect Responses to Male and Female Leaders: Implications for Leadership Evaluations," 58 J. Personality & Social Psychology 48 (1990). Social psychologists Doré Butler and Florence Geis studied perception of women and men in leadership roles to see if automatic expectations for women were still dominated by traditional stereotypes.

Male and female subjects participated in four-person discussions in which male or female confederates assumed leadership. The leadership roles were predetermined by a script which called either for "leader" and "non-leader" or "co-leader" roles. Male and female confederates would switch roles for consecutive trials, and the subjects' nonverbal responses were recorded from behind one-way mirrors during the discussions. Female leaders received more negative than positive non-verbal responses, in contrast to male leaders, who received at least as many positive as negative responses. In a survey following the discussion, female leaders received more negative ratings, such as being "bossy and dominating," than their male counterparts.

Butler and Geis found their results supported the premise that "intellectual assertiveness by women in mixed-sex discussions elicits visible cues of negative affect." They argue that this result has implications for hiring, salary, and promotion, which often depend on recognition of the individual as an emergent leader. The results suggest that training women to be "more assertive" (or less assertive, for that matter) in leadership will not eliminate discrimination.

Does this change your perception of the result in Price Waterhouse? How do you interpret Hopkins' evaluations and co-workers' comments about her technique and personality?

10. A discrimination plaintiff need not demonstrate that she was replaced by a person outside her protected class to establish that her dismissal was a consequence of unlawful sex discrimination. Stella v. Mineta, 284 F.3d 135 (D.C.Cir.2002).

11. Lautermilch, a male, was not hired as a substitute public school teacher. The court said: "Lautermilch attempts to base his entire case on one off-hand comment by Principal Crates (that he was 'too macho') * * *. The comment was critical of Lautermilch's behavior, not his sex or gender." The dissenting judge wrote: "The commonplace usage of the word 'macho' refers exclusively to behavior or qualities associated with the male gender." He cited *Price Waterhouse* and its holding that Hopkins should not be punished for being insufficiently "feminine." Lautermilch v. Findlay City Schools, 314 F.3d 271 (6th Cir. 2003), cert. denied, 540 U.S. 813 (2003).

12. Joe's Stone Crab, a famous restaurant in Miami Beach, committed intentional disparate treatment discrimination by maintaining "the ethos that female food servers were not to be hired * * * and, in fact, they were not." Women were excluded "based on a sexual stereotype which simply associated 'fine-dining ambience' with all-male food service * * * Joe's sought to emulate Old World traditions by creating an ambience in which tuxedo-clad men served its distinctive menu." EEOC v. Joe's Stone Crab, Inc., 136 F.Supp.2d 1311 (S.D.Fla.2001), partially affirmed, 296 F.3d 1265 (11th Cir. 2002). See also the earlier court of appeals decision reversing a holding that the restaurant's policies were unlawful disparate impact discrimination. EEOC v. Joe's Stone Crab, Inc., 220 F.3d 1263 (11th Cir. 2000).

McDonnell Douglas and Beyond

The *McDonnell Douglas* standard has evolved significantly since the original decision. Originally, *McDonnell Douglas* required a plaintiff to show that unlawful discrimination was the but-for cause of an adverse employment action. In practice, the need to show but-for causation often created an uphill battle for plaintiffs because the defendant-employer could usually point to some consideration, such as poor job performance, that would have triggered the adverse employment action even in the absence of unlawful discrimination. The Supreme Court clarified this position in Texas Dep't of Community Affairs v. Burdine, 450 U.S. 248 (1981). In *Burdine*, the Court stated that "[t]he defendant need not persuade the court that it was actually motivated by the proferred reasons" in order to overcome the plaintiff's prima facie case. Rather, the defendant needed only to raise "a genuine issue of fact as to whether it discriminated against the plaintiff." The Court concluded that "[t]he ultimate burden of persuading the trier of fact that the defendant intentionally discriminated against the plaintiff remains at all times with the plaintiff." In St. Mary's Honor Center v. Hicks, 509 U.S. 502 (1993), the Court further clarified the plaintiff's burden by holding that "Title VII does not award damages against employers who cannot prove a nondiscriminatory reason for adverse employment action." Liability did not exist unless the defendant was "proven [by the plaintiff] to have taken [an] adverse employment action by reason of * * * race [or some other unlawful motive]."

Price Waterhouse v. Hopkins, supra, p. 227, opened a wider door to mixed-motive claims. In Price Waterhouse, a four-justice plurality stated that "since we know that the words 'because of' [in Title VII] do not mean 'solely because of,' we also know that Title VII meant to condemn even those decisions based on a mixture of legitimate and illegitimate considerations." Justice O'Connor provided the fifth vote, but her concurrence qualified the plurality's view by requiring plaintiffs to "show by direct evidence that an illegitimate criterion was a substantial factor in the decision." Although the precise nature of Justice O'Connor's "direct evidence" has been the subject of extensive debate, its basic purpose was to require plaintiffs to produce something more than the circumstantial evidence that would ordinarily prove but-for causation.

Congress responded to *Price Waterhouse* by enacting the Civil Rights Act of 1991, which stated that "an unlawful employment practice is established when the complaining party demonstrates that race, color, [or other unlawful consideration] was a motivating factor for any employment practice, even though other factors also motivated the practice." Crucially, however, the Act failed to define the distinction between circumstantial evidence and direct evidence. It was silent as to whether a "demonstration" of unlawful motivating factors must be founded on direct evidence. Following the Act, lower courts continued to apply Justice O'Connor's direct-evidence requirement to claims based on motivating factors. Although a plaintiff could theoretically prevail by showing that unlawful discrimination was a motivating factor—as opposed to the but-for cause—of an adverse employment action, the unclear nature of the direct-evidence requirement complicated this strategy.

The Court finally settled these evidentiary issues in Desert Palace, Inc. v. Costa, 539 U.S. 90 (2003). In *Desert Palace*, the Court abrogated Justice O'Connor's direct-evidence requirement from *Price Waterhouse*. The Court stated that the Act "does not mention, much less require, that a plaintiff make a heightened showing through direct evidence." The Court further observed that "if Congress intended the term 'demonstrates' [in the Civil Rights Act of 1991] to require * * * direct evidence or some other heightened showing, it could have made that intent clear by including language to that effect." As a result, plaintiffs can now advance their claims by using circumstantial evidence to prove that unlawful discrimination was a motivating factor for an adverse employment action.

After *Desert Palace*, courts have struggled to decide when a case should be analyzed at the pretrial stage using the *McDonnell Douglas* framework and when it should be analyzed using the mixed motives framework from *Price Waterhouse*. See Coleman v. Donohue, 667 F.3d 835 (7th Cir. 2012) (Wood, J., concurring) (arguing that the two tests should be collapsed at the pretrial stage of a case, as they have been at the trial stage of a case, and the plaintiff should simply be required to present evidence showing that "the employer took . . . adverse action on account of her protected class"). In University of Texas Southwestern Medical Center v. Nassar, 570 U.S. 338 (2013), the Supreme Court in dicta suggested that such a collapse of the two evidentiary frameworks was appropriate when it explained that the mixed-motive evidentiary framework "is not itself a substantive bar on discrimination. Rather, it is a rule that establishes the causation standard for proving a violation defined elsewhere in Title VII." In Quigg v. Thomas Cnty. Sch. Dist., 814 F.3d 1227 (11th Cir. 2016), the Eleventh Circuit joined the Second, Third, Fourth, Fifth, Sixth, Seventh, Ninth, and Tenth Circuits in holding that at summary judgment, mixed motive claims involving circumstantial evidence should not be evaluated using the *McDonnell Douglas* standard. Instead, summary judgment should be denied in such cases if the plaintiff raises a genuine issue of material fact as to whether a protected characteristic was a motivating factor for the defendant's adverse employment action. Only the Eighth Circuit has continued to hold, post *Desert Palace*, that the *McDonnell Douglas* approach is appropriate at the summary judgment stage for mixed motive cases. See Griffin v. City of Des Moines, 387 F.3d 733 (8th Cir. 2004).

NOTE

The Supreme Court held in Gross v. FBL Financial Services, 557 U.S. 167 (2009), that a plaintiff bringing a claim under the Age Discrimination in Employment Act (ADEA) must show that age discrimination was a but-for cause of any adverse employment action. In refusing to apply *Price Waterhouse* and *Desert Palace* to ADEA claims, the Court effectively turned back the clock to the original *McDonnell Douglas* decision for ADEA plaintiffs. Professor Michael Harper has criticized *Gross* for straining against the intent of Congress and for interfering with doctrinal coherence among the federal anti-discrimination statutes. Michael C. Harper, Gross v. FBL Financial Services, Inc., and the Unfulfilled Promise of the Civil Rights Act of 1991, 58 Buff. L. Rev. 69 (2010).

The Court's focus in *Gross* was on the evidentiary burden born by the plaintiff at trial with the Court making clear that the plaintiff retains the burden of proving "but-for" causation in ADEA claims. *Gross* did not address the evidentiary framework applicable to a motion for summary judgment. In Shelly v. Green, 666 F.3d 599 (9th Cir. 2012), the Ninth Circuit held that it was appropriate for courts to continue using the *McDonnell Douglas* burden shifting framework, as they had prior to *Gross*, to decide summary judgment motions in ADEA cases. The court rejected the district court's conclusion that because *Gross* required a plaintiff to prove "but-for" causation to win at trial, the *McDonnell Douglas* burden shifting framework was no longer appropriate at summary judgment.

Preston v. Wisconsin Health Fund

397 F.3d 539 (7th Cir. 2005).

■ POSNER, CIRCUIT JUDGE.

Jay Preston, a dentist, charges that the Wisconsin Health Fund, his former employer, discriminated against him on account of his sex in violation of Title VII of the Civil Rights Act of 1964, when they replaced him as director of the Fund's dental clinic with Linda Hamilton (not to be confused with the female lead in the first two *Terminator* movies). Preston further argues that in procuring this substitution, Bruce Trojak, the Fund's chief executive officer, conspired with Hamilton to destroy Preston's contractual relationship with the Fund, in violation of Wisconsin's common law of tortious interference with contract. The district court granted summary judgment for the defendants.

The fund is a Teamsters Health and Welfare Fund that provides health services directly in clinics that it owns, as well as indirectly by paying for medical or dental treatment that its participants obtain outside the Fund's clinics. The Fund had been hemorrhaging money for many years when Trojak became its chief executive officer in 1998. The dental clinic alone, under Preston, its long-time director, lost $1 million the following year. Preston presented ideas for stemming the flow to Trojak in a well-written business plan (Preston has an M.B.A. as well as a dental degree), despite which Trojak fired him and replaced him with Hamilton, a much younger dentist who had no apparent credentials for the job except eagerness for it. Trojak testified at his deposition that Preston's ideas were too few and too late and that he was impressed by Hamilton's "can do" attitude. This may be true but it may also be true, as Preston claims, that Trojak favored Hamilton for personal reasons. There were rumors, although unsubstantiated, that they were having an affair. They frequently dined together and sometimes after dinner would repair to his apartment for—according to their not terribly credible deposition testimony—platonic sessions solely devoted to disinterested discussion of the future of the dental clinic, though Hamilton did acknowledge indicating at these sessions her desire to be promoted to dental director.

Trojak is no longer with the Fund, and Hamilton is no longer the dental director. But the circumstances of their departures are obscure, and both are represented in this lawsuit by the Fund's law firm.

A male executive's romantically motivated favoritism toward a female subordinate is not sex discrimination even when it disadvantages a male competitor of the woman. Such favoritism is not based on a belief that women are better workers, or otherwise deserve to be treated better, than men; indeed, it is entirely consistent with the opposite opinion. The effect on the composition of the workplace is likely to be nil, especially since the disadvantaged competitor is as likely to be another woman as a man—were Preston a woman, Trojak would still have fired her to make way for Hamilton unless Trojak was romantically entangled with both of them. Neither in purpose nor in consequence can favoritism resulting from a personal relationship be equated to sex discrimination.

Preston tries to bolster his case by pointing to the fact that Trojak gave large raises to several women and by noting that there was even talk in the workplace of "Bruce and his harem." But he provides no details that would enable a trier of fact to infer that the raises were motivated by the recipients' sex. All we know is the amount of the raises, the number of recipients, and the sex ratio of the recipients—five women to two men. To infer discrimination we would need to know more. We would need to know the sex composition of the Fund's workforce, whether there were men who had jobs comparable to those of the five women but didn't get similar raises, and whether the raises were due to the women's being promoted to new jobs and if so whether men had a fair opportunity to compete for those promotions. There are some answers in the record but Preston makes nothing of them. He insists that the bare fact that more women than men got large raises, together with the favoritism shown Linda Hamilton, is enough to get him to a jury.

One reason it is not enough is that the courts take a realistic view of the circumstances in which an inference that men are discriminating in favor of rather than against women is plausible. It is not surprising when women discriminate in favor of women any more than it is surprising when men discriminate in favor of men. It is surprising, in many though not all cases, when men discriminate against men in favor of women. Two situations have been identified in the cases where it is not surprising. The first is where the men running the company are under pressure from affirmative action plans, customers, public opinion, the EEOC, a judicial decree, or corporate superiors imbued with the belief in "diversity" to increase the proportion of women in the company's workforce. The second situation is where the jobs in question are traditional "women's work," such as nursing, which the men running the company believe women can do better than men; fixated on this stereotype they refuse to make an individualized assessment of male applicants.

There may be other situations as well in which it is plausible to expect that men might discriminate against men an in favor of women;

the list is not a closed one. But when as in this case no reason is given why men might be expected to discriminate against men, the plaintiff, to raise a triable issue of discrimination, must present some evidence beyond the bare fact that a woman got a job that a man wanted to get or keep. A gross disparity in qualifications might be such evidence—but for the fact in this case that the plaintiff himself is insisting that the reason the less-qualified Hamilton was given the job of the more-qualified Preston was personal and, as we have explained, unrelated to sex discrimination. All that is left is the undeveloped evidence of the raises given to the other women. The district judge was correct, therefore, to grant summary judgment for the Fund on Preston's Title VII claim.

NOTES

1.   *Preston* is a good example of the limited nature of Title VII: it does not aim to prohibit all unfair employment decisions; only those that impermissibly discriminate based on proscribed criteria. One plausible explanation for the restrained character of federal employment law is the tradition of at-will employment in the United States, discussed earlier in Chapter 3 and fully treated in Chapter 10. See generally, Anita Bernstein, Foreword: What We Talk About When We Talk About Workplace Privacy, 66. La.L.Rev. (2006).

2.   Maelynn Tenge, "the highest paid employee" at Phillips, worked closely with Scott Phillips, owner of the company. Lori Phillips, Scott's wife, saw inappropriate behavior between Tenge and Scott in a bar and encouraged Scott to fire Tenge, which he did. Tenge testified that Scott told her that Lori was "making me choose between my best employee or her and the kids." Held: This was not sex discrimination, and the district court was correct to dismiss Title VII actions against Scott and the company and to dismiss Tenge's state-law action against Lori for tortious interference with her employment status. Tenge v. Phillips Modern Ag. Co., 446 F.3d 903 (8th Cir. 2006). May a male employer terminate a female employee because the employer's wife finds the employee to be a threat to their marriage even in the absence of any inappropriate behavior on the part of the employee? See Nelson v. Knight, 2012 WL 6652747 (Iowa, Dec. 21, 2012) (finding no sex discrimination but noting that "[i]f an employer repeatedly took adverse employment actions against persons of a particular gender because of alleged personal relationship issues, it might well be possible to infer that gender and not the relationship was a motivating factor").

3.   Employees were fired because they were dating each other in violation of the employer's antinepotism policy. The Washington Supreme Court said that "marital status" protection did not apply to cohabiting or dating relationships. Waggoner v. Ace Hardware Corp., 953 P.2d 88 (Wash.1998).

4.   Keith Vaughn worked on grounds and buildings maintenance for Lawrenceburg Power System. Jennifer Paige began work as a cashier at LPS. Keith and Jennifer became engaged. The LPS manual said "it is the policy of the system to employ only one member of a family * * *. When two employees * * * are subsequently married, one must terminate employment."

A supervisor met with Keith and suggested that there would be no problem if Keith and Jennifer lived together. "The Vaughns are reluctant to pursue this option, in large part because Jennifer has become pregnant * * *." The court of appeals found no legal problem with the no marriage rule. "[T]he policy did not bar Jennifer or Keith from getting married, nor did it prevent them marrying a large portion of population even in Lawrence County [Tennessee]." Vaughn v. Lawrenceburg Power Sys., 269 F.3d 703 (6th Cir. 2001).

5.   In Miller v. Department of Corrections, 115 P.3d 77 (Cal. 2005), a prison warden demonstrated favoritism towards three female employees with whom he had previously had sexual affairs. The California Supreme Court held that "when such sexual favoritism in a workplace is sufficiently widespread it may create an actionable hostile work environment in which the demeaning message is conveyed to female employees that they are viewed by management as 'sexual playthings' or that the way required for women to get ahead is to engage in sexual conduct with their supervisors * * *."

Implicit Bias

In recent years, antidiscrimination law scholars have written extensively about the theory of "implicit," or unconscious, bias. Professors Christine Jolls and Cass Sunstein explain that the theory is rooted in cognitive psychology research:

> Much evidence of these forms of implicit bias comes from the Implicit Association Test (IAT), which has been taken by large and diverse populations on the Internet and elsewhere. The IAT asks individuals to perform the seemingly straightforward task of categorizing a series of words or pictures into groups. Two of the groups are racial or other categories, such as "black" and "white," and two of the groups are the categories "pleasant" and "unpleasant." * * * The IAT is rooted in the very simple hypothesis that people will find it easier to associate pleasant words with white faces and names than with African-American faces and names—and that the same pattern will be found for other traditionally disadvantaged groups.

> In fact, implicit bias as measured by the IAT has proven to be extremely widespread. Most people tend to prefer white to African-American, young to old, and heterosexual to gay. Strikingly, members of traditionally disadvantaged groups tend to show the same set of preferences.

> It might not be so disturbing to find implicit bias in experimental settings if the results did not predict actual behavior, and in fact the relationship between IAT scores and behavior remains an active area of research. . . . For example, there is strong evidence that scores on the IAT and similar tests are correlated with third parties' ratings of the degree of general

friendliness individuals show to members of another race. More particularly, "larger IAT effect scores predicted greater speaking time, more smiling, [and] more extemporaneous social comments" in interactions with whites as compared to African-Americans. And it is reasonable to speculate that such uneasy interactions are associated with biased behavior. In the employment context in particular, even informal differences in treatment may have significant effects on employment outcomes, particularly in today's fluid work-places. If this is so, then the importance to legal policy is clear. If people are treated differently, and worse, because of their race or another protected trait, then the principle of antidiscrimination has been violated, even if the source of the differential treatment is implicit rather than conscious bias.

Christine Jolls & Cass R. Sunstein, The Law of Implicit Bias, 94 Cal. L. Rev. 969 (2006).

Research in cognitive psychology has shown that IAT bias scores are not fixed; in fact, they appear to be quite malleable. In one study, individuals exhibited decreased levels of bias against African Americans after being shown a photograph of [a prominent African-American athlete]. See Nilankana Dasgupta & Anthony G. Greenwald, On the Malleability of Automatic Attitudes: Combating Automatic Prejudice with Images of Admired and Disliked Individuals, 81 J. Personality & Soc. Psychol. 800, 803–04 (2001). These lower bias levels remained unchanged twenty-four hours later when the same subjects underwent a second test. In another study, subjects had lower IAT bias scores when an African-American administered the test. See Brian S. Lowery, Curtis D. Hardin & Stacey Sinclair, Social Influence Effects on Automatic Racial Prejudice, 81 J. Personality & Soc. Psychol. 842, 844–45, 846–47 (2001). These results beg an obvious question: if levels of implicit bias are affected by current social and political environments, does the government have a duty to alter those environments and "de-bias" its citizens? Should we instead leave it to culture and the media to shift our unconscious biases? Is there a way in which "de-biasing" would amount to governmental thought control? Does the malleability of implicit bias provide a new defense for affirmative action? See Jerry Kang & Mahzarin R. Banaji, Fair Measures: A Behavioral Realist Revision of "Affirmative Action," 94 Cal. L. Rev. 1063 (2006).

Critics of the significance of implicit bias, however, worry that judges and legislators might heed political calls to reform the law without realizing that they stand on shaky scientific ground. Professors Gregory Mitchell and Philip E. Tetlock argue that using questionable research findings to fashion legal rules could lead to untoward results:

Our fear is that the stage has been set for an epistemic disaster of minor-epic proportions. Throughout this Article, we have seen how rarely IAT researchers temper their enthusiasm for ferreting out unconscious prejudice with offsetting concerns about the dangers of making false accusations of prejudice * * *. If the knowledge claims of IAT advocates are as exaggerated as we maintain, IAT advocates are already causing substantial harm to American society by: (a) stimulating excessive suspicion of Whites among Blacks, suspicion that can crystallize into conspiracy theories that poison race relations; (b) convincing Blacks that they are held in contempt, thereby inducing "stereotype threat" and "social-identity threat" that, respectively, increase the likelihood of self-fulfilling prophecies in which Blacks act in ways that confirm the ill opinions they imagine others hold and heighten preconscious attention to subtle cues that confirm the devalued role of minority groups; (c) providing authoritative-sounding but false feedback to a million-plus visitors to IAT websites that they are prejudiced; and (d) providing authoritative-sounding but false grounds for commonality-of-cause requirements in class action litigation.

Gregory Mitchell & Philip E. Tetlock, Antidiscrimination Law and the Perils of Mindreading, 67 Ohio St. L.J. 1023 (2006).

Should lawmakers and judges hesitate to fashion legal rules on the basis of social science research? Professors Linda Krieger and Susan Fiske note that our legal system values predictability and the principle of stare decisis, whereas the social sciences are more welcoming of innovation, revision, and creativity. See Linda Hamilton Krieger & Susan T. Fiske, Behavioral Realism in Employment Discrimination Law: Implicit Bias and Disparate Treatment, 94 Cal. L. Rev. 997 (2006). How can we reconcile these conflicting impulses? In the natural sciences, a hypothesis does not become a "law" until many successful experiments have been completed over a long period of time. Should we apply the same rigorous test to conclusions drawn from social science before permitting them to modify legal doctrines? Is it possible to develop a jurisprudential model for incorporating social scientific research into legal construction and interpretation? Does the influence of a social science such as economics on the law suggest that we already have developed such a model?

NOTES

1.   Employment-discrimination plaintiffs tend to fare significantly less well than plaintiffs in other types of cases. *See* Kevin M. Clermont & Stewart J. Schwab, Employment Discrimination Plaintiffs in Federal Court: From Bad to Worse?, 3 Harv. L. & Pol'y Rev. 103 (2009). Analyzing cases decided between the early 1970s and early 2000s, Professors Clermont and Schwab have noticed a consistent "anti-plaintiff effect" that is especially pronounced at the appellate level. Their data show that defendants obtain reversals in 30 to 50 percent of employment-discrimination cases whereas plaintiffs obtain reversals in only 10 to 20 percent of cases. Clermont and Schwab

suggest that one explanation for this disparity may lie in the tendency of appellate judges to perceive lower courts as pro-plaintiff and therefore to "harshly scrutiniz[e] employees' victories below while gazing benignly at employers' victories."

2.   Professor Russell Robinson has suggested that racial differences in the perception of discrimination may partly explain plaintiffs' low chances of prevailing on employment-discrimination claims. Russell K. Robinson, Perceptual Segregation, 108 Colum. L. Rev. 1093 (2008). Robinson argues that whites tend strongly to demand "smoking gun" evidence when identifying instances of discrimination whereas racial minorities tend to detect discrimination even when it is masked by ambiguity. In one example of such subtextual discrimination, Robinson states that a black person may interpret praise for being "articulate" as reflecting the "assumption * * * that blacks generally have difficulty speaking proper English." As overt discrimination becomes increasingly rare, what implications do Robinson's observations have for evidentiary standards in discrimination claims?

Systemic Discrimination/Statistical Proof

In International Bhd. of Teamsters v. United States, 431 U.S. 324 (1977), the Supreme Court approved the use of statistics to prove discrimination. The government had sued T.I.M.E.-D.C., Inc., a motor freight carrier, and the Teamsters for discriminating against minorities in hiring, job assignment, and promotions and transfers. As to whether the government had made a prima facie case that the company had discriminated, the Court stated:

> We agree with the District Court and the Court of Appeals that the Government carried its burden of proof. As of March 31, 1971, shortly after the Government filed its complaint alleging systemwide discrimination, the company had 6,472 employees. Of these, 314 (5%) were Negroes and 257 (4%) were Spanish-surnamed Americans. Of the 1,828 line drivers, however, there were only 8 (0.4%) Negroes and 5 (0.3%) Spanish-surnamed persons, and all of the Negroes had been hired after the litigation had commenced. With one exception a man who worked as a line driver at the Chicago terminal from 1950 to 1959—the company and its predecessors *did not employ a Negro on a regular basis as a line driver until 1969.* And, as the Government showed, even in 1971 there were terminals in areas of substantial Negro population where all of the company's line drivers were white.[6] A great majority of the Negroes (83%) and

---

[6]   In Atlanta, for instance, Negroes composed 22.35% of the population in the surrounding metropolitan area and 51.31% of the population in the city proper. The company's Atlanta terminal employed 57 line drivers. All were white. In Los Angeles, 10.84% of the greater metropolitan population and 17.88% of the city population were Negro. But at the company's two Los Angeles terminals there was not a single Negro among the 374 line drivers. The proof showed similar disparities in San Francisco, Denver, Nashville, Chicago, Dallas, and at several other terminals.

Spanish-surnamed Americans (78%) who did work for the company held the lower-paying city operations and serviceman jobs, whereas only 39% of the nonminority employees held jobs in those categories.

The Government bolstered its statistical evidence with the testimony of individuals who recounted over 40 specific instances of discrimination.

* * *

The company's principal response to this evidence is that statistics can never in and of themselves prove the existence of a pattern or practice of discrimination, or even establish a prima facie case shifting to the employer the burden of rebutting the inference raised by the figures. But, as even our brief summary of the evidence shows, this was not a case in which the Government relied on "statistics alone." The individuals who testified about their personal experiences with the company brought the cold numbers convincingly to life.

In any event, our cases make it unmistakably clear that "[s]tatistical analyses have served and will continue to serve an important role" in cases in which the existence of discrimination is a disputed issue. We have repeatedly approved the use of statistical proof, where it reached proportions comparable to those in this case, to establish a prima facie case of racial discrimination in jury selection cases. Statistics are equally competent in proving employment discrimination.[7] We caution only that statistics are not irrefutable; they come in infinite variety and, like any other kind of evidence, they may be rebutted. In short, their usefulness depends on all of the surrounding facts and circumstances. 431 U.S. at 337–40.

The Court further delineated the appropriate role of statistics in establishing adverse impact in Hazelwood School District v. United States, 433 U.S. 299 (1977), when it narrowed the application of statistical data to the "relevant labor market." In *Teamsters,* the government had compared the employer's hiring record to the percentage of blacks in the population in the surrounding area. In *Hazelwood,* the Court distinguished the

---

[7] Petitioners argue that statistics, at least those comparing the racial composition of an employer's work force to the composition of the population at large, should never be given decisive weight in a Title VII case. * * *

* * * Statistics showing racial or ethnic imbalance are probative in a case such as this one only because such imbalance is often a telltale sign of purposeful discrimination; absent explanation, it is ordinarily to be expected that nondiscriminatory hiring practices will in time result in a work force more or less representative of the racial and ethnic composition of the population in the community from which employees are hired. Evidence of longlasting and gross disparity between the composition of a work force and that of the general population thus may be significant even though § 703(j) makes clear that Title VII imposes no requirement that a work force mirror the general population.

job requirement in *Teamsters* the ability to drive, which is widely held in the adult population from the more specialized job requirement in *Hazelwood* of having a teaching certificate. In *Hazelwood,* the "relevant labor market" was not the general population in the greater St. Louis area, but the population of individuals having teaching certificates.

NOTES AND QUESTIONS

1.   In addition to the statistical evidence about the company's hiring and selection practices, the Court in *Teamsters* also had before it testimony from a number of individual African Americans who had been discriminated against. Would statistical evidence alone be sufficient to establish a prima facie case against the employer even if there were no individual testimony to support the statistics? On what basis?

2.   The employer's workforce data in *Teamsters* was compared to the percentage of blacks in the general population, whereas *Hazelwood* focused on comparisons between the School District's hiring data and the "relevant labor market." Under what circumstances are general population comparisons still useful? What factors determine the "relevant labor market"?

3.   Another possible data base to use is "applicant flow data." What advantages and disadvantages does such information present for a court charged with the task of determining whether the employer's hiring practices have had an adverse impact on a protected group?

4.   Once the proper quantitative data comparison has been established, some measure of the qualitative usefulness of the data is necessary before a court can conclude that a particular hiring pattern has an "adverse impact" within the meaning of the law. In *Hazelwood,* the Supreme Court endorsed the use of standard deviations, a mathematical measure of statistical significance, to determine whether data has legal significance as well. Standard deviations measure the likelihood that a particular set of numbers is the result of chance rather than what one would expect to occur naturally as a result of the employer's selection processes. What the Supreme Court has not done, however, is indicate precisely what level of statistical significance is legally determinative. As a result, many complex adverse impact cases have involved sophisticated statistical battles between mathematical experts debating the relative merits of various measures of significance, particularly multiple regression analysis.

5.   Sample size is an important component of statistical probability analysis. The fewer employment decisions an employer makes, the more difficult it is to conclude that differences in selection rates are meaningful. How does one prove discrimination in such cases? The First Circuit has offered guidance on this problem:

> Widely accepted statistical techniques have been developed to determine the likelihood an observed disparity resulted from mere chance. Where a plaintiff relies exclusively on a narrow base of

data, * * * it is crucial for the court to consider the possibility that chance could account for the observed disparity.

We think that in cases involving a narrow data base, the better approach is for the courts to require a showing that the disparity is statistically significant, or unlikely to have occurred by chance, applying basic statistical tests as the method of proof. When statistical tests sufficiently diminish chance as a likely explanation, it can then be presumed that an apparently substantial difference in pass rates is attributable to discriminatory bias, thus shifting the burden to defendants to show job relatedness. If the probability is sufficiently high that the disparity resulted from chance, the plaintiff must present additional evidence of disproportionate impact in order to establish a prima facie case.

Fudge v. Providence Fire Dep't, 766 F.2d 650 (1st Cir. 1985). An additional problem surfaces when an employer changes its testing procedures, making it impossible to compare test results from one time period to another.

Wal-Mart Stores, Inc. v. Dukes
564 U.S. 338 (2011).

■ JUSTICE SCALIA delivered the opinion of the Court.

We are presented with one of the most expansive class actions ever. The District Court and the Court of Appeals approved the certification of a class comprising about one and a half million plaintiffs, current and former female employees of petitioner Wal-Mart who allege that the discretion exercised by their local supervisors over pay and promotion matters violates Title VII by discriminating against women. In addition to injunctive and declaratory relief, the plaintiffs seek an award of backpay. We consider whether the certification of the plaintiff class was consistent with Federal Rules of Civil Procedure 23(a) and (b)(2).

Petitioner Wal-Mart is the Nation's largest private employer. It operates four types of retail stores throughout the country: Discount Stores, Supercenters, Neighborhood Markets, and Sam's clubs. Those stores are divided into seven nationwide divisions, which in turn comprise 41 regions of 80 to 85 stores apiece. Each store has between 40 and 53 separate departments and 80 to 500 staff positions. In all, Wal-Mart operates approximately 3,400 stores and employs more than one million people.

Pay and promotion decisions at Wal-Mart are generally committed to local managers' broad discretion, which is exercised "in a largely subjective manner." Local store managers may increase the wages of hourly employees (within limits) with only limited corporate oversight. As for salaried employees, such as store managers and their deputies, higher corporate authorities have discretion to set their pay within preestablished ranges.

Promotions work in a similar fashion. Wal-Mart permits store managers to apply their own subjective criteria when selecting candidates as "support managers," which is the first step on the path to management. Admission to Wal-Mart's management training program, however, does require that a candidate meet certain objective criteria, including an above-average performance rating, at least one year's tenure in the applicant's current position, and a willingness to relocate. But except for those requirements, regional and district managers have discretion to use their own judgment when selecting candidates for management training. Promotion to higher office—e.g., assistant manager, co-manager, or store manager—is similarly at the discretion of the employee's superiors after prescribed objective factors are satisfied.

The named plaintiffs in this lawsuit, representing the 1.5 million members of the certified class, are three current or former Wal-Mart employees who allege that the company discriminated against them on the basis of their sex by denying them equal pay or promotions, in violation of Title VII of the Civil Rights Act of 1964.

Betty Dukes began working at a Pittsburgh, California, Wal-Mart in 1994. She started as a cashier, but later sought and received a promotion to customer service manager. After a series of disciplinary violations, however, Dukes was demoted back to cashier and then to greeter. Dukes concedes she violated company policy, but contends that the disciplinary actions were in fact retaliation for invoking internal complaint procedures and that male employees have not been disciplined for similar infractions. Dukes also claims two male greeters in the Pittsburgh store are paid more than she is.

Christine Kwapnoski has worked at Sam's Club stores in Missouri and California for most of her adult life. She has held a number of positions, including a supervisory position. She claims that a male manager yelled at her frequently and screamed at female employees, but not at men. The manager in question "told her to 'doll up,' to wear some makeup, and to dress a little better."

The final named plaintiff, Edith Arana, worked at a Wal-Mart store in Duarte, California, from 1995 to 2001. In 2000, she approached the store manager on more than one occasion about management training, but was brushed off. Arana concluded she was being denied opportunity for advancement because of her sex. She initiated internal complaint procedures, whereupon she was told to apply directly to the district manager if she thought her store manager was being unfair. Arana, however, decided against that and never applied for management training again. In 2001, she was fired for failure to comply with Wal-Mart's timekeeping policy.

These plaintiffs, respondents here, do not allege that Wal-Mart has any express corporate policy against the advancement of women. Rather, they claim that their local managers' discretion over pay and promotions is exercised disproportionately in favor of men, leading to an unlawful disparate impact on female employees. And, respondents say, because Wal-Mart is aware of this effect, its refusal to cabin its managers' authority amounts to disparate treatment. Their complaint seeks injunctive and declaratory relief, punitive damages, and backpay. It does not ask for compensatory damages.

Importantly for our purposes, respondents claim that the discrimination to which they have been subjected is common to all Wal-Mart's female employees. The basic theory of their case is that a strong and uniform "corporate culture" permits bias against women to infect, perhaps subconsciously, the discretionary decisionmaking of each one of Wal-Mart's thousands of managers—thereby making every woman at the company the victim of one common discriminatory practice. Respondents therefore wish to litigate the Title VII claims of all female employees at Wal-Mart's stores in a nationwide class action.

* * *

The class action is "an exception to the usual rule that litigation is conducted by and on behalf of the individual named parties only." In order to justify a departure from that rule, "a class representative must be part of the class and 'possess the same interest and suffer the same injury' as the class members." Rule 23(a) ensures that the named plaintiffs are appropriate representatives of the class whose claims they wish to litigate. The Rule's four requirements—numerosity, commonality, typicality, and adequate representation—"effectively 'limit the class claims to those fairly encompassed by the named plaintiff's claims.'"

The crux of this case is commonality—the rule requiring a plaintiff to show that "there are questions of law or fact common to the class." That language is easy to misread, since "[a]ny competently crafted class complaint literally raises common 'questions.'" For example: Do all of us plaintiffs indeed work for Wal-Mart? Do our managers have discretion over pay? Is that an unlawful employment practice? What remedies should we get? Reciting these questions is not sufficient to obtain class certification. Commonality requires the plaintiff to demonstrate that the class members "have suffered the same injury," This does not mean merely that they have all suffered a violation of the same provision of law. Title VII, for example, can be violated in many ways—by intentional discrimination, or by hiring and promotion criteria that result in disparate impact, and by the use of these practices on the part of many different superiors in a single company. Quite obviously, the mere claim by employees of the same company that they have suffered a Title VII injury, or even a disparate-impact Title VII injury, gives no cause to believe that all their claims can productively be litigated at once. Their claims must depend upon a common contention—for example, the assertion of discriminatory bias on the part of the same supervisor. That common contention, moreover, must be of such a nature that it is capable of classwide resolution—which means that determination of its truth or falsity will resolve an issue that is central to the validity of each one of the claims in one stroke.

"What matters to class certification . . . is not the raising of common 'questions'—even in droves—but, rather the capacity of a classwide proceeding to generate common answers apt to drive the resolution of the litigation. Dissimilarities within the proposed class are what have the potential to impede the generation of common answers."

* * *

In this case, proof of commonality necessarily overlaps with respondents' merits contention that Wal-Mart engages in a pattern or practice of discrimination. That is so because, in resolving an individual's Title VII claim, the crux of the inquiry is "the reason for a particular employment decision." Here respondents wish to sue about literally millions of employment decisions at once. Without some glue holding the alleged reasons for all those decisions together, it will be impossible to say that examination of all the class members' claims for relief will produce a common answer to the crucial question why *was I disfavored*.

* * *

The second manner of bridging the gap requires "significant proof" that Wal-Mart "operated under a general policy of discrimination." That is entirely absent here. Wal-Mart's announced policy forbids sex discrimination, and as the District Court recognized the company imposes penalties for denials of equal employment opportunity. The only evidence of a general policy of discrimination respondents produced was the testimony of Dr. William Bielby, their sociological expert. Relying on "social framework" analysis, Bielby testified that Wal-Mart has a "strong corporate culture," that makes it " 'vulnerable' " to "gender bias". He could not, however, determine with any specificity how regularly stereotypes play a meaningful role in employment decisions at Wal-Mart. At his deposition . . . Dr. Bielby conceded that he could not calculate whether 0.5 percent or 95 percent of the employment decisions at Wal-Mart might be determined by stereotyped thinking.

The only corporate policy that the plaintiffs' evidence convincingly establishes is Wal-Mart's "policy" of allowing discretion by local supervisors over employment matters. On its face, of course, that is just the opposite of a uniform employment practice that would provide the commonality needed for a class action; it is a policy against having uniform employment practices. It is also a very common and presumptively reasonable way of doing business—one that we have said "should itself raise no inference of discriminatory conduct."

To be sure, we have recognized that, "in appropriate cases," giving discretion to lower-level supervisors can be the basis of Title VII liability under a disparate-impact theory—since "an employer's undisciplined system of subjective decisionmaking [can have] precisely the same effects as a system pervaded by impermissible intentional discrimination." But the recognition that this type of Title VII claim "can" exist does not lead to the conclusion that every employee in a company using a system of discretion has such a claim in common. To the contrary, left to their own devices most managers in any corporation—and surely most managers in a corporation that forbids sex discrimination—would select sex-neutral, performance-based criteria for hiring and promotion that produce no actionable disparity at all. Others may choose to reward various attributes that produce disparate impact—such as scores on general aptitude tests or educational achievements. And still other managers may be guilty of intentional discrimination that produces a sex-based disparity. In such a company, demonstrating the invalidity of one manager's use of discretion will do nothing to demonstrate the invalidity of another's. A party seeking to certify a nationwide class will be unable to show that all the employees' Title VII claims will in fact depend on the answers to common questions.

Respondents have not identified a common mode of exercising discretion that pervades the entire company—aside from their reliance on Dr. Bielby's social frameworks analysis that we have rejected. In a company of Wal-Mart's size and geographical scope, it is quite unbelievable that all managers would exercise their discretion in a common way without some common direction. Respondents attempt to make that showing by means of statistical and anecdotal evidence, but their evidence falls well short.

The statistical evidence consists primarily of regression analyses performed by Dr. Richard Drogin, a statistician, and Dr. Marc Bendick, a labor economist. Drogin conducted his analysis region-by-region, comparing the number of women promoted into management positions with the percentage of women in the available pool of hourly workers. After considering regional and national data, Drogin concluded that "there are statistically significant disparities between men and women at Wal-Mart ... [and] these disparities ... can be explained only by gender discrimination." Bendick compared work-force data from Wal-Mart and competitive retailers and concluded that Wal-Mart "promotes a lower percentage of women than its competitors."

Even if they are taken at face value, these studies are insufficient to establish that respondents' theory can be proved on a classwide basis.

* * *

There is another, more fundamental, respect in which respondents' statistical proof fails. Even if it established (as it does not) a pay or promotion pattern that differs from the nationwide figures or the regional figures in all of Wal-Mart's 3,400 stores, that would still not demonstrate that commonality of issue exists. Some managers will claim that the availability of women, or qualified women, or interested women, in their stores' area does not mirror the national or regional statistics. And almost all of them will claim to have been applying some sex-neutral, performance-based criteria—whose nature and effects will differ from store to store. In the landmark case of ours which held that giving discretion to lower-level supervisors can be the basis of Title VII liability under a disparate-impact theory, the plurality opinion conditioned that holding on the corollary that merely proving that the discretionary system has produced a racial or sexual disparity is not enough. "[T]he plaintiff must begin by identifying the specific employment practice that is challenged." That is all the more necessary when a class of plaintiffs is sought to be certified. Other than the bare existence of delegated discretion, respondents have identified no "specific employment practice"—much less one that ties all their 1.5 million claims together. Merely showing that Wal-Mart's policy of discretion has produced an overall sex-based disparity does not suffice.

Respondents' anecdotal evidence suffers from the same defects, and in addition is too weak to raise any inference that all the individual, discretionary personnel decisions are discriminatory.

* * *

In sum, we agree with Chief Judge Kozinski that the members of the class:

> "held a multitude of different jobs, at different levels of Wal-Mart's hierarchy, for variable lengths of time, in 3,400 stores, sprinkled across 50 states, with a kaleidoscope of supervisors (male and female), subject to a variety of regional policies that all differed. . . . Some thrived while others did poorly. They have little in common but their sex and this lawsuit."

* * *

. . . Wal-Mart is entitled to individualized determinations of each employee's eligibility for backpay. Title VII includes a detailed remedial scheme. If a plaintiff prevails in showing that an employer has discriminated against him in violation of the statute, the court "may enjoin the respondent from engaging in such unlawful employment practice, and order such affirmative action as may be appropriate, [including] reinstatement or hiring of employees, with or without backpay or any other equitable relief as the court deems appropriate." But if the employer can show that it took an adverse employment action against an employee for any reason other than discrimination, the court cannot order the "hiring, reinstatement, or promotion of an individual as an employee, or the payment to him of any backpay."

We have established a procedure for trying pattern-or-practice cases that gives effect to these statutory requirements. When the plaintiff seeks individual relief such as reinstatement or backpay after establishing a pattern or practice of discrimination, "a district court must usually conduct additional proceedings . . . to determine the scope of individual relief." At this phase, the burden of proof will shift to the company, but it will have the right to raise any individual affirmative defenses it may have, and to "demonstrate that the individual applicant was denied an employment opportunity for lawful reasons."

The Court of Appeals believed that it was possible to replace such proceedings with Trial by Formula. A sample set of the class members would be selected, as to whom liability for sex discrimination and the backpay owing as a result would be determined in depositions supervised by a master. The percentage of claims determined to be valid would then be applied to the entire remaining class, and the number of (presumptively) valid claims thus derived would be multiplied by the average backpay award in the sample set to arrive at the entire class recovery—without further individualized proceedings. We disapprove that novel project. Because the Rules Enabling Act forbids interpreting Rule 23 to "abridge, enlarge or modify any substantive right," a class cannot be certified on the premise that Wal-Mart will not be entitled to litigate its statutory defenses to individual claims. And because the necessity of that litigation will prevent backpay from being "incidental" to the classwide injunction, respondents' class could not be certified even assuming, arguendo, that "incidental" monetary relief can be awarded to a 23(b)(2) class.

* * *

The judgment of the Court of Appeals is reversed.

■ JUSTICE GINSBURG, with whom JUSTICE BREYER, JUSTICE SOTOMAYOR, and JUSTICE KAGAN join, concurring in part and dissenting in part.

The class in this case, I agree with the Court, should not have been certified under Federal Rule of Civil Procedure 23(b)(2). The plaintiffs, alleging discrimination in violation of Title VII, seek monetary relief that is not merely incidental to any injunctive or declaratory relief that might be available. A putative class of this type may be certifiable under Rule 23(b)(3), if the plaintiffs show that common class questions "predominate" over issues affecting individuals—e.g., qualification for, and the amount of, backpay or compensatory damages—and that a class action is "superior" to other modes of adjudication.

Whether the class the plaintiffs describe meets the specific requirements of Rule 23(b)(3) is not before the Court, and I would reserve that matter for consideration and decision on remand. The Court, however, disqualifies the class at the starting gate, holding that the plaintiffs cannot cross the "commonality" line set by Rule 23(a)(2). In so ruling, the Court imports into the Rule 23(a) determination concerns properly addressed in a Rule 23(b)(3) assessment.

Rule 23(a)(2) establishes a preliminary requirement for maintaining a class action: "[T]here are questions of law or fact common to the class." The Rule "does not require that all questions of law or fact raised in the litigation be common," indeed, "[e]ven a single question of law or fact common to the members of the class will satisfy the commonality requirement."

* * *

The District Court certified a class of "[a]ll women employed at any Wal-Mart domestic retail store at any time since December 26, 1998." The named plaintiffs, led by Betty Dukes, propose to litigate, on behalf of the class, allegations that Wal-Mart discriminates on the basis of gender in pay and promotions. They allege that the company "[r]eli[es] on gender stereotypes in making employment decisions such as . . . promotion[s][and] pay." Wal-Mart permits those prejudices to infect personnel decisions, the plaintiffs contend, by leaving pay and promotions in the hands of "a nearly all male managerial workforce" using "arbitrary and subjective criteria." Further alleged barriers to the advancement of female employees include the company's requirement, "as a condition of promotion to management jobs, that employees be willing to relocate." Absent instruction otherwise, there is a risk that managers will act on the familiar assumption that women, because of their services to husband and children, are less mobile than men.

Women fill 70 percent of the hourly jobs in the retailer's stores but make up only "33 percent of management employees." "[T]he higher one looks in the organization the lower the percentage of women." The plaintiffs' "largely uncontested descriptive statistics" also show that women working in the company's stores "are paid less than men in every region" and "that the salary gap widens over time even for men and women hired into the same jobs at the same time."

The District Court identified "systems for . . . promoting in-store employees" that were "sufficiently similar across regions and stores" to conclude that "the manner in which these systems affect the class raises issues that are common to all class members." The selection of employees for promotion to in-store management "is fairly characterized as a 'tap on the shoulder' process," in which managers have discretion about whose shoulders to tap. Vacancies are not regularly posted; from among those employees satisfying minimum qualifications, managers choose whom to promote on the basis of their own subjective impressions.

Wal-Mart's compensation policies also operate uniformly across stores, the District Court found. The retailer leaves open a $2 band for every position's hourly pay rate. Wal-Mart provides no standards or criteria for setting wages within that band, and thus does nothing to counter unconscious bias on the part of supervisors.

Wal-Mart's supervisors do not make their discretionary decisions in a vacuum. The District Court reviewed means Wal-Mart used to maintain a "carefully constructed . . . corporate culture," such as frequent meetings to reinforce the common way of thinking, regular transfers of managers between stores to ensure uniformity throughout the company, monitoring of stores "on a close and constant basis," and "Wal-Mart TV," "broadcas[t] . . . into all stores."

The plaintiffs' evidence, including class members' tales of their own experiences, suggests that gender bias suffused Wal-Mart's company culture. Among illustrations, senior management often refer to female associates as "little Janie Qs."

* * *

The District Court's identification of a common question, whether Wal-Mart's pay and promotions policies gave rise to unlawful discrimination, was hardly infirm. The practice of delegating to supervisors large discretion to make personnel decisions, uncontrolled by formal standards, has long been known to have the potential to produce disparate effects. Managers, like all humankind, may be prey to biases of which they are unaware. The risk of discrimination is heightened when those managers are predominantly of one sex, and are steeped in a corporate culture that perpetuates gender stereotypes.

* * *

The plaintiffs' allegations state claims of gender discrimination in the form of biased decisionmaking in both pay and promotions. The evidence reviewed by the District Court adequately demonstrated that resolving those claims would necessitate examination of particular policies and practices alleged to affect, adversely and globally, women employed at Wal-Mart's stores. Rule 23(a)(2), setting a necessary but not a sufficient criterion for class-action certification, demands nothing further.

* * *

Wal-Mart's delegation of discretion over pay and promotions is a policy uniform throughout all stores. The very nature of discretion is that people will exercise it in various ways. A system of delegated discretion is a practice actionable under Title VII when it produces discriminatory outcomes. A finding that Wal-Mart's pay and promotions practices in fact violate the law would be the first step in the usual order of proof for plaintiffs seeking individual remedies for company-wide discrimination. That each individual employee's unique circumstances will ultimately determine whether she is entitled to backpay or damages, should not factor into the Rule 23(a)(2) determination.

NOTE

The *Dukes* case raised the bar on class certification in systemic discrimination cases by emphasizing the narrowness of the commonality requirement needed to obtain class certification under Federal Rule of Civil Procedure 23(a)(2). The Court's opinion, which was divided 5–4 in this part, indicated that commonality could be found by pointing to a uniform biased testing procedure or to a general policy of discrimination. The "bare existence of delegated discretion" the Court made clear is insufficient to establish commonality. The Court was unanimous, however in its opinion that individualized claims for monetary damages, including backpay, could not be certified under Rule 23(b)(2) and instead needed to be certified, if at all, under the more onerous requirements of Rule 23(b)(3). The opinion has been the subject of substantial commentary as well as numerous proposals for legislative reform. Some scholars have argued that the Court's holding regarding the commonality requirement cripples large class action challenges to the employment practices—particularly subjective practices—of large employers. See generally Catherine Fisk & Erwin Chemerinsky, The Failing Faith in Class Actions: Wal-Mart v. Dukes and AT&T Mobility v. Concepcion, 7 Duke J. Const. L. & Pub. Pol'y 73 (2011); John M. Husband and Bradford J. Williams, Wal-Mart v. Dukes Redux: The Future of the Sprawling Class Action, 40 Colo. Law. 53 (Sept. 2011). Other scholars have argued, however, that the case's holding on the commonality requirement has actually had less impact on subsequent case law than has the Court's ruling on the limited remedies available under Rule 23(b)(2). See Elizabeth Tippett, Robbing a Barren Vault: the Implications of Dukes v. Wal-Mart for Cases Challenging Subjective Employment Practices, 29 Hofstra Lab. & Emp. L. J. 433 (2012); Melissa Hart, Civil Rights and Systemic Wrongs, 32 Berk. J. of Emp. & Lab. Law, 455 (2011). Moreover, in EEOC v. Bass Pro Outdoor World, L.L.C., 826 F.3d 791, 797–98 (5th Cir. 2016), the Fifth Circuit held that the EEOC was not required to meet the Rule 23 prerequisites of numerosity, commonality, typicality, and adequacy of representation when bringing an enforcement action in its own name because " '[w]hen the EEOC acts, albeit at the behest of and for the benefit of specific individuals, it acts also to vindicate the public interest in preventing employment discrimination.' "

(i) Harassment

The social and legal unacceptability of sexual harassment in the workplace and other settings (e.g., education, the military) is such an established part of our culture it is easy to forget its relatively recent development. The legal doctrine of sexual harassment emerged in the mid-1970s. In 1980, the EEOC issued guidelines specifying that sexual harassment constituted a form of sex discrimination prohibited by Title VII. The term sexual harassment was defined as "[u]nwelcome sexual advances, requests for sexual favors, and other verbal or physical conduct of a sexual nature." Regardless of whether the harassment is an economic quid pro quo, it will violate Title VII if the "conduct has the purpose or effect of unreasonably interfering with an individual's work performance or creating an intimidating, hostile, or offensive working environment." 29 C.F.R. § 1604.11.

The two types of sexual harassment defined by the EEOC have been recognized by the courts. Quid pro quo sexual harassment occurs when agreement to engage in sexual activity is made a condition of employment. Hostile environment sexual harassment exists when statements or conduct of a sexual nature creates an environment of intimidation, insult, or ridicule. In the Supreme Court's first sexual harassment case, Meritor Sav. Bank, FSB v. Vinson, 477 U.S. 57 (1986), a unanimous Court recognized both forms of sexual harassment and further held that "unwelcomeness" and not "consent" is the standard for determining whether unlawful harassment had occurred.

Although courts continue to apply both theories, as a practical matter, the overwhelming majority of sexual harassment cases involve conduct that allegedly creates a hostile environment. Indeed, it may be fair to say that the term "sexual harassment" is somewhat misleading in that the typical case consists of gender-based harassment in which speech or conduct of a sexual nature often plays an important part. Thus, sexual harassment is less about sex than harassment and therefore is closely related to harassment based on race, color, religion, or national origin, which are also prohibited by Title VII.

Vicki Schultz, Talking About Harassment[*]
9 J.L. & Pol'y 417, 418–420 (2001).

I have come to believe that we need to fundamentally change the way we think about harassment. In my view, we need to move away from the model that has prevailed over the last twenty-years. In an earlier work I have referred to this model as the sexual desire-dominance model, but today I am going to call it the sexual model for short.

Under the sexual model, the quintessential case of harassment involves a powerful, typically older male boss who makes unwanted sexual advances toward a less powerful female subordinate. * * * I have come to believe that this is a fundamentally misguided way to think about sex harassment.

* * *

One problem with the sexual model is that it is top-down; indeed, the entire conception of dominance and subordination that is used in some of the literature is top-down. Top-down models assume that power follows from formal roles and that it flows from those who occupy higher positions down onto those who occupy lower positions. Yet power is not always contained in formal structures, and it can circulate in many unexpected directions. In the workplace, many women (and men) experience horizontal harassment that involves exclusion by peers, not simply vertical harassment that involves coercion from bosses. Indeed, the day-to-day interactions through which co-workers create relationships that mark some people as insiders and other people as outsiders are a crucial part of the dynamic that sustains sex segregation and hierarchy in the workplace. Harassment is not always about who is on top and who is on bottom; it is also about who is "in" and who is "out."

I want to move our legal and cultural understanding of sex harassment toward a model that places exclusion from work, rather than abuse of sexuality, at the forefront. The sexual model treats harassment

[*] Reprinted by permission.

as a way for men to use *work* to appropriate *sex* from women. But we can see harassment as a way for men (or women) to use *sex* to appropriate *work* for themselves. Some men resort to sexual assault, along with other behaviors that intimidate and exclude women, as a way to claim the best jobs as masculine terrain.

Work is one of the most important distributional goods that exists in our society; it provides the foundation for citizenship, economic security, community, and self-esteem. Indeed, work is central to most people's sense of themselves, including their sense of themselves as men or women. So, it should not surprise us that some men will try to monopolize good jobs to safeguard their economic superiority and to secure their manly identities. Male workers can define their jobs as the domain of those who are suitably "masculine," for example, by driving away the women and even men who do not fit the projected masculine image, or by marking those who remain as different and inferior.

Harris v. Forklift Systems, Inc.
510 U.S. 17 (1993).

■ JUSTICE O'CONNOR delivered the opinion of the Court.

In this case we consider the definition of a discriminatorily "abusive work environment" (also known as a "hostile work environment") under Title VII of the Civil Rights Act of 1964.

Teresa Harris worked as a manager at Forklift Systems, Inc., an equipment rental company, from April 1985 until October 1987. Charles Hardy was Forklift's president.

The Magistrate found that, throughout Harris' time at Forklift, Hardy often insulted her because of her gender and often made her the target of unwanted sexual innuendos. Hardy told Harris on several occasions, in the presence of other employees, "You're a woman, what do you know" and "We need a man as the rental manager"; at least once, he told her she was "a dumb ass woman." Again in front of others, he suggested that the two of them "go to the Holiday Inn to negotiate [Harris'] raise." Hardy occasionally asked Harris and other female employees to get coins from his front pants pocket. He threw objects on the ground in front of Harris and other women, and asked them to pick the objects up. He made sexual innuendos about Harris' and other women's clothing.

In mid-August 1987, Harris complained to Hardy about his conduct. Hardy said he was surprised that Harris was offended, claimed he was only joking, and apologized. He also promised he would stop, and based on this assurance Harris stayed on the job. But in early September, Hardy began anew: While Harris was arranging a deal with one of Forklift's customers, he asked her, again in front of other employees,

"What did you do, promise the guy * * * some [sex] Saturday night?" On October 1, Harris collected her paycheck and quit.

Harris then sued Forklift, claiming that Hardy's conduct had created an abusive work environment for her because of her gender. The United States District Court for the Middle District of Tennessee, adopting the report and recommendation of the Magistrate, found this to be "a close case," but held that Hardy's conduct did not create an abusive environment. The court found that some of Hardy's comments "offended [Harris], and would offend the reasonable woman," but that they were not

> "so severe as to be expected to seriously affect [Harris'] psychological well-being. A reasonable woman manager under like circumstances would have been offended by Hardy, but his conduct would not have risen to the level of interfering with that person's work performance.

> "Neither do I believe that [Harris] was subjectively so offended that she suffered injury * * *. Although Hardy may at times have genuinely offended [Harris], I do not believe that he created a working environment so poisoned as to be intimidating or abusive to [Harris]."

In focusing on the employee's psychological well-being, the District Court was following Circuit precedent. See Rabidue v. Osceola Refining Co., 805 F.2d 611, 620 (C.A.6 1986), cert. denied, 481 U.S. 1041 (1987). The United States Court of Appeals for the Sixth Circuit affirmed in a brief unpublished decision.

We granted certiorari to resolve a conflict among the Circuits on whether conduct, to be actionable as "abusive work environment" harassment (no *quid pro quo* harassment issue is present here), must "seriously affect [an employee's] psychological well-being" or lead the plaintiff to "suffe[r] injury." Compare *Rabidue* (requiring serious effect on psychological well-being); Vance v. Southern Bell Telephone & Telegraph Co., 863 F.2d 1503, 1510 (C.A.11 1989) (same); and Downes v. FAA, 775 F.2d 288, 292 (C.A.Fed. 1985) (same), with Ellison v. Brady, 924 F.2d 872, 877–878 (C.A.9 1991) (rejecting such a requirement).

Title VII of the Civil Rights Act of 1964 makes it "an unlawful employment practice for an employer * * * to discriminate against any individual with respect to his compensation, terms, conditions, or privileges of employment, because of such individual's race, color, religion, sex, or national origin." As we made clear in Meritor Savings Bank v. Vinson, 477 U.S. 57 (1986), this language "is not limited to 'economic' or 'tangible' discrimination. The phrase 'terms, conditions, or privileges of employment' evinces a congressional intent 'to strike at the entire spectrum of disparate treatment of men and women' in employment," which includes requiring people to work in a discriminatorily hostile or abusive environment. When the workplace is permeated with "discriminatory intimidation, ridicule, and insult," that is "sufficiently severe or pervasive to alter the conditions of the victim's employment and create an abusive working environment," Title VII is violated.

This standard, which we reaffirm today, takes a middle path between making actionable any conduct that is merely offensive and requiring the conduct to cause a tangible psychological injury. As we pointed out in *Meritor,* "mere utterance of an * * * epithet which engenders offensive feelings in a employee," does not sufficiently affect the conditions of employment to implicate Title VII. Conduct that is not severe or pervasive enough to create an objectively hostile or abusive work environment—an environment that a reasonable person would find hostile or abusive—is beyond Title VII's purview. Likewise, if the victim does not subjectively perceive the environment to be abusive, the conduct has not actually altered the conditions of the victim's employment, and there is no Title VII violation.

But Title VII comes into play before the harassing conduct leads to a nervous breakdown. A discriminatorily abusive work environment, even one that does not seriously affect employees' psychological well-being, can and often will detract from employees' job performance, discourage employees from remaining on the job, or keep them from advancing in their careers. Moreover, even without regard to these tangible effects, the very fact that the discriminatory conduct was so severe or pervasive that it created a work environment abusive to employees because of their race, gender, religion, or national origin offends Title VII's broad rule of workplace equality. The appalling conduct alleged in *Meritor,* and the reference in that case to environments " 'so heavily polluted with discrimination as to destroy completely the emotional and psychological stability of minority group workers,' " merely present some especially egregious examples of harassment. They do not mark the boundary of what is actionable.

We therefore believe the District Court erred in relying on whether the conduct "seriously affect[ed] plaintiff's psychological well-being" or led her to "suffe[r] injury." Such an inquiry may needlessly focus the factfinder's attention on concrete psychological harm, an element Title VII does not require. Certainly Title VII bars conduct that would seriously affect a reasonable person's psychological well-being, but the statute is not limited to such conduct. So long as the environment would reasonably be perceived, and is perceived, as hostile or abusive, there is no need for it also to be psychologically injurious.

This is not, and by its nature cannot be, a mathematically precise test. We need not answer today all the potential questions it raises, nor specifically address the EEOC's new regulations on this subject, see 58 Fed.Reg. 51266 (1993) (proposed 29 CFR §§ 1609.1, 1609.2); see also 29 CFR § 1604.11 (1993). But we can say that whether an environment is "hostile" or "abusive" can be determined only by looking at all the circumstances. These may include the frequency of the discriminatory conduct; its severity; whether it is physically threatening or humiliating, or a mere offensive utterance; and whether it unreasonably interferes with an employee's work performance. The effect on the employee's psychological well-being is, of course, relevant to determining whether the plaintiff actually found the environment abusive. But while psychological harm, like any other relevant factor, may be taken into account, no single factor is required.

Forklift, while conceding that a requirement that the conduct seriously affect psychological well-being is unfounded, argues that the District Court nonetheless correctly applied the *Meritor* standard. We disagree. Though the District Court did conclude that the work environment was not "intimidating or abusive to [Harris]," it did so only after finding that the conduct was not "so severe as to be expected to seriously affect plaintiff's psychological well-being," and that Harris was not "subjectively so offended that she suffered injury," *ibid.* The District Court's application of these incorrect standards may well have influenced its ultimate conclusion, especially given that the court found this to be a "close case."

We therefore reverse the judgment of the Court of Appeals, and remand the case for further proceedings consistent with this opinion.

■ JUSTICE SCALIA, concurring.

Meritor Savings Bank v. Vinson, 477 U.S. 57 (1986), held that Title VII prohibits sexual harassment that takes the form of a hostile work environment. The Court stated that sexual harassment is actionable if it is "sufficiently severe or pervasive 'to alter the conditions of [the victim's] employment and create an abusive work environment.'" Today's opinion elaborates that the challenged conduct must be severe or pervasive enough "to create an objectively hostile or abusive work environment— an environment that a reasonable person would find hostile or abusive."

"Abusive" (or "hostile," which in this context I take to mean the same thing) does not seem to me a very clear standard—and I do not think clarity is at all increased by adding the adverb "objectively" or by appealing to a "reasonable person's" notion of what the vague word means. Today's opinion does list a number of factors that contribute to abusiveness, but since it neither says how much of each is necessary (an impossible task) nor identifies any single factor as determinative, it thereby adds little certitude. As a practical matter, today's holding lets virtually unguided juries decide whether sex-related conduct engaged in (or permitted by) an employer is egregious enough to warrant an award of damages. One might say that what constitutes "negligence" (a traditional jury question) is not much more clear and certain than what constitutes "abusiveness." Perhaps so. But the class of plaintiffs seeking to recover for negligence is limited to those who have suffered harm, whereas under this statute "abusiveness" is to be the test of whether legal harm has been suffered, opening more expansive vistas of litigation.

Be that as it may, I know of no alternative to the course the Court today has taken. One of the factors mentioned in the Court's nonexhaustive list—whether the conduct unreasonably interferes with an employee's work performance—would, if it were made an absolute test, provide greater guidance to juries and employers. But I see no basis for such a limitation in the language of the statute. Accepting *Meritor*'s interpretation of the term "conditions of employment" as the law, the test is not whether work has been impaired, but whether working conditions have been discriminatorily altered. I know of no test more faithful to the inherently vague statutory language than the one the Court today adopts. For these reasons, I join the opinion of the Court.

■ JUSTICE GINSBURG, concurring.

Today the Court reaffirms the holding of Meritor Savings Bank v. Vinson, 477 U.S. 57, 66 (1986): "[A] plaintiff may establish a violation of Title VII by proving that discrimination based on sex has created a hostile or abusive work environment." The critical issue, Title VII's text indicates, is whether members of one sex are exposed to disadvantageous terms or conditions of employment to which members of the other sex are not exposed. As the Equal Employment Opportunity Commission emphasized, the adjudicator's inquiry should center, dominantly, on whether the discriminatory conduct has unreasonably interfered with the plaintiff's work performance. To show such interference, "the plaintiff need not prove that his or her tangible productivity has declined as a result of the harassment." It suffices to prove that a reasonable person subjected to the discriminatory conduct would find, as the plaintiff did, that the harassment so altered working conditions as to "ma[k]e it more difficult to do the job." * * *

The Court's opinion, which I join, seems to me in harmony with the view expressed in this concurring statement.

NOTES AND QUESTIONS

1. The Court in *Harris* resolved the issue of whether the plaintiff must show severe psychological distress in a sexual harassment case. Another vexing issue is whether the "reasonable person" or the "reasonable woman" standard should be applied. See Ellison v. Brady, 924 F.2d 872 (9th Cir. 1991). Without specifically addressing this issue, all three opinions in *Harris* refer to the "reasonable person."

2. A former employee brought an action against her former employer alleging sexual harassment and retaliation. The employee claimed damages for both past and ongoing emotional distress. Is the employer entitled to conduct a psychological examination of her? See Jansen v. Packaging Corp. of America, 158 F.R.D. 409 (N.D.Ill.1994) (held: yes, but it did not have the right to use an expert of its own choice). How far should the employer's right of discovery extend? What are the dangers?

In Beckford v. Department of Corrections, 605 F.3d 951 (11th Cir. 2010), 14 female former employees at a state correctional facility sued the state based on pervasive sexual harassment perpetrated by male inmates. The Eleventh Circuit held that the defendant made almost no effort to protect the women employees and that reasonable remedial measures were available, including referring the incidents for criminal prosecution.

3. Justice Ginsburg's concurring opinion suggests that the focus should be on "whether the discriminatory conduct has unreasonably interfered with the plaintiff's work performance." This does not require a loss of productivity; it can be established by an alteration of working conditions that simply makes it "more difficult to do the job." How is the court to determine when a job has been made more difficult?

4. To be actionable under Title VII, hostile environment sexual harassment must be pervasive. In Clark County Sch. Dist. v. Breeden, 532 U.S. 268 (2001), an employee complained about one isolated sexually suggestive comment by her supervisor. Shortly thereafter, the employee was transferred, which she claimed was an act of retaliation. In her action under Title VII she asserted that her sexual harassment complaint was protected because she reasonably believed that the complained-of conduct was unlawful even though it was not. The Supreme Court held that because no one could reasonably believe that the conduct was actionable, her complaint was unprotected, thereby declining to address the broader issue of whether her conduct would have been protected if it were reasonable.

5. The EEOC Guidelines state that an employer "may also be responsible for the acts of non-employees, with respect to sexual harassment of employees in the workplace, where the employer (or its agents or supervisory employees) knows or should have known of the conduct and fails to take immediate and appropriate corrective action." 29 C.F.R. § 1604.11(e). To what extent is the employer liable for sexual harassment by customers? In Lockard v. Pizza Hut, Inc., 162 F.3d 1062 (10th Cir. 1998), the failure of a supervisor to address sexual harassment of a waitress by customers established employer liability. According to the court, an employer that tolerates sexual harassment on its premises "should be held liable regardless of whether the environment was created by a co-employee or nonemployee, since the employer ultimately controls the conditions of the work environment."

6. In addition to Title VII remedies the victim of sexual harassment may be able to proceed on a breach of contract theory, see Monge v. Beebe Rubber Co., 316 A.2d 549 (N.H.1974), or a tort theory, see Phillips v. Smalley Maint. Servs., 435 So.2d 705 (Ala.1983). Sexual harassment also may support tort actions for assault, battery, and intentional infliction of emotional distress. See Rojo v. Kliger, 801 P.2d 373 (Cal.1990); Ford v. Revlon, Inc., 734 P.2d 580 (Ariz.1987); Johnson v. Ramsey County, 424 N.W.2d 800 (Minn.App.1988). See generally Regina Austin, Employer Abuse, Worker Resistance, and the Tort of Intentional Infliction of Emotional Distress, 41 Stan.L.Rev. 1 (1988).

7. The courts have resisted attempts to extend sexual harassment theory to a wider range of allegedly unfair treatment. For example, in DeClue v. Central Illinois Light Co., 223 F.3d 434 (7th Cir. 2000), the Seventh Circuit held that a female lineman could not maintain a hostile environment sexual harassment claim based on her employer's failure to provide restroom facilities for her. The majority said that a claim for disparate impact sex discrimination would lie, but this was not raised by the plaintiff. In her partial dissent, Judge Ilana Diamond Rovner asserted that the employer's failure to remedy the problem despite repeated attempts could be viewed as subjecting her to a hostile work environment.

8.   Harassment may be based on a variety of factors other than sex. It may be based on race, Swinton v. Potomac Corp., 270 F.3d 794 (9th Cir. 2001), national origin, Erebia v. Chrysler Plastic Prods. Corp., 772 F.2d 1250 (6th Cir.1985), cert. denied, 475 U.S. 1015 (1986), religion, Weiss v. United States, 595 F.Supp. 1050 (E.D.Va.1984), age, Crawford v. Medina Gen. Hosp., 96 F.3d 830 (6th Cir. 1996), or disability, Fox v. General Motors, 247 F.3d 169 (4th Cir. 2001). These other forms of harassment are invariably of the "abusive environment" variety.

Oncale v. Sundowner Offshore Services, Inc.
523 U.S. 75 (1998).

■ JUSTICE SCALIA delivered the opinion of the Court.

This case presents the question whether workplace harassment can violate Title VII's prohibition against "discriminat[ion] . . . because of . . . sex," 42 U.S.C. § 2000e–2(a)(1), when the harasser and the harassed employee are of the same sex.

I

The District Court having granted summary judgment for respondent, we must assume the facts to be as alleged by petitioner Joseph Oncale. The precise details are irrelevant to the legal point we must decide, and in the interest of both brevity and dignity we shall describe them only generally. In late October 1991, Oncale was working for respondent Sundowner Offshore Services on a Chevron U.S.A., Inc., oil platform in the Gulf of Mexico. He was employed as a roustabout on an eight-man crew which included respondents John Lyons, Danny Pippen, and Brandon Johnson. Lyons, the crane operator, and Pippen, the driller, had supervisory authority. On several occasions, Oncale was forcibly subjected to sex-related, humiliating actions against him by Lyons, Pippen and Johnson in the presence of the rest of the crew. Pippen and Lyons also physically assaulted Oncale in a sexual manner, and Lyons threatened him with rape.

Oncale's complaints to supervisory personnel produced no remedial action; in fact, the company's Safety Compliance Clerk, Valent Hohen, told Oncale that Lyons and Pippen "picked [on] him all the time too," and called him a name suggesting homosexuality. Oncale eventually quit—asking that his pink slip reflect that he "voluntarily left due to sexual harassment and verbal abuse." When asked at his deposition why he left

Sundowner, Oncale stated "I felt that if I didn't leave my job, that I would be raped or forced to have sex."

Oncale filed a complaint against Sundowner in the United States District Court for the Eastern District of Louisiana, alleging that he was discriminated against in his employment because of his sex. Relying on the Fifth Circuit's decision in Garcia v. Elf Atochem North America, 28 F.3d 446, 451–452 (C.A.5 1994), the district court held that "Mr. Oncale, a male, has no cause of action under Title VII for harassment by male co-workers." On appeal, a panel of the Fifth Circuit concluded that *Garcia* was binding Circuit precedent, and affirmed. We granted certiorari.

II

Title VII of the Civil Rights Act of 1964 provides, in relevant part, that "[i]t shall be an unlawful employment practice for an employer . . . to discriminate against any individual with respect to his compensation, terms, conditions, or privileges of employment, because of such individual's race, color, religion, sex, or national origin." We have held that this not only covers "terms" and "conditions" in the narrow contractual sense, but "evinces a congressional intent to strike at the entire spectrum of disparate treatment of men and women in employment." Meritor Savings Bank, FSB v. Vinson, 477 U.S. 57, 64 (1986) (citations and internal quotation marks omitted). "When the workplace is permeated with discriminatory intimidation, ridicule, and insult that is sufficiently severe or pervasive to alter the condition of the victim's employment and create an abusive working environment, Title VII is violated." Harris v. Forklift Systems Inc., 510 U.S. 17, 21 (1993) (citations and internal quotation marks omitted.)

Title VII's prohibition of discrimination "because of . . . sex" protects men as well as women, and in the related context of racial discrimination in the workplace we have rejected any conclusive presumption that an employer will not discriminate against members of his own race. "Because of the many facets of human motivation, it would be unwise to presume as a matter of law that human beings of one definable group will not discriminate against other members of that group." In Johnson v. Transportation Agency, Santa Clara Cty., 480 U.S. 616 (1987), a male employee claimed that his employer discriminated against him because of his sex when it preferred a female employee for promotion. Although we ultimately rejected the claim on other grounds, we did not consider it significant that the supervisor who made that decision was also a man. If our precedents leave any doubt on the question, we hold today that nothing in Title VII necessarily bars a claim of discrimination "because of . . . sex." merely because the plaintiff and the defendant (or the person charged with acting on behalf of the defendant) are of the same sex.

Courts have had little trouble with that principle in cases like *Johnson,* where an employee claims to have been passed over for a job or promotion. But when the issue arises in the context of a "hostile environment" sexual harassment claim, the state and federal courts have taken a bewildering variety of stances. Some, like the Fifth Circuit in this case, have held that same-sex sexual harassment claims are never cognizable under Title VII. Other decisions say that such claims are actionable only if the plaintiff can prove that the harasser is homosexual (and thus presumably motivated by sexual desire). Still others suggest that workplace harassment that is sexual in content is always actionable, regardless of the harasser's sex, sexual orientation, or motivations.

We see no justification in the statutory language or our precedents for a categorical rule excluding same-sex harassment claims from the coverage of Title VII. As some courts have observed, male-on-male sexual harassment in the workplace was assuredly not the principal evil Congress was concerned with when it enacted Title VII. But statutory prohibitions often go beyond the principal evil to cover reasonably comparable evils, and it is ultimately the provisions of our laws rather than the principal concerns of our legislators by which we are governed. Title VII prohibits "discriminat[ion] . . . because of . . . sex" in the "terms" or "conditions" of employment. Our holding that this includes sexual harassment must extend to sexual harassment of any kind that meets the statutory requirements.

Respondents and their amici contend that recognizing liability for same-sex harassment will transform Title VII into a general civility code for the American workplace. But that risk is no greater for same-sex than for opposite-sex harassment, and is adequately met by careful attention to the requirements of the statute. Title VII does not prohibit all verbal or physical harassment in the workplace; it is directed only at "*discriminat[ion]* . . . because of . . . sex." We have never held that workplace harassment, even harassment between men and women, is automatically discrimination because of sex merely because the words used have sexual content or connotations. "The critical issue, Title VII's text indicates, is whether members of one sex are exposed to disadvantageous terms or conditions of employment to which members of the other sex are not exposed."

Courts and juries have found the inference of discrimination easy to draw in most male-female sexual harassment situations, because the challenged conduct typically involves explicit or implicit proposals of sexual activity; it is reasonable to assume those proposals would not have been made to someone of the same sex. The same chain of inference would be available to a plaintiff alleging same-sex harassment, if there were credible evidence that the harasser was homosexual. But harassing conduct need not be motivated by sexual desire to support an inference of discrimination on the basis of sex. A trier of fact might reasonably find such discrimination, for example, if a female victim is harassed in such sex-specific and derogatory terms by another woman as to make it clear that the harasser is motivated by general hostility to the presence of women in the workplace. A same-sex harassment plaintiff may also, of course, offer direct comparative evidence about how the alleged harasser treated members of both sexes in a mixed-sex workplace. Whatever evidentiary route the plaintiff chooses to follow, he or she must always prove that the conduct at issue was not merely tinged with offensive sexual connotations, but actually constituted *"discrimina[tion] . . . because of . . . sex."*

And there is another requirement that prevents Title VII from expanding into a general civility code: As we emphasized in *Meritor* and *Harris,* the statute does not reach genuine but innocuous differences in the ways men and women routinely interact with members of the same sex and of the opposite sex. The prohibition of harassment on the basis of sex requires neither asexuality nor androgyny in the workplace; it forbids only behavior so objectively offensive as to alter the "conditions" of the victim's employment. "Conduct that is not severe or pervasive enough to create an objectively hostile or abusive work environment—an environment that a reasonable person would find hostile or abusive—is beyond Title VII's purview." We have always regarded that requirement as crucial, and as sufficient to ensure that courts and juries do not mistake ordinary socializing in the workplace—such as male-on-male horseplay or intersexual flirtation—for discriminatory "conditions of employment."

We have emphasized, moreover, that the objective severity of harassment should be judged from the perspective of a reasonable person in the plaintiff's position, considering "all the circumstances." In same-sex (as in all) harassment cases, that inquiry requires careful consideration of the social context in which particular behavior occurs and is experienced by its target. A professional football player's working environment is not severely or pervasively abusive, for example, if the coach smacks him on the buttocks as he heads onto the field—even if the same behavior would reasonably be experienced as abusive by the coach's secretary (male or female) back at the office. The real social impact of workplace behavior often depends on a constellation of surrounding circumstances, expectations, and relationships which are not fully captured by a simple recitation of the words used or the physical acts performed. Common sense, and an appropriate sensitivity to social context, will enable courts and juries to distinguish between simple teasing or roughhousing among members of the same sex, and conduct which a reasonable person in the plaintiff's position would find severely hostile or abusive.

Because we concluded that sex discrimination consisting of same-sex sexual harassment is actionable under Title VII, the judgment of the Court of Appeals for the Fifth Circuit is reversed, and the case is remanded for further proceedings consistent with this opinion.

It is so ordered.

■ JUSTICE THOMAS, concurring.

I concur because the Court stresses that in every sexual harassment case, the plaintiff must plead and ultimately prove Title VII's statutory requirement that there be discrimination "because of . . . sex."

NOTE

The Supreme Court in *Oncale* made clear that although same sex harassment could be actionable, the harassment had to be "because of" sex. The Court discussed several ways that a plaintiff could show that harassment was because of sex. Although the Supreme Court in *Oncale* did not explicitly mention sex stereotyping, plaintiffs after *Oncale* have regularly relied on the sex stereotyping logic of *Price Waterhouse* to prove that harassment was because of sex. See Nichols v. Azteca Restaurant Enter., Inc., 256 F.3d 864 (9th Cir. 2001).

Pennsylvania State Police v. Suders

542 U.S. 129 (2004).

■ JUSTICE GINSBURG delivered the opinion of the Court.

Plaintiff-respondent Nancy Drew Suders alleged sexually harassing conduct by her supervisors, officers of the Pennsylvania State Police (PSP), of such severity she was forced to resign. The question presented concerns the proof burdens parties bear when a sexual harassment/ constructive discharge claim of that character is asserted under Title VII of the Civil Rights Act of 1964.

To establish hostile work environment, plaintiffs like Suders must show harassing behavior "sufficiently severe or pervasive to alter the conditions of [their] employment." Meritor Savings Bank, FSB v. Vinson, 477 U.S. 57, 67 (1986); see Harris v. Forklift Systems, Inc., 510 U.S. 17, 22 (1993). Beyond that, we hold, to establish "constructive discharge," the plaintiff must make a further showing: She must show that the abusive working environment became so intolerable that her resignation qualified as a fitting response. An employer may defend against such a claim by showing both (1) that it had installed a readily accessible and effective policy for reporting and resolving complaints of sexual harassment, and (2) that the plaintiff unreasonably failed to avail herself of that employer-provided preventive or remedial apparatus. This affirmative defense will not be available to the employer, however, if the plaintiff quits in reasonable response to an employer-sanctioned adverse action officially changing her employment status or situation, for example, a humiliating demotion, extreme cut in pay, or transfer to a position in which she would face unbearable working conditions. In so ruling today, we follow the path marked by our 1998 decisions in Burlington Industries, Inc. v. Ellerth, 524 U.S. 742 (1998) and Faragher v. Boca Raton, 524 U.S. 775 (1998).

I

Because this case was decided against Suders in the District Court on the PSP's motion for summary judgment, we recite the facts, as summarized by the Court of Appeals, in the light most favorable to Suders. In March 1998, the PSP hired Suders as a police communications operator for the McConnellsburg barracks. Suders' supervisors were Sergeant Eric D. Easton, Station Commander at the McConnellsburg barracks, Patrol Corporal William D. Baker, and Corporal Eric B. Prendergast. Those three supervisors subjected Suders to a continuous barrage of sexual harassment that ceased only when she resigned from the force.

Easton "would bring up [the subject of] people having sex with animals" each time Suders entered his office. He told Prendergast, in front of Suders, that young girls should be given instruction in how to gratify men with oral sex. Easton also would sit down near Suders, wearing spandex shorts, and spread his legs apart. Apparently imitating a move popularized by television wrestling, Baker repeatedly made an obscene gesture in Suders' presence by grabbing his genitals and shouting out a vulgar comment inviting oral sex. Baker made this gesture as many as five-to-ten times per night throughout Suders' employment at the barracks. Suders once told Baker she " 'd[id]n't think [he] should be doing this' "; Baker responded by jumping on a chair and again performing the gesture, with the accompanying vulgarity. Further, Baker would "rub his rear end in front of her and remark 'I have a nice ass, don't I?' " Prendergast told Suders " 'the village idiot could do her job' "; wearing black gloves, he would pound on furniture to intimidate her.

Nancy Drew Suders

Photo courtesy of the Associated Press.

In June 1998, Prendergast accused Suders of taking a missing accident file home with her. After that incident, Suders approached the

PSP's Equal Employment Opportunity Officer, Virginia Smith-Elliott, and told her she "might need some help." Smith-Elliott gave Suders her telephone number, but neither woman followed up on the conversation. On August 18, 1998, Suders contacted Smith-Elliott again, this time stating that she was being harassed and was afraid. Smith-Elliott told Suders to file a complaint, but did not tell her how to obtain the necessary form. Smith-Elliott's response and the manner in which it was conveyed appeared to Suders insensitive and unhelpful.

Two days later, Suders' supervisors arrested her for theft, and Suders resigned from the force. The theft arrest occurred in the following circumstances. Suders had several times taken a computer-skills exam to satisfy a PSP job requirement. Each time, Suders' supervisors told her that she had failed. Suders one day came upon her exams in a set of drawers in the women's locker room. She concluded that her supervisors had never forwarded the tests for grading and that their reports of her failures were false. Regarding the tests as her property, Suders removed them from the locker room. Upon finding that the exams had been removed, Suders' supervisors devised a plan to arrest her for theft. The officers dusted the drawer in which the exams had been stored with a theft-detection powder that turns hands blue when touched. As anticipated by Easton, Baker, and Prendergast, Suders attempted to return the tests to the drawer, whereupon her hands turned telltale blue. The supervisors then apprehended and handcuffed her, photographed her blue hands, and commenced to question her. Suders had previously prepared a written resignation, which she tendered soon after the supervisors detained her. Nevertheless, the supervisors initially refused to release her. Instead, they brought her to an interrogation room, gave her warnings under Miranda v. Arizona, 384 U.S. 436 (1966), and continued to question her. Suders reiterated that she wanted to resign, and Easton then let her leave. The PSP never brought theft charges against her.

In September 2000, Suders sued the PSP in Federal District Court, alleging, *inter alia*, that she had been subjected to sexual harassment and constructively discharged, in violation of Title VII of the Civil Rights Act of 1964. At the close of discovery, the District Court granted the PSP's motion for summary judgment. Suders' testimony, the District Court recognized, sufficed to permit a trier of fact to conclude that the supervisors had created a hostile work environment. The court nevertheless held that the PSP was not vicariously liable for the supervisors' conduct.

In so concluding, the District Court referred to our 1998 decision in *Faragher*. In *Faragher*, along with *Ellerth* decided the same day, the Court distinguished between supervisor harassment unaccompanied by an adverse official act and supervisor harassment attended by "a tangible employment action." Both decisions hold that an employer is strictly liable for supervisor harassment that "culminates in a tangible employment action, such as discharge, demotion, or undesirable reassignment." But when no tangible employment action is taken, both decisions also hold, the employer may raise an affirmative defense to liability, subject to proof by a preponderance of the evidence: "The defense comprises two necessary elements: (a) that the employer exercised reasonable care to prevent and correct promptly any sexually harassing behavior, and (b) that the plaintiff employee unreasonably failed to take advantage of any preventive or corrective opportunities provided by the employer or to avoid harm otherwise."

Suders' hostile work environment claim was untenable as a matter of law, the District Court stated, because she "unreasonably failed to avail herself of the PSP's internal procedures for reporting any harassment." Resigning just two days after she first mentioned anything about harassment to Equal Employment Opportunity Officer Smith-Elliott, the court noted, Suders had "never given [the PSP] the opportunity to respond to [her] complaints." The District Court did not address Suders' constructive discharge claim.

The Court of Appeals for the Third Circuit reversed and remanded the case for disposition on the merits. The Third Circuit agreed with the District Court that Suders had presented evidence sufficient for a trier of fact to conclude that the supervisors had engaged in a "pattern of sexual harassment that was pervasive and regular." But the appeals court disagreed with the District Court in two fundamental respects. First, the Court of Appeals held that, even assuming the PSP could assert the affirmative defense described in *Ellerth* and *Faragher*, genuine issues of material fact existed concerning the effectiveness of the PSP's "program . . . to address sexual harassment claims." Second, the appeals court held that the District Court erred in failing to recognize that Suders had stated a claim of constructive discharge due to the hostile work environment.

* * *

II

Under the constructive discharge doctrine, an employee's reasonable decision to resign because of unendurable working conditions is assimilated to a formal discharge for remedial purposes. The inquiry is objective: Did working conditions become so intolerable that a reasonable person in the employee's position would have felt compelled to resign?

* * *

Although this Court has not had occasion earlier to hold that a claim for constructive discharge lies under Title VII, we have recognized constructive discharge in the labor-law context. Furthermore, we have stated that "Title VII is violated by either explicit or constructive alterations in the terms or conditions of employment." We agree with the lower courts and the EEOC that Title VII encompasses employer liability for a constructive discharge.

This case concerns an employer's liability for one subset of Title VII constructive discharge claims: constructive discharge resulting from sexual harassment, or "hostile work environment," attributable to a supervisor. Our starting point is the framework *Ellerth* and *Faragher* established to govern employer liability for sexual harassment by supervisors. As earlier noted, those decisions delineate two categories of hostile work environment claims: (1) harassment that "culminates in a tangible employment action," for which employers are strictly liable, and (2) harassment that takes place in the absence of a tangible employment action, to which employers may assert an affirmative defense. With the background set out above in mind, we turn to the key issues here at stake: Into which *Ellerth/Faragher* category do hostile-environment constructive discharge claims fall—and what proof burdens do the parties bear in such cases.

In *Ellerth* and *Faragher*, the plaintiffs-employees sought to hold their employers vicariously liable for sexual harassment by their supervisors, even though the plaintiffs "suffer[ed] no adverse, tangible job consequences." Setting out a framework for employer liability in those decisions, this Court noted that Title VII's definition of "employer" includes the employer's "agent[s]." We viewed that definition as a direction to "interpret Title VII based on agency principles." The Restatement (Second) of Agency (1957) (hereinafter Restatement), the Court noted, states (in its black-letter formulation) that an employer is liable for the acts of its agent when the agent " 'was aided in accomplishing the tort by the existence of the agency relation.' "

We then identified "a class of cases where, beyond question, more than the mere existence of the employment relation aids in commission of the harassment: when a supervisor takes a tangible employment action against the subordinate." A tangible employment action, the Court explained, "constitutes a significant change in employment status, such as hiring, firing, failing to promote, reassignment with significantly different responsibilities, or a decision causing a significant change in benefits." Unlike injuries that could equally be inflicted by a co-worker, we stated, tangible employment actions "fall within the special province of the supervisor," who "has been empowered by the company as . . . [an] agent to make economic decisions affecting other employees under his or her control." The tangible employment action, the Court elaborated, is, in essential character, "an official act of the enterprise, a company act." It is "the means by which the supervisor brings the official power of the enterprise to bear on subordinates." Often, the supervisor will "use [the company's] internal processes" and thereby "obtain the imprimatur of the enterprise." Ordinarily, the tangible employment decision "is documented in official company records, and may be subject to review by higher level supervisors." In sum, we stated, "when a supervisor takes a tangible employment action against a subordinate[,] . . . it would be implausible to interpret agency principles to allow an employer to escape liability."

When a supervisor's harassment of a subordinate does not culminate in a tangible employment action, the Court next explained, it is "less obvious" that the agency relation is the driving force. We acknowledged that a supervisor's "power and authority invests his or her harassing conduct with a particular threatening character, and in this sense, a supervisor always is aided by the agency relation." But we also recognized that "there are acts of harassment a supervisor might commit which might be the same acts a coemployee would commit, and there may be some circumstances where the supervisor's status [would] mak[e] little difference."

An "aided-by-the-agency-relation" standard, the Court suggested, was insufficiently developed to press into service as the standard governing cases in which no tangible employment action is in the picture. Looking elsewhere for guidance, we focused on Title VII's design "to encourage the creation of antiharassment policies and effective grievance mechanisms." The Court reasoned that tying the liability standard to an employer's effort to install effective grievance procedures would advance Congress' purpose "to promote conciliation rather than litigation" of Title VII controversies. At the same time, such linkage of liability limitation to effective preventive and corrective measures could serve Title VII's deterrent purpose by "encourag[ing] employees to report harassing conduct before it becomes severe or pervasive." Accordingly, we held that when no tangible employment action is taken, the employer may defeat vicarious liability for supervisor harassment by establishing, as an affirmative defense, both that "the employer exercised reasonable care to prevent and correct promptly any sexually harassing behavior," and that "the plaintiff employee unreasonably failed to take advantage of any preventive or corrective opportunities provided by the employer or to avoid harm otherwise."

* * *

The constructive discharge here at issue stems from, and can be regarded as an aggravated case of, sexual harassment or hostile work environment. For an atmosphere of sexual harassment or hostility to be actionable, we reiterate, the offending behavior "must be sufficiently severe or pervasive to alter the conditions of the victim's employment and create an abusive working environment." A hostile-environment constructive discharge claim entails something more: A plaintiff who advances such a compound claim must show working conditions so intolerable that a reasonable person would have felt compelled to resign.

Suders' claim is of the same genre as the hostile work environment claims the Court analyzed in *Ellerth* and *Faragher*. Essentially, Suders presents a "worse case" harassment scenario, harassment ratcheted up to the breaking point. Like the harassment considered in our pathmarking decisions, harassment so intolerable as to cause a resignation may be effected through co-worker conduct, unofficial supervisory conduct, or official company acts. Unlike an actual termination, which is always effected through an official act of the company, a constructive discharge need not be. A constructive discharge involves both an employee's decision to leave and precipitating conduct: The former involves no official action; the latter, like a harassment claim without any constructive discharge assertion, may or may not involve official action.

To be sure, a constructive discharge is functionally the same as an actual termination in damages-enhancing respects. As the Third Circuit observed, both "en[d] the employer-employee relationship," and both "inflic[t] . . . direct economic harm." But when an official act does not underlie the constructive discharge, the *Ellerth* and *Faragher* analysis, we here hold, calls for extension of the affirmative defense to the employer. As those leading decisions indicate, official directions and declarations are the acts most likely to be brought home to the employer, the measures over which the employer can exercise greatest control. Absent "an official act of the enterprise," as the last straw, the employer ordinarily would have no particular reason to suspect that a resignation is not the typical kind daily occurring in the work force. And as *Ellerth* and *Faragher* further point out, an official act reflected in company records—a demotion or a reduction in compensation, for example—shows "beyond question" that the supervisor has used his managerial or controlling position to the employee's disadvantage. Absent such an official act, the extent to which the supervisor's misconduct has been aided by the agency relation, as we earlier recounted, is less certain. That uncertainty, our precedent establishes, justifies affording the employer the chance to establish, through the *Ellerth/Faragher* affirmative defense, that it should not be held vicariously liable.

* * *

We agree with the Third Circuit that the case, in its current posture, presents genuine issues of material fact concerning Suders' hostile work environment and constructive discharge claims. We hold, however, that the Court of Appeals erred in declaring the affirmative defense described in *Ellerth* and *Faragher* never available in constructive discharge cases. Accordingly, we vacate the Third Circuit's judgment and remand the case for further proceedings consistent with this opinion.

■ JUSTICE THOMAS, dissenting.

* * *

NOTES AND QUESTIONS

1.   As the Court notes, *Suders* involves two related issues: (1) employer liability for harassment by supervisors and (2) constructive discharge. On which issue does the plaintiff have the more difficult burden of proof? See

generally Stephen F. Befort & Sarah J. Gorajski, When Quitting is Fitting:
The Need for a Reformulated Sexual Harassment/Constructive Discharge
Standard in the Wake of Pennsylvania State Police v. Suders, 67 Ohio St.
L.J. 593 (2006).

2. Assuming that her allegations are true, are the reasons for the
harassment of Nancy Drew Suders a mystery? In what types of jobs do you
think sexual harassment is most prevalent? Does *Suders* support the model
of sexual harassment suggested by Professor Schultz? If so, is sexual
harassment less about sex and more about bullying?

3. In the absence of statutory protection, the only possible remedies for
workplace bullying are common law actions for assault, intentional infliction
of emotional distress, and similar causes of action against the alleged bully.
For example, in Raess v. Doescher, 883 N.E.2d 790 (Ind. 2008), an operating
room perfusionist sued a cardiovascular surgeon for assault and intentional
infliction of emotional distress stemming from alleged workplace bullying.
The Supreme Court of Indiana upheld a jury award of $325,000 for assault
after the defendant "rapidly advanced on the plaintiff with clenched fists,
piercing eyes, beet-red face, popping veins, and screaming and swearing at
him," and then told the plaintiff "you're finished, you're history." The court
held that workplace bullying was an appropriate factor for the jury to
consider in evaluating the plaintiff's claims.

An important issue is whether an employer can be held liable for the
bullying of one employee by another. In Wheeler v. Marathon Printing, Inc.,
974 P.2d 207 (Or. Ct. App. 1998), the court held that the employer could not
be held directly liable for tolerating the bullying by one of its employees,
which the court characterized as "sadistic" and "extraordinarily vicious,"
resulting in the other employee's attempted suicide. Cf. Cavicchi v. Chertoff
ex rel. United States Bureau of Customs & Border Protection, 2008 WL
239157 (S.D. Fla. 2008) (toleration of bullying does not constitute an adverse
employment action under Title VII). What about an action based on vicarious
liability? What about negligent retention? See generally David C. Yamada,
The Phenomenon of "Workplace Bullying" and the Need for Status-Blind
Hostile Work Environment Protection, 88 Geo. L.J. 475 (2000).

4. As discussed in *Suders*, in Faragher v. City of Boca Raton, 524 U.S. 775
(1998), and Burlington Indus., Inc. v. Ellerth, 524 U.S. 742 (1998), the
Supreme Court delineated the burden of proof in cases of sexual harassment
by supervisors. An employer is vicariously liable for the sexual harassment
of a supervisor. When the supervisor's action culminates in a tangible
employment action, such as discharge, demotion, or undesirable
reassignment, there is no defense available to the employer. When the
employee suffers no tangible, adverse employment action, the employer may
defend by showing that it exercised reasonable care to prevent and correct
promptly any sexually harassing behavior and the employee unreasonably
failed to take advantage of the preventive or corrective opportunity provided
by the employer or to avoid harm otherwise. The lower courts have applied
this doctrine to a wide range of factual situations. For example, in
Brenneman v. Famous Dave's of Am., Inc., 507 F.3d 1139 (8th Cir. 2007), the
Eighth Circuit held that an employee who quit without giving the employer

a reasonable opportunity to resolve the problem was not subject to an adverse employment action. The court held the employer satisfied elements of *Ellerth-Faragher* based upon evidence it had a valid anti-harassment policy, employees received training about the policy, employees were given the number of a hotline to complain of harassment, and the employer investigated the complaint promptly and offered to take corrective measures, but the employee quit before such measures could be implemented. As a result of *Ellerth* and *Faragher,* most employers have implemented sexual harassment training and procedures, in effect, adding a judicially "encouraged" requirement when there was no prior statutory or regulatory obligation. For a discussion of whether this approach has been successful, see Joanna L. Grossman, The Culture of Compliance: The Final Triumph of Form over Substance in Sexual Harassment Law, 26 Harv. Women's L.J. 3 (2003).

5. In Vance v. Ball State University, 570 U.S. 421 (2013), the Supreme Court addressed the question of who is a "supervisor" for the purposes of a *Faragher*-type analysis. The Supreme Court explained that an employee is a "supervisor" under Title VII only if he or she is "empowered by the employer to take tangible employment actions against the victim." Following the Supreme Court's holding in *Vance,* the Sixth Circuit in Hylko v. Hemphill, 698 Fed. Appx. 298 (6th Cir. 2017), emphasized that "colloquial uses of 'supervisor' do not control the question of whether an employee is one," instead " '[s]upervisor' has various meanings in business settings, but has a specific meaning for the purposes of Title VII."

6. State courts are free to impose more stringent standards on employers based on state human rights laws. For example, in VECO, Inc. v. Rosebrock, 970 P.2d 906 (Alaska 1999), the Supreme Court of Alaska held "that an employer is vicariously liable for the hostile work environment created by its supervisors regardless of whether management-level employees know or should have known of the harassment, and regardless of whether the supervisors were acting within the scope of their employment."

7. The EEOC guidelines on sex discrimination include a section on sexual harassment. 29 C.F.R. § 1604.11(a) provides:

> Unwelcome sexual advances, requests for sexual favors, and other verbal or physical conduct of a sexual nature constitute sexual harassment when (1) submission to such conduct is made either explicitly or implicitly a term or condition of an individual's employment, (2) submission to or rejection of such conduct by an individual is used as the basis for employment decisions affecting such individual, or (3) such conduct has the purpose or effect of unreasonably interfering with an individual's work performance or creating an intimidating, hostile, or offensive working environment.

8. In *Suders,* the Court held that the crude and sexually-oriented language and behavior, if proved at trial, could establish a case of hostile environment sexual harassment. Will such behavior always result in liability? Consider Lyle v. Warner Bros. TV, 132 P.3d 211 (Cal. 2006). The plaintiff was a comedy writers' assistant who worked on the television show *Friends*. Before she was hired, she was told that the show dealt with sexual matters and that the comedy writers would be discussing sexual jokes and sexual activities. After four months of employment, the plaintiff was fired because of problems with her typing and transcription. In an action for sexual harassment brought under California's Fair Employment and Housing Act (FEHA), the record demonstrated that the plaintiff was exposed to a pervasive atmosphere of "sexually coarse and vulgar language." Nevertheless, the Supreme Court of California held that the plaintiff could not establish a prima facie case of hostile environment sexual harassment. But cf. Reeves v. C.H. Robinson Worldwide, Inc., 594 F.3d 798 (11th Cir. 2010) (en banc) (pervasive verbal harassment of female employee with sexually-charged coarse language was unlawful).

9. In Meritor Sav. Bank v. Vinson, 477 U.S. 57 (1986), the first Supreme Court case dealing with sexual harassment, the Court rejected the argument that "consent" is a defense to sexual harassment. Instead, the Court said that the standard is whether the conduct is "unwelcome," regardless of whether the harassment establishes a "hostile environment" or constitutes a "quid pro quo"—in which acquiescence to sexual demands is made a condition of employment or advancement.

10. Although sexual harassment cases overwhelmingly involve women harassed by men, there are cases involving men harassed by women. In EEOC v. Prospect Airport Services, Inc., 621 F.3d 991 (9th Cir. 2010), a male employee, a recent widower, alleged he was relentlessly pursued by a married female coworker, who left him notes and constantly demanded a sexual relationship. Despite clearly indicating his lack of interest and repeatedly complaining to management, the harassment continued, leading to severe stress, poor work performance, and eventual discharge. The Ninth Circuit reversed summary judgment for the defendant and held the allegations stated a valid claim.

11. Can the plaintiff's off-work conduct be used to show that the alleged harassing conduct was "welcome"? In Burns v. McGregor Electronic Indus., Inc., 989 F.2d 959 (8th Cir. 1993), a female employee alleged hostile environment sexual harassment. The district court found that while a reasonable person would consider the complained of conduct to constitute sexual harassment, it did not constitute sexual harassment as to the plaintiff. It further stated that because the plaintiff had posed nude for *Easyriders* magazine, the uninvited sexual advances and crude behavior toward her were not offensive to her. The Eighth Circuit reversed. "The plaintiff's choice to pose nude for a magazine outside work hours is not material to the issue of whether plaintiff found her employer's work-related conduct offensive. * * * Her private life, regardless of how reprehensible the trier of fact might find it to be, did not provide lawful acquiescence to unwanted sexual advances at her workplace by her employer."

California Evidence Code § 1106 provides that in a sexual harassment action, "opinion evidence, reputation evidence, and evidence of specific instances of plaintiff's sexual conduct, or any of such evidence, is not admissible by the defendant to prove consent by the plaintiff or the absence of injury to the plaintiff * * *." A key exception allows for admission of evidence of "the plaintiff's sexual conduct with the alleged perpetrator." Does this provision, applicable to sexual assaults as well as sexual harassment, further the aims of the law? For judicial construction, see Rieger v. Arnold, 128 Cal.Rptr.2d 295 (Cal.Ct.App.2002) (evidence of plaintiff's sexual conduct with named defendants admissible).

12. If the relationship is truly consensual, an action for hostile environment sexual harassment will not lie. See Herman v. Western Fin. Corp., 869 P.2d 696 (Kan.1994). Nevertheless, many companies have adopted policies which forbid even consensual relationships between employees, especially where one of the employees has supervisory authority over the other.

13. Ordinarily, if a supervisor gives preferential treatment to an employee with whom he or she is romantically involved, the courts hold that the other employees have not been subjected to sex discrimination. See Preston v. Wisconsin Health Fund, 397 F.3d 539 (7th Cir. 2005), p. 242 supra. In Miller v. Department of Corrections, 115 P.3d 77 (Cal. 2005), however, the facts were more complicated. The plaintiffs were former prison employees who claimed that the warden gave unwarranted favorable treatment to numerous female employees with whom he was having sexual affairs. In ruling on an action brought under the California Fair Employment and Housing Act, the court held that "when such sexual favoritism in a workplace is sufficiently widespread it may create an actionable hostile work environment in which the demeaning message is conveyed to female employees that they are viewed by management as 'sexual playthings' or that the way required for women to get ahead in the workplace is to engage in sexual conduct with their supervisors or the management." 115 P.3d at 80.

(ii) Because of Race

Disparate treatment claims based on race require the plaintiff to prove that discrimination is "because of race." Such proof is not difficulty when an employer excludes all workers of a particular race. The question becomes more difficult, however, when an employer excludes some members of a particular racial group while including others, and distinguishes between the two groups based upon the presence or absence of a racially associated trait or attribute.

Rogers v. American Airlines, Inc.

527 F.Supp. 229 (S.D. N.Y. 1981).

■ SOFAER, DISTRICT JUDGE.

Plaintiff is a black woman who seeks $10,000 damages, injunctive, and declaratory relief against enforcement of a grooming policy of the defendant American Airlines that prohibits employees in certain employment categories from wearing an all-braided hairstyle. Plaintiff has been an American Airlines employee for approximately eleven years, and has been an airport operations agent for over one year. Her duties involve extensive passenger contact, including greeting passengers, issuing boarding passes, and checking luggage. She alleges that the policy violates her rights under the Thirteenth Amendment of the United States Constitution, under Title VII of the Civil Rights Act, 42 U.S.C. s 2000e et seq. (1976), and under 42 U.S.C. s 1981 (1976), in that it discriminates against her as a woman, and more specifically as a black woman. She claims that denial of the right to wear her hair in the "corn row" style intrudes upon her rights and discriminates against her. Plaintiff has exhausted her administrative remedies and has been issued a right to sue letter by the Equal Employment Opportunity Commission ("EEOC").

Defendants move to dismiss plaintiff's claims. Insofar as the motion is addressed to the claim under the Thirteenth Amendment, it is meritorious. That provision prohibits practices that constitute a "badge of slavery" and, unless a plaintiff alleges she does not have the option of leaving her job, does not support claims of racial discrimination in employment. Plaintiff has made no such allegation.

The motion is also meritorious with respect to the statutory claims insofar as they challenge the policy on its face. The statutory bases alleged, Title VII and section 1981, are indistinguishable in the circumstances of this case, and will be considered together. The policy is addressed to both men and women, black and white. Plaintiff's assertion that the policy has practical effect only with respect to women is not supported by any factual allegations. Many men have hair longer than many women. Some men have hair long enough to wear in braids if they choose to do so. Even if the grooming policy imposed different standards for men and women, however, it would not violate Title VII. It follows, therefore, that an even-handed policy that prohibits to both sexes a style more often adopted by members of one sex does not constitute prohibited sex discrimination. This is because this type of regulation has at most a negligible effect on employment opportunity. It does not regulate on the basis of any immutable characteristic of the employees involved. It concerns a matter of relatively low importance in terms of the constitutional interests protected by the Fourteenth Amendment and Title VII, rather than involving fundamental rights such as the right to have children or to marry. The complaint does not state a claim for sex discrimination.

The considerations with respect to plaintiff's race discrimination claim would clearly be the same, except for plaintiff's assertion that the "corn row" style has a special significance for black women. She contends that it "has been, historically, a fashion and style adopted by Black American women, reflective of cultural, historical essence of the Black women in American society." Plaintiff's Memo. in Opposition to Motion to Dismiss, p. 4. "The style was 'popularized' so to speak, within the larger society, when Cicely Tyson adopted the same for an appearance on nationally viewed Academy Awards presentation several years ago. . . . It was and is analogous to the public statement by the late Malcolm X regarding the Afro hair style. . . . At the bottom line, the completely braided hair style, sometimes referred to as corn rows, has been and continues to be part of the cultural and historical essence of Black American women." Id. at 4–5. "There can be little doubt that, if American adopted a policy which foreclosed Black women/all women from wearing hair styled as an 'Afro/bush,' that policy would have very pointedly racial dynamics and consequences reflecting a vestige of slavery unwilling to die (that is, a master mandate that one wear hair divorced from ones historical and cultural perspective and otherwise consistent with the 'white master' dominated society and preference thereof)." Id. at 14–15.

Plaintiff is entitled to a presumption that her arguments, largely repeated in her affidavit, are true. But the grooming policy applies equally to members of all races, and plaintiff does not allege that an all-braided hair style is worn exclusively or even predominantly by black people. Moreover, it is proper to note that defendants have alleged without contravention that plaintiff first appeared at work in the all-braided hairstyle on or about September 25, 1980, soon after the style had been popularized by a white actress in the film "10." Affidavit of Robert Zurlo. Plaintiff may be correct that an employer's policy prohibiting the "Afro/bush" style might offend Title VII and section 1981. But if so, this chiefly would be because banning a natural hairstyle would implicate the policies underlying the prohibition of discrimination on the basis of immutable characteristics. In any event, an all-braided hairstyle is a different matter. It is not the product of natural hair growth but of artifice. An all-braided hair style is an "easily changed characteristic," and, even if socioculturally associated with a particular race or nationality, is not an impermissible basis for distinctions in the application of employment practices by an employer. The Fifth Circuit recently upheld, without requiring any showing of business purpose, an employer's policy prohibiting the speaking of any language but English in the workplace, despite the importance of Spanish to the ethnic identity of Mexican-Americans. Gloor v. Garcia, supra, 618 F.2d at 267–69. The court stated that Title VII

> is directed only at specific impermissible bases of discrimination-race, color, religion, sex, or national origin. National origin must not be confused with ethnic or sociocultural traits. . . . Save for religion, the discriminations on which the Act focuses its laser of prohibition are those that are either beyond the victim's power to alter, or that impose a burden on an employee on one of the prohibited bases. . . . "(A) hiring policy that distinguishes on some other ground, such as grooming codes or length of hair, is related more closely to the employer's choice of how to run his business than to equality of employment opportunity."

Id. at 269 (footnotes and citations omitted).

Although the Act may shield "employees' psychological as well as economic fringes" from employer abuse, plaintiff's allegations do not amount to charging American with "a practice of creating a working environment heavily charged with ethnic or racial discrimination," or one "so heavily polluted with discrimination as to destroy completely the emotional and psychological stability of minority group workers. . . ." Id. If an even-handed English-only policy that has the effect of prohibiting a Mexican-American from speaking Spanish during working hours is valid without a showing of business purpose, the policy at issue here, even if ill-advised, does not offend the law.

Moreover, the airline did not require plaintiff to restyle her hair. It suggested that she could wear her hair as she liked while off duty, and permitted her to pull her hair into a bun and wrap a hairpiece around the bun during working hours. A similar policy was approved in Carswell v. Peachford Hospital, supra. Plaintiff has done this, but alleges that the hairpiece has caused her severe headaches. A larger hairpiece would seem in order. But even if any hairpiece would cause such discomfort, the policy does not offend a substantial interest.

Plaintiff has failed to allege sufficient facts to require defendants to demonstrate that the policy has a bona fide business purpose. In this regard, however, plaintiff does not dispute defendant's assertion that the policy was adopted in order to help American project a conservative and business-like image, a consideration recognized as a bona fide business purpose. Rather she objects to its impact with respect to the "corn row" style, an impact not protected against by Title VII or section 1981.

* * *

NOTES AND QUESTIONS

1. The court in Rogers blurs and rejects both Rogers's disparate treatment and disparate impact arguments. The court refuses to equate cornrows with race itself for the purposes of disparate treatment analysis. Moreover, the court says that even if a no cornrows policy disproportionately affects black women, it is not an impermissible distinction under disparate impact analysis. Any disparate impact caused by the policy is not, in effect, legally cognizable. As a result, although American Airlines did in fact state a business justification for the policy, it was not required to do so.

2. The mutability of the trait at issue in this case is important to the court. It refers to cornrows as an "easily changed characteristic" and distinguishes a prohibition on cornrows from a prohibition on an Afro hairstyle, by suggesting that the latter is an immutable characteristic. A prohibition on an Afro hairstyle, the court says, might violate Title VII. Is an Afro hairstyle immutable? What factors other than relative mutability might be driving the court to view a prohibition on an Afro hairstyle as more about race, and more likely actionable, than a prohibition on cornrows? Trait mutability was also critical to the Eleventh Circuit's decision in EEOC v. Catastrophe Management Solutions, 852 F.3d 1018 (11th Cir. 2016). In *Catastrophe*

Management, the Eleventh Circuit affirmed the district court's dismissal of plaintiff's disparate treatment claim of race discrimination challenging her employer's no dreadlocks policy. Title VII, the Eleventh Circuit held, prohibits only discrimination based on immutable traits.

3. The *Rogers* court emphasizes that the policy in effect was facially neutral and applied equally to both sexes and all races. Many scholars have disagreed about the neutrality of dress and grooming policies contending that they implicitly enforce culturally white norms. See Devon W. Carbado and Mitu Gulati, Acting White?: Rethinking Race in Post-Racial America (2013); Angela Onwuachi-Willig, Another Hair Piece: Exploring New Strands of Analysis Under Title VII, 98 Geo. L.J. 1079 (2010).

4. While courts routinely dismiss race discrimination claims challenging dress and grooming codes, one exception has been cases brought by black men challenging no beard rules by employers. Such plaintiffs have, in some instances, been able to win their claims of race discrimination by showing that because of their race they were much more likely to be affected by a skin disease called Psuedofolliculitis barbae (PFB), which can make shaving very painful. See University of Maryland at Baltimore v. Boyd, 612 A.2d 305 (Md. 1992); Richardson v. Quick Trip, 591 F.Supp. 1151 (S.D. Iowa 1984). What explains courts' more sympathetic response to the plaintiffs in PFB cases than the plaintiff in Rogers? Is the distinction justified?

5. In Village of Freeport v. Barella, 814 F.3d 594 (2d Cir. 2016), the Second Circuit did not take on the big question of what is race, but did hold that "Hispanic" is a "race" for the purposes of Title VII, and, more generally, that Title VII's definition of race encompasses ethnicity.

(iii) Because of Sex

The critical question in disparate treatment cases alleging sex discrimination is whether an employer made an adverse employment decision "because of sex." As with race discrimination, this determination was simple and uncontroversial in the early years after Title VII's passage when employers frequently excluded all women from particular job categories. The determination of whether conduct is because of sex has become much more controversial in recent years as the nature of discrimination has changed. Categorical discrimination has been largely eradicated, more common are instances in which not all women (or men) are adversely treated, but only those with particular characteristics—for example, those who are gender nonconforming, those who are pregnant, or those with caregiving responsibilities. Determining when adverse employment actions of this sort are discrimination because of sex has become a fertile ground of litigation and scholarly writing. See Joan C. Williams, The Evolution of "FRED"; Family Responsibilities Discrimination and Developments in the Law of Stereotyping and Implicit Bias, 59 Hastings L.J. 1311 (2008); Kimberly A. Yuracko, Trait Discrimination as Sex Discrimination: An Argument Against Neutrality, 83 Tex. L. Rev. 167 (2006).

(a) Sex Stereotyping

In Price Waterhouse v. Hopkins, the Supreme Court not only established the mixed motives framework for disparate treatment claims, it also made clear that discrimination based on sex stereotypes was an actionable form of sex discrimination. The Supreme Court explained:

As for the legal relevance of sex stereotyping, we are beyond the day when an employer could evaluate employees by assuming or insisting that they matched the stereotype associated with their group, for " '[i]n forbidding employers to discriminate against individuals because of their sex, Congress intended to strike at the entire spectrum of disparate treatment of men and women resulting from sex stereotypes.' " 490 U.S. 228, 251 (1988).

What followed the Court's pronouncement has been significant litigation by gender nonconformists, or those perceived as such, to determine the meaning and scope of the law's prohibition on sex stereotyping.

Smith v. City of Salem, Ohio
378 F.3d 566 (6th Cir. 2004).

■ COLE, CIRCUIT JUDGE.

Smith is—and has been, at all times relevant to this action—employed by the city of Salem, Ohio, as a lieutenant in the Salem Fire Department (the "Fire Department"). Prior to the events surrounding this action, Smith worked for the Fire Department for seven years without any negative incidents. Smith—biologically and by birth a male—is a transsexual and has been diagnosed with Gender Identity Disorder ("GID"), which the American Psychiatric Association characterizes as a disjunction between an individual's sexual organs and sexual identity. After being diagnosed with GID, Smith began "expressing a more feminine appearance on a full-time basis"—including at work—in accordance with international medical protocols for treating GID. Soon thereafter, Smith's co-workers began questioning him about his appearance and commenting that his appearance and mannerisms were not "masculine enough." As a result, Smith notified his immediate supervisor, Defendant Thomas Eastek, about his GID diagnosis and treatment. He also informed Eastek of the likelihood that his treatment would eventually include complete physical transformation from male to female. Smith had approached Eastek in order to answer any questions Eastek might have concerning his appearance and manner and so that Eastek could address Smith's co-workers' comments and inquiries. Smith specifically asked Eastek, and Eastek promised, not to divulge the substance of their conversation to any of his superiors, particularly to Defendant Walter Greenamyer, Chief of the Fire Department. In short order, however, Eastek told Greenamyer about Smith's behavior and his GID.

Greenamyer then met with Defendant C. Brooke Zellers, the Law Director for the City of Salem, with the intention of using Smith's transsexualism and its manifestations as a basis for terminating his employment. On April 18, 2001, Greenamyer and Zellers arranged a meeting of the City's executive body to discuss Smith and devise a plan for terminating his employment. The executive body included Defendants Larry D. DeJane, Salem's mayor; James A. Armeni, Salem's auditor; and Joseph S. Julian, Salem's service director. Also present was Salem Safety Director Henry L. Willard, now deceased, who was never a named defendant in this action.

* * *

Two days after the meeting, on April 20, 2001, Smith's counsel telephoned DeJane to advise him of Smith's legal representation and the potential legal ramifications for the City if it followed through on the plan devised by Defendants during the April 18 meeting. On April 22, 2001, Smith received his "right to sue" letter from the U.S. Equal Employment Opportunity Commission ("EEOC"). Four days after that, on April 26, 2001, Greenamyer suspended Smith for one twenty-four hour shift, based on his alleged infraction of a City and/or Fire Department policy.

At a subsequent hearing before the Salem Civil Service Commission (the "Commission") regarding his suspension, Smith contended that the suspension was a result of selective enforcement in retaliation for his having obtained legal representation in response to Defendants' plan to terminate his employment because of his transsexualism and its manifestations. * * * The Commission ultimately upheld Smith's suspension. Smith appealed to the Columbiana County Court of Common Pleas, which reversed the suspension, finding that "[b]ecause the regulation [that Smith was alleged to have violated] was not effective[,] [Smith] could not be charged with violation of it."

Smith then filed suit in the federal district court. In his complaint, he asserted Title VII claims of sex discrimination and retaliation, along with claims pursuant to 42 U.S.C. § 1983 and state law claims of invasion of privacy and civil conspiracy. In a Memorandum Opinion and Order dated February 26, 2003, the district court dismissed the federal claims and granted judgment on the pleadings to Defendants pursuant to Federal Rule of Civil Procedure 12(c). The district judge also dismissed the state law claims without prejudice, having declined to exercise supplemental jurisdiction over them pursuant to 28 U.S.C. § 1367(c)(3).

II. ANALYSIS

On appeal, Smith contends that the district court erred in holding that: (1) he failed to state a claim of sex stereotyping; (2) Title VII protection is unavailable to transsexuals; (3) even if he had stated a claim of sex stereotyping, he failed to demonstrate that he suffered an adverse employment action; and (4) he failed to state a claim based on the deprivation of a constitutional or federal statutory right, pursuant to 42 U.S.C. § 1983.

* * *

A. *Title VII*

The parties disagree over two issues pertaining to Smith's Title VII claims: (1) whether Smith properly alleged a claim of sex stereotyping, in violation of the Supreme Court's pronouncements in *Price Waterhouse v. Hopkins,* 490 U.S. 228 (1989); and (2) whether Smith alleged that he suffered an adverse employment action.

* * *

1. *Sex Stereotyping*

Title VII of the Civil Rights Act of 1964 provides, in relevant part, that "[i]t shall be an unlawful employment practice for an employer . . . to discriminate against any individual with respect to his compensation, terms, conditions, or privileges of employment because of such individual's race, color, religion, sex, or national origin." 42 U.S.C. § 2000e–2(a).

In his complaint, Smith asserts Title VII claims of retaliation and employment discrimination "because of . . . sex." The district court dismissed Smith's Title VII claims on the ground that he failed to state a claim for sex stereotyping pursuant to Price Waterhouse v. Hopkins, 490 U.S. 228 (1989). The district court implied that Smith's claim was disingenuous, stating that he merely "invokes the term-of-art created by *Price Waterhouse,* that is, 'sex-stereotyping,' " as an end run around his "real" claim, which, the district court stated, was "based upon his transsexuality." The district court then held that "Title VII does not prohibit discrimination based on an individual's transsexualism."

Relying on *Price Waterhouse*—which held that Title VII's prohibition of discrimination "because of . . . sex" bars gender discrimination, including discrimination based on sex stereotypes—Smith contends on appeal that he was a victim of discrimination "because of . . . sex" both because of his gender non-conforming conduct and, more generally, because of his identification as a transsexual.

We first address whether Smith has stated a claim for relief, pursuant to *Price Waterhouse'* s prohibition of sex stereotyping, based on his gender non-conforming behavior and appearance. In *Price Waterhouse,* the plaintiff, a female senior manager in an accounting firm, was denied partnership in the firm, in part, because she was considered "macho." 490 U.S. at 235. She was advised that she could improve her chances for partnership if she were to take "a course at charm school," "walk more femininely, talk more femininely, dress more femininely, wear make-up, have her hair styled, and wear jewelry." *Id.* (internal quotation marks omitted). Six members of the Court agreed that such comments bespoke gender discrimination, holding that Title VII barred not just discrimination because Hopkins was a woman, but also sex stereotyping—that is, discrimination because she failed to *act* like a woman. * * * The Supreme Court made clear that in the context of Title VII, discrimination because of "sex" includes gender discrimination: "In the context of sex stereotyping, an employer who acts on the basis of a belief that a woman cannot be aggressive, or that she must not be, has acted on the basis of gender." *Price Waterhouse*, 490 U.S. at 250. The Court emphasized that "we are beyond the day when an employer could evaluate employees by assuming or insisting that they matched the stereotype associated with their group." *Id.* at 251.

Smith contends that the same theory of sex stereotyping applies here. His complaint sets forth the conduct and mannerisms which, he alleges, did not conform with his employers' and co-workers' sex stereotypes of how a man should look and behave. Smith's complaint states that, after being diagnosed with GID, he began to express a more feminine appearance and manner on a regular basis, including at work. The complaint states that his co-workers began commenting on his appearance and mannerisms as not being masculine enough; and that his supervisors at the Fire Department and other municipal agents knew about this allegedly unmasculine conduct and appearance. The complaint then describes a high-level meeting among Smith's supervisors and other municipal officials regarding his employment. Defendants allegedly schemed to compel Smith's resignation by forcing him to undergo multiple psychological evaluations of his gender non-conforming behavior. The complaint makes clear that these meetings took place soon after Smith assumed a more feminine appearance and manner and after his conversation about this with Eastek. In addition, the complaint alleges that Smith was suspended for twenty-four hours for allegedly violating an unenacted municipal policy, and that the suspension was ordered in retaliation for his pursuing legal remedies after he had been informed about Defendants' plan to intimidate him into resigning. In short, Smith claims that the discrimination he experienced was based on his failure to conform to sex stereotypes by expressing less masculine, and more feminine mannerisms and appearance.

Having alleged that his failure to conform to sex stereotypes concerning how a man should look and behave was the driving force behind Defendants' actions, Smith has sufficiently pleaded claims of sex stereotyping and gender discrimination.

In so holding, we find that the district court erred in relying on a series of pre-*Price Waterhouse* cases from other federal appellate courts holding that transsexuals, as a class, are not entitled to Title VII protection because "Congress had a narrow view of sex in mind" and "never considered nor intended that [Title VII] apply to anything other than the traditional concept of sex." * * *

However, the approach in *Holloway, Sommers,* and *Ulane*—and by the district court in this case—has been eviscerated by *Price Waterhouse.*
* * *

After *Price Waterhouse,* an employer who discriminates against women because, for instance, they do not wear dresses or makeup, is engaging in sex discrimination because the discrimination would not occur but for the victim's sex. It follows that employers who discriminate against men because they *do* wear dresses and makeup, or otherwise act femininely, are also engaging in sex discrimination, because the discrimination would not occur but for the victim's sex.

Yet some courts have held that this latter form of discrimination is of a different and somehow more permissible kind. For instance, the man who acts in ways typically associated with women is not described as engaging in the same activity as a woman who acts in ways typically associated with women, but is instead described as engaging in the different activity of being a transsexual (or in some instances, a homosexual or transvestite). Discrimination against the transsexual is then found not to be discrimination "because of . . . sex," but rather, discrimination against the plaintiff's unprotected status or mode of self-identification. In other words, these courts superimpose classifications such as "transsexual" on a plaintiff, and then legitimize discrimination based on the plaintiff's gender non-conformity by formalizing the non-conformity into an ostensibly unprotected classification.

Such was the case here: despite the fact that Smith alleges that Defendants' discrimination was motivated by his appearance and mannerisms, which Defendants felt were inappropriate for his perceived sex, the district court expressly declined to discuss the applicability of *Price Waterhouse.* The district court therefore gave insufficient consideration to Smith's well-pleaded claims concerning his contra-gender behavior, but rather accounted for that behavior only insofar as it confirmed for the court Smith's status as a transsexual, which the district court held precluded Smith from Title VII protection.

Such analyses cannot be reconciled with *Price Waterhouse,* which does not make Title VII protection against sex stereotyping conditional or provide any reason to exclude Title VII coverage for non sex-stereotypical behavior simply because the person is a transsexual. As such, discrimination against a plaintiff who is a transsexual—and therefore fails to act and/or identify with his or her gender—is no different from the discrimination directed against Ann Hopkins in *Price Waterhouse,* who, in sex-stereotypical terms, did not act like a woman. Sex stereotyping based on a person's gender non-conforming behavior is impermissible discrimination, irrespective of the cause of that behavior; a label, such as "transsexual," is not fatal to a sex discrimination claim where the victim has suffered discrimination because of his or her gender non-conformity. Accordingly, we hold that Smith has stated a claim for relief pursuant to Title VII's prohibition of sex discrimination.

Finally, we note that, in its opinion, the district court repeatedly places the term "sex stereotyping" in quotation marks and refers to it as a "term of art" used by Smith to disingenuously plead discrimination because of transsexualism. Similarly, Defendants refer to sex stereotyping as "the *Price Waterhouse* loophole." (Appellees' Brief at 6.) These characterizations are almost identical to the treatment that Price Waterhouse itself gave sex stereotyping in its briefs to the U.S. Supreme Court. As we do now, the Supreme Court noted the practice with disfavor, stating:

> In the specific context of sex stereotyping, an employer who acts on the basis of a belief that a woman cannot be aggressive, or that she must not be, has acted on the basis of gender. Although the parties do not overtly dispute this last proposition, the placement by Price Waterhouse of "sex stereotyping" in quotation marks throughout its brief seems to us an insinuation either that such stereotyping was not present in this case or that it lacks legal relevance. We reject both possibilities.

Price Waterhouse, 490 U.S. at 250.

* * *

NOTES AND QUESTIONS

1. Several years before *Smith*, the Supreme Court in Oncale v. Sundowner Offshore Services, Inc., 523 U.S. 75 (1998), held that same-sex harassment could be discrimination because of sex. The Court outlined several ways that a plaintiff could show that same sex harassment was because of sex, namely: 1. Show that the harasser was homosexual and the harassing conduct was motivated by sexual attraction; 2. Show that the harassment was in "such sex-specific and derogatory terms" "as to make it clear that the harasser is motivated by general hostility to the presence" of people of a particular sex in the workplace; or 3. "offer direct comparative evidence about how the alleged harasser treated members of both sexes in a mixed-sex workplace." Id. at 80–81. Interestingly, however, the Supreme Court did not name sex stereotyping as a means by which Oncale could show his harassment was because of sex. Nonetheless, and despite the Supreme Court's silence in *Oncale*, the sex stereotyping prohibition has been critically important to plaintiffs seeking protection from same-sex sexual harassment.

2. *Smith* was the first time a circuit court had held that discrimination against a transsexual worker because of gender nonconformity constituted actionable sex discrimination. The Sixth Circuit relied on and affirmed its holding in *Smith* by holding in EEOC v. R.G. & G.R. Harris Funeral Homes, Inc. 884 F.3d 560 (6th Cir. 2018) that discrimination against a transsexual employee for transitioning from male to female in her appearance at work was discrimination because of sex. Traditionally, discrimination based on an individual's transsexualism was not prohibited under Title VII. The Seventh Circuit explained the reason for such exclusion in blunt terms in Ulane v. Eastern Airlines, 742 F.2d 1081 (7th Cir. 1984). According to the court, "The

phrase in Title VII prohibiting discrimination based on sex, in its plain meaning, implies that it is unlawful to discriminate against women because they are women and against men because they are men. The words of Title VII do not outlaw discrimination against a person who has a sexual identity disorder." Id. at 1085. In recent years, however, courts have increasingly followed the Sixth Circuit in holding that discrimination against transsexual workers who are transitioning from one sex to the other violates the prohibition on sex stereotyping articulated by the Supreme Court in *Price Waterhouse*. See, e.g., Glenn v. Brumby, 663 F.3d 1312 (11th Cir. 2011) (holding that discriminating against someone on the basis of his or her gender non-conformity constitutes sex-based discrimination under the Equal Protection Clause); Macy v. Holder, Appeal No. 0120120821, 2012 WL 1435995 (EEOC April 20, 2012) (holding that discrimination against transgendered individuals constitutes sex discrimination under Title VII).

Recently there has been a great deal of attention to the question of whether Title VII's antidiscrimination mandate requires that transgender workers be permitted to use the bathroom associated with their gender rather than their biological sex. The EEOC has ruled that an employer violates Title VII if it denies a transgender employee access to the restroom corresponding to the employee's gender identity. See Lusardi v. Dep't of the Army, 2015 WL 1607756 (April 1, 2015). Federal courts have not yet followed the EEOC's lead. In Etsitty v. Utah Transit Auth., 502 F.3d 1215 (10th Cir. 2007), for example, a bus driver informed her employer that she was transgender and would begin to present as female at work and use female restrooms while on her route. Her employer terminated her because it was unable to accommodate her restroom needs. The Tenth Circuit held that Etsitty was not entitled to protection under Title VII because the employer's concern about potential liability stemming from her use of female restrooms, while still biologically male, was a legitimate business justification for burdening the plaintiff's gender expression. See also Kastle v. Maricopa County Commun. Coll. Dist., 325 Fed. Appx. 492 (9th Cir. 2009) (explaining that "after *Hopkins* and *Schwenk*, it is unlawful to discriminate against a transgender (or any other person) because he or she does not behave in accordance with an employer's expectations for men or women," but holding that the employer's ban on a transgender plaintiff's use of restroom for safety reasons did not constitute sex discrimination). Courts interpreting Title IX's prohibition on sex discrimination in the context of education have interpreted that statute to require that transgender students be permitted to use the bathroom associated with their gender identity. In G.G. ex rel. Grimm v. Gloucester Sch. Bd., 822 F.3d 709 (4th Cir. 2016), for example, the Fourth Circuit held that the prohibition on sex discrimination under Title IX requires educational institutions to give transgender students restroom access consistent with their gender identity. In reaching its conclusion, the court relied heavily on guidances to this effect offered by the Obama Administration. In March 2017, the Supreme Court vacated and remanded the case to the Fourth Circuit in light of the fact that the Department of Education and Department of Justice under the Trump Administration had withdrawn the relevant guidances. See Gloucester Cty Sch. Bd v. GG, 137 S.Ct 1239 (2017). More recently, the Seventh Circuit in Whitaker v. Kenosha

Unified Sch. Dist., 858 F.3d 1034 (7th Cir. 2017), held that a transgender student was likely to succeed on the merits of his Title IX claim alleging that his school's refusal to allow him to use the bathroom associated with his gender identity constituted sex discrimination. What may explain courts' reluctance to extend the sex stereotyping logic to cases involving individuals' choice of restroom? Is there any reason to interpret Title VII's antidiscrimination mandate differently from Title IX's in this regard?

3. Transgendered individuals have also been held to be protected under at least one state sex discrimination law. See, e.g., Enriquez v. West Jersey Health Sys., 777 A.2d 365 (N.J.App.Div.2001), cert. denied, 785 A.2d 439 (N.J.2001). See generally Ann C. McGinley, Erasing Boundaries: Masculinities, Sexual Minorities, and Employment Discrimination, 43 U. Mich. J. L Reform 713 (2010).

4. While most courts, as will be discussed at the end of the chapter, continue to hold that discrimination based on sexual orientation per se is not an actionable form of sex discrimination under Title VII, the Second Circuit in Christiansen v. Omnicom Group, Inc., 852 F.3d 195, 200–01 (2d. Cir. 2017), made clear that "gay, lesbian, and bisexual individuals do not have *less* protection under *Price Waterhouse* against traditional gender stereotype discrimination than do heterosexual individuals."

Jespersen v. Harrah's Operating Co., Inc.
444 F.3d 1104 (9th Cir. 2006) (en banc).

■ SCHROEDER, CHIEF JUDGE.

I.   BACKGROUND

Plaintiff Darlene Jespersen worked successfully as a bartender at Harrah's for twenty years and compiled what by all accounts was an exemplary record. During Jespersen's entire tenure with Harrah's, the company maintained a policy encouraging female beverage servers to wear makeup. The parties agree, however, that the policy was not enforced until 2000. In February 2000, Harrah's implemented a "Beverage Department Image Transformation" program at twenty Harrah's locations, including its casino in Reno. Part of the program consisted of new grooming and appearance standards, called the "Personal Best" program. The program contained certain appearance standards that applied equally to both sexes, including a standard uniform of black pants, white shirt, black vest, and black bow tie. Jespersen has never objected to any of these policies. The program also contained some sex-differentiated appearance requirements as to hair, nails, and makeup.

Darlene Jespersen

Photo courtesy of Andrew Barbano and Darlene Jespersen.

In April 2000, Harrah's amended that policy to require that women wear makeup. Jespersen's only objection here is to the makeup requirement. The amended policy provided in relevant part:

> All Beverage Service Personnel, in addition to being friendly, polite, courteous and responsive to our customer's needs, must possess the ability to physically perform the essential factors of the job set forth in the standard job descriptions. They must be well groomed, appealing to the eye, be firm and body toned, and be comfortable with maintaining this look while wearing the specified uniform. Additional factors to be considered include, but are not limited to, hair styles, overall body contour, and degree of comfort the employee projects while wearing the uniform.
>
> * * *
>
> Beverage Bartenders and Barbacks will adhere to these additional guidelines:
>
> - Overall Guidelines (applied equally to male/female):
>   - Appearance: Must maintain Personal Best image portrayed at time of hire.
>   - Jewelry, if issued, must be worn. Otherwise, tasteful and simple jewelry is permitted; no large chokers, chains or bracelets.
>   - No faddish hairstyles or unnatural colors are permitted.
> - Males:
>   - Hair must not extend below top of shirt collar. Ponytails are prohibited.

- Hands and fingernails must be clean and nails trimmed at all times. No colored polish is permitted.

- Eye and facial makeup is not permitted.

- Shoes will be solid black leather type with rubber (non skid) soles.

- Females:

  - Hair must be teased, curled, or styled every day you work. Hair must be worn down at all times, no exceptions.

  - Stockings are to be of nude or natural color consistent with employee's skin tone. No runs.

  - Nail polish can be clear, white, pink, or red color only. No exotic nail art or length.

  - Shoes will be solid black leather or leather type with rubber (non skid) soles.

  - *Make up (face powder, blush and mascara) must be worn and applied neatly in complimentary colors. Lip color must be worn at all times.*

  (emphasis added).

Jespersen did not wear makeup on or off the job, and in her deposition stated that wearing it would conflict with her self-image. It is not disputed that she found the makeup requirement offensive, and felt so uncomfortable wearing makeup that she found it interfered with her ability to perform as a bartender. Unwilling to wear makeup, and not qualifying for any open positions at the casino with a similar compensation scale, Jespersen left her employment with Harrah's.

After exhausting her administrative remedies with the Equal Employment Opportunity Commission and obtaining a right to sue notification, Jespersen filed this action in July 2001. In her complaint, Jespersen sought damages as well as declaratory and injunctive relief for discrimination and retaliation for opposition to discrimination, alleging that the "Personal Best" policy discriminated against women by "(1) subjecting them to terms and conditions of employment to which men are not similarly subjected, and (2) requiring that women conform to sex-based stereotypes as a term and condition of employment."

Harrah's moved for summary judgment, supporting its motion with documents giving the history and purpose of the appearance and grooming policies. Harrah's argued that the policy created similar standards for both men and women, and that where the standards differentiated on the basis of sex, as with the face and hair standards, any burdens imposed fell equally on both male and female bartenders.

In her deposition testimony, attached as a response to the motion for summary judgment, Jespersen described the personal indignity she felt as a result of attempting to comply with the makeup policy. Jespersen testified that when she wore the makeup she "felt very degraded and very demeaned." In addition, Jespersen testified that "it prohibited [her] from doing [her] job because 'it affected [her] self-dignity . . . [and] took away [her] credibility as an individual and as a person.' " Jespersen made no cross-motion for summary judgment, taking the position that the case should go to the jury. Her response to Harrah's motion for summary judgment relied solely on her own deposition testimony regarding her subjective reaction to the makeup policy, and on favorable customer feedback and employer evaluation forms regarding her work.

The record therefore does not contain any affidavit or other evidence to establish that complying with the "Personal Best" standards caused burdens to fall unequally on men or women, and there is no evidence to suggest Harrah's motivation was to stereotype the women bartenders. Jespersen relied solely on evidence that she had been a good bartender, and that she had personal objections to complying with the policy, in order to support her argument that Harrah's " 'sells' and exploits its women employees." Jespersen contended that as a matter of law she had made a prima facie showing of gender discrimination, sufficient to survive summary judgment on both of her claims.

The district court granted Harrah's motion for summary judgment on all of Jespersen's claims. In this appeal, Jespersen maintains that the record before the district court was sufficient to create triable issues of material fact as to her unlawful discrimination claims of unequal burdens and sex stereotyping. We deal with each in turn.

II.   UNEQUAL BURDENS

* * *

In Gerdom v. Cont'l Airlines, Inc. 692 F.2d 602 (9th Cir. 1982), we considered the Continental Airlines policy that imposed strict weight restrictions on female flight attendants, and held it constituted a violation of Title VII. We did so because the airline imposed no weight restriction whatsoever on a class of male employees who performed the same or similar functions as the flight attendants. Indeed, the policy was touted by the airline as intended to "create the public image of an airline which offered passengers service by thin, attractive women, whom executives referred to as Continental's 'girls.' " In fact, Continental specifically argued that its policy was justified by its "desire to compete [with other airlines] by featuring attractive female cabin attendants[,]" a justification which this court recognized as "discriminatory on its face." The weight restriction was part of an overall program to create a sexual image for the airline.

In contrast, this case involves an appearance policy that applied to both male and female bartenders, and was aimed at creating a professional and very similar look for all of them. All bartenders wore the same uniform. The policy only differentiated as to grooming standards.

* * *

We have long recognized that companies may differentiate between men and women in appearance and grooming policies, and so have other circuits. The material issue under our settled law is not whether the policies are different, but whether the policy imposed on the plaintiff creates an "unequal burden" for the plaintiff's gender.

Not every differentiation between the sexes in a grooming and appearance policy creates a "significantly greater burden of compliance[.]" For example, this court upheld [an employer's] enforcement of its sex-differentiated appearance standard, including its requirement that male employees wear ties, because the company's actions in enforcing the regulations were not "overly burdensome to its employees[.]" Similarly, as the Eighth Circuit has recognized, "where, as here, such [grooming and appearance] policies are reasonable and are imposed in an evenhanded manner on all employees, slight differences in the appearance requirements for males and females have only a negligible effect on employment opportunities." Under established equal burdens analysis, when an employer's grooming and appearance policy does not unreasonably burden one gender more than the other, that policy will not violate Title VII.

* * *

III. SEX STEREOTYPING

In Price Waterhouse v. Hopkins, the Supreme Court considered a mixed-motive discrimination case. 490 U.S. 228 (1989). There, the plaintiff, Ann Hopkins, was denied partnership in the national accounting firm of Price Waterhouse because some of the partners found her to be too aggressive. While some partners praised Hopkins's " 'strong character, independence and integrity[,]' " others commented that she needed to take " 'a course at charm school[.]' " The Supreme Court determined that once a plaintiff has established that gender played "a motivating part in an employment decision, the defendant may avoid a finding of liability only by proving by a preponderance of the evidence that it would have made the same decision even if it had not taken the plaintiff's gender into account."

* * *

The stereotyping in *Price Waterhouse* interfered with Hopkins' ability to perform her work; the advice that she should take "a course at charm school" was intended to discourage her use of the forceful and aggressive techniques that made her successful in the first place. Impermissible sex stereotyping was clear because the very traits that she was asked to hide were the same traits considered praiseworthy in men.

Harrah's "Personal Best" policy is very different. The policy does not single out Jespersen. It applies to all of the bartenders, male and female. It requires all of the bartenders to wear exactly the same uniforms while interacting with the public in the context of the entertainment industry. It is for the most part unisex, from the black tie to the non-skid shoes. There is no evidence in this record to indicate that the policy was adopted to make women bartenders conform to a commonly-accepted stereotypical image of what women should wear. The record contains nothing to suggest the grooming standards would objectively inhibit a woman's ability to do the job. The only evidence in the record to support the stereotyping claim is Jespersen's own subjective reaction to the makeup requirement.

* * *

We emphasize that we do not preclude, as a matter of law, a claim of sex-stereotyping on the basis of dress or appearance codes. Others may well be filed, and any bases for such claims refined as law in this area evolves. This record, however, is devoid of any basis for permitting this particular claim to go forward, as it is limited to the subjective reaction of a single employee, and there is no evidence of a stereotypical motivation on the part of the employer. This case is essentially a challenge to one small part of what is an overall apparel, appearance, and grooming policy that applies largely the same requirements to both men and women. A makeup requirement must be seen in the context of the overall standards imposed on employees in a given workplace.

AFFIRMED.

■ KOZINSKI, CIRCUIT JUDGE, with whom JUDGES GRABER and W. FLETCHER join, dissenting:

* * *

It might have been tidier if Jespersen had introduced evidence as to the time and cost associated with complying with the makeup requirement, but I can understand her failure to do so, as these hardly seem like questions reasonably subject to dispute. We could—and should—take judicial notice of these incontrovertible facts.

Alternatively, Jespersen did introduce evidence that she finds it burdensome to *wear* makeup because doing so is inconsistent with her self-image and interferes with her job performance. My colleagues dismiss this evidence, apparently on the ground that wearing makeup does not, as a matter of law, constitute a substantial burden. This presupposes that Jespersen is unreasonable or idiosyncratic in her discomfort. Why so? Whether to wear cosmetics—literally, the face one presents to the world—is an intensely personal choice. Makeup, moreover, touches delicate parts of the anatomy—the lips, the eyes, the cheeks—and can cause serious discomfort, sometimes even allergic reactions for someone unaccustomed to wearing it. If you are used to wearing makeup—as most American women are—this may seem like no big deal. But those of us not used to wearing makeup would find a requirement that we do so highly intrusive. Imagine, for example, a rule that all judges wear face powder, blush, mascara and lipstick while on the bench. Like Jespersen, I would find such a regime burdensome and demeaning; it would interfere with my job performance. I suspect many of my colleagues would feel the same way.

Everyone accepts this as a reasonable reaction from a man, but why should it be different for a woman? It is not because of anatomical differences, such as a requirement that women wear bathing suits that cover their breasts. Women's faces, just like those of men, can be perfectly presentable without makeup; it is a cultural artifact that most women raised in the United States learn to put on—and presumably enjoy wearing—cosmetics. But cultural norms change; not so long ago a man wearing an earring was a gypsy, a pirate or an oddity. Today, a man wearing body piercing jewelry is hardly noticed. So, too, a large (and perhaps growing) number of women choose to present themselves to the world without makeup. I see no justification for forcing them to conform to Harrah's quaint notion of what a "real woman" looks like.

* * *

NOTES AND QUESTIONS

1.   The court rejected both the "unequal burdens" and "sex stereotyping" theories of the plaintiff. As to the former, the court refused to take judicial notice of the time and expense of buying and applying makeup. As to the latter, the court noted that the case did not involve appearance standards designed to be sexually provocative, sexual harassment, or unequal application of its rules. What type of evidence do you think a plaintiff would have to introduce to prevail in a case such as this? The *Jespersen* opinion has not been free from criticism from other courts. In EEOC v. R.G. & G.R. Harris Funeral Homes, Inc., 201 F.Supp.3d 837, 853 (E.D. Mich. 2016), the court noted that it agreed with the dissent rather than the majority in *Jespersen* and held that an employer could not shield itself from liability under the sex stereotyping theory "simply by virtue of having put its gender-based stereotypes into a formal policy."

2.   The case involved a bartender at Harrah's casino in Reno, Nevada. Do you think the same analysis should apply to a bartender at Joe's Corner Bar?

3.   Harrah's "Personal Best Program" also said that employees must be "firm and body toned." Can you think of a possible legal basis for challenging this provision?

4.   At the end of the dissent, Judge Kozinski wrote: "Having won the legal battle, I hope that Harrah's will now do the generous and decent thing by offering Jespersen her job back, and letting her give it her personal best—without the makeup." If you were in Reno or Las Vegas, how would you bet on this proposition? For a further discussion, see Dianne Avery & Marion Crain, Branded: Corporate Image, Sexual Stereotyping, and the New Face of Capitalism, 14 Duke J. Gender L. & Pol'y 13 (2007). Women's appearances may be deemed problematic for different reasons. In Edwards v. Nicolai, 153 A.D. 3d 440 (N.Y. App. Div. 2017), a New York Appeals Court held that a woman who alleged she was fired because she was "too cute" could sue for

gender discrimination under New York state law. When should appearance demands by employers be permissible and when impermissible? Should appearance policing when applied to women always be treated as a form of sex discrimination? If so, why?

5. Hooters restaurants have been the subject of several lawsuits alleging sex discrimination and sexual harassment. The suits usually charge that the plaintiffs were required to wear sexually provocative outfits and that they had to endure sexually offensive remarks and contact. Both customers and supervisors have been alleged to have made unwelcome remarks of a sexual nature as well as unwelcome touching. Have the women servers "assumed the risk" of this conduct by going to work for such an employer? See Kelly Ann Cahill, Hooters: Should There Be an Assumption of Risk Defense to Some Hostile Work Environment Sexual Harassment Claims?, 48 Vand.L.Rev. 1107 (1995). What is the essence of the business? If you think that the conduct of Hooters is unlawful, would it be unlawful if the employer were a topless bar? Should it matter if Hooters calls itself a "family restaurant?" Can you formulate some workable legal doctrine to cover "mixed essence" businesses?

6. As *Jespersen* makes clear, not all forms of sex-based differentiation violate Title VII. In Bauer v. Lynch, 812 F.3d 340, 351 (4th Cir. 2016), the Fourth Circuit held that an employer, in this case the Federal Bureau of Investigation, did not violate Title VII when it required male candidates seeking to become agents to complete 30 push ups as part of their physical fitness test, but required female candidates to complete only 14. In Frank v. United Airlines, Inc., 216 F.3d 845 (9th Cir. 2000), the court held that an employer can require all employees to wear sex-differentiated uniforms, but it would violate Title VII for the employer to require only female employees to wear uniforms.

7. Would an employer violate Title VII by prohibiting women employees from wearing pants in the executive offices? See Lanigan v. Bartlett & Co. Grain, 466 F.Supp. 1388 (W.D.Mo.1979) (held: no). California law makes it illegal for an employer to prohibit female employees from wearing pants to work, unless special clothing is required as a uniform or costume. Cal. Gov't Code § 12947.5. Would a public employer's "pants-only" rule, based on safety considerations, violate a female driver's First Amendment right of freedom of expression? See Zalewska v. Sullivan County, 316 F.3d 314 (2d Cir. 2003) (held no).

(b) Pregnancy

In 1974, the Supreme Court ruled in Geduldig v. Aiello, 417 U.S. 484 (1974), that excluding pregnancy coverage from the list of compensable disabilities under the California Disability Plan did not constitute sex discrimination. "While it is true that only women can become pregnant . . . the program divides potential recipients into two groups—pregnant women and nonpregnant persons. While the first group is exclusively female, the second includes members of both sexes. The fiscal and actuarial benefits of the program thus accrue to members of both sexes."

General Elec. v. Gilbert, 429 U.S. 125 (1976), found no violation when a health insurance plan provided to employees by an employer did not cover pregnancy.

In response to the public outcry that followed these decisions, Congress enacted the Pregnancy Discrimination Act of 1978 ("PDA"), amending Title VII to provide:

> The terms "because of sex" or "on the basis of sex" include, but are not limited to, because of or on the basis of pregnancy, childbirth, or related medical conditions; and women affected by pregnancy, childbirth, or related medical conditions shall be treated the same for all employment-related purposes, including receipt of benefits under fringe benefit programs, as other persons not so affected but similar in their ability to work.

Young v. United Parcel Service, Inc.
575 U.S. 206 (2015).

■ JUSTICE BREYER delivered the opinion of the Court.

The Pregnancy Discrimination Act makes clear that Title VII's prohibition against sex discrimination applies to discrimination based on pregnancy. It also says that employers must treat "women affected by pregnancy . . . the same for all employment-related purposes . . . as other persons not so affected but similar in their ability or inability to work." We must decide how this latter provision applies in the context of an employer's policy that accommodates many, but not all, workers with nonpregnancy-related disabilities.

* * *

We begin with a summary of the facts. The petitioner, Peggy Young, worked as a part-time driver for the respondent, United Parcel Service (UPS). Her responsibilities included pickup and delivery of packages that had arrived by air carrier the previous night. In 2006, after suffering several miscarriages, she became pregnant. Her doctor told her that she should not lift more than 20 pounds during the first 20 weeks of her pregnancy or more than 10 pounds thereafter. UPS required drivers like Young to be able to lift parcels weighing up to 70 pounds (and up to 150 pounds with assistance). UPS told Young she could not work while under a lifting restriction. Young consequently stayed home without pay during most of the time she was pregnant and eventually lost her employee medical coverage.

Young subsequently brought this federal lawsuit. We focus here on her claim that UPS acted unlawfully in refusing to accommodate her pregnancy-related lifting restriction. Young said that her co-workers were willing to help her with heavy packages. She also said that UPS accommodated other drivers who were "similar in their . . . inability to work." She accordingly concluded that UPS must accommodate her as well.

UPS responded that the "other persons" whom it had accommodated were (1) drivers who had become disabled on the job, (2) those who had lost their Department of Transportation (DOT) certifications, and (3) those who suffered from a disability covered by the Americans with Disabilities Act of 1990 (ADA). UPS said that, since Young did not fall within any of those categories, it had not discriminated against Young on the basis of pregnancy but had treated her just as it treated all "other" relevant "persons."

* * *

The District Court granted UPS' motion for summary judgment. It concluded that Young could not show intentional discrimination through direct evidence. Nor could she make out a prima facie case of discrimination under McDonnell Douglas. The court wrote that those with whom Young compared herself—those falling within the on-the-job, DOT, or ADA categories—were too different to qualify as "similarly situated comparator [s]." The court added that, in any event, UPS had offered a legitimate, nondiscriminatory reason for failing to accommodate pregnant women, and Young had not created a genuine issue of material fact as to whether that reason was pretextual.

On appeal, the Fourth Circuit affirmed. It wrote that "UPS has crafted a pregnancy-blind policy" that is "at least facially a 'neutral and legitimate business practice,' and not evidence of UPS's discriminatory animus toward pregnant workers." It also agreed with the District Court that Young could not show that "similarly-situated employees outside the protected class received more favorable treatment than Young." Specifically, it believed that Young was different from those workers who were "disabled under the ADA" (which then protected only those with permanent disabilities) because Young was "not disabled"; her lifting limitation was only "temporary and not a significant restriction on her ability to perform major life activities." Young was also different from those workers who had lost their DOT certifications because "no legal obstacle stands between her and her work" and because many with lost DOT certifications retained physical (i.e., lifting) capacity that Young lacked. And Young was different from those "injured on the job because, quite simply, her inability to work [did] not arise from an on-the-job injury." Rather, Young more closely resembled "an employee who injured his back while picking up his infant child or . . . an employee whose lifting limitation arose from her off-the-job work as a volunteer firefighter," neither of whom would have been eligible for accommodation under UPS' policies.

* * *

II

The parties disagree about the interpretation of the Pregnancy Discrimination Act's second clause. As we have said, * * * the Act's first clause specifies that discrimination " 'because of sex' " includes discrimination "because of . . . pregnancy." But the meaning of the second clause is less clear; it adds: "[W]omen affected by pregnancy, childbirth, or related medical conditions shall be treated the same for all employment-related purposes . . . as *other persons* not so affected but *similar in their ability or inability to work.*" Does this clause mean that courts must compare workers only in respect to the work limitations that they suffer? Does it mean that courts must ignore all other similarities or differences between pregnant and nonpregnant workers? Or does it mean that courts, when deciding who the relevant "other persons" are, may consider other similarities and differences as well? If so, which ones?

* * *

The parties propose very different answers to this question. Young and the United States believe that the second clause of the Pregnancy Discrimination Act "requires an employer to provide the same accommodations to workplace disabilities caused by pregnancy that it provides to workplace disabilities that have other causes but have a similar effect on the ability to work." In other words, Young contends that the second clause means that whenever "an employer accommodates only a subset of workers with disabling conditions," a court should find a Title VII violation if "pregnant workers who are similar in the ability to work" do not "receive the same [accommodation] even if still other non-pregnant workers do not receive accommodations."

UPS takes an almost polar opposite view. It contends that the second clause does no more than define sex discrimination to include pregnancy discrimination. Under this view, courts would compare the accommodations an employer provides to pregnant women with the accommodations it provides to others within a facially neutral category (such as those with off-the-job injuries) to determine whether the employer has violated Title VII.

A

We cannot accept either of these interpretations. Young asks us to interpret the second clause broadly and, in her view, literally. As just noted, she argues that, as long as "an employer accommodates only a subset of workers with disabling conditions," "pregnant workers who are similar in the ability to work [must] receive the same treatment even if still other nonpregnant workers do not receive accommodations." She adds that, because the record here contains "evidence that pregnant and nonpregnant workers were not treated the same," that is the end of the matter, she must win; there is no need to refer to *McDonnell Douglas.*

The problem with Young's approach is that it proves too much. It seems to say that the statute grants pregnant workers a "most-favored-nation" status. As long as an employer provides one or two workers with an accommodation—say, those with particularly hazardous jobs, or those whose workplace presence is particularly needed, or those who have worked at the company for many years, or those who are over the age of 55—then it must provide similar accommodations to all pregnant workers (with comparable physical limitations), irrespective of the nature of their jobs, the employer's need to keep them working, their ages, or any other criteria.

* * *

We agree with UPS to this extent: We doubt that Congress intended to grant pregnant workers an unconditional most-favored-nation status. The language of the statute does not require that unqualified reading. The second clause, when referring to nonpregnant persons with similar disabilities, uses the open-ended term "other persons." It does not say that the employer must treat pregnant employees the "same" as "any other persons" (who are similar in their ability or inability to work), nor does it otherwise specify which other persons Congress had in mind.

* * *

III

The statute lends itself to an interpretation other than those that the parties advocate and that the dissent sets forth. Our interpretation minimizes the problems we have discussed, responds directly to *Gilbert*, and is consistent with longstanding interpretations of Title VII.

In our view, an individual pregnant worker who seeks to show disparate treatment through indirect evidence may do so through application of the *McDonnell Douglas* framework. That framework requires a plaintiff to make out a prima facie case of discrimination. But it is "not intended to be an inflexible rule." Furnco Constr. Corp. v. Waters, 438 U.S. 567, 575 (1978). Rather, an individual plaintiff may establish a prima facie case by "showing actions taken by the employer from which one can infer, if such actions remain unexplained, that it is more likely than not that such actions were based on a discriminatory criterion illegal under" Title VII. The burden of making this showing is "not onerous." In particular, making this showing is not as burdensome as succeeding on "an ultimate finding of fact as to" a discriminatory employment action. Neither does it require the plaintiff to show that those whom the employer favored and those whom the employer disfavored were similar in all but the protected ways.

Thus, a plaintiff alleging that the denial of an accommodation constituted disparate treatment under the Pregnancy Discrimination Act's second clause may make out a prima facie case by showing, as in *McDonnell Douglas*, that she belongs to the protected class, that she sought accommodation, that the employer did not accommodate her, and that the employer did accommodate others "similar in their ability or inability to work."

The employer may then seek to justify its refusal to accommodate the plaintiff by relying on "legitimate, nondiscriminatory" reasons for denying her accommodation. But, consistent with the Act's basic objective, that reason normally cannot consist simply of a claim that it is more expensive or less convenient to add pregnant women to the category of those ("similar in their ability or inability to work") whom the employer accommodates. After all, the employer in *Gilbert* could in all likelihood have made just such a claim.

If the employer offers an apparently "legitimate, nondiscriminatory" reason for its actions, the plaintiff may in turn show that the employer's proffered reasons are in fact pretextual. We believe that the plaintiff may reach a jury on this issue by providing sufficient evidence that the employer's policies impose a significant burden on pregnant workers, and that the employer's "legitimate, nondiscriminatory" reasons are not sufficiently strong to justify the burden, but rather—when considered along with the burden imposed—give rise to an inference of intentional discrimination.

The plaintiff can create a genuine issue of material fact as to whether a significant burden exists by providing evidence that the employer accommodates a large percentage of nonpregnant workers while failing to accommodate a large percentage of pregnant workers. Here, for example, if the facts are as Young says they are, she can show that UPS accommodates most nonpregnant employees with lifting limitations while categorically failing to accommodate pregnant employees with lifting limitations. Young might also add that the fact that UPS has multiple policies that accommodate nonpregnant employees with lifting restrictions suggests that its reasons for failing to accommodate pregnant employees with lifting restrictions are not sufficiently strong—to the point that a jury could find that its reasons for failing to accommodate pregnant employees give rise to an inference of intentional discrimination.

* * *

IV

Under this interpretation of the Act, the judgment of the Fourth Circuit must be vacated. A party is entitled to summary judgment if there is "no genuine dispute as to any material fact and the movant is entitled to judgment as a matter of law." Fed. Rule Civ. Proc. 56(a). We have already outlined the evidence Young introduced. Viewing the record in the light most favorable to Young, there is a genuine dispute as to whether UPS provided more favorable treatment to at least some employees whose situation cannot reasonably be distinguished from Young's. In other words, Young created a genuine dispute of material fact as to the fourth prong of the *McDonnell Douglas* analysis.

* * *

We do not determine whether Young created a genuine issue of material fact as to whether UPS' reasons for having treated Young less favorably than it treated these other nonpregnant employees were pretextual. We leave a final determination of that question for the Fourth Circuit to make on remand, in light of the interpretation of the Pregnancy Discrimination Act that we have set out above.

* * *

For the reasons above, we vacate the judgment of the Fourth Circuit and remand the case for further proceedings consistent with this opinion.

It is so ordered.

NOTES

1.   For a discussion of the PDA as it affects health benefits, see infra, Chapter 6.

2.   In *Young*, the Supreme Court made clear that the PDA does not grant pregnant workers a "most-favored-nation status" entitling them to the very best treatment that the employer provides to another group of employees similar in their ability or inability to work. Nonetheless, the Court also explained that an employer cannot always protect itself from liability simply by pointing to some other group of workers similar in their ability or inability to work that it treats similarly to pregnant workers. Instead, a plaintiff may still win if she can convince a jury that there is no legitimate non-discriminatory reason for the employer's policies treating pregnant workers less favorably than other similarly situated categories of non-pregnant workers. For large employers who distinguish between many types of disabled workers, how much guidance does the Court's ruling in *Young* provide about which particular subset of employees pregnant women will be compared to and when an employer will be found in violation of Title VII? State law may provide pregnant workers with greater protection. In January 2014, New Jersey amended its Law Against Discrimination to not only explicitly prohibit discrimination against pregnant women but also to require employers to make reasonable accommodations available to pregnant workers. N.J.S.A. 10:5–12. However, should an employer choose to provide special accommodations to pregnant employees, it may not necessarily be able to force the employees to accept the accommodations. This is particularly relevant when accommodations involve a reduction in hours or responsibilities resulting in a lower salary. In EEOC v. Catholic Healthcare W., 530 F.Supp.2d 1096 (C.D. Cal. 2008), a federal district court applied the BFOQ test to Catholic Healthcare's unsolicited transfer of a pregnant radiology technologist to a different area of work. Catholic Healthcare's transfer was found to be discriminatory.

3.   Loyal American Life Insurance Company offered Margaret Ahmad employment as a medical claims examiner but withdrew its offer two days later when it learned that she was four months pregnant. Loyal American contended that Ms. Ahmad's anticipated leave of absence would interfere with her four to five month long training program. Ms. Ahmad sued alleging pregnancy discrimination. The court found for the employer and held that the insurance company had a legitimate concern in only hiring employees who could begin processing claims immediately after training. Ahmad v. Loyal Am. Life Ins. Co., 767 F.Supp. 1114 (S.D.Ala.1991). Do you agree that a company may consider a pregnant applicant's anticipated maternity leave in denying her employment? Could an employer also inquire about an applicant's plans to raise a family? What if the employee changes her mind? Cf. Lulaj v. Wackenhut Corp., 512 F.3d 760 (6th Cir. 2008) (plaintiff made out prima facie case of discrimination where she was promised a promotion to supervisor but was offered a lesser promotion after her employer learned she was pregnant).

4. A collective bargaining agreement at Lucky Stores provided one year of leave for work-related illnesses or injuries and six months for disabilities including pregnancy that are not caused by work. This satisfied the California and U.S. rules for family leave, but the distinction between work-related absences and pregnancy absences was challenged as a violation of state anti-discrimination law. The court found no violation. Spaziano v. Lucky Stores, Inc., 81 Cal.Rptr.2d 378 (Cal.App. 1999). Recent decisions by courts have generally allowed a similar distinction between work-related disabilities and pregnancy. See Serednyj v. Beverly Healthcare, LLC, 656 F.3d 540 (7th Cir. 2011); Urbano v. Continental Airlines, Inc., 138 F.3d 204 (5th Cir. 1998), cert. denied, 525 U.S. 1000 (1998); Young v. United Parcel Serv., Inc., 2011 WL 665321 (D. Md. Feb. 14, 2011); Brophy v. Day & Zimmerman Hawthorne Corp., 799 F.Supp.2d 1185 (D. Nev. 2011); Cunningham v. Dearborn Bd. of Educ., 246 Mich. App. 621, 633 N.W.2d 481 (2001).

5. Plaintiff, a truck driver whose responsibilities included occasional heavy lifting and loading of trucks, was terminated due to a lifting restriction imposed by her physician because of her pregnancy. She asserted a violation of the PDA. The court of appeals held that the PDA was not violated even though the employer provided an accommodation of light-duty work to workers injured on the job but not to pregnant workers. Reeves v. Swift Trans. Co., Inc., 446 F.3d 637 (6th Cir. 2006). See also Spivey v. Beverly Enter., Inc., 196 F.3d 1309 (11th Cir. 1999). In Stansfield v. O'Reilly Auto., Inc., 2006 WL 1030010 (S.D.Tex. 2006), however, the court denied the employer's motion for summary judgment, finding a prima facie case of discrimination in violation of the PDA when the employer refused to apply its lifting policy for female employees asking male employees for assistance to the plaintiff when she announced that she was pregnant.

6. In the case of religious institutions, pregnant women may be terminated not for the pregnancy itself but rather for premarital sex. In 1996, Leigh Cline's teaching contract with the Catholic Diocese of Toledo was not renewed because Cline's due date was only five months after her wedding. The court of appeals reversed an award of summary judgment for the defendant. By engaging in premarital sex, Cline violated her duties to uphold the school's religious teachings; however, "a school cannot use the mere observation or knowledge of pregnancy as its sole method of detecting violations of its premarital sex policy." Cline v. Catholic Diocese of Toledo,

206 F.3d 651, 667 (6th Cir. 2000). In a similar case, Jarretta Hamilton was fired from Southland Christian School after informing the school administrator that she had engaged in premarital sex. In 2012, the court of appeals reversed an award of summary judgment for the school, finding "a genuine issue of material fact about the reason that Southland fired her." Hamilton v. Southland Christian Sch., Inc., 680 F.3d 1316 (11th Cir. 2012).

7.　　Plaintiff was a probationary employee for her first ninety days. The employer maintained a strict attendance policy: Anyone missing more than three days during the probationary period was terminated. Plaintiff experienced early labor and a miscarriage. She missed two weeks of work and was fired. Held: no violation of the Pregnancy Discrimination Act. Absences for pregnancy were treated the same as absences for other reasons. "The PDA does not require preferential treatment of pregnant employees and does not require employers to treat pregnancy related absences more leniently than other absences * * *. To hold otherwise would be to transform the PDA into a guarantee of medical leave for pregnant employees * * *." Stout v. Baxter Healthcare Corp., 282 F.3d 856 (5th Cir. 2002).

8.　　What, if any, rights should men have under the PDA? A farm owned by an order of Catholic nuns fired two employees on the same day, a man and his girlfriend, who had become pregnant and suffered two miscarriages while working on the farm. The employer claimed that it terminated the male employee because of dissatisfaction with the way he ran the farm's internship program and the female employee because her services were no longer needed. However, the director of the farm had also expressed concerns about the employees' openness with their relationship and their "behavior contrary to Roman Catholic teachings." The employees, acting pro se, argued that the employer's explanations were pretextual and that the PDA protects males and females equally for "exercising their reproductive rights." The Seventh Circuit disagreed, upholding summary judgment for the employer. Although the PDA's language and purpose speak to discrimination against women, men can still be successful PDA plaintiffs, but their claims must allege discrimination because of sex. Griffin v. Sisters of St. Francis, 489 F.3d 838 (7th Cir. 2007). For a discussion of the PDA and discrimination in benefits, see Ch. 6.

9.　　The PDA says that "because of sex" includes "pregnancy, childbirth, or related medical conditions." The EEOC guidelines say: "A woman is therefore protected against such practices as being fired * * * merely because she is pregnant or has had an abortion." See, e.g., Doe v. C.A.R.S. Protection Plus, Inc., 527 F.3d 358 (3d Cir. 2008).

10.　Before enactment of the PDA in 1978, discrimination on the basis of pregnancy was not a violation of Title VII. At that time, AT & T's pension system gave less retirement credit for pregnancy leave than for medical leave generally. After the PDA took effect in 1979, the company equalized treatment of pregnancy leave. The Supreme Court decided in 2009 that the PDA did not apply retroactively, so current pensions affected by the pre-1979 discrimination do not violate Title VII. Justices Ginsburg and Breyer dissented. AT & T Corp. v. Hulteen, 556 U.S. 701 (2009). For a further discussion of pensions, see Ch. 13.

11. Cheryl Hall said she was fired for taking time off from work to undergo in vitro fertilization. The district court dismissed a PDA claim, saying infertility is a gender-neutral condition. The court of appeals reversed. The procedure Hall underwent is performed only on women. "Hall was terminated not for the gender-neutral condition of infertility, but rather for the gender-specific quality of childbearing capacity." Hall v. Nalco Co., 534 F.3d 644 (7th Cir. 2008). For a discussion of health benefits for infertility treatments, see Ch. 6.

12. The PDA has generally not been interpreted to extend protection to women who seek to breastfeed at work. See, e.g., Wallace v. Pyro Mining Co., 951 F.2d 351 (6th Cir. 1991) (PDA did not give employee right to breastfeed at work because doing so was not a medical necessity); Barrash v. Bowen, 846 F.2d 927, 931 (4th Cir. 1988) (plaintiff could not establish disparate impact claim based on denial of breastfeeding leave because the PDA applied only to incapacitating illnesses). Recently, the Fifth Circuit held that lactation was a related medical condition of pregnancy for purposes of the PDA and that discrimination against a woman because she is lactating or expressing breast milk violates Title VII and the PDA. Importantly, however, the plaintiff in the case did not seek any accommodation to breastfeed and was allegedly fired simply for raising the issue of breastfeeding at work with her employer. See EEOC v. Houston Funding II, 717 F.3d 425 (2013). The Patient Protection and Affordable Care Act, H.R. 3590, which President Obama signed into law on March 23, 2010, does provide some limited protection to breastfeeding mothers. The Act amended the Fair Labor Standards Act of 1938 (29 U.S.C. § 207) to require an employer to provide reasonable break time for a nonexempt employee to express breast milk for one year after a child's birth. As of 2014, twenty-five states also have laws providing some protection for breastfeeding in the workplace. See National Conference of State Legislatures, available at http://www.ncsl.org/issues-research/health/breastfeeding-state-laws.aspx (last visited July 30, 2014).

(c)   Caregiver Discrimination

Back v. Hastings on Hudson Union Free School District

365 F.3d 107 (2d Cir. 2004).

■ CALABRESI, CIRCUIT JUDGE.

In 1998, Plaintiff Appellant Elana Back was hired as a school psychologist at the Hillside Elementary School on a three-year tenure track. At the end of that period, when Back came up for review, she was denied tenure and her probationary period was terminated. Back subsequently brought this lawsuit, seeking damages and injunctive relief under 42 U.S.C. § 1983 (2000). She alleged that the termination violated her constitutional right to equal protection of the laws. Defendant-Appellees contend that Back was fired because she lacked organizational and interpersonal skills. Back asserts that the real reason she was let go was that the defendants presumed that she, as a young mother, would not continue to demonstrate the necessary devotion to her job, and indeed that she could not maintain such devotion while at the same time being a good mother.

This appeal thus poses an important question, one that strikes at the persistent "fault line between work and family precisely where sex-based overgeneralization has been and remains strongest." It asks whether stereotyping about the qualities of mothers is a form of gender discrimination, and whether this can be determined in the absence of evidence about how the employer in question treated fathers. We answer both questions in the affirmative.

* * *

As the school psychologist at Hillside Elementary School, Elana Back counseled and conducted psychological evaluations of students, prepared reports for the Committee on Special Education, assisted teachers in dealing with students who acted out in class, worked with parents on issues related to their children, and chaired the "Learning Team," a group made up of specialists and teachers which conducted intensive discussions about individual students. Defendant-Appellee Marilyn Wishnie, the Principal of Hillside, and defendant-appellee Ann Brennan, the Director of Pupil Personnel Services for the District, were Back's supervisors. They were responsible for establishing performance goals for her position, and evaluating Back's work against these standards.

In the plaintiff's first two years at Hillside, Brennan and Wishnie consistently gave her excellent evaluations. In her first annual evaluation, on a scale where the highest score was "outstanding," and the second highest score was "superior," Back was deemed "outstanding" and "superior" in almost all categories, and "average" in only one. "Superior" was, according to the performance instrument, the "standard for consideration for obtaining tenure in Hastings." Narrative evaluations completed by Wishnie and Brennan during this time were also uniformly positive, attesting, for example, that Back had "served as a positive child advocate throughout the year," and had "successfully adjusted to become a valued and valuable member of the school/community."

In her second year at Hillside, Back took approximately three months of maternity leave. After she returned, she garnered another "outstanding" evaluation from Brennan, who noted that she was "very pleased with Mrs. Back's performance during her second year at Hillside." Other contemporaneous observations also resulted in strongly positive feedback, for example, that Back "demonstrate[d] her strong social/emotional skills in her work with parents and teachers, and most especially with students," and that she was "a positive influence in many areas, and continues to extend a great deal of effort and commitment to our work." In her annual evaluation, Back received higher marks than the previous year, with more "outstandings" and no "averages." The narrative comments noted that she "continues to serve in an outstanding manner and provides excellent support for our students," and that her "commitment to her work and to her own learning is outstanding." At the beginning of Back's third year at Hillside, she again received "outstanding" and "superior" evaluations from both Brennan and Wishnie.

* * *

Back asserts that things changed dramatically as her tenure review approached. The first allegedly discriminatory comments came in spring 2000, when Back's written evaluations still indicated that she was a very strong candidate for tenure. At that time, shortly after Back had returned from maternity leave, the plaintiff claims that Brennan, (a) inquired about how she was "planning on spacing [her] offspring," (b) said " '[p]lease do not get pregnant until I retire,' " and (c) suggested that Back "wait until [her son] was in kindergarten to have another child."

Then, a few months into Back's third year at Hillside, on December 14, 2000, Brennan allegedly told Back that she was expected to work until 4:30 p.m. every day, and asked "What's the big deal. You have a nanny. This is what you [have] to do to get tenure." Back replied that she did work these hours. And Brennan, after reportedly reassuring Back that there was no concern about her job performance, told her that Wishnie expected her to work such hours. But, always according to Back, Brennan also indicated that Back should "maybe * * * reconsider whether [Back] could be a mother and do this job which [Brennan] characterized as administrative in nature," and that Brennan and Wishnie were "concerned that, if [Back] received tenure, [she] would work only until 3:15 p.m. and did not know how [she] could possibly do this job with children."

A few days later, on January 8, 2001, Brennan allegedly told Back for the first time that she might not support Back's tenure because of what Back characterizes as minor errors that she made in a report. According to Back, shortly thereafter Principal Wishnie accused her of working only from 8:15 a.m. to 3:15 p.m. and never working during lunch. When Back disputed this, Wishnie supposedly replied that "this was not [Wishnie's] impression and * * * that she did not know how she could perform my job with little ones. She told me that she worked from 7 a.m. to 7 p.m. and that she expected the same from me. If my family was my priority, she stated, maybe this was not the job for me." A week later, both Brennan and Wishnie reportedly told Back that this was perhaps not the job or the school district for her if she had "little ones," and that it was "not possible for [her] to be a good mother and have this job." The two also allegedly remarked that it would be harder to fire Back if she had tenure, and wondered "whether my apparent commitment to my job was an act. They stated that once I obtained tenure, I would not show the same level of commitment I had shown because I had little ones at home. They expressed concerns about my child care arrangements, though these had never caused me conflict with school assignments." They did not—as Back told the story—discuss with her any concerns with her performance at that time.

Back claims that in March, Brennan and Wishnie reiterated that her job was "not for a mother," that they were worried her performance was "just an 'act' until I got tenure," and that "because I was a young mother, I would not continue my commitment to the work place." On April 30, 2001, Brennan and Wishnie purportedly repeated the same concerns about her ability to balance work and family, and told Back that they would recommend that she not be granted tenure and that Superintendent Russell would follow their recommendation. They reportedly also "stated they wanted another year to assess the child care situation."

Brennan and Wishnie both testified in depositions that they never questioned Back's ability to combine work and motherhood, and did not insinuate that they thought the commitment that Back had previously demonstrated was an "act." They contended, instead, that Back was told at these meetings that both had concerns about her performance, and that she would need to make progress in certain areas in order to receive tenure.

Back retained counsel in response to Brennan and Wishnie's alleged statements, and in a letter dated May 14, 2001, informed Russell of these comments, and of her fear that they reflected attitudes that would improperly affect her tenure review. On May 29, 2001, Brennan and Wishnie sent a formal memo to Russell informing him that they could not recommend Back for tenure. Their reasons included (a) that although their formal reports had been positive, their informal interactions with her had been less positive, (b) that there were "far too many" parents and teachers who had "serious issues" with the plaintiff and did not wish to work with her, and (c) that she had persistent difficulties with the planning and organization of her work, and with inaccuracies in her reports, and that she had not shown improvement in this area, despite warnings.

* * *

On or around June 13, 2001, Wishnie and Brennan filed the first negative evaluation of Back, which gave her several "below average" marks and charged her with being inconsistent, defensive, difficult to supervise, the source of parental complaints, and inaccurate in her reports. Their evaluation, which was submitted to Russell, concluded that Back should not be granted tenure. Around the same time, several parents who had apparently complained about Back were encouraged by Russell to put their concerns in writing. Several parents submitted letters, reporting a range of complaints about Back's work, including that she was defensive, immature, unprofessional, and had misdiagnosed children.

On June 18, 2001, Russell informed Back by letter that he had received Wishnie and Brennan's annual evaluation, and was recommending to the Board of Education that her probationary appointment be terminated. The union filed a grievance on Back's behalf, claiming that Brennan and Wishnie's discriminatory comments tainted the termination decision. The grievance review process first involved an evaluation by Wishnie, who denied making any comments about the incompatibility of Back's work and motherhood, and concluded that the union grievance was without merit. At the second stage of the process, a panel, consisting of two teachers in the district and an administrator, was convened by the Board of Education. The group examined the plaintiff's file, interviewed Back, Brennan, and Wishnie, and reported to Russell in July that it agreed with his recommendation not to grant plaintiff tenure. In September 2001, the Board notified Back that her probationary appointment would be terminated.

* * *

Individuals have a clear right, protected by the Fourteenth Amendment, to be free from discrimination on the basis of sex in public employment * * *. Back does not allege a violation of Title VII, nor does she allege that the defendants violated her constitutional rights to have and care for children. We therefore consider only whether she has alleged facts that can support a finding of gender discrimination under the Equal Protection Clause.

To make out such a claim, the plaintiff must prove that she suffered purposeful or intentional discrimination on the basis of gender.

To show sex discrimination, Back relies upon a Price Waterhouse v. Hopkins, 490 U.S. 228 (1989) "stereotyping" theory. * * * The instant case, however, foregrounds a crucial question: What constitutes a "gender-based stereotype"? *Price Waterhouse* suggested that this question must be answered in the particular context in which it arises, and without undue formalization. We have adopted the same approach, as have other circuits. Just as "[i]t takes no special training to discern sex stereotyping in a description of an aggressive female employee as requiring 'a course at charm school,' so it takes no special training to discern stereotyping in the view that a woman cannot 'be a good mother' " and have a job that requires long hours, or in the statement that a mother who received tenure "would not show the same level of commitment [she] had shown because [she] had little ones at home." These are not the kind of "innocuous words" that we have previously held to be insufficient, as a matter of law, to provide evidence of discriminatory intent.

* * *

The defendants argue that stereotypes about pregnant women or mothers are not based upon gender, but rather, "gender plus parenthood," thereby implying that such stereotypes cannot, without comparative evidence of what was said about fathers, be presumed to be "on the basis of sex." Nevada Department of Human Resources v. Hibbs, 538 U.S. 721 (2003), makes pellucidly clear, however, that, at least where stereotypes are considered, the notions that mothers are insufficiently devoted to work, and that work and motherhood are incompatible, are properly considered to be, themselves, gender-based. *Hibbs* explicitly called the stereotype that "women's family duties trump those of the workplace" a "*gender* stereotype," and cited a number of state pregnancy and family leave acts including laws that provided *only* pregnancy leave as evidence of "pervasive sex-role stereotype that caring for family members is women's work,"

Defendants are thus wrong in their contention that Back cannot make out a claim that survives summary judgment unless she demonstrates that the defendants treated similarly situated men differently. Back has admittedly proffered no evidence about the treatment of male administrators with young children. Although her case would be stronger had she provided or alleged the existence of such evidence, there is no requirement that such evidence be adduced.

* * *

Defendants also fail in their claim that they are immune from Back's allegations simply because, in the year that Back was hired, 85% of the teachers employed at Hillside were women, and 71% of these women had children. As *Brown* indicates, although the jury is surely allowed to consider such comparative evidence, what matters is how *Back* was treated. Furthermore, the defendants make no mention of the number of men or women in *administrative* positions, nor of the age of any of the relevant children. Both details are essential if the comparative evidence adduced by the defendants is to be given any weight.

* * *

Applying [legal doctrine] to the facts before us, we hold that Back has clearly produced sufficient evidence to defeat summary judgment as to Brennan and Wishnie. She has made out her prima facie case by offering evidence of discriminatory comments, which can constitute "direct evidence," and are adequate to make out a prima facie case, even where uncorroborated. The nondiscriminatory reasons proffered by Brennan and Wishnie for their negative evaluations namely, Back's poor organizational skills and her negative interactions with parents are in no way dispositive. Viewing the evidence in the light most favorable to Back, a jury could find that the administrative deficiencies cited by the defendants were minor, and unimportant to the defendants before the development of the purported discriminatory motive. As for the parental complaints, it is unclear which of these Brennan and Wishnie were aware of at the time of their negative recommendations and evaluations. But Back's allegations, in any event, are sufficient to allow a jury to find that these complaints were not the real reason for their proffered criticisms of Back. Back asserts, for example, that "[i]n even the most supportive school setting, whether dealing with a teacher or provider of special services, as I was, a small minority of parents will always be critical of the professional. I had very minor skirmishes with several parents while in Hastings. But * * * Brennan and Wishnie always emphasized to me that I was doing an excellent job and that the complaining parent had her own problems coping with the reality of having a classified child." If some of these "skirmishes" were in Back's first two years, as she alleges, then her performance evaluations conducted by Brennan and Wishnie also tend to support her version of events. Similarly, although Back's second year evaluations indicated that she faced some challenges in dealing with teachers and parents who were resistant to her advocacy for students, they also noted that Back was aware of these issues and working to "enhance" this area. Back also alleges that Brennan and Wishnie instructed her not to have parents or supporters submit positive letters for her file. This, and the sudden decline in performance evaluations that occurred between the beginning and end of Back's third year that is, only after the alleged discriminatory comments began support a conclusion of pretext.

We conclude that a jury could find, on the evidence proffered, that Brennan and Wishnie's cited justifications for their adverse recommendation and evaluation were pretextual, and that discrimination was one of the "motivating" reasons for the recommendations against Back's tenure.

* * *

Municipalities and other local government bodies, including school districts, are considered "persons" within the meaning of § 1983. But a municipality cannot be held liable pursuant to § 1983 solely because of the discriminatory actions of one of its employees. The District can therefore only be held liable if its "policy or custom, whether made by its lawmakers or by those whose edicts or acts may fairly be said to represent official policy, inflicts the injury." Back makes no allegation that the District engaged in a "custom" of sex discrimination. There is, that is, no claim of a "relevant practice [that] is so widespread as to have the force of law" with regard to mothers of young children in positions like Back's.

* * *

We find that the plaintiff adduced facts sufficient to allow a jury to determine that defendants Brennan and Wishnie discriminated against Back on the basis of gender, and that qualified immunity should not attach to their behavior. Accordingly we VACATE the district court's grant of summary judgment, and REMAND the case for trial with respect to them. We also hold that no material facts support the conclusion that the School District or Superintendent Russell acted with the requisite intent to discriminate against the plaintiff. We therefore AFFIRM summary judgment as applied to these two defendants only.

NOTES

1. Plaintiff Back was not successful in her jury trial. Back v. Hastings on Hudson, 161 F. App'x 96 (2d Cir. 2005).

2. Cynthia Fisher sued Vassar when she was denied tenure, alleging violations of Title VII and the Age Discrimination in Employment Act (ADEA) under the theory of "sex plus" discrimination, which was recognized by the Supreme Court in Phillips v. Martin Marietta Corp., 400 U.S. 542 (1971).

Fisher had spent eight years away from the teaching profession while caring for her two children. She alleged that "it was her decision to be a wife, mother and a scientist before seeking tenure at Vassar that resulted in the denial of [her] tenure application" and "claim[ed] that despite her qualifications and her progress in becoming current in her field, her absence from academia was held against her as an insurmountable barrier."

The district court found for plaintiff and criticized Vassar's "acceptance of a stereotype and bias: that a married woman with an active and on-going family life cannot be a productive scientist and, therefore, is not one despite much evidence to the contrary."

A panel of the court of appeals for the second circuit reversed: "In making tenure decisions, it is perfectly reasonable to consider as a factor the candidate's prolonged absence from academia in making hiring and promotion decisions. The law does not prevent employers from considering such things. Moreover, the choice of remaining at home for an extended period following the birth of a child 'is not the inevitable consequence of a medical condition related to pregnancy.' A policy may discriminate between those employees who take off long periods of time in order to raise children and those who either do not have children or are able to raise them without an appreciable career interruption. That is not inherently sex specific and does not give rise to a claim under Title VII." Fisher v. Vassar College, 70 F.3d 1420, 1448 (2d Cir.), aff'd en banc, 114 F.3d 1332 (1997).

Who was right, the district or the circuit court? Compare Cynthia Fisher to Ann Hopkins. Is it possible that Professor Fisher was too "feminine" when she took a leave of absence from her career to raise a family, while Ms. Hopkins was too "masculine" because she was aggressive at work?

3. Professor Christine Littleton rejects what she terms a "symmetrical" approach to sex discrimination, which assumes that there are no differences between men's and women's ability to perform in the workplace. Littleton instead argues in favor of an "asymmetrical" model of sexual equality, one which recognizes both biological and social differences between the sexes: "If women currently tend to assume primary responsibility for childrearing, we should not ignore that fact in an attempt to prefigure the rosy day when parenting is fully shared. We should instead figure out how to assure that equal resources, status, and access to social decision-making flow to those women (and few men) who engage in this socially female behavior." Christine A. Littleton, Reconstructing Sexual Equality, 75 Cal.L.Rev. 1279 (1987).

4.   Courts appear far more wary of finding Title VII violations in cases involving academic tenure, preferring instead to defer to the judgment of tenure-review committees regarding the credentials of their candidates. Why does this "academic deference" phenomenon exist, and is there any reason this deference is reserved for academia? Professor Scott A. Moss argues for abolishing what he views as an arbitrary exception in employment discrimination litigation. See Scott A. Moss, Against "Academic Deference": How Recent Developments in Employment Discrimination Law Undercut An Already Dubious Doctrine, 27 Berkeley J. Emp. & Lab. L. 1 (2006).

5.   Some sociological studies support the proposition that mothers are at a severe disadvantage in the job market when compared with other female job applicants. One Cornell study found that employers consistently viewed mothers as less competent or committed and held them to higher standards of performance and punctuality than non-mothers. On average, mothers were 80 percent less likely to be hired and were offered a starting salary $11,000 lower than non-mothers, while fathers were offered the highest salaries of all. Eyal Press, Family-Leave Values, N.Y. Times, July 29, 2007 (citing study by Shelley Correll published in American Journal of Sociology).

6.   The EEOC officially recognized a "connection between parenthood, especially motherhood, and employment discrimination" when it issued an enforcement guidance titled Unlawful Disparate Treatment of Workers with Caregiving Responsibilities in 2007. "An employer may violate Title VII when it takes actions or limits opportunities for employees because of beliefs that the employer has about mothers and caretakers that are linked to sex," said EEOC Commissioner Stuart J. Ishimaru. The enforcement guidance is available at www.eeoc.gov/policy/docs/caregiving.html. See also Joan C. Williams and Stephanie Bornstein, The Evolution of "FRED": Family Responsibilities Discrimination and Developments in the Law of Stereotyping and Implicit Bias, 59 Hastings L.J. 1311 (2008).

b.   DISPARATE IMPACT/ADVERSE IMPACT

Even if no intentional discrimination is evident, some facially neutral employment practices are proscribed by Title VII. Prerequisites such as high school diplomas, standardized tests, and height and weight requirements may violate the law if they have a disparate impact on groups of individuals protected by Title VII. At the same time, such tests are common in fields such as medicine, law enforcement, and business. So when are facially neutral employment policies unlawful discrimination?

Griggs v. Duke Power Co.
401 U.S. 424 (1971).

■ MR. CHIEF JUSTICE BURGER delivered the opinion of the Court.

We granted the writ in this case to resolve the question whether an employer is prohibited by the Civil Rights Act of 1964, Title VII, from requiring a high school education or passing of a standardized general intelligence test as a condition of employment in or transfer to jobs when (a) neither standard is shown to be significantly related to successful job performance, (b) both requirements operate to disqualify Negroes at a substantially higher rate than white applicants, and (c) the jobs in question formerly had been filled only by white employees as part of a longstanding practice of giving preference to whites.

Congress provided, in Title VII of the Civil Rights Act of 1964, for class actions for enforcement of provisions of the Act and this proceeding was brought by a group of incumbent Negro employees against Duke Power Company. All the petitioners are employed at the Company's Dan River Steam Station, a power generating facility located at Draper, North Carolina. At the time this action was instituted, the Company had 95 employees at the Dan River Station, 14 of whom were Negroes; 13 of these are petitioners here.

The District Court found that prior to July 2, 1965, the effective date of the Civil Rights Act of 1964, the Company openly discriminated on the basis of race in the hiring and assigning of employees at its Dan River plant. The plant was organized into five operating departments: (1) Labor, (2) Coal Handling, (3) Operations, (4) Maintenance, and (5) Laboratory and Test. Negroes were employed only in the Labor Department where the highest paying jobs paid less than the lowest paying jobs in the other four "operating" departments in which only whites were employed.[2] Promotions were normally made within each department on the basis of job seniority. Transferees into a department usually began in the lowest position.

In 1955 the Company instituted a policy of requiring a high school education for initial assignment to any department except Labor, and for transfer from the Coal Handling to any "inside" department (Operations, Maintenance, or Laboratory). When the Company abandoned its policy of restricting Negroes to the Labor Department in 1965, completion of high school also was made a prerequisite to transfer from Labor to any other department. From the time the high school requirement was instituted to the time of trial, however, white employees hired before the time of the high school education requirement continued to perform satisfactorily and achieve promotions in the "operating" departments. Findings on this score are not challenged.

The Company added a further requirement for new employees on July 2, 1965, the date on which Title VII became effective. To qualify for placement in any but the Labor Department it became necessary to register satisfactory scores on two professionally prepared aptitude tests, as well as to have a high school education. Completion of high school alone continued to render employees eligible for transfer to the four

---

[2] A Negro was first assigned to a job in an operating department in August 1966, five months after charges had been filed with the Equal Employment Opportunity Commission. The employee, a high school graduate who had begun in the Labor Department in 1953, was promoted to a job in the Coal Handling Department.

desirable departments from which Negroes had been excluded if the incumbent had been employed prior to the time of the new requirement. In September 1965 the Company began to permit incumbent employees who lacked a high school education to qualify for transfer from Labor or Coal Handling to an "inside" job by passing two tests—the Wonderlic Personnel Test, which purports to measure general intelligence, and the Bennett Mechanical Comprehension Test. Neither was directed or intended to measure the ability to learn to perform a particular job or category of jobs. The requisite scores used for both initial hiring and transfer approximated the national median for high school graduates.[3]

* * *

The Court of Appeals was confronted with a question of first impression, as are we, concerning the meaning of Title VII. After careful analysis a majority of that court concluded that a subjective test of the employer's intent should govern, particularly in a close case, and that in this case there was no showing of a discriminatory purpose in the adoption of the diploma and test requirements. On this basis, the Court of Appeals concluded there was no violation of the Act.

The Court of Appeals reversed the District Court in part, rejecting the holding that residual discrimination arising from prior employment practices was insulated from remedial action. The Court of Appeals noted, however, that the District Court was correct in its conclusion that there was no showing of a racial purpose or invidious intent in the adoption of the high school diploma requirement or general intelligence test and that these standards had been applied fairly to whites and Negroes alike. It held that, in the absence of a discriminatory purpose, use of such requirements was permitted by the Act. In so doing, the Court of Appeals rejected the claim that because these two requirements operated to render ineligible a markedly disproportionate number of Negroes, they were unlawful under Title VII unless shown to be job related. We granted the writ on these claims.

The objective of Congress in the enactment of Title VII is plain from the language of the statute. It was to achieve equality of employment opportunities and remove barriers that have operated in the past to favor an identifiable group of white employees over other employees. Under the Act, practices, procedures, or tests neutral on their face, and even neutral in terms of intent, cannot be maintained if they operate to "freeze" the status quo of prior discriminatory employment practices.

The Court of Appeals' opinion, and the partial dissent, agreed that, on the record in the present case, "whites register far better on the Company's alternative requirements" than Negroes.[4] This consequence

---

[3]   The test standards are thus more stringent than the high school requirement, since they would screen out approximately half of all high school graduates.

[4]   In North Carolina, 1960 census statistics show that, while 34% of white males had completed high school, only 12% of Negro males had done so. U.S. Bureau of the Census, U.S. Census of Population: 1960, Vol. 1, Characteristics of the Population, pt. 35, Table 47.

would appear to be directly traceable to race. Basic intelligence must have the means of articulation to manifest itself fairly in a testing process. Because they are Negroes, petitioners have long received inferior education in segregated schools and this Court expressly recognized these differences in Gaston County v. United States, 395 U.S. 285 (1969). There, because of the inferior education received by Negroes in North Carolina, this Court barred the institution of a literacy test for voter registration on the ground that the test would abridge the right to vote indirectly on account of race. Congress did not intend by Title VII, however, to guarantee a job to every person regardless of qualifications. In short, the Act does not command that any person be hired simply because he was formerly the subject of discrimination, or because he is a member of a minority group. Discriminatory preference for any group, minority or majority, is precisely and only what Congress has proscribed. What is required by Congress is the removal of artificial, arbitrary, and unnecessary barriers to employment when the barriers operate invidiously to discriminate on the basis of racial or other impermissible classification.

Congress has now provided that tests or criteria for employment or promotion may not provide equality of opportunity merely in the sense of the fabled offer of milk to the stork and the fox. On the contrary, Congress has now required that the posture and condition of the job-seeker be taken into account. It has—to resort again to the fable—provided that the vessel in which the milk is proffered be one all seekers can use. The Act proscribes not only overt discrimination but also practices that are fair in form, but discriminatory in operation. The touchstone is business necessity. If an employment practice which operates to exclude Negroes cannot be shown to be related to job performance, the practice is prohibited.

On the record before us, neither the high school completion requirement nor the general intelligence test is shown to bear a demonstrable relationship to successful performance of the jobs for which it was used. Both were adopted, as the Court of Appeals noted, without meaningful study of their relationship to job-performance ability. Rather, a vice president of the Company testified, the requirements were instituted on the Company's judgment that they generally would improve the overall quality of the work force.

The evidence, however, shows that employees who have not completed high school or taken the tests have continued to perform satisfactorily and make progress in departments for which the high school and test criteria are now used. The promotion record of present employees who would not be able to meet the new criteria thus suggests the possibility that the requirements may not be needed even for the

---

Similarly, with respect to standardized tests, the EEOC in one case found that use of a battery of tests, including the Wonderlic and Bennett tests used by the Company in the instant case, resulted in 58% of whites passing the tests, as compared with only 6% of the blacks.

limited purpose of preserving the avowed policy of advancement within the Company. In the context of this case, it is unnecessary to reach the question whether testing requirements that take into account capability for the next succeeding position or related future promotion might be utilized upon a showing that such long-range requirements fulfill a genuine business need. In the present case the Company has made no such showing.

The Court of Appeals held that the Company had adopted the diploma and test requirements without any "intention to discriminate against Negro employees." We do not suggest that either the District Court or the Court of Appeals erred in examining the employer's intent; but good intent or absence of discriminatory intent does not redeem employment procedures or testing mechanisms that operate as "built-in headwinds" for minority groups and are unrelated to measuring job capability.

The Company's lack of discriminatory intent is suggested by special efforts to help the undereducated employees through Company financing of two-thirds the cost of tuition for high school training. But Congress directed the thrust of the Act to the *consequences* of employment practices, not simply the motivation. More than that, Congress has placed on the employer the burden of showing that any given requirement must have a manifest relationship to the employment in question.

The facts of this case demonstrate the inadequacy of broad and general testing devices as well as the infirmity of using diplomas or degrees as fixed measures of capability. History is filled with examples of men and women who rendered highly effective performance without the conventional badges of accomplishment in terms of certificates, diplomas, or degrees. Diplomas and tests are useful servants, but Congress has mandated the commonsense proposition that they are not to become masters of reality.

* * *

Nothing in the Act precludes the use of testing or measuring procedures; obviously they are useful. What Congress has forbidden is giving these devices and mechanisms controlling force unless they are demonstrably a reasonable measure of job performance. Congress has not commanded that the less qualified be preferred over the better qualified simply because of minority origins. Far from disparaging job qualifications as such, Congress has made such qualifications the controlling factor, so that race, religion, nationality, and sex become irrelevant. What Congress has commanded is that any tests used must measure the person for the job and not the person in the abstract.

The judgment of the Court of Appeals is, as to that portion of the judgment appealed from, reversed.

NOTES AND QUESTIONS

1. Do you believe the company intentionally discriminated against African Americans? The Supreme Court regarded itself as bound by the trial judge's conclusion that no intentional discrimination occurred.

2. What standard does the Court establish for employers that want to avoid liability for facially neutral selection practices that have an adverse impact on categories of individuals protected by Title VII? What was wrong with the employer's efforts to meet that standard in *Griggs*?

3. What is wrong with an employer seeking to upgrade its workforce? Why should the law constrain the employer's determination of the qualifications it seeks in its employees? Does Title VII prohibit an employer from hiring an "overqualified" workforce?

4. Assuming that Duke Power had acted in good faith in implementing the testing and diploma requirements, should this be a defense? Duke Power offered to finance two-thirds of the cost of tuition for high school training for any of its employees who wanted to complete their education on their own time. What effect should that program have on the Court's evaluation of Duke Power's liability under the law?

5. The Court takes judicial notice of the inferior education received by African Americans in North Carolina in the early 1960s to establish the adverse impact of the high school diploma requirement for plaintiffs, in a context where the Court concluded that a diploma requirement was not job related. In other circumstances, courts have been willing to take judicial notice of the job relatedness of an education requirement. See, e.g., Aguilera v. Cook County Police & Corrections Merit Board, 760 F.2d 844 (7th Cir.), cert. denied, 474 U.S. 907 (1985):

> Sometimes the appropriateness of an educational requirement is sufficiently obvious to allow dispensing with empirical validation. No one would insist that a law school validate statistically the "business need" behind requiring that its faculty members have law degrees (which might, indeed, be quite difficult to do), or that a hospital validate a requirement that its doctors have medical degrees. * * * [T]here has now been enough judicial and professional experience with educational requirements in law enforcement to establish a presumption in civil rights cases that a high school education is an appropriate requirement for anyone who is going to be a policeman, * * * and therefore to excuse civil rights defendants from having to prove, over and over again, that such requirements really are necessary for such jobs.

Is this holding wrong? That is, should all diploma and test requirements be subjected to a strict test of business necessity?

6. The I.Q. Taxi Company had a policy of hiring only unemployed Ph.D.s. In its advertising, I.Q. urged customers to ride in I.Q. cabs and "have an intellectual discussion with our drivers on the way to the airport or wherever you may be going." In a Title VII challenge to I.Q.'s hiring (based on alleged disparate impact race discrimination), can the hiring policy be sustained?

Should it matter whether I.Q. charged more than other taxis, advertised the education of its drivers, or required a high school diploma instead of a Ph.D.? Cf. Wileman v. Frank, 979 F.2d 30, 37 (4th Cir. 1992) (reversing the district court's holding that any consideration of educational differences beyond minimum requirements was per se pretextual, the Fourth Circuit held that "[w]hen two applicants meet the minimum educational qualifications of a position, Title VII does not prevent an employer from preferring the applicant who has educational qualifications which surpass the minimum requirements of the position."). Does this mean that Duke Power Co. could not *require* a high school diploma, but could *prefer* applicants who had one?

7. What of a discriminatory impact that results from the policy of a religious group whose activities are constitutionally protected? See Murphy v. Derwinski, 776 F.Supp. 1466 (D.Colo. 1991), affirmed, 990 F.2d 540 (10th Cir. 1993), holding that a Veteran's Administration requirement that chaplains be ordained discriminated against women who cannot be ordained by the Catholic Church but who can, instead, be "endorsed" by an ecclesiastical agency.

8. The California Basic Education Skills Test is a prerequisite for employment in a variety of positions in the state's public schools. The test is pass-fail. The passing score is 123. The "scaling" system allows a "pass" to a test-taker who gets 28 out of 40 right answers in reading and 26 out of 40 in math. Minority candidates disproportionately receive failing scores. The test survived Title VII review in the U.S. court of appeals, the majority accepting district court conclusions that the test is a valid measure of job-related skills, that the test is a valid measure of job-related minimum levels of basic knowledge, and that plaintiffs failed to show the existence of other, equally effective screening devices. Association of Mex.-Am. Educators v. California, 231 F.3d 572 (9th Cir. 2000) (en banc, 7–3). Judge Reinhardt, dissenting, wrote: "As a result of this ruling, qualified minority educators * * * will be denied the opportunity to work in California's severely understaffed public schools, simply because they failed to pass a test that concededly has a disparate impact on minority group members." The dissenters' strongest argument was that no single test that has a differential impact on minority applicants is an acceptable standard for the wide range of jobs to which this test is applied.

9. Since a race-based disparate impact claim requires proof that those of a particular race are disproportionately excluded by a particular practice, plaintiffs must have some way of identifying or determining the race of those individuals who are and are not excluded by the challenged practice. In EEOC v. Kaplan Higher Education Corp., 748 F.3d 749 (2014), the Sixth Circuit dismissed the EEOC's disparate impact challenge to Kaplan's credit check policy for new employees on the grounds that the testimony presented by the EEOC's expert regarding racially disparate impact, which was based on a visual race rating of applicants, was inadmissible under Daubert v. Merrell Dow Pharmaceuticals, Inc., 509 U.S. 579 (1993). Without such expert testimony, the EEOC could not show race based impact. How could the EEOC have established the race of the relevant applicants so as to establish its disparate impact claim?

Costs of Antidiscrimination Law

What are the costs of antidiscrimination law? Who bears the burden? Professor Christine Jolls argues that many of the costs associated with disparate impact liability are in fact accommodation costs. Employers are often required by disparate impact law to incur special costs in response to the distinctive needs or circumstances (measured against existing market structures) of particular groups, and these requirements may arise in situations in which the employer had no intention of treating the group differently on the basis of group membership. Thus, important aspects of disparate impact law are in fact accommodation requirements. As one example, Professor Jolls argues that when employers are forbidden to use job selection criteria, they are effectively forced to accommodate certain applicants. In Lanning v. Southeastern Pa. Transp. Auth., 181 F.3d 478 (3d Cir. 1999), cert. denied, 528 U.S. 1131 (2000), female plaintiffs challenged a requirement that applicants to the transit police force run 1.5 miles in twelve minutes under a disparate impact theory. The employer responded that there was a business necessity to use the test because it accurately measured aerobic ability, which the employer further demonstrated correlates well to arrests. The Third Circuit reversed a lower court judgment for the employer and held that the test might not constitute a business necessity. Professor Jolls makes the point that, if the test is invalidated on remand, the court will have imposed on the employer the costs of finding an equally effective test that does not have a disparate impact on female applicants. In other words, if the employer adopted this requirement with no intention to discriminate against women, the court is in some ways ordering the employer to accommodate female applicants. On remand, the district court held that the aerobic capacity test was valid, and the decision was affirmed on appeal. Lanning v. Southeastern Pa. Transp. Auth., 308 F.3d 286 (3d Cir. 2002).

Under the Americans with Disabilities Act, employers must extend reasonable accommodations to individuals with disabilities. The costs of accommodation are borne by the individual employer and will be equitably shared by all employees, both disabled and nondisabled. In the context of disparate impact law, however, Professor Jolls argues that sometimes these costs will be imposed upon precisely those whom the antidiscrimination laws mean to protect.

> The result I wish to highlight here involves the case in which limits on both wage and employment differentials are fully binding on employers. In this case, antidiscrimination law's restrictions on differential job conditions—like requirements of accommodation—ordinarily will make disadvantaged employees better off because the costs of the intervention will be partially shifted to nondisadvantaged employees. This outcome, of course, is not surprising and is presumably the point of the intervention. However, the interesting result I wish to

emphasize here is that in certain cases the restrictions on differential job conditions imposed by antidiscrimination law will actually make disadvantaged employees worse off, even though limits on wage and employment differentials between disadvantaged and nondisadvantaged groups are fully binding. This will occur if the disadvantaged group comprises a large fraction of the relevant labor pool and the cost of the legal intervention to employers exceeds its value to disadvantaged employees by a sufficient margin. The intuition here is that if the disadvantaged group comprises a large fraction of the relevant labor pool, then there is not a large group of nondisadvantaged employees to help share the costs of the legal intervention. With such limited prospects for cost-shifting, and with costs of the intervention in excess of the value of the intervention to the disadvantaged group, the disadvantaged group can be made worse off by the legal intervention even though limits on wage and employment differentials are fully binding.

Christine Jolls, Antidiscrimination and Accommodation, 115 Harv. L. Rev. 642 (2001).

Should disparate impact law take account of differences in the make-up of labor pools? If a disadvantaged group constitutes a large enough fraction of a labor pool, such that there are too few nondisadvantaged employees on whom to spread the costs, should disparate impact still protect that pool? Would such a numerical cut-off for liability function like a quota defense? Finally, does this economic analysis suggest that employees who are entitled to accommodations for religious practices, pregnancy, or physical disabilities might shoulder a disproportionately large fraction of the associated costs and thereby be made "worse off" by regulations that are intended to protect and support these employees?

Proving Disparate Impact

Proof of discrimination in disparate impact (or adverse impact) cases takes a much different form from disparate treatment cases. Intent is relatively unimportant: because the challenged selection criteria like the high school diploma requirement in *Griggs* apply equally to all employees or applicants for employment, any discrimination which occurs may be unintentional. This is the importance of *Griggs*; it recognizes even unintentional discrimination as unlawful. In contrast to disparate treatment cases, the critical questions in disparate impact cases are: What constitutes a "disparate impact" sufficient to be considered discrimination? What constitutes "job relatedness" or "business necessity," the defenses mentioned by the Supreme Court in *Griggs*? And finally, what level of proof must the parties establish in order to prevail at trial?

An employer's selection process must be shown to have a disparate impact along a dimension proscribed under Title VII before any liability can be found. Although the concept is an easy one to understand, what actually constitutes disparate impact has been the subject of considerable litigation. The Equal Employment Opportunity Commission has issued official Guidelines for its agents to follow in conducting compliance checks of large employers.

Uniform Guidelines on Employee Selection Procedures (1978)
29 C.F.R. § 1607.4D.

Adverse impact and the "four-fifths rule." A selection rate for any race, sex, or ethnic group which is less than four-fifths (4/5) will generally be regarded by the Federal enforcement agencies as evidence of adverse impact, while a greater than four-fifths rate will generally not be regarded by Federal enforcement agencies as evidence of adverse impact. Smaller differences in selection rate may nevertheless constitute adverse impact, where they are significant in both statistical and practical terms or where a user's actions have discouraged applicants disproportionately on grounds of race, sex, or ethnic group. Greater differences in selection rate may not constitute adverse impact where the differences are based on small numbers and are not statistically significant, or where special recruiting or other programs cause the pool of minority or female candidates to be atypical of the normal pool of applicants from that group. Where the user's evidence concerning the impact of a selection procedure indicates adverse impact but is based upon numbers which are too small to be reliable, evidence concerning the impact of the procedure over a longer period of time and/or evidence concerning the impact which the selection procedure had when used in the same manner in similar circumstances elsewhere may be considered in determining adverse impact.

* * *

Although the EEOC Guidelines have received deference from the courts as an interpretation of the law from the agency charged by Congress with enforcing the statute, they are not binding on the federal courts, nor is an EEOC finding of reasonable cause to believe that discrimination has or has not occurred. In Jones v. City of Boston, 845 F.3d 28, 31 (1st Cir. 2016) for example, the First Circuit deviated from the standard four-fifths rule of thumb to find an actionable disparate impact in a case involving a hair drug test that resulted in 99% of whites testing negative and 98% of blacks testing negative because "the difference in exam results by race was indisputably statistically significant."

Wards Cove Packing Co. v. Atonio
490 U.S. 642 (1989).

■ JUSTICE WHITE delivered the opinion of the Court.

Title VII of the Civil Rights Act of 1964 makes it an unfair employment practice for an employer to discriminate against any individual with respect to hiring or the terms and condition of employment because of such individual's race, color, religion, sex, or national origin; or to limit, segregate or classify his employees in ways that would adversely affect any employee because of the employee's race, color, religion, sex, or national origin. Griggs v. Duke Power Co. construed Title VII to proscribe "not only overt discrimination but also practices that are fair in form but discriminatory in practice." Under this basis for liability, which is known as the "disparate impact" theory and which is involved in this case, a facially neutral employment practice may be deemed violative of Title VII without evidence of the employer's subjective intent to discriminate that is required in a "disparate treatment" case.

* * *

The claims before us are disparate-impact claims, involving the employment practices of petitioners, two companies that operate salmon canneries in remote and widely separated areas of Alaska. The canneries operate only during the salmon runs in the summer months. They are inoperative and vacant for the rest of the year. In May or June of each year, a few weeks before the salmon runs begin, workers arrive and prepare the equipment and facilities for the canning operation. Most of these workers possess a variety of skills. When salmon runs are about to begin, the workers who will operate the cannery lines arrive, remain as long as there are fish to can, and then depart. The canneries are then closed down, winterized, and left vacant until the next spring. During the off season, the companies employ only a small number of individuals at their headquarters in Seattle and Astoria, Oregon, plus some employees at the winter shipyard in Seattle.

The length and size of salmon runs vary from year to year and hence the number of employees needed at each cannery also varies. Estimates are made as early in the winter as possible; the necessary employees are hired, and when the time comes, they are transported to the canneries. Salmon must be processed soon after they are caught, and the work during the canning season is therefore intense. For this reason, and because the canneries are located in remote regions, all workers are housed at the canneries and have their meals in company-owned mess halls.

Jobs at the canneries are of two general types: "cannery jobs" on the cannery line, which are unskilled positions; and "noncannery jobs," which fall into a variety of classifications. Most noncannery jobs are classified as skilled positions. Cannery jobs are filled predominantly by nonwhites,

Filipinos and Alaska Natives. The Filipinos are hired through and dispatched by Local 37 of the International Longshoremen Workers Union pursuant to a hiring hall agreement with the Local. The Alaska Natives primarily reside in villages near the remote cannery locations. Noncannery jobs are filled with predominantly white workers, who are hired during the winter months from the companies' offices in Washington and Oregon. Virtually all of the noncannery jobs pay more than cannery positions. The predominantly white noncannery workers and the predominantly nonwhite cannery employees live in separate dormitories and eat in separate mess halls.

In 1974, respondents, a class of nonwhite cannery workers who were (or had been) employed at the canneries, brought this Title VII action against petitioners. Respondents alleged that a variety of petitioners' hiring/promotion practices e.g., nepotism, a rehire preference, a lack of objective hiring criteria, separate hiring channels, a practice of not promoting from within were responsible for the racial stratification of the work force, and had denied them and other nonwhites employment as noncannery workers on the basis of race. Respondents also complained of petitioners' racially segregated housing and dining facilities. . . .[4]

In holding that respondents had made out a prima facie case of disparate impact, the court of appeals relied solely on respondents' statistics showing a high percentage of nonwhite workers in the cannery jobs and a low percentage of such workers in the noncannery positions. Although statistical proof can alone make out a prima facie case, the Court of Appeals' ruling here misapprehends our precedents and the purposes of Title VII, and we therefore reverse.

"There can be no doubt," . . . "that the . . . comparison . . . fundamentally misconceived the role of statistics in employment discrimination cases." The "proper comparison [is] between the racial composition of [the at-issue jobs] and the racial composition of the qualified * * * population in the relevant labor market." It is such a comparison between the racial composition of the qualified persons in the labor market and the persons holding at-issue jobs—that generally forms

---

[4] The fact that neither the District Court, nor the Ninth Circuit *en banc*, nor the subsequent Court of Appeals panel ruled for respondents on their disparate treatment claims— i.e., their allegations of intentional racial discrimination warrants particular attention in light of the dissents' comment that the canneries "bear an unsettling resemblance to aspects of a plantation economy."

Whatever the "resemblance," the unanimous view of the lower courts in this litigation has been that respondents did not prove that the canneries practice intentional racial discrimination. Consequently, Justice Blackmun's hyperbolic allegation that our decision in this case indicates that this Court no longer "believes that race discrimination . . . against nonwhites . . . is a problem in our society," is inapt. Of course, it is unfortunately true that race discrimination exists in our country. That does not mean, however, that it exists at the canneries—or more precisely, that it has been proven to exist at the canneries.

Indeed, Justice Stevens concedes that respondents did not press before us the legal theories under which the aspects of cannery life that he finds to most resemble a "plantation economy" might be unlawful. Thus, the question here is not whether we "approve" of petitioners' employment practices or the society that exists at the canneries, but rather, whether respondents have properly established that these practices violate Title VII.

the proper basis for the initial inquiry in a disparate impact case. Alternatively, in cases where such labor market statistics will be difficult if not impossible to ascertain, we have recognized that certain other statistics such as measures indicating the racial composition of "otherwise-qualified applicants" for at-issue jobs are equally probative for this purpose.

It is clear to us that the Court of Appeals' acceptance of the comparison between the racial composition of the cannery work force and that of the noncannery work force, as probative of a prima facie case of disparate impact in the selection of the latter group of workers, was flawed for several reasons. Most obviously, with respect to the skilled noncannery jobs at issue here, the cannery work force in no way reflected "the pool of *qualified* job applicants" or the "*qualified* population in the labor force." Measuring alleged discrimination in the selection of accountants, managers, boat captains, electricians, doctors, and engineers and the long list of other "skilled" noncannery positions found to exist by the District Court by comparing the number of nonwhites occupying these jobs to the number of nonwhites filling cannery worker positions is nonsensical. If the absence of minorities holding such skilled positions is due to a dearth of qualified nonwhite applicants (for reasons that are not petitioners' fault), petitioners' selection methods or employment practices cannot be said to have had a "disparate impact" on nonwhites.

Such a result cannot be squared with our cases or with the goals behind the statute. The Court of Appeals' theory, at the very least, would mean that any employer who had a segment of his work force that was for some reason—racially imbalanced, could be haled into court and forced to engage in the expensive and time-consuming task of defending the "business necessity" of the methods used to select the other members of his work force. The only practicable option for many employers will be to adopt racial quotas, insuring that no portion of his work force deviates in racial composition from the other portions thereof; this is a result that Congress expressly rejected in drafting Title VII. The Court of Appeals' theory would "leave the employer little choice . . . but to engage in a subjective quota system of employment selection. This, of course, is far from the intent of Title VII." . . .

Consequently, we reverse the Court of Appeals' ruling that a comparison between the percentage of cannery workers who are nonwhite and the percentage of noncannery workers who are nonwhite makes out a prima facie case of disparate impact. Of course, this leaves unresolved whether the record made in the District Court will support a conclusion that a prima facie case of disparate impact has been established on some basis other than the racial disparity between cannery and noncannery workers. This is an issue that the Court of Appeals or the District Court should address in the first instance.

Since the statistical disparity relied on by the Court of Appeals did not suffice to make out a prima facie case, any inquiry by us into whether the specific challenged employment practices of petitioners caused that disparity is pretermitted, as is any inquiry into whether the disparate impact that any employment practice may have had was justified by business considerations. Because we remand for further proceedings, however, on whether a prima facie case of disparate impact has been made in defensible fashion in this case, we address two other challenges petitioners have made to the decision of the Court of Appeals.

First is the question of causation in a disparate-impact case.

* * *

Our disparate-impact cases have always focused on the impact of *particular* hiring practices on employment opportunities for minorities. Just as an employer cannot escape liability under Title VII by demonstrating that, "at the bottom line," his work force is racially balanced (where particular hiring practices may operate to deprive minorities of employment opportunities), a Title VII plaintiff does not make out a case of disparate impact simply by showing that, "at the bottom line," there is racial *imbalance* in the work force. As a general matter, a plaintiff must demonstrate that it is the application of a specific or particular employment practice that has created the disparate impact under attack. Such a showing is an integral part of the plaintiff's prima facie case in a disparate-impact suit under Title VII.

Here, respondents have alleged that several "objective" employment practices (e.g., nepotism, separate hiring channels, rehire preferences), as well as the use of "subjective decision making" to select noncannery workers, have had a disparate impact on nonwhites. Respondents base this claim on statistics that allegedly show a disproportionately low percentage of nonwhites in the at-issue positions. However, even if on remand respondents can show that nonwhites are underrepresented in the at-issue jobs in a manner that is acceptable under the standards set forth in Part II, this alone will *not* suffice to make out a prima facie case of disparate impact. Respondents will also have to demonstrate that the disparity they complain of is the result of one or more of the employment practices that they are attacking here, specifically showing that each challenged practice has a significantly disparate impact on employment opportunities for whites and nonwhites. To hold otherwise would result in employers being potentially liable for "the myriad of innocent causes that may lead to statistical imbalances in the composition of their work forces."

* * *

Consequently, on remand, the courts below are instructed to require, as part of respondents' prima facie case, a demonstration that specific elements of the petitioners' hiring process have a significantly disparate impact on nonwhites.

If, on remand, respondents meet the proof burdens outlined above, and establish a prima facie case of disparate impact with respect to any of petitioners' employment practices, the case will shift to any business justification petitioners offer for their use of these practices. This phase of the disparate-impact case contains two components: first, a consideration of the justifications an employer offers for his use of these practices; and second, the availability of alternate practices to achieve the same business ends, with less racial impact. We consider these two components in turn.

Though we have phrased the query differently in different cases, it is generally well-established that at the justification stage of such a disparate impact case, the dispositive issue is whether a challenged practice serves, in a significant way, the legitimate employment goals of the employer. The touchstone of this inquiry is a reasoned review of the employer's justification for his use of the challenged practice. A mere insubstantial justification in this regard will not suffice, because such a low standard of review would permit discrimination to be practiced through the use of spurious, seemingly neutral employment practices. At the same time, though, there is no requirement that the challenged practice be "essential" or "indispensable" to the employer's business for it to pass muster: this degree of scrutiny would be almost impossible for most employers to meet, and would result in a host of evils we have identified above. In this phase, the employer carries the burden of producing evidence of a business justification for his employment practice. The burden of persuasion, however, remains with the disparate-impact plaintiff. * * *

Finally, if on remand the case reaches this point, and respondents cannot persuade the trier of fact on the question of petitioners' business necessity defense, respondents may still be able to prevail. To do so, respondents will have to persuade the factfinder that "other tests or selection devices, without a similarly undesirable racial effect, would also serve the employer's legitimate [hiring] interest[s];" by so demonstrating, respondents would prove that "[petitioners were] using [their] tests merely as a 'pretext' for discrimination." If respondents, having established a prima facie case, come forward with alternatives to petitioners' hiring practices that reduce the racially-disparate impact of practices currently being used, and petitioners refuse to adopt these alternatives, such a refusal would belie a claim by petitioners that their incumbent practices are being employed for nondiscriminatory reasons.

Of course, any alternative practices which respondents offer up in this respect must be equally effective as petitioners' chosen hiring procedures in achieving petitioners' legitimate employment goals. Moreover, "[f]actors such as the cost or other burdens of proposed alternative selection devices are relevant in determining whether they would be equally as effective as the challenged practice in serving the employer's legitimate business goals." "Courts are generally less competent than employers to restructure business practices;" consequently, the judiciary should proceed with care before mandating that an employer must adopt a plaintiff's alternate selection or hiring practice in response to a Title VII suit.

For the reasons given above, the judgment of the Court of Appeals is reversed, and the case is remanded for further proceedings consistent with this opinion.

It is so ordered.

■ JUSTICE STEVENS, with whom JUSTICE BRENNAN, JUSTICE MARSHALL, and JUSTICE BLACKMUN join, dissenting.

Fully 18 years ago, this Court unanimously held that Title VII of the Civil Rights Act of 1964 prohibits employment practices that have discriminatory effects as well as those that are intended to discriminate. Griggs v. Duke Power Co. Federal courts and agencies consistently have enforced that interpretation, thus promoting our national goal of eliminating barriers that define economic opportunity not by aptitude and ability but by race, color, national origin, and other traits that are easily identified but utterly irrelevant to one's qualification for a particular job. Regrettably, the Court retreats from these efforts in its review of an interlocutory judgment respecting the "peculiar facts" of this lawsuit. Turning a blind eye to the meaning and purpose of Title VII, the majority's opinion perfunctorily rejects a longstanding rule of law and underestimates the probative value of evidence of a racially stratified work force.[4] I cannot join this latest sojourn into judicial activism.

* * *

In a disparate treatment case there is no "discrimination" within the meaning of Title VII unless the employer intentionally treated the employee unfairly because of race. Therefore, the employee retains the burden of proving the existence of intent at all times.

* * *

---

[4] Respondents comprise a class of present and former employees of petitioners, two Alaskan salmon canning companies. The class members, described by the parties as "nonwhite," include persons of Samoan, Chinese, Filipino, Japanese, and Alaska Native descent, all but one of whom are United States citizens. Fifteen years ago they commenced this suit, alleging that petitioners engage in hiring, job assignment, housing, and messing practices that segregate nonwhites from whites, in violation of Title VII. Evidence included this response in 1971 by a foreman to a college student's inquiry about cannery employment:

> "We are not in a position to take many young fellows to our Bristol Bay canneries as they do not have the background for our type of employees. Our cannery labor is either Eskimo or Filipino and we do not have the facilities to mix others with these groups."

Some characteristics of the Alaska salmon industry described in this litigation: in particular, the segregation of housing and dining facilities and the stratification of jobs along racial and ethnic lines—bear an unsettling resemblance to aspects of a plantation economy. Indeed the maintenance of inferior, segregated facilities for housing and feeding nonwhite employees, strikes me as a form of discrimination that, although it does not necessarily fit neatly into a disparate impact or disparate treatment mold, nonetheless violates Title VII. Respondents, however, do not press this theory before us.

In contrast, intent plays no role in the disparate impact inquiry. The question, rather, is whether an employment practice has a significant, adverse effect on an identifiable class of workers regardless of the cause or motive for the practice. The employer may attempt to contradict the factual basis for this effect; that is, to prevent the employee from establishing a prima facie case. But when an employer is faced with sufficient proof of disparate impact, its only recourse is to justify the practice by explaining why it is necessary to the operation of business. Such a justification is a classic example of an affirmative defense. * * *

Also troubling is the Court's apparent redefinition of the employees' burden of proof in a disparate impact case. No prima facie case will be made, it declares, unless the employees " 'isolat[e] and identif[y] the specific employment practices that are allegedly responsible for any observed statistical disparities.' " This additional proof requirement is unwarranted. It is elementary that a plaintiff cannot recover upon proof of injury alone; rather, the plaintiff must connect the injury to an act of the defendant in order to establish prima facie that the defendant is liable. Although the causal link must have substance, the act need not constitute the sole or primary cause of the harm. Thus in a disparate impact case, proof of numerous questionable employment practices ought to fortify an employee's assertion that the practices caused racial disparities. Ordinary principles of fairness require that Title VII actions be tried like "any lawsuit." The changes the majority makes today, tipping the scales in favor of employers, are not faithful to those principles.

* * *

Evidence that virtually all the employees in the major categories of at-issue jobs were white, whereas about two-thirds of the cannery workers were nonwhite, may not by itself suffice to establish a prima facie case of discrimination. But such evidence of racial stratification puts the specific employment practices challenged by respondents into perspective. Petitioners recruit employees for at-issue jobs from outside the work force rather than from lower-paying, overwhelmingly nonwhite, cannery worker positions. Information about availability of at-issue positions is conducted by word of mouth; therefore, the maintenance of housing and mess halls that separate the largely white noncannery work force from the cannery workers, coupled with the tendency toward nepotistic hiring, are obvious barriers to employment opportunities for nonwhites. Putting to one side the issue of business justifications, it would be quite wrong to conclude that these practices have no discriminatory consequence. Thus I agree with the Court of Appeals that when the District Court makes the additional findings prescribed today, it should treat the evidence of racial stratification in the work force as a significant element of respondents' prima facie case.

The majority's opinion begins with recognition of the settled rule that "a facially neutral employment practice may be deemed violative of

Title VII without evidence of the employer's subjective intent to discriminate that is required in a 'disparate treatment' case." It then departs from the body of law engendered by this disparate impact theory, reformulating the order of proof and the weight of the parties' burdens. Why the Court undertakes these unwise changes in elementary and eminently fair rules is a mystery to me.

I respectfully dissent.

■ JUSTICE BLACKMUN, with whom JUSTICE BRENNAN and JUSTICE MARSHALL join, dissenting.

I fully concur in Justice Stevens' analysis of this case. * * *

The harshness of these results is well demonstrated by the facts of this case. The salmon industry as described by this record takes us back to a kind of overt and institutionalized discrimination we have not dealt with in years: a total residential and work environment organized on principles of racial stratification and segregation, which, as Justice Stevens points out, resembles a plantation economy. This industry long has been characterized by a taste for discrimination of the old-fashioned sort: a preference for hiring nonwhites to fill its lowest-level positions, on the condition that they stay there. The majority's legal rulings essentially immunize these practices from attack under a Title VII disparate-impact analysis.

Sadly, this comes as no surprise. One wonders whether the majority still believes that race discrimination—or, more accurately, race discrimination against nonwhites—is a problem in our society, or even remembers that it ever was.

NOTES AND COMMENTS

1.   On the strongest reading of *Griggs,* an employer with a smaller minority or female workforce than the appropriate labor pool had to show a business necessity for its selection processes. Thus, companies had to "validate" their procedures or else demonstrate numerically satisfactory results. *Wards Cove* rejected (or, according to some commentators, changed) that statement of Title VII law:

a)   The plaintiff must specify a particular selection practice, and show its relevance to the numerical results;

b)   The employer must show a "business justification," and not that a challenged practice is "essential" or "indispensable";

c)   The plaintiff bears the burden of showing that alternative selection practices would work just as well and produce more jobs for minorities or women.

The argument between the two positions was rehearsed, and in some ways more effectively joined, in Watson v. Fort Worth Bank & Trust, 487 U.S. 977 (1988), where each side had four votes (because Justice Kennedy had not yet been seated). *Watson* held unanimously that subjective or discretionary employment practices are subject to attack under disparate impact analysis. Justice O'Connor's opinion in *Watson* said that an employer seeking to justify a selection method (even one that has a statistical impact on the race or gender distribution of those hired) need only show "a manifest relationship to the employment in question." She said that formal validation studies are not required.

2. If the *Wards Cove* burden of proof had been applied in *Griggs,* would the plaintiffs have prevailed?

3. According to Professor Cass Sunstein:

Although the issue is complex, one might start by observing that discriminatory purpose is exceptionally difficult to show even when it exists. A test that makes discriminatory effects probative of discriminatory purpose might invalidate some practices that should, given perfect implementing devices, be upheld. *Wards Cove,* however, will validate many practices that should, given such devices, be struck down. Moreover, discrimination exists when an employer has been nonneutral in the sense that it has adopted a practice having a discriminatory effect on blacks that it would not have adopted if the burden had been imposed on whites; *Wards Cove* will not reach this form of discrimination. For these reasons, *Wards Cove* will produce substantial underenforcement of the law. By contrast, systemic barriers to the implementation of antidiscrimination statutes make any concern about overenforcement highly speculative. No approach is perfect in this situation, but *Griggs* was probably a better method of implementing the statutory proscription.

Cass R. Sunstein, Interpreting Statutes in the Regulatory State, 103 Harv.L.Rev. 405, 485 (1989). Do you agree?

4. Is the result in *Wards Cove* consistent with *Price Waterhouse,* supra p. 227? There, Justice O'Connor cast the decisive vote for requiring employers to demonstrate in a mixed-motive case that the improper consideration did not influence the hiring result. In *Wards Cove,* she supported the majority result that the plaintiff must prove that alternatives are available to a selection process that results in a numerically unbalanced labor force. Is it easier for Supreme Court justices to identify with a worker denied a partnership at an accounting firm than with Asian cannery workers in Alaska?

Why not analyze *Wards Cove* (and perhaps all disparate impact cases) as mixed-motive cases, similar to *Price Waterhouse*? If *Wards Cove* is approached that way, who wins?

5. The two-tier structure at Wards Cove arguably represents job channeling at a fairly obvious level. If the difference in wages and benefits between the cannery and noncannery jobs (i.e., between white and non-white workers) is not sufficient to establish a prima facie case of disparate impact, what would be? What is the evidentiary significance of the racial stratification at Wards Cove?

6. In light of the majority opinion, what is the role of statistics in proving violations of Title VII? Note, as discussed below, that Congress subsequently enacted the Civil Rights Act of 1991, which overrides much of the majority opinion with respect to race and gender discrimination. Would statistics other than internal work force statistics suffice to establish a prima facie case of discrimination? As a practical matter, where would one find "relevant labor market" statistics for the seasonal salmon industry in Alaska?

7. See Lynch v. Freeman, 817 F.2d 380 (6th Cir. 1987), holding that furnishing unsanitary toilets to both men and women is unlawful sex discrimination because biology makes clean toilets more important to women. See also EEOC v. Warshawsky & Co., 768 F.Supp. 647 (N.D.Ill.1991), concluding that it is differential impact discrimination against females to require employees to work at least one year before becoming eligible for sick leave because of the effect of the policy on pregnant women.

8. The degree to which a strict job-relatedness requirement is applied to all hiring criteria depends on the nature of the job involved. This is particularly true with regard to jobs in which public safety is an issue. For example, United Airlines required that its flight officers have a college degree (in addition to a commercial pilot's license and instrument rating). This requirement had a disparate impact upon blacks and, in fact, only nine of United's 5900 flight officers were black. Nevertheless, the college degree requirement was upheld:

> When a job requires a small amount of skill and training and the consequences of hiring an unqualified applicant are insignificant, the courts should examine closely any pre-employment standard or criteria which discriminate against minorities. In such a case, the employer should have a heavy burden to demonstrate to the court's satisfaction that his employment criteria are job-related. On the other hand, when the job clearly requires a high degree of skill and the economic and human risks involved in hiring an unqualified applicant are great, the employer bears a correspondingly lighter burden to show that his employment criteria are job-related.

Spurlock v. United Airlines, Inc., 475 F.2d 216, 219 (10th Cir. 1972). A similar approach has been taken in cases decided under age and disability discrimination laws, discussed later in this chapter. Different circuits disagree on the appropriate standard, however. See Lanning v. Southeastern Pa. Trans. Auth., 181 F.3d 478 (3d Cir. 1999).

In contrast, Professor Elizabeth Bartholet is critical of what she perceives as varying levels of judicial scrutiny applied to different "levels" of positions. Professor Bartholet points out that, although courts have insisted employers modify or justify testing standards that exclude minorities in lower level, blue collar positions, they are reluctant to challenge hiring tests in "upper level" positions, such as teachers, lawyers and managers. Professor Bartholet argues that this subverts the underlying purpose of Title VII and should have no legal basis. Do you agree? Elizabeth Bartholet, Application of Title VII to Jobs in High Places, 95 Harv. L. Rev. 945 (1982).

9. Courts are split on the issue of whether supervisors should be individually liable for claims of discrimination in the workplace. Some have held that no individual liability exists under Title VII. See, e.g., Miller v. Maxwell's Int'l, Inc., 991 F.2d 583 (9th Cir. 1993), cert. denied, 510 U.S. 1109 (1994). Others have held that supervisors, as agents of employers, are themselves "employers" for purposes of Title VII liability. The Supreme Court has yet to resolve the debate. In contrast, supervisors can be held individually liable for sexual harassment if employers can affirmatively establish they exercised "reasonable care" to prevent a hostile work environment. This affirmative defense against vicarious liability is not available if the supervisor's action resulted in "a tangible employment action, such as discharge, demotion, or undesirable reassignment." See Faragher v. City of Boca Raton, 524 U.S. 775 (1998); Burlington Indus., Inc. v. Ellerth, 524 U.S. 742 (1998).

10. In what the court of appeals called "the final chapter" in a litigation that lasted 27 years, defendants finally prevailed on all counts in Atonio v. Wards Cove Packing Co., 275 F.3d 797 (9th Cir. 2001). In particular, the appellate court upheld a finding that the workers' suggested alternative to segregated housing would not be as effective in meeting the employer's legitimate business goals. The decision has little precedential value because Congress specifically made the Civil Rights Act of 1991 inapplicable to this dispute. Note this paragraph from the final district court opinion:

> While references to "Filipino," "Alaska Native," and "Eskimo" were frequent, inappropriate, and offensive to this court, these are not physically threatening or humiliating references. The evidence established that the class members themselves made references to, for example, the "Filipino Bunkhouse." The union negotiators took great pride in the fact that the "Filipino crews" at the canneries were the best fish crews. The Superintendent of Wards Cove attempted to get a Filipino manager to avoid using the term "Filipino Bunkhouse" to no avail.

275 F.3d at 802.

NOTE ON THE CIVIL RIGHTS ACT OF 1991

The Civil Rights Act of 1991 was enacted in substantial part as a response to the Supreme Court's decision in *Wards Cove*. The preamble states: "The purposes of this Act are * * * (2) to codify the concepts of 'business necessity' and 'job related' enunciated by the Supreme Court in Griggs v. Duke Power Co., and in the other Supreme Court decisions prior to Wards Cove Packing Co. v. Atonio; (3) to confirm statutory authority and provide statutory guidelines for the adjudication of disparate impact suits under title VII * * *; (4) to respond to recent decisions of the Supreme Court by expanding the scope of relevant civil rights statutes * * *."

The 1991 Act overturned *Wards Cove*'s formulation of the burden of proof and the types of proof necessary to show disparate impact discrimination. Under the Act, an employee must still attempt to show which employment practice has caused the disparate impact. If, however, the practices are impossible to disaggregate, courts must analyze the decisionmaking process as one practice. In addition, Congress increased the burden on the employer in demonstrating that a challenged practice is job-related. Now, the employer must show that "the challenged practice is job-related for the position in question and consistent with business necessity." The burden of persuasion remains with the employer to prove business necessity. See Kingsley R. Browne, The Civil Rights Act of 1991: A "Quota Bill," A Codification of *Griggs,* A Partial Return to *Wards Cove,* or All of the Above?, 43 Case W. Res. L. Rev. 287 (1993).

In Bradley v. Pizzaco of Neb., Inc., 7 F.3d 795 (8th Cir. 1993), the court struck down Domino's Pizza's no-beard policy because the policy had a differential impact on black males, half of whom suffer from the skin condition pseudofolliculitis barbae ("PFB"). The district court had found for defendant on the question of business justification under *Wards Cove.* It was reversed by the court of appeals which applied the 1991 Act rather than *Wards Cove* because the EEOC sought only prospective relief to enjoin Domino's no-beard policy. The court rejected Domino's claim that it was "common sense" that "the better our people look, the better our sales will be," as speculative and conclusory. The court also rejected the relevance of a consumer preference for smooth-shaven pizza delivery persons, even if such consumer preference could be shown.

NOTE

The Eighth Circuit has held that "subjective promotion policies" can support liability for disparate impact. McClain v. Lufkin Indus., Inc., 519 F.3d 264 (5th Cir. 2008), cert. denied, 555 U.S. 881 (2008). Employees of Lufkin Industries challenged the company's system for awarding promotions on the ground that supervisors had used the system to entertain racial preferences. Although the system ostensibly awarded promotions on the basis of seniority and ability, the plaintiff employees produced evidence showing that "promotions [were] not rigidly awarded according to seniority" and that "supervisors did not always truly evaluate ability when awarding promotions." The plaintiffs showed that African-American employees had been "bypassed for promotion in favor of [ ] less senior white employee[s]" and that the company "permitted its managers to apportion training opportunities subjectively [in a way] that disadvantaged black employees who sought promotions."

3.   THE BONA FIDE OCCUPATIONAL QUALIFICATION DEFENSE

Section 703(e) of Title VII provides it is not unlawful for an employer to differentiate in hiring on the basis of religion, sex, or national origin "in those certain instances where religion, sex, or national origin is a bona fide occupational qualification reasonably necessary to the normal operation of that particular business or enterprise."

According to the EEOC's guidelines on sex as a BFOQ, 29 C.F.R. § 1604.2, the following situations do *not* warrant the application of the BFOQ exception: (1) refusal to hire a woman is based on the assumption of employment characteristics of women in general (e.g., turnover rate higher among women); (2) refusal to hire is based on sex stereotypes (e.g., women cannot be aggressive salespersons); (3) refusal to hire is based on the preferences of co-workers, clients, customers, or the employer; and (4) the fact that the employer may have to provide separate facilities.

State laws prohibiting women from working certain hours or lifting certain weights ("women's protective laws") are proscribed by Title VII and, under the supremacy clause, have been struck down. See Rosenfeld v. Southern Pac. Co., 444 F.2d 1219 (9th Cir. 1971).

The leading Supreme Court case on this topic is Dothard v. Rawlinson, 433 U.S. 321 (1977), in which the plaintiff claimed that Alabama's height (5'2") and weight (120 pounds) requirements for correctional officers, and its rule forbidding women from "contact positions" in maximum security male penitentiaries, were unlawful under Title VII. The Court held that Alabama's height and weight requirements discriminated impermissibly, but also held that the state could refuse to hire women for "contact positions" even though the rule excluded women from 75 percent of jobs in the Alabama prison system.

It said "the BFOQ exception was in fact meant to be an extremely narrow exception to the general prohibition of discrimination on the basis of sex," but that Alabama met that test because a woman's relative ability to maintain order in a male, maximum-security, unclassified penitentiary of the type Alabama now runs could be directly reduced by her womanhood. There is a basis in fact for expecting that sex offenders who have criminally assaulted women in the past would be moved to do so again if access to women were established within the prison. There would also be a real risk that other inmates, deprived of a normal heterosexual environment, would assault women guards because they were women. In a prison system where violence is the order of the day, where inmate access to guards is facilitated by dormitory living arrangements, where every institution is understaffed, and where a substantial portion of the inmate population is composed of sex offenders mixed at random with other prisoners, there are a few visible deterrents to inmate assaults on women custodians.

Justice Marshall, in a dissent joined by Justice Brennan, said:

> what would otherwise be considered unlawful discrimination against women is justified by the Court, however, on the basis of the "barbaric and inhumane" conditions in Alabama prisons, conditions so bad that state officials have conceded that they violate the Constitution. To me, this analysis sounds distressingly like saying two wrongs make a right. * * * The effect of the decision, made I am sure with the best of intentions, is to punish women because their very presence might provoke sexual assaults. It is women who are made to pay the price in lost job opportunities for the threat of depraved conduct by prison inmates. Once again, "[t]he pedestal upon which women have been placed has * * *, upon closer inspection, been revealed

as a cage." Sail'er Inn, Inc. v. Kirby, 5 Cal.3d 1, 20, 485 P.2d 529, 541 (1971). It is particularly ironic that the cage is erected here in response to feared misbehavior by imprisoned criminals.

Dothard was cited in a decision holding that female gender is a BFOQ for serving as a correctional officer at a female prison that had had "rampant sexual abuse of * * * prisoners." Everson v. Michigan Dep't of Corrections, 391 F.3d 737 (6th Cir. 2004), cert. denied, 546 U.S. 825 (2005).

Wilson v. Southwest Airlines Co.

517 F.Supp. 292 (N.D. Tex. 1981).

■ PATRICK E. HIGGINBOTHAM, DISTRICT JUDGE.

This case presents the important question whether femininity, or more accurately female sex appeal, is a bona fide occupational qualification ("BFOQ") for the jobs of flight attendant and ticket agent with Southwest Airlines. Plaintiff Gregory Wilson and the class of over 100 male job applicants he represents have challenged Southwest's open refusal to hire males as a violation of Title VII of the Civil Rights Act of 1964. The class further alleges that Southwest's published height-weight requirement for flight attendants operates to exclude from eligibility a greater proportion of male than female applicants.

At the phase one trial on liability, Southwest conceded that its refusal to hire males was intentional. The airline also conceded that its height-weight restrictions would have an adverse impact upon male applicants, if actually applied. Southwest contends, however, that the BFOQ exception to Title VII's ban on sex discrimination justifies its hiring only females for the public contact positions of flight attendant and ticket agent. The BFOQ window through which Southwest attempts to fly permits sex discrimination in situations where the employer can prove that sex is a "bona fide occupational qualification reasonably necessary to the normal operation of that particular business or enterprise." Southwest reasons it may discriminate against males because its attractive female flight attendants and ticket agents personify the airline's sexy image and fulfill its public promise to take passengers skyward with "love." Defendant claims maintenance of its females-only hiring policy is crucial to the airline's continued financial success.

Since it has been admitted that Southwest discriminates on the basis of sex, the only issue to decide is whether Southwest has proved that being female is a BFOQ reasonably necessary to the normal operation of its particular business.

* * *

Barely intact, Southwest, in early 1971, called upon a Dallas advertising agency, the Bloom Agency, to develop a winning marketing strategy. Planning to initiate service quickly, Southwest needed instant recognition and a "catchy" image to distinguish it from its competitors.

The Bloom Agency evaluated both the images of the incumbent competitor airlines as well as the characteristics of passengers to be served by a commuter airline. Bloom determined that the other carriers serving the Texas market tended to project an image of conservatism. The agency also determined that the relatively short haul commuter market which Southwest hoped to serve was comprised of predominantly male businessmen. Based on these factors, Bloom suggested that Southwest break away from the conservative image of other airlines and project to the traveling public an airline personification of feminine youth and vitality. A specific female personality description was recommended and adopted by Southwest for its corporate image:

> This lady is young and vital . . . she is charming and goes through life with great flair and exuberance . . . you notice first her exciting smile, friendly air, her wit . . . yet she is quite efficient and approaches all her tasks with care and attention. . . .

From the personality description suggested by The Bloom Agency, Southwest developed its now famous "Love" personality. Southwest projects an image of feminine spirit, fun and sex appeal. Its ads promise to provide "tender loving care" to its predominantly male, business passengers.[3] The first advertisements run by the airline featured the slogan, "AT LAST THERE IS SOMEBODY ELSE UP THERE WHO LOVES YOU." Variations on this theme have continued through newspaper, billboard, magazine and television advertisements during the past ten years.[4] Bloom's "Love" campaign was given a boost in 1974–1975 when the last of Southwest's competitors moved its operations to the new Dallas/Fort Worth Regional Airport, leaving Southwest as the only heavy carrier flying out of Dallas' convenient and fortuitously named, Love Field.

Over the years, Southwest gained national and international attention as the "love airline." Southwest Airlines' stock is traded on the New York Stock Exchange under the ticker symbol "LUV". During 1977 when Southwest opened five additional markets in Texas, the love theme was expanded to "WE'RE SPREADING LOVE ALL OVER TEXAS."

As an integral part of its youthful, feminine image, Southwest has employed only females in the high customer contact positions of ticket

---

[3] According to an October, 1979 on-board marketing survey commissioned before this lawsuit was filed, 69.01% of the respondents were male, while 58.41% of all respondents listed their occupation as either professional/technical, manager/administrator, or sales. Only 49.75% of the passengers surveyed, however, gave "business" as the reason for their trip.

[4] Unabashed allusions to love and sex pervade all aspects of Southwest's public image. Its T.V. commercials feature attractive attendants in fitted outfits, catering to male passengers while an alluring feminine voice promises in-flight love. On board, attendants in hot-pants (skirts are now optional) serve "love bites" (toasted almonds) and "love potions" (cocktails). Even Southwest's ticketing system features a "quickie machine" to provide "instant gratification."

agent and flight attendant. From the start, Southwest's attractive personnel, dressed in high boots and hot-pants, generated public interest and "free ink." Their sex appeal has been used to attract male customers to the airline. Southwest's flight attendants, and to a lesser degree its ticket agents, have been featured in newspaper, magazine, billboard and television advertisements during the past ten years. Some attendants assist in promotional events for other businesses and civic organizations. Southwest flight attendants and ticket agents are featured in the company's in-flight magazine and have received notice in numerous other national and international publications. The airline also encourages its attendants to entertain the passengers and maintain an atmosphere of informality and "fun" during flights. According to Southwest, its female flight attendants have come to "personify" Southwest's public image.

Southwest has enjoyed enormous success in recent years.

* * *

In evaluating Southwest's BFOQ defense, the Court proceeds on the basis that "love," while important, is not everything in the relationship between Defendant and its passengers. Still, it is proper to infer from the airline's competitive successes that Southwest's overall "love image" has enhanced its ability to attract passengers. To the extent the airline has successfully feminized its image and made attractive females an integral part of its public face, it also follows that femininity and sex appeal are qualities related to successful job performance by Southwest's flight attendants and ticket agents. The strength of this relationship has not been proved. It is with this factual orientation that the Court turns to examine Southwest's BFOQ defense.

* * *

To date, the [EEOC] has steadfastly adhered to its position that customer preference gives rise to a bona fide occupational qualification for sex in one instance only, "[w]here it is necessary for the purpose of authenticity or genuineness * * * e.g. an actor or actress." This exception is analogous to the example of a BFOQ for a French Cook in a French restaurant suggested by the Senate Floor Managers in their Interpretative Memorandum. * * *

Those courts which have analyzed Title VII's BFOQ exception, however, have broadened its sweep. Consistent with the language of § 703(e), courts have held, or stated, that customer preference for one sex may be taken into account in those limited instances where satisfying customer preference is "reasonably necessary to the normal operation of the particular business or enterprise."

This Circuit's decisions in Weeks v. Southern Bell Tel. & Tel. Co., 408 F.2d 228 (5th Cir. 1969) and Diaz v. Pan American World Airways, Inc., 442 F.2d 385 (5th Cir.) cert. denied 404 U.S. 950 (1971) have given rise to a two step BFOQ test: (1) does the particular *job* under consideration require that the worker be of one sex only; and if so, (2) is that requirement reasonably necessary to the "essence" of the employer's business. The first level of inquiry is designed to test whether sex is so essential to job performance that a member of the opposite sex simply could not do the same job. The second level is designed to assure that the qualification being scrutinized is one so important to the operation of the business that the business would be undermined if employees of the "wrong" sex were hired.

Southwest concedes with respect to the *Weeks* test that males are able to perform safely and efficiently all the basic, mechanical functions required of flight attendants and ticket agents.

* * *

Southwest's position, however, is that females are required to fulfill certain non-mechanical aspects of these jobs: to attract those male customers who prefer female attendants and ticket agents, and to preserve the authenticity and genuineness of Southwest's unique, female corporate personality.

A similar, though not identical, argument that females could better perform certain non-mechanical functions required of flight attendants was rejected in *Diaz*. There, the airline argued and the trial court found that being female was a BFOQ because women were superior in "providing reassurance to anxious passengers, giving courteous personalized service and, in general, making flights as pleasurable as possible within the limitations imposed by aircraft operations." Although it accepted the trial court findings, the Court of Appeals reversed, holding that femininity was not a BFOQ, because catering to passengers' psychological needs was only "tangential" to what was "reasonably *necessary*" for the business involved (original emphasis). Characterizing the "essence" or "primary function" of Pan American's business as the safe transportation of passengers from one point to another, the court explained:

> While a pleasant environment, enhanced by the obvious cosmetic effect that female stewardesses provide as well as, according to the findings of the trial court, their apparent ability to perform the non-mechanical functions of the job in a more effective manner than most men, may all be important, they are tangential to the essence of the business involved. No one has suggested that having male stewards will so seriously affect the operation of the airline as to jeopardize or even minimize its ability to provide safe transportation from one place to another.

Similar reasoning underlay the appellate court's rejection of Pan American's claim that its customers' preference for female attendants justified its refusal to hire males. Because the non-mechanical functions that passengers preferred females to perform were tangential to the airline's business, the court held, "the fact that customers prefer [females] cannot justify sex discrimination." The Fifth Circuit in *Diaz* did not hold that customer preference could never give rise to a sex BFOQ. Rather, consistent with the EEOC's exception for authenticity and genuineness, the Court allowed that customer preference could "be taken into account only when it is based on the company's inability to perform the primary function or service it offers," that is, where sex or sex appeal is itself the dominant service provided.

Diaz and its progeny establish that to recognize a BFOQ for jobs requiring multiple abilities, some sex-linked and some sex-neutral, the sex-linked aspects of the job must predominate. Only then will an employer have satisfied *Weeks'* requirement that sex be so essential to successful job performance that a member of the opposite sex could not perform the job. An illustration of such dominance in sex cases is the exception recognized by the EEOC for authenticity and genuineness. In the example given in § 1604.B2(a)(2), that of an actor or actress, the primary function of the position, its essence, is to fulfill the audience's expectation and desire for a particular role, characterized by particular physical or emotional traits. Generally, a male could not supply the authenticity required to perform a female role. Similarly, in jobs where sex or vicarious sexual recreation is the primary service provided, e.g. a social escort or topless dancer, the job automatically calls for one sex exclusively; the employee's sex and the service provided are inseparable. Thus, being female has been deemed a BFOQ for the position of a Playboy Bunny, female sexuality being reasonably necessary to perform the dominant purpose of the job which is forthrightly to titillate and entice male customers. One court has also suggested, without holding, that the authenticity exception would give rise to a BFOQ for Chinese nationality where necessary to maintain the authentic atmosphere of an ethnic Chinese restaurant. Consistent with the language of *Diaz,* customer preference for one sex only in such a case would logically be so strong that the employer's ability to perform the primary function or service offered would be undermined by not hiring members of the authentic sex or group exclusively.

The Court is aware of only one decision where sex was held to be a BFOQ for an occupation not providing primarily sex oriented services. In Fernandez v. Wynn Oil Co., 20 FEP Cases 1162 (C.D.Cal.1979), the court approved restricting to males the job of international marketing director for a company with extensive overseas operations. The position involved primarily attracting and transacting business with Latin American and Southeast Asian customers who would not feel comfortable doing business with a woman. The court found that the customers' attitudes, customs, and mores relating to the proper business roles of the sexes created formidable obstacles to successful job performance by a woman. South American distributors and customers, for example, would have been offended by a woman conducting business meetings in her hotel room. Applying the *Diaz* test, the court concluded that hiring a female as international marketing director "would have totally subverted any business [defendant] hoped to accomplish in those areas of the world." Because hiring a male was *necessary* to the Defendant's ability to continue its foreign operations, sex was deemed a BFOQ for the marketing position.

Applying the first level test for a BFOQ, with its legal gloss, to Southwest's particular operations results in the conclusion that being female is not a qualification required to perform successfully the jobs of flight attendant and ticket agent with Southwest.

* * *

While possession of female allure and sex appeal have been made qualifications for Southwest's contact personnel by virtue of the "love" campaign, the functions served by employee sexuality in Southwest's operations are not dominant ones. * * * Accordingly, the ability of the airline to perform its primary business function, the transportation of passengers, would not be jeopardized by hiring males.

It is also relevant that Southwest's female image was adopted at its discretion, to promote a business unrelated to sex. Contrary to the unyielding South American preference for males encountered by the Defendant company in *Fernandez,* Southwest exploited, indeed nurtured, the very customer preference for females it now cites to justify discriminating against males. Moreover, the fact that a vibrant marketing campaign was necessary to distinguish Southwest in its early years does not lead to the conclusion that sex discrimination was then, or is now, a business *necessity.* Southwest's claim that its female image will be tarnished by hiring males is, in any case, speculative at best.

* * *

One final observation is called for. This case has serious underpinnings, but it also has disquieting strains. These strains, and they were only that, warn that in our quest for non-racist, non-sexist goals, the demand for equal rights can be pushed to silly extremes. The rule of law in this country is so firmly embedded in our ethical regimen that little can stand up to its force—except literalistic insistence upon one's rights. And such inability to absorb the minor indignities suffered daily by us all without running to court may stop it dead in its tracks. We do not have such a case here—only warning signs rumbling from the facts.

NOTES AND QUESTIONS

1.   One issue posed by the BFOQ defense is individualized determination. Consider the following situation: An employer has a job opening on its loading dock and the workers need to be able to lift and load 150 pound boxes. Could the employer interview only men for the job or would the employer be required to test each female applicant (as well as male) to see if she could lift the 150 pounds? Would there be any obligation to use 50 pound boxes so that more women could lift them? Suppose an employer has a 50 pound lifting

requirement, which a woman applicant can meet. She is then refused employment because the dock foreman says: "Big deal, she can lift one box. There's no way she can do it all day long." In a Title VII case, what result? Suppose that a woman of small stature applies for a job on the loading dock, attempts to lift a heavy box, and injures her back. Is the employer liable? See Legault v. aRusso, 842 F.Supp. 1479 (D.N.H.1994), granting preliminary injunction in favor of plaintiff because a fire department testing procedure which included a physical agility test that no woman applicant could pass was discriminatory.

2.   The second issue raised by BFOQ cases is "essence of the job." Are you persuaded by the court's conclusion that attracting airline passengers with sex-linked ads is not the essence of the job Southwest Airlines is filling? Is the court invalidating use of sex (and appearance) in hiring models, cocktail waitresses, and Las Vegas hostesses? If not, is the court second-guessing the airline's judgment about how to survive in its competitive market?

3.   How should a business respond to customers who articulate openly racial preferences regarding its employees? Consider the situation that arose in Chaney v. Plainfield Healthcare Center, 612 F.3d 908 (7th Cir. 2010). Chaney was an African-American certified nursing assistant (CNA) at the Plainfield Healthcare Center. When a patient at the Healthcare Center expressed the desire to avoid receiving care from black staff members, the Center responded by issuing "assignment sheets" that "bann[ed]" Chaney from assisting that patient. Although the Healthcare Center tried to characterize the work assignments as an attempt to conform to patients' preferences and state regulations, the Seventh Circuit reiterated that "a company's desire to cater to the perceived racial preferences of its customers is not a defense under Title VII for treating employees differently based on race." The court emphasized that "[the relevant state] regulations do not say that a patient's preference for white aides * * * trumps [the Healthcare Center's] duty to its employees to abstain from race-based work assignments."

4.   Jean Rae Sutton, a woman, worked as a security guard at a distillery in Cincinnati, Ohio. To prevent the theft of tools and small bottles of liquor ("miniatures") the company began having the security guards conduct pat-down searches of employees as they left the distillery. Some of the 500 male workers and their wives objected to the searches by a woman guard and she was transferred. Has the employer violated Title VII? See Sutton v. National Distillers Prods. Co., 445 F.Supp. 1319 (S.D.Ohio 1978), affirmed, 628 F.2d 936 (6th Cir. 1980) (held: no violation).

5.   In Healey v. Southwood Psych. Hosp., 78 F.3d 128 (3d Cir. 1996), the Third Circuit found that a psychiatric hospital treating emotionally disturbed and sexually abused children had established that gender is a bona fide occupational qualification necessary for normal business operation. If members of both sexes were not present on a shift, the court found, Southwood's ability to provide therapeutic care to sexually abused patients who feel comfortable talking only to a staff member of the same sex would be hindered, disrupting the normal operation of its particular business. Thus, although the night shift was a less desirable shift because of added

housekeeping duties and less patient contact, the court held that the hospital did not discriminate unlawfully against a female employee by assigning her to that shift. The Third Circuit has not yet decided whether concern for the privacy needs of the patients justifies the use of sex as a BFOQ. Particularly in cases involving touching or viewing of naked bodies, however, courts have regularly deferred to customer preferences for privacy and held sex to be a BFOQ. See Backus v. Baptist Medical Center, 510 F.Supp. 1191 (E.D. Ark. 1981) (sex a BFOQ in hiring of hospital obstetrics and gynecology nurses); Jones v. Hinds Gen. Hosp., 666 F.Supp. 933, 935 (S.D. Miss. 1987) (finding sex a BFOQ for hiring female nurse assistants and male orderlies since such jobs often required the employee to "view or touch the private parts of their patients"); Fesel v. Masonic Home of Del., Inc., 447 F.Supp. 1346 (D. Del. 1978) (finding sex a BFOQ in hiring nurse to care for elderly female residents of retirement home). See generally Kimberly A. Yuracko, Private Nurses and Playboy Bunnies: Explaining Permissible Sex Discrimination, 92 Cal. L. Rev. 147 (2004) (explaining that courts are far more deferential to employer BFOQ claims responding to customer privacy preferences than to those responding to customer preferences for sexual titillation).

6. The job of "counselor" at a chain of weight loss centers includes taking tape measurements of customers every two weeks and taking body-fat measurements with calipers every six. Can the employer refuse to hire males for the position because its mostly female clientele has, in the past, refused to accept counseling services from males? See EEOC v. Hi 40 Corp., Inc., 953 F.Supp. 301 (W.D.Mo.1996) (held: no).

7. The court in *Wilson* distinguishes Fernandez v. Wynn Oil Co., allowing selection of a male to work with Latin American and Asian customers. The *Fernandez* decision was reversed, 653 F.2d 1273 (9th Cir. 1981). Could discriminatory preferences of foreigners ever be more worthy of legal respect than the preferences of American customers? Would this mean that an overseas airline could hire only female cabin attendants? What about refusing to assign a Jewish anesthesiologist to work at a hospital in Saudi Arabia? See Abrams v. Baylor Coll. of Med., 805 F.2d 528 (5th Cir. 1986) (held: illegal discrimination on the basis of religion). But cf. Kern v. Dynalectron Corp., 577 F.Supp. 1196 (N.D.Tex. 1983), affirmed, 746 F.2d 810 (5th Cir. 1984), which upheld a BFOQ defense for an employer's requirement that helicopter pilots hired to fly into Mecca be Moslem. The court wrote: "Dynalectron has proven a factual basis for believing that *all* non-Moslems would be unable to perform this job safely. Specifically, non-Moslems flying into Mecca are, if caught, beheaded. * * * Thus, the essence of Dynalectron's business would be undermined by the beheading of all the non-Moslem pilots based in Jeddah."

8. In Dothard v. Rawlinson, 433 U.S. 321 (1977), discussed *supra* on page 340, the Court struck down the use of height and weight requirements because of the disparate impact on women. Roadway Express would not hire anyone taller than 6′4″ as a truckdriver. Plaintiff, a 6′7″ male, sued, saying that .9% of adult men are taller than 6′4″ and only .3% of adult women are 6′ or taller. The court decided for the employer, saying height rules should be scrutinized carefully on behalf of historically disfavored groups but not on behalf of a formerly preferred group. The court noted that under the allegedly anti-male system Roadway had hired 189 male drivers and 2 females. Livingston v. Roadway Express, Inc., 802 F.2d 1250 (10th Cir. 1986).

9.   What about cultural differences between men and women?

a.   American Airlines required cabin attendants who became mothers to switch to ground duty positions, but it imposed no such rule on fathers. This was held to violate Title VII, In re Consolidated Pretrial Proceedings, 582 F.2d 1142 (7th Cir. 1978). The court said, "[A]ttributes that are culturally more common to one sex than the other are an insufficient basis for a BFOQ. Cultural stereotypes should not be employed to justify sex discrimination * * *. To accept [the view that a mother would be preoccupied with her parental duties and so be deficient in assisting safe transport] requires acquiescence in assumptions steeped in cultural stereotypes, such as that female parents have a more intense concern for their children than male parents, assumptions that are inconsistent with the purposes of the Act." Did the Supreme Court disagree when it upheld special treatment for pregnancy in California Fed. Sav. & Loan Ass'n v. Guerra, 479 U.S. 272 (1987)?

b.   Defendant company violates Title VII by requiring male employees but not female employees to keep their hair a certain length, "since this disparate treatment is based on the sex stereotype that men should have short hair." Longo v. Carlisle DeCoppet & Co., 403 F.Supp. 692 (S.D.N.Y.1975), reversed, 537 F.2d 685 (2d Cir. 1976). But see Willingham v. Macon Tel. Pub. Co., 507 F.2d 1084 (5th Cir. 1975), holding that Title VII does not bar different hair lengths for males and females because such a rule is discrimination "based not upon sex, but rather upon grooming standards," and because Title VII does not bar distinctions between men and women "on the basis of something other than immutable or protected characteristics." (Macon community disapproval of long-haired males had recently been exacerbated by an "International Pop Festival" at Byron, Georgia.) For a further discussion of grooming, see Ch. 7.

c.   Devine v. Lonschein, 621 F.Supp. 894 (S.D.N.Y.1985), affirmed without opinion, 800 F.2d 1127 (2d Cir. 1986), upheld a rule requiring male attorneys before a court (and not female attorneys) to wear neckties. Concerning uniforms and other sex-differentiated dress requirements see Ch. 7.

See Katharine Bartlett, Only Girls Wear Barrettes: Dress and Appearance Standards, Community Norms, and Workplace Equality, 92 Mich. L. Rev. 2541 (1994):

> [C]ourts should approach challenges to practices grounded in community norms by attempting to identify the cultural meanings underlying them and determining to what extent they impose burdens that disadvantage members of one sex in relation to the other. For example, in reviewing the apparently "trivial" rule that women wear skirts, a court must ask whether there is something in the cultural coding of skirts that disadvantages their wearers by making them seem, say, less professional and more ornamental or

vulnerable than those who wear pants. In answering this question, it is useful to inquire whether it would be considered equally trivial if men in the same workplace were required to wear skirts. * * * When such status distinctions are revealed, rules built on them must be carefully scrutinized for job-relatedness under the BFOQ exception to Title VII. Likewise, weight restrictions grounded in the community's expectations that women be thinner than men must be examined to determine whether these expectations are tied to, and help to sustain, gender disadvantage. Biological explanations for women's lower average weights might help to establish that different weight standards impose no extra actual burden on women. * * * average weight tables, it turns out, demonstrate only what average women and men actually weigh, not what they would weigh without societal pressures, placed disproportionately on women, to be thin * * *

Is it possible to have it both ways, that is, to preserve the fun, creative, and even subversive potential of dress and appearance without at the same time strengthening its potential to oppress?

See also Deborah Rhode, The Beauty Bias: The Injustice of Appearance in Life and Law (2010):

> Part of the problem is that attractiveness and grooming standards fall along a continuum. How would employers or courts determine what aspects of appearance are entitled to protection? As one judge put it, "No Court can be expected to create a standard on such vagaries as attractiveness." Will there be a national standard of attractiveness established by EEOC rulemaking? * * * Commentators from all points on the political spectrum worry that appearance-discrimination statutes will result in "litigiousness run wild," impose "untold costs" on businesses, and erode support for other legislation prohibiting "truly invidious discrimination."
>
> * * *
>
> Although such concerns are not without force, neither do they justify the prevailing tolerance for appearance discrimination in contemporary legal doctrine and social practices. An initial difficulty lies in critics' assumption that prejudice based on appearance is more natural and harder to eradicate than other forms of bias. In fact, considerable evidence suggests that in-group favoritism—the preferences that individuals feel for those who are like them in salient respects such as race, sex, and ethnicity, are also deeply rooted. Plessy v. Ferguson, the shameful 1896 Supreme Court decision that affirmed "separate but equal" racial policies, assumed that segregation was a natural desire. Opponents of civil rights statutes in the 1960s similarly insisted that "you can't legislate morality" on matters like racial tolerance. But we can legislate conduct, and a half century's experience makes clear that changes in attitudes can follow.
>
> * * *

The point is [ ] that even forms of prejudice assumed to be hardwired have in fact been profoundly influenced by law. There is no reason to believe that appearance discrimination would be different.

10. A major test of the intersection between culture and antidiscrimination law arose when the EEOC sued Sears Roebuck, asserting that women did not hold their share of better paid commission sales positions. The litigation took many procedural turns but in the end a court of appeals accepted, as a legally sufficient explanation for statistical disparity between men and women, Sears' argument that "women were not as interested in commission sales positions as were men. * * * [W]omen were generally more interested in product lines like clothing, jewelry, and cosmetics that were usually sold on a noncommission basis, than they were in product lines involving commission selling like automobiles, roofing, and furnaces." Judge Cudahy, dissenting in part, said that "the stereotype of women as less greedy and daring than men is one that the sex discrimination laws were intended to address. * * * There are abundant indications that women lack neither the desire to compete strenuously for financial gain nor the capacity to take risks." EEOC v. Sears, Roebuck & Co., 839 F.2d 302 (7th Cir. 1988).

For insightful discussion of the *Sears* litigation, see Lucinda Finley, Choice and Freedom: Elusive Issues in the Search for Gender Justice, 96 Yale L.J. 914, 937–40 (1987):

> The statement of qualifications for [the higher paid positions at Sears] reads like a description of the stereotypical male: someone who is aggressive, competitive, has lots of drive, physical vigor, and social dominance, someone with technical knowledge and fluency, someone who could frequently work odd evening or weekend hours. People with prior experience selling technical product lines were preferred, and personnel interviewers often evaluated candidates according to how closely they matched those already doing the job, a comparison group that was almost totally male. Perhaps recognizing how unlike their conceptions of themselves these very male job descriptions were, most women who did apply to be sellers for Sears stated a preference for selling noncommissioned and very female products jewelry, lingerie, cosmetics, and women's apparel. * * *

> The court finds that women also do not like to accept financial risk as much as men; this is perhaps because their economic dependence and their principal responsibility for children can make monetary risk a suicidal course. Women's education makes it less likely that they will have the requisite technical background, comfort, or confidence in their ability to master technical information. For all these reasons, it was not surprising that Sears encountered difficulties in attempting to convince women to apply for positions selling machinery, home improvement devices, and automotive products.

[According to some commentators,] the argument based on women's nature ends the inquiry. Men and women simply are different, and that means they have different interests. Government should do nothing to disturb these natural preferences. But instead of satisfying these choice advocates, these supposedly preference-based disparities between men and women could lead to profoundly important inquiries about liberty. These inquiries would suggest how men and women could be liberated from the powerful constraints set by the social construction of gender roles. First, rather than blaming women and their nature for their underrepresentation in the high paying jobs, why not reexamine the jobs and their values? It may not be necessary for a salesperson to be an aggressive hustler willing to pester the customer to sell the commissioned items successfully. * * * Second, is the qualifications personality profile really geared to the needs of the job, or does it merely describe those who have been doing the job and the way they have been doing it? * * * Finally, should it be of any concern to an equal liberty advocate that when a woman sees the male bias in the job itself, she may sense that she is not wanted or would suffer isolation and hazing on the job, and instead may cope with the odds against her by convincing herself that she really does not want what she probably would not get? A woman's "choice" to accept a traditionally female sales position may not be such a free one, after all. * * *

On the assumption that people exposed to new possibilities begin to change their attitudes, government might require employers to grant parenting leave and create incentives for men to take it. Employers might need to restructure their advancement tracks, so that those of either sex who assume parenting obligations need not sacrifice their careers. Employers might need to reevaluate the skills or traits currently considered desirable for certain jobs. Government could provide incentives to try things in new ways. It might even inaugurate affirmative action for men in traditionally female jobs, as well as for women in traditionally male jobs. Such significant departures from existing practices would be much more likely to result in * * * a world in which men and women can exercise the full range of options previously available primarily to the other sex, without risking undue economic loss or social disapprobation for nontraditional choices, and a world in which one's gender is not as determinative as it is now of what one can do or wants to do.

In *Sears,* the defendant prevailed by arguing that women lack interest in "male" jobs. Gender plaintiffs have been less likely to prevail against the lack of interest defense than race plaintiffs. A comparison of the content and strength of race and sex discrimination cases concluded that sex discrimination cases are not weaker than race cases to a degree sufficient to explain the disparity in success rates of plaintiffs. Vicki Schultz, Race, Gender, Work, and Choice: An Empirical Study of the Lack of Defense in

Title VII Cases Challenging Job Segregation, 59 U.Chi.L.Rev. 1073 (1992). Professor Schultz found that judges regularly accepted the premise that a woman's work aspirations have been shaped through socialization or innate predisposition and not artificially limited because of a discriminatory market.

In Stender v. Lucky Stores, Inc., 803 F.Supp. 259 (N.D.Cal.1992), plaintiffs introduced statistical evidence to show a significant disparity in job distribution and job promotion between male and female employees. Expert testimony showed that ambiguous job qualifications coupled with the secrecy of the decision-making process led test subjects to recommend candidates of their own sex. When evaluative criteria were clear and the decision-making process public, sex was less likely to be a factor in selection. Defendants used the lack of interest defense to explain the statistical disparity. This argument was rejected by the court:

> Even in a situation where gender stereotypes about work interest patterns reflect reality, it is unlawful for an employer to discriminate against those whose work interests deviate from the stereotype. Therefore, the court holds that job interest surveys cannot be used as a defense in disparate treatment cases. Defendant's survey only has evidentiary weight as a rebuttal to plaintiff's statistical argument in its disparate impact claim. In rebuttal, interest surveys may be used to explain the statistical disparities between men and women which plaintiff alleges. However, anecdotal evidence of disparate treatment or of disparate impact cannot be rebutted by job interest surveys. Generalizations about women's job interests cannot be used to trump the testimony of individual women about their job interests.

11. How much of stereotypes, such as different "work interests" of men and women, is reinforced by current prevailing attitudes about cultural norms and assumptions of their roles? How much does unconscious bias or stereotyping against plaintiffs play into reestablishing these roles, first in employer decisions, and then once again in employment discrimination litigation? Assuming these unconscious bias exist, could they and should they be overcome? For recent scholarship on this discussion, see Melissa Hart, Subjective Decisionmaking and Unconscious Discrimination, 56 Ala. L. Rev. 741 (2005) and Audrey J. Lee, Unconscious Bias in Employment Discrimination Litigation, 40 Harv. C.R.-C.L. L. Rev. 481 (2005).

12. On February 27, 1997, the Vienna Philharmonic Orchestra ended its men-only policy and voted to accept women as members. The first woman to be admitted was a female harpist who had played for the Philharmonic for 26 years.

Just one week prior to the announcement, the orchestra director argued that an orchestra containing women would be paralyzed by mass pregnancy and long maternity leaves. According to the new rules, any player absent more than 24 months will have to audition for his or her place again.

Some of the musicians have complained that admitting women will change the dynamic of the orchestra, which is its traditional deep strings.

Perhaps they should consider blind auditions, a technique that has become popular with United States orchestras.

Economists Claudia Goldin of Harvard and Cecelia Rouse of Princeton conducted a study of auditions for American orchestras. They found that when judges could not see auditioners, and musicians auditioned behind a heavy cloth suspended from the ceiling, the odds of a woman getting the job were boosted by 50 percent.

With the switch to blind auditions, the percentage of female musicians in the top five orchestras in the United States increased from five percent in 1970 to 25 percent in 1996. Thirty-five percent of the new hires for the Boston and Chicago symphonies were women, while less than 10 percent of the new hires in years prior to the use of blind auditions were women. Wall Street Journal, March 7, 1997, B6B.

13. Issues of fetal vulnerability (employer arguments that women of child-bearing age must be excluded from certain jobs because of health risks to unborn or unconceived children) are considered in Chapter 8.

14. Taylor, a Postal Service superintendent, was demoted during a massive reorganization. She said that her supervisor told her that he had to pick between her and a male employee, and that he chose the male because he had a wife and children and needed the money. The Eleventh Circuit said the jury should be allowed to decide whether the statement, if made, constituted unlawful gender discrimination. Taylor v. Runyon, 175 F.3d 861 (11th Cir. 1999).

15. Plaintiff, reorganized out of his job as a social worker, said it was unlawful sex discrimination because several women were retained. He showed notes on the file of a female worker saying "smiles warm," and said there was no similar note in his file. The court said that even if smiling is more common among women, paying attention to a smile is not unlawful because smiling is an appropriate trait for a social worker. Scott v. Parkview Mem. Hosp., 175 F.3d 523 (7th Cir. 1999).

Ferrill v. Parker Group, Inc.
168 F.3d 468 (11th Cir. 1999).

■ ALAIMO, SENIOR DISTRICT JUDGE:

Appellant, The Parker Group, Inc. ("TPG"), appeals the District Court's order granting summary judgment to plaintiff-appellee, Shirley Ferrill, on Ferrill's claim of race discrimination in job assignment in violation of Title 42 of the United States Code, section 1981. TPG argues that the District Court erred in finding TPG liable under § 1981 despite the District Court's finding that TPG had no racial animus. TPG also appeals the jury award of compensatory and punitive damages.

Because this appeal involves the grant of a motion for summary judgment, we review the facts in the light most favorable to TPG, the non-moving party on this motion.

TPG is a telephone marketing corporation, often hired to perform work for political candidates. The conduct at issue in this case involves TPG's work making "get-out-the-vote" calls for various political candidates preceding the November 1994 election. About 60% of TPG's overall business is pre-election "get-out-the-vote" calling. Approximately 10% of such calling is race-matched, such that black voters are called by black TPG employees who use the "black" script, while white voters are called by white TPG employees who use a different, "white" script.[1] Race-matched calling apparently is used only when specifically requested by customers. TPG employees doing the race-matched calling in 1994 were assigned separate calling areas and separate scripts according to race. To facilitate supervision, TPG also physically segregated employees who worked at race-matched calling.[2] Black callers were segregated into one room, and white callers segregated into another.

Ferrill, an African-American woman, was hired as a temporary employee to fill TPG's pre-election staffing needs from September through November 1994.[4] She worked primarily on Jim Folsom's gubernatorial campaign, making race-matched "get-out-the-vote" calls. Ferrill was laid off during a "reduction in force" ("RIF") immediately after the election.

Ferrill filed this action under 42 U.S.C. § 1981, as amended by the Civil Rights Act of 1991, alleging race discrimination in her termination and job assignment. Ferrill and TPG filed cross-motions for summary judgment. The District Court granted TPG's Motion for Summary Judgment on the unlawful termination claim because Ferrill failed to rebut TPG's proffered legitimate nondiscriminatory reason for the termination, namely, a RIF. The District Court granted Ferrill's Motion for Summary Judgment on the unlawful job assignment claim. TPG appeals this grant of summary judgment to Ferrill.

After granting Ferrill's Motion for Summary Judgment and finding TPG liable on the unlawful job assignment claim, the District Court struck a jury to decide damages. The jury awarded Ferrill $500 in compensatory damages and $4000 in punitive damages. TPG also appeals this award of compensatory and punitive damages.

* * *

A showing of disparate impact through a neutral practice is insufficient to prove a § 1981 violation because proof of discriminatory intent is essential.

---

[1] TPG apparently also tries to match other characteristics. For example, TPG claims that it attempts to match callers with Midwestern accents with Midwestern voters.

[2] TPG asserts that it has now abandoned the practice of physical segregation. Through use of computers and other technological innovations, it is now possible to supervise callers effectively even if callers on different projects work side by side.

[4] Ferrill was not a TPG employee, but rather was employed by a temporary placement agency. Thus, she was precluded from suing TPG under Title VII.

* * *

TPG has admitted that the 1994 assignments of "get-out-the-vote" calls and scripts were made on the basis of race and that TPG employees were segregated on the basis of race. TPG's admission is direct evidence of disparate treatment on the basis of race and sustains Ferrill's prima facie case. The District Court relied on that unrebutted evidence to find TPG liable for intentional race discrimination in job assignments in violation of § 1981.

Implicit in the District Court's finding is the notion that racial animus and intent to discriminate are not synonymous. In its Memorandum Opinion, the District Court stated that there is "no evidence" that TPG acted with any racial animus. The crucial issue then is whether a defendant who acts with no racial animus but makes job assignments on the basis of race can be held liable for intentional discrimination under § 1981. Clearly, the answer is yes.

* * *

Discrimination in employment on the basis of protected traits such as sex, religion, age, national origin, or race, may be permissible in at least three circumstances. First, disparate treatment on the basis of religion, sex, or national origin is allowed where a particular religion, sex, or national origin is deemed a qualification reasonably necessary to the functioning of a business (a "bona fide occupational qualification"). Secondly, facially neutral employer practices that disparately impact protected classes may be justified by "business necessity." Finally, under the aegis of "affirmative action," employers may engage in disparate treatment in favor of a protected class for the purpose of remedying past discrimination.

An employer may intentionally discriminate "on the basis of * * * religion, sex, or national origin in those certain instances where religion, sex, or national origin is a bona fide occupational qualification reasonably necessary to the normal operation of that particular business or enterprise * * * " 42 U.S.C. § 2000eB2(e)(1). The bona fide occupational qualification ("BFOQ") defense is an extremely narrow exception, and is not available for racial discrimination. Because § 1981 proscribes discrimination solely on the basis of race, and the BFOQ defense does not apply to racial discrimination, the BFOQ defense is never available to the § 1981 defendant.

An employer may assert "business necessity" as a defense to claims that facially neutral employment practices have discriminatory effects. The business necessity defense originally had no textual basis but evolved primarily from Griggs v. Duke Power Co., as a defense to claims that facially neutral employment practices have discriminatory effects. In 1991, Congress codified the business necessity defense as articulated by the Court in *Griggs*. When a facially neutral practice is challenged for its disparate impact, an employer need not assert a BFOQ for justification, but may argue instead that the practice is grounded in a legitimate, job-related purpose. Because § 1981 liability must be grounded on intentional discrimination, and the neutral practice mode of proof is inapposite in § 1981 cases, the business necessity defense is not available to the § 1981 defendant.

In sum, then, it is clear that the BFOQ and business necessity defenses are not available to a defendant who, like TPG, is accused of intentional discrimination on the basis of race in violation of § 1981.[10]

Neither is Title VII's "affirmative action" exception available to TPG. Although discrimination to remedy the effects of past discrimination is permitted under Title VII, and this defense is available to the § 1981 defendant, the defense is not applicable to the case at bar. Ferrill's assignment to call African Americans "was not affirmative action, or benign discrimination, intended to correct racial imbalance. Rather, it was based on a racial stereotype that blacks" would respond to blacks and "on the premise that [Ferrill's] race was directly related to her ability to do the job."

Recently, the Seventh Circuit adopted a narrow, judicially-crafted racial BFOQ in Wittmer v. Peters, 87 F.3d 916 (7th Cir. 1996). In Wittmer, white boot camp correctional officers denied promotions to lieutenant sued for race discrimination in violation of the Equal Protection Clause. Applying strict scrutiny, the Seventh Circuit held that preference given to a black applicant on the basis of his race did not violate equal protection because expert evidence suggested that black boot camp inmates would not participate in the correctional game of "brutal drill sergeant" unless there were some black officers in authority positions at the camp. Subsequently, in McNamara v. City of Chicago, 138 F.3d 1219 (7th Cir. 1998), the Seventh Circuit declined to extend this racial BFOQ to firefighters because there was no compelling evidence that white firefighters could not be effective as firefighters.

---

[10] The District Court expressed some concern that its decision "might well prevent advertisers from employing, based on race, actors to solicit products to a certain group." This conclusion, however, does not necessarily follow. A film director casting a movie about African-American slaves may not exclude Caucasians from the auditions, but the director may limit certain roles to persons having the physical characteristics of African-Americans. Indeed, the drafters of Title VII expressly anticipated this issue. In their interpretative memorandum, Senators Case and Clark explained that

> [a]lthough there is no exemption in Title VII for occupations in which race might be deemed a bona fide job qualification, a director of a play or movie who wished to cast an actor in the role of a Negro, could specify that he wished to hire someone with the physical appearance of a Negro.

110 Cong. Rec. 7213, 7217 (1964) (emphasis added). See also Miller, 615 F.2d at 654 (suggesting that a director wishing to cast the role of Henry VIII may announce that only applicants of sufficient physical likeness to Henry VIII will be considered). As applied here, TPG could have legally assigned jobs based on accent, speech pattern or dialect, but not expressly on race. Although the statutory language allows gender to be a valid BFOQ for hiring an actor or actress where it is necessary for the "purpose of authenticity or genuineness," see 29 C.F.R. § 1604.2(a)(2), Congress specifically rejected race as a BFOQ. See generally 110 Cong. Rec. 2550–63 (1964) (House discussion on inclusion of race and color in the BFOQ exception).

Although two cases from the former Fifth Circuit suggest in dicta that such a defense may be justified in certain circumstances, this circuit has never adopted a racial BFOQ. In Baker v. City of St. Petersburg, 400 F.2d 294 (5th Cir. 1968), the former Fifth Circuit suggested that race may be considered for "the undercover infiltration of an all-Negro criminal organization or plainclothes work in an area where a white man could not pass without notice. Special assignments [on the basis of race] might also be justified during brief periods of unusually high racial tension." Id. at 301 n. 10 (emphasis added). Similarly, in Miller, 615 F.2d 650, the former Fifth Circuit stated that a "business necessity defense may also be appropriate in the selection of actors to play certain roles," but explicitly recognized that "the black on black assignments tentatively approved in Baker may be prohibited unless a business or similar exception is recognized for such intentional discrimination." No such business or similar exception has been recognized by this Circuit, and we decline to do so today.

TPG raises for the first time on appeal their argument that their practice of using race-matched calling is political speech protected by the First and Fourteenth Amendments. Specifically, TPG argues that its clients, political candidates, should be able to choose the particular mode of political expression, i.e., race-matched get-out-the-vote calling.

* * *

[B]ecause TPG did not present a First Amendment argument in the district court, we decline to consider this issue on appeal.

* * *

This Court affirms the District Court's finding that TPG intentionally discriminated on the basis of race in violation of § 1981. In addition, we affirm the award of compensatory damages in the amount of $500. However, because the record is devoid of evidence of the ill will required to support the imposition of punitive damages, we reverse on that issue.

AFFIRMED in part and REVERSED in part.

NOTES AND QUESTIONS

1. Section 703(e) of Title VII does *not* include race among the classifications for which a BFOQ defense may be raised. Can race ever be a BFOQ? Consider the following case: A county's civil service commission assigned a black personnel specialist to minority recruitment against his wishes. The commission argued that it was trying to attract more minority applicants to the civil service and it believed that a black personnel specialist would be better able to develop a rapport with potential black applicants. Is the county's rationale a valid defense to a charge of race discrimination? See Knight v. Nassau County Civil Serv. Comm'n, 649 F.2d 157 (2d Cir. 1981), cert. denied, 454 U.S. 818 (1981) (held: no). Does this mean that a police department in assigning officers partners and "beats" could not consider the

race of the officers? Are there valid interests served by assuring that at least some minority officers are assigned to patrol in minority neighborhoods?

2. The BFOQ defense is not available to defendants accused of discrimination based on race. However, there has been tacit acceptance of race as a BFOQ in jobs where the authenticity of an actor in a role is central: from the straightforward scenario of Hollywood casting breakdowns to settings such as police undercover operations. Should this be made explicitly permissible? In the case of casting, should First Amendment freedom of expression trump Equal Employment protections of Title VII? For a walk-through on the available arguments and defenses based on prior Title VII and First Amendment jurisprudence and a compelling argument that Title VII should prevail over First Amendment considerations, see Russell K. Robinson, Casting and Caste-ing: Reconciling Artistic Freedom and Antidiscrimination Norms, 95 Cal. L. Rev. 1 (2007).

3. Illinois opened a "boot camp" for young criminals. Although 68 percent of the inmates were black, the correctional officers, lieutenants, and captains were overwhelmingly white. Is it permissible for the state to use race as a factor in the promotion of correctional officers on the belief that they will be more effective? See Wittmer v. Peters, cited in *Ferrell*, supra (held: promotion of black officer over higher ranked white officers was constitutional). In *Wittmer*, Judge Posner wrote:

> Plaintiffs * * * claim that the black man who was made a lieutenant was less qualified than they and received the appointment only because of his race. He ranked forty-second in the test * * * while the plaintiffs ranked third, sixth, and eighth * * *. While we may assume that a practice that is subject to the skeptical, questioning, beady-eyed scrutiny that the law requires when public officials use race to allocate burdens or benefits is not illegal per se, it can survive that intense scrutiny only if the defendants can show that they are motivated by a truly powerful and worthy concern and that the racial measure that they have adopted is a plainly apt response to that concern * * * The black lieutenant is needed because the black inmates are believed unlikely to play the correctional game of brutal drill sergeant and brutalized recruit unless there are some blacks in authority in the camp * * * If academic research is required to validate any departure from strict racial neutrality, social experimentation in the area of race will be impossible despite its urgency * * *.

4. Was the law violated when New York transferred 22 "black and black-Hispanic" police officers to the 70th precinct following the torture and beating of Abner Louima? The court upheld a jury verdict that the city's race-based transfers were not narrowly tailored to meet a compelling state interest and approved an award of $50,000 in damages per plaintiff. Patrolmen's Benevolent Ass'n v. New York, 310 F.3d 43 (2d Cir. 2002), cert. denied, 538 U.S. 1032 (2003).

B. PROCEDURE

1. FILING A CHARGE OF EMPLOYMENT DISCRIMINATION

Section 706 of Title VII describes enforcement procedures. The statute is administered by the Equal Employment Opportunity Commission (EEOC), an independent federal agency with five presidentially-appointed members who serve five-year terms. Violations of the statute are brought to the EEOC's attention by agency investigation and individual complaints.

A charge must be filed with the EEOC within 180 days after the "occurrence" of the alleged unlawful employment practice, unless there is a state or local antidiscrimination law similar to Title VII (and virtually every state has one), with its own procedure for investigating and resolving complaints. In those cases, the procedure is modified, to encourage resolution of claims at the local level. Charges may be filed with either the EEOC or the state or local agency. If the charge is initially filed with the state or local agency, an EEOC charge may be filed up to 300 days after the occurrence of the alleged discrimination or 30 days after notice of termination of local proceedings, whichever comes first. If the charge is filed first with EEOC, it must defer to local proceedings for 60 days before undertaking its own investigation.

Federal employees must file a charge with the EEOC within 45 days of the "date of the matter alleged to be discriminatory" in order to preserve the right to sue in federal court for a violation of Title VII. In Green v. Brennan, 136 S.Ct. 1769 (2016), the Supreme Court held that for an employee alleging "constructive discharge" in violation of Title VII, the statutory period begins to run only after the employee resigns, not, as some circuits had previously held, at the time of the employer's last allegedly discriminatory act giving rise to the resignation. After a Title VII charge has been filed, the EEOC must serve notice of the charge on the respondent within ten days. The EEOC then investigates and determines if there is reasonable cause to believe discrimination has occurred. If cause is found, the EEOC attempts conciliation. If no conciliation can be reached, the EEOC may bring a civil action in United States district court. If no cause is found, or if within 180 days of the filing of the charge there has been no conciliation or civil action filed by the EEOC, the EEOC notifies the complainant in a "right to sue" letter. The charging party has 90 days after receipt of the right to sue letter to bring a civil action in federal district court.

All district court proceedings under Title VII are de novo. If the court finds an unlawful employment practice, it may enjoin the practice and grant affirmative relief including reinstatement, retroactive seniority, and back pay. Compensatory and punitive damages also may be awarded, up to $300,000 for companies with more than 500 employees. Section 706(g) limits back pay to two years before the filing of the charge with the EEOC. The court may also award attorneys' fees to prevailing parties.

In Walters v. Metropolitan Educ. Enter., Inc., 519 U.S. 202 (1997), the Supreme Court agreed with the EEOC's "payroll" approach, under which all employees on the payroll are counted toward meeting the jurisdictional minimum, regardless of whether every employee worked or was compensated on any given day.

For a detailed discussion of Title VII procedures, see Barbara Lindemann & Paul Grossman, Employment Discrimination Law, Chs. 29–37 (5th ed. 2012).

NOTES AND QUESTIONS

1. Although a plaintiff employee must pass muster under the *McDonnell Douglas* standard to prevail on the merits of an employment-discrimination claim, the standard does not apply when the court is merely evaluating whether a complaint is sufficient to overcome a motion to dismiss. The Supreme Court held in Swierkiewicz v. Sorema N.A., 534 U.S. 506 (2002), that "an employment discrimination complaint need not include such facts [as required by the *McDonnell Douglas* standard] and instead must contain only 'a short and plain statement of the claim showing that the pleader is entitled to relief.' "

2. Title VII has a short statute of limitations (charges must be filed within 180 or 300 days "after the alleged unlawful employment practice occurred.") But in a hostile environment case, "provided that an act contributing to the claim occurs within the filing period, the entire time period of the hostile environment may be considered by a court for the purposes of determining liability." National R.R. Passenger Corp. v. Morgan, 536 U.S. 101 (2002) (5–4).

3. Title VII protects only employees and not a volunteer attorney participating for no pay in a bar association committee. To be a covered employee, a plaintiff must receive "financial benefit" which can include benefits such as health insurance. Clerical support and networking opportunities are insufficient. York v. Association of the Bar of the City of New York, 286 F.3d 122 (2d Cir. 2002), cert. denied, 537 U.S. 1089 (2002).

4. The threshold for Title VII liability is 15 employees during 20 weeks of a year. Plaintiff sued her employer, The Moonlight Café in New Orleans, charging sexual harassment in violation of Title VII and related state law violations. After Plaintiff won $40,000 in a jury trial and the district court entered judgment, defendant asserted for the first time that it had fewer than 15 employees because eight delivery workers were independent contractors and the owners of the café and their wives should not count even though the wives receive a salary and have taxes deducted from their wages. The district court and the court of appeals agreed that the 15-employee requirement was jurisdictional and dismissed the case. The Supreme Court reversed, holding that the 15-employee threshold is substantive, not jurisdictional. Thus the plaintiff's judgment on the state law issues survives defendant's demonstration that it is not subject to Title VII liability. Arbaugh v. Y & H Corp., 546 U.S. 500 (2006).

5. In Halpert v. Manhattan Apts., Inc., 580 F.3d 86 (2d Cir. 2009), the Second Circuit held that an employer may not escape liability for discriminatory acts by delegating those acts to an ostensibly independent agent. After Halpert applied for a position at Manhattan Apartments, he completed an interview with a "hiring agent" named Brooks. Halpert sued after Brooks allegedly told him during the interview that he was "too old" for the position. Ruling in favor of Halpert, the court found that Brooks was "acting as the hiring agent or apparent hiring agent [of Manhattan Apartments]" as opposed to "hiring on his own account."

2. DAMAGES

NOTES AND QUESTIONS

1. Congress has established limits on compensatory damages for employment discrimination. 42 U.S.C. § 1981a(b)(3). These limits do not apply to "back pay," or compensation the plaintiff would have received if the employment discrimination had not taken place. 42 U.S.C. § 1981a(b)(2). The statute, however, was silent as to whether it similarly exempted "front pay," or compensation withheld from the plaintiff pending adjudication of the claim. The Supreme Court exempted front pay from statutory limits in Pollard v. E.I. du Pont de Nemours & Co., 532 U.S. 843 (2001).

2. *Pollard* does not alter a discrimination plaintiff's duty to mitigate damages, often an employer's main defense to front or back pay relief.

3. The 1972 amendments to Title VII authorize the EEOC to order federal agencies to pay compensatory damages as well as back pay to U.S. employees who are victims of discrimination. West v. Gibson, 527 U.S. 212 (1999).

4. The Civil Rights Act of 1991 provides for both compensatory and punitive damages in Title VII cases. Compensatory damages are limited to conduct that is intentional on the part of the defendant (as opposed to disparate impact). The total amount of damages for combined compensatory and punitive damages is based on a sliding scale tied to the size of the defendant. For defendants with 15–100 employees, the maximum is $50,000; for 101–200 employees, the maximum is $100,000; for 201–500 employees, the maximum is $200,000; for 501 or more employees, the maximum is $300,000. Back pay, however, is not subject to the cap.

5. Kolstad v. American Dental Ass'n, 527 U.S. 526 (1999), discussed the standard for awarding punitive damages. The plaintiff must show "malice" or "reckless indifference," and the employer's conduct need not reach the level of "egregious" to be held liable for punitive damages. The Court also held that good faith employer efforts to enforce anti-discrimination policies can be a defense to punitive damages.

6. The D.C. Circuit upheld an award of punitive damages, in addition to back pay and compensatory damages, to an African-American hospital administrator who was not hired by a medical management company because of his race because the plaintiff was able to show an "evil motive or intent" to violate his civil rights. Barbour v. Merrill, 48 F.3d 1270 (D.C.Cir.1995), cert. dismissed, 516 U.S. 1155 (1996).

7.   Circuits are split on whether plaintiffs are able to recover supplemental Title VII damages in federal court if successful proceedings in state court or state administrative bodies do not yield complete relief. The Second Circuit joined the Seventh and Eighth Circuits in Nestor v. Pratt & Whitney, 466 F.3d 65 (2d Cir. 2006), allowing plaintiffs to proceed in federal court for supplemental Title VII damages. The Fourth Circuit, on the other hand, held that federal courts had no subject matter jurisdiction to hear claims in federal court solely for attorneys fees and costs after state administrative proceedings. Chris v. Tenet, 221 F.3d 648 (4th Cir. 2000), cert. denied, 531 U.S. 1191 (2001).

3. PROVING DISCRIMINATION

Staub v. Proctor Hospital
562 U.S. 411 (2011).

■ JUSTICE SCALIA, delivered the opinion of the Court.

We consider the circumstances under which an employer may be held liable for employment discrimination based on the discriminatory animus of an employee who influenced, but did not make, the ultimate employment decision.

Petitioner Vincent Staub worked as an angiography technician for respondent Proctor Hospital until 2004, when he was fired. Staub and Proctor hotly dispute the facts surrounding the firing, but because a jury found for Staub in his claim of employment discrimination against Proctor, we describe the facts viewed in the light most favorable to him.

While employed by Proctor, Staub was a member of the United States Army Reserve, which required him to attend drill one weekend per month and to train full time for two to three weeks a year. Both Janice Mulally, Staub's immediate supervisor, and Michael Korenchuk, Mulally's supervisor, were hostile to Staub's military obligations. Mulally scheduled Staub for additional shifts without notice so that he would " 'pa[y] back the department for everyone else having to bend over backwards to cover [his] schedule for the Reserves.' " She also informed Staub's co-worker, Leslie Sweborg, that Staub's " 'military duty had been a strain on th[e] department,' " and asked Sweborg to help her " 'get rid of him.' " Korenchuk referred to Staub's military obligations as " 'a b[u]nch of smoking and joking and [a] waste of taxpayers['] money.' " He was also aware that Mulally was " 'out to get' " Staub.

In January 2004, Mulally issued Staub a "Corrective Action" disciplinary warning for purportedly violating a company rule requiring him to stay in his work area whenever he was not working with a patient. The Corrective Action included a directive requiring Staub to report to

Mulally or Korenchuk " 'when [he] ha[d] no patients and [the angio] cases [we]re complete[d].' " According to Staub, Mulally's justification for the Corrective Action was false for two reasons: First, the company rule invoked by Mulally did not exist; and second, even if it did, Staub did not violate it.

On April 2, 2004, Angie Day, Staub's co-worker, complained to Linda Buck, Proctor's vice president of human resources, and Garrett McGowan, Proctor's chief operating officer, about Staub's frequent unavailability and abruptness. McGowan directed Korenchuk and Buck to create a plan that would solve Staub's " 'availability' problems." But three weeks later, before they had time to do so, Korenchuk informed Buck that Staub had left his desk without informing a supervisor, in violation of the January Corrective Action. Staub now contends this accusation was false: he had left Korenchuk a voice-mail notification that he was leaving his desk. Buck relied on Korenchuk's accusation, however, and after reviewing Staub's personnel file, she decided to fire him. The termination notice stated that Staub had ignored the directive issued in the January 2004 Corrective Action.

Staub challenged his firing through Proctor's grievance process, claiming that Mulally had fabricated the allegation underlying the Corrective Action out of hostility toward his military obligations. Buck did not follow up with Mulally about this claim. After discussing the matter with another personnel officer, Buck adhered to her decision.

Staub sued Proctor under the Uniformed Services Employment and Reemployment Rights Act of 1994, claiming that his discharge was motivated by hostility to his obligations as a military reservist. His contention was not that Buck had any such hostility but that Mulally and Korenchuk did, and that their actions influenced Buck's ultimate employment decision. A jury found that Staub's "military status was a motivating factor in [Proctor's] decision to discharge him," and awarded $57,640 in damages.

The Seventh Circuit reversed, holding that Proctor was entitled to judgment as a matter of law. The court observed that Staub had brought a " 'cat's paw' case," meaning that he sought to hold his employer liable for the animus of a supervisor who was not charged with making the ultimate employment decision.[1] It explained that under Seventh Circuit precedent, a "cat's paw" case could not succeed unless the nondecisionmaker exercised such " 'singular influence' " over the decisionmaker that the decision to terminate was the product of "blind reliance." It then noted that "Buck looked beyond what Mulally and

---

[1] The term "cat's paw" derives from a fable conceived by Aesop, put into verse by La Fontaine in 1679, and injected into United States employment discrimination law by Posner in 1990. In the fable, a monkey induces a cat by flattery to extract roasting chestnuts from the fire. After the cat has done so, burning its paws in the process, the monkey makes off with the chestnuts and leaves the cat with nothing. A coda to the fable (relevant only marginally, if at all, to employment law) observes that the cat is similar to princes who, flattered by the king, perform services on the king's behalf and receive no reward.

Korenchuk said," relying in part on her conversation with Day and her review of Staub's personnel file. The court "admit[ted] that Buck's investigation could have been more robust," since it "failed to pursue Staub's theory that Mulally fabricated the write-up." But the court said that the " 'singular influence' " rule "does not require the decisionmaker to be a paragon of independence": "It is enough that the decisionmaker is not wholly dependent on a single source of information and conducts her own investigation into the facts relevant to the decision." Because the undisputed evidence established that Buck was not wholly dependent on the advice of Korenchuk and Mulally, the court held that Proctor was entitled to judgment.

* * *

The Uniformed Services Employment and Reemployment Rights Act (USERRA) provides in relevant part as follows:

"A person who is a member of . . . or has an obligation to perform service in a uniformed service shall not be denied initial employment, reemployment, retention in employment, promotion, or any benefit of employment by an employer on the basis of that membership, . . . or obligation."

It elaborates further:

"An employer shall be considered to have engaged in actions prohibited . . . under subsection (a), if the person's membership . . . is a motivating factor in the employer's action, unless the employer can prove that the action would have been taken in the absence of such membership."

The statute is very similar to Title VII, which prohibits employment "discrimination because of . . . race, color, religion, sex, or national origin" and states that such discrimination is established when one of those factors "was a motivating factor for any employment practice, even though other factors also motivated the practice."

The central difficulty in this case is construing the phrase "motivating factor in the employer's action." When the company official who makes the decision to take an adverse employment action is personally acting out of hostility to the employee's membership in or obligation to a uniformed service, a motivating factor obviously exists. The problem we confront arises when that official has no discriminatory animus but is influenced by previous company action that is the product of a like animus in someone else.

* * *

Staub contends that the fact that an unfavorable entry on the plaintiff's personnel record was caused to be put there, with discriminatory animus, by Mulally and Korenchuk, suffices to establish the tort, even if Mulally and Korenchuk did not intend to cause his dismissal. But discrimination was no part of Buck's reason for the dismissal; and while Korenchuk and Mulally acted with discriminatory animus, the act they committed—the mere making of the reports—was not a denial of "initial employment, reemployment, retention in employment, promotion, or any benefit of employment," as liability under USERRA requires. If dismissal was not the object of Mulally's and Korenchuk's reports, it may have been their result, or even their foreseeable consequence, but that is not enough to render Mulally or Korenchuk responsible.

Here, however, Staub is seeking to hold liable not Mulally and Korenchuk, but their employer. Perhaps, therefore, the discriminatory motive of one of the employer's agents (Mulally or Korenchuk) can be aggregated with the act of another agent (Buck) to impose liability on Proctor. When a decision to fire is made with no unlawful animus on the part of the firing agent, but partly on the basis of a report prompted (unbeknownst to that agent) by discrimination, discrimination might perhaps be called a "factor" or a "causal factor" in the decision; but it seems to us a considerable stretch to call it a motivating factor.

Proctor, on the other hand, contends that the employer is not liable unless the de facto decisionmaker (the technical decisionmaker or the agent for whom he is the "cat's paw") is motivated by discriminatory animus. This avoids the aggregation of animus and adverse action, but it seems to us not the only application of general tort law that can do so. Animus and responsibility for the adverse action can both be attributed to the earlier agent (here, Staub's supervisors) if the adverse action is the intended consequence of that agent's discriminatory conduct. So long as the agent intends, for discriminatory reasons, that the adverse action occur, he has the scienter required to be liable under USERRA. And it is axiomatic under tort law that the exercise of judgment by the decisionmaker does not prevent the earlier agent's action (and hence the earlier agent's discriminatory animus) from being the proximate cause of the harm. Proximate cause requires only "some direct relation between the injury asserted and the injurious conduct alleged," and excludes only those "link[s] that are too remote, purely contingent, or indirect." We do not think that the ultimate decisionmaker's exercise of judgment automatically renders the link to the supervisor's bias "remote" or "purely contingent." The decisionmaker's exercise of judgment is also a proximate cause of the employment decision, but it is common for injuries to have multiple proximate causes. Nor can the ultimate decisionmaker's judgment be deemed a superseding cause of the harm. A cause can be thought "superseding" only if it is a "cause of independent origin that was not foreseeable."

Moreover, the approach urged upon us by Proctor gives an unlikely meaning to a provision designed to prevent employer discrimination. An employer's authority to reward, punish, or dismiss is often allocated among multiple agents. The one who makes the ultimate decision does so on the basis of performance assessments by other supervisors.

Proctor's view would have the improbable consequence that if an employer isolates a personnel official from an employee's supervisors, vests the decision to take adverse employment actions in that official, and asks that official to review the employee's personnel file before taking the adverse action, then the employer will be effectively shielded from discriminatory acts and recommendations of supervisors that were designed and intended to produce the adverse action. That seems to us an implausible meaning of the text, and one that is not compelled by its words.

Proctor suggests that even if the decisionmaker's mere exercise of independent judgment does not suffice to negate the effect of the prior discrimination, at least the decisionmaker's independent investigation (and rejection) of the employee's allegations of discriminatory animus ought to do so. We decline to adopt such a hard-and-fast rule. As we have already acknowledged, the requirement that the biased supervisor's action be a causal factor of the ultimate employment action incorporates the traditional tort-law concept of proximate cause. Thus, if the employer's investigation results in an adverse action for reasons unrelated to the supervisor's original biased action (by the terms of USERRA it is the employer's burden to establish that), then the employer will not be liable. But the supervisor's biased report may remain a causal factor if the independent investigation takes it into account without determining that the adverse action was, apart from the supervisor's recommendation, entirely justified. We are aware of no principle in tort or agency law under which an employer's mere conduct of an independent investigation has a claim-preclusive effect. Nor do we think the independent investigation somehow relieves the employer of "fault." The employer is at fault because one of its agents committed an action based on discriminatory animus that was intended to cause, and did in fact cause, an adverse employment decision.

We therefore hold that if a supervisor performs an act motivated by antimilitary animus that is intended by the supervisor to cause an adverse employment action, and if that act is a proximate cause of the ultimate employment action, then the employer is liable under USERRA.

Applying our analysis to the facts of this case, it is clear that the Seventh Circuit's judgment must be reversed. Both Mulally and Korenchuk were acting within the scope of their employment when they took the actions that allegedly caused Buck to fire Staub. A "reprimand . . . for workplace failings" constitutes conduct within the scope of an agent's employment. As the Seventh Circuit recognized, there was evidence that Mulally's and Korenchuk's actions were motivated by hostility toward Staub's military obligations. There was also evidence that Mulally's and Korenchuk's actions were causal factors underlying Buck's decision to fire Staub. Buck's termination notice expressly stated that Staub was terminated because he had "ignored" the directive in the Corrective Action. Finally, there was evidence that both Mulally and

Korenchuk had the specific intent to cause Staub to be terminated. Mulally stated she was trying to " 'get rid of' " Staub, and Korenchuk was aware that Mulally was " 'out to get' " Staub. Moreover, Korenchuk informed Buck, Proctor's personnel officer responsible for terminating employees, of Staub's alleged noncompliance with Mulally's Corrective Action, and Buck fired Staub immediately thereafter; a reasonable jury could infer that Korenchuk intended that Staub be fired. The Seventh Circuit therefore erred in holding that Proctor was entitled to judgment as a matter of law.

NOTE

The claim in *Staub* was for discrimination on the basis of association with the military. The court described a cat's-paw claim as an argument that the ultimate decision-maker exhibited "blind reliance" on a subordinate employee whose motives were unlawfully discriminatory. To what extent does this standard of proof allow an employer to escape liability when the supervisor conducts a perfunctory "independent" investigation? In Vasquez v. Empress Ambulance Service, 835 F.3d 267, 272–73 (2d Cir. 2016), the Second Circuit held that "the 'cat's paw' theory may also be used to support recovery for claims of retaliation in violation of Title VII."

C. RETALIATION

Title VII also protects employees from retaliation by their employers as punishment for exercising their rights and seeking protection under the statute. For instance, in Robinson v. Shell Oil Co., 519 U.S. 337 (1997), an African-American sales representative was fired and sued unsuccessfully under Title VII. When he applied for another job, the prospective employer received an unfavorable reference. Robinson then sued Shell for retaliation. The Supreme Court read section 704(a) as prohibiting retaliation against former employees as well as current ones.

Yanowitz v. L'Oreal USA, Inc.
116 P.3d 1123 (Cal. 2005).

■ GEORGE, C.J.—Plaintiff Elysa J. Yanowitz was a regional sales manager employed by defendant L'Oreal USA, Inc. (L'Oreal), a prominent cosmetics and fragrance company. Yanowitz alleges that after she refused to carry out an order from a male supervisor to terminate the employment of a female sales associate who, in the supervisor's view, was not sufficiently sexually attractive or "hot," she was subjected to heightened scrutiny and increasingly hostile adverse treatment that undermined her relationship with the employees she supervised and caused severe emotional distress that led her to leave her position. In bringing this action against L'Oreal, Yanowitz contended, among other matters, that L'Oreal's actions toward her constituted unlawful retaliation in violation of the provisions of Government Code section

12940, subdivision (h) (section 12940(h)), which forbids employers from retaliating against employees who have acted to protect the rights afforded by the California Fair Employment and Housing Act (FEHA) (Gov. Code, § 12900 et seq.).

Section 12940(h) makes it an unlawful employment practice for an employer "to discharge, expel, or otherwise discriminate against any person because the person has opposed any practices forbidden under this part or because the person has filed a complaint, testified, or assisted in any proceeding under this part." In this case, we are presented with an array of issues regarding the proper legal standards to apply in determining whether an allegedly retaliatory action by an employer is actionable under section 12940(h). First, we must decide whether an employee's refusal to follow a supervisor's order (to discharge a subordinate) that the employee reasonably believes to be discriminatory constitutes "protected activity" under the FEHA for which the employee may not properly be subjected to retaliation, when the employee objects to the supervisor's order but does not explicitly tell the supervisor or the employer that she (the employee) believes the order violates the FEHA or is otherwise discriminatory.

* * *

For the reasons set forth below, we conclude that an employee's refusal to follow a supervisor's order that she reasonably believes to be discriminatory constitutes protected activity under the FEHA and that an employer may not retaliate against an employee on the basis of such conduct when the employer, in light of all the circumstances, knows that the employee believes the order to be discriminatory, even when the employee does not explicitly state to her supervisor or employer that she believes the order to be discriminatory.

* * *

Yanowitz began her employment with the predecessor of L'Oreal as a sales representative in 1981 and was promoted to regional sales manager for Northern California and the Pacific Northwest in 1986. As regional sales manager, Yanowitz was responsible for managing L'Oreal's sales team and dealing with the department and specialty stores that sold L'Oreal's fragrances. From 1986 to 1996, Yanowitz's performance as a regional sales manager consistently was judged as "Above Expectation" and in some instances fell close to "Outstanding," the highest possible rating, although her reviews over this period also consistently contained some criticism of her "listening" and "communication" skills.

In early 1997, Yanowitz was named L'Oreal's regional sales manager of the year (for 1996). She received a Cartier watch and a congratulatory note from human resources manager Jane Sears praising her leadership, loyalty, motivation, and ability to inspire team spirit. Yanowitz's bonuses for the years 1996 and 1997 were the highest paid to any regional sales manager in her division.

Beginning in 1996, Yanowitz's immediate supervisor was Richard Roderick, the vice-president of sales for the designer fragrance division. Roderick reported directly to Jack Wiswall, the general manager of the designer fragrance division. Roderick and Wiswall worked out of New York, and Yanowitz was based in San Francisco.

In June 1997, Roderick wrote a memorandum to Yanowitz's personnel file in which he criticized Yanowitz's listening skills and characterized her attitude as "negative." He also noted that he had received complaints about Yanowitz's attitude from several retailers. In August 1997, Roderick wrote a memorandum to Sears, L'Oreal's human resources manager, in which he again criticized Yanowitz for her listening skills and her "negative" attitude, noting that several accounts also had complained about Yanowitz's attitude. Roderick stated in this memorandum that "Elysa does a terrific job as a regional manager, however, she must become a better listener and she must not put a gun to the heads of the retailers in order to get them to do what needs to be done."

In the fall of 1997, L'Oreal restructured the designer fragrance division, merging the division with the Ralph Lauren fragrance division. Although some regional sales managers were laid off after the restructuring, L'Oreal retained Yanowitz and increased her responsibilities. After the merger and restructuring, Yanowitz was assigned to supervise the personnel who formerly worked for the Ralph Lauren division, and to supervise the marketing of Ralph Lauren fragrances in her region.

Shortly after Yanowitz assumed responsibility for the Ralph Lauren sales force and marketing campaigns in the fall of 1997, Wiswall and Yanowitz toured the Ralph Lauren Polo installation at Macy's in the Valley Fair Shopping Center in San Jose. After the tour, Wiswall instructed Yanowitz to terminate the employment of a dark-skinned female sales associate because he did not find the woman to be sufficiently physically attractive. Wiswall expressed a preference for fair-skinned blondes and directed Yanowitz to "[g]et me somebody hot," or words to that effect. On a return trip to the store, Wiswall discovered that the sales associate had not been dismissed. He reiterated to Yanowitz that he wanted the associate terminated and complained that Yanowitz had failed to do so. He passed "a young attractive blonde girl, very sexy," on his way out, turned to Yanowitz, and told her, "God damn it, get me one that looks like that." Yanowitz asked Wiswall for an adequate justification before she would terminate the associate. On several subsequent occasions, Wiswall asked Yanowitz whether the associate had been dismissed. On each occasion, Yanowitz asked Wiswall to provide adequate justification for dismissing the associate. In March 1998, in the midst of Yanowitz's conversations with Wiswall regarding the termination of the sales associate, Yanowitz learned that the sales associate in question was among the top sellers of men's fragrances in the Macy's West chain. Ultimately, Yanowitz refused to carry out Wiswall's order and did not terminate the sales associate. She never complained to her immediate supervisor or to the human resources department that Wiswall was pressuring her to fire the sales associate, however, nor did she explicitly tell Wiswall that she believed his order was discriminatory.

In April 1998, Roderick began soliciting negative information about Yanowitz from her subordinates. Roderick called Christine DeGracia, who reported to Yanowitz, and asked her about any "frustrations" she had with Yanowitz. When DeGracia said she had had some, Roderick asked her to hold her thoughts so that the matter could be discussed with human resources. Roderick and Sears then called back DeGracia to discuss those issues. When Roderick asked DeGracia whether any other persons were having problems with Yanowitz, DeGracia did not provide any names. Two weeks later, Roderick called DeGracia again and told her it was urgent that she help him persuade individuals to come forward with their problems concerning Yanowitz. In early June 1998, Roderick again asked DeGracia to notify him of negative incidents involving Yanowitz and other account executives.

On May 13, 1998, Roderick summoned Yanowitz to L'Oreal's home office in New York. Roderick opened the meeting by asking whether she thought she had been brought in to be terminated, then criticized Yanowitz for her "dictatorial" management style with regard to two account executives. He closed the meeting by saying, "It would be a shame to end an eighteen-year career this way." During May and June 1998, Roderick and Wiswall obtained Yanowitz's travel and expense reports and audited them.

On June 19, 1998, a representative for Macy's West, one of Yanowitz's accounts, wrote to Roderick to complain about the handling of a Polo Sport promotion, which Yanowitz's team was responsible for coordinating. In June 1998, Yanowitz met with Wiswall, Roderick, and various account executives and regional sales managers responsible for the Macy's account. Wiswall screamed at Yanowitz in front of her staff, told her he was "sick and tired of all the fuckups" on the Macy's account, and said that Yanowitz could not get it right. In July 1998, the Macy's account executive wrote to Roderick and again complained about the handling of a different promotion by Yanowitz's team.

On June 22, 1998, Yanowitz wrote Roderick, advising him that her Macy's West team was disturbed about certain issues. Wiswall, who had been sent a copy, wrote a note to Roderick on Yanowitz's memo: "Dick— She is writing everything! Are you!!! ___ " One week after Wiswall's note, Roderick prepared three memos to human resources documenting the meeting with Yanowitz on May 13, 1998, a conversation with DeGracia on June 4, 1998, and a visit to Yanowitz's market area in early June 1998.

These memos were critical of Yanowitz; the memo discussing the May 13 meeting criticized her for being too assertive.

On July 16, 1998, Roderick prepared a more elaborate memorandum and delivered it to Yanowitz. The memorandum criticized Yanowitz's handling of a Polo Sport promotion, a Picasso promotion, coordination of advertising with others, handling of the Sacramento market, and the length and substance of a March 1998 business trip to Hawaii. Roderick closed, "I have yet to see evidence that you took [the May 13] conversation seriously and made the necessary style modifications. Elysa, I am quite surprised that a person with so many years of experience and so many years with Cosmair could become so ineffective so quickly. Our business is changing daily and we all must learn to adapt to those changes or we will fail as individuals and as a company. Your changes must start immediately. I expect a reply to this memo within one week of receipt."

Yanowitz viewed the memorandum as an expression of intent to develop pretextual grounds and then terminate her. She suggested the parties meet to discuss a severance package, but also indicated she first wanted to prepare her written response to the July 16, 1998, memorandum.

Carol Giustino, Sears's replacement as human resources director, set up a meeting for July 22 and rejected Yanowitz's request that the meeting be postponed. Giustino also denied Yanowitz's request to have Yanowitz's attorney-husband present at the meeting, citing company policy. During the July 22 meeting, Roderick and Giustino questioned Yanowitz about the accusations in the July 16 memorandum without reading her written response. Yanowitz, who was being treated for nervous anxiety allegedly brought on by the situation at work, broke down in tears. During the meeting, Roderick imposed a new travel schedule on Yanowitz, a schedule that regulated precisely how often she should visit each market in her territory. Two days after the meeting, Yanowitz departed on disability leave due to stress. She did not return, and L'Oreal replaced her in November 1998.

Yanowitz filed a discrimination charge with the Department of Fair Employment and Housing (DFEH) on June 25, 1999. She alleged that L'Oreal had discriminated against her on the basis of sex, age (Yanowitz was 53), and religion (Yanowitz is Jewish). She also alleged that L'Oreal had retaliated against her for refusing to terminate the female employee whom Wiswall considered unattractive.

* * *

As a threshold matter, L'Oreal does not dispute that an employee's conduct may constitute protected activity for purposes of the antiretaliation provision of the FEHA not only when the employee opposes conduct that ultimately is determined to be unlawfully discriminatory under the FEHA, but also when the employee opposes conduct that the employee reasonably and in good faith believes to be discriminatory, whether or not the challenged conduct is ultimately found to violate the FEHA. It is well established that a retaliation claim may be brought by an employee who has complained of or opposed conduct that the employee reasonably believes to be discriminatory, even when a court later determines the conduct was not actually prohibited by the FEHA.

Strong policy considerations support this rule. Employees often are legally unsophisticated and will not be in a position to make an informed judgment as to whether a particular practice or conduct actually violates the governing anti-discrimination statute. A rule that permits an employer to retaliate against an employee with impunity whenever the employee's reasonable belief turns out to be incorrect would significantly deter employees from opposing conduct they believe to be discriminatory. By the same token, a rule that would allow retaliation against an employee for opposing conduct the employee reasonably and in good faith believed was discriminatory, whenever the conduct subsequently was found not to violate the FEHA, would significantly discourage employees from opposing incidents of discrimination, thereby undermining the fundamental purposes of the antidiscrimination statutes.

In the present case, in her opposition to L'Oreal's motion for summary judgment, Yanowitz presented evidence that she reasonably believed that Wiswall's order constituted unlawful sex discrimination, because she thought the order represented the application of a different standard for female sales associates than for male sales associates. Yanowitz stated in this regard that she had hired and supervised both male and female sales associates for a number of years, and never had been asked to fire a male sales associate because he was not sufficiently attractive. Because a trier of fact could find from this evidence that Yanowitz believed Wiswall's order was discriminatory as reflecting an instance of disparate treatment on the basis of sex, we have no occasion in this case to determine whether a gender-neutral requirement that a cosmetic sales associate be physically or sexually attractive would itself be violative of the FEHA or could reasonably be viewed by an employee as unlawfully discriminatory. Courts in other jurisdictions have uniformly held that an appearance standard that imposes more stringent appearance requirements on employees of one sex than on employees of the other sex constitutes unlawful sexual discrimination unless such differential treatment can be justified as a bona fide occupational qualification. We believe it is clear that such unjustified disparate treatment also would constitute unlawful sex discrimination under the FEHA.

L'Oreal does not claim that such disparate treatment on the basis of sex is permissible under the FEHA, but maintains that the evidence presented at the summary judgment motion was insufficient to support a reasonable belief that Wiswall's order represented an instance of impermissible disparate treatment on the basis of sex. We disagree.

Yanowitz presented evidence that Wiswall ordered her to terminate a female sales associate simply because he felt the associate was "not good looking enough," and directed her to "[g]et me someone hot." On a subsequent visit to the Macy's store, when Wiswall discovered Yanowitz had not terminated the sales associate, he pointed out a young attractive blonde woman and stated, "God damn it, get me one that looks like that." Although Yanowitz repeatedly requested that Wiswall provide her with "adequate justification" for the dismissal, he failed to respond to the request. As noted, Yanowitz additionally stated that she had hired and supervised both male and female sales associates for a number of years, and never had been asked to fire a male sales associate because he was not sufficiently attractive.

Moreover, L'Oreal failed to present any evidence in the summary judgment proceedings to counter the claim that Wiswall's order constituted an instance of disparate treatment on the basis of sex. It introduced no evidence suggesting that Wiswall's order was based upon the particular sales associate's performance or sales record, or, indeed, that Wiswall had any knowledge of such matters. In addition, L'Oreal did not establish that the company maintained a general policy requiring cosmetic sales associates to be physically or sexually attractive, or that such a policy was routinely applied to both male and female sales associates.

* * *

We agree with Yanowitz that when the circumstances surrounding an employee's conduct are sufficient to establish that an employer knew that an employee's refusal to comply with an order was based on the employee's reasonable belief that the order is discriminatory, an employer may not avoid the reach of the FEHA's antiretaliation provision by relying on the circumstance that the employee did not explicitly inform the employer that she believed the order was discriminatory.

* * *

In sum, we conclude that the evidence presented by Yanowitz would permit—although it certainly would not compel—a reasonable trier of fact to find that, in view of the nature of Wiswall's order, Yanowitz's refusal to implement the order, coupled with her multiple requests for "adequate justification," sufficiently communicated to Wiswall that she believed that his order was discriminatory. Thus, we conclude that Yanowitz presented sufficient evidence to satisfy the protected activity element of her prima facie case.

* * *

■ CHIN, J.—I dissent.

* * *

Employees should be able to complain about what they believe to be unlawful employment practices without fear of retaliation. But it makes no sense to extend whistleblower protection to someone, like plaintiff, who did not make any complaint, did not engage in any meaningful communication, did not seek any informal dispute resolution in the workplace, and did nothing to try to cause L'Oreal to take voluntary steps to avoid or remedy a perceived FEHA violation.

Although section 12940(h)'s language requires the person seeking its protection to oppose "any practices forbidden under" the FEHA—which seems to require that the practices actually be forbidden—courts have expanded the statute beyond its language to permit a retaliation claim by an employee "who has complained of or opposed conduct that the employee reasonably believes to be discriminatory, even when a court later determines the conduct was not actually prohibited by the FEHA." I agree with this expansion and the policy behind it. But if we are to interpret the statute as not requiring conduct that was actually illegal but merely conduct the employee believes to be illegal, then surely we must require that the plaintiff communicate this belief to the employer. It makes no sense to hold both that the conduct need not be unlawful and that the plaintiff need not complain of it.

* * *

To receive the special protection that section 12940(h) gives to whistleblowers, one must blow the whistle not in any technical way, but in some way. Plaintiff did not do so. Hence, I would reverse the judgment of the Court of Appeal, which reversed summary judgment in defendant's favor.

NOTES AND QUESTIONS

1.   Does the disagreement between the majority and the dissent hinge on the purpose of the anti-retaliation statute? What is its purpose? Is it primarily to encourage internal reform when workplace discrimination is brought to light, or is it to protect whistleblowers, even those who do not voice their discrimination-specific concerns to upper management?

2.   Do you agree that not being "hot" is a proscribed basis of termination because it is a form of sex discrimination? Should physical appearance be explicitly excluded from the BFOQ doctrine?

Crawford v. Metropolitan Government of Nashville
555 U.S. 271 (2009).

■ JUSTICE SOUTER delivered the opinion of the Court.

Title VII of the Civil Rights Act of 1964 forbids retaliation by employers against employees who report workplace race or gender discrimination. The question here is whether this protection extends to an employee who speaks out about discrimination not on her own initiative, but in answering questions during an employer's internal investigation. We hold that it does.

In 2002, respondent Metropolitan Government of Nashville and David-son County, Tennessee (Metro), began looking into rumors of sexual harassment by the Metro School District's employee relations director, Gene Hughes. When Veronica Frazier, a Metro human resources officer, asked petitioner Vicky Crawford, a 30-year Metro employee, whether she had witnessed "inappropriate behavior" on the part of Hughes, Crawford described several instances of sexually harassing behavior: once, Hughes had answered her greeting, " 'Hey Dr. Hughes, what's up?,' " by grabbing his crotch and saying " '[Y]ou know what's up' "; he had repeatedly " 'put his crotch up to [her] window' "; and on one occasion he had entered her office and " 'grabbed her head and pulled it to his crotch.' " Two other employees also reported being sexually harassed by Hughes. Although Metro took no action against Hughes, it did fire Crawford and the two other accusers soon after finishing the investigation, saying in Crawford's case that it was for embezzlement. Crawford claimed Metro was retaliating for her report of Hughes's behavior and filed a charge of a Title VII violation with the Equal Employment Opportunity Commission (EEOC), followed by this suit in the United States District Court for the Middle District of Tennessee.

The Title VII antiretaliation provision has two clauses, making it "an unlawful employment practice for an employer to discriminate against any of his employees . . . [1] because he has opposed any practice made an unlawful employment practice by this subchapter, or [2] because he has made a charge, testified, assisted, or participated in any manner in an investigation, proceeding, or hearing under this subchapter." The one is known as the "opposition clause," the other as the "participation clause," and Crawford accused Metro of violating both.

The District Court granted summary judgment for Metro. It held that Crawford could not satisfy the opposition clause because she had not "instigated or initiated any complaint," but had "merely answered questions by investigators in an already-pending internal investigation, initiated by someone else." It concluded that her claim also failed under the participation clause, which Sixth Circuit precedent confined to protecting " 'an employee's participation in an employer's internal investigation . . . where that investigation occurs pursuant to a pending EEOC charge' " (not the case here).

The Court of Appeals affirmed on the same grounds, holding that the opposition clause " 'demands active, consistent "opposing" activities to warrant . . . protection against retaliation,' " whereas Crawford did "not claim to have instigated or initiated any complaint prior to her participation in the investigation, nor did she take any further action following the investigation and prior to her firing." Again like the trial judge, the Court of Appeals understood that Crawford could show no violation of the participation clause because her " 'employer's internal investigation' " was not conducted " 'pursuant to a pending EEOC charge.' "

* * *

The opposition clause makes it "unlawful . . . for an employer to discriminate against any . . . employe[e] . . . because he has opposed any practice made . . . unlawful . . . by this subchapter." The term "oppose" being left undefined by the statute, carries its ordinary meaning, "to resist or antagonize . . . ; to contend against; to confront; resist; withstand," Webster's New International Dictionary 1710 (2d ed. 1958). Although these actions entail varying expenditures of energy, "RESIST frequently implies more active striving than OPPOSE." see also Random House Dictionary of the English Language 1359 (2d ed. 1987) (defining "oppose" as "to be hostile or adverse to, as in opinion").

The statement Crawford says she gave to Frazier is thus covered by the opposition clause, as an ostensibly disapproving account of sexually obnoxious behavior toward her by a fellow employee, an answer she says antagonized her employer to the point of sacking her on a false pretense. Crawford's description of the louche goings-on would certainly qualify in the minds of reasonable jurors as "resist[ant]" or "antagoni[stic]" to Hughes's treatment, if for no other reason than the point argued by the Government and explained by an EEOC guideline: "When an employee communicates to her employer a belief that the employer has engaged in . . . a form of employment discrimination, that communication" virtually always "constitutes the employee's opposition to the activity." It is true that one can imagine exceptions, like an employee's description of a supervisor's racist joke as hilarious, but these will be eccentric cases, and this is not one of them.

* * *

"Oppose" goes beyond "active, consistent" behavior in ordinary discourse, where we would naturally use the word to speak of someone who has taken no action at all to advance a position beyond disclosing it. Countless people were known to "oppose" slavery before Emancipation, or are said to "oppose" capital punishment today, without writing public letters, taking to the streets, or resisting the government. And we would call it "opposition" if an employee took a stand against an employer's discriminatory practices not by "instigating" action, but by standing pat, say, by refusing to follow a supervisor's order to fire a junior worker for discriminatory reasons. There is, then, no reason to doubt that a person can "oppose" by responding to someone else's question just as surely as by provoking the discussion, and nothing in the statute requires a freakish rule protecting an employee who reports discrimination on her own initiative but not one who reports the same discrimination in the same words when her boss asks a question.

* * *

If it were clear law that an employee who reported discrimination in answering an employer's questions could be penalized with no remedy, prudent employees would have a good reason to keep quiet about Title VII offenses against themselves or against others. This is no imaginary horrible given the documented indications that "[f]ear of retaliation is the leading reason why people stay silent instead of voicing their concerns about bias and discrimination." The appeals court's rule would thus create a real dilemma for any knowledgeable employee in a hostile work environment if the boss took steps to assure a defense under our cases. If the employee reported discrimination in response to the enquiries, the employer might well be free to penalize her for speaking up. But if she kept quiet about the discrimination and later filed a Title VII claim, the employer might well escape liability, arguing that it "exercised reasonable care to prevent and correct [any discrimination] promptly" but "the plaintiff employee unreasonably failed to take advantage of . . . preventive or corrective opportunities provided by the employer." Nothing in the statute's text or our precedent supports this catch-22.

* * *

The judgment of the Court of Appeals for the Sixth Circuit is reversed, and the case is remanded for further proceedings consistent with this opinion.

■ JUSTICE ALITO, with whom JUSTICE THOMAS joins, concurring in the judgment.

The question in this case is whether Title VII of the Civil Rights Act of 1964 prohibits retaliation against an employee who testifies in an internal investigation of alleged sexual harassment. I agree with the Court that the "opposition clause" prohibits retaliation for such conduct. I also agree with the Court's primary reasoning, which is based on the point argued by the Government and explained by an EEOC guideline: "When an employee communicates to her employer a belief that the employer has engaged in . . . a form of employment discrimination, that communication virtually always 'constitutes the employee's opposition to the activity.'" I write separately to emphasize my understanding that the Court's holding does not and should not extend beyond employees who testify in internal investigations or engage in analogous purposive conduct.

Petitioner contends that the statutory term "oppose" means "taking action (including making a statement) to end, prevent, redress, or correct unlawful discrimination."

In order to decide the question that is before us, we have no need to adopt a definition of the term "oppose" that is broader than the definition that petitioner advances. But in dicta, the Court notes that the fourth listed definition in the Random House Dictionary of the English Language goes further, defining "oppose" to mean " 'to be hostile or adverse to, as in opinion.'" Thus, this definition embraces silent opposition.

While this is certainly an accepted usage of the term "oppose," the term is not always used in this sense, and it is questionable whether silent opposition is covered by the opposition clause of 42 U.S.C. § 2000e–3(a). It is noteworthy that all of the other conduct protected by this provision—making a charge, testifying, or assisting or participating in an investigation, proceeding, or hearing—requires active and purposive conduct.

An interpretation of the opposition clause that protects conduct that is not active and purposive would have important practical implications. It would open the door to retaliation claims by employees who never expressed a word of opposition to their employers. To be sure, in many cases, such employees would not be able to show that management was aware of their opposition and thus would not be able to show that their opposition caused the adverse actions at issue. But in other cases, such employees might well be able to create a genuine factual issue on the question of causation. Suppose, for example, that an employee alleges that he or she expressed opposition while informally chatting with a co-worker at the proverbial water cooler or in a workplace telephone conversation that was overheard by a co-worker. Or suppose that an employee alleges that such a conversation occurred after work at a restaurant or tavern frequented by co-workers or at a neighborhood picnic attended by a friend or relative of a supervisor. Some courts hold that an employee asserting a retaliation claim can prove causation simply by showing that the adverse employment action occurred within a short time after the protected conduct. The number of retaliation claims filed with the EEOC has proliferated in recent years. An expansive interpretation of protected opposition conduct would likely cause this trend to accelerate.

The question whether the opposition clause shields employees who do not communicate their views to their employers through purposive conduct is not before us in this case; the answer to that question is far from clear; and I do not understand the Court's holding to reach that issue here. For present purposes, it is enough to hold that the opposition clause does protect an employee, like petitioner, who testifies about unlawful conduct in an internal investigation.

NOTE

In University of Texas Southwestern Medical Center v. Nassar, 570 U.S. 338 (2013), the Supreme Court held that plaintiffs bringing retaliation claims under Title VII were required to prove that the desire to retaliate was the "but for" cause of the challenged employment action. Such plaintiffs could not rely on the mixed-motive framework available for status-based discrimination claims. In explaining the different causation standards, the Court emphasized that Title VII's antiretaliation provision appears in a different section from its status-based discrimination ban and that the retaliation provision uses the same critical "because" language used in the ADEA, which the Court in Gross v. FBL Fin. Servs., Inc., 557 U.S. 167 (2009) had interpreted as requiring but for causation. The Court in *Nassar* was silent on how its ruling affected summary judgment standards, and a circuit split has emerged on the issue. Compare Foster v. University of Maryland-Eastern Shore, 787 F.3d 243 (4th Cir. 2015) (holding that *Nassar* did not change the plaintiff's burden of proof regarding the prima facie case and the need to present evidence of pretext in order to survive summary judgment on a retaliation claim brought under the *McDonnell Douglas* standard) with EEOC v. Ford Motor Co., 782 F.3d 753 (6th Cir. 2015) (requiring evidence of but for causation as part of plaintiff's prima facie case in order for plaintiff to survive summary judgment on her retaliation claim).

Burlington Northern & Santa Fe Railway Co. v. White
548 U.S. 53 (2006).

■ JUSTICE BREYER delivered the opinion of the Court.

Title VII of the Civil Rights Act of 1964 forbids employment discrimination against "any individual" based on that individual's "race, color, religion, sex, or national origin." A separate section of the Act—its anti-retaliation provision—forbids an employer from "discriminat[ing] against" an employee or job applicant because that individual "opposed any practice" made unlawful by Title VII or "made a charge, testified, assisted, or participated in" a Title VII proceeding or investigation. The Courts of Appeals have come to different conclusions about the scope of the Act's anti-retaliation provision, particularly the reach of its phrase "discriminate against." Does that provision confine actionable retaliation to activity that affects the terms and conditions of employment? And how harmful must the adverse actions be to fall within its scope? We conclude that the anti-retaliation provision does not confine the actions and harms it forbids to those that are related to employment or occur at the workplace. We also conclude that the provision covers those (and only those) employer actions that would have been materially adverse to a reasonable employee or job applicant. In the present context that means that the employer's actions must be harmful to the point that they could well dissuade a reasonable worker from making or supporting a charge of discrimination.

* * *

This case arises out of actions that supervisors at petitioner Burlington Northern & Santa Fe Railway Company took against respondent Sheila White, the only woman working in the Maintenance of Way department at Burlington's Tennessee Yard. In June 1997, Burlington's roadmaster, Marvin Brown, interviewed White and expressed interest in her previous experience operating forklifts.

Burlington hired White as a "track laborer," a job that involves removing and replacing track components, transporting track material, cutting brush, and clearing litter and cargo spillage from the right-of-way. Soon after White arrived on the job, a co-worker who had previously operated the forklift chose to assume other responsibilities. Brown immediately assigned White to operate the forklift. While she also performed some of the other track laborer tasks, operating the forklift was White's primary responsibility. In September 1997, White complained to Burlington officials that her immediate supervisor, Bill Joiner, had repeatedly told her that women should not be working in the Maintenance of Way department. Joiner, White said, had also made insulting and inappropriate remarks to her in front of her male colleagues. After an internal investigation, Burlington suspended Joiner for 10 days and ordered him to attend a sexual-harassment training session.

On September 26, Brown told White about Joiner's discipline. At the same time, he told White that he was removing her from forklift duty and assigning her to perform only standard track laborer tasks. Brown explained that the reassignment reflected coworker's complaints that, in fairness, a " 'more senior man' " should have the "less arduous and cleaner job" of forklift operator. On October 10, White filed a complaint with the Equal Employment Opportunity Commission. She claimed that the reassignment of her duties amounted to unlawful gender-based discrimination and retaliation for her having earlier complained about Joiner. In early December ... White and her immediate supervisor, Percy Sharkey, disagreed about which truck should transport White from one location to another. The specific facts of the disagreement are in dispute, but the upshot is that Sharkey told Brown later that afternoon that White had been insubordinate. Brown immediately suspended White without pay. White invoked internal grievance procedures. Those procedures led Burlington to conclude that White had not been insubordinate. Burlington reinstated White to her position and awarded her backpay for the 37 days she was suspended. White filed an additional retaliation charge with the EEOC based on the suspension.

* * *

After exhausting administrative remedies, White filed this Title VII action against Burlington in federal court. As relevant here, she claimed that Burlington's actions (1) changing her job responsibilities, and (2) suspending her for 37 days without pay amounted to unlawful retaliation in violation of Title VII. A jury found in White's favor on both of these claims. It awarded her $43,500 in compensatory damages, including $3,250 in medical expenses.

Title VII's anti-retaliation provision forbids employer actions that "discriminate against" an employee (or job applicant) because he has "opposed" a practice that Title VII forbids or has "made a charge, testified, assisted, or participated in" a Title VII "investigation, proceeding, or hearing." No one doubts that the term "discriminate against" refers to distinctions or differences in treatment that injure protected individuals. But different Circuits have come to different conclusions about whether the challenged action has to be employment or workplace related and about how harmful that action must be to constitute retaliation.

* * *

Petitioner and the Solicitor General both argue that the Sixth Circuit is correct to require a link between the challenged retaliatory action and the terms, conditions, or status of employment. They note that Title VII's substantive anti-discrimination provision protects an individual only from employment-related discrimination. They add that the anti-retaliation provision should be read in pari materia with the anti-discrimination provision. And they conclude that the employer actions prohibited by the anti-retaliation provision should similarly be limited to conduct that "affects the employee's 'compensation, terms, conditions, or privileges of employment.' "

We cannot agree. The language of the substantive provision differs from that of the anti-retaliation provision in important ways.

* * *

The underscored words in the substantive provision "hire," "discharge," "compensation, terms, conditions, or privileges of employment," "employment opportunities," and "status as an employee" explicitly limit the scope of that provision to actions that affect employment or alter the conditions of the workplace. No such limiting words appear in the anti-retaliation provision. Given these linguistic differences, the question here is not whether identical or similar words should be read in pari materia to mean the same thing. Rather, the question is whether Congress intended its different words to make a legal difference. We normally presume that, where words differ as they differ here, " 'Congress acts intentionally and purposely in the disparate inclusion or exclusion.' " There is strong reason to believe that Congress intended the differences that its language suggests, for the two provisions differ not only in language but in purpose as well. The anti-discrimination provision seeks a workplace where individuals are not discriminated against because of their racial, ethnic, religious, or gender-based status. The anti-retaliation provision seeks to secure that primary objective by preventing an employer from interfering (through retaliation) with an employee's efforts to secure or advance enforcement of the Act's basic guarantees. The substantive provision seeks to prevent injury to individuals based on who they are, i.e., their status. The anti-retaliation provision seeks to prevent harm to individuals based on what they do, i.e., their conduct.

To secure the first objective, Congress did not need to prohibit anything other than employment-related discrimination. The substantive provision's basic objective of "equality of employment opportunities" and the elimination of practices that tend to bring about "stratified job environments," would be achieved were all employment-related discrimination miraculously eliminated.

But one cannot secure the second objective by focusing only upon employer actions and harm that concern employment and the workplace. Were all such actions and harms eliminated, the anti-retaliation provision's objective would not be achieved. An employer can effectively retaliate against an employee by taking actions not directly related to his employment or by causing him harm outside the workplace. A provision limited to employment-related actions would not deter the many forms that effective retaliation can take. Hence, such a limited construction would fail to fully achieve the anti-retaliation provision's "primary purpose," namely, "[m]aintaining unfettered access to statutory remedial mechanisms."

Thus, purpose reinforces what language already indicates, namely, that the anti-retaliation provision, unlike the substantive provision, is not limited to discriminatory actions that affect the terms and conditions of employment * * *.

The anti-retaliation provision protects an individual not from all retaliation, but from retaliation that produces an injury or harm. As we have explained, the Courts of Appeals have used differing language to describe the level of seriousness to which this harm must rise before it becomes actionable retaliation * * * In our view, a plaintiff must show that a reasonable employee would have found the challenged action materially adverse, "which in this context means it well might have 'dissuaded a reasonable worker from making or supporting a charge of discrimination.' " We speak of material adversity because we believe it is important to separate significant from trivial harms. Title VII, we have said, does not set forth "a general civility code for the American workplace." An employee's decision to report discriminatory behavior cannot immunize that employee from those petty slights or minor annoyances that often take place at work and that all employees experience. The anti-retaliation provision seeks to prevent employer interference with "unfettered access" to Title VII's remedial mechanisms. It does so by prohibiting employer actions that are likely "to deter victims of discrimination from complaining to the EEOC," the courts, and their employers. And normally petty slights, minor annoyances, and simple lack of good manners will not create such deterrence.

We refer to reactions of a reasonable employee because we believe that the provision's standard for judging harm must be objective. An objective standard is judicially administrable. It avoids the uncertainties and unfair discrepancies that can plague a judicial effort to determine a plaintiff's unusual subjective feelings. We have emphasized the need for objective standards in other Title VII contexts, and those same concerns animate our decision here. We phrase the standard in general terms because the significance of any given act of retaliation will often depend upon the particular circumstances. Context matters. "The real social impact of workplace behavior often depends on a constellation of surrounding circumstances, expectations, and relationships which are not fully captured by a simple recitation of the words used or the physical acts performed." A schedule change in an employee's work schedule may make little difference to many workers, but may matter enormously to a young mother with school age children. A supervisor's refusal to invite an employee to lunch is normally trivial, a nonactionable petty slight. But to retaliate by excluding an employee from a weekly training lunch that contributes significantly to the employee's professional advancement might well deter a reasonable employee from complaining about discrimination. Hence, a legal standard that speaks in general terms rather than specific prohibited acts is preferable, for an "act that would be immaterial in some situations is material in others."

Finally, we note that . . . this standard does not require a reviewing court or jury to consider "the nature of the discrimination that led to the filing of the charge." Rather, the standard is tied to the challenged retaliatory act, not the underlying conduct that forms the basis of the Title VII complaint. By focusing on the materiality of the challenged action and the perspective of a reasonable person in the plaintiff's position, we believe this standard will screen out trivial conduct while effectively capturing those acts that are likely to dissuade employees from complaining or assisting in complaints about discrimination.

Applying this standard to the facts of this case, we believe that there was a sufficient evidentiary basis to support the jury's verdict on White's retaliation claim. The jury found that two of Burlington's actions amounted to retaliation: the reassignment of White from forklift duty to standard track laborer tasks and the 37-day suspension without pay. Burlington does not question the jury's determination that the motivation for these acts was retaliatory. But it does question the statutory significance of the harm these acts caused. The District Court instructed the jury to determine whether respondent "suffered a materially adverse change in the terms or conditions of her employment," and the Sixth Circuit upheld the jury's finding based on that same stringent interpretation of the anti-retaliation provision (the interpretation that limits § 704 to the same employment-related conduct forbidden by § 703). Our holding today makes clear that the jury was not required to find that the challenged actions were related to the terms or conditions of employment. And insofar as the jury also found that the actions were "materially adverse," its findings are adequately supported.

First, Burlington argues that a reassignment of duties cannot constitute retaliatory discrimination where, as here, both the former and present duties fall within the same job description. We do not see why that is so. Almost every job category involves some responsibilities and duties that are less desirable than others. Common sense suggests that one good way to discourage an employee such as White from bringing discrimination charges would be to insist that she spend more time performing the more arduous duties and less time performing those that are easier or more agreeable. * * *

Second, Burlington argues that the 37-day suspension without pay lacked statutory significance because Burlington ultimately reinstated White with backpay. Burlington says that "it defies reason to believe that Congress would have considered a rescinded investigatory suspension with full back pay" to be unlawful, particularly because Title VII, throughout much of its history, provided no relief in an equitable action for victims in White's position. We do not find Burlington's last mentioned reference to the nature of Title VII's remedies convincing. After all, throughout its history, Title VII has provided for injunctions to "bar like discrimination in the future," And we have no reason to believe that a court could not have issued an injunction where an employer suspended an employee for retaliatory purposes, even if that employer later provided backpay. In any event, Congress amended Title VII in 1991 to permit victims of intentional discrimination to recover compensatory (as White received here) and punitive damages, concluding that the additional remedies were necessary to " 'help make victims whole.' " We would undermine the significance of that congressional judgment were we to conclude that employers could avoid liability in these circumstances.

Neither do we find convincing any claim of insufficient evidence. White did receive backpay. But White and her family had to live for 37 days without income. They did not know during that time whether or when White could return to work. Many reasonable employees would find a month without a paycheck to be a serious hardship. And White described to the jury the physical and emotional hardship that 37 days of having "no income, no money" in fact caused. ("That was the worst Christmas I had out of my life. No income, no money, and that made all of us feel bad. * * * I got very depressed"). Indeed, she obtained medical treatment for her emotional distress. A reasonable employee facing the choice between retaining her job (and paycheck) and filing a discrimination complaint might well choose the former. That is to say, an indefinite suspension without pay could well act as a deterrent, even if the suspended employee eventually received backpay. Thus, the jury's conclusion that the 37-day suspension without pay was materially adverse was a reasonable one.

For these reasons, the judgment of the Court of Appeals is affirmed.

NOTES AND QUESTIONS

1.   Sheila White, the plaintiff in this case, was hired by Burlington Northern in 1997 as an experienced forklift operator and was the only woman in the workplace. According to White, her co-workers immediately let her know that she was not welcome. "They showed it more than they expressed it . . . it was rough, I'm just going to say, it was rough. I had to

pray every night." White recalled being singled out by the foreman on her first day. "He said, 'Sheila, when you come on your period, let us know and we'll make your job lighter' . . . I overlooked that. I didn't know I'd be going through much more later on." Interestingly, it was the government-mandated flier that her employer had posted promising a workplace free of discrimination on the basis of race, creed or sex that inspired Ms. White throughout the litigation process. "I can always visualize that," she said. "But I never thought that would happen to me." N.Y. Times, June 24, 2006, p. A12.

2. An alleged harasser testified involuntarily against his employer when his victim brought suit against the company. When the company subsequently fired the harasser, the court of appeals found that his termination was unlawful retaliation for his testimony. However, the court was quick to point out that the employer was free to fire him on grounds of sexual harassment. Merritt v. Dillard Paper Co., 120 F.3d 1181 (11th Cir. 1997).

3. Can litigious conduct, such as lawsuits, counter-claims, or EEOC activity, be considered retaliatory conduct under the *Burlington* standard? Plaintiff filed a sexual harassment lawsuit against her employer and lost in court. When the employer responded by filing a tort claim alleging, among other things, abuse of process, malicious prosecution, and intentional infliction of emotional distress, the employee countered by filing a claim of retaliation. The Ohio Supreme Court held that the employer's counterclaim was not per se retaliatory, because it was not objectively baseless, and employers have a First Amendment right to seek relief in court. See Greer-Burger v. Temesi, 879 N.E.2d 174 (Ohio 2007).

4. Can an employer be liable for retaliation against an employee based on the protected activities of a third party? A 16-year-old girl working at a Burger King restaurant was being sexually harassed by her 35-year-old manager. After the employee's mother visited the restaurant to complain of her daughter's harassment, the harassing supervisor fired the employee. The Seventh Circuit referred to this as "third party retaliation": someone other than the victim complains about the harassment, and the employer responds by retaliating against the victim. If the third party is a "bystander" or "stranger" to the harassment, then the victim has no remedy for retaliation. However, if the third party is an agent of the victim, such as an attorney or, as in this case, a minor's parent or guardian, then the complaining party's actions may be attributed to the victim, and therefore the retaliation against the victim is actionable. See EEOC v. V & J Foods, 507 F.3d 575 (7th Cir. 2007). See also Baird ex rel. Baird v. Rose, 192 F.3d 462 (4th Cir. 1999) (permitting a claim on behalf of the child for retaliation based on parent-guardian conduct). The court in V & J Foods declined to decide whether an "intermediate" type of third-party retaliation, involving an informal representative or ad hoc agent of the victim, would be actionable.

5. Can an employee claim retaliation if he or she is neither the victim nor the opposer of the original alleged act of discrimination? Both Eric Thompson and his fiancée, Miriam Regalado, were employees of North American Stainless. Regalado filed a charge with the EEOC alleging sex discrimination. Three weeks later, NAS fired Thompson. The Sixth Circuit, en banc, held that Thompson "is not included in the class of persons for whom Congress created a retaliation cause of action." The Supreme Court unanimously reversed, relying heavily on *Burlington Northern*, supra p. 380: "We think it obvious that a reasonable worker might be dissuaded from engaging in protected activity if she knew that her fiancé would be fired." Thompson v. North American Stainless, LP, 562 U.S. 170 (2011).

6.   Plaintiff, a black man, filed EEOC complaints against the Veterans Administration. Supervisors "overrated him on his performance evaluations" to avoid further complaints. An accurate performance rating would have made plaintiff eligible for remedial training, but as plaintiff could not demonstrate accurate rating and training would have led to his promotion, the court of appeals found no retaliation. Giving plaintiff a higher rating than he deserved "may have been a poor and even dishonest policy, but it was not unlawful retaliation." Cullom v. Brown, 209 F.3d 1035 (7th Cir. 2000).

7.   Courts must decide whether specific discrimination statutes create a cause of action for retaliation when the statutory text is silent on the question. In 2008, the Supreme Court interpreted two important statutes as granting such a right. The Court held that 42 U.S.C. § 1981, which grants "[a]ll persons * * * the same right * * * to make and enforce contracts . . . as is enjoyed by white citizens," encompasses retaliation claims. Justice Breyer's opinion for the majority relied heavily on stare decisis. Justice Thomas, in a dissent joined by Justice Scalia, argued that section 1981 only bars racial discrimination and that, for example, an employer who retaliates against both an African American and a white employee who each complain of racial discrimination would not be discriminating on the basis of race. CBOCS West, Inc. v. Humphries, 553 U.S. 442 (2008). On the same day the Court held that the Age Discrimination in Employment Act also covers retaliation by the federal government. Gomez-Perez v. Potter, 553 U.S. 474 (2008).

8.   Retaliation plays a large part in many workplace harassment claims. Both causes of action can be supported by overlapping evidence, which causes problems for plaintiffs, courts, and scholars. For instance, if a female employee is denied a raise, brings suit against her employer, and then is subjected to severe and pervasive harsh treatment based on her sex, the later discrimination is at once retaliation and harassment. Some scholars suggest changing the doctrine to allow plaintiffs to bring hybrid harassment/ retaliation claims, so that they can seek more complete relief. See, e.g., Eisha Jain, Note, Realizing the Potential of the Joint Harassment/Retaliation Claim, 117 Yale L.J. 120 (2007).

9.   Retaliation is one of the most common employment discrimination charges filed. About 40% of all EEOC charges filed include retaliation claims— an increase from 25.4% in 1999 to 41.1% in 2013. The total number of employment discrimination charges has risen from 75,768 in 2006 to 93,727 in 2013. Why might these numbers be rising? See Charge Statistics From The U.S. Equal Employment Opportunity Commission FY 1997, available at http:// eeoc.gov/eeoc/statistics/enforcement/charges.cfm.

D. AFFIRMATIVE ACTION AND REVERSE DISCRIMINATION

In addition to the legal standards which employers must meet in hiring employees and the obligations which may be imposed on employers who violate those standards, there are numerous instances where an employer undertakes voluntarily to alter the mix of employees which its applicant pool and existing selection methods would otherwise produce. Usually such a change takes the form of an "affirmative action program" under which the employer seeks to recruit minorities or sets aside a specific number or percentage of job vacancies for blacks, women, or some other group. Such plans have been challenged by individuals, usually white males, who claim that the program shuts them out of employment opportunities as a result of their race or sex, and that they are the victims of "reverse discrimination" under section 703(j) of Title VII, which states:

> Nothing contained in this title shall be interpreted to require any employer, employment agency, labor organization, or joint labor-management committee subject to this title to grant preferential treatment to any individual or to any group because of the race, color, religion, sex, or national origin of such individual or group.

Ricci v. DeStefano
557 U.S. 557 (2009).

■ JUSTICE KENNEDY delivered the opinion of the Court.

When the City of New Haven undertook to fill vacant lieutenant and captain positions in its fire department (Department), the promotion and hiring process was governed by the city charter, in addition to federal and state law. The charter establishes a merit system. That system requires the City to fill vacancies in the classified civil-service ranks with the most qualified individuals, as determined by job-related examinations. After each examination, the New Haven Civil Service Board (CSB) certifies a ranked list of applicants who passed the test. Under the charter's "rule of three," the relevant hiring authority must fill each vacancy by choosing one candidate from the top three scorers on the list. Certified promotional lists remain valid for two years.

The City's contract with the New Haven firefighters' union specifies additional requirements for the promotion process. Under the contract, applicants for lieutenant and captain positions were to be screened using written and oral examinations, with the written exam accounting for 60 percent and the oral exam 40 percent of an applicant's total score. To sit for the examinations, candidates for lieutenant needed 30 months' experience in the Department, a high-school diploma, and certain vocational training courses. Candidates for captain needed one year's service as a lieutenant in the Department, a high-school diploma, and certain vocational training courses.

After reviewing bids from various consultants, the City hired Industrial/Organizational Solutions, Inc. (IOS) to develop and administer the examinations, at a cost to the City of $100,000. IOS is an Illinois company that specializes in designing entry-level and promotional examinations for fire and police departments.

* * *

Candidates took the examinations in November and December 2003. Seventy-seven candidates completed the lieutenant examination—43 whites, 19 blacks, and 15 Hispanics. Of those, 34 candidates passed—25 whites, 6 blacks, and 3 Hispanics. Eight lieutenant positions were vacant at the time of the examination. As the rule of three operated, this meant that the top 10 candidates were eligible for an immediate promotion to lieutenant. All 10 were white. Subsequent vacancies would have allowed at least 3 black candidates to be considered for promotion to lieutenant.

Forty-one candidates completed the captain examination—25 whites, 8 blacks, and 8 Hispanics. Of those, 22 candidates passed—16 whites, 3 blacks, and 3 Hispanics. Seven captain positions were vacant at the time of the examination. Under the rule of three, 9 candidates were eligible for an immediate promotion to captain—7 whites and 2 Hispanics.

The City's contract with IOS contemplated that, after the examinations, IOS would prepare a technical report that described the examination processes and methodologies and analyzed the results. But in January 2004, rather than requesting the technical report, City officials, including the City's counsel, Thomas Ude, convened a meeting with IOS Vice President Chad Legel. (Legel was the leader of the IOS team that developed and administered the tests.) Based on the test results, the City officials expressed concern that the tests had discriminated against minority candidates. Legel defended the examinations' validity, stating that any numerical disparity between white and minority candidates was likely due to various external factors and was in line with results of the Department's previous promotional examinations.

* * *

At the close of witness testimony, the CSB voted on a motion to certify the examinations. With one member recused, the CSB deadlocked 2 to 2, resulting in a decision not to certify the results. Explaining his vote to certify the results, Chairman Segaloff stated that "nobody convinced me that we can feel comfortable that, in fact, there's some likelihood that there's going to be an exam designed that's going to be less discriminatory."

The CSB's decision not to certify the examination results led to this lawsuit. The plaintiffs—who are the petitioners here—are 17 white firefighters and 1 Hispanic firefighter who passed the examinations but were denied a chance at promotions when the CSB refused to certify the test results. They include the named plaintiff, Frank Ricci, who addressed the CSB at multiple meetings.

* * *

Petitioners allege that when the CSB refused to certify the captain and lieutenant exam results based on the race of the successful candidates, it discriminated against them in violation of Title VII's disparate-treatment provision. The City counters that its decision was permissible because the tests "appear[ed] to violate Title VII's disparate-impact provisions."

Our analysis begins with this premise: The City's actions would violate the disparate-treatment prohibition of Title VII absent some valid defense. All the evidence demonstrates that the City chose not to certify the examination results because of the statistical disparity based on race—i.e., how minority candidates had performed when compared to white candidates. As the District Court put it, the City rejected the test results because "too many whites and not enough minorities would be promoted were the lists to be certified." Without some other justification, this express, race-based decisionmaking violates Title VII's command that employers cannot take adverse employment actions because of an individual's race.

* * *

We consider, therefore, whether the purpose to avoid disparate-impact liability excuses what otherwise would be prohibited disparate-treatment discrimination. Courts often confront cases in which statutes and principles point in different directions. Our task is to provide guidance to employers and courts for situations when these two prohibitions could be in conflict absent a rule to reconcile them. In providing this guidance our decision must be consistent with the important purpose of Title VII—that the workplace be an environment free of discrimination, where race is not a barrier to opportunity.

* * *

In searching for a standard that strikes a more appropriate balance, we note that this Court has considered cases similar to this one, albeit in the context of the Equal Protection Clause of the Fourteenth Amendment. The Court has held that certain government actions to remedy past racial discrimination—actions that are themselves based on race—are constitutional only where there is a "strong basis in evidence" that the remedial actions were necessary. Richmond v. J. A. Croson Co., 488 U.S. 469, 500 (1989). This suit does not call on us to consider whether the statutory constraints under Title VII must be parallel in all respects to those under the Constitution. That does not mean the constitutional authorities are irrelevant, however. Our cases discussing constitutional principles can provide helpful guidance in this statutory context.

Writing for a plurality in Wygant [v. Jackson Bd. of Ed., 476 U.S. 267 (1986)] and announcing the strong-basis-in-evidence standard, Justice Powell recognized the tension between eliminating segregation and discrimination on the one hand and doing away with all governmentally imposed discrimination based on race on the other. The plurality stated that those "related constitutional duties are not always harmonious," and that "reconciling them requires . . . employers to act with extraordinary care." The plurality required a strong basis in evidence because "[e]videntiary support for the conclusion that remedial action is warranted becomes crucial when the remedial program is challenged in court by nonminority employees." The Court applied the same standard in Croson, observing that "an amorphous claim that there has been past discrimination . . . cannot justify the use of an unyielding racial quota."

The same interests are at work in the interplay between the disparate-treatment and disparate-impact provisions of Title VII. Congress has imposed liability on employers for unintentional discrimination in order to rid the workplace of "practices that are fair in form, but discriminatory in operation." But it has also prohibited employers from taking adverse employment actions "because of" race. Applying the strong-basis-in-evidence standard to Title VII gives effect to both the disparate-treatment and disparate-impact provisions, allowing violations of one in the name of compliance with the other only in certain, narrow circumstances. The standard leaves ample room for employers' voluntary compliance efforts, which are essential to the statutory scheme and to Congress's efforts to eradicate workplace discrimination. And the standard appropriately constrains employers' discretion in making race-based decisions: It limits that discretion to cases in which there is a strong basis in evidence of disparate-impact liability, but it is not so restrictive that it allows employers to act only when there is a provable, actual violation. Resolving the statutory conflict in this way allows the disparate-impact prohibition to work in a manner that is consistent with other provisions of Title VII, including the prohibition on adjusting employment-related test scores on the basis of race. Examinations like those administered by the City create legitimate expectations on the part of those who took the tests. As is the case with any promotion exam, some of the firefighters here invested substantial time, money, and personal commitment in preparing for the tests. Employment tests can be an important part of a neutral selection system that safeguards against the very racial animosities Title VII was intended to prevent. Here, however, the firefighters saw their efforts invalidated by the City in sole reliance upon race-based statistics.

* * *

Title VII does not prohibit an employer from considering, before administering a test or practice, how to design that test or practice in order to provide a fair opportunity for all individuals, regardless of their race. And when, during the test-design stage, an employer invites comments to ensure the test is fair, that process can provide a common ground for open discussions toward that end. We hold only that, under Title VII, before an employer can engage in intentional discrimination for the asserted purpose of avoiding or remedying an unintentional disparate impact, the employer must have a strong basis in evidence to believe it will be subject to disparate-impact liability if it fails to take the race-conscious, discriminatory action.

* * *

The racial adverse impact here was significant, and petitioners do not dispute that the City was faced with a prima facie case of disparate-impact liability. On the captain exam, the pass rate for white candidates was 64 percent but was 37.5 percent for both black and Hispanic candidates. On the lieutenant exam, the pass rate for white candidates was 58.1 percent; for black candidates, 31.6 percent; and for Hispanic candidates, 20 percent. The pass rates of minorities, which were approximately one-half the pass rates for white candidates, fall well below the 80-percent standard set by the EEOC to implement the disparate-impact provision of Title VII. Based on how the passing candidates ranked and an application of the "rule of three," certifying the examinations would have meant that the City could not have considered black candidates for any of the then-vacant lieutenant or captain positions.

Based on the degree of adverse impact reflected in the results, respondents were compelled to take a hard look at the examinations to determine whether certifying the results would have had an impermissible disparate impact. The problem for respondents is that a prima facie case of disparate-impact liability—essentially, a threshold showing of a significant statistical disparity, and nothing more—is far from a strong basis in evidence that the City would have been liable under Title VII had it certified the results. That is because the City could be liable for disparate-impact discrimination only if the examinations were not job related and consistent with business necessity, or if there existed an equally valid, less-discriminatory alternative that served the City's needs but that the City refused to adopt. We conclude there is no strong basis in evidence to establish that the test was deficient in either of these respects

* * *

The record in this litigation documents a process that, at the outset, had the potential to produce a testing procedure that was true to the promise of Title VII: No individual should face workplace discrimination based on race. Respondents thought about promotion qualifications and relevant experience in neutral ways. They were careful to ensure broad racial participation in the design of the test itself and its administration. As we have discussed at length, the process was open and fair.

The problem, of course, is that after the tests were completed, the raw racial results became the predominant rationale for the City's refusal to certify the results. The injury arises in part from the high, and justified, expectations of the candidates who had participated in the testing process on the terms the City had established for the promotional process. Many of the candidates had studied for months, at considerable personal and financial expense, and thus the injury caused by the City's reliance on raw racial statistics at the end of the process was all the more severe. Confronted with arguments both for and against certifying the test results—and threats of a lawsuit either way—the City was required to make a difficult inquiry. But its hearings produced no strong evidence of a disparate-impact violation, and the City was not entitled to disregard the tests based solely on the racial disparity in the results.

*　*　*

Petitioners are entitled to summary judgment on their Title VII claim, and we therefore need not decide the underlying constitutional question. The judgment of the Court of Appeals is reversed, and the cases are remanded for further proceedings consistent with this opinion.

*　*　*

■ JUSTICE SCALIA, concurring.

I join the Court's opinion in full, but write separately to observe that its resolution of this dispute merely postpones the evil day on which the Court will have to confront the question: Whether, or to what extent, are the disparate-impact provisions of Title VII of the Civil Rights Act of 1964 consistent with the Constitution's guarantee of equal protection? The question is not an easy one.

*　*　*

The Court's resolution of these cases makes it unnecessary to resolve these matters today. But the war between disparate impact and equal protection will be waged sooner or later, and it behooves us to begin thinking about how—and on what terms—to make peace between them.

*　*　*

■ JUSTICE GINSBURG, with whom JUSTICE STEVENS, JUSTICE SOUTER, and JUSTICE BREYER join, dissenting.

In assessing claims of race discrimination, "[c]ontext matters." Grutter v. Bollinger, 539 U.S. 306, 327 (2003). In 1972, Congress extended Title VII of the Civil Rights Act of 1964 to cover public employment. At that time, municipal fire departments across the country, including New Haven's, pervasively discriminated against minorities. The extension of Title VII to cover jobs in firefighting effected no overnight change. It took decades of persistent effort, advanced by Title VII litigation, to open firefighting posts to members of racial minorities.

The white firefighters who scored high on New Haven's promotional exams understandably attract this Court's sympathy. But they had no vested right to promotion. Nor have other persons received promotions in preference to them. New Haven maintains that it refused to certify the test results because it believed, for good cause, that it would be vulnerable to a Title VII disparate-impact suit if it relied on those results. The Court today holds that New Haven has not demonstrated "a strong basis in evidence" for its plea. In so holding, the Court pretends that "[t]he City rejected the test results solely because the higher scoring candidates were white." That pretension, essential to the Court's disposition, ignores substantial evidence of multiple flaws in the tests New Haven used. The Court similarly fails to acknowledge the better tests used in other cities, which have yielded less racially skewed outcomes.

By order of this Court, New Haven, a city in which African-Americans and Hispanics account for nearly 60 percent of the population, must today be served—as it was in the days of undisguised discrimination—by a fire department in which members of racial and ethnic minorities are rarely seen in command positions. In arriving at its order, the Court barely acknowledges the pathmarking decision in Griggs v. Duke Power Co., 401 U.S. 424 (1971), which explained the centrality of the disparate-impact concept to effective enforcement of Title VII. The Court's order and opinion, I anticipate, will not have staying power.

* * *

Neither Congress' enactments nor this Court's Title VII precedents (including the now-discredited decision in Wards Cove [v. Atonio, 490 U.S. 642 (1989)]) offer even a hint of "conflict" between an employer's obligations under the statute's disparate-treatment and disparate-impact provisions. Standing on an equal footing, these twin pillars of Title VII advance the same objectives: ending workplace discrimination and promoting genuinely equal opportunity. Yet the Court today sets at odds the statute's core directives. When an employer changes an employment practice in an effort to comply with Title VII's disparate-impact provision, the Court reasons, it acts "because of race"—something Title VII's disparate-treatment provision, generally forbids. This characterization of an employer's compliance-directed action shows little attention to Congress' design or to the Griggs line of cases Congress recognized as pathmarking.

* * *

In codifying the Griggs and Albemarle [Paper Co. v. Moody, 422 U.S. 405 (1975)] instructions, Congress declared unambiguously that selection criteria operating to the disadvantage of minority group members can be retained only if justified by business necessity. In keeping with Congress' design, employers who reject such criteria due to reasonable doubts about their reliability can hardly be held to have engaged in discrimination "because of" race. A reasonable endeavor to comply with the law and to ensure that qualified candidates of all races have a fair opportunity to compete is simply not what Congress meant to interdict. I would therefore hold that an employer who jettisons a selection device when its disproportionate racial impact becomes apparent does not violate Title VII's disparate-treatment bar automatically or at all, subject to this key condition: The employer must have good cause to believe the device would not withstand examination for business necessity.

* * *

Our precedents defining the contours of Title VII's disparate-treatment prohibition further confirm the absence of any intra-statutory discord. In Johnson v. Transportation Agency, Santa Clara Cty., 480 U.S. 616 (1987), we upheld a municipal employer's voluntary affirmative-action plan against a disparate-treatment challenge. Pursuant to the plan, the employer selected a woman for a road-dispatcher position, a job category traditionally regarded as "male." A male applicant who had a slightly higher interview score brought suit under Title VII. This Court rejected his claim and approved the plan, which allowed consideration of gender as "one of numerous factors." Such consideration, we said, is "fully consistent with Title VII" because plans of that order can aid "in eliminating the vestiges of discrimination in the workplace."

This litigation does not involve affirmative action. But if the voluntary affirmative action at issue in Johnson does not discriminate within the meaning of Title VII, neither does an employer's reasonable effort to comply with Title VII's disparate-impact provision by refraining from action of doubtful consistency with business necessity.

The Court's decision in this litigation underplays a dominant Title VII theme. This Court has repeatedly emphasized that the statute "should not be read to thwart" efforts at voluntary compliance. Such compliance, we have explained, is "the preferred means of achieving [Title VII's] objectives." The strong-basis-in-evidence standard, however, as barely described in general, and cavalierly applied in this case, makes voluntary compliance a hazardous venture.

As a result of today's decision, an employer who discards a dubious selection process can anticipate costly disparate-treatment litigation in which its chances for success—even for surviving a summary-judgment motion—are highly problematic. Concern about exposure to disparate-impact liability, however well grounded, is insufficient to insulate an employer from attack. Instead, the employer must make a "strong" showing that (1) its selection method was "not job related and consistent with business necessity," or (2) that it refused to adopt "an equally valid, less-discriminatory alternative." It is hard to see how these requirements differ from demanding that an employer establish "a provable, actual violation" against itself. There is indeed a sharp conflict here, but it is not the false one the Court describes between Title VII's core provisions. It is, instead, the discordance of the Court's opinion with the voluntary compliance ideal.

* * *

Relying heavily on written tests to select fire officers is a questionable practice, to say the least. Successful fire officers, the City's description of the position makes clear, must have the "[a]bility to lead personnel effectively, maintain discipline, promote harmony, exercise sound judgment, and cooperate with other officials." These qualities are not well measured by written tests. Testifying before the CSB, Christopher Hornick, an exam-design expert with more than two decades of relevant experience, was emphatic on this point: Leadership skills, command presence, and the like "could have been identified and evaluated in a much more appropriate way."

* * *

This case presents an unfortunate situation, one New Haven might well have avoided had it utilized a better selection process in the first place. But what this case does not present is race-based discrimination in violation of Title VII. I dissent from the Court's judgment, which rests on the false premise that respondents showed "a significant statistical disparity," but "nothing more."

NOTES

1. The majority asserted there is a serious conflict between the disparate impact and disparate treatment branches of Title VII doctrine, a point strongly contested by the dissent. Congress specifically approved of the Supreme Court-developed disparate impact doctrine when it enacted the Civil Rights Act of 1991. Would you favor a congressional response to *Ricci*?

2. Suppose the City of Old Haven, concerned about possible bias in its promotion examination, received "provisional" test results without any names, but containing a breakdown of scores by race/ethnicity. The examinees received the same results. The city, upon seeing the disparate impact, decides not to use the results because it considers them invalid, not job-related, and unacceptably skewed by race and ethnicity. Concern for potential liability is not a factor. Could the white firefighters prevail in a lawsuit to discover their scores and to require the tests to be used in determining promotions? Can you distinguish *Ricci*?

3. What does *Ricci* portend for the future of *Griggs*? Justice Scalia strongly hints at his view that the disparate impact doctrine is unconstitutional under the Equal Protection clause. Do you agree?

4. Consider the difficulties facing an employer seeking to avoid disparate-impact liability stemming from employment tests. On the one hand, the

Supreme Court established in *Ricci* that an employer generally may not preemptively abandon test results that seem to exhibit racial skewing. The Court stated that an employer must have a "strong basis in evidence" for suspecting disparate impact before it can invalidate a test, but the Court warned that a "threshold showing of a significant statistical disparity" does not constitute such a basis. On the other hand, the Court suggested in Lewis v. Chicago, 559 U.S. 932 (2010), that racially skewed results such as those in Ricci constitute a prima facie showing of disparate impact. In Lewis, the plaintiffs argued that a hiring test administered by the Chicago Fire Department disproportionately eliminated minority candidates. The Court found that statistical evidence similar to that in Ricci supported a "cognizable claim" of disparate impact. To what extent do the combined holdings of Ricci and Lewis make it difficult for an employer to forestall a disparate-impact lawsuit?

5. According to Richard Primus, The Future of Disparate Impact, 108 Mich. L. Rev. 1341 (2010):

> At the heart of the New Haven decision lies an idea that we can call the *Ricci* premise: that the city's suspension of the written test would constitute disparate treatment under Title VII unless suspending the test were justified by Title VII's provisions regarding disparate impact. In other words, *Ricci* portrayed disparate impact doctrine as creating an exception to Title VII's prohibition on formal or intentional discrimination. The view that disparate impact doctrine constitutes an exception to disparate treatment doctrine entails the view that the two doctrines are conceptually in conflict—or, more precisely, that they would be in conflict if one were unable to carve itself out of the other. The Court articulated this vision as a matter of statutory construction, but it clearly implies a constitutional proposition as well. For these purposes, Title VII's prohibition of disparate treatment and the Fourteenth Amendment's guarantee of equal protection are substantively interchangeable. A conflict between disparate impact and disparate treatment is also a conflict between disparate impact and equal protection. And that makes things look bleak for the disparate impact standard. A Title VII doctrine can stand its ground against another Title VII doctrine, but not against the Constitution.

> * * *

> [T]he *Ricci* premise means that the actions necessary to remedy a disparate impact violation are per se in conceptual conflict with the demands of disparate treatment doctrine (and, implicitly, the demands of equal protection). Disparate impact doctrine is race conscious; equal protection requires racial neutrality; the two are not compatible. * * * The general reading is plausible, straightforward, and likely fatal for disparate impact doctrine. But it is not the only reading available, and it may not be the best one.

The institutional reading of the *Ricci* premise focuses on a difference between courts and public employers. On this view, a municipal employer's attempt to implement a disparate impact remedy is in conceptual conflict with the prohibition on disparate treatment (and implicitly with the requirements of equal protection) not because any disparate impact remedy is discriminatory but because public employers, unlike courts, are not authorized to engage in the race-conscious decisionmaking that disparate impact remedies entail. Judges are responsible for remedying racial discrimination, and that task requires more leeway to take note of race than other public officials have. (A requirement of complete judicial colorblindness would undermine all of antidiscrimination law, because courts cannot assess garden-variety discrimination claims without knowing the race of the parties involved.) Conversely, public employers face pressures that make it unwise to leave them with too much discretion to invoke disparate impact doctrine to justify racially conscious hiring decisions. If the *Ricci* premise is read through this institutional lens, courts can continue to enforce Title VII's disparate impact doctrine, even if public employers will have to tread more carefully.

Third and last, there is a visible-victims reading. It holds that the problem in New Haven's case was not the race-consciousness of the city's decision per se but the fact that the decision disadvantaged determinate and visible innocent third parties—that is, the white firefighters. Most disparate impact remedies avoid creating such victims. And within the category of formally race-neutral actions intended to improve the position of disadvantaged racial groups, equal protection doctrine may well distinguish between those that have visible victims and those whose costs are more diffuse.

Many people to both the left and the right of the Supreme Court may consider this distinction unprincipled. If race-conscious decisionmaking is objectionable, one might contend, then it is objectionable whether its allocative effects are visible or not. Conversely, if some race-conscious decisionmaking is permissible, its permissibility should not depend on its being kept secret. These objections have force. That said, the distinction between more and less visible race-conscious interventions is already present in equal protection caselaw, and it may well be defensible, or even wise. If the Court ultimately reads Ricci through a visible-victims prism, Title VII's disparate impact doctrine can survive, because the standard judicial remedies all avoid creating visible victims: the *Ricci* plaintiffs suffered in the New Haven case only because the city acted more aggressively than a court enforcing a disparate impact order would have.

6. See also Wygant v. Jackson Bd. of Educ., 476 U.S. 267 (1986), holding unconstitutional a remedial affirmative action plan that was not shown to be intended to remedy past or present discrimination by that particular employer. *Wygant* concerned layoffs and rejected the argument that African American role models were a sufficient reason to lay off whites with more seniority than African Americans who were kept. Affirmative action plans also raise issues under Title VII. In Steelworkers v. Weber, 443 U.S. 193 (1979), the Supreme Court held that Title VII does not condemn all voluntary race-conscious affirmative action plans. Kaiser Aluminum had few African American workers in high-paying craft positions, though it was not clear whether there had been specific discrimination. A new collective bargaining agreement reserved 50% of the openings in a training program for African-American employees until their percentage reached their share of the local labor force. The Supreme Court declared that Congress had not intended to prohibit private programs directed toward the goal of Title VII—the eradication of discrimination and its effects. In Johnson v. Transportation Agency, 480 U.S. 616 (1987), the Court followed *Weber* and upheld a plan seeking "an equitable representation of minorities, women and handicapped persons." The Agency had 238 road dispatchers, none of them female. A vacancy was filled by hiring a qualified female and rejecting a qualified male. The employer was not required to show that it had discriminated in the past; "manifest imbalance" and "traditionally segregated job category" were sufficient.

7. Sharon Taxman, who was white, and Debra Williams, who was black, both started work as teachers at Piscataway High School, N.J. on the same day. When the faculty had to be reduced due to cut-backs, the School Board decided to break the tie in seniority between Taxman and Williams using affirmative action, retaining Williams and firing Taxman. Taxman brought an employment discrimination suit under Title VII and won on summary judgment. The court of appeals affirmed, ruling that the School Board violated Title VII when it used its affirmative action plan to grant a non-remedial work force preference in order to promote "racial diversity." Taxman v. Board of Educ., 91 F.3d 1547 (3d Cir. 1996) (en banc), cert. dismissed, 522 U.S. 1010 (1997).

8. A reverse discrimination case concluded that Miami had unlawfully promoted two African American police officers. The district court awarded "make-whole" relief to all "adversely affected" white and Hispanic officers, as if each of these officers would have received one of the two promotions. The court of appeals vacated, concluding that the monetary value of the two positions should be divided pro rata among the class of eligible candidates. United States v. City of Miami, 195 F.3d 1292 (11th Cir. 1999), cert. denied sub nom. Fraternal Order of Police v. United States, 531 U.S. 815 (2000).

9. Major League Baseball created a medical and supplemental income plan for former Negro League players who were barred by racial discrimination from playing in the major leagues. White former players who played less than four years and thus did not qualify for the regular pension and medical plan for retired players sued. The court of appeals decided that MLB had a legitimate non-discriminatory reason for its actions and upheld dismissal of the lawsuit. "To the extent that MLB sought to remedy in part its past discriminatory conduct, it acted honorably and decently and not out of an improper or invidious motive. MLB has thus shown a legitimate, non-

discriminatory reason for its decision to provide benefits to former Negro League Players, a reason that is not pretextual in any respect." Moran v. Selig, 447 F.3d 748, 757 (9th Cir. 2006).

10. What are the larger social ramifications of affirmative action and reverse discrimination? Besides the obvious impact on non-favored groups, how does affirmative action affect those groups it attempts to benefit? Justice Thomas, in his dissent to Grutter v. Bollinger, 539 U.S. 306 (2003), wrote:

> I believe what lies beneath the Court's decision today are the benighted notions that one can tell when racial discrimination benefits (rather than hurts) minority groups . . . It is uncontested that each year, the Law School admits a handful of blacks who would be admitted in the absence of racial discrimination. Who can differentiate between those who belong and those who do not? The majority of blacks are admitted to the Law School because of discrimination, and because of this policy all are tarred as undeserving. This problem of stigma does not depend on determinacy as to whether those stigmatized are actually the "beneficiaries" of racial discrimination. When blacks take positions in the highest places of government, industry, or academia, it is an open question today whether their skin color played a part in their advancement. The question itself is the stigma because either racial discrimination did play a role, in which case the person may be deemed "otherwise unqualified," or it did not, in which case asking the question itself unfairly marks those blacks who would succeed without discrimination.

11. Can extra-judicial solutions supplement judicial enforcement of Title VII in propagating fair employment practices? Given more recent findings of unconscious bias and stereotyping that may stymie the natural progression of workplace equality, there has been a resurgence of the advocacy of structural solutions. One leading advocate is Professor Susan Sturm, who encourages the use of neutral figures such as lawyers and educators to play a more active role in encouraging employers to improve employment equality, thereby fostering a community internalization of social equality.

The following is an excerpt from her article, Second Generation Employment Discrimination: A Structural Approach, 101 Colum. L. Rev. 458 (2001):

> Over the last decade, an interesting and complex regulatory pattern has emerged. Multiple public, private, and nongovernmental actors are actively and interactively developing systems to address sexual harassment, glass ceiling, and other second generation problems. Each of these institutional actors has begun to approach these questions as posing essentially issues of problem solving. Each has, to varying degrees, linked its anti-bias efforts with the more general challenge of enhancing institutional capacity to manage complex workplace relationships. These multiple actors have, perhaps unwittingly, begun to carve out distinctive roles and relationships that form the outlines of a

dynamic regulatory system for addressing second generation discrimination * * *. This regulatory approach shifts the emphasis away from primary reliance on after-the-fact enforcement of centrally defined, specific commands. Instead, normative elaboration occurs through a fluid, interactive relationship between problem solving and problem definition within specific workplaces and in multiple other arenas, including but not limited to the judiciary. In this framework, compliance is achieved through, and evaluated in relation to, improving institutional capacity to identify, prevent, and redress exclusion, bias, and abuse. This approach expands the field of "regulatory" participants to include the long-neglected activities of legal actors within workplaces and significant nongovernmental organizations, such as professional associations, insurance companies, brokers, research consortia, and advocacy groups. These actors have already begun to play a significant role in pooling information, developing standards of effectiveness, and evaluating the adequacy of local problem-solving efforts.

The motif of this second generation regulatory approach is that of structuralism. By this, I mean an approach that encourages the development of institutions and processes to enact general norms in particular contexts. "Legality" emerges from an interactive process of information gathering, problem identification, remediation, and evaluation. Regulation fosters dynamic interactions that cut across established conceptual, professional, and organizational boundaries in reaction to observed problems. This approach encourages experimentation with respect to information gathering, organizational design, incentive structures, measures of effectiveness, and methods of institutionalizing accountability as part of an explicit system of legal regulation. Workplaces and nongovernmental institutions influencing workplace practice are treated within this regulatory regime as lawmaking bodies, rather than simply as objects of state or market regulation.

Courts, employers, and nongovernmental actors each play an important part in fostering this shift toward structuralism. Recent Supreme Court decisions can—I do not say must—be read to encourage workplace structures that provide for contextual norm elaboration and problem solving. At least in some contexts, these cases have converged with a more structural and dynamically oriented approach to second generation bias within workplaces as well. Some employers have responded to patterns of bias, exclusion, turnover, and glass ceiling by redesigning their systems of decisionmaking, work assignment, and conflict resolution to simultaneously address concerns about equity and effectiveness. Sexual harassment and glass ceiling jurisprudence has encouraged and reinforced widespread organizational development of internal problem-solving and dispute resolution processes.

* * *

The architecture of a multi-sector regulatory system for addressing second generation workplace problems is emerging through the interplay among the judiciary, workplaces, and nongovernmental actors playing an intermediary role ... Responsive employers have instituted internal systems for preventing and remedying problems stemming from complex workplace relationships. These systems develop the information and capacity necessary to understand the nature of the problem, respond at the appropriate organizational level to remedy it, and learn from previous problem-solving efforts. These pathbreaking organizations demonstrate that internal dispute resolution and problem-solving systems can be robust, if they are designed to provide for accountability and effectiveness. They also provide a starting point for systematic reflection about the meaning of legitimacy and accountability in these internal workplace problem-solving regimes.

Critics of the structural approach, however, are pessimistic about the success of such structural approaches. Professor Samuel Bagenstos writes:

I believe that the structural turn in employment discrimination scholarship is best understood as highlighting the limits of antidiscrimination law. Perhaps paradoxically, I believe so in part because I find the case for a structural approach to employment discrimination law so compelling. Unconscious bias, interacting with today's "boundaryless workplace," generates inequalities that our current antidiscrimination law is not well equipped to solve. In spite of its limits, a structural approach to employment discrimination law may be the best hope for addressing those inequalities.

But there are significant obstacles to the success of a structural approach to antidiscrimination law. In spite of doctrines that already seem to impose on courts the obligation to police workplace structures that might facilitate discrimination, judges have proven unwilling or unable to discharge that responsibility with rigor. The new proposals seek to sidestep that history, but they do so largely by urging judicial deference to professional communities such as those of human relations professionals and lawyers that are as likely to subvert as to promote norms of workplace equality.

These difficulties are mere symptoms of a deeper problem: structural employment inequalities cannot be solved without going beyond the generally accepted normative underpinnings of antidiscrimination law. Because courts and legislatures have proven unable or unwilling to take that step, structural discrimination advocates essentially proceed by indirection. They seek to develop rules that will empower workplace constituencies who will internalize and advance the correct vision of equality. But unless courts have some normative idea of what workplace equality should mean, they will be unable to ensure that those workplace constituencies will serve the purposes of antidiscrimination law.

Samuel R. Bagenstos, The Structural Turn and the Limits of Antidiscrimination Law, 94 Cal. L. Rev. 1 (2006). To read a response to Professor Bagenstos' and others' criticisms, see Sturm, The Architecture of Inclusion: Advancing Workplace Equity in Higher Education, 29 Harv. J. L. & Gender 247 (2006).

E. DISCRIMINATION BASED ON FACTORS OTHER THAN RACE OR SEX

1. RELIGION

Reed v. Great Lakes Cos.
330 F.3d 931 (7th Cir. 2003).

■ POSNER, CIRCUIT JUDGE. Melvin Reed, the plaintiff in this Title VII religious-discrimination suit, appeals from the grant of summary judgment to his former employer, Great Lakes, and from the imposition of sanctions on him. His lawyer wants the $500 sanction imposed on her also reversed, but she failed to file a notice of appeal and the notice of appeal that she filed on behalf of Reed does not mention her sanction. Although Fed. R. App. P. 3(c)(4) provides that an appeal should not be dismissed "for failure to name a party whose intent to appeal is otherwise clear from the notice [of appeal]," the lawyer's intent to appeal is not clear from the notice of appeal—indeed is not so much as hinted at in it—and as a result we lack jurisdiction over her challenge to the sanction that was imposed on her.

Construed as favorably to Reed as the record permits, the facts of the case are as follows. He was hired to be the executive housekeeper of a newly opened Holiday Inn that Great Lakes operates in Milwaukee. One of his duties was to see to it that a copy of the Bible, supplied free of charge to the hotel by the Gideons, was placed in every room. It is customary for representatives of management to meet with the Gideons when they deliver Bibles to a newly opened hotel. Reed had been working for Great Lakes for less than a month when the Gideons showed up to deliver the Bibles. A few days before their scheduled arrival, the manager of the Holiday Inn had told Reed in a joking manner that they were going to "pray with the Gideons," which Reed understood to mean that, given his responsibility for the distribution of the Bibles to the rooms, he was to accompany the manager to the meeting at which they would receive the Bibles from the Gideons. Reed did not object to attending the meeting. But, to the manager's surprise, at the meeting the Gideons, besides delivering Bibles, did some Bible reading and some praying. Reed was offended by the religious character of the meeting and left in the middle, to the manager's chagrin. Later in the day, the manager ran into Reed and told him: "Don't do that again, you embarrassed me." Reed riposted: "You can't compel me to a religious event," to which the manager replied that Reed would do what he was told to do. Reed responded, "Oh, hell no, you won't, not when it comes to my spirituality," whereupon the manager fired him for insubordination.

Oddly, Reed at his deposition refused to indicate what if any religious affiliation or beliefs (or nonbeliefs) he has; refused even to deny that he might be a Gideon! His position was that Title VII forbids an employer to require an employee to attend a religious meeting, period.

Title VII does forbid an employer, unless it is a religious organization, which Great Lakes is not, to discriminate against an employee on the basis of the employee's religion. And for these purposes, as assumed by the parties, as strongly intimated in EEOC v. Townley Engineering & Mfg. Co., 859 F.2d 610, 613–14 n. 5 (9th Cir. 1988), and Young v. Southwestern Savings & Loan Ass'n, 509 F.2d 140, 142 (5th Cir. 1975), and as supported by analogy to cases under the free-exercise clause of the First Amendment,—cases which hold that religious freedom includes the freedom to reject religion—"religion" includes antipathy to religion. And so an atheist (which Reed may or may not be) cannot be fired because his employer dislikes atheists. If we think of religion as taking a position on divinity, then atheism is indeed a form of religion.

But there is no indication that Reed was fired because of his religious beliefs, identity, or observances or because of his aversion to religion, to Christianity, or to the Gideons, whatever the case may be (remember that we don't know anything about his religion or lack of religion). Great Lakes accepts Bibles from the Gideons because the Bibles are free, not because any of Great Lakes' owners or managers, including the manager of the Holiday Inn who fired Reed, is a Gideon. So far as appears, none is. The manager's joking reference to "praying with the Gideons" makes it pretty clear that he is not one of them; anyway there is no contention that he is. For that matter, there is no evidence that he expected to encounter prayers and Bible reading at the meeting with them. At previous such meetings the Gideons had handed over the Bibles and the manager had thanked them, and that was that. The religious service was a surprise. It is apparent that the manager fired Reed because Reed's sudden departure from the meeting was embarrassing to the manager, who would be in trouble with his superiors if the Gideons became huffy and cut off the supply of free Bibles to Great Lakes hotels, and also because Reed's refusal to see the manager's point of view indicated that he was unlikely to be a cooperative employee.

The manager *must* have been indifferent to Reed's religious views, because Reed never expressed them to the manager; to this day we do not know what his religion is, as he refused to say at his deposition. It is difficult to see how an employer can be charged with discrimination on the basis of an employee's religion when he doesn't know the employee's religion (or lack thereof, which, as we have noted, is in the eyes of the law a form of religion), though the employee can survive summary judgment if, while declining to specify his religious beliefs, he attests that they differ from his employer's and that that is why he was fired.

Reed has utterly failed to make a prima facie case of intentional religious discrimination. But he has another string to his bow. Besides forbidding intentional discrimination, Title VII requires an employer to try to accommodate the religious needs of its employees, that is, to try to adjust the requirements of the job so that the employee can remain employed without giving up the practice of his religion, provided the adjustment would not work an undue hardship on the employer. And again for these purposes hostility to religion counts as a form of religion. So if attending a meeting at which Gideons might pray or read from the Bible would offend Reed's religious or antireligious sensibilities, he might be entitled to an accommodation.

We say "might be" rather than "would be" for two reasons. First, the duty to accommodate is not absolute; the cost to the employer must be considered. Second, an employee is not permitted to redefine a purely personal preference or aversion as a religious belief. Otherwise he could announce without warning that white walls or venetian blinds offended his "spirituality," and the employer would have to scramble to see whether it was feasible to accommodate him by repainting the walls or substituting curtains for venetian blinds. This case is not so extreme, because compelled attendance at sectarian religious services is the sort of thing that is likely to offend someone who does not belong to the sect in question, though we repeat that for all we know Reed is a Gideon and his claim for accommodation therefore completely spurious.

But putting that possibility to one side, and assuming that it would have been no sort of hardship for Great Lakes to have excused Reed from attendance at meetings with the Gideons, who are hardly likely to ask, "Why isn't the executive housekeeper here?" we think the district court was right to grant summary judgment for Great Lakes with respect to this claim as well as the disparate-treatment claim. There is a line, indistinct but important, between an employee who seeks an accommodation to his religious faith and an employee who asserts as Reed did an unqualified right to disobey orders that he deems inconsistent with his faith though he refuses to indicate at what points that faith intersects the requirements of his job. Today he storms out of a meeting with the Gideons; tomorrow he may refuse to place their Bibles in the rooms; the day after that he may announce that he will not come to work on the day when the Gideons visit. Reed failed to give any indication of what future occurrences at the Holiday Inn would impel him to make a scene embarrassing to the manager and potentially injurious to the employer. Title VII imposes a duty on the employer but also a reciprocal duty on the employee to give fair warning of the employment practices that will interfere with his religion and that he therefore wants waived or adjusted. A person's religion is not like his sex or race—something obvious at a glance. Even if he wears a religious symbol, such as a cross or a yarmulka, this may not pinpoint his particular beliefs and observances; and anyway employers are not charged with detailed knowledge of the beliefs and observances associated with particular sects. Suppose the employee is an Orthodox Jew and believes that it is deeply sinful to work past sundown on Friday. He does not tell his employer, the owner of a hardware store that is open from 9 a.m. to 6 p.m. on Fridays, who leaves the employee in sole charge of the store one Friday afternoon in mid-winter, and at 4 p.m. the employee leaves the store. The employer could fire him without being thought guilty of failing to accommodate his religious needs. This case is similar.

We turn to the propriety of the sanctions that the district judge imposed on Reed for filing a frivolous claim, which is an apt description of his claim to having been intentionally discriminated against on account of his religion. The judge ordered him to pay Great Lakes $1,000 and write a letter of apology to Great Lakes, and also forbade him to file any further lawsuits until he complies with the rest of the order. If the sanction had consisted merely of a monetary penalty for filing a frivolous claim, we would affirm. The fact that Reed's accommodation claim, while it has failed, was not frivolous would be no bar to imposing sanctions for putting his opponent to the expense of opposing a frivolous claim (or defense) just because he had a nonfrivolous claim as well. But the district judge's basis for imposing the sanctions he did on Reed was different; it was that in the past 15 years Reed had worked for 25 different employers, often (as in this case) for a month or less, and had filed 13 employment discrimination suits in the federal district court in Milwaukee. He had won a partial victory in one of the suits but had lost all the rest, some of them through abandonment. The judge inferred that Reed is engaged in a pattern of extortion, working for an employer just long enough to obtain a pretext for suing him.

There is indeed something amiss in Reed's employment and litigation history, though extortion doesn't seem the word for it. Were he engaged in extortion he would have dropped his suits in exchange for nuisance-suit settlements. So far as appears, his 15-year campaign of "extortion" hasn't yielded him a penny, except in his one victory, where he obtained damages in a trial and not by way of a settlement, nuisance or otherwise. It seems more likely that he has a psychological problem than that he has been committing extortion for the last 15 years with nothing to show for it.

Even so, a judge can sanction a litigant for filing a frivolous suit or claim regardless of the motives for such filing, and in deciding whether to sanction such a litigant he can take into account a history of frivolous litigation. The fact that the previous suits were the result of an unbalanced mind rather than an extortionate one would be no defense. Yet, odd as it may seem, none of Reed's previous cases has been adjudged frivolous. Nor did the district judge find that any of them had been frivolous. The sanctions order thus appears to rest on nothing more solid than the judge's speculation that Reed is an extortionist. The speculation is too thin to sustain that order. The order must therefore be vacated and the matter returned to the judge for reconsideration in light of this opinion; but the grant of summary judgment to Great Lakes is affirmed.

AFFIRMED IN PART, VACATED IN PART, AND REMANDED.

■ RIPPLE, CIRCUIT JUDGE, concurring in part and dissenting in part. I agree that Mr. Reed has failed to establish a case of intentional discrimination on the basis of religion. Nor has he established a case of failure to accommodate his religious beliefs on the part of Great Lakes. The deposition testimony of Mr. Reed makes it clear that he was quite unwilling to enter into a dialogue with his employer on that matter.

I do not, however, regard either of the allegations made by Mr. Reed to be frivolous. Accordingly, I would reverse that part of the judgment of the district court that imposes sanctions.

NOTES AND QUESTIONS

1. Should a plaintiff have to indicate his or her religious beliefs at a deposition or trial to claim that he or she found it offensive to be compelled to attend a meeting where prayers were said?

2. To what degree, if any, is Mr. Reed's extensive litigation history relevant to the merits of *this* case? Do you think Mr. Reed's lawyer should be subject to a $500 sanction?

3. In *Reed,* the promotion of religion by the employer was inadvertent. Suppose it is intended by the employer? The results have varied. Where religious observance plays an ancillary part in a business activity, the activity may still be lawful. For example, in Kolodziej v. Smith, 588 N.E.2d 634 (Mass.1992), it was lawful for an employer to require that management employees attend a week-long seminar on "interpersonal relationships," which drew heavily on the scriptures. On the other hand, if employee religious concerns may be easily accommodated, the employer may be required to do so. An employer who forced an employee to answer the telephone "Merry Christmas" against her religious beliefs, when it would have been easy to accommodate her, was found in violation of Title VII. Kentucky Comm'n on Human Rights v. Lesco Mfg. & Design Co., Inc., 736 S.W.2d 361 (Ky. Ct. App.1987).

4. Doyle Ollis, a Protestant, was a sales associate for a homebuilding company. John Smith, the owner of the company, believed in reincarnation and that a person's traumas in past lives can explain his or her behavior in the present. The company required employees to attend sessions of Mind Body Energy (MBE) to cleanse their negative energy. They were also encouraged to read Buddhist and Hindu teachings. Ollis complained to his supervisor and to senior management that these sessions conflicted with his religion and made him uncomfortable. After a complaint of sexual harassment was lodged against him (by a female employee later discharged

for removing her clothing at a golf outing and doing cartwheels naked on the golf course), Ollis was fired for "poor leadership and lack of judgment." Ollis brought actions for religious discrimination and retaliatory discharge. The jury found in his favor and awarded him $1 in nominal damages, and the court awarded him attorney fees and costs. The Eighth Circuit affirmed. See Ollis v. HearthStone Homes, Inc., 495 F.3d 570 (8th Cir. 2007).

5. Unlike *Reed*, where the employee objected to the religious conduct in the workplace, many cases involve employees who seek to practice their religion in the workplace. For public employers, it is often a difficult task balancing the First Amendment's Free Exercise and Establishment clauses. In Berry v. Department of Soc. Servs., 447 F.3d 642 (9th Cir. 2006), Daniel Berry was employed at the state division of employment services, which administered state unemployment compensation claims. He described himself as "an evangelical Christian who holds sincere religious beliefs that require him to share his faith, when appropriate, and to pray with other Christians." Id. at 646. He alleged that his employer violated Title VII and his First Amendment rights when it prohibited him from discussing religion with his clients, displaying religious items in his cubicle where he interviewed clients, and using a conference room for prayer meetings. The Ninth Circuit affirmed the grant of summary judgment to the employer, holding, among other things, that the employer's action was reasonable because it only restricted personal religious displays in areas in which clients visited and that other areas besides the conference room were available to employees for prayer and other meetings during nonworking time.

6. A private sector case comparable to *Berry* is Moranski v. General Motors Corp., 433 F.3d 537 (7th Cir. 2005). General Motors (GM) established a voluntary "affinity group" program, which it supported through company resources. Some of the approved affinity groups were those comprised of people with disabilities, veterans, and employees of African ancestry. GM had a policy of not approving a group that promotes or advocates a particular religious or political position. Does the program constitute religious discrimination under Title VII? Held: no. The court said that it did not discriminate on the basis of religion because it treated all religions alike—including atheism and agnosticism—by excluding them.

7. Some workplace conduct may be so closely tied to religious beliefs as to implicate Title VII religious discrimination. For example, in Turic v. Holland Hospitality, Inc., 842 F.Supp. 971 (W.D.Mich.1994), when a pregnant waitress told some coworkers that she was considering having an abortion, some of the "very Christian" staff became upset, and she was later discharged for allegedly poor performance. The trial court denied the defendant's motion for summary judgment and held that the plaintiff had alleged sufficient facts to establish Title VII religious discrimination as well as a violation of the Pregnancy Discrimination Act. In another abortion-related case, Wilson v. U.S. West Commc'ns, Inc., 58 F.3d 1337 (8th Cir. 1995), the court held that the discharge of an information specialist who refused to stop wearing or cover up an anti-abortion pin depicting a fetus did not violate Title VII because it was disturbing, disruptive, and offensive to other employees. Similarly, in Rodriguez v. City of Chicago, 156 F.3d 771

(7th Cir. 1998), cert. denied, 525 U.S. 1144 (1999), the Seventh Circuit affirmed the dismissal of a claim of religious discrimination filed by a Catholic police officer who asserted that protecting an abortion clinic conflicted with his religious beliefs. The court held that the officer could have transferred to another district without an abortion clinic.

8. An apprentice electrician, a devout Roman Catholic, believed that commercial nuclear power threatens the environment and future generations. Did an apprenticeship training council have an obligation to accommodate his beliefs by not assigning him to work at a nuclear power plant? See Best v. California Apprenticeship Council, 207 Cal.Rptr. 863 (Cal. Ct.App.1984) (held: yes). Why? Is opposition to nuclear power part of Catholic theology? Would the same holding be applied to an agnostic or atheist? Suppose the apprentice belonged to a religion that did oppose nuclear power as a part of its religious tenets? Is there a difference between religious beliefs and moral beliefs? Would it violate Title VII for an employer to force an employee to resign because of his membership in and presidency of a church-affiliated organization that advocated gay marriage?

9. Section 701(j) protects "all aspects of religious observance and practice, *as well as belief * * * *"* (emphasis added). Thus, even highly personal and idiosyncratic beliefs may be protected, as long as they fall under the umbrella of a religious belief. The issue often involves whether employees can refuse to perform certain job requirements on the ground that they violate the individual's religion. For example, a high school biology teacher refused to teach evolution. He argued that evolutionism was part of the religion of "secular humanism," and therefore to require him to teach this "religion" violated the First Amendment. Has the school district violated the Establishment Clause of the First Amendment? See Peloza v. Capistrano Unified Sch. Dist., 37 F.3d 517 (9th Cir. 1994), cert. denied, 515 U.S. 1173 (1995) (held: no). But see Peterson v. Wilmur Commc'ns, Inc., 205 F.Supp.2d 1014 (E.D.Wis. 2002) (white supremacist belief system called "Creativity" was a religion and therefore demotion based on adherence to these beliefs violated Title VII).

10. Title VII prohibits invidious, overt discrimination in employment based on religion. See, e.g., Shapolia v. Los Alamos Nat'l Lab., 992 F.2d 1033 (10th Cir. 1993). Much of the case law, however, focuses on the duty of reasonable accommodation. Frequently, the cases involve adjusting work schedules to permit religious observances. In the leading case, Trans World Airlines, Inc. v. Hardison, 432 U.S. 63 (1977), the Supreme Court construed the employer's obligations quite narrowly and held that requiring employers to bear more than a de minimis cost to accommodate an employee would impose an undue hardship. Similarly, in Ansonia Bd. of Educ. v. Philbrook, 479 U.S. 60 (1986), the Court held that an employer must offer an employee reasonable accommodation but need not show that each of the employee's proposed alternatives would result in undue hardship. A violation will be found only where the employer refuses to make de minimis efforts at accommodation, such as in Smith v. Pyro Mining Co., 827 F.2d 1081 (6th Cir. 1987), cert. denied, 485 U.S. 989 (1988), where the employer required the employee to find his own replacement when it could have done so without undue hardship by placing a notice in the company newspaper or on its bulletin board.

11. In *Hardison,* the plaintiff sought preferential scheduling to accommodate his Saturday Sabbath beliefs. In other cases, the courts have found violations of Title VII where employers failed to revise an employee's schedule to accommodate an employee's regular religious observance, EEOC v. Arlington Transit Mix, Inc., 957 F.2d 219 (6th Cir. 1991), or specific holidays or observances, EEOC v. Ilona of Hungary, Inc., 97 F.3d 204 (7th Cir. 1996); Heller v. EBB Auto Co., 8 F.3d 1433 (9th Cir.1993). Many of the reasonable accommodation cases continue to grapple with the question of modifying employee work schedules to accommodate religious observances. In general, the courts have held that employers need not accede completely to an employee's requested accommodation, even if doing so would not be an undue hardship, so long as the employer makes a reasonable effort to eliminate the conflict between work and religious practices. See, e.g., EEOC v. Firestone Fibers & Textiles Co., 515 F.3d 307 (4th Cir. 2008) (employee absences); Morrissette-Brown v. Mobile Infirmary Med. Ctr., 506 F.3d 1317 (11th Cir. 2007) (swapping schedules with other employees).

12. An applicant for the position of truck driver, who was a member of the Native American Church, was denied a position because his occasional (twice within the six-month period before applying for the job) use of peyote in religious ceremonies precluded him from safely driving for 24 hours after ingestion. Does the employer have a duty to accommodate the applicant's religious use of peyote? See Toledo v. Nobel-Sysco, Inc., 892 F.2d 1481 (10th Cir. 1989), cert. denied, 495 U.S. 948 (1990) (held: yes).

13. A long haul truck driver notified his supervisor that he could not accept overnight runs where he would be paired with a female driver, because it would violate his Jehovah's Witness religious beliefs. Does the employer have a duty to accommodate his religious beliefs by pairing him only with male drivers on overnight runs? See Weber v. Roadway Express, 199 F.3d 270 (5th Cir. 2000) (held: no, citing *Hardison*). Compare *Toledo*, note 12.

14. In Endres v. Indiana State Police, 349 F.3d 922 (7th Cir. 2003), cert. denied, 541 U.S. 989 (2004), a Baptist police officer, who was assigned to work at a casino, sought a transfer to another position because of his religious opposition to gambling. The court held that the state police had no duty to accommodate his religious opposition to the assignment.

15. In Walden v. CDC, 669 F.3d 1277 (11th Cir. 2012), the plaintiff worked as an Employee Assistance Program (EAP) counselor for Computer Sciences Corporation (CSC), a contractor supplying EAP services to the CDC. The plaintiff is a devout Christian who believes it is immoral to engage in same-sex relationships. After she refused to provide relationship counseling to a CDC employee engaged in a same-sex relationship, a CDC official asked CSC to remove the plaintiff from the contract, and the CSC did so by placing the plaintiff on layoff status pending reassignment. Affirming summary judgment for the defendants on the plaintiff's Title VII religious discrimination claim, the Eleventh Circuit held that "CSC reasonably accommodated Ms. Walden when it encouraged her to obtain new employment with the company and offered her assistance in obtaining a new position."

16. What must an employee do to trigger an employer's duty to accommodate her religion? In EEOC v. Abercrombie & Fitch, 135 S.Ct. 2028 (2015) (see also case excerpt in Chapter 7), the Supreme Court distinguished between motive and knowledge, making clear that a disparate treatment claim may succeed if an employer acts with the motive of avoiding accommodation even if the employer lacks actual knowledge that the applicant in fact needs a religious accommodation. In other words, an applicant need not provide explicit notification to a prospective employer that a particular practice is religiously motivated and would require accommodation in order to trigger the employer's duty to provide religious accommodation. An employer may be found liable if its motive is to avoid accommodation even if the employer is acting on no more than "an unsubstantiated suspicion" that religious accommodation would be needed. Consistent with the Court's ruling in *Abercrombie & Fitch*, is the earlier decision by the Seventh Circuit in Adeyeye v. Heartland Sweeteners, LLC, 721 F.3d 444 (7th Cir. 2013), in which the court held that an employee's request to take unpaid leave to attend the funeral ceremonies of his father in Nigeria was sufficient to put the employer on notice of the religious nature of the request. The court explained that even though the plaintiff's religious beliefs and practices were unfamiliar to most Americans, his request for leave gave sufficient notice of the religious nature of the leave by referring to "a funeral ceremony,' a 'funeral rite,' and animal sacrifice." Moreover, the court explained that "[i]f the managers who considered the request had questions about whether the request was religious, nothing would have prevented them from asking Adeyeye to explain a little more about the nature of his request. . . ."

17. If an individual quits or is discharged because performing certain work activities would violate his or her religion, what effect does this have on eligibility for unemployment insurance? In Employment Div. v. Smith, 494 U.S. 872 (1990), a county employee whose job was an alcohol abuse counselor was discharged because of his off-duty use of peyote. The Supreme Court, six-to-three, found no violation of the free exercise clause of the First Amendment in denying him unemployment compensation for work-related misconduct. *Smith* was superseded by the Religious Freedom Restoration Act of 1993, 42 U.S.C. §§ 2000bb et seq., but the statute was held to be unconstitutional in City of Boerne v. Flores, 521 U.S. 507 (1997). This issue is further discussed in Chapter 12.

18. Section 702 of Title VII contains a religious exemption that, as interpreted by the courts, applies to two discrete situations. First, religious institutions are exempt from Title VII's ban on religious discrimination, even as to non-religious personnel. In Corporation of the Presiding Bishop v. Amos, 483 U.S. 327 (1987), an employee of a gymnasium run by the church was discharged because he was no longer a member in good standing in the church. The plaintiff argued that the exemption of a church's secular enterprises has the effect of "establishing" religion in violation of the First Amendment. The Court disagreed, holding that section 702 is a valid attempt by Congress to avoid entanglement of the courts in distinctions between religious and nonprofit secular activities. See LeBoon v. Lancaster Jewish Cmty. Ctr. Ass'n, 503 F.3d 217 (3d Cir. 2007) (nonprofit organization with mission "to enhance and promote Jewish life, identity, and community" was exempt). Second, religious institutions are exempt from other forms of discrimination banned by Title VII (race, color, sex, and national origin) involving religious personnel, such as priests, ministers, and rabbis. The courts have held that this "ministerial exemption" is robust and that a church need not proffer any religious explanation for its conduct. EEOC v. Roman Catholic Diocese, 213 F.3d 795 (4th Cir. 2000). See Petruska v. Gannon Univ., 462 F.3d 294 (3d Cir. 2006) (sex discrimination and retaliation claims brought by a chaplain against a Catholic university were barred). On the other hand, the ministerial exemption does not apply where an employee's job is primarily secular (e.g., teaching) and only involves incidentally imparting church doctrine. EEOC v. Fremont Christian School, 781 F.2d 1362 (9th Cir. 1986). See generally Note, The Ministerial Exception to Title VII: The Case for a Deferential Primary Duties Test, 121 Harv. L. Rev. 1776 (2008). For a further discussion, see *Curay-Cramer*, infra p. 727.

19. In addition to the religious exemptions to Title VII found in Section 702, the Religious Freedom Restoration Act provides additional protection for employers. In Burwell v. Hobby Lobby, 134 S.Ct 2751, 2761 (2014) (p. 613), the Supreme Court held that persons or "closely held" companies were entitled to exemption under RFRA from neutral laws of general applicability that burdened the exercise of religion unless the government demonstrated that the application of the burden "1) is in furtherance of a compelling governmental interest; and 2) is the least restrictive means of furthering that compelling interest." Relying on *Hobby Lobby*, the court in EEOC v. R.G. & B.R. Harris Funeral Homes, 201 F.Supp.3d 837, 842 (E.D. Mich. 2016), held that a funeral home was entitled to a RFRA exemption from "Title VII, and the body of sex-stereotyping case law that has developed under it."

20. Since the mid-1990s, the federal government has supported "faithbased initiatives" to supply federally-funded social services (e.g., substance abuse treatment) through religious-affiliated organizations. These efforts have become known as "Charitable Choice," to emphasize that the recipient has a choice of secular or religious social service providers. See https://www.samhsa.gov/sites/default/files/charchoice_assurance.pdf. The courts have not ruled on whether the religious groups may use religion as a criterion in hiring employees who provide these services. Title VII case law suggests that the ministerial exception of Title VII would not apply, but the Bush Administration took the opposite view.

Hosanna-Tabor Evangelical Lutheran Church & School v. EEOC
565 U.S. 171 (2012).

■ CHIEF JUSTICE ROBERTS delivered the opinion of the Court.

Certain employment discrimination laws authorize employees who have been wrongfully terminated to sue their employers for reinstatement and damages. The question presented is whether the Establishment and Free Exercise Clauses of the First Amendment bar such an action when the employer is a religious group and the employee is one of the group's ministers.

Petitioner Hosanna-Tabor Evangelical Lutheran Church and School is a member congregation of the Lutheran Church-Missouri Synod, the second largest Lutheran denomination in America. Hosanna-Tabor operated a small school in Redford, Michigan, offering a Christ-centered education to students in kindergarten through eighth grade.

The Synod classifies teachers into two categories: "called" and "lay." "Called" teachers are regarded as having been called to their vocation by God through a congregation. To be eligible to receive a call from a congregation, a teacher must satisfy certain academic requirements. One way of doing so is by completing a "colloquy" program at a Lutheran college or university. The program requires candidates to take eight courses of theological study, obtain the endorsement of their local Synod district, and pass an oral examination by a faculty committee. A teacher who meets these requirements may be called by a congregation. Once called, a teacher receives the formal title "Minister of Religion, Commissioned." A commissioned minister serves for an open-ended term; at Hosanna-Tabor, a call could be rescinded only for cause and by a supermajority vote of the congregation.

"Lay" or "contract" teachers, by contrast, are not required to be trained by the Synod or even to be Lutheran. At Hosanna-Tabor, they were appointed by the school board, without a vote of the congregation, to one-year renewable terms. Although teachers at the school generally performed the same duties regardless of whether they were lay or called, lay teachers were hired only when called teachers were unavailable.

Respondent Cheryl Perich was first employed by Hosanna-Tabor as a lay teacher in 1999. After Perich completed her colloquy later that school year, Hosanna-Tabor asked her to become a called teacher. Perich accepted the call and received a "diploma of vocation" designating her a commissioned minister.

Perich taught kindergarten during her first four years at Hosanna-Tabor and fourth grade during the 2003–2004 school year. She taught math, language arts, social studies, science, gym, art, and music. She also taught a religion class four days a week, led the students in prayer and devotional exercises each day, and attended a weekly school-wide chapel service. Perich led the chapel service herself about twice a year.

Perich became ill in June 2004 with what was eventually diagnosed as narcolepsy. Symptoms included sudden and deep sleeps from which she could not be roused. Because of her illness, Perich began the 2004–2005 school year on disability leave. On January 27, 2005, however, Perich notified the school principal, Stacey Hoeft, that she would be able to report to work the following month. Hoeft responded that the school had already contracted with a lay teacher to fill Perich's position for the remainder of the school year. Hoeft also expressed concern that Perich was not yet ready to return to the classroom.

On January 30, Hosanna-Tabor held a meeting of its congregation at which school administrators stated that Perich was unlikely to be physically capable of returning to work that school year or the next. The congregation voted to offer Perich a "peaceful release" from her call, whereby the congregation would pay a portion of her health insurance premiums in exchange for her resignation as a called teacher. Perich refused to resign and produced a note from her doctor stating that she would be able to return to work on February 22. The school board urged Perich to reconsider, informing her that the school no longer had a position for her, but Perich stood by her decision not to resign.

On the morning of February 22—the first day she was medically cleared to return to work—Perich presented herself at the school. Hoeft asked her to leave but she would not do so until she obtained written documentation that she had reported to work. Later that afternoon, Hoeft called Perich at home and told her that she would likely be fired. Perich responded that she had spoken with an attorney and intended to assert her legal rights.

Following a school board meeting that evening, board chairman Scott Salo sent Perich a letter stating that Hosanna-Tabor was reviewing the process for rescinding her call in light of her "regrettable" actions. Salo subsequently followed up with a letter advising Perich that the congregation would consider whether to rescind her call at its next meeting. As grounds for termination, the letter cited Perich's "insubordination and disruptive behavior" on February 22, as well as the damage she had done to her "working relationship" with the school by "threatening to take legal action." The congregation voted to rescind Perich's call on April 10, and Hosanna-Tabor sent her a letter of termination the next day.

Perich filed a charge with the Equal Employment Opportunity Commission, alleging that her employment had been terminated in violation of the Americans with Disabilities Act. The ADA prohibits an employer from discriminating against a qualified individual on the basis of disability. It also prohibits an employer from retaliating "against any individual because such individual has opposed any act or practice made unlawful by [the ADA] or because such individual made a charge, testified, assisted, or participated in any manner in an investigation, proceeding, or hearing under [the ADA]."

The EEOC brought suit against Hosanna-Tabor, alleging that Perich had been fired in retaliation for threatening to file an ADA lawsuit. Perich intervened in the litigation, claiming unlawful retaliation under both the ADA and the Michigan Persons with Disabilities Civil Rights Act. The EEOC and Perich sought Perich's reinstatement to her former position (or frontpay in lieu thereof), along with backpay, compensatory and punitive damages, attorney's fees, and other injunctive relief.

Hosanna-Tabor moved for summary judgment. Invoking what is known as the "ministerial exception," the Church argued that the suit was barred by the First Amendment because the claims at issue concerned the employment relationship between a religious institution and one of its ministers. According to the Church, Perich was a minister, and she had been fired for a religious reason—namely, that her threat to sue the Church violated the Synod's belief that Christians should resolve their disputes internally.

The District Court agreed that the suit was barred by the ministerial exception and granted summary judgment in Hosanna-Tabor's favor.

* * *

The Court of Appeals for the Sixth Circuit vacated and remanded, directing the District Court to proceed to the merits of Perich's retaliation claims.

* * *

We granted certiorari.

The First Amendment provides, in part, that "Congress shall make no law respecting an establishment of religion, or prohibiting the free exercise thereof." We have said that these two Clauses "often exert conflicting pressures," and that there can be "internal tension ... between the Establishment Clause and the Free Exercise Clause." Not so here. Both Religion Clauses bar the government from interfering with the decision of a religious group to fire one of its ministers.

* * *

It was against this background that the First Amendment was adopted. Familiar with life under the established Church of England, the founding generation sought to foreclose the possibility of a national church. By forbidding the "establishment of religion" and guaranteeing the "free exercise thereof," the Religion Clauses ensured that the new Federal Government—unlike the English Crown—would have no role in filling ecclesiastical offices. The Establishment Clause prevents the Government from appointing ministers, and the Free Exercise Clause prevents it from interfering with the freedom of religious groups to select their own.

* * *

Until today, we have not had occasion to consider whether this freedom of a religious organization to select its ministers is implicated by a suit alleging discrimination in employment. The Courts of Appeals, in contrast, have had extensive experience with this issue. Since the passage of Title VII of the Civil Rights Act of 1964 and other employment discrimination laws, the Courts of Appeals have uniformly recognized the existence of a "ministerial exception," grounded in the First Amendment, that precludes application of such legislation to claims concerning the employment relationship between a religious institution and its ministers.

We agree that there is such a ministerial exception. The members of a religious group put their faith in the hands of their ministers. Requiring a church to accept or retain an unwanted minister, or punishing a church for failing to do so, intrudes upon more than a mere employment decision. Such action interferes with the internal governance of the church, depriving the church of control over the selection of those who will personify its beliefs. By imposing an unwanted minister, the state infringes the Free Exercise Clause, which protects a religious group's right to shape its own faith and mission through its appointments. According the state the power to determine which individuals will minister to the faithful also violates the Establishment Clause, which prohibits government involvement in such ecclesiastical decisions.

The EEOC and Perich acknowledge that employment discrimination laws would be unconstitutional as applied to religious groups in certain circumstances. They grant, for example, that it would violate the First Amendment for courts to apply such laws to compel the ordination of women by the Catholic Church or by an Orthodox Jewish seminary. According to the EEOC and Perich, religious organizations could successfully defend against employment discrimination claims in those circumstances by invoking the constitutional right to freedom of association—a right "implicit" in the First Amendment. The EEOC and Perich thus see no need—and no basis—for a special rule for ministers grounded in the Religion Clauses themselves.

We find this position untenable. The right to freedom of association is a right enjoyed by religious and secular groups alike. It follows under the EEOC's and Perich's view that the First Amendment analysis should be the same, whether the association in question is the Lutheran Church, a labor union, or a social club. That result is hard to square with the text of the First Amendment itself, which gives special solicitude to the rights of religious organizations. We cannot accept the remarkable view that the Religion Clauses have nothing to say about a religious organization's freedom to select its own ministers.

The EEOC and Perich also contend that our decision in Employment Div., Dept. of Human Resources of Ore. v. Smith, 494 U.S. 872 (1990), precludes recognition of a ministerial exception. In *Smith*, two members of the Native American Church were denied state unemployment benefits after it was determined that they had been fired from their jobs for ingesting peyote, a crime under Oregon law. We held that this did not violate the Free Exercise Clause, even though the peyote had been ingested for sacramental purposes, because the "right of free exercise does not relieve an individual of the obligation to comply with a valid and neutral law of general applicability on the ground that the law proscribes (or prescribes) conduct that his religion prescribes (or proscribes)."

It is true that the ADA's prohibition on retaliation, like Oregon's prohibition on peyote use, is a valid and neutral law of general applicability. But a church's selection of its ministers is unlike an individual's ingestion of peyote. Smith involved government regulation of only outward physical acts. The present case, in contrast, concerns government interference with an internal church decision that affects the faith and mission of the church itself. The contention that Smith forecloses recognition of a ministerial exception rooted in the Religion Clauses has no merit.

Having concluded that there is a ministerial exception grounded in the Religion Clauses of the First Amendment, we consider whether the exception applies in this case. We hold that it does.

Every Court of Appeals to have considered the question has concluded that the ministerial exception is not limited to the head of a religious congregation, and we agree. We are reluctant, however, to adopt a rigid formula for deciding when an employee qualifies as a minister. It is enough for us to conclude, in this our first case involving the ministerial exception, that the exception covers Perich, given all the circumstances of her employment.

To begin with, Hosanna-Tabor held Perich out as a minister, with a role distinct from that of most of its members. When Hosanna-Tabor extended her a call, it issued her a diploma of vocation according her the title "Minister of Religion, Commissioned." She was tasked with performing that office "according to the Word of God and the confessional standards of the Evangelical Lutheran Church as drawn from the Sacred Scriptures." The congregation prayed that God "bless [her] ministrations to the glory of His holy name, [and] the building of His church." In a supplement to the diploma, the congregation undertook to periodically review Perich's "skills of ministry" and "ministerial responsibilities," and to provide for her "continuing education as a professional person in the ministry of the Gospel."

* * *

Perich held herself out as a minister of the Church by accepting the formal call to religious service, according to its terms. She did so in other ways as well. For example, she claimed a special housing allowance on her taxes that was available only to employees earning their compensation " 'in the exercise of the ministry.' " In a form she submitted to the Synod following her termination, Perich again indicated that she regarded herself as a minister at Hosanna-Tabor, stating: "I feel that God is leading me to serve in the teaching ministry. . . . I am anxious to be in the teaching ministry again soon."

Perich's job duties reflected a role in conveying the Church's message and carrying out its mission. Hosanna-Tabor expressly charged her with "lead[ing] others toward Christian maturity" and "teach[ing] faithfully the Word of God, the Sacred Scriptures, in its truth and purity and as set forth in all the symbolical books of the Evangelical Lutheran Church." In fulfilling these responsibilities, Perich taught her students religion four days a week, and led them in prayer three times a day. Once a week, she took her students to a school-wide chapel service, and—about twice a year—she took her turn leading it, choosing the liturgy, selecting the hymns, and delivering a short message based on verses from the Bible. During her last year of teaching, Perich also led her fourth graders in a brief devotional exercise each morning. As a source of religious instruction, Perich performed an important role in transmitting the Lutheran faith to the next generation.

In light of these considerations—the formal title given Perich by the Church, the substance reflected in that title, her own use of that title, and the important religious functions she performed for the Church—we conclude that Perich was a minister covered by the ministerial exception.

* * *

Although the Sixth Circuit did not adopt the extreme position pressed here by the EEOC, it did regard the relative amount of time Perich spent performing religious functions as largely determinative. The issue before us, however, is not one that can be resolved by a stopwatch. The amount of time an employee spends on particular activities is relevant in assessing that employee's status, but that factor cannot be considered in isolation, without regard to the nature of the religious functions performed and the other considerations discussed above.

* * *

The EEOC and Perich foresee a parade of horribles that will follow our recognition of a ministerial exception to employment discrimination suits. According to the EEOC and Perich, such an exception could protect religious organizations from liability for retaliating against employees for reporting criminal misconduct or for testifying before a grand jury or in a criminal trial. What is more, the EEOC contends, the logic of the exception would confer on religious employers "unfettered discretion" to violate employment laws by, for example, hiring children or aliens not authorized to work in the United States.

Hosanna-Tabor responds that the ministerial exception would not in any way bar criminal prosecutions for interfering with law enforcement investigations or other proceedings. Nor, according to the Church, would the exception bar government enforcement of general laws restricting eligibility for employment, because the exception applies only to suits by or on behalf of ministers themselves. Hosanna-Tabor also notes that the ministerial exception has been around in the lower courts for 40 years.

The case before us is an employment discrimination suit brought on behalf of a minister, challenging her church's decision to fire her. Today we hold only that the ministerial exception bars such a suit. We express no view on whether the exception bars other types of suits, including actions by employees alleging breach of contract or tortious conduct by their religious employers. There will be time enough to address the applicability of the exception to other circumstances if and when they arise.

* * *

The interest of society in the enforcement of employment discrimination statutes is undoubtedly important. But so too is the interest of religious groups in choosing who will preach their beliefs, teach their faith, and carry out their mission. When a minister who has been fired sues her church alleging that her termination was discriminatory, the First Amendment has struck the balance for us. The church must be free to choose those who will guide it on its way.

The judgment of the Court of Appeals for the Sixth Circuit is reversed.

It is so ordered.

■ JUSTICE THOMAS, concurring.

I join the Court's opinion. I write separately to note that, in my view, the Religion Clauses require civil courts to apply the ministerial exception and to defer to a religious organization's good-faith understanding of who qualifies as its minister. As the Court explains, the Religion Clauses guarantee religious organizations autonomy in matters of internal governance, including the selection of those who will minister the faith. A religious organization's right to choose its ministers would be hollow, however, if secular courts could second-guess the organization's sincere determination that a given employee is a "minister" under the organization's theological tenets. Our country's religious landscape includes organizations with different leadership structures and doctrines that influence their conceptions of ministerial status. The question whether an employee is a minister is itself religious in nature, and the answer will vary widely. Judicial attempts to fashion a civil definition of "minister" through a bright-line test or multi-factor analysis risk disadvantaging those religious groups whose beliefs, practices, and membership are outside of the "mainstream" or unpalatable to some.

■ JUSTICE ALITO, with whom JUSTICE KAGAN joins, concurring.

I join the Court's opinion, but I write separately to clarify my understanding of the significance of formal ordination and designation as a "minister" in determining whether an "employee" of a religious group falls within the so-called "ministerial" exception. The term "minister" is commonly used by many Protestant denominations to refer to members of their clergy, but the term is rarely if ever used in this way by Catholics, Jews, Muslims, Hindus, or Buddhists. In addition, the concept of ordination as understood by most Christian churches and by Judaism has no clear counterpart in some Christian denominations and some other religions. Because virtually every religion in the world is represented in the population of the United States, it would be a mistake if the term "minister" or the concept of ordination were viewed as central to the important issue of religious autonomy that is presented in cases like this one. Instead, courts should focus on the function performed by persons who work for religious bodies.

NOTE

Relying on *Hosanna-Tabor*, the Fifth Circuit in Cannata v. Catholic Diocese of Austin, 700 F.3d 169 (5th Cir. 2012), held that the ministerial exception barred an ADEA claim by the church's music director because by playing the piano during services he "furthered the mission of the church and helped convey its message to the congregants." Id. at 177. The court emphasized that in determining when the ministerial exception applies "the *Hosanna-Tabor* Court engaged in a fact-intensive inquiry and explicitly rejected the adoption of a 'rigid formula' or bright-line test." Id. at 176. See also Fisher v. Archdiocese of Cincinnati, 6 N.E.3d 1254 (Ohio Ct. App., 2014) (relying on Hosanna-Tabor to conclude that employee at Catholic cemetery was a "ministerial" employee whose age discrimination claim was barred).

2. NATIONAL ORIGIN

Fragante v. City & County of Honolulu
888 F.2d 591 (9th Cir. 1989), cert. denied, 494 U.S. 1081 (1990).

■ TROTT, CIRCUIT JUDGE:

Manuel Fragante applied for a clerk's job with the City and County of Honolulu (Defendants). Although he placed high enough on a civil service eligible list to be chosen for the position, he was not selected because of a perceived deficiency in relevant oral communication skills caused by his "heavy Filipino accent." Fragante brought suit, alleging that the defendants discriminated against him on the basis of his national origin, in violation of Title VII of the Civil Rights Act. At the conclusion of a trial, the district court found that the oral ability to communicate effectively and clearly was a legitimate occupational qualification for the job in question. This finding was based on the court's understanding that an important aspect of defendant's business—for which a clerk would be responsible—involved the providing of services and assistance to the general public. The court also found that defendant's failure to hire Fragante was explained by his deficiencies in the area of oral communication, not because of his national origin. Finding no proof of a discriminatory intent or motive by the defendant the court dismissed Fragante's complaint, and he appeals. We have jurisdiction under 28 U.S.C. § 1291, and we affirm.

In April 1981, at the age of sixty, Fragante emigrated from the Philippines to Hawaii. In response to a newspaper ad, he applied in November of 1981 for the job at issue in this appeal—an entry level Civil Service Clerk SR-8 job for the City of Honolulu's Division of Motor Vehicles and Licensing. The SR-8 clerk position involved such tasks as filing, processing mail, cashiering, orally providing routine information to the "sometimes contentious" public over the telephone and at an information counter, and obtaining supplies. Fragante scored the highest of 721 test takers on the written SR-8 Civil Service Examination which tested, among other things, word usage, grammar and spelling. Accordingly, he was ranked first on a certified list of eligibles for two SR-8 clerk positions, an achievement of which he is understandably quite proud.

Fragante then was interviewed in the normal course of the selection process—as were other applicants—by George Kuwahara, the assistant licensing administrator, and Kalani McCandless, the division secretary. Both Kuwahara and McCandless were personally familiar with the demands of the position at issue, and both had extensive experience interviewing applicants to the division. During the interview, Kuwahara stressed that the position involved constant public contact and that the ability to speak clearly was one of the most important skills required for the position.

Both Kuwahara and McCandless had difficulty understanding Fragante due to his pronounced Filipino accent, and they determined on the basis of the oral interview that he would be difficult to understand both at the information counter and over the telephone. Accordingly, both interviewers gave Fragante a negative recommendation. They noted he had a very pronounced accent and was difficult to understand. It was their judgment that this would interfere with his performance of certain aspects of the job. As a consequence, Mr. Fragante dropped from number one to number three on the list of eligibles for the position.

Under the city's civil service rules, the Department of Motor Vehicles and Licensing, as the appointing authority, is allowed discretion in selecting applicants for the clerk vacancies. City Civil Service Rule 4.2(d) allows the defendants to select any of the top five eligibles without regard to their rank order. The essence of this rule was clearly stated in the employment announcement posted for the SR-8 position:

> The names of the "top five" qualified applicants with the highest examination grades will be referred to the employing agency in the order of their examination grade and availability for employment according to Civil Service Rules. The employing agency may select any one of the eligibles referred. Those not selected will remain on the list for at least one year for future referrals.

In accord with this process, the two other applicants who were judged more qualified than Fragante and who therefore placed higher than he on the final list got the two available jobs, and he was so notified by mail.

After exhausting administrative remedies, Fragante filed a claim under Title VII of the Civil Rights Act against the City and County of Honolulu, alleging he was discriminated against because of his accent. The district court relied on the results of the oral interview and found that Fragante's oral skills were "hampered by his accent or manner of speaking." The court found no evidence of unlawful discrimination in violation of Title VII, concluding that Fragante lacked the "bona fide occupational requirement" of being able to communicate effectively with the public, and dismissed his claim.

* * *

Title VII prohibits employment discrimination on the basis of race, color, sex, religion and national origin. 42 U.S.C. § 2000e–2(a)(1) (1982). A plaintiff may bring an action against an employer under a disparate treatment and/or disparate impact theory. Fragante's action was brought under the disparate treatment theory.

* * *

Defendants first argue Fragante failed to meet his burden of proving a prima facie case because he failed to show he was actually qualified for the SR-8 clerk position, a position which requires the applicant to be able to communicate clearly and effectively. Fragante, on the other hand, contends he was qualified for the position. As proof he points to his exceptional score on the objective written examination, and he argues that his speech, though heavily accented, was deemed comprehensible by two expert witnesses at trial. Fragante's position is supported by the approach taken by the Equal Employment Opportunity Commission which submits that a plaintiff who proves he has been discriminated against solely because of his accent does establish a prima facie case of national origin discrimination. This contention is further supported by EEOC guidelines which define discrimination to include "the denial of equal employment opportunity * * * because an individual has the * * * linguistic characteristics of a national origin group." 29 C.F.R. § 1606.1 (1988). Furthermore, Fragante was never advised that he was not qualified for the job; he was only told that he was less-qualified than his competition.

Because we find that Fragante did not carry the ultimate burden of proving national origin discrimination, however, the issue of whether Fragante established a prima facie case of discrimination is not significant, and we assume without deciding that he did.

Preliminarily, we do well to remember that this country was founded and has been built in large measure by people from other lands, many of whom came here—especially after our early beginnings—with a limited knowledge of English. This flow of immigrants has continued and has been encouraged over the years. From its inception, the United States of

America has been a dream to many around the world. We hold out promises of freedom, equality, and economic opportunity to many who only know these words as concepts. It would be more than ironic if we followed up our invitation to people such as Manuel Fragante with a closed economic door based on national origin discrimination. It is no surprise that Title VII speaks to this issue and clearly articulates the policy of our nation: unlawful discrimination based on national origin shall not be permitted to exist in the workplace. But, it is also true that there is another important aspect of Title VII: the "preservation of an employer's remaining freedom of choice."

* * *

We turn our discussion to whether defendants articulated a legitimate, nondiscriminatory reason for Fragante's nonselection. We find that they did, but to this finding we add a note of caution to the trial courts. Accent and national origin are obviously inextricably intertwined in many cases. It would therefore be an easy refuge in this context for an employer unlawfully discriminating against someone based on national origin to state falsely that it was not the person's national origin that caused the employment or promotion problem, but the candidate's inability to measure up to the communications skills demanded by the job. We encourage a very searching look by the district courts at such a claim.

An adverse employment decision may be predicated upon an individual's accent when—but only when—it interferes materially with job performance. There is nothing improper about an employer making an *honest* assessment of the oral communications skills of a candidate for a job when such skills are reasonably related to job performance.

The defendants advertised for applicants to fill SR-8 vacancies. The initial job announcement listed the ability to "deal tactfully and effectively with the public" as one of the areas to be tested. There is no doubt from the record that the oral ability to communicate effectively in English is reasonably related to the normal operation of the clerk's office. A clerk must be able to respond to the public's questions in a manner which the public can understand. In this regard, the district court in its Findings of Fact and Conclusions of Law and Order made the following significant observations:

> The job is a difficult one because it involves dealing with a great number of disgruntled members of the public. The clerk must deal with 200–300 people a day, many of whom are angry or complaining and who do not want to hear what the clerk may have to explain concerning their applications or an answer to their questions. It is a high turnover position where people leave quickly because of the high stress involving daily contact with contentious people.

What must next be determined is whether defendants established a factual basis for believing that Fragante would be hampered in performing this requirement. Defendants submit that because his accent made Fragante difficult to understand as determined by the interview, he would be less able to perform the job than other applicants. Fragante, on the other hand, contends he is able to communicate effectively in English as established by two expert witnesses at trial and by his responses in open court. In essence, he argues his non-selection was effectively based upon national origin discrimination.

After the interview, Kuwahara and McCandless scored Fragante on a rating sheet that was used for all applicants. Applicants were scored in the categories of appearance, speech, self-confidence, emotional control, alertness, initiative, personality, attitude, work experience, and overall fitness for the job. A scale of 1–10 was used. Kuwahara gave Fragante a score of 3 for speech, and noted: "very pronounced accent, difficult to understand." Although McCandless did not enter a score in the speech category, she noted: "Heavy Filipino accent. Would be difficult to understand over the telephone."

After the interviews were scored, Kuwahara and McCandless reviewed the scores, discussed the applicants, and decided on their hiring recommendation to finance director Peter Leong. In making the recommendation, written examination scores were given no consideration. Kuwahara prepared the written recommendation to Leong, dated April 13, 1982, recommending two others for selection. Fragante in his position as Number 3 on the final list was described as follows:

> 3. Manuel Fragante—Retired Phillippine (sic) army officer. Speaks with very pronounced accent which is difficult to understand. He has 37 years of experience in management administration and appears more qualified for professional rather than clerical work. However, because of his accent, I would not recommend him for this position.

McCandless then notified Fragante that he was not selected for either of the clerk position vacancies. Pursuant to a request from Fragante, Kuwahara then reduced the matter to writing. In a letter, dated June 28, 1982, the reasons why he was not selected were articulated as follows:

> As to the reason for your non-selection, we felt the two selected applicants were both superior in their verbal communication ability. As we indicated in your interview, our clerks are constantly dealing with the public and the ability to speak clearly is one of the most important skills required for the position. Therefore, while we were impressed with your educational and employment history, we felt the applicants selected would be better able to work in our office because of their communication skills.

Thus, the interviewers' record discloses Fragante's third place ranking was based on his "pronounced accent which is difficult to understand." Indeed, Fragante can point to no facts which indicate that his ranking was based on factors other than his inability to communicate effectively with the public. This view was shared by the district court.

Although the district court determined that the interview lacked some formality as to standards, instructions, guidelines, or criteria for its conduct and that the rating sheet was inadequate, the court also found that these "insufficiencies" were irrelevant with respect to plaintiff's complaint of unlawful discrimination. A review of the record reveals nothing that would impeach this assessment. Kuwahara and McCandless recorded their evaluation of Fragante's problem in separate written remarks on their rating sheets. As such, a legitimate factual basis for this conclusion that Fragante would be less able than his competition to perform the required duties was established.

Fragante argues the district court erred in considering "listener prejudice" as a legitimate, nondiscriminatory reason for failure to hire. We find, however, that the district court did not determine defendants refused to hire Fragante on the basis that some listeners would "turn off" a Filipino accent. The district court after trial noted that: "Fragante, in fact, has a difficult manner of pronunciation and the Court further finds as a fact from his general testimony that he would often not respond directly to the questions as propounded. He maintains much of his military bearing." We regard the last sentence of the court's comment to be little more than a stray remark of no moment.

We do not find the court's conclusion clearly erroneous. We find support for our view in Fernandez v. Wynn Oil, 653 F.2d 1273, 1275 (9th Cir. 1981), where this court held inability to communicate effectively to be one valid ground for finding a job applicant not qualified.

Having established that defendants articulated a legitimate reason for Fragante's non-selection, our next inquiry is whether the reason was a mere pretext for discrimination. Fragante essentially argues that defendant's selection and evaluation procedures were so deficient as to render the proffered reason for non-selection nothing more than a pretext for national origin discrimination. The problem with this argument, however, is that on examination it is only a charge without substance. The process may not have been perfect, but it reveals no discriminatory motive or intent. Search as we have, we have not been able to find even a hint of a mixed motive such as existed in *Price Waterhouse*. Instead, it appears that defendants were motivated exclusively by reasonable business necessity.

Fragante's counsel attempts to cast this case as one in which his client was denied a job simply because he had a difficult accent. This materially alters what actually happened. Fragante failed to get the job because two competitors had superior qualifications with respect to a relevant task performed by a government clerk. Insofar as this implicates "the interest of the State, as an employer, in promoting the efficiency of the public services it performs through its employees * * *," it is not something we are permitted to ignore. Title VII does not stand for the proposition that a person in a protected class—or a person with a foreign accent—shall enjoy a position of advantage thereby when competing for a job against others not similarly protected. And, the record does not show that the jobs went to persons less qualified than Fragante: to the contrary.

Under our holding in Ward v. Westland Plastics, Inc., 651 F.2d 1266, 1269 (9th Cir. 1980), "[a]n employer's decision may be justified by the hired employee's superior qualifications unless the purported justification is a pretext for invidious discrimination." In this case, there is simply no proof whatsoever of pretext, and we do not find the district court's finding of "no discrimination" to be clearly erroneous.

In sum, the record conclusively shows that Fragante was passed over because of the deleterious *effect* of his Filipino accent on his ability to communicate orally, not merely because he had such an accent.

The district court is

AFFIRMED.

NOTES AND QUESTIONS

1. According to the court, must the defendant prove that customers or the public would not want to listen to the plaintiff's accent or that they would not be able to understand it?

2. Should the same standard be applied to coworkers as is applied to customers or the public in determining whether they can understand the plaintiff? What steps did the court take to make sure that its holding is limited to the facts of this case?

3. Professor Mari Matsuda, who served as volunteer appellate counsel for Mr. Fragante, writes critically of the level of scrutiny given by the trial court to the employer's assertion that Fragante could not be understood.

> The evaluation of Fragante was shoddy. Given the care and effort put into the civil service examination process, the cursory interview by untrained office workers seems an irrational allocation of resources. The interviewers who found Fragante's accent "difficult" did not identify any incidences of misunderstanding during the interview. The lack of standard interview questions, the irrationality of the rating sheet, and the absence in the interview process of training or instruction in either speech assessment or the obligation of nondiscrimination, reveal a weak system of evaluation. This weakness is unjustified given the size and the resources of the employer, and the regular turnover in the job. Significantly, the evaluation process did not include a functional component. That is, Fragante's speech was never tested in a real or simulated job setting. There was no evidence other than

presumption that Fragante could not communicate with customers at the DMV.

> The evaluation process invited discretion and subjective judgment. As the sociolinguistic evidence would have predicted, a candidate with an accent identified as foreign and inferior is unlikely to survive such a subjective process. The interviewers concluded that a person with a heavy Filipino accent could not function in the job. The expert/linguist concluded the opposite. He testified that the unprejudiced listener would have no trouble understanding Fragante. There is significant evidence on the record that every listener in the courtroom could understand Mr. Fragante during direct and cross-examinations, which required speech more complex than that described by the employer as necessary for the job. A reviewing court could easily find, on this record, an absence of fair evaluation. At a minimum, a reviewing court should require that trial courts scrutinize the fairness of the evaluation process.

Professor Matsuda further raises the issue of the role of accent in the "culture of domination."

> Unmasking the false neutrality of accent discrimination raises a deeper set of questions: Why are employers so willing to discriminate on the basis of accent, and why are courts so willing to allow this? Why does accent discrimination seem like an employer's entitlement, such that employers willingly confess to intentional discrimination on the basis of accent? The answer may be that we are acculturated to domination.

Mari J. Matsuda, Voices of America: Accent, Antidiscrimination Law, and a Jurisprudence for the Last Reconstruction, 100 Yale L.J. 1329, 1384–85 (1991).

4. In Xieng v. Peoples Nat'l Bank, 844 P.2d 389 (Wash.1993), the Washington Supreme Court affirmed the holding that a Seattle bank committed national origin discrimination by refusing to promote an employee because of his Cambodian accent. The employee, a bank teller, successfully completed a management training program and also took additional English classes. He was told that he could not be promoted because he could not speak "American." The court rejected the bank's argument that it acted in good faith belief that the plaintiff's lack of communication skills would materially interfere with his job performance. The court stated that such a subjective standard "could easily become a refuge for unlawful national origin discrimination."

For an interesting article arguing that Title VII should be amended to prohibit discrimination based on "ethnicity" rather than "national origin," see Juan F. Perea, Ethnicity and Prejudice: Reevaluating "National Origin" Discrimination Under Title VII, 35 Wm. & Mary L.Rev. 805 (1994). For an alternative view see James Leonard, The Zero-Sum Game of Language Accommodations in the Workplace, 33 Cardozo L. Rev. 1 (2011).

5. The term "national origin" has been held to include the country of one's ancestors, even if that country no longer exists. See Pejic v. Hughes

Helicopters, 840 F.2d 667 (9th Cir. 1988) (employee of Serbian ancestry filed Title VII action after his discharge). At the time of the case, Serbia, had not existed as a separate political entity in more than 70 years. The court found that animosity based on national origin can outlast political boundaries and held that statutory protection is not limited to nations with modern boundaries or nations that have existed for a set period of time. See Janko v. Illinois State Toll Highway Auth., 704 F.Supp. 1531 (N.D.Ill.1989) ("Gypsy" is a national origin for Title VII purposes).

6.   *Fragante* held that if the ability to speak English is job related, the employer may require it of prospective employees. But may an employer forbid employees from speaking their native language on the job? In Garcia v. Spun Steak Co., 998 F.2d 1480 (9th Cir. 1993), the Ninth Circuit held that an English-only rule in the workplace did not impose significant adverse effects on the terms, conditions, or privileges of employment of employees. See Montes v. Vail Clinic, Inc., 497 F.3d 1160 (10th Cir. 2007) (upholding hospital's English-only rule which prohibited housekeepers from speaking Spanish for job-related discussions while working in operating room department). On the other hand, in Maldonado v. City of Altus, 433 F.3d 1294 (10th Cir. 2006), the Tenth Circuit reversed a grant of summary judgment to the defendant, noting that the English-only policy created a hostile atmosphere for Hispanics in the workplace and exposed them to taunting and harassment. EEOC guidance on English-only rules provides that if such a rule applies at all times it is presumptively a violation of Title VII, but a limited rule justified by business necessity will be upheld. 29 C.F.R. § 1606.7.

7.   EEOC's regulations on national origin indicate that Title VII protection extends to the following:

(1)   Marriage or association with a person of a specific national origin;

(2)   Membership in, or association with, an organization identified with or seeking to promote the interests of national groups;

(3)   Attendance at, or participation in, schools, churches, temples, or mosques generally used by persons of a national origin group;

(4)   Use of an individual's or spouse's name which is associated with a national origin group.

29 C.F.R. § 1606.1.

8.   In Cortezano v. Salin Bank & Trust Co., 680 F.3d 936 (7th Cir. 2012), the plaintiff alleged she was discharged because she was married to a Mexican citizen and therefore this was national origin discrimination in violation of Title VII. The court disagreed. "[A]ny discrimination . . . was not based on [her husband's] race or national origin, but rather his status as an alien who lacked permission to be in the country."

9.   Because they adversely affect Asians and Hispanics, height and weight requirements have been held to constitute disparate impact national origin discrimination. See Craig v. Los Angeles, 626 F.2d 659 (9th Cir. 1980), cert. denied, 450 U.S. 919 (1981).

10. Section 703(e) of Title VII provides that BFOQ is a defense to national origin discrimination. There are few cases. The legislative history suggests that BFOQ would permit a restaurant to advertise for or hire only a French or Italian chef. If so, this is a more expansive definition of BFOQ than has been used in religion and sex cases and one that may not be job related. Should a French restaurant be permitted to refuse to hire Emeril Lagasse because he is not French? Can you think of a more justifiable national origin BFOQ?

11. Title VII applies to the United States operations of foreign companies. If a foreign company discriminates against United States citizens (usually this has involved senior level positions), does this discrimination violate Title VII? See Chaiffetz v. Robertson Research Holding, Ltd., 798 F.2d 731 (5th Cir. 1986) (held: yes). See generally Note, Title VII, United States Citizenship, and American National Origin, 60 N.Y.U.L.Rev. 245 (1985). In EEOC v. Arabian Am. Oil Co., 499 U.S. 244 (1991), the Supreme Court held that Title VII does not apply extraterritorially to regulate employment practices of U.S. employers that employ U.S. citizens abroad. This decision was overturned by the Civil Rights Act of 1991. Both Title VII and the Americans with Disabilities Act now apply to American citizens working for American businesses abroad.

12. A number of states have enacted statutes that restrict access to certain jobs to citizens and, in some instances, lawfully admitted aliens who have applied for citizenship. See Chapter 3, p. 94 supra. In a series of cases, the Supreme Court has held that the U.S. Constitution prohibits many such laws. In Application of Griffiths, 413 U.S. 717 (1973), the Court invalidated a state statute that excluded aliens from eligibility for membership in the state bar. In Sugarman v. Dougall, 413 U.S. 634 (1973), the Court held that the fourteenth amendment prohibited barring aliens from a broad range of state jobs. A similar holding in Hampton v. Mow Sun Wong, 426 U.S. 88 (1976), based on the due process clause of the fifth amendment, invalidated across-the-board bans on hiring aliens for permanent positions in the civil service, while recognizing that there is a compelling governmental interest in barring aliens from some positions. In Foley v. Connelie, 435 U.S. 291 (1978), the Court held that a state could require citizenship for "important nonelective positions" held by "officers who participate directly in the formulation, execution, or review of broad public policy." Id. at 291 (quoting *Sugarman*). Subsequent cases have further defined the parameters of *Foley,* generally limiting the broad holdings of *Sugarman* and *Hampton.* In Ambach v. Norwick, 441 U.S. 68 (1979), the Court upheld a Connecticut statute prohibiting aliens from teaching in the public schools, although they could teach in private schools or be elected to the School Board. In Cabell v. Chavez-Salido, 454 U.S. 432 (1982), the Court upheld a California statute requiring probation officers and their deputies to be citizens, although an alien could be appointed as chief probation officer, could serve as attorney in a case before the probation board, or could serve as a state Superior Court judge or Supreme Court justice. In Bernal v. Fainter, 467 U.S. 216 (1984), the Court struck down a Texas statute which prohibited aliens from becoming notaries public.

A NOTE ON NATIONAL ORIGIN DISCRIMINATION UNDER IRCA

Section 102 of the Immigration Reform and Control Act, 8 U.S.C. § 1324b, makes it an "unfair immigration-related employment practice" to discriminate in hiring, recruitment, or discharge against a lawfully admitted alien because of the individual's national origin, or in the case of a citizen or "intending citizen," because of the individual's citizenship status. IRCA does not prohibit discrimination in wages, promotions, fringe benefits, or other terms and conditions of employment, although Title VII may afford additional protection to some individuals.

IRCA applies to all employers that employ four or more employees. 8 U.S.C. § 1324b(a)(2)(A). Thus, it provides additional and exclusive protection for applicants and employees of small employers not covered by Title VII. The EEOC, however, has exclusive jurisdiction of any case in which an individual alleges national origin discrimination and the employer is covered under Title VII. 8 U.S.C. § 1324b(a)(2)(B).

IRCA contains two exceptions to the nondiscrimination provision. It is not unlawful to prefer a U.S. citizen over an alien if the two individuals are equally qualified. 28 C.F.R. § 44.200(b)(2). Nevertheless, such a policy may constitute national origin discrimination under Title VII if the purpose or effect is discriminatory. In addition, an employer may hire only citizens or may otherwise discriminate in favor of citizens if required to do so by a law or governmental contract. 28 C.F.R. § 44.200(b)(1)(iii).

IRCA provides that "immigration-related unfair employment practices" are investigated by a "special counsel" in the Department of Justice. 28 C.F.R. § 0.53. There is a 180-day statute of limitations. 8 U.S.C. § 1324b(d)(3). If the special counsel fails to resolve the matter or bring a complaint within 120 days, the individual may file a complaint directly with an administrative law judge of the ICE. After a hearing, as provided for in the regulations, the ALJ is authorized to award, among other things, hiring, reinstatement, back pay for up to two years, and attorney fees. Civil penalties of $100 to $1,000 for each individual discriminated against (or $2,000 to $5,000 each for repeat offenders) also may be assessed. 8 U.S.C. § 1324b(g)(2)(B). Appeals from ALJ decisions go to the United States Court of Appeals for the circuit in which the violation occurred or in which the employer resides or transacts business.

3. AGE

Smith v. City of Jackson
544 U.S. 228 (2005).

■ JUSTICE STEVENS delivered the opinion of the Court.

Petitioners, police and public safety officers employed by the city of Jackson, Mississippi (hereinafter City), contend that salary increases received in 1999 violated the Age Discrimination in Employment Act of 1967 (ADEA) because they were less generous to officers over the age of 40 than to younger officers. Their suit raises the question whether the "disparate-impact" theory of recovery announced in Griggs v. Duke Power Co., 401 U.S. 424 (1971), for cases brought under Title VII of the Civil Rights Act of 1964, is cognizable under the ADEA. Despite the age of the ADEA, it is a question that we have not yet addressed.

I.

On October 1, 1998, the City adopted a pay plan granting raises to all City employees. The stated purpose of the plan was to "attract and retain qualified people, provide incentive for performance, maintain competitiveness with other public sector agencies and ensure equitable compensation to all employees regardless of age, sex, race and/or disability." On May 1, 1999, a revision of the plan, which was motivated, at least in part, by the City's desire to bring the starting salaries of police officers up to the regional average, granted raises to all police officers and police dispatchers. Those who had less than five years of tenure received proportionately greater raises when compared to their former pay than those with more seniority. Although some officers over the age of 40 had less than five years of service, most of the older officers had more.

Petitioners are a group of older officers who filed suit under the ADEA claiming both that the City deliberately discriminated against them because of their age (the "disparate-treatment" claim) and that they were "adversely affected" by the plan because of their age (the "disparate-impact" claim). The District Court granted summary judgment to the City on both claims. The Court of Appeals held that the ruling on the former claim was premature because petitioners were entitled to further discovery on the issue of intent, but it affirmed the dismissal of the disparate-impact claim. Over one judge's dissent, the majority concluded that disparate-impact claims are categorically unavailable under the ADEA. Both the majority and the dissent assumed that the facts alleged by petitioners would entitle them to relief under the reasoning of *Griggs*.

We granted the officers' petition for certiorari, and now hold that the ADEA does authorize recovery in "disparate-impact" cases comparable to *Griggs*. Because, however, we conclude that petitioners have not set forth a valid disparate-impact claim, we affirm.

II.

During the deliberations that preceded the enactment of the Civil Rights Act of 1964, Congress considered and rejected proposed amendments that would have included older workers among the classes protected from employment discrimination. Congress did, however, request the Secretary of Labor to "make a full and complete study of the factors which might tend to result in discrimination in employment because of age and of the consequences of such discrimination on the economy and individuals affected." The Secretary's report, submitted in response to Congress' request, noted that there was little discrimination arising from dislike or intolerance of older people, but that "arbitrary" discrimination did result from certain age limits. Moreover, the report observed that discriminatory effects resulted from "[i]nstitutional arrangements that indirectly restrict the employment of older workers."

In response to that report Congress directed the Secretary to propose remedial legislation, and then acted favorably on his proposal. As enacted in 1967, § 4(a)(2) of the ADEA, now codified as 29 U.S.C. § 623(a)(2), provided that it shall be unlawful for an employer "to limit, segregate, or classify his employees in any way which would deprive of tend to deprive any individual of employment opportunities or otherwise adversely affect his status as an employee, because of such individual's age. . . ." Except for substitution of the words "race, color, religion, sex, or national origin," the language of that provision in the ADEA is identical to that found in § 703(a)(2) of the Civil Rights Act of 1964 (Title VII). Other provisions of the ADEA also parallel the earlier statute. Unlike Title VII, however, § 4(f)(1) of the ADEA, contains language that significantly narrows its coverage by permitting any "otherwise prohibited" action "where the differentiation is based on reasonable factors other than age" (hereinafter RFOA provision).

III.

In determining whether the ADEA authorizes disparate-impact claims, we begin with the premise that when Congress uses the same language in two statutes having similar purpose, particularly when one is enacted shortly after the other, it is appropriate to presume that Congress intended that text to have the same meaning in both statutes. We have consistently applied that presumption to language in the ADEA that was "derived in haec verba from Title VII." Our unanimous interpretation of § 703(a)(2) of Title VII in *Griggs* is therefore a precedent of compelling importance.

* * *

While our opinion in *Griggs* relied primarily on the purpose of the Act, buttressed by the fact that the EEOC had endorsed the same view, we have subsequently noted that our holding represented the better reading of the statutory text as well. Neither § 703(a)(2) nor the comparable language in the ADEA simply prohibits actions that "limit, segregate, or classify" persons; rather the language prohibits such actions that "deprive any individual of employment opportunities or otherwise adversely affect his status as an employee, because of such individual's" race of age. Thus the text focuses on the effects of the action on the employee rather than the motivation for the action of the employer.

Griggs, which interpreted the identical text at issue here, thus strongly suggests that a disparate-impact theory should be cognizable under the ADEA. Indeed, for over two decades after our decision in *Griggs*, the Courts of Appeal uniformly interpreted the ADEA as authorizing recovery on a "disparate-impact" theory in appropriate cases. It was only after our decision in Hazen Paper Co. v. Biggins, 507 U.S. 604

(1993), that some of those courts concluded that the ADEA did not authorize a disparate-impact theory of liability. Our opinion in *Hazen Paper*, however, did not address or comment on the issue we decide today. In that case, we held that an employee's allegation that he was discharged shortly before his pension would have vested did not state a cause of action under a disparate-treatment theory. The motivating factor was not, we held, the employee's age, but rather his years of service, a factor that the ADEA did not prohibit an employer from considering when terminating an employee. While we noted that disparate-treatment "captures the essence of what Congress sought to prohibit in the ADEA," we were careful to explain that we were not deciding "whether a disparate impact theory of liability is available under the ADEA. . . ." In sum, there is nothing in our opinion in *Hazen Paper* that precludes an interpretation of the ADEA that parallels our holding in *Griggs*.

Two textual differences between the ADEA and Title VII make it clear that even though both statutes authorize recovery on a disparate-impact theory, the scope of disparate-impact liability under ADEA is narrower than under Title VII. The first is the RFOA provision, which we have already identified. The second is the amendment to Title VII contained in the Civil Rights Act of 1991. One of the purposes of that amendment was to modify the Court's holding in Wards Cove Packing Co. v. Atonio, 490 U.S. 642 (1989), a case in which we narrowly construed the employer's exposure to liability on a disparate-impact theory. While the relevant 1991 amendments expanded the coverage of Title VII, they did not amend the ADEA or speak to the subject of age discrimination. Hence *Wards Cove's,* pre-1991 interpretation of Title VII's identical language remains applicable to the ADEA. Congress' decision to limit the coverage of the ADEA by including the RFOA provision is consistent with the fact that age, unlike race or other classifications protected by Title VII, not uncommonly has relevance to an individual's capacity to engage in certain types of employment. To be sure, Congress recognized that this is not always the case, and that society may perceive those differences to be larger or more consequential that they are in fact. However, as Secretary Wirtz noted in his report, "certain circumstances . . . unquestionably affect older workers more strongly, as a group, than they do younger workers." Thus, it is not surprising that certain employment criteria that are routinely used may be reasonable despite their adverse impact on older workers as a group. Moreover, intentional discrimination on the basis of age has not occurred at the same levels as discrimination against those protected by Title VII. While the ADEA reflects Congress' intent to give older workers employment opportunities whenever possible, the RFOA provision a reflects this historical difference.

Turning to the case before us, we initially note that petitioners have done little more than point out that the pay plan at issue is relatively less generous to older workers than to younger workers. They have not identified any specific test, requirement, or practice within the pay plan that has an adverse impact on older workers. As we held in *Wards Cove*, it is not enough to simply allege that there is a disparate impact on workers, or point to a generalized policy that leads to such an impact. Rather, the employee is " 'responsible for isolating and identifying the specific employment practices that are allegedly responsible for any observed statistical disparities.' " Their failure to identify the specific practice being challenged is the sort of omission that could "result in employers being potentially liable for 'the myriad of innocent causes that may lead to statistical imbalances. . . .' " In this case not only did petitioners thus err by failing to identify the relevant practice, but it is also clear from the record that the City's plan was based on reasonable factors other than age.

* * *

Thus, the disparate impact is attributable to the City's decision to give raises based on seniority and position. Reliance on seniority and rank is unquestionably reasonable given the City's goal of raising employees' salaries to match those in surrounding communities. In sum, we hold that the City's decision to grant a larger raise to lower echelon employees for the purpose of bringing salaries in line with that of surrounding police forces was a decision based on a "reasonable factor other than age" that responded to the City's legitimate goal of retaining police officers.

Accordingly, while we do not agree with the Court of Appeals' holding that the disparate-impact theory of recovery is never available under the ADEA, we affirm its judgement.

It is so ordered.

NOTES AND QUESTIONS

1.   After *Wards Cove*, plaintiffs' lawyers lamented that the decision was tantamount to overruling *Griggs* by making disparate impact cases under Title VII virtually impossible to win. In the context of the ADEA, have potential disparate impact plaintiffs "won the battle and lost the war"?

2.   The Age Discrimination in Employment Act (ADEA), 29 U.S.C. §§ 621–634, originally enacted in 1967, prohibits age discrimination in the employment, discharge, promotion, or treatment of persons over the age of 40. (As originally enacted, persons were protected between age 40 and 65.) A 1986 amendment to the Act prohibits all mandatory retirement. However, an exception exists that allows state and local governments to set mandatory retirement ages for firefighters and law enforcement officers. See Sadi v. City of Cleveland, 718 F.3d 596 (6th Cir. 2013) (finding no ADEA violation when police officers were forced to retire pursuant to mandatory retirement law). Retirement is considered in Chapter 13.

3.   In General Dynamics Land Systems, Inc. v. Cline, 540 U.S. 581 (2004), the company eliminated health care benefits for retirees below the age of 50.

Affected employees ages 40–49 claimed this was overt age discrimination and brought suit under the ADEA. The Supreme Court held that the ADEA does not prohibit an employer from favoring an older employee over a younger one.

4.   The ADEA applies to every employer engaged in an enterprise affecting commerce that has 20 or more employees for each working day in each of 20 or more calendar weeks in the current or preceding calendar year. The ADEA also applies to employment agencies, unions, state and local political subdivisions, and the federal government. There is disagreement, however, about whether the ADEA's requirement that employers have 20 or more employees also applies to state and local employers. In Guido v. Mount Lemmon Fire District, 859 F.3d 1168 (9th Cir. 2017), the Ninth Circuit held that there is no small employer exception for state and local employers and hence that the ADEA applies to all such employers regardless of size. The Sixth, Seventh, Eighth and Tenth Circuits have disagreed. The Supreme Court has recently granted cert. in Mount Lemmon Fire District v. Guido, 138 S.Ct. 1165 (2018).

5.   Although the ADEA was passed as an amendment to the Fair Labor Standards Act, with enforcement vested in the Department of Labor, since 1978 responsibility for enforcing the ADEA has been assigned to the EEOC. Private actions also may be brought by aggrieved individuals. In addition to the ADEA, most states have laws prohibiting age discrimination in employment. Procedures under the ADEA are similar to those under Title VII, except that there is a right to a jury trial under the ADEA. There is also a wide range of relief available, including reinstatement, injunctive and declaratory relief, and attorney fees. Liquidated damages in the amount of backpay are available in cases in which an employer's violation of the Act is "willful." 29 U.S.C. § 626(b). See Miller v. Raytheon Co., 716 F.3d 145 (5th Cir. 2013) ("A violation of the ADEA is willful, and liquidated damages may be awarded, when an employer must have 'kn[own] or show[n] reckless disregard for the matter of whether its conduct was prohibited by the ADEA.' ").

6.   In Kimel v. Florida Bd. of Regents, 528 U.S. 62 (2000), the plaintiffs sued their state employers seeking money damages for alleged age discrimination. The Supreme Court, five-to-four, held that Congress exceeded its authority under section five of the Fourteenth Amendment by abrogating the states' immunity. Because age is not a suspect classification under the equal protection clause, and there was no evidence that the states were unconstitutionally discriminating against their employees on the basis of age, applying the ADEA to the states is "so out of proportion to a supposed remedial or preventive object that it cannot be understood as responsive to, or designed to prevent, unconstitutional behavior." Id. at 64. The ADEA may not, however, be the exclusive remedy for workers alleging age discrimination. In Levin v. Madigan, 692 F.3d 607 (7th Cir. 2012), the Seventh Circuit permitted a state employee to bring an equal protection claim for age discrimination under 42 U.S.C. § 1983. While several district courts have ruled similarly, the other circuit courts to consider the issue have held that the ADEA is the exclusive remedy for age discrimination claims.

Compare Shapiro v. N.T. City Dep't of Educ., 561 F.Supp.2d 413 (S.D.N.Y. 2008) (ADEA does not preclude a § 1983 claim) and Mustafa v. State of Neb. Dep't of Corr. Servs., 196 F.Supp.2d 945 (D. Neb. 2002) (same) with Hildebrand v. Allegheny Cnty., 757 F.3d 99 (3d Cir. 2014) (holding that a state or local government employee may not maintain an age discrimination claim under § 1983, but must instead proceed under the ADEA); Zombro v. Baltimore City Police Dep't, 868 F.2d 1364 (4th Cir. 1989) (same); Ahlmeyer v. Nev. Sys. of Higher Ed., 555 F.3d 1051 (9th Cir. 2009) (same); Tapia-Tapia v. Potter, 322 F.3d 742 (1st Cir. 2003) (same); Lafleur v. Tex. Dep't of Health, 126 F.3d 758 (5th Cir. 1997) (same); Chennareddy v. Bowsher, 935 F.2d 315 (D.C. Cir. 191) (same). The Supreme Court accepted cert in Madigan v. Levin for the 2013 term, but then dismissed it as improvidently granted, 571 U.S. 1 (2013).

7.   Generally speaking, the courts have applied the *McDonnell Douglas* test to disparate treatment age discrimination cases. See, e.g., Sutton v. Atlantic Richfield Co., 646 F.2d 407 (9th Cir. 1981). The burden then shifts to the defendant to prove a lawful, nondiscriminatory reason for the plaintiff's adverse treatment.

Section 4(f) of the ADEA sets forth five affirmative defenses:

It shall not be unlawful for an employer, employment agency or labor organization—

(1)   to take any action otherwise prohibited * * * where age is a bona fide occupational qualification reasonably necessary to the normal operation of the particular business. * * *

(2)   to take any action otherwise prohibited * * * where the different action is based on reasonable factors other than age. * * *

(3)   to observe the terms of a bona fide seniority system. * * *

(4)   to observe the terms of * * * any bona fide employee benefit plan. * * *

(5)   to discharge or otherwise discipline an individual for good cause.

With regard to BFOQ, EEOC has issued the following interpretive regulation, 29 C.F.R. § 1625.6(b):

An employer asserting a BFOQ defense has the burden of proving that

(1)   the age limit is reasonably necessary to the essence of the business, and either

(2)   that all or substantially all individuals excluded from the job involved are in fact disqualified or

(3)   that some of the individuals so excluded possess a disqualifying trait that cannot be ascertained except by reference to age.

If the employer's objective in asserting a BFOQ is the goal of public safety, the employer must prove that the challenged practice does indeed effectuate that goal and that there is no acceptable alternative which would better advance it with less discriminatory impact.

8. Only a few of the circuits have explicitly ruled on whether a claim for hostile work environment is cognizable under the ADEA. In Dediol v. Best Chevrolet, Inc., 655 F.3d 435 (5th Cir. 2011), the Fifth Circuit recognized such an action. Adopting the reasoning of the Sixth Circuit in Crawford v. Medina Gen. Hosp., 96 F.3d 830 (6th Cir. 1996), the Fifth Circuit said that an employee-plaintiff must prove that (1) the employee is 40 or older; (2) the employee was subjected to harassment based on age, either through words or actions; (3) the harassment created an objectively intimidating, hostile, or offensive work environment; and (4) there exists some basis for liability on the part of the employer.

9. In Gross v. FBL Fin. Servs., 557 U.S. 157 (2009), the Supreme Court, 5–4, held that the mixed motive analysis of Price Waterhouse v. Hopkins (p. 227), as amended by the Civil Rights Act of 1991 (p. 238), does not apply to age discrimination cases. For ADEA cases, the plaintiff must prove that age discrimination was a "but-for" cause of the adverse employment action and not merely a "motivating factor" as is the law for Title VII cases. According to Justice Thomas, the fact that Congress did not include the ADEA when it clarified the burden of proving mixed motive cases in the 1991 Civil Rights Act is dispositive. In the absence of congressional action, "the burden of persuasion necessary to establish employer liability is the same in alleged mixed-motive cases as in any other ADEA disparate-treatment action." In dissent, Justice Stevens noted that the majority in *Price Waterhouse* rejected the "but-for" approach even before Congress expressly repudiated it in the Civil Rights Act of 1991. "*Price Waterhouse* repudiated that standard 20 years ago, and Congress' response to our decision further militates against the crabbed interpretation the Court adopts today." In a separate dissent, Justice Breyer argued that the "but-for" test is appropriate for the physical causation issues in torts, but it is inappropriate for the "mind-related characterizations that constitute motive."

10. In Karlo v. Pittsburgh Glass Works, 849 F.3d 61 (3d Cir. 2017), the Third Circuit held that plaintiffs could show a disparate impact under the ADEA based on subgroup comparisons and were not limited to comparisons simply between employees age 40 and above and those under 40. Which party should bear the burden of persuasion in establishing "reasonable factors other than age" in a disparate impact claim under the ADEA? In Meacham v. Knolls Atomic Power Lab., 554 U.S. 84 (2008), the Court held that an employer defending a disparate impact claim under the ADEA bears both the burden of production and the burden of persuasion for the RFOA defense. The Court held that the business necessity defense is inapplicable under the ADEA.

11. Is salary a "reasonable factor other than age"? May an employer replace older, more expensive employees with younger, less expensive employees? Is it permissible for an employer to reduce the benefits of workers when doing so has a disparate impact on older workers who are eligible for more benefits? In Finnegan v. TWA, 967 F.2d 1161 (7th Cir. 1992), the airline made cuts in wages and benefits to avoid bankruptcy. One cut put a cap on vacations, allowing a maximum of four weeks vacation. Previously, workers with more than 16 years of service were entitled to longer vacations, such that a 30-year employee was entitled to seven weeks. The court held that the change in benefits did not violate the ADEA, even though it adversely affected older workers. "Practices so tenuously related to discrimination, so remote from the objectives of the civil rights law, do not reach the prima facie threshold." Id. at 1165. However, in Tramp v. Associated Underwriters, 768 F3d 793 (8th Cir. 2014), a disparate treatment case, the Eighth Circuit held that an employer's consideration of health care costs in making decisions about which employees to terminate could constitute age discrimination if the employer "supposes a correlation" between costs and age "and acts accordingly." Id. at 802.

12. In 2016, the Eleventh Circuit vacated its prior decision in Villarreal v. R.J. Reynolds Tobacco Co, 806 F.3d 1288 (11th Cir. 2015), in which a panel of the Eleventh Circuit held that job seekers—not just employees—may bring disparate impact claims under the ADEA. Rehearing the case en banc, the Eleventh Circuit held that the text of the ADEA "makes clear that an applicant for employment cannot sue an employer for disparate impact because the applicant has no 'status as an employee.' " 839 F.3d 958 (11th Cir. 2016) (en banc). Recently, the Seventh Circuit reached the opposite conclusion in Kleber v. CareFusion Corp., 888 F.3d 868 (7th Cir. 2018), in which it held that job applicants are protected under the ADEA.

13. A 61-year-old insurance manager was denied a promotion based on, among other things, an "unimpressive" interview. The poor interview was attributed to the employee's asserted lack of aggressiveness in answering some questions. Because there is a stereotype that older people are not as aggressive as younger people, does the employer's reliance on aggressiveness help support the plaintiff's case of age discrimination under the ADEA? See Chapman v. AI Transp., 229 F.3d 1012 (11th Cir. 2000) (held: no). "In the rough and tumble, highly competitive business world, aggressiveness can be a valuable and much sought after trait. Just because a sought after trait is linked by stereotype to an impermissible consideration does not mean an employer cannot search for and consider the trait itself independently from the stereotype. . . . In this case, the decisionmakers considered Chapman's lack of aggressiveness because he was not aggressive in the interview, not because of his age." What is the employer's burden of proof? Is it (1) that the preference for aggressiveness was applied in a nondiscriminatory manner, (2) that aggressiveness is an essential component of the job, or (3) that aggressiveness at an interview is predictive of aggressiveness on the job?

14. In O'Connor v. Consolidated Coin Caterers Corp., 517 U.S. 308 (1996), a 56-year-old employee was fired and replaced by a 40-year-old. The Fourth Circuit held that there was no violation of the ADEA because the employee was replaced by another individual in the protected class. The Supreme Court unanimously reversed. According to Justice Scalia:

> [The ADEA] does not ban discrimination against employees because they are aged 40 or older; it bans discrimination against employees because of their age, but limits the protected class to

those who are 40 or older. * * * [T]he fact that a replacement is substantially younger than the plaintiff is a far more reliable indicator of age discrimination than is the fact that the plaintiff was replaced by someone outside the protected class.

Id. at 1312. How should the lower courts determine when the replacement is "substantially younger"? Is this a question of fact or a question of law? According to the Supreme Judicial Court of Massachusetts, a prima facie case of age discrimination under state law requires an age disparity of at least five years between the favored and disfavored individual. Knight v. Avon Prods., 780 N.E.2d 1255 (Mass.2003). Is this a better solution?

15. In Sprint/United Mgmt. Co. v. Mendelsohn, 552 U.S. 379 (2008), the plaintiff sought to support his age discrimination claim by introducing "me, too" evidence testimony by his co-workers that they were also discriminated against on the basis of age by other supervisors. The Supreme Court held that "me, too" evidence is not subject to a per se rule of admissibility under the ADEA. The district court must consider many factors in determining relevance and balancing the probative value against the possible prejudicial effect of the evidence.

16. Employers refusing to hire older workers because of concerns for public safety have more often found the courts to be sympathetic. For example, in Usery v. Tamiami Trail Tours, Inc., 531 F.2d 224 (5th Cir.1976), the employer refused to consider applications from individuals over age 40 to be intercity bus drivers. In sustaining the employer's BFOQ defense the court stated: "[S]afety to fellow employees is of such humane importance that the employer must be afforded substantial discretion in selecting specific standards which, if they err at all, should err on the [side of] preservation of life and limb." Id. at 238. In Enlow v. Salem-Keizer Yellow Cab Co., 389 F.3d 802 (9th Cir. 2004), cert. denied, 544 U.S. 974 (2005), however, the Ninth Circuit held that the temporary or permanent discharge of a 73-year-old taxi driver because the company's insurance did not cover drivers over 70 was direct evidence of age discrimination.

17. The Glee Club is a large, way-out hipster bar. Its customers are almost exclusively 21–25 year hipsters, many of whom have taken to outlandish dress and grooming styles. The bar has several openings for bartenders, food servers, receptionists, and other positions. Several of the applicants are over 40 years of age. Although these people are qualified, the bar does not want to hire them because it will destroy the image the bar is trying to project. Can the bar restrict its hiring to people under the age of 25? In a recently filed case, Communication Workers of America v. T-Mobile U.S. (N.D. Cal. 2017) (No. 5:17-cv-07232), the plaintiffs argue that the defendants, which includes hundreds of major American employers and employment agencies, violated the ADEA by excluding older workers from receiving their employment and recruiting ads on Facebook.

18. Between 1946 and 1964, 78.2 million "Baby Boomers" were born in the United States. In 2011, the first of this cohort reached age 65, the traditional retirement age. Because of the recession, many of these people will postpone retirement and remain in the job market, protected from age discrimination by the ADEA. What effect will their continued presence in the labor force have on the employment opportunities of younger workers and the economy in general? For a further discussion of age discrimination issues in retirement, see Ch. 13 infra.

4. DISABILITY

The first major law prohibiting discrimination in employment on the basis of disability (originally "handicap") was the Rehabilitation Act of 1973, 29 U.S.C. §§ 701–796. It prohibits discrimination by federal government agencies (§ 501), federal contractors (§ 503), and recipients of federal financial assistance (§ 504). The Rehabilitation Act served as the basis for state anti-discrimination laws, and virtually every state has enacted a law prohibiting disability-based discrimination in employment. The Rehabilitation Act also served as the model for the Americans with Disabilities Act of 1990, 42 U.S.C. §§ 12101–12213 (ADA), the nation's first comprehensive law prohibiting disability-based discrimination in employment, public services, public accommodations, and telecommunications.

Title I of the ADA, dealing with employment, applies to employers with 15 or more employees, the same coverage as Title VII of the Civil Rights Act of 1964. It also has the same procedures and remedies as Title VII. Section 102(a) of the ADA contains the general prohibition on employment discrimination. "No covered entity shall discriminate against a qualified individual with a disability on the basis of the disability of such individual in regard to job application procedures, the hiring, advancement, or discharge of employees, employee compensation, job training, and other terms, conditions, and privileges of employment." The definition of disability in § 3(2) relies on the Rehabilitation Act and its three-part definition of a disability as a physical or mental impairment that substantially limits one or more of the major life activities of the individual, a record of such an impairment, or being regarded as having such an impairment.

Sutton v. United Air Lines, Inc.

527 U.S. 471 (1999).

■ JUSTICE O'CONNOR delivered the opinion of the Court.

Petitioners are twin sisters, both of whom have severe myopia. Each petitioner's uncorrected visual acuity is 20/200 or worse in her right eye and 20/400 or worse in her left eye, but "[w]ith the use of corrective lenses, each . . . has vision that is 20/20 or better." Consequently, without corrective lenses, each "effectively cannot see to conduct numerous activities such as driving a vehicle, watching television or shopping in public stores," but with corrective measures, such as glasses or contact lenses, both "function identically to individuals without a similar impairment."

In 1992, petitioners applied to respondent for employment as commercial airline pilots. They met respondent's basic age, education, experience, and FAA certification qualifications. After submitting their applications for employment, both petitioners were invited by respondent to an interview and to flight simulator tests. Both were told during their interviews, however, that a mistake had been made in inviting them to interview because petitioners did not meet respondent's minimum vision requirement, which was uncorrected visual acuity of 20/100 or better. Due to their failure to meet this requirement, petitioners' interviews were terminated, and neither was offered a pilot position.

In light of respondent's proffered reason for rejecting them, petitioners filed a charge of disability discrimination under the ADA with the Equal Employment Opportunity Commission (EEOC).

* * *

The ADA prohibits discrimination by covered entities, including private employers, against qualified individuals with a disability. Specifically, it provides that no covered employer "shall discriminate against a qualified individual with a disability because of the disability of such individual in regard to job application procedures, the hiring, advancement, or discharge of employees, employee compensation, job training, and other terms, conditions, and privileges of employment." A "qualified individual with a disability" is identified as "an individual with a disability who, with or without reasonable accommodation, can perform the essential functions of the employment position that such individual holds or desires." § 12111(8). In turn, a "disability" is defined as:

"(A) a physical or mental impairment that substantially limits one or more of the major life activities of such individual;

"(B) a record of such an impairment; or

"(C) being regarded as having such an impairment." § 12102(2).

Accordingly, to fall within this definition one must have an actual disability (subsection (A)), have a record of a disability (subsection (B)), or be regarded as having one (subsection (C)).

* * *

With this statutory and regulatory framework in mind, we turn first to the question whether petitioners have stated a claim under subsection (A) of the disability definition, that is, whether they have alleged that they possess a physical impairment that substantially limits them in one or more major life activities. Because petitioners allege that with corrective measures their vision "is 20/20 or better," they are not actually disabled within the meaning of the Act if the "disability" determination is made with reference to these measures. Consequently, with respect to subsection (A) of the disability definition, our decision turns on whether disability is to be determined with or without reference to corrective measures.

Petitioners maintain that whether an impairment is substantially limiting should be determined without regard to corrective measures. They argue that, because the ADA does not directly address the question at hand, the Court should defer to the agency interpretations of the statute, which are embodied in the agency guidelines issued by the EEOC and the Department of Justice. These guidelines specifically direct that the determination of whether an individual is substantially limited in a major life activity be made without regard to mitigating measures.

Respondent, in turn, maintains that an impairment does not substantially limit a major life activity if it is corrected. It argues that the Court should not defer to the agency guidelines cited by petitioners because the guidelines conflict with the plain meaning of the ADA. The phrase "substantially limits one or more major life activities," it explains, requires that the substantial limitations actually and presently exist. Moreover, respondent argues, disregarding mitigating measures taken by an individual defies the statutory command to examine the effect of the impairment on the major life activities "of such individual." And even if the statute is ambiguous, respondent claims, the guidelines' directive to ignore mitigating measures is not reasonable, and thus this Court should not defer to it.

We conclude that respondent is correct that the approach adopted by the agency guidelines—that persons are to be evaluated in their hypothetical uncorrected state—is an impermissible interpretation of the ADA. Looking at the Act as a whole, it is apparent that if a person is taking measures to correct for, or mitigate, a physical or mental impairment, the effects of those measures—both positive and negative—must be taken into account when judging whether that person is "substantially limited" in a major life activity and thus "disabled" under the Act. The dissent relies on the legislative history of the ADA for the contrary proposition that individuals should be examined in their uncorrected state. Because we decide that, by its terms, the ADA cannot be read in this manner, we have no reason to consider the ADA's legislative history.

* * *

The agency guidelines' directive that persons be judged in their uncorrected or unmitigated state runs directly counter to the individualized inquiry mandated by the ADA. The agency approach would often require courts and employers to speculate about a person's condition and would, in many cases, force them to make a disability determination based on general information about how an uncorrected impairment usually affects individuals, rather than on the individual's actual condition. For instance, under this view, courts would almost certainly find all diabetics to be disabled, because if they failed to monitor their blood sugar levels and administer insulin, they would almost certainly be substantially limited in one or more major life activities. A diabetic whose illness does not impair his or her daily activities would therefore be considered disabled simply because he or she has diabetes. Thus, the guidelines approach would create a system in which persons often must be treated as members of a group of people with similar impairments, rather than as individuals. This is contrary to both the letter and the spirit of the ADA.

The guidelines approach could also lead to the anomalous result that in determining whether an individual is disabled, courts and employers could not consider any negative side effects suffered by an individual resulting from the use of mitigating measures, even when those side effects are very severe. This result is also inconsistent with the individualized approach of the ADA.

Finally, and critically, findings enacted as part of the ADA require the conclusion that Congress did not intend to bring under the statute's protection all those whose uncorrected conditions amount to disabilities. Congress found that "some 43,000,000 Americans have one or more physical or mental disabilities, and this number is increasing as the population as a whole is growing older." § 12101(a)(1). This figure is inconsistent with the definition of disability pressed by petitioners.

* * *

Because it is included in the ADA's text, the finding that 43 million individuals are disabled gives content to the ADA's terms, specifically the term "disability." Had Congress intended to include all persons with corrected physical limitations among those covered by the Act, it undoubtedly would have cited a much higher number of disabled persons in the findings. That it did not is evidence that the ADA's coverage is restricted to only those whose impairments are not mitigated by corrective measures.

The dissents suggest that viewing individuals in their corrected state will exclude from the definition of "disab[led]" those who use prosthetic limbs, or take medicine for epilepsy or high blood pressure. This suggestion is incorrect. The use of a corrective device does not, by itself, relieve one's disability. Rather, one has a disability under subsection A if, notwithstanding the use of a corrective device, that individual is substantially limited in a major life activity. For example, individuals who use prosthetic limbs or wheelchairs may be mobile and capable of functioning in society but still be disabled because of a substantial limitation on their ability to walk or run. The same may be true of individuals who take medicine to lessen the symptoms of an impairment so that they can function but nevertheless remain substantially limited. Alternatively, one whose high blood pressure is "cured" by medication may be regarded as disabled by a covered entity, and thus disabled under subsection C of the definition. The use or nonuse of a corrective device does not determine whether an individual is disabled; that determination depends on whether the limitations an individual with an impairment actually faces are in fact substantially limiting.

Applying this reading of the Act to the case at hand, we conclude that the Court of Appeals correctly resolved the issue of disability in respondent's favor. As noted above, petitioners allege that with corrective measures, their visual acuity is 20/20, and that they "function identically to individuals without a similar impairment." In addition, petitioners concede that they "do not argue that the use of corrective lenses in itself demonstrates a substantially limiting impairment." Accordingly, because we decide that disability under the Act is to be determined with reference to corrective measures, we agree with the courts below that petitioners have not stated a claim that they are substantially limited in any major life activity.

* * *

For these reasons, the decision of the Court of Appeals for the Tenth Circuit is affirmed.

It is so ordered.

■ JUSTICE GINSBURG, concurring.

* * *

■ JUSTICE STEVENS, with whom JUSTICE BREYER joins, dissenting.

* * *

■ JUSTICE BREYER, dissenting.

* * *

Beyond *Sutton*

There were two companion cases decided the same day as *Sutton*. In Murphy v. UPS, Inc., 527 U.S. 516 (1999), the Court held that a truck mechanic with high blood pressure should be considered, for ADA purposes, in his medicated state. In Albertson's, Inc. v. Kirkingburg, 527 U.S. 555 (1999), the Court held that an employer did not violate the ADA when it refused to hire a truck driver with monocular vision, even though DOT's experimental waiver program would have permitted the hiring.

The facts in *Sutton*, commercial airline pilot candidates with uncorrected vision far less than 20/20, might suggest that deference should be given to the airline's determination of the need for visual acuity. Yet, in deciding the case on the question of coverage under the statute rather than as an employer's defense ("direct threat," discussed at p. 452 infra), the effect of *Sutton* was devastating to ADA plaintiffs, especially those with medical impairments (as opposed to, for example, mobility impairments). If medications or medical devices controlled their condition, then they were not covered by the ADA; if the measures failed to control their condition, then they were often held not to be qualified for the position. See, e.g., Orr v. Wal-Mart Stores, Inc., 297 F.3d 720 (8th Cir. 2002) (diabetes); Hein v. All Am. Plywood Co., Inc., 232 F.3d 482 (6th Cir. 2000) (hypertension); Ivy v. Jones, 192 F.3d 514 (5th Cir. 1999) (hearing impairment); Muller v. Costello, 187 F.3d 298 (2d Cir. 1999) (asthma); Spades v. City of Walnut Ridge, 186 F.3d 897 (8th Cir. 1999) (depression).

To be a disability, the impairment must substantially limit a "major life activity," originally defined in the EEOC regulations as including, but not limited to, "caring for oneself, performing manual tasks, walking, seeing, hearing, speaking, breathing, learning, and working." Three years after *Sutton*, in Toyota Motor Mfg., Ky., Inc. v. Williams, 534 U.S. 184 (2002), the Supreme Court considered the issue of when working is a major life activity. The Court unanimously held that an individual's inability to perform manual tasks associated with her job, due to work-induced carpal tunnel syndrome, did not constitute a substantial limitation of the major life activity of working. It is not enough that an individual is prevented from performing tasks associated with a particular job. The individual must be prevented from performing "a variety of tasks central to most people's daily lives." Justice O'Connor's opinion said that "major life activities" must be strictly construed to effectuate the congressional intent that the ADA has limited coverage.

Sutton and *Toyota* were leading forces in creating a judicially inhospitable atmosphere to enforcement of the ADA. Indeed, between 1999 and 2008, plaintiffs lost over 90 percent of ADA cases, and the leading reason was the plaintiff's failure to establish coverage under the definition of disability. See Sharona Hoffman, Settling the Matter: Does Title I of the ADA Work?, 59 Ala. L. Rev. 305 (2008). By 2008, Congress realized it was necessary to amend the ADA to reestablish the federal law of workplace nondiscrimination on the basis of disability.

ADA Amendments Act of 2008

The ADA Amendments Act of 2008, P.L. 110–325 (2008) (ADAAA), was enacted to overturn the Supreme Court decisions that narrowly interpreted the definition of an individual with a disability. The essence of the amendments is captured in the following rule of construction: "The definition of a disability in this Act shall be construed in favor of broad coverage of individuals under this Act, to the maximum extent permitted by the terms of this Act." ADAAA § 3(4)(A). The amendments address many of the key controversies of the ADA.

Mitigating measures

Section 3(4)(E)(i) of the ADAAA provides that "[t]he determination of whether an impairment substantially limits a major life activity shall be made without regard to the ameliorative effects of mitigating measures such as medication, medical supplies, equipment; * * * assistive technology; reasonable accommodations or auxiliary aids or services; or learned behavioral or adaptive neurological modifications." Interestingly, the ameliorative effects of ordinary eyeglasses and contact lenses "shall be considered." ADAAA § 3(4)(E)(ii). Thus, the result in *Sutton* would be the same under the new provisions, but the doctrine established by the case has been expressly overruled.

Major life activity

Section 3(2)(A) of the ADAAA expands on the list of major life activities originally listed in the EEOC regulations. "[M]ajor life activities include, but are not limited to, caring for oneself, performing manual tasks, seeing, hearing, eating, sleeping, walking, standing, lifting, bending, speaking, breathing, learning, reading, concentrating, thinking, communicating, and working." In addition, "a major life activity also includes the operation of a major bodily function, including but not limited to, functions of the immune system, normal cell growth, digestive, bowel, bladder, neurological, brain, respiratory, circulatory, endocrine, and reproductive functions." ADAAA § 3(2)(B). In Norton v. Assisted Living Concepts, Inc., 786 F.Supp.2d 1173 (E.D. Tex. 2011), the court held that under the ADAAA cancer at any stage substantially limits the major life activity of cell growth. The case illustrates the effect of the amendments, as pre-ADAAA numerous cases had held that various plaintiffs with cancer were not covered under the ADA because they did not have a substantial limitation of a major life activity.

Working as a major life activity

Section 3(4) of the ADAAA declares that one purpose of the Act was "to reject the standards enunciated by the Supreme Court in *Toyota* * * * that to be substantially limited in performing a major life activity under the ADA 'an individual must have an impairment that prevents or severely restricts that individual from doing activities that are of central importance to most people's daily lives.' "

Minor and transitory impairments

Minor and transitory impairments are excluded from the definition of disability in the ADA. The ADAAA clarifies that a transitory impairment is "an impairment with an actual or expected duration of 6 months or less." Nonetheless, in Summers v. Altarum Institute, Corp., 740 F.3d 325 (4th Cir. 2014), the Fourth Circuit held that a temporary impairment, albeit one lasting more than six months, was not excluded from the definition of disability under the ADAAA.

Episodic conditions and conditions in remission

Is an individual with cancer covered by the ADA when the cancer is in remission? Lower courts had reached conflicting results. Similarly, lower courts reached different results regarding "episodic conditions" that flared up periodically. The ADAAA clarifies that "[a]n impairment that is episodic or in remission is a disability if it would substantially limit a major life activity when active." ADAAA § 3(4)(D).

Regarded as having an impairment

The ADAAA specifically rejects the other part of *Sutton's* holding in which the Court adopted a narrow interpretation of the "regarded as" prong of the definition of disability. To be covered under this part of the ADA, *Sutton* said the condition the individual is regarded as having must be substantially limiting. One of the most perplexing sections of the ADAAA is § 3(3).

> (A) An individual meets the requirement of "being regarded as having such an impairment" if the individual establishes that he or she has been subjected to an action prohibited under this Act because of an actual or perceived physical or mental impairment whether or not the impairment limits or is perceived to limit a major life activity.

> (B) Paragraph 1(C) [definition of regarded as having an impairment] shall not apply to impairments that are transitory and minor. A transitory impairment is an impairment with an actual or expected duration of 6 months or less.

Note there is no definition of "minor impairment" in the ADAAA. It remains to be seen if the courts will construe the coverage of the ADA as broadly as this section of the ADAAA has been drafted.

A NOTE ON THE ADA COVERAGE CONUNDRUM

Title VII applies to all victims of discrimination in employment. Despite some loose language in cases and commentaries, there are no "protected classes" under Title VII. People of all races, colors, religions, and national origins, and both sexes are protected when they are subject to discrimination on the basis of statutorily proscribed criteria. The ADEA was the first federal employment discrimination law to use a "protected class" model. As amended, the ADEA prohibits age discrimination in employment against individuals age 40 and over, thereby dividing the population into two categories. Those under 40 are not covered; those 40 and above are protected.

The ADA, borrowing heavily from the Rehabilitation Act, uses an even more complicated model of protected class. Title I of the ADA does not and was not intended to prohibit all discrimination in employment on the basis of an individual's physical or mental condition. It was intended to prohibit discrimination against a discrete group of "Americans with disabilities." By statute, these are individuals with substantially limiting impairments. The distinction was logically based, because people who use wheelchairs, have severe visual or hearing impairments, or similar conditions historically have been subject to discrimination.

In effect, the ADA divides the population of individuals with physical or mental impairments into three classes. Individuals with minor or temporary impairments are not covered. Individuals who are so severely impaired they cannot perform the job even with reasonable accommodation also are not protected by the ADA. On a continuum of impairment severity, between the two excluded categories (too mild and too severe) are individuals who have an impairment that constitutes a substantial limitation of a major life activity but who can perform the essential functions of the job with or without reasonable accommodation.

Not long after the ADA's enactment it became clear there were two main problems with the ADA's coverage model. First, the line between uncovered minor conditions and substantially limiting impairments was unclear. For example, many common health conditions, such as asthma, cancer, diabetes, epilepsy, heart disease, and hypertension, vary widely in severity. Based on the statute and EEOC regulations, it was not clear to employers, employees and applicants, and the courts whether an individual was covered under the ADA. Second, judicial decisions such as *Sutton* and *Toyota* expanded the category of conditions that were not severe enough to be covered, thereby substantially limiting the ADA's protections.

There were several options available to Congress in restoring broader coverage to the ADA, including the following. First, Congress could prohibit discrimination in employment on the basis of any non-job-related health status. This would eliminate the coverage issue, but extending to the entire population a law intended to redress discrimination against a discrete class of individuals with a history of discrimination likely would be politically untenable. Second, Congress could prohibit discrimination against individuals with certain specified disabilities. In 2007, Maine amended its Human Relations Act to cover 27 listed impairments, regardless of their severity (e.g., cancer, diabetes, epilepsy, heart disease, HIV/AIDS, mental retardation). Me. Rev. Stat. Ann. § 4553–A. This would add clarity, but it would have involved Congress at an uncomfortable level of detail in choosing which conditions to declare per se covered by the law. Third, Congress could borrow from Social Security Disability Insurance and prohibit discrimination against individuals who meet medically-determined criteria of severity for their condition. This would add objectivity and clarity, but it would require detailed rulemaking. See Mark A. Rothstein, Serge A. Martinez, & W. Paul McKinney, Using Established Medical Criteria to Define Disability: A Proposal to Amend the Americans with Disabilities Act, 80 Wash. U.L.Q. 243 (2002).

In the ADAAA Congress chose a different path. It indicated its intent to legislatively overrule *Sutton* and *Toyota* while retaining the general coverage structure of the ADA. "The definition of disability in this Act shall be construed in favor of broad coverage of individuals under this Act, to the maximum extent permitted by the terms of this Act." ADAAA § 4(a)(4)(A). Although the ADAAA restored coverage, the line between minor conditions and covered conditions remains fuzzy. The courts have yet to determine whether, in the absence of congressional intent, certain conditions will be deemed covered without further inquiry. The EEOC is promulgating regulations that would list certain conditions as always being covered, despite the absence of express congressional intent to do so.

Congress also confusingly broadened the "regarded as" prong of the definition. An individual is "regarded as" having a disability if he or she has been subject to discrimination "because of an actual or perceived physical or mental impairment whether or not the impairment limits or is perceived to limit a major life activity." ADAAA § 4(a)(3)(A). This provision does not apply to minor or temporary conditions, ADAAA § 4(a)(3)(B), and no reasonable accommodation is required. Does it create another category of conditions that are not minor but not substantially limiting? If so, why? If not, are these new provisions superfluous? See the Problem infra.

Has Congress struck the right balance in restoring the coverage of the ADA, or has it gone too far, not far enough, or in the wrong direction?

PROBLEM FOR DISCUSSION

John Knice, the owner of a manufacturing company with 75 employees, is walking through the plant one day with production manager Harry Grimes when they come across a new employee hard at work. Joe Smith, an at-will employee, is a 35-year old skilled mechanic. Mr. Knice orders Grimes to fire Smith immediately. Which of the following possible reasons for firing Smith would violate the ADA, as amended? In particular, consider the amended "regarded as" clause.

1. "I hate people with glasses."

2. "I hate bald guys."

3. "That short guy looks like a jockey, and jockeys have cost me a lot of money at the track."

4. "That guy has his arm in a sling."

5. "That cross-eyed guy gives me the creeps."

6. "That fat guy looks out of shape."

7. "The rash on that guy's arm is really gross."

8. "That guy has awful teeth."

9. "That guy's shirt reads 'Viva Viagra.' "

10. "That bald guy with glasses reminds me of my father, and I hated my father."

Has the amended "regarded as" clause of the ADA become a way to challenge a wide range of arbitrary or unreasonable employer actions? Is this a good development or a bad development?

NOTES AND QUESTIONS

1. Section 511 of the ADA expressly excludes from coverage the following conditions: homosexuality, bisexuality, transvestism, transsexualism, pedophilia, exhibitionism, voyeurism, gender identity disorders not resulting from physical impairments, other sexual behavior disorders, compulsive gambling, kleptomania, pyromania, and psychoactive substance use disorders resulting from current illegal use of drugs. However, in Blatt v. Cabela's Retail, Inc., No. 5:14-cv-04822-JFL (E.D. Pa., filed Aug. 15, 2014), a transgender plaintiff argued that the ADA's exclusion of gender identity disorders violates the Equal Protection Clause of the U.S. Constitution. On September 21, 2015, the district court ordered the Department of Justice to intervene or file a supplemental statement of interest regarding the constitutionality of the gender identity disorder exclusion in the ADA. Subsequently, the *Blatt* court held that it could avoid the constitutional issue if it interpreted the term "gender identity disorders" in the ADA "narrowly to refer to simply the condition of identifying with a different gender, not to exclude from ADA coverage disabling conditions that persons who identify with a different gender may have—such as Blatt's gender dysphoria, which substantially limits her major life activities of interacting with others, reproducing, and social and occupational functioning." Given this interpretation of the ADA, the court concluded that Blatt's gender dysphoria was not excluded from protection and denied the defendant's motion to dismiss. Blatt v. Cabela's Retail, Inc., 2017 WL 2178123 (E.D. Pa., May 18, 2017).

2.   Section 104 of the ADA also excludes from coverage any employee or applicant who is currently engaging in the illegal use of drugs. Individuals who are not currently engaged in the illegal use of drugs are covered if they have been rehabilitated, are currently participating in rehabilitation, or are erroneously regarded as engaging in drug use. It is not clear when individuals are no longer engaging in drug use (i.e., for how long do they have to be "clean"). It is also unclear whether individuals with a false-positive drug test are "erroneously regarded" as engaging in the illegal use of drugs. The ADA is neutral on the issue of drug testing, neither requiring nor prohibiting it. See *Harrison* supra p. 167.

3.   An assistant football coach at the University of Tennessee is fired after he is arrested for driving under the influence. He claims that he is an alcoholic and therefore is protected against discrimination based on his disability of alcoholism. What result? See Maddox v. University of Tenn., 62 F.3d 843 (6th Cir. 1995) (held: employer may lawfully discharge an employee for conduct-related offenses, even where the proscribed conduct is caused by alcoholism).

4.   In Raytheon Co. v. Hernandez, 540 U.S. 44 (2003), a 25-year employee of the company was required to take a drug test when he was suspected of being under the influence of drugs or alcohol. When the test was positive, he was forced to resign. Two years later, after completing a rehabilitation program, he applied for his former position but was denied employment because of an unwritten company rule prohibiting the rehire of individuals who left the company for violating personal conduct rules. The Ninth Circuit held that, as applied to the plaintiff, the rule had a disparate impact on substance abusers who were later rehabilitated. The Supreme Court held that the Ninth Circuit erred in deciding the case on a disparate impact theory that was not pled timely and in failing to resolve the case on the disparate treatment claim. It reversed and remanded. The unresolved issue in the case, the validity of the employer's no-rehire policy, is important to consider. Although there is a facial justification for the rule, if Raytheon can refuse to rehire its former employees who were terminated for violations, then it would seem that other employers could adopt an even broader policy of not hiring any individual who was discharged for cause (including violating a substance abuse policy) by itself or *any other* employer. Such a result, however, would undermine the intent of section 510(b)(1) of the ADA, which provides that the protections of the ADA apply to an individual who "has successfully completed a supervised drug rehabilitation program and is no longer engaging in the illegal use of drugs, or has otherwise been rehabilitated successfully and is no longer engaging in such use. * * * "

5. In Bragdon v. Abbott, 524 U.S. 624 (1998), the Supreme Court held that asymptomatic HIV infection is a disability under the ADA. "In light of the immediacy with which the virus begins to damage the infected person's white blood cells and the severity of the disease, we hold it is an impairment from the moment of infection." Id. at 637. The Court further held that HIV infection was a substantial limitation on the major life activity of reproduction. Although *Bragdon* was a Title III ADA case involving the public accommodation of a dentist's services, it undoubtedly applies to employment.

6. Section 102(b)(4) of the ADA provides that it is unlawful to discriminate against a qualified individual "because of the known disability of an individual with whom the qualified individual is known to have a relationship or association." Although the provision was included in the ADA because of discrimination against individuals who associated with HIV-positive individuals, there are three categories of cases arising under this provision: increased health care expenses caused by an individual's dependents; disability by association; and distraction, such as where a parent has a child with special needs. See Larimer v. IBM Corp., 370 F.3d 698 (7th Cir.), cert. denied, 543 U.S. 984 (2004).

EEOC v. Schneider National, Inc.
481 F.3d 507 (7th Cir. 2007).

■ POSNER, CIRCUIT JUDGE.

In 2002, shortly after receiving an award from his employer, the Schneider trucking company, for having driven a million miles for the company without an avoidable accident, Jerome Hoefner had a fainting spell and was diagnosed with a condition called "neurocardiogenic syncope." This is a disorder of the nervous system that can produce a sudden drop in blood pressure that in turn reduces the amount of blood reaching the brain, causing the person with the disorder to faint. Schneider's policy is (with a possible exception discussed later in this opinion) not to employ a truck driver who has the disorder, although it is treatable with medicines such as Florinef and does not prevent a person from satisfying the safety standards required by federal law of anyone who drives, on a public highway, a truck that weighs (with its load) at least 26,001 pounds or is used to transport hazardous materials or at least 16 passengers.

After being dismissed by Schneider, Hoefner obtained a similar job with another trucking company. Nevertheless the EEOC brought suit on Hoefner's behalf against Schneider, contending that the company had fired him because it mistakenly believes that neurocardiogenic syncope is a disabling condition within the meaning of the Americans with

Disabilities Act, which among other things forbids discrimination in employment against persons mistakenly believed to be disabled. The district court granted summary judgment for Schneider, precipitating this appeal.

* * *

The Commission's case relies primarily on statements by a nurse who heads Schneider's occupational health unit and believes that anyone with Hoefner's condition should be disqualified from driving Schneider's trucks as "a matter of safety and direct threat." But the reason for this belief, as she further explained and the Commission does not question, is that two years before Hoefner's fainting spell another driver for Schneider, Michael Kupsky, whom Schneider had hired shortly after Kupsky had been diagnosed with neurocardiogenic syncope while driving for another trucking company, had driven a Schneider truck off a bridge and been killed. Schneider was "advised that it appeared that [Kupsky] may have fallen asleep" at the wheel. The incident precipitated the company's adoption of a "zero tolerance" policy for drivers with neurocardiogenic syncope. The nurse stated that "Schneider made the right decision after the Kupsky accident. . . . [W]e don't know what caused that accident. We'll never know. And Schneider is not going to take the chance that . . . that horrible accident happens to anybody else." The executive who fired Hoefner echoed what the nurse had said: "we simply cannot take the risk that while driving, you would lose consciousness."

There is nothing to suggest that Schneider has a mistaken understanding of neurocardiogenic syncope. It simply is unwilling to risk a repetition (a possible repetition, since Kupsky's autopsy could not determine whether he had fainted and if so whether that was why he had veered off the road) of the Kupsky calamity. The risk is not zero, as the EEOC suggests, even if Florinef is totally efficacious, because Hoefner could forget to take his medicine. Anyway the drug is not totally efficacious. It merely reduces the risk of dehydration, and that is only one risk factor for neurocardiogenic syncope.

No doubt the risk that a person afflicted with this disorder will faint while driving is small, as otherwise Hoefner wouldn't be allowed to drive big trucks, as he is, for the trucking company that with full knowledge of his medical history hired him after Schneider fired him. But Schneider is entitled to determine how much risk is too great for it to be willing to take. "[A]n employer is free to decide that physical characteristics or medical conditions that do not rise to the level of an impairment—such as one's height, build, or singing voice—are preferable to others, just as it is free to decide that some limiting, but not substantially limiting, impairments make individuals less than ideally suited for a job." The fact that another employer and, as in all such cases, the worker himself are willing to assume a risk does not compel the worker's current employer to do likewise.

Schneider is the nation's largest truck company, employing 13,000 drivers. The more drivers a company employs, the greater the likelihood of the kind of accident that befell Kupsky and could befall Hoefner. Suppose Schneider had no policy against hiring drivers with neurocardiogenic syncope. Then some number of the 13,000 would have the condition. The EEOC presented no estimate of what that number would be, but syncope is common, "accounting for 3 percent of emergency room visits and 6 percent of hospital admissions." Suppose 2 percent of Schneider's drivers had it; that would be 260. The risk that at least one of them would have a Kupsky-type accident could not be thought wholly negligible, and the liability implications for Schneider (should there be an accident that killed or injured someone other than the driver, whose rights against Schneider would be limited to workers' compensation) could be calamitous. The victim's lawyers would wave the Kupsky accident in front of the jury, asking it to award punitive damages because the company had continued to employ drivers with neurocardiogenic syncope after having been warned by Kupsky's accident. The argument for punitive damages would be that employing Hoefner in the wake of Kupsky's accident showed that Schneider had acted in the face of a known risk and was therefore reckless.

The argument might not succeed; the risk might not be deemed big enough to make Schneider reckless for not eliminating it by barring drivers who have neurocardiogenic syncope. But once burned, twice shy. Because of Kupsky's unfortunate accident, Schneider may be excessively risk averse, as United Air Lines and other airlines (Sutton v. United Air Lines, Inc., 130 F.3d 893, 903–04 (10th Cir. 1997), aff'd 527 U.S. 471 (1999)) may be in refusing to hire pilots who do not have at least 20–100 uncorrected vision. But as there is no evidence that Schneider exaggerates the severity of Hoefner's condition and the risk he poses as a driver, there is no violation of the Americans with Disabilities Act.

The EEOC has confused risk with risk aversion. Two companies might each correctly believe that the risk of a particular type of accident was 1 in 10,000, yet one company, perhaps because it was small, financially fragile, owned by a trust, or as in this case had had an experience of the risk materializing, might be unwilling to assume the risk. That would be a decision irrelevant to liability under the Americans with Disabilities Act, even if that company's degree of risk aversion was "unique" in its industry.

* * *

Affirmed.

NOTES AND QUESTIONS

1.   The court views the direct threat defense as subjective, meaning that a particular employer, such as Schneider National, with a history of a fatality involving a truck driver with the same medical condition could adopt more

risk averse medical standards than other trucking companies. Is this correct? What are the implications? Could all trucking companies in the area with knowledge of the prior fatality adopt the same rule? Could any trucking company with a prior suspected medical fatality adopt risk averse medical standards?

2. The ADA prohibits discrimination against a "qualified individual with a disability," 42 U.S.C. § 12112, defined as someone who, "with or without reasonable accommodation, can perform the essential functions of the employment position that such individual holds or desires." 42 U.S.C. § 12111(8). The ADA further provides that an employer is not permitted to use a qualification standard that tends to screen out an individual with a disability unless it "is shown to be job-related for the position in question and is consistent with business necessity." Id.

3. Section 103(b) provides that "[t]he term 'qualification standards' may include a requirement that an individual shall not pose a direct threat to the health and safety of other individuals in the workplace." Although the language is narrow and does not include harm to the individual employee with a disability, the interpretive regulation of the EEOC is broader. It defines "direct threat" to include the affected individual, as well. 29 C.F.R. § 1630.2(r).

In Chevron U.S.A., Inc. v. Echazabal, 536 U.S. 73 (2002), an employee who had worked for independent contractors at a Chevron Oil refinery applied for a job with Chevron. On two prior occasions the employer withdrew conditional offers of employment following medical examinations which indicated that Echazabal had chronic hepatitis C. Although he had worked at the Chevron facility for over 20 years without experiencing any health problems, Echazabal was denied employment by Chevron on the ground that exposure to toxic chemicals at the refinery would damage his liver. He was laid off by his contractor-employer when Chevron requested that he be removed from further exposures. Echazabal then sued under the ADA. The Supreme Court unanimously upheld the validity of the EEOC interpretation of the direct threat provision, saying that the "other individuals" in section 103(b) is only an example of the type of direct threat that could disqualify an employee under the ADA.

4. To be actionable discrimination under the ADA an individual with a disability must suffer an "adverse employment action" because of the disability. In EEOC v. C.R. England, Inc., 644 F.3d 1028 (10th Cir. 2011), the plaintiff worked as a driver-trainer for a trucking company. Because he was HIV-positive the employer required employees training with the plaintiff to sign an acknowledgment of the trainer's HIV status. The Tenth Circuit held that on the present record the plaintiff did not prove that any of his employment opportunities were limited and thus there was no violation of the ADA. The court stated it was not sanctioning a "co-worker preference" defense and that under different facts an employer's use of a co-worker consent policy could be actionable.

Lyons v. Legal Aid Society

68 F.3d 1512 (2d Cir. 1995).

■ KEARSE, CIRCUIT JUDGE:

Plaintiff Beth Lyons, a staff attorney employed by defendant Legal Aid Society ("Legal Aid"), appeals from a judgment of the United States District Court for the Southern District of New York, Kevin Thomas Duffy, Judge, dismissing her complaint alleging that Legal Aid violated her rights under, inter alia, the Americans with Disabilities Act of 1990, and the Rehabilitation Act of 1973 ("Rehabilitation Act") (collectively the "federal disability statutes"), principally by failing to provide her with a parking space near work. The district court, holding that the federal disability statutes imposed no such duty, dismissed Lyons's federal claims pursuant to Fed.R.Civ.P. 12(b)(6) for failure to state a claim on which relief can be granted.

* * *

Since September 1987, Lyons has been employed as an attorney in the Criminal Defense Division of Legal Aid in its office in lower Manhattan. Taking all of the factual allegations in the complaint as true, the pertinent events were as follows.

In January 1989, an automobile struck Lyons as she was leaving her parked car and dragged her some twenty feet, inflicting near-fatal injuries that included torn muscles, other hard—and soft—tissue wounds, and a dislocated left knee. From the date of the accident until June 1993, Lyons was on disability leave from Legal Aid; she underwent multiple reconstructive surgeries and received "constant" physical therapy. Since the accident, Lyons has been able to walk only by "us[ing] walking devices, including walkers, canes and crutches." Her physician has prescribed several exercise sessions each week in order for Lyons to maintain her ability to walk.

Lyons was able to return to work at Legal Aid in June 1993 and has since then performed her job duties successfully. She has continued, however, to suffer from various physical impairments. She wears a brace on her left knee; she cannot stand for extended periods, and she cannot climb or descend stairs without difficulty. Her condition "severely limits her ability to walk long distances either at one time or during the course of a day" and her general physical stamina is "significantly less than normal"

Before returning to work, Lyons asked Legal Aid to accommodate her disability by "pay[ing] for a parking space near her office and the courts in which she would practice." She stated that she would be unable to take public transportation from her home in New Jersey to the Legal Aid office in Manhattan because such "commuting would require her to walk distances, climb stairs, and on occasion to remain standing for extended periods of time," thereby "overtax[ing] her limited physical capabilities." Lyons's physician, an orthopedic and reconstructive plastic surgeon, advised Legal Aid by letter that such a parking space was "necessary to enable [Lyons] to return to work."

Legal Aid informed Lyons that it would not pay for a parking space for her. Accordingly, since returning to work, Lyons has spent $300–$520 a month, representing 15–26 percent of her monthly net salary, for a parking space adjacent to her office building.

Prior to returning to work, Lyons had also requested that Legal Aid accord her seniority increases for the entire 4 1/2-year period of her disability leave. Under Legal Aid's internal policies, management had "discretion to adjust the seniority of employees who have not been actively employed for an extended period." Legal Aid agreed to increase Lyons's seniority level, but only by one year rather than by 4 1/2. Accordingly, Lyons has received lower compensation than she would have received had she been accorded full seniority increases for the entire period of her disability leave.

* * *

The ADA prohibits an employer from discriminating against an employee "because of the disability of such individual in regard to job application procedures, the hiring, advancement, or discharge of employees, employee compensation, job training, and other terms, conditions, and privileges of employment." As defined by the ADA, "discrimination" includes, inter alia,

> not making reasonable accommodations to the known physical or mental limitations of an otherwise qualified individual with a disability who is an applicant or employee, unless . . . [the employer] can demonstrate that the accommodation would impose an undue hardship on the operation of the . . . [employer's] business.

42 U.S.C. § 12112(b)(5)(A) (emphasis added). "[O]therwise qualified" means that the individual, "with or without reasonable accommodation, can perform the essential functions of the employment position that such individual holds or desires." Id. § 12111(8) (emphasis added).

The Rehabilitation Act, which prohibits disability-based discrimination by government agencies and other recipients of federal funds, is similar. Section 504(a) of the Rehabilitation Act provides:

> No otherwise qualified individual with a disability . . . shall, solely by reason of her or his disability, be excluded from the participation in, be denied the benefits of, or be subjected to discrimination under any program or activity receiving Federal financial assistance. . . .

29 U.S.C. § 794(a) Regulations promulgated under this statute by the Department of Health and Human Services define a "qualified" person with a disability as one "who, with reasonable accommodation, can

perform the essential function of the job in question," 45 C.F.R. § 84.3(k)(1) (1994) (emphasis added), and require recipients of federal funds to "make reasonable accommodation to the known physical or mental limitations of an otherwise qualified handicapped ... employee unless the recipient can demonstrate that the accommodation would impose an undue hardship on the operation of its program," § 84.12(a) (emphasis added).

Thus, under either the ADA or the Rehabilitation Act, a plaintiff can state a claim for discrimination based upon her employer's failure to accommodate her handicap by alleging facts showing (1) that the employer is subject to the statute under which the claim is brought, (2) that she is an individual with a disability within the meaning of the statute in question, (3) that, with or without reasonable accommodation, she could perform the essential functions of the job, and (4) that the employer had notice of the plaintiff's disability and failed to provide such accommodation. There is no question here with respect to the first, second, and fourth elements. The only question is whether Lyons's request that Legal Aid provide her with a parking space near work is, as a matter of law, not a request for a "reasonable" accommodation.

Neither the ADA nor the Rehabilitation Act provides a closed-end definition of "reasonable accommodation." The ADA sets out a nonexclusive list of different methods of accommodation encompassed by that term, stating that

> [t]he term "reasonable accommodation" may include—

> (A) making existing facilities used by employees readily accessible to and usable by individuals with disabilities; and

> (B) job restructuring, part-time or modified work schedules, reassignment to a vacant position, acquisition or modification of equipment or devices, appropriate adjustment or modifications of examinations, training materials or policies, the provision of qualified readers or interpreters, and other similar accommodations for individuals with disabilities.

* * *

In support of the order of dismissal in the present case, Legal Aid argues that Lyons's claim for financial assistance in parking her car amounts to a demand for unwarranted preferential treatment because the requested accommodation is merely "a matter of personal convenience that she uses regularly in daily life." Legal Aid asserts that it does not provide parking facilities or any other commuting assistance to its nondisabled employees and that Lyons's special needs in getting to work must therefore lie outside the scope of its obligations under the federal disability statutes. We find Legal Aid's contentions to be an inappropriate foundation for the Rule 12(b)(6) dismissal.

First, Legal Aid's assertion that it does not provide parking assistance to any other employee goes beyond the face of the complaint. This assertion cannot be the basis for a dismissal for failure to state a claim.

Further, even if that assertion were established as a matter of fact, it would not dispose of the issue of whether provision of a parking space would be a reasonable accommodation. It is clear that an essential aspect of many jobs is the ability to appear at work regularly and on time, and that Congress envisioned that employer assistance with transportation to get the employee to and from the job might be covered. Thus, the report of the House of Representatives Committee on Education and Labor noted that a qualified person with a disability seeking employment at a store that is "located in an inaccessible mall" would be entitled to reasonable accommodation in helping him "get to the job site." H.R.Rep. No. 485, 101st Cong., 2d Sess., pt. 2, at 61 (1990), reprinted in 1990 U.S.C.C.A.N. 303, 343. Similarly, the EEOC has stated that possible required accommodations other than those specifically listed in the statute include "making employer provided transportation accessible, and providing reserved parking spaces." So far as we are aware, there has been no judicial interpretation of this EEOC guideline, which may have been intended to mean that the provision of parking spaces can be required, or that the reservation of employer-provided parking spaces can be required, or both.

Whatever the guideline intended, we think that the question of whether it is reasonable to require an employer to provide parking spaces may well be susceptible to differing answers depending on, e.g., the employer's geographic location and financial resources, and that the determination of the reasonableness of such a requirement will normally require some development of a factual record. Further, we have noted that while reasonableness depends upon "a common-sense balancing of the costs and benefits" to both the employer and the employee, an accommodation may not be considered unreasonable merely because it requires the employer "to assume more than a de minimis cost," or because it will cost the employer more overall to obtain the same level of performance from the disabled employee.

Finally, we reject Legal Aid's contention that Lyons's request for a parking space amounts to no more than a demand for an additional fringe benefit in the nature of a "personal amenity" unrelated to the "essential functions" of her job. According to the complaint, whose factual allegations must be taken as true, Lyons cannot fulfill her responsibilities as a staff attorney at Legal Aid without being able to park her car adjacent to her office. Lyons's ability to reach her office and the courts is an essential prerequisite to her work in that position. There is no suggestion in the complaint that the requested parking space near the Legal Aid office and the courts was sought for any purpose other than to allow Lyons to reach and perform her job.

Plainly there is nothing inherently unreasonable, given the stated views of Congress and the agencies responsible for overseeing the federal disability statutes, in requiring an employer to furnish an otherwise qualified disabled employee with assistance related to her ability to get to work. We conclude that Lyons's complaint stated a claim on which relief can be granted under the ADA and the Rehabilitation Act. We express no view as to whether Legal Aid may be able to develop an evidentiary record prior to trial that is sufficient to demonstrate the unreasonableness of the requested accommodation as a matter of law. At this juncture, we note only that, in light of the need to develop a factual record, it was inappropriate to dismiss the complaint summarily by granting defendant's motion pursuant to Rule 12(b)(6).

NOTES AND QUESTIONS

1. An employer's duty of accommodation only extends to *reasonable* accommodations. The accommodation need not be ideal. McAdams v. UPS, 30 F.3d 1027 (8th Cir. 1994). The burden of proof is on the individual to prove that an accommodation exists that will permit him or her to perform the essential functions of the job. White v. York Int'l Corp., 45 F.3d 357 (10th Cir. 1995). Accommodations that pose an undue hardship or expense are not required. For example, a medical group had no duty to hire an assistant to help an internist with reflex sympathetic dystrophy perform the physical tasks related to practicing medicine. Reigel v. Kaiser Fdn. Health Plan, 859 F.Supp. 963 (E.D.N.C.1994).

2. One frequently requested accommodation is unpaid leave to obtain medical treatment. In general, courts have held that leaves of absence are reasonable accommodations. See Schmidt v. Safeway, Inc., 864 F.Supp. 991 (D.Or.1994); Eisfelder v. Michigan Dep't of Natural Res., 847 F.Supp. 78 (W.D.Mich.1993). On the other hand, an employer did not have a duty to grant an employee indefinite leave at half salary while he recovered from chronic heart disease, hypertension, phlebitis, and diabetes. Myers v. Hose, 50 F.3d 278 (4th Cir. 1995). See generally Stephen F. Befort, The Most Difficult ADA Reasonable Accommodation Issues: Reassignment and Leaves of Absence, 37 Wake Forest L. Rev. 439 (2002).

3. A contentious issue in reasonable accommodation is the employer's duty to reassign an individual to another position. There is no duty to reassign an individual where there is no vacant position. Fedro v. Reno, 21 F.3d 1391 (7th Cir. 1994). Where there is only one vacant position, does an employer have a duty to reassign the employee with a disability or the employee with the most seniority, based on the terms of a collective bargaining agreement? See Aka v. Washington Hosp. Ctr., 156 F.3d 1284 (D.C.Cir.1998) (held: no per se rule; conflict with collective bargaining agreement should be considered as one factor in evaluating reasonableness of accommodation).

4. In US Airways, Inc. v. Barnett, 535 U.S. 391 (2002), the Supreme Court held that, when an employee's request for reassignment to another position as a reasonable accommodation under the ADA conflicts with the employer's unilaterally-imposed seniority rules, the employer's rules presumptively will prevail. To rebut this presumption, the employee must prove the existence of "special circumstances," such as where the seniority policy is changed so frequently as to reduce employee expectations. The result is that the employee with the most seniority, rather than an employee with a disability, ordinarily will be awarded the position. Justice Breyer's plurality opinion produced separate concurrences by Justices Stevens and O'Connor and separate dissents. Justices Scalia and Thomas wrote that the employer's seniority rule should always take precedence over the ADA requirements. Justices Souter and Ginsburg wrote that seniority systems should be merely "a factor" in determining whether the accommodation is reasonable. The Seventh Circuit has interpreted *Barnett* as contradicting its prior precedent regarding reassignments under the ADA. In EEOC v. Humiston-Keeling, 227 F.3d 1024 (7th Cir. 2000), the Seventh Circuit had held that a competitive transfer policy did not violate the ADA. In EEOC v. United Airlines, 693 F.3d 760 (7th Cir. 2012), the Seventh Circuit held that *Humiston-Keeling* could not survive *Barnett* and ruled that the ADA does "mandate that an employer appoint employees with disabilities to vacant positions for which they are qualified, provided that such accommodations would be ordinarily reasonable and would not present an undue hardship to that employer." Id. at 761.

5.   Is permitting an individual to work full-time at home a reasonable accommodation? The courts generally are willing to consider this accommodation a possibility under extraordinary circumstances, but they almost always hold it is unreasonable because of the lack of supervision and the inability to participate in activities requiring teamwork. See Rauen v. U.S. Tobacco Mfg. Ltd. Partnership, 319 F.3d 891 (7th Cir. 2003). Ongoing technological advancements may, however, make such an accommodation seem more reasonable to courts in the future. See Core v. Champaign County Bd. of County Com'rs, 2012 WL 3073418 (S.D. Ohio 2012). As the Sixth Circuit explained in EEOC v. Ford Motor Co., 752 F.3d 634 (6th Cir. 2014): "When we first developed the principle that attendance is an essential requirement of most jobs, technology was such that the workplace and an employer's brick-and-mortar location were synonymous. However, as technology has advanced in the intervening decades, and an ever-greater number of employers and employees utilize remote work arrangements, attendance at the workplace can no longer be assumed to mean attendance at the employer's physical location." 752 F.3d at 641.

6.   Employers are permitted to refuse to employ individuals with disabilities who are unable, even with reasonable accommodation, to perform the essential functions of the job. What is an essential function of a job varies, of course, depending on the context. In Samper v. Providence St. Vincent Medical Ctr., 675 F.3d 1233 (9th Cir. 2013), the Ninth Circuit held that a neonatal intensive care unit nurse who could not meet her employer's attendance requirements, even with accommodation, was not a qualified individual under the ADA because "on-site regular attendance is an essential job function" for such a position. In Tardie v. Rehabilitation Hosp. of R.I., 168 F.3d 538 (1st Cir. 1999), the First Circuit held that the ability to work in excess of 40 hours per week was an essential function of the position of

human resources director. Based on this decision, would it be lawful for a law firm to refuse to hire an associate whose disability prevented him or her from working long hours each week?

7. What defenses are available? Two of the most common defenses asserted in disability discrimination cases are the following:

(a) *Employee misconduct.* Employee discharges have been upheld where they were the result of misconduct, such as shoplifting, Harris v. Polk County, 103 F.3d 696 (8th Cir. 1996), fighting, Johnson v. New York Hosp., 96 F.3d 33 (2d Cir. 1996), and making threats, Palmer v. Circuit Court, 117 F.3d 351 (7th Cir. 1997).

(b) *Customer/coworker preference.* In race, sex, and other discrimination cases this defense has failed. The courts may not reject it out of hand in disability cases, however. Does a gourmet restaurant have to hire "Elephant Man" to be head waiter? Cf. Chico Dairy Co. v. West Virginia Human Rights Comm'n, 382 S.E.2d 75 (W.Va.1989) (employee who had prosthetic eye and disfigured eye socket did not have a "handicap," and Human Rights Commission lacked authority to interpret state law to cover "perceived handicaps," thus employer's refusal to promote employee to manager at a food store because of her "unsavory appearance" was not unlawful).

In Martinson v. Kinney Shoe Corp., 104 F.3d 683 (4th Cir. 1997), a shoe salesperson had uncontrolled epileptic seizures, which caused him to lose consciousness. When this occurred, he would fall to the floor, causing coworkers to rush to his assistance and customers to become upset. After 16 seizures in a six-month period, he was discharged. The district court held that there was no violation of the ADA, that the employer did not discriminate because of the employee's epilepsy but because of the effects of the epilepsy. It cautioned, however, that its holding was limited to the facts and was not an endorsement of a "customer preference" defense. The Fourth Circuit rejected this reasoning, but affirmed on the ground that the employee, who sometimes worked alone, could not maintain security at the time of a seizure.

8. Following the Supreme Court's ruling in Gross v. FBL Fin. Servs., Inc., 557 U.S. 167 (2009), in which the Supreme Court held that the mixed motives framework did not apply to ADEA claims, the Seventh Circuit has held that the mixed motives framework similarly does not apply to ADA claims. See Serwatka v. Rockwell Automation, Inc., 591 F.3d 957, 962 (7th Cir. 2010) (explaining that "in the absence of a cross-reference to Title VII's mixed-motive liability language or comparable stand-alone language in the ADA itself, a plaintiff complaining of discriminatory discharge under the ADA must show that his or her employer would not have fired him but for his actual or perceived disability; proof of mixed motives will not suffice").

One open question after the passage of the ADA was whether the Act's protection could extend to individuals discriminated against on the basis of race. In 1995, the EEOC issued a non-binding interpretation of the ADA in which it declared that individuals who are discriminated against on the basis of "genetic information relating to illness, disease, or other disorders" are being regarded as having a disability. The ADA Amendments Act did not address the issue of genetic discrimination. This may have been because several months before the ADA Amendments Act was signed into law, Congress enacted the Genetic Information Act of 2008 (GINA). GINA expressly prohibited employers from requesting, requiring, or purchasing genetic information about employees, applicants, or their family members (§ 202(b)). For a discussion of the implications of genetic information on legal notions of equality see Mark A. Rothstein, Legal Conceptions of Equality in the Genomic Age, 25 Law and Inequality 429 (2007). See Chapter 3 for a more extensive discussion of GINA.

5. SEXUAL ORIENTATION

Hively v. Ivy Tech Community College of Indiana

853 F.3d 339 (7th Cir. 2017) (en banc).

■ WOOD, CHIEF JUDGE.

Title VII of the Civil Rights Act of 1964 makes it unlawful for employers subject to the Act to discriminate on the basis of a person's "race, color, religion, sex, or national origin. . . ." 42 U.S.C. § 2000e–2(a). For many years, the courts of appeals of this country understood the prohibition against sex discrimination to exclude discrimination on the basis of a person's sexual orientation. The Supreme Court, however, has never spoken to that question. In this case, we have been asked to take a fresh look at our position in light of developments at the Supreme Court extending over two decades. We have done so, and we conclude today that discrimination on the basis of sexual orientation is a form of sex discrimination. We therefore reverse the district court's judgment dismissing Kimberly Hively's suit against Ivy Tech Community College and remand for further proceedings.

I

Hively is openly lesbian. She began teaching as a part-time, adjunct professor at Ivy Tech Community College's South Bend campus in 2000. Hoping to improve her lot, she applied for at least six full-time positions between 2009 and 2014. These efforts were unsuccessful; worse yet, in July 2014 her part-time contract was not renewed. Believing that Ivy Tech was spurning her because of her sexual orientation. . . .

After receiving a right-to-sue letter, she filed this action in the district court (again acting pro se). Ivy Tech responded with a motion to dismiss for failure to state a claim on which relief can be granted. It argued that sexual orientation is not a protected class under Title VII. . . . Relying on a line of this court's cases exemplified by Hamner v. St. Vincent Hosp. and Health Care Ctr., Inc., 224 F.3d 701 (7th Cir. 2000), the district court granted Ivy Tech's motion and dismissed Hively's case with prejudice.

Now represented by the Lambda Legal Defense & Education Fund, Hively has appealed to this court. After an exhaustive exploration of the law governing claims involving discrimination based on sexual orientation, the panel affirmed. Hively v. Ivy Tech Cmty. Coll., 830 F.3d 698 (7th Cir. 2016). It began its analysis by noting that the idea that discrimination based on sexual orientation is somehow distinct from sex discrimination originated with dicta in Ulane v. Eastern Airlines, Inc., 742 F.2d 1081 (7th Cir. 1984). *Ulane* stated (as if this resolved matters) that Title VII's prohibition against sex discrimination "implies that it is unlawful to discriminate against women because they are women and against men because they are men." *Id.* at 1085. From this truism, we deduced that "Congress had nothing more than the traditional notion of 'sex' in mind when it voted to outlaw sex discrimination. . . ." Doe v. City of Belleville, Ill., 119 F.3d 563, 572 (7th Cir. 1997), *cert. granted, judgment vacated sub nom.* City of Belleville v. Doe, 523 U.S. 1001, *abrogated by* Oncale v. Sundowner Offshore Servs., Inc., 523 U.S. 75 (1998).

Later cases in this court, including Hamm v. Weyauwega Milk Prods., 332 F.3d 1058 (7th Cir. 2003), *Hamner*, and Spearman v. Ford Motor Co., 231 F.3d 1080, 1085 (7th Cir. 2000), have accepted this as settled law. Almost all of our sister circuits have understood the law in the same way. See, e.g., Higgins v. New Balance Athletic Shoe, Inc., 194 F.3d 252, 259 (1st Cir. 1999); Dawson v. Bumble & Bumble, 398 F.3d 211, 217 (2d Cir. 2005); Prowel v. Wise Bus. Forms, Inc., 579 F.3d 285, 290 (3d Cir. 2009); Wrightson v. Pizza Hut of Am., Inc., 99 F.3d 138, 143 (4th Cir. 1996); Blum v. Gulf Oil Corp., 597 F.2d 936, 938 (5th Cir. 1979); Kalich v. AT&T Mobility, LLC, 679 F.3d 464, 471 (6th Cir. 2012); Williamson v. A.G. Edwards & Sons, Inc., 876 F.2d 69, 70 (8th Cir. 1989); Medina v. Income Support Div., 413 F.3d 1131, 1135 (10th Cir. 2005); Fredette v. BVP Mgmt. Assocs., 112 F.3d 1503, 1510 (11th Cir. 1997). A panel of the Eleventh Circuit, recognizing that it was bound by the Fifth Circuit's precedent in *Blum*, 597 F.2d 936, recently reaffirmed (by a 2–1 vote) that it could not recognize sexual orientation discrimination claims under Title VII. Evans v. Georgia Reg'l Hosp., 850 F.3d 1248, 1255–57 (11th Cir. 2017). On the other hand, the Second Circuit recently found that an openly gay male plaintiff pleaded a claim of gender stereotyping that was sufficient to survive dismissal. The court observed that one panel lacked the power to reconsider the court's earlier decision holding that sexual orientation discrimination claims were not cognizable under Title VII. Christiansen v. Omnicom Group, Inc., 852 F.3d 195 (2d Cir. 2017) (per curiam). Nonetheless, two of the three judges, relying on many of the same arguments presented here, noted in concurrence that they thought their court ought to consider revisiting that precedent in an appropriate case. *Id.* at 198–99 (Katzmann, J., concurring). Notable in its absence from the debate over the proper interpretation of the scope of Title VII's ban on sex discrimination is the United States Supreme Court.

That is not because the Supreme Court has left this subject entirely to the side. To the contrary, as the panel recognized, over the years the Court has issued several opinions that are relevant to the issue before us. Key among those decisions are Price Waterhouse v. Hopkins, 490 U.S. 228 and Oncale v. Sundowner Offshore Servs., Inc., 523 U.S. 75 (1998). *Price Waterhouse* held that the practice of gender stereotyping falls within Title VII's prohibition against sex discrimination, and *Oncale* clarified that it makes no difference if the sex of the harasser is (or is not) the same as the sex of the victim. Our panel frankly acknowledged how difficult it is "to extricate the gender nonconformity claims from the sexual orientation claims." That effort, it commented, has led to a "confused hodge-podge of cases." It also noted that "all gay, lesbian and bisexual persons fail to comply with the sine qua non of gender stereotypes—that all men should form intimate relationships only with women, and all women should form intimate relationships only with men." *Id.* Especially since the Supreme Court's recognition that the Due Process and Equal Protection Clauses of the Constitution protect the right of same-sex couples to marry, Obergefell v. Hodges, ___ U.S. ___, 135 S.Ct. 2584 (2015), bizarre results ensue from the current regime. As the panel noted, it creates "a paradoxical legal landscape in which a person can be married on Saturday and then fired on Monday for just that act." Finally, the panel highlighted the sharp tension between a rule that fails to recognize that discrimination on the basis of the sex with whom a person associates is a form of sex discrimination, and the rule, recognized since Loving v. Virginia, 388 U.S. 1 (1967), that discrimination on the basis of the race with whom a person associates is a form of racial discrimination.

Despite all these problems, the panel correctly noted that it was bound by this court's precedents, to which we referred earlier. It thought that the handwriting signaling their demise might be on the wall, but it did not feel empowered to translate that message into a holding. "Until the writing comes in the form of a Supreme Court opinion or new legislation," it felt bound to adhere to our earlier decisions. In light of the importance of the issue, and recognizing the power of the full court to overrule earlier decisions and to bring our law into conformity with the Supreme Court's teachings, a majority of the judges in regular active service voted to rehear this case en banc.

II

A

The question before us is not whether this court can, or should, "amend" Title VII to add a new protected category to the familiar list of "race, color, religion, sex, or national origin." 42 U.S.C. § 2000e–2(a). Obviously that lies beyond our power. We must decide instead what it means to discriminate on the basis of sex, and in particular, whether actions taken on the basis of sexual orientation are a subset of actions taken on the basis of sex. This is a pure question of statutory interpretation and thus well within the judiciary's competence.

* * *

Ivy Tech sets great store on the fact that Congress has frequently considered amending Title VII to add the words "sexual orientation" to the list of prohibited characteristics, yet it has never done so. Many of our sister circuits have also noted this fact. In our view, however, it is simply too difficult to draw a reliable inference from these truncated legislative initiatives to rest our opinion on them. The goalposts have been moving over the years, as the Supreme Court has shed more light on the scope of the language that already is in the statute: no *sex* discrimination.

The dissent makes much of the fact that Congresses acting more than thirty years after the passage of Title VII made use of the term "sexual orientation" to prohibit discrimination or violence on that basis in statutes such as the Violence Against Women Act and the federal Hate Crimes Act. But this gets us no closer to answering the question at hand, for Congress may certainly choose to use both a belt and suspenders to achieve its objectives, and the fact that "sex" and "sexual orientation" discrimination may overlap in later statutes is of no help in determining whether sexual orientation discrimination is discrimination on the basis of sex for the purposes of Title VII. See, e.g., McEvoy v. IEI Barge Servs., Inc., 622 F.3d 671, 677 (7th Cir. 2010) ("Congress may choose a belt-and-suspenders approach to promote its policy objectives. . . .").

Moreover, the agency most closely associated with this law, the Equal Employment Opportunity Commission, in 2015 announced that it now takes the position that Title VII's prohibition against sex discrimination encompasses discrimination on the basis of sexual orientation. See Baldwin v. Foxx, EEOC Appeal No. 0120133080, 2015 WL 4397641 (July 15, 2015). Our point here is not that we have a duty to defer to the EEOC's position. We assume for present purposes that no such duty exists. But the Commission's position may have caused some in Congress to think that legislation is needed to carve sexual orientation *out* of the statute, not to put it *in*. In the end, we have no idea what inference to draw from congressional inaction or later enactments, because there is no way of knowing what explains each individual member's votes, much less what explains the failure of the body as a whole to change this 1964 statute.

* * *

It is therefore neither here nor there that the Congress that enacted the Civil Rights Act in 1964 and chose to include sex as a prohibited basis for employment discrimination (no matter why it did so) may not have realized or understood the full scope of the words it chose. Indeed, in the years since 1964, Title VII has been understood to cover far more than the simple decision of an employer not to hire a woman for Job A, or a man for Job B. The Supreme Court has held that the prohibition against sex discrimination reaches sexual harassment in the workplace, see Meritor Sav. Bank, FSB v. Vinson, 477 U.S. 57 (1986), including same-sex workplace harassment, see *Oncale*; it reaches discrimination based on actuarial assumptions about a person's longevity, see City of Los Angeles, Dep't of Water and Power v. Manhart, 435 U.S. 702 (1978); and it reaches discrimination based on a person's failure to conform to a certain set of gender stereotypes, see *Hopkins*. It is quite possible that these interpretations may also have surprised some who served in the 88th Congress. Nevertheless, experience with the law has led the Supreme Court to recognize that each of these examples is a covered form of sex discrimination.

B

Hively offers two approaches in support of her contention that "sex discrimination" includes discrimination on the basis of sexual orientation. The first relies on the tried-and-true comparative method in which we attempt to isolate the significance of the plaintiff's sex to the employer's decision: has she described a situation in which, holding all other things constant and changing only her sex, she would have been treated the same way? The second relies on the Loving v. Virginia, 388 U.S. 1, 87 S.Ct. 1817, 18 L.Ed.2d 1010 (1967), line of cases, which she argues protect her right to associate intimately with a person of the same sex. Although the analysis differs somewhat, both avenues end up in the same place: sex discrimination.

1

* * *

Hively alleges that if she had been a man married to a woman (or living with a woman, or dating a woman) and everything else had stayed the same, Ivy Tech would not have refused to promote her and would not have fired her. . . . This describes paradigmatic sex discrimination. To use the phrase from *Ulane*, Ivy Tech is disadvantaging her *because she is a woman*. Nothing in the complaint hints that Ivy Tech has an anti-marriage policy that extends to heterosexual relationships, or for that matter even an anti-partnership policy that is gender-neutral.

Viewed through the lens of the gender non-conformity line of cases, Hively represents the ultimate case of failure to conform to the female stereotype (at least as understood in a place such as modern America, which views heterosexuality as the norm and other forms of sexuality as exceptional): she is not heterosexual. Our panel described the line between a gender nonconformity claim and one based on sexual orientation as gossamer-thin; we conclude that it does not exist at all. Hively's claim is no different from the claims brought by women who were rejected for jobs in traditionally male workplaces, such as fire departments, construction, and policing. The employers in those cases were policing the boundaries of what jobs or behaviors they found acceptable for a woman (or in some cases, for a man).

* * *

The virtue of looking at comparators and paying heed to gender non-conformity is that this process sheds light on the interpretive question raised by Hively's case: is sexual-orientation discrimination a form of sex discrimination, given the way in which the Supreme Court has interpreted the word "sex" in the statute? The dissent criticizes us for not trying to *rule out* sexual-orientation discrimination by controlling for it in our comparator example and for not placing any weight on the fact that if someone had asked Ivy Tech what its reasons were at the time of the discriminatory conduct, it probably would have said "sexual orientation," not "sex." We assume that this is true, but this thought experiment does not answer the question before us—instead, it begs that question. It commits the logical fallacy of assuming the conclusion it sets out to prove. It makes no sense to control for or rule out discrimination on the basis of sexual orientation if the question before us is *whether* that type of discrimination is nothing more or less than a form of sex discrimination. Repeating that the two are different, as the dissent does at numerous points, also does not advance the analysis.

2

As we noted earlier, Hively also has argued that action based on sexual orientation is sex discrimination under the associational theory. It is now accepted that a person who is discriminated against because of the protected characteristic of one with whom she associates is actually being disadvantaged because of her own traits. This line of cases began with *Loving*, in which the Supreme Court held that "restricting the freedom to marry solely because of racial classifications violates the central meaning of the Equal Protection Clause." The Court rejected the argument that miscegenation statutes do not violate equal protection because they "punish equally both the white and the Negro participants in an interracial marriage." When dealing with a statute containing racial classifications, it wrote, "the fact of equal application does not immunize the statute from the very heavy burden of justification" required by the Fourteenth Amendment for lines drawn by race.

* * *

The dissent would instead have us compare the treatment of men who are attracted to members of the male sex with the treatment of women who are attracted to members of the female sex, and ask whether an employer treats the men differently from the women. But even setting to one side the logical fallacy involved, *Loving* shows why this fails. In the context of interracial relationships, we could just as easily hold constant a variable such as "sexual or romantic attraction to persons of a different race" and ask whether an employer treated persons of different races who shared that propensity the same. That is precisely the rule that *Loving* rejected, and so too must we, in the context of sexual associations.

The fact that *Loving* . . . dealt with racial associations, as opposed to those based on color, national origin, religion, or sex, is of no moment. The text of the statute draws no distinction, for this purpose, among the different varieties of discrimination it addresses—a fact recognized by the *Hopkins* plurality. This means that to the extent that the statute prohibits discrimination on the basis of the race of someone with whom the plaintiff associates, it also prohibits discrimination on the basis of the national origin, or the color, or the religion, or (as relevant here) the sex of the associate. No matter which category is involved, the essence of the claim is that the *plaintiff* would not be suffering the adverse action had his or her sex, race, color, national origin, or religion been different.

III

Today's decision must be understood against the backdrop of the Supreme Court's decisions, not only in the field of employment discrimination, but also in the area of broader discrimination on the basis of sexual orientation. We already have discussed the employment cases, especially *Hopkins* and *Oncale.* The latter line of cases began with Romer v. Evans, 517 U.S. 620 (1996), in which the Court held that a provision of the Colorado Constitution forbidding any organ of government in the state from taking action designed to protect "homosexual, lesbian, or bisexual" persons, *id.* at 624, violated the federal Equal Protection Clause. *Romer* was followed by Lawrence v. Texas, 539 U.S. 558 (2003), in which the Court found that a Texas statute criminalizing homosexual intimacy between consenting adults violated the liberty provision of the Due Process Clause. Next came United States v. Windsor, ___ U.S. ___, 133 S.Ct. 2675 (2013), which addressed the constitutionality of the part of the Defense of Marriage Act (DOMA) that excluded a same-sex partner from the definition of "spouse" in other federal statutes. The Court held that this part of DOMA "violate[d] basic due process and equal protection principles applicable to the Federal Government." Finally, the Court's decision in *Obergefell, supra,* held that the right to marry is a fundamental liberty right, protected by the Due Process and Equal Protection Clauses of the Fourteenth Amendment. The Court wrote that "[i]t is now clear that the challenged laws burden the liberty of same-sex couples, and it must be further acknowledged that they abridge central precepts of equality."

It would require considerable calisthenics to remove the "sex" from "sexual orientation." The effort to do so has led to confusing and contradictory results, as our panel opinion illustrated so well. The EEOC concluded, in its *Baldwin* decision, that such an effort cannot be reconciled with the straightforward language of Title VII. Many district courts have come to the same conclusion. See, *e.g.*, Boutillier v. Hartford Pub. Sch., No. 3:13-CV-01303-WWE, ___ F.Supp.3d ___, 2016 WL 6818348 (D. Conn. Nov. 17, 2016); *U.S.* Equal Emp't Opportunity

Comm'n v. Scott Med. Ctr., P.C., No. CV 16-225, ___ F.Supp.3d ___, 2016 WL 6569233 (W.D. Pa. Nov. 4, 2016); Winstead v. Lafayette Cnty. Bd. of Cnty. Comm'rs, 197 F.Supp.3d 1334 (N.D. Fla. 2016); Isaacs v. Felder Servs., LLC, 143 F.Supp.3d 1190 (M.D. Ala. 2015); see also Videckis v. Pepperdine Univ., 150 F.Supp.3d 1151 (C.D. Cal. 2015) (Title IX case, applying Title VII principles and *Baldwin*). Many other courts have found that gender-identity claims are cognizable under Title VII. See, *e.g.*, Rosa v. Park W. Bank & Tr. Co., 214 F.3d 213, 215–16 (1st Cir. 2000) (claim for sex discrimination under Equal Credit Opportunity Act, analogizing to Title VII); Schwenk v. Hartford, 204 F.3d 1187, 1201–02 (9th Cir. 2000) (relying on Title VII cases to conclude that violence against a transsexual was violence because of gender under the Gender Motivated Violence Act); Barnes v. City of Cincinnati, 401 F.3d 729 (6th Cir. 2005); Smith v. City of Salem, Ohio, 378 F.3d 566 (6th Cir. 2004); Fabian v. Hosp. of Cent. Conn., 172 F.Supp.3d 509 (D. Conn. 2016); Schroer v. Billington, 577 F.Supp.2d 293, 308 (D.D.C. 2008).

* * *

. . . We hold only that a person who alleges that she experienced employment discrimination on the basis of her sexual orientation has put forth a case of sex discrimination for Title VII purposes. It was therefore wrong to dismiss Hively's complaint for failure to state a claim. The judgment of the district court is REVERSED and the case is REMANDED for further proceedings.

NOTES AND QUESTIONS

1.   Traditionally, federal courts have distinguished discrimination based on sex from discrimination based on sexual orientation and held that the latter did not constitute discrimination based on sex. Under the Obama Administration, the EEOC pushed the argument that discrimination based on sexual orientation is a form of discrimination based on sex. See EEOC Press Release, EEOC Files First Suits Challenging Sexual Orientation Discrimination as Sex Discrimination (3/1/16), available at https://www.eeoc.gov/eeoc/newsroom/release/3-1-16.cfm. In Baldwin v. Foxx, EEOC Doc. 0120133080, 2015 WL 4397641 (July 15, 2015), the EEOC collapsed the distinction between sex and sexual orientation discrimination holding that discrimination based on sexual orientation is a form of sex discrimination. The Trump Administration rescinded Obama era guidances regarding the scope of sex discrimination law and has taken the position that discrimination based on sexual orientation does not constitute discrimination because of sex under Title VII. See U.S. Dep'ts of Educ. & Justice, Dear Colleague Letter (Feb. 22, 2017), https://www2.ed.gov/about/offices/list/ocr/letters/colleague-201702-title-ix.pdf.

2.   In *Hively*, the en banc Seventh Circuit reversed its own precedent to become the first circuit court to agree with the EEOC and hold that discrimination based on sexual orientation is actionable sex discrimination. See also Zarda v. Altitude Express, 883 F.3d 100 (2d Cir. 2018) (en banc)

(holding that discrimination based on sex encompasses discrimination based on sexual orientation), *cert. granted* Altitude Express, Inc. v. Zarda, 139 S.Ct. 1599 (2019). Other courts have maintained the distinction between sex and sexual orientation holding that only the former is actionable under Title VII. See Evans v. Georgia Reg'l Hosp., 850 F.3d 1248 (11th Cir. 2017) (holding that discrimination based on sexual orientation is not actionable under Title VII, though discrimination based on failure to conform to a gender stereotype is); Hinton v. Virginia Union Univ., 185 F.Supp.3d 807 (E.D.Va. 2016) (holding that "Title VII does not encompass sexual orientation discrimination claims, and cannot be supplanted by the merely persuasive power of the EEOC's decision"); Simonton v. Runyon, 232 F.3d 33, 35 (2d Cir. 2000) (rejecting plaintiff's argument that discrimination based on sex includes discrimination based on sexual orientation); but see Franchina v. City of Providence, 881 F.3d 32 (1st Cir. 2018) (holding that Title VII does not "foreclose[ ] a plaintiff in our Circuit from bringing sex-plus claims under Title VII where in addition to the sex-based charge, the "plus" factor is the plaintiff's status as a gay or lesbian individual"). From the perspective of legal logic, does it make sense to treat discrimination based on sexual orientation as a form of sex discrimination or as a distinct form of discrimination? From a policy standpoint, which approach is most appropriate?

3.   In October 2019, the Supreme Court held oral arguments in two cases addressing the scope of Title VII's sex discrimination prohibition. Zarda v. Altitude Express raised the question of whether Title VII's prohibition on discrimination because of sex encompasses discrimination because of sexual orientation. Altitude Express, Inc. v. Zarda, 883 F.3d 100 (2d Cir. 2018) (en banc), cert. granted, Altitude Express, Inc. v. Zarda, 139 S.Ct. 1599 (2019). R.G. and G.R. Harris Funeral Homes v. EEOC, raised the question of whether Title VII's prohibition on discrimination because of sex prohibits discrimination because of transgender status. EEOC v. R.G. & G.R. Harris Funeral Homes, Inc., 884 F.3d 560 (6th Cir. 2018), cert granted R.G. & G.R. Harris Funeral Homes, Inc. v. EEOC, 139 S.Ct. 1599 (2019).

4.   Employees have also been unsuccessful establishing a Title VII violation for religious discrimination based on sexual orientation discrimination. See Prowel v. Wise Bus. Forms, Inc., 579 F.3d 285 (3d Cir. 2009) (held: no claim for religious discrimination under Title VII where homosexual employee claimed he was harassed for failing to conform to his employer's religious beliefs).

5.   Although courts have held that discrimination based on sexual orientation does not violate Title VII, sexual orientation does not preclude an employee from establishing a valid Title VII claim for harassment based on sex where the alleged harasser is of the same sex. See Ellsworth v. Pot Luck Enters., Inc., 624 F.Supp.2d 868 (M.D. Tenn. 2009).

6.   About half of the states, the District of Columbia, and numerous cities have enacted laws prohibiting discrimination in private employment on the basis of sexual orientation. In Underwood v. Archer Mgmt. Servs. Inc., 857 F.Supp. 96 (D.D.C. 1994), the court held that the District of Columbia's law prohibiting discrimination based on sexual orientation did not extend to transsexuals, although a discharge based on the plaintiff's masculine appearance stated a claim for discrimination based on the D.C. statute prohibiting discrimination based on personal appearance.

7.   In Romer v. Evans, 517 U.S. 620 (1996), the Supreme Court, 6–3, held that Colorado's "Amendment 2" was unconstitutional. The amendment invalidated all existing and *future* state and local legislative, executive, or judicial action in Colorado, including those dealing with employment, that protect homosexuals from discrimination. In holding that Amendment 2 violated Equal Protection, Justice Kennedy wrote that Amendment 2 "seems inexplicable by anything but animus toward the class it affects." State efforts to limit the expansion of antidiscrimination protection have not ended however, but only changed forms. In 2015, Arkansas passed the Intrastate Commerce Improvement Act prohibiting local governments from providing protections against discrimination that exceeded those provided by state law. Ark. Code § 14–1–403. The Act was passed in response to a City of Fayetteville ordinance prohibiting discrimination in employment and housing based on sexual orientation and gender identity. Tennessee passed similar legislation, the Equal Access to Intrastate Commerce Act, in 2011. T.C.A. § 7–51–1801. In Howe v. Haslam, 2014 WL 5698877 (Tenn. Ct. App., Nov. 4, 2014), the Tennessee Court of Appeals upheld that state's law against an equal protection challenge and distinguished the law from that at issue in *Romer*. In 2016, North Carolina passed a law preempting any local workplace anti-discrimination ordinances. See H.R. 2, 2016 Gen. Assemb., 2d Extra Sess. (N.C. 2016).

8.   In Goins v. West Group, 635 N.W.2d 717 (Minn. 2001), however, a former employee was unsuccessful in a claim of sexual orientation discrimination under state law. The Minnesota Supreme Court held that an employer did not violate the law's prohibition on sexual orientation discrimination by designating employee restroom use on the basis of biological gender rather than "self-image" gender.

PART III

TERMS AND CONDITIONS OF EMPLOYMENT

CHAPTER 5

WAGES AND HOURS

A. FEDERAL AND STATE WAGE AND HOUR REGULATION

Direct government regulation of wages and hours has existed in America since colonial times; in 1630, the Massachusetts General Court placed a wage cap of two shillings a day on the work of carpenters, bricklayers, thatchers, and other craftsmen, and under threat of a heavy fine, forbade them to charge, or anyone to pay, more. The shortage of skilled workers in the colonies had resulted in high wages, with colonial craftsmen earning up to 100 percent above what their peers in England received for the same work. Even common laborers typically earned a wage premium of 30 percent over contemporary English wages. Concern over protective working conditions surfaced as early as the eighteenth century when Philadelphia carpenters advocating a ten-hour day engaged in a work stoppage. Regulating working hours was also a way of limiting workers' exposure to hazardous conditions associated with certain industries and of protecting women and children from overwork. Government interference with the private right of contract, however, was subject to challenge and, in many cases, judicial hostility, despite the progressive ends usually sought by such legislation.

Lochner v. New York

198 U.S. 45 (1905).

■ MR. JUSTICE PECKHAM delivered the opinion of the court:

The indictment, it will be seen, charges that the plaintiff in error violated the 110th section of article 8, chapter 415, of the Laws of 1897, known as the labor law of the state of New York, in that he wrongfully and unlawfully required and permitted an employee working for him to work more than sixty hours in one week. * * * The mandate of the statute, that "no employee shall be required or permitted to work," is the substantial equivalent of an enactment that "no employee shall contract or agree to work," more than ten hours per day; and, as there is no provision for special emergencies, the statute is mandatory in all cases. It is not an act merely fixing the number of hours which shall constitute a legal day's work, but an absolute prohibition upon the employer permitting, under any circumstances, more than ten hours' work to be done in his establishment. The employee may desire to earn the extra money which would arise from his working more than the prescribed time, but this statute forbids the employer from permitting the employee to earn it.

The statute necessarily interferes with the right of contract between the employer and employees, concerning the number of hours in which the latter may labor in the bakery of the employer. The general right to make a contract in relation to his business is part of the liberty of the individual protected by the 14th Amendment of the Federal Constitution. Under that provision no state can deprive any person of life, liberty, or property without due process of law. The right to purchase or to sell labor is part of the liberty protected by this amendment, unless there are circumstances which exclude the right. There are, however, certain powers, existing in the sovereignty of each state in the Union, somewhat vaguely termed police powers, the exact description and limitation of which have not been attempted by the courts. Those powers, broadly stated, and without, at present, any attempt at a more specific limitation, relate to the safety, health, morals, and general welfare of the public. Both property and liberty are held on such reasonable conditions as may be imposed by the governing power of the state in the exercise of those powers, and with such conditions the 14th Amendment was not designed to interfere.

The state, therefore, has power to prevent the individual from making certain kinds of contracts, and in regard to them the Federal Constitution offers no protection. If the contract be one which the state, in the legitimate exercise of its police power, has the right to prohibit, it is not prevented from prohibiting it by the 14th Amendment.

* * *

It must, of course, be conceded that there is a limit to the valid exercise of the police power by the state. There is no dispute concerning this general proposition. * * * In every case that comes before this court, therefore, where legislation of this character is concerned, and where the protection of the Federal Constitution is sought, the question necessarily arises: Is this a fair, reasonable, and appropriate exercise of the police power of the state, or is it an unreasonable, unnecessary, and arbitrary interference with the right of the individual to his personal liberty, or to enter into those contracts in relation to labor which may seem to him appropriate or necessary for the support of himself and his family? Of course the liberty of contract relating to labor includes both parties to it. The one has as much right to purchase as the other to sell labor.

* * *

The question whether this act is valid as a labor law, pure and simple, may be dismissed in a few words. There is no reasonable ground for interfering with the liberty of person or the right of free contract, by determining the hours of labor, in the occupation of a baker. There is no contention that bakers as a class are not equal in intelligence and capacity to men in other trades or manual occupations, or that they are not able to assert their rights and care for themselves without the protecting arm of the state, interfering with their independence of judgment and of action. They are in no sense wards of the state. Viewed in the light of a purely labor law, with no reference whatever to the question of health, we think that a law like the one before us involves neither the safety, the morals, nor the welfare, of the public, and that the interest of the public is not in the slightest degree affected by such an act. The law must be upheld, if at all, as a law pertaining to the health of the individual engaged in the occupation of a baker. It does not affect any other portion of the public than those who are engaged in that occupation. Clean and wholesome bread does not depend upon whether the baker works but ten hours per day or only sixty hours a week.

* * *

We think the limit of the police power has been reached and passed in this case. There is, in our judgment, no reasonable foundation for holding this to be necessary or appropriate as a health law to safeguard the public health, or the health of the individuals who are following the trade of a baker. * * * It might be safely affirmed that almost all occupations more or less affect the health. There must be more than the mere fact of the possible existence of some small amount of unhealthiness to warrant legislative interference with liberty. It is unfortunately true that labor, even in any department, may possibly carry with it the seeds of unhealthiness. But are we all, on that account, at the mercy of legislative majorities? A printer, a tinsmith, a locksmith, a carpenter, a cabinetmaker, a dry goods clerk, a bank's, a lawyer's, or a physician's clerk, or a clerk in almost any kind of business, would all come under the power of the legislature, on this assumption. No trade, no occupation, no mode of earning one's living, could escape this all-pervading power, and the acts of the legislature in limiting the hours of labor in all employments would be valid, although such limitation might seriously cripple the ability of the laborer to support himself and his family. In our large cities there are many buildings into which the sun penetrates for but a short time in each day, and these buildings are occupied by people carrying on the business of bankers, brokers, lawyers, real estate, and many other kinds of business, aided by many clerks, messengers, and other employees. Upon the assumption of the validity of this act under review, it is not possible to say that an act, prohibiting lawyers' or bank clerks, or others, from contracting to labor for their employers more than eight hours a day would be invalid. It might be said that it is unhealthy to work more than that number of hours in an apartment lighted by artificial light during the working hours of the day; that the occupation of the bank clerk, the lawyer's clerk, the real-estate clerk, or the broker's clerk, in such offices is therefore unhealthy, and the legislature, in its paternal wisdom, must, therefore, have the right to legislate on the subject of, and to limit, the hours for such labor; and, if it exercises that power, and its validity be questioned, it is sufficient to say, it has reference to the public health; it has reference to the health of the employees condemned to labor day after day in buildings where the sun never shines; it is a health law, and therefore it is valid, and cannot be questioned by the courts.

* * *

It is manifest to us that the limitation of the hours of labor as provided for in this section of the statute under which the indictment was found, and the plaintiff in error convicted, has no such direct relation to, and no such substantial effect upon, the health of the employee, as to justify us in regarding the section as really a health law. It seems to us that the real object and purpose were simply to regulate the hours of labor between the master and his employees (all being men, sui juris), in a private business, not dangerous in any degree to morals, or in any real and substantial degree to the health of the employees. Under such circumstances the freedom of master and employee to contract with each other in relation to their employment, and in defining the same, cannot be prohibited or interfered with, without violating the Federal Constitution.

Reversed.

■ MR. JUSTICE HARLAN (with whom MR. JUSTICE WHITE and MR. JUSTICE DAY concurred) dissenting:

* * *

It is plain that this statute was enacted in order to protect the physical well-being of those who work in bakery and confectionery establishments. It may be that the statute had its origin, in part, in the belief that employers and employees in such establishments were not upon an equal footing, and that the necessities of the latter often compelled them to submit to such exactions as unduly taxed their strength. Be this as it may, the statute must be taken as expressing the belief of the people of New York that, as a general rule, and in the case of the average man, labor in excess of sixty hours during a week in such establishments may endanger the health of those who thus labor. * * * I find it impossible, in view of common experience, to say that there is here no real or substantial relation between the means employed by the state and the end sought to be accomplished by its legislation. * * *

Professor Hirt in his treatise on the "Diseases of the Workers" has said: "The labor of the bakers is among the hardest and most laborious imaginable, because it has to be performed under conditions injurious to the health of those engaged in it. It is hard, very hard, work, not only because it requires a great deal of physical exertion in an overheated workshop and during unreasonably long hours, but more so because of the erratic demands of the public, compelling the baker to perform the greater part of his work at night, thus depriving him of an opportunity to enjoy the necessary rest and sleep,—a fact which is highly injurious to his health." Another writer says: "The constant inhaling of flour dust causes inflammation of the lungs and of the bronchial tubes. The eyes also suffer through this dust, which is responsible for the many cases of running eyes among the bakers. The long hours of toil to which all bakers are subjected produce rheumatism, cramps, and swollen legs. The intense heat in the workshops induces the workers to resort to cooling drinks, which, together with their habit of exposing the greater part of their bodies to the change in the atmosphere, is another source of a number of diseases of various organs. Nearly all bakers are pale-faced and of more delicate health than the workers of other crafts, which is chiefly due to their hard work and their irregular and unnatural mode of living, whereby the power of resistance against disease is greatly diminished. The average age of a baker is below that of other workman; they seldom live over their fiftieth year, most of them dying between the ages of forty and fifty. During periods of epidemic diseases the bakers are generally the first to succumb to the disease, and the number swept away during such periods far exceeds the number of other crafts in comparison to the men employed in the respective industries. When, in 1720, the plague visited the city of Marseilles, France, every baker in the city succumbed to the epidemic, which caused considerable excitement in the neighboring cities and resulted in measures for the sanitary protection of the bakers."

* * *

We judicially know that the question of the number of hours during which a workman should continuously labor has been, for a long period, and is yet, a subject of serious consideration among civilized peoples, and by those having special knowledge of the laws of health. Suppose the statute prohibited labor in bakery and confectionery establishments in excess of eighteen hours each day. No one, I take it, could dispute the power of the state to enact such a statute. * * *

* * * We cannot say that the state has acted without reason, nor ought we to proceed upon the theory that its action is a mere sham. Our duty, I submit, is to sustain the statute as not being in conflict with the Federal Constitution, for the reason—and such is an all-sufficient reason—it is not shown to be plainly and palpably inconsistent with that instrument. Let the state alone in the management of its purely domestic affairs, so long as it does not appear beyond all question that it has violated the Federal Constitution. This view necessarily results from the principle that the health and safety of the people of a state are primarily for the state to guard and protect.

NOTES AND QUESTIONS

1.   The majority in *Lochner* recognized that there were circumstances under which the state could legitimately regulate private contracts. Can you think of any employment setting in which the *Lochner* majority would have upheld such legislation? Suppose the state had tried to limit the number of hours worked by underground miners or steelworkers? Hospital workers? Airline pilots? Why? See Holden v. Hardy, 169 U.S. 366 (1898) (upholding

constitutionality of law setting maximum hours for workers in mines and refineries).

2.	If, as Justice Harlan pointed out, the Court would not have overturned a statute prohibiting an 18-hour day, why did it overturn the New York statute? What about a 16-hour day? 14? 12? Do you agree with Justice Harlan's argument that the employers and employees do not have equal bargaining power over hours worked, or with the majority's freedom of contract argument?

3.	Nominally, *Lochner* is a case about maximum working hours in the baking industry. It has also been characterized as the paradigm constitutional law case, for its holding on the permissible reach of state action, for the extent of judicial activism engaged in by the majority in striking down the New York statute, and for its unspoken, but unquestioning, approval of the existing distribution of wealth and entitlements. For a discussion of the larger constitutional issues, see, e.g., Cass R. Sunstein, Lochner's Legacy, 87 Colum. L. Rev. 873 (1987). Courts now acknowledge that economic regulations will be sustained against substantive due process challenges provided the regulation has a rational basis. See Matter of Gifford, 688 F.2d 447, 453 (7th Cir. 1982) (upholding constitutionality of provision in bankruptcy code retroactively cancelling lender's security interest in borrower's household goods).

4.	As the length of the "standard" working day was gradually reduced from 12 hours to eight hours in the early part of the twentieth century, the shorter work day became a more intense, concentrated work day with a shorter time for meal breaks and few, if any, rest breaks. For many workers, ranging from nurses and school teachers to manufacturing and agricultural workers, this situation still pertains today. Meal and rest breaks, to the extent they are mandated at all by law, are the province of state laws. Most states require employers to offer lunch breaks, typically 30 minutes for a work day longer than six hours. Many fewer states require rest breaks, typically 10 minutes every four hours. Threatened with being fired for going to the bathroom, a surprisingly large number of workers suffer discomfort and humiliation—as well as damage to their kidneys, bladder, and cardiovascular system—from not being able to use the bathroom as needed. For a further discussion, see Marc Linder & Ingrid Nygaard, Void Where Prohibited: Rest Breaks and the Right to Urinate on Company Time (1998).

———

Until the Depression, the state legislatures were much more successful than the federal government in regulating working conditions. As *Lochner* illustrates, the rationale most frequently cited for government interference with the employment relationship was public health. If state regulation was an impermissible infringement on freedom of contract, federal regulation was seen as even worse. The widespread unemployment of the 1930s, however, cast a new perspective on wage and hour laws in which minimum wage regulation was perceived as necessary to guarantee "the minimum standard of living necessary for health, efficiency, and general well-being of workers," and hour regulation as an important way to spread a scarce commodity—employment—among distressed American workers. After several unsuccessful attempts to establish a comprehensive legislative scheme, Congress finally passed the Fair Labor Standards Act (FLSA) in 1938. In passing the FLSA, however, Congress did not preempt the states' ability to regulate employment as well, and to this day state law plays an important role in protecting workers' rights. For example, state minimum wage laws may be higher than the federal standard and may apply to workers not covered by the federal law. In addition, state law provides a means for employees who have not been paid their full wages, regardless of how much they earn, to recover unpaid compensation from their employers.

1.   FEDERAL WAGE AND HOUR REGULATION: THE FAIR LABOR STANDARDS ACT

a.   LEGISLATIVE HISTORY

Bernard Schwartz, Statutory History of the United States: Labor Organization*
396–399 (Robert F. Koretz ed. 1970).

The Wagner Act, of course, was but one of a number of statutes passed during the New Deal focusing on labor conditions. But, in a sense, it was a culmination of years of employee attempts to establish minimum wages and maximum hours. As early as 1868, Congress had established a ten-hour day for employees on public works. Subsequently, the government's efforts to establish labor standards related largely to work conditions under public contract and to interstate mail transportation, although Congress did attempt to control child labor through its commerce and taxing powers. The idea was for the government to set an example for private employers to follow. But the inability to establish minimum working conditions through Congress also reflected labor's national political weakness. Workingmen's organizations were often much more successful at the state level. Child labor laws, for example, were enacted in the six New England states by the mid-nineteenth century, and by 1900 some twenty-eight states had at least minimal protection for child workers. Today, there exists in every state a considerable body of law covering the employment of women and children, sanitation, and safety. Much of this sort of legislation, both state and federal, was challenged in the courts by employers and often declared unconstitutional. Thus, the Supreme Court upheld in 1898 a state statute fixing maximum hours for male miners (Holden v. Hardy, 169 U.S. 366), but subsequently decided in 1905 that it was unconstitutional for a state to limit work hours in bakeries (Lochner v.

---

*   Reprinted by permission of Chelsea House Publishers.

New York, 198 U.S. 45). The Court similarly struck down in 1923 state legislation fixing minimum wages in Adkins v. Children's Hospital, 261 U.S. 525. Federal regulation fared no better. An effort to control child labor was nullified by the Court in 1922 (Bailey v. Drexel Furniture Company, 259 U.S. 20). Further, the early efforts of the New Deal to regulate labor standards through the National Industrial Recovery Act [A.L.A. Schechter Poultry Corp. v. United States, 295 U.S. 495 (1935)] and the Bituminous Coal Conservation Act [Carter v. Carter Coal Co., 298 U.S. 238 (1936)] suffered the same fate. But in 1937, the Court sustained the constitutionality of the Wagner Act and upheld a state minimum wage law, in West Coast Hotel Company v. Parrish, 300 U.S. 379. Decisions such as these quite plainly forecast Court approval of federal legislation in the area of wages and hours. * * *

On May 24, 1937, President Roosevelt, whose Administration consistently urged wage and hour legislation as an anti-depression measure, sent Congress a special message: "To conserve our primary resources of manpower, Government must have some control over maximum hours, minimum wages, the evil of child labor, and the exploitation of unorganized labor." The President argued that Congress' power to act in these matters rested on the Constitution's commerce clause. On the same day, Senator Eugene Black (Dem., Tex.) and Representative Lawrence Connery (Dem., Mass.) introduced bills to implement the Presidential request. But more than a year of legislative activity passed before a law was enacted. * * *

The new statute created a Wage and Hour Division in the Department of Labor under the supervision of an administrator. The statute regulated wages, hours, and child labor. More specifically, it provided for a minimum hourly wage of twenty-five cents for the first year, and thirty cents for the second year. A minimum of forty cents was to become effective after seven years, and a wage between thirty and forty cents could be ordered during the first seven years. As to hours, it sought to spread employment by overtime penalties: for the first year maximum straight-time hours were forty-four; for the second year, forty-two; and thereafter forty. The child labor provisions, similar to those previously declared unconstitutional by the Supreme Court, prohibited the interstate shipment of goods produced in an establishment employing child labor.

Consistent with the constitutional philosophy exhibited in the Supreme Court's decisions to uphold the Wagner and Railway Labor Acts, the Court, in United States v. Darby, 312 U.S. 100 (1941), sustained the constitutionality of the act against attacks based upon the commerce clause and due process clause of the Fifth Amendment.

In the meantime, a number of proposals had been made for revision of the act. These culminated in what was called the "Fair Labor Standards Amendments of 1949." * * * It has been pointed out that "the Amendments of 1949 were a compromise between President Truman's desire for a broader law to cover all employees of employers engaged in covered business, raise standards, and restrict exemptions, and the aims of those who wished to narrow the coverage, broaden the exemptions, and tie the minimum wage to the cost-of-living index." In brief, the 1949 amendments narrowed the coverage of the statute, strengthened the child labor prohibitions, set forth in greater detail the overtime standards, revised certain exemptions, made certain administrative changes, and increased the minimum wage to seventy-five cents.

There have been a number of amendments since 1949, the most important of which have increased the minimum wage and broadened statutory coverage. Coverage was extended by the 1961 amendments through a new concept, the covering of specified business enterprises as well as the activities of individual employees; in 1966 the enterprise concept was utilized to further broaden coverage. In 1963 equal pay provisions were added to the act for the purpose of eliminating wage differentials based upon sex.

b.   BASIC PROVISIONS OF THE FAIR LABOR STANDARDS ACT

The basic scheme of the Fair Labor Standards Act, 29 U.S.C. § 201, is quite simple: it establishes a minimum wage applicable to all employees of covered employers and it provides for mandatory overtime payment for covered employees who work more than 40 hours a week. The statutory scheme has remained practically unchanged since its original passage, except for updates to bring the minimum wage into parity with wage inflation. Currently, the Act covers more than 130 million full-time and part-time workers in the public and private sector.

(i) Minimum Wage

The Fair Minimum Wage Act of 2007 raised the federal minimum wage in three increments, concluding at $7.25 per hour effective July 24, 2009. As of 2014, the mean hourly earnings for a U.S. worker were just below $25. The protection of the statute's minimum wage provisions has its greatest impact on wage rates for low-level, unskilled jobs; the national economic shift from manufacturing to services has resulted in larger numbers of such jobs.

Section 206(a) of the FLSA is the basic minimum wage provision. It provides:

> Every employer shall pay to each of his employees who in any workweek is engaged in commerce or in the production of goods for commerce, or is employed in an enterprise engaged in commerce or in the production of goods for commerce, wages at the following rates: (1) except as otherwise provided in this section, not less than—* * * (C) $7.25 an hour, beginning [on July 24, 2009.]

The balance of section 206 illustrates the particularized nature of some sections of the statute, enumerating special provisions for domestic workers, seamen on American vessels, and other workers. Section 206(d) prohibits sex discrimination in wages for male and female employees performing equal work (See Part B., infra.).

"Tipped employees," such as restaurant wait staff, are entitled to receive a lower cash minimum wage of $2.13 per hour if their employers claim a tip credit against their minimum wage obligation. If an employee's tips combined with the employer's cash wage of at least $2.13 per hour do not equal the minimum hourly wage, the employer must make up the difference. Certain other conditions must also be met.

STATE MINIMUM WAGE LAWS

As of January 2020, 29 states and the District of Columbia have minimum wages higher than that required by federal law, and 17 of them have hourly minimums of $10 or more. Further, a list of cities have higher minimum wages than the states in which they are located; for example, the city of SeaTac, Washington was the first city in the country to adopt a $15/hour minimum wage, in late 2013. However, as discussed at greater length later in the chapter, states may preempt local wage laws.

Beginning with Baltimore in 1994, several cities around the country have enacted "living wage" ordinances to attempt to assist low-income families. Other cities with these ordinances include Boston, Detroit, Los Angeles, Miami, New Orleans, and New York. Living wage ordinances impose a wage floor that is higher than traditional federal and state minimum wages. Living wage levels are often set to the wage level needed for a family to reach the federal poverty line. Coverage under living wage ordinances is often restricted to businesses that contract with the city. David Neumark argues that such living wage legislation has the same positive and negative effects as federal and state minimum wage laws despite its limited coverage, however the negative effects are slightly weaker. Despite this positive outcome, Neumark urges caution with the "living wage." Only certain cities with very specific coverage rules had success in reducing poverty through use of a living wage ordinance, so many questions remain unanswered. For more information, see David Neumark, Raising Incomes by Mandating Higher Wages, NBER Reporter (Fall 2002). The validity of a city minimum wage ordinance was challenged in RUI One Corp. v. City of Berkeley, 371 F.3d 1137 (9th Cir. 2004), and the court upheld the constitutionality under California law of such municipal "living wage" legislation. In 2007, Maryland became the first state to require a living wage. Maryland currently requires employers with state contracts to pay workers a minimum living wage—$13.96 an hour in the Baltimore-Washington corridor and $10.49 an hour in the rural counties, where wages and prices are usually lower. Md. Code, State Finance and Procurement, § 18–101 through § 18–109. Proposals for a federal "living wage" law have been introduced in Congress, but (thus far) have garnered little support.

(ii) Overtime

The overtime provisions of the FLSA, which do not limit the number of hours employees may work but merely require overtime pay after a certain number of hours, have more general applicability than the wage provisions. The child labor provisions of the Act regulate employment of children. Generally, the statute prohibits employing children under the age of 14, with special exceptions for certain types of agricultural work, babysitting and other chores, employment in a parents' business, and for actors and performers. The Department of Labor has also issued regulations that limit the kinds of work children over 14 may perform as well as the hours they may work.

Section 207(a)(1) of the FLSA concerns maximum hours:

Except as otherwise provided in this section, no employer shall employ any of his employees who in any workweek is engaged in commerce or in the production of goods for commerce, or is employed in an enterprise engaged in commerce or in the production of goods for commerce, for a workweek longer than forty hours unless such employee receives compensation for his employment in excess of the hours above specified at a rate not less than one and one-half times the regular rate at which he is employed.

The rest of section 207 addresses special conditions for hours worked pursuant to a collective bargaining agreement, piece workers, hospital workers, police and firefighters, and transit workers, many of whose traditional work days or work weeks do not fit the typical "eight hours a day/40 hours a week" configuration. The 1989 amendments added section 207(q), a maximum hour exemption for up to ten hours in any workweek for remedial education offered by the employer to employees who lack a high school diploma or education at the eighth-grade level.

The Wage and Hour Division of the Department of Labor, the federal agency responsible for enforcing the FLSA, remains active in policing violations. In fiscal year 2008, the Wage and Hour Division received more than 28,000 complaints and collected more than $185 million in back wages for more than 228,000 employees. The agency collected a total of more than $1.4 billion in back wages from 2001 to 2008. Further, violators are not limited to sweat shops and day labor camps. In 1982, the United States Postal Service entered into a settlement agreement with the Department of Labor under which it agreed to pay $400 million for overtime and premium pay violations committed during the period 1974–1978. Approximately 550,000 current and former employees were entitled to receive amounts up to $765 each to resolve their claims; the settlement was the largest ever achieved in an FLSA case.

NOTES

1. There are a number of employment practices that the FLSA does not regulate. For example, the FLSA does *not* require vacation, holiday, severance, or sick pay; meal or rest periods; premium pay for weekend or holiday work; pay raises or fringe benefits; and a discharge notice, reason for discharge, or immediate payment of final wages to terminated employees.

Additionally, the FLSA does not limit the number of hours in a day or days in a week an employee may be required or scheduled to work, including overtime hours, if the employee is at least 16 years old.

2. The proportionality of the minimum wage to the national average has not been constant. When originally enacted, the minimum wage was set at about half the national average wage. When the minimum wage was amended in 1989, it dropped to about one-third the national average wage. After legislation in 1996, the minimum wage increased to $5.15—almost half the national average wage of $11.76. By 2014, the minimum wage was about one-third of the national average wage.

3. California has a "day of rest" statute. That law prohibits an employer from "causing employees to work more than six days in seven" but does not apply "when the total hours of employment do not exceed 30 hours in any week or six hours in any one day thereof." If the employer fails to comply, it will have to pay the relevant workers an "overtime premium." For interpretation of the complicated ambiguities of this statute, some sections of which go back to 1858, see Mendoza v. Nordstrom, Inc., 393 P.3d 375 (Cal. 2017).

4. A handful of cities have enacted what are sometimes called "secure scheduling laws," which are aimed at promoting predictable and stable work schedules for low wage workers. For example, in 2015, San Francisco enacted a law requiring "formula retail" businesses to pay workers a premium for last-minute schedule changes or for requiring workers to be "on call."

c.   COVERAGE

(i)   Who Is Covered by the FLSA?

The Act's Coverage is extensive. A business is covered if it meets the definition of "enterprise," as defined by section 203 of the Act. In addition, employees who are engaged in commerce are covered even if their employers do not qualify as enterprises. To meet the commerce test, goods or services produced by the business must cross state lines, but this requirement has been broadly construed (e.g., a laundry facility using soap that has been shipped across state lines is a covered employer). Employees or businesses that are not covered by the FLSA may, however, be regulated by similar state legislation.

Section 203 of the Act defines an enterprise to exclude certain types of small businesses according to their gross sales. The 1989 Amendments streamlined the section 203(s) definition of an "enterprise engaged in commerce or in the production of goods for commerce," by replacing a diversity of industry-specific gross annual sales limits with a more uniform coverage floor of $500,000 annual gross volume of sales made or business done. Hospitals, schools, and public agencies are covered regardless of their financial size; any business that employs only members of the immediate family of the owner are exempted regardless of size. Under section 203(r), the gross sales of separate businesses having unified operations or under common control may be aggregated to bring a business within the Act's coverage.

To determine whether nominally separate companies qualify as a single enterprise, courts apply a three-part test. The company must (1) perform related activities (2) under unified operations or common control (3) for a common business purpose. See Martin v. Deiriggi, 985 F.2d 129, 133 (4th Cir. 1992) (motel and on-premises restaurant were single entity under FLSA). The judiciary has liberally interpreted the "enterprise" definition of the FLSA in favor of coverage, particularly where "separate" businesses which individually are too small to be covered by the Act are owned and operated by the same individual or parent corporation. In Donovan v. Grim Hotel Co., 747 F.2d 966 (5th Cir. 1984), cert. denied, 471 U.S. 1124 (1985), the court found that five separate hotel corporations were a single "enterprise" where they were all virtually controlled by a single individual, members of his family owned the shares that he did not, the corporations shared the same officers, and a related company provided bookkeeping and financial services for the group.

NOTES

1.   In 1976, the Supreme Court held that the application of the provisions of the FLSA to state and local governments constituted a violation of the Tenth Amendment. National League of Cities v. Usery, 426 U.S. 833 (1976). Nine years later, in Garcia v. San Antonio Metro. Transit Auth., 469 U.S. 528 (1985), the Court overruled *National League of Cities* and held, five-to-four, that nothing in the minimum wage and overtime provisions of the Act violated any constitutional provision. Congress promptly passed the Fair Labor Standards Amendments of 1985, permitting state and local government employers to substitute compensatory time off for the mandatory overtime provisions of the FLSA, eliminating volunteers and state and local legislative employees from coverage, and minimizing employers' liability for unpaid wages prior to April 15, 1986 (the effective date of the Amendments). "Comp time" in lieu of overtime must accrue at the time-and-a-half rate for overtime set forth in the Act, however. The 1985 Amendments were upheld in Rhinebarger v. Orr, 839 F.2d 387 (7th Cir. 1988), cert. denied, 488 U.S. 824 (1988).

2.   Despite the fact that the FLSA is applicable to state governments, such bodies may be immune from lawsuits brought under the Act. In Alden v. Maine, 527 U.S. 706 (1999), the Court held that Maine was immune from a lawsuit brought in state court by probation officers seeking money damages for alleged violations of the overtime provisions of the Fair Labor Standards Act. Federal court actions against states are barred by Seminole Tribe of

Florida v. Florida, 517 U.S. 44 (1996), unless the state has waived sovereign immunity. The *Alden* decision would not prevent an action against a local government or a quasi-independent authority created by the state; subordinate units do not have the state's sovereign immunity. It would not bar an action against the state seeking a declaration of the plaintiffs' rights, or an action for damages against an individual state official who made or implemented decisions that interfered with plaintiffs' federal statutory rights. Also, the *Alden* opinion specifically says that FLSA enforcement actions for money damages can be brought by the United States Department of Labor. But suits seeking money damages brought by citizens of the state (or other states) cannot be brought in federal or state courts unless the state has explicitly waived its sovereign immunity.

Alden drew a distinction between FLSA actions and, on the other hand, private lawsuits seeking to enforce federal anti-discrimination statutes enacted pursuant to congressional power granted by section 5 of the Fourteenth Amendment. Nevertheless, *Alden* is an important decision because it affects five million state employees, requiring Congress to tailor carefully the remedial structures for federal regulation of these employees' workplace conditions. For example, *Alden* would be an important precedent if Congress decided to extend OSHA coverage (see Chapter 8) or ERISA pension regulation (see Chapter 13) to state employees. While the border between "mere" economic regulation of work and Fourteenth Amendment civil rights enforcement is murky, *Alden* may bar private money damage actions by state employees enforcing regulatory rules as to hours, child labor, family leave, and—if a federal right were ever created—wrongful discharge.

The decision in *Alden* was by a vote of 5–4. The dissenting opinion by Justice Souter compared the Court's decision to its earlier invalidation of federal power to adopt minimum wage and maximum hour provisions. In *Alden*, Justice Souter wrote, referring to *Lochner*, supra p. 475: "I expect the Court's late essay into immunity doctrine will prove the equal of its earlier experiment in laissez-faire, the one being as unrealistic as the other, as indefensible, and probably as fleeting."

3.   In Thompson v. Real Estate Mortgage Network, 748 F.3d 142 (3d Cir. 2014), the Third Circuit determined for the first time that a successor-employer may be held financially accountable for its predecessor's wage-and-hour violations under the FLSA. Instead of applying the New Jersey state law test for determining whether successor liability applied, the court applied the federal common law test, which allowed for a lower bar to relief. It requires consideration of the following factors in determining whether successor liability should be imposed: "(1) continuity in operations and work force of the successor and predecessor employers; (2) notice to the successor-employer of its predecessor's legal obligations; and (3) ability of the predecessor to provide adequate relief directly." By contrast, under New Jersey law, successor companies are considered legally distinct from their predecessors and do not assume any debts or obligations of the successor unless: (1) the successor agrees to assume such liabilities; (2) the transaction amounts to a consolidation or merger of the buyer and seller; (3) the purchasing company is merely a "continuation" of the selling company; or (4) the transaction was consummated to fraudulently escape its liabilities and debts.

4. A federal law, the Aviation Administrative Authorization Act of 1994, preempts state regulation of motor carriers. California nonetheless sought to apply to truck drivers its meal and rest break laws. Held, California can do that because the state laws at issue are not "related to prices, routes, or services, and therefore are not preempted." Dilts v. Penske Logistics LLC, 769 F.3d 637 (9th Cir. 2014).

Another preemption question—perhaps a more obscure one—arose in Parker Drilling Management Services v. Newton, 139 S.Ct. 1881 (2019). In that case, the Court interpreted the Outer Continental Shelf Lands Act to conclude that federal and not (more employee-protective) California law controlled whether workers had to be paid for their "controlled standby" time.

5. What happens when there is more than one entity that is arguably responsible for complying with the FLSA? In Hall v. DIRECTV, 846 F.3d 757 (4th Cir. 2017), the court considered whether DIRECTV or one of its subsidiaries was a "joint employer" of the plaintiffs, who were technicians charged with installing satellite TV systems. According to the complaint in the case, DIRECTV contracted with "Home Service Providers," which in turn contracted with subcontractors, which then hired the technicians. However, the complaint further alleged that DIRECTV controlled nearly every aspect of the technicians' work, including the uniforms they wore, their training, and their work assignments. The Fourth Circuit held that the plaintiffs had stated a claim that DIRECTV was their joint employer under its test, which considers whether the putative joint employer "(1) had the power to hire and fire the employee; (2) supervised and controlled employee work schedules or conditions of employment; (3) determined the rate and method of payment; and (4) maintained employment records.

(ii) Who Is a Covered Employee?

Even though an enterprise may be covered by the FLSA, not all of the individuals who work there necessarily are.

(a) Who Is an Employee?

First, the FLSA only covers employees. Section 203 (e) (1) defines an employee as "any individual employed by an employer," and section 203 (g) defines employ as "to suffer or permit to work." The concept of employment in the FLSA is very broad and is tested by "economic reality." Most notably, the economic reality test for the FLSA means that it does not cover workers who are considered independent contractors. Courts have identified a number of factors which may be useful in distinguishing employees from independent contractors under the FLSA.

Donovan v. DialAmerica Marketing, Inc.

757 F.2d 1376 (3d Cir.), cert. denied, 474 U.S. 919 (1985).

■ BECKER, CIRCUIT JUDGE:

This opinion concerns an appeal by the Secretary of Labor (the "Secretary") from the district court's judgment for defendant, DialAmerica Marketing, Inc., in an action brought by the Secretary under the Fair Labor Standards Act, 29 U.S.C. §§ 201–219 (1982) (the "FLSA"). The Secretary alleged that DialAmerica had failed to comply with the minimum-wage and record-keeping provisions of the FLSA. The district court determined that the two groups of workers in question, persons who research telephone numbers for DialAmerica in their homes and those who also distribute telephone-research work to other home researchers ("distributors"), are independent contractors, not "employees" subject to the provisions of the FLSA. * * *

Because we believe the district court misapplied the relevant legal test for determining "employee" status under the FLSA, we hold that the court erred in concluding that the home researchers were not employees of DialAmerica. On the other hand, we hold that the district court did not err in its conclusion that the distributors were independent contractors rather than employees. * * *

DialAmerica Marketing, Inc., is a telephone marketing firm that operates in twenty states and maintains its principal place of business in Teaneck, New Jersey. A major aspect of DialAmerica's business is the sale of magazine renewal subscriptions by telephone to persons whose subscriptions have expired or are near expiration. Under this "expire" program, publishers supply DialAmerica with the names and addresses of subscribers, and DialAmerica locates phone numbers for these subscribers and telephones them in an effort to sell renewal subscriptions.

Initially, DialAmerica located subscribers' phone numbers by employing in-house researchers who would find numbers by consulting telephone books and calling directory-assistance operators. In 1976, DialAmerica initiated its home-researcher program as a method of increasing its capacity to locate needed telephone numbers. Under the program, persons would travel to DialAmerica's office in Teaneck and pick up cards, each of which contained the name and address of a subscriber whose telephone number was needed. They would then take these cards home, use telephone books or operators to locate the telephone numbers of the persons listed, write the numbers on the cards in a specified manner, and then return the completed cards to DialAmerica's office. The home-research program remained in effect until 1982, when it was discontinued.

In June 1979, DialAmerica began a computerized telephone-number search operation. During the period from 1979 to 1982, this operation accounted for the locating of about 50% of all telephone numbers searched by DialAmerica. Another 20% of the numbers were located by the company's in-house researchers. The home-research program accounted for the discovery of about 4%–5% of all numbers sought; the remainder apparently were never found.

Upon deciding to begin the home-research program, DialAmerica sought researchers by placing a total of five newspaper advertisements, the last of which ran in May 1979. After that date, prospective home researchers approached DialAmerica after learning about the program from others. Those desiring such work met with an officer of the company. During the meeting, they were instructed how properly to complete the magazine expire cards, and they were asked to sign a document labeled an "Independent Contractor's Agreement." DialAmerica never rejected anyone who applied for such work, although it did subsequently discharge some home researchers who performed their work inadequately.

Upon signing the agreement to do home-research work, a worker was given an initial box of 500 cards to be researched. The worker was expected to set up an appointment to return the cards one week later. Appointments were designed to prevent too many of the home researchers (generally women some of whom brought their small children along) from being present in the office at one time.

Home researchers were free to choose the weeks and hours they wanted to work and the number of cards they wished to research (subject to a 500-card minimum per batch and to the sometimes-limited availability of cards). DialAmerica instructed the researchers not to look for the phone numbers of schools, libraries, government installations, or hospitals. The researchers were instructed to keep all duplicate cards separate. DialAmerica required the use of a black ink or Flair pen and sold such pens to the researchers. The researchers were required to place their initials and the letter "H" (for home researcher) on each card they completed. When DialAmerica installed a machine to read and process the completed cards automatically, DialAmerica required that the home researchers place numbers on the cards by writing them in ink around dots pre-printed on the cards. Finally, the home researchers were instructed not to wear shorts when they came to the office to pick up or deliver cards. DialAmerica did not, however, require the home researchers to keep records of the hours that they worked.

* * *

When the program began in 1976, DialAmerica paid its home researchers five cents for every completed telephone-number card. At the same time, DialAmerica was paying its in-house researchers the minimum-wage hourly rate. The piece rate paid to home researchers was eventually raised to seven cents and then to ten cents per card. On special projects, DialAmerica set the piece rate higher to compensate for the lower percentage of correct numbers that were likely to be found.

Generally, one week after a home researcher had returned a group of cards, DialAmerica would make payment to that researcher of a check equal to the piece rate times the number of cards completed. DialAmerica made no deductions from these checks. Distributors were paid a lump sum equivalent to one cent more than the going piece rate for every completed card they returned to DialAmerica, regardless of whether the card had been completed by them or their distributees. Initially, DialAmerica instructed the distributors to pay distributees the going piece rate and to keep the remaining one cent per card for themselves. Later, however, DialAmerica gave no instructions as to the amount to be paid to distributees, allowing the distributors to negotiate their own piece rates.

* * *

Congress and the courts have both recognized that, of all the acts of social legislation, the Fair Labor Standards Act has the broadest definition of "employee." In determining whether a worker is an "employee" of another person or organization within the purview of the FLSA, the Supreme Court, in Rutherford Food Corp. v. McComb, 331 U.S. 722 (1947), emphasized that the circumstances of the whole activity should be examined rather than any one particular factor.

In *Rutherford,* the Court held that boners who worked in a slaughterhouse were employees under the FLSA, even though they were paid collectively on a piece-rate basis, owned their own tools, and worked under individual employment contracts. Specific factors examined by the *Rutherford* Court in rendering its decision included:[whether the work being done is part of the integrated unit of production: whether the workers shift from one workplace to another as a unit; whether managers from the alleged employer keep in close touch with the workers; and whether the work is more like piecework than an enterprise dependent for success on the workers' initiative, judgment or foresight.]

Recently, the Court of Appeals for the Ninth Circuit, in Donovan v. Sureway Cleaners, 656 F.2d 1368 (9th Cir. 1981), refined the test for "employee" status originally set forth initially by the Supreme Court in *Rutherford.* This test lists six specific factors for determining whether a worker is an "employee":

[1) the degree of the alleged employer's right to control the manner in which the work is to be performed; 2) the alleged employee's opportunity for profit or loss depending upon his managerial skill; 3) the alleged employee's investment in equipment or materials required for his task, or his employment of helpers; 4) whether the service rendered requires a special skill; 5) the degree of permanence of the working relationship; 6) whether the service rendered is an integral part of the alleged employer's business.]

In addition, *Sureway Cleaners* instructs that neither the presence nor absence of any particular factor is dispositive and that courts should examine the "circumstances of the whole activity,", and should consider whether, as a matter of economic reality, the individuals "are dependent upon the business to which they render service." The *Sureway Cleaners* test has been previously cited with approval by this court in dicta. We now adopt it as the standard for determining "employee" status under the FLSA, and we will proceed to analyze the district court's decision in relation thereto.

* * *

In its opinion, the district court conceded that three of the six *Sureway Cleaners* factors, when applied to the home researchers, weighed in favor of the conclusion that they were "employees." As the district court stated:

> It cannot be denied that, for the most part, the investment of these workers was not great, the opportunity for profit and loss was small and the skills required were few.

These findings are not only supported in the record, they are clearly correct. DialAmerica had contended that some of the home researchers made a significant investment in their business, particularly in the purchase of speed dialers and telephone directories.

The district court devoted most of its discussion, however, to explaining that defendant had very little control over the manner in which the home researchers did their work. The court emphasized that the home researchers had the freedom to work at any time and for as many hours as they desired, and that they were not directly supervised by defendant. Had the district court been analyzing the status of a group of in-house workers, the court's emphasis on these facts would have been appropriate. But in the context of this case—one involving homeworkers—the court's emphasis was misplaced. * * *

That the home researchers could generally choose the times during which they would work and were subject to little direct supervision inheres in the very nature of home work. Yet, courts have held consistently that the fact that one works at home is not dispositive of the issue of "employee" status under the FLSA. In a seminal decision, Goldberg v. Whitaker House Cooperative, 366 U.S. 28 (1961), the Supreme Court held that members of a cooperative who made knitted goods in their homes and were paid on a piece-rate basis, were "employees" under the FLSA. The Court examined, *inter alia*, the legislative history of the FLSA and determined that, in general, homeworkers were intended to be encompassed by the Act. The Court then examined the specific homeworkers at issue and, upon analyzing the economic reality of their whole situation, concluded that they were indeed "employees":

The members are not self-employed; nor are they independent, selling their products on the market for whatever price they can command. They are regimented under one organization, manufacturing what the organization desires and receiving the compensation the organization dictates. Apart from formal differences, they are engaged in the same work they would be doing whatever the outlet for their products. The management fixes the piece rates at which they work; the management can expel them for substandard work or for failure to obey the regulations. The management, in other words, can hire or fire the homeworkers.

Other federal court rulings have been consistent with *Goldberg*, holding that homeworkers in various situations were "employees" under the FLSA. Thus, the facts relied on by the district court in concluding that defendant had only a slight degree of control over the manner in which the home researchers did their work were, to a large extent, insignificant. The district court therefore misapplied and overemphasized the right-to-control factor in its analysis.

The district court did not apply two other factors specified in the *Sureway Cleaners* test: the degree of permanence of the working relationship and whether the service rendered is an integral part of the alleged employer's business. The working relationship between the home researchers and DialAmerica was, for the most part, not a transitory one. Although there was testimony presented that several researchers performed telephone calling services for other organizations following the termination of their work for the defendant, this was not true generally. Moreover, there was no evidence to show that more than three among dozens of home researchers performed similar services for another organization while he or she was working for the defendant. In short, the home researchers did not transfer their services from place to place, as do independent contractors. Each worked continuously for the defendant, and many did so for long periods of time. As such, the permanence-of-working-relationship factor indicates that the home researchers were "employees" of the defendant.

The district court also did not expressly consider whether the service rendered by the home researchers was an integral part of the defendant's business. Given the evidence in the record, we conclude that it was. * * *

In this case, the primary work of the defendant is locating phone numbers of various people and calling them to sell particular products. The home researchers were engaged in the location of phone numbers, and their work was therefore an integral part of defendant's business. Thus, consideration of the integral-economic-relationship factor also weighs in favor of the conclusion that the home researchers were "employees" of the defendant.

The final consideration included within the *Sureway Cleaners* test is whether, as a matter of economic reality, the workers at issue " 'are dependent upon the business to which they render service.'" The district court clearly misinterpreted and misapplied this part of the analysis. The court reasoned that, because many of the home researchers used the money they earned from their work only as a secondary source of income for their households, they were not economically dependent upon DialAmerica. There is no legal basis for this position. The economic-dependence aspect of the *Sureway Cleaners* test does not concern whether the workers at issue depend on the money they earn for obtaining the necessities of life, as the district court suggests. Rather, it examines whether the workers are dependent on a particular business or organization for their continued employment. * * *

The home researchers in this case were not in a position to offer their services to many different businesses and organizations. They worked on a continuous basis with DialAmerica and were able to work only when and if DialAmerica was in need of their services. Consequently, the home researchers were economically dependent on DialAmerica, indicating that they were indeed "employees" of the defendant under the FLSA.

In summary, of the six factors and one general consideration identified by *Sureway Cleaners* as the basis for determining "employee" status, only one factor weighs in favor of the conclusion that the home researchers were not "employees." And that factor, the right-to-control factor, was overemphasized by the district court because homeworkers by their very nature are generally subject to little supervision and control by an alleged employer. Federal courts have consistently held homeworkers of many varieties to be "employees" under the FLSA.

* * *

The district court concluded that the six or seven home researchers who distributed telephone-number research cards to the other home researchers were also not "employees" under the FLSA. In reaching its decision, the court again did not consider all of the factors specified in the *Sureway Cleaners* test for determining "employee" status. Nevertheless, upon application of the entire *Sureway Cleaners* test, we agree that the distributors were not "employees" and were not subject to the minimum-wage protection of the FLSA for their work in delivering cards to and from other home researchers. We recognize that the distributors performed home research work for DialAmerica in addition to their distribution work. We hold that, while performing home research for DialAmerica, these persons were "employees" under the FLSA and entitled to payment of the minimum wage.

With respect to the right-to-control factor, the district court correctly found that the defendant exercised little control over the distributors' delivery of cards. The distributors were permitted to recruit their own distributees, and some of them did so. Although the defendant initially kept records of all distributees, it eventually relied on the distributors to maintain those records.

Moreover, we also defer to the district court's finding that the distributors risked financial loss if they did not manage their distribution network properly. The distributors were responsible for paying all of their expenses, which consisted primarily of transportation expenses. And each distributor had the authority to set the rate at which its distributees would be paid. Thus, theoretically at least, distributors could lose money if their expenses outweighed their revenues. * * *

The distributors also had to make an investment in their business. Again, this investment consisted primarily of transportation expenses. One distributor also used paid advertising in an effort to gain more distributees. Consideration of the investment factor, therefore, supports the conclusion that the distributors were independent contractors.

* * *

Finally, the *Sureway Cleaners* test examines the circumstances of the whole activity and considers whether, in this case, the distributors are economically dependent on the defendant. It is more likely than not that the distributors were economically dependent. Although defendant did not prohibit these persons from performing distribution work for other organizations, there was no evidence that any of them did so, either during or following the period in which they worked for the defendant. Presumably, all of the distributors ceased doing distribution work when defendant ceased providing such work for them. Thus, for the most part, the distributors were dependent on DialAmerica for continuing their work as distributors.

In summary, all of the factors in the *Sureway Cleaners* test, when applied to the distributors, do not lead to the same conclusion. Having considered the evidence with appropriate deference to the district court's fact-finding, we note that some factors support the conclusion that the distributors are "employees," while others do not. Although the question is admittedly close, we hold that the distributors *qua* distributors were not employees under the FLSA because they operated more like independent contractors than like employees of DialAmerica. The distributors were subject to minimal oversight or control over their distribution activities. Moreover, they faced a real opportunity for either a profit or loss in their operations, depending upon the amount of their investment and their skills in management. Finally, their work as distributors was not an integral part of DialAmerica's business and thus was less likely to be performed by an "employee" of DialAmerica.

* * *

In summary, therefore, we hold that the persons who performed telephone-number research at home were "employees" of DialAmerica under the FLSA. DialAmerica was obligated to pay them the applicable minimum wage and to comply with the other provisions of the Act. Those home researchers who also distributed telephone-number research cards to other home researchers were not "employees" while they were engaged in the act of distributing. Therefore, they were not entitled to the minimum-wage protection of the FLSA for their distribution work. * * *

NOTES AND QUESTIONS

1. The "economic realities" test applied by the court is in extensive use. An employer-employee relationship has been found even where the parties explicitly agreed in writing to an independent contractor relationship and the employer did not intend to create an employment relationship. *See* Donovan v. Sandy Retreat Beach Club, 95 Lab.Cas. ¶ 34,239 (S.D.Tex. 1982) (applying economic realities test, salespeople were employees despite contract language stating they were independent contractors).

2. Consider the following fact pattern: Mr. W owns 100 fireworks stands located and operated across South Texas. Texas law permits the sale of fireworks only during a 13-day season ending January 1 and during an 11-day season ending July 4 each year. Mr. W. Fireworks operates an office and warehouse in Somerset, Texas, from which it buys and imports from Asia the fireworks it sells, recruits operators, acquires land for fireworks stands, constructs the stands and paints them in uniform colors with a standard Mr. W logo, employs 5 or 6 routemen to supply the stands with fireworks, and advertises. Mr. W procures licenses and insurance for all the stands; it also pays for electrical service at all the stands, and it pays a commission to the operators of the stands. The operators are responsible for trash collection, pay for renting portable toilets (the stands are permanent), and pay for various devices to improve business conditions, security, and the personal living environment at the stands. All operators sign standard form contracts with Mr. W that set stand hours and prices, and prohibit the sale of other merchandise by the operators. The contracts, however, refer to the stand operators as independent contractors and give them sole control over day-to-day operations of their stands. Are the operators employees or independent contractors? See Brock v. Mr. W Fireworks, 814 F.2d 1042 (5th Cir. 1987), cert. denied, 484 U.S. 924 (1987) (stand operators are "employees" due to owners' control and investment).

3. Prisoners may be "employees" under the FLSA, depending on their employers. Prisoners working under prison programs are not subject to the FLSA. McMaster v. State of Minn., 30 F.3d 976 (8th Cir. 1994), cert. denied, 513 U.S. 1157 (1995). However, some work performed for private employers may fall within the scope of FLSA. See Henthorn v. Department of Navy, 29 F.3d 682 (D.C.Cir. 1994) (voluntary work for a private employer is subject to FLSA unless wages are paid by prison). Thus prisoners are not entirely excluded from the FLSA. Vanskike v. Peters, 974 F.2d 806 (7th Cir. 1992), cert. denied, 507 U.S. 928 (1993).

4. The Immigration Reform and Control Act of 1986 (IRCA), supra pp. 93–113 made it unlawful to hire undocumented aliens and provides sanctions against employers that do so. Is an undocumented alien who has been unlawfully hired under IRCA an "employee" within the meaning of the FLSA and entitled to its protection? See Patel v. Quality Inn South, 846 F.2d 700 (11th Cir. 1988), cert. denied, 489 U.S. 1011 (1989) (undocumented alien was "employee" under FLSA and can sue for unpaid wages). Congress's purposes in enacting the FLSA and the IRCA are in harmony. The IRCA unambiguously prohibits hiring unauthorized aliens, and the FLSA unambiguously requires that any unauthorized aliens—hired in violation of federal immigration law—be paid minimum and overtime wages. Holding employers that violate federal immigration law and federal employment law liable for both violations advances the purpose of federal immigration policy by deterring employers from hiring undocumented aliens for their most attractive quality: their willingness to work for less than the minimum wage. Lucas v. Jerusalem Café, LLC, 721 F.3d 927 (8th Cir. 2013). Undocumented alien workers are included in Title VII's definition of "employee." 42 U.S.C. § 2000e(f), (i); EEOC v. Tortilleria "La Mejor," 758 F.Supp. 585, 586 (E.D.Cal.1991). Despite legal protections, however, undocumented aliens have little incentive to report FLSA violations by employers due to fear of deportation. In Making Strange Bedfellows: Enlisting the Cooperation of Undocumented Employees in the Enforcement of Employer Sanctions, 110 Colum. L. Rev. 1526 (2010), Farhang Heydari described the possibility and implications of a cooperative model of employer sanctions enforcement by encouraging unauthorized workers to come forward with information about potential employer violations. Heydari argued that legislative reform, such as implementing whistleblower protections, modifying existing visas, and creating a new Employee-Cooperator visa, could provide law enforcement with the tools required to make the cooperative model a reality and incentivize employers to raise the conditions in which unauthorized employees work.

5.   Courts disagree about whether the FLSA requires employers to pay for travel from home to place of work and for visa fees for temporary, seasonal workers (also called "guest workers") coming from other countries to work legally in the U.S. Arriaga v. Florida Pac. Farms, LLC, 305 F.3d 1228 (11th Cir. 2002), held that employers do need to pay visa, immigration, and travel-from-home fees for H-2A workers because those costs are for the benefit of the employer. But see Castellanos-Contreras v. Decatur Hotels, LLC, 622 F.3d 393 (5th Cir. 2010), reaching the opposite conclusion for H-2B workers. The two decisions agreed that employers do not have to reimburse the fees paid by guest workers to Mexican recruiters.

6.   Some courts in the past found migrant workers not to be employees of the farms where they worked, but employees instead of their crew leaders, who were classified as independent contractors to the farms. This resulted in large numbers of agricultural workers not being covered by the statute. Recent cases have focused more stringently on the "economic realities" test, specifically in finding crew leaders and farms to be joint employers within the meaning of the Act. See Secretary of Labor v. Lauritzen, 835 F.2d 1529 (7th Cir. 1987), cert. denied, 488 U.S. 898 (1988) (migrant cucumber pickers not independent contractors; see Judge Easterbrook's concurrence, advocating abandonment of fact-bound factors test in favor of more focused statutory test). Cf. Donovan v. Brandel, 736 F.2d 1114 (6th Cir. 1984) (migrant cucumber farmers not employees). See also Real v. Driscoll Strawberry Assoc., Inc., 603 F.2d 748 (9th Cir. 1979) (expansive definition of

employer and employee); Haywood v. Barnes, 109 F.R.D. 568 (E.D.N.C.1986) (owners and operators are joint employers); Mendez v. Brady, 618 F.Supp. 579 (W.D.Mich. 1985) (blueberry harvesters are employees).

7. Are unpaid internships win-win solutions, or illegal employment practices that violate minimum wage laws? The legal status of unpaid internships turns on the question whether an intern is an employee under the FLSA. The Supreme Court held in Walling v. Portland Terminal Co., 330 U.S. 148 (1947), that when trainees did not displace any regular employees and the employer received no immediate advantage from the trainees' work, the trainees were not employees under the FLSA because "the definition 'suffer or permit to work' was obviously not intended to stamp all persons as employees who, without any express or implied compensation agreement, might work for their own advantage on the premises of another."

The Wage and Hour Division of the Department of Labor derived a six-factor test from the *Walling* decision that provides guidance about the legality of trainee programs, and in 2010 it extended that test to unpaid internships. An unpaid internship is illegal under the FLSA unless all six criteria are satisfied: (1) the training, even though it includes actual operation of the facilities of the employer, is similar to that which would be given in a vocational school; (2) the training is for the benefit of the trainee; (3) the trainees do not displace regular employees, but work under close observation; (4) the employer that provides the training derives no immediate advantage from the activities of the trainees and on occasion the employer's operations may actually be impeded; (5) the trainees are not necessarily entitled to a job at the completion of the training period; and (6) the employer and the trainee understand that the trainees are not entitled to wages for the time spent in training. U.S. Wage and Hour Division, Fact Sheet #71: Internship Programs Under The Fair Labor Standard Act, Department of Labor (April 2010) at http://www.dol.gov/whd/regs/compliance/whdfs71.htm. Although WHD's interpretation of the FLSA does not bind the courts, it is entitled to deference. If the six-factor test is applied strictly, can you think of an example of a legal unpaid internship? Would employers have enough incentives to keep most of today's internship programs?

Circuit courts split on the interpretation of the FLSA in the context of training programs. Some courts apply *Walling* or the six factors the DOL derived from *Walling*. See, e.g., Donovan v. Am. Airlines, Inc., 686 F.2d 267 (5th Cir. 1982) (relying on *Walling* to determine whether airline trainees were employees for the purposes of the FLSA); Hawkins v. Securitas Sec. Services USA, 2013 WL 1337158 (N.D. Ill. 2013) ("A trainee's entitlement to wages for time spent in training is governed by a six-part test developed by the Department of Labor and derived from Walling v. Portland Terminal Co.").Others consider the "economic realities" of the situation and look at the totality of the circumstances, sometimes considering the DOL guidelines. See, e.g., Kaplan v. Code Blue Billing & Coding, Inc., 504 Fed. Appx. 831, 834–35 (11th Cir. 2013) (stating that to determine whether a trainee is an employee a court must consider "the economic realities of the relationship, including whether a person's work confers an economic benefit on the entity for whom they are working" and considering the DOL guidelines as "guidance"). Still others apply the primary benefit test, in which they ask whether the employer or the trainees principally benefited from the work the trainees did. See, e.g., Solis v. Laurelbrook Sanitarium & Sch., Inc., 642 F.3d 518 (6th Cir. 2011) ("the proper approach for determining whether an employment relationship exists in the context of a training or learning situation is to ascertain which party derives the primary benefit from the relationship").

In the case that follows, the Second Circuit addressed whether or not to apply the WHD's six factor test to decide whether an unpaid intern qualified as an employee.

Glatt v. Fox Searchlight Pictures, Inc.

811 F.3d 528 (2d Cir. 2016).

■ JOHN M. WALKER, JR., CIRCUIT JUDGE:

Plaintiffs, who were hired as unpaid interns, claim compensation as employees under the Fair Labor Standards Act and New York Labor Law. Plaintiffs Eric Glatt and Alexander Footman moved for partial summary judgment on their employment status. Plaintiff Eden Antalik moved to certify a class of all New York interns working at certain of defendants' divisions between 2005 and 2010 and to conditionally certify a nationwide collective of all interns working at those same divisions between 2008 and 2010. The district court granted Glatt and Footman's motion for partial summary judgment, certified Antalik's New York class, and conditionally certified Antalik's nationwide collective. On defendants' interlocutory appeal, we VACATE the district court's order granting partial summary judgment to Glatt and Footman, VACATE its order certifying Antalik's New York class, VACATE its order conditionally certifying Antalik's nationwide collective, and REMAND for further proceedings.

Plaintiffs worked as unpaid interns either on the Fox Searchlight-distributed film *Black Swan* or at the Fox corporate offices in New York City. They contend that the defendants, Fox Searchlight and Fox Entertainment Group, violated the Fair Labor Standards Act (FLSA) by failing to pay them as employees during their internships as required by the FLSA's and NYLL's minimum wage and overtime provisions. The following background facts are undisputed except where noted.

Eric Glatt graduated with a degree in multimedia instructional design from New York University. Glatt was enrolled in a non-matriculated (non-degree) graduate program at NYU's School of Education when he started working on *Black Swan*. His graduate program did not offer him credit for his internship.

From December 2, 2009, through the end of February 2010, Glatt interned in *Black Swan's* accounting department under the supervision of Production Accountant Theodore Au. He worked from approximately

9:00 a.m. to 7:00 p.m. five days a week. As an accounting intern, Glatt's responsibilities included copying, scanning, and filing documents; tracking purchase orders; transporting paperwork and items to and from the *Black Swan* set; maintaining employee personnel files; and answering questions about the accounting department.

Glatt interned a second time in *Black Swan's* post-production department from March 2010 to August 2010, under the supervision of Post Production Supervisor Jeff Robinson. Glatt worked two days a week from approximately 11:00 a.m. until 6:00 or 7:00 p.m. His post-production responsibilities included drafting cover letters for mailings; organizing filing cabinets; filing paperwork; making photocopies; keeping the take-out menus up-to-date and organized; bringing documents to the payroll company; and running errands, one of which required him to purchase a non-allergenic pillow for Director Darren Aronofsky.

Alexander Footman graduated from Wesleyan University with a degree in film studies. He was not enrolled in a degree program at the time of his *Black Swan* internship. From September 29, 2009, through late February or early March 2010, Footman interned in the production department under the supervision of Production Office Coordinator Lindsay Feldman and Assistant Production Office Coordinator Jodi Arneson. Footman worked approximately ten-hour days. At first, Footman worked five days a week, but, beginning in November 2009, he worked only three days a week. After this schedule change, *Black Swan* replaced Footman with another unpaid intern in the production department.

Footman's responsibilities included picking up and setting up office furniture; arranging lodging for cast and crew; taking out the trash; taking lunch orders; answering phone calls; watermarking scripts; drafting daily call sheets; photocopying; making coffee; making deliveries to and from the film production set, rental houses, and the payroll office; accepting deliveries; admitting guests to the office; compiling lists of local vendors; breaking down, removing, and selling office furniture and supplies at the end of production; internet research; sending invitations to the wrap party; and other similar tasks and errands, including bringing tea to Aronofsky and dropping off a DVD of *Black Swan* footage at Aronofsky's apartment.

Eden Antalik worked as an unpaid publicity intern in Fox Searchlight's corporate office in New York from the beginning of May 2009 until the second week of August 2009. During her internship, Antalik was enrolled in a degree program at Duquesne University that required her to have an internship in order to graduate.

Antalik was supposed to receive credit for her internship at Fox Searchlight, but, for reasons that are unclear from the record, she never actually received the credit. Antalik began work each morning around 8:00 a.m. by assembling a brief, referred to as "the breaks," summarizing mentions of various Fox Searchlight films in the media. She also made travel arrangements, organized catering, shipped documents, and set up rooms for press events.

* * *

On June 11, 2013, the district court concluded that Glatt and Footman had been improperly classified as unpaid interns rather than employees and granted their partial motion for summary judgment. The district court also granted Antalik's motions to certify the class of New York interns and to conditionally certify the nationwide FLSA collective.

* * *

At its core, this interlocutory appeal raises the broad question of under what circumstances an unpaid intern must be deemed an "employee" under the FLSA and therefore compensated for his work. That broad question underlies our answers to the three specific questions on appeal. First, did the district court apply the correct standard in evaluating whether Glatt and Footman were employees, and, if so, did it reach the correct result? Second, did the district court err by certifying Antalik's class of New York interns? Third, did the district court err by conditionally certifying Antalik's nationwide collective?

* * *

With certain exceptions not relevant here, the FLSA requires employers to pay all employees a specified minimum wage, and overtime of time and one-half for hours worked in excess of forty hours per week. NYLL requires the same, except that it specifies a higher wage rate than the federal minimum. An employee cannot waive his right to the minimum wage and overtime pay because waiver "would nullify the purposes of the [FLSA] and thwart the legislative policies it was designed to effectuate."

The strictures of both the FLSA and NYLL apply only to employees. The FLSA unhelpfully defines "employee" as an "individual employed by an employer." "Employ" is defined as "to suffer or permit to work." New York likewise defines "employee" as "any individual employed, suffered or permitted to work by an employer." Because the statutes define "employee" in nearly identical terms, we construe the NYLL definition as the same in substance as the definition in the FLSA.

The Supreme Court has yet to address the difference between unpaid interns and paid employees under the FLSA. In 1947, however, the Court recognized that unpaid railroad brakemen trainees should not be treated as employees, and thus that they were beyond the reach of the FLSA's minimum wage provision. The Court adduced several facts. First, the brakemen-trainees at issue did not displace any regular employees, and their work did not expedite the employer's business. Second, the brakemen-trainees did not expect to receive any compensation and would not necessarily be hired upon successful completion of the course. Third, the training course was similar to one offered by a vocational school.

Finally, the employer received no immediate advantage from the work done by the trainees.

In 1967, the Department of Labor ("DOL") issued informal guidance on trainees as part of its Field Operations Handbook. The guidance enumerated six criteria and stated that the trainee is not an employee only if all of the criteria were met. In 2010, the DOL published similar guidance for unpaid interns working in the for-profit private sector. This Intern Fact Sheet provides that an employment relationship does not exist if all of the following factors apply:

1. The internship, even though it includes actual operation of the facilities of the employer, is similar to training which would be given in an educational environment;

2. The internship experience is for the benefit of the intern;

3. The intern does not displace regular employees, but works under close supervision of existing staff;

4. The employer that provides the training derives no immediate advantage from the activities of the intern; and on occasion its operations may actually be impeded;

5. The intern is not necessarily entitled to a job at the conclusion of the internship; and

6. The employer and the intern understand that the intern is not entitled to wages for the time spent in the internship.

The district court evaluated Glatt's and Footman's employment using a version of the DOL's six-factor test. However, the district court, unlike the DOL, did not explicitly require that all six factors be present to establish that the intern is not an employee and instead balanced the factors. The district court found that the first four factors weighed in favor of finding that Glatt and Footman were employees and the last two factors favored finding them to be trainees. As a result, the district court concluded that Glatt and Footman had been improperly classified as unpaid interns and granted their motion for partial summary judgment.

The specific issue we face—when is an unpaid intern entitled to compensation as an employee under the FLSA?—is a matter of first impression in this Circuit. When properly designed, unpaid internship programs can greatly benefit interns. For this reason, internships are widely supported by educators and by employers looking to hire well-trained recent graduates. However, employers can also exploit unpaid interns by using their free labor without providing them with an appreciable benefit in education or experience. Recognizing this concern, all parties agree that there are circumstances in which someone who is labeled an unpaid intern is actually an employee entitled to compensation under the FLSA. All parties also agree that there are circumstances in which unpaid interns are not employees under the FLSA. They do not agree on what those circumstances are or what standard we should use to identify them.

The plaintiffs urge us to adopt a test whereby interns will be considered employees whenever the employer receives an immediate advantage from the interns' work. Plaintiffs argue that focusing on any immediate advantage that accrues to the employer is appropriate because, in their view, the Supreme Court in [1947] rested its holding on the finding that the brakemen trainees provided no immediate advantage to the employer.

The defendants urge us to adopt a more nuanced primary beneficiary test. Under this standard, an employment relationship is created when the tangible and intangible benefits provided to the intern are greater than the intern's contribution to the employer's operation. They argue that the primary beneficiary test best reflects the economic realities of the relationship between intern and employer. They further contend that a primary beneficiary test that considers the totality of the circumstances is in accordance with how we decide whether individuals are employees in other circumstances.

DOL, appearing as amicus curiae in support of the plaintiffs, defends the six factors enumerated in its Intern Fact Sheet and its requirement that every factor be present before the employer can escape its obligation to pay the worker. DOL argues (1) that its views on employee status are entitled to deference because it is the agency charged with administering the FLSA and (2) that we should use the six factors because they come directly from [the Supreme Court].

We decline DOL's invitation to defer to the test laid out in the Intern Fact Sheet.

* * *

Instead, we agree with defendants that the proper question is whether the intern or the employer is the primary beneficiary of the relationship. The primary beneficiary test has two salient features. First, it focuses on what the intern receives in exchange for his work. Second, it also accords courts the flexibility to examine the economic reality as it exists between the intern and the employer.

Although the flexibility of the primary beneficiary test is primarily a virtue, this virtue is not unalloyed. The defendants' conception of the primary beneficiary test requires courts to weigh a diverse set of benefits to the intern against an equally diverse set of benefits received by the employer without specifying the relevance of particular facts.

In somewhat analogous contexts, we have articulated a set of non-exhaustive factors to aid courts in determining whether a worker is an employee for purposes of the FLSA. In the context of unpaid internships, we think a non-exhaustive set of considerations should include:

1. The extent to which the intern and the employer clearly understand that there is no expectation of compensation. Any promise of compensation, express or implied, suggests that the intern is an employee—and vice versa.

2. The extent to which the internship provides training that would be similar to that which would be given in an educational environment, including the clinical and other hands-on training provided by educational institutions.

3. The extent to which the internship is tied to the intern's formal education program by integrated coursework or the receipt of academic credit.

4. The extent to which the internship accommodates the intern's academic commitments by corresponding to the academic calendar.

5. The extent to which the internship's duration is limited to the period in which the internship provides the intern with beneficial learning.

6. The extent to which the intern's work complements, rather than displaces, the work of paid employees while providing significant educational benefits to the intern.

7. The extent to which the intern and the employer understand that the internship is conducted without entitlement to a paid job at the conclusion of the internship.

Applying these considerations requires weighing and balancing all of the circumstances. No one factor is dispositive and every factor need not point in the same direction for the court to conclude that the intern is not an employee entitled to the minimum wage. In addition, the factors we specify are non-exhaustive—courts may consider relevant evidence beyond the specified factors in appropriate cases.

* * *

The approach we adopt also reflects a central feature of the modern internship—the relationship between the internship and the intern's formal education. The purpose of a bona-fide internship is to integrate classroom learning with practical skill development in a real-world setting, and, * * * all of the plaintiffs were enrolled in or had recently completed a formal course of post-secondary education. By focusing on the educational aspects of the internship, our approach better reflects the role of internships in today's economy than the DOL factors, which were derived from a 68-year old Supreme Court decision that dealt with a single training course offered to prospective railroad brakemen.

In sum, we agree with the defendants that the proper question is whether the intern or the employer is the primary beneficiary of the relationship, and we propose the above list of non-exhaustive factors to aid courts in answering that question. The district court limited its review to the six factors in DOL's Intern Fact Sheet. Therefore, we vacate the district court's order granting partial summary judgment to Glatt and Footman and remand for further proceedings. On remand, the district court may, in its discretion, permit the parties to submit additional evidence relevant to the plaintiffs' employment status, such as evidence on Glatt's and Footman's formal education. Of course, we express no opinion with respect to the outcome of any renewed motions for summary judgment the parties might make based on the primary beneficiary test we have set forth.

* * *

For the foregoing reasons, the district court's orders are VACATED and the case REMANDED for further proceedings consistent with this opinion.

NOTES AND QUESTIONS

1.   The *Glatt* lawsuit was part of a flood of lawsuits from unpaid interns seeking back wages. These lawsuits could have significant consequences for unpaid internships. A pending lawsuit has already led magazine publisher Condé Nast to end its internship program entirely. Cara Buckley, Sued Over Pay, Condé Nast Ends Internship Program, N.Y. Times (Oct. 23, 2013).

The uncertain legality of unpaid internships is problematic. The problems are exacerbated by the large number of students who intern during college. The consulting company Accenture found that 72% of students who graduated from college in 2011 and 2012 had interned at some point during college. More than half of those internships were unpaid, Accenture, 2013 College Graduate Employment Survey 5.

2.   In Berger v. National Collegiate Athletic Ass'n, 843 F.3d 285 (7th Cir. 2016), the court declined to follow *Glatt*'s multi-factor test in a case involving an FLSA claim filed by student athletes. The court wrote that "We have declined to apply multifactor tests in the employment setting when they 'fail to capture the true nature of the relationship' between the alleged employee and the alleged employer." Instead, the court relied in part on the "tradition of amateurism" in college sports to hold that the student athletes were not entitled to FLSA protections.

3.   In Acosta v. Cathedral Buffet, 887 F.3d 761 (6th Cir. 2018), the court held that unpaid church members who worked at a church-operated restaurant were not employees because they did not expect to be paid. The possibility that church members worked in the restaurant due to "spiritual coercion"—they were reportedly told that refusing to volunteer was an "unforgivable sin"—was not enough to qualify as an expectation of remuneration.

4.   Note that not all federal laws share common definitions of an employee. Therefore a determination of employment status must be made separately under each law.

(b) Exempt Employees

Even those who are "employees" under section 203(e)(1) may be excluded from coverage under the FLSA under section 213. Excluded from the FLSA's coverage are such diverse types of employees as summer camp counselors (seasonal recreational establishments), professional crabbers (employees engaged in fishing), the Saturday night babysitter (casual babysitters and companions to the elderly and infirm), and journalists on local newspapers with circulation less than 4,000. The FLSA also exempts from its overtime provisions certain occupations whose hours do not traditionally fit a standard eight-hour working day, such as taxi drivers, employees at movie theatres, radio or television news announcers, local agricultural workers, and a variety of employees engaged in transportation. Other types of employees are partially exempted from the overtime pay provisions: for instance, certain retail employees paid on a commission basis, private hospital and nursing home employees, and law enforcement and firefighting personnel. The single most significant exemption from the statute's general coverage, however, is for executive, administrative, and professional employees.

Christopher v. Smithkline Beecham Corp.

567 U.S. 142 (2012).

■ JUSTICE ALITO delivered the opinion of the Court.

The Fair Labor Standards Act (FLSA) imposes minimum wage and maximum hours requirements on employers, but those requirements do not apply to workers employed "in the capacity of outside salesman." This case requires us to decide whether the term "outside sales man," as defined by Department of Labor (DOL or Department) regulations, encompasses pharmaceutical sales representatives whose primary duty is to obtain nonbinding commitments from physicians to prescribe their employer's prescription drugs in appropriate cases. We conclude that these employees qualify as "outside salesm[e]n."

* * *

Congress did not define the term "outside salesman," but it delegated authority to the DOL to issue regulations "from time to time" to "defin[e] and delimi[t]" the term. The DOL promulgated such regulations in 1938, 1940, and 1949. In 2004, following notice-and comment procedures, the DOL reissued the regulations with minor amendments. The current regulations are nearly identical in substance to the regulations issued in the years immediately following the FLSA's enactment.

* * *

The general regulation sets out the definition of the statutory term "employee employed in the capacity of outside salesman." It defines the term to mean "any employee . . . [w]hose primary duty is . . . making sales within the meaning of [29 U.S.C. § 203(k)]" and "[w]ho is customarily and regularly engaged away from the employer's place or places of business in performing such primary duty." The referenced statutory provision states that " '[s]ale' or 'sell' includes any sale, exchange, contract to sell, consignment for sale, shipment for sale, or other disposition." Thus, under the general regulation, an outside salesman is any employee whose primary duty is making any sale, exchange, contract to sell, consignment for sale, shipment for sale, or other disposition.

The sales regulation restates the statutory definition of sale discussed above and clarifies that "[s]ales within the meaning of [29 U.S.C. § 203(k)] include the transfer of title to tangible property, and in certain cases, of tangible and valuable evidences of intangible property."

Finally, the promotion-work regulation identifies "[p]romotion-work" as "one type of activity often performed by persons who make sales, which may or may not be exempt outside sales work, depending upon the circumstances under which it is performed." Promotion work that is "performed incidental to and in conjunction with an employee's own outside sales or solicitations is exempt work," whereas promotion work that is "incidental to sales made, or to be made, by someone else is not exempt outside sales work."

* * *

Respondent SmithKline Beecham Corporation is in the business of developing, manufacturing, and selling prescription drugs. The prescription drug industry is subject to extensive federal regulation, including the now-familiar requirement that prescription drugs be dispensed only upon a physician's prescription. In light of this requirement, pharmaceutical companies have long focused their direct marketing efforts, not on the retail pharmacies that dispense prescription drugs, but rather on the medical practitioners who possess the authority to prescribe the drugs in the first place. Pharmaceutical companies promote their prescription drugs to physicians through a process called "detailing," whereby employees known as "detailers" or "pharmaceutical sales representatives" provide information to physicians about the company's products in hopes of persuading them to write prescriptions for the products in appropriate cases. The position of "detailer" has existed in the pharmaceutical industry in substantially its current form since at least the 1950's, and in recent years the industry has employed more than 90,000 detailers nationwide.

Respondent hired petitioners Michael Christopher and Frank Buchanan as pharmaceutical sales representatives in 2003. During the roughly four years when petitioners were employed in that capacity, they were responsible for calling on physicians in an assigned sales territory to discuss the features, benefits, and risks of an assigned portfolio of respondent's prescription drugs. Petitioners' primary objective was to obtain a nonbinding commitment from the physician to prescribe those drugs in appropriate cases, and the training that petitioners received underscored the importance of that objective.

Petitioners spent about 40 hours each week in the field calling on physicians. These visits occurred during normal business hours, from about 8:30 a.m. to 5 p.m. Outside of normal business hours, petitioners spent an additional 10 to 20 hours each week attending events, reviewing product information, returning phone calls, responding to e-mails, and performing other miscellaneous tasks. Petitioners were not required to punch a clock or report their hours, and they were subject to only minimal supervision.

Petitioners were well compensated for their efforts. On average, Christopher's annual gross pay was just over $72,000, and Buchanan's was just over $76,000.[7] Petitioners' gross pay included both a base salary and incentive pay. The amount of petitioners' incentive pay was based on the sales volume or market share of their assigned drugs in their assigned sales territories, and this amount was uncapped. Christopher's incentive pay exceeded 30 percent of his gross pay during each of his years of employment; Buchanan's exceeded 25 percent. It is undisputed that respondent did not pay petitioners time-and-a half wages when they worked in excess of 40 hours per week.

* * *

The DOL first announced its view that pharmaceutical detailers are not exempt outside salesmen in an amicus brief filed in the Second Circuit in 2009, and the Department has subsequently filed similar amicus briefs in other cases, including the case now before us. While the DOL's ultimate conclusion that detailers are not exempt has remained unchanged since 2009, the same cannot be said of its reasoning. In both the Second Circuit and the Ninth Circuit, the DOL took the view that "a 'sale' for the purposes of the outside sales exemption requires a consummated transaction directly involving the employee for whom the exemption is sought." Perhaps because of the nebulous nature of this "consummated transaction" test, the Department changed course after we granted certiorari in this case. The Department now takes the position that "[a]n employee does not make a 'sale' for purposes of the 'outside salesman' exemption unless he actually transfers title to the property at issue." Petitioners and the DOL assert that this new interpretation of the regulations is entitled to controlling deference.

* * *

In this case, there are strong reasons for withholding the deference that Auer v. Robbins, 519 U.S. 452 (1997), generally requires. Petitioners invoke the DOL's interpretation of ambiguous regulations to impose potentially massive liability on respondent for conduct that occurred well before that interpretation was announced. To defer to the agency's

---

[7]   The median pay for pharmaceutical detailers nationwide exceeds $90,000 per year.

interpretation in this circumstance would seriously undermine the principle that agencies should provide regulated parties "fair warning of the conduct [a regulation] prohibits or requires."

This case well illustrates the point. Until 2009, the pharmaceutical industry had little reason to suspect that its longstanding practice of treating detailers as exempt outside salesmen transgressed the FLSA. The statute and regulations certainly do not provide clear notice of this. The general regulation adopts the broad statutory definition of "sale," and that definition, in turn, employs the broad catchall phrase "other disposition." This catchall phrase could reasonably be construed to encompass a nonbinding commitment from a physician to prescribe a particular drug, and nothing in the statutory or regulatory text or the DOL's prior guidance plainly requires a contrary reading. Even more important, despite the industry's decades long practice of classifying pharmaceutical detailers as exempt employees, the DOL never initiated any enforcement actions with respect to detailers or otherwise suggested that it thought the industry was acting unlawfully. We acknowledge that an agency's enforcement decisions are informed by a host of factors, some bearing no relation to the agency's views regarding whether a violation has occurred. But where, as here, an agency's announcement of its interpretation is preceded by a very lengthy period of conspicuous inaction, the potential for unfair surprise is acute.

* * *

Accordingly, whatever the general merits of Auer deference, it is unwarranted here. We instead accord the Department's interpretation a measure of deference proportional to the " 'thoroughness evident in its consideration, the validity of its reasoning, its consistency with earlier and later pronouncements, and all those factors which give it power to persuade.' "

* * *

We begin with the text of the FLSA. Although the provision that establishes the overtime salesman exemption does not furnish a clear answer to the question before us, it provides at least one interpretive clue: It exempts anyone "employed . . . in the capacity of [an] outside salesman." "Capacity," used in this sense, means "[o]utward condition or circumstances; relation; character; position." The statute's emphasis on the "capacity" of the employee counsels in favor of a functional, rather than a formal, inquiry, one that views an employee's responsibilities in the context of the particular industry in which the employee works.

* * *

Petitioners made sales for purposes of the FLSA and therefore are exempt outside salesmen within the meaning of the DOL's regulations. Obtaining a nonbinding commitment from a physician to prescribe one of respondent's drugs is the most that petitioners were able to do to ensure the eventual disposition of the products that respondent sells. This kind of arrangement, in the unique regulatory environment within which pharmaceutical companies must operate, comfortably falls within the catch-all category of "other disposition."

That petitioners bear all of the external indicia of salesmen provides further support for our conclusion. Petitioners were hired for their sales experience. They were trained to close each sales call by obtaining the maximum commitment possible from the physician. They worked away from the office, with minimal supervision, and they were rewarded for their efforts with incentive compensation. It would be anomalous to require respondent to compensate petitioners for overtime, while at the same time exempting employees who function identically to petitioners in every respect except that they sell physician administered drugs, such as vaccines and other inject able pharmaceuticals, that are ordered by the physician directly rather than purchased by the end user at a pharmacy with a prescription from the physician.

Our holding also comports with the apparent purpose of the FLSA's exemption for outside salesmen. The exemption is premised on the belief that exempt employees "typically earned salaries well above the minimum wage" and enjoyed other benefits that "se[t] them apart from the nonexempt workers entitled to overtime pay." It was also thought that exempt employees performed a kind of work that "was difficult to standardize to any time frame and could not be easily spread to other workers after 40 hours in a week, making compliance with the overtime provisions difficult and generally precluding the potential job expansion intended by the FLSA's time and-a-half overtime premium." Petitioners—each of whom earned an average of more than $70,000 per year and spent between 10 and 20 hours outside normal business hours each week performing work related to his assigned portfolio of drugs in his assigned sales territory—are hardly the kind of employees that the FLSA was intended to protect. And it would be challenging, to say the least, for pharmaceutical companies to compensate detailers for overtime going forward without significantly changing the nature of that position.

* * *

For these reasons, we conclude that petitioners qualify as outside salesmen under the most reasonable interpretation of the DOL's regulations. The judgment of the Court of Appeals is *Affirmed.*

■ JUSTICE BREYER, with whom JUSTICE GINSBURG, JUSTICE SOTOMAYOR, and JUSTICE KAGAN join, dissenting.

* * *

Unless we give the words of the statute and regulations some special meaning, a detailer's primary duty is not that of "making sales" or the equivalent. A detailer might convince a doctor to prescribe a drug for a particular kind of patient. If the doctor encounters such a patient, he might prescribe the drug. The doctor's client, the patient, might take the prescription to a pharmacist and ask the pharmacist to fill the prescription. If so, the pharmacist might sell the manufacturer's drug to the patient, or might substitute a generic version. But it is the pharmacist, not the detailer, who will have sold the drug.

To put the same fairly obvious point in the language of the regulations and of § 3(k) of the FLSA, the detailer does not "sell" anything to the doctor. Nor does he, during the course of that visit or immediately thereafter, "exchange" the manufacturer's product for money or for anything else. He enters into no "contract to sell" on behalf of anyone. He "consigns" nothing "for sale." He "ships" nothing for sale. He does not "dispose" of any product at all.

What the detailer does is inform the doctor about the nature of the manufacturer's drugs and explain their uses, their virtues, their drawbacks, and their limitations. The detailer may well try to convince the doctor to prescribe the manufacturer's drugs for patients. And if the detailer is successful, the doctor will make a "nonbinding commitment" to write prescriptions using one or more of those drugs where appropriate. If followed, that "nonbinding commitment" is, at most, a nonbinding promise to consider advising a patient to use a drug where medical indications so indicate (if the doctor encounters such a patient), and to write a prescription that will likely (but may not) lead that person to order that drug under its brand name from the pharmacy. (I say "may not" because 30% of patients in a 2-year period have not filled a prescription given to them by a doctor. And when patients do fill prescriptions, 75% are filled with generic drugs.

Where in this process does the detailer *sell* the product? At most he obtains from the doctor a "nonbinding commitment" to advise his patient to take the drug (or perhaps a generic equivalent) as well as to write any necessary prescription. I put to the side the fact that neither the Court nor the record explains exactly what a "nonbinding commitment" is. Like a "definite maybe," an "impossible solution," or a "theoretical experience," a "nonbinding commitment" seems to claim more than it can deliver. Regardless, other than in colloquial speech, to obtain a commitment to *advise* a client to buy a product is not to obtain a commitment to *sell* that product, no matter how often the client takes the advice (or the patient does what the doctor recommends).

* * *

Taken together, the statute, regulations, ethical codes, and Labor Department Reports indicate that the drug detailers do not promote their "own sales," but rather "sales made, or to be made, by someone else." Therefore, detailers are not "outside salesmen." And the detailers do not fall within that category. For these reasons, with respect, I dissent.

* * *

The following case made two trips to the Supreme Court. This is the most recent opinion, issued in 2018.

Encino Motorcars v. Navarro
138 S.Ct. 1134 (2018).

■ JUSTICE THOMAS delivered the opinion of the Court.

The Fair Labor Standards Act (FLSA), 52 Stat. 1060, as amended, 29 U.S.C. § 201 et seq., requires employers to pay overtime compensation to covered employees. The FLSA exempts from the overtime-pay requirement "any salesman, partsman, or mechanic primarily engaged in selling or servicing automobiles" at a covered dealership. § 213(b)(10)(A). We granted certiorari to decide whether this exemption applies to service advisors—employees at car dealerships who consult with customers about their servicing needs and sell them servicing solutions. We conclude that service advisors are exempt.

I.

A.

Enacted in 1938, the FLSA requires employers to pay overtime to covered employees who work more than 40 hours in a week. 29 U.S.C. § 207(a). But the FLSA exempts many categories of employees from this requirement. See § 213. Employees at car dealerships have long been among those exempted.

Congress initially exempted all employees at car dealerships from the overtime-pay requirement. See Fair Labor Standards Amendments of 1961, § 9. Congress then narrowed that exemption to cover "any salesman, partsman, or mechanic primarily engaged in selling or servicing automobiles, trailers, trucks, farm implements, or aircraft." Fair Labor Standards Amendments of 1966, § 209. In 1974, Congress enacted the version of the exemption at issue here. It provides that the FLSA's overtime-pay requirement does not apply to "any salesman, partsman, or mechanic primarily engaged in selling or servicing automobiles, trucks, or farm implements, if he is employed by a nonmanufacturing establishment primarily engaged in the business of selling such vehicles or implements to ultimate purchasers." § 213(b)(10)(A).

This language has long been understood to cover service advisors. Although the Department of Labor initially interpreted it to exclude them, the federal courts rejected that view. After these decisions, the Department issued an opinion letter in 1978, explaining that service advisors are exempt in most cases. From 1978 to 2011, Congress made no changes to the exemption, despite amending § 213 nearly a dozen times. . . .

In 2011, however, the Department reversed course. It issued a rule that interpreted "salesman" to exclude service advisors. 76 Fed. Reg.

18832, 18859 (2011) (codified at 29 C.F.R. § 779.372(c)). That regulation prompted this litigation.

B.

Petitioner Encino Motorcars, LLC, is a Mercedes-Benz dealership in California. Respondents are current and former service advisors for petitioner. Service advisors "interact with customers and sell them services for their vehicles." Encino Motorcars, LLC v. Navarro, 136 S.Ct. 2117, 2121 (2016) (*Encino I*). They "mee[t] customers; liste[n] to their concerns about their cars; sugges[t] repair and maintenance services; sel[l] new accessories or replacement parts; recor[d] service orders; follo[w] up with customers as the services are performed (for instance, if new problems are discovered); and explai[n] the repair and maintenance work when customers return for their vehicles."

In 2012, respondents sued petitioner for backpay. Relying on the Department's 2011 regulation, respondents alleged that petitioner had violated the FLSA by failing to pay them overtime. Petitioner moved to dismiss, arguing that service advisors are exempt under § 213(b)(10)(A). The District Court agreed with petitioner and dismissed the complaint, but the Court of Appeals for the Ninth Circuit reversed. Finding the text ambiguous and the legislative history "inconclusive," the Ninth Circuit deferred to the Department's 2011 rule under Chevron U.S.A. Inc. v. Natural Resources Defense Council, Inc., 467 U.S. 837 (1984).

We granted certiorari and vacated the Ninth Circuit's judgment. We explained that courts cannot defer to the 2011 rule because it is procedurally defective. Specifically, the regulation undermined significant reliance interests in the automobile industry by changing the treatment of service advisors without a sufficiently reasoned explanation. But we did not decide whether, without administrative deference, the exemption covers service advisors. We remanded that issue for the Ninth Circuit to address in the first instance.

C.

On remand, the Ninth Circuit again held that the exemption does not include service advisors. The Court of Appeals agreed that a service advisor is a " 'salesman' " in a "generic sense," and is " 'primarily engaged in . . . servicing automobiles' " in a "general sense." Nonetheless, it concluded that "Congress did not intend to exempt service advisors."

The Ninth Circuit began by noting that the Department's 1966–1967 Occupational Outlook Handbook listed 12 job titles in the table of contents that could be found at a car dealership, including "automobile mechanics," "automobile parts countermen," "automobile salesmen," and "automobile service advisors." Because the FLSA exemption listed three of these positions, but not service advisors, the Ninth Circuit concluded that service advisors are not exempt. The Ninth Circuit also determined that service advisors are not primarily engaged in "servicing" automobiles, which it defined to mean "only those who are actually occupied in the repair and maintenance of cars." And the Ninth Circuit further concluded that the exemption does not cover salesmen who are primarily engaged in servicing. In reaching this conclusion, the Ninth Circuit invoked the distributive canon. See A. Scalia & B. Garner, Reading Law 214 (2012) ("Distributive phrasing applies each expression to its appropriate referent"). It reasoned that "Congress intended the gerunds—selling and servicing—to be distributed to their appropriate subjects—salesman, partsman, and mechanic. A salesman sells; a partsman services; and a mechanic services." Finally, the Court of Appeals noted that its interpretation was supported by the principle that exemptions to the FLSA should be construed narrowly, and the lack of any "mention of service advisors" in the legislative history.

We granted certiorari, and now reverse.

II.

The FLSA exempts from its overtime-pay requirement "any salesman, partsman, or mechanic primarily engaged in selling or servicing automobiles, trucks, or farm implements, if he is employed by a nonmanufacturing establishment primarily engaged in the business of selling such vehicles or implements to ultimate purchasers." § 213(b)(10)(A). The parties agree that petitioner is a "nonmanufacturing establishment primarily engaged in the business of selling [automobiles] to ultimate purchasers." The parties also agree that a service advisor is not a "partsman" or "mechanic," and that a service advisor is not "primarily engaged . . . in selling automobiles." The question, then, is whether service advisors are "salesm[e]n . . . primarily engaged in . . . servicing automobiles." We conclude that they are. Under the best reading of the text, service advisors are "salesm[e]n," and they are "primarily engaged in . . . servicing automobiles." The distributive canon, the practice of construing FLSA exemptions narrowly, and the legislative history do not persuade us otherwise.

A.

A service advisor is obviously a "salesman." The term "salesman" is not defined in the statute, so "we give the term its ordinary meaning." The ordinary meaning of "salesman" is someone who sells goods or services. Service advisors do precisely that. As this Court previously explained, service advisors "sell [customers] services for their vehicles."

B.

Service advisors are also "primarily engaged in . . . servicing automobiles." § 213(b)(10)(A). The word "servicing" in this context can mean either "the action of maintaining or repairing a motor vehicle" or "[t]he action of providing a service." Service advisors satisfy both definitions. Service advisors are integral to the servicing process. They "mee[t] customers; liste[n] to their concerns about their cars; sugges[t] repair and maintenance services; sel[l] new accessories or replacement parts; recor[d] service orders; follo[w] up with customers as the services are performed (for instance, if new problems are discovered); and explai[n] the repair and maintenance work when customers return for their vehicles." If you ask the average customer who services his car, the primary, and perhaps only, person he is likely to identify is his service advisor.

True, service advisors do not spend most of their time physically repairing automobiles. But the statutory language is not so constrained. All agree that partsmen, for example, are "primarily engaged in . . . servicing automobiles." . . . In other words, the phrase "primarily engaged in . . . servicing automobiles" must include some individuals who do not physically repair automobiles themselves but who are integrally involved in the servicing process. That description applies to partsmen and service advisors alike.

C.

The Ninth Circuit concluded that service advisors are not covered because the exemption simply does not apply to "salesm[e]n . . . primarily engaged in . . . servicing automobiles." The Ninth Circuit invoked the distributive canon to reach this conclusion. Using that canon, it matched "salesman" with "selling" and "partsma[n] [and] mechanic" with "servicing." We reject this reasoning.

The text of the exemption covers "any salesman, partsman, or mechanic primarily engaged in selling or servicing automobiles, trucks, or farm implements." § 213(b)(10)(A). The exemption uses the word "or" to connect all of its nouns and gerunds, and "or" is "almost always disjunctive." Thus, the use of "or" to join "selling" and "servicing" suggests that the exemption covers a salesman primarily engaged in either activity.

Unsurprisingly, statutory context can overcome the ordinary, disjunctive meaning of "or." The distributive canon, for example, recognizes that sometimes "[w]here a sentence contains several antecedents and several consequents," courts should "read them distributively and apply the words to the subjects which, by context, they seem most properly to relate."

But here, context favors the ordinary disjunctive meaning of "or" for at least three reasons. First, the distributive canon has the most force when the statute allows for one-to-one matching. But here, the distributive canon would mix and match some of three nouns—"salesman, partsman, or mechanic"—with one of two gerunds—"selling or servicing." § 213(b)(10)(A). We doubt that a legislative drafter would leave it to the reader to figure out the precise combinations. Second, the distributive canon has the most force when an ordinary, disjunctive reading is linguistically impossible. But as explained above, the phrase "salesman . . . primarily engaged in . . . servicing automobiles" not only makes sense; it is an apt description of a service advisor. Third, a narrow distributive phrasing is an unnatural fit here because the entire exemption bespeaks breadth. It begins with the word "any." And it uses the disjunctive word "or" three times. In fact, all agree that the third list in the exemption—"automobiles, trucks, or farm implements"—modifies every other noun and gerund. But it would be odd to read the exemption as starting with a distributive phrasing and then, halfway through and without warning, switching to a disjunctive phrasing—all the while using the same word ("or") to signal both meanings. The more natural reading is that the exemption covers any combination of its nouns, gerunds, and objects.

D.

The Ninth Circuit also invoked the principle that exemptions to the FLSA should be construed narrowly. We reject this principle as a useful guidepost for interpreting the FLSA. Because the FLSA gives no "textual indication" that its exemptions should be construed narrowly, "there is no reason to give [them] anything other than a fair (rather than a 'narrow') interpretation." Scalia, Reading Law, at 363. The narrow-construction principle relies on the flawed premise that the FLSA " 'pursues' " its remedial purpose " 'at all costs.' " But the FLSA has over two dozen exemptions in § 213(b) alone, including the one at issue here. Those exemptions are as much a part of the FLSA's purpose as the overtime-pay requirement. We thus have no license to give the exemption anything but a fair reading.

* * *

In sum, we conclude that service advisors are exempt from the overtime-pay requirement of the FLSA because they are "salesm[e]n . . . primarily engaged in . . . servicing automobiles." § 213(b)(10)(A). Accordingly, we reverse the judgment of the Court of Appeals and remand the case for further proceedings consistent with this opinion.

It is so ordered.

■ JUSTICE GINSBURG, with whom JUSTICE BREYER, JUSTICE SOTOMAYOR, and JUSTICE KAGAN join, dissenting.

Diverse categories of employees staff automobile dealerships. Of employees so engaged, Congress explicitly exempted from the Fair Labor Standards Act hours requirements only three occupations: salesmen, partsmen, and mechanics. The Court today approves the exemption of a fourth occupation: automobile service advisors. In accord with the judgment of the Court of Appeals for the Ninth Circuit, I would not enlarge the exemption to include service advisors or other occupations outside Congress' enumeration.

* * *

"Where Congress explicitly enumerates certain exceptions . . ., additional exceptions are not to be implied, in the absence of evidence of a contrary legislative intent." The Court thus has no warrant to add to the three explicitly exempt categories (salesmen, partsmen, and mechanics) a fourth (service advisors) for which the Legislature did not provide. . . .

Had the § 213(b)(10)(A) exemption covered "any salesman or mechanic primarily engaged in selling or servicing automobiles," there could be no argument that service advisors fit within it. Only "salesmen" primarily engaged in "selling" automobiles and "mechanics" primarily engaged in "servicing" them would fall outside the Act's coverage. Service advisors, defined as "*salesmen* primarily engaged in the *selling of services*," plainly do not belong in either category. . . .

Petitioner stakes its case on Congress' addition of the "partsman" job to the exemption. That inclusion, petitioner urges, has a vacuum effect: It draws into the exemption job categories other than the three for which Congress provided, in particular, service advisors. Because partsmen, like service advisors, neither "sell" nor "service" automobiles in the conventional sense, petitioner reasons, Congress must have intended the word "service" to mean something broader than repair and maintenance.

To begin with, petitioner's premise is flawed. Unlike service advisors, partsmen " 'get their hands dirty' by 'working as a mechanic's right-hand man or woman.' " As the Solicitor General put it last time this case was before the Court, a mechanic "might be able to obtain the parts to complete a repair without the real-time assistance of a partsman by his side." But dividing the "key [repair] tasks . . . between two individuals" only "reinforces" "that both the mechanic and the partsman are . . . involved in repairing ('servicing') the vehicle." Service advisors, in contrast, "*sell . . . services* [to customers] for their vehicles," services that are later performed by mechanics and partsmen.

Adding partsmen to the exemption, moreover, would be an exceptionally odd way for Congress to have indicated that "servicing" should be given a meaning deviating from its ordinary usage. There is a more straightforward explanation for Congress' inclusion of partsmen alongside salesmen and mechanics: Common features of the three enumerated jobs make them unsuitable for overtime pay.

* * *

Unlike salesmen, partsmen, and mechanics, service advisors "wor[k] ordinary, fixed schedules on-site." Respondents, for instance, work *regular* 11-hour shifts, at all times of the year, for a weekly minimum of 55 hours. Service advisors thus do not implicate the concerns underlying the § 213(b)(10)(A) exemption. Indeed, they are precisely the type of workers Congress intended the FLSA to shield "from the evil of overwork."

* * *

Petitioner contends that "affirming the decision below would disrupt decades of settled expectations" while exposing "employers to substantial retroactive liability." "[M]any dealerships," petitioner urges, "have offered compensation packages based primarily on sales commissions," in reliance on court decisions and agency guidance ranking service advisors as exempt.

Congress . . . has spoken directly to the treatment of *commission-*based workers. The FLSA exempts from its overtime directives any employee of a "retail or service establishment" who receives more than half of his or her pay on commission, so long as the employee's "regular rate of pay" is more than 1 ½ times the minimum wage. § 207(i). Thus, even without the § 213(b)(10)(A) exemption, many service advisors compensated on commission would remain ineligible for overtime remuneration.

In crafting the commission-pay exemption, Congress struck a deliberate balance: It exempted *higher* paid commissioned employees, perhaps in recognition of their potentially irregular hours, but it maintained protection for *lower* paid employees, to vindicate the Act's "principal . . . purpose" of shielding "workers from substandard wages and oppressive working hours."

This Court once recognized that the "particularity" of FLSA exemptions "preclude[s] their enlargement by implication." . . . The Court today, in adding an exemption of its own creation, veers away from that comprehension of the FLSA's mission.

NOTES

1. The Seventh Circuit considered overtime eligibility for another group of pharmaceutical sales representatives and avoided the issue of the "outside sales exemption" by holding that the representatives meet the requirements for the "administrative exemption." This means that the sales reps' "primary duty includes the exercise of discretion and independent judgment with respect to matters of significance." Schaefer-LaRose v. Eli Lilly & Co., 679 F.3d 560 (7th Cir. 2012).

2. In 2004, the Department of Labor revised regulation 29 C.F.R. § 541, which describes how an employee may be exempt under the FLSA. An employee—not a position—must meet all the requirements of the applicable exemption test to be exempt. That said, an employee who changes positions may change from being exempt to nonexempt (or vice versa) based on the duties of the new job.

The five categories in which a worker may qualify as exempt are: executive, administrative, professional (learned or creative), computer or outside sales. The Department of Labor has established tests to determine whether an employee fits into one of the five groups. Formerly, the DOL had two tests—a "short" and "long" test of job duties and salary requirements—to determine whether an employee was exempt. However, the new revision created one standardized test for each exemption, and also increased the weekly salary for the salary basis. This test has three parts: the Salary Limit Test, the Salary Basis Test, and the Duties Test.

The Salary Limit Test is the same for all of the exemption categories except outside sales. The 2004 regulations raised the salary limit from $155 per week to $455 per week ($23,660 per year), and beginning in January 2020, the limit was raised again to $684 per week ($35,568 per year). Thus, under this test, any employee earning less than $35,568 per year is classified as nonexempt, regardless of duties performed.

The Salary Basis Test mandates that an exempt employee must be paid on a salaried basis. To be "salaried," an employee must be paid the full salary for the workweek regardless of the number of hours worked, the quality or quantity of work performed. The only exception to this is the computer professional, who does not have to be paid on a salaried basis.

Finally, the new regulations formulated a standard (as opposed to "short" and "long") Duties Test for each exemption.

Executive Exemption: To satisfy the Executive Exemption, an employee must have the primary duty of managing the enterprise or a recognized department or subdivision. To qualify as a manager, the employee should have the authority to hire or fire other employees, or make recommendations as to the hiring, firing, advancement, promotion or any other change of status of other employees which must be given particular weight. The employee must also routinely direct the work of at least two other full-time employees.

Administrative Exemption: To meet the Administrative Exemption, an employee's primary duty must be the performance of office or nonmanual work directly related to management policies or general business operations of the employer or the employer's customers. The employee must exercise discretion and independent judgment with respect to matters of significance. When drafting the new regulations, the Department of labor provided examples of jobs that may meet the Administrative Exemption: insurance claims adjusters, employees in the financial services industry, executive assistants to a business owner or senior executive of a large business, human resources managers, purchasing agents, or buyers. The DOL also provided examples of jobs that do not meet the duties test for the Administrative Exemption: employees that grade lumber, comparison shoppers, and public sector inspectors.

Professional Exemption: The DOL published two different exemption tests under the umbrella of the Professional Exemption—the "learned professional" and the "creative professional" (formerly artistic professional) tests. To satisfy the Learned Professional Exemption, an employee's work must require advanced knowledge, be predominantly intellectual in nature and require consistent exercise of discretion and judgment instead of routine and manual work. The DOL specifically states that this type of advanced knowledge cannot be attained at the high school level, and must be acquired by "prolonged course of specialized intellectual instruction." Examples of fields that satisfy these criteria are law, medicine, theology, accounting, actuarial computation, engineering, architecture, teaching, physical, chemical, and biological sciences, and pharmacy. To satisfy the Creative Professional Exemption, the primary duties performed must require invention, imagination, originality or talent in a recognized field of artistic endeavor. This can include actors, musicians, composers, conductors, soloists, painters, cartoonists, novelists, or journalists.

Computer Employees: Because there are too many variations in the types of work performed by computer programmers and systems analysts, they do not qualify as a profession under one of the other exemptions. To alleviate this problem, the Computer Employee Exemptions were created for employees whose primary duty is to perform work requiring theoretical and practical application of highly specialized knowledge in computer systems analysis, programming and software engineering. This exemption only applies to computer systems analysts and computer programmers, and does not apply to employees who specialize in manufacturing or repairing computers.

Outside Sales: The final DOL exemption is for outside salespeople whose primary duty is making sales (any sale, exchange, contract to sell, consignment for sales, shipment for sale or other disposition, including the transfer of title to tangible property and, in certain cases, of tangible valuable evidences of intangible property), or obtaining orders or contracts for services or for the use of facilities for which a consideration will be paid by the client or customer. This employee must be customarily and regularly engaged away from the employer's place or places of business.

The Obama Administration pursued a misclassification initiative to fight against wrongful FLSA exemptions. However, the Trump Administration has not continued to pursue this initiative. Shortly after Secretary of Labor Alex Acosta was confirmed, he withdrew the Obama-era Administrator Interpretation entitled The Application of the Fair Labor Standards Act's 'Suffer or Permit' Standard in the Identification of Employees Who Are Misclassified as Independent Contractors, which had sought to define relatively broadly the scope of "employee" under the FLSA.

Another policy shift between the Obama and Trump Administrations involves the salary limit. On May 18, 2016, the Department of Labor announced a raise in the salary threshold for mandatory overtime pay from $23,660 to $47,476. The rule was blocked by a U.S. District Court. Nevada v. United States Department of Labor, 218 F.Supp.3d 520 (E.D. Tex. 2016). The Trump Administration filed an appeal, which was stayed as of June 2018 while the Administration pursues a new rulemaking. That rulemaking is expected to set the threshold of $35,568.

3. The Department of Labor stated that the 2004 DOL exemption regulations guarantee overtime protection to an additional 1.3 million workers who were previously denied protection. The changes also are estimated to exclude 640,000 additional executive, administrative, and professional workers from coverage. Based on the regulations, those earning more than $100,000 per year have difficulty qualifying.

The changes to the exemption regulations were attacked by Democrats and some Republicans as unfairly removing protection from a significant group of employees. In July 2004, the Economic Policy Institute (EPI) released a somewhat controversial report concluding that at least 6 million American workers would lose their right to overtime pay under the new regulations. EPI found that the original version of these rules, proposed by the Bush Administration in March 2003, would have stripped overtime protection from eight million workers. In the face of widespread public opposition, the administration revised its regulations so that police, firefighters, and emergency medical technicians would continue to get overtime.

4. The so-called "white-collar" exemptions (described above) may have made more sense when the FLSA was originally enacted. During the 1930s and 1940s, when the Act was passed, the United States had a principally agrarian and manufacturing-oriented economy where the white-collar exemptions were easy to administer. "White-collar workers had clearly defined decision making responsibilities, were closer to management, and were paid better than they are today. * * * These workers were middle class in income, outlook, attitude, and life style." Regan Rowan, Solving the Bluish Collar Problem: An Analysis of the DOL'S Modernization of the Exemptions to the Fair Labor Standards Act, 7 U. Pa. J. Lab. & Emp. L. 119, 120 (2004). By contrast, today's economy is service oriented, and white-collar workers are no longer middle class managers, but are more likely to share class traits typically associated with their blue-collar counterparts. "Modern white-collar jobs involve repetitive, mechanical duties, rather than intellectual or creative responsibilities. Moreover, since most white-collar workers today 'earn less than unionized blue-collar factory workers and skilled craftsmen,' their exemption from the FLSA is arguably in conflict with Congress' original intent in enacting the statute." Id.

In Solving the Bluish Collar Problem: An Analysis of the DOL's Modernization of the Exemptions to the Fair Labor Standards Act, Rowan argues that despite the modern day problems with the white-collar exemption, the new regulations may bring the FLSA more in line with Congress's original intent. According to Rowan, the FLSA was enacted primarily to provide a minimum subsistence wage and protection against oppressive working hours to those employees with little bargaining power. Because it was enacted during the Great Depression, the over overtime pay provisions were designed to advance three main policy goals: a shorter workweek, compensation for overworked employees, and spreading work to a larger number of citizens. This was accomplished by requiring employers to pay a premium for having employees work overtime. Id. at 123–124. The legislative history of the FLSA contains no explanation for the white-collar exemptions, but Rowan claims that the FLSA was never intended to cover all employees. Instead, they were possibly used as a line-drawing tool between those workers in who had so little bargaining power that they needed government intervention, and those who had sufficient bargaining power to protect themselves. Id. at 124–125.

The Second Circuit confronted the "bluish collar problem" in two cases, both decided before the *Encino Motorcars* Court admonished that FLSA exemptions should be "fairly read." The court narrowly construed the exemptions from the FLSA's overtime-pay requirements against the employers. In Davis v. J.P. Morgan Chase & Co., 587 F.3d 529 (2d Cir. 2009), an underwriter whose job was to evaluate whether to issue loans to individual applicants was found to be outside the FLSA's administrative exemption, since his work constituted "production" of loans for the bank. Similarly, the court held in Young v. Cooper Cameron Corp., 586 F.3d 201 (2d Cir. 2009), that a product design specialist was not within the professional exemption from the FLSA's overtime-pay provision because the position required no formal advanced education and knowledge required for the job was not customarily acquired by a prolonged course of specialized intellectual instruction. However that same court held that entry-level accountants were "learned professionals" and so not eligible for overtime pay because they were "employed in a field of science and learning, . . . relied on knowledge customarily acquired by prolonged specialized instruction, and that their work involved consistent exercise of professional judgment . . ." Pippins v. KPMG LLP, 759 F.3d 235 (2014).

5.   The FLSA contains an overtime exemption for commissioned employees who work for a retail or service employer, as long as two requirements are met: first, the employee's regular pay rate is more than one and one-half times the minimum wage rate in weeks in which the employee works overtime hours; and second, more than half the employee's total earnings in a representative pay period consists of commissions. Regarding the relationship between employees paid "commissions" and wage and hour rules, see Klinedinst v. Swift Investments, Inc., 260 F.3d 1251 (11th Cir. 2001) (payment by auto repair shop to painter of a flat rate based on the number of hours included for painting in estimate given to customers was a commission); Mechmet v. Four Seasons Hotels, Ltd., 825 F.2d 1173 (7th Cir. 1987) (payment by hotel to waiters of flat rate based on service charge added to banquet bills was a commission).

6.   Employers are exempt from the FLSA's maximum hours requirement for employees "in domestic service * * * to provide companionship services for individuals who * * * are unable to care for themselves * * *." The regulation says domestic service means work "in or about a private home * * *." Beginning in 1975, the Department of Labor's interpretation of the statutory exemption from FLSA protections for certain "domestic service" workers included caretakers employed by third-party agencies. The Supreme Court addressed this issue in Long I. Care at Home, Ltd. v. Coke, 551 U.S. 158 (2007). The Court confirmed the validity of the FLSA's companionship service exemption, holding that the exemption applies to services rendered in an individual's home by a person employed by a social service agency. In 2013, the DOL changed its interpretation to restrict the exemption to workers hired directly by the home care recipients and their families. The

D.C. Circuit held that DOL's change in the law's coverage was reasonable and therefore within its authority. Home Care Ass'n of America v. Weil, 799 F.3d 1084 (D.C. Cir. 2015), cert. denied, 136 S.Ct. 2506 (2016).

The exemption has been strictly limited to domestic services. For example, in Chao v. Gotham Registry, Inc., 514 F.3d 280 (2d Cir. 2008), a temporary staffing agency required nurses to get approval before working overtime at any facility. This proved difficult as the nurses typically did not know when facilities would request overtime. If the nurses worked overtime without approval of the agency, they were paid overtime only if the agency was able to negotiate a premium price from the facility requesting additional nursing care. Most of the time, the agency was not successful. The Second Circuit held that the agency did not satisfy its obligation under the FLSA, regardless of whether the nurse voluntarily agreed to work overtime at the facility's request without permission and regardless of the agency's lack of control over the nurse's decision to accept overtime work. Do you think the burden on the agency is appropriate considering its lack of power to control overtime? On the other hand, didn't Congress enact the FLSA to help people like these nurses receive fair pay for their work?

7. In 2010, New York State enacted a "Nanny Bill of Rights" law that requires overtime pay, a day of rest every seventh day, and three paid days of rest per year. Since then, several additional states have enacted similar laws. In 2013, New York City enacted a requirement of paid sick time for workers. This law was strengthened in 2014.

8. Exotic dancers are often employees and not independent contractors. E.g., McFeeley v. Jackson Street Entertainment, LLC, 825 F.3d 235 (4th Cir. 2016).

9. An interesting dispute is whether minor league baseball players should be covered by the FLSA or whether they are "professionals." See Senne v. Kansas City Royals Baseball Corp., 934 F.3d 918 (9th Cir. 2019). See Lucas J. Carney, Major League Baseball's 'Foul Ball': Why Minor League Baseball Players are Not Exempt Employees under the Fair Labor Standards Act, 41 J. Corp. L. 283 (2015). For another context involving the exemption for professional employees, see the following case.

Lola v. Skadden, Arps, Slate, Meagher & Flom
620 Fed. Appx. 37 (2d Cir. 2015).

■ POOLER, CIRCUIT JUDGE.

David Lola, on behalf of himself and all others similarly situated, appeals from the September 16, 2014 opinion and order of the United States District Court for the Southern District of New York (Sullivan, J.) dismissing his putative collective action seeking damages from Skadden, Arps, Slate, Meagher & Flom LLP and Tower Legal Staffing, Inc. for violations of the overtime provision of the Fair Labor Standards Act, 29 U.S.C. §§ 201 et seq. ("FLSA"), arising out of Lola's work as a contract attorney in North Carolina. We agree with the district court's conclusion that: (1) state, not federal, law informs FLSA's definition of "practice of law;" and (2) North Carolina, as the place where Lola worked and lived, has the greatest interest in this litigation, and thus we look to North Carolina law to determine if Lola was practicing law within the meaning of FLSA. However, we disagree with the district court's conclusion, on a motion to dismiss, that by undertaking the document review Lola allegedly was hired to conduct, Lola was necessarily "practicing law" within the meaning of North Carolina law. We find that accepting the allegations as pleaded, Lola adequately alleged in his complaint that his document review was devoid of legal judgment such that he was not engaged in the practice of law, and remand for further proceedings.

* * *

Lola, a North Carolina resident, alleges that beginning in April 2012, he worked for Defendants for fifteen months in North Carolina. He conducted document review for Skadden in connection with a multi-district litigation pending in the United States District Court for the Northern District of Ohio. Lola is an attorney licensed to practice law in California, but he is not admitted to practice law in either North Carolina or the Northern District of Ohio.

Lola alleges that his work was closely supervised by the Defendants, and his "entire responsibility . . . consisted of (a) looking at documents to see what search terms, if any, appeared in the documents, (b) marking those documents into the categories predetermined by Defendants, and (c) at times drawing black boxes to redact portions of certain documents based on specific protocols that Defendants provided." Lola further alleges that Defendants provided him with the documents he reviewed, the search terms he was to use in connection with those documents, and the procedures he was to follow if the search terms appeared. Lola was paid $25 an hour for his work, and worked roughly forty-five to fifty-five hours a week. He was paid at the same rate for any hours he worked in excess of forty hours per week. Lola was told that he was an employee of Tower, but he was also told that he needed to follow any procedures set by Skadden attorneys, and he worked under the supervision of Skadden attorneys. Other attorneys employed to work on the same project performed similar work and were likewise paid hourly rates that remained the same for any hours worked in excess of forty hours per week.

* * *

Pursuant to FLSA, employers must generally pay employees working overtime one and one-half times the regular rate of pay for any hours worked in excess of forty a week. However, employees "employed in a bona fide . . . professional capacity" are exempt from that requirement. The statute does not provide a definition of "professional capacity," instead delegating the authority to do so to the Secretary of the Department of Labor ("DOL"), who defines "professional employees" to include those employees who are:

(1) Compensated on a salary or fee basis at a rate of not less than $455 per week . . .; and

(2) Whose primary duty is the performance of work:

(i) Requiring knowledge of an advanced type in a field of science or learning customarily acquired by a prolonged course of intellectual instruction; or

(ii) Requiring invention, imagination, originality or talent in a recognized field of artistic or creative endeavor.

These requirements, however, do not apply to attorneys engaged in the practice of law. Instead, attorneys fall under 29 C.F.R. § 541.304, which exempts from the overtime requirement:

Any employee who is the holder of a valid license or certificate permitting the practice of law or medicine or any of their branches and is actually engaged in the practice thereof[.]

While it is undisputed that Lola is an attorney licensed to practice law in California, the parties dispute whether the document review he allegedly performed constitutes "engaging in the practice of law."

Lola urges us to fashion a new federal standard defining the "practice of law" within the meaning of Section 541.304. We decline to do so because we agree with the district court that the definition of "practice of law" is "primarily a matter of state concern."

* * *

Just as "there is no federal law of domestic relations," here there is no federal law governing lawyers. Regulating the "practice of law" is traditionally a state endeavor. No federal scheme exists for issuing law licenses. As the district court aptly observed, "[s]tates regulate almost every aspect of legal practice: they set the eligibility criteria and oversee the admission process for would-be lawyers, promulgate the rules of professional ethics, and discipline lawyers who fail to follow those rules, among many other responsibilities." The exemption in FLSA specifically relies on the attorney possessing "a valid license . . . permitting the practice of law." The regulation's history indicates that the DOL was well aware that such licenses were issued by the states. In rejecting a proposal to exempt librarians from the overtime rules, the DOL noted that "states do not generally license the practice of library science, so that in this respect . . . the profession is not comparable to that of law or medicine." A similar distinction was drawn in a discussion of extending the exemption to architects and engineers:

The practice of law and medicine has a long history of state licensing and certification; the licensing of engineers and architects is relatively recent. While it is impossible for a doctor or lawyer legally to practice his profession without a certificate or license, many architects and engineers perform work in these fields without possessing licenses, although failure to hold a license may limit their permissible activities to those of lesser responsibilities.

We thus find no error with the district court's conclusion that we should look to state law in defining the "practice of law."

We turn to the question of which state's law to apply. "Where jurisdiction is based on the existence of a federal question . . . we have not hesitated to apply a federal common law choice of law analysis." * * * Here, there are four possible forum states: North Carolina (where Lola worked and lived); Ohio (where the underlying litigation is venued); California (where Lola is barred); and New York (where Skadden is located).

* * *

Here, the services were rendered in North Carolina. Moreover, as the state where Lola resides, North Carolina possesses a strong interest in making sure Lola is fairly paid. We find no error in the district court's decision to apply North Carolina law.

North Carolina defines the "practice of law" in its General Statutes, Section 84–2.1, which provides that:

> The phrase "practice law" as used in this Chapter is defined to be performing any legal service for any other person, firm or corporation, with or without compensation, specifically including . . . the preparation and filing of petitions for use in any court, including administrative tribunals and other judicial or quasi-judicial bodies, or assisting by advice, counsel, or otherwise in any legal work; and to advise or give opinion upon the legal rights of any person, firm or corporation. . . .

North Carolina courts typically read Section 84–2.1 in conjunction with Section 84–4, which defines the unauthorized practice of law as follows:

> Except as otherwise permitted by law, . . . it shall be unlawful for any person or association of persons except active members of the Bar, for or without a fee or consideration, to give legal advice or counsel, [or] perform for or furnish to another legal services. . . .

The North Carolina General Statutes do not clarify whether "legal services" includes the performance of document review. Nevertheless, the North Carolina State Bar issued a formal ethics opinion shedding light on what is meant by "legal services." The question considered in the ethics opinion was: "May a lawyer ethically outsource legal support services abroad, if the individual providing the services is either a nonlawyer or a lawyer not admitted to practice in the United States (collectively 'foreign assistants')?" In its opinion, the Bar's Ethics Committee opined that:

A lawyer may use foreign assistants for administrative support services such as document assembly, accounting, and clerical support. A lawyer may also use foreign assistants for limited legal support services such as reviewing documents; conducting due diligence; drafting contracts, pleadings, and memoranda of law; and conducting legal research. Foreign assistants may not exercise independent legal judgment in making decisions on behalf of a client. . . . The limitations on the type of legal services that can be outsourced, in conjunction with the selection and supervisory requirements associated with the use of foreign assistants, insures that the client is competently represented. *See* Rule 5.5(d). Nevertheless, when outsourcing legal support services, lawyers need to be mindful of the prohibitions on unauthorized practice of law in Chapter 84 of the General Statutes and on the prohibition on aiding the unauthorized practice of law in Rule 5.5(d).

The district court found that (1) under North Carolina law, document review is considered "legal support services," along with "drafting contracts, pleadings, and memoranda of law[,] and conducting legal research;" (2) the ethics opinion draws a clear line between legal support services, like document review, and "administrative support services," like "document assembly, accounting, and clerical support;" and (3) by emphasizing that only lawyers may undertake legal work, the ethics opinion makes clear that "document review, like other legal support services, constitutes the practice of law and may be lawfully performed by a non-lawyer only if that non-lawyer is supervised by a licensed attorney." Thus, the district court concluded, any level of document review is considered the "practice of law" in North Carolina. The district court also concluded that because FLSA's regulatory scheme carves doctors and lawyers out of the salary and duty analysis employed to discern if other types of employees fall within the professional exemption, a fact-intensive inquiry is at odds with FLSA's regulatory scheme.

We disagree. The district court erred in concluding that engaging in document review per se constitutes practicing law in North Carolina. The ethics opinion does not delve into precisely what type of document review falls within the practice of law, but does note that while "reviewing documents" may be within the practice of law, "[f]oreign assistants may not exercise independent legal judgment in making decisions on behalf of a client." The ethics opinion strongly suggests that inherent in the definition of "practice of law" in North Carolina is the exercise of at least a modicum of independent legal judgment.

* * *

The gravamen of Lola's complaint is that he performed document review under such tight constraints that he exercised no legal judgment whatsoever—he alleges that he used criteria developed by others to simply sort documents into different categories. Accepting those allegations as true, as we must on a motion to dismiss, we find that Lola adequately alleged in his complaint that he failed to exercise any legal judgment in performing his duties for Defendants. A fair reading of the complaint in the light most favorable to Lola is that he provided services that a machine could have provided. The parties themselves agreed at oral argument that an individual who, in the course of reviewing discovery documents, undertakes tasks that could otherwise be performed entirely by a machine cannot be said to engage in the practice of law. We therefore vacate the judgment of the district court and remand for further proceedings consistent with this opinion.

NOTE

The plaintiffs and Skadden, Arps settled the Lola lawsuit and the U.S. District Judge approved the settlement. Lola v. Skadden, Arps, Slate, Meagher & Flom LLP, 2016 WL 922223 (S.D.N.Y. 2016).

d.   WAGES

As previously stated, as of July 24, 2009, the federal minimum wage was $7.25 an hour. The FLSA itself and regulations issued by the Department of Labor specify how the wage actually received by employees should be computed. Employees need not actually be paid on an hourly basis. For example, piece work rates, such as those which are common in the garment industry, are permissible as long as employees in fact receive at least the minimum wage for time worked. Similarly, fixed weekly or monthly salaries are permissible, as long as the average weekly salary equals or exceeds the minimum wage. Minimum wage compliance is determined on a weekly basis; employers who pay on a semi-monthly or monthly basis may not pay more in one week to make up for a prior underpayment, unless a statutory exception exists.

Wages need not be in cash. Noncash payments may be credited toward the minimum wage if certain conditions are met. Employers may credit toward the minimum wage the reasonable cost (not retail value) to the employer of meals, lodging, and other facilities provided by the employer for the employees' benefit—not the employer's. The facility must be of a kind typically provided by the employer (e.g., meals from a restaurant), employees must be told that the value is being deducted from their wages, and acceptance by employees must be voluntary. The cost of facilities which are provided primarily for the employer's benefit may not be included in computing wages; this would include the cost of uniforms which the employer requires employees to wear, safety equipment required by law, or medical services and hospitalization that the employer is required by law to furnish. Offsets for debts owed to the employer by the employee (i.e. cash or merchandise shortages) may not be applied if the resulting wage would be below the statutory minimum.

The employee's "regular rate of pay" is important for purposes of determining how much must be paid when overtime is due. Under section 207(e) of the Act, exclusions from regular rates of pay include gifts or bonuses; vacation, holiday or sick pay, when no work is performed; irrevocable contributions to pension or insurance plans; premium pay for hours worked in excess of the employee's normal or regular working hours or pursuant to a collective bargaining agreement. Such premium rate compensation may also be credited toward overtime payment under the Act.

NOTES AND QUESTIONS

1.　The employer may be able to deduct from wages the cost of meals even where the employee does not take advantage of them. Melton v. Round Table Restaurants, Inc., 20 Wage & Hour Cases (BNA) 532 (N.D.Ga.1971). Furthermore, the employer need not give employees a choice between cash and meals or board. See Davis Bros., Inc. v. Donovan, 700 F.2d 1368 (11th Cir. 1983); Morrison, Inc. v. Donovan, 700 F.2d 1374 (11th Cir. 1983) (cafeterias may credit toward minimum cash wages the cost of meals provided to employees; "customarily furnished" language of statute means "regularly provided" by employer, not "voluntarily accepted" by employee).

2.　The Second Circuit ruled that housing furnished to migrant farmworkers was presumptively for the benefit of the workers rather than the employer and thus includable as wages under the FLSA. Soler v. G. & U., Inc., 833 F.2d 1104 (2d Cir. 1987), cert. denied, 488 U.S. 832 (1988). But see Osias v. Marc, 700 F.Supp. 842 (D.Md.1988) (employer not entitled to housing credit where facilities provided were substandard).

3.　Setoffs against any back pay due as a result of an action to enforce the Act are prohibited. In Brennan v. Heard, 491 F.2d 1, 7 (5th Cir. 1974), the court held that such offsets were impermissible in an action to enforce the Act:

> Congress has determined that the individual worker should have both the freedom and the responsibility to allocate his minimum wage among competing economic and personal interests. * * * The FLSA decrees a minimum unconditional payment and the commands of that Act are not to be vitiated by an employer * * *. The federal courts were not designated by the FLSA to be either collection agents or arbitrators for an employee's creditors. Their sole function and duty under the Act is to assure to the employees of a covered company a minimum level of wages. Arguments and disputations over claims against those wages are foreign to the genesis, history, interpretation, and philosophy of the Act. The only economic feud contemplated by the FLSA involves the employer's obedience to minimum wage and overtime standards. To clutter these proceedings with the minutiae of other employer-employee relationships would be antithetical to the purpose of the Act. Set-offs against back pay awards deprive the employee of the "cash in

> hand" contemplated by the Act, and are therefore inappropriate in
> any proceeding brought to enforce the FLSA.

Suppose employees of an employer that has been found guilty of violating the Act owe the employer money for goods purchased at a company store. If the employer is not entitled to set off against its penalties the amount of money owed to it by its employees, how will it recover the money owed to it? Under what circumstances may an employer properly set off debts owed it by an employee? Why should it make a difference if, for instance, food is furnished to employees by the employer as meals, which are a proper offset against wages, or if the employer permits employees to select food of their choice at a company-owned store? In Blanton v. City of Murfreesboro, 856 F.2d 731 (6th Cir. 1988), the court found that the city's downward adjustment of firefighters' base wage rate to offset the increased cost imposed by the Act violated the FLSA regardless of the city's good faith.

4. Employers may not shift the burden of business losses to their employees by deducting them from pay. A California appellate court held illegal Neiman Marcus's practice of deducting from sales associates' commissions a percentage of merchandise returns. Hudgins v. Neiman Marcus Grp., Inc., 41 Cal.Rptr.2d 46 (Ct.App.1995).

5. Radio Shack paid its store managers "a base salary as straight time pay for all hours worked each workweek" and "overtime at one-half the calculated regular rate * * * for all hours worked over forty in any workweek." The company calculated the "regular rate" by "dividing the number of hours worked in the workweek into the weekly base salary amount." The workweek fluctuated, so the hourly rate on which overtime was calculated varied. The Washington Supreme Court said this way of calculating overtime pay did not violate the state's wage and hour law. Inniss v. Tandy Corp., 7 P.3d 807 (Wash.2000).

6. An employee who worked at a Wendy's restaurant for $5.50 per hour, got into a dispute with a manager and quit. Under Oregon law her final wages were due on January 17, five days (excluding weekends and holidays) after her notice. On January 14, she returned to the restaurant and was told the check would be available in a day or two. The employee asked the assistant manager to telephone her when the check was ready. The paycheck arrived at the restaurant on January 24, no one contacted the former employee, and she did not get the check until she came to the restaurant on February 8. An appellate court imposed on Wendy's Oregon's stiff penalties for not paying an employee within the prescribed period. Wales v. Walt Stallcup Enter., 2 P.3d 944 (Or.Ct.App.2000).

7. A bonus is not "wages" within the meaning of the New York statute. Thus the employer could enforce its policy of paying a 1997 bonus in quarterly installments through 1998 and of not making bonus payments due after the employee resigned. "An employee's entitlement to a bonus is governed by the terms of the employer's bonus plan." Truelove v. Northeast Capital & Advisory, Inc., 738 N.E.2d 770 (N.Y.2000). But see Fiorenti v. Central Emergency Physicians, P.L.L.C., 723 N.Y.S.2d 851 (N.Y. Sup.Ct. 2001) (a potential bonus, as outlined in contract between employees and employer, constituted "wages" within definition of wage payment statute, assuming requirements for bonus were satisfied, where bonus plan was predicated on employees' personal productivity and the objective success of the employer).

8.   Restaurant servers alleged that their employers showed service charges on customers' bills but did not give the servers the money. Their salaries were above minimum wage. New York law forbids an employer from retaining "any charge purported to be a gratuity." The state's highest court held that this provision applies not only to tips presented by the customer, but also to a service charge shown on the bill that the customer is likely to think is a tip. Samiento v. World Yacht Inc., 883 N.E.2d 990 (N.Y. 2008).

See also Matamoros v. Starbucks Corp., 699 F.3d 129 (1st Cir. 2012), holding that Massachusetts' "Tips Act" does not permit Starbucks to share customer gratuities with "shift supervisors" as well as with baristas because the shift supervisors perform a small degree of supervisory work.

If a restaurant is paying legal (non-tipped) minimum wage or more to both servers and kitchen employees, can it require tips received by servers to be shared with both groups of workers? An Obama-era DOL regulation said that servers should get all the tip money. The regulation was upheld by the Ninth Circuit in Oregon Restaurant & Lodging Ass'n v. Perez, 816 F.3d 1080 (9th Cir. 2017). However, the Tenth Circuit reached the opposite conclusion. Marlow v. New Food Guy, 861 F.3d 1157 (10th Cir. 2017) (employee who made above the minimum wage was not entitled to tips under FLSA, and DOL did not have the authority to promulgate a rule to the contrary). But in December 2017, the WHD issued a notice of proposed rulemaking that would allow employers that do not pay the full minimum wage to tipped workers to distribute customer tips within a tip pool that includes non-tipped workers.

Another issue involving tips concerns when an employee who performs some tipped work and some non-tipped work is entitled to be paid the full minimum wage for the time spent doing the non-tipped work. In Marsh v. J. Alexander's, the court wrote that an employee stated a claim that he had "dual jobs" (triggering the employer's obligation to pay the minimum wage for the employee's time spent performing the non-tipped job) based on his allegation that he had to spend more than twenty percent of his time performing intermittent tasks such as cleaning or making tea during the course of a restaurant server job. In reaching that conclusion, the court deferred to the DOL's interpretation of its dual jobs regulation. 905 F.3d 610 (9th Cir. 2018) (rehearing en banc granted).

9.   The Los Angeles Living Wage Ordinance requires contractors who operate at the city's airports to pay their employees $14.89 per hour, or $10.30 per hour if the contractor provides health benefits. See Calop Bus. Sys., Inc. v. City of Los Angeles, 614 Fed. Appx. 867 (9th Cir. 2015).

Seattle raised minimum wages more for large employers and classified certain franchisees as large employers. The new policy survived legal challenges. International Franchise Ass'n v. City of Seattle, 803 F.3d 389 (9th Cir. 2015), cert. denied, 136 S.Ct. 1838 (2016).

Efforts by cities to raise the minimum wage are not always successful, however. In at least seventeen states, state legislatures have prohibited localities from enacting minimum wage ordinances. In April 2015, the Birmingham, Alabama City Council adopted a series of ordinances enacting a local minimum wage. Shortly thereafter, the Alabama state legislature passed the Alabama Uniform Minimum Wage and Right-to-Work Act. Ala. Code §§ 25–7–40 (2016). A purported effort to increase state uniformity in labor policy, the Act gave the legislature complete control over minimum wage policy and a host of other labor policy issues. Birmingham workers then brought suit in district court. They lost on a motion to dismiss, but the 11th Circuit initially reversed in part, holding that that plaintiffs had stated a plausible equal protection claim because they had plausibly alleged that the state preemption law has a racially discriminatory impact, and was enacted with an intent to discriminate based on race. Lewis v. Governor of Alabama, 896 F.3d 1282 (11th Cir. 2018). However, the Eleventh Circuit then reheard the case en banc, and held that the plaintiffs lacked standing because they sued the state Attorney General, rather than their employers.

e. HOURS

The FLSA requires that employees be paid for all hours worked, at minimum wage for the first 40 hours worked in a week and at time and a half their regular rate of pay for all hours in excess of 40 per week. What constitutes compensable hours is subject to debate. Employees must be paid for all time they are engaged in "principal" job activities, as well as "incidental" activities which are an integral part of their work. However, the Portal-to-Portal Act excludes preliminary and postliminary activity ("waiting to be engaged") from compensable time. Generally, time spent in such activities as coffee breaks of up to 20 minutes, waiting, staff meetings, fire drills, and grievance adjustment during working hours ("engaged to be waiting") are compensable. Meal periods of one-half hour or more during which the employee is relieved of all duties, scheduled maintenance shutdowns, union meetings for internal union affairs, voting time (unless compensation required by state law), and absences for illness, holiday, or vacation are examples of noncompensable time.

IBP, Inc. v. Alvarez

546 U.S. 21 (2005).

■ JUSTICE STEVENS delivered the opinion of the court:

These consolidated cases raise questions concerning the coverage of the Fair Labor Standards Act of 1938 (FLSA), as amended by the Portal-to-Portal Act of 1947, with respect to activities of employees who must don protective clothing on the employer's premises before they engage in the productive labor for which they are primarily hired. The principal question, which is presented in both cases, is whether the time employees spend walking between the changing area and the production area is compensable under the FLSA. * * * In No. 03–1238, the Court of Appeals for the Ninth Circuit answered "yes" * * * the Court of Appeals for the First Circuit answered "no". We granted certiorari to resolve the conflict.

I.

As enacted in 1938, the FLSA required employers engaged in the production of goods for commerce to pay their employees a minimum wage of "not less than 25 cents an hour," and prohibited the employment of any person for workweeks in excess of 40 hours after the second year following the legislation "unless such employee receives compensation for his employment in excess of [40] hours * * * at a rate not less than one and one-half times the regular rate at which he is employed." Neither "work" nor "workweek" is defined in the statute. The most pertinent definition provides: " 'Employ' includes to suffer or permit to work."

Our early cases defined those terms broadly. In Tennessee Coal, Iron & R. Co. v. Muscoda Local No. 123, we held that time spent traveling from iron ore mine portals to underground working areas was compensable; relying on the remedial purposes of the statute and Webster's Dictionary, we described "work or employment" as "physical or mental exertion (whether burdensome or not) controlled or required by the employer and pursued necessarily and primarily for the benefit of the employer and his business." The same year, in *Armour & Co. v. Wantock*, we clarified that "exertion" was not in fact necessary for an activity to constitute "work" under the FLSA. We pointed out that "an employer, if he chooses, may hire a man to do nothing, or to do nothing but wait for something to happen." Two years later, in *Anderson v. Mt. Clemens Pottery Co.*, we defined "the statutory workweek" to "include all time during which an employee is necessarily required to be on the employer's premises, on duty or at a prescribed workplace." Accordingly, we held that the time necessarily spent by employees walking from time clocks near the factory entrance gate to their workstations must be treated as part of the workweek.

The year after our decision in *Anderson*, Congress passed the Portal-to-Portal Act, amending certain provisions of the FLSA. Based on findings that judicial interpretations of the FLSA had superseded "long-established customs, practices, and contracts between employers and employees, thereby creating wholly unexpected liabilities, immense in amount and retroactive in operation," it responded with two statutory remedies, the first relating to "existing claims," and the second to "future claims," Both remedies distinguish between working time that is compensable pursuant to contract or custom and practice, on the one hand, and time that was found compensable under this Court's expansive reading of the FLSA, on the other. Like the original FLSA, however, the Portal-to-Portal Act omits any definition of the term "work."

With respect to existing claims, the Portal-to-Portal Act provided that employers would not incur liability on account of their failure to pay minimum wages or overtime compensation for any activity that was not compensable by either an express contract or an established custom or practice. With respect to "future claims," the Act preserved potential liability for working time not made compensable by contract or custom but narrowed the coverage of the FLSA by excepting two activities that had been treated as compensable under our cases: walking on the employer's premises to and from the actual place of performance of the principal activity of the employee, and activities that are "preliminary or postliminary" to that principal activity.

Specifically, Part III of the Portal-to-Portal Act, entitled "FUTURE CLAIMS," provides in relevant part:

"Sec. 4. Relief from Certain Future Claims Under the Fair Labor Standards Act of 1938 . . .—

"(a) Except as provided in subsection (b) [which covers work compensable by contract or custom], no employer shall be subject to any liability or punishment under the Fair Labor Standards Act of 1938, as amended, . . . on account of the failure of such employer to pay an employee minimum wages, or to pay an employee overtime compensation, for or on account of any of the following activities of such employee engaged in on or after the date of the enactment of this Act—

"(1) walking, riding, or traveling to and from the actual place of performance of the principal activity or activities which such employee is employed to perform, and

"(2) activities which are preliminary to or postliminary to said principal activity or activities, which occur either prior to the time on any particular workday at which such employee commences, or subsequent to the time on any particular workday at which he ceases, such principal activity or activities."

Other than its express exceptions for travel to and from the location of the employee's "principal activity," and for activities that are preliminary or postliminary to that principal activity, the Portal-to-Portal Act does not purport to change this Court's earlier descriptions of the terms "work" and "workweek," or to define the term "workday." A regulation promulgated by the Secretary of Labor shortly after its enactment concluded that the statute had no effect on the computation of hours that are worked "within" the workday. That regulation states: "[T]o the extent that activities engaged in by an employee occur after the employee commences to perform the first principal activity on a particular workday and before he ceases the performance of the last principal activity on a particular workday, the provisions of [§ 4] have no application" Similarly, consistent with our prior decisions interpreting the FLSA, the Department of Labor has adopted the continuous workday rule, which means that the "workday" is generally defined as "the period between the commencement and completion on the same workday of an employee's principal activity or activities." These regulations have remained in effect since 1947, and no party disputes the validity of the continuous workday rule.

In 1955, eight years after the enactment of the Portal-to-Portal Act and the promulgation of these interpretive regulations, we were confronted with the question whether workers in a battery plant had a statutory right to compensation for the "time incident to changing clothes at the beginning of the shift and showering at the end, where they must make extensive use of dangerously caustic and toxic materials, and are compelled by circumstances, including vital considerations of health and hygiene, to change clothes and to shower in facilities which state law requires their employers to provide. . . ." After distinguishing "changing clothes and showering under normal conditions" and stressing the important health and safety risks associated with the production of batteries, the Court endorsed the Court of Appeals' conclusion that these activities were compensable under the FLSA.

In reaching this result, we specifically agreed with the Court of Appeals that "the term 'principal activity or activities' in Section 4 [of the Portal-to-Portal Act] embraces all activities which are an 'integral and indispensable part of the principal activities,' and that the activities in question fall within this category." Thus, activities, such as the donning and doffing of specialized protective gear, that are "performed either before or after the regular work shift, on or off the production line, are compensable under the portal-to-portal provisions of the Fair Labor Standards Act if those activities are an integral and indispensable part of the principal activities for which covered workmen are employed and are not specifically excluded by Section 4(a)(1)."

The principal question presented by these consolidated cases—both of which involve required protective gear that the courts below found integral and indispensable to the employees' work—is whether postdonning and predoffing walking time is specifically excluded by § 4(a)(1). We conclude that it is not.

II.

Petitioner is a large producer of fresh beef, pork, and related products. At its plant in Pasco, Washington, it employs approximately 178 workers in 113 job classifications in the slaughter division and 800 line workers in 145 job classifications in the processing division. All production workers in both divisions must wear outer garments, hardhats, hairnets, earplugs, gloves, sleeves, aprons, leggings, and boots. Many of them, particularly those who use knives, must also wear a variety of protective equipment for their hands, arms, torsos, and legs; this gear includes chain link metal aprons, vests, plexiglass armguards, and special gloves. IBP requires its employees to store their equipment and tools in company locker rooms, where most of them don their protective gear.

Production workers' pay is based on the time spent cutting and bagging meat. Pay begins with the first piece of meat and ends with the last piece of meat. Since 1998, however, IBP has also paid for four minutes of clothes-changing time. In 1999, respondents, IBP employees, filed this class action to recover compensation for preproduction and postproduction work, including the time spent donning and doffing protective gear and walking between the locker rooms and the production floor before and after their assigned shifts.

After a lengthy bench trial, the District Court for the Eastern District of Washington held that donning and doffing of protective gear that was unique to the jobs at issue were compensable under the FLSA because they were integral and indispensable to the work of the employees who wore such equipment. Moreover, consistent with the continuous workday rule, the District Court concluded that, for those employees required to don and doff unique protective gear, the walking time between the locker room and the production floor was also compensable because it occurs during the workday. The court did not, however, allow any recovery for ordinary clothes changing and washing, or for the "donning and doffing of hard hat[s], ear plugs, safety glasses, boots [or] hairnet[s]."

The District Court proceeded to apply these legal conclusions in making detailed factual findings with regard to the different groups of employees. For example, the District Court found that, under its view of what was covered by the FLSA, processing division knife users were entitled to compensation for between 12 and 14 minutes of preproduction and postproduction work, including 3.3 to 4.4 minutes of walking time.

IBP does not challenge the holding below that the donning and doffing of unique protective gear are "principal activities" under § 4 of the Portal-to-Portal Act. Thus, the only question for us to decide is whether the Court of Appeals correctly rejected IBP's contention that the walking between the locker rooms and the production areas is excluded from FLSA coverage by § 4(a)(1) of the Portal-to-Portal Act.

IBP argues that the text of § 4(a)(1), the history and purpose of its enactment, and the Department of Labor's interpretive guidance compel the conclusion that the Portal-to-Portal Act excludes this walking time from the scope of the FLSA. We find each of these arguments unpersuasive.

* * *

IBP emphasizes that our decision in *Anderson v. Mt. Clemens Pottery Co.,* may well have been the proximate cause of the enactment of the Portal-to-Portal Act. In that case we held that the FLSA mandated compensation for the time that employees spent walking from time clocks located near the plant entrance to their respective places of work prior to the start of their productive labor. In IBP's view, Congress' forceful repudiation of that holding reflects a purpose to exclude what IBP regards as the quite similar walking time spent by respondents before and after their work slaughtering cattle and processing meat. Even if there is ambiguity in the statute, we should construe it to effectuate that important purpose.

This argument is also unpersuasive. There is a critical difference between the walking at issue in *Anderson* and the walking at issue in this case. In *Anderson* the walking preceded the employees' principal activity; it occurred before the workday began. The relevant walking in this case occurs after the workday begins and before it ends. Only if we were to endorse IBP's novel submission that an activity can be sufficiently "principal" to be compensable, but not sufficiently so to start the workday, would this case be comparable to *Anderson*. * * *

For the foregoing reasons, we hold that any activity that is "integral and indispensable" to a "principal activity" is itself a "principal activity" under § 4(a) of the Portal-to-Portal Act. Moreover, during a continuous workday, any walking time that occurs after the beginning of the employee's first principal activity and before the end of the employee's last principal activity is excluded from the scope of that provision, and as a result is covered by the FLSA.

* * *

NOTES AND QUESTIONS

1.   Should employees who are "on-call" be paid overtime for the time spent having to respond to their pagers? In Adair v. Charter County of Wayne, 452 F.3d 482 (6th Cir. 2006), cert. denied, 549 U.S. 1279 (2007), the court held that airport police officers were not entitled to overtime pay under the Fair Labor Standards Act (FLSA) for time off duty when they were required to carry pagers.

In Owens v. Local No. 169, Ass'n of W. Pulp & Paper Workers, 971 F.2d 347 (9th Cir. 1992), the Ninth Circuit ruled that off-duty time spent on-call by pulp mill mechanics was not compensable. The court, under the standard articulated in Armour & Co. v. Wantock, 323 U.S. 126 (1944), looked to see if employees had freedom to engage in personal activities while on call and whether there was an agreement between the parties. Answering both questions in the affirmative, the court reversed the grant of summary judgment for the plaintiffs and remanded for summary judgment for the defendants.

California law requires employers to permit their employees to take off-duty rest periods. The California Supreme Court decided that employers may not require employees to remain "on call" during these rest periods. Thus, ABM Security Services cannot require guards to keep their pagers and radio phones on during rest periods and to "remain vigilant and responsive to calls when needs arose." Augustus v. ABM Security Services, Inc., 347 P.3d 89 (Cal. 2016) (5–2).

2.   Generally, meal times of one-half hour or more are considered noncompensable, provided the employee is relieved of all duties during the

break. However, it is possible for an employer to put so many restrictions on employees' right to take a meal break that it becomes compensable, either under the FLSA or equivalent state laws, because the meal time benefits the employer. In Reich v. Southern New Eng. Telecomms. Corp., 121 F.3d 58 (2d Cir. 1997), the court held that the employer's requirement that employees working on outside work sites remain on site during lunch breaks to provide security and ensure safety at the sites transformed otherwise uncompensable breaks into compensable work periods. In Avery v. City of Talladega, 24 F.3d 1337 (11th Cir. 1994), however, the court held that police officers' meal breaks were not spent predominantly for benefit of city, and, therefore, were not compensable, where employees were free to spend their meal breaks in any way they wished even though they were required to remain in uniform, leave their radios on, and were not permitted to leave the jurisdiction. In Department of Labor v. American Future Systems, 873 F.3d 420 (3d Cir. 2017), the Third Circuit held that employers were required to compensate employees for breaks of up to 20 minutes.

3. Plaintiff sought overtime wages for the large amounts of time he spent driving between his home and the Grand Union stores where he performed mechanical services. He lived in Long Island and was assigned to stores in Connecticut and New York, including some in upstate New York. He was paid for daytime travel between job sites but not for travel between his home and the first or last job of the day. The court of appeals said that Grand Union's treatment of plaintiff was "inequitable" but not in violation of the Portal-to-Portal Act, which declines coverage for "normal travel" between home and work. The dissenting judge said "this interpretation * * * cannot be right. The FLSA was intended to invalidate 'customs and contracts which allow an employer to claim all of an employee's time while compensating him for only a part of it.' " Kavanagh v. Grand Union Co., 192 F.3d 269 (2d Cir. 1999).

New York City fire alarm inspectors go directly from home to the places they will inspect and return home at the end of the workday. Thus, they must pick up inspection documents on Friday at the office and carry them back and forth from home to their inspection locations. Held: The city need not pay the inspectors for their commuting time, although they must bring documents with them. The instructors had argued that commuting sometimes took longer because carrying a briefcase caused them to miss a train or bus. Singh v. City of New York, 524 F.3d 361 (2d Cir. 2008).

4. Agricultural employees were subject to the employer's "control" during time spent traveling to and from fields on employer-provided buses, so the travel time was compensable as "hours worked." The court said that in interpreting the California statute it would give no deference to doctrine developed by federal courts under the FLSA and the Portal-to-Portal Act. Morillion v. Royal Packing Co., 995 P.2d 139 (Cal.2000).

5. K-9 police officer sought overtime pay for the 44 hours per week he spent at home caring for "Bandit." The town's policy was to pay K-9 officers for two hours of overtime per week. The court said that "at some point, an officer's attention to his assigned dog may not be provided primarily for the employer's benefit but rather out of the caretaker's own sense of love and devotion to the animal in his charge." It called for a jury instruction that would ask how much of the dog-care time was required by the employer and whether time spent was primarily for the benefit of the employer. It recognized that the consequence of applying the overtime statute might be to make it uneconomic for municipalities to use police dogs. Holzapfel v. Town of Newburgh, 145 F.3d 516 (2d Cir. 1998), cert. denied, 525 U.S. 1055 (1998).

6. Operating room employees in a hospital are required to work "on-premises-on-call" overtime, during which they have to remain at the hospital, although they are not on active duty until called. When they are on active duty, they perform their regular jobs and are paid one and one-half their regular shift rate. During waiting periods, employees have no assigned duties and are free to sleep, watch television, and otherwise occupy themselves. Employees are paid one and one-half times the federal minimum wage for waiting periods, an amount considerably less than their usual rate. Does the employer violate the FLSA with this two-rate wage structure? Not necessarily, held the Third Circuit in Townsend v. Mercy Hosp., 862 F.2d 1009 (3d Cir. 1988). Under section 7(g)(2) of the FLSA, an employer and employee may agree to a "bona fide rate" that is different from the employee's regular rate of pay and is applicable to work performed only during overtime hours. Typically, the parties agree to two rates when the employee performs two or more kinds of work in the ordinary course of working, with the two-rate structure being carried over to overtime. In *Townsend,* the employer did not pay two different wages for active duty and waiting periods during employees' regular hours; the two-rate structure applied only to "on-call-on-premises" overtime. The Third Circuit held no violation, finding that in addition to there being agreement between the parties, there was a qualitative difference between "idle time" during regular shift hours, when employees were constrained in what they could do (e.g., no sleeping or watching television), and the separately compensable "waiting time" that occurred during the on-call shifts.

When the employer is a hospital or an establishment engaged in care of sick, aged or mentally ill, the FLSA requires the employer to pay its employees at one-and-one-half times the employees' "regular rate" for any "employment in excess of eight hours in any workday and in excess of eighty hours in [a] fourteen-day period." 29 U.S.C. § 207(j). The Ninth Circuit has held that when an employer changes its shift schedule to accommodate its employees' scheduling desires, the mere fact that pay rates changed, altering the old and new scheduling schemes in an attempt to keep overall pay revenue-neutral, does not violate the FLSA's overtime pay requirements. Parth v. Pomona Valley Hosp., 584 F.3d 794 (9th Cir. 2009). In response to the nurses' request, the Pomona Valley Hospital Medical Center developed and implemented an optional 12-hour shift schedule and pay plan that provided nurses the option of working a 12-hour shift schedule in exchange for receiving a lower base hourly salary and time-and-a-half pay for hours worked in excess of eight per day. Many nurses opted to work the 12-hour shift because it provides them more scheduling flexibility and allows them to spend less time commuting to work. As a result, nurses who volunteered for the 12-hour shift schedule would make approximately the same amount of money as they made on the 8-hour shift schedule while working the same number of hours. Are the base hourly pay rate differences between the 8-hour and 12-hour shifts justified, considering that nurses working both shifts perform the same job duties? Is the 12-hour base pay rate an unlawful "artifice" designed to avoid the FLSA's overtime and maximum hours requirements?

7. Work sharing and flextime have been suggested as possible ways to enhance the quality of work life for some employees, especially women with small children. What special modifications, if any, would need to be made in the FLSA's wage and hour provisions to accommodate and to promote such nontraditional working conditions? In 2010, section 4207 of the Patient Protection and Affordable Care Act amended the FLSA to require an employer to provide reasonable break time for an employee to express breast milk for her nursing child for one year after the child's birth each time such employee has need to express milk. The employer is not required to compensate an employee receiving reasonable break time for any work time spent for such purpose. However, the employer must also provide a place, other than a bathroom, for the employee to express breast milk. If these requirements impose undue hardship, an employer that employs less than 50 employees is not subject to them. In addition, these requirements do not preempt a state law that provides greater protections to employees. As of 2014, 29 states, the District of Columbia, and Puerto Rico have laws related to breastfeeding in the workplace.

8. Are Department of Justice attorneys entitled to overtime pay? In Doe v. United States, 463 F.3d 1314 (Fed. Cir. 2006), cert. denied, 549 U.S. 1321 (2007), plaintiff John Doe and a class of similarly situated attorneys brought a claim for administratively uncontrollable overtime (AUO) pay under the Federal Employees Pay Act of 1945. The court ruled against the unhappy attorneys, holding that "attorney" was not one of the limited positions subject to overtime compensation under the act.

9. Will the prevalence of smart phones create potential liability for employers? Although there are presently no cases in the U.S. alleging FLSA wage and hour violations with respect to the use of smart phones outside of work, experts believe that it is only a matter of time before such a claim is filed. In Controlling Smart-Phone Abuse, Sean L. McLaughlin suggests that the de minimis doctrine, the Portal-to-Portal Act, and the on-call case law provide an analytical framework for courts to evaluate smart-phone claims and separate the legitimate claims from the frivolous ones. Employers may actively seek to avoid the potential for liability by eliminating smart phones for non-exempt workers and setting strict guidelines on their use through written contracts. See Sean L. McLaughlin, Controlling Smart-Phone Abuse: The Fair Labor Standards Act's Definition of "Work" in Non-Exempt Employee Claims for Overtime, 58 U. Kan. L. Rev. 737 (2010). At the beginning of 2017, France adopted a "right to disconnect," which requires larger companies to negotiate an out-of-office email policy with their staffs. Some large European countries limit employees' abilities to access their work email outside of work time.

10. In Sandifer v. United States Steel Corp., the Supreme Court unanimously decided that the statutory provision discussed in *Alvarez* meant that a class of steelworkers need not be paid for time spent changing into and out of protective gear. Justice Scalia discussed in detail the possible meanings of the statutory word "clothes," in the context of the workers' protective gear: "a flame-retardant jacket, pair of pants, and hood; a hardhat; a 'snood'; 'wristlets'; work gloves . . . safety glasses, earplugs; and a respirator." Judge Richard Posner's decision in the court of appeals, reaching the result that the Supreme Court affirmed, had included a photograph of one of his law clerks modeling these items. Justice Scalia also discussed the meaning of "changing," saying that "layer[ing] garments" is covered as is taking off one item of clothing and replacing it with another. He said that glasses, earplugs, and a respirator are not "clothes," but that adding those items takes little time so the additional seconds or minutes need not be compensated. Sandifer v. United States Steel Corp., 571 U.S. 220 (2014).

11. West Yellowstone, Montana, employed a police force of four. They worked 12-hour shifts but had to be on-call for the 12 hours preceding a shift. When on call they had to stay within cell phone access and keep the ringer loud enough to wake them if they were asleep. If called, the officer would get a minimum of 2.5 hours of overtime pay. A jury, influenced by evidence that Sergeant Stubblefield was in fact called out only 18 times in 609 on-call shifts (with similar numbers for two other officers), ruled for the town and the Montana Supreme Court refused to overturn the jury verdict. Stubblefield v. Town of West Yellowstone, 298 P.3d 419 (Mont. 2013).

12. In Busk v. Integrity Staffing Solutions, 713 F.3d 525 (9th Cir. 2013), a Ninth Circuit panel held that employees at a warehouse where Amazon orders were filled had a right to be paid for time spent on line waiting for security clearance at the end of their shifts but not for their 30 minute lunch period, of which ten minutes were spent walking to and from the cafeteria and (again) surviving a security check. The court also held that an opt-in federal FLSA collective action and an opt-out Nevada class action are compatible and can proceed together. The Supreme Court reversed, holding that by enacting the Portal-to-Portal Act, Congress cut back on the broad judicial interpretation given to the FLSA's undefined terms "work" and "workweek." The Court unanimously held that employers do not have to pay for "activities which are preliminary to or postliminary to" the principal activities that an employee is hired to perform. Integrity Staffing Solutions, Inc. v. Busk, 135 S.Ct. 513 (2014).

13. In 1999 and 2001, the Department of Labor said that mortgage-loan officers are not administrators exempt from overtime pay requirements. In 2006, the Department said they were exempt as administrators. In 2010, the Department withdrew the 2006 letter and restored overtime pay to them. The Mortgage Bankers Association sued, arguing that the 2010 action did not meet the procedural requirements of the Administrative Procedure Act. The Supreme Court said the Department's 2010 action did satisfy the APA. Perez v. Mortgage Bankers Ass'n, 135 S.Ct. 1199 (2015).

14. Should the hours worked by employees employed by two companies be aggregated for the purposes of the FLSA? The pivotal question to answer in such cases is whether the employees are jointly or separately employed. An employer of a separately employed employee can disregard the work the employee performs for the other employer. If the employee is jointly employed, however, then the work the employee performs for both employers is aggregated when determining compliance of both employers with the FLSA. 29 C.F.R. § 791.2 (1961).

The Fourth Circuit recently took up this issue in Salinas v. Commercial Interiors, Inc. 848 F.3d 125 (4th Cir. 2017). There, a host of plaintiffs employed as dry wall installers for both J.I., a dry wall installation subcontractor, and Commercial, a general contracting company, sued the two companies, arguing that the hours they worked for both companies be aggregated to assess the companies' compliance with the FLSA. The district court granted summary judgment to Commercial, finding that joint employment did not exist because the agreement entered into between the two companies was a traditionally recognized contractor-subcontractor relationship, and the companies did not intent to avoid compliance with the FLSA. The Fourth Circuit reversed and remanded, holding:

> Joint employment exists when (1) two or more persons or entities share, agree to allocate responsibility for, or otherwise codetermine—formally or informally, directly or indirectly—the essential terms and conditions of a worker's employment and (2) the two entities' combined influence over the essential terms and conditions of the worker's employment render the worker an employee as opposed to an independent contractor. 848 F.3d at 130.

Applying this test, the court found that the undisputed facts in the case established that the J.I. and Commercial shared authority over and codetermined the terms and conditions of the plaintiffs' employment. Commercial actively supervised the work of J.I.'s employees, provided all the tools needed for the work, coordinated staffing hours and pay with J.I., and, on at least one occasion, required J.I. employees to apply for employment with Commercial. The court affirmed the district court's finding that the plaintiffs were employees and not independent contractors using the economic realities test.

15. A group of Tyson Foods employees brought a class action against the company, asserting that their FLSA rights were violated when Tyson failed to provide overtime compensation for donning and doffing protective equipment and clothing before work, before and after lunch, and at the end of the workday. The Supreme Court affirmed a $5.7 million jury verdict for the class, concluding that statistical evidence derived from studying a sample of the plaintiffs was an adequate basis for the class action. The Court was influenced by the fact that the employer had not kept records adequate for challenging the plaintiffs' sample evidence. The employees had done similar work and were paid under the same policy, a reason for distinguishing this case from Wal-Mart Stores, Inc. v. Dukes, p. 251. The Supreme Court affirmed a jury verdict of $5.7 million for the class. Chief Justice Roberts, joined by Justice Alito, concurred but expressed his "concern that the District Court may not be able to fashion a method for awarding damages only to those class members who suffered an actual injury." Tyson Foods, Inc. v. Bouaphakeo, 136 S.Ct. 1036 (2016) (6–2).

f.   CHILD LABOR

In addition to the minimum wage and overtime provisions of the FLSA, the Act also restricts the employment of children under the age of 18 and limits the conditions under which they may work. Specifically, the FLSA dictates that employees must be at least 16 years old to work in most non-farm jobs and at least 18 to work in non-farm jobs declared hazardous. Youths 14 and 15 years old may work outside school hours in various non-manufacturing, non-mining, non-hazardous jobs under specified conditions.

A significant number of young people are employed. Nearly half of 16 and 17 year olds are employed, though more than three-quarters of them hold part-time jobs. From April to July 2014, the number of employed youths 16 to 24 years old rose by 2.1 million to 20.1 million. (See also Chapter 2.)

Child labor laws evolved in the twentieth century in part in response to intolerable and abusive working conditions for children.

M. Neil Browne et al., Universal Moral Principles and the Law: The Failure of One-Size-Fits-All Child Labor Laws
27 Hous. J. Int'l L. 1 (2004).

* * *

II.   Evolution of Anti-Child Labor Sentiment in the United States

"If there is any matter upon which civilized countries have agreed— far more unanimously than they have with regard to . . . some other matters . . . it is the evil of premature and excessive child labor."

From the contemporary perspective of developed nations, one might wonder why it took so long for anti-child labor sentiment to become visible and popular. To begin, we should note that historically the only children who have needed to work have been poor children. Not surprisingly, such children tended to be overlooked by those in society with the power to stop such practices. In addition, as a popular pro-child labor argument contended, work saved children from the "sin of idleness." It was easy for bored children to get into trouble, and work kept them busy. This idea was popular among Puritans and Quakers and spread to the New World when colonization of the Americas began.

In North American colonies, children were an asset—free labor to their families and their new farms. Child labor was seen as a tool to keep children from idleness, as well as a necessity for starting a successful colony and farm. However, as part of the changes necessitated by the American colonists' desire to be independent from England, Americans needed to start producing their own goods, such as clothing. To facilitate this manufacture, the first children began working in American textile and clothing shops. Children were ideal for working in these factories because they worked for a fraction of the cost of comparable adult workers. They also were quick to learn, and their small hands could create the intricate details in the fabrics.

Because children worked long days, they were often uneducated due to a lack of time to attend school. One of the early arguments against child labor focused on the need for children to receive more education. Ironically, it was the Puritans who pushed for children to work less and receive an education, despite the fact that it was also the Puritans who believed that work was a tool to fight the sin of idleness. The Puritans' reasoning for education was that children needed to learn to read in order to read the Bible and be able to save themselves from sin.

Legislatively, during the Industrial Revolution the country was increasingly active in protecting child workers. In 1892, the Democratic Party officially announced that they were against the employment of children under the age of fifteen. In 1893, the Illinois Factory Act allowed for state control of industries. Then, in 1904, the Socialist Party fought for a complete ban on child labor. Because of these endorsements by political parties, such legal reforms began to build momentum.

Yet, passage of a law was only a first step toward resolving the problem addressed by the legislation. For example, a Boston law in 1902 enforced an age limit of eleven years old for boys and fourteen years old for girls for the jobs of boot blacking and selling anything. Such laws took years to create but were so specific and contained such minimal authority that the battle to protect children seemed futile.

Until 1938, the laws that were passed were either state or local statutes; victories were few. But the prospects for child labor legislation changed dramatically during the Great Depression when eradicating child labor provided the promise of supplying unemployed adults with the jobs heretofore held by children. When child labor began to have a negative effect on the welfare of adults, the nation began to take notice. In the depths of the Great Depression the Fair Labor Standards Act of 1938 (FLSA) was passed. This law prohibited children under sixteen from working during the school year and prohibited children from working at specific dangerous jobs all year round. This law was a landmark in the child labor battle because it has endured and, unlike its predecessors, was not found unconstitutional.

Although the FLSA was very beneficial to children's welfare, it was hardly all encompassing in protecting child labor. One of the largest loopholes in the law was its lack of applicability agricultural employment. For decades after the FLSA was passed, children continued to work on farms during the harvest season. Furthermore, children who worked in agriculture were not required to attend school.

World War II revolutionized American industry in many ways. Machines were created to do many of the tedious, monotonous jobs that children once did, and the people who were required to run the machines needed increasingly more and more education. States responded to the decline in child labor by lengthening the school year, requiring more years of education, and enforcing the truancy laws more effectively. In 1949, Congress amended the FLSA to include businesses that were not previously covered. These measures drastically lowered the number of children working.

One of the only areas in the United States where child labor still thrived in the last half of the twentieth century was in the population of poor, migrant farmers. Their frequent moves across the country and problems with their questionable legal status made them particularly susceptible to market pressures encouraging child labor. In addition, this industry had no special need for highly educated workers nor were unions being formed to protect their rights and raise working standards.

The economic plight of the migrant workers often made it crucial for the children to work. The conditions of migrant workers in the 1950s served as a reminder of what life was like for almost all American children when the nation was less affluent. Migrant children were vital providers of income. As before, efforts to reform this situation in the fields were rebutted by references to the fact that child labor teaches children valuable life lessons, such as: the value of a dollar, pride in a job well done, and the joy of recreation outdoors.

Currently, both state and federal laws restrict the work and the occupations or industries in which children can work. Yet certain exceptions remain. The governing sections of the FLSA outline the general guidelines and exceptions in the regulation of child labor.

* * *

NOTE

Although child labor problems are not as extensive today, they still exist. After a steep increase in child labor violations in the 1980s, a study by the Wage and Hour Division of the DOL showed that the number of violations of the FLSA's child labor provisions fell from 5,889 in 1990 to 233 in 2013. The number of young workers affected by those violations fell from 40,000 in 1990 to 1,393 in 2013. Child labor violations not only disrupt school and other opportunities of children, they are responsible for death, injury, and illness. Children often are given the dirtiest and least safe and healthful jobs to perform, they may be too small to work with tools properly, or they may lack the experience and judgment to work with machinery. In 2013, 14 adolescents under the age of 18 were fatally injured at work; thousands more suffered non-fatal injuries. Bureau of Labor Statistics, Census of Fatal Occupational Injuries Summary 2013, Table 4 (2013). Agriculture and restaurant work have the most reported injuries, illnesses, and fatalities, although the lack of good data remains a problem.

Seymour Moskowitz, Malignant Indifference: The Wages of Contemporary Child Labor in the United States

57 Okla. L. Rev. 465 (2004).

The problems associated with child labor in underdeveloped countries have captured our nation's attention. Legislatures have passed statutes and resolutions, citizen coalitions have organized, and the media has devoted extensive coverage to the issue. School classes have petitioned Disney and Nike to stop employing child workers in their overseas factories. Global Exchange protestors recently rallied in front of M & M's World store in Las Vegas to protest Mars's use of cocoa harvested with child labor. Even portfolio managers are under investor pressure not to invest in foreign companies using child labor. Only one thing is missing from this wave of moral outrage and activism-attention to the problems of child labor here at home.

In 2001, more than 3.7 million American youths worked. Employment in the United States poses substantial, immediate, and long-term risks for youthful workers. Many are killed and injured each year. The total number of occupational fatalities from 1992–1998 for youths under eighteen was 468. An estimated 200,000 young people are injured on the job annually.

In addition to health risks, youth employment fails to teach children the skills they need to become responsible adults. Instead of using their wages to support their families, teens typically spend their wages on luxury items. Contemporary American teens are avid consumers, spending $170 billion in 2002. Moreover, today's workplace encourages

> [y]oung people [to] perform tasks and use skills * * * that few will perform or use again in work settings after they cease to be adolescents * * * [These jobs provide] little meaningful contact with adults who have a stake in their socialization for the future * * *. [E]conomic rewards . . . typically are used for . . . records, movies, designer clothing, fast food, alcohol, drugs—and not for long-term "adult" investments, such as college, or for increasing the adolescent's ability to establish an independent household. This premature affluence has its own risks.

A child's employment status also negatively affects school work and social behavior, particularly when a child works excessive hours. Scholars define "high-intensity work" as twenty or more hours per week. Generally, high school students engaged in high-intensity work have lower grade point averages than students who do not work at all or who work fewer hours. In addition to lower grades, these student-workers are more likely to be suspended from school, use cigarettes and other substances, and experience a wide variety of other negative outcomes. Subgroups of youth workers, such as agricultural workers or teens in lower social and economic groups, are at even greater health and educational risks.

Contemporary U.S. child labor law and enforcement reflects a malignant indifference to the plight of American youth in the workplace. American law generally does not permit minors to make decisions with long-term consequences on their own. Yet the federal Fair Labor Standards Act (FLSA) requires no consent from—or even notification to—parents before a child may work. While some minimal hour limits are set for youths under sixteen in nonagricultural employment, only jobs or equipment designated "hazardous" by the Department of Labor (DOL) are off limits for children sixteen or older. Remarkably, those hazardous designations have remained largely unchanged for decades. The DOL, moreover, has imposed no other hour or place restrictions on the work of sixteen- and seventeen-year-olds.

The FLSA also has huge gaps in coverage, and private enforcement of the statute—typical of other civil rights and protective legislation—is unavailable. Despite DOL's monopoly on enforcement, its performance is extraordinarily ineffectual. In the last decade, the federal courts decided only six lawsuits involving child labor violations. The DOL underestimates the numbers of illegally employed children and rarely initiates investigations of statutory violations.

States also regulate child labor, although most states follow the pattern of the federal FLSA. State child labor laws are also closely connected to compulsory school attendance laws, which determine the minimum permissible age for leaving school. While many states give parents the right to notice and consent concerning a child's decision to drop out of school, other states leave the decision to the child once they attain a minimum age. The decision to work, however, is almost always left to the child. * * *

In an attempt to rally public support for legislative reforms, the National Child Labor Committee, in the early 1900s, used dramatic visual images to document the horrors and negative social effects of unrestricted child labor. Louis Hine, a photographer and social reformer who worked for the Committee, photographed children in textile mills, the tobacco industry, and a variety of other settings. These images were immensely important in changing public opinion. * * *

NOTE

Do you agree that teenage employment has a negative impact on the lives of American youths? The Secretary of Labor claims that early work experiences can be rewarding for young workers, proving them with opportunities to learn important job skills and eventually integrate into the American workforce. For more information, see http://www.youthrules.dol.gov/.

NOTES AND QUESTIONS

1. "The Amish just want to be let alone, [the Amish furniture maker] said, but the federal government is meddling in the lives and livelihoods by fining Amish sawmills and woodworking shops that employ teenagers, in violation of child labor law." Amish religious rules require children to leave school after eighth grade and then learn a trade. N.Y. Times, Oct. 18 2003, p. 1.

2. Under the FLSA, children between the ages of 14 and 16 may be employed if employment takes place outside of school hours. While school is in session, children may not work more than 18 hours a week and no more than three hours a day. While school is out of session, children may not work more than 40 hours a week and no more than 8 hours a day. In addition, employment must be between 7 a.m. and 7 p.m., or until 9 p.m. when school is not in session. See Thomas v. Brock, 617 F.Supp. 526 (W.D.N.C.1985), modified and remanded to correct order, 810 F.2d 448 (4th Cir. 1987) (regulations violated where children between the ages of 14 and 16 sold candy door to door until 11:30 p.m. or midnight). See also Echaveste v. Q & D, 2 Wage & Hour Cases 2d (BNA) 726 (E.D.Pa.1994) (upholding violation where tavern employed four minors under age 14 to bus tables).

3. The FLSA not only regulates the hours that children may work, but also protects them from dangerous working conditions. Regulations issued by the Department of Labor cover 17 hazardous occupations plus agriculture and prohibit all work in certain occupations, such as mining, roofing, and excavation, as well as work with such equipment as power saws, metal presses, and meat slicers and grinders in groceries, delicatessens, and fast food restaurants. Minors are also prohibited from operating freight elevators and hoisting apparatuses such as forklift trucks. See Breitwieser v. KMS Indus., Inc., 467 F.2d 1391 (5th Cir. 1972), cert. denied, 410 U.S. 969 (1973), where a 16 year-old boy hired to drive a forklift for a construction company was killed when the forklift flipped over.

4. Section 213(c) of the FLSA provides exemptions from the Act's coverage, such as for children who are employed by their parents in agriculture, except in situations declared hazardous by the Secretary of Labor. Other exemptions include minors employed as actors or as newspaper deliverers. State laws may provide coverage in these areas, however, for instance, where state law prohibits the selling of alcoholic beverages or employment in a tavern by anyone under age 21.

5. While the employment of children under the age of 12 is generally forbidden under the Act, section 213(c)(4)(A) permits employers to apply for a waiver from the Secretary of Labor for children age 10 and 11 to work as hand harvesters for not more than eight weeks in a calendar year to pick what are known as "short season" crops (e.g., strawberries). The Secretary of Labor may not grant any waivers unless certain statutorily specified conditions are met, and any waivers granted are subject to other limitations, such as no employment during school hours.

In the past, controversy arose over the Secretary's right to issue waivers where certain chemicals and pesticides have been used on crops shortly before harvest. A waiver may issue only where the Secretary has found, "based on objective data," that employment will not be "deleterious" to the health and well-being of the children. Because of the lack of specific data on the health effects on children of certain commonly used agricultural chemicals, the Department of Labor in 1978 proposed a rule that would apply the EPA, OSHA, and NIOSH standards to establish safe exposure levels for minors entering sprayed fields. Following bitter litigation against the Department by both state farm bureaus and child advocacy representatives, the rule was ultimately modified to provide that waivers could only be issued to growers who do not use pesticides or those who provide sufficient data to the Secretary to establish safe reentry times. See Washington State Farm Bureau v. Marshall, 625 F.2d 296 (9th Cir. 1980); National Ass'n of Farmworkers Orgs. v. Marshall, 628 F.2d 604 (D.C.Cir.1980); 29 C.F.R. § 575.5(d) (1982). Congress is considering whether to rewrite the law to ban the hiring of 12- and 13-year-olds, cap working hours by 14- and 15-year-olds, and keep teenagers out of hazardous jobs. The Obama administration has opened a broad campaign of enforcement against farmers who employ children. In June 2010, the Department of Labor increased the fines that farmers can face for employing children from about $1,000 to as much as $11,000 per child. Erik Eckholm, U.S. Cracks Down on Farmers Who Hire Children, N.Y. Times, June 18, 2010 at A1.

6. Every state also regulates child labor; in enacting the FLSA, Congress provided that the federal law would not preempt state law but that whichever standard provided greater protection to the child would apply. There is no clear pattern of state regulation: some states have higher standards than the FLSA and others have lower ones. Local conditions are often reflected in state regulations: Maine has special laws regarding the employment of children in the ski industry, while Nevada has specific restrictions on employment in casinos.

g.   ENFORCEMENT OF THE FLSA

Stephen G. Wood & Mary Anne Q. Wood, The Fair Labor Standards Act: Recommendations to Improve Compliance

1983 Utah L. Rev. 529 (1983).

Five enforcement actions are possible under the FLSA: The Secretary of Labor may commence either an action for civil liability, an action for civil money penalties for making use of oppressive child labor or an action for an injunction; one or more employees may seek civil damages; and the Department of Justice may bring an action for criminal penalties.

The Secretary of Labor may bring an action for civil liability to recover the amount of back wages and an additional equal amount as liquidated damages. Any sums recovered by the Secretary are held in a special deposit account and are paid directly to the affected employee or employees. Any sums not paid to an employee because the Department of Labor is unable to locate him or her within a period of three years are paid into the Treasury of the United States.

The Secretary of Labor may bring an action for civil money penalties against any person who violates the provisions prohibiting oppressive child labor. The Secretary of Labor determines the amount of the civil penalty. That amount is final unless the person charged with the violation takes exception. If that person protests, a final determination of the civil penalty is made in a Department of Labor administrative proceeding before an administrative law judge. The Secretary of Labor also may seek an injunction to restrain violations of section 215, and to order the payment of back wages found by the court to be due to employees under the FLSA.

Employees can seek back pay and damages for minimum wage or overtime compensation violations through a civil action against their employer. An action for civil liability also can be brought against any employer who discharges an employee in retaliation for instituting an FLSA suit. In that action, the employer is liable for such legal or equitable relief as may be appropriate, including, without limitation, employment reinstatement, promotion, back wages and an additional equal amount as liquidated damages. Either of those actions for civil liability can be maintained in any federal or state court of competent jurisdiction. The employee's right to bring such an action, however, terminates upon the filing of (1) a complaint by the Secretary of Labor in an action for an injunction in which either restraint is sought of any further delay in the payment of back wages or legal or equitable relief is sought as a result of an alleged attempt by an employer to discharge or in any other manner discriminate against any employee (section 217 action) or (2) a complaint by the Secretary in which recovery is sought of back wages or liquidated or other damages due such employees, unless such action is dismissed without prejudice on motion of the Secretary of Labor (section 216(c) action).

An action for criminal penalties brought by the Department of Justice is another enforcement tool available under the FLSA. That action can be brought against any person who willfully violates any of the provisions in section 215. If convicted, the person is subject to a fine of not more than $10,000, imprisonment for not more than six months or both.

NOTES AND QUESTIONS

1.   The statute of limitations for filing an action under the FLSA presents a recurrent enforcement issue for the courts. Ordinarily, the limitations period is two years, unless the employer's violation is "willful," in which case a three-year period applies. But what is "willful" conduct under the Act? In McLaughlin v. Richland Shoe Co., 486 U.S. 128 (1988), the Court held that an employer did not commit a willful violation of the Act unless it "either knew or showed reckless disregard for the matter of whether its conduct was

prohibited by the statute." Why should an employer that acts "unreasonably, but not recklessly" be subject to the same (shorter) statute of limitations as the reasonable employer? Does the Court give full weight to the congressional intent regarding "willful" violations of the FLSA? The Court interprets "willful" not only for the FLSA, but also for the ADEA, Equal Pay Act, Davis-Bacon Act, and Walsh-Healey Act. What considerations under each statute might suggest different standards of willfulness?

2.   The Act also provides for both civil and criminal penalties, although the criminal penalties are almost never used. A study by the Government Accounting Office of the Department of Labor's FLSA enforcement practices indicated that regional directors in at least four regions could not recall having filed a criminal suit under the Act in more than ten years. Imprisonment is available only after a second criminal conviction, and the maximum prison term is six months.

3.   What effect does the existence of a collective bargaining agreement have on the employees' FLSA claim? Can a union, bargaining in good faith on behalf of employees, agree to wage or hour terms different from those specified in the Act? For instance, instead of time and a half for overtime, could the union instead agree that overtime would be compensated by single time pay and double compensatory time off (for each hour of overtime, the employee would receive his regular rate of pay plus two hours time off)? In Bailey v. Karolyna Co., 50 F.Supp. 142 (S.D.N.Y. 1943), the court held that employees cannot bargain away their rights under the FLSA or release their employers from paying full amount due thereunder. However, some cities have adopted minimum wage laws that explicitly allow for unions and employers to agree to a wage rate lower than the city minimum wage.

In Wheeler v. Hampton Twp., 399 F.3d 238 (3d Cir. 2005), police officers sued to recover overtime pay under the FLSA. They argued that the Township's method of calculating overtime had shortchanged them, even though they had agreed to the method in the collective bargaining agreement in exchange for additional vacation time and other "non work pay." The court held that plain text of the statute prohibited the Township from taking a credit from the "non work pay" to offset the lesser overtime pay.

4.   It is open to question whether the U.S. Department of Labor is enforcing the FLSA effectively. From 1997 to 2007, the number of WHD enforcement actions decreased by more than a third, from approximately 47,000 in 1997 to just under 30,000 in 2007. In 2008 and 2009, the U.S. Government Accountability Office ("GAO") released four reports finding that the WHD frequently failed to uphold and enforce FLSA regulations. The GAO found that the WHD's investigations were often delayed by months or years. Under the FLSA, the statute of limitations is two years from the date of the violation, meaning that every day that the WHD delays an investigation, the complainant's risk of becoming ineligible to collect back wages increases. The GAO also identified many cases closed based on unverified information provided by the employer and cases dropped when the employer did not return phone calls. The GAO's overall assessment of the WHD complaint intake, conciliation, and investigation processes found an ineffective system that discourages wage theft complaints. See, e.g., GAO, Department of

Labor: Wage and Hour Division Needs Improved Investigative Processes and Ability to Suspend Statute of Limitations to Better Protect Workers Against Wage Theft (2009); GAO, Department of Labor: Wage and Hour Division's Complaint Intake and Investigative Processes Leave Low Wage Workers Vulnerable To Wage Theft (2009); GAO, Department of Labor: Case Studies from Ongoing Work Show Examples in Which Wage and Hour Division Did Not Adequately Pursue Labor Violations (2008). GAO, Fair Labor Standards Act: Better Use of Available Resources and Consistent Reporting Could Improve Compliance (2008). Peter Romer-Friedman argues:

> * * * [T]he U.S. Department of Labor's Wage and Hour Division ("WHD") has not had sufficient resources or successful strategies for wage and hour enforcement. From the 1950s to the late-1990s, the ratio of WHD investigators to American workers declined from one investigator for every 46,000 workers to one investigator for every 150,000 workers. Also, in a troubling report, the General Accounting Office has identified major problems with the WHD's enforcement, such as visiting fewer worksites, giving employers advance notice of visits, conducting investigations over the phone, and "focusing on a single worker, a single minor violation, or a particular timeframe." For example, in 2005, the DOL's Inspector General severely criticized the WHD for entering into a compliance agreement with Wal-Mart, giving Wal-Mart fifteen days of advanced notice for inspections. Another concern is that the WHD is often uninterested in litigating small, individual wage claims, while state agencies are more willing to litigate such claims.

Peter Romer-Friedman, Eliot Spitzer Meets Mother Jones: How State Attorneys General Can Enforce State Wage and Hour Laws, 39 Colum. J.L. & Soc. Probs. 495, 506 (2006).

5. The FLSA's anti-retaliation provision forbids employers from discharging or discriminating against any employee because, *inter alia*, the employee "filed any complaint" against such employer. Fair Labor Standards Act, 29 U.S.C. § 215(a)(3). In Kasten v. Saint-Gobain Performance Plastics Corp., 131 S.Ct. 1325 (2011), the Supreme Court considered whether the statutory phrase "filed any complaint" applies to oral as well as written complaints. On several occasions Kevin Kasten complained to his employers that the position of the timeclocks between the area where workers donned and doffed work-related protective gear violated the FLSA. Kasten argued that the oral complaints led the company to discipline him and eventually dismiss him. The Supreme Court held that the FLSA's anti-retaliation provision protects both oral and written complaints. Although the statutory text alone was inconclusive on the subject, Justice Breyer reasoned that both congressional intent to protect oral complaints and deference to an EEOC interpretation finding that oral complaints were covered weighed in favor of the holding. The Court limited protection to oral complaints which a reasonable, objective person would have understood as putting the employer on notice that the employee was asserting statutory rights under the Act. In a dissenting opinion, Justice Scalia, joined by Justice Thomas, argued that the plain meaning of the statutory phrase "filed any complaint" applied only to complaints filed with a government body and not complaints delivered from an employee to an employer. The majority declined to reach the issue addressed by the dissent, since the issue was not raised in the certiorari petitions.

6. Does a lawsuit become moot when one party (usually the defendant) offers to pay everything the plaintiff requested? Compare *Genesis Healthcare Corp. v. Symczyk*, 569 U.S. 66 (2013)(5–4), an FLSA case, with *Campbell-Ewald Co. v. Gomez*, 136 S.Ct. 663 (2016)(6–3), not an employment law case. The two cases found different reasons for concluding that the plaintiff's case was not mooted.

h. THE ECONOMICS AND POLITICS OF MINIMUM WAGE LAWS

The purpose of the minimum wage, according to the FLSA's drafters, was to provide a "minimum standard of living necessary for health, efficiency and general well-being of workers * * *." Does the law accomplish what Congress originally intended? At the time of its passage more than 50 years ago, the minimum wage was 25 cents an hour. Beginning July 24, 2009, the minimum wage increased to $7.25 an hour. At that rate, an individual working full-time (40 hours a week, 50 weeks a year) would earn $14,500. In 2014, the federal poverty level for a family of three was $17,790. Is it accurate to say that the minimum wage currently does not provide that minimum decent standard of living originally envisioned by Congress?

Further, for years economists have debated whether raising the minimum wage may actually have adverse employment effects, such as lowering employment or raising inflation. Consider the following analysis:

Richard B. Freeman, The Minimum Wage As a Redistributive Tool
106 Econ. J. 639 (1996).

* * *

Minimum wages do not increase the pay of workers by magic. Save in the case of monopsony, they do not raise national output, but rather take money from some citizens and pay it to others. Even in the monopsony case, moreover, there is redistribution from the firm to workers and consumers.

Who pays for the higher pay of minimum wage workers depends on the labour and product market conditions in sectors of the economy where those workers are employed and on the social welfare benefits which they receive. Putting aside for the moment social welfare benefits, consider the market factors that determine who pays for a given minimum. There are three potential groups of payers.

First are consumers of the products of minimum wage employees. These consumers will pay higher prices for those goods or services, proportional to the minimum wage workers' share of the cost of production. The minimum-wage-induced change in relative prices will affect the distribution of who pays depending on the income of those purchasers. If the wealthy disproportionately buy minimum wage goods/services, the wealthy will be the primary payers for the redistribution. Conversely, if the poor disproportionately buy those goods/services. In the absence of a definitive study of the distribution of income of consumers of minimum wage goods, the most plausible assumption is that the incidence is roughly neutral by income class. Minimum wage workers produce low-price goods, which may be bought disproportionately by the poor, but they often work in service sectors— restaurants, hotels, etc.—that are disproportionately used by higher-income citizens.

Whether the burden of paying for the minimum falls more on the wealthy or the poor, the fact that consumers foot some (perhaps most) of the cost of the minimum raises the question of whether consumers as a group are willing to pay higher prices to "subsidize" minimum wage workers. * * *

Another group who may pay for a minimum wage are stakeholders in businesses that raise hourly rates to meet the minimum (or to keep rates above the minimum). If the business has some "rents" to distribute, the minimum will force it to share those rent with low paid workers. Research on pay differentials in the United States suggests that economic rent is common, so that if minimum wage workers were employed in rent-paying sectors, reduced rents to other groups could finance much of the minimum. But rents are most prevalent in capital-intensive large firms which pay good wages, so that it is unlikely that much of the incidence of paying for a minimum will fall on the stakeholders in the firm. If the firm is a monopsony, not only does it pay for the increased minimum, but output will also rise given a judiciously chosen minimum.

The third group who may pay for the minimum are low-wage workers, or some subset thereof, through loss of jobs. If the elasticity of demand for minimum wage workers exceeds one, the minimum will reduce rather than increase the share of earnings going to the low-paid. Research on the employment effects of the US minimum and of wages councils minima in the United Kingdom has shown that the elasticity of demand for minimum wage workers hovers around zero. Some well-constructed studies in the United States find employment growing modestly in impacted sectors after a minimum wage increase. Careful British studies found that abolition of wages councils reduced pay but did not raise employment in affected occupations. No study in the United States or the United Kingdom has found that increases in minimum wages reduce total employment with an elasticity near unity: the debate over the employment effects of the minimum is a debate of values around zero. Absence of noticeable employment losses in these studies does not, of course, imply that minimum wages much higher than those observed may not risk large job losses nor that minimum wages may not cause employment disasters in particular sectors, such as apparel, or in particular firms. It does imply that at some levels little of the cost of the minimum is borne by low-wage workers.

Still, if even a few workers are disemployed by the minimum, the minimum may have undesirable redistributive effects. Employed low-paid workers benefit from the minimum, but the disemployed lose. In the United States, where job turnover is high and durations of joblessness relatively short, this is unlikely to be a serious problem. Low-paid workers will effectively "share" the benefits of higher-paid minimum wage work through normal mobility and turnover. In continental OECD-Europe, where durations of joblessness are long, the risk that a minimum will divide the low-paid work force into lucky winners and unlucky losers is more serious. Higher duration of joblessness in the United Kingdom puts it closer to the European countries in this dimension.

There is another way in which a minimum wage may have some undesirable distributional consequences. Consider the following scenario. The United Kingdom enacts a minimum wage that raises the pay in a particular occupation from £3 to £4. At £3, middle-class women and teenagers found the work unattractive, but at £4, they are willing to take minimum wage jobs. Analogously, at £3, they are willing to work at the job for only a few hours a week, but at £4 they may want to work more hours. The minimum thus increases the supply of labour. But it does not increase the demand. If employers prefer middle-class job applicants to lower-income applicants (for productivity reasons or for other reasons), the consequence for distribution will be perverse: the distribution of minimum wage jobs will shift from the poor to the middle class. In this case, the group the minimum tried to help would be harmed, not because of any reduction in minimum wage employment, but because middle-class secondary earners responded to the improved earnings opportunity.

That the supply side responses of middle-class competitors may reduce the employment of some persons whom the minimum was designed to benefit does not mean that the minimum is undesirable, any more than does the finding that a minimum costs some jobs through demand responses. The issue is whether the gains to the bulk of minimum wage workers offset the losses to some.

Notes and Questions

1.   In The Minimum Wage as a Redistributive Tool, Freeman also examines who benefits from an increase in the minimum wage.

Beneficiaries of the minimum wage are not, in general, the lowest-income families. The minimum targets the employed, whereas the lowest-income families are largely families with no employed workers. In the United States poverty is concentrated among children, particularly children in single-parent homes on welfare. Poverty is also high among the disabled, whose physical condition prevents them from working. In the United Kingdom poverty is significant among families whose chief breadwinner is long-term unemployed as well as among non-working lone parents. A minimum wage will not help these persons or groups. Neither will any in-work benefits programme such as the British Family Tax Credit or the American Earned Income Tax Credit.

Richard B. Freeman, The Minimum Wage as a Redistributive Tool, 106 Econ. J. 639, 643 (1996).

2. According to the Bureau of Labor Statistics, 75.3 million American workers age 16 and over were paid at hourly rates, representing 58.2 percent of all wage and salary workers. Among those paid by the hour, 286,000 earned exactly the prevailing federal minimum wage in 2008. About 1.9 million had wages below the minimum. Together, these 2.2 million workers with wages at or below the minimum—generally young, unmarried, and without a high school diploma—made up three percent of all hourly-paid workers. A comprehensive study of low-wage workers in Chicago, Los Angeles, and New York in 2008 found that the percentage of workers who said they were paid less than the minimum wage varied by industry. More than 40 percent of those who work in the apparel and textile manufacturing industry, the personal and repair services industry, and private households said that they were paid less than the minimum wage. The study also found that women were far more likely to suffer minimum wage violations than men, with the highest prevalence among women who were illegal immigrants. Among American-born workers, African-Americans had a violation rate nearly triple that for whites. Steven Greenhouse, Low-Wage Workers Are Often Cheated, Study Says, N.Y. Times, Sept. 2, 2009 at A11.

3. Is the minimum wage fair? Does it even really effect what most employers will pay their employees? Often employers will agree to pay their employees more than the minimum that the employees would accept for the job. This may be because employers feel that such "fair" treatment will encourage employees to perform their job duties better. In Fairness, Minimum Wage Law, and Employee Benefits, Christine Jolls examines the legal implications of this "fairness dynamic." Fairness behavior is more significant when employees are difficult to monitor. Once the fairness dynamic is taken into account, the argument for the minimum wage is undercut, particularly in situations where employees are relatively difficult to monitor, as fairness considerations will tend to drive the wage up regardless. See Christine Jolls, Fairness, Minimum Wage Law, and Employee Benefits, 77 N.Y.U. L. Rev. 47 (2002).

4. In Do Minimum Wages Affect Non-Wage Job Attributes? Evidence on Fringe Benefits, Simon and Kaestner examine the effects of raising the minimum wage on non-wage compensation (i.e., health insurance), job safety, and training. Their study suggests that despite the fact that most fringe benefit programs are voluntary from the standpoint of the employer, minimum wages have no discernible impact on the availability of such benefits to such employees. For more information, see Kosali Ilayperuma Simon & Robert Kaestner, Do Minimum Wages Affect Non-Wage Job Attributes? Evidence on Fringe Benefits?, 58 Indus. & Lab. Rel. Rev. 52 (2004).

5. One possible alternative to a minimum wage would be a wage subsidy for individuals who earned less than a certain wage. (The Earned Income Tax Credit performs this function to a degree.) What economic effect would a wage subsidy have? Would it be preferable to a mandatory minimum wage?

6. Studies measuring the unemployment effects of the minimum wage show that it hits hardest at teenagers, one estimate being that a ten percent increase in the minimum wage induces a one percent increase in teenage unemployment (and less than half that for adults). The teenage unemployment rate is already considerably higher than any older segment of the workforce. One proposed solution to the unemployment effect of the minimum wage would be a subminimum wage for youth, which would establish a new, lower minimum wage rate for teenagers. Proponents of the youth subminimum argue that it would encourage employers to hire teenagers, who tend to be unskilled and in need of substantial job training, and thus enable teenagers to escape the Catch-22 cycle of "employers won't hire you if you don't have experience, and how will you get experience if no one will hire you?" What are the potential dangers of the subminimum wage? See David H. Solomon, Note: A Model Youth Differential Amendment: Reducing Youth Unemployment Through A Lower Minimum Wage for the Young, 19 Harv.J. on Legis. 143 (1982).

i.   MODERNIZING THE FLSA FOR THE TWENTY-FIRST CENTURY

Scott D. Miller, Revitalizing the FLSA
19 Hofstra Lab. & Emp. L.J. 1 (2001).

* * * [T]he first half of the twentieth century also saw widespread predictions that work would disappear and that technological and economic progress would steadily reduce work hours. Social critics such as George Bernard Shaw predicted a two-hour workday by the twenty-first century. Experts estimated that by the 1990s, the United States would have either a twenty-two hour workweek, a six-month work year, or standardize the retirement age at thirty-eight. Academia developed leisure studies programs to prepare for the onslaught of free time that would otherwise stultify the masses.

The United States, at the beginning of the twenty-first century, has turned the twentieth century work hours/technological and economic progress conundrum on its head. The nation is currently confronting technological, political, social, and economic changes paralleling the eras that produced maximum hour labor standards. Technological and economic progress has, however, increased, not decreased, work hours. Home computers and faxes, voice and e-mail, beepers, and cell and car phones have lured workers into a 24/7 marketplace workweek. Non-marketplace household work hours have also increased as washing machines, vacuum cleaners, and other labor saving devices created higher expectations for household cleanliness.

There are no mass movements today addressing increasing work hours. Instead, the issue has become a staple of mass media and academic debate. This is particularly true regarding the phenomenon called "time-squeeze," the shortage of leisure time resulting from long work hours. In addition, there is substantial debate regarding, and empirical evidence supporting, the thesis that Americans have become "overworked" since the 1970s.

There is also a growing body of research arguing that time-squeeze and overwork are better understood by examining the household, not the individual, level. "Dual-earner" households (working couples) currently outnumber "single-earner" households. This trend corresponds with the dramatic increase of women in the workforce. In addition, dual-earner households work more combined hours than the sum increase of working spouses. This development escapes the protective scope of the FLSA maximum hours labor standards. The standards, their white-collar exemptions, and the USDOL's regulations delineating and defining the exemptions, were designed to address the single-earner household model. Under this model, a breadwinner (particularly exempt white-collar male employees) perform long hours of marketplace work, enabled by a stay-at-home spouse (female) performing the non-marketplace work for the household. This model has a detrimental effect on many dual-earner households where both partners are often exempt white-collar workers who come home from their first shift marketplace work hours to a second shift of non-marketplace household work.

While Americans work double shifts (market and non-market work), trying to balance their jobs and personal lives, and the media and academia ponder the existence of time-squeeze, Congress debates the continued relevance of overtime pay under the FLSA. The most vocal proponents for revamping the maximum hours labor standards argue business and labor must form a new paradigm recognizing the need for flexibility to address the rapid changes in employment and the economy that have occurred since the enactment of the FLSA. The existing model is an outdated system produced from an agrarian and manufacturing economy. They further argue that the USDOL must comprehensively review and adjust the regulations for the white-collar exemptions. The current "regulatory structure is a minefield which employers attempting to create more efficient workplaces cross at their peril."

Opponents of changing maximum hours labor standards respond that the politics of overtime have not changed in over sixty years. Employers seek more exemptions from, and workers seek more inclusion within, the labor standards. The standards are not broken—so do not fix them.

* * *

It is time to revitalize the FLSA. It is time to reconfirm the policies and purposes of maximum hours labor standards, protecting individual and dual-earner households from time-squeeze, and providing employers and the judiciary with clear, comprehensive and up-to-date standards. This article recommends:

1. Replacing the current minimum wage provision (which, through lack of Congressional action, has failed to keep pace with increasing prices, poverty thresholds and average wages) with no less than a $7.25 per hour minimum living wage [this took place in 2009] that automatically increases on an annual basis, along with the consumer price index for urban wage earners and clerical workers (CPI-W), as calculated by the Bureau of Labor Statistics (BLS). The new provision will reestablish the minimum wage as a maximum hours labor standard supporting minimum living standards, redistributing wealth, and shortening the workweek.

2. Capping work hours at eight hours per day, forty hours per week, dropping to thirty hours per week within ten years, with no loss of pay and a right to refuse work over the daily and weekly standard protected by the anti-retaliation provisions of FLSA section 15(a)(3). This proposal provides overtime pay at time and one-half the regular rate for all hours worked over the daily and weekly standards (not to exceed forty-eight, dropping to thirty-eight, hours per week) and USDOL supervised waivers for flexible work hours (allowing compressed work schedules, such as four ten hour days, etc., not exceeding the weekly overtime ceiling) similar to USDOL supervised settlements under FLSA section 16(b). This will make the FLSA a true maximum hours statute.

3. Replacing the three white-collar exemptions with one exemption for the top 10% of an employer's workforce, analogous to the FMLA "key employee" exemption. This provides maximum hours protection for all workers except: (a) those highly paid individuals at the top of the corporate ladder who run the business (not the mid-level managers and administrator, or the low-income supervisors exempt in Donovan [Donovan v. Burger King Corp., 672 F.2d 221 (1st Cir. 1982)]); and (b) the independent and/or self-employed generalists addressed in the 1954 rules defining exempt bona fide professionals (not the burgeoning class of time-starved dual-income households who work as specialists within public and private bureaucracies). By harmonizing the FLSA with the FMLA, this proposal also provides one simple and uniform standard for employers and the judiciary to follow for the two primary federal work reduction statutes.

4. Requiring employers to provide employees with four weeks of paid vacation per calendar year. This proposal addresses two of the

primary reasons for the increase in work hours: steadier year-round work since the 1960s and reductions in employer provided paid time off since the 1980s (such as vacation time, holidays, sick pay, and other paid absences).

* * *

Time-squeeze adversely affects family and community life. Business Week observed in 2000, " '[w]e watch TV, and we go to work' * * *. 'The front porch is empty.' " Living and working under these conditions, it becomes increasingly clear that the FLSA maximum hours labor standards are as relevant today, and in the foreseeable future, as they were when enacted in 1938 as a means to advance society's quality of life. This vision incorporates a living standard that provides meaningful time from work for a personal, home, community, and cultural life, not just enough time to passively watch television and go to sleep after work. Revitalizing the FLSA maximum hours labor standards will provide a good start for making this vision a reality in the twenty-first century.

* * *

NOTE

When Congress enacted the FLSA in 1938, American workers showed up at an employer's place of business to perform work. More than 70 years later, a large number of workers perform work in cyberspace using a computer and the Internet. In Working For (Virtually) Minimum Wage: Applying the Fair Labor Standards Act in Cyberspace, Miriam A. Cherry argued that although the line between work and leisure is somewhat blurred in the realm of virtual work, "the economic and equitable purposes of the FLSA are best served by ensuring that the statute is construed broadly so that clickworkers—the new virtual workers—receive the federal minimum wage." 60 Ala. L. Rev. 1077 (2009). Cherry used Facebook as an example:

As for the distinction between volunteer work and paid work, consider Facebook, currently a prominent social-networking site. There is no doubt that meeting, "friending," "poking" other Facebook members, and updating one's own profile on one's "wall" is a recreational and fun activity. Recently, however, Facebook has asked its users to translate various pages, instructions, and other information into other languages, so that Facebook can expand into additional countries. Some users, however, have resisted and indeed have been critical of the effort:

[A Facebook user], a Californian who teaches English in Seoul, South Korea, has volunteered in the past to translate for the nonprofit Internet encyclopedia Wikipedia but said he won't do it for Facebook. "[Wikipedia is] an altruistic, charitable, information-sharing, donation-supported cause," [he] told The Associated Press in a Facebook message. "Facebook is not. Therefore, people should not be tricked into donating their time and energy to a multimillion-dollar company so that the company can make millions more—at least not without some type of compensation."

2. MISCELLANEOUS FEDERAL STATUTES

In addition to the Fair Labor Standards Act, other federal statutes govern wage rates in specific industries, primarily for government contractors. All of these statutes attempt to guarantee wage rates for employees on government projects at a level commensurate with prevailing local wage rates. Employment at 85 percent of the minimum wage may be permitted for students in retail or service establishments, agriculture, or in their schools. Section 214(b)(1–3). This subminimum wage rate may be applied if approved by the Wage-Hour Administrator.

The Walsh-Healey Public Contracts Act, 41 U.S.C. §§ 35–45, establishes basic labor standards for work done on U.S. government contracts in excess of $10,000 in value for materials, supplies, articles, equipment, or naval vessels. All persons engaged in the manufacture or furnishing of contracted items are covered, except those in executive, administrative, or professional positions, or those performing office, custodial, or maintenance work.

The Davis-Bacon Act, 40 U.S.C. §§ 3141 to 3148, covers construction, alteration, or repair of federal buildings or other public works for contracts in excess of $2000. It applies to all agencies of the federal government and the District of Columbia. Davis-Bacon requires federal contractors to pay wages on construction work that are equivalent to the prevailing wages for corresponding types of workers on similar construction in the locality where the work is performed. It also provides for the determination of prevailing fringe benefits. The Secretary of Labor is charged with making the determination of what are prevailing wages. Employee complaints may be filed with the contracting agency or with the Department of Labor. The Miller Act of 1935, 40 U.S.C. §§ 270 et seq., is an important adjunct to the Davis-Bacon Act; it requires construction contractors to execute a payment bond to protect the wages of employees providing labor before any contract covered by its provisions is awarded. The law applies to contracts over $2000 for the construction, alteration, or repair of any public building or public work of the United States; it does not apply to federal aid projects but only to direct federal contracts.

The McNamara-O'Hara Service Contract Act of 1965, 41 U.S.C. §§ 351–358, establishes labor standards for federal contracts in excess of $2500 for the provision of services through the use of service employees. This includes employees in a wide variety of occupations: cafeteria and food service, maintenance and guard service, linen supply services, warehousing or storage services, laundry and dry-cleaning, and secretarial services. As with the Walsh-Healey Act, executive, administrative, and professional employees are exempted.

NOTES AND QUESTIONS

1.   The "prevailing wage" acts have been criticized by both politicians and economists for their inflationary economic effects, and numerous unsuccessful attempts have been made to modify or eliminate the Davis-Bacon Act in particular. See Robert S. Goldfarb & John F. Morrell, The Davis-Bacon Act: An Appraisal of Recent Studies, 34 Indus. & Lab. Rel. Rev. 191 (1981); John Warner, Congressional and Administrative Efforts to Modify or Eliminate the Davis-Bacon Act, 10 W. St. U. L. Rev. 1 (1982).

Why enact such legislation? The economic efficiency arguments are weak. One possible rationale is to prevent the government from abusing its tremendous economic power, but government effectively competes with private employers for employees. Another is to eliminate any incentive for contractors bidding on government contracts to cut costs ("wage busting" particularly) to the point where project quality deteriorates. The most likely rationale is that it is designed to redistribute or stabilize income in the construction trades. The Department of Labor has stated that the Davis-Bacon Act's purpose is "to protect prevailing living standards of the construction workers, to provide equality of opportunity for contractors, and to prevent the disturbance of the local economy." Comments in U.S. General Accounting Office, Report: The Davis-Bacon Act Should Be Repealed 203 (1979).

Some studies indicate that the inflationary effect of the Davis-Bacon Act is much less than earlier thought. See Steven G. Allen, Much Ado About Davis-Bacon: A Critical Review and New Evidence, 26 J. Law & Econ. 707 (1983).

2.   The Walsh-Healey and Service Contract Acts have been subjected to the same criticisms as the Davis-Bacon Act, but have exhibited a similar political resilience. For a thorough cost-benefit analysis of the Service Contract Act, see Robert G. Goldfarb & John S. Heywood, An Economic Evaluation of the Service Contract Act, 36 Indus. & Lab. Rel. Rev. 56 (1982).

3.   The Walsh-Healey Act and the Contract Work Hours and Safety Standards Act were amended in December 1985 by P.L. 99–145. Effective January 1, 1986, employees of government contractors no longer have to be paid a daily overtime premium for work over eight hours a day; instead, overtime will be due only after 40 hours a week.

B.   WHAT IS A JOB WORTH?

1.   THE ECONOMICS OF WAGE DETERMINATION

Whether an individual is paid minimum wage or more than a million dollars a year is determined by some measure of the value of the individual's labor. But what is a job "worth"? To some extent, that depends on whose perspective is used to determine the worth or value of a job. Some employers set wages by looking externally at the "market rate" for similar work at other enterprises. Others engage industrial engineers to conduct sophisticated internal job evaluations, which peg the relative value to the employer of different jobs within the same enterprise. From the employee's perspective, both monetary and nonmonetary factors affect individual determinations of what a job is "worth."

Robert J. Flanagan, The Price of Labor and Its Value, The Park City Papers—Papers Presented at the Labor Law Group Conference on Labor and Employment Law in Park City, Utah

293–303 (1985).

The price of labor is determined by supply and demand. So, in some important but sometimes subtle ways is the value. The answer is of no help, nor are the subtleties obvious, however, until one explores the meaning of that well-worn phrase, "the forces of supply and demand," in the labor market. Nevertheless, I believe that there are only three basic ideas, which, once understood, give the fundamental analytical power to labor market analysis. These three ideas pertain to (a) the employer's side of the market (demand), (b) the worker's side of the market (supply), and (c) the interaction of the two sides of the market (equilibrium).

The Employer's Side: The Tradeoff Between Wages and Employment

The first basic idea is that on the demand side of the market there is a tradeoff between the rate of compensation and the level of employment. An increase in the wage rate induces a reduction in employment (other things held equal) and conversely. Technically, this is sometimes referred to as the "law of downward sloping demand for labor." This is a proposition of fundamental importance and one for which there is considerable empirical support. Consider two of the most obvious implications. Increases in the wage rate via collective bargaining or minimum wage statutes will induce reductions in employment. (This behavioral response is behind the skepticism of most economists concerning the efficacy of minimum wages as a device to reduce poverty.) Conversely, a wage subsidy policy may be a good way to expand the employment opportunities of the unemployed.

Where does this scientific "law" come from? What is its behavioral basis? We are dealing with the employer side of the market, so we must begin with the employer's objectives. This is usually taken to be profit maximization. Profit maximization yields one important decision rule: Take any action that adds more to revenues than it does to costs—i.e., any action that increases profits. The corollary is: Stop taking any action (e.g., the hiring of workers) at the point at which the additional revenues obtained from the action just equal the additional costs incurred. It is the application of this decision rule that is implied by the profit maximization objective that yields the tradeoff between the wage rate and the level of employment on the employer's side of the market.

To see this, simply apply the decision rule to the labor hiring decision. Initially, assume that the additional (marginal) cost of hiring another worker is the wage rate. What is the additional (marginal) revenue from hiring another worker? The additional revenue consists of the additional production that is attributable to the hiring of another employee multiplied by the price at which the new output can be sold. A profit-maximizing firm will hire workers up to the point at which the revenue received from hiring one more worker just equals the wage of the worker. But—getting back to the basic question—why does the application of the decision rule of a profit-maximizing firm result in a tradeoff between wages and employment? In a competitive labor market, the wage paid will not vary as a firm hires more workers. Likewise, in a competitive product market, the price at which the product is sold will remain constant as the firm sells more output (produced by additional workers). The key question, then, is how the output per worker changes as more workers are hired. Here we run into the law of diminishing returns: As more and more workers are added to a fixed capital stock or plant, their productivity (although positive) will begin to diminish at some point. It is usually easiest to think of this as the problem of not enough machines and equipment to use labor resources efficiently. With each new worker producing less, the additional revenue to hiring workers is falling. When it falls to the wage rate, the firm stops hiring labor.

From an employer's point of view, the "value" of labor is the market value of the additional output produced by adding the last worker (technically referred to as the value of the marginal product of labor), and this is the same as the wage rate. Thus, the value and the price of labor are the same.

Now consider the dynamics of this situation. Initially, an employer applies the decision rule discussed above to maximize profits. Then a wage increase (e.g., as the result of a minimum wage increase or collective bargaining settlement) raises the employer's marginal costs above the value of labor's marginal product. Profits are no longer maximized. In order to set marginal revenue equal to marginal costs again (as the decision rule requires) the employer must raise the marginal productivity of labor, and the only way to do this is to reduce employment (relative to capital, materials, etc.). Thus, it is the technical relationships that induce diminishing marginal productivity that produce the tradeoff between wages and employment.

The Worker Side: Compensating Wage Differentials

The second basic idea is that the wage rates that we observe in the labor market tend to compensate for variations in the nonmonetary conditions of jobs. This idea goes back to Adam Smith over 200 years ago—a relatively long period of time for a scientific idea to survive. It is important to note at the outset that the nonmonetary working conditions can be good or bad (e.g., a very safe or a very unsafe work environment).

The key fact that differentiates labor from other productive resources is the fact that it can have preferences concerning the work environment, and any serious analysis of the labor market must cope with this. Adam Smith's durable theory was deceptively simple, and it involves both a *process* and a *result*. The process is this: Workers select jobs that maximize their "net advantage" (i.e., the combination of monetary and nonmonetary aspects of a job). Therefore, they move between jobs until the net advantage of different jobs is equalized—i.e., there is no job change worth making.

The result of this process is a system of "compensating" or "equalizing" wage differentials between jobs. To see that this is the result, recall that (a) if net advantage (the sum of wage and nonwage job elements) is equalized and (b) the nonwage characteristics of jobs differ across jobs, then (c) the wage of the jobs must also differ in offsetting directions. In effect, a worker "buys" agreeable working conditions by accepting a relatively low wage (other factors, including skill, held constant). Alternatively, a worker is bribed to accept relatively poor working conditions by being offered a relatively high wage. Thus, for a given skill, there will be a spectrum of wages and working conditions, reflecting the dispersion of tastes among workers for the mix of pecuniary and nonpecuniary compensation.

What does this imply for our discussion of the value and price of labor? Obviously, the notion of compensation that is appropriate for labor supply decisions is much broader than the "price" of labor that is commonly reported in wage and fringe benefit statistics. When benefits are relatively congenial, the value of a job will exceed the observed price (because some of the worker's potential money wage has been "spent" on good working conditions). When job conditions are very poor, the value of the job may be less than the observed wage—i.e., the nonmonetary aspects are effectively negative.

* * *

Both Sides of the Labor Market: Equilibrium

Economic analysis is distinguished from most other work in the social sciences by the notion of *equilibrium*—there are forces that drive the system toward a resting point. These forces are the supply and demand factors discussed above. This is the third basic idea in discussing the price and value of labor. In the context of a labor market, equilibrium is the rate of compensation and level of employment from which there is no tendency for the system to move in the absences of some disturbance on the demand or supply side. It is the outcome of the interaction of the two sets of motivations discussed above: the employer's drive to maximize profits and the worker's drive to maximize net advantage.

A key feature of the equilibrium notion is that there are two sets of motivations operating simultaneously—i.e., on the two sides of the market. Some of the most persistent economic fallacies arise from arguments that address the response on one side of the market while ignoring the simultaneous responses on the other side of the market. Consider the earlier minimum wage example. Those who argue that increasing the minimum wage is desirable because it will draw individuals off of welfare and into the labor force are more or less correct about the supply response if there was a certain prospect of employment, but are completely overlooking the demand side of the market, where the effect of an increased minimum wage would be to reduce the probability that new labor force entrants would find a job.

The presence of an equilibrium greatly simplifies the study of the effect of institutional impacts (e.g., statutes or collective bargaining) on the price and value of labor, because the effect of such an impact is normally to change the equilibrium wage and employment levels.

* * *

My first examples come from EEO law. When applied to wage discrimination in a class action context, these laws raise the following question: Is the work of some groups undervalued in comparison to that of other groups? A standard of value is needed to answer this question, and the touchstone for developing the standard is the compensating differentials idea that each aspect of a job has a price. This has two roles in employment discrimination litigation, one apparently much less obvious than the other.

The more obvious role is the statistical implementation of the idea that there is a specific monetary return to education, training, stable job attendance, etc. Every class action begins with a showing that the average wage of racial minorities or women is less than the average wage of whites or men that is countered by the defendant's claim that there are skill differences or other "business necessity" explanations for the average wage differences. Who is right? With a large sample of individuals, one can implement the compensating differentials idea by estimating a statistical relationship that effectively describes the "price" of each job or personal attribute *and* also permits a test of whether the plaintiff's class is disadvantaged *after* controlling for the effects of the factors that the defendant claims explain the average wage difference.

Suppose a statistically significant wage difference associated with race or sex remains? Does this reflect discrimination? Absent additional evidence, many judges presumably would accept this as evidence of "adverse impact"—it would be seen as the result of something the employer is doing to the worker. Often that is exactly what is going on. But is it always? This is where a more subtle implication of the compensating differential idea may be important. Suppose that the group with the relatively low average wage has chosen jobs with relatively attractive nonmonetary working conditions more frequently than the group with the relatively high average wage. The observed wage differential may be nothing more than compensation for unobserved differences in nonmonetary compensation. Absent some demonstration that the two groups do systematically make different job choices in this manner (a showing that might require data from a job bidding system), the "adverse impact" interpretation might erroneously be accepted, solely because the overly limited measure of monetary compensation was used.

NOTES AND QUESTIONS

1.   If, as Professor Flanagan suggests, individuals value working conditions as well as monetary reward, why are menial jobs, which very few individuals would choose to work, so low-paid, while jobs with better working conditions are higher paid? If Flanagan is correct, should we not expect the opposite economic effect?

2.   What does the economic theory of the price and value of labor suggest for labor and employment *law?* Elsewhere in the article, Flanagan states:

> [T]here is nothing inherently desirable from a distributional perspective about the structure of wages or income that results from the unfettered operation of a market economy. Whatever the efficiency attributes of such a system, the resulting distribution of income and degree of inequality will depend in important ways on the initial endowments of assets.

> Second, while there is nothing inherently desirable about the income distribution that results from a market wage structure, direct action against the wage structure is often an inefficient way to attain distributional objectives. * * * Precisely because direct action against (relative) wages tends to induce opposite employment reactions, the correlation between policy-induced changes in wages and policy-induced changes in income is weak and, under certain circumstances, can be negative.

3.   The traditional neoclassical model of the labor market posited by Professor Flanagan has been criticized as unrealistic. What real-life impediments to free functioning of the market exist? What are their implications for employment law and policy?

2. WAGE COMPARABILITY FOR INDIVIDUALS: THE QUEST FOR PAY EQUITY

Even where employees perform the same job, different employees are paid different wages, no matter how one determines the abstract "value" of the job. As Professor Flanagan suggests, a number of factors are used to justify wage differentials: seniority, qualifications, education, prior experience, better bargaining power, and a host of others. Unequal access to many of these factors contributes to race and gender earnings gaps; implicit and explicit bias on the part of employers also often contributes to those gaps. Figures from the Bureau of Labor Statistics for 2017 show that the median weekly earnings for full-time wage and salary workers were: $971 for white men; $710 for black men; $1,043 for Asian men; $690 for Hispanic men; $743 for white women; $657 for black women; $903 for Asian women; $603 for Hispanic women. Bureau of Labor Statistics, Household Data, Annual Averages (2018). On average, women who work full-time earn roughly 82% of what their male counterparts earn. That percentage has remained relatively constant for several decades, although it has shown some upward movement in recent years. While the difference in pay between genders has narrowed, it is still pronounced, especially in certain fields. For example, data from Harvard University economist Claudia Goldin shows that in 2014, female physicians and surgeons earned only 71% of what males made in the same positions. Claire Miller, Pay Gap Is Because of Gender, Not Jobs, New York Times, Apr. 24, 2014, at B3. Women continue to be concentrated disproportionately in the lowest paying occupations. The existence of such a significant sex-based wage gap has resulted in substantial litigation, as women have sought to redress perceived discrimination in salaries paid to women and in occupations traditionally dominated by women.

NOTE

According to a Pew Research Center analysis, while the gender wage disparity has shrunk from 36 cents on the dollar in 1980 to 17 cents in 2015, certain groups have seen notable differences. For young women ages 25–34, the wage gap with young men has decreased from 37 cents in 1980 to 10 cents in 2015. By race, the disparity is also striking. Compared to white males, the wage gap between 1980 and 2015 among white women decreased by 22 cents; for black women, 9 cents; for Asian women, the records only start after 1980 but are approximately the same as for white women; for Hispanic women, 5 cents. Pew Research Center tabulations of Current Population Survey data, 2015.

a. THE EQUAL PAY ACT

The Equal Pay Act of 1963, passed as an amendment to the Fair Labor Standards Act, prohibits sex-based wage discrimination. 29 U.S.C. § 206(d)(1) provides:

> No employer having employees subject to any provisions of this section shall discriminate, within any establishment in which such employees are employed, between employees on the basis of sex by paying wages to employees in such establishment at a rate less than the rate at which he pays wages to employees of the opposite sex in such establishment for equal work on jobs the performance of which requires equal skill, effort, and responsibility, and which are performed under similar working conditions, except where such payment is made pursuant to (i) a seniority system; (ii) a merit system; (iii) a system which measures earnings by quantity or quality of production; or (iv) a differential based on any other factor other than sex: *Provided,* That an employer who is paying a wage rate differential in

violation of this subsection shall not, in order to comply with the provisions of this subsection, reduce the wage rate of any employee.

But what are "equal" jobs? Must they be absolutely identical? What are "equal skill, effort and responsibility" and "similar working conditions"?

Wernsing v. Department of Human Services
427 F.3d 466 (7th Cir. 2005).

■ EASTERBROOK, CIRCUIT JUDGE.

This appeal presents the question whether a common personnel-management practice violates the Equal Pay Act of 1963. Like many employers both public and private, the Department of Human Services in Illinois gives lateral entrants a salary at least equal to what they had been earning, plus a raise if that is possible under the scale for the new job. Jenny Wernsing contends that the normal raise at the Office of the Inspector General, where she works, is 10%. This practice, Wernsing maintains, discriminates against women and thus violates federal law. When Wernsing was hired in 1998 as an "Internal Security Investigator II," the civil service classification of that job allowed a monthly pay from $2,478 to $4,466, depending on prior experience and years of service. Wernsing, who had been earning $1,925 monthly as a Special Agent with the Southern Illinois Enforcement Group, started with the Department at $2,478, a raise of almost 30%. People who came to the Department from more remunerative positions landed higher salaries (though lower percentage raises). For example, Charles Bingaman, hired contemporaneously with Wernsing, had a prior salary of $3,399 monthly as a Child Welfare Specialist III at the state's Department of Children and Family Services. He received a monthly salary of $3,739 to start his new job, a 10% raise. Wernsing and Bingaman do the same work but at substantially different pay as a result of this process for determining initial salaries. Annual raises preserve the relative gap until employees reach the maximum of the pay scale. Bingaman will top out years before Wernsing does. Section 206(d)(1) establishes this rule: "No employer . . . shall discriminate . . . between employees on the basis of sex by paying wages to employees in such establishment at a rate less than the rate at which he pays wages to employees of the opposite sex in such establishment for equal work on jobs the performance of which requires equal skill, effort, and responsibility, and which are performed under similar working conditions". Wernsing observes that she performs the same tasks as Bingaman, under the same working conditions, yet is paid substantially less; it follows, she contends, that the Department must raise her salary. The difficulty with this argument is that § 206(d)(1) forbids differences "on the basis of sex" rather than differences that have other origins—and § 206(d)(1)(iv) drives this home by exempting any pay "differential based on any other factor other than sex". Wages at one's prior employer are a "factor other than sex" and so, the district judge held, an employer may use them to set pay consistently with the Act.

Although three decisions of this court have held that prior wages are a "factor other than sex"—Wernsing contends that we should rule in her favor anyway. She advances two principal arguments: first that the Department lacks an "acceptable business reason" for its approach; second that because all pay systems discriminate on account of sex, any use of prior pay to set salary must be discriminatory. We start with the first of these contentions.

* * *

Wernsing insists that Illinois lacks an "acceptable" reason—despite the evident benefit of making the job more attractive to the best candidates—because the state's civil service criteria call for more attention to employees' background and skills than to the market. New employees are supposed to start at the bottom of the range, with higher salary only if justified by "directly related training and experience." Making a public salary track wages elsewhere is faithless to civil-service principles, Wernsing insists. Yet the Equal Pay Act is not a back-door means to enforce civil-service laws; if Wernsing thinks the Department's practice bad under state law, she is in the wrong court. (Given the eleventh amendment and principles of state sovereign immunity, federal courts cannot enforce state law against the state itself.)

Section 206(d) does not authorize federal courts to set their own standards of "acceptable" business practices. The statute asks whether the employer has a reason other than sex—not whether it has a "good" reason. Congress has not authorized federal judges to serve as personnel managers for America's employers. As we say frequently when dealing with equivalent questions under other federal statutes, such as Title VII of the Civil Rights Act of 1964: "A district judge does not sit in a court of industrial relations. No matter how medieval a firm's practices, no matter how high-handed its decisional process, no matter how mistaken the firm's managers, Title VII and § 1981 do not interfere."

Employment-discrimination statutes forbid reliance on criteria such as race and sex. Provided that they avoid these, employers are free to set their own standards. Under Title VII and other anti-discrimination statutes, once the plaintiff makes a prima facie case of discrimination, all the employer need do is articulate a ground of decision that avoids reliance on the forbidden grounds. The plaintiff then bears the burden to show that the stated reason is a pretext for a decision really made on prohibited criteria. Proof that the actual reason disserves the employer's interests does not discharge that burden, as long as the employer does not rely on one of the forbidden grounds.

Kouba, 691 F.2d 873 (9th Cir. 1982), which originated the "acceptable business reason" requirement, did not explain its genesis; it was advanced as ukase. The ninth circuit proceeded as if the Equal Pay Act worked like the disparate-impact theory under Title VII: if the plaintiff shows that an employment practice adversely affects protected workers as a group, then the employer must provide a strong reason ("business necessity") for the practice. An analogy to disparate-impact litigation under Title VII does not justify a "business reason" requirement under the Equal Pay Act, however, because the Equal Pay Act deals exclusively with disparate treatment. It does not have a disparate-impact component. And in disparate-treatment litigation under other employment-discrimination statutes, the rule is the one we have already summarized: the employer may act for any reason, good or bad, that is not one of the prohibited criteria such as race, sex, age, or religion.

Circuits that have followed the ninth likewise do not locate an acceptable-business-reason requirement in either the statutory text or the rules developed under other similar statutes. The eleventh circuit, for example, asserted (again as a ukase) that employers are forbidden to set salaries based on competitive markets, and as prior salary reflects economic competition it is off limits to employers. The eleventh circuit recognized that it was disagreeing with our holding in *Covington*, 816 F.2d 317 (7th Cir.1987), and stated: "The flaws of the Covington decision are that the Seventh Circuit implicitly used the market force theory to justify the pay disparity and that the Seventh Circuit ignored congressional intent as to what is a 'factor other than sex.' Consequently, we reject Covington because it ignores that prior salary alone cannot justify pay disparity." We're not sure what "congressional intent" the eleventh circuit thought we had ignored; Congress makes legal rules through statutes rather than pure "intent" demonstrated by statements in committee reports or on the floor. The Equal Pay Act forbids sex discrimination, an intentional wrong, while markets are impersonal and have no intent. To the extent other circuits believe that employers must disregard wages set in markets, they have adopted a variant of the comparable-worth doctrine—the view that wages must be based on "merit" rather than forces of supply and demand. This circuit rejected the comparable-worth theory in American Nurses' Ass'n v. Illinois, 783 F.2d 716 (7th Cir. 1986), and we have been given no reason to reconsider that decision.

* * *

Thus we turn to Wernsing's second argument: that because women earn less than men from private employment, all market wages must be discriminatory and therefore must be ignored when setting salaries. The premise is correct; many empirical studies show that women's wages are less than men's on average. But the conclusion is a non-sequitur. Wages rise with experience as well as with other aspects of human capital. That many women spend more years in child-rearing than do men thus implies that women's market wages will be lower on average, but such a difference does not show discrimination.

Wage patterns in some lines of work could be discriminatory, but this is something to be proved rather than assumed. Wernsing has not offered expert evidence (or even a citation to the literature of labor economics) to support a contention that the establishments from which the Department recruits its employees use wage scales that violate the Equal Pay Act and thus discriminate against women. If sex discrimination led to lower wages in the "feeder" jobs, then using those wages as the base for pay at the Department would indeed perpetuate discrimination and violate the Equal Pay Act. But as the record is silent about this possibility, and plaintiffs bear the burden of persuasion in civil litigation, the Department is entitled to the summary judgment it received.

When Wernsing asked the Department for a raise to match Bingaman, the reason she gave is that her prior salary had been lower than his because she had worked for a small, nonprofit employer; she did not suggest that either her former employer or Bingaman's was out of compliance with the Equal Pay Act. Indeed, she has not even tried to show disparate impact; for all this record shows, the Department's female internal security investigators make as much on average as the men. Wernsing's position from the beginning has been that the Department's salary-setting practices hurt her, not that they harm women generally. (Wernsing demonstrated on the record that four other men holding the Internal Security Investigator II position also are paid more than she is because they came to the Department from higher-paying positions. She contends that the district court should have let her make a similar demonstration for other men, but the absolute number is beside the point and so the ruling in limine, right or wrong, does not affect the judgment.)

In lieu of proof, Wernsing relies on a statement that a Senate committee made 42 years ago: that "the wage structure of 'many segments of American industry has been based on an ancient but outmoded belief that a man, because of his role in society, should be paid more than a woman even though his duties are the same.' " That was indeed the view of many employers in 1963, the year the Equal Pay Act came into force, one year before Title VII forbade sex discrimination in private employment, and nine years before Title VII was extended to public employment. But what relevance can this have now that anti-discrimination statutes have been in force for more than two generations? It remains possible that pay differences between men and women reflect discrimination rather than choices made about allocating time between family and market endeavors, and some industries may have been successful in disguising their discrimination. But if this is so it must be established by evidence rather than assumed. Wernsing has abjured her opportunity to supply evidence.

NOTES AND QUESTIONS

1. Judge Easterbrook claims that "markets are impersonal and have no intent," yet he also concedes that "some industries may have been successful in disguising their discrimination." The Equal Pay Act was passed in order to allow two people performing the same work to collect the same pay, regardless of gender. Here, both internal security investigators completed the same tasks. How can the difference in their wages be reconciled with the purpose of the Act? Is the use of an employee's previous salary a means of disguising discrimination?

2. What are "equal skill, effort and responsibility"? Consider the following case: An employer had previously hired Female Selector-Packers to pack glassware it manufactured, at $2.14 an hour. Snap-up Boys were males who performed lifting, errands, and clean-up tasks in the same department, at $2.16 an hour. Male Selector-Packers performed the same work as the Female Selector-Packers, plus occasional snap-up work, at $2.36 an hour. The employer's justification for the difference in the male and female selector-packer rates was that the males performed additional tasks and that the extra flexibility that the employer had in assigning them work was a differential based on "a factor other than sex" under the Act. Is this permissible under the Act? See Shultz v. Wheaton Glass Co., 421 F.2d 259 (3d Cir.), cert. denied, 398 U.S. 905 (1970) (held: flexibility factor did not justify wage differential of 22 cents per hour when snap-up work paid only two cents more per hour than female selector-packer). What standards should be used to determine what constitutes "equal" work?

In EEOC v. Madison Commun. Unit Sch. Dist. No. 12, 818 F.2d 577 (7th Cir. 1987), the employer school district had paid female athletic coaches of girls' sports teams less than it had male athletic coaches of boys' teams. In upholding the district court's finding that the school district had violated the Equal Pay Act, Judge Posner addressed the problem of determining similarity of jobs:

> * * * [T]he jobs that are compared must be in some sense the same to count as "equal work" under the Equal Pay Act; and here we come to the main difficulty in applying the Act; whether two jobs are the same depends on how fine a system of job classification the courts will accept. If coaching an athletic team in the Madison, Illinois school system is considered a single job rather than a congeries of jobs, the school district violated the Equal Pay Act prima facie by paying female holders of this job less than male holders * * * If on the other hand coaching the girls' tennis team is considered a different job from coaching the boys' tennis team, and a fortiori if coaching the girls' volleyball or basketball team is considered a different job (or jobs) from coaching the boys' soccer team, there is no prima facie violation. So the question is how narrow a definition of job the courts should be using in deciding whether the Equal Pay Act is applicable.
>
> We can get some guidance from the language of the Act. The Act requires that the jobs compared have "similar working conditions,"

not the same working conditions. This implies that some comparison of different jobs is possible. It is true that the similarity of working conditions between the jobs being compared is not enough to bring the Act into play—the work must be "equal" and the jobs must require "equal" skill, effort, and responsibility, as well as similar working conditions. But since the working conditions need not be "equal," the jobs need not be completely identical * * *.

818 F.2d at 580. See also Brock v. Georgia S.W. Coll., 765 F.2d 1026 (11th Cir. 1985) (need to show that jobs are "substantially equal," not the skills and qualifications of the individual employees holding those jobs).

3. A clothing store employs only men as sales clerks in the men's department and women as sales clerks for women's clothing. The male sales clerks are paid more than the female clerks; the employer's justification is that the men's department is more profitable than the women's. Is this a violation of the Equal Pay Act? See Hodgson v. Robert Hall Clothes, Inc., 473 F.2d 589 (3d Cir.), cert. denied, 414 U.S. 866 (1973) (held: no violation; exception for "any other factor other than sex" included greater profits earned in men's department). Cf. Bence v. Detroit Health Corp., 712 F.2d 1024 (6th Cir. 1983), cert. denied, 465 U.S. 1025 (1984) (male and female managers of health spas received substantially equal total compensation, but female managers were paid lower membership commissions; held: lower commissions not justified, because female managers generated more profit than male counterparts.) See also EEOC v. Hay Assoc., 545 F.Supp. 1064 (E.D.Pa.1982) (violation of Equal Pay Act for employer to base different starting salaries for male and female employees solely on expectation that male's work would be more profitable than female's.) Cf. Hein v. Oregon Coll. of Educ., 718 F.2d 910 (9th Cir. 1983) (different male and female starting salaries no violation of Equal Pay Act if difference can be justified under one of the four exceptions to the Act). Peters v. Shreveport, 818 F.2d 1148 (5th Cir. 1987) (no violation of Equal Pay Act where employer paid male-dominated fire communications officers 40% more than female-dominated police communications officers for substantially equal work because sex was not a significant factor).

4. One of the most difficult elements of an Equal Pay Act case is determining what constitutes a legitimate "factor other than sex." For example, in Kouba v. Allstate Ins. Co., 691 F.2d 873 (9th Cir. 1982), the employer computed the minimum salary guaranteed to new sales agents on the basis of ability, education, experience, and prior salary. As a result of its practice, female sales agents, on average, made less than their male counterparts. Lola Kouba, a female sales agent, sued under Title VII, alleging that the company's use of prior salaries, in particular, caused the wage differential and constituted unlawful sex discrimination, because of historic sex-based wage discrimination against women in the labor market. In rejecting Kouba's claim, the Ninth Circuit addressed the company's "factor other than sex" defense, incorporated into Title VII wage discrimination claims by the Bennett Amendment (infra, p. 586):

> * * * Kouba insists that in order to give the Act its full remedial force, employers cannot use any factor that perpetuates historic sex

discrimination. * * * But while Congress fashioned the Equal Pay Act to help cure long-standing societal ills, it also intended to exempt factors such as training and experience that may reflect opportunities denied to women in the past. * * *

* * * The Equal Pay Act concerns business practices. It would be nonsensical to sanction the use of a factor that rests on some consideration unrelated to business. An employer thus cannot use a factor which causes a wage differential between male and female employees absent an acceptable business reason. Conversely, a factor used to effectuate some business policy is not prohibited simply because a wage differential results.

* * *

691 F.2d at 876. But see Glenn v. General Motors Corp., 841 F.2d 1567 (11th Cir. 1988) (employer's reliance on market force theory failed to justify pay disparity between male and female clerks), cert. denied, 488 U.S. 948 (1988); Price v. Lockheed Space Operations Co., 856 F.2d 1503 (11th Cir. 1988) (prior salary alone insufficient to justify pay differential). See generally, Note, When Prior Pay Isn't Equal Pay: A Proposed Standard for the Identification of "Factors Other than Sex" under the Equal Pay Act, 89 Colum. L. Rev. 1085 (1989).

In Rizo v. Yovino, the Ninth Circuit held that an employer could not justify a gender wage differential by relying on the fact that the employees had different salaries at their previous jobs. 887 F.3d 453 (9th Cir. 2018). The Court wrote that "to allow employers to capitalize on the persistence of the wage gap and perpetuate that gap *ad infinitum* [ ] would be contrary to the text and history of the Equal Pay Act, and would vitiate the very purpose for which the Act stands." However, that en banc decision was authored by Judge Reinhardt, who both cast the deciding vote in the case, and died just before the Court's decision was filed. The Supreme Court vacated the decision, writing that "federal judges are appointed for life, not for eternity." Yovino v. Rizo, 139 S.Ct. 706 (2019).

5. Consider in the following hypotheticals whether the distinguishing factors used by the employers to justify different salaries for males and females warrant an exception to the Act, keeping in mind that, by definition, the males and the females are performing essentially the same job.

a. A municipal employer calculates starting salaries according to a standardized pay classification system, resulting in different starting salaries for individual male and female employees. See Maxwell v. Tucson, 803 F.2d 444 (9th Cir. 1986) (employer's pay classification system did not establish a merit system defense to the Equal Pay Act); Parker v. Burnley, 693 F.Supp. 1138 (N.D.Ga. 1988) (employer violated Equal Pay Act by paying female employee less than male predecessor for substantially equal work).

b. A woman is hired at a salary less than her male predecessor, or a male replacement is hired at a higher salary than the woman who just retired from the position. See Parker v. Burnley, supra; Ciardella v. Carson City Sch. Dist., 671 F.Supp. 699 (D.Nev.1987). Is the size of the differential important? Suppose it is an increase for the male of $5,000 over a salary of

$60,000. Is an increase of $12,000 over a salary of $24,000 qualitatively different?

c.   The employer uses a "head of the household" eligibility test for medical and dental benefits. (Benefits are considered "compensation" under the Act.) See EEOC v. J.C. Penney Co., 843 F.2d 249 (6th Cir. 1988) (" 'factor other than sex' defense does not include literally *any* other factor, but a factor that, at a minimum, was adopted for a legitimate business reason").

d.   An employer pays women less than men because hiring women increases its costs for unemployment compensation, workers' compensation, and group health insurance. See Wirtz v. Midwest Mfg. Corp., 9 FEP Cases 483 (S.D.Ill.1968) (held: unlawful). Why would this case be decided differently from *Robert Hall Clothes,* supra note 3? Both cases involve an "economic benefit" for the employer, don't they? (For a discussion of differential insurance rates in the context of retirement annuities, see City of Los Angeles Dep't of Water & Power v. Manhart, infra, p. 1217.)

e.   A federal employer hires a man with disabilities and four women and proceeds to pay the male employee significantly more. The male employee's eligibility for a special exception to normal Civil Service hiring criteria was found to be a factor other than sex. Girdis v. EEOC, 688 F.Supp. 40 (D.Mass.1987), affirmed, 851 F.2d 540 (1st Cir. 1988).

6.   The employer justifies a higher salary to a man, John, because "he's married with a new baby"; Mary, a single woman, receives lower pay. Would this be a violation of the Act if John and Mary perform the same job? What if there are three individuals performing the same job—John, Mary and Elmer, who is also single and without family responsibilities—and Mary and Elmer are paid the same salary. Violation of the Act? Should the employer's liability under the Act depend on the composition of its work force? On the other hand, should Mary have a cause of action for wage discrimination while Elmer has none?

7.   The employer offers two openings for similar jobs to Robert and Sally, both at a starting salary of $40,000 per year. Sally accepts the offer immediately. Robert says, "I'd like to work for you, but I think I'm worth $50,000." They bargain, and agree on a salary for Robert of $45,000. Must the employer now raise Sally's salary to match Robert's? Same situation, but Robert says, "I have an outstanding offer from another firm for $40,000, and you'll have to pay me $45,000 for me to accept your offer rather than theirs." The company complies.

8.   As noted in Chapter 3, some cities have barred employers from asking about job candidates' prior salaries. One of these laws has been challenged under the First Amendment.

9.   When the House of Representatives approved the Ledbetter amendment in January 2009, infra p. 599 it separately approved the Paycheck Fairness Act (H.R. 12). In his 2010 State of the Union address, President Obama brought the issue to a national audience, asserting that "we're going to crack down on violations of equal pay laws—so that women get equal pay for an equal day's work." The White House also announced the establishment of a National Equal Pay Enforcement Task Force to improve compliance, public education, and enforcement of equal pay laws. However, as of July 1, 2010, the Senate had not considered the Paycheck Fairness Act (S. 182). Among other provisions, the House-approved PFA would amend the Equal Pay Act to:

(1) replace the EPA's exemption for wage rate differentials "based on any other factor other than sex" with an exemption only for "bona fide factors, such as education, training or experience";

(2) limit the bona fide defense to employer demonstrations that the factor is not derived from a sex-based differential, is job-related with respect to the position in question, and is consistent with business necessity; in addition, the employee would be able to show that an alternative employment practice would serve the same business purposes without producing a gendered differential in pay;

(3) prohibit retaliation against employees who inquire about, discuss, or disclose wages with other workers as part of a sex discrimination inquiry.

b.   Title VII of the Civil Rights Act of 1964

The Equal Pay Act requires equal pay for equal work. In addition, it is unlawful under Title VII of the Civil Rights Act of 1964 to discriminate in wage rates on the basis of Title VII's protected categories. Section 703(a)(1) provides: "It shall be an unlawful employment practice for an employer * * * to discriminate against any individual with respect to his compensation * * * because of such individual's race, color, religion, sex, or national origin."

The Equal Pay Act only applies to circumstances in which employees are performing "substantially equal" work; it does not apply to situations where men and women perform work *similar* in "skill, effort, and responsibility" and are not paid equally. Nor can it be used to attack an employer's decision to pay a female-dominated occupation less than it would pay a male-dominated occupation; this common situation is the target of "comparable worth" advocates.

The "comparable worth" or "pay equity" movement has engendered substantial debate between employee advocates and feminists, on the one hand, and management representatives on the other. The debate has largely centered on whether pervasive sex-based wage discrimination in the workplace actually exists, its sources in the economics and politics of the labor market, and the appropriateness of legal efforts to change practices so deeply rooted in social and cultural norms.

Arguments have been made that application of disparate impact analysis, see Griggs v. Duke Power Co., supra page 318, would lead to a conclusion that gender-based pay scales violate Title VII's ban on discrimination on the basis of sex, but the legislative history of the Civil Rights Act of 1991 specifically disclaimed such arguments. See H.R.Rep. No. 40(1), 102d Cong., 1st Sess., 1991 U.S.C.C.A.N. 549 (1991):

"Additionally, concerns have been raised that applying disparate impact analysis to terms and conditions of employment somehow implicates 'comparable worth' claims. That concern is unfounded. The legislation does not provide any basis for challenges based on disparate impact that did not exist prior to Wards Cove."

National gross earnings data clearly indicate, at an aggregate level, the existence of a substantial earnings gap between men and women. At the level of specific occupations, however, the differences are smaller. Studies by the Bureau of Labor Statistics and by the National Academy of Sciences conclude that while some of the differential in gross earnings is due to recognized distinguishing factors, such as differences in education levels, not all of it can be explained by such factors. Others have attempted to control for occupation and job tenure and have concluded that women occupying the same jobs as men for the same length of time earn approximately the same wage or salary, undercutting the notion of a serious "earnings gap" problem.

Sources of the Wage Gap

What are the sources of the earnings gap? Figure 5–1 illustrates the wage gap between men and women conceptually.

FIGURE 5-1

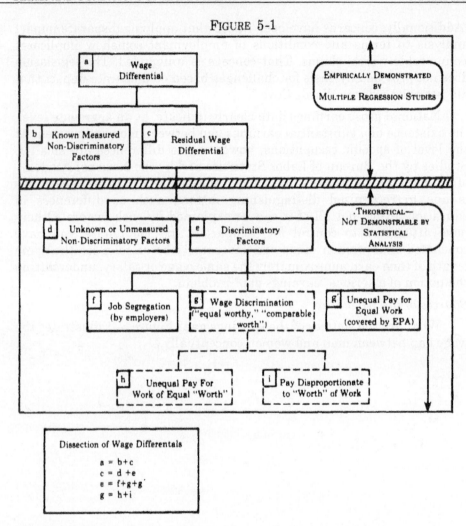

From Bruce A. Nelson, Edward M. Opton, & Thomas E. Wilson, Wage Discrimination and the "Comparable Worth" Theory in Perspective, 13 Mich. J. L. Ref. 231 (1980)

The "wage differential" (a) in Figure 5–1 is the gross difference in wages between men and women. Econometric studies have separated the differential into two components: Known measured nondiscriminatory factors (b) and the residual wage difference (c). Known measured nondiscriminatory factors include seniority, education, and experience, all of which men tend to have more of than women. The residual wage difference can be divided into two more components, unknown or unmeasured nondiscriminatory factors (d) and discriminatory factors (e).

Unknown and unmeasured nondiscriminatory factors (d) include, for instance, voluntary job segregation by employees: how many women with children choose lower level, less demanding jobs in order to have time and energy for family responsibilities? Or refuse to work voluntary overtime for the same reason? The more demanding a job is, the more it tends to pay. Alternatively, studies on occupational preferences show that women in general prefer jobs that are not as dirty or risky as some traditionally male jobs which pay better than traditionally female jobs such as secretary. Also, parents and schools may encourage young women to pursue educational programs different from those toward which they push young men, with the result that men have educational backgrounds more highly valued in the employment market. Societal sex typing conventions play a role in individual choice here, but it is not clear that it is possible or practical to measure their effect. And because such choices are voluntary, they are categorized as nondiscriminatory factors, not subject to "correction" by the law.

Discriminatory factors (e) can be broken down into job segregation by employers (f) and wage discrimination (g) and (g%21). Women may be in lower paying jobs because of unequal access to high-paying jobs. Job segregation may be voluntary or involuntary; furthermore, job segregation alone does not necessarily produce wage discrimination. For example, in baseball, only about 9 percent of all pitchers are black, while 53 percent of outfielders are black. There would appear to be job segregation, but statistics show that there is no wage discrimination which accompanies the job segregation: many outfielders make as much as or more than pitchers, depending on their batting and fielding skills. Job channelling, as it is also known, may give rise to a cause of action under Title VII, however, so that women who are routinely assigned to low level (and legitimately low-paid) jobs without regard to their qualifications could sue, not for direct wage discrimination, but for discriminatory job assignment. If successful, they would be entitled to back pay and increased future wages as part of their remedy.

Wage discrimination takes two forms: unequal pay for equal work (g), which is unlawful under the Equal Pay Act, and wage discrimination in jobs which are not readily identifiable as "equal" (g). Category (g) represents the target of pay equity litigation, and it subsumes two different forms of discrimination: unequal pay for jobs which are comparable but not, strictly speaking, equal (h), and disproportionately low pay for jobs which are in some sense "worth" more than what they are paid (i).

How Real Is the Wage Gap?

Depending on what set of data one uses, estimates are that women earn, on average, somewhere between 75 and 77 percent of what men earn. The measure of actual sex-based wage differentials is probably somewhere between the no-gap proponents who claim that the entire differential is due to such known, identifiable nondiscriminatory factors as education and experience, and those who claim that all women only earn a portion of what men earn, because of deliberate discrimination against women. Recent studies show that over the past decade, occupational sex-segregation has decreased, primarily because the proportion of both men and women in sex-neutral occupations like sales has increased. The largest percentage occupational increase for women has been in the category of executive, administrative, and managerial occupations. The proportion of women in many formerly male-dominated occupations is rising, albeit slowly in most areas. Women in both the formerly male-dominated and sex-neutral fields, at least at entry levels, earn about the same as similarly situated males.

More sobering are the data which indicate that women are not achieving upper-level positions in these occupations at the same rate as their male cohorts. In addition, while some "male" occupations are being "feminized" by the entry of women, there is no significant comparable "masculinization" of such traditionally female—and low-paid— occupations as secretary, private household services, and nursing. Consequently, both *inter*-occupational and *intra*-occupational segregation still account for some amount of the male-female wage gap. The mere existence of a gap is not necessarily unlawful, but given the statutory prohibitions against sex-based wage discrimination, the persistence of the earnings gap is troubling.*

Pay Equity

A certain amount of doctrinal confusion pervades discussion of pay equity. There are actually two distinct types of alleged wage discrimination which arise in the workplace, both of which pay equity advocates would like to eliminate. (See boxes (h) and (i) in Figure 5–1.) The first is where male and female employees are performing what is essentially "comparable work" and being paid different wages. This situation is typified by the *Gunther* case, below, where Washington County had separate job categories for male jail wardens and female jail wardens. Even though the work performed by both was comparable, it did not meet the "substantially equal" standard of the Equal Pay Act and was not actionable under that statute.

The second type of problem presented in pay equity cases is more subtle and complex, and presents a more fundamental challenge to the economics and wage structure of the workplace as we know it. Women occupy eight out of ten jobs in the lowest paying occupations and only three out of ten in the highest. Is the concentration of women in low-paying jobs an accident, or does it reflect wage discrimination against various occupations, not because of their intrinsic value or "worth" to an employer but because they are female-dominated and our society undervalues women and their work? This theory of sex-based wage

---

* Sources: Rytina & Bianchi, Occupational Reclassification and Changes in Distribution by Gender, Monthly Labor Rev., March 1984, at 11; Mellor, Investigating the Differences in Weekly Earnings of Women and Men, Monthly Labor Rev., June 1984, at 17 (especially Table 2, at 20–22, detailing male-female wage differentials in a number of specific occupations); Seiling, Staffing Patterns Prominent in Female-Male Earnings Gap, id., at 29.

discrimination takes the first theory a step further, in looking less at "comparable work" than at "comparable worth."

NOTE

In 1951, women earned 73.9% of men's salaries. In 2012 the percentage was between 75 and 78% for women older than 34. Among workers between age 16 and age 34, the women were paid 90% of men's salaries. Many employers use formal job evaluation systems to determine wage scales; evaluation systems attempt to measure the "value" of a job based on a number of factors. But measures of "value" as determined by such a system are only as good as the system itself. The following excerpt both describes and questions the operation of common job evaluation techniques.

Michele Andrisin Wittig & Gillian Turner, Implementing Comparable Worth: Some Measurement and Conceptual Issues in Job Evaluation, Comparable Worth, Pay Equity, and Public Policy
143–145 (Rita Mae Kelly & Jane Bayes, eds. 1988).

* * *

JOB EVALUATION

The tool of comparable worth is job evaluation, which attempts to compare dissimilar jobs and rank them hierarchically in a particular firm or industry. Critics disparage comparable worth job evaluation as an attempt to compare "apples and oranges," either because it involves comparing jobs of dissimilar content on each of several compensable factors and/or because it usually gives equal weight to each of these compensable factors. However, the practice of establishing common criteria by which to compare jobs of different content and structure, then weighing and summing the respective point values for each job, is an inherent aspect of job evaluation systems. Such procedures, originally developed by industrial-organization psychologists during World War II, have been widely accepted in the public and private sectors since that time (Ferraro, 1984).

In job evaluation, jobs are assessed on a set of compensable factors (usually including skill, responsibility, effort, and working conditions) to produce a total job-worth score. The Equal Pay Act of 1963 stipulates that for two jobs to be considered similar, they must have the same score on each of the compensable factors. In contrast, according to the comparable worth approach, two jobs are similar if their composite scores are the same (Campbell, 1983).

Because job evaluation involves judgments about which compensable factors to use and how to weight them, discriminatory elements may be incorporated (Treiman and Hartmann, 1981; Remick,

1978; Thomsen, 1978). Even guidelines that have been developed to reduce such discriminatory elements (Remick, 1978; Thomsen, 1978) cannot remove the subjectivity inherent in job evaluation. For example, if most women, but few men, know how to sew, then female-dominated jobs requiring this skill may be weighted low on "need for training." However, the same job, if male-dominated, may be scored higher on need for training simply because men ordinarily have not already acquired this skill. Ferraro (1984) reports just such a case of job evaluation bias concerning bookbinder in the U.S. Government Printing Office.

MEASUREMENT ISSUES

A number of measurement and statistical problems arise in modeling the relationship between various worker characteristics, job requirements, and wages. One problem concerns gender and race differences in the fit between operational definitions and their theoretical constructs. For example, when seniority is used as the measure of on-the-job experience, it may be defined as the number of continuous days worked at a particular job. However, an alternative measure of the same theoretical construct is the total number of days worked at the job, regardless of continuity. Both measures are useful proxies for theoretical construct "on-the-job experience," but the "fit" of the former measure to men's actual job experience is likely to be greater than to women's, and the reverse is likely for the latter definition. Continuous days worked and total number of days worked may each contribute positively to on-the-job experience. However, the two measures may introduce distinct biases, causing the regression lines relating job experience to salary to be displaced for different groups of workers. Measures of continuous service may underestimate the actual experience of workers who have interrupted their labor force participation for childrearing or military duty. On the other hand, total number of days worked may overestimate the useful experience of such workers relative to their continuously working counterparts because of the disruptive effect of suspension of labor force participation in job categories for which start-up time is a factor in performance.

Furthermore, the reasons for a worker's labor force interruption can introduce secondary effects apart from the actual time lost. For example, while some types of military duty are more life-threatening than is childbearing, the former is paid work and the free training associated with it is more likely to increase the worker's later civilian employability than does maternity. Such differential spin-offs undermine simplistic interpretations of the role of seniority as a predictor of wages.

A second type of measurement problem involves statistical interactions between gender or race and measures of worker characteristics. Specifically, when the direction of the relationship between a given predictor and salary is equal for the two sex or race groups, but opposite in direction, the importance of that variable may be completely obscured when the respective effects of sex and race are combined in a common regression equation. For example, the relationship of marital status to wages may be opposite in direction for men and women workers, such that being married contributes positively to wage increments for males, but negatively for females. In such a case, with approximately equal numbers of males and females in a sample, combining the data for both genders and attempting to fit one regression equation could result in these two effects cancelling each other out, so that marital status does not contribute significantly to the prediction of wages. However, separate regression equations by gender would show a significant weight or "effect" of marital status, opposite in direction for each sex, for these same data. * * *

NOTES AND QUESTIONS

1. The importance of job evaluations in proving wage discrimination cannot be overstated. In some wage discrimination cases, employers are forced to attack their own previously conducted studies; in others, a battle of the experts develops over plaintiffs' independently conducted evaluation. The courts have shown a definite disinclination to examine competing evaluations, on the grounds that they are complicated (and, implicitly, beyond the court's expertise) and that it is inappropriate for the judiciary to second-guess the employer. It should be kept in mind, however, that courts routinely evaluate very complex matters in a variety of cases: antitrust, other race and sex discrimination cases, rate-fixing in a number of regulated industries, and the like. What is different about a case of wage discrimination, especially given the availability, familiarity, and near-universal use in industry of job evaluation systems?

2. In its first important case on pay equity, County of Wash. v. Gunther, 452 U.S. 161 (1981), the Supreme Court was faced with the question whether Title VII of the Civil Rights Act of 1964 provided a cause of action for sex-based wage discrimination separate from the Equal Pay Act, or whether section 703(h) of Title VII limited Title VII's applicability in such cases. The relevant portion of section 703(h), also known as the Bennett Amendment, had been inserted into Title VII to harmonize that statute with the Equal Pay Act, which had been passed a year earlier. The Bennett Amendment states:

> It shall not be an unlawful employment practice under this title for any employer to differentiate upon the basis of sex in determining the amount of the wages or compensation paid to employees of such employer if such differentiation is authorized by the provisions of Section 6(d) of the Fair Labor Standards Act of 1938 as amended (29 U.S.C. § 206(d)) [the Equal Pay Act].

The County of Washington, Oregon, paid female guards in the female section of the county jail substantially lower wages ($525–$668 per month in 1973) than it paid male guards in the male section ($701–$940 per month). State law required that female prisoners be guarded solely by women, and women were not employed to guard male prisoners. The plaintiffs sued, alleging that they were paid unequal wages for work substantially equal to that performed by male guards and, in the alternative, that because of intentional discrimination, the county set the pay scale for female guards, but not for male guards, at a level lower than that warranted by its own wage survey. According to the plaintiffs, the survey indicated that the female guards' job was worth approximately 95 percent of the male guard's job. It was paid 70 percent as much, while male guards received the full amount indicated in the survey. The two jobs were not identical: the males guarded ten times more prisoners than the women, and the women performed more clerical duties than the males. The plaintiffs' Equal Pay Act claim was rejected under the "equal skill, effort, and responsibility" standard. The county further argued that a sex-based wage discrimination claim under Title VII also had to satisfy the equal work standard of the Equal Pay Act, because the Bennett Amendment, which read into Title VII all of the provisions of the Equal Pay Act, limited Title VII claims to those which could also be brought under the Equal Pay Act.

In a five to four decision, the Court held that the Bennett Amendment was a "technical amendment" intended only to harmonize potential conflicts between Title VII and the Equal Pay Act. Thus, section 703(h)'s effect was to incorporate only the affirmative defenses of the Equal Pay Act (seniority system, merit system, quantity or quality of production system, and "any other factor other than sex"); it did not usurp an independent claim for sex-based wage discrimination that could arise under Title VII. In its opinion, the majority was clearly concerned about undermining Title VII:

> Our interpretation of the Bennett Amendment draws additional support from the remedial purposes of Title VII and the Equal Pay Act. Section 703(a) of Title VII makes it unlawful for an employer "to fail or refuse to hire or to discharge any individual, or *otherwise to discriminate* against any individual with respect to his compensation, terms, conditions, or privileges of employment" because of such individual's sex. As Congress itself has indicated, a "broad approach" to the definition of equal employment opportunity is essential to overcoming and undoing the effect of discrimination. We must therefore avoid interpretations of Title VII that deprive victims of discrimination of a remedy, without clear congressional mandate.

> Under petitioner's reading of the Bennett Amendment, only those sex-based wage discrimination claims that satisfy the "equal work" standard of the Equal Pay Act could be brought under Title VII. In practical terms, this means that a woman who is discriminatorily underpaid could obtain no relief—no matter how egregious the discrimination might be—unless her employer also employed a man in an equal job in the same establishment, at a higher rate of pay. Thus, if an employer hired a woman for a unique position in the company and then admitted that her salary would have been higher had she been male, the woman would be unable to obtain legal redress under petitioner's interpretation. Similarly, if an employer used a transparently sex-biased system for wage determination, women holding jobs not equal to those held by men

would be denied the right to prove that the system is a pretext for discrimination. * * * Congress surely did not intend the Bennett Amendment to insulate such blatantly discriminatory practices from judicial redress under Title VII.

In the majority opinion, Justice Brennan emphasized the "narrowness" of the question before the Court, noting that "respondents" suit does not require a court to make its own subjective assessment of the value of the male and female guard jobs, or to attempt by statistical technique or other method to quantify the effect of sex discrimination on the wage rates. In fact, the Court rejected the notion that *Gunther* was a "comparable worth" case, "under which plaintiffs might claim increased compensation on the basis of a comparison of the intrinsic worth or difficulty of their job with that of other jobs in the same organization or community."

In a strong dissent, Justice Rehnquist rejected the majority's opinion as a misinterpretation of the legislative history of Title VII and the political compromises which were made to ensure the passage of Title VII:

> In rejecting [the County's] argument, the Court ignores traditional canons of statutory construction and relevant legislative history. Although I had thought it well settled that the legislative history of a statute is a useful guide to the intent of Congress, the Court today claims that the legislative history "has no bearing on the meaning of the Act," "does not provide a solution to our present problem," and is simply of "no weight." Instead, the Court rests its decision on its unshakable belief that any other result would be unsound public policy. It insists that there simply *must* be a remedy for wage discrimination beyond that provided in the Equal Pay Act. The Court does not explain *why* that must be so, nor does it explain *what* the remedy might be. And, of course, the Court cannot explain why it and not Congress is charged with determining what is and what is not sound public policy. [Emphasis in original.]

Although *Gunther* was viewed as a victory for the advocates of pay equity, it did not address how the lower federal courts should treat other pay equity cases, particularly the application of Title VII theory to such cases. Perhaps the most problematic issue has been the appropriateness of the employer's "market rate" defense.

3.   In 2004, a female school nutrition director sued her school district for violation of the Equal Pay Act. Although she had been performing the same work as the male director of maintenance and had been receiving the same wages for 10 years, the maintenance director had received a salary increase of almost $10,000 while the nutrition director's salary remained the same. The school district admitted that the two directors performed equal work but claimed that its salary decisions were "based on a statistical survey of salaries which satisfies the 'factor other than sex' exception to the equal pay act." Does a survey of salaries satisfy the exception, or does it simply profit from historically low wages for women? See Hudon v. West Valley Sch. Dist. No. 208, 97 P.3d 39 (Wash.Ct.App.2004).

AFSCME v. Washington
578 F.Supp. 846 (W.D. Wash. 1983).

[Two unions representing 15,500 state employees in jobs primarily held by females initiated a class action against the state of Washington for discriminatory implementation and application of its compensation system. In 1973, the state had conducted a study of male and female compensation that suggested the existence of a wage gap between job classes held predominately by men and those filled predominately by women, a gap that could not be explained solely by "job worth." Subsequently, in 1974 the state engaged an independent consulting firm to perform a more complete study. "Men's" or "women's" jobs were defined as jobs with 70% men or women. The study concluded that there was a tendency for women's job classes to be paid less than men's job classes for jobs of comparable worth; overall, the disparity was about 20 percent, and the amount of disparity increased as the job value increased. In December 1976, then-Governor Evans included a $7 million budget appropriation to begin the process of eradicating sex-based wage discrimination in state employment. That same month, the State Personnel Board adopted a resolution stating its support for the correction of disparities identified by the study. In 1977, a new Governor eliminated the appropriation from that year's budget, even though the state had a budget surplus; the state legislature authorized continuing study of compensation differentials and instructed two state agencies to furnish the governor with supplementary data on compensation differentials, in the form of a separate salary schedule.

District Judge Jack Tanner concluded that the state was guilty of intentional discrimination against employees in predominately female job classifications. The evidence established a pattern of sex discrimination in employment by the state, in that it historically failed to pay predominately female jobs their full evaluated worth as established by the state's own job evaluation studies; further, the state failed to rebut the plaintiffs' prima facie case by producing credible evidence demonstrating a legitimate and overriding business justification.]

The Defendant, State of Washington, has set forth a number of reasons injunctive relief should not be formulated and enforced by this Court: (1) the tremendous costs involved; (2) lack of revenue because of the depressed economy nationally, and more particularly in the State of Washington (i.e., high unemployment and recession in the forest industry which provides much of the State tax revenues); (3) prior State revenue commitments to education, prisons, and social services; (4) the State Constitution's mandated balanced budget; (5) disruption in the State's work force, and of the State's compensation scheme; (6) the State Legislature has already initiated a remedy which will eliminate the sex discrimination by no later than 1993; and (7) the Tenth Amendment to the United States Constitution. This Court finds that Defendant's reasons are without merit and unpersuasive, for the following reasons:

First, Title VII does not contain "* * * a cost-justification defense comparable to the affirmative defense available in a price discrimination suit. (footnote omitted) * * * neither Congress nor the Courts have recognized such a defense under Title VII. (footnote omitted)." Los Angeles Dept. of Water and Power v. Manhart, 435 U.S. 702, 716–17 (1978).

Second, Defendant's shortage of revenue, prior revenue commitments, and constitutionally mandated balanced budget defenses, cannot withstand the evidence produced at trial herein. It was uncontroverted that in the 1976–77 biennium the State of Washington had a surplus budget, was cognizant of the disparity which is the subject of this lawsuit, and did not consider the acknowledged discrimination enough of a priority to divert the surplus to the victims of the discrimination. The bad faith of Defendant's action is patent, and cannot be overcome at this late date with arguments that sound in equity.

Third, any disruption full implementation of the proposed injunctive relief would effect, is a direct result of the discrimination Defendant created and has maintained. Sound reasoning dictates that in any cause-effect analysis one cannot be heard to argue the effect is the evil to be eradicated.

Fourth, the belated May 1983 appropriation did not purport to eliminate discrimination. At best, it indicated a change in attitude by the Defendant.

Further, were the Court to adopt the May 1983 act of the Washington legislature as the injunctive remedy herein, this Court would be endorsing a compensation plan that works a grave injustice to the discriminatees. Injunctive orders couched in terms of "with all deliberate speed" result in non-action. This Court sees no credible distinction between endorsing a remedy to be phased in over a ten (10) year period and an injunction ordering compliance "with all deliberate speed."

It is time, *right now* for a remedy. Defendant's preoccupation with its budget constraints pales when compared with the invidiousness of the impact ongoing discrimination has upon the Plaintiffs herein.

* * *

There is little doubt that had the State produced evidence that the unlawful discrimination was other than in "bad faith", the *Manhart* and *Norris* decisions would have persuaded this court that back pay would not have been an appropriate remedy. The devastating cost to a Defendant who did not act in bad faith would then, and only then, become relevant. However, the record herein does not lend itself to a finding that the State was acting in good faith by not paying Plaintiffs their evaluated worth. Rather, the persistent and intransigent conduct of Defendant in refusing to pay Plaintiffs indicates "bad faith." * * *

This Court finds that the State had knowledge of the sex discrimination in employment before and after the March 24, 1972 amendment to Title VII; that the evidence shows the discrimination is pervasive and intentional and is still being practiced by the State; and that the State is adhering to a practice of sex discrimination in violation of the terms of Title VII with full knowledge of, and indifference to, its effect upon the Plaintiffs.

AFSCME v. Washington
770 F.2d 1401 (9th Cir. 1985).

■ KENNEDY, CIRCUIT JUDGE:

In this class action affecting approximately 15,500 of its employees, the State of Washington was sued in the United States District Court for the Western District of Washington. The district court found the State discriminated on the basis of sex in violation of Title VII of the Civil Rights Act of 1964, 42 U.S.C. § 2000e–2(a) (1982), by compensating employees in jobs where females predominate at lower rates than employees in jobs where males predominate, if these jobs, though dissimilar, were identified by certain studies to be of comparable worth. The State appeals. We conclude a violation of Title VII was not established here, and we reverse.

The State of Washington has required salaries of state employees to reflect prevailing market rates. Throughout the period in question, comprehensive biennial salary surveys were conducted to assess prevailing market rates. The surveys involved approximately 2,700 employers in the public and private sectors. The results were reported to state personnel boards, which conducted hearings before employee representatives and agencies and made salary recommendations to the State Budget Director. The Director submitted a proposed budget to the Governor, who in turn presented it to the state legislature. Salaries were fixed by enactment of the budget.

In 1974 the State commissioned a study by management consultant Norman Willis to determine whether a wage disparity existed between employees in jobs held predominantly by women and jobs held predominantly by men. The study examined sixty-two classifications in which at least seventy percent of the employees were women, and fifty-nine job classifications in which at least seventy percent of the employees were men. It found a wage disparity of about twenty percent, to the disadvantage of employees in jobs held mostly by women, for jobs considered of comparable worth. * * * The State of Washington conducted similar studies in 1976 and 1980, and in 1983 the State enacted legislation providing for a compensation scheme based on comparable worth. The scheme is to take effect over a ten-year period. * * *

AFSCME alleges sex-based wage discrimination throughout the state system, but its explanation and proof of the violation is, in essence, Washington's failure as early as 1979 to adopt and implement at once a comparable worth compensation program. The trial court adopted this theory as well. The comparable worth theory, as developed in the case before us, postulates that sex-based wage discrimination exists if employees in job classifications occupied primarily by women are paid less than employees in job classifications filled primarily by men, if the jobs are of equal value to the employer, though otherwise dissimilar. * * *

We must determine whether comparable worth, as presented in this case, affords AFSCME a basis for recovery under Title VII.

* * *

In the instant case, the district court found a violation of Title VII, premised upon both the disparate impact and the disparate treatment theories of discrimination. Under the disparate impact theory, discrimination may be established by showing that a facially neutral employment practice, not justified by business necessity, has a disproportionately adverse impact upon members of a group protected under Title VII. Proof of an employer's intent to discriminate in adopting a particular practice is not required in a disparate impact case. The theory is based in part on the rationale that where a practice is specific and focused we can address whether it is a pretext for discrimination in light of the employer's explanation for the practice. Under the disparate treatment theory, in contrast, an employer's intent or motive in adopting a challenged policy is an essential element of liability for a violation of Title VII. It is insufficient for a plaintiff alleging discrimination under the disparate treatment theory to show the employer was merely aware of the adverse consequences the policy would have on a protected group. The plaintiff must show the employer chose the particular policy because of its effect on members of a protected class.

* * *

The trial court erred in ruling that liability was established under a disparate impact analysis. The precedents do not permit the case to proceed upon that premise. AFSCME's disparate impact argument is based on the contention that the State of Washington's practice of taking prevailing market rates into account in setting wages has an adverse impact on women, who, historically, have received lower wages than men in the labor market. Disparate impact analysis is confined to cases that challenge a specific, clearly delineated employment practice applied at a single point in the job selection process. Atonio v. Wards Cove Packing Co., 768 F.2d 1120, 1130 (9th Cir. 1985); see also *Dothard*, 433 U.S. at 328–29 (height and weight requirement disproportionately excluded women); *Griggs,* 401 U.S. at 430–31 (requirement of high school diploma or satisfactory performance on standardized tests disproportionately affected minorities). The instant case does not involve an employment practice that yields to disparate impact analysis. As we noted in an earlier case, the decision to base compensation on the competitive market, rather than on a theory of comparable worth, involves the assessment of a number of complex factors not easily ascertainable, an assessment too multifaceted to be appropriate for disparate impact analysis. In the case before us, the compensation system in question resulted from surveys, agency hearings, administrative recommendations, budget proposals, executive actions, and legislative enactments. A compensation system that is responsive to supply and demand and other market forces is not the type of specific, clearly delineated employment policy contemplated by *Dothard* and *Griggs;* such a compensation system, the result of a complex of market forces, does not constitute a single practice that suffices to support a claim under disparate impact theory. Such cases are controlled by disparate treatment analysis. Under these principles and precedents, we must reverse the district court's determination of liability under the disparate impact theory of discrimination.

We consider next the allegations of disparate treatment. Under the disparate treatment theory, AFSCME was required to prove a prima facie case of sex discrimination by a preponderance of the evidence. Our review of the record, however, indicates failure by AFSCME to establish the requisite element of intent by either circumstantial or direct evidence.

AFSCME contends discriminatory motive may be inferred from the Willis study, which finds the State's practice of setting salaries in reliance on market rates creates a sex-based wage disparity for jobs deemed of comparable worth. AFSCME argues from the study that the market reflects a historical pattern of lower wages to employees in positions staffed predominantly by women; and it contends the State of Washington perpetuates that disparity, in violation of Title VII, by using market rates in the compensation system. The inference of discriminatory motive which AFSCME seeks to draw from the State's participation in the market system fails, as the State did not create the market disparity and has not been shown to have been motivated by impermissible sex-based considerations in setting salaries.

The requirement of intent is linked at least in part to culpability. That concept would be undermined if we were to hold that payment of wages according to prevailing rates in the public and private sectors is an act that, in itself, supports the inference of a purpose to discriminate. Neither law nor logic deems the free market system a suspect enterprise. Economic reality is that the value of a particular job to an employer is but one factor influencing the rate of compensation for that job. Other considerations may include the availability of workers willing to do the job and the effectiveness of collective bargaining in a particular industry. We find nothing in the language of Title VII or its legislative history to indicate Congress intended to abrogate fundamental economic principles such as the laws of supply and demand or to prevent employers from competing in the labor market.

While the Washington legislature may have the discretion to enact a comparable worth plan if it chooses to do so, Title VII does not obligate it to eliminate an economic inequality that it did not create. Title VII was enacted to ensure equal opportunity in employment to covered individuals, and the State of Washington is not charged here with barring access to particular job classifications on the basis of sex.

We have recognized that in certain cases an inference of intent may be drawn from statistical evidence. We have admonished, however, that statistics must be relied on with caution. Though the comparability of wage rates in dissimilar jobs may be relevant to a determination of discriminatory animus, job evaluation studies and comparable worth statistics alone are insufficient to establish the requisite inference of discriminatory motive critical to the disparate treatment theory. The weight to be accorded such statistics is determined by the existence of independent corroborative evidence of discrimination. We conclude the independent evidence of discrimination presented by AFSCME is insufficient to support an inference of the requisite discriminatory motive under the disparate treatment theory.

AFSCME offered proof of isolated incidents of sex segregation as evidence of a history of sex-based wage discrimination. The evidence consists of "help wanted" advertisements restricting various jobs to members of a particular sex. These advertisements were often placed in separate "help wanted—male" and "help wanted—female" columns in state newspapers between 1960 and 1973, though most were discontinued when Title VII became applicable to the states in 1972. * * * However, none of the individually named plaintiffs in the action ever testified regarding specific incidents of discrimination. The isolated incidents alleged by AFSCME are insufficient to corroborate the results of the Willis study and do not justify an inference of discriminatory motive by the State in the setting of salaries for its system as a whole. * * * We also reject AFSCME's contention that, having commissioned the Willis study, the State of Washington was committed to implement a new system of compensation based on comparable worth as defined by the study. Whether comparable worth is a feasible approach to employee compensation is a matter of debate. Assuming, however, that like other job evaluation studies it may be useful as a diagnostic tool, we reject a rule that would penalize rather than commend employers for their effort and innovation in undertaking such a study. The results of comparable worth studies will vary depending on the number and types of factors measured and the maximum number of points allotted to each factor. A study that indicates a particular wage structure might be more equitable should not categorically bind the employer who commissioned it. The employer should also be able to take into account market conditions, bargaining demands, and the possibility that another study will yield different results. * * * We hold there was a failure to establish a violation of Title VII under the disparate treatment theory of discrimination, and reverse the district court on this aspect of the case as well. The State of Washington's initial reliance on a free market system in which employees in male-dominated jobs are compensated at a higher rate than employees in dissimilar female-dominated jobs is not in and of itself a violation of Title VII, notwithstanding that the Willis study deemed the positions of comparable worth. Absent a showing of discriminatory motive, which has not been made here, the law does not permit the federal courts to interfere in the market-based system for the compensation of Washington's employees.

REVERSED.

Notes and Questions

1.   For other post-*Gunther* decisions illustrating the mixed results in pay equity cases, see: Wiley v. American Elec. Power Servs. Corp., 287 F.App'x 335 (5th Cir. 2008) (admission to the employer's profit-sharing plan was based on factors other than sex, precluding female employees' disparate pay claim); Stanley v. USC, 13 F.3d 1313 (9th Cir. 1994) (no discrimination because the men's basketball coach engaged in more promotional and revenue-raising activities than the women's basketball coach, which resulted in revenue 90 times greater than that generated by the women's team); Lanegan-Grimm v. Library Ass'n, 560 F.Supp. 486 (D.Or.1983) (library discriminated when it paid female driver of mobile library less than male delivery truck driver); Briggs v. City of Madison, 536 F.Supp. 435 (W.D.Wis.1982).

2.   The Ninth Circuit firmly rejected the use of the disparate impact theory to prove the existence of sex-based wage discrimination. Is the disparate impact model in fact limited only to employer selection processes, as the opinion stated? (Hint: see City of L.A. Dep't of Water & Power v. Manhart, infra, p. 1217.) Disparate impact analysis is typically used in other systemic discrimination cases. Why did the court reject its use in *AFSCME II*?

Following *AFSCME II,* comparable worth litigation has almost uniformly met with failure in the federal courts. See UAW v. Michigan, 886 F.2d 766 (6th Cir. 1989); EEOC v. Sears, Roebuck & Co., 839 F.2d 302 (7th Cir. 1988); American Nurses' Ass'n v. Illinois, 783 F.2d 716 (7th Cir. 1986) (particularly notable for its discussion of the labor market defense by Judge Posner); California State Employees' Ass'n v. State of Cal., 724 F.Supp. 717 (N.D.Cal.1989); Manuel v. WSBT, Inc., 706 F.Supp. 654 (N.D.Ind.1988); Beard v. Whitley County REMC, 656 F.Supp. 1461 (N.D.Ind.1987), affirmed, 840 F.2d 405 (7th Cir. 1988). But in Denny v. Westfield State Coll., 669 F.Supp. 1146 (D.Mass.1987), 880 F.2d 1465 (1st Cir. 1989), female faculty members successfully sued for sex-based wage discrimination under Title VII when they proved that they received significantly lower salaries than male faculty members and the college failed to provide a legitimate nondiscriminatory reason for the difference; the court rejected explanations for the difference based on departmental affiliation and exceptional performance.

3. In trying to prove a case of disparate treatment, how can plaintiffs establish an employer's intent to discriminate in wages? In *AFSCME I,* Judge Tanner looked at direct and circumstantial evidence of historical discrimination against women, job segregation, and overtly discriminatory behavior and statements by state officials. Why is that not enough for the Court of Appeals? What additional evidence would support a finding of "intent"? In deciding the question of "intent" in favor of plaintiffs, the court in Taylor v. Charley Bros. Co., 25 F.E.P. Cases 602 (W.D.Pa.1981), noted the following: the employer's failure to conduct a job evaluation; its practice of segregating women within one department in the company (a large warehousing operation); its practice of only considering women job applicants for openings in that department; and discriminatory remarks made by company officials. In general, what *minimal* evidence would be necessary to establish intent?

4. The Ninth Circuit relied heavily on the defendant's "market rate" theory to hold that the plaintiffs failed to establish intent, a requisite part of their prima facie disparate treatment case. Review the burdens of proof for establishing discrimination under Title VII. Given the inference of intent that can be drawn from the employer's wage statistics, should not the court have recognized that plaintiffs established a prima facie case and then evaluated the market rate argument as the employer's defense to the prima facie case? What difference would this make?

The market rate defense has proved powerful in post-*Gunther* litigation. Opponents of legal intervention on behalf of pay equity argue that any intrusion into the free workings of the labor market is unwarranted. This same argument can be made about almost any statute, however; Title VII constitutes a deliberate intrusion into the "free market", as do the FLSA, OSH Act, and other statutes establishing minimum working standards. Similarly, antitrust or environmental laws interfere with the free operation of the market in areas outside employment. What role should "the market" play in cases of alleged wage discrimination?

5. If comparable worth theories were successfully used to increase wages in traditionally female-dominated jobs, wouldn't those higher wages encourage women to stay in (or enter) those jobs and thus perpetuate occupational segregation? Is that a result we want to encourage?

6. What applicability, if any, does comparable worth analysis have for eliminating race discrimination?

7. For economic analysis, both theoretical and empirical, see the exchange: Richard A. Posner, An Economic Analysis of Sex Discrimination Laws, 56 U. Chi. L.Rev. 1311 (1989), and John J. Donohue, Prohibiting Sex Discrimination in the Workplace: An Economic Perspective, 56 U. Chi. L. Rev. 1337 (1989). See also George Johnson & Gary Solon, The Attainment of Pay Equity Between the Sexes by Legal Means: An Economic Analysis, 20 U. Mich. J.L. Ref. 183 (1986) (entire issue devoted to comparable worth).

8.   The Canadian Human Rights Act commits all provinces to a policy of comparable worth. One consequence of this legislation has been an onslaught of litigation against employers. For example, union clerical workers whose pay was lower than that of technicians have won large comparable worth claims against Bell Canada, Canada's largest telephone company. As a result, Bell Canada has had to pay considerable back pay damages. The company has outsourced many of its jobs to the United States to avoid Canada's comparable worth laws. Operators at Bell Canada in Canada may have higher wages, but Bell Canada is creating fewer jobs in Canada. See Bell Canada v. Canada (Human Rights Commission), [2001] 3 F.C. 481 (F.C.A.); Bell Canada v. Canadian Tel. Employees Ass'n., [1998] 3 F.C. 244 (T.D.); Morley Gunderson & W. Craig Riddell, *Comparable Worth:* Canada's Experience, 10 Contemporary Economic Policy, n. 3, July 1992, 85–94; Beth Bilson, A Colloquy on Employment and Labour Law and Policy for the New Millennium: Promises and Paradoxes: The Ravages of Time: The Work of the Federal Pay Equity Task Force and Section 11 of the Canadian Human Rights Act, 67 Sask. L. Rev. 525 (2004).

9.   The EU has mandated equal pay for men and women for equal work in Article 141 of the European Economic Community Treaty. This article requires that "each Member State shall ensure that the principle of equal pay for male and female workers for equal work or work of equal value is applied." Unlike the Equal Pay Act, Article 141 contains the comparable worth standard whereby equal pay is given for equal value rather than the equal pay for equal work standard. See Treaty Establishing the European Community, Feb. 7, 1992, O.J. (C 224) 1 (1992), [1992] 1 C.M.L.R. 573 (1992), art. 141 (as in effect in 1999).

Carin Clauss, Comparable Worth—The Theory, Its Legal Foundation, and the Feasibility of Implementation
20 U. Mich. J.L. Ref. 7 (1986).

A major difficulty in discussing the legal status of comparable worth, as well as its economic cost and administrative feasibility, is that the phrase "comparable worth" is used interchangeably to refer to many different concepts. Comparable worth may mean (1) a requirement that compensation be proportional to the intrinsic worth of the job, (2) a pay system under which all jobs of equal value are paid the same, (3) a procedure that permits the comparison of job content and compensation across job families (i.e., work that is dissimilar), (4) evidence used in a wage discrimination case to demonstrate that the difference in wages is due to sex and not to any difference in job value, (5) a requirement that female-dominated jobs be paid the same as male-dominated jobs of equal value, (6) a requirement that the wage rates for female-dominated jobs be established using the same criteria as are used in establishing the wage rates for male-dominated jobs, and (7) a requirement that wage disparities based on sex (or race) be eliminated.

The important distinction in these various meanings is between an equal value concept (items (1), (2), and (5) above), under which the employer is required to pay the same wage rate for all jobs of equal or comparable value, and a nondiscrimination concept (items (3), (4), (6), and (7)), under which the employer is prohibited from using different standards in establishing the rates for male- and female-dominated jobs, or from otherwise basing wages on sex. Unlike an equal value concept, nondiscrimination does not mandate equal wages for work of equal value but instead prohibits disparate wage treatment on the basis of sex or race.

The legal and moral justifications for these two distinct concepts vary considerably. Most people would probably agree that wage discrimination offends a basic civil liberty and is thus properly dealt with by our legal system—as witnessed by the widespread support for the Equal Pay Act and the nondiscrimination in pay provisions of Title VII of the Civil Rights Act. By the same token, there are probably very few people who would agree that equal pay for work of equal value (without regard to discrimination) is a basic civil liberty—whatever their view might be as to the fairness of such a system. Indeed, there are a great many compensation systems in both the private and public sectors that do not pay all jobs of equal or comparable value at the same rate, regardless of whether those jobs are male or female. In these systems, male-dominated jobs are paid less than other male-dominated jobs even though the work content of the jobs might be of "equal" or "comparable" value. For example, the average wage for architects is less than the average wage for engineers, although the educational and skill requirements for the two jobs are very much the same. Similar disparities also exist among female jobs.

The reasons for such disparities could be several: individual employers, or society as a whole, may reward certain skills more than others (e.g., managerial skills over artistic skills, or technical skills over administrative skills); wages may be inflated by the unionization of specific occupations, or by restrictions on entry into particular occupations; or wages may be influenced by tradition and custom. Whatever the reason, such disparities are commonplace. It is not the wage disparity in jobs of equal value that invokes the charge of discrimination; rather, it is the use of different standards—i.e., disparate treatment—in establishing the wage rates for the male- and female-dominated jobs.

This distinction between an equal value concept and a theory of nondiscrimination is critical, not only because it establishes the legal and moral justification for comparable worth, but also because it answers three of the more common criticisms directed at comparable worth. First, comparable worth does not mandate an "equality of results" for employees in male- and female-dominated jobs. Those individuals who make this argument suggest that comparable worth proponents want to eliminate the earnings gap between men and women by compelling employers to increase the wage rates for female-dominated jobs even if these jobs are less skilled or are located in the more marginal firms or industries—what the chairman of the United States Civil Rights Commission calls "reparations for middle-class white women" or a "financial quota system."

But comparable worth, as defined here, and as used by litigators and legislators, does not seek to raise the wage rates of less skilled or less productive female jobs to equal those of higher skilled or more productive male jobs, or to ensure that women obtain the same economic benefits from a day's labor as do men. It may be that the high concentration of women in less skilled and less productive jobs is the result of discrimination, but discrimination in employment, not pay. Comparable worth is only concerned with pay discrimination. So, for example, if it were shown that a publishing company had channeled women college graduates into clerical jobs and men college graduates into editorial positions, or that a bank had assigned women applicants to teller positions and men with equivalent education and experience to officer trainee positions, the remedy would be to allow women to transfer into the "male" positions, not to increase the wage rates for clerical and teller positions to equal the wage rates for editorial assistants and officer trainees. On the other hand, if it were shown that the clerical jobs and teller positions were paid less than male-dominated jobs of comparable or lesser value, the remedy would be to reassess the wage rates for the female-dominated jobs using the same criteria as were used in establishing the wage rates for the male-dominated jobs—i.e., equal treatment, not equal results.

Second, because comparable worth is based on a theory of discrimination (disparate treatment) and not on some ill-defined notion of public justice, it does not attempt to eliminate all wage disparities existing within an employing unit, but only those resulting from the application of different standards in establishing the wage rates for female-dominated jobs. Thus, it would not affect any differentials existing between male-dominated jobs, where certain male-dominated jobs are paid more than others of comparable or equal value. Nor would comparable worth affect any disparities existing between female-dominated jobs of equal value. Such disparities may be the result of market forces or of long-standing custom, or they may just be the result of a random wage structure. But they are not the result of prohibited disparate treatment. The fact that disparate treatment must be based on sex, race, color, religion, or national origin—and not just on custom or chance—should satisfy the frequently expressed concern that comparable worth will open the floodgates to large numbers of suits challenging the relative ranking of jobs.

And finally, because comparable worth is not concerned with just any wage disparity, but only those disparities that are the result of sex-based wage discrimination, the degree of government or judicial intervention into an employer's wage practice will be much more limited than the critics suggest. Bureaucrats and judges would not, for example, be authorized to determine what the fair wage should be for any male-dominated or integrated job. These decisions would all be made by the employer. Nor would the government or courts be able to alter the ranking of these jobs. Comparable worth does not require an employer to pay more to those who perform work of greater value, or less to those who perform work of lesser value; the employer is free to pay all employees the same rate, or to pay different rates for work of equal value. The employer can choose to give greater monetary weight to artistic or creative skills than to managerial skills, or it can give little or no weight to such skills. Similarly, it can give greater weight to responsibility than to skill, or, alternatively, greater weight to skill than to responsibility. The only requirement of comparable worth is that the employer use the same standards in establishing the pay rates for female-dominated jobs, and for black and Hispanic jobs, as it uses in establishing the pay rates for male-dominated and integrated jobs. Where it can be shown that the employer has used different standards, the doctrine of comparable worth requires that the employer adjust the wage rates for the female-dominated jobs so that these jobs will occupy the same relative position that they would have occupied had they been male-dominated or integrated jobs.

c.   THE LILLY LEDBETTER FAIR PAY ACT

The Lilly Ledbetter Fair Pay Act of 2009 ("FPA"), one of the first statutes signed by President Obama, overturned the Supreme Court decision, Ledbetter v. Goodyear Tire & Rubber Co., Inc., 550 U.S. 618 (2007) (5–4). It amended Title VII, the ADEA, and the ADA "to clarify that a discriminatory compensation decision * * * occurs each time compensation is paid pursuant to the discriminatory compensation decision." For Title VII actions, a successful plaintiff will be entitled to back pay for up to two years preceding the filing of the charge.

Lilly Ledbetter

Lilly Ledbetter worked for Goodyear as one of the few female area managers at its Alabama plant from 1979 until her retirement in 1998. Initially, Ledbetter's salary was in line with the salaries of men performing substantially similar work. However, Goodyear changed to a performance-based pay system. Because of Goodyear's policy to keep employee compensation strictly confidential, Ledbetter did not know that there was a substantial disparity between her pay and the pay of male employees doing the same job. By the end of 1997, Ledbetter was paid $3,727 per month; the lowest paid male area manager received $4,286 per month, the highest paid, $5,236. After receiving an anonymous note informing her of the pay disparity shortly before her retirement, Ledbetter filed a charge with the EEOC. At trial, the jury found Ledbetter had been discriminated against and awarded her $3 million in compensatory and punitive damages. The trial judge reduced the damage award to the Title VII statutory cap of $300,000. On appeal, Goodyear argued that Ledbetter's pay discrimination claim was time-barred with respect to all pay decisions made more than 180 days before the filing of her EEOC claim and that no discriminatory act relating to Ledbetter's pay occurred after that date. The Eleventh Circuit agreed and reversed the lower court's decision, holding that Ledbetter's award could not stand because the claim was filed after the statute of limitations had run. The United States Supreme Court affirmed.

Justice Alito wrote the majority opinion, which held that the continuing effects of the prior discrimination did not make out a present violation:

> [A] discriminatory act which is not made the basis for a timely
> charge * * * is merely an unfortunate event in history which has
> no present legal consequences * * * Ledbetter's attempt to take
> the intent associated with the prior pay decisions and shift it to
> the 1998 pay decision is unsound. It would shift intent from one
> act (the act that consummates the discriminatory employment
> practice) to a later act that was not performed with bias or
> discriminatory motive. The effect of this shift would be to impose
> liability in the absence of the requisite intent.

He stressed the importance of repose because of the potential harm that
"tardy lawsuits" could bring to employers:

> Ledbetter's claims of sex discrimination turned principally on
> the misconduct of a single Goodyear supervisor, who, Ledbetter
> testified, retaliated against her when she rejected his sexual
> advances during the early 1980's, and did so again in the mid-
> 1990's when he falsified deficiency reports about her work. His
> misconduct, Ledbetter argues, was "a principal basis for [her]
> performance evaluation in 1997." Yet, by the time of trial, this
> supervisor had died and therefore could not testify. A timely
> charge might have permitted his evidence to be weighed
> contemporaneously.

Justice Ginsburg wrote a strong dissent and read it from the bench.
She argued that:

> [E]ach paycheck that offers a woman less pay than a similarly
> situated man because of her sex is a separate violation of Title
> VII with its own limitations period, regardless of whether the
> paycheck simply implements a prior discriminatory decision
> made outside the limitations period . . . Pay disparities, of the
> kind Ledbetter experienced, have a closer kinship to hostile
> work environment claims than to charges of a single episode of
> discrimination. Ledbetter's claim rested not on one particular
> paycheck, but on the "cumulative effect of individual acts." * * *
> This is not the first time the Court has ordered a cramped
> interpretation of Title VII, incompatible with the statute's broad
> remedial purpose. Once again, the ball is in Congress' court. As
> in 1991, the Legislature may act to correct this Court's
> parsimonious reading of Title VII.

The FPA implemented the kind of legislative override that Justice
Ginsburg predicted. While it only dealt with the procedural issue of
statute of limitations, some scholars think that the FPA has the potential
to change radically the landscape for litigating claims under Title VII and
other antidiscrimination laws.

NOTE

The Texas Supreme Court held that since the Texas Legislature has enacted nothing comparable to the Lily Ledbetter Act, a plaintiff suing pursuant to the Texas Commission on Human Rights Act, modeled after Title VII, must file a claim within 180 days of the date the employee learns what his or her pay will be. Prairie View A&M University v. Chatha, 381 S.W.3d 500 (Tex. 2012). Chief Justice Jefferson, dissenting, said: "This [decision] creates innumerable problems, not the least of which are the elimination of equitable defenses and a divergence between the Act and the statute it was enacted to promote. . . . I would hold that the 180-day period . . . is not a statutory prerequisite to suit."

Charles A. Sullivan, Raising the Dead?: The Lilly Ledbetter Fair Pay Act

84 Tulane L. Rev. 499 (2010).

* * *

President Obama's signing of the Lilly Ledbetter Fair Pay Act marked an important moment for antidiscrimination law and for the relationship between Court and Congress in their ongoing tug of war over the meaning of civil rights statutes. * * * The new statute seems likely to have wide-ranging effects with regard to the timeliness of suits under all the modern antidiscrimination laws. * * *

A. An Overview of the Amendment

The Lilly Ledbetter Fair Pay Act of 2009 amends Title VII to provide:

an unlawful employment practice occurs, with respect to discrimination in compensation in violation of this title, when a discriminatory compensation decision or other practice is adopted, when an individual becomes subject to a discriminatory compensation decision or other practice, or when an individual is affected by application of a discriminatory compensation decision or other practice, including each time wages, benefits, or other compensation is paid, resulting in whole or in part from such a decision or other practice.

The LLFPA similarly amended the other antidiscrimination laws, including the ADEA and ADA. The effect on all these statutes is to codify a version of the "paycheck" rule—a plaintiff who suffers discrimination in compensation can file a timely charge, inter alia, within 180/300 days of receiving a paycheck that is lower than it would have been but for the discrimination. Unlike lower court authorities, however, the FPA appears to allow suit for any discriminatory adverse employment action with an effect on compensation, not merely attacks on compensation decisions per se.

However, the LLFPA makes a limited accommodation to employer interests by an express limit on back pay recovery to no more than two years prior to the filing of a charge, although even that provision is somewhat odd. Title VII has so limited recovery since its enactment in 1964. Indeed, the two year limit has been argued to be the strongest textual basis for rejecting the entire notice of decision rule. In any event, the limitation prevents the LLFPA from imposing potentially enormous liabilities, although the calculation of recovery back to two years before the charge was filed will reflect the ripple effects of discrimination over the years. For example, and using Justice Alito's hypothetical, a plaintiff who was discriminatorily denied a $1,000 raise 20 years before her charge is filed, and assuming a 3% cost of living increase and no further discrimination, would have lost $26,870.37 at the point she filed her charge. She would, however, be entitled only to the last two years' lost backpay, a total of $3,455.94 (in addition, of course, to any further backpay lost from the time of filing to the date of judgment). Thus, the vast majority of plaintiff's lost wages ($23,414.43) is not recoverable even under the new Act.

* * *

B.   Discrimination in Compensation

At first glance, the Lilly Ledbetter Fair Pay Act seems to consign to the scrap heap the Supreme Court's prior timeliness jurisprudence. Clearly, compensation decisions with present consequences on pay are actionable. Some have suggested that the amendment reaches beyond compensation decisions to all acts of discrimination because of the references to "other practices." However, a careful reading of the language suggests a more limited, but still broad, interpretation: the actionable discrimination must be "with respect to discrimination in compensation in violation of this title," although such discrimination may be "a discriminatory compensation decision or other practice." In other words, as long as it results in "discrimination in compensation," the statute on its face reaches any employer "practice," which is the word Title VII uses to describe any violation of its prohibitions. Thus, for example, a denial of promotion is actionable to the extent, as will almost always be the case, it results in lower compensation. In short, any policy that effects compensation is within the expanded FPA notion of "occurrence," but any policy that does not is not.

An example of the potential reach of the statute can be drawn from Jackson v. City of Chicago [552 F.3d 619 (7th Cir. 2009)], where promotions had been denied because the plaintiff lacked skills due to the discriminatory denial of training opportunities. Applying pre-FPA law, the Seventh Circuit held that plaintiff had no cause of action; the promotion denials, as such, were nondiscriminatory and the denial of training was time-barred. In the wake of the Fair Pay Act, ultimate compensation consequences would seem to require the claim to be revived.

Undoubtedly, employers will argue for a more limited reading. Looking to Justice Ginsburg's dissent, they may claim that the Act reaches only practices that, like the raises denied Ms. Ledbetter, were either or both (1) not apparently discriminatory at the time, perhaps because the employee lacked any basis to compare her treatment with that of others; (2) relatively insignificant viewed individually but cumulatively ripening over time into a substantial disadvantage.

Even stating the argument this way shows its flaw: it is impossible to reconcile either of these complicated concepts with the straightforward statutory language. Justice Ginsburg's dissent may have been the catalyst for the Fair Pay Act, but it appears that Congress chose not to limit its legislative fix to the situation that was at issue in the Ledbetter case. Nor is that unusual. As Justice Scalia reminded us in another Title VII case, "statutory prohibitions often go beyond the principal evil to cover reasonably comparable evils, and it is ultimately the provisions of our laws rather than the principal concerns of our legislators by which we are governed." Further, Justice Alito wrote firmly in Ledbetter, "We apply the statute as written," and any attempt to find limiting principles in the legislative history of the Act or the Ginsburg dissent that triggered it would not only require him and the other justices in the majority to abandon their textualist proclivities but it would also likely be futile.

To the extent the legislative history bears on the question, it supports a broad view of "other practices." There are no committee reports for the 2009 version of the act, so no help can be found there, but House Report for the 2007 version, which is framed identically to the enacted statute, suggests a broad reading. Further, there were floor debates on the 2009 debates which provide a number of indications of a broad approach. Ironically, in one of the debates, then Republican Senator Specter of Pennsylvania offered a limiting amendment eliminating the "other practices" language to avoid a parade of horribles while predicting that its eventual defeat (which in fact occurred) would result in "lawyers * * * citing this argument to say, well, if the amendment offered by Arlen Specter was defeated, it must mean that all of those other practices are included, and then some, which is not my intent." The Democratic response was basically that the language was necessary to reverse Ledbetter.

This suggests that any limitation on the sweep of the Fair Pay Act must come from the word "compensation," not the word "practice." But the courts have been expansive in their approach to similar terms under Title VII, and the Fair Pay Act itself suggests a broad view by speaking of "each time wages, benefits, or other compensation is paid." The one possible limitation found in the language of the statute is § 2(4), which, as part of Congress' findings, states, "[n]othing in this Act is intended to change current law treatment of when pension distributions are considered paid." This language is cryptic. It does not undercut the reality that pension contributions are compensation, and the discrimination questions for pension benefits in an era of defined contribution plans are much more likely to be contribution questions than distribution questions.

* * *

NOTE

A new California law prohibits employers from paying different wages to employees who do "substantially similar work." The law also prohibits retaliation against employees who inquire about their colleagues' salaries. The California law is a version of the Paycheck Fairness Act that the U.S. Congress declined to enact in 2014. Cal. Lab. Code § 1197.5 (2016).

In 2016, Massachusetts became the first state to amend their equal pay laws by prohibiting employers from inquiring about an applicant's current or previous salary. In 2017, Philadelphia became the first city to implement laws with similar prohibitions, followed by the city of New York. The Massachusetts amendment also follows several other states in providing employees the right to discuss their salary with other employees, free from retaliation by the employer. Additionally, Massachusetts has struck out any definition of "Woman" (previously "a female 18 or older"), and uses the term "gender" in regard to pay discrimination, with no mention of "male" or "female." While some states' equal pay acts continue to prohibit wage discrepancy between men and women, or to include phrases such as "the opposite gender," the use of non-binary terms has increased as further laws are being passed.

CHAPTER 6

HEALTH BENEFITS

A. INTRODUCTION

For many Americans with employment-based health care, the debate over access to health care, consumer choice of health care providers, and health care quality is in many respects a debate about the role of employers in funding, controlling access to, administering, and containing the costs of employer-sponsored health insurance. The modest role originally assumed by some employers during World War II has dramatically expanded in scope and cost. In 2013, 158 million nonelderly Americans had health coverage through an employer-sponsored group health plan.

The magnitude of the benefit obligations of employers is staggering and continues to grow. Health insurance is the fastest growing fringe benefit expense for employers. As of 2013, the average annual cost of covering a family of four was approximately $16,000. Wage levels have remained virtually unchanged for over two decades, with almost all of the increased compensation costs going to health benefits. Thus, in a real sense, supposedly employer-funded health insurance is really employer- and employee-funded health insurance.

The Patient Protection and Affordable Care Act of 2010 (ACA) made sweeping reforms to the U.S. health care system. The law builds upon the system of employer-sponsored health insurance and is phased-in over a period of eight years. Therefore, this chapter contains materials reflecting the statutory and case law applicable today and the new requirements of tomorrow.

This chapter considers in some detail the Employee Retirement Income Security Act (ERISA) and its effect on health benefits. It also considers discrimination in benefits and the consequences for employers of changing societal norms. This chapter focuses on an area of employment law that is front-page news on a daily basis, and that will continue to be extremely important for the foreseeable future.

A Brief History of the Employer Role in Health Care Finance

In the United States today, employers play a vital role in sponsoring, subsidizing, and administering health benefit plans, but it was not always this way. Medicine did not become a science-based profession until the twentieth century. In the first half of the twentieth century, medicine was practiced largely by physicians (mostly generalists) who worked alone and were paid in cash for their services. Hospitals were usually single entities, as opposed to chains, and either publicly owned or not-for-profit (often owned by religious entities). The pharmaceutical industry was small, commercial health insurance nonexistent, and employers' involvement in health care consisted almost exclusively of providing medical examinations before hiring to determine fitness for duty and supplying first aid after an injury on the job.

In 1929, to ensure essential operating capital, the American Hospital Association launched a fixed premium, community-rated, nonprofit insurance system for hospital expenses called Blue Cross. When this social insurance system proved successful, Blue Shield plans were initiated in the 1940s by physicians' associations to cover the cost of medical services. Although Theodore Roosevelt had unsuccessfully campaigned for a national health system in 1912 and European countries beginning with Germany had adopted national health insurance plans, the United States lagged behind. During the New Deal, President Franklin Roosevelt declined to advocate for a larger federal government role in health care, choosing to focus on other economic and social priorities. The private sector, particularly employers, would fill the vacuum.

The greatest impetus for expanding the role of employers in health benefits was World War II. With a decreased supply of available labor and a scarcity of consumer goods during the war, to prevent inflation the federal government enacted wage and price controls. Employers were not permitted to increase the salaries of workers, but they were permitted to increase the level of benefits. Consequently, employers, especially large, unionized employers, began offering health benefits, beginning with hospitalization coverage. After the war, coverage expanded to physician fees, prescription drugs, dependent coverage, retiree coverage, and other benefits. An especially important aspect of these benefits is that they were and still are not subject to income tax. Thus, a dollar of health benefits is worth more to an employee than a dollar in wages.

The post-war industrial and baby booms helped fuel a boom in health insurance as well. By the mid-1950s, 45 percent of the population had hospital insurance; coverage soared to 77 percent by 1963. By 1963, more than half the population had coverage for regular medical expenses, and almost one-fourth had major medical insurance. Today, there are over 850 health insurance companies in the United States.

The next major piece of the health finance puzzle was put into place in 1965 with the enactment of Medicare and Medicaid. These federal government programs for the elderly and indigent had a major effect on the rest of the health care system. By moving a population of the highest cost users of health care to the government-funded rolls, health insurance premiums were reduced for the rest of the insured population. Medicare and Medicaid also expanded the market of regular consumers of health care, thereby supporting greater concentration of health care entities, greater specialization of health professionals, and increased demand for pharmaceutical and other health care products.

ERISA

The Employee Retirement Income Security Act of 1974 (ERISA), 29 U.S.C. §§ 1001–1461, is the primary federal law of employee benefits. Although the law was enacted mainly to combat abuses in the administration and investment of private pensions, ERISA also applies to other employer-sponsored or employer-provided benefits. ERISA does not require employers to provide pensions or any other benefits, but if they do, the benefit plan must satisfy minimum standards to protect employees and other beneficiaries.

There are two main types of benefit plans under ERISA. First, pension benefit plans are covered in Chapter 13. Second, "welfare benefit plans" are broadly defined under ERISA and include the following: medical, surgical, or hospital care or benefits; benefits in the event of sickness, accident, disability, death, or unemployment; vacation benefits; apprenticeship or training programs; day care centers; scholarship funds; prepaid legal services; and other benefits allowed under section 302(c) of the Labor-Management Relations Act.

ERISA has been especially important to large employers whose employees often work in numerous states. ERISA provides that employers with welfare plans regulated by the Department of Labor do not have to comply with state laws regulating health insurance policies sold in the state. The ERISA preemption provision has been a source of much important case law covered later in the chapter. When health reform legislation was enacted in 2010 (discussed below), the basic structure and legal effect of ERISA was retained.

ERISA has been amended several times. Two of the most important amendments are the Comprehensive Omnibus Budget Reconciliation Act of 1985 (COBRA) and the Health Insurance Portability and Accountability Act of 1996 (HIPAA). Both of these laws are discussed below in this introductory text. ERISA case law is discussed in sections B and C of this chapter.

COBRA

The Comprehensive Omnibus Budget Reconciliation Act of 1985 (COBRA), 29 U.S.C. §§ 1161–1168, requires employers with 20 or more employees that offer health benefits to offer continued coverage to former employees, their spouses, and dependent children for 18 or 36 months or until coverage begins under another plan. Employers can charge no more than 102 percent of the average cost to the employer of providing coverage to all of its employees.

COBRA obligations are triggered by a "qualifying event," which includes termination for any reason other than discharge for "gross misconduct" or a reduction of hours. The term "gross misconduct" is not defined in the statute, and some courts have looked to interpretations of the term under state unemployment insurance laws. The length of coverage depends on the qualifying event. For example, the normal period of 18 months is extended to 36 months upon the death of the employee, divorce or separation, loss of dependent child status, or eligibility for Medicare. Coverage offered under COBRA must be identical to the coverage available to the beneficiary immediately before the qualifying event. Employers must provide employees with notice of their COBRA rights in accordance with statutory notice provisions.

According to provisions of the ACA (discussed below), the importance of COBRA was supposed to end in 2014. In that year, employers with 50 or more employees were to be subject to a tax if they did not offer health benefits to their full-time employees; individuals were required to purchase coverage (which may be subsidized by the government, depending on income) or pay a tax penalty; and health exchanges were to be established in all states. As a result, instead of temporary coverage, workers who no longer qualify for employer-sponsored health benefits will have more flexibility and greater security in their health coverage. The employer mandate, scheduled to begin on January 1, 2014, was postponed until January 1, 2015, and for employers with 51–100 employees, it was postponed until January 1, 2016. http://www.treasury.gov/connect/blog/Pages/Continuing-to-Implement-the-ACA-in-a-Careful-Thoughtful-Manner-.aspx. The operation of health exchanges is also discussed below.

HIPAA

The Health Insurance Portability and Accountability Act of 1996 (HIPAA) 42 U.S.C. § 300gg et seq., applies to employer-based group health plans (ERISA qualified employee welfare plans) and commercially issued, employment-based, group health insurance (previously the exclusive subject of state insurance regulation). HIPAA curtails the use of exclusions for preexisting conditions. Employers and insurers may apply a maximum, one-time 12-month exclusion to illnesses that were diagnosed or treated within the six months prior to enrollment, but individuals must be given a credit for time they were covered under another plan. Therefore, an individual with at least one year's continuous coverage who changes jobs is eligible immediately for health benefits. No exclusions at all may be applied for pregnancy, newborns, or adopted children. Genetic information may not be treated as a preexisting condition in the absence of a diagnosis of the condition and therefore there may be no exclusions for genetic predisposition.

An individual who is leaving a group health plan must first use COBRA continuation coverage. Thereafter, the individual is eligible for individual insurance without an exclusion for preexisting conditions. Although the individual insurance is "guaranteed issue," there is no limitation on the premiums that may be charged. This provision has been superseded by the ACA.

Individuals in a group health plan may not be subject to discrimination based on health status in their eligibility, enrollment, or premium contributions. Individuals cannot be charged higher premiums than other "similarly situated individuals," which refers to full-time/part-time status or geographic location. An insurer that issues group health plans to the small employer market must accept all applying small employers and all eligible employees. The insurer also must renew insurance coverage to small and large employers.

The law is not comprehensive. It does not apply to individuals who are unemployed. It does not require that employers provide health insurance coverage or any specific benefits package. Employers may place restrictions or limitations on the amount, level, or nature of the benefits. There are no restrictions on the amount an insurer may charge an employer or the premiums that may be charged employees. These provisions also have been superseded by the ACA.

HIPAA prohibits group health plans and health insurers connected with group health plans from using an individual's health history or risk factors in denying eligibility or setting individual premiums. By regulation, there also can be no discrimination because of an individual's participation in risky activities, such as motorcycling, snowmobiling, all-terrain vehicle riding, horseback riding, and skiing. A plan may exclude coverage for some types of conditions resulting from some risky activities (e.g., alligator wrestling). See Interim Rules for Nondiscrimination in Health Coverage in the Group Health Market, 66 Fed. Reg. 1378 (2001).

Perhaps the most notorious part of HIPAA is its Privacy Rule, 45 C.F.R. Parts 160, 164. Because the Privacy Rule is linked to provisions in HIPAA that regulate the electronic transfer of health claims information, it applies only to three classes of covered entities involved in the health claims process: health providers, health plans, and health clearinghouses (which standardize formats for billing), and as of 2013, their business associates. Employers are not considered covered entities, but employer benefit plans are covered entities. Consequently, employers are required to build a "fire wall" between employee health benefit information (e.g., health claims) and other employment records. Employer health plans also have a responsibility to safeguard the privacy and security of personally identifiable health information through a variety of measures spelled out in the Privacy Rule and the HIPAA Security Rule, 45 C.F.R. Parts 160, 162, 164.

Patient Protection and Affordable Care Act of 2010

Two contentious and complicated laws were enacted in early 2010 to reform the American health care system. On March 30, 2010, President Barack Obama signed the Health Care and Education Reconciliation Act, P.L. 111–152, also known as the "Reconciliation Act," making changes to the Patient Protection and Affordable Care Act, P.L. 111–148, also known as "ACA" and the "Affordable Care Act," passed one week earlier. The Acts collectively make numerous changes to existing laws and add a variety of new programs in an effort to expand access to health care, improve quality, prohibit discriminatory practices by insurers, and reduce costs. The legislation was designed to augment rather than supplant employer-based group health plans, and in several ways the new laws attempt to promote and support the role of employers in health care finance.

President Obama signing into law the Patient Protection and
Affordable Care Act of 2010, March 23, 2010.

The health reform law is a famously long and complicated piece of legislation. The following discussion focuses on a selection of key issues of relevance to employers and employees.

EMPLOYER RESPONSIBILITIES

Large Employer Penalty. Under the new laws, employers are not required to provide health insurance coverage; however, supposedly beginning in 2014, but extended now through 2020 (for employers with 51–100 employees), employers that do not offer health insurance to their employees will be penalized. Section 1513 of the ACA provides that "applicable large employers" that do not offer minimum essential health coverage under an eligible employer-sponsored plan, and that have at least one full-time employee who enrolls in a plan on the state health exchange using a federal premium tax credit or costsharing reduction, will be liable for a penalty. This penalty is also known as the "play-or-pay" mandate and the "free rider penalty." ACA § 1513 imposes a penalty in the amount of $2,000 on large employers that do not offer minimum essential health coverage each year (or $166.67 for each month the employer does not provide a plan), multiplied by the number of full-time employees. The first 30 employees do not count towards the penalty.

An "applicable large employer" is defined as an employer with at least 50 full-time employees on business days during the preceding calendar year. A "full-time employee" is defined as an employee who works an average of at least 30 hours per week. "Essential health benefits" includes the following non-comprehensive list of features:

(A) Ambulatory patient services;

(B) Emergency services;

(C) Hospitalization;

(D) Maternity and newborn care;

(E) Mental health and substance use disorder services, including behavioral health treatment;

(F) Prescription drugs;

(G) Rehabilitative and habilitative services and devices;

(H) Laboratory services;

(I) Preventive and wellness services and chronic disease management;

and

(J) Pediatric services, including oral and vision care.

The Department of Health and Human Services (HHS) issued regulations in 2012 holding that the ACA provision requiring health plans to cover "preventive health services without cost sharing," 42 U.S.C. § 300gg–13(a)(4), included all FDA-approved contraceptive methods and sterilization procedures, including the "morning-after pill." 77 Fed. Reg. 8725 (2012). There is a "religious employers" exemption, 45 C.F.R. § 147.130(a)(1)(iv)(A)–(B), but the exemption does not apply to for-profit businesses. In Burwell v. Hobby Lobby, 134 S.Ct. 2751 (2014), the Supreme Court, five-to-four, held that "closely held," for-profit companies run on religious principles can challenge government actions pursuant to the Religious Freedom Restoration Act and that such companies can seek an exemption from the birth control mandate of the ACA. The Obama Administration previously had provided an accommodation to permit employees of religious-affiliated nonprofits to obtain insurance coverage without direct employer involvement, by authorizing insurers to provide the coverage directly. It is likely that this provision will be extended to religiously oriented, for-profit companies. Notwithstanding the decision in *Hobby Lobby*, laws in 28 states provide that health insurance policies covering prescription drugs are required to cover all FDA-approved contraceptive drugs and devices. Most recently, the Supreme Court accepted certiorari in yet another contraceptive case in 2020. In Trump v. Pennsylvania, the issue is whether the birth control mandate of the ACA violates religious freedom laws and whether proposed exemptions pushed by the Trump administration that have so far been blocked by lower courts can stand. The ACLU and other groups say the religious exemptions amount to discrimination. They also see it as an attack on access to reproductive choice.

Large employers that offer coverage described above but whose coverage is not "affordable" or whose coverage does not provide a certain value must pay an additional penalty. To be "affordable" the premium of the employer-sponsored plan must cost less than 9.5% of the employee's household income. The plan must also provide a minimum value of at least 60% of the coverage (i.e., the employer's share must constitute 60% of the employee's covered medical expenses). If the large employer does not meet either of these minimum requirements of coverage, the employer will be liable for a penalty in the amount of $3,000 per year for each full-time employee (or $250 each month that the employer offers coverage below these levels). ACA § 1513(c)(2) provides a limitation on this penalty, which cannot exceed $2,000 per full-time employee per year (or $166.67 for each month), and the first 30 employees will not count towards the penalty.

Exempt from these penalties are large employers with seasonal workers and large employers that have over 50 full-time employees for only 120 days or less out of the calendar year, and the employees in excess of the 50 employees during that 120-day period are seasonal workers. A "seasonal worker" is defined as a "worker who performs labor or services on a seasonal basis as defined by the Secretary of Labor," and retail workers employed exclusively during holiday seasons.

Automatic Enrollment. The ACA amended the Fair Labor Standards Act (FLSA) to impose another duty on larger employers. Employers with more than 200 full-time employees and offer group health plans are required to enroll automatically new full-time employees in a health benefits plan. They are also required to continue the enrollment of current employees. On November 2, 2015, the Bipartisan Budget Act of 2015 was enacted which, among other things, repealed the automatic enrollment requirement.

Lifetime and Annual Limits. There is a prohibition on lifetime limits on the dollar value of benefits, and annual limits may only be restricted to the dollar value of "essential health benefits" (effective six months after enactment, or September 23, 2010). Beginning in 2014, annual limits are prohibited altogether.

Rescissions. There is a prohibition on rescissions of coverage for enrollees once they are covered except in cases where the current enrollee has committed fraud or made an intentional misrepresentation of material fact as prohibited by the terms of the plan or coverage (effective six months after enactment).

Coverage of Dependents. Individual and group health plans that provide coverage to dependents must continue to make coverage available to adult dependents up to age 26, regardless of marriage status (effective six months after enactment).

Coverage of Individuals with Preexisting Conditions. The Public Health Service Act is amended to prohibit exclusions with respect to children up to age 18 with preexisting conditions (effective six months after enactment). The prohibition with respect to preexisting conditions was extended to adults beginning in 2014.

Appeals Process. An internal and external appeals process must be established for appeals of coverage determinations and claims. The plan must allow an enrollee to review his or her file, present evidence and testimony, and receive continued coverage pending the outcome of the appeals process. Notice of the available internal and external processes must be given to enrollees (effective six months after enactment). The internal process and external process both must meet requirements under certain state and/or federal law, and both processes must be updated with any new standards published by the Secretary of HHS.

Nondiscrimination. The ACA has a number of provisions designed to prohibit discrimination, shaping rules ranging from enrollment eligibility to marketing. Insurers are prohibited from having eligibility rules for enrollment based on health status, medical condition (including physical or mental illnesses) or medical history, claims experience, receipt of health care, genetic information, disability, evidence of insurability, or any factor determined appropriate by HHS (effective 2014). In addition, there is a prohibition on eligibility rules based on wages, or rules that otherwise have the effect of discriminating in favor of higher wage employees (effective six months after enactment). Insurers are also prohibited from utilizing discriminatory premium rates. Premium rates may only vary based only on the following factors: family composition, age, tobacco use, and geographic area. No rating variation is allowed based on health, race, or gender (effective 2014). Insurers may not employ marketing practices that have the effect of discouraging enrollment by individuals with significant health needs.

Immigrants. In October 2019, President Trump issued a proclamation that will deny visas to immigrants who cannot prove they will obtain health insurance or can cover medical costs. This proclamation will require immigrants to prove they will either obtain health insurance within 30 days of entering the country or prove they are able to cover "reasonably foreseeable" medical costs. Those who do not meet the requirement will be denied visas. Immigrants will also be denied a visa if they use the Affordable Care Act's subsidies to obtain insurance.

INDIVIDUAL RESPONSIBILITY

Concurrent with the employer's obligations under the ACA, beginning in 2014, individuals are required to maintain minimal essential health care coverage for themselves and their dependents. Individuals who fail to maintain such coverage were subject initially to a penalty under the ACA to be included in their tax return. That provisions is currently being litigated as to its constitutionality. The penalty will be either a percentage of the individual's household income, or a flat dollar amount for each year the individual fails to maintain coverage, whichever is greater.

The new law exempts certain individuals from coverage, including individuals who object to health care coverage on religious grounds, who are not lawfully present in the United States, or who are incarcerated. The new law also provides exceptions from the penalty for certain low income individuals, including individuals who cannot afford coverage (defined as individuals whose required contribution for coverage would exceed 8% of household income for the taxable year) and individuals whose income is less than 100% of the federal poverty line, members of Indian tribes, and individuals who suffer hardship.

Beginning in 2014, individuals were required to maintain minimal essential health care coverage for themselves and their dependents. Individuals who failed to maintain such coverage were subject to a penalty to be included in their tax return. The penalty was to be either a percentage of the individual's household income or a flat dollar amount for each year the individual failed to maintain coverage, whichever was greater.

This so-called "individual mandate" exempted certain individuals from coverage, including individuals who object to health care coverage on religious grounds, who were not lawfully present in the United States, or who were incarcerated. The law also provided exceptions to the penalty for certain low income individuals, including individuals who could not afford coverage and individuals whose income was less than 100% of the federal poverty level, members of Indian tribes, and individuals who suffered hardship.

Congress completely repealed the financial penalties associated with the individual mandate of the ACA as part of a comprehensive tax reform package in December 2017, and this law went into effect January 1, 2019. It is unclear, at this time, how significant an impact this loss of members from the health insurance risk pool will have on the overall working of the ACA or how many more people will now end up without health insurance. The Congressional Budget Office has predicted that the loss of the individual mandate will lead to 4 million people deciding to forgo insurance in 2019 and 13 million people dropping coverage by 2027. Another possible consequence is that the repeal will raise healthcare insurance premiums and cause the ACA's health insurance exchanges (discussed below) to fall part.

An additional blow to the individual mandate was struck by a district court in Texas in December 2018 when it held that the ACA is unconstitutional because the 2017 GOP tax law phased out the individual mandate penalty. With no fine for those who refuse to buy insurance, the court found that the mandate is now unconstitutional, and since it's a central part of the law, so is the entire ACA. The Fifth Circuit Court of Appeals, 2–1, in December of 2019 then affirmed the holding on the unconstitutionality of the individual mandate and remanded the case back to the district court to see if the rest of the ACA could be saved. The U.S. Supreme Court refused to expedite an appeal of the Fifth Circuit decision in January 2020, and the case is now back in front of the original district court for further consideration of the decision's impact on the ACA as a whole.

All that being said, some individuals will still have to pay penalties for not carrying insurance, at least at the state level. New Jersey, the District of Columbia, and Massachusetts impose penalties for not maintaining insurance. Vermont intends to jump on the bandwagon in 2020 as the result of legislation passed in 2018. Lawmakers in Rhode Island voted to adopt a similar provision in July 2019, also effective January 1, 2020.

HEALTH EXCHANGES

Under the ACA, by January 1, 2014, states were required to establish an "American Health Benefit Exchange" or state health exchange, where individuals who do not have coverage under their employer can purchase qualified health plans. As of 2014, there are state exchanges in sixteen states and the District of Columbia. In the remaining states individuals can purchase insurance through the federal exchange. Individuals with incomes below 400% of the federal poverty level may qualify for reduced premiums via tax credits. Those making below 250% of the federal poverty level may qualify for premium subsidies. Those making below 138% of the federal poverty level may qualify for Medicaid if their state has implemented Medicaid expansion.

The U.S. Supreme Court agreed to hear a new case on whether insurance companies are due health care subsidies from the administration in June 2019. In the consolidated cases of Maine Community Health Options v. U.S., Moda Health Plan v. U.S., Land of Lincoln Mutual Health Insurance Co. v. U.S., the Court hear argument in December 2019 a challenge from health insurers who argue the federal government owes them hefty Obamacare payments, stoking the possibility the Trump administration could be forced to pay out billions of dollars for a law it's tried to dismantle. More specifically, the Court will decide whether insurers are due money from an Obamacare program helping companies that attracted sick and expensive customers in the early years of the law's insurance marketplaces (so-called "risk corridor programs"). A decision is expected by the summer of 2020.

TIMELINE

The provisions of the laws are being phased in between 2010 and 2018. The following implementation timeline includes some selected provisions affecting employers and employees.

2010

- *Eliminating Lifetime Limits.* Effective six months after enactment, lifetime limits on benefits are prohibited.

- *Regulating Use of Lifetime and Annual Limits.* Effective six months after enactment and pursuant to regulations issued by the Secretary of HHS, all employer-sponsored plans are prohibited in their use of lifetime limits and restricted in their use of annual limits. When exchanges became operational in 2014, the use of annual limits were prohibited completely.

- *Coverage of Dependents.* Effective six months after enactment, group health plans providing dependent coverage for children must make coverage available until the child becomes 26 years of age. In addition, individual and group health plans are prohibited from excluding children on the basis of a preexisting condition.

- *Preexisting Conditions.* Individual and group health plans are prohibited from excluding children up to age 18 on the basis of a preexisting condition. Exclusion on the basis of preexisting conditions was extended to adults in 2014.

- *Rescission.* Effective six months after enactment, individual and group health plans are prohibited from rescinding coverage, except in cases of fraud or intentional misrepresentation of material fact.

2011

- *Disclosure of Health Benefits.* Effective January 1, 2011, employers are required to disclose on Form W-2 the value of the benefit provided for health insurance coverage.

2013

- *Flexible Savings Accounts.* The amount of employee contributions to flexible health savings accounts was reduced to $2,500, indexed to the consumer price index in future years. This provision has been postponed until 2015 or 2016 (for employers with 51–100 employees).

2014

- *Employer Mandate.* Employers with 50 or more employees that do not offer health benefits to their full-time employees are subject to a $2000 per employee tax penalty.

- *Automatic Enrollment.* This provisions has been eliminated as of 2015.

- *Health Exchanges.* Health exchanges are established to provide access to health insurance at competitive rates; individuals with incomes up to 400% of the poverty level will be eligible for subsidies, as well as eligible small employers.

- *Waiting Periods.* Individual and group health plans may not impose waiting periods exceeding 90 days.

2018

• *High Cost Plan Excise Tax.* Originally, an excise tax of 40% was to be imposed on the amount of the premium costs in excess of $10,200 for individuals and $27,500 for families. The so-called "Cadillac Tax" was originally scheduled to become effective in 2018, but as of December 20, 2019, the Cadillac Tax was completely eliminated by the Setting Every Community Up for Retirement Enhancement (Secure) Act.

• *Association Health Plans (AHPs).* On June 21, 2018, the U.S. Department of Labor released a final rule, "Definition of 'Employer' Under Section 3(5) of ERISA—Association Health Plans," 83 Fed. Reg. 28912 (June 21, 2018). The AHP Final Rule expands the universe of arrangements that can qualify as an AHP for purposes of ERISA and also applies large group treatment to qualifying AHP coverage. The AHP Final Rule achieves this by broadening the criteria under ERISA for determining when employers may join together in an association that is treated as the ERISA "employer" of a single group health plan and by allowing certain self-employed persons to be treated as employers under appropriate circumstances.

In March 2019, the expansion of the commonality requirement to allow employers in similar geographical areas to pool health insurance was rejected by being beyond the scope of the DOL's authority by the D.C. District Court in New York v. U.S. Department of Labor, 363 F. Supp. 3d 109 (D. D.C. 2019). In this vein, the Court stated, "that the geography standard under the Final Rule fails to account in any way for employers' commonality of interest. This standard effectively eviscerates the genuine commonality of interest required under ERISA, thereby expanding the scope of the statute beyond what ERISA intended." Id. at 134. That case involved the final rule by DOL instituting AHPs. This AHP case is now pending on appeal in front of the D.C. Circuit as this edition of the book goes to press in 2020.

The Affordable Care Act (ACA) has been subject to several judicial challenges alleging the statute is unconstitutional. The cases were consolidated in a much-anticipated Supreme Court decision in June 2012. In National Federation of Independent Business v. Sebelius, 567 U.S. 519 (2012), the Supreme Court, five-to-four, in an opinion by Chief Justice Roberts, rejected challenges to the constitutionality of the ACA. There were two main issues. First, the challengers asserted that the individual mandate is not a valid exercise of congressional power under the Commerce Clause. Although a majority of the Court agreed that the Commerce Clause did not permit regulation of individuals who were doing nothing (i.e., not buying health insurance), a majority held that the individual mandate was a legitimate exercise of Congress' taxing power. Second, a majority of the Court held that the Medicaid expansion violates the Spending Clause of the Constitution by threatening states with the loss of their existing Medicaid funding if they decline to participate in the expansion. Nevertheless, the Court held that the constitutional violation is fully remedied by precluding the Secretary of Health and Human Services from withdrawing current Medicaid funding from any state electing not to participate in the expansion. Under the ACA states are eligible for 100 percent federal funding for three years to increase Medicaid eligibility to individuals with incomes below 138 percent of the federal poverty level ($30,657 for a family of four). After three years the federal payment drops to 90 percent.

Although the specific provisions applicable to employers were not the basis of the challenges to the ACA, employers certainly were interested in the outcome of the case. The effect of the Court's decision is to confirm the obligations of employers, including reporting of the value of health coverage on employees' Form W-2 (beginning 2013), limiting to $2,500 the amount of employer contributions to employees' flexible health care spending accounts (beginning 2013), and the employer mandate. The mandate for all employers, originally scheduled to take effect on January 1, 2014, was delayed until January 1, 2015. The mandate for mid-size employers (51–100 employees) was delayed until January 1, 2016.

Another Supreme Court case challenging the legality of the ACA is King v. Burwell, 135 S.Ct. 2480 (2015). The plaintiffs lived in Virginia, a state that has not created a state exchange and whose residents therefore used the federal exchange to purchase individual health insurance. The plaintiffs argued that there was no statutory basis for the IRS to give tax credits for use on the federal exchange because section 36B of the ACA only describes tax credits for exchanges "established by the State." The Supreme Court, 6–3, rejected the plaintiffs' argument. In an opinion by Chief Justice Roberts, the Court held that the challenged portion of the text needs to be considered in light of the ACA's context and structure. The majority noted that the lack of a state *and* federal exchange in any state would deny tax credits and health coverage, thereby threatening the basic goals of the law.

> Congress passed the Affordable Care Act to improve health insurance markets, not to destroy them. If at all possible, we must interpret the Act in a way that is consistent with the former, and avoids the latter. Section 36B can fairly be read consistent with what we see as Congress's plan, and that is the reading we adopt.

135 S.Ct. at 2496. In a characteristically animated dissent, Justice Scalia wrote:

> The Act that Congress passed makes tax credits available only on an "Exchange established by the State." This Court, however, concludes that this limitation would prevent the rest of the Act from working as well as hoped. So it rewrites the law to make tax credits available everywhere. We should start calling this law SCOTUScare.

135 S.Ct. at 2506.

In Zubik v. Burwell, 136 S.Ct. 444 (2016), nonprofit organizations that provide health insurance to their employees challenged a regulation promulgated to implement the ACA requiring them to provide certain contraceptive services as part of their health plans unless they submit a form either to their insurer or to the federal government indicating that they object on religious grounds. The organizations alleged that submitting the notice substantially burdens the exercise of their religion in violation of the Religious Freedom Restoration Act of 1993, 42 U.S.C. § 2000bb et seq. In a per curiam opinion, the Court vacated decisions of the lower courts and remanded the case to allow the parties to resolve the issues themselves. Many commentators believed that this action was to avoid a four-to-four split by the justices caused by the death of Justice Scalia.

Although not technically an employee benefits case, the public accommodations case, Masterpiece Cake v. Colorado Civil Rights Commission, 138 S.Ct. 1719 (2018), may have employment benefit law implications. *Masterpiece Cakeshop* deals with a cake shop owner's claim that his religious freedom should allow him to refuse customers who wanted a cake for a same-sex wedding. The Supreme Court reversed a state commission's decision against the shop owner, holding that the decision violated the cake shop owner's right to free expression. But the decision is narrower than it may first appear. In particular, the Court appeared to hinge the decision on the state commission's decision in the case, which it viewed as being impermissibly hostile to religion (this may have led to the 7–2 lineup at the Court).

The Court seemed to duck the underlying issue about free expression versus antidiscrimination laws. Employers will no doubt try to use *Masterpiece* as a defense. Its value will depend on employers' ability to couch their employment discrimination as expression because one of the unique aspects of *Masterpiece* was that the shop owner claimed that making cakes was artistic—that is, constitutionally protected expression. Because of that, and the Court's criticism of the state anti-discrimination commission, it may be that most employers will not be able to make an argument like *Masterpiece*. There will no doubt be exceptions—maybe a religious-themed artist that hires assistants—but there are not a lot of businesses that involve both the level of expression needed for such a claim, as well as the level of hostility that the Court perceived. So stay tuned to see if *Masterpiece* is not cited in the next significant ERISA same-sex benefits case. The ability of private employers to assert religious or moral objections to providing contraceptive coverage may only be the start of attempts to assert such objections to the provision of other employee benefits. This trend may affect the provision of medical benefits for transgender employees, coverage for same-sex spouses in health plans, fertility benefits for employees in same-sex relationships, and medical marijuana.

A NOTE ON EMPLOYER-SPONSORED WELLNESS PROGRAMS

In an attempt to reduce the cost of preventable illnesses, the Patient Protection and Affordable Care Act of 2010 (ACA) expanded the HIPAA and ERISA regulations dealing with wellness programs. The prior laws prohibited discrimination in benefits, premiums, and contributions based on health status, but contained an exception for wellness programs. Employers were allowed to offer rewards up to 20 percent of the premium costs to employees for participating in wellness programs. This can be a substantial savings, and it has been especially difficult to resist for lower income workers. The ACA increases the amount of incentives up to 30 percent and permits the Secretaries of HHS, Labor, and Treasury, which jointly enforce these provisions, to increase the reward to 50 percent if they determine that an increase is appropriate and not a subterfuge for discriminating based on health status. The ACA also provides for grants to small employers to establish wellness programs.

The regulations for employer-sponsored wellness plans define two types of wellness programs. The first, participatory wellness programs, entitle the participant to a reward merely for joining the program. The second, health-contingent wellness programs, give rewards only if certain health goals are met. These latter programs are more closely regulated and must comply with the following requirements: (1) it must give eligible individuals an opportunity to qualify for a reward at least once a year; (2) the reward is limited to 30% of the total cost of the employee—only coverage under the plan or 50% to the extent the program is designed to prevent or reduce tobacco use; (3) the reward must be available to all similarly situated individuals (and waive the requirements for those who are medically unable to comply); (4) the program must be reasonably designed to promote health or prevent disease; and (5) the plan must disclose in all plan materials the means for qualifying or the possibility of a waiver. 78 Fed. Reg. 33,158 (2013).

At first glance, it seems that such programs are win-win propositions, improving health and reducing costs. The peer-reviewed literature, however, is not nearly so positive in evaluating the success of these programs or in comparing their success with wellness programs directed by the individuals' own physicians. Among other things, there are extremely high relapse rates in smoking cessation, weight loss, and similar programs by employees. Furthermore, there are concerns about discrimination based on income (where higher paid employees can afford to pay a "privacy tax" to avoid participation) and privacy violations in obtaining and sharing sensitive information. It remains to be seen whether expansion of workplace wellness programs will be worth the effort and how greater employer involvement in health risk reduction will be received by employees.

Employers are displaying a keen interest in offering these programs. According to a 2012 report by the Society for Human Resource Management, the percentage of companies offering health insurance premium discounts for (1) participating in a weight loss program increased from 4% in 2009 to 9% in 2012; (2) not using tobacco products increased from 8% in 2009 to 20%

in 2012; and (3) getting an annual health risk assessment increased from 10% in 2009 to 21% in 2012.

When employee wellness programs ask for individual and family medical histories they may implicate the ADA and GINA. Provisions of these two laws permit employer-sponsored wellness programs to request medical or genetic information, but only if participation in the programs is voluntary. Under the final rule issued by the EEOC, 81 Fed. Reg. 31126 (2016), employers are able to award an "incentive" of up to 30% of the total cost of self-only coverage or as high as 50% of the total cost of self-only coverage to implement a smoking cessation program. The average cost of a self-only plan in 2015 was $6251 per year. The EEOC rejected the argument that the amount of the "incentive" (or "penalty" for those who refuse to participate), was so high as to be coercive for lower paid employees who, for all practical purposes, have no choice but to submit their health information and that of their spouse.

In January 2018, the U.S. District Court for the District of Columbia vacated the EEOC's wellness rule effective Jan. 1, 2019, instructing the agency that its goal of revising the rule by 2021 was too slow. *AARP v. EEOC*, No. 16-2113 (D.D.C. Dec. 20, 2017).

The issue of incentives for employees to participate in employer-sponsored wellness programs continues to generate substantial scholarly interest. See Jennifer S. Bard, When Public Health and Genetic Privacy Collide: Positive and Normative Theories Explaining How ACA's Expansion of Corporate Wellness Programs Conflicts with GINA's Privacy Rules, 39 J.L. Med. & Ethics 469 (2011); Kristin M. Madison, Kevin G. Volpp, & Scott D. Halpern, The Law, Policy, and Ethics of Employers' Use of Financial Incentives to Improve Health, 39 J.L. Med. & Ethics 450 (2011); Mark A. Rothstein & Heather L. Harrell, Health Risk Reduction Programs in Employer-Sponsored Health Plans: Part I—Efficacy, 51 J. Occup. & Envtl. Med. 943 (2009); Mark A. Rothstein & Heather L. Harrell, Health Risk Reduction Programs in Employer-Sponsored Health Plans: Part II—Law and Ethics, 51 J. Occup. & Envtl. Med. 951 (2009); Harald Schmidt, Wellness Incentives, Equity, and the 5 Groups Problem, 102 Am. J. Pub. Health 49 (2012).

Defined Contribution Plans: The Future of Health Benefits?

Employers are still trying to assess the effects of the ACA on their businesses, including the short- and long-term costs of their health plans. Costs, although moderating from the days of double-digit yearly increases, continue to be unpredictable and subject to the effects of new drugs, technologies, and health care organizational models. At the same time, because of the ACA, employees have more options for health insurance without any exclusions based on preexisting conditions. In this new environment, it is fair to ask whether employers increasingly will shift their health plans from defined benefit to defined contribution plans. A parallel change already has occurred in employer-sponsored pension plans, which used to be overwhelmingly defined benefit plans (i.e., retirees get a set payment each month) and now overwhelmingly are defined contribution plans (especially in the private sector). As further discussed in Chapter 13, under a defined contribution pension plan, employers provide a set amount of money each month (usually a percentage of wages or salary, which the employee can supplement with pretax dollars), and the employee decides how to invest the money from approved options.

Under a defined contribution health plan, employers would give employees a set amount of money each month and employees could use that money (plus their own contributions) to purchase health insurance through a health exchange. The employee could choose the plan that provided the best benefits at the lowest cost. What are the pros and cons of such a system of health care coverage? Do you think this change is likely? Why or why not? What effect would such a change have on employers, employees, and the law of employer-sponsored health benefits?

B. ERISA—SUBSTANTIVE PROVISIONS

1. DENIAL OF BENEFITS

Salley v. E.I. Dupont de Nemours & Co.

966 F.2d 1011 (5th Cir. 1992).

■ JERRE S. WILLIAMS, CIRCUIT JUDGE:

Danielle Salley was a psychiatric patient at DePaul Hospital. DuPont paid for her treatment under an ERISA plan it had established. DuPont concluded that Danielle's treatment was no longer medically necessary and terminated the benefits. Salley and her father brought suit to recover the costs of Danielle's hospitalization. The district court ruled in their favor. DuPont appeals the decision, claiming the district court erred both in holding that the plan administrators abused their discretion and in applying the treating physician rule. DuPont also appeals the court's decision to award attorney's fees, and the Salleys contest the court's calculation of the fees. We affirm the district court's ruling.

DuPont established its Hospital Medical-Surgical Coverage Policy (the "Plan") in accordance with the Employee Retirement Income Security Act of 1974, 29 U.S.C. § 1001, et seq. ("ERISA"). At all relevant times, Connecticut General administered the Plan, and DuPont reimbursed Connecticut General the full costs of medical claims. DuPont also contracted with Preferred Health Care ("Preferred") to manage the individual cases.

Danielle Salley is a fifteen-year-old girl with a history of emotional disabilities, drug abuse, and depression. Her father, Jack Salley, is a retired DuPont employee and continues to participate in the Plan under which Danielle is covered as his dependent. Danielle has been an in-patient three times at DePaul Northshore Hospital in Covington, Louisiana. Each time, she has been under the care of Dr. Gordon Blundell, a psychiatrist in charge of the hospital's adolescent unit. The present litigation concerns DuPont's termination of benefits during the third admission in the hospital.

During her first two visits, Danielle was an extremely troubled child. She displayed suicidal tendencies, attempted to escape, and experienced episodes of head-banging. She, however, improved during each visit, but as soon as she was released, she "recompensated"—i.e. reverted back to her previous behavior. Dr. Blundell thus determined that Danielle could not live with her parents and attend public schools.

Dr. Blundell was concerned about Danielle's continual admissions and releases from the hospital, a problem he referred to as her "revolving door admissions." In an attempt to eliminate the revolving door admissions, Dr. Blundell worked with Plan administrators to "flex" the benefits. A "benefits flex" is a health insurance industry practice in which the parties amend or modify the policy's coverage benefits in order to accommodate a contingency that the original contract did not address specifically. Although the policy does not in terms permit the treatment provided, the treatment is mutually beneficial because the insured receives the coverage desired while the insurer reduces its payout expense through less expensive treatment.

Beginning in Danielle's second admission at DePaul Hospital, the Salleys and hospital employees attempted to locate a less restrictive treatment for Danielle, including several boarding schools. They, however, were unable to find a facility capable to meet Danielle's particular needs. Unable to find such a facility, the hospital released Danielle to attend public school. She subsequently recompensated.

On September 10, 1990, Danielle was readmitted to DePaul Hospital. As the hospital's records evidence, she quickly restabilized. In fact, Dr. Blundell wrote in his October 5, 1990 Progress Notes that Danielle was beginning "to function at the highest level she ever has in life."

On September 28, 1990, Dr. Blundell conversed on the telephone with Ron Schlegel, a Preferred case manager, regarding Danielle's condition. Schlegel was knowledgeable about Danielle's case because he had been involved with it since her first admission. Dr. Blundell apprised Schlegel of Danielle's dramatic improvement but also informed Schlegel that although Danielle was currently stable, he did not think he could release her because she would quickly regress. Schlegel advised Dr. Blundell that Dr. Satwant Ahluwalia, in accordance with Preferred procedures, would review the case to determine medical necessity. The Plan pays only for expenses that are "medically necessary," although the Plan never defines the phrase.

Dr. Ahluwalia, a psychiatrist and regional director at Preferred, also had been involved with the case since Danielle's first admission. She, however, never had examined Danielle nor reviewed the medical records from the second or third admission. She had reviewed the records from Danielle's first admission.

Dr. Blundell and Dr. Ahluwalia discussed Danielle's treatment on the telephone on October 2, 1990. Dr. Blundell told Dr. Ahluwalia that Danielle was stabilizing and would be able to leave the hospital soon, but he did not want to repeat the revolving door of admissions. Dr. Ahluwalia instructed Dr. Blundell that DuPont would terminate the benefits for in-patient hospitalization on October 11, 1990. She testified at trial that she knew Dr. Blundell did not agree with this date for release.

The Salleys brought suit challenging DuPont's termination of benefits from October 11, 1990 through January 25, 1991.[1] Dr. Blundell discharged Danielle on January 25, 1991. She has since enrolled in the Darrow School in New York.

The district court concluded that DuPont abused its discretion when it terminated benefits for Danielle's in-patient hospitalization. Consequently, the court found DuPont liable for Danielle's hospital bills from October 11, 1990 through January 25, 1991. * * * DuPont appeals the district court's ruling.

We first address the standard of review we employ in evaluating DuPont's decision to terminate benefits under the terms of the ERISA benefit plan. The Supreme Court holds that the denial of benefits "is to be reviewed under a de novo standard unless the benefit plan gives the administrator or fiduciary discretionary authority to determine eligibility for benefits or to construe the terms of the plan." Firestone Tire and Rubber Co. v. Bruch, 489 U.S. 101, 115 (1989). If the plan gives the administrator or fiduciary discretionary authority, then we apply an abuse of discretion standard. In applying the abuse of discretion standard, we analyze whether the plan administrator acted arbitrarily or capriciously.

The Policy states "The [DuPont] Employee Relations Department shall be responsible for development of procedures to implement the policy, for interpretation of policy, and for coordination of administration." Similar language has led this Court to apply the abuse of discretion standard.

The Salleys assert two reasons why we should not apply the abuse of discretion standard. First, DuPont contracted with Preferred Health Care for medical necessity reviews. DuPont, therefore, was not exercising its discretion as the Plan envisioned. We disagree. The contract between DuPont and Preferred explicitly states, "DUPONT reserves final

---

[1] In accordance with an agreement between the parties, DuPont paid Danielle's hospitalization expenses through November 20, 1990, although DuPont challenges whether the Plan required it to make the payments.

authority to authorize or deny payment for services to beneficiaries of a Plan." Moreover, counsel for DuPont stated that DuPont exercised final authority in the case at hand. As long as a company maintains the ultimate decision on denial of benefits, it can be beneficial for it to have experienced agents assist in the determination.

DuPont's conflict of interest also concerns the Salleys. DuPont funds the Plan from current operating revenues, giving it an apparent incentive to deny benefits. The alleged conflict, however, does not change the standard of review. "[I]f a benefit plan gives discretion to an administrator or fiduciary who is operating under a conflict of interest, that conflict must be weighed as a 'factor[ ] in determining whether there is an abuse of discretion.'" Firestone, 489 U.S. at 115 (citation omitted). Accordingly, we apply an abuse of discretion standard to DuPont's benefits termination decision.

Analyzing the record before us, we conclude the district court correctly ruled that DuPont abused its discretion when it terminated benefits for Danielle's in-patient hospitalization. DuPont argues that this Court's decision whether the Plan administrator abused his discretion must be based upon the facts known to the administrator at the time the decision was made. Although we generally decide abuse of discretion based upon the information known to the administrator at the time he made the decision, the administrator can abuse his discretion if he fails to obtain the necessary information. In the present case, neither Schlegel nor Dr. Ahluwalia ever examined Danielle, nor had either one obtained the records from the second or third admissions to DePaul Hospital.

The Plan administrators may rely on the treating physician's advice, or it can independently investigate the treatment's medical necessity. In the present case, the Plan administrators apparently relied on Dr. Blundell's description that Danielle was no longer suicidal or out of control. The administrators, however, cannot rely on part of Dr. Blundell's advice and ignore his other advice. Dr. Blundell also warned Dr. Ahluwalia that he could release Danielle only if there was an "iron-clad plan in hand that would assure her structure, safety, and well being." Such a plan had not been found.

The hospital records from the third admission would have demonstrated to the administrators the medical necessity of Danielle's in-patient hospitalization. Danielle was stable when she was in the hospital, but as soon as she was released into her former environment, she began to deteriorate. The doctors who examined Danielle and carefully evaluated her case were confident release into the improper environment would lead to recompensation.

DuPont maintains that options other than just hospitalization or release to her former environment existed. It suggests, for example, that a residential care treatment would have satisfied Danielle's needs. In reality, hospitalization and release to her former environment were the only options available at the time in question. Dr. Blundell agreed a less restrictive environment could be beneficial to Danielle, but he felt releasing Danielle was inappropriate until a proper program and environment was found. Such a program had not been discovered at the time in question. Therefore, if Dr. Blundell had released Danielle, of necessity she would have returned to her former environment.

Both the Salleys and the hospital spent significant time trying to find a less restrictive environment for Danielle. The evidence indicates they acted in good faith and without any unnecessary delay. In fact, the Salleys eventually found an appropriate environment for Danielle at Darrow School, where she enrolled in January 1991.

We further note that the issue of a less restrictive environment has nothing to do with money. One of the issues the district court addressed was whether DuPont would pay for the alternative treatment. The district court held DuPont did not have to pay for the costs of Darrow School, and the Salleys have not appealed this issue. Whether DuPont would pay for the alternative treatment, however, is irrelevant. If the requisite facility had been found, then hospitalization would not have been medically necessary. On the other hand, until the facility was found, hospitalization was medically necessary.

We hold that although DuPont followed the prescribed procedures, it abused its discretion in relying upon the Schlegel and Dr. Ahluwalia recommendation to terminate Danielle's benefits. Because they chose to follow Dr. Blundell's diagnosis, Schlegel and Dr. Ahluwalia were required, absent independent inquiry, to follow all his advice, not just part of it. If they decided to deviate from his diagnosis, they were required to investigate further the medical necessity of in-patient hospitalization. Whether this investigation included an examination of Danielle or an analysis of hospital records depended on the particulars of each case. At the very least, however, administrators relying on hospital records obviously must review the most recent records. The case administrator and the physician conceded at trial that they did not do so.

During the trial, the judge stated, "I am certainly going to give deference to the treating physician." Moreover, the court's opinion stated, "In light of Dr. Blundell's testimony in this matter, and the deference to be shown him as the patient's treating physician, the Court concludes that the continued inpatient psychiatric hospitalization * * * was 'medically necessary' * * *" DuPont maintains that applying the "treating physician rule" is improper in ERISA cases.

The "treating physician rule" requires the court, in appropriate circumstances, to defer to a patient's treating physician's testimony unless substantial evidence contradicts the testimony. We have recognized the use of the rule in cases involving termination of social security benefits. Courts have also applied the rule in suits brought under the Federal Tort Claims Act. But we declined to apply the rule when a handicapped child's treating physician testified regarding the appropriate education for the child.

This Court has not addressed the propriety of the "treating physician rule" in ERISA cases. We have considerable doubt about holding the rule applicable in ERISA cases. Under it, the treating physician would stand to profit greatly if the court were to find benefits should not be terminated. There is a clear and strong conflict of interest, and we are doubtful that a court should defer automatically to his or her testimony.

The district court did apply the "treating physician rule." But even assuming this was error, the error was harmless. Although the court announced it was applying the "treating physician rule," it later stated in its opinion that "of all the witnesses heard, the one most interested in the welfare of this patient, and not in the insurer's pocketbook, was the treating physician." Assuming it is error to grant a presumption in favor of the treating physician in an ERISA case, the district court nevertheless may properly assess each case's individual circumstances and evaluate the witnesses' credibility. If a court believes the treating physician is more credible than other witnesses, it is entitled to give greater weight to his or her testimony. The record here is clear that the court made the decision as to credibility and properly relied heavily upon the testimony of the treating physician.

* * *

AFFIRMED.

NOTES AND QUESTIONS

1. The basis of the denial of the claim in *Salley* was that the hospitalization was "not medically necessary." Who has the burden of proving medical necessity? What should the standard be for making the determination? What should the standard be for reviewing determinations by plan administrators?

2. *Salley* also raises the issue of whether deference should be given to the medical opinions of the individual's treating physician. In Black & Decker Disab. Plan v. Nord, 538 U.S. 822 (2003), the Supreme Court rejected the claimant's argument that the opinion of his treating physician should be given the same controlling weight as afforded in Social Security cases. The Court held that ERISA's requirement of a "full and fair consideration" of the claim did not mandate application of this rule. The Social Security rule was distinguished as being necessary for the efficient operation of a large benefit system, whereas deference to the treating physician was not necessary in considering claims filed under diverse employee benefit plans.

3. Another line of cases addresses the other main reason for denial of medical benefits under ERISA-qualified plans—that the treatment was "experimental." A number of cases have concerned the issue of high dose chemotherapy with autologous bone marrow transplants, a procedure once thought to hold promise in treating advanced cases of breast cancer and costing upwards of $150,000. Most of the cases held that the procedure was experimental. See, e.g., Harris v. Mutual of Omaha Cos., 992 F.2d 706 (7th Cir. 1993); Holder v. Prudential Ins. Co. of Am., 951 F.2d 89 (5th Cir. 1992). Other procedures held to be experimental include a Jarvik-7 artificial heart,

Loyola Univ. of Chicago v. Humana Ins. Co., 996 F.2d 895 (7th Cir. 1993), stem cell transplant to treat chronic lymphocytic leukemia, Klein v. Central States, S.E. & S.W. Areas Health & Welfare Plan, 346 Fed. Appx. 1 (6th Cir. 2009), lung volume reduction surgery for treatment of emphysema, Kilar v. Blue Cross Blue Shield Ass'n, 195 Fed. Appx. 547 (9th Cir. 2006), and hyperbaric oxygen therapy for quadriplegia, Washington v. Winn-Dixie of La., Inc., 736 F.Supp. 1418 (E.D.La.1990).

4.   Procedurally, the cases may be brought as actions for injunctive relief, where the plaintiff is seeking a court order directing the approval of certain treatment. They also may be brought after the treatment has been provided, and the action seeks reimbursement. In the latter action, what relevance, if any, should evidence that the procedure was successful (or unsuccessful) have on whether it was "not medically necessary" or "experimental"? Some cases have alleged that delay or failure to provide coverage by a health plan administrator was the proximate cause of injury or death. These claims have been held to be preempted by ERISA. For example, in McDonald v. Household Int'l, Inc., 425 F.3d 424 (7th Cir. 2005), claims of negligence and breach of contract brought by a beneficiary who suffered a stroke after a delay in treatment for high blood pressure were held to be preempted by ERISA. Similarly, in Marks v. Watters, 322 F.3d 316 (4th Cir. 2003), a beneficiary's estate claimed a health plan administrator was responsible for the premature release of the beneficiary from a mental health care facility and poor follow-up, resulting in the beneficiary murdering his wife and daughter, injuring his son, and committing suicide. The court held the action was preempted by ERISA.

5.   Beneficiaries of an ERISA plan normally must exhaust their internal plan remedies before seeking judicial relief. An exception exists where using internal remedies would be futile. See Sibley-Schreiber v. Oxford Health Plans, Inc., 62 F.Supp.2d 979 (E.D.N.Y.1999) (beneficiary had made numerous unsuccessful attempts to get exception to health plan's six-pills-per-month rule for Viagra).

6.   In Great-West Life & Annuity Ins. Co. v. Knudson, 534 U.S. 204 (2002), the Supreme Court, 5–4, held that § 502(2)(a)(3) of ERISA, which authorizes plan participants and fiduciaries to bring civil actions to obtain "appropriate equitable relief," did not authorize a plan to bring an action for specific performance of the reimbursement provision of the plan. Justice Scalia's majority opinion viewed the lawsuit as a claim for money due and therefore an action "at law" rather than an action for "equitable relief." Justice Ginsburg's dissent argued that there was no evidence that Congress intended to rely on such "archaic" notions to limit the available relief. But see Sereboff v. Mid Atl. Med. Servs., Inc., 547 U.S. 356 (2006) (Roberts, C.J.), allowing a health insurer to recover funds it had paid to a beneficiary when the beneficiary achieved a tort settlement from a third party for the injury that led to the expenses. The health plan clearly provided for reimbursement in these circumstances.

"Cases awarding money damages * * * exist in profusion in trust remedy law. Accordingly, money damages were and are as much an equitable remedy as a legal remedy. Justice Scalia was correct to say that 'money damages are

* * * the classic form of legal relief,' but flatly wrong to assert that money damages are not equally characteristic of equity when it enforces equity-based causes of action such as those arising from breach of trust." John H. Langbein, What ERISA Means by "Equitable": The Supreme Court's Trail of Error in *Russell, Mertens,* and *Great-West,* 103 Colum. L. Rev. 1317, 1337 (2003).

7. An employee was seriously injured in a car accident and the administrator of his ERISA-qualified health plan paid $66,866 for his medical expenses. In a subsequent lawsuit the employee recovered $110,000 from third parties. The plan administrator then brought an action to recover full payment from the employee, even though it was more than his net recovery (less attorney fees and costs). The Supreme Court held that general equitable principles, such as unjust enrichment, are inapplicable to an action under section 502(a)(3) of ERISA based on equitable lien by agreement. Although the ERISA plan's terms govern, equitable principles may be used in construing the contract terms. Because the plan is silent about allocating the costs of recovery, it is reasonable to apply the "common fund rule" as the default position. The effect of the rule is to allocate a portion of the attorney fees to US Airways. US Airways, Inc. v. McCutchen, 133 S.Ct. 1537 (2013).

8. Does section 502(a)(3) of ERISA authorize recovery of damages in the form of payment of a life insurance benefit that would have accrued but for a breach of duty by the fiduciary? Amschwand was on sick leave when Sopherion Corp. changed life insurance companies to Aetna. A Spherion executive told Amschwand he could keep his benefit even if he did not return to work for one day as the policy provided. But Spherion never put Amschwand's name on the list given to Aetna of individuals for whom the one-day-of-work requirement was being waived. Amschwand paid the premium until his death. His widow sued for the life insurance benefit. (The company did return the premium payments that had been made by Amschwand.) The court of appeals applied *Great-West,* said this would be "legal" relief, and denied the widow's claim. Amschwand v. Spherion Corp., 505 F.3d 342 (5th Cir. 2007), cert. denied, 554 U.S. 932 (2008).

9. ERISA distinguishes between welfare benefit plans and pension plans, providing more stringent protections for the latter. The statute expressly excludes welfare plans from the stringent minimum vesting, participation, and funding standards imposed on pension plans. ERISA §§ 201(1), 301(a)(1), 29 U.S.C. §§ 1051(1), 1081(a)(1).

10. Sometimes courts have been faced with welfare plans that have no explicit provision reserving the right to the employer to reduce or eliminate benefits. In the case of collectively bargained benefits, the court will look to normal contract principles to determine the continuation of retiree medical benefits based on its decision in M&G Polymers USA v. Tackett, 574 U.S. 527 (2015). In other words, unlike before, no inferences from the context of labor negotiations are to be applied in determining whether collective bargaining agreements created a vested right to lifetime contribution-free health care benefits.

11. In Stiltner v. Beretta U.S.A. Corp., 74 F.3d 1473 (4th Cir. 1996) (en banc), cert. denied, 519 U.S. 810 (1996), the plaintiff was an employee who was disabled by a heart condition. The employer threatened to cut off his free health insurance unless he dropped his lawsuit seeking $332,000 in long-term disability benefits. The plaintiff then sued under § 510 of ERISA, asserting that the threat to terminate his health insurance was an "interference" with his benefits. The Fourth Circuit held, eight-to-five, that ERISA does not prevent employers from revoking gratuitous benefits. The dissent argued that § 510 bars all retaliation, regardless of whether the benefits are gratuitous.

12. Section 501(c)(3) of the Americans with Disabilities Act (ADA) provides that the employment discrimination title of the Act shall not be construed to prohibit an employer "from establishing, sponsoring, observing or administering the terms of a bona fide benefit plan that is not subject to State laws that regulate insurance." In other words, the ADA does not appear to regulate the terms of the health benefits plans of self-insured employers, so long as the plan is not a "subterfuge" to avoid the ADA. A June 1993 statement by the EEOC, however, asserts that it violates the ADA for an employer to offer any health benefit plan that discriminates on the basis of disability or fails to afford equal access to health benefits unless justified by actuarial considerations. "Employees with disabilities must be accorded 'equal access' to whatever health insurance the employer provides to employees without disabilities." Employers may not set lower benefit levels for particular conditions, such as AIDS, cancer, or heart disease, although broad distinctions applying to numerous disorders may be permissible. EEOC Interim Guidance on Application of the ADA to Health Insurance (1993). See generally Sharona Hoffman, AIDS Caps, Contraceptive Coverage, and the Law: An Analysis of the Federal Anti-Discrimination Statutes' Applicability to Health Insurance, 23 Cardozo L. Rev. 1315 (2002).

2. DISCRIMINATION

Phelps v. Field Real Estate Co.

991 F.2d 645 (10th Cir. 1993).

■ WESLEY E. BROWN, SENIOR DISTRICT JUDGE.

Plaintiff-Appellant John Phelps (Phelps) sought recovery for an alleged violation of Section 510 of ERISA, 29 U.S.C. § 1140, which prohibits discrimination against participants of any employee benefit plan for the purpose of interfering with rights under such plan. He also sought damages for alleged discrimination under a Colorado statute prohibiting employer discrimination against those with handicaps, C.R.S. § 24–34–402(1)(a).

Phelps began work as a commercial real estate division manager for defendant Field Real Estate Company in February, 1985. In November, 1986, he learned that he had tested positive for the virus which causes the disease Acquired Immuno-Deficiency Syndrome (AIDS). On August

4, 1989, Phelps was discharged from his employment, and this resulted in his loss of insurance benefits.

The district court found that Phelps had failed to prove the requisite intent to violate 29 U.S.C. § 1140 and that he had likewise failed to prove that he was discharged or discriminated against in violation of Colorado law. Phelps v. Field Real Estate, 793 F.Supp. 1535 (D.Colo.1991).

Phelps contends that the district court misconstrued the nature of the showing required for liability under ERISA § 510, and that under the facts found by the trial court, Phelps met his statutory burden of proof under the Colorado handicap discrimination statute. In this respect, Phelps accepts the findings of fact as found by the district court, but contends that its conclusions of law from those facts are erroneous.

A summary of the district court's findings of fact establishes this sequence of events:

> Prior to February, 1985, when he began working for defendant Field Real Estate, Phelps had obtained an M.B.A. from Arizona State University, served two years in Vietnam, and began work as a real estate salesman in Pueblo, Colorado, in 1974. In 1979, he began work with Fuller & Company in Denver, selling commercial real estate, including undeveloped land. He obtained a real estate broker's license in 1983 but wanted to move into management; and, following an interview with Ray Stanley, then president of Field Real Estate Company, in February, 1985, he entered the Field organization as vice president of the commercial real estate division at $60,000 per year plus 3.5% commission with a guarantee of $82,000 during the first two years. At this time, W. Douglas Poole was chairman of the board and chief executive officer of Field.

When Phelps began work, a job specification was created for the commercial real estate division manager. Under this, the position was described as general management of the division without any direct selling, in accordance with Phelps' wishes.

The commercial real estate division was divided into a commercial sales division and a commercial leasing division. Phelps was manager of commercial sales and reported directly to Poole, while Ray Stanley was manager of commercial leasing.

At the outset, there was some conflict with Poole as to the expected volume of business which would be generated. Phelps believed that each sales agent could be expected to generate $2 million in sales per year, while Poole stated he expected $8 million per agent in each year. Poole's background was in retail sales, and he had had no experience in the real estate business. However, the two appeared to get along well; and Poole felt that Phelps did a good job in 1986 and 1987.

In November, 1986, Phelps learned that he was infected with the AIDS virus; but he was not ill, he had no symptoms of disease, and his condition did not interfere with his ability to perform his job. He kept his infection secret and did not disclose his medical condition to anyone.

By letter dated January 22, 1987, Poole extended Phelps' employment letter with the same compensation and benefits except that Phelps was to be granted listing agreements, beginning with the "Midland Building." Additional listing agreements were to be selected by Poole.

Annual performance evaluations were made by Poole, rating employees from 5 down. Poole gave Phelps mostly 3's for the 1986 evaluation. The only written comment under "areas for growth" was "needs to take a more hands-on approach to job."

On May 8, 1987, Phelps and Norman Marsh, manager of accounting, administration and personnel and assistant to Poole, were made senior vice presidents of Field.

In the annual review for 1987, Phelps was given mostly 4's, with note that Phelps needed "more personal involvement in development of third party business," and that he needed to reduce his outside activities in order to concentrate on developing the commercial sales division. Poole resented the time that Phelps spent away from the office, but he and Phelps continued to have a good working relationship.

In March, 1988, Poole found an anonymous note on his desk from "Members of the Staff," advising that Phelps had a fatal blood disease and requesting that he be transferred. When Phelps was shown the note, he told Poole that the note was true, that he had kept his condition a secret, and that he was concerned about his job and keeping his insurance. Poole assured Phelps that the matter would be kept in confidence and that, so long as Phelps was at Field, he had nothing to worry about.

Poole was concerned about Phelps' condition; the matter was discussed at a board meeting on May 3, 1988, and Poole and Phelps had another meeting on May 24, 1988. Phelps spoke of his disease as "diminished lymphoma," a phrase with no medical meaning, and told Poole that it involved a dormancy period of 8 to 10 years, and that when the disease became active, there would be 2 to 3 years of productivity and then death. Poole was concerned with corporate liability; and, because there was a possibility Field might be sold, there could be a problem about securing "key man" insurance for Phelps.

In June, 1988, Phelps went to see Dr. Kerr about the problem of obtaining insurance and obtained a letter from him which concealed more than it revealed.[4] The doctor's letter stated in pertinent part that:

---

[4] At the doctor's request, Phelps drafted this letter and, after making some changes, the doctor signed it. There was no mention of the AIDS virus, and all references to future risk were related to an example based upon blood tests relating to the presence of "Agent Orange".

> The tests for which I am aware of in (Phelps') case indicate that, although currently able to perform all the duties of your occupation, owing to your past exposure to potentially injurious agents, you are at increased risk for certain types of cancers and other conditions. It is my opinion that the agents detected by the tests which I am aware of are likely to be discovered in the course of the routine tests that are generally administered to determine an individual's insurability, and that it is highly likely that an insurer would decline to issue a policy to you on this basis.

> Again, I would wish to emphasize that, from a medical standpoint, you are presently able to satisfactorily perform all of the duties of your current position, and that your condition does not pose any health threat to anyone whom you may encounter in the workplace.

The doctor's letter was given to Poole, and Poole stated that he was "completely satisfied" that Phelps was capable of doing his job.

On July 10, 1988, Poole placed a blind classified ad for a "real estate commercial division manager." The job description was applicable to Phelps' position, and also to Stanley's position, the leasing manager. Other anonymous notes appeared; there was some conflict between Poole and Phelps, and on July 23 and 24, Poole met with managers and real estate agents and informed them he was considering a new division to handle "REO properties," properties with defaulted loans. One agent asked Poole why he had called the meeting. Poole stated "that some people thought Phelps' job was in jeopardy, but it wasn't."

In January, 1989, there was another annual evaluation of employees. Phelps was given 4's on all categories, but under "performance" Poole wrote the following:

> The Commercial Sales division's development over the past three years has been very poor—both from the standpoint of recruiting productive agents as well as meeting Company objectives growthwise.

Phelps was allowed to write and place a rebuttal of this evaluation in his file. In this rebuttal, Phelps admitted that the Commercial Division had lost money in 1988, but he attributed the loss to three external causes—a decline in Denver's overall economy; market prices declining below Bank Western's inventory prices; and loss of confidence by the sales force due to the classified ad for a "commercial division manager," which resulted in the loss of two sales agents.

* * *

Marsh and Poole met with Phelps on August 4, 1989, to tell him he was being discharged because of poor performance of the division and because of the reorganization. Phelps asked if they knew they were firing someone with AIDS and that terminating his job would also terminate his insurance benefits. Poole's response was that he was sorry, and Poole and Marsh both stated that they did not know that Phelps had AIDS. Marsh suggested that Phelps could stay on as a real estate agent, working on commissions, and then he could continue his insurance at his own expense. Phelps declined to do so. This offer was repeated by letter of August 17, 1989, but it was rejected and Phelps filed this action on November 21, 1989.

The ERISA Claim

Section 510 of ERISA, 29 U.S.C. § 1140, provides in part that:

It shall be unlawful for any person to discharge, fine, suspend, expel, discipline, or discriminate against a participant or beneficiary for exercising any right to which he is entitled under the provisions of an employee benefit plan * * * *for the purpose of interfering with the attainment of any right to which such participant may become entitled under the plan* * * *. (Emphasis supplied)

As noted by the district court, Phelps was required to prove, by a preponderance of the evidence, that his discharge was motivated by an intent to interfere with employee benefits protected by ERISA. In order to establish this intent, the courts have looked to circumstantial evidence surrounding the employment decision because there is rarely direct evidence of wrongful intent.

Since Poole was the one who personally made the decision to discharge Phelps, the question thus was whether Poole fired Phelps because "at least in part," Poole wanted to protect the benefit plans from the effect of Phelps' health condition. As noted by the district court, "(p)ut bluntly, was Poole motivated to save the costs of health care, disability and death benefits as the expected consequences of the plaintiff's developing AIDS?"

Phelps contends that his appeal "is based entirely, and only, upon the facts found and accepted by the trial court". As a part of its findings, the district court determined that Poole in fact was aware that Phelps had AIDS, but that this was not the motivating factor for Phelps' discharge. In this respect, the district court found that "sales performance was a serious problem in the summer of 1988," and that placement of the ad for a new manager on July 12, 1988, "was an awkward effort to motivate Phelps to resign." The court found that "(f)or whatever reason, Poole failed to confront Phelps directly about his health. The lack of candor between these two men affected the working relationship between them. Yet, a failure of leadership or ineffective management of this difficult situation is not equivalent to discriminatory treatment for the purpose of protecting the assets of the employee plans."

While there was evidence concerning the possible effect of an AIDS patient on benefit plans, the record supports the district court's conclusion that there was "no evidence that Poole, Marsh or anyone else in Field's management made any such calculations or even expressed any awareness of such consequences," and we agree that it is also significant that Phelps' termination was not made until more than fourteen months after he first disclosed his medical condition. In addition, the evidence was that the commercial sales division failed to meet the expectations of Poole and his board of directors. Whether or not this was in fact Phelps' fault, the fact remains that the commercial sales and leasing department was completely reorganized into three divisions, with new employees heading the industrial and office divisions, with Ray Stanley in charge of the retail division. It is significant that Stanley was warned that his future was limited and that he, too, left the company soon after the reorganization.

Under this evidence, the district court's conclusion that Phelps had failed to prove the intent required by Section 510 of ERISA was correct.

NOTES AND QUESTIONS

1. What factors in the case most strongly suggest that the employer did not engage in discrimination? Suppose that the employee had an 18-year record of excellent evaluations, he was discharged for allegedly poor performance shortly after notifying the employer that he had multiple sclerosis, the employer failed to follow its normal procedure of probation before discharge, and the employer had a strong financial incentive to fire him because its medical and disability plans were self-funded. Would these facts create an inference of discrimination? See Folz v. Marriott Corp., 594 F.Supp. 1007 (W.D.Mo.1984) (held: defendant violated section 510). See also Holtzclaw v. DSC Communications Corp., 255 F.3d 254 (5th Cir. 2001) (no violation where plaintiff failed to prove he was qualified for the position); Tracy v. Financial Ins. Mgmt. Corp., 458 F.Supp.2d 734 (S.D. Ind. 2006) (no violation where employee discharged for poor performance and lack of professionalism).

2. Discrimination under section 510 is broadly defined to include not only the discharge of an employee to prevent benefit accrual, but discrimination against any beneficiary for asserting rights under ERISA, as well as retaliating against an employee for exercising rights under the statute. See, e.g., Fleming v. Ayers & Assoc., 948 F.2d 993 (6th Cir. 1991) (discharge of employee because of expected high medical costs of her infant child).

3. In Inter-Modal Rail Employees Ass'n v. Atchison, Topeka & Santa Fe Ry. Co., 520 U.S. 510 (1997), the Supreme Court held that section 510 prohibits interference with both pension plans and welfare plans. On the issue of interference with pension plans, see Chapter 13. In addition, section 510 applies to a variety of welfare plan benefits, including long-term and short-term disability benefits. See Parker v. Cooper Tire & Rubber Co., 546 F. Appx. 522 (5th Cir. 2014), cert. denied, 135 S.Ct. 167 (2014).

C. ERISA—PREEMPTION OF STATE ACTIONS

ERISA contains an extremely broad preemption provision. Section 514(a) of ERISA, 29 U.S.C. § 1144(a), preempts "any and all State laws insofar as they may now or hereafter relate to any employee benefit plan" covered by the Act. It bars state regulation of benefit plans, both pension and welfare. ERISA, however, contains substantive federal standards only for pension plans. Nevertheless, ERISA preempts state regulation of welfare plans, even though there is no comparable federal regulation. Among the exceptions to this provision include state laws that regulate insurance, banking, or securities; generally applicable criminal laws; and qualified domestic relations orders.

New York State Conference of Blue Cross & Blue Shield Plans v. Travelers Insurance Co.
514 U.S. 645 (1995).

■ JUSTICE SOUTER delivered the opinion of the Court.

A New York statute requires hospitals to collect surcharges from patients covered by a commercial insurer but not from patients insured by a Blue Cross/Blue Shield plan, and it subjects certain health maintenance organizations (HMO's) to surcharges that vary with the number of Medicaid recipients each enrolls. These cases call for us to decide whether [ERISA] pre-empts the state provisions for surcharges on bills of patients whose commercial insurance coverage is purchased by employee health-care plans governed by ERISA, and for surcharges on HMO's insofar as their membership fees are paid by an ERISA plan. We hold that the provisions for surcharges do not "relate to" employee benefit plans within the meaning of ERISA's pre-emption provision, and accordingly suffer no pre-emption.

New York's Prospective Hospital Reimbursement Methodology (NYPHRM) regulates hospital rates for all in-patient care, except for services provided to Medicare beneficiaries. The scheme calls for patients to be charged not for the cost of their individual treatment, but for the average cost of treating the patient's medical problem, as classified under one or another of 794 Diagnostic Related Groups (DRGs). The charges allowable in accordance with DRG classifications are adjusted for a specific hospital to reflect its particular operating costs, capital investments, bad debts, costs of charity care, and the like.

Patients with Blue Cross/Blue Shield coverage, Medicaid patients, and HMO participants are billed at a hospital's DRG rate. Others, however, are not. Patients served by commercial insurers providing inpatient hospital coverage on an expense-incurred basis, by self-insured funds directly reimbursing hospitals, and by certain workers' compensation, volunteer firefighters' benefit, ambulance workers' benefit, and no-fault motor vehicle insurance funds, must be billed at the

DRG rate plus a 13% surcharge to be retained by the hospital. For the year ending March 31, 1993, moreover, hospitals were required to bill commercially insured patients for a further 11% surcharge to be turned over to the State, with the result that these patients were charged 24% more than the DRG rate.

New York law also imposes a surcharge on HMOs, which varies depending on the number of eligible Medicaid recipients an HMO has enrolled, but which may run as high as 9% of the aggregate monthly charges paid by an HMO for its members' in-patient hospital care. This assessment is not an increase in the rates to be paid by an HMO to hospitals, but a direct payment by the HMO to the State's general fund. * * *

On the claimed authority of ERISA's general pre-emption provision, several commercial insurers, acting as fiduciaries of ERISA plans they administer, joined with their trade associations to bring actions against state officials in United States District Court seeking to invalidate the 13%, 11%, and 9% surcharge statutes. The New York State Conference of Blue Cross and Blue Shield plans, Empire Blue Cross and Blue Shield (collectively the Blues), and the Hospital Association of New York State intervened as defendants, and the New York State Health Maintenance Organization Conference and several HMO's intervened as plaintiffs. The District Court consolidated the actions and granted summary judgment to the plaintiffs. * * * The Court of Appeals for the Second Circuit affirmed. [We] now reverse and remand.

Our past cases have recognized that the Supremacy Clause may entail pre-emption of state law either by express provision, by implication, or by a conflict between federal and state law. And yet, despite the variety of these opportunities for federal preeminence, we have never assumed lightly that Congress has derogated state regulation, but instead have addressed claims of pre-emption with the starting presumption that Congress does not intend to supplant state law. Indeed, in cases like this one, where federal law is said to bar state action in fields of traditional state regulation, we have worked on the "assumption that the historic police powers of the States were not to be superseded by the Federal Act unless that was the clear and manifest purpose of Congress."

Since pre-emption claims turn on Congress's intent, we begin as we do in any exercise of statutory construction with the text of the provision in question, and move on, as need be, to the structure and purpose of the Act in which it occurs. The governing text of ERISA is clearly expansive. Section 514(a) marks for pre-emption "all state laws insofar as they . . . relate to any employee benefit plan" covered by ERISA, and one might be excused for wondering, at first blush, whether the words of limitation ("insofar as they . . . relate") do much limiting. If "relate to" were taken to extend to the furthest stretch of its indeterminacy, then for all practical purposes pre-emption would never run its course, for "really, universally, relations stop nowhere." But that, of course, would be to read Congress's words of limitation as mere sham, and to read the presumption against pre-emption out of the law whenever Congress speaks to the matter with generality. That said, we have to recognize that our prior attempt to construe the phrase "relate to" does not give us much help drawing the line here.

In *Shaw* [Shaw v. Delta Air Lines, Inc. 463 U.S. 85 (1983)], we explained that "[a] law 'relates to' an employee benefit plan, in the normal sense of the phrase, if it has a connection with or reference to such a plan." The latter alternative, at least, can be ruled out. The surcharges are imposed upon patients and HMO's, regardless of whether the commercial coverage or membership, respectively, is ultimately secured by an ERISA plan, private purchase, or otherwise, with the consequence that the surcharge statutes cannot be said to make "reference to" ERISA plans in any manner. But this still leaves us to question whether the surcharge laws have a "connection with" the ERISA plans, and here an uncritical literalism is no more help than in trying to construe "relate to." For the same reasons that infinite relations cannot be the measure of pre-emption, neither can infinite connections. We simply must go beyond the unhelpful text and the frustrating difficulty of defining its key term, and look instead to the objectives of the ERISA statute as a guide to the scope of the state law that Congress understood would survive.

As we have said before, § 514 indicates Congress's intent to establish the regulation of employee welfare benefit plans "as exclusively a federal concern." We have found that in passing § 514(a), Congress intended

> "to ensure that plans and plan sponsors would be subject to a uniform body of benefits law; the goal was to minimize the administrative and financial burden of complying with conflicting directives among States or between States and the Federal Government ..., [and to prevent] the potential for conflict in substantive law ... requiring the tailoring of plans and employer conduct to the peculiarities of the law of each jurisdiction."

* * * The basic thrust of the pre-emption clause, then, was to avoid a multiplicity of regulation in order to permit the nationally uniform administration of employee benefit plans.

Accordingly in *Shaw*, for example, we had no trouble finding that New York's "Human Rights Law, which prohibited employers from structuring their employee benefit plans in a manner that discriminated on the basis of pregnancy, and [New York's] Disability Benefits Law, which required employers to pay employees specific benefits, clearly 'related to' benefit plans." These mandates affecting coverage could have been honored only by varying the subjects of a plan's benefits whenever New York law might have applied, or by requiring every plan to provide all beneficiaries with a benefit demanded by New York law if New York law could have been said to require it for any one beneficiary. Similarly, Pennsylvania's law that prohibited "plans from ... requiring reimbursement [from the beneficiary] in the event of recovery from a third party" related to employee benefit plans within the meaning of § 514(a). The law "prohibited plans from being structured in a manner requiring reimbursement in the event of recovery from a third party" and "required plan providers to calculate benefit levels in Pennsylvania based on expected liability conditions that differ from those in States that have not enacted similar antisubrogation legislation," thereby "frustrating plan administrators' continuing obligation to calculate uniform benefit levels nationwide." Pennsylvania employees who recovered in negligence actions against tortfeasors would, by virtue of the state law, in effect have been entitled to benefits in excess of what plan administrators intended to provide, and in excess of what the plan provided to employees in other States. Along the same lines, New Jersey could not prohibit plans from setting workers' compensation payments off against employees' retirement benefits or pensions, because doing so would prevent plans from using a method of calculating benefits permitted by federal law. In each of these cases, ERISA pre-empted state laws that mandated employee benefit structures or their administration. Elsewhere, we have held that state laws providing alternative enforcement mechanisms also relate to ERISA plans, triggering pre-emption.

Both the purpose and the effects of the New York surcharge statute distinguish it from the examples just given. The charge differentials have been justified on the ground that the Blues pay the hospitals promptly and efficiently and, more importantly, provide coverage for many subscribers whom the commercial insurers would reject as unacceptable risks. The Blues' practice, called open enrollment, has consistently been cited as the principal reason for charge differentials, whether the differentials resulted from voluntary negotiation between hospitals and payers as was the case prior to the NYPHRM system, or were created by the surcharges as is the case now. Since the surcharges are presumably passed on at least in part to those who purchase commercial insurance or HMO membership, their effects follow from their purpose. Although there is no evidence that the surcharges will drive every health insurance consumer to the Blues, they do make the Blues more attractive (or less unattractive) as insurance alternatives and thus have an indirect economic effect on choices made by insurance buyers, including ERISA plans.

An indirect economic influence, however, does not bind plan administrators to any particular choice and thus function as a regulation of an ERISA plan itself; commercial insurers and HMOs may still offer more attractive packages than the Blues. Nor does the indirect influence of the surcharges preclude uniform administrative practice or the provision of a uniform interstate benefit package if a plan wishes to provide one. It simply bears on the costs of benefits and the relative costs of competing insurance to provide them. It is an influence that can affect a plan's shopping decisions, but it does not affect the fact that any plan will shop for the best deal it can get, surcharges or no surcharges.

There is, indeed, nothing remarkable about surcharges on hospital bills, or their effects on overall cost to the plans and the relative attractiveness of certain insurers. Rate variations among hospital providers are accepted examples of cost variation, since hospitals have traditionally "attempted to compensate for their financial shortfalls by adjusting their price . . . schedules for patients with commercial health insurance." Charge differentials for commercial insurers, even prior to state regulation, "varied dramatically across regions, ranging from 13 to 36 percent," presumably reflecting the geographically disparate burdens of providing for the uninsured.

If the common character of rate differentials even in the absence of state action renders it unlikely that ERISA pre-emption was meant to bar such indirect economic influences under state law, the existence of other common state action with indirect economic effects on a plan's costs leaves the intent to pre-empt even less likely. Quality standards, for example, set by the State in one subject area of hospital services but not another would affect the relative cost of providing those services over others and, so, of providing different packages of health insurance benefits. Even basic regulation of employment conditions will invariably affect the cost and price of services.

Quality control and workplace regulation, to be sure, are presumably less likely to affect premium differentials among competing insurers, but that does not change the fact that such state regulation will indirectly affect what an ERISA or other plan can afford or get for its money. Thus, in the absence of a more exact guide to intended pre-emption than § 514, it is fair to conclude that mandates for rate differentials would not be pre-empted unless other regulation with indirect effects on plan costs would be superseded as well. The bigger the package of regulation with indirect effects that would fall on the respondents' reading of § 514, the less likely it is that federal regulation of benefit plans was intended to eliminate state regulation of health care costs.

Indeed, to read the pre-emption provision as displacing all state laws affecting costs and charges on the theory that they indirectly relate to ERISA plans that purchase insurance policies or HMO memberships that would cover such services would effectively read the limiting language in § 514(a) out of the statute, a conclusion that would violate basic principles of statutory interpretation and could not be squared with our prior pronouncement that "pre-emption does not occur * * * if the state law has only a tenuous, remote, or peripheral connection with covered plans, as is the case with many laws of general applicability" * * * [and] nothing in the language of the Act or the context of its passage indicates that Congress chose to displace general health care regulation, which historically has been a matter of local concern. * * *

In sum, cost uniformity was almost certainly not an object of pre-emption, just as laws with only an indirect economic effect on the relative costs of various health insurance packages in a given State are a far cry from those "conflicting directives" from which Congress meant to insulate ERISA plans. Such state laws leave plan administrators right where they would be in any case, with the responsibility to choose the best overall coverage for the money. We therefore conclude that such state laws do not bear the requisite "connection with" ERISA plans to trigger pre-emption.

It remains only to speak further on a point already raised, that any conclusion other than the one we draw would bar any state regulation of hospital costs. The basic DRG system (even without any surcharge), like any other interference with the hospital services market, would fall on a theory that all laws with indirect economic effects on ERISA plans are pre-empted under § 514(a). This would be an unsettling result and all the more startling because several States, including New York, regulated hospital charges to one degree or another at the time ERISA was passed. And yet there is not so much as a hint in ERISA's legislative history or anywhere else that Congress intended to squelch these state efforts.

That said, we do not hold today that ERISA pre-empts only direct regulation of ERISA plans, nor could we do that with fidelity to the views expressed in our prior opinions on the matter. We acknowledge that a state law might produce such acute, albeit indirect, economic effects, by intent or otherwise, as to force an ERISA plan to adopt a certain scheme of substantive coverage or effectively restrict its choice of insurers, and that such a state law might indeed be pre-empted under § 514. But as we have shown, New York's surcharges do not fall into either category; they affect only indirectly the relative prices of insurance policies, a result no different from myriad state laws in areas traditionally subject to local regulation, which Congress could not possibly have intended to eliminate.

The judgment of the Court of Appeals is therefore reversed, and the cases are remanded for further proceedings consistent with this opinion.

NOTES AND QUESTIONS

1. Courts use two somewhat overlapping tests to determine whether a law "relates to" an ERISA plan: the "reference to" and "connection with" tests. Under the "reference to" test, state laws are preempted if they refer to an ERISA plan. State laws have the necessary reference if they act "immediately and exclusively upon ERISA plans * * * or where the existence of ERISA plans is essential to the law's operation." California Div. of Labor Stds. Enforcement v. Dillingham Constr., N.A., 519 U.S. 316, 325 (1997).

For example, in District of Columbia v. Greater Wash. Bd. of Trade, 506 U.S. 125 (1992), the Court held that ERISA preempted a D.C. law that provided that "[a]ny employer who provides health insurance coverage for an employee shall provide * * * coverage equivalent to the existing * * * coverage of the employee while the employee receives or is eligible to receive workers' compensation benefits." The Court stated that:

> [The Act] specifically refers to welfare benefit plans regulated by ERISA and on that basis alone is pre-empted. The health insurance coverage that § 2(c)(2) requires employers to provide for eligible employees is measured by reference to "the existing health insurance coverage" provided by the employer and "shall be at the same benefit level." * * * The employee's "existing health insurance coverage," in turn, is a welfare benefit plan under [ERISA], because it involves a fund or program maintained by an employer for the purpose of providing health benefits for the employee "through the purchase of insurance or otherwise." Such employer-sponsored health insurance programs are subject to ERISA regulation, and any state law imposing requirements by reference to such covered programs must yield to ERISA.

By contrast, the Court in *Travelers* quickly rejected the argument that the surcharge satisfied the "reference to" test, probably because the surcharge did not refer only to ERISA plans but instead applied more broadly to all commercial health insurance. Similarly, in Pharmaceutical Care Mgmt. Ass'n v. Rowe, 429 F.3d 294 (1st Cir. 2005), the First Circuit held that a Maine law that did not single out ERISA plans did not satisfy the "reference to" test. The law regulated pharmacy benefit managers (PBMs), companies that act as go-betweens between pharmaceutical companies and health care providers. The law, which imposed disclosure requirements and banned self-dealing, applied to PBMs that dealt with "covered entities"— meaning health care providers, including insurance companies, the state Medicaid program, and employer health plans (some covered by ERISA). The court reasoned that this law did not satisfy the "reference to" test because it applied to PBMs that dealt with a wide variety of health care providers; it did not single out PBMs that only dealt with ERISA plans.

2.   The "connection with" test, the focus of *Travelers*, is somewhat more vague. The other leading "connection with" case is Egelhoff v. Egelhoff, 532 U.S. 141 (2001). Mr. Egelhoff designated his wife as the beneficiary of his pension plan. They divorced but he died shortly thereafter without changing that designation. A Washington law provided that, unless a plan specifically states otherwise, a designation of a spouse as a beneficiary to a non-probate asset is invalidated when a couple divorces. The Court held that ERISA preempted the state law in part because allowing such state laws to survive preemption would reduce the uniformity of laws governing ERISA pensions. The Court also reasoned that the law regulated the payment of benefits, which was a core concern of ERISA; more specifically, the Court noted that the state law "runs counter to ERISA's commands that a plan shall 'specify the basis on which payments are made to and from the plan,' and that the fiduciary shall administer the plan 'in accordance with the documents and instruments governing the plan,' making payments to a 'beneficiary' who is 'designated by a participant, or by the terms of [the] plan.' "

By contrast, in Hattem v. Schwarzenegger, 449 F.3d 423 (2d Cir. 2006), the court found that ERISA did not preempt a state tax on the business-related income of non-profit corporations' trusts. The court reasoned that the tax did not govern an area traditionally found to be at the core of ERISA (such as the payment of benefits). The court also noted that the tax applied to a wide range of non-ERISA trusts.

In Pharmaceutical Care Mgmt. Ass'n v. District of Columbia, 613 F.3d 179 (D.C. Cir. 2010), the D.C. Circuit held that a District of Columbia statute requiring employee benefit plans that outsourced administration of their pharmaceutical benefits to do so in a particular way "related to" an employee benefit plan and therefore was preempted by ERISA.

3. For years before *Travelers*, the Supreme Court emphasized the breadth of ERISA preemption. See, e.g., FMC Corp. v. Holliday, 498 U.S. 52, 58 (1990) (noting that the "pre-emption clause is conspicuous for its breadth"). Many commentators think that in *Travelers* the Supreme Court signaled that it now viewed ERISA preemption as narrower. One court has even gone so far as to label *Travelers* a "sea change." Whitt v. Sherman Int'l Corp., 147 F.3d 1325, 1333 (11th Cir. 1998).

4. In *Travelers*, the Supreme Court also noted that it would be less willing to find that ERISA preempts a state law when the state law deals with traditional subjects of state regulation. ERISA, however, has often been found to preempt state laws dealing with matters usually thought to be well within state police powers.

For example, consider the case of MacLean v. Ford Motor Co., 831 F.2d 723 (7th Cir. 1987). During his employment with Ford, David Pithie participated in Ford's Savings and Stock Investment Plan (SSIP). The Plan's 1983 prospectus provided that if an employee failed to file a written document with administrators of the Plan designating a beneficiary, the employee would be deemed to have designated as beneficiary the person who was entitled to receive the proceeds of the employee's company life insurance policy. Pithie never filed the required documentation identifying a beneficiary for his SSIP but had designated his son, Allen Pithie, as the beneficiary of the company life policy. David Pithie's will, however, included the SSIP as part of his estate, only one quarter of which was to be distributed to his son, the balance going to his sister. Following Pithie's death, the executor of his estate sued Ford to collect the assets accumulated in Pithie's SSIP in order to distribute them pursuant to the terms of the will. The court of appeals held that the assets must be distributed in accordance with the terms of the SSIP:

> [W]e must determine whether ERISA preempts state testamentary transfer law in determining the beneficiary of the decedent's SSIP assets. We agree with the district court that the state law "relate[s] to" the terms of the SSIP and, therefore, the state law is preempted.
>
> In this situation, the state testamentary law has "a connection with or reference to [the SSIP]," * * * because, if applied, the state law would determine the distribution of assets under the Plan. The SSIP includes a specific method of identifying the designated beneficiary. Applying state testamentary transfer law to determine the beneficiary under the terms of the decedent's will would not

only relate to the Plan, but would interfere with the administration of the Plan and violate its terms. When, as here, the terms of an employee pension plan under ERISA provide a valid method for determining the beneficiary, that mechanism cannot be displaced by the provisions of a will.

By contrast, a district court held that ERISA did not preempt the New York law prohibiting a killer from profiting from her crime. Mendez-Bellido v. Board of Trustees, 709 F.Supp. 329 (E.D.N.Y.1989) (first wife of a deceased pension plan participant had brought an action to declare the decedent's second wife disqualified due to her conviction for manslaughter of the decedent).

5. In Montanile v. Bd. of Trustees, 136 S.Ct. 651 (2016), Montanile was seriously injured by a drunk driver, and his ERISA plan paid more than $120,000 for his medical expenses. Montanile sued the drunk driver and obtained a $500,000 settlement. Pursuant to the plan's subrogation clause the plan administrator sued to recover the funds expended for Montanile's care. Because of the delay in asserting the claim, Montanile spent all of the money on "nontraceable items," such as services or food. The Court held that when the participant dissipates the whole settlement on nontraceable items, the fiduciary cannot bring an action to attach the participant's general assets because the suit is not one for "appropriate equitable relief" under ERISA § 502(a)(3). Because it was unclear whether the participant dissipated all of the settlement in this manner, the case was remanded.

6. Gobeille v. Liberty Mut. Ins. Co., 136 S.Ct. 936 (2016), involved a challenge to a Vermont law requiring health insurers to report health care claims and other information to a state agency for compilation in an all-inclusive health care database. These "all-payer claims databases" have been enacted in 18 states, and they attempt to generate data on the cost and effectiveness of health care. The Supreme Court held that the Vermont law was preempted by ERISA because ERISA requires plans to file detailed reports with the Secretary of Labor (although different data than required by Vermont) and therefore reporting is a fundamental ERISA function. "Any difference in purpose does not transform this direct regulation of a 'central matter of plan administration,' into an innocuous and peripheral set of additional rules." 136 S.Ct. at 940.

7. In Coventry Health Care of Missouri, Inc. v. Nevils, 137 S.Ct. 1190 (2017), Jody Nevils, a federal employee, was insured under a health plan pursuant to the Federal Employees Health Benefits Act (FEHBA). Nevils was injured in an auto accident and Coventry paid his medical expenses. After Nevil obtained a settlement against the driver of the other car, Coventry asserted a lien against part of the settlement. Nevils satisfied the lien and then sued in Missouri state court asserting that the lien violated Missouri law. The Missouri Supreme Court held that Missouri law applied and prohibited the lien, but the Supreme Court reversed, holding that the Missouri law was preempted. The Court noted that the preemption language in the FEHBA, prohibiting contractual provisions for subrogation that "relate to" benefits, is the same language that has been broadly construed to require preemption under ERISA.

8. ERISA provides for several statutory exceptions to its broad preemption provision. For example, ERISA was amended to save substantive portions of the Hawaii Prepaid Health Care Act after that Act was held to be preempted by ERISA in Standard Oil Co. v. Agsalud, 442 F.Supp. 695 (N.D.Cal.1977), affirmed, 633 F.2d 760 (9th Cir. 1980), affirmed mem., 454 U.S. 801 (1981). Also, ERISA does not preempt "generally applicable criminal laws of a state." 29 U.S.C. § 1144(b)(4).

Domestic relations orders, if they meet certain requirements, are not subject to ERISA's anti-alienation provision and are not preempted by ERISA. ERISA defines "domestic relations orders" as orders that relate to "the provision of child support, alimony payments, or marital property rights to a spouse, former spouse, child, or other dependent of a participant, and are made pursuant to a State domestic relations law (including a community property law)." 29 U.S.C. § 1056(d)(3)(B)(ii). Thus, for example, a state court can order a retiree to give half of his benefits from an ERISA pension plan to his ex-wife as part of their divorce settlement. This provision, usually referred to as the QDRO exception (for "Qualified Domestic Relations Orders"), is the main exception to ERISA's anti-alienation provision, which states that "[e]ach pension plan shall provide that benefits provided under the plan may not be assigned or alienated." 29 U.S.C. § 1056(d)(1).

A NOTE ON THE INSURANCE EXCEPTION

ERISA does not preempt any laws that "regulate insurance." 29 U.S.C. § 1144(b)(2)(A). This provision, also known as the "insurance savings clause," was meant to reconcile ERISA with the policy of the McCarran-Ferguson Act of 1945, 15 U.S.C. §§ 1011–1015, which sought to maintain the regulation of insurance as a province of the states.

The insurance savings clause has prompted litigation over which laws were considered to "regulate insurance" for the purposes of ERISA preemption. One of the early cases to deal with this issue was Metropolitan Life Ins. Co. v. Massachusetts, 471 U.S. 724 (1985). That case concerned the question of whether ERISA preempted a Massachusetts statute that required that health insurance policies provide certain minimum mental-health-care benefits. The Court found that the Massachusetts law—one of many so-called state mandate laws that required health insurance companies to provide certain types of care to their beneficiaries—"relates to" insurance, but that it was saved from preemption by the insurance savings clause:

> To state the obvious, § 47B regulates the terms of certain insurance contracts, and so seems to be saved from preemption as a law which "regulates insurance." This common-sense view of the matter, moreover, is reinforced by the language of the subsequent subsection of ERISA, the "deemer clause," which states that an employee-benefit plan shall not be deemed to be an insurance company "for purposes of any law of any State purporting to regulate insurance companies, *insurance contracts*, banks, trust companies, or investment companies." § 514(b)(2)(B), 29 U. S. C.

§ 1144(b)(2)(B) (emphasis added). By exempting from the saving clause laws regulating insurance contracts that apply directly to benefit plans, the deemer clause makes explicit Congress' intention to include laws that regulate insurance contracts within the scope of the insurance laws preserved by the saving clause. Unless Congress intended to include laws regulating insurance contracts within the scope of the insurance saving clause, it would have been unnecessary for the deemer clause explicitly to exempt such laws from the saving clause when they are applied directly to benefit plans.

The insurers nonetheless argue that § 47B is in reality a health law that merely operates on insurance contracts to accomplish its end, and that it is not the kind of traditional insurance law intended to be saved by § 514(b)(2)(A). We find this argument unpersuasive.

Appellants assert that state laws that directly regulate the insurer, and laws that regulate such matters as the way in which insurance may be sold, are traditional laws subject to the clause, while laws that regulate the substantive terms of insurance contracts are recent innovations more properly seen as health laws rather than as insurance laws, which § 514(b)(2)(A) does not save. This distinction reads the saving clause out of ERISA entirely, because laws that regulate only the insurer, or the way in which it may sell insurance, do not "relate to" benefit plans in the first instance. Because they would not be pre-empted by § 514(a), they do not need to be "saved" by § 514(b)(2)(A). * * *

Moreover, it is both historically and conceptually inaccurate to assert that mandated-benefit laws are not traditional insurance laws. As we have indicated, state laws regulating the substantive terms of insurance contracts were commonplace well before the mid-70's, when Congress considered ERISA. The case law concerning the meaning of the phrase "business of insurance" in the McCarran-Ferguson Act strongly supports the conclusion that regulation regarding the substantive terms of insurance contracts falls squarely within the saving clause as laws "which regulate insurance."

Cases interpreting the scope of the McCarran-Ferguson Act have identified three criteria relevant to determining whether a particular practice falls within that Act's reference to the "business of insurance": "*first*, whether the practice has the effect of transferring or spreading a policyholder's risk; *second*, whether the practice is an integral part of the policy relationship between the insurer and the insured; and *third*, whether the practice is limited to entities within the insurance industry." Application of these principles suggests that mandated-benefit laws are state regulation of the "business of insurance."

Section 47B obviously regulates the spreading of risk: as we have indicated, it was intended to effectuate the legislative judgment that the risk of mental-health care should be shared. It is also evident that mandated-benefit laws directly regulate an integral part of the relationship between the insurer and the policyholder by limiting the type of insurance that an insurer may sell to the policyholder. Finally, the third criterion is present here, for mandated-benefit statutes impose requirements only on insurers, with the intent of affecting the relationship between the insurer and the policyholder. Section 47B, then, is the very kind of regulation that this Court has identified as a law that relates to the regulation of the business of insurance as defined in the McCarran-Ferguson Act.

The Supreme Court later sought to downplay the significance of the three McCarran-Ferguson factors identified in *Metropolitan Life*. In UNUM Life Ins. Co. of Am. v. Ward, 526 U.S. 358 (1999), the Court held that the insurance savings clause saved from ERISA preemption a California law that barred insurers from denying benefits based on an insured's untimely notice of claim unless the insurer could show prejudice from the delay. The Court first found that the California law regulated insurance "as a matter of common sense." Next, in its discussion of the McCarran-Ferguson factors, the Court stated:

Preliminarily, we reject UNUM's assertion that a state regulation must satisfy all three McCarran-Ferguson factors in order to "regulate insurance" under ERISA's saving clause. Our precedent is more supple than UNUM conceives it to be. We have indicated that the McCarran-Ferguson factors are "considerations [to be] weighed" in determining whether a state law regulates insurance and that "none of these criteria is necessarily determinative in itself." In *Metropolitan Life*, the case in which we first used the McCarran-Ferguson formulation to assess whether a state law "regulates insurance" for purposes of ERISA's saving clause, we called the McCarran-Ferguson factors "relevant"; we did not describe them as "required."

The Court then found that there was some uncertainty as to whether the California law satisfied the first McCarran-Ferguson factor (whether the law spread or transferred risk), but that that uncertainty did not need to be resolved because the law obviously satisfied the other two factors.

Similarly, in Rush Prudential HMO, Inc. v. Moran, 536 U.S. 355 (2002), the Court found that ERISA did not preempt an Illinois law that provided HMO beneficiaries a right to independent review of denials of benefits. As in *UNUM*, the Court did not resolve the question of whether the law satisfied the first McCarran-Ferguson factor when it thought that the other two were clearly satisfied.

The Court also attempted to clarify its approach to determining when, as a matter of common sense, a law regulates insurance:

The common-sense enquiry focuses on "primary elements of an insurance contract [which] are the spreading and underwriting of a policyholder's risk." * * * Rush contends that seeing an HMO as an insurer distorts the nature of an HMO, which is, after all, a health care provider, too. This, Rush argues, should determine its characterization, with the consequence that regulation of an HMO is not insurance regulation within the meaning of ERISA. The answer to Rush is, of course, that an HMO is both: it provides health care, and it does so as an insurer. Nothing in the saving clause requires an either-or choice between health care and insurance in deciding a preemption question, and as long as providing insurance fairly accounts for the application of state law, the saving clause may apply.

Not satisfied with an approach dominated by "common sense" and the McCarran-Ferguson factors, the court again modified its "regulates insurance" doctrine a year later in the following case.

Kentucky Association of Health Plans, Inc. v. Miller
538 U.S. 329 (2003).

■ JUSTICE SCALIA delivered the opinion of the Court.

Kentucky law provides that "[a] health insurer shall not discriminate against any provider who is located within the geographic coverage area of the health benefit plan and who is willing to meet the terms and conditions for participation established by the health insurer, including the Kentucky state Medicaid program and Medicaid partnerships." Moreover, any "health benefit plan that includes chiropractic benefits shall . . . permit any licensed chiropractor who agrees to abide by the terms, conditions, reimbursement rates, and standards of quality of the health benefit plan to serve as a participating primary chiropractic provider to any person covered by the plan." We granted certiorari to decide whether [ERISA] pre-empts either, or both, of these "Any Willing Provider" (AWP) statutes.

* * * ERISA pre-empts all state laws "insofar as they may now or hereafter relate to any employee benefit plan," but state "laws . . . which regulate insurance, banking, or securities" are saved from pre-emption. The District Court concluded that although both AWP statutes "relate to" employee benefit plans, each law "regulates insurance" and is therefore saved from pre-emption. [The Sixth Circuit also found that the statutes regulated insurance and were therefore not preempted]

To determine whether Kentucky's AWP statutes are saved from preemption, we must ascertain whether they are "laws . . . which regulate insurance." * * *

Petitioners contend that Kentucky's AWP laws fall outside the scope of [the insurance savings clause] for two reasons. First, because Kentucky has failed to "specifically direct" its AWP laws towards the insurance industry; and second, because the AWP laws do not regulate an insurance practice. We find neither contention persuasive.

Petitioners claim that Kentucky's statutes are not "specifically directed toward" insurers because they regulate not only the insurance industry but also doctors who seek to form and maintain limited provider networks with HMOs. That is to say, the AWP laws equally prevent *providers* from entering into limited network contracts with *insurers,* just as they prevent insurers from creating exclusive networks in the first place. We do not think it follows that Kentucky has failed to specifically direct its AWP laws at the insurance industry.

Neither of Kentucky's AWP statutes, by its terms, imposes any prohibitions or requirements on health-care providers. And Kentucky health-care providers are still capable of entering exclusive networks with insurers who conduct business outside the Commonwealth of Kentucky or who are otherwise not covered by [the statutes]. Kentucky's statutes are transgressed only when a "health insurer" or a "health benefit plan that includes chiropractic benefits" excludes from its network a provider who is willing and able to meet its terms.

It is of course true that as a *consequence* of Kentucky's AWP laws, entities outside the insurance industry (such as health-care providers) will be unable to enter into certain agreements with Kentucky insurers. But the same could be said about the state [law] we held saved from preemption in [*Rush*]. Illinois' requirement that HMOs provide independent review of whether services are "medically necessary" likewise excluded insureds from joining an HMO that would have withheld the right to independent review in exchange for a lower premium. Yet [*Rush* did not find] the effects of these laws on noninsurers, significant though they may have been, inconsistent with the requirement that laws saved from pre-emption by [the insurance savings clause] be "specifically directed toward" the insurance industry. Regulations "directed toward" certain entities will almost always disable other entities from doing, with the regulated entities, what the regulations forbid; this does not suffice to place such regulation outside the scope of ERISA's savings clause.

Petitioners claim that the AWP laws do not regulate insurers with respect to an insurance practice because, unlike the state laws we held saved from pre-emption in *Metropolitan Life Ins., UNUM,* and *Rush Prudential,* they do not control the actual terms of insurance policies. Rather, they focus upon the relationship between an insurer and *third-party providers*—which in petitioners' view does not constitute an "insurance practice."

In support of their contention, petitioners rely on Group Life & Health Ins. Co. v. Royal Drug Co., 440 U.S. 205 (1979), which held that third-party provider arrangements between insurers and pharmacies were not "the 'business of insurance'" under § 2(b) of the McCarran-Ferguson Act. ERISA's savings clause, however, is not concerned (as is the McCarran-Ferguson Act provision) with how to characterize *conduct* undertaken by private actors, but with how to characterize *state laws* in regard to what they "regulate." It does not follow from *Royal Drug* that a law mandating certain insurer-provider relationships fails to "regulate insurance." Suppose a state law required all licensed attorneys to participate in 10 hours of continuing legal education (CLE) each year. This statute "regulates" the practice of law—even though sitting through 10 hours of CLE classes does not constitute the practice of law—because the state has *conditioned* the right to practice law on certain requirements, which substantially affect the product delivered by lawyers to their clients. Kentucky's AWP laws operate in a similar manner with respect to the insurance industry: Those who wish to provide health insurance in Kentucky (any "health insurer") may not discriminate against any willing provider. This "regulates" insurance by imposing conditions on the right to engage in the business of insurance; whether or not an HMO's contracts with providers constitute "the business of insurance" under *Royal Drug* is beside the point.

We emphasize that conditions on the right to engage in the business of insurance must also substantially affect the risk pooling arrangement between the insurer and the insured to be covered by ERISA's savings clause. Otherwise, any state law aimed at insurance companies could be deemed a law that "regulates insurance," contrary to our interpretation of [the insurance savings clause] in *Rush Prudential*. A state law requiring all insurance companies to pay their janitors twice the minimum wage would not "regulate insurance," even though it would be a prerequisite to engaging the business of insurance, because it does not substantially affect the risk pooling arrangement undertaken by insurer and insured. Petitioners contend that Kentucky's AWP statutes fail this test as well, since they do not alter or affect the terms of insurance policies, but concern only the relationship between insureds and third-party providers. We disagree. We have never held that state laws must alter or control the actual terms of insurance policies to be deemed "laws . . . which regulate insurance" under § 1144(b)(2)(A); it suffices that they substantially affect the risk pooling arrangement between insurer and insured. By expanding the number of providers from whom an insured may receive health services, AWP laws alter the scope of permissible bargains between insurers and insureds in a manner similar to the mandated-benefit laws we upheld in *Metropolitan Life*, the notice-prejudice rule we sustained in *UNUM*, and the independent-review provisions we approved in *Rush Prudential*. No longer may Kentucky insureds seek insurance from a closed network of health-care providers in exchange for a lower premium. The AWP prohibition substantially affects the type of risk pooling arrangements that insurers may offer.

Our prior decisions have relied, to varying degrees, on our cases interpreting §§ 2(a) and 2(b) of the McCarran-Ferguson Act. In determining whether certain practices constitute "the *business of* insurance" under the McCarran-Ferguson Act, our cases have looked to three factors: "*first*, whether the practice has the effect of transferring or spreading a policyholder's risk; *second*, whether the practice is an integral part of the policy relationship between the insurer and the insured; and *third*, whether the practice is limited to entities within the insurance industry."

We believe that our use of the McCarran-Ferguson case law in the ERISA context has misdirected attention, failed to provide clear guidance to lower federal courts, and, as this case demonstrates, added little to the relevant analysis. That is unsurprising, since the statutory language of § 1144(b)(2)(A) differs substantially from that of the McCarran-Ferguson Act. Rather than concerning itself with whether certain practices constitute "the business of insurance," or whether a state law was "enacted . . . *for the purpose of* regulating the business of insurance," 29 U.S.C. § 1144(b)(2)(A) asks merely whether a state law is a "law . . . which regulates insurance, banking, or securities." What is more, the McCarran-Ferguson factors were developed in cases that characterized *conduct* by private actors, not state laws.

Our holdings in *UNUM* and *Rush Prudential*—that a state law may fail the first McCarran-Ferguson factor yet still be saved from preemption under § 1144(b)(2)(A)—raise more questions than they answer and provide wide opportunities for divergent outcomes. May a state law satisfy *any* two of the three McCarran-Ferguson factors and still fall under the savings clause? Just one? What happens if two of three factors are satisfied, but not "securely satisfied" or "clearly satisfied," as they were in *UNUM* and *Rush Prudential*? * * *

Today we make a clean break from the McCarran-Ferguson factors and hold that for a state law to be deemed a "law . . . which regulates insurance," it must satisfy two requirements. First, the state law must be specifically directed toward entities engaged in insurance. Second, as explained above, the state law must substantially affect the risk pooling arrangement between the insurer and the insured. Kentucky's law satisfies each of these requirements.

For these reasons, we affirm the judgment of the Sixth Circuit.

NOTES AND QUESTIONS

1.   Has the Supreme Court's tinkering with the insurance savings clause clarified it? Is there any practical difference between the "directed towards entities engaged in insurance" and the "common sense" test?

2.   Although the Court has endorsed a different test than those used by *Rush, UNUM,* and *Metropolitan Life,* are the ultimate holdings of those cases still good law? Does ERISA still preempt state mandate laws, laws requiring independent review of benefit denials, and laws requiring insurers to prove prejudice before denying claims of late filers? Few cases have clarified these issues, perhaps because it seems probable that these laws are "directed

towards entities engaged in insurance" and "affect the risk pooling arrangement." Also, *Miller's* discussion of these cases does not seem too critical of their outcome, even if it does declare a "clean break" with the McCarran-Ferguson factors.

3. When an employer self-insures, its plan is not covered by the insurance savings clause and ERISA still preempts state laws that relate to the employer plan. See 29 U.S.C. § 1144(b)(2)(B) ("[A]n employee benefit plan * * * [shall not] be deemed to be an insurance company or other insurer, bank, trust company, or investment company or to be engaged in the business of insurance or banking for purposes of any law of any State purporting to regulate insurance companies, insurance contracts, banks, trust companies, or investment companies"). By freeing self-insured health care plans from costly state regulation, this so-called "deemer clause" provides an incentive for employers to self-insure. For large employers, self-insurance is not too difficult, but it can be risky for small companies. Some small employers attempt to solve this problem by purchasing "stop-loss" insurance, which insures the employer against health care costs that exceed a certain dollar value. Are small employers that self-fund and purchase stop-loss insurance still self-funded for the purposes of ERISA? So far, the courts that have considered the issue appear to have found that such employers are self-funded and that, therefore, ERISA preemption saves them from state regulation. See, e.g., Lincoln Mut. Cas. Co. v. Lectron Prods., Inc., 970 F.2d 206 (6th Cir. 1992). See generally Russell Karobkin, The Battle Over Self-Insured Health Plans, or "One Good Loophole Deserves Another," 5 Yale J. Health Pol'y, L. & Ethics 89 (2005).

D. FAMILY AND MEDICAL LEAVE

The Family and Medical Leave Act of 1993, 29 U.S.C. §§ 2601–2654, requires that employers provide leaves of absence for childbirth or the care of children or other family members. Employers of 50 or more employees must permit eligible workers to take up to 12 weeks of unpaid leave in any 12-month period for the birth or adoption of a child, to care for a child, spouse, or parent with a serious health condition, or for the worker's own serious health condition that makes him or her unable to perform the job. Only workers who have been employed by the employer for at least 12 months and have at least 1,250 hours of service during that period are eligible for statutory leave. "Serious health condition" is defined as an illness, injury, impairment, or physical or mental condition that involves inpatient care or continuing treatment by a health care provider. An employer may require medical certification, including a second or third opinion at its expense, of the need for a leave to care for a sick relative or for the employee's own illness.

An employee may elect, or the employer may require the employee to substitute, any accrued paid vacation leave, personal or family leave, or medical or sick leave for any part of the 12-week leave provided by the Act. When leave for childbirth or adoption is foreseeable, the employee must give at least 30 days' notice of his or her intention to take a leave;

when medical leave is foreseeable because of a planned treatment, the employee must make a reasonable effort to schedule the treatment in a manner that will not unduly disrupt the employer's operations, and the employee must give 30 days' notice if possible. If a husband and wife work for the same employer, the employer may limit their aggregate number of weeks of leave for birth, adoption, or care of a sick parent to 12 in a 12-month period.

During the leave the employer must continue to provide health care benefits at the same level and under the same conditions as if the employee were actively at work. If the employee fails to return from leave for a reason other than the continuation, recurrence, or onset of a serious health condition that would entitle the employee to leave under the Act, or for some other reason beyond the employee's control, the employer may recover any premium it paid to maintain the employee's coverage during the leave. When the employee returns from leave, the employer must restore him or her to the same or an equivalent position, with no loss of employment benefits accrued before the date the leave began. The employer may, however, deny restoration of employment to a salaried employee who is among the highest paid ten percent of its workforce, if the denial is "necessary to prevent substantial and grievous economic injury" to its operations, and the employer notifies the employee of its determination.

The enforcement mechanisms of the Act are similar to those under the Fair Labor Standards Act. The Act may be enforced through suit in either federal or state court by employees individually or on behalf of themselves and other similarly situated employees, or by the Secretary of Labor. An employee's right to bring suit terminates if the Secretary brings an action on his or her behalf. The statute of limitations is two years from the last event constituting a violation and three years for willful violations. The Department of Labor may receive and investigate employee complaints, but, as under the FLSA, there is no administrative prerequisite to suit.

Remedies for violations of the Act include lost wages and benefits plus interest, or, if the employee has not lost any wages or benefits, any actual monetary losses the employee sustained as a direct result of the violation, plus interest. The statute mentions the cost of providing care as an example of these non-wage losses. In addition, plaintiffs may recover an amount equal to the monetary recovery as liquidated damages, subject to reduction by the court if the employer proves it acted in good faith and with reasonable grounds for believing it was not in violation of the Act. The court must award a victorious plaintiff reasonable attorney's fees, reasonable witness fees, and costs. Because the statute speaks only of fee awards from defendants to plaintiffs, fee awards under the Act are not available to prevailing defendants.

Over half the states have their own family and medical leave laws, some applicable to the public and private sectors and others applicable only in the public sector. The states vary in whether they require leave for the birth of a child, adoption, family illness (including the employee's own illness), or some combination of the three. The duration of the leave ranges from six weeks to two years. Most state laws provide that employees on leave can continue group health and other benefits at their own expense, while some states also specify which benefits must be extended and at what cost to the employee. Legislation in California provides for up to six weeks of *paid* family leave. Cal. Unemp. Ins. Code §§ 3300–3306.

For examples of judicial construction of state family leave laws, see e.g., Portland Gen. Elec. Co. v. Bureau of Labor & Indus., 859 P.2d 1143 (Or.1993) (state parental leave statute allowed employee to use accrued leave during parental leave, even if employee did not meet eligibility criteria under collective bargaining agreement); Butzlaff v. Wisconsin Personnel Comm'n, 480 N.W.2d 559 (Wis. Ct. App.1992) (employee need not work for same employer for 52 consecutive weeks prior to leave).

From a policy standpoint, there are two areas in which family and medical leave laws are the most likely to be extended. First, new laws could mandate *paid* family and medical leave. See Gillian Lester, A Defense of Paid Family Leave, 28 Harv. J.L. & Gender 1 (2005). Second, laws could expand the categories of family and medical leave beyond childbirth and adoption, illness of a family member, or illness of an employee. Several states already have enacted parental leave laws that prohibit discrimination against employees who take time off from work to attend parent-teacher conferences or other school-related activities (see West's Ann. Cal. Lab. Code § 230.8), or to accompany a minor child to a juvenile court appearance (see Utah Code Ann. § 78–3a–507). Other laws grant employees a certain number of unpaid personal leave days to attend to personal matters, such as medical appointments, court appearances, and funerals. See Ohio Rev. Code § 124.386 (applicable to public employees).

Ballard v. Chicago Park District

741 F.3d 838 (7th Cir. 2014).

■ FLAUM, CIRCUIT JUDGE.

The Family and Medical Leave Act gives eligible employees a right to twelve workweeks of leave "[i]n order to care for the spouse, or a son, daughter, or parent, of the employee, if such spouse, son, daughter, or parent has a serious health condition." 29 U.S.C. § 2612(a)(1)(C). This case is about what qualifies as "caring for" a family member under the Act. In particular, it is about whether the FMLA applies when an employee requests leave so that she can provide physical and psychological care to a terminally ill parent while that parent is traveling away from home. For the reasons set forth below, we conclude that such an employee is seeking leave "to care for" a family member within the meaning of the FMLA.

I. Background

Beverly Ballard is a former Chicago Park District employee. In April 2006, Beverly's mother, Sarah, was diagnosed with end-stage congestive heart failure and began receiving hospice support through Horizon Hospice & Palliative Care. Beverly lived with Sarah and acted as her primary caregiver; among other things, she cooked her mother's meals, administered insulin and other medication, drained fluids from her heart, bathed and dressed her, and prepared her for bed. In 2007, Sarah and a Horizon Hospice social worker met to discuss Sarah's end-of-life goals. Sarah said that she had always wanted to take a family trip to Las Vegas. The social worker was able to secure funding from the Fairygodmother Foundation, a nonprofit that facilitated these sorts of opportunities for terminally ill adults. The six-day trip was scheduled for January 2008.

Ballard requested unpaid leave from the Chicago Park District so that she could accompany her mother to Las Vegas. (The parties dispute many particulars of Ballard's request, including whether Ballard gave the Park District sufficient notice, but these issues are not germane to this appeal and we will ignore them.) The Park District ultimately denied the request, although Ballard maintains that she was not informed of the denial prior to her trip.

Ballard and her mother traveled to Las Vegas as planned, where they spent time together and participated in typical tourist activities. Beverly continued to serve as her mother's caretaker during the trip. In addition to performing her usual responsibilities, Beverly drove her mother to a hospital when a fire unexpectedly prevented them from reaching their hotel room, where Sarah's medicine was stored.

Several months later, the Chicago Park District terminated Ballard for unauthorized absences accumulated during her trip. Ballard filed suit under the FMLA. The Park District moved for summary judgment, arguing in part that Ballard did not "care for" her mother in Las Vegas because she was already providing Sarah with care at home and because the trip was not related to a continuing course of medical treatment. The district court denied the motion, explaining that "[s]o long as the employee provides 'care' to the family member, where the care takes place has no bearing on whether the employee receives FMLA protections." The Park District moved for an interlocutory appeal.

II. Discussion

We begin with the text of the statute: an eligible employee is entitled to leave "[i]n order to care for" a family member with a "serious health condition." 29 U.S.C. § 2612(a)(1)(C). The Park District does not dispute that Sarah Ballard suffered from a serious health condition. Instead, it claims that Beverly did not "care for" Sarah in Las Vegas. It would have us read the FMLA as limiting "care," at least in the context of an away-from-home trip, only to services provided in connection with ongoing medical treatment.

One problem with the Park District's argument is that § 2612(a)(1)(C) speaks in terms of "care," not "treatment." The latter term does appear in other subsections of § 2612, but Ballard does not rely on those provisions for her leave, and the Park District does not argue that they are implicated in this case. Furthermore, the Park District does not explain why participation in ongoing treatment is required when the employee provides away-from-home care, but not when she provides at-home care. Certainly we see no textual basis for that distinction in the statute.

Another problem is that the FMLA's text does not restrict care to a particular place or geographic location. For instance, it does not say that an employee is entitled to time off "to care *at home* for" a family member. The only limitation it places on care is that the family member must have a serious health condition. We are reluctant, without good reason, to read in another limitation that Congress has not provided.

Still, the FMLA does not define "care," so perhaps there is room to disagree about whether Ballard can be said to have cared for her mother in Las Vegas. We therefore turn to the Department of Labor's regulations to clear away any lurking ambiguity. There are no regulations specifically interpreting 29 U.S.C. § 2612(a)(1)(C). There are, however, regulations interpreting a closely related provision concerning health-care provider certification. Those regulations state:

What does it mean that an employee is "needed to care for" a family member?

(a) The medical certification provision that an employee is "needed to care for" a family member encompasses both physical and psychological care. It includes situations where, for example, because of a serious health condition, the family member is unable to care for his or her own basic medical, hygienic, or nutritional needs or safety, or is unable to transport himself or herself to the doctor, etc. The term also includes providing psychological comfort and reassurance which would be beneficial to a child, spouse or parent with a serious health condition who is receiving inpatient or home care.

* * *

29 C.F.R. § 825.116 (2008).

We see nothing in these regulations to support the Park District's argument, either. The first sentence defines "care" expansively to include "physical and psychological care"—again without any geographic limitation. The only part of the regulations suggesting that the location of care might make a difference is the statement that psychological care "includes providing psychological comfort and reassurance to [a family member] . . . who is *receiving inpatient or home care*." Even so, as the district court correctly observed, this example of what constitutes psychological care does not purport to be exclusive. Moreover, this example only concerns psychological care. The examples of what constitutes physical care use no location-specific language whatsoever.

Sarah's basic medical, hygienic, and nutritional needs did not change while she was in Las Vegas, and Beverly continued to assist her with those needs during the trip. In fact, as the district court observed, Beverly's presence proved quite important indeed when a fire at the hotel made it impossible to reach their room, requiring Beverly to find another source of insulin and pain medicine. Thus, at the very least, Ballard requested leave in order to provide physical care. That, in turn, is enough to satisfy 29 U.S.C. § 2612(a)(1)(C).

The Park District nevertheless argues that any care Ballard provided in Las Vegas needed to be connected to ongoing medical treatment in order for her leave to be protected by the FMLA. But, like the statute itself, the regulations never use the term "treatment" in their definition of care. Rather, they speak in terms of basic medical, hygienic, and nutritional needs—needs that, as in this case, do not change merely because a person is not undergoing active medical treatment. And it would be odd to read an ongoing-treatment requirement into the definition of "care" when the definition of "serious health condition" explicitly states that active treatment is *not* a prerequisite.

In support of its ongoing-treatment argument, the Park District principally relies on out-of-circuit case law construing 29 U.S.C. § 2612(a)(1)(C). First, it cites a pair of Ninth Circuit cases holding that "caring for a family member with a serious health condition 'involves some level of participation in ongoing treatment of that condition.' " Tellis v. Alaska Airlines, Inc., 414 F.3d 1045, 1047 (9th Cir.2005) (quoting Marchisheck v. San Mateo Cnty., 199 F.3d 1068, 1076 (9th Cir.1999)). *Tellis* involved an employee who flew cross-country to pick up a car and drive it back to his pregnant wife; *Marchisheck* involved an employee who brought her son to the Philippines because she worried that his social environment in Los Angeles was unhealthy. Next, the Park District cites a First Circuit case about an employee who took leave to accompany her seriously ill husband on a "healing pilgrimage" to the Philippines. Tayag v. Lahey Clinic Hosp., Inc., 632 F.3d 788 (1st Cir.2011). Before considering whether the pilgrimage qualified as medical care under the FMLA, the *Tayag* court noted that the employee "properly does not claim that caring for her husband would itself be protected leave" if the pair traveled "for reasons unrelated to medical treatment of [her husband's] illnesses."

We respectfully part ways with the First and Ninth Circuits on this point. The only one of these cases that purports to ground its conclusion in the text of the statute or regulations is *Marchisheck*. However, as explained above, we do not see how that conclusion follows. The relevant rule says that, so long as the employee attends to a family member's basic medical, hygienic, or nutritional needs, that employee is caring for the family member, even if that care is not part of ongoing treatment of the condition. Furthermore, none of the cases explain why certain services provided to a family member at home should be considered "care," but those same services provided away from home should not be. Again, we see no basis for that distinction in either the statute or the regulations.

At points in its briefing, the Park District describes Ballard's travel as a "recreational trip" or a "non-medically related pleasure trip." It also raises the specter that employees will help themselves to (unpaid) FMLA leave in order to take personal vacations, simply by bringing seriously ill family members along. So perhaps what the Park District means to argue is that the real reason Beverly requested leave was in order to take a free pleasure trip, and not in order to care for her mother. Whether that sort of argument is borne out by the record—which suggests that Sarah arranged the trip with her social worker as part of her end-of-life hospice planning, that Beverly consulted with Sarah's doctor about what would be required on the trip, and that Beverly did in fact provide care in Las Vegas—is not for us to decide at this stage. However, we note that an employer concerned about the risk that employees will abuse the FMLA's leave provisions may of course require that requests be certified by the family member's health care provider. And any worries about opportunistic leave-taking in this case should be tempered by the fact that this dispute arises out of the hospice and palliative care context.

If Beverly had sought leave to care for her mother in Chicago, her request would have fallen within the scope of the FMLA. So too if Sarah had lived in Las Vegas instead of with her daughter, and Beverly had requested leave to care for her mother there. Ultimately, other than a concern that our straightforward reading will "open the door to increased FMLA requests," the Park District gives us no reason to treat the current scenario any differently. Yet even if we credit the Park District's policy concern, "[d]esire for what we may consider a more sensible result cannot justify a judicial rewrite" of the FMLA.

III. Conclusion

We AFFIRM the judgment of the district court.

NOTES AND QUESTIONS

1.   The court noted that the Park District's main objection was that Ballard was seeking to take a recreational trip that was not medically necessary. Do you think part of the Park District's concern was about avoiding the "slippery slope" of FMLA leave takers? If so, is it realistic to assume there will be other requests for "recreational" leave?

2.   As discussed in *Ballard,* to qualify for FMLA leave to "care for" a seriously ill family member, what "caring" activities must the employee

undertake? In Tellis v. Alaska Airlines, Inc., 414 F.3d 1045 (9th Cir. 2005), the Ninth Circuit held that an airline mechanic's cross-country trip to get a more reliable family car for his pregnant wife and his regular telephone calls to her during the trip did not constitute "caring for" her. See also Fioto v. Manhattan Woods Golf Enters., LLC, 270 F.Supp.2d 401 (S.D.N.Y. 2003) (merely visiting a sick relative does not qualify as providing care).

3. The Wage and Hour Division of the Labor Department issued final regulations implementing the Family and Medical Leave Act in early 1995. 60 Fed.Reg. 2180, codified at 29 C.F.R. Part 825. The regulations provide that to be a "serious health condition," there must be a period of incapacity of more than three days. According to the Labor Department, the FMLA was not intended to cover short-term conditions for which treatment and recovery are very brief because Congress expected that such conditions would be covered by "even the most modest of employer sick leave policies." Some critics of the "more than three day" rule argued unsuccessfully that it encourages employees to remain absent from work longer than necessary in order to qualify for statutory protection. Other critics, however, have contended that "more than three days" is too short and that the FMLA was not intended to cover short-term absences caused by routine illnesses, but only long-term absences caused by serious health conditions.

The Secretary of Labor's FMLA regulations, 29 C.F.R. Part 825, were overhauled and reissued at the end of 2008. Among the numerous changes are the following: (1) if an employee submits insufficient medical documentation of the need for leave, specifically-designated parties (health care provider, human resources professional, leave administrator, or management official other than the employee's supervisor) may call the employee's health care provider for the purpose of clarifying and authenticating the employee's leave request; (2) whereas the prior version of the regulation provided that an employee had two business days after an absence to notify his or her employer of the need for FMLA leave, the new version requires the employee to use the employer's customary call-in procedures unless there are abnormal circumstances; and (3) the time spent by an employee performing light duty work does not count against the employee's FMLA leave entitlement.

4. Other cases on the issue of what is a "serious health condition" include: Pollard v. NY Methodist Hospital, 861 F.3d 374 (2d Cir. 2017) (finding genuine issue of material fact existed precluding summary judgment as to whether employee's foot growth was serious health condition requiring multiple treatments); Novak v. MetroHealth Med. Ctr., 503 F.3d 572 (6th Cir. 2007) (temporary post-partum depression not a serious health condition); Miller v. AT & T Corp., 250 F.3d 820 (4th Cir. 2001) (under certain circumstances seasonal flu can be a serious health condition); Oswalt v. Sara Lee Corp., 74 F.3d 91 (5th Cir. 1996) (food poisoning not a serious illness); Godwin v. Rheem Mfg. Co., 15 F.Supp.2d 1197 (M.D.Ala.1998) (poison ivy not a serious health condition); Manuel v. Westlake Polymers Corp., 66 F.3d 758 (5th Cir. 1995) (ingrown toenail was a serious illness); Bauer v. Dayton-Walther Corp., 910 F.Supp. 306 (E.D.Ky.1996) (rectal bleeding not a serious health condition); Brannon v. OshKosh B'Gosh, 897 F.Supp. 1028

(M.D.Tenn.1995) (gastroenteritis and upper respiratory infection not a serious health condition).

5. An employee who, as a result of injury or illness, is unable to perform the essential functions of a job has no FMLA entitlement to "work harden" on a reduced schedule, gradually working up to full time. Hatchett v. Philander Smith Coll., 251 F.3d 670 (8th Cir. 2001). The employee may have such a right as a "reasonable accommodation" under the ADA. Because of the difficulty of meeting the definition of "individual with a disability," however, the ADA route may be foreclosed to many individuals with temporarily disabling conditions.

6. Under the FMLA, an employee is required to provide the employer with notice of a request for leave. It is not necessary that the employee mention the FMLA in the request, but merely stating that he or she is sick is insufficient. In Burnett v. LFW, Inc., 472 F.3d 471 (7th Cir. 2006), the employee stated that he was sick and "wanted to go home." The Seventh Circuit held that this was adequate notice because the employer had been made aware over a four-month period that the employee was being treated for possible prostate cancer. But see Pollard v. New York Methodist Hospital, 861 F.3d 374 (2d Cir. 2017) (holding that state agency's finding in awarding unemployment insurance benefits to former employee that employee provided notice to former employer of surgery "as soon as was practicable" did not preclude employer from challenging whether employee provided adequate notice of her request for FMLA leave).

7. In Coutard v. Municipal Credit Union, 848 F.3d 102 (2d Cir. 2017), the plaintiff alleged that his employer violated the FMLA by refusing to permit him to take leave to care for his seriously ill grandfather, who, in loco parentis, had raised him as a child. The FMLA provides for leave under these circumstances, but in requesting leave the plaintiff did not specifically mention the loco parentis relationship. The Second Circuit held that when the employee requested leave, the employer had an obligation to specific any additional information it needed to determine whether the employee was eligible for leave.

8. Employees may bring FMLA actions for "interference" with their statutory rights or "retaliation" for exercising those rights. In either type of case the employer may defend by proving it had an independent reason for taking the adverse action, such as discharging the employee. If the employer has an "honest belief" in its legitimate reason for the adverse action there will be no liability under the FMLA, even if the employer's reason is ultimately found to be mistaken. See Jaszczyszyn v. Advantage Health Physician Network, 504 Fed. Appx. 440) (6th Cir. 2012). Accord Capps v. Mendelez Global, LLC, 847 F.3d 144 (3d Cir. 2017) (applying "honest belief" standard).

9. An employee loses the protection of the FMLA if he or she is unable to return to work at the end of the 12-week leave period. It has even been held not to violate the FMLA to discharge an employee before the end of the leave period (for a lawful reason) when the individual is unable to return after the end of the leave. Edgar v. JAC Prods., Inc., 443 F.3d 501 (6th Cir. 2006).

10. Alan McFarland, a maintenance director at a nursing home, suffered a stroke and was placed on FMLA leave by his employer. When McFarland sought to return to work, his employer refused to reinstate him because his doctor imposed a 20-pound lifting restriction. McFarland alleged an FMLA violation. The employer introduced evidence that while McFarland was off work he collected short-term disability benefits because "he was unable to perform the material duties of his regular occupation." The Third Circuit, in upholding the district court's dismissal and summary judgment on all claims, applied judicial estoppel to prevent the plaintiff from asserting he was able to work. The court also noted that employers have no duty of reasonable accommodation under the FMLA. Macfarlan v. Ivy Hall SNF, LLC, 675 F.3d 266 (3d Cir. 2012).

11. In Seeger v. Cincinnati Bell Tel. Co., 681 F.3d 274 (6th Cir. 2012), an employee on FMLA leave for a herniated disc and sciatica was observed by coworkers walking at the Oktoberfest in downtown Cincinnati. When this was reported to management, the employee was discharged for filing a fraudulent FMLA (and paid disability leave) claim. In upholding the employer, the Sixth Circuit applied the "honest belief" test, under which the employer merely needs to act in good faith, as opposed to an objective test, under which the employer needs to be correct in its factual conclusions. What are the advantages and disadvantages of each approach?

12. A provision of the Defense Authorization Act of 2008 amends the FMLA to permit a "spouse, son, daughter, parent, or next of kin" to take up to 26 weeks of leave to care for a member of the Armed Forces, including a member of the National Guard or Reserves, who is undergoing medical treatment, recuperation, or therapy, is otherwise in outpatient status, or is otherwise on the temporary disability retired list, for a serious injury or illness.

13. The FMLA provides that any employer that violates the statute shall be liable for "any wages, salary, employment benefits, or other compensation denied or lost to such employee by reason of the violation." 29 U.S.C.A. § 2617(a)(1)(A)(i)(I). Is a prevailing plaintiff entitled to out-of-pocket expenses, such as moving and job search expenses? See Nero v. Indus. Molding Corp., 167 F.3d 921 (5th Cir. 1999) (held: no).

14. In Nevada Dep't of Human Resources v. Hibbs, 538 U.S. 721 (2003), the Supreme Court held that the FMLA's abrogation of state immunity under the Eleventh Amendment was a valid exercise of congressional power under Section 5 of the Fourteenth Amendment. In reaching a result at odds with the trend in Eleventh Amendment case law involving employment law, the Court traced legislative findings of gender discrimination in workplace leave policies. It determined that the FMLA is "congruent and proportional to the targeted violation."

By creating an across-the-board, routine employment benefit for all eligible employees, Congress sought to ensure that family-care leave would no longer be stigmatized as an inordinate drain on the workplace caused by female employees, and that employers could not evade leave obligations simply by hiring men. By setting a minimum standard of family leave for *all* eligible employees, irrespective of gender, the FMLA attacks the formerly state-sanctioned stereotype that only women are responsible for family care-giving, thereby reducing employers' incentives to engage in discrimination by basing hiring and promotion decisions on stereotypes.

In Coleman v. Court of Appeals of Maryland, 566 U.S. 30 (2012), an employee of the court brought an action under the FMLA alleging his employer denied him leave necessitated by his own serious health condition. The Supreme Court distinguished *Hibbs* and held that, unlike the FMLA's "family-care" provisions designed to redress a history of sex discrimination in leave policies, the "self-care" provision did not validly abrogate the state's immunity from suit. Therefore, subjecting states to FMLA suits for damages violated § 5 of the Fourteenth Amendment.

15. In June 2013, the New York City Council overrode Mayor Bloomberg's veto and approved a bill (effective April 1, 2014) requiring businesses with 20 or more employees (15 or more as of October 1, 2015) to provide employees with five days of paid sick leave per year. Paid sick leave laws also have been enacted in Seattle, and Washington, D.C. In 2011, Connecticut became the first state to enact a paid sick leave law.

A related issue is paid family leave. According to the Bureau of Labor Statistics, 11% of private sector employees and 16% of state and local government employees have access to some paid family leave. Legislation in California, Oregon, New Jersey, and New York provides some family leave benefits. California also requires 30 days of paid leave for an employee who is an organ donor. Cal. Lab. Code §§ 1508–1513. Under California law, Cal. Gov't Code § 12945.2, workers are entitled to paid parental leave for six weeks at 55% of their pay, paid for by employee-financed public disability insurance. In 2016, San Francisco enacted a law mandating full pay for parental leave, with the 45% difference being paid by employers. S.F. Police Code art. 33H. New Jersey, N.J. Pub. L. 1948, ch. 110, § 2, and Rhode Island, R.I. Gen. Laws § 28–48, also provide for paid parental leave, but not at full pay, and also financed by employee-funded insurance.

On June 28, 2018, Massachusetts Governor Baker signed a law affecting all employers in the Commonwealth by creating a paid family and medical leave program funded by a state payroll tax. Beginning in 2021, eligible employees will be allowed to take the following leave in a benefit year: (1) Up to 20 weeks of job-protected paid medical leave to care for their own serious health condition; (2) Up to 12 weeks of job-protected paid family leave to care for a family member with a serious health condition, to bond with the employee's child during the first 12 months after the child's birth or the first 12 months after the placement of the child for adoption or foster care with the employee; and (3) Up to 26 weeks of job-protected paid family leave to care for a covered servicemember. To be eligible for paid family and medical leave, an employee must meet the financial eligibility requirements for receiving unemployment compensation under Massachusetts law.

E. NONDISCRIMINATION IN BENEFITS

1. PREGNANCY

Title VII of the Civil Rights Act of 1964 prohibits discrimination with respect to all terms and conditions of employment, including benefits. One of the most controversial and heavily litigated subjects under Title VII's prohibition against sex discrimination in benefits has been the provision of pregnancy benefits for female employees. The Supreme Court first held in Geduldig v. Aiello, 417 U.S. 484 (1974), that a state law that excluded from disability benefits a temporary disability arising from a normal pregnancy did not violate the Equal Protection clause of the Fourteenth Amendment. Then in General Elec. Co. v. Gilbert, 429 U.S. 125 (1976), the Court held that an employer's disability plan which covered all disabilities except those associated with or arising out of pregnancy was not a violation of Title VII. The Court reasoned that discrimination on the basis of pregnancy was not sex-based discrimination, since at any given time there were both men and (non-pregnant) women who benefited fully from the disability plan.

A year later, in Nashville Gas Co. v. Satty, 434 U.S. 136 (1977), the Court reviewed an employer policy that required pregnant women to take a formal leave of absence during pregnancy but provided no disability benefits to them, and then stripped them of their accrued company seniority for competitive bidding purposes upon their return from maternity leave. The company did not hold jobs for women on maternity leave nor did it guarantee them a job when they returned. A woman who wanted to return to work had to apply for a new job, and permanent positions were not always available. The Court upheld the disability exclusion under its reasoning in *Gilbert,* but distinguished the mandatory forfeiture of seniority:

> In *Gilbert,* there was no showing that General Electric's policy of compensating for all non-job-related disabilities except pregnancy favored men over women. No evidence was produced to suggest that men received more benefits from General Electric's disability insurance fund than did women; both men and women were subject generally to the disabilities covered and presumably drew similar amounts from the insurance fund. We therefore upheld the plan under Title VII.
>
> * * *
>
> Here, by comparison, petitioner has not merely refused to extend to women a benefit that men cannot and do not receive, but has imposed on women a substantial burden that men need not suffer. The distinction between benefits and burdens is more than one of semantics. We held in *Gilbert* that § 703(a)(1) did not require that greater economic benefits be paid to one sex or the other "because of their differing roles in 'the scheme of

human existence,' " 429 U.S. at 139 n. 17. But that holding does not allow us to read § 703(a)(2) to permit an employer to burden female employees in such a way as to deprive them of employment opportunities because of their significant role.

434 U.S. at 139–42. The Court pointed out that the employer had the opportunity to establish the existence of a business necessity which would justify its policy, but that Nashville Gas Company had not submitted such proof.

Following *Gilbert* and *Satty,* Congress amended Title VII by adding the Pregnancy Discrimination Act of 1978, codified as § 701(k) of Title VII. It provides:

> The terms "because of sex" or "on the basis of sex" include, but are not limited to, because of or on the basis of pregnancy, childbirth, or related medical conditions, and women affected by pregnancy, childbirth, or related medical conditions shall be treated the same for all employment-related purposes, including receipt of benefits under fringe benefit programs, as other persons not so affected but similar in their ability or inability to work, and nothing in section 703(h) of this title shall be interpreted to permit otherwise. * * *

Section 701(k) "undoes" *Gilbert* by making it clear that an employer must treat pregnant employees the same as nonpregnant employees. That is, the employer may not maintain a policy that adversely affects pregnant employees relative to other employees, unless it can establish a business necessity or BFOQ defense.

As a result of the passage of § 701(k), a number of employers amended their health insurance plans to cover pregnancy-related conditions of female employees to the same extent as other medical conditions. In Newport News Shipbuilding & Dry Dock Co. v. EEOC, 462 U.S. 669 (1983), a male employee alleged that his employer unlawfully refused to provide full insurance coverage for the hospitalization costs associated with his wife's pregnancy. The Supreme Court held that the employer's plan was a violation of Title VII, because under the plan, married male employees received less comprehensive coverage than married female employees.

Lang v. Star Herald
107 F.3d 1308 (8th Cir. 1997), cert. denied, 522 U.S. 839 (1997).

■ HANSEN, CIRCUIT JUDGE.

Jodee Lang appeals from the district court's grant of summary judgment to the *Star Herald* in this Title VII case, in which Lang alleges gender discrimination on the basis of her pregnant status. We affirm.

Viewed in the light most favorable to Lang, the record reveals the following facts. Jodee Lang began working as a part-time employee for the *Star Herald* in April of 1991 and moved to full-time status in November of 1992. Under the *Star Herald's* employee benefits policy, which is outlined in an employee handbook, Lang accumulated vacation time and sick leave based upon the number of hours she worked.

In early May 1993, Lang informed her supervisor, Scott Walker, that she was pregnant. She continued working during her pregnancy until she took one week of vacation from June 7 through 11. During her vacation, Lang experienced some bleeding associated with her pregnancy and was advised by her physician not to return to work until it stopped.

On Monday, June 14, 1993, Lang left a message for Walker, stating that she would not be in because she had a medical appointment. The next day, Lang phoned Walker and read him a note from her doctor, which recommended rest for two weeks. During this conversation, she asked Walker whether the *Star Herald* had a short-term disability policy; he replied that he would find out for her. Lang was absent from work the entire week of June 14–18 and was paid with the balance of her accrued sick leave and vacation time.

Walker phoned Lang on June 23 and informed her that her sick leave had expired and she had no remaining paid vacation time. He also reported that the *Star Herald* did not have a short-term disability policy. Walker said he would have to let her go but agreed not to take any action until after Friday, June 25.

That Friday, Lang told Walker that her doctor had told her not to resume work because she was still incurring pregnancy-related problems. Lang said she would know after her medical appointment on Monday, June 28, when she could return to work. Walker promised not to take any action until after that time.

On June 28, Lang's doctor recommended that she take additional time off from her job and said he could not predict when she could resume work. When Lang informed Walker of the doctor's recommendation, Walker explained the *Star Herald's* policy for unpaid leaves of absence. The policy provides that an employee who has exhausted her paid leave time can apply for an unpaid leave of absence, but the *Star Herald* does not guarantee that it will hold open the employee's position during her absence. Walker asked Lang to apply for an indefinite leave of absence, but Lang refused to do so because she would not be guaranteed re-employment. As a result of her refusal, her employment with the *Star Herald* was terminated.

Lang filed a charge of discrimination with the Equal Employment Opportunity Commission and then timely filed this suit. The *Star Herald* filed a motion for summary judgment, which was eventually granted by the district court. This appeal followed.

Title VII makes it "an unlawful employment practice for an employer to fail or refuse to hire or to discharge any individual, or otherwise to discriminate against any individual with respect to his compensation, terms, conditions, or privileges of employment, because of such individual's . . . sex." 42 U.S.C. § 2000e–2(a) (1994). In 1978, Congress enacted the Pregnancy Discrimination Act (PDA), amending the definitional provision of Title VII to clarify that discrimination "on the basis of pregnancy, childbirth, or related medical conditions" is sex discrimination under Title VII. *Id.* § 2000e(k).

Lang claims that the *Star Herald* illegally discriminated against her on the basis of her pregnancy by denying her an indefinite leave of absence with a guarantee that she could return to her position. Lang appeals the district court's grant of the *Star Herald's* motion for summary judgment, arguing that her Title VII claim should survive under the theories of disparate treatment and disparate impact.

* * *

Lang argues that the policy was in fact discriminatory. She first points to a nonpregnant coworker, Peggy Carbojol, who allegedly was given indefinite time off for personal reasons. The benefit Carbojol received was quite different, however, from the one Lang sought. Carbojol's absence, which amounted to only one day, was covered by her accrued paid leave time. The evidence of Carbojol's leave does not show that Carbojol or any employee was granted unpaid leave time with a guarantee of re-employment as Lang sought, nor does it establish that Lang was qualified to receive that benefit.

Lang also makes a comparison to another nonpregnant coemployee, Teresa Martinez, who was granted a variance from the leave policy. According to Lang's brief, Martinez asked for and received three to four days off without pay at the commencement of her employment period. The benefit Martinez received differs significantly from the one Lang sought in that Martinez's period of unpaid leave was definite in duration—four days at the most. Like the Carbojol evidence, this evidence of Martinez's leave does not advance Lang's case.

Because Lang has produced no evidence to show that the *Star Herald's* indefinite-leave-of-absence policy was different for her than it was for nonpregnant employees, we conclude that Lang failed to establish a prima facie case. Lang has not submitted evidence showing that she is qualified to receive an unpaid indefinite leave of absence with a guarantee of returning to her position or that the *Star Herald* has ever granted such a benefit to other employees.

Lang maintains that the fact that she asked for indefinite leave is unimportant, because coworkers could have covered for her. The relevant question, however, is whether the *Star Herald* treated Lang differently than nonpregnant employees on an indefinite leave of absence, not whether the *Star Herald* could have made more concessions for Lang. We emphasize again that Title VII does not create rights to preferential treatment.

Finally, Lang contends that she actually had five remaining unpaid vacation days to use at the time she was discharged. She points to a policy provision in the employee handbook, which states: "All employees eligible for vacation who have not earned two weeks of vacation during the year may take unpaid time off in addition to their paid vacation time off up to a total of two weeks off during the year." Lang contends that because she had only accumulated 40 hours (5 days) of vacation time at the time she was terminated (June), she could have taken 5 unpaid days under this provision.

We agree with the district court that this provision applies only to newly hired employees who have not yet worked for the *Star Herald* for one year. At the time Lang was discharged, she had worked for the *Star Herald* for more than two years. The provision is therefore inapplicable here.

We do not address Lang's arguments that the *Star Herald's* proffered reason for its employment decision was pretext for discrimination, because her failure to establish her prima facie case means that the burden of production of the employer's allegedly nondiscriminatory reason never arises.

Lang also argues her case under the theory of disparate impact. The district court dismissed Lang's disparate impact claim because she had not specifically alleged in her pleadings that the *Star Herald's* unpaid leave policy has a disproportionate impact on pregnant women. Because Lang's disparate impact claim fails as a matter of law, we decline to address the pleading issue. To establish a prima facie case of disparate impact, Lang must show that the *Star Herald's* facially neutral policy is in fact unjustifiably more harsh on pregnant women than on other people. To prove this, Lang "must offer 'statistical evidence of a kind and degree sufficient to show that the practice in question has caused the exclusion' of benefits because the beneficiaries would be women." Lang has provided no statistical support for her claim, and in fact concedes in her brief that "there is no evidence of statistical imbalance with this small [of] an employer." As a result, there is no evidence in this record of a disproportionately adverse impact on pregnant women, and we affirm the district court's judgment because Lang cannot establish a prima facie case of disparate impact.

For the above reasons, we affirm the judgment of the district court.

NOTES AND QUESTIONS

1.   Could a state enact a law mandating more generous leave policies for pregnant employees than other nonpregnant employees? See California Fed. Sav. & Loan Ass'n v. Guerra, 479 U.S. 272 (1987) (upholding California law). In the absence of a statutory requirement, would it be lawful for an employer to treat pregnant employees more favorably? See Harness v. Hartz Mtn. Corp., 877 F.2d 1307 (6th Cir. 1989) (upholding employer's preferential leave

policy). For discussion of the PDA as antidiscrimination statute, see Chapter 4, pp. 302–310.

2. In Young v. United Parcel Service, 135 S. Ct. 1338 (2015), supra p. 302 the Supreme Court held that a plaintiff could make out a disparate treatment pregnancy discrimination case based on an employer's failure to provide reasonable accommodation when other employees with similar inability to work were accommodated. Although the case did not involve discrimination in benefits, it could well presage a more sympathetic view of the needs of pregnant employees in general, including in the realm of health benefits.

On the issue of mandatory coverage of contraceptives, see Burwell v. Hobby Lobby, 134 S. Ct. 2751 (2014).

3. On the issue of possible discrimination in employee benefits in light of religious free exercise rights of employees, see Masterpiece Cake v. Colorado Civil Rights Commission, 138 S. Ct. 1719 (2018).

4. Employers are not required to provide pregnant employees with light duty work, Ensley-Gaines v. Runyon, 100 F.3d 1220 (6th Cir. 1996), nor to engage in reasonable accommodation for their pregnancy. For a discussion of occupational safety and health issues related to fertile and pregnant women employees, see Chapter 8, infra.

2. MARITAL STATUS

Braatz v. Labor & Industry Review Commission
496 N.W.2d 597 (Wis. 1993).

■ STEINMETZ, JUSTICE.

The issue in this case is whether the Labor and Industry Review Commission ("LIRC") properly concluded that the marital status provisions of the Wisconsin Fair Employment Act ("WFEA") permit the school district of Maple's health insurance nonduplication policy. The circuit court answered in the negative, and LIRC appealed from the judgment. The court of appeals affirmed the circuit court's judgment in Braatz v. LIRC, 168 Wis.2d 124, 483 N.W.2d 246 (Ct.App.1992).

We affirm the court of appeals reversal of LIRC's decision. The school district of Maple's nonduplication policy constitutes marital status discrimination which is prohibited under the WFEA. Health insurance is not excepted from this prohibition, expressly or implicitly.

The facts of this case are not in dispute. The plaintiffs are teachers employed by the Maple School District. Each teacher is married; each teacher's spouse is employed; and each spouse's employer offers health insurance benefits to the spouse.

The 1986–87 collective bargaining agreement between the Maple Federation of Teachers and the Maple Board of Education provides as follows:

Article VBA. Insurance. Health, Life, Dental and Long Term Disability.

Section 1.   Health and Hospitalization Insurance Coverage:

Hospital, medical and major medical coverage for the employees and their family will be provided if requested by the employee through the existing contract with the insurance company presently providing coverage to district employees. All requests for hospital, medical, and major medical will be subjected to the limitations outlined in a, b, c and d below:

a.   All single employees may request single coverage under this plan.

b.   Unmarried person who has the care custody or support of any minor children of said unmarried person is eligible for family coverage if the policy so warrants.

c.   A married employee is entitled to family coverage.

d.   A married teacher who [sic] spouse is eligible for family coverage at his/her place of work shall have the option of carrying either the district's policy or the spouse's policy but not both. If the spouse carries a single plan, the employee of the district shall be eligible for a single plan through the district.

(1) Employees who are presently duplicating insurance coverage who do not fall into the above guidelines would be allowed to do so if they notify the school district that they wish to have the premium for health insurance deducted from their paycheck. Employees who do not fall into the above guidelines who are duplicating insurance and do not wish to have the premium deducted from their paycheck will have to notify the school district that they wish to have their health coverage with the district terminated.

(2) The Board would allow duplicate coverage if the employee's other insurance policy provided significantly less coverage than the School District of Maple's policy. This would be determined by the school administration.

The LIRC describes this condition of employment as simply a "health insurance non-duplication policy." However, it is a non-duplication policy applicable only to married employees. Married employees, with employed spouses who are covered by comparable employer provided health insurance, are forced to elect the district's policy or the spouse's policy. The plaintiffs in this case were forced to make this election.

The WFEA prohibits employers from "discriminat[ing] against any individual in promotion, compensation or in terms, conditions or privileges of employment" on the basis of marital status. Section 111.322(1); sec. 111.321, Stats. Section 111.32(12) defines marital status as "the status of being married, single, divorced, separated or widowed."

There is only one express exception to this prohibition against marital status discrimination. It provides as follows: "Notwithstanding 111.322, it is not employment discrimination because of marital status to prohibit an individual from directly supervising or being directly supervised by his or her spouse." Section 111.345, Stats.

The declaration of policy in sec. 111.31(3), Stats., mandates liberal construction of the WFEA:

> In the interpretation and application of this subchapter, and otherwise, it is declared to be the public policy of the state to encourage and foster to the fullest extent practicable the employment of all properly qualified individuals regardless of * * * marital status * * *. This subchapter shall be liberally construed for the accomplishment of this purpose.

LIRC argues that the school district of Maple's policy does not discriminate based on marital status. Instead, application of the policy is triggered by the conduct of an employee's spouse (choosing to work, accepting health insurance benefits from an employer, etc.) rather than marital status. Because LIRC did not rely on this rationale in its decision, we review this interpretation of the school district's policy de novo.

We disagree with LIRC's interpretation. The school district's policy constitutes marital status discrimination. It is only married employees with duplicate coverage who must make a choice between the district's policy or the policy provided by their spouse's employer. Single employees who have health insurance coverage from another source are not forced to choose between that coverage and the district's coverage.

Moreover, the choice required by the district's policy does not account for an employee's death or divorce, which may terminate the former spouse's coverage through the district and leave him or her unable to obtain a single or family policy elsewhere, especially if not qualifying healthwise. This problem would not exist if spouses were allowed to accept their employer-provided health insurance in addition to the district's coverage.

Also, insurance companies consider double policies within a family by allowing coverage only by a primary carrier. The policy can state that it is secondary to any other coverage and therefore the premium can be lower. This, of course, will raise an issue of which policy is primary coverage.

In its decision, LIRC concluded that the school district's policy did not violate the WFEA because health insurance benefits are implicitly excepted from the WFEA's prohibition against marital status discrimination. In support of its implied exception theory, LIRC argues that the fact that the state of Wisconsin, as an employer and by statute, offers different health insurance benefits to married and single employees evinces a legislative intent to allow employers in general to do the same.

LIRC specifically refers to two state practices. First, the state offers dependent health insurance benefits to an employee's spouse but not to an employee's adult companion, although dependant in fact. See sec. 40.02(20), Stats.; Phillips v. Wisconsin Personnel Commission, 167 Wis.2d 205, 482 N.W.2d 121 (Ct.App.1992). Second, if both spouses are state employees and one spouse elects family coverage, the state provides coverage to the other spouse as a dependant but prohibits that spouse from electing other coverage.

Because LIRC's decision was based on this implied exception theory, this court will uphold LIRC's interpretation of the WFEA if it is reasonable and not clearly contrary to legislative intent. Interpretation of a statute and application of that statute to undisputed facts presents a question of law. Generally, an agency's conclusion of law is reviewed *de novo*. However, in this case we give deference to LIRC's conclusion because LIRC has experience in interpreting the marital status discrimination provision of the WFEA.

Health insurance benefits are not implicitly excepted from the WFEA's prohibition against marital status discrimination. There is no reasonable basis to support LIRC's conclusion. LIRC's conclusion is simply contrary to the intent of the legislature.

The fact that the state offers dependant health insurance benefits to an employee's spouse but not to an employee's adult companion does not support LIRC's implied exception theory. *Phillips* held that this practice does not constitute marital status discrimination. The court reasoned that "[i]t is only where similarly situated persons are treated differently that discrimination is an issue." Even though an employee and an adult companion may "have a committed relationship that partakes of many of the attributes of marriage in the traditional sense," a spouse and a companion are not similarly situated. This is so because Wisconsin law imposes a mutual duty of general support upon married couples, but there is no comparable duty of support imposed upon adult companions.

In effect, the plaintiff in *Phillips* wanted something not even married employees got: reimbursement for medical expenses that she had no obligation to pay. *Phillips* and the policy reviewed therein are not relevant to this case.

The state's policy of prohibiting duplication of health insurance by married couples employed by the state also does not support LIRC's position. Even if we assume *arguendo* that this policy indicates that there is an implied exception to the WFEA's prohibition against marital status discrimination, the school district of Maple's policy would not fall within this exception. The state's policy is not the same as the Maple policy. The state's policy only applies where both spouses are employed by the state. Maple's policy applies no matter where the employee's spouse is employed.

Further support for our conclusion that health insurance benefits are not excepted from the WFEA's prohibition against marital status discrimination is found in sec. 111.33(2)(d), Stats. That section excepts health insurance from the WFEA's prohibition against age discrimination. It states that it is not age discrimination "[t]o apply varying insurance coverage according to an employee's age." This exception indicates that the legislature considered the WFEA's effect on health insurance issues, chose to create an exception for age discrimination, but chose not to create an exception for marital status discrimination.

Finally, our conclusion is supported by the WFEA's liberal construction clause, referred to above. Limiting the reach of the WFEA's prohibition against marital status discrimination with an implied exception is certainly not liberal construction.

We hold that the district's policy violates the WFEA. The policy constitutes marital status discrimination and does not fall within an exception, express or implied, to the WFEA's prohibition against such discrimination.

The decision of the court of appeals is affirmed.

* * *

As discussed in the following section, the law of employee health benefits has been changed substantially by striking down state prohibitions on same-sex marriage. In states where same-sex marriage was illegal, some employers extended eligibility for health benefits to domestic partnerships or other non-marital arrangements of same-sex partners, but not opposite-sex partners, on the ground that opposite-sex partners could marry and same-sex partners could not. Now that same-sex marriage is legal in all states, many employers have restructured their benefits to apply to all married couples, but not to any couples in non-marital arrangements. There have been no reported cases as yet by non-marital couples, including by same-sex unmarried couples who lost benefits. Could such a couple argue that if there is a right to marry, there is also a right not to marry, and therefore it is unlawful to deny otherwise available benefits to couples, both same-sex and opposite-sex, that in all other respects are the same as married couples? What arguments, pro and con, would you make in the public sector and the private sector?

3. SEXUAL ORIENTATION

In 1996, Congress overwhelmingly enacted, and President Clinton signed, the Defense of Marriage Act (DOMA), which provided that "the word 'marriage' means only a legal union between one man and one woman as husband and wife, and the word 'spouse' refers only to a person of the opposite sex who is a husband or a wife." DOMA § 3. In United States v. Windsor, 133 S. Ct. 2675 (2013), a lawsuit was brought by a surviving same-sex spouse whose inheritance was taxed as if she were unmarried, and thus at a higher rate. The Supreme Court, five-to-four, held that section 3 of DOMA was unconstitutional as a violation of "the liberty of the person protected by the Fifth Amendment."

Later in 2013, the Department of Labor provided guidance to plans, plan sponsors, fiduciaries, participants, and beneficiaries on the Windsor decision's impact on ERISA. According to DOL Technical Release No. 2013–04, generally the terms "spouse" and "marriage" in ERISA include same-sex couples who are legally married in any state or foreign jurisdiction that recognizes such marriages, regardless of where the couple currently resides. Windsor and the DOL's guidance established a conflict between state law (many of which prohibited same-sex marriage) and federal law, which provided that same-sex benefits had to be treated equally under ERISA.

In Obergefell v. Hodges, 135 S. Ct. 2584 (2015), the Supreme Court held, five-to-four, with Justice Kennedy writing for the majority, the right to marry is a fundamental right inherent in the liberty of the person, and under the Due Process and Equal Protection clauses of the Fourteenth Amendment couples of the same sex may not be deprived of that right and liberty. Also, states must recognize same-sex marriages performed in other states.

In a sense, the *Obergefell* case simplifies health benefits because there is only one rule that applies to all employees in all states. Nevertheless, there is still a level of uncertainty or confusion. Although the Affordable Care Act requires employers to offer coverage to employees (or they will be assessed a penalty), employers are not required to offer health plan coverage to spouses. Also, a spouse who is covered by an employee's health insurance is entitled to 36 months of health care continuation (at no more than 102% of cost) in the event of the participant's termination of employment, or the couple's divorce or legal separation under COBRA.

CHAPTER 7

EMPLOYEE LIBERTY

Wages, hours, and health benefits—the subjects of the preceding two chapters—are often thought to be the most important aspects of the employment relationship. Although certainly important, these elements are merely the starting points in assessing terms and conditions of employment. From an employee perspective, the degree of employee liberty greatly affects the quality of working life. From an employer perspective, employee liberty needs to be balanced with management prerogatives to control essential aspects of the work relationship.

In nonunionized workplaces, employers traditionally had wide latitude in determining the method of operation and the working conditions of employees. Employees who were unhappy with their working conditions could request a modification or seek employment elsewhere. New Deal legislation addressed some issues, such as child labor, wages, and hours. (see Chapter 5). In 1964, Title VII of the Civil Rights Act prohibited discrimination in terms or conditions of employment on the basis of race, color, religion, sex, and national origin. Prohibitions on discrimination based on age (1967) and disability (1973, 1990) were added later. In 1970, the Occupational Safety and Health Act required employers to provide a safe and healthy workplace. The courts also have begun to recognize additional sources of protection in common law torts and contracts and, for public employees, in the United States Constitution.

The issues in this chapter exemplify a recurring theme in employment law: the struggle for control of the workplace. Traditionally, the employer could freely dictate any and all working conditions. Above all else, the law protected the employer's property rights, managerial prerogatives, and right to direct the workforce as it saw fit. Today, society recognizes other values, such as privacy, freedom of expression, and freedom from sexual harassment. Increased employee liberty epitomizes changing perceptions of the proper relationship between employers and employees.

It is sometimes said that "the Bill of Rights stops at the plant gate." Assuming this is true, at least with regard to the private sector, should the freedom of expression, the right of privacy, and other similar concepts be applied in the workplace? If so, what is the legal authority for these rights? What are the limits? What procedures should be used in their enforcement? What is the cost of establishing them?

As you read the cases and materials in this chapter, notice how the method of analysis and the outcome are affected by whether the employer is public or private, union or nonunion, and by whether the source of the relevant law is constitutional, statutory (federal or state), regulatory, or common law. Try to assess whether the outcomes and doctrines are consistent, the level of legal intervention in a particular setting is appropriate, and the means chosen for achieving desired ends are feasible.

Employee liberty is a recurring theme in this book, and it is also explored in other chapters. For example, it is covered in Chapter 3 (e.g., pre-hire employer inquiries and testing); Chapter 4 (e.g., sex discrimination caused by appearance requirements reflecting sex stereotyping); and Chapter 10 (e.g., wrongful discharge cases alleging violations of public policy for diverse deprivations of employee liberty).

A. Appearance

1. Grooming

Kelley v. Johnson

425 U.S. 238 (1976).

■ Mr. Justice Rehnquist delivered the opinion of the Court.

* * *

In 1971 respondent's predecessor, individually and as president of the Suffolk County Patrolmen's Benevolent Association, brought this action under the Civil Rights Act of 1871, 42 U.S.C. § 1983, against petitioner's predecessor, the Commissioner of the Suffolk County Police Department. The Commissioner had promulgated Order No. 71–1, which established hair-grooming standards applicable to male members of the police force. The regulation was directed at the style and length of hair, sideburns, and mustaches; beards and goatees were prohibited, except for medical reasons; and wigs conforming to the regulation could be worn for cosmetic reasons. The regulation was attacked as violative of respondent patrolman's right of free expression under the First Amendment and his guarantees of due process and equal protection under the Fourteenth Amendment, in that it was "not based upon the generally accepted standard of grooming in the community" and placed "an undue restriction" upon his activities therein.

* * *

Section 1 of the Fourteenth Amendment to the United States Constitution provides in pertinent part:

"No State shall * * * deprive any person of life, liberty, or property, without due process of law."

This section affords not only a procedural guarantee against the deprivation of "liberty," but likewise protects substantive aspects of liberty against unconstitutional restrictions by the State.

The "liberty" interest claimed by respondent here, of course, is distinguishable from the interests protected by the Court in Roe v. Wade, Eisenstadt v. Baird, Stanley v. Illinois, Griswold v. Connecticut, and Meyer v. Nebraska. Each of those cases involved a substantial claim of infringement on the individual's freedom of choice with respect to certain basic matters of procreation, marriage, and family life. But whether the citizenry at large has some sort of "liberty" interest within the Fourteenth Amendment in matters of personal appearance is a question on which this Court's cases offer little, if any, guidance. We can, nevertheless, assume an affirmative answer for purposes of deciding this case, because we find that assumption insufficient to carry the day for respondent's claim.

Respondent has sought the protection of the Fourteenth Amendment, not as a member of the citizenry at large, but on the contrary as an employee of the police department of Suffolk County, a subdivision of the State of New York. While the Court of Appeals made passing reference to this distinction, it was thereafter apparently ignored. We think, however, it is highly significant. In Pickering v. Board of Education, 391 U.S. 563 (1968), after noting that state employment may not be conditioned on the relinquishment of First Amendment rights, the Court stated that "[a]t the same time it cannot be gainsaid that the State has interests as an employer in regulating the speech of its employees that differ significantly from those it possesses in connection with regulation of the speech of the citizenry in general." More recently, we have sustained comprehensive and substantial restrictions upon activities of both federal and state employees lying at the core of the First Amendment. If such state regulations may survive challenges based on the explicit language of the First Amendment, there is surely even more room for restrictive regulations of state employees where the claim implicates only the more general contours of the substantive liberty interest protected by the Fourteenth Amendment.

The hair-length regulation here touches respondent as an employee of the county and, more particularly, as a policeman. Respondent's employer has, in accordance with its well-established duty to keep the peace, placed myriad demands upon the members of the police force, duties which have no counterpart with respect to the public at large. Respondent must wear a standard uniform, specific in each detail. When in uniform he must salute the flag. He may not take an active role in local political affairs by way of being a party delegate or contributing or soliciting political contributions. He may not smoke in public. All of these and other regulations of the Suffolk County Police Department infringe on respondent's freedom of choice in personal matters, and it was apparently the view of the Court of Appeals that the burden is on the State to prove a "genuine public need" for each and every one of these regulations.

This view was based upon the Court of Appeals' reasoning that the "unique judicial deference" accorded by the judiciary to regulation of members of the military was inapplicable because there was no historical or functional justification for the characterization of the police as "paramilitary." But the conclusion that such cases are inapposite, however correct, in no way detracts from the deference due Suffolk County's choice of an organizational structure for its police force. Here the county has chosen a mode of organization which it undoubtedly deems the most efficient in enabling its police to carry out the duties assigned to them under state and local law. Such a choice necessarily gives weight to the overall need for discipline esprit de corps, and uniformity.

The county's choice of an organizational structure, therefore, does not depend for its constitutional validity on any doctrine of historical prescription. Nor, indeed has respondent made any such claim. His argument does not challenge the constitutionality of the organizational structure, but merely asserts that the present hair-length regulation infringes his asserted liberty interest under the Fourteenth Amendment. We believe, however, that the hair-length regulation cannot be viewed in isolation, but must be rather considered in the context of the county's chosen mode of organization for its police force.

The promotion of safety of persons and property is unquestionably at the core of the State's police power, and virtually all state and local governments employ a uniform police force to aid in the accomplishment of that purpose. Choice of organization, dress, and equipment for law enforcement personnel is a decision entitled to the same sort of presumption of legislative validity as are state choices designed to promote other aims within the cognizance of the State's police power. Having recognized in other contexts the wide latitude accorded the government in the "dispatch of its own internal affairs," Cafeteria Workers v. McElroy, 367 U.S. 886 (1961), we think Suffolk County's police regulations involved here are entitled to similar weight. Thus the question is not, as the Court of Appeals conceived it to be, whether the State can "establish" a "genuine public need" for the specific regulation. It is whether respondent can demonstrate that there is no rational connection between the regulation, based as it is on the county's method of organizing its police force, and the promotion of safety of persons and property.

We think the answer here is so clear that the District Court was quite right in the first instance to have dismissed respondent's complaint. Neither this Court, the Court of Appeals, nor the District Court is in a position to weigh the policy arguments in favor of and against a rule regulating hairstyles as a part of regulations governing a uniformed civilian service. The constitutional issue to be decided by these courts is whether petitioner's determination that such regulations should be enacted is so irrational that it may be branded "arbitrary," and therefore a deprivation of respondent's "liberty" interest in freedom to choose his own hairstyle. The overwhelming majority of state and local police of the present day are uniformed. This fact itself testifies to the recognition by those who direct those operations, and by the people of the States and localities who directly or indirectly choose such persons, that similarity in appearance of police officers is desirable. This choice may be based on a desire to make police officers readily recognizable to the members of the public, or a desire for the esprit de corps which such similarity is felt to inculcate within the police force itself. Either one is a sufficiently rational justification for regulations so as to defeat respondent's claim based on the liberty guarantee of the Fourteenth Amendment.

* * *

The regulation challenged here did not violate any right guaranteed respondent by the Fourteenth Amendment to the United States Constitution, and the Court of Appeals was therefore wrong in reversing the District Court's original judgment dismissing the action. The judgment of the Court of Appeals is

Reversed.

* * *

■ MR. JUSTICE MARSHALL, with whom MR. JUSTICE BRENNAN joins, dissenting.

The Court today upholds the constitutionality of Suffolk County's regulation limiting the length of a policeman's hair. While the Court only assumes for purposes of its opinion that "the citizenry at large has some sort of 'liberty' interest within the Fourteenth Amendment in matters of personal appearance * * *," I think it clear that the Fourteenth Amendment does indeed protect against comprehensive regulation of what citizens may or may not wear. And I find that the rationales offered by the Court to justify the regulation in this case are insufficient to demonstrate its constitutionality. Accordingly, I respectfully dissent.

As the Court recognizes, the Fourteenth Amendment's guarantee against the deprivation of liberty "protects substantive aspects of liberty against unconstitutional restriction by the State." And we have observed that "[l]iberty under law extends to the full range of conduct which the individual is free to pursue." It seems to me manifest that that "full range of conduct" must encompass one's interest in dressing according to his own taste. An individual's personal appearance may reflect, sustain, and nourish his personality and may well be used as a means of expressing his attitude and lifestyle. In taking control over a citizen's personal appearance, the government forces him to sacrifice substantial elements of his integrity and identity as well. To say that the liberty guarantee of the Fourteenth Amendment does not encompass matters of personal appearance would be fundamentally inconsistent with the values of privacy, self-identity, autonomy, and personal integrity that I have always assumed the Constitution was designed to protect.

To my mind, the right in one's personal appearance is inextricably bound up with the historically recognized right of "every individual to the possession and control of his own person," Union Pacific R. Co. v. Botsford, 141 U.S. 250, 251 (1891), and, perhaps even more fundamentally, with "the right to be let alone—the most comprehensive of rights and the right most valued by civilized men." Olmstead v. United States, 277 U.S. 438, 478 (1928) (Brandeis, J., dissenting). In an increasingly crowded society in which it is already extremely difficult to maintain one's identity and personal integrity, it would be distressing, to say the least, if the government could regulate our personal appearance unconfined by any constitutional strictures whatsoever.

Acting on its assumption that the Fourteenth Amendment does encompass a right in one's personal appearance, the Court justifies the challenged hair-length regulation on the grounds that such regulations may "be based on a desire to make police officers readily recognizable to the members of the public, or a desire for the esprit de corps which such similarity is felt to inculcate within the police force itself." While fully accepting the aims of "identifiability" and maintenance of esprit de corps, I find no rational relationship between the challenged regulation and these goals.

As for the first justification offered by the Court, I simply do not see how requiring policemen to maintain hair of under a certain length could rationally be argued to contribute to making them identifiable to the public as policemen. Surely, the fact that a uniformed police officer is wearing his hair below his collar will make him no less identifiable as a policeman. And one cannot easily imagine a plainclothes officer being readily identifiable as such simply because his hair does not extend beneath his collar.

As for the Court's second justification, the fact that it is the president of the Patrolmen's Benevolent Association, in his official capacity, who has challenged the regulation here would seem to indicate that the regulation would if anything, decrease rather than increase the police force's esprit de corps. And even if one accepted the argument that substantial similarity in appearance would increase a force's esprit de corps, I simply do not understand how implementation of this regulation could be expected to create any increment in similarity of appearance among members of a uniformed police force. While the regulation prohibits hair below the ears or the collar and limits the length of sideburns, it allows the maintenance of any type of hairstyle, other than a ponytail. Thus, as long as their hair does not go below their collars, two police officers, with an "Afro" hairstyle and the other with a crewcut could both be in full compliance with the regulation.

The Court cautions us not to view the hair-length regulation in isolation, but rather to examine it "in the context of the county's chosen mode of organization for its police force." While the Court's caution is well taken, one should also keep in mind, as I fear the Court does not, that what is ultimately under scrutiny is neither the overall structure of the police force nor the uniform and equipment requirements to which its members are subject, but rather the regulation which dictates acceptable hair lengths. The fact that the uniform requirement, for instance, may be rationally related to the goals of increasing police officer "identifiability" and the maintenance of esprit de corps does absolutely nothing to establish the legitimacy of the hair-length regulation. I see no connection between the regulation and the offered rationales and would accordingly affirm the judgment of the Court of Appeals.

NOTES AND QUESTIONS

1. The police department argued that the hair length and grooming regulations were needed to protect the police officers, to achieve esprit de corps, and to maintain uniformity. Which of these arguments is the strongest? Why? What else could have been argued?

2. If you agree with the dissent that the police department failed to justify the need for the regulation, would there be a justification for prohibiting officers from wearing jewelry, using excessive makeup or cosmetics, or wearing unusual eyeglasses? What about the police department's prohibition on officers smoking in public?

3. In *Kelley*, because the police department-employer was a government entity, the First Amendment applied to its actions, including the hair length regulation. First Amendment protections are not applicable in the private sector. Accordingly, most hair length cases in private employment have been brought under a Title VII sex discrimination theory. The plaintiffs have argued that employer rules prohibiting men but not women from having long hair discriminate on the basis of sex. Generally, plaintiffs have been unsuccessful for two reasons. First, it has been held that Title VII was designed only to prohibit discrimination based on *immutable* characteristics. Fagan v. National Cash Register Co., 481 F.2d 1115 (D.C.Cir. 1973). Second, the cases have declared that hair length regulations do not inhibit employment *opportunity*. Willingham v. Macon Telegraph Publ'g Co., 507 F.2d 1084 (5th Cir. 1975) (en banc). Implicit in both theories are the ideas that differential hair length is a social norm, that grooming regulations seek to project a favorable company image to the public, and that "Congress sought only to give all persons equal access to the job market, not to limit an employer's right to exercise his informed judgment as to how best to run his shop." Id. at 1092. See Tavora v. New York Mercantile Exch., 101 F.3d 907 (2d Cir. 1996), cert. denied, 520 U.S. 1229 (1997) (hair length restriction applied only to male employees does not violate Title VII).

4. Sing Sing Prison in New York had a grooming rule that prohibited prison guards from having spikes, tails, or names shaved into their hair. Two prison guards became members of the Rastafarian religion and started wearing their hair in dreadlocks. The prison ordered them to cut their hair because it allegedly was unprofessional and created a risk to safety. Has the prison violated Title VII? See Francis v. Keane, 888 F.Supp. 568 (S.D.N.Y. 1995) (denying the state's motion for summary judgement). Compare Webb

v. City of Philadelphia, 562 F.3d 256 (3d Cir. 2009) (no Title VII violation where police department could not accommodate an officer's request to wear a Muslim headscarf without undue hardship) with Francis v. Keane, 888 F.Supp. 568 (S.D.N.Y.1995) (held: yes). See also Fraternal Order of Police Newark Lodge No. 12 v. City of Newark, 170 F.3d 359 (3d Cir. 1999), cert. denied, 528 U.S. 817 (1999) (police department's failure to grant exemption to no-beard rule for Muslim police officers who desire to wear beards for religious reasons violates the free exercise clause of the First Amendment).

5. In EEOC v. Catastrophe Management Solutions, 852 F.3d 1018 (11th Cir. 2016), Chastity Jones was hired as a customer service representative, a position that did not have contact with the public. Her offer was rescinded, however, when she refused to cut her dreadlocks. The employer's grooming policy called for hairstyle to reflect a "business/professional image." The EEOC alleged that the employer's policy constituted race discrimination because "dreadlocks are a manner of wearing hair that is physiologically and culturally associated with people of African descent." The Eleventh Circuit affirmed dismissal of the case on the ground that race discrimination does not entail cultural practices.

6. A black man applied for a job as a bus driver. The bus company had a no-beard policy for its bus drivers. The man asserted that he suffered from pseudofolliculitis barbae, a skin disorder resulting from ingrown hair which is aggravated by shaving. He demonstrated that this condition affects 25 percent of black males but less than one percent of white males. In a Title VII race discrimination action, what result? See EEOC v. Trailways, Inc., 530 F.Supp. 54 (D.Colo.1981) (held: employer failed to rebut prima facie case). See also Bradley v. Pizzaco of Nebraska, Inc., 7 F.3d 795 (8th Cir. 1993) (employer failed to accommodate workers with pseudofolliculitis barbae). Cf. EEOC v. UPS, 94 F.3d 314 (7th Cir. 1996) (no-beard rule may constitute religious discrimination). But see Fitzpatrick v. City of Atlanta, 2 F.3d 1112 (11th Cir. 1993) (upholding no-beard rule for firefighters because beard interfered with respirator use).

7. In 2019, California, New York, and New Jersey became the first states to enact laws prohibiting employment discrimination on the basis of natural hairstyles, such as braids, Bantu knots, and twists. The laws were enacted after highly publicized incidents of discrimination against African Americans in employment, education, and other settings.

Cloutier v. Costco Wholesale Corp.

390 F.3d 126 (1st Cir. 2004).

* * *

■ LIPEZ, CIRCUIT JUDGE.

Kimberly Cloutier alleges that her employer, Costco Wholesale Corp. (Costco), failed to offer her a reasonable accommodation after she alerted it to a conflict between the "no facial jewelry" provision of its dress code and her religious practice as a member of the Church of Body Modification. She argues that this failure amounts to religious discrimination in violation of Title VII, 42 U.S.C. § 2000e–2(a), and the corresponding Massachusetts statute, Mass. Gen. Laws ch. 151B, § 4(1A). The district court granted summary judgment for Costco, concluding that Costco reasonably accommodated Cloutier by offering to reinstate her if she either covered her facial piercing with a band-aid or replaced it with a clear retainer. We affirm the grant of summary judgment, but on a different basis. We hold that Costco had no duty to accommodate Cloutier because it could not do so without undue hardship.

I.

* * *

Kimberly Cloutier began working at Costco's West Springfield, Massachusetts store in July 1997. Before her first day of work, Cloutier received a copy of the Costco employment agreement, which included the employee dress code. When she was hired, Cloutier had multiple earrings and four tattoos, but no facial piercings.

Cloutier moved from her position as a front-end assistant to the deli department in September 1997. In 1998, Costco revised its dress code to prohibit food handlers, including deli employees, from wearing any jewelry. Cloutier's supervisor instructed her to remove her earrings pursuant to the revised code, but Cloutier refused. Instead, she requested to transfer to a front-end position where she would be permitted to continue wearing her jewelry. Cloutier did not indicate at the time that her insistence on wearing her earrings was based on a religious or spiritual belief.

Costco approved Cloutier's transfer back to a front-end position in June 1998, and promoted her to cashier soon thereafter. Over the ensuing two years, she engaged in various forms of body modification including facial piercing and cutting. Although these practices were meaningful to Cloutier, they were not motivated by a religious belief.

In March 2001, Costco further revised its dress code to prohibit all facial jewelry, aside from earrings, and disseminated the modified code to its employees. Cloutier did not challenge the dress code or seek an accommodation, but rather continued uneventfully to wear her eyebrow piercing for several months.

Costco began enforcing its no-facial-jewelry policy in June 2001. On June 25, 2001, front-end supervisors Todd Cunningham and Michele Callaghan informed Cloutier and another employee, Jennifer Theriaque, that they would have to remove their facial piercings. Cloutier and Theriaque did not comply, returning to work the following day still wearing their piercings. When Callaghan reiterated the no-facial-jewelry policy, Cloutier indicated for the first time that she was a member of the Church of Body Modification (CBM), and that her eyebrow piercing was part of her religion.

The CBM was established in 1999 and counts approximately 1000 members who participate in such practices as piercing, tattooing, branding, cutting, and body manipulation. Among the goals espoused in the CBM's mission statement are for its members to "grow as individuals through body modification and its teachings," to "promote growth in mind, body and spirit," and to be "confident role models in learning, teaching, and displaying body modification." The church's website, apparently its primary mode for reaching its adherents, did not state that members' body modifications had to be visible at all times or that temporarily removing body modifications would violate a religious tenet. Still, Cloutier interprets the call to be a confident role model as requiring that her piercings be visible at all times and precluding her from removing or covering her facial jewelry. She does not extend this reasoning to the tattoos on her upper arms, which were covered at work by her shirt.

After reviewing information that Cloutier provided from the CBM website, Callaghan's supervisor, Andrew Mulik, instructed Cloutier and Theriaque to remove their facial jewelry. They refused. The following day, Cloutier filed a religious discrimination complaint with the Equal Employment Opportunity Commission (EEOC), which is empowered to enforce Title VII. 42 U.S.C. § 2000e–5.

* * *

The district court granted Costco's motion to dismiss Cloutier's state civil rights claim but allowed the federal and state discrimination claims to proceed. Costco then moved for summary judgment on the discrimination claims.

* * *

The court ultimately avoided ruling on whether the CBM is a religion or whether Cloutier's interpretation of the CBM tenets is protected by Title VII. Instead, the court concluded that even if Cloutier had met her prima facie case, Costco should prevail because it fulfilled its obligations under the second part of the Title VII framework. Specifically, the court found that Costco met its burden of showing that it had offered Cloutier a reasonable accommodation of her religious practice:

> Costco's offer of accommodation was manifestly reasonable as a matter of law. The temporary covering of plaintiff's facial piercings during working hours impinges on plaintiff's religious scruples no more than the wearing of a blouse, which covers plaintiff's tattoos. The alternative of a clear plastic retainer does not even require plaintiff to cover her piercings. Neither of these alternative accommodations will compel plaintiff to violate any of the established tenets of the CBM.

Cloutier v. Costco Wholesale, 311 F.Supp.2d 190, 199 (D.Mass.2004).

In granting summary judgment on the Title VII claim, the court stressed that "the search for a reasonable accommodation goes both ways. Although the employer is required under Title VII to accommodate an employee's religious beliefs, the employee has a duty to cooperate with the employer's good faith efforts to accommodate." The court also noted that Title VII does not require Costco to grant Cloutier's preferred accommodation, but merely a reasonable one. While Costco's suggested accommodation balanced Cloutier's beliefs with its interest in presenting a professional appearance, Cloutier "offered no accommodation whatsoever."

* * *

Having resolved the federal claim, the court turned to Cloutier's state law claim under Mass. Gen. Laws ch. 151B § 4(1A), which has been interpreted largely to mirror Title VII. Wheatley v. AT & T, 418 Mass. 394, 397, 636 N.E.2d 265, 268 (1994). The statute prevents employers from imposing a condition of employment which "would require [an employee] to violate, or forego the practice of, his creed or religion as required by that creed or religion."

* * *

Under the foregoing framework, the district court concluded that summary judgment for Costco was appropriate. Although it noted the possibility that the state statute "casts a broader net than Title VII in covering purely personal beliefs that may be entitled to protection from discrimination," the court relied on its previous finding that Costco's offer to let Cloutier return to work wearing a band-aid or plastic retainer was "reasonable as a matter of law."

* * *

On appeal, Cloutier vigorously asserts that her insistence on displaying all her facial jewelry at all times is the result of a sincerely held religious belief. Determining whether a belief is religious is "more often than not a difficult and delicate task," one to which the courts are ill-suited. Fortunately, as the district court noted, there is no need for us to delve into this thorny question in the present case. Even assuming, arguendo, that Cloutier established her prima facie case, the facts here do not support a finding of impermissible religious discrimination.

Although the district court's decision rested on the conclusion that Costco had offered Cloutier a reasonable accommodation, "[w]e may affirm . . . on any grounds supported by the record." We find dispositive that the only accommodation Cloutier considers reasonable, a blanket exemption from the no-facial-jewelry policy, would impose an undue hardship on Costco. In such a situation, an employer has no obligation to offer an accommodation before taking an adverse employment action.

* * *

Cloutier asserts that the CBM mandate to be a confident role model requires her to display all of her facial piercings at all times. In her view, the only reasonable accommodation would be exemption from the no-facial-jewelry policy. Costco maintains that such an exemption would cause it to suffer an undue hardship, and that as a result it had no obligation to accommodate Cloutier.

An accommodation constitutes an "undue hardship" if it would impose more than a de minimis cost on the employer. Trans World Airlines, Inc. v. Hardison, 432 U.S. 63, 84 (1977). This calculus applies both to economic costs, such as lost business or having to hire additional employees to accommodate a Sabbath observer, and to non-economic costs, such as compromising the integrity of a seniority system.

Cloutier argues that Costco has not met its burden of demonstrating that her requested accommodation would impose an undue hardship. She asserts that she did not receive complaints about her facial piercings and that the piercings did not affect her job performance. Hence, she contends that any hardship Costco posits is merely hypothetical and therefore not sufficient to excuse it from accommodating her religious practice under Title VII.

Courts are "somewhat skeptical of hypothetical hardships that an employer thinks might be caused by an accommodation that never has been put into practice." "Nevertheless, it is possible for an employer to prove undue hardship without actually having undertaken any of the possible accommodations. . . ." It can do so by "examining the specific hardships imposed by specific accommodation proposals." Here, Costco has only one proposal to evaluate (allowing Cloutier to wear and display her body jewelry as she demands) and has determined that it would constitute an undue hardship.

The district court acknowledged that "Costco has a legitimate interest in presenting a workforce to its customers that is, at least in Costco's eyes, reasonably professional in appearance." Costco's dress code, included in the handbook distributed to all employees, furthers this interest. The preface to the code explains that, "Appearance and perception play a key role in member service. Our goal is to be dressed in professional attire that is appropriate to our business at all times. . . . All Costco employees must practice good grooming and personal hygiene to convey a neat, clean and professional image."

It is axiomatic that, for better or for worse, employees reflect on their employers. This is particularly true of employees who regularly interact with customers, as Cloutier did in her cashier position. Even if Cloutier did not personally receive any complaints about her appearance, her facial jewelry influenced Costco's public image and, in Costco's calculation, detracted from its professionalism.

Costco is far from unique in adopting personal appearance standards to promote and protect its image. As the D.C. Circuit noted, "Perhaps no facet of business life is more important than a company's place in public estimation. . . . Good grooming regulations reflect a company's policy in our highly competitive business environment. Reasonable requirements in furtherance of that policy are an aspect of managerial responsibility." Courts have long recognized the importance of personal appearance regulations, even in the face of Title VII challenges.

Courts considering Title VII religious discrimination claims have also upheld dress code policies that, like Costco's, are designed to appeal to customer preference or to promote a professional public image.

* * *

Cloutier's insistence on a wholesale exemption from the no-facial-jewelry policy precludes Costco from using its managerial discretion to search for a reasonable accommodation. Exempting Cloutier from the dress code would have imposed more than a de minimis burden on Costco for the reasons outlined above. Her refusal to consider anything less means that Costco could not offer a reasonable accommodation without incurring an undue hardship.

Affirmed.

NOTES AND QUESTIONS

1. The court observes that policies like Costco's have been upheld on the basis of "customer preference or to promote a professional image." Is this an objective standard, i.e., what customers actually prefer in terms of employee grooming? Or is it a subjective standard, i.e., what the employer believes customers prefer? Does this matter? What are the limits of the "employer image" defense?

2. San Francisco has a law that prohibits discrimination based on size. S.F. Admin. Code chs. 12A–C; S.F. Police Code art. 33 (enacted 2000)). When Jennifer Portnick, a 240 pound, 5-foot-8 aerobics teacher was denied a Jazzercise franchise, she was told in her rejection letter: "Jazzercise sells fitness. Consequently, a Jazzercise applicant must have a high muscle-to-fat ratio and look leaner than the public." After she sued under the San Francisco size discrimination law, Jazzercise settled. In a statement, the company said: "Recent studies document that it may be possible for people of varying weights to be fit." Patricia Leigh Brown, Jazzercise Relents to Plus-Size Pressure, N.Y. Times, May 8, 2002, at A18. Cf. Goodman v. L.A. Weight Loss Centers, Inc., 2005 WL 241180 (E.D. Pa. 2005) (weight loss center did not violate the ADA when it refused to hire a morbidly obese applicant for a sales counselor position because the applicant failed to show that he was an individual with a disability under the ADA; it was not unlawful to refuse to hire the applicant for fear that his appearance was not in accord with the center's image).

3. According to the Food and Drug Administration, more than 45 million Americans have at least one tattoo. Younger people are more likely to have one. According to a 2010 study by the Pew Research Center, 15 percent of Baby Boomers (born 1946 to 1964) have tattoos; 32 percent of Gen X (born

1965 to 1976) have tattoos; and 38 percent of Millennials (born 1977–1997) have tattoos. Is it lawful for an employer to refuse to hire someone with a tattoo? See Jon D. Bible, Tattoos and Body Piercings: New Terrain for Employers and Courts, 61 Lab. L.J. 109 (2010).

2. DRESS

EEOC v. Abercrombie & Fitch Stores, Inc.
575 U.S. 768 (2015).

■ JUSTICE SCALIA delivered the opinion of the Court.

Title VII of the Civil Rights Act of 1964 prohibits a prospective employer from refusing to hire an applicant in order to avoid accommodating a religious practice that it could accommodate without undue hardship. The question presented is whether this prohibition applies only where an applicant has informed the employer of his need for an accommodation.

I

We summarize the facts in the light most favorable to the Equal Employment Opportunity Commission (EEOC), against whom the Tenth Circuit granted summary judgment. Respondent Abercrombie & Fitch Stores, Inc., operates several lines of clothing stores, each with its own "style." Consistent with the image Abercrombie seeks to project for each store, the company imposes a Look Policy that governs its employees' dress. The Look Policy prohibits "caps"—a term the Policy does not define—as too informal for Abercrombie's desired image.

Samantha Elauf is a practicing Muslim who, consistent with her understanding of her religion's requirements, wears a headscarf. She applied for a position in an Abercrombie store, and was interviewed by Heather Cooke, the store's assistant manager. Using Abercrombie's ordinary system for evaluating applicants, Cooke gave Elauf a rating that qualified her to be hired; Cooke was concerned, however, that Elauf's headscarf would conflict with the store's Look Policy.

Cooke sought the store manager's guidance to clarify whether the headscarf was a forbidden "cap." When this yielded no answer, Cooke turned to Randall Johnson, the district manager. Cooke informed Johnson that she believed Elauf wore her headscarf because of her faith. Johnson told Cooke that Elauf's headscarf would violate the Look Policy, as would all other headwear, religious or otherwise, and directed Cooke not to hire Elauf.

Samantha Elauf

The EEOC sued Abercrombie on Elauf's behalf, claiming that its refusal to hire Elauf violated Title VII. The District Court granted the EEOC summary judgment on the issue of liability, 798 F.Supp.2d 1272 (N.D.Okla.2011), held a trial on damages, and awarded $20,000. The Tenth Circuit reversed and awarded Abercrombie summary judgment. 731 F.3d 1106 (2013). It concluded that ordinarily an employer cannot be liable under Title VII for failing to accommodate a religious practice until the applicant (or employee) provides the employer with actual knowledge of his need for an accommodation. We granted certiorari.

II

Title VII of the Civil Rights Act of 1964, as amended, prohibits two categories of employment practices. It is unlawful for an employer:

"(1) to fail or refuse to hire or to discharge any individual, or otherwise to discriminate against any individual with respect to his compensation, terms, conditions, or privileges of employment, because of such individual's race, color, religion, sex, or national origin; or

(2) to limit, segregate, or classify his employees or applicants for employment in any way which would deprive or tend to deprive any individual of employment opportunities or otherwise adversely affect his status as an employee, because of such individual's race, color, religion, sex, or national origin."

These two proscriptions, often referred to as the "disparate treatment" (or "intentional discrimination") provision and the "disparate impact" provision, are the only causes of action under Title VII. The word "religion" is defined to "includ[e] all aspects of religious observance and practice, as well as belief, unless an employer demonstrates that he is unable to reasonably accommodate to" a "religious observance or practice without undue hardship on the conduct of the employer's business."

Abercrombie's primary argument is that an applicant cannot show disparate treatment without first showing that an employer has "actual knowledge" of the applicant's need for an accommodation. We disagree. Instead, an applicant need only show that his need for an accommodation was a motivating factor in the employer's decision.

The disparate-treatment provision forbids employers to: (1) "fail . . . to hire" an applicant (2) "because of" (3) "such individual's . . . religion" (which includes his religious practice). Here, of course, Abercrombie (1) failed to hire Elauf. The parties concede that (if Elauf sincerely believes that her religion so requires) Elauf's wearing of a headscarf is (3) a "religious practice." All that remains is whether she was not hired (2) "because of" her religious practice.

The term "because of" appears frequently in antidiscrimination laws. It typically imports, at a minimum, the traditional standard of but-for causation. Title VII relaxes this standard, however, to prohibit even making a protected characteristic a "motivating factor" in an employment decision. "Because of" in § 2000e–2(a)(1) links the forbidden consideration to each of the verbs preceding it; an individual's actual religious practice may not be a motivating factor in failing to hire, in refusing to hire, and so on.

It is significant that § 2000e–2(a)(1) does not impose a knowledge requirement. As Abercrombie acknowledges, some antidiscrimination statutes do. For example, the Americans with Disabilities Act of 1990 defines discrimination to include an employer's failure to make "reasonable accommodations to the known physical or mental limitations" of an applicant. Title VII contains no such limitation.

Instead, the intentional discrimination provision prohibits certain motives, regardless of the state of the actor's knowledge. Motive and knowledge are separate concepts. An employer who has actual knowledge of the need for an accommodation does not violate Title VII by refusing to hire an applicant if avoiding that accommodation is not his motive. Conversely, an employer who acts with the motive of avoiding accommodation may violate Title VII even if he has no more than an unsubstantiated suspicion that accommodation would be needed.

Thus, the rule for disparate-treatment claims based on a failure to accommodate a religious practice is straightforward: An employer may not make an applicant's religious practice, confirmed or otherwise, a factor in employment decisions. For example, suppose that an employer thinks (though he does not know for certain) that a job applicant may be an orthodox Jew who will observe the Sabbath, and thus be unable to work on Saturdays. If the applicant actually requires an accommodation of that religious practice, and the employer's desire to avoid the prospective accommodation is a motivating factor in his decision, the employer violates Title VII.

Abercrombie urges this Court to adopt the Tenth Circuit's rule "allocat[ing] the burden of raising a religious conflict." This would require the employer to have actual knowledge of a conflict between an applicant's religious practice and a work rule. The problem with this approach is the one that inheres in most incorrect interpretations of statutes: It asks us to add words to the law to produce what is thought to be a desirable result. That is Congress's province. We construe Title VII's silence as exactly that: silence. Its disparate-treatment provision prohibits actions taken with the motive of avoiding the need for accommodating a religious practice. A request for accommodation, or the employer's certainty that the practice exists, may make it easier to infer motive, but is not a necessary condition of liability.

Abercrombie argues in the alternative that a claim based on a failure to accommodate an applicant's religious practice must be raised as a disparate-impact claim, not a disparate-treatment claim. We think not. That might have been true if Congress had limited the meaning of "religion" in Title VII to religious belief—so that discriminating against a particular religious practice would not be disparate treatment though it might have disparate impact. In fact, however, Congress defined "religion," for Title VII's purposes, as "includ[ing] all aspects of religious observance and practice, as well as belief." Thus, religious practice is one of the protected characteristics that cannot be accorded disparate treatment and must be accommodated.

Nor does the statute limit disparate-treatment claims to only those employer policies that treat religious practices less favorably than similar secular practices. Abercrombie's argument that a neutral policy cannot constitute "intentional discrimination" may make sense in other contexts. But Title VII does not demand mere neutrality with regard to religious practices—that they be treated no worse than other practices. Rather, it gives them favored treatment, affirmatively obligating employers not "to fail or refuse to hire or discharge any individual . . . because of such individual's" "religious observance and practice." An employer is surely entitled to have, for example, a no-headwear policy as an ordinary matter. But when an applicant requires an accommodation as an "aspec[t] of religious . . . practice," it is no response that the subsequent "fail[ure] . . . to hire" was due to an otherwise-neutral policy. Title VII requires otherwise-neutral policies to give way to the need for an accommodation.

* * *

The Tenth Circuit misinterpreted Title VII's requirements in granting summary judgment. We reverse its judgment and remand the case for further consideration consistent with this opinion.

It is so ordered.

JUSTICE ALITO, concurring in the judgment.

* * *

JUSTICE THOMAS, concurring in the judgment.

* * *

I would hold that Abercrombie's conduct did not constitute "intentional discrimination." Abercrombie refused to create an exception to its neutral Look Policy for Samantha Elauf's religious practice of wearing a headscarf. In doing so, it did not treat religious practices less favorably than similar secular practices, but instead remained neutral with regard to religious practices. To be sure, the effects of Abercrombie's neutral Look Policy, absent an accommodation, fall more harshly on those who wear headscarves as an aspect of their faith. But that is a classic case of an alleged disparate impact. It is not what we have previously understood to be a case of disparate treatment because Elauf received the same treatment from Abercrombie as any other applicant who appeared unable to comply with the company's Look Policy. Because cannot classify Abercrombie's conduct as "intentional discrimination," I would affirm.

NOTES AND QUESTIONS

1. Suppose the employer's agent, unaware of the likely religious significance of the headscarf she wore to the interview, refused to hire Elauf because she thought the color of Elauf's headscarf "clashed" with her dress and therefore she believed Elauf lacked the sense of style to be a sales associate for Abercrombie & Fitch. Would this be actionable religious discrimination? How would you apply the reasoning of the majority?

2. Suppose the employer's agent knew that another applicant was not a Muslim and refused to hire her because he thought it was "wrong" for a non-Muslim to wear an assumedly Muslim headscarf. Would this violate Title VII?

3. Suppose yet another applicant was not a Muslim and wore a headscarf simply because she liked the way it looked. Further suppose that the employer refused to hire her because it erroneously believed she was a Muslim. Would this be a violation of Title VII? Compare the "regarded as" provision of the ADA. Does there need to be a "regarded as" provision for Title VII?

4. For a further discussion of *Abercrombie*, see Jeffrey M. Hirsch, EEOC v. Abercrombie & Fitch Stores, Inc.: Mistakes, Same-Sex Marriage, and Unintended Consequences, 94 Tex. L. Rev. 95 (2016); Michael C. Harper, Confusion on the Court: Distinguishing Disparate Treatment from Disparate Impact in Young v. UPS and EEOC v. Abercrombie & Fitch, Inc., 96 B.U.L. Rev. 543 (2016).

B. PRIVACY

1. VISUAL

Hernandez v. Hillsides, Inc.
211 P.3d 1063 (Cal. 2009).

■ BAXTER, CIRCUIT JUDGE:

Defendants Hillsides, Inc., and Hillsides Children Center, Inc. (Hillsides) operated a private nonprofit residential facility for neglected and abused children, including the victims of sexual abuse. Plaintiffs Abigail Hernandez (Hernandez) and Maria-Jose Lopez (Lopez) were employed by Hillsides. They shared an enclosed office and performed clerical work during daytime business hours. Defendant John M. Hitchcock (Hitchcock), the director of the facility, learned that late at night, after plaintiffs had left the premises, an unknown person had repeatedly used a computer in plaintiffs' office to access the Internet and view pornographic Web sites. Such use conflicted with company policy and with Hillsides' aim of providing a safe haven for the children.

Concerned that the culprit might be a staff member who worked with the children, and without notifying plaintiffs, Hitchcock set up a hidden camera in their office. The camera could be made operable from a remote location, at any time of day or night, to permit either live viewing or videotaping of activities around the targeted workstation. It is undisputed that the camera was not operated for either of these purposes during business hours, and, as a consequence, that plaintiffs' activities in the office were not viewed or recorded by means of the surveillance system. Hitchcock did not expect or intend to catch plaintiffs on tape.

Nonetheless, after discovering the hidden camera in their office, plaintiffs filed this tort action alleging, among other things, that defendants intruded into a protected place, interest, or matter, and violated their right to privacy under both the common law and the state Constitution. The trial court granted defendants' motion for summary judgment and dismissed the case. The Court of Appeal reversed, finding triable issues that plaintiffs had suffered (1) an intrusion into a protected zone of privacy that (2) was so unjustified and offensive as to constitute a privacy violation.

* * *

Beginning in 2001, plaintiffs shared an office in the administrative building at Hillsides. Each woman had her own desk and computer workstation. The office had three windows on exterior walls. Blinds on the windows could be opened and closed. The office also had a door that could be closed and locked. A "doggie" door near the bottom of the office door was missing its flap, creating a small, low opening into the office. Several people, besides plaintiffs, had keys to their office: five administrators, including Hitchcock, and all of the program directors. Hernandez estimated that there were five program directors. Hitchcock counted eight of them.

According to plaintiffs, they occasionally used their office to change or adjust their clothing. Hernandez replaced her work clothes with athletic wear before leaving Hillsides to exercise at the end of the day. Two or three times, Lopez raised her shirt to show Hernandez her postpregnancy figure. Both women stated in their declarations that the blinds were drawn and the door was closed when this activity occurred. Hernandez also recalled the door being locked when she changed clothes.

In order to ensure compliance with Hillsides' computer policy and restrictions, Foster, the computer specialist, could retrieve and print a list of all Internet Web sites accessed from every computer on the premises. The network server that recorded and stored such information could pinpoint exactly when and where such Web access had occurred. In July 2002, Foster determined that numerous pornographic Web sites had been viewed in the late-night and early-morning hours from at least two different computers. One of them was located in the computer laboratory, or classroom. The other one sat on the desk Lopez used in the office she shared with Hernandez.

The evidence indicated that Lopez's computer could have been accessed after hours by someone other than her, because she did not always log off before going home at night. Hitchcock explained in his deposition that employees were expected to turn off their computers when leaving work at the end of the day, that a personal password was required to log onto the computer again after it had been turned off, and that this policy was communicated orally to employees when their computers were first assigned. He admitted that he did not remind plaintiffs of this procedure before taking the surveillance steps at issue here. Nonetheless, Lopez noted in her declaration that "[o]nce [her] computer at Hillsides was turned off, it required the input of a secret password in order to be accessed again."

Foster told defendant Hitchcock about the inappropriate Internet use, and showed him printouts listing the pornographic Web sites that had been accessed. Given the odd hours at which such activity had occurred, Hitchcock surmised that the perpetrator was a program director or other staff person who had unfettered access to Hillsides in the middle of the night. Hitchcock did not blame any of the children, because they would have been under supervision and asleep in the residence halls at the time. Nor did he suspect plaintiffs. They typically were gone from the premises when the impermissible nighttime computer use occurred.

In light of these circumstances, Hitchcock decided to use video equipment Hillsides already had in its possession to record the perpetrator in the act of using the computers at night. He told other administrators about the problem and his surveillance plan. Hitchcock explained in both his deposition and declaration that he sought to protect the children from any staff person who might expose them to pornography, emphasizing the harm they had endured before entering Hillsides.

* * *

Hitchcock rarely activated the camera and motion detector in plaintiffs' office, and never did so while they were there. His deposition testimony addressed these circumstances as follows: On three occasions, Hitchcock connected the wireless receptors to the television in the storage room after plaintiffs left work for the day, and then disconnected the receptors the next morning, before plaintiffs returned to work. On one such morning, he also removed the camera from the office, and returned it later, when plaintiffs were gone for the night. In short, the camera and motion detector were always disabled during the workday, such that "there was no picture showing" and "no recording going on" while plaintiffs were in their office. Hitchcock further stated that between installation of the equipment in early October 2002, and his decision to remove it three weeks later, no one was videotaped or caught using the computer in plaintiffs' office. He assumed that the culprit had learned about the camera and stopped engaging in unauthorized activity.

Meanwhile, about 4:30 p.m. on Friday, October 25, 2002, plaintiffs discovered the video equipment in their office. A red light on the motion detector flashed at the time. The cord attached to the camera was plugged into the wall and was hot to the touch.

* * *

A privacy violation based on the common law tort of intrusion has two elements. First, the defendant must intentionally intrude into a place, conversation, or matter as to which the plaintiff has a reasonable expectation of privacy. Second, the intrusion must occur in a manner highly offensive to a reasonable person. These limitations on the right to privacy are not insignificant. Nonetheless, the cause of action recognizes a measure of personal control over the individual's autonomy, dignity, and serenity. The gravamen is the mental anguish sustained when both conditions of liability exist.

As to the first element of the common law tort, the defendant must have "penetrated some zone of physical or sensory privacy . . . or obtained unwanted access to data" by electronic or other covert means, in violation of the law or social norms. In either instance, the expectation of privacy must be "objectively reasonable." In Sanders v. American Broadcasting Companies (1999) 20 Cal.4th 907, (*Sanders*), a leading case on workplace privacy that we discuss further below, this court linked the reasonableness of privacy expectations to such factors as (1) the identity of the intruder, (2) the extent to which other persons had access to the subject place, and could see or hear the plaintiff, and (3) the means by which the intrusion occurred.

The second common law element essentially involves a "policy" determination as to whether the alleged intrusion is "highly offensive" under the particular circumstances. Relevant factors include the degree and setting of the intrusion, and the intruder's motives and objectives. Even in cases involving the use of photographic and electronic recording devices, which can raise difficult questions about covert surveillance, "California tort law provides no bright line on ['offensiveness']; each case must be taken on its facts."

* * *

The present case, of course, does not involve an imposter or "stranger to the workplace" who surreptitiously recorded and videotaped conversations that were later published without the speaker's consent. Nor does it involve commercial interactions between the representatives of a business and its customers or other members of the public. Rather, defendants represent a private employer accused of installing electronic equipment that gave it the capacity to secretly watch and record employee activities behind closed doors in an office to which the general public had limited access. As we discuss later with respect to the "offensiveness" element of plaintiffs' claim, an employer may have sound reasons for monitoring the workplace, and an intrusion upon the employee's reasonable privacy expectations may not be egregious or actionable under the particular circumstances. However, on the threshold question whether such expectations were infringed, decisional law suggests that is the case here.

Consistent with *Sanders*, which asks whether the employee could be "overheard or observed" by others when the tortious act allegedly occurred, courts have examined the physical layout of the area intruded upon, its relationship to the workplace as a whole, and the nature of the activities commonly performed in such places. At one end of the spectrum are settings in which work or business is conducted in an open and accessible space, within the sight and hearing not only of coworkers and supervisors, but also of customers, visitors, and the general public.

At the other end of the spectrum are areas in the workplace subject to restricted access and limited view, and reserved exclusively for performing bodily functions or other inherently personal acts.

The present scenario falls between these extremes.

Plaintiffs plausibly claim that Hillsides provided an enclosed office with a door that could be shut and locked, and window blinds that could be drawn, to allow the occupants to obtain some measure of refuge, to focus on their work, and to escape visual and aural interruptions from other sources, including their employer. Such a protective setting generates legitimate expectations that not all activities performed behind closed doors would be clerical and work related. As suggested by the evidence here, employees who share an office, and who have four walls that shield them from outside view (albeit, with a broken "doggie" flap on the door), may perform grooming or hygiene activities, or conduct personal conversations, during the workday. Privacy is not wholly lacking because the occupants of an office can see one another, or because colleagues, supervisors, visitors, and security and maintenance personnel have varying degrees of access.

Regarding another relevant factor in *Sanders*, the "means of intrusion," employees who retreat into a shared or solo office, and who perform work and personal activities in relative seclusion there, would not reasonably expect to be the subject of televised spying and secret filming by their employer. As noted, in assessing social norms in this regard, we may look at both the "common law" and "statutory enactment."

Courts have acknowledged the intrusive effect for tort purposes of hidden cameras and video recorders in settings that otherwise seem private. It has been said that the "unblinking lens" can be more penetrating than the naked eye with respect to "duration, proximity, focus, and vantage point." Such monitoring and recording denies the actor a key feature of privacy—the right to control the dissemination of his image and actions. We have made clear that the " 'mere fact that a person can be seen by someone does not automatically mean that he or she can legally be forced to be subject to being seen by everyone.' "

Not surprisingly, we discern a similar legislative policy against covert monitoring and recording that intrudes—or threatens to intrude—upon visual privacy. Some statutes criminalize the use of camcorders, motion picture cameras, or photographic cameras to violate reasonable expectations of privacy in specified areas in which persons commonly undress or perform other intimate acts. Liability exists, under certain circumstances, where the lens allows the intruder to "look" into or "view" the protected area. Of course, the intruder also cannot "secretly videotape, film, photograph, or record" anyone in that private place where various conditions exist.

* * *

As emphasized by defendants, the evidence shows that Hitchcock never viewed or recorded plaintiffs inside their office by means of the equipment he installed both there and in the storage room. He also did not intend or attempt to do so, and took steps to avoid capturing them on camera and videotape. While such factors bear on the offensiveness of the challenged conduct, as discussed below, we reject the defense suggestion that they preclude us from finding the requisite intrusion in the first place.

In particular, Hitchcock hid the video equipment in plaintiffs' office from view in an apparent attempt to prevent anyone from discovering, avoiding, or dismantling it. He used a camera and motion detector small enough to tuck inside and around decorative items perched on different bookshelves, both high and low. Plaintiffs presumably would have been caught in the camera's sights if they had returned to work after hours, or if Hitchcock had been mistaken about them having left the office when he activated the system. Additionally, except for the one day in which Hitchcock removed the camera from plaintiffs' office, the means to activate the monitoring and recording functions were available around the clock, for three weeks, to anyone who had access to the storage room. Assuming the storage room was locked, as many as eight to 11 employees had keys under plaintiffs' version of the facts (depending upon the total number of program directors at Hillsides).

* * *

In sum, the undisputed evidence seems clearly to support the first of two basic elements we have identified as necessary to establish a violation of privacy as alleged in plaintiffs' complaint. Defendants secretly installed a hidden video camera that was both operable and operating (electricity-wise), and that could be made to monitor and record activities inside plaintiffs' office, at will, by anyone who plugged in the receptors, and who had access to the remote location in which both the receptors and recording equipment were located. The workplace policy, that by means within the computer system itself, plaintiffs would be monitored about the pattern and use of Web sites visited, to prevent abuse of Hillsides' computer system, is distinguishable from and does not necessarily create a social norm that in order to advance that same interest, a camera would be placed inside their office, and would be aimed toward a computer workstation to capture all human activity occurring there. Plaintiffs had no reasonable expectation that their employer would intrude so tangibly into their semi-private office.

Plaintiffs must show more than an intrusion upon reasonable privacy expectations. Actionable invasions of privacy also must be "highly offensive" to a reasonable person and "sufficiently serious" and unwarranted as to constitute an "egregious breach of the social norms." Defendants claim that, in finding a triable issue in this regard, the Court of Appeal focused too narrowly on the mere presence of a functioning camera in plaintiffs' office during the workday, and on the inchoate risk that someone would sneak into the locked storage room and activate the monitoring and recording devices. Defendants imply that under a broader view of the relevant circumstances, no reasonable jury could find in plaintiffs' favor and impose liability on this evidentiary record. We agree.

* * *

We appreciate plaintiffs' dismay over the discovery of video equipment—small, blinking, and hot to the touch—that their employer had hidden among their personal effects in an office that was reasonably secluded from public access and view. Nothing we say here is meant to encourage such surveillance measures, particularly in the absence of adequate notice to persons within camera range that their actions may be viewed and taped.

Nevertheless, considering all the relevant circumstances, plaintiffs have not established, and cannot reasonably expect to establish, that the particular conduct of defendants that is challenged in this case was highly offensive and constituted an egregious violation of prevailing social norms. We reach this conclusion from the standpoint of a reasonable person based on defendants' vigorous efforts to avoid intruding on plaintiffs' visual privacy altogether. Activation of the surveillance system was narrowly tailored in place, time, and scope, and was prompted by legitimate business concerns. Plaintiffs were not at risk of being monitored or recorded during regular work hours and were never actually caught on camera or videotape.

We therefore reverse the judgment of the Court of Appeal insofar as it reversed and vacated the trial court's order granting defendants' motion for summary judgment on all counts alleged in the complaint.

NOTES AND QUESTIONS

1. What facts are most helpful to the defendant's case? No doubt, the employees were hurt, insulted, angry, and embarrassed, but the court is clear that for either common law or state constitutional invasion of privacy based on intrusion, there must be substantial evidence of objective, unreasonable conduct on the part of the defendant.

2. Surveillance of workers on the job is increasing in an effort to improve efficiency and reduce theft. Does the use of TV cameras, microphones, metal detectors, mirrors, one-way mirrors, or other devices invade any legitimate interests of employees? Does the reasonableness of such measures depend on the employer's justifications, the consent of the workers, or some other factors? See Sacramento County Deputy Sheriffs' Ass'n v. Sacramento County, 59 Cal.Rptr.2d 834 (Ct.App.1996) (placement of video camera in county jail's release office did not violate deputy sheriff's Fourth Amendment rights). See also Cowles v. Alaska, 23 P.3d 1168 (Alaska 2001), cert. denied, 534 U.S. 1131 (2002) (placing video camera without sound in ceiling above a desk visible to the public to determine reason for cash shortages did not violate Alaska Constitution).

3. Some employers also have engaged in surveillance of employees at home and other off-work locations to investigate whether workers' compensation claims were fraudulently filed, whether trade secrets were being disclosed to competitors, and for various other reasons. See generally Daniel P. O'Gorman, Looking Out for Your Employees: Employers' Surreptitious Physical Surveillance of Employees and the Tort of Invasion of Privacy, 85 Neb. L. Rev. 212 (2006).

2. ELECTRONIC

City of Ontario v. Quon
560 U.S. 746 (2010).

■ JUSTICE KENNEDY delivered the opinion of the Court.

This case involves the assertion by a government employer of the right, in circumstances to be described, to read text messages sent and received on a pager the employer owned and issued to an employee. The employee contends that the privacy of the messages is protected by the ban on "unreasonable searches and seizures" found in the Fourth Amendment to the United States Constitution, made applicable to the States by the Due Process Clause of the Fourteenth Amendment. Though the case touches issues of far reaching significance, the Court concludes it can be resolved by settled principles determining when a search is reasonable.

The City of Ontario (City) is a political subdivision of the State of California. The case arose out of incidents in 2001 and 2002 when respondent Jeff Quon was employed by the Ontario Police Department (OPD). He was a police sergeant and member of OPD's Special Weapons and Tactics (SWAT) Team.

* * *

In October 2001, the City acquired 20 alphanumeric pagers capable of sending and receiving text messages. Arch Wireless Operating Company provided wireless service for the pagers. Under the City's service contract with Arch Wireless, each pager was allotted a limited number of characters sent or received each month. Usage in excess of that amount would result in an additional fee. The City issued pagers to Quon and other SWAT Team members in order to help the SWAT Team mobilize and respond to emergency situations.

Before acquiring the pagers, the City announced a "Computer Usage, Internet and E-Mail Policy" (Computer Policy) that applied to all employees. Among other provisions, it specified that the City "reserves the right to monitor and log all network activity including e-mail and Internet use, with or without notice. Users should have no expectation of privacy or confidentiality when using these resources." In March 2000, Quon signed a statement acknowledging that he had read and understood the Computer Policy.

The Computer Policy did not apply, on its face, to text messaging. Text messages share similarities with e-mails, but the two differ in an important way. In this case, for instance, an e-mail sent on a City computer was transmitted through the City's own data servers, but a text message sent on one of the City's pagers was transmitted using wireless radio frequencies from an individual pager to a receiving station owned by Arch Wireless. It was routed through Arch Wireless' computer network, where it remained until the recipient's pager or cellular telephone was ready to receive the message, at which point Arch Wireless transmitted the message from the transmitting station nearest to the recipient. After delivery, Arch Wireless retained a copy on its computer servers. The message did not pass through computers owned by the City.

Although the Computer Policy did not cover text messages by its explicit terms, the City made clear to employees, including Quon, that the City would treat text messages the same way as it treated e-mails. At an April 18, 2002, staff meeting at which Quon was present, Lieutenant Steven Duke, the OPD officer responsible for the City's contract with Arch Wireless, told officers that messages sent on the pagers "are considered e-mail messages. This means that [text] messages would fall under the City's policy as public information and [would be] eligible for auditing." Duke's comments were put in writing in a memorandum sent on April 29, 2002, by Chief Scharf to Quon and other City personnel.

Within the first or second billing cycle after the pagers were distributed, Quon exceeded his monthly text message character allotment. Duke told Quon about the overage, and reminded him that messages sent on the pagers were "considered e-mail and could be audited." Duke said, however, that "it was not his intent to audit [an] employee's text messages to see if the overage [was] due to work related transmissions." Duke suggested that Quon could reimburse the City for the overage fee rather than have Duke audit the messages. Quon wrote a check to the City for the overage. Duke offered the same arrangement to other employees who incurred overage fees.

Over the next few months, Quon exceeded his character limit three or four times. Each time he reimbursed the City. Quon and another officer again incurred overage fees for their pager usage in August 2002. At a meeting in October, Duke told Scharf that he had become " 'tired of being a bill collector.' " Scharf decided to determine whether the existing character limit was too low—that is, whether officers such as Quon were having to pay fees for sending work-related messages—or if the overages were for personal messages. Scharf told Duke to request transcripts of text messages sent in August and September by Quon and the other employee who had exceeded the character allowance.

At Duke's request, an administrative assistant employed by OPD contacted Arch Wireless. After verifying that the City was the subscriber on the accounts, Arch Wireless provided the desired transcripts. Duke reviewed the transcripts and discovered that many of the messages sent and received on Quon's pager were not work related, and some were sexually explicit. Duke reported his findings to Scharf, who, along with Quon's immediate supervisor, reviewed the transcripts himself. After his review, Scharf referred the matter to OPD's internal affairs division for an investigation into whether Quon was violating OPD rules by pursuing personal matters while on duty.

The officer in charge of the internal affairs review was Sergeant Patrick McMahon. Before conducting a review, McMahon used Quon's work schedule to redact the transcripts in order to eliminate any messages Quon sent while off duty. He then reviewed the content of the messages Quon sent during work hours. McMahon's report noted that Quon sent or received 456 messages during work hours in the month of August 2002, of which no more than 57 were work related; he sent as many as 80 messages during a single day at work; and on an average workday, Quon sent or received 28 messages, of which only 3 were related to police business. The report concluded that Quon had violated OPD rules. Quon was allegedly disciplined.

Raising claims under Rev. Stat. § 1979, 42 U.S.C. § 1983; 18 U.S.C. § 2701 et seq., popularly known as the Stored Communications Act (SCA); and California law, Quon filed suit against petitioners in the United States District Court for the Central District of California. * * * Among the allegations in the complaint was that petitioners violated respondents' Fourth Amendment rights and the SCA by obtaining and reviewing the transcript of Jeff Quon's pager messages and that Arch Wireless had violated the SCA by turning over the transcript to the City.

* * *

The Fourth Amendment states: "The right of the people to be secure in their persons, houses, papers, and effects, against unreasonable searches and seizures, shall not be violated. . . ." It is well settled that the Fourth Amendment's protection extends beyond the sphere of criminal investigations. Camara v. Municipal Court of City and County of San Francisco, 387 U.S. 523, 530 (1967). "The Amendment guarantees the privacy, dignity, and security of persons against certain arbitrary and invasive acts by officers of the Government," without regard to whether the government actor is investigating crime or performing another function. Skinner v. Railway Labor Executives' Assn., 489 U.S. 602, 613–614 (1989). The Fourth Amendment applies as well when the Government acts in its capacity as an employer. Treasury Employees v. Von Raab, 489 U.S. 656, 665 (1989).

The Court discussed this principle in O'Connor [v. Ortega, 480 U.S. 709 (1987)]. There a physician employed by a state hospital alleged that hospital officials investigating workplace misconduct had violated his Fourth Amendment rights by searching his office and seizing personal items from his desk and filing cabinet. All Members of the Court agreed with the general principle that "[i]ndividuals do not lose Fourth Amendment rights merely because they work for the government instead of a private employer." A majority of the Court further agreed that " 'special needs, beyond the normal need for law enforcement,' " make the warrant and probable-cause requirement impracticable for government employers.

* * *

Later, in the *Von Raab* decision, the Court explained that "operational realities" could diminish an employee's privacy expectations, and that this diminution could be taken into consideration when assessing the reasonableness of a workplace search. In the two decades since *O'Connor*, however, the threshold test for determining the scope of an employee's Fourth Amendment rights has not been clarified further. Here, though they disagree on whether Quon had a reasonable expectation of privacy, both petitioners and respondents start from the premise that the *O'Connor* plurality controls. It is not necessary to resolve whether that premise is correct. The case can be decided by determining that the search was reasonable even assuming Quon had a reasonable expectation of privacy.

* * *

The Court must proceed with care when considering the whole concept of privacy expectations in communications made on electronic equipment owned by a government employer. The judiciary risks error by elaborating too fully on the Fourth Amendment implications of emerging technology before its role in society has become clear. * * * It is not so clear that courts at present are on so sure a ground. Prudence counsels caution before the facts in the instant case are used to establish far-reaching premises that define the existence, and extent, of privacy expectations enjoyed by employees when using employer-provided communication devices.

Rapid changes in the dynamics of communication and information transmission are evident not just in the technology itself but in what society accepts as proper behavior. As one *amici* brief notes, many employers expect or at least tolerate personal use of such equipment by employees because it often increases worker efficiency. Another *amicus* points out that the law is beginning to respond to these developments, as some States have recently passed statutes requiring employers to notify employees when monitoring their electronic communications. At present, it is uncertain how workplace norms, and the law's treatment of them, will evolve.

Even if the Court were certain that the *O'Connor* plurality's approach were the right one, the Court would have difficulty predicting how employees' privacy expectations will be shaped by those changes or the degree to which society will be prepared to recognize those expectations as reasonable. Cell phone and text message communications are so pervasive that some persons may consider them to be essential means or necessary instruments for self-expression, even self-identification. That might strengthen the case for an expectation of privacy. On the other hand, the ubiquity of those devices has made them generally affordable, so one could counter that employees who need cell phones or similar devices for personal matters can purchase and pay for their own. And employer policies concerning communications will of course shape the reasonable expectations of their employees, especially to the extent that such policies are clearly communicated.

A broad holding concerning employees' privacy expectations vis-à-vis employer-provided technological equipment might have implications for future cases that cannot be predicted. It is preferable to dispose of this case on narrower grounds. For present purposes we assume several propositions *arguendo*: First, Quon had a reasonable expectation of privacy in the text messages sent on the pager provided to him by the City; second, petitioners' review of the transcript constituted a search within the meaning of the Fourth Amendment; and third, the principles applicable to a government employer's search of an employee's physical office apply with at least the same force when the employer intrudes on the employee's privacy in the electronic sphere.

Even if Quon had a reasonable expectation of privacy in his text messages, petitioners did not necessarily violate the Fourth Amendment by obtaining and reviewing the transcripts. Although as a general matter, warrantless searches "are *per se* unreasonable under the Fourth Amendment," there are "a few specifically established and well-delineated exceptions" to that general rule. The Court has held that the " 'special needs' " of the workplace justify one such exception.

Under the approach of the *O'Connor* plurality, when conducted for a "noninvestigatory, work-related purpos[e]" or for the "investigatio[n] of work-related misconduct," a government employer's warrantless search is reasonable if it is " 'justified at its inception' " and if " 'the measures adopted are reasonably related to the objectives of the search and not excessively intrusive in light of' " the circumstances giving rise to the search. The search here satisfied the standard of the *O'Connor* plurality and was reasonable under that approach.

The search was justified at its inception because there were "reasonable grounds for suspecting that the search [was] necessary for a noninvestigatory work-related purpose." As a jury found, Chief Scharf ordered the search in order to determine whether the character limit on the City's contract with Arch Wireless was sufficient to meet the City's needs. This was, as the Ninth Circuit noted, a "legitimate work-related rationale." The City and OPD had a legitimate interest in ensuring that employees were not being forced to pay out of their own pockets for work-related expenses, or on the other hand that the City was not paying for extensive personal communications.

As for the scope of the search, reviewing the transcripts was reasonable because it was an efficient and expedient way to determine whether Quon's overages were the result of work-related messaging or personal use. The review was also not " 'excessively intrusive.' " Although Quon had gone over his monthly allotment a number of times, OPD requested transcripts for only the months of August and September 2002. While it may have been reasonable as well for OPD to review transcripts of all the months in which Quon exceeded his allowance, it was certainly reasonable for OPD to review messages for just two months in order to obtain a large enough sample to decide whether the character limits were efficacious. And it is worth noting that during his internal affairs investigation, McMahon redacted all messages Quon sent while off duty, a measure which reduced the intrusiveness of any further review of the transcripts.

Furthermore, and again on the assumption that Quon had a reasonable expectation of privacy in the contents of his messages, the extent of an expectation is relevant to assessing whether the search was too intrusive. Even if he could assume some level of privacy would inhere in his messages, it would not have been reasonable for Quon to conclude that his messages were in all circumstances immune from scrutiny. Quon was told that his messages were subject to auditing. As a law enforcement officer, he would or should have known that his actions were likely to come under legal scrutiny, and that this might entail an analysis of his on-the-job communications. Under the circumstances, a reasonable employee would be aware that sound management principles might require the audit of messages to determine whether the pager was being appropriately used.

* * *

Because the search was reasonable, petitioners did not violate respondents' Fourth Amendment rights, and the court below erred by concluding otherwise. The judgment of the Court of Appeals for the Ninth Circuit is reversed, and the case is remanded for further proceedings consistent with this opinion.

■ JUSTICE STEVENS, concurring.

* * *

■ JUSTICE SCALIA, concurring in part and concurring in the judgment.

* * *

NOTES AND QUESTIONS

1. Does the ubiquity of pagers, e-mail, cell phones, and similar forms of communications technology suggest that employees have lesser expectations of privacy in their communications? To what extent is your answer influenced by the public/private nature of the employment or more specific facts of a particular job?

2. In its decision, the Ninth Circuit held that the search was unreasonable. It pointed to less intrusive methods of reviewing Quon's pager use, including reminding him that he was forbidden from using his pager for personal communications and that the contents would be subject to audit, to ensure that the pager was only used for work-related purposes. It also suggested that it could have asked Quon to count the characters himself or asked him to redact personal messages and grant the OPD permission to review the redacted transcript. The Supreme Court held this was unnecessary. "Even

assuming there were ways that OPD could have performed the search that would have been less intrusive, it does not follow that the search was unreasonable." Do you agree?

3. In his opinion, Justice Kennedy was careful to avoid stating principles of electronic communication privacy in the workplace more broadly. He noted that the world of communications technology is changing rapidly. Is the Court being too timid and too limited in its pronouncements to afford sufficient guidance or is it being wise and cautious? See generally Paul M. Secunda, Privatizing Workplace Privacy, 88 Notre Dame L. Rev. 277 (2012).

4. Title I of the Electronic Communications Privacy Act of 1986, 18 U.S.C. § 2510 et seq., prohibits interception, defined as the acquisition, of the contents of any wire, electronic, or oral communication through the use of an electronic, mechanical, or other device at the time the communication is transmitted. Title II of the Act creates civil liability for the unauthorized access of a facility through which electronic communications services are provided, and thereby obtains, alters, or prevents electronic storage of the communications. There is an exception for the seizure of e-mails authorized by the person or entity providing the wire or electronic communications service. Courts have held that where an employer provides an e-mail server, the provider exception precludes civil liability for accessing the communications stored therein, including employee e-mails. Fraser v. Nationwide Mut. Ins. Co., 334 F. Supp. 2d 755 (E.D. Pa. 2004)

5. Employers have wide leeway to monitor a variety of electronic on-line activities by employees, including their use of the internet. They also can use various technologies to accomplish the monitoring, including data recovery from a hard drive, spyware, or other electronic means. The information from monitoring may lead to disciplinary action. See Urofsky v. Gilmore, 216 F.3d 401 (4th Cir. 2000), cert. denied, 531 U.S. 1070 (2001) (upholding constitutionality of Virginia law restricting state employees from accessing sexually explicit material on computers owned or leased by the state).

6. Employees whose jobs require them to be online to deal with customers may be subject to extensive computer monitoring to measure productivity and quality. For example, some airline reservation computers closely measure how long individual clerks take to handle each customer, the amount of time between calls, lunch hours, coffee breaks, and even trips to the bathroom. At least 14 million workers are subject to "continuous" computer monitoring. Employees complain about the increased stress of working while being monitored. Employers assert that they have a legitimate interest in measuring productivity. See Jay P. Kesan, Cyber-Working or Cyber-Shirking?: A First Principles Examination of Electronic Privacy in the Workplace, 54 Fla. L. Rev. 289 (2002).

7. Other monitoring technologies, including radio frequency identification devices (RFID) and global positioning systems (GPS), have important implications for the workplace. Employers can track employee movements wherever they go during work time or off-work hours, especially when they are using company-owned vehicles. Do you think the workplace application of this technology should be regulated? If so, why and how? See Jill Yung,

Big Brother IS Watching: How Employee Monitoring in 2004 Brought Orwell's 1984 to Life and What the Law Should Do About It, 36 Seton Hall L. Rev. 163 (2005) (recommending legislation to deal with the after-hours location-based tracking of employees).

8. For a proposal to enact federal legislation in the area, see Ariana R. Levinson, Carpe Diem: Privacy Protection in Employment Act, 43 Akron L. Rev. 331 (2010). For a compilation of state laws dealing with electronic surveillance, see Corey A. Ciocchetti, The Eavesdropping Employer: A Twenty-first Century Framework for Employee Monitoring, 48 Am. Bus. L.J. 285 (2011).

A NOTE ON EMPLOYMENT RECORDS

An individual's employment record or personnel file is important to that person's present and future employment opportunities. With the computer age, these records are even more important because of the ease with which the information can be compiled, sorted, stored, and disseminated.

From a legal standpoint, two main questions have arisen. First, what rights do individuals have to inspect and correct their own files? Second, are there any restrictions on an employer's freedom to communicate or use employment record information?

Most of the regulation of employment records involves state law. About one-fourth of the states have enacted laws giving employees such rights as access to their files, the right to correct their files, the right to receive notice prior to release of information, and the right to have employers refrain from maintaining records about their nonemployment activities. See, e.g., Cal. Lab. Code § 1198.5 (right to see personnel files); Ohio Rev. Code Ann. § 4113.23 (right to see medical records).

Employees also have certain access rights under federal statutes and regulations. For example, under OSHA employees exposed to toxic substances or harmful physical agents have a right of access to their exposure and medical records. 29 C.F.R. § 1910.20. For a further discussion, see Chapter 8.

The Privacy Act of 1974, 5 U.S.C. § 522a, requires federal agencies to keep their records with due regard for the privacy of the subjects of the records. Among other things, the law requires the agencies to: (1) keep only relevant and necessary information; (2) give individuals an opportunity to examine their own files; (3) permit individuals to request amendment of the files; and (4) limit disclosure of the records without consent. A number of proposals have been made to extend these rights to private sector records, but as yet there has been no action. A number of states, however, have enacted privacy laws regulating records collected and maintained by the state government. See, e.g., Minn. Stat .Ann. § 13.02; Utah Code Ann. §§ 63G–2–101. Would it violate the Privacy Act for a federal agency to release personnel records to the union? See Andrews v. Veterans Admin., 838 F.2d 418 (10th Cir. 1988) (held: no violation absent willful or intentional conduct).

The Family Educational Rights and Privacy Act of 1974, 20 U.S.C. § 1232g, and its implementing regulations, 34 C.F.R. Part 99, provide, among other things, that students at educational institutions receiving federal funds have a right of access to their educational records and have a right to challenge the contents of their records. Should employees have a similar right? What about applicants?

Three common law theories have been used by employees who believe their employment records have been misused: defamation, invasion of privacy, and negligence. Defamation is discussed in Chapter 3. The common law tort of invasion of privacy is comprised of four separate kinds of tortious acts: (1) appropriation, for the defendant's benefit or advantages, of the plaintiff's name or likeness; (2) unreasonable and highly offensive intrusion upon the seclusion of another; (3) public disclosure of embarrassing private facts about the plaintiff; and (4) publicity which places the plaintiff in a false light in the public eye. W. Page Keeton, et al., Prosser and Keeton on the Law of Torts ch. 20 (5th ed. 1984). A theory commonly used in invasion of privacy actions is that there has been a public disclosure of private facts. Thus, issues often arise as to whether certain facts are "private" and whether they have been disclosed publicly.

C. FREEDOM OF EXPRESSION

Legal regulation of employee speech, inside the workplace or out, depends to a large extent on whether the employer is private or public. Where government is the employer, the U.S. Constitution protects employees from arbitrary "state action" adversely affecting their job status. The Fourteenth Amendment ensures government employees "due process" protection against discipline or discharge, while the First Amendment provides at least limited substantive protection. In Perry v. Sindermann, 408 U.S. 593 (1972), the Supreme Court stated:

> For at least a quarter century, this Court has made clear that even though a person has no "right" to a valuable governmental benefit and even though the government may deny him the benefit for any number of reasons, there are some reasons upon which the government may not rely. It may not deny a benefit to a person on a basis that infringes his constitutionally protected interests—especially, his interest in freedom of speech. For if the government could deny a benefit to a person because of his constitutionally protected speech or associations, his exercise of those freedoms would in effect be penalized and inhibited. * * * Such interference with constitutional rights is impermissible.

Id. at 597. As developed by the courts, however, the individual's freedom to speak out on the job is not unlimited.

The procedural limits on the government employer's ability to discharge public and private sector employees are discussed in Chapter 10.

1. PUBLIC SECTOR

Pickering v. Board of Education
391 U.S. 563 (1968).

■ JUSTICE MARSHALL delivered the opinion of the Court.

Appellant Marvin L. Pickering, a teacher in Township High School District 205, Will County, Illinois, was dismissed from his position by the appellee Board of Education for sending a letter to a local newspaper in connection with a recently proposed tax increase that was critical of the way in which the Board and the district superintendent of schools had handled past proposals to raise new revenue for the schools. Appellant's dismissal resulted from a determination by the Board, after a full hearing, that the publication of the letter was 'detrimental to the efficient operation and administration of the schools of the district' and hence, under the relevant Illinois statute, that 'interests of the schools require(d) (his dismissal).'

Appellant's claim that his writing of the letter was protected by the First and Fourteenth Amendments was rejected. Appellant then sought review of the Board's action in the Circuit Court of Will County, which affirmed his dismissal on the ground that the determination that appellant's letter was detrimental to the interests of the school system was supported by substantial evidence and that the interests of the schools overruled appellant's First Amendment rights. On appeal, the Supreme Court of Illinois, two Justices dissenting, affirmed the judgment of the Circuit Court. We noted probable jurisdiction of appellant's claim that the Illinois statute permitting his dismissal on the facts of this case was unconstitutional as applied under the First and Fourteenth Amendments. For the reasons detailed below we agree that appellant's rights to freedom of speech were violated and we reverse.

I.

In February of 1961 the appellee Board of Education asked the voters of the school district to approve a bond issue to raise $4,875,000 to erect two new schools. The proposal was defeated. Then, in December of 1961, the Board submitted another bond proposal to the voters which called for the raising of $5,500,000 to build two new schools. This second proposal passed and the schools were built with the money raised by the bond sales. In May of 1964 a proposed increase in the tax rate to be used for educational purposes was submitted to the voters by the Board and was defeated. Finally, on September 19, 1964, a second proposal to increase the tax rate was submitted by the Board and was likewise defeated. It was in connection with this last proposal of the School Board that appellant wrote the letter to the editor (which we reproduce in an Appendix to this opinion) that resulted in his dismissal.

Prior to the vote on the second tax increase proposal a variety of articles attributed to the District 205 Teachers' Organization appeared in the local paper. These articles urged passage of the tax increase and stated that failure to pass the increase would result in a decline in the quality of education afforded children in the district's schools. A letter from the superintendent of schools making the same point was published in the paper two days before the election and submitted to the voters in mimeographed form the following day. It was in response to the foregoing material, together with the failure of the tax increase to pass, that appellant submitted the letter in question to the editor of the local paper.

The letter constituted, basically, an attack on the School Board's handling of the 1961 bond issue proposals and its subsequent allocation of financial resources between the schools' educational and athletic programs. It also charged the superintendent of schools with attempting to prevent teachers in the district from opposing or criticizing the proposed bond issue.

The Board dismissed Pickering for writing and publishing the letter. Pursuant to Illinois law, the Board was then required to hold a hearing on the dismissal. At the hearing the Board charged that numerous statements in the letter were false and that the publication of the statements unjustifiably impugned the 'motives, honesty, integrity, truthfulness, responsibility and competence' of both the Board and the school administration. The Board also charged that the false statements damaged the professional reputations of its members and of the school administrators, would be disruptive of faculty discipline, and would tend to foment 'controversy, conflict and dissension' among teachers, administrators, the Board of Education, and the residents of the district. Testimony was introduced from a variety of witnesses on the truth or falsity of the particular statements in the letter with which the Board took issue. The Board found the statements to be false as charged. No evidence was introduced at any point in the proceedings as to the effect of the publication of the letter on the community as a whole or on the administration of the school system in particular, and no specific findings along these lines were made.

The Illinois courts reviewed the proceedings solely to determine whether the Board's findings were supported by substantial evidence and whether, on the facts as found, the Board could reasonably conclude that appellant's publication of the letter was 'detrimental to the best interests of the schools.' Pickering's claim that his letter was protected by the First Amendment was rejected on the ground that his acceptance of a teaching position in the public schools obliged him to refrain from making statements about the operation of the schools 'which in the absence of such position he would have an undoubted right to engage in.' It is not altogether clear whether the Illinois Supreme Court held that the First Amendment had no applicability to appellant's dismissal for writing the letter in question or whether it determined that the particular statements made in the letter were not entitled to First Amendment protection.

In any event, it clearly rejected Pickering's claim that, on the facts of this case, he could not constitutionally be dismissed from his teaching position.

II.

To the extent that the Illinois Supreme Court's opinion may be read to suggest that teachers may constitutionally be compelled to relinquish the First Amendment rights they would otherwise enjoy as citizens to comment on matters of public interest in connection with the operation of the public schools in which they work, it proceeds on a premise that has been unequivocally rejected in numerous prior decisions of this Court. '(T)he theory that public employment which may be denied altogether may be subjected to any conditions, regardless of how unreasonable, has been uniformly rejected.' At the same time it cannot be gainsaid that the State has interests as an employer in regulating the speech of its employees that differ significantly from those it possesses in connection with regulation of the speech of the citizenry in general. The problem in any case is to arrive at a balance between the interests of the teacher, as a citizen, in commenting upon matters of public concern and the interest of the State, as an employer, in promoting the efficiency of the public services it performs through its employees.

III.

The Board contends that 'the teacher by virtue of his public employment has a duty of loyalty to support his superiors in attaining the generally accepted goals of education and that, if he must speak out publicly, he should do so factually and accurately, commensurate with his education and experience.' Appellant, on the other hand, argues that the test applicable to defamatory statements directed against public officials by persons having no occupational relationship with them, namely, that statements to be legally actionable must be made 'with knowledge that (they were) * * * false or with reckless disregard of whether (they were) * * * false or not,' New York Times Co. v. Sullivan, 376 U.S. 254, 280 (1964), should also be applied to public statements made by teachers. Because of the enormous variety of fact situations in which critical statements by teachers and other public employees may be thought by their superiors, against whom the statements are directed to furnish grounds for dismissal, we do not deem it either appropriate or feasible to attempt to lay down a general standard against which all such statements may be judged. However, in the course of evaluating the conflicting claims of First Amendment protection and the need for orderly school administration in the context of this case, we shall indicate some of the general lines along which an analysis of the controlling interests should run.

An examination of the statements in appellant's letter objected to by the Board reveals that they, like the letter as a whole, consist essentially of criticism of the Board's allocation of school funds between educational and athletic programs, and of both the Board's and the superintendent's methods of informing, or preventing the informing of, the district's taxpayers of the real reasons why additional tax revenues were being sought for the schools. The statements are in no way directed towards any person with whom appellant would normally be in contact in the course of his daily work as a teacher. Thus no question of maintaining either discipline by immediate superiors or harmony among coworkers is presented here. Appellant's employment relationships with the Board and, to a somewhat lesser extent, with the superintendent are not the kind of close working relationships for which it can persuasively be claimed that personal loyalty and confidence are necessary to their proper functioning. Accordingly, to the extent that the Board's position here can be taken to suggest that even comments on matters of public concern that are substantially correct, such as statements (1)–(4) of appellant's letter, may furnish grounds for dismissal if they are sufficiently critical in tone, we unequivocally reject it.

We next consider the statements in appellant's letter which we agree to be false. The Board's original charges included allegations that the publication of the letter damaged the professional reputations of the Board and the superintendent and would foment controversy and conflict among the Board, teachers, administrators, and the residents of the district. However, no evidence to support these allegations was introduced at the hearing. So far as the record reveals, Pickering's letter was greeted by everyone but its main target, the Board, with massive apathy and total disbelief. The Board must, therefore, have decided, perhaps by analogy with the law of libel, that the statements were per se harmful to the operation of the schools.

However, the only way in which the Board could conclude, absent any evidence of the actual effect of the letter, that the statements contained therein were per se detrimental to the interest of the schools was to equate the Board members' own interests with that of the schools. Certainly an accusation that too much money is being spent on athletics by the administrators of the school system (which is precisely the import of that portion of appellant's letter containing the statements that we have found to be false,) cannot reasonably be regarded as per se detrimental to the district's schools. Such an accusation reflects rather a difference of opinion between Pickering and the Board as to the preferable manner of operating the school system, a difference of opinion that clearly concerns an issue of general public interest.

In addition, the fact that particular illustrations of the Board's claimed undesirable emphasis on athletic programs are false would not normally have any necessary impact on the actual operation of the schools, beyond its tendency to anger the Board. For example, Pickering's letter was written after the defeat at the polls of the second proposed tax increase. It could, therefore, have had no effect on the ability of the school district to raise necessary revenue, since there was no showing that there was any proposal to increase taxes pending when the letter was written.

More importantly, the question whether a school system requires additional funds is a matter of legitimate public concern on which the judgment of the school administration, including the School Board, cannot, in a society that leaves such questions to popular vote, be taken as conclusive. On such a question free and open debate is vital to informed decision-making by the electorate. Teachers are, as a class, the members of a community most likely to have informed and definite opinions as to how funds allotted to the operations of the schools should be spent. Accordingly, it is essential that they be able to speak out freely on such questions without fear of retaliatory dismissal.

In addition, the amounts expended on athletics which Pickering reported erroneously were matters of public record on which his position as a teacher in the district did not qualify him to speak with any greater authority than any other taxpayer. The Board could easily have rebutted appellant's errors by publishing the accurate figures itself, either via a letter to the same newspaper or otherwise. We are thus not presented with a situation in which a teacher has carelessly made false statements about matters so closely related to the day-to-day operations of the schools that any harmful impact on the public would be difficult to counter because of the teacher's presumed greater access to the real facts. Accordingly, we have no occasion to consider at this time whether under such circumstances a school board could reasonably require that a teacher make substantial efforts to verify the accuracy of his charges before publishing them.

What we do have before us is a case in which a teacher has made erroneous public statements upon issues then currently the subject of public attention, which are critical of his ultimate employer but which are neither shown nor can be presumed to have in any way either impeded the teacher's proper performance of his daily duties in the classroom or to have interfered with the regular operation of the schools generally. In these circumstances we conclude that the interest of the school administration in limiting teachers' opportunities to contribute to public debate is not significantly greater than its interest in limiting a similar contribution by any member of the general public.

IV.

The public interest in having free and unhindered debate on matters of public importance—the core value of the Free Speech Clause of the First Amendment—is so great that it has been held that a State cannot authorize the recovery of damages by a public official for defamatory statements directed at him except when such statements are shown to have been made either with knowledge of their falsity or with reckless disregard for their truth or falsity. The same test has been applied to suits for invasion of privacy based on false statements where a 'matter of public interest' is involved. It is therefore perfectly clear that, were appellant a member of the general public, the State's power to afford the appellee Board of Education or its members any legal right to sue him for writing the letter at issue here would be limited by the requirement that the letter be judged by the standard laid down in *New York Times*.

This Court has also indicated, in more general terms, that statements by public officials on matters of public concern must be accorded First Amendment protection despite the fact that the statements are directed at their nominal superiors. Garrison v. State of Louisiana, 379 U.S. 64 (1964). In *Garrison*, the *New York Times* test was specifically applied to a case involving a criminal defamation conviction stemming from statements made by a district attorney about the judges before whom he regularly appeared.

While criminal sanctions and damage awards have a somewhat different impact on the exercise of the right to freedom of speech from dismissal from employment, it is apparent that the threat of dismissal from public employment is nonetheless a potent means of inhibiting speech. We have already noted our disinclination to make an across-the-board equation of dismissal from public employment for remarks critical of superiors with awarding damages in a libel suit by a public official for similar criticism. However, in a case such as the present one, in which the fact of employment is only tangentially and insubstantially involved in the subject matter of the public communication made by a teacher, we conclude that it is necessary to regard the teacher as the member of the general public he seeks to be.

In sum, we hold that, in a case such as this, absent proof of false statements knowingly or recklessly made by him, a teacher's exercise of his right to speak on issues of public importance may not furnish the basis for his dismissal from public employment. Since no such showing has been made in this case regarding appellant's letter, his dismissal for writing it cannot be upheld and the judgment of the Illinois Supreme Court must, accordingly, be reversed and the case remanded for further proceedings not inconsistent with this opinion. It is so ordered.

Judgment reversed and case remanded with directions.

NOTES AND QUESTIONS

1. For a discussion of *Pickering* and its implications, see Paul M. Secunda, Neoformalism and the Reemergence of the Right-Privilege Distinction in Public Employment Law, 48 San Diego L. Rev. 907 (2011).

2. In Rankin v. McPherson, 483 U.S. 378 (1987), Ardith McPherson was a 19 year-old, probationary clerical employee with the title "deputy constable," who was working in the office of the Harris County, Texas, constable's office.

On March 30, 1981, McPherson and some fellow employees heard on an office radio that there had been an attempt to assassinate President Ronald Reagan. McPherson and her boyfriend, Lawrence Jackson, both of whom are African American, had a brief, private discussion about President Reagan's policies of cutting back on food stamps, Medicaid, and other programs, in which McPherson said, "if they go for him again, I hope they get him." The remark was overheard by another deputy constable, who reported it to Constable Rankin, and McPherson was fired. In an action brought under 42 U.S.C. § 1983, the Supreme Court, 5–4, held that McPherson's statement was protected by the First Amendment. Applying the *Pickering* balancing test, Justice Marshall wrote that the statement was on a matter of public concern, and that despite its "inappropriate or controversial" nature, McPherson's interest in making the statement outweighed Rankin's interest in the effective functioning of his office in light of the nature of her position and the circumstances surrounding the statement. In dissent, Justice Scalia wrote that McPherson's statement was unprotected and that Rankin's interest in the law enforcement duties of his office outweighed McPherson's free speech rights.

3. In Waters v. Churchill, 511 U.S. 661 (1994), a nurse working at a public hospital was fired because of statements she made to coworkers during a dinner break that were critical of the hospital. It was disputed whether the statements were "disruptive." The district court granted summary judgment for the hospital and the Seventh Circuit reversed. The Supreme Court, seven-to-two, vacated the judgment and remanded the case for trial. Writing for a four-justice plurality, Justice O'Connor, relying on Connick v. Myers, 461 U.S. 138 (1983), held that the government's interests are greater when it acts as an employer than when it acts as a sovereign. Therefore, it may restrict more of employee speech in the interest of efficiency. In reviewing the facts, the key is what the employer reasonably believed was said, rather than what the trier of fact ultimately determined was said. The public employer must merely proceed with reasonable care to determine the facts and act in good faith. In a concurring opinion for three justices, Justice Scalia asserted that a public employer's disciplining of an employee violates the First Amendment only if it is in retaliation for the employee's speech on a matter of public concern. An investigation is not necessary before taking disciplinary action. Thus, only the employer's motive is relevant. In dissent, Justices Stevens and Blackmun argued that nondisruptive speech on a matter of public concern is protected, and whether it is protected should not turn on whether the employer believed the speech was protected.

Garcetti v. Ceballos

547 U.S. 410 (2006).

■ JUSTICE KENNEDY delivered the opinion of the Court.

It is well settled that "a State cannot condition public employment on a basis that infringes the employee's constitutionally protected interest in freedom of expression." Connick v. Myers, 461 U.S. 138, 142 (1983). The question presented by the instant case is whether the First

Amendment protects a government employee from discipline based on speech made pursuant to the employee's official duties.

I

Respondent Richard Ceballos has been employed since 1989 as a deputy district attorney for the Los Angeles County District Attorney's Office. During the period relevant to this case, Ceballos was a calendar deputy in the office's Pomona branch, and in this capacity he exercised certain supervisory responsibilities over other lawyers. In February 2000, a defense attorney contacted Ceballos about a pending criminal case. The defense attorney said there were inaccuracies in an affidavit used to obtain a critical search warrant. The attorney informed Ceballos that he had filed a motion to traverse, or challenge, the warrant, but he also wanted Ceballos to review the case. According to Ceballos, it was not unusual for defense attorneys to ask calendar deputies to investigate aspects of pending cases.

After examining the affidavit and visiting the location it described, Ceballos determined the affidavit contained serious misrepresentations. The affidavit called a long driveway what Ceballos thought should have been referred to as a separate roadway. Ceballos also questioned the affidavit's statement that tire tracks led from a stripped-down truck to the premises covered by the warrant. His doubts arose from his conclusion that the roadway's composition in some places made it difficult or impossible to leave visible tire tracks.

Ceballos spoke on the telephone to the warrant affiant, a deputy sheriff from the Los Angeles County Sheriff's Department, but he did not receive a satisfactory explanation for the perceived inaccuracies. He relayed his findings to his supervisors, petitioners Carol Najera and Frank Sundstedt, and followed up by preparing a disposition memorandum. The memo explained Ceballos' concerns and recommended dismissal of the case. On March 2, 2000, Ceballos submitted the memo to Sundstedt for his review. A few days later, Ceballos presented Sundstedt with another memo, this one describing a second telephone conversation between Ceballos and the warrant affiant.

Based on Ceballos' statements, a meeting was held to discuss the affidavit. Attendees included Ceballos, Sundstedt, and Najera, as well as the warrant affiant and other employees from the sheriff's department. The meeting allegedly became heated, with one lieutenant sharply criticizing Ceballos for his handling of the case.

Despite Ceballos' concerns, Sundstedt decided to proceed with the prosecution, pending disposition of the defense motion to traverse. The trial court held a hearing on the motion. Ceballos was called by the defense and recounted his observations about the affidavit, but the trial court rejected the challenge to the warrant.

Ceballos claims that in the aftermath of these events he was subjected to a series of retaliatory employment actions. The actions included reassignment from his calendar deputy position to a trial deputy position, transfer to another courthouse, and denial of a promotion. Ceballos initiated an employment grievance, but the grievance was denied based on a finding that he had not suffered any retaliation. Unsatisfied, Ceballos sued in the United States District Court for the Central District of California, asserting, as relevant here, a claim under 42 U.S.C. § 1983. He alleged petitioners violated the First and Fourteenth Amendments by retaliating against him based on his memo of March 2.

Petitioners responded that no retaliatory actions were taken against Ceballos and that all the actions of which he complained were explained by legitimate reasons such as staffing needs. They further contended that, in any event, Ceballos' memo was not protected speech under the First Amendment. Petitioners moved for summary judgment, and the District Court granted their motion.

* * *

The Court of Appeals for the Ninth Circuit reversed, holding that "Ceballos's allegations of wrongdoing in the memorandum constitute protected speech under the First Amendment." In reaching its conclusion the court looked to the First Amendment analysis set forth in Pickering v. Board of Educ., 391 U.S. 563 (1968), and *Connick*.

* * *

We granted certiorari, and we now reverse.

II

As the Court's decisions have noted, for many years "the unchallenged dogma was that a public employee had no right to object to conditions placed upon the terms of employment—including those which restricted the exercise of constitutional rights." That dogma has been qualified in important respects. The Court has made clear that public employees do not surrender all their First Amendment rights by reason of their employment. Rather, the First Amendment protects a public employee's right, in certain circumstances, to speak as a citizen addressing matters of public concern.

Pickering provides a useful starting point in explaining the Court's doctrine. There the relevant speech was a teacher's letter to a local newspaper addressing issues including the funding policies of his school board. "The problem in any case," the Court stated, "is to arrive at a balance between the interests of the teacher, as a citizen, in commenting upon matters of public concern and the interest of the State, as an employer, in promoting the efficiency of the public services it performs through its employees." The Court found the teacher's speech "neither [was] shown nor can be presumed to have in any way either impeded the teacher's proper performance of his daily duties in the classroom or to have interfered with the regular operation of the schools generally."

Thus, the Court concluded that "the interest of the school administration in limiting teachers' opportunities to contribute to public debate is not significantly greater than its interest in limiting a similar contribution by any member of the general public."

Pickering and the cases decided in its wake identify two inquiries to guide interpretation of the constitutional protections accorded to public employee speech. The first requires determining whether the employee spoke as a citizen on a matter of public concern. If the answer is no, the employee has no First Amendment cause of action based on his or her employer's reaction to the speech. If the answer is yes, then the possibility of a First Amendment claim arises. The question becomes whether the relevant government entity had an adequate justification for treating the employee differently from any other member of the general public. This consideration reflects the importance of the relationship between the speaker's expressions and employment. A government entity has broader discretion to restrict speech when it acts in its role as employer, but the restrictions it imposes must be directed at speech that has some potential to affect the entity's operations.

To be sure, conducting these inquiries sometimes has proved difficult. This is the necessary product of "the enormous variety of fact situations in which critical statements by teachers and other public employees may be thought by their superiors . . . to furnish grounds for dismissal." The Court's overarching objectives, though, are evident.

When a citizen enters government service, the citizen by necessity must accept certain limitations on his or her freedom. Government employers, like private employers, need a significant degree of control over their employees' words and actions; without it, there would be little chance for the efficient provision of public services. Public employees, moreover, often occupy trusted positions in society. When they speak out, they can express views that contravene governmental policies or impair the proper performance of governmental functions.

At the same time, the Court has recognized that a citizen who works for the government is nonetheless a citizen. The First Amendment limits the ability of a public employer to leverage the employment relationship to restrict, incidentally or intentionally, the liberties employees enjoy in their capacities as private citizens. So long as employees are speaking as citizens about matters of public concern, they must face only those speech restrictions that are necessary for their employers to operate efficiently and effectively.

* * *

III

With these principles in mind we turn to the instant case. Respondent Ceballos believed the affidavit used to obtain a search warrant contained serious misrepresentations. He conveyed his opinion and recommendation in a memo to his supervisor. That Ceballos expressed his views inside his office, rather than publicly, is not dispositive. Employees in some cases may receive First Amendment protection for expressions made at work. Many citizens do much of their talking inside their respective workplaces, and it would not serve the goal of treating public employees like "any member of the general public," to hold that all speech within the office is automatically exposed to restriction.

The memo concerned the subject matter of Ceballos' employment, but this, too, is nondispositive. The First Amendment protects some expressions related to the speaker's job. As the Court noted in *Pickering:* "Teachers are, as a class, the members of a community most likely to have informed and definite opinions as to how funds allotted to the operation of the schools should be spent. Accordingly, it is essential that they be able to speak out freely on such questions without fear of retaliatory dismissal." The same is true of many other categories of public employees.

The controlling factor in Ceballos' case is that his expressions were made pursuant to his duties as a calendar deputy. That consideration— the fact that Ceballos spoke as a prosecutor fulfilling a responsibility to advise his supervisor about how best to proceed with a pending case— distinguishes Ceballos' case from those in which the First Amendment provides protection against discipline. We hold that when public employees make statements pursuant to their official duties, the employees are not speaking as citizens for First Amendment purposes, and the Constitution does not insulate their communications from employer discipline.

Ceballos wrote his disposition memo because that is part of what he, as a calendar deputy, was employed to do. It is immaterial whether he experienced some personal gratification from writing the memo; his First Amendment rights do not depend on his job satisfaction. The significant point is that the memo was written pursuant to Ceballos' official duties. Restricting speech that owes its existence to a public employee's professional responsibilities does not infringe any liberties the employee might have enjoyed as a private citizen. It simply reflects the exercise of employer control over what the employer itself has commissioned or created. Contrast, for example, the expressions made by the speaker in *Pickering*, whose letter to the newspaper had no official significance and bore similarities to letters submitted by numerous citizens every day.

Ceballos did not act as a citizen when he went about conducting his daily professional activities, such as supervising attorneys, investigating charges, and preparing filings. In the same way he did not speak as a citizen by writing a memo that addressed the proper disposition of a pending criminal case. When he went to work and performed the tasks he was paid to perform, Ceballos acted as a government employee. The fact that his duties sometimes required him to speak or write does not mean his supervisors were prohibited from evaluating his performance.

* * *

IV

Exposing governmental inefficiency and misconduct is a matter of considerable significance. As the Court noted in *Connick*, public employers should, "as a matter of good judgment," be "receptive to constructive criticism offered by their employees." The dictates of sound judgment are reinforced by the powerful network of legislative enactments—such as whistle-blower protection laws and labor codes—available to those who seek to expose wrongdoing. Cases involving government attorneys implicate additional safeguards in the form of, for example, rules of conduct and constitutional obligations apart from the First Amendment. These imperatives, as well as obligations arising from any other applicable constitutional provisions and mandates of the criminal and civil laws, protect employees and provide checks on supervisors who would order unlawful or otherwise inappropriate actions.

We reject, however, the notion that the First Amendment shields from discipline the expressions employees make pursuant to their professional duties. Our precedents do not support the existence of a constitutional cause of action behind every statement a public employee makes in the course of doing his or her job.

The judgment of the Court of Appeals is reversed, and the case is remanded for proceedings consistent with this opinion.

It is so ordered.

■ JUSTICE STEVENS, dissenting.

* * *

As Justice Souter explains, public employees are still citizens while they are in the office. The notion that there is a categorical difference between speaking as a citizen and speaking in the course of one's employment is quite wrong. Over a quarter of a century has passed since then-Justice Rehnquist, writing for a unanimous Court, rejected "the conclusion that a public employee forfeits his protection against governmental abridgment of freedom of speech if he decides to express his views privately rather than publicly." Givhan v. Western Line Consol. School Dist., 439 U.S. 410, 414 (1979). We had no difficulty recognizing that the First Amendment applied when Bessie Givhan, an English teacher, raised concerns about the school's racist employment practices to the principal. Our silence as to whether or not her speech was made pursuant to her job duties demonstrates that the point was immaterial. That is equally true today, for it is senseless to let constitutional protection for exactly the same words hinge on whether they fall within a job description. Moreover, it seems perverse to fashion a new rule that provides employees with an incentive to voice their concerns publicly before talking frankly to their superiors.

■ JUSTICE SOUTER, with whom JUSTICE STEVENS and JUSTICE GINSBURG join, dissenting.

The Court holds that "when public employees make statements pursuant to their official duties, the employees are not speaking as citizens for First Amendment purposes, and the Constitution does not insulate their communications from employer discipline." I respectfully dissent. I agree with the majority that a government employer has substantial interests in effectuating its chosen policy and objectives, and in demanding competence, honesty, and judgment from employees who speak for it in doing their work. But I would hold that private and public interests in addressing official wrongdoing and threats to health and safety can outweigh the government's stake in the efficient implementation of policy, and when they do public employees who speak on these matters in the course of their duties should be eligible to claim First Amendment protection.

* * *

As all agree, the qualified speech protection embodied in *Pickering* balancing resolves the tension between individual and public interests in the speech, on the one hand, and the government's interest in operating efficiently without distraction or embarrassment by talkative or headline-grabbing employees. The need for a balance hardly disappears when an employee speaks on matters his job requires him to address; rather, it seems obvious that the individual and public value of such speech is no less, and may well be greater, when the employee speaks pursuant to his duties in addressing a subject he knows intimately for the very reason that it falls within his duties.

* * *

Nothing, then, accountable on the individual and public side of the *Pickering* balance changes when an employee speaks "pursuant" to public duties. On the side of the government employer, however, something is different, and to this extent, I agree with the majority of the Court. The majority is rightly concerned that the employee who speaks out on matters subject to comment in doing his own work has the greater leverage to create office uproars and fracture the government's authority to set policy to be carried out coherently through the ranks. "Official communications have official consequences, creating a need for substantive consistency and clarity. Supervisors must ensure that their employees' official communications are accurate, demonstrate sound judgment, and promote the employer's mission," Up to a point, then, the majority makes good points: government needs civility in the workplace, consistency in policy, and honesty and competence in public service.

But why do the majority's concerns, which we all share, require categorical exclusion of First Amendment protection against any official retaliation for things said on the job? Is it not possible to respect the unchallenged individual and public interests in the speech through a

Pickering balance without drawing the strange line I mentioned before? This is, to be sure, a matter of judgment, but the judgment has to account for the undoubted value of speech to those, and by those, whose specific public job responsibilities bring them face to face with wrongdoing and incompetence in government, who refuse to avert their eyes and shut their mouths. And it has to account for the need actually to disrupt government if its officials are corrupt or dangerously incompetent. It is thus no adequate justification for the suppression of potentially valuable information simply to recognize that the government has a huge interest in managing its employees and preventing the occasionally irresponsible one from turning his job into a bully pulpit. Even there, the lesson of *Pickering* (and the object of most constitutional adjudication) is still to the point: when constitutionally significant interests clash, resist the demand for winner-take-all; try to make adjustments that serve all of the values at stake.

■ JUSTICE BREYER, dissenting.

This case asks whether the First Amendment protects public employees when they engage in speech that both (1) involves matters of public concern and (2) takes place in the ordinary course of performing the duties of a government job. I write separately to explain why I cannot fully accept either the Court's or Justice Souter's answer to the question presented.

* * *

Like the majority, I understand the need to "affor[d] government employers sufficient discretion to manage their operations." And I agree that the Constitution does not seek to "displac[e] ... managerial discretion by judicial supervision." Nonetheless, there may well be circumstances with special demand for constitutional protection of the speech at issue, where governmental justifications may be limited, and where administrable standards seem readily available—to the point where the majority's fears of department management by lawsuit are misplaced. In such an instance, I believe that courts should apply the *Pickering* standard, even though the government employee speaks upon matters of public concern in the course of his ordinary duties.

This is such a case. The respondent, a government lawyer, complained of retaliation, in part, on the basis of speech contained in his disposition memorandum that he says fell within the scope of his obligations under Brady v. Maryland, 373 U.S. 83 (1963). The facts present two special circumstances that together justify First Amendment review.

First, the speech at issue is professional speech—the speech of a lawyer. Such speech is subject to independent regulation by canons of the profession. Those canons provide an obligation to speak in certain instances. And where that is so, the government's own interest in forbidding that speech is diminished.

Second, the Constitution itself here imposes speech obligations upon the government's professional employee. A prosecutor has a constitutional obligation to learn of, to preserve, and to communicate with the defense about exculpatory and impeachment evidence in the government's possession. So, for example, might a prison doctor have a similar constitutionally related professional obligation to communicate with superiors about seriously unsafe or unsanitary conditions in the cellblock.

Where professional and special constitutional obligations are both present, the need to protect the employee's speech is augmented, the need for broad government authority to control that speech is likely diminished, and administrable standards are quite likely available. Hence, I would find that the Constitution mandates special protection of employee speech in such circumstances. Thus I would apply the *Pickering* balancing test here.

While I agree with much of Justice Souter's analysis, I believe that the constitutional standard he enunciates fails to give sufficient weight to the serious managerial and administrative concerns that the majority describes. The standard would instruct courts to apply *Pickering* balancing in all cases, but says that the government should prevail unless the employee (1) "speaks on a matter of unusual importance," and (2) "satisfies high standards of responsibility in the way he does it." Justice Souter adds that "only comment on official dishonesty, deliberately unconstitutional action, other serious wrongdoing, or threats to health and safety can weigh out in an employee's favor."

There are, however, far too many issues of public concern, even if defined as "matters of unusual importance," for the screen to screen out very much. Government administration typically involves matters of public concern. Why else would government be involved? And "public issues," indeed, matters of "unusual importance," are often daily bread-and-butter concerns for the police, the intelligence agencies, the military, and many whose jobs involve protecting the public's health, safety, and the environment. This aspect of Justice Souter's "adjustment" of "the basic *Pickering* balancing scheme" is similar to the Court's present insistence that speech be of "legitimate news interest" when the employee speaks only as a private citizen. It gives no extra weight to the government's augmented need to direct speech that is an ordinary part of the employee's job-related duties.

NOTES AND QUESTIONS

1.   *Garcetti* affords less protection to statements made in the course of a public employee's official duties, but *Pickering* said that the free speech rights of teachers to discuss issues related to schools was especially important because of their expertise. Is it possible to reconcile these two positions?

2. How far should *Garcetti* extend? David Weintraub, a fifth grade public school teacher in Brooklyn, New York, was discharged after he filed a grievance over his employer's refusal to discipline a student who threw a book at him on two consecutive days. *Garcetti* held that the First Amendment does not protect speech made pursuant to an employee's official duties. The Board of Education argued that Weintraub's filing of the grievance was "speech in furtherance of official duties" and therefore was not protected by the First Amendment. See Weintraub v. Board of Education, 593 F.3d 196 (2d Cir. 2010) (upholding dismissal). If, instead of filing a grievance, Weintraub had led a protest march through the streets of Brooklyn, would his actions have been protected?

3. A police sergeant with 25 years of service posted on her Facebook page comments highly critical of the police chief because he did not permit officers to use their police cars to attend the funeral of an officer killed in the line of duty in a surrounding town. Are the postings protected under *Garcetti*, thereby allowing her to challenge her subsequent discharge? See Graziosi v. City of Greenville, 775 F.3d 731 (5th Cir. 2015) (held: no; speech was not on a matter of public concern). See also Brown v. Chicago Board of Educ., 824 F.3d 713 (7th Cir. 2016) (statements made in classroom by a teacher are within official duties and therefore not about a public concern); Rock v. Levinski, 791 F.3d 1215 (10th Cir. 2015) (statement by school principal opposing school district's plan to close her school was not protected because it was a statement by a policymaking individual with the potential to have a detrimental impact on close working relationships).

4. In Lane v. Franks, 134 S. Ct. 2369 (2014), the director of a program for underprivileged youth at a community college testified under subpoena in court about the financial improprieties of a state representative who was on the payroll of the program. Following his testimony, the director was discharged. The Supreme Court held, based on *Garcetti,* that an individual's sworn testimony in court about matters outside the scope of his ordinary job duties is entitled to First Amendment protection. The Court observed that sworn testimony in a judicial proceeding is a "quintessential example of citizen speech."

5. The limits of the First Amendment's protection extend beyond employee criticism of employer policies to such matters as political activity. Although most government employees are limited in the kinds of political activity in which they may actively engage by the Hatch Act, 5 U.S.C. §§ 1501–1508, 7321–7326, and state "little Hatch Acts," employment decisions may not be made on the basis of party affiliation alone except for confidential or policymaking positions. Branti v. Finkel, 445 U.S. 507 (1980); Elrod v. Burns, 427 U.S. 347 (1976). It also has been held that statements on matters of public concern before the legislature may not serve as the basis for discharge where the statements do not pertain to a political party. See State v. Haley, 687 P.2d 305 (Alaska 1984).

6. In Liverman v. City of Petersburg, 844 F.3d 400 (4th Cir. 2016), the Fourth Circuit held that the police department's social media policy, prohibiting all posts that tended to discredit or reflect unfavorably on the department, was overbroad. "The advent of social media does not provide cover for the airing of purely personal grievances, but neither can it provide a pretext for shutting off meaningful discussion of larger public issues in this new public sphere." Id. at 414.

7.   Freedom of association and the right to privacy also protect certain extra-employment activities for public employees, although the employer's interest is often found to outweigh the individual's rights where other employees or clients are also involved. See Barry v. City of New York, 712 F.2d 1554 (2d Cir.), cert. denied, 464 U.S. 1017 (1983) (family financial disclosure law for public employees upheld); Shawgo v. Spradlin, 701 F.2d 470 (5th Cir. 1983), cert. denied, 464 U.S. 965 (1983) (12-day suspension upheld for two police officers found to be living together, even though no rule expressly prohibited cohabitation); Naragon v. Wharton, 572 F.Supp. 1117 (M.D.La.1983), affirmed, 737 F.2d 1403 (5th Cir. 1984) (demotion of teacher having lesbian affair with pupil upheld). See also D'Angelo v. School Board, 497 F.3d 1203 (11th Cir. 2007) (*Garcetti* applies to freedom to petition and freedom of association cases).

2.   PRIVATE SECTOR

Curay-Cramer v. Ursuline Academy
450 F.3d 130 (3d Cir. 2006).

■ ROTH, CIRCUIT JUDGE:

Michele Curay-Cramer, a teacher at the Ursuline Academy, a private, Catholic school, was fired after she signed her name to a pro-choice advertisement in the local newspaper. Curay-Cramer asserts both that signing the advertisement was conduct protected by 42 U.S.C. § 2000e–3(a) and that she was fired for conduct less egregious under Catholic doctrine than conduct of male employees who were treated less harshly. The District Court granted defendants' motions to dismiss under FED. R. CIV. P. 12(b)(6). We will affirm but, in doing so, we do not adopt all of the District Court's reasoning.

I.   Factual Background

Ursuline Academy is a private, non-diocesan Catholic school in Wilmington, Delaware. Students range in grade from pre-kindergarten to high school. Ursuline provides college preparatory education from a Catholic perspective. In June of 2001, Curay-Cramer began teaching four English classes and a Religion class to 7th and 8th graders at Ursuline. Eighteen months later, on the thirtieth anniversary of the Supreme Court's decision in Roe v. Wade, 410 U.S. 113 (1973), she lent her name to an advertisement in support of that decision, signed by some six hundred individuals and organizations. The advertisement, which ran in the *News-Journal*, a newspaper of general circulation in Wilmington, Delaware, stated:

> Thirty years ago today, the U.S. Supreme Court in Roe v. Wade
> guaranteed a woman's right to make her own reproductive

choices. That right is under attack. We, the undersigned individuals and organizations, reaffirm our commitment to protecting that right. We believe that each woman should be able to continue to make her own reproductive choices, guided by her conscience, ethical beliefs, medical advice and personal circumstances. We urge all Delawareans and elected officials at every level to be vigilant in the fight to ensure that women now and in the future have the right to choose.

Following the text were the names of the individuals endorsing it, including Curay-Cramer.

On the day the advertisement appeared, Curay-Cramer was called into the office of Barbara C. Griffin, the President of Ursuline. Griffin informed Curay-Cramer that the school was deeply troubled by her public support of a position inimical to accepted Catholic doctrine and that Griffin was considering terminating Curay-Cramer's employment with the school. In response, Curay-Cramer asserted her right to protest without retribution the school's stance on abortion. She also informed Griffin that she had volunteered for Planned Parenthood and distributed pamphlets that she believed contained important information related to reproductive options.

Curay-Cramer alleges that Griffin then consulted with Bishop Michael Saltarelli, who ratified the school's decision to terminate her.

A few days later, Curay-Cramer was again summoned to Griffin's office. She was informed that Ursuline had decided to terminate her employment but was offering her an opportunity to resign. She was given the weekend to think it over. The following week, Curay-Cramer met with Griffin and the head of Ursuline's Religion Department. Curay-Cramer told them that it was illegal to fire her for opposing the school's illegal employment practices. She also asserted that she had never said or done anything in class that was contrary to Ursuline's pedagogic philosophy. Griffin responded that Curay-Cramer could keep her job if she immediately and publicly recanted her support of the advertisement and stated unequivocally that she was pro-life. Curay-Cramer refused. She was then fired.

II. Procedural History

After she was fired, Curay-Cramer filed suit against Ursuline, Griffin, Jerry Botto (Ursuline's Director of Communications), Bishop Saltarelli, and the Diocese of Wilmington. Curay-Cramer included six counts in her Complaint: three federal claims and three state-law claims. Of the federal claims, Count One focuses on the advertisement in the *News-Journal* and alleges that it was a violation of Title VII and the Pregnancy Discrimination Act (PDA) to fire Curay-Cramer for opposing Ursuline's illegal employment practice of firing anyone who has or contemplates an abortion.[1] Count Two is based on the advertisement and associated advocacy for, and association with, persons protected by Title VII and the PDA. In Count Three, Curay-Cramer avers that she was fired because she is a woman and that similarly situated male employees have been treated less harshly for substantially similar conduct.

* * *

Curay-Cramer contends that Title VII's opposition clause protects any employee who has had an abortion, who contemplates having an abortion, or who supports the rights of women who do so. This Court has not ruled on this issue. However, even if we were to assume that properly structured opposition and association activity, directed toward an employer's policy or practice of discriminating against women who have or contemplate abortions, can fall within the ambit of Title VII, still we conclude that Curay-Cramer has failed to state a claim in Counts One and Two.

A.   Counts One and Two

* * *

Title VII's anti-retaliation provisions protect employees who participate in Title VII's statutory processes or who otherwise oppose employment practices made illegal by Title VII. Defendants Ursuline, the Diocese, and Bishop Saltarelli argue, however, that basic pro-choice advocacy does not constitute opposition to an illegal employment practice. We agree.

* * *

The *News-Journal* advertisement stated that the right to abortion was "under attack" and urged "Delawareans and elected officials at every level to be vigilant in the fight to ensure that women now and in the future have the right to choose." This language cannot be construed as opposition to Ursuline's alleged policy and practice of terminating women who have or contemplate abortions. The advertisement did not mention gender discrimination, pregnancy discrimination, or employment practices. It did not mention Ursuline or any other schools or employers. To turn pro-choice advocacy, unconnected to employment practices, into conduct protected by Title VII would inappropriately stretch the concept of protected activity.

As written and under the circumstances in which it appeared, the advertisement simply is not protected opposition activity. Moreover, there is no context from which one could reasonably conclude that Curay-Cramer's signature at the bottom of the advertisement was in response to Ursuline's alleged illegal policy or practice. Instead, context suggests that the advertisement was a public endorsement of the Supreme Court's decision in Roe v. Wade, running, as it did, on the thirtieth anniversary

---

[1]   Curay-Cramer alleges that Ursuline has such a policy and practice; for purposes of reviewing this motion to dismiss, we accept that assertion.

of that decision. Having failed to mention discrimination in any way, let alone employment discrimination, and absent any context from which it is reasonable to conclude that the advertisement was directed at employers generally or at Ursuline specifically, Curay-Cramer did not engage in activity protected by Title VII when she lent her name to the pro-choice position articulated by the advertisement.

* * *

B. Count Three

Turning to Count Three, we agree with the District Court's determination that applying the PDA and Title VII raises a substantial constitutional question under the First Amendment's Religion Clauses. Curay-Cramer contends that she was fired because she is a woman and that similarly situated male employees have been treated less harshly for substantially similar conduct. In order to assess this claim of the relative harshness of penalties for "similar conduct," we would have to measure the degree of severity of various violations of Church doctrine.

* * *

Here, however, with the allegation that male employees, who committed substantially similar offenses, were treated differently than was Curay-Cramer, we would have to assess the relative severity of offenses. This exercise would violate the First Amendment. In this case, Curay-Cramer alleges that similarly situated male employees were treated differently, but points only to men who are Jewish or oppose the war in Iraq.

* * *

We conclude that if we were to consider whether being Jewish or opposing the war in Iraq is as serious a challenge to Church doctrine as is promoting a woman's right to abortion, we would infringe upon the First Amendment Religion clauses. Thus, having reached the conclusion that it would raise serious constitutional questions to apply Title VII to this case, we turn to * * * whether Congress has manifested an intent to have Title VII apply to teachers in religious schools in this context.

We note that the courts that have addressed this issue have held that, under most circumstances, Title VII's substantive provisions, with the exception of the prohibition against religious discrimination, apply to religious employers. Nevertheless, we do not assume that Title VII applies in all contexts and under all fact scenarios.

* * *

Nevertheless, there are circumstances in which Congress' intention to apply Title VII to religious employers is less clear. These cases tend to involve the interplay of Title VII's exemption for religious employers and the application of Title VII's remaining substantive provisions. The conflict is presented because the text and legislative history of § 2000e–

2(e)(2) show that "Congress intended the explicit exemptions of Title VII to enable religious organizations to create and maintain communities composed solely of individuals faithful to their doctrinal practices," whether or not every individual plays a direct role in the organizations' religious activities.

In this context, there are circumstances, like those presented here, where a religious institution's ability to "create and maintain communities composed solely of individuals faithful to their doctrinal practices" will be jeopardized by a plaintiff's claim of gender discrimination.

We distinguish this case from one in which a plaintiff avers that truly comparable employees were treated differently following substantially similar conduct. In such a case, * * * the interests of the exemption for religious employers from religious discrimination claims are [not] raised. Requiring a religious employer to explain why it has treated two employees who have committed essentially the same offense differently poses no threat to the employer's ability to create and maintain communities of the faithful.

* * *

We caution religious employers against over-reading the impact of our holding. It is by no means the case that all claims of gender discrimination against religious employers are impermissible. Indeed, as we have discussed above, many such claims may not raise serious constitutional questions. If a religious employer does not offer a religious justification for an adverse employment action against a non-ministerial employee, it is unlikely that serious constitutional questions will be raised by applying Title VII.

NOTES AND QUESTIONS

1. Do you agree with the court's balancing of the employee interests in nondiscrimination with the employer's interest in promulgation of its religious doctrine? The plaintiff in the case was a secular employee. Should that matter? Should it matter what subjects she taught or whether her students were aware of the newspaper ad?

2. In Novosel v. Nationwide Ins. Co., 721 F.2d 894 (3d Cir. 1983), the Third Circuit held that the discharge of an employee for refusing to lobby the Pennsylvania Legislature on a pending bill could constitute wrongful discharge in violation of the public policy of freedom of expression. A controversial and singular decision, *Novosel* has been criticized as, in effect, extending constitutional protection to private sector employees and abrogating the state action doctrine. See generally Lisa B. Bingham, Employee Free Speech in the Workplace: Using the First Amendment as Public Policy for Wrongful Discharge Actions, 55 Ohio St. L.J. 341 (1994).

3. "Free speech" may apply to speech in the workplace as well as speech outside of work. Private sector employees' free speech rights often depend on the type of speech at issue.

Internal speech—Employees who have been discharged because of internal speech have alleged that their discharge violated a public policy in favor of free speech or some more specific public policy based on the nature of the speech. Often, these cases have concerned complaints to management about certain practices in the company. Most courts have held for the employer. See Suchodolski v. Michigan Consol. Gas Co., 316 N.W.2d 710 (Mich.1982) (complaints to management about internal accounting practices; discharge upheld); Keneally v. Orgain, 606 P.2d 127 (Mont.1980) (complaints to supervisors about inadequate service to customers; discharge upheld); Geary v. United States Steel Corp., 319 A.2d 174 (Pa.1974) (complaints to supervisors about defective products; discharge upheld). But see Grant-Burton v. Covenant Care, Inc., 122 Cal.Rptr.2d 204 (Ct.App.2002) (statutory right of employees to discuss their compensation with other employees provided support for claim of wrongful discharge in violation of public policy).

External speech—Employees are more likely to be protected when their speech is outside the workplace. As discussed in Chapter 10, many of the early cases to recognize wrongful discharge actions involved the exercise of statutorily created rights by employees, such as the filing of workers' compensation claims. Whether other forms of external communications are protected usually depends on the public policy implicated by the speech activity. Compare Rozier v. St. Mary's Hosp., 411 N.E.2d 50 (Ill.Ct.App.1980) (reporting incidents at local hospital to newspaper; discharge upheld) with Palmateer v. International Harvester Co., 421 N.E.2d 876 (Ill.1981) (reporting suspected criminal activity of another employee to police; discharge unlawful).

4. Private sector employees may be extended free speech rights in the workplace by state statute. See, e.g., Trusz v. UBS Realty Investors, LLC, 123 A.3d 1212 (Conn. 2015).

A NOTE ON EMPLOYEE USE OF SOCIAL MEDIA

Many individuals use social media to post information about their private lives as well as opinions about their work experiences, including their feelings about coworkers or managers. Some employers have exhibited a keen interest in both types of information. Thus, they not only monitor publicly available information about applicants and employees on social media, but they make disclosure of individual passwords a condition of employment or they gain access to social media sites without a password by obtaining the contents from another "trusted" person. In 2012, Maryland became the first state to prohibit employers from requesting or requiring access to an applicant's or employee's password. Md. Code Ann., Lab. & Empl. § 3–712. As of 2018, eleven other states had enacted similar laws.

With regard to the posting of work-related information, there have been few reported cases. In Konop v. Hawaiian Airlines, 302 F.3d 868 (9th Cir. 2002), a pilot maintained a restricted access, employee-only website on which he posted remarks criticizing airline management and the union. A company vice president got permission from two other pilots to use their passwords to gain access to the site. The plaintiff-pilot sued the airline under the federal Wiretap Act and the Stored Communications Act (SCA). The Ninth Circuit held that there was no violation of the Wiretap Act because an unlawful "interception" must be contemporaneous with the transmission. It remanded the case, however, on the SCA claim to determine whether the two pilots had used the site. If so, as "users," they could give authorization to a third party to use the site.

In many incidents reported in newspapers and on-line, but not the subject of litigation, employers have discharged employees because their on-line activities allegedly damaged the employer's business or reputation. Undoubtedly, this will be a fertile source of litigation and commentary in the years ahead. For a further discussion, see generally Paul S. Gutman, Say What? Blogging and Employment Law in Conflict, 27 Colum. J.L. & Arts 145 (2003); Henry Hoang Pham, Note and Comment, Bloggers and the Workplace: The Search for a Legal Solution to the Conflict Between Employee Blogging and Employers, 26 Loy. L.A. Ent. L. Rev. 207 (2005/2006).

D. BULLYING

David Yamada, The Phenomenon of "Workplace Bullying" and the Need for Status-Blind Hostile Work Environment Protection*
88 Geo. L. J. 475, 477–478 (2000).

They sometimes are called "bullies," "tyrants," or "jerks." However, regardless of how they are described (usually) out of earshot, bosses and others who inflict psychological abuse on their coworkers constitute one of the most common and serious problems facing employees in today's workplace. Of course, to many who have toiled for years in America's offices and factories, this observation simply states the obvious: intimidating, mean-spirited, manipulative, and sometimes high-decibel behaviors are not unusual workplace occurrences, especially from supervisors or managers. The unfortunate targets of abuse usually have to chalk up their experiences to bad luck and the ordinary costs of being employed.

In recent years, however, we have begun to gain a more sophisticated understanding of the phenomenon called "workplace bullying." In particular, scholars, therapists, and industrial psychologists have begun to create a conceptual framework for analyzing workplace bullying. It is now possible to generalize about the types of bullies that exist, the tactics they use, the targets they tend to seek out, and the individual and systemic consequences of their behavior. The emerging literature on

---

*   Reprinted with permission of the publisher, Georgetown Law Journal ©2000.

workplace bullying confirms that this behavior inflicts harmful, even devastating, effects on its targets and can sabotage employee morale in ways that severely undercut productivity and loyalty.

Given the negative ramifications workplace bullying has for employees and employers, one might naturally look to the legal system to encourage employers to prevent and punish bullying behavior and to provide relief to employees when it occurs. Unfortunately, the growing body of statutory and common-law protections for workers-particularly status-based employment discrimination laws and tort claims for emotional distress-have not been effective against workplace bullying. Consistent with the law's historic reluctance to regulate the everyday employment arena, workplace bullying has yet to be fully recognized and addressed by the American legal system. For example, as will be discussed below, claims for intentional infliction of emotional distress (IIED) arising out of the workplace are seldom successful, and many courts have held that these claims are preempted by workers' compensation statutes. Furthermore, bullying behavior fueled by discriminatory intent often falls outside the protections of the hostile work environment doctrine promulgated under employment discrimination statutes. For now, abusive behavior that is considered harmful to employees and employers alike is rarely illegal.

NOTES AND QUESTIONS

1. According to a 2017 survey released by the Workplace Bullying Institute, 19 percent of U.S. workers reported experiencing abusive conduct in the past, and another 19 percent witnessed it. The survey reported that 61 percent of respondents said bosses were the main bullies; 70 percent said the bullies were men, who mostly (60 percent) bullied women.

2. Is recognizing a cause of action for workplace bullying, especially intentional infliction of emotional distress, tantamount to creating a legal basis for white, male, at-will employees to challenge their discharges (actual or constructive)? See Dennis P. Duffy, Intentional Infliction of Emotional Distress and Employment at Will: The Case against the "Tortification" of Labor and Employment Law, 74 B.U.L. Rev. 387 (1994).

Caldera v. Department of Corrections and Rehabilitation
235 Cal. Rptr. 3d 262 (Cal. Ct. App. 2018).

■ MOORE, ACTING P.J.:

* * *

FACTS AND PROCEDURAL BACKGROUND

In July 1994, Caldera began working as correctional officer in Imperial County. About a year later he transferred to the California State Institute for Men in Chino. At the time of trial Caldera was still employed as a correctional officer and had been working at the state prison in Chino for 20 years. Caldera stutters when he speaks.

Starting in 2006, Caldera began working as a mental health escort officer within the administrative segregation unit (Ad Seg) of the prison. The Ad Seg unit is an area where inmates with disciplinary issues or mental health needs are housed. The Ad Seg unit consists of two to three "halls," or housing facilities. Caldera's primary duties were to transport inmates to and from their mental health appointments.

Between 2006 and 2008, Sergeant Grove and Officer Caldera largely worked in two different halls within the Ad Seg unit. At some point, Grove began mocking or mimicking Caldera's stutter. Caldera did not document what occurred; Caldera never imagined he would have to testify in court. Grove always mimicked Caldera's stutter when other employees were present. According to Caldera, "Whatever [words] I stuttered on, Grove would sit back and repeat what I stuttered." Caldera felt that Grove's conduct "was demeaning. It was embarrassing, ... definitely harmful." Caldera also described the conduct as "really hurtful." A psychologist testified at trial that Caldera had experienced psychological disorders as a result of the mimicking of his stutter. When asked to estimate how many times Grove had mocked or mimicked his stutter, Caldera said, "More than 5, less than 15."

On one particular occasion (date unknown), Grove mimicked Caldera's stutter over the prison's radio system. After Caldera had broadcasted an announcement, Grove got on the radio and mimicked what Caldera had said. The transmission could be heard by about 50 employees. Officer Robert Konrad was on duty with Caldera at the time; Konrad saw that Caldera's "facial expression was in shock, saddened." Konrad later discussed the incident with Caldera. Konrad "said, that's kind of f***ed up, on the radio, like that. [Caldera] said, yeah, I get it all the time. . . ."

In 2008, Dr. Victor Jordan worked as a psychologist supervisor in the Ad Seg unit. Dr. Jordan had worked closely with Caldera and regarded him as an "outstanding" correctional officer. At the time of trial in 2015, Dr. Jordan had been working at the Chino prison for over 23 years and had been promoted to chief psychologist and chief of mental health. Dr. Jordan described Caldera's disability as a: "Speech impairment, stuttering, specifically, stammering." Dr. Jordan testified that he personally heard prison employees mock or mimic Caldera's stutter on many occasions. When asked to "estimate over the years" how many times he had witnessed this, he replied, "I'm sure a dozen times that I've paid attention to." He agreed that there was "a culture of joking" at the prison about Caldera's stutter. Dr. Jordan said that Caldera's reactions varied; at times Caldera laughed, at times Caldera reacted by "firing back," and at times Caldera appeared embarrassed by the conduct.

On September 2, 2008, Sergeant Grove, Officer Caldera, and Dr. Jordan were all present in a main corridor of the prison during a busy shift change, which occurred at about 2:00 p.m. At that time, there were about 24 correctional officers in the general area. Caldera said something to Grove and he responded by saying, " 'F-f-f-f**k you.' " Caldera threatened to file a formal complaint. Grove then responded by saying, "I don't give a F-f-f. Make sure you get my name right." Later that day, Caldera went to the prison's Equal Employment Opportunity (EEO) office and obtained a form to file a complaint. Sergeant Grove went to his supervisor and self-reported the encounter.

On September 9, 2008, Caldera filed an EEO complaint against Grove. Two days later, Caldera learned that Grove was to be reassigned to the same Ad Seg hall where he had been working (although they had separate chains of command). Caldera went to several superiors, including the warden, to express his concerns about Grove's upcoming reassignment. One of the superiors said that Caldera was "almost to the point of tears when he spoke about" the shift change incident and that Caldera "felt really degraded" by what Grove had said to him in front of his fellow correctional officers.

Several days later, the prison reassigned Grove to the same Ad Seg hall where Caldera had been working. Caldera learned from others that Grove was continuing to mock and mimic his stutter. Caldera felt that Grove treated him differently than the other correctional officers.

On October 3, 2008, there was a training class for the prison's supervisors. Sergeant Jessie Lara was in attendance, as was Grove. Before the class, Lara had heard about the shift change incident involving Grove and Caldera. At some point during the class, Grove was again mimicking Caldera's "speech impediment and basically saying he didn't give a f**k about him. Saying it with the speech, I don't give a f**k." Lara said that Grove mimicked Caldera's stutter "throughout the whole conversation."

Court Proceedings

Caldera filed a complaint in the superior court alleging various causes of action against defendants including disability harassment, failure to prevent harassment, and retaliation. The trial court granted defendants' summary judgment motion, which this court reversed in an unpublished opinion. This court held that as to each cause of action there were triable issues of material fact.

The matter then went to trial. The jury returned the following special verdicts: Caldera was subjected to unwanted harassing conduct based on his disability; the harassment was severe; the harassment was pervasive; a reasonable person in Caldera's position would have considered the work environment to be hostile or abusive; a supervisor participated in, assisted, or encouraged the harassing conduct; the harassing conduct was a substantial factor in causing harm; the CDCR had failed to take all reasonable steps to prevent the harassment; and the CDCR's failure to prevent the harassment was a substantial factor in causing Caldera harm. The jury did not find true Caldera's claim that he had been subjected to adverse employment actions (retaliation).

The jury determined that Caldera was entitled to $500,000 in noneconomic damages.

II

DISCUSSION

Defendants contend there was insufficient evidence to support the jury's factual findings and the trial court committed two instructional and one evidentiary error. Caldera contends the trial court's order granting defendants' motion for new trial should be reversed. We shall address each of the parties' contentions in turn.

A. Defendants' Sufficiency of the Evidence Claims

The trial court instructed the jury: "Harassing conduct may include: verbal harassment, such as obscene language, demeaning comments, slurs, threats, or mocking and mimic of [Caldera's] stutter." (CACI No. 2523.) Defendants do not argue there is insufficient evidence of "harassing conduct." Rather, defendants argue there is insufficient evidence the harassing conduct was either severe or pervasive. The CDCR further argues there is insufficient evidence that it failed to take all reasonable steps to prevent the harassment. We disagree.

* * *

1. Severe or Pervasive Harassment

* * *

As far as the harassing conduct being severe, Caldera described the conduct he was subjected to as: demeaning, embarrassing, harmful, and hurtful. Caldera testified that every time Grove mocked or mimicked his stutter, he did so in front of others. Grove's harassing conduct over the prison's radio system was heard by about 50 employees and appears to have been particularly egregious. The shift change incident occurred in front of about 24 employees. The training incident occurred in front of an unknown number of supervisors. Dr. Jordan testified that the harassing conduct was at times done in a mean spirited and harmful manner. A psychologist testified that the harassment caused Caldera to experience psychological disorders. Based on the totality of circumstances, a jury could reasonably find that the harassing conduct was "severe."

As far as the harassing conduct being pervasive, Dr. Jordan said that he witnessed the harassing conduct on at least 12 occasions. Caldera estimated that Grove had mocked or mimicked his stutter anywhere from five to 15 times. Although neither Dr. Jordan nor Caldera provided exact dates as to when each incident occurred, their testimony reasonably indicates that the harassing conduct roughly took place over a two-year time frame from 2006 to 2008.

Dr. Jordan further testified the harassing conduct was so pervasive that he regarded it as part of the culture at the prison. Dr. Jordan's testimony was also bolstered by the testimony of Sergeant Lara, who witnessed the harassing conduct during the training class. It seems striking to us that the harassment was so pervasive within the institution that Grove apparently felt he could openly mimic Caldera's stutter in front of his peers (a group of prison supervisors) without any sense of shame or fear of reprisal. It appears plain to us there was sufficient evidence upon which the jury could reasonably determine that the harassing conduct was "pervasive."

In sum, there was sufficient evidence—the testimony of several witnesses—to support the jury's factual determination that the harassing conduct in Caldera's workplace was both severe *and* pervasive (again, the jury only needed to find the harassing conduct to be either severe *or* pervasive).

NOTES AND QUESTIONS

1.   In Madani v. Kendall Ford, Inc., 818 P.2d 930 (Or. 1991), a car salesperson was discharged when he refused to pull down his pants and expose himself in view of other employees and the public. He sued for wrongful discharge and intentional infliction of emotional distress. The Supreme Court of Oregon held that there was no intentional infliction of emotional distress in the firing because the motive for the firing was irrelevant, the method of firing was not abusive, and the plaintiff was distressed only by being fired.

2.   In another Oregon case, Wheeler v. Marathon Printing, Inc., 974 P.2d 207 (Or. Ct. App. 1998), the Oregon Court of Appeals held that an employer was not liable for intentional infliction of emotional distress because it failed to stop a "sadistic bully," whose actions caused a coworker to attempt suicide. The court held that an employer cannot be liable based on "nonresponsiveness." Damages against the bullying coworker, however, were affirmed. See also Cavicchi v. Chertoff ex rel. United States Bureau of Customs & Border Protection, 2008 WL 139157 (S.D. Fla. 2008) (holding toleration of bullying does not constitute an adverse employment action under Title VII).

3.   In Wagenseller v. Scottsdale Memorial Hosp., 710 P.2d 1025 (Ariz. 1985), the Arizona Supreme Court held that a nurse who was discharged as a result of refusing to engage in an act of indecent exposure stated a claim for relief under the public policy exception to the at-will doctrine. The Arizona Legislature, however, responded to this decision by enacting a statute to bar the state courts from establishing the contours of the public policy exception. Ariz. Rev. Stat. Ann. § 23–1501.

4.   Over half the states have considered legislation to prevent workplace bullying. California's Healthy Workplace Law, Cal. Lab. Code § 245, enacted

in 2014, added "abusive conduct" to the required biannual, two-hour training in sexual harassment for supervisors at employers with 50 or more employees. "Abusive conduct" is defined as "conduct of an employer or employee in the workplace, with malice, that a reasonable person would find hostile, offensive, and unrelated to an employer's legitimate business interests. Abusive conduct may include repeated infliction of verbal abuse, such as the use of derogatory remarks, insults, and epithets, verbal or physical conduct that a reasonable person would find threatening, intimidating, or humiliating, or the gratuitous sabotage or undermining of a person's work performance. A single act shall not constitute abusive conduct, unless especially severe and egregious." There is no private right of action established by the law.

5.   In the absence of statutory protection, the only possible remedies for workplace bullying are common law actions for assault, intentional infliction of emotional distress, and similar causes of action against the alleged bully. For example, in Raess v. Doescher, 883 N.E.2d 790 (Ind. 2008), an operating room perfusionist sued a cardiovascular surgeon for assault and intentional infliction of emotional distress stemming from alleged workplace bullying. The Supreme Court of Indiana upheld a jury award of $325,000 for assault after the defendant "rapidly advanced on the plaintiff with clenched fists, piercing eyes, beet-red face, popping veins, and screaming and swearing at him," and then told the plaintiff "you're finished, you're history." The court held that workplace bullying was an appropriate factor for the jury to consider in evaluating the plaintiff's claims.

E. REGULATION OF OFF-WORK ACTIVITY

An employer's control over its employees extends even beyond the workplace. In this section, the cases and materials address three areas of employer control: personal associations, political activity, and lifestyle.

The first limitations imposed upon employer control of off-work activities of employees were the constitutional protections afforded public employees. Recently, certain protections have been given to private sector employees, but these are limited and depend on collective bargaining agreements, implied contract rights, and other sources.

As you read the cases and materials in this section try to decide when an employer may have a legitimate interest in regulating its employees' off-work activities and how the balance should be struck between employee and employer concerns.

1. PERSONAL ASSOCIATIONS

Rulon-Miller v. IBM Corp.

208 Cal.Rptr. 524 (Cal. Ct. App. 1984).

■ RUSHING, ASSOCIATE JUSTICE.

International Business Machines (IBM) appeals from the judgment entered against it after a jury awarded $100,000 compensatory and $200,000 punitive damages to respondent (Virginia Rulon-Miller) on claims of wrongful discharge and intentional infliction of emotional distress. Rulon-Miller was a low-level marketing manager at IBM in its office products division in San Francisco. Her termination as a marketing manager at IBM came about as a result of an accusation made by her immediate supervisor, defendant Callahan, of a romantic relationship with the manager of a rival office products firm, QYX.

* * *

IBM knew about respondent's relationship with Matt Blum well before her appointment as a manager. Respondent met Blum in 1976 when he was an account manager for IBM. That they were dating was widely known within the organization. In 1977 Blum left IBM to join QYX, an IBM competitor, and was transferred to Philadelphia. When Blum returned to San Francisco in the summer of 1978, IBM personnel were aware that he and respondent began dating again. This seemed to present no problems to respondent's superiors, as Callahan confirmed when she was promoted to manager. Respondent testified: "Somewhat in passing, Phil said: I heard the other day you were dating Matt Blum, and I said: Oh. And he said, I don't have any problem with that. You're my number one pick. I just want to assure you that you are my selection." The relationship with Blum was also known to Regional Manager Gary Nelson who agreed with Callahan. Neither Callahan nor Nelson raised any issue of conflict of interest because of the Blum relationship.

Respondent flourished in her management position, and the company, apparently grateful for her efforts, gave her a $4,000 merit raise in 1979 and told her that she was doing a good job. A week later, her manager, Phillip Callahan, left a message that he wanted to see her.

When she walked into Callahan's office he confronted her with the question of whether she was *dating* Matt Blum. She wondered at the relevance of the inquiry and he said the dating constituted a "conflict of interest," and told her to stop dating Blum or lose her job and said she had a "couple of days to a week" to think about it.

The next day Callahan called her in again, told her "he had made up her mind for her," and when she protested, dismissed her. IBM and Callahan claim that he merely "transferred" respondent to another division.

Respondent's claims of wrongful discharge and intentional infliction of emotional distress were both submitted to the jury. * * *

The initial discussion between Callahan and respondent of her relationship with Blum is important. We must accept the version of the facts most favorable to the respondent herein. When Callahan questioned her relationship with Blum, respondent invoked her right to privacy in her personal life relying on existing IBM policies. A threshold inquiry is thus presented whether respondent could reasonably rely on those policies for job protection. Any conflicting action by the company would be wrongful in that it would constitute a violation of her contract rights.

Under the common law rule codified in Labor Code section 2922, an employment contract of indefinite duration is, in general, terminable at "the will" of either party. This common law rule has been considerably altered by the recognition of the Supreme Court of California that implicit in any such relationship or contract is an underlying principle that requires the parties to deal openly and fairly with one another. * * * The duty of fair dealing by an employer is, simply stated, a requirement that like cases be treated alike. Implied in this, of course, is that the company, if it has rules and regulations, apply those rules and regulations to its employees as well as affording its employees their protection.

* * *

In this case, there is a close question of whether those rules or regulations permit IBM to inquire into the purely personal life of the employee. If so, an attendant question is whether such a policy was applied consistently, particularly as between men and women. The distinction is important because the right of privacy, a constitutional right in California, could be implicated by the IBM inquiry. Much of the testimony below concerned what those policies were. The evidence was conflicting on the meaning of certain IBM policies. We observe ambiguity in the application but not in the intent. The "Watson Memo" (so called because it was signed by a former chairman of IBM) provided as follows:

"TO ALL IBM MANAGERS:

"The line that separates an individual's on-the-job business life from his other life as a private citizen is at times well-defined and at other times indistinct. But the line does exist, and you and I, as managers in IBM, must be able to recognize that line.

"I have seen instances where managers took disciplinary measures against employees for actions or conduct that are not rightfully the company's concern. These managers usually justified their decisions by citing their personal code of ethics and morals or by quoting some fragment of company policy that seemed to support their position. Both arguments proved unjust on close examination. What we need, in every case, is balanced judgment which weighs the needs of the business and the rights of the individual.

"Our primary objective as IBM managers is to further the business of this company by leading our people properly and measuring quantity and quality of work and effectiveness on the job against clearly set standards of responsibility and compensation. This is performance—and performance is, in the final analysis, the one thing that the company can insist on from everyone.

"We have concern with an employee's off-the-job behavior only when it reduces his ability to perform regular job assignments, interferes with the job performance of other employees, or if his outside behavior affects the reputation of the company in a major way. When on-the-job performance is acceptable, I can think of few situations in which outside activities could result in disciplinary action or dismissal.

"When such situations do come to your attention, you should seek the advice and counsel of the next appropriate level of management and the personnel department in determining what action—if any—is called for. Action should be taken only when a legitimate interest of the company is injured or jeopardized. Furthermore the damage must be clear beyond reasonable doubt and not based on hasty decisions about what one person might think is good for the company.

"IBM's first basic belief is respect for the individual, and the essence of this belief is a strict regard for his right to personal privacy. This idea should never be compromised easily or quickly.

"/s/ Tom Watson, Jr."

It is clear that this company policy insures to the employee both the right of privacy and the right to hold a job even though "off-the-job behavior" might not be approved of by the employee's manager.

IBM had adopted policies governing employee conduct. Some of those policies were collected in a document known as the "Performance and Recognition" (PAR) Manual. IBM relies on the following portion of the PAR Manual:

"A conflict of interest can arise when an employee is involved in activity for personal gain, which for any reason is in conflict with IBM's business interests. Generally speaking, 'moonlighting' is defined as working at some activity for personal gain outside of your IBM job. If you do perform outside work, you have a special responsibility to avoid any conflict with IBM's business interests.

"Obviously, you cannot solicit or perform in competition with IBM product or service offerings. Outside work cannot be performed on IBM time, including 'personal' time off. You cannot use IBM equipment, materials, resources, or 'inside' information for outside work. Nor should you solicit business or clients or perform outside work on IBM premises.

"Employees must be free of any significant investment or association of their own or of their immediate family's [sic], in competitors or suppliers, which might interfere or be thought to interfere with the independent exercise of their judgment in the best interests of IBM."

This policy of IBM is entitled "Gifts" and appears to be directed at "moonlighting" and soliciting outside business or clients on IBM premises. It prohibits "significant investment" in competitors or suppliers of IBM. It also prohibits "association" with such persons "which might interfere or be thought to interfere with the independent exercise of their judgment in the best interests of IBM."

Callahan based his action against respondent on a "conflict of interest." But the record shows that IBM did not interpret this policy to prohibit a romantic relationship. Callahan admitted that there was no company rule or policy requiring an employee to terminate friendships with fellow employees who leave and join competitors.[4] Gary Nelson, Callahan's superior, also confirmed that IBM had no policy against employees socializing with competitors.

This issue was hotly contested with respondent claiming that the "conflict of interest" claim was a pretext for her unjust termination. Whether it was presented a fact question for the jury.

Do the policies reflected in this record give IBM a right to terminate an employee for a conflict of interest? The answer must be yes, but whether respondent's conduct constituted such was for the jury. We observe that while respondent was successful, her primary job did not give her access to sensitive information which could have been useful to competitors. She was, after all, a seller of typewriters and office equipment. Respondent's brief makes much of the concession by IBM that there was no evidence whatever that respondent had given any information or help to IBM's competitor QYX. It really is no concession at all; she did not have the information or help to give. Even so, the question is one of substantial evidence. The evidence is abundant that there was no conflict of interest by respondent.

It does seem clear that an overall policy established by IBM chairman Watson was one of no company interest in the outside activities of an employee so long as the activities did not interfere with the work of the employee. Moreover, in the last analysis, it may be simply a question for the jury to decide whether, in the application of these policies, the right was conferred on IBM to inquire into the personal or romantic relationships its managers had with others. This is an important question because IBM, in attempting to reargue the facts to us, casts this

---

[4] An interesting side issue to this point is that Blum continued to play on an IBM softball team while working for QYX.

argument in other terms, namely: that it had a right to inquire even if there was no evidence that such a relationship interfered with the discharge of the employee's duties *because* it had the effect of diminishing the morale of the employees answering to the manager. This is the "Caesar's wife" argument; it is merely a recast of the principal argument and asks the same question in different terms.[5] The same answer holds in both cases: there being no evidence to support the more direct argument, there is no evidence to support the indirect argument.

Moreover, the record shows that the evidence of rumor was not a basis for any decline in the morale of the employees reporting to respondent. Employees Mary Hrize and Wayne Fyvie, who reported to respondent's manager that she was seen at a tea dance at the Hyatt Regency with Matt Blum and also that she was not living at her residence in Marin, did not believe that those rumors in any way impaired her abilities as a manager. In the initial confrontation between respondent and her superior the assertion of the right to be free of inquiries concerning her personal life was based on substantive direct contract rights she had flowing to her from IBM policies. Further, there is no doubt that the jury could have so found and on this record we must assume that they did so find.

The judgment is affirmed.

NOTES AND QUESTIONS

1.   On what legal theory did the court uphold the verdict for the plaintiff? Was it contract, tort, or some other basis? In a subsequent California case, Barbee v. Household Automotive Finance Corp., 6 Cal.Rptr.3d 406 (Cal.Ct. App.2003), the employer had a clearly expressed policy of not permitting employees to date subordinate employees. The court upheld the discharge of the employee against a challenge based on the California Constitution's right to privacy and various state statutes.

2.   Ironically, IBM is a company well known for its commitment to employee rights and dignity—as evidenced in the "Watson memo." To what extent do you think IBM actually was disadvantaged in the case by its policy of tolerance of employee off-work activities? Would this fact tend to make IBM or other companies *less* tolerant in the future?

3.   A romantic involvement with a competitor has the potential to be a conflict of interest for the employee and to have a negative effect on the company. At what point would a company be justified in attempting to regulate an employee's relationship with a competitor? What degree of proof of actual harm to the company is necessary before the employer can take

---

[5]   What we mean by that is that if you charge that an employee is passing confidential information to a competitor, the question remains whether the charge is true on the evidence available to the person deciding the issue, in this case, the respondent's managers at IBM. If you recast this argument in the form of the "Caesar's wife" argument attempted by IBM, it will be seen that exactly the same question arises, namely, "is it true?" Indeed, the import of the argument is that the rumor, or an unfounded allegation, could serve as a basis for the termination of the employee.

action? See Salazar v. Furr's, Inc., 629 F.Supp. 1403 (D.N.M.1986) (employee failed to state claim of abusive discharge on ground that she was discharged because she was married to employee of her employer's competitors).

4. Following an extramarital affair by two employees, an employer discharged the female employee but retained the male employee. The evidence indicated that the employer knew of 12 other employees who engaged in extramarital affairs and did not discipline either employee. The employer discharged the female employee because of fear that her husband might cause a disruption at the workplace, and the male employee was a top producer. In a Title VII case alleging sex discrimination, what result? See Hossack v. Floor Covering Assocs. of Joliet, Inc., 492 F.3d 853 (7th Cir. 2007) (held: no violation; plaintiff failed to introduce sufficient evidence of intentional discrimination).

5. Randolph Starling, a "rescue captain" with the Palm Beach County Fire Rescue Department, sued under 42 U.S.C. § 1983 alleging he was denied his First Amendment right to intimate association when he was demoted for having an extramarital affair with Carolyn Smith, one of his subordinates. The Eleventh Circuit upheld the public employer's action because its interest in discouraging intimate association between supervisors and subordinates was so critical to the effective functioning of the fire department that it outweighed Starling's interest. Starling v. Board of County Comm'ners, 602 F.3d 1257 (11th Cir. 2010).

6. When would a public employer be justified in regulating the associational rights of its employees? Would it be lawful for a sheriff to order his deputy to stop "associating" with the wife of a reputed mobster? See Baron v. Meloni, 556 F.Supp. 796 (W.D.N.Y.1983), affirmed mem., 779 F.2d 36 (2d Cir. 1985) (held: no). What about a police department regulation prohibiting fraternization with known felons? See Morrisette v. Dilworth, 454 N.Y.S.2d 864 (App.Div.1982), affirmed, 452 N.E.2d 1222 (N.Y.1983) (held: no). Would it violate the First Amendment for a city to discipline a police officer who was a part owner of a video store that rented nonobscene, sexually explicit videotapes? See Flanagan v. Munger, 890 F.2d 1557 (10th Cir. 1989) (held: yes).

7. A New York statute prohibits employers from discriminating against employees for a range of off-duty recreational activities, including sports, games, hobbies, exercise, and movies. Does the law prohibit an employer from discharging employees for violating the company's ban on dating between married employees and employees other than their spouses? See State v. Wal-Mart Stores, Inc., 621 N.Y.S.2d 158 (App.Div.1995) (held: no— "To us, dating is entirely distinct from and, in fact, bears little resemblance to 'recreational activity' "). Accord, McCavitt v. Swiss Reins. America Corp., 237 F.3d 166 (2d Cir. 2001). See generally Stephen D. Sugarman, "Lifestyle" Discrimination in Employment, 24 Berkeley J. Lab. & Emp. L. Rev. 377 (2003).

2. POLITICAL ACTIVITY

Nelson v. McClatchy Newspapers, Inc.
936 P.2d 1123 (Wash. 1997).

■ SANDERS, JUSTICE.

* * *

FACTS

Sandra Nelson began working as a reporter for [The News Tribune] TNT in 1983, three years before McClatchy Newspapers, Inc., purchased it. When McClatchy acquired TNT in 1986 it retained Nelson as a reporter. Nelson covered the "education beat" and focused on Tacoma schools as well as regional and state educational issues and, by all accounts, did a good job.

A fundamental goal of TNT, as a news publication, is to appear objective in the eyes of its readers. As part of this effort, TNT management put forth an ethics code in 1987 regulating activity deemed to present apparent or actual conflicts of interest. The ethics code defines conflicts of interest to include all situations in which readers might be led to believe that the news reporting is biased, including situations in which reporters participate in high profile political activity. Nelson's admitted violation of this code of ethics led to her transfer and the present suit.

Journalistic codes of ethics are common. In fact, most newspapers in the country have some form of code of conduct to minimize conflicts of interest. A 1983 study indicates that 75 percent of news organizations have similar codes in place. For example, *The Washington Post* has a code nearly identical to TNT's stating in part that newsroom employees must " 'avoid active involvement in any partisan causes—politics, community affairs, social action, demonstrations—that could compromise or seem to compromise our ability to report and edit fairly.' " Similarly, the Associated Press has a code containing nearly identical provisions including "Involvement in politics, demonstrations and social causes that could cause a conflict of interest, or the appearance of such conflict should be avoided." The code of ethics of the Society of Professional Journalists is also similar.

Nelson is a self-professed lesbian who spends much of her off-duty hours serving as a political activist. She attends political fora, demonstrations, and classes for political causes including highly visible support for gay and lesbian rights, feminist issues, and abortion rights. Nelson is also a member of and organizer for Tacoma Radical Women, a feminist socialist organization, and the Freedom Socialist Party. Much of her political activism has been supported by this party and has been in support of its party platform. McClatchy knew of Nelson's political activities when it chose to retain her.

In 1987, Nelson was seen by a TNT reporter and photographer as she was picketing for abortion rights outside a local hospital. TNT management told her such activity compromised the paper's appearance of objectivity. Nelson responded she would continue her public political activity anyway.

In 1989, Nelson helped launch a ballot initiative to have an antidiscrimination ordinance reinstated following its repeal. Throughout 1990 she visibly promoted the initiative by organizing volunteers, soliciting support from various groups, arranging for community speakers, organizing rallies, and collecting signatures for the initiative. The initiative battle remained a major political story throughout the year and increasingly so as the fall election approached. On August 15, 1990, TNT's editors informed Nelson that she would be transferred from her position as education reporter to swing shift copy editor until after the November election. TNT stated that Nelson's activities violated the ethics code and raised concern about TNT's appearance of objectivity.

A swing shift copy editor is a nonmanagerial position requiring the same general qualifications as a reporter. Nelson maintained her salary, benefits, and seniority and edited a wide variety of local and national stories. However, she was required to work nights and weekends and was no longer a beat reporter investigating and writing stories. Nelson's transfer became permanent when she refused to promise future conformity with the ethics code.

Nelson remained politically active. For example in 1994 she actively opposed a ballot initiative which would have prevented municipalities from extending civil rights to gays and lesbians. Also in 1994 she testified before the state Legislature on behalf of the "Stonewall Committee" in support of a gay and lesbian civil rights bill. The story received front page coverage in TNT and most other state newspapers. TNT was initially alerted by a legislator who knew Nelson as a TNT employee and contacted TNT to ask if Nelson was lobbying the Legislature on TNT's behalf. TNT's editors wrote to Nelson that "We are dismayed and concerned that you have taken your political activism to a new and larger arena." The editors also wrote that such activity jeopardized the credibility of TNT in the eyes of its readers and the Legislature alike. They told Nelson that their discomfort had nothing to do with the content of her politics as, indeed, TNT has on several occasions adopted pro-gay positions in its editorial. TNT concluded by informing Nelson that if her political activism further compromised the paper's credibility, it would be forced to "further isolate" her and to "take appropriate disciplinary action."

Nelson requested TNT to reinstate her as reporter. In October 1993 she wrote to her supervisor requesting her reinstatement and she later applied for a position as reporter. In January 1995 she sent TNT a letter asking to be considered for what she asserted was an unannounced opening as education reporter. Since Nelson's transfer, TNT has hired nine reporters to cover various topics. Nelson alleged that it was made clear that the positions would remain closed to her so long as she continued her high profile political activism. TNT responded that Nelson never applied for any open position; however, for the purpose of this opinion we will assume the truth of Nelson's allegations.

After unsuccessfully pursuing redress in a federal forum, Nelson filed suit in Pierce County Superior Court alleging TNT improperly stripped her of her position as reporter. Nelson alleged TNT: (a) violated RCW 42.17.680(2) of the Fair Campaign Practices Act, which Nelson claims prohibits employers from discriminating against employees based on their support of initiatives, political parties or political committees; (b) violated several provisions of the state constitution including article I, section 5 (free speech), article I, section 4 (freedom to assemble and petition government), article I, section 19 (guarantee of free elections), and article II, section 1 (popular right to initiative); (c) breached her employment contract because she was transferred without good cause; and (d) wrongfully transferred her because it is against public policy to forbid employees from participating in off-duty political activity. The trial court granted summary judgment to TNT on Nelson's claim under RCW 42.17.680 and on all her constitutional claims. The remaining breach of employment and wrongful transfer claims survived and are scheduled for trial on remand. Thus, the issue before this court is the propriety of the trial court's summary judgment dismissal of Nelson's statutory and constitutional claims.

DOES RCW 42.17.680(2) APPLY?

Nelson asserts that RCW 42.17.680(2) applies. We agree.

RCW 42.17.680(2) states in full:

No employer or labor organization may discriminate against an officer or employee in the terms or conditions of employment for (a) the failure to contribute to, (b) the failure in any way to support or oppose or (c) *in any way supporting or opposing a candidate, ballot proposition, political party, or political committee.*

(Emphasis added.)

Nelson asserts the statute is clear on its face and applies in her case. A fundamental rule of construction is, absent ambiguity, the plain wording of the statute controls. Thus, the statute prohibits discrimination based on an employee's "supporting or opposing a candidate, ballot proposition, political party, or political committee."

The issue is whether an employee who is discriminated against for refusing to abstain from political involvement fits within the statutory language of someone removed for "supporting or opposing" a ballot initiative, political party or committee. There is little outside guidance on the meaning of the provision in question and there is no case law interpreting the statute. The original version of the initiative came out of the state senate as Engrossed Substitute Senate Bill 5864, and the legislative history of intent is scarce there as well. A staff memo circulated to the senate committee originally overseeing the bill stated that, amongst other things, the bill would prohibit employers from "discriminat[ing] against employees on the basis of their political activity." Newspaper articles and editorials published during the 1992 election season uniformly fail to mention this particular provision nor does the voter's pamphlet in its description of or the statements for and against the law. In all, the provision now before the court seems to have gone largely unnoticed.

Nelson urges that the plain language of the statute supports her position. And, in circumspect, one may also find support for her position in the subsection preceding the one at issue. Subsection (2)(b) states that no employer may discriminate against an employee for the "failure in any way to support or oppose" a candidate, ballot proposition, political party, or political committee. Subsection (2)(c), at issue here, states that no employer may discriminate against an employee for "in any way supporting or opposing a candidate, ballot proposition, political party, or political committee." Logically, subsection (2)(b) would apply when the employee fails to adopt and support the employer's political position, whereas subsection (2)(c) would apply when the employee refuses to abstain from political activity. It is difficult to imagine what subsection (2)(c) would mean if not what Nelson claims. Adopting TNT's reading that the statute does not apply when the employer merely requires political abstinence is contrary to the text of subsection (2)(c).

TNT, on the other hand, asserts that the provision should be read in context. TNT asserts that when read in context, the provision has a narrower meaning and will apply only when an employer attempts to strong-arm an employee into adopting its political position. The trial court agreed with TNT and held the statute applies only when the employer requires an employee to adopt its political position and does not apply when the employer merely requires political neutrality of its employees.

Initiative 134 which contains the provision in question was aimed at repairing the political process through campaign finance reform. The primary change proposed by the initiative was the imposition of contribution limits that individuals and entities could give per candidate per election. The initiative also sought to prohibit contributions from one candidate's campaign to another, forbid public funding of campaigns, limit the repayment of loans taken out while campaigning, and prohibit fundraising by legislators during session. The official ballot title asked:

> Shall campaign contributions be limited; public funding of state and local campaigns be prohibited; and campaign related activities be restricted?

1992 Voters Pamphlet, *Initiative Measure 134,* at 8.

One of the stated purposes of the initiative was to prevent financially strong organizations from exercising a disproportionate or controlling influence on elections. RCW 42.17.610(1). In 1993, the initiative became codified under the heading of *Campaign Contribution Limitations* under chapter 42.17 RCW, the public disclosure act, the purpose of which is to inform the public of campaign and lobbying contributions and to help ensure, through disclosure, the integrity of government.

TNT argues the statutory provision in question was not intended to apply as Nelson asserts. Washington already has a labor law statute forbidding discrimination against an employee on the basis of age, sex, marital status, race, creed, color, national origin, or physical handicap. Nelson's reading, TNT argues, in effect creates an additional category, that of political activist, but would locate it in the campaign finance reform law rather than in labor or other civil rights laws. TNT argues if creation of such a broad right was intended, why was it quietly slipped into campaign finance reform?

But TNT's interpretation does not track the text of the act. When read in context this law has a clear relation to the rest of the campaign finance reform act; it is meant to prevent employers from wielding their might to influence politics and elections. The law is part of campaign finance, not civil rights or labor law. Taken as a whole, the provision in question means that employers may not disproportionately influence politics by forcing their employees to support their position or by attempting to force political abstinence on politically active employees. The law is designed to restrict organizations from wielding political influence by manipulating the political influence of their employees through employment decisions. Moreover, TNT's reading essentially renders the provision in question meaningless as RCW 42.17.680(2)(b) already covers the interpretation urged by TNT.

We hold RCW 42.17.680(2) applies to the present case and substantial evidence supports its application.

We now turn to the constitutional issue which we find dispositive.

DOES RCW 42.17.680(2) UNCONSTITUTIONALLY INFRINGE ON TNT'S RIGHT TO FREEDOM OF THE PRESS?

We hold that RCW 42.17.680(2) unconstitutionally infringes on TNT's right to freedom of the press.

TNT asserts that RCW 42.17.680(2) as applied to it violates the First Amendment to the United States Constitution and article I, section 5, of the state constitution. In particular, TNT asserts that the free press clause of both constitutions guarantees it editorial discretion to control the content of its publication. TNT further asserts that controlling the newspaper's credibility is an integral component of this. TNT argues its conflict of interest policies are designed to control its credibility and are a reflection of its content. TNT concludes that requiring its reporters to abide by its no-conflict-of-interest policy is necessary to uphold its editorial integrity, which TNT asserts is constitutionally protected. Accordingly, TNT claims that RCW 42.17.680(2) does not apply to it in this case. On the contrary, Nelson asserts that what TNT's reporters do on their own time has nothing to do with the content or credibility of the newspaper and accordingly the free press clauses of the federal and state constitutions are irrelevant. While the trial court dismissed Nelson's statutory claim holding the statute inapplicable, it redundantly ruled in TNT's favor on this point as well, reasoning:

> The First Amendment and the Washington Constitution protect Defendants' editorial discretion. Under the First Amendment and the Washington Constitution, Defendants have a right to protect the newspaper's unbiased content, both its facts and as perceived by its readers, its sources and its advertisers. In order to protect the newspaper's credibility, Defendants may enforce the political neutrality of reporters.

We agree with TNT and affirm the trial court on this ground.

The free speech clauses of the federal and state constitutions have always held a revered position in our society. Laurence Tribe, a preeminent constitutional law scholar, has characterized free speech as "the Constitution's most majestic guarantee." Free speech is a fundamental right on its own as well as a keystone right enabling us to preserve all other rights. As one federal judge has noted, "Free speech is the single most important element upon which this nation has thrived."

The Supreme Court has observed "the Founders . . . felt that a free press would advance 'truth, science, morality, and arts in general' as well as responsible government." From the start we have acknowledged that active protection from governmental abridgment is essential. Upon presenting the Bill of Rights to Congress in 1789 James Madison declared "the liberty of the press is expressly declared to be *beyond the reach of this government.* . . ."

* * *

When addressing whether a governmental regulation or action affecting the press is violative of its constitutional free press protection, we begin by noting the two governing polar principles and then consider where the complained action falls. On one extreme is the general principle that a newspaper has "no special immunity from the application of general laws" simply because it is the press. Associated Press v. N.L.R.B., 301 U.S. 103 (1937). On the opposite side is the principle that the government absolutely may not regulate the content of a newspaper. Miami Herald Publishing Co. v. Tornillo, 418 U.S. 241 (1974).

Miami Herald Publishing is the seminal case on the issue. In *Miami Herald* the United States Supreme Court held that the state absolutely may not regulate the content of a newspaper. At issue was the constitutionality of a Florida "right-of-access" statute which forced newspapers to publish responses of politicians who had been criticized by the paper. At the heart of *Miami Herald* is the notion that in order to uphold the circulation of ideas the editors of a newspaper must be free to exercise editorial control and discretion. The court held that " '[l]iberty of the press is in peril as soon as the government tries to compel what is to go into a newspaper.' " The court concluded because the state law deprived the paper of its editorial discretion, it was necessarily unconstitutional as applied to the newspaper.

Thus, *Miami Herald* clearly establishes that editorial control is a necessary component of the free press and a state law infringing thereon will be unconstitutional as applied.

* * *

Here, TNT implemented a code of ethics which it designed in good faith to foster the newspaper's integrity and credibility. Case law unambiguously allows a news publication to follow a code designed to limit conflicts of interest which may diminish publication credibility. TNT adopted such a code. Freedom of the press leaves such decisions to the press, not the legislature or the courts. The code is facially designed to uphold the appearance of impartiality. Indeed, the code seems representative of those in place at 75 percent of our nation's newspapers. In fact, as stated earlier, it is nearly identical to those employed by the Associated Press, *The Washington Post,* and the Society of Professional Journalists.

* * *

CONCLUSION

We recognize Nelson's statutory right to avoid workplace discrimination based on her politics. Since this right is established by the statute we need not consider whether it is also established by the state constitution. However, the First Amendment freedom of the press is the constitutional minimum regardless of the legal source of government abridgment. Choosing an editorial staff is a core press function, at least when that choice is based on editorial considerations. That is the case here. This statute has been unconstitutionally applied. The trial court's summary judgment dismissal of statutory claims is affirmed and McClatchy shall recover its costs on appeal. The case is remanded for further appropriate proceedings.

NOTES AND QUESTIONS

1.   "Political expression laws" protecting private sector employees have been enacted in slightly more than half of the states. California's law dates back to 1915. Cal. Lab. Code § 1102. Without statutory protection and before the erosion of the at will doctrine employers could not only refuse to permit employees to engage in their own political activities, but could insist on employees engaging in certain political activity. For example, in Bell v. Faulkner, 75 S.W.2d 612 (Mo.Ct.App.1934), an employee alleged that he was

discharged because he would not vote for certain candidates in a city election and would not coerce family members to vote for them. Even though a specific Missouri statute prohibited coercion of workers to vote for political candidates the court held that the only remedy was imprisonment of offenders and therefore no private right of action for damages would lie.

2. For public employees it is important to distinguish between partisan and nonpartisan political activities. Whereas nonpartisan political activities are almost always protected under the First Amendment, partisan activity may be regulated more closely.

The Hatch Act, 5 U.S.C. § 7324(a), prohibits federal employees from taking an active part in political campaigns. Similar state laws limit the political activities of state and local employees. In United States Civil Serv. Comm'n v. National Ass'n of Letter Carriers, 413 U.S. 548 (1973), the Supreme Court spelled out the range of partisan political activities that can be regulated:

> We unhesitatingly reaffirm the *Mitchell* [United Public Workers v. Mitchell, 330 U.S. 75 (1947)] holding that Congress had, and has, the power to prevent Mr. Poole and others like him from holding a party office, working at the polls, and acting as party paymaster for other party workers. An Act of Congress going no farther would in our view unquestionably be valid. So would it be if, in plain and understandable language, the statute forbade activities such as organizing a political party or club; actively participating in fund-raising activities for a partisan candidate or political party; becoming a partisan candidate for, or campaigning for, an elective public office; actively managing the campaign of a partisan candidate for public office; initiating or circulating a partisan nominating petition or soliciting votes for a partisan candidate for public office; or serving as a delegate, alternate or proxy to a political party convention. Our judgment is that neither the First Amendment nor any other provision of the Constitution invalidates a law barring this kind of partisan political conduct by federal employees.

Id. at 556. See Developments in the Law—Public Employment, 97 Harv.L. Rev. 1611, 1651–57 (1984).

3. Heffernan v. City of Paterson, 136 S. Ct. 1412 (2016), involved a police officer working in the office of the chief of police of Paterson, New Jersey. Both the chief of police and Heffernan's supervisor had been appointed by the mayor, who was running for re-election against Spagnola, a good friend of Heffernan's. Heffernan was not involved in Sapgnola's campaign in any capacity. As a favor to his bedridden mother, Heffernan agreed to pick up a Spagnola campaign yard sign to replace one that had been stolen. When Heffernan was observed by other police officers while holding a Spagnola yard sign, word spread throughout the force and Heffernan was demoted from a detective to a patrol officer because of his "overt involvement" in Spagnola's campaign. Heffernan brought suit under section 1983, arguing that he had been demoted in violation of his First Amendment rights. The district court and the Third Circuit held that Heffernan's case was actionable only if his employer's conduct was prompted by his actual, rather than his perceived, exercise of free-speech rights. The Supreme Court, 6–2, reversed in an opinion by Justice Breyer. "When an employer demotes an employee out of a desire to prevent the employee from engaging in political activity that the First Amendment protects, the employee is entitled to challenge that unlawful action under the First Amendment and 42 U.S.C. § 1983— even if, as here, the employer makes a factual mistake about the employee's behavior." 136 S. Ct. at 1418. In dissent, Justice Thomas (with Justice Alito) argued, as had the Third Circuit, that Heffernan had no cause of action because his constitutional rights had not been violated.

4. Political appointments (the hiring of non-civil service employees) raise a series of First Amendment issues. In Elrod v. Burns, 427 U.S. 347 (1976), the Supreme Court held that patronage dismissals had to be limited to policymaking and confidential positions. Thus, political party affiliation could not be used as the basis for hiring or retention for most non-civil service positions. Is the job of assistant public defender policymaking or confidential? See Branti v. Finkel, 445 U.S. 507 (1980) (held: no).

5. Many governmental entities require employees to take or sign loyalty oaths, pledging loyalty to the United States. Would an oath declaring that the individual is not a member of the Communist Party be valid? In Baggett v. Bullitt, 377 U.S. 360 (1964), the Supreme Court held that such an oath was unconstitutionally vague. To be valid, the oath must state that the individual did not have a specific intent to further illegal aims. Would an oath be valid if it stated that the individual opposed the overthrow of the government of the United States by force, violence, or by any illegal or unconstitutional method? See Cole v. Richardson, 405 U.S. 676 (1972) (held: yes).

6. Section 501(b) of the Ethics in Government Act of 1978, as amended, 5 U.S.C. App. IV § 502, prohibits a member of Congress, federal officer, or other federal government employee from accepting an honorarium for making an appearance or speech or writing an article. In United States v. National Treasury Employees Union, 514 U.S. 1002 (1995), a class action of federal government employees below the grade of GS-16 who had previously received honoraria for speeches and articles on nongovernmental topics such as history, religion, and dance challenged the law. The Supreme Court held that the statute was overbroad and violated the First Amendment.

7. In Greenwell v. Parsley, 541 F.3d 401 (6th Cir. 2008), the Sixth Circuit upheld the discharge of a deputy sheriff when the sheriff read in the newspaper that the deputy was planning to run against him in the next election. The court noted that the firing was not based on political beliefs or affiliations.

CHAPTER 8

OCCUPATIONAL SAFETY AND HEALTH

The possibility of death, injury, or illness on the job is a stark reality to millions of American workers in a variety of jobs. According to the latest compilation of data by the Bureau of Labor Statistics, in 2018, a total of 5,250 U.S. workers died from work-related injuries. There were 2.8 million nonfatal work-related injuries and illnesses in the private sector and over 700,000 in state and local government. OSHA estimates that workplace injuries and illnesses cost businesses at least $60 billion a year.

This chapter is important, therefore, because of the gravity of its subject matter. Beyond that, however, it is important as a vehicle for studying the effectiveness of pervasive regulation of the workplace and a unique administrative framework established to implement national occupational safety and health policy. As you read the cases and materials in this chapter, consider (1) whether the federal regulatory approach adopted under the Occupational Safety and Health Act (OSH Act), 29 U.S.C. §§ 651–678 is the most effective and efficient way of achieving the goal of occupational safety and health; (2) whether the economic and noneconomic costs of regulation are justified by gains in employee safety and health; and (3) whether the courts and administrative bodies possess the technical expertise and have adopted the appropriate procedural mechanisms to decide these complex scientific and regulatory issues.

A. INTRODUCTION

1. BACKGROUND

Eric Schlosser, Fast Food Nation: The Dark Side of the All-American Meal*
187–190 (2002).

Kenny Dobbins was a Monfort employee almost sixteen years. He was born in Keokuk, Iowa, had a tough childhood and an abusive stepfather, left home at the age of thirteen, went in and out of various schools, never learned to read, did various odd jobs, and wound up at the Monfort slaughterhouse in Grand Island, Nebraska. He started working there in 1979, right after the company bought it from Swift. He was

---

twenty-four. He worked in the shipping department at first, hauling boxes that weighed as much as 120 pounds. Kenny could handle it, though. He was a big man, muscular and six-foot-five, and nothing in his life had ever been easy.

One day Kenny heard someone yell, "Watch out!" then turned around and saw a ninety-pound box falling from an upper level of the shipping department. Kenny caught the box with one arm, but the momentum threw him against a conveyor belt, and the metal rim of the belt pierced his lower back. The company doctor bandaged Kenny's back and said the pain was just a pulled muscle. Kenny never filed for workers' comp, stayed home for a few days, then returned to work. He had a wife and three children to support. For the next few months, he was in terrible pain. "It hurt so fucking bad you wouldn't believe it," he told me. He saw another doctor, got a second opinion. The new doctor said Kenny had a pair of severely herniated disks. Kenny had back surgery, spent a month in the hospital, got sent to a pain clinic when the operation didn't work. His marriage broke up amid the stress and financial difficulty. Fourteen months after the injury, Kenny returned to the slaughterhouse. "GIVE UP AFTER BACK SURGERY? NOT KEN DOBBINS!!" a Monfort newsletter proclaimed. "Ken has learned how to handle the rigors of working in a packing plant and is trying to help others do the same. Thanks, Ken, and keep up the good work."

Kenny felt a strong loyalty to Monfort. He could not read, possessed few skills other than his strength, and the company had still given him a job. When Monfort decided to reopen its Greeley plant with a non-union workforce, Kenny volunteered to go there and help. He did not think highly of labor unions. His supervisors told him that unions had been responsible for shutting down meatpacking plants all over the country. When the UFCW tried to organize the Greeley slaughterhouse, Kenny became an active and outspoken member of an anti-union group.

At the Grand Island facility, Kenny had been restricted to light duty after his injury. But his supervisor in Greeley said that old restrictions didn't apply in this new job. Soon Kenny was doing tough, physical labor once again, wielding a knife and grabbing forty-to fifty-pound pieces of beef off a table. When the pain became unbearable, he was transferred to ground beef, then to rendering. According to a former manager at the Greeley plant, Monfort was trying to get rid of Kenny, trying to make his work so unpleasant that he'd quit. Kenny didn't realize it. "He still believes in his heart that people are honest and good," the former manager said about Kenny. "And he's wrong."

As part of the job in rendering, Kenny sometimes had to climb into gigantic blood tanks and gut bins, reach to the bottom of them with his long arms, and unclog the drains. One day he was unexpectedly called to work over the weekend. There had been a problem with *Salmonella* contamination. The plant needed to be disinfected, and some of the maintenance workers had refused to do it. In his street clothes, Kenny began cleaning the place, climbing into tanks and spraying a liquid chlorine mix. Chlorine is a hazardous chemical that can be inhaled or absorbed through the skin, causing a litany of health problems. Workers who spray it need to wear protective gloves, safety goggles, a self-contained respirator, and full coveralls. Kenny's supervisor gave him a paper dust mask to wear, but it quickly dissolved. After eight hours of working with the chlorine in unventilated areas, Kenny went home and fell ill. He was rushed to the hospital and placed in an oxygen tent. His lungs had been burned by the chemicals. His body was covered in blisters. Kenny spent a month in the hospital.

Kenny eventually recovered from the overexposure to chlorine, but it left his chest feeling raw, made him susceptible to colds and sensitive to chemical aromas. He went back to work at the Greeley plant. He had remarried, didn't know what other kind of work to do, still felt loyal to the company. He was assigned to an early morning shift. He had to drive an old truck from one part of the slaughterhouse complex to another. The truck was filled with leftover scraps of meat. The headlights and the wipers didn't work. The windshield was filthy and cracked. One cold, dark morning in the middle of winter, Kenny became disoriented while driving. He stopped the truck, opened the door, got out to see where he was—and was struck by a train. It knocked his glasses off, threw him up in the air, and knocked both of his work boots off. The train was moving slowly, or he would've been killed. Kenny somehow made it back to the plant, barefoot and bleeding from deep gashes in his back and his face. He spent two weeks at the hospital, then went back to work.

One day, Kenny was in rendering and saw a worker about to stick his head into a pre-breaker machine, a device that uses hundreds of small hammers to pulverize gristle and bone into a fine powder. The worker had just turned the machine off, but Kenny knew the hammers inside were still spinning. It takes fifteen minutes for the machine to shut down completely. Kenny yelled, "Stop!" but the worker didn't hear him. And so Kenny ran across the room, grabbed the man by the seat of his pants, and pulled him away from the machine an instant before it would have pulverized him. To honor this act of bravery, Monfort gave Kenny an award for "Outstanding Achievement in CONCERN FOR FELLOW WORKERS." The award was a paper certificate, signed by his supervisor and the plant safety manager.

Kenny later broke his leg stepping into a hole in the slaughterhouse's concrete floor. On another occasion he shattered an ankle, an injury that required surgery and the insertion of five steel pins. Now Kenny had to wear a metal brace on one leg in order to walk, an elaborate, spring-loaded brace that cost $2000. Standing for long periods caused him great pain. He was given a job recycling old knives at the plant. Despite his many injuries, the job required him to climb up and down three flights of narrow stairs carrying garbage bags filled with knives. In December of 1995 Kenny felt a sharp pain in his chest while lifting some boxes. He thought it was a heart attack. His union steward took him to see the nurse, who said it was just a pulled muscle and sent Kenny home. He was indeed having a massive heart attack. A friend rushed Kenny to a nearby hospital. A stent was inserted in his heart, and the doctors told Kenny that he was lucky to be alive.

While Kenny Dobbins was recuperating, Monfort fired him. Despite the fact that Kenny had been with the company for almost sixteen years, despite the fact that he was first in seniority at the Greeley plant, that he'd cleaned blood tanks with his bare hands, fought the union, done whatever the company had asked him to do, suffered injuries that would've killed weaker men, nobody from Monfort called him with the news. Nobody even bothered to write him. Kenny learned that he'd been fired when his payments to the company health insurance plan kept being returned by the post office.

* * *

"They used me to the point where I had no body parts left to give," Kenny said, struggling to maintain his composure. "Then they just tossed me into the trash can." Once strong and powerfully built, he now walks with difficulty, tires easily, and feels useless, as though his life were over. He is forty-six years old.

The Regulatory Approach to Occupational Safety and Health

The U.S. government can approach the problem of workplace safety and health in any of three ways. First, it can leave the problem to employers and employees. This approach is supported by the following rationales: (a) under contract principles, employers with unsafe conditions would have to pay their employees higher wages; employees could "purchase" more safety by working for safer employers at presumably lower wages; (b) reliance should be placed on employers that, acting in their own enlightened self-interest, would improve safety and health; (c) safety and health issues should be resolved by collective bargaining; and (d) workers' compensation rates and the fear of personal injury litigation are adequate incentives in promoting occupational safety and health.

A second possible approach to the problem is to leave occupational safety and health regulation to the states. Although, in general, this approach was rejected by Congress in 1970 as having been tried and failed, the OSH Act allows states to adopt their own versions of the statute—"state plans"—which preempt federal activity.

The third approach, adopted by Congress in 1970 with the enactment of the OSH Act, was enactment of federal legislation. Congress opted for a standards/enforcement model. The initial safety and health standards were industry-developed consensus standards and federal standards already established by other, less comprehensive laws. New standards were to be promulgated through informal notice and comment rulemaking by the Secretary of Labor, with only the vaguest statutory directions as to the level of protection to be afforded to workers and the costs to be imposed on the economy.

The OSH Act requires preinspection compliance by employers and provides penalties for noncompliance detected during an inspection. Thus, the Act contemplates an important role for safety and health inspectors (compliance officers). When the Act was passed, however, there was an acute shortage of trained inspectors. In fact, in 1970 there were twice as many fish and game wardens in the U.S. as safety and health inspectors. By 1973, there were still only about 500 inspectors to serve 5 million workplaces and 75 million workers. (Today, there are about 8 million workplaces and 130 million workers.) Even worse, many of the inspectors initially hired lacked a formal education in safety or industrial hygiene, were poorly trained by OSHA, and had a "traffic cop" mentality in which the more violations cited, the better. (Today there are still fewer than 1,900 federal and state inspectors, although they have better education and training.)

Poor quality initial standards (discussed infra) and often incompetent inspectors led to OSHA's negative image as nitpicking, harassing, and ineffective. Although these early problems have been resolved, there are three reasons why OSHA continues to be an unpopular agency with business. First, OSHA has broad jurisdiction. The FAA, FCC, ICC, and other agencies each regulate a particular industry. OSHA regulates virtually all industries. Managers who are opposed to federal regulation will invariably have a common nemesis in OSHA. Second, OSHA is intrusive. Few business executives like the FTC, SEC, or IRS. But, generally speaking, these agencies do not show up at the door unannounced, demand to be let in, inspect the workplace, and then require a company to change the way it has been doing business for years. Third, OSHA-mandated compliance measures may be costly and infringe upon management prerogatives. OSHA seemingly intrudes into labor-management relations on the side of labor and requires, among other things, that workers be allowed to see their medical records and be permitted to refuse to work when conditions are extremely hazardous.

Mark A. Rothstein, Occupational Safety and Health Law[*]

3–11 (2020 ed.).

In 1936 Congress enacted the Walsh-Healey Public Contracts Act, which limited working hours, child and convict labor, and set mild standards for working conditions in factories. The Act required that

---

[*]   Reprinted by permission of Thomson/Reuters.

contracts entered into by any agency of the United States for the manufacture or furnishing of materials in any amount exceeding $10,000 must contain a stipulation that the working conditions of the contractor's employees must not be unsanitary, hazardous, or dangerous to health and safety. The Walsh-Healey Act, however, had limited coverage and failed to provide and enforce strict industrial health and safety standards.

The Labor Management Relations Act (Taft-Hartley Act), passed in 1947 over President Truman's veto, contained a provision (§ 502) permitting employees to walk off a job if it was "abnormally dangerous." In 1948 President Truman attempted to remedy industrial accidents by calling the first Presidential Conference on Industrial Safety. Although these meetings continued to take place throughout the Eisenhower years, the only noticeable outcome of the conferences was a bill introduced by Senator Hubert Humphrey in 1951. The Humphrey Bill, which attempted to establish an accident prevention bureau, led Congresswoman Lenore K. Sullivan to ask Labor Secretaries James P. Mitchell and Willard Wirtz for their support of legislation to ensure proper standards for handling hazardous materials in industry.

In the area of mine safety, Congress was more inclined to take action after the occurrence of a tragic accident. For example, the death of 119 miners in West Frankfort, Illinois in December, 1951 led to the passage of a Coal Mine Safety Act in 1952. Six years later, the Maritime Safety Act was passed, which amended the Longshoremen's and Harbor Workers' Compensation Act.

During the mid and late 1960s Congress continued to enact specialized or limited safety statutes. In 1965 the McNamara-O'Hara Public Service Contract Act was passed to provide labor standards for the protection of employees of contractors who performed maintenance service for federal agencies. Also in 1965 the National Foundation on the Arts and Humanities Act was passed, conditioning receipt of federal grants on the maintenance of safe and healthful working conditions for performers, laborers, and mechanics.

Congress took its first significant step in job safety and health when it passed the Metal and Nonmetallic Mine Safety Act of 1966. In January, 1968, President Johnson proposed the nation's first comprehensive occupational safety and health program. Although this bill never reached a vote, a later version of the bill was reported out of the House Education and Labor Committee's Select Subcommittee on Labor.

Later in 1968, a coal mine explosion in Farmington, West Virginia, killed 78 men and shocked Congress into realizing the need for new job safety legislation. Congress reacted by passing the Coal Mine Health and Safety Act of 1969. The Contract Work Hours and Safety Standards Act of 1969 (also known as the Construction Safety Act) established federal standards for construction on public works. In 1970 Congress enacted the

Federal Railway Safety Act, which was designed primarily for passenger safety, but also contained employee safety provisions.

By 1970, interest in job safety and health had reached new heights. The initial industry-specific legislation had already been passed and many members of Congress were ready to give serious consideration to more comprehensive federal regulations in industrial safety and health. The result was the passage of the Occupational Safety and Health Act of 1970 (OSH Act).

* * *

The Act covers employment in every state, the District of Columbia, Puerto Rico, and all American territories, an estimated 8 million workplaces and 130 million employees. The Act does not apply to working conditions of employees over whom other state and federal agencies exercise statutory authority to prescribe or enforce standards or regulations affecting occupational safety or health.

Among other requirements, each employer must comply with two provisions of the Act. First, § 5(a)(1) requires the employer to keep its place of employment free from recognized hazards that are causing or likely to cause death or serious physical harm to its employees. Second, § 5(a)(2) requires the employer to comply with promulgated OSHA standards.

The Act provides for the promulgation of standards in three ways. Under § 6(a), the Secretary of Labor was authorized to adopt national consensus standards and established federal standards without lengthy rulemaking procedures for two years from the effective date of the Act. This authority ended April 27, 1973. Section 6(b) sets out the procedures to be followed in modifying, revoking, or issuing new standards. The Secretary may also promulgate an emergency temporary standard pursuant to § 6(c). An emergency temporary standard may be established if the Secretary determines that employees are subject to grave danger from exposure to substances or agents known to be toxic or physically harmful and that an emergency standard is necessary to protect employees from danger. These standards are effective upon publication in the Federal Register but remain in effect only for six months.

Pursuant to § 6(d), an employer may petition the Secretary for an order granting a variance from any standard promulgated under § 6. The main types of variances are temporary and permanent. A temporary variance may be issued if the employer is unable to comply with a standard because of unavailability of workers, facilities, or equipment; is taking all available steps to protect its employees from the hazards covered by the standard; and has an effective program for coming into compliance as soon as possible. A permanent variance will be issued only if the Secretary determines that the workplace is as safe and healthful as it would be by compliance with the established standard.

All enforcement functions of the Act rest with the Occupational Safety and Health Administration (OSHA) of the Labor Department. OSHA compliance officers (COs) are empowered by § 8(a) to inspect any workplace covered by the Act. The CO must present his or her credentials to the owner, operator, or agent in charge before proceeding with the inspection tour. The employer and an employee representative have a right to accompany the inspector. After the inspection a closing conference is held, during which the CO and employer representative discuss safety and health conditions and possible violations. Most COs cannot issue citations "on the spot," but must confer with the OSHA area director.

After the CO files a report, the area director decides whether to issue a citation, computes any penalties to be assessed, and sets the date for abatement of each alleged violation. If a citation is issued, it is mailed to the employer as soon as possible after the inspection, but in no event can it be more than six months after the alleged violation occurred. Citations must be in writing and must describe with particularity the violations alleged, including the relevant standards and regulations.

Section 701 of the Bipartisan Budget Act of 2015 (Pub. L. No. 114–74) contains a provision requiring OSHA to increase the maximum penalties through a one-time "catch-up" increase based on the Consumer Price Index (CPI) since 1990. From 1990 to 2015 the CPI increased 82%. OSHA is also required to increase maximum penalties by the amount of inflation in the prior year. As of January 2020, the maximum OSHA penalties are as follows:

De Minimis Notice	$0
Nonserious	$0–$13,494
Serious	$1–$13,494
Repeated	$0–$134,937
Willful	$9,639–$134,937
Failure to abate	$0–$13,494 per day

The good faith of the employer, the gravity of the violation, the employer's past history of compliance, and the size of the employer are all considered in penalty assessment. In addition to the above-mentioned civil penalties, there are criminal sanctions for willful violations that have caused the death of one or more employees.

Under the Act, an employer, an employee, or authorized employee representative (union) have 15 working days in which to file a notice of contest. If the employer does not contest the violation, abatement date, or proposed penalty, the citation becomes final and not subject to review by any court or agency. Contrarily, if a notice of contest is filed in good faith, the abatement requirement is tolled and a hearing is scheduled. An employer may also file a petition for modification of abatement (PMA), if unable to comply with any abatement requirement that has become a final order. If the Secretary or an employee contests the PMA, a hearing is held to determine whether any abatement requirement, even if part of an uncontested citation, should be modified.

The Secretary must immediately forward any notice of contest to the Occupational Safety and Health Review Commission (OSHRC). The Commission is a quasi-judicial, independent administrative agency comprised of three Presidentially-appointed Commissioners who serve staggered six year terms. In cases before the Commission, the Secretary is usually referred to as the complainant, and has the burden of proving the violation; the employer is usually called the respondent. The hearing is presided over by an administrative law judge (ALJ) of the Commission. After the hearing the ALJ renders a decision, affirming, modifying, or vacating the citation, penalty, or abatement date. The ALJ's decision then automatically goes before the OSHRC. An aggrieved party may file a petition for discretionary review (PDR), asking that the ALJ's decision be reviewed, but even without a PDR any Commission member may direct review of any part or all of the ALJ's decision. In this event, the Commission reconsiders the evidence and issues a new decision. If, however, no member of the Commission directs review within 30 days, the decision of the ALJ is final.

Any person adversely affected by a final order of the Commission may file a petition for review in the United States court of appeals for the circuit in which the violation is alleged to have occurred or in the United States Court of Appeals for the District of Columbia Circuit. The affected party must file within 60 days of the final order.

NOTES

1. The Occupational Safety and Health Act (OSH Act) created three new government agencies: the National Institute for Occupational Safety and Health (NIOSH), located in the Department of Health and Human Services, is charged with scientific research on matters of occupational safety and health; the Occupational Safety and Health Administration (OSHA), located in the Department of Labor, is responsible for promulgating new standards and enforcement; and the Occupational Safety and Health Review Commission (OSHRC), an independent agency, adjudicates administrative cases arising under the Act. This compartmentalization of functions differs from the traditional administrative model and resulted from congressional concern about maintaining the separation of functions and assuring employers that these functions would, in fact, be separate and neutral.

2. Before 1977, miners were protected by two separate laws: the Federal Metal and Nonmetallic Mine Safety Act of 1966 and the Federal Coal Mine Health and Safety Act of 1969. Both laws were enforced by the Mining Enforcement and Safety Administration (MESA), part of the Department of the Interior. Also within the Department of the Interior was the Bureau of Mines charged with promoting mine production. (Before 1973, when MESA

was established, the Bureau of Mines also was responsible for safety.) Besides this conflict of interest and a history of poor enforcement, neither act had provisions covering toxic substances and neither required specific training for inexperienced miners. In addition, there were jurisdictional conflicts between OSHA and MESA.

To remedy these and other problems, Congress enacted the Federal Mine Safety and Health Act of 1977 (Mine Safety Act), 30 U.S.C. §§ 801–962. All mining activity is now covered by one law, enforced by the Mine Safety and Health Administration (MSHA), within the Department of Labor. The Mine Safety and Health Review Commission (MSHRC) was established to adjudicate contested mining cases.

The Mine Safety Act was based on the OSH Act model, but there are several differences reflecting the smaller number of sites covered (13,000 mines versus 8,000,000 workplaces), the hazardous nature of mining, and the experience with some problem areas under the OSH Act. Some of the unique features of the Mine Safety Act are the following:

(1) All underground mines must be inspected at least four times a year and all surface mines must be inspected at least twice a year. § 103(a), 30 U.S.C. § 813.

(2) All inexperienced miners must receive forty hours of training before working underground, § 115(a)(1), or twenty-four hours of training before working in a surface mine, § 115(a)(2), 30 U.S.C. § 825(a).

(3) Inspectors may issue orders calling for the immediate withdrawal of miners. § 104(b), 30 U.S.C. § 814.

(4) There is no general duty clause.

(5) There are no state plans, but existing state laws are not automatically superseded.

(6) Miners may refuse to work if there are extremely hazardous conditions. § 103(g), 30 U.S.C. § 813.

(7) There is no difference between serious and nonserious violations. Penalties up to $10,000 may be assessed for violations; $25,000 and up to one year in jail for a willful violation; and $50,000 and up to five years in jail for a second willful violation.

(8) Employees filing nonfrivolous complaints alleging that they were discriminated against for exercising rights under MSHA are entitled to temporary reinstatement pending adjudication of the merits. § 105(c), 30 U.S.C. § 815.

(9) Discrimination cases are heard initially by the Commission, with a right of appeal to district court. Miners may proceed on their own behalf if the Secretary declines to proceed. § 105(c), 30 U.S.C. § 815.

(10) The MSHRC is comprised of five members, with two votes needed to direct review of an ALJ's decision. § 113(a), 30 U.S.C. § 823.

2. JURISDICTION

Chao v. OSHRC (Eric K. Ho)

401 F.3d 355 (5th Cir. 2005).

■ DeMoss, Circuit Judge:

This appeal stems from a final order of Respondent Occupational Safety and Health Review Commission (the "Commission"), which vacated in part citations issued by Petitioner—Cross-Respondent Elaine Chao, Secretary of Labor (the "Secretary"), against Respondents—Cross-Petitioners Eric K. Ho ("Ho"), et al. (together, "Ho Respondents"). For the following reasons, we DENY the petitions for review and AFFIRM the decision of the Commission.

BACKGROUND

The penalties assessed by the Secretary and mostly affirmed by the Administrative Law Judge ("ALJ") and the Commission against Ho for various violations of the Occupational Safety and Health Act, 29 U.S.C. §§ 651–678 ("OSH Act"), and associated safety and health regulations all concern his behavior as proprietor of a worksite where workers were exposed to asbestos in the course of a project to renovate a building. On October 27, 1997, Ho individually purchased a defunct hospital and medical office building in Houston to develop the property as residential housing. Ho knew there was asbestos onsite. He was also aware that any alteration to asbestos-containing materials was to be handled by personnel licensed and registered with the Texas Department of Health ("TDH"). Ho instead hired Manuel Escobedo ("Escobedo") and Corston Tate ("Tate"), whose work he had previously used, to do the renovations. Escobedo hired 11 Mexican nationals, who were illegal immigrants, to assist. Renovations, including the removal of asbestos, started in January 1998.

At most, the workers were occasionally given dust masks not suitable for protection against asbestos. They were not issued protective clothing. Ho also did not provide a respiratory protection program, conduct medical surveillance, conduct asbestos monitoring, implement adequate ventilation or debris removal, inform the workers of the presence and hazards of asbestos, or provide any training whatsoever. There is no dispute that Ho was aware of the worksite conditions; he visited almost every day.

On February 2, 1998, a city inspector visited the worksite. After observing the conditions, he issued a stop-work order citing the possibility of exposure to asbestos, requiring that city approval be given before work could resume. Ho then began negotiating with a licensed contractor, Alamo Environmental ("Alamo"), to remove the asbestos. Alamo prepared an abatement estimate in accordance with Occupational Safety and Health Administration ("OSHA"), amongst other federal, guidelines. On March 27, 1998, Ho notified Alamo by fax that he agreed to their proposal.

However, during this period of negotiation, Ho had resumed work at the site under the same conditions, except that he directed all work be performed at night. The workers ate, and some lived, at the site. The workers had no potable water and only one portable toilet. Tate sometimes allowed workers to leave the property to use the restroom at a nearby commercial establishment; and Tate would purchase and bring back food for the workers when they gave him money. Ho continued to visit the worksite and was aware of these conditions.

Asbestos removal continued in this fashion until March 10, 1998. On March 11, 1998, as Ho had directed, daytime work resumed at the site. Ho had been informed that either the sprinkler system or fire hydrant valves had not been turned off and thus remained available for use. To wash out the building, Ho directed Tate to tap into an unmarked valve believed to be a water line. It turned out to be a gas line. An explosion later occurred when Tate started his truck; it injured Tate and two workers. On March 12, 1998, workers were summoned to Ho's office where they were given releases to sign, acknowledging receipt of $1000 as full payment for their work, and acknowledging receipt of $100 to release Ho from any claims that might arise from the explosion and fire. The releases were written in English, but an interpreter translated them for the workers.

After the explosion, TDH conducted an investigation. Samples of debris and the ambient air at the worksite showed levels of asbestos in excess of federal and state standards. The state notified Ho that the site remained unsafe and needed to be sealed by qualified personnel. Again, Ho used the same workers to install plywood over the windows and did not give them any protective equipment.

OSHA also conducted an investigation. As a result, the Secretary issued a total of 10 serious and 29 willful violations against Ho Respondents; these charges included 11 willful violations of 29 C.F.R. § 1926.1101(h)(1)(i) for failing to provide respirators to 11 employees removing asbestos and 11 willful violations of 29 C.F.R. § 1926.1101(k)(9)(i) and (viii) for failing to train the 11 employees on the hazards of asbestos and safety precautions. The Secretary also charged Ho Respondents with willfully violating the OSH Act's general duty clause, 29 U.S.C. § 654(a)(1), by ordering Tate to tap into the unmarked pipeline. Ho was also convicted of criminal violations of the Clean Air Act ("CAA"). This Court upheld his conviction. United States v. Ho, 311 F.3d 589, 611 (5th Cir. 2002).

Ho conceded before the ALJ that he violated the asbestos respirator and training standards. Ho argued that he was not subject to the OSH Act's requirements because he was not engaged in a business affecting interstate commerce and that the corporate Ho Respondents should be dismissed because they were not employers of the employees engaged in asbestos removal. He also challenged the per-employee citations of the respirator and training violations. Finally, Ho contended he did not violate the general duty clause of the OSH Act, or if he had violated it, that such violation was not willful.

* * *

DISCUSSION

Whether the Commission's factual finding that Ho's illegal asbestos abatement activities at the hospital worksite affected interstate commerce was supported by substantial evidence.

The OSH Act applies to employers, defined as "persons engaged in a business affecting commerce who have employees." 29 U.S.C. § 652 (5) (1970). By enacting the OSH Act, Congress intended to exercise the full extent of the authority granted by the Commerce Clause. Austin Road Co. v. OSHRC, 683 F.2d 905, 907 (5th Cir. 1982). "Accordingly, an employer comes under the aegis of the [OSH] Act by merely affecting commerce; it is not necessary that the employer be engaged directly in interstate commerce."

The Secretary bears "the burden of showing that the employer's activities affect interstate commerce." This burden is "modest, if indeed not light." On appeal, this Court only reviews the Commission's findings of fact to ensure they are "supported by substantial evidence in the record considered as a whole." Substantial evidence is "such relevant evidence as a reasonable mind might accept as adequate to support a conclusion."

Ho Respondents argue that the Secretary put forth no evidence to support the Commission's finding that the building renovation was a business affecting interstate commerce. Because the Secretary failed to provide jurisdictional evidence, Ho Respondents contend none of them was subject to the OSH Act. Moreover, Ho Respondents charge the Secretary cannot rely on the Commission's finding of fact because the Commission relied on an inapplicable Ninth Circuit per se rule, see Usery v. Lacy, 628 F.2d 1226, 1229 (9th Cir. 1980) (extending OSH Act reach over employers in the construction industry "whose activities in the aggregate affect commerce"), and a nonpreclusive jurisdictional finding of this Court in the criminal action against Ho based on the "aggregate" effect on interstate commerce of asbestos removal violations under the CAA.

The Secretary responds that she provided evidence that Ho was engaged in a business affecting interstate commerce and was therefore subject to the OSH Act. The Secretary points out Ho had a majority interest in two interstate trucking firms (Ho Ho Express being one). Alternatively, the Secretary argues Ho's asbestos abatement activities at the hospital site constituted a business affecting interstate commerce. The Secretary notes this Court has previously held that Ho's illicit asbestos operations at the hospital site, when aggregated, affected the interstate markets in asbestos removal services and commercial real estate in the context of Ho's CAA criminal case. The Secretary maintains Ho's activities at the hospital were specifically found to affect interstate commerce substantially enough to support federal regulation; this issue cannot be relitigated. The Secretary also argues Ho misreads *Austin Road* to impose an evidentiary hurdle to defeat even normal application of collateral estoppel.

Even if this Court does not find jurisdiction based on collateral estoppel, the Secretary stresses she presented evidence showing that, by failing to comply with the OSH Act requirements, Ho gained a competitive advantage over licensed asbestos firms, including Alamo, and deprived them of a commercial business opportunity in the national market for asbestos removal. Moreover, the Secretary argues Ho's illicit asbestos removal project also would increase asbestos removal costs for law-abiding commercial property owners.

This Court in Ho's criminal appeal clearly indicated that his specific illicit construction activities concerning asbestos abatement, when considered in the aggregate, directly affected interstate commerce in the national market of asbestos removal. In finding that the challenged provisions of the CAA constitutionally reached Ho under the Commerce Clause, we stated that "a national market exists for asbestos removal services" and that "Ho's activities would injure this market." We also stated that Ho's illegal asbestos abatement activities in the aggregate "posed a threat to the interstate commercial real estate market" because they "would reduce the number of companies providing asbestos removal services" and "conscientious property owners would have more trouble locating licensed abatement companies and likely would have to pay higher prices."

Here, though we are informed by the aggregation principle's application to asbestos removal activities outlined in *Ho*, as the Commission was also so informed, we do not rest the instant jurisdictional result based on collateral estoppel or issue preclusion from Ho's criminal CAA case. Nor do we have before us the constitutionality of any provision of the OSH Act or accompanying regulation. We also do not recognize the Ninth Circuit per se construction rule Ho Respondents insist was adopted by the Commission in its decision. Instead, pursuant to *Austin Road*, we consider whether the Commission's factual finding that Ho's illegal asbestos abatement activities at the hospital worksite affected interstate commerce was supported by substantial evidence in the record.

Despite Ho Respondents' arguments, there is sufficient record evidence that Ho specifically deprived the asbestos removal firm Alamo of a legitimate commercial job to remove asbestos from the hospital site in accordance with the OSH Act. Ho negotiated with, but did not actually employ, Alamo to perform the licensed abatement. Instead, Ho hired illegal immigrants to remove the asbestos for $1000 each before he ever agreed to Alamo's proposal. This evidence indicates in the context of the

OSH Act, similar to what this Court has already analyzed in the context of the CAA, that Ho's asbestos removal activities affected interstate commerce by depriving legitimate commercial asbestos abatement firms of the opportunity to perform the work at the site. Ho's deliberate decision to have unlicensed workers perform the asbestos abatement project sidestepped, and thus supplanted, a commercial firm that operates within the legitimate national market for asbestos removal services, a licensed firm which adheres to OSH Act provisions and regulations. We find Ho's illegal asbestos activities sufficiently affected interstate commerce so as to be subject to the OSH Act. Unlike in *Austin Road*, here the essential fact that Ho's abatement activities affected interstate commerce is not speculative and conclusionary, but rather is established in the record.

The Secretary thus met her modest jurisdictional burden under the OSH Act. Therefore, on this record, we find substantial evidence exists to support the Commission's factual finding that Ho's activities sufficiently affected interstate commerce to support the OSH Act's jurisdictional reach over Ho as an employer per § 652(5).

NOTES AND QUESTIONS

1. In *Ho*, the court relied on the effect of the unlawful asbestos removal operation on legitimate asbestos companies engaged in interstate commerce to find jurisdiction. In another leading case, Usery v. Lacy, 628 F.2d 1226 (9th Cir.1980), the court held that it was appropriate for the Commission to take official notice that the employer used tools and materials that had moved in commerce. Thus, it is relatively easy for the Secretary to prove that the cited employer is covered by the OSH Act.

2. Section 3(5) of the OSH Act excludes states and political subdivisions of states from the definition of "employer." It is not always clear, however, whether a quasi-public entity is covered. For example, in Brock v. Chicago Zoological Soc'y, 820 F.2d 909 (7th Cir. 1987), the court held that the zoo was not a political subdivision of the state of Illinois. Even though over half of its funding was public, the zoo was operated by trustees who were private citizens and zoo employees were not covered by any laws applicable to public employees.

3. An important jurisdictional provision of the OSH Act is section 4(b)(1), which provides that the Act does not apply to "working conditions of employees with respect to which other Federal agencies * * * exercise statutory authority to prescribe or enforce standards or regulations affecting occupational safety and health." Congress sought to avoid duplication of enforcement by OSHA and other federal agencies, but section 4(b)(1) has posed a number of legal issues. Decisions of the OSHRC suggest a three-part test to determine whether the Act is preempted from exercising authority by virtue of section 4(b)(1):

> (1) The employer is covered by another federal act directed exclusively at employee safety and health or directed at public

safety and health and employees directly receive the protection the act is intended to provide.

(2)   The other federal agency has exercised its statutory grant of authority.

(3)   The other federal agency has acted in such a manner as to exempt the cited working conditions from OSHA jurisdiction.

See Northwest Airlines, Inc., 8 OSHC 1982, 1980 OSHD ¶ 24,751 (1980).

4.   In section 4(b)(1) cases, employers typically argue that they are exempt from the OSH Act because they are regulated by another agency. Cf. Old Dominion Power Co. v. Donovan, 772 F.2d 92 (4th Cir. 1985) (in defending MSHA citation employer successfully argued that OSHA rather than MSHA had jurisdiction). Why would employers prefer to be regulated by an agency other than OSHA, such as the FAA, USDA, DOT, or FRA?

5.   The OSH Act preempts all state occupational safety and health legislation. Pursuant to section 18, however, if a state has an OSHA approved "state plan," with comparable standards, enforcement, and adjudicatory functions, jurisdiction may be ceded back to the state. There are currently 22 approved state plans.

States without approved plans retain jurisdiction in certain areas. States may enforce standards, such as state and local fire regulations, which are designed to protect a wider class of persons than employees. They may conduct consultation, training, and safety information activities; and they may enforce standards to protect state and local government employees. A variety of other state laws have been held not to be preempted by the OSH Act, including local zoning ordinances, drinking water and toilet facilities laws, injury reporting laws, criminal laws, and common law damage and indemnity actions.

6.   In Gade v. National Solid Wastes Mgmt. Ass'n, 505 U.S. 88 (1992), the Supreme Court addressed whether two Illinois laws requiring state licensing of hazardous waste workers were preempted by the OSH Act. The dual purposes of the state laws were to protect employees and the general public. A detailed OSHA standard also addressed training requirements for hazardous waste workers. The Supreme Court held that the OSH Act "precludes any state regulation of an occupational safety and health issue with respect to which a federal standard has been established, unless a state plan has been submitted and approved pursuant to § 18(b)." Id. at 102.

7.   In Ramsey Winch, Inc. v. Henry, 555 F.3d 1199 (10th Cir. 2009), several employers challenged an Oklahoma law requiring property owners to permit firearms on their property. The district court held that the law is preempted by the OSH Act, which generally requires employers to prevent workplace hazards. The Tenth Circuit reversed, noting that OSHA has declined to adopt any standard dealing with firearms in the workplace. But cf. Plona v. United Parcel Service, Inc., 558 F.3d 478 (6th Cir. 2009) (employer's discharge of an employee for possessing firearm in vehicle in company parking lot did not violate a clear public policy in Ohio). See generally Dayna B. Royal, Take Your Gun to Work and Leave It in the Parking Lot: Why the

OSH Act Does Not Preempt State Guns-at-Work Laws, 61 Fla. L. Rev. 475 (2009).

SeaWorld of Florida, LLC v. Perez

748 F.3d 1202 (D.C. Cir. 2014).

■ ROGERS, CIRCUIT JUDGE: SeaWorld of Florida, LLC, operates a theme park in Orlando, Florida, that is designed to entertain and educate paying customers by displaying and studying marine animals. Following the death of one of SeaWorld's trainers while working in close contact with a killer whale during a performance, the Occupational Safety and Health Review Commission found that SeaWorld had violated the general duty clause, § 5(a)(1) of the Occupational Safety and Health Act of 1970, 29 U.S.C. § 654(a)(1), by exposing the trainers to recognized hazards when working in close contact with killer whales during performances, and that the abatement procedures recommended by the Secretary of Labor were feasible. SeaWorld challenges the order with respect to one citation. Concluding its challenges are unpersuasive, we deny the petition for review.

I.

On February 24, 2010, SeaWorld trainer Dawn Brancheau was interacting with Tilikum, a killer whale, during a performance before a live audience in a pool at Shamu Stadium in Orlando. Ms. Brancheau was reclined on her back on a platform a few inches below the water surface. Tilikum was supposed to mimic her behavior by rolling over. Instead, the killer whale grabbed her and pulled her off the platform into the pool, refusing to release her. She suffered traumatic injuries and drowned as a result of Tilikum's actions.

The Secretary of Labor issued three citations to SeaWorld after an investigation by an Occupational Safety and Health Administration ("OSHA") compliance officer. Only the second citation is at issue. It alleged two instances of a "willful" violation of the general duty clause for exposing animal trainers to the recognized hazards of drowning or injury when working with killer whales during performances. The first instance related to animal trainers working with Tilikum being exposed to "struck-by and drowning hazards" by being "allowed unprotected contact with Tilikum" while conducting " 'drywork' performances on pool ledges, slideouts and platforms." In SeaWorld's terms, when trainers are out of the pool or on submerged ledges called "slideouts" in water no deeper than their knees, their interactions with killer whales are called "drywork." Any interaction in deeper water is "waterwork." According to the Secretary, "[a]mong other methods, one feasible and acceptable means of abatement would be to not allow animal trainers to have any contact with Tilikum unless they are protected by a physical barrier. . . ." The second instance concerned animal trainers working with killer whales other than Tilikum who were exposed to struck-by and drowning hazards when they were "allowed to engage in 'waterwork' and 'drywork' performances with the killer whales without adequate protection." The Secretary listed as possible abatement methods "prohibit[ing] animal trainers from working with killer whales, including 'waterwork' or 'dry work,' unless the trainers are protected through the use of physical barriers or through the use of decking systems, oxygen supply systems or other engineering or administrative controls that provide the same or greater level of protection for the trainers." The Secretary proposed a penalty of $70,000.

* * *

II.

The general duty clause, § 5(a)(1) of the Occupational Safety and Health Act, provides: "Each employer [ ] shall furnish to each of his employees employment and a place of employment which are free from recognized hazards that are causing or are likely to cause death or serious physical harm to his employees."

* * *

"To establish a violation of the General Duty Clause, the Secretary must establish that: (1) an activity or condition in the employer's workplace presented a hazard to an employee, (2) either the employer or the industry recognized the condition or activity as a hazard, (3) the hazard was likely to or actually caused death or serious physical harm, and (4) a feasible means to eliminate or materially reduce the hazard existed." Fabi Constr. Co. v. Sec'y of Labor, 508 F.3d 1077, 1081 (D.C.Cir.2007) Tempering the range of potential remedies that might be imposed upon finding a violation of the clause, the court explained: "In other words, 'the *Secretary* must prove that a reasonably prudent employer familiar with the circumstances of the industry would have protected against the hazard in the manner specified by the Secretary's citation.' "

SeaWorld contests only the second and fourth elements regarding recognized hazard and feasibility. In challenging the general duty citation, SeaWorld does not perforce contend that the Secretary of Labor or the Occupational Safety and Health Review Commission lack legal authority to require employers to provide a reasonably safe working environment for employees. Rather, SeaWorld takes issue with the interpretation by these officials of what constitutes a recognized hazard that would subject an employer to citation under the Occupational Safety and Health Act. First, SeaWorld contends that the finding that it exposed its employees to a "recognized hazard" is unsupported by substantial evidence. Second, it contends that "when some risk is inherent in a business activity, that risk cannot constitute a 'recognized hazard.' " Third, it contends that the ALJ's decision was based on unreliable expert testimony about the extent of killer whale predictability after SeaWorld's training and precautions. As regards the feasibility of physical barriers and minimum distances SeaWorld contends that the Secretary failed to prove feasible abatement methods (or that SeaWorld had already implemented these measures), and that the ALJ failed to consider evidence these abatement measures present additional hazards and erred because eliminating close contact changes the nature of a trainer's job.

* * *

A.

Whether a work condition poses a recognized hazard is a question of fact. Substantial evidence supports the finding that "drywork" and "waterwork" with killer whales were recognized hazards. Tilikum is a 32-year-old male killer whale with known aggressive tendencies who in 1991 killed a whale trainer at a marine park in Vancouver, British Columbia. SeaWorld had established special protocols for Tilikum, which prohibited "waterwork" and, among other things, required non-killer whale personnel and guests to stay five feet behind pool walls or three feet from Tilikum's head, indicating that SeaWorld recognized the possibility of harm to people standing outside of the pool on land. Although "drywork" with Tilikum continued, SeaWorld limited it to a team of experienced trainers who used extra caution. The caution with which SeaWorld treated Tilikum even when trainers were poolside or on "slideouts" in the pool indicates that it recognized the hazard the killer whale posed, not that it considered its protocols rendered Tilikum safe.

As to other killer whales, SeaWorld suggests that close contact with these whales was not a recognized hazard because all whales behave differently and its incident reports help SeaWorld improve training. But SeaWorld's incident reports demonstrate that it recognized the danger its killer whales posed to trainers notwithstanding its protocols. At the time of Ms. Brancheau's death, seven killer whales were at the Orlando park. Even though SeaWorld had not recorded incident reports on all of its killer whales, a substantial portion of SeaWorld's killer whale population had at least one reported incident. The ALJ also relied on the many comments by SeaWorld management personnel, including corporate curators of animal training, who described the need for caution around killer whales generally, not only around certain killer whales. Killer whales bit trainers' body parts on several occasions (although not generally puncturing skin) and in 2006 a killer whale pulled a trainer underwater by the foot and submerged him repeatedly for approximately 10 minutes. Although this incident occurred during "waterwork," substantial evidence supports the finding with regard to "drywork" as well. On numerous occasions, trainers fell or were pulled into the water, as later happened with Tilikum and Ms. Brancheau, or killer whales lunged out of the water toward trainers. These incidents constitute substantial evidence to support the ALJ's finding that "drywork" was also a recognized hazard.

* * *

SeaWorld's suggestion that because trainers "formally accepted and controlled their own exposure to . . . risks," the hazard of close contact with killer whales cannot be recognized, contravenes Congress's decision to place the duty to ensure a safe and healthy workplace on the employer, not the employee. This court has long held "this duty is not qualified by such common law doctrines as assumption of risk, contributory negligence, or comparative negligence."

* * *

The Secretary and the Commission could also reasonably determine that the remedy does not go to the essence of SeaWorld's productions. SeaWorld has had no "waterwork" performances since Ms. Brancheau's death in 2010, and it temporarily suspended "waterwork" after other incidents, such as the killing of a trainer by a killer whale in 2009 at a non SeaWorld park in Spain. With distance and physical barriers between Tilikum and trainers during drywork, Tilikum can still perform almost the same behaviors performed when no barriers were present. The nature of SeaWorld's workplace and the unusual nature of the hazard to its employees performing in close physical contact with killer whales do not remove SeaWorld from its obligation under the General Duty Clause to protect its employees from recognized hazards.

* * *

C.

Substantial evidence supports the ALJ's findings that it was feasible for SeaWorld to abate the hazard to its employees by using barriers or minimum distance between trainers and killer whales, most notably because SeaWorld has implemented many of these measures on its own. When an employer has existing safety procedures, the burden is on the Secretary to show that those procedures are inadequate. The record evidence showed that SeaWorld's training and protocols did not prevent continued incidents, including the submerging and biting of one trainer in 2006, the killing of a trainer by a SeaWorld-trained and—owned killer whale in 2009 at an amusement park in Spain, and Ms. Brancheau's death in 2010. SeaWorld employees repeatedly acknowledged the unpredictability of its killer whales. This record evidence supports the ALJ's finding that existing protocols were inadequate to eliminate or materially reduce the hazard to SeaWorld's trainer employees performing with killer whales.

Abatement is "feasible" when it is "economically and technologically capable of being done." After Ms. Brancheau's death, SeaWorld required that all trainers work with Tilikum from a minimum distance or behind a barrier, and "waterwork" ceased with all of its killer whales. As the ALJ noted, SeaWorld had not argued the Secretary's proposed abatement was not economically or technologically feasible and had already implemented abatement for at least one of its killer whales and needed only to apply the same or similar protective contact measures it used with Tilikum to other killer whales. Consequently, the Secretary was not required to specify the precise manner in which abatement should be implemented.

* * *

Accordingly, we deny the petition for review.

■ KAVANAUGH, CIRCUIT JUDGE, dissenting: Many sports events and entertainment shows can be extremely dangerous for the participants. Football. Ice hockey. Downhill skiing. Air shows. The circus. Horse racing. Tiger taming. Standing in the batter's box against a 95 mile per hour fastball. Bull riding at the rodeo. Skydiving into the stadium before a football game. Daredevil motorcycle jumps. Stock car racing. Cheerleading vaults. Boxing. The balance beam. The ironman triathlon. Animal trainer shows. Movie stunts. The list goes on.

* * *

The broad question implicated by this case is this: When should we as a society paternalistically decide that the participants in these sports and entertainment activities must be protected from themselves—that the risk of significant physical injury is simply too great even for eager and willing participants? And most importantly for this case, *who decides* that the risk to participants is too high?

* * *

In my view, the Department of Labor either has authority to regulate sports and entertainment so as to prevent injuries to participants, or it does not. The fact that the Department expressly disclaims its authority over the NFL and NASCAR, and that the Department goes to such lengths to draw head-scratching distinctions between sports events on the one hand and entertainment shows on the other, shows that something is up. What's up is that the Department is treating similar cases dissimilarly, the paradigmatic arbitrary and capricious agency action.

* * *

To the extent sports or entertainment activities raise concern about the risk of injury to the participants, several extant legal bodies possess significant authority to clamp down on unreasonable dangers: Congress, state legislatures, state regulators, courts applying state tort law. I take no position here on whether SeaWorld—or for that matter the NFL or NASCAR—should be subject to more stringent government regulation or liability, or otherwise should voluntarily make its activities safer. That *policy* question is not before us. My *legal* disagreement with the majority opinion boils down to one basic question: Who decides? Under current law, it is not the Department of Labor. I respectfully dissent.

NOTES AND QUESTIONS

1. Tilikum, who died in 2017, was not just any killer whale; he was the largest killer whale in captivity. Despite a series of behavioral problems, Tilikum was reportedly very valuable to Sea World's breeding program. In 2013, a controversial documentary, *Blackfish*, chronicled the 2010 incident and other killer whale attacks. It is not clear why Tilikum attacked Dawn Brancheau, but one theory is that she had run out of the food used to reward him for performing certain tricks.

2. The majority argued that there is a difference between the sports and entertainment industries, and that OSHA has been used to regulate entertainment. The dissent merged sports and entertainment to argue that Congress did not intend to regulate such sports as NASCAR or the NFL and, in any event, the employees in those fields assumed the risk of injury. In 2017, the NFL Players' Association, concerned about a rise in concussions, asked OSHA to take action. David Michaels, head of OSHA under President Obama, said OSHA should not act. "Even if OSHA could issue regulations to reduce the risk of concussions, OSHA would be a target of widespread derision and there would be accusations of interference in areas where it is not necessary." A contrary view was expressed by Adam Finkel, a former director of OSHA health standards. "If OSHA ran away every time an industry said 'leave us alone,' it would accomplish nothing." What are your views?

3. The general duty clause, section 5(a)(1), the basis of citation in *Sea World*, was included in the OSH Act because Congress realized that it would be impossible to promulgate a standard dealing with every conceivable workplace hazard. Therefore, alleged violations of the general duty clause originally tended to focus on distinct hazards, such as where an employee was suffocated by the cave-in of stored cottonseed, Southern Soya Corp., 1 OSHC 1412, 1973–74 OSHD ¶ 16,957 (1973), and where an employee was killed while cleaning the inside of cement mixer, Richmond Block, Inc., 1 OSHC 1505, 1973–74 OSHD ¶ 17,137 (1974).

4. Because it is worded so broadly, Congress attempted to restrict the types of cases in which section 5(a)(1) could be used. First, the hazard must be "recognized," which means that the cited employer or the employer's industry regards the condition as a hazard. Second, section 5(a)(1) only applies to serious violations. Third, the general duty clause may be cited only where the violation creates a risk of harm to employees of the cited employer.

5. The Secretary's burden of proof is greater in cases brought under section 5(a)(1) than those brought under section 5(a)(2). In National Realty & Constr. Co. v. OSHRC, 489 F.2d 1257 (D.C.Cir. 1973), the D.C. Circuit held that to prove a violation of section 5(a)(1) the Secretary must prove: (1) that the employer failed to render its workplace free of a hazard which was (2) recognized and (3) causing or likely to cause death or serious physical harm, and (4) the Secretary must specify the particular steps the cited employer should have taken to avoid citation and to demonstrate the feasibility and likely utility of these measures.

B. PROMULGATION OF STANDARDS

The Occupational Safety and Health Act does not describe the specific hazards to be regulated or the methods to reduce or eliminate the hazards. The responsibility for all rulemaking activity was delegated to the Secretary of Labor (and the administrator of OSHA). OSHA standards may be promulgated in three ways: (a) from 1971 to 1973, OSHA was empowered to adopt existing standards under other federal laws and privately developed standards; (b) OSHA can promulgate new standards or revise or revoke existing OSHA standards by following the rulemaking procedures set out in section 6(b); and (c) OSHA can promulgate emergency standards in accordance with section 6(c).

Numerous technical, policy, and legal issues have arisen under each of the rulemaking methods. Under section 6(a), there have been questions of the applicability or scope of standards and the interpretation of vague language. Under section 6(b), there have been questions about the certainty and severity of the risk needed to justify regulation, the adequacy of the evidence about the benefits to be achieved by the standards, and the economic and technological feasibility of the standards. Under section 6(c), the most common question has been whether an emergency temporary standard is needed to alleviate a "grave danger."

1. INITIAL STANDARDS

Mark A. Rothstein, OSHA After Ten Years: A Review and Some Proposed Reforms[*]
34 Vand.L.Rev. 71, 73–74 (1981).

Under section 6(a) of the Act the Secretary of Labor was initially authorized to adopt, as the agency's own regulations governing workplace conditions, "national consensus standards"[6] and "established federal standards"[7] without having first to comply with the lengthy rulemaking procedures of either section 6(b) or the Administrative Procedure Act. This special authority, which expired after two years, was

---

[*]　Reprinted by permission.

[6]　29 U.S.C. § 652(9) (1976) defines "national consensus standard" as follows:

　　The term "national consensus standard" means any occupational safety and health standard or modification thereof which (1), has been adopted and promulgated by a nationally recognized standards-producing organization under procedures whereby it can be determined by the Secretary that persons interested and affected by the scope of provisions of the standard have reached substantial agreement on its adoption, (2) was formulated in a manner which afforded an opportunity for diverse views to be considered and (3) has been designated as such a standard by the Secretary, after consultation with other appropriate Federal agencies.

[7]　29 U.S.C. § 652(10) (1976) defines "established federal standard" as follows:

　　The term "established Federal standard" means any operative occupational safety and health standard established by any agency of the United States and presently in effect, or contained in any Act of Congress in force on December 29, 1970.

included in the Act to assure that workers would be protected as soon as possible after the statute's effective date. Because they were adopted without the burden of rulemaking procedures, the standards did provide immediate coverage to millions of employees across the nation. Unfortunately, because the standards were adopted so quickly, they became the source of numerous problems and legal controversies. This was especially true for the national consensus standards.

Most of the difficulties with national consensus standards can be traced to the fact that they were privately adopted, optional measures. Many of the standards were poorly drafted, extremely general, vague, redundant, contradictory, or hopelessly outdated. The requirements were usually couched as specification standards[8] rather than as more flexible performance standards.[9] Other standards were advisory, directory, or precatory and were never intended to be given binding effect.

In its haste to promulgate an initial standards package, OSHA did not review the standards carefully. Consequently, some of the national consensus standards adopted under section 6(a) were trivial, outdated, and even ludicrous. For example, two of the more notorious standards adopted by OSHA were a prohibition on the use of ice in drinking water[10] and a requirement that all workplace toilet seats be "open-front."[11] Although these and similar questionable standards were not zealously enforced, they were the source of embarrassment to OSHA and contributed greatly to the Agency's developing image of over-enforcement of the Act and of nitpicking.

NOTES AND QUESTIONS

1. Courts reviewing OSHA cases brought under section 6(a) were not sympathetic to the agency. For example, in Usery v. Kennecott Copper Corp., 577 F.2d 1113 (10th Cir. 1977), the Tenth Circuit held that a standard requiring guardrails and toeboards on construction above 10 feet in the air was unenforceable because, in promulgating the standard, the Secretary of Labor had changed the wording of the industry-developed "national consensus standard", from "should" to "shall." According to the court, the Secretary was not authorized to make any changes without resort to the rulemaking procedures of section 6(b). On the other hand, if the Secretary did not make the change, the "should" standard would be optional and unenforceable. In 1984, OSHA simply revoked 153 "should" standards.

2. In Kiewit Power Constructors Co., 27 OSHC 1445, 2018 OSHD ¶ 33,689 (2018), the Occupational Safety and Health Review Commission considered the long-dormant issue of whether, in adopting an "established federal

---

[8] E.g., Ladder rungs must be made of wood and must be one inch in diameter.

[9] E.g., Ladder rungs must be capable of supporting 500 pounds.

[10] 29 C.F.R. § 1910.141(b)(1)(iii) (1972), revised, 38 Fed.Reg. 10,932 (1973). The standard was directed at the nineteenth century practice of obtaining and storing ice cut from rivers and lakes that might be polluted.

[11] 29 C.F.R. § 1910.141(c)(3)(iii) (1972), revised, 38 Fed.Reg. 10,933 (1973).

standard" from the Walsh-Healey Public Contracts Act pursuant to section 6(a), the Secretary of Labor was authorized to expand the scope of the standard from manufacturing to all industries, including construction. The Commission held that the adoption of established federal standards and national consensus standards without rulemaking was justified because affected industries had the opportunity to participate in the original rulemaking, an opportunity not afforded to newly covered industries if the scope of the standard could be altered by the Secretary. It is not clear how many other construction standards adopted from the Walsh-Healey Act were rendered invalid by this decision.

3. The most troubling part of the section 6(a) standards controversy is that the section 6(a) health standards are not automatically updated. There are about 450 health standards, which were adopted in 1971 as established federal standards, and which are based on 1968 American Conference of Governmental Industrial Hygienists (ACGIH) threshold limit values (TLVs). The standards set exposure levels, but do not require medical examinations, biological monitoring, or other compliance measures. The ACGIH revises its TLVs annually, but OSHA is required to use section 6(b) procedures to revise its standards, and since 1971 OSHA has promulgated only about two dozen new or revised health standards. As a result, many OSHA standards permit exposures at levels no longer considered safe by experts.

2. NEW STANDARDS

Industrial Union Department v. American Petroleum Institute (The Benzene Case)
448 U.S. 607 (1980).

[Benzene is a clear, highly flammable liquid hydrocarbon compound that is widely used in industry as a chemical intermediate, component of motor fuels, and solvent. While benzene had long been known to cause death within minutes at very high levels of concentration, studies in the early and mid-1970s demonstrated that lower concentration levels of benzene over an extended period of time caused leukemia.]

[In 1971 OSHA adopted the American National Standards Institute (ANSI) recommendation of a threshold limit value (TLV) of ten ppm. After an earlier unsuccessful attempt to promulgate an emergency temporary standard (ETS), on May 27, 1977, OSHA proposed a new standard of one ppm and also called for extensive monitoring, medical examinations, labeling, record-keeping, and other requirements. After a three week hearing featuring 95 witnesses, 1400 comments and exhibits, and a transcript of 3500 pages, on February 3, 1978, OSHA promulgated a permanent standard with an effective date of March 13, 1978. The Fifth Circuit struck down the standard, holding that OSHA failed to prove by substantial evidence that a reduction in the permissible exposure limit (PEL) would result in appreciable benefits. American Petroleum Institute v. OSHA, 581 F.2d 493 (5th Cir. 1978).]

■ MR. JUSTICE STEVENS announced the judgment of the Court and delivered an opinion in which THE CHIEF JUSTICE and MR. JUSTICE STEWART join and in Parts of which MR. JUSTICE POWELL joins.

* * *

Our resolution of the issues in this case turns, to a large extent, on the meaning of and the relationship between § 3(8), which defines a health and safety standard as a standard that is "reasonably necessary and appropriate to provide safe or healthful employment," and § 6(b)(5), which directs the Secretary in promulgating a health and safety standard for toxic materials to "set the standard which most adequately assures, to the extent feasible, on the basis of the best available evidence, that no employee will suffer material impairment of health or functional capacity * * *."

In the Government's view, § 3(8)'s definition of the term "standard" has no legal significance or at best merely requires that a standard not be totally irrational. It takes the position that § 6(b)(5) is controlling and that it requires OSHA to promulgate a standard that either gives an absolute assurance of safety for each and every worker or that reduces exposures to the lowest level feasible. The Government interprets "feasible" as meaning technologically achievable at a cost that would not impair the viability of the industries subject to the regulation. The respondent industry representatives, on the other hand, argue that the Court of Appeals was correct in holding that the "reasonably necessary and appropriate" language of § 3(8), along with the feasibility requirement of § 6(b)(5), requires the Agency to quantify both the costs and the benefits of a proposed rule and to conclude that they are roughly commensurate.

In our view, it is not necessary to decide whether either the Government or industry is entirely correct. For we think it is clear that § 3(8) does apply to all permanent standards promulgated under the Act and that it requires the Secretary, before issuing any standard, to determine that it is reasonably necessary and appropriate to remedy a significant risk of material health impairment. Only after the Secretary has made the threshold determination that such a risk exists with respect to a toxic substance, would it be necessary to decide whether § 6(b)(5) requires him to select the most protective standard he can consistent with economic and technological feasibility, or whether, as respondents argue, the benefits of the regulation must be commensurate with the costs of its implementation. Because the Secretary did not make the required threshold finding in this case, we have no occasion to determine whether costs must be weighed against benefits in an appropriate case.

Under the Government's view, § 3(8), if it has any substantive content at all, merely requires OSHA to issue standards that are reasonably calculated to produce a safer or more healthy work environment. Apart from this minimal requirement of rationality, the Government argues that § 3(8) imposes no limits on the Agency's power, and thus would not prevent it from requiring employers to do whatever would be "reasonably necessary" to eliminate all risks of any harm from their workplaces. With respect to toxic substances and harmful physical agents, the Government takes an even more extreme position. Relying on § 6(b)(5)'s direction to set a standard "which most adequately assures * * * that no employee will suffer material impairment of health or functional capacity," the Government contends that the Secretary is required to impose standards that either guarantee workplaces that are free from any risk of material health impairment, however small, or that come as close as possible to doing so without ruining entire industries.

If the purpose of the statute were to eliminate completely and with absolute certainty any risk of serious harm, we would agree that it would be proper for the Secretary to interpret §§ 3(8) and 6(b)(5) in this fashion. But we think it is clear that the statute was not designed to require employers to provide absolutely risk-free workplaces whenever it is technologically feasible to do so, so long as the cost is not great enough to destroy an entire industry. Rather, both the language and structure of the Act, as well as its legislative history, indicate that it was intended to require the elimination, as far as feasible, of significant risks of harm.

By empowering the Secretary to promulgate standards that are "reasonably necessary or appropriate to provide safe or healthful employment and places of employment," the Act implies that, before promulgating any standard, the Secretary must make a finding that the workplaces in question are not safe. But "safe" is not the equivalent of "risk-free." There are many activities that we engage in every day—such as driving a car or even breathing city air—that entail some risk of accident or material health impairment; nevertheless, few people would consider these activities "unsafe." Similarly, a workplace can hardly be considered "unsafe" unless it threatens the workers with a significant risk of harm.

Therefore, before he can promulgate *any* permanent health or safety standard, the Secretary is required to make a threshold finding that a place of employment is unsafe—in the sense that significant risks are present and can be eliminated or lessened by a change in practices. This requirement applies to permanent standards promulgated pursuant to § 6(b)(5), as well as to other types of permanent standards. For there is no reason why § 3(8)'s definition of a standard should not be deemed incorporated by reference into § 6(b)(5). The standards promulgated pursuant to § 6(b)(5) are just one species of the genus of standards governed by the basic requirement. That section repeatedly uses the term "standard" without suggesting any exception from, or qualification of, the general definition; on the contrary, it directs the Secretary to select "*the* standard"—that is to say, one of various possible alternatives that satisfy the basic definition in § 3(8)—that is most protective. Moreover, requiring the Secretary to make a threshold finding of significant risk is consistent with the scope of the regulatory power granted to him by § 6(b)(5), which empowers the Secretary to promulgate standards, not for chemicals and physical agents generally, but for "*toxic* chemicals" and "*harmful* physical agents."

* * *

Given the conclusion that the Act empowers the Secretary to promulgate health and safety standards only where a significant risk of harm exists, the critical issue becomes how to define and allocate the burden of proving the significance of the risk in a case such as this, where scientific knowledge is imperfect and the precise quantification of risks is therefore impossible. The Agency's position is that there is substantial evidence in the record to support its conclusion that there is no absolutely safe level for a carcinogen and that, therefore, the burden is properly on industry to prove, apparently beyond a shadow of a doubt, that there *is* a safe level for benzene exposure. The Agency argues that, because of the uncertainties in this area, any other approach would render it helpless, forcing it to wait for the leukemia deaths that it believes are likely to occur before taking any regulatory action.

We disagree. As we read the statute, the burden was on the Agency to show, on the basis of substantial evidence, that it is at least more likely than not that long-term exposure to 10 ppm of benzene presents a significant risk of material health impairment. Ordinarily, it is the proponent of a rule or order who has the burden of proof in administrative proceedings. In some cases involving toxic substances, Congress has shifted the burden of proving that a particular substance is safe onto the party opposing the proposed rule. The fact that Congress did not follow this course in enacting OSHA indicates that it intended the Agency to bear the normal burden of establishing the need for a proposed standard.

In this case OSHA did not even attempt to carry its burden of proof. The closest it came to making a finding that benzene presented a significant risk of harm in the workplace was its statement that the benefits to be derived from lowering the permissible exposure level from 10 to 1 ppm were "likely" to be "appreciable." The Court of Appeals held that this finding was not supported by substantial evidence. Of greater importance, even if it were supported by substantial evidence, such a finding would not be sufficient to satisfy the Agency's obligations under the Act.

* * *

Contrary to the Government's contentions, imposing a burden on the Agency of demonstrating a significant risk of harm will not strip it of its ability to regulate carcinogens, nor will it require the Agency to wait for deaths to occur before taking any action. First, the requirement that a "significant" risk be identified is not a mathematical straitjacket. It is the Agency's responsibility to determine, in the first instance, what it considers to be a "significant" risk. Some risks are plainly acceptable and others are plainly unacceptable. If, for example, the odds are one in a billion that a person will die from cancer by taking a drink of chlorinated water, the risk clearly could not be considered significant. On the other hand, if the odds are one in a thousand that regular inhalation of gasoline vapors that are two percent benzene will be fatal, a reasonable person might well consider the risk significant and take appropriate steps to decrease or eliminate it. Although the Agency has no duty to calculate the exact probability of harm, it does have an obligation to find that a significant risk is present before it can characterize a place of employment as "unsafe."

Second, OSHA is not required to support its finding that a significant risk exists with anything approaching scientific certainty. Although the Agency's findings must be supported by substantial evidence, § 6(b)(5) specifically allows the Secretary to regulate on the basis of the "best available evidence." As several courts of appeals have held, this provision requires a reviewing court to give OSHA some leeway where its findings must be made on the frontiers of scientific knowledge. Thus, so long as they are supported by a body of reputable scientific thought, the Agency is free to use conservative assumptions in interpreting the data with respect to carcinogens, risking error on the side of over-protection rather than under-protection.

Finally, the record in this case and OSHA's own rulings on other carcinogens indicate that there are a number of ways in which the Agency can make a rational judgment about the relative significance of the risks associated with exposure to a particular carcinogen.

It should also be noted that, in setting a permissible exposure level in reliance on less-than-perfect methods, OSHA would have the benefit of a backstop in the form of monitoring and medical testing. Thus, if OSHA properly determined that the permissible exposure limit should be set at 5 ppm, it could still require monitoring and medical testing for employees exposed to lower levels. By doing so, it could keep a constant check on the validity of the assumptions made in developing the permissible exposure limit, giving it a sound evidentiary basis for decreasing the limit if it was initially set too high. Moreover, in this way it could ensure that workers who were unusually susceptible to benzene could be removed from exposure before they had suffered any permanent damage.

Because our review of this case has involved a more detailed examination of the record than is customary, it must be emphasized that we have neither made any factual determinations of our own, nor have we rejected any factual findings made by the Secretary. We express no opinion on what factual findings this record might support, either on the basis of empirical evidence or on the basis of expert testimony; nor do we express any opinion on the more difficult question of what factual determinations would warrant a conclusion that significant risks are present which make promulgation of a new standard reasonably necessary or appropriate. The standard must, of course, be supported by the findings actually made by the Secretary, not merely by findings that we believe he might have made.

In this case the record makes it perfectly clear that the Secretary relied squarely on a special policy for carcinogens that imposed the burden on industry of proving the existence of a safe level of exposure, thereby avoiding the Secretary's threshold responsibility of establishing the need for more stringent standards. In so interpreting his statutory authority, the Secretary exceeded his power.

* * *

The judgment of the Court of Appeals remanding the petition for review to the Secretary for further proceedings is affirmed.

It is so ordered.

■ [CHIEF JUSTICE BURGER filed a separate concurring opinion.]

■ [JUSTICE POWELL filed a separate opinion concurring in part and in the judgment.]

■ MR. JUSTICE REHNQUIST, concurring in the judgment.

* * *

I believe that the legislative history demonstrates that the feasibility requirement, as employed in § 6(b)(5), is a legislative mirage, appearing to some members but not to others, and assuming any form desired by the beholder. I am unable to accept MR. JUSTICE MARSHALL'S argument that, by changing the phrasing of § 6(b)(5) from "most adequately and feasibly assures" to "most adequately assures, to the extent feasible," the Senate injected into that section something that wasn't already there.

■ MR. JUSTICE MARSHALL, with whom MR. JUSTICE BRENNAN, MR. JUSTICE WHITE, and MR. JUSTICE BLACKMUN join, dissenting.

* * *

The plurality is insensitive to three factors which, in my view, make judicial review of occupational safety and health standards under the substantial evidence test particularly difficult. First, the issues often reach a high level of technical complexity. In such circumstances the courts are required to immerse themselves in matters to which they are unaccustomed by training or experience. Second, the factual issues with which the Secretary must deal are frequently not subject to any definitive resolution. Often "the factual finger points, it does not conclude." Causal connections and theoretical extrapolations may be uncertain. Third, when the question involves determination of the acceptable level of risk, the ultimate decision must necessarily be based on considerations of policy as well as empirically verifiable facts. Factual determinations can at most define the risk in some statistical way; the judgment whether that risk is tolerable cannot be based solely on a resolution of the facts.

The decision to take action in conditions of uncertainty bears little resemblance to the sort of empirically verifiable factual conclusions to which the substantial evidence test is normally applied. Such decisions were not intended to be unreviewable; they too must be scrutinized to ensure that the Secretary has acted reasonably and within the boundaries set by Congress. But a reviewing court must be mindful of the limited nature of its role. It must recognize that the ultimate decision cannot be based solely on determinations of fact, and that those factual conclusions that have been reached are ones which the courts are ill-equipped to resolve on their own.

NOTES AND QUESTIONS

1. Section 3(8) defines the term "occupational safety and health standard" as "a standard which requires conditions, or the adoption or use of one or more practices, means, methods, operations, or processes, reasonably necessary *or* appropriate to provide safe or healthful employment and places of employment." (emphasis added). Justice Stevens misquotes this section as requiring that standards be "reasonably necessary *and* appropriate." How, if at all, does this interpretation affect the plurality's theory of significant risk?

2. What is the authority for Justice Stevens' "significant risk" and "more likely than not" requirements? Did Congress intend section 3(8) to have the importance Justice Stevens attributes to it?

3. When is a risk significant? Does Justice Stevens help to illustrate the concept?

> Having ordered OSHA to apply a "significant risk" threshold test, the court gave very little indication of how the agency should go about meeting its burden, and the one example that the plurality opinion provided, demonstrated rather clearly that the author of the opinion did not understand the concept of environmental risk assessment. Justice Stevens, by way of explanation, offered the following example:

> "Some risks are plainly acceptable and others are plainly unacceptable. If, for example, the odds are one in 1 billion that a person will die from cancer by taking a drink of chlorinated water, the risk clearly could not be considered significant. On the other hand, if the odds are one in a thousand that regular inhalation of gasoline vapors that are two percent benzene will be fatal, a reasonable person might well consider the risk significant and take appropriate steps to decrease or eliminate it."

> The example is an ideal illustration of a confused approach to risk assessment in the public health context. Drinking chlorinated water is an activity engaged in by practically everyone in American society. If 250 million Americans drink 4 glasses of water a day and are exposed to a 1 in 1 billion risk each time, then an average of 1 cancer per day will result. This amounts to about 365 cancers per year, a number that reasonable people might find "significant."

> Justice Stevens's example of a significant risk is harder to address from a public health perspective, because he neglected to provide two important pieces of information: the length of exposure that would result in a cancer and the number of persons who regularly breath gasoline vapors. If we assume that exposure for a year presents the 1 in 1,000 risk and that 2 employees in each of the approximately 200,000 service stations in America are regularly exposed to benzene (an estimate that is, by the way, on the high side), then a 1 in 1,000 risk would yield 400 cancers per year, a number that is not meaningfully different from the 365 cancers per year that Justice Stevens found to be clearly insignificant.

Thomas O. McGarity & Sidney A. Shapiro, Workers at Risk: The Failed Promise of the Occupational Safety and Health Administration 56–57 (1993).

4. Who should have the burden of proof when the health effects of occupational hazards are uncertain? Should OSHA have to prove that there are risks or should the industry have to prove the absence of risks? OSHA adopted the policy that there are no known safe levels at which humans can be exposed to a carcinogen, and therefore exposures must be reduced to their lowest feasible levels. How did the plurality view this policy? What does Justice Marshall think about the burden of proof?

5. In National Cottonseed Prods. Ass'n v. Brock, 825 F.2d 482 (D.C.Cir.1987), cert. denied, 485 U.S. 1020 (1988), the D.C. Circuit held that the Secretary's failure to find that dust in cottonseed mills presents a significant risk of harm will not prevent the agency from requiring medical surveillance of employees. The *Cottonseed* court acknowledged that the Supreme Court in the *Benzene* case had required that OSHA make a threshold finding of significant risk in promulgating standards for toxic substances. The court, however, relied on dicta in *Benzene* that the agency may require medical monitoring as a backstop to ensure that workers will not be exposed to dangerous conditions.

In American Textile Mfrs. Inst., Inc. v. Donovan (The Cotton Dust Case), 452 U.S. 490 (1981), the Supreme Court addressed the issue of cost-benefit analysis it had avoided the year before when it decided *The Benzene Case.* In a five-to-three decision, the Court rejected the industry argument that the Act requires the use of cost-benefit analysis. Relying on the plain meaning of the word "feasible" in section 6(b)(5) as "capable of being done," the Court held that imposing a cost-benefit requirement would be inconsistent with the mandate of Congress.

> Congress itself defined the basic relationship between costs and benefits, by placing the "benefit" of worker health above all considerations save those making attainment of this "benefit" unachievable. * * * Thus, cost-benefit analysis by OSHA is not required by the statute because feasibility analysis is.

452 U.S. at 509 (footnote omitted).

The Court observed that when Congress has intended that an agency engage in cost-benefit analysis, it has clearly indicated such an intent on the face of the statute. Neither the language of the Act nor its legislative history indicates such a congressional intent. Moreover, the general definitional language of section 3(8) cannot be used to impose a cost-benefit requirement and thereby "eviscerate" the "to the extent feasible" language of section 6(b)(5).

According to the majority opinion of Justice Brennan, "feasible," as used in section 6(b)(5), includes economic feasibility. After reviewing the record, the Court concluded that the D.C. Circuit did not err in holding that the Secretary's finding that compliance with the cotton dust standard was economically feasible was supported by substantial evidence. Even though no specific economic studies were performed on the final standard, there were studies that showed that compliance with a stricter and more costly standard was feasible.

The five-Justice majority in *Cotton Dust* consisted of the four dissenters from *Benzene* and Justice Stevens. Justice Powell took no part in the decision. Justice Stewart filed a separate dissent. Justice Rehnquist, joined by Chief Justice Burger, dissented along the lines of his dissent in *Benzene*.

NOTES AND QUESTIONS

1. Professor William Rodgers has suggested that economic cost consideration models exist on a continuum from the least to the most rigorous:

> (a) *cost-oblivious*—adoption of standards without regard for any cost-benefit consideration because of a moral and policy judgment that concerns about efficiency are inappropriate in some areas of regulation.

> (b) *cost-effective*—use of a formal analysis to determine the most efficient means for attaining a regulatory goal.

> (c) *cost sensitive*—costs, along with other economic factors, must be considered by the agency, but not necessarily with a formal cost-benefit analysis.

> (d) *strict cost-benefit*—regulatory activity is limited to those areas where the calculable costs do not exceed the calculable benefits.

Based on the *Cotton Dust* case, which model, if any, is OSHA required to follow? Which of these models do you believe is most appropriate for OSHA? Why? See William H. Rodgers, Benefits, Costs, and Risks: Oversight of Health and Environmental Decisionmaking, 4 Harv.Envtl.L.Rev. 191 (1980).

2. In many instances the cost-benefit issue arises in the context of the method of compliance to be used. Engineering controls (e.g., ventilation systems) are much more expensive than personal protective equipment (e.g., respirators). According to the industrial hygiene principle of hierarchy of controls, however, engineering controls are preferred because they control a

hazard at its source. Respirators often do not protect workers adequately; they may fit poorly and need frequent cleaning; they often are hot and uncomfortable, encouraging some workers to remove them.

3. EMERGENCY TEMPORARY STANDARDS

Section 6(c)(1) provides that if the Secretary determines that employees are "exposed to grave danger from exposure to substances or agents determined to be toxic or physically harmful or from new hazards," an emergency temporary standard (ETS) may be issued. These standards, promulgated without detailed rulemaking, are effective immediately upon publication in the Federal Register. Under section 6(c)(3) an ETS may remain in effect for only six months; thereafter, the Secretary must promulgate a permanent standard under section 6(b). In this event the ETS serves as the proposed rule.

In 1983, OSHA promulgated an ETS for asbestos, lowering the permissible exposure limit (PEL) from 2.0 fibers per cubic centimeter (f/cc) to 0.5 f/cc. The ETS was based on a new quantitative risk assessment showing that reducing the PEL for six months would save 40 to 80 lives. OSHA had performed a detailed quantitative risk assessment and developed a dose-response curve from epidemiological studies of exposed workers rather than by relying on animal data. This assessment was made specifically to satisfy the "significant risk" requirement of the Supreme Court's *Benzene* decision and the "grave danger" language of section 6(c). A group of asbestos products manufacturers sought judicial review of the ETS in the Fifth Circuit.

In Asbestos Info. Ass'n/N. Am. v. OSHA, 727 F.2d 415 (5th Cir. 1984), the Fifth Circuit held that the ETS was invalid and stayed its enforcement. The court's analysis focused on whether OSHA had proved the need to adopt an ETS for asbestos rather than modifying the existing standard after notice and comment rulemaking. The Fifth Circuit was troubled by the possibility of inaccuracy in using risk assessment for a six-month exposure period. Moreover, the court noted that the mathematical extrapolations had not been the subject of "peer reviews." "Precisely because the data has not been scrutinized, however, the court has particular interest in having access to both favorable and unfavorable peer reviews." Id. at 421 n. 15.

Did the court confuse "peer review" with "notice and comment" rulemaking? All of the studies relied upon by OSHA were "peer reviewed"—they were scrutinized and analyzed by other scientific experts. The type of peer review deemed essential by the court is the right of interested parties to comment upon and rebut OSHA's evidence. Such a procedure, specified under section 6(b), was specifically rejected by Congress in section 6(c). Indeed, the entire purpose of the ETS provision was to avoid the lengthy rulemaking that would preclude a swift, emergency regulation. Has the Fifth Circuit, in effect, written section 6(c) out of the statute?

Each year between 8200 and 9700 people die from asbestos exposure and the total will continue for years based on the long latency period. By the year 2000, more than 200,000 people had died from asbestos exposure since the 1940s. The court found that the Secretary's estimate that the ETS would save 80 lives in six months was too high. Should it matter whether the actual number is 60 or 40 or 35?

C. ENFORCEMENT

The threat of an OSHA inspection and citation is intended to encourage employers to meet their preinspection duty to comply with the Act. For noncomplying employers, the enforcement process involves the government's effort to penalize prior dereliction and to require the prompt correction of existing hazards.

OSHA inspections may be divided into four categories, which have been assigned the following priority: (1) imminent dangers; (2) fatality and catastrophe investigations; (3) investigation of employee complaints; and (4) regional programmed inspections. The first three categories are referred to as unprogrammed inspections because they are scheduled quickly in response to a particular concern. The fourth category, programmed inspections, concentrates on establishments in high hazard industries and with large numbers of employees.

Brennan v. OSHRC (Republic Creosoting Co.)
501 F.2d 1196 (7th Cir. 1974).

■ PELL, CIRCUIT JUDGE.

The Secretary of Labor appeals from a decision of the Occupational Safety and Health Review Commission, which found that the respondent Republic Creosoting Company had not committed any violations of the Occupational Safety and Health Act. The underlying facts are not in dispute on appeal, these facts being either stipulated by the parties or testified to at the hearing before the administrative law judge.

Republic Creosoting Company (Republic), a division of Reilly Tar and Chemical Corporation, operated five railroad tie marshalling yards in southern Indiana, including one in Jeffersonville, Indiana. Despite its name, Republic did not at the Jeffersonville yard engage in the creosoting process but it did, upon the acquisition of newly cut or "green" ties, undertake the first step of seasoning or drying the wood for its eventual use. Republic ultimately resold the ties to railroad companies. These ties weighed approximately 150 to 235 pounds each.

The truckloads of ties arriving at the Jeffersonville yard were secured by chains to the transporting trucks. In twenty to twenty-five percent of the truckloads, the ties were bound together into packages, with each package held together by a single narrow steel band. Each package contained 25 to 45 ties, five ties high, five to nine ties across and one tie in length. The packaged ties were loaded lengthwise along the length of the truck, generally one package high and two packages across.

Republic unloaded the truckloads of banded ties in the following manner. The truckdriver ordinarily removed the chains holding the packages of ties onto the truck. The unloader operator (an employee of Republic) then moved the unloader (a forklift truck) into position so that it supported a package of banded ties. Only after the unloader was supporting a package, did the truckdriver, standing on an adjacent package, cut the band on the package to be unloaded. Under no circumstances would the band be cut before the unloader was in position. The unloader then removed the loosened ties from the truck. This process was repeated package by package until the truck was completely unloaded. During the entire operation, all Republic employees, other than the unloader operator, remained a safe distance from the truck.

On July 9, 1971, a truckload of banded ties was delivered to the Jeffersonville yard. Raymond Davis, a new employee working his fourth day for Republic, was present at the yard on that date. Davis had been hired to sort and stack ties after the completion of the unloading process. The unloader operator, James Wiseman, suggested to Davis on the day in question that he come to the unloading so that he could help sort the ties after they had been unloaded. Davis had never witnessed the unloading operation before nor had it been described to him. The field superintendent, Wallace Worley, however, when hiring Davis had told him "not to get around no trucks; the unloader done all the unloading."

Davis was originally standing some distance from the truck and Worley and Wiseman expected him to remain there until the unloading was completed. The chains had, at this time, already been removed from the truck but the unloader had not yet been moved into position. Without being ordered to do so and without informing anyone of what he intended to do, Davis went up to the truck and while standing on the ground next to the truck, cut the steel band on a package of ties with an ax. As a result, five of the ties fell on Davis, fatally injuring him.

On July 30, 1971, a compliance officer for the Secretary of Labor conducted an inspection of the Jeffersonville yard. On the basis of the inspection, the Secretary issued two citations to Republic for alleged violations of the Occupational Safety and Health Act: a "Citation for Serious Violation" based on the Davis accident; a "Citation" based on the lack of warning signs and barricades around the piles of ties in the yard.

Republic filed a notice of contest and a hearing was held before an administrative law judge, who affirmed both citations but raised the second citation from a nonserious to a serious violation. The total penalty imposed was $1300.

Republic petitioned for discretionary review by the Occupational Safety and Health Review Commission. The Commission (with one

Commissioner dissenting) reversed the administrative law judge and vacated the citations.

* * *

The citation issued to Republic on the basis of the Davis accident alleged a serious violation of the "general duty clause" of the Act, which provides:

> "Each employer (1) shall furnish to each of his employees employment and a place of employment which are free from recognized hazards that are causing or are likely to cause death or serious physical harm to his employees. * * * "

A "serious violation" is present only where there is "a substantial probability that death or serious physical harm could result from a condition which exists or from one or more practices, means, methods, operations, or processes which have been adopted or are in use, in such place of employment unless the employer did not, and could not with the exercise of reasonable diligence, know of the presence of the violations." Republic does not dispute that the cutting of the band before the unloader was in place gave rise to "a substantial probability that death or serious physical harm could result." The issue on appeal is whether an employer, using reasonable diligence, would have foreseen the danger in question.

The Secretary contends that where an inexperienced, untrained employee is placed at the site of a potentially dangerous operation, the employer should foresee that the employee is likely, because of his ignorance of the safe procedures, to injure himself. Davis, the Secretary points out, was a new employee, working his fourth day for Republic. He had neither seen the unloading operation nor had it described to him. Davis was, nonetheless, asked by the unloader operator to be present at the place of the unloading. Since Davis did not know what the safe procedure for unloading the ties was, it was foreseeable, the Secretary argues, that Davis would do something unsafe and, thereby, injure himself—even if the exact nature of his unsafe actions, i.e., cutting the band, could not have been foreseen. The fact that Davis was not assigned to assist in the actual unloading operation itself is irrelevant, according to the Secretary, since Davis was requested to be present at the unloading site. In such a situation, it is argued, the employee should be instructed in the safe procedure for the operation which is going on in his presence.

The Commission rejected the Secretary's argument on the theory that the Act does not require that a new employee always be trained in proper procedures for a task simply because he is required to be present at the place of the operation in question in which he is not a participant. We agree with the Commission's interpretation of the Act. The Act clearly requires that, for a serious-violation citation to be sustained, the danger must be one of which the employer knew or, with reasonable diligence, could have known. Whether training is necessary and the amount of any training required will depend on a number of factors, such as the experience of the employee in the particular field of work, the extent of the employee's participation in the operation in question, and the complexity and danger involved in the operation. Where an employee is directly participating in a job, the employer may well, as the Commission noted, have a duty under the Act to instruct him on the safe procedure for handling the job. On the other hand, the Commission accurately recognized that training may be unnecessary for an employee who is wholly disassociated with the operation in question and who would not be foreseeably exposed to danger.

The instruction given to Davis was general but explicit and unambiguous. Worley testified: "I told him not to get around no trucks; the unloader done all the unloading." We find that, under these circumstances, this instruction was sufficient to satisfy the employer's duty under the Act. It is true that the unloading could be dangerous if the proper procedure was not followed. Davis' relationship with the trucks and the unloading, however, was very simple: he merely had to stay away from the trucks. This he was clearly told to do. The fact that he did not know the correct procedure for unloading a truck is immaterial since *his own* position with respect to the trucks had been stated in no uncertain terms: he was to stay away. In this situation, we agree with the Commission that a reasonably diligent employer would not have foreseen that Davis would injure himself.

NOTES AND QUESTIONS

1.   Would there have been a violation if Davis had not been told anything?

2.   In what possible ways could Davis have construed the warning he was given? In other words, aside from safety considerations, why might he be told not to do any unloading?

3.   Should the employer be required to tell the employee *why* he should not get too close to the trucks? How important a consideration is the employee's experience, training, skill, and degree of supervision? What about the severity of the hazard?

4.   In essence, the employer's position was that the warning was adequate and that it took all necessary steps to eliminate *preventable* hazards. Therefore, the employee's act of cutting the bonds was unpreventable employee misconduct. Although the issue was raised here in the context of a section 5(a)(1) violation, the identical defense is recognized under section 5(a)(2). According to the Commission, an employer must satisfy a four-part test to invoke the unpreventable employee misconduct defense: (1) the employer has established work rules designed to prevent the violation; (2) it has adequately communicated these rules to its employees; (3) it has taken steps to discover violations; and (4) it has effectively enforced the rules when violations have been discovered. Jensen Constr. Co., 7 OSHC 1477, 1979 OSHD ¶ 23,664 (1979).

5. Unpreventable employee misconduct is the most important substantive defense, but there are many others, including vagueness of the standard, infeasibility of compliance, and that compliance would cause a greater hazard. For a discussion of these and other defenses, see Mark A. Rothstein, Occupational Safety and Health Law §§ 5:19 to 5:34 (2020). Common law defenses, such as contributory negligence and assumption of the risk do not apply to OSHA. Why?

6. During an OSHA inspection of a stevedoring company the compliance officer observed nearly all of the longshore workers without hard hats. (OSHA requires hard hats to protect against serious head injuries from falling objects.) In defending against the subsequent OSHA citation under section 5(a)(2), the employer claimed that it did all that it could to obtain compliance, but the employees refused. Specifically, the employer had furnished the required hard hats, had encouraged their use at regular safety meetings, had posted hard hat signs, had used payroll envelope stuffers to advocate hard hat wearing, and had placed hard hat safety messages on hiring tapes. The employer feared that sanctioning employees would cause a wildcat strike, which had already occurred at another port. Is the employer in violation of the Act? What else should the employer have to do? Is there any way for OSHA to cite the *employees?* Should the workers be permitted to assume the risk? See Atlantic & Gulf Stevedores, Inc. v. OSHRC, 534 F.2d 541 (3d Cir. 1976). (no authority to cite employees, but court may consider refusal by employees to wear hard hats, despite employer's best efforts, when reviewing sanctions against employer).

7. Section 5(b) of the OSH Act provides that "Each employee shall comply with occupational safety and health standards and all rules, regulations, and orders issued pursuant to this Act which are applicable to his own actions and conduct." This provision, however, is not enforceable by the government. In Atlantic & Gulf Stevedores, Inc. v. OSHRC, 534 F.2d 541 (3d Cir. 1976), the court held that neither OSHA nor the Commission could sanction disobedient employees nor order their compliance. Employers have the duty to ensure the compliance of their employees.

Although enforcement action may not be directed at them, employees are the intended beneficiaries of the Act's protections. Congress sought to ensure employee participation at all stages of OSHA proceedings. At the rulemaking stage, employees may petition for adoption of a standard (section 6(b)(1)), serve on standards advisory committees (section 7(b)), and seek judicial review of new standards (section 6(f)). At the enforcement stage, employees may file a complaint with OSHA (section 8(f)(1)), bring a mandamus action in district court to compel an inspection when there are imminent dangers (section 13(d)), participate in the inspection tour (section 8(e)), and have the employer post copies of all citations (section 9(b)). At the adjudicatory stage, employees may file a notice of contest to the abatement period in the citation (section 10(c)), elect party status in contests initiated by the employer (section 10(c)), and seek judicial review of Commission decisions (section 11(a)).

D. NON-OSHA SAFETY AND HEALTH LAW

Section 4(b)(4) of the Act provides in pertinent part:

Nothing in this Act shall be construed to supersede or in any manner affect any workmen's compensation law or to enlarge or diminish or affect in any manner the common law or statutory rights, duties, or liabilities of employers and employees. * * *

Despite this language, the OSH Act has had significant effects on a number of areas of employment law. Some of these areas are discussed in other chapters of this book. For example, wage and hour law requirements for the payment of wages for time spent donning protective gear are discussed in Chapter 5; the OSH Act's effect on workers' compensation and personal injury litigation are discussed in Chapter 9; and wrongful discharge based on safety and health complaints is discussed in Chapter 10. The issues surrounding collective bargaining for safety and health are beyond the scope of this book.

Among the most contentious issues are the real (or merely alleged) conflicts between antidiscrimination laws and the OSH Act. Public policy supports equal employment opportunity, but it also supports safe and healthful workplaces. In cases involving claims of discrimination based on disability, gender, and religion the courts have been called upon to decide how to balance these interests.

International Union, UAW v. Johnson Controls, Inc.
499 U.S. 187 (1991).

■ JUSTICE BLACKMUN delivered the opinion of the Court.

In this case we are concerned with an employer's gender-based fetal-protection policy. May an employer exclude a fertile female employee from certain jobs because of its concern for the health of the fetus the woman might conceive?

I.

Respondent Johnson Controls, Inc., manufactures batteries. In the manufacturing process, the element lead is a primary ingredient. Occupational exposure to lead entails health risks, including the risk of harm to any fetus carried by a female employee.

Before the Civil Rights Act of 1964 became law, Johnson Controls did not employ any woman in a battery-manufacturing job. In June 1977, however, it announced its first official policy concerning its employment of women in lead-exposure work:

"[P]rotection of the health of the unborn child is the immediate and direct responsibility of the prospective parents. While the medical profession and the company can support them in the exercise of this responsibility, it cannot assume it for them without simultaneously infringing their rights as persons.

* * *

"* * * Since not all women who can become mothers wish to become mothers (or will become mothers), it would appear to be illegal discrimination to treat all who are capable of pregnancy as though they will become pregnant."

Consistent with that view, Johnson Controls "stopped short of excluding women capable of bearing children from lead exposure," but emphasized that a woman who expected to have a child should not choose a job in which she would have such exposure. The company also required a woman who wished to be considered for employment to sign a statement that she had been advised of the risk of having a child while she was exposed to lead. The statement informed the woman that although there was evidence "that women exposed to lead have a higher rate of abortion," this evidence was "not as clear * * * as the relationship between cigarette smoking and cancer," but that it was, "medically speaking, just good sense not to run that risk if you want children and do not want to expose the unborn child to risk, however small * * *."

Five years later, in 1982, Johnson Controls shifted from a policy of warning to a policy of exclusion. Between 1979 and 1983, eight employees became pregnant while maintaining blood lead levels in excess of 30 micrograms per deciliter. This appeared to be the critical level noted by the Occupational Health and Safety Administration (OSHA) for a worker who was planning to have a family. The company responded by announcing a broad exclusion of women from jobs that exposed them to lead:

> "* * * [I]t is [Johnson Controls'] policy that women who are pregnant or who are capable of bearing children will not be placed into jobs involving lead exposure or which could expose them to lead through the exercise of job bidding, bumping, transfer or promotion rights."

The policy defined "women * * * capable of bearing children" as "[a]ll women except those whose inability to bear children is medically documented." It further stated that an unacceptable work station was one where, "over the past year," an employee had recorded a blood lead level of more than 30 micrograms per deciliter or the work site had yielded an air sample containing a lead level in excess of 30 micrograms per cubic meter.

II.

In April 1984, petitioners filed in the United States District Court for the Eastern District of Wisconsin a class action challenging Johnson Controls' fetal-protection policy as sex discrimination that violated Title VII of the Civil Rights Act of 1964, as amended. Among the individual plaintiffs were petitioners Mary Craig, who had chosen to be sterilized in order to avoid losing her job, Elsie Nason, a 50-year-old divorcee, who had suffered a loss in compensation when she was transferred out of a job where she was exposed to lead, and Donald Penney, who had been denied a request for a leave of absence for the purpose of lowering his lead level because he intended to become a father. Upon stipulation of the parties, the District Court certified a class consisting of "all past, present and future production and maintenance employees" in United Auto Workers bargaining units at nine of Johnson Controls' plants "who have been and continue to be affected by [the employer's] Fetal Protection Policy implemented in 1982."

The District Court granted summary judgment for defendant-respondent Johnson Controls.

* * *

The Court of Appeals for the Seventh Circuit, sitting en banc, affirmed the summary judgment by a 7-to-4 vote. The majority held that the proper standard for evaluating the fetal-protection policy was the defense of business necessity; that Johnson Controls was entitled to summary judgment under that defense; and that even if the proper standard was a BFOQ, Johnson Controls still was entitled to summary judgment.

* * *

III.

The bias in Johnson Controls' policy is obvious. Fertile men, but not fertile women, are given a choice as to whether they wish to risk their reproductive health for a particular job. Section 703(a) of the Civil Rights Act of 1964 prohibits sex-based classifications in terms and conditions of employment, in hiring and discharging decisions, and in other employment decisions that adversely affect an employee's status. Respondent's fetal-protection policy explicitly discriminates against women on the basis of their sex. The policy excludes women with childbearing capacity from lead-exposed jobs and so creates a facial classification based on gender. Respondent assumes as much in its brief before this Court.

Nevertheless, the Court of Appeals assumed, as did the two appellate courts who already had confronted the issue, that sex-specific fetal-protection policies do not involve facial discrimination. These courts analyzed the policies as though they were facially neutral, and had only a discriminatory effect upon the employment opportunities of women. Consequently, the courts looked to see if each employer in question had established that its policy was justified as a business necessity. The business necessity standard is more lenient for the employer than the statutory BFOQ defense. The Court of Appeals here went one step further and invoked the burden-shifting framework set forth in Wards Cove Packing Co. v. Atonio, 490 U.S. 642 (1989), thus requiring petitioners to bear the burden of persuasion on all questions. The court assumed that because the asserted reason for the sex-based exclusion (protecting women's unconceived offspring) was ostensibly benign, the policy was not sex-based discrimination. That assumption, however, was incorrect.

First, Johnson Controls' policy classifies on the basis of gender and childbearing capacity, rather than fertility alone. Respondent does not seek to protect the unconceived children of all its employees. Despite evidence in the record about the debilitating effect of lead exposure on the male reproductive system, Johnson Controls is concerned only with the harms that may befall the unborn offspring of its female employees. Accordingly, it appears that Johnson Controls would have lost in the Eleventh Circuit under Hayes because its policy does not "effectively and equally protec[t] the offspring of all employees." This Court faced a conceptually similar situation in Phillips v. Martin Marietta Corp., 400 U.S. 542 (1971), and found sex discrimination because the policy established "one hiring policy for women and another for men—each having pre-school-age children." Johnson Controls' policy is facially discriminatory because it requires only a female employee to produce proof that she is not capable of reproducing.

Our conclusion is bolstered by the Pregnancy Discrimination Act of 1978 (PDA), 42 U.S.C. § 2000e(k), in which Congress explicitly provided that, for purposes of Title VII, discrimination "on the basis of sex" includes discrimination "because of or on the basis of pregnancy, childbirth, or related medical conditions."[3] "The Pregnancy Discrimination Act has now made clear that, for all Title VII purposes, discrimination based on a woman's pregnancy is, on its face, discrimination because of her sex." In its use of the words "capable of bearing children" in the 1982 policy statement as the criterion for exclusion, Johnson Controls explicitly classifies on the basis of potential for pregnancy. Under the PDA, such a classification must be regarded, for Title VII purposes, in the same light as explicit sex discrimination. Respondent has chosen to treat all its female employees as potentially pregnant; that choice evinces discrimination on the basis of sex.

We concluded above that Johnson Controls' policy is not neutral because it does not apply to the reproductive capacity of the company's male employees in the same way as it applies to that of the females. Moreover, the absence of a malevolent motive does not convert a facially discriminatory policy into a neutral policy with a discriminatory effect. Whether an employment practice involves disparate treatment through explicit facial discrimination does not depend on why the employer discriminates but rather on the explicit terms of the discrimination.

---

[3]   The Act added subsection (k) to § 701 of the Civil Rights Act of 1964 and reads in pertinent part:

> "The terms 'because of sex' or 'on the basis of sex' (in Title VII) include, but are not limited to, because of or on the basis of pregnancy, childbirth, or related medical conditions; and women affected by pregnancy, childbirth, or related medical conditions shall be treated the same for all employment-related purposes as other persons not so affected but similar in their ability or inability to work * * *."

* * *

In sum, Johnson Controls' policy "does not pass the simple test of whether the evidence shows 'treatment of a person in a manner which but for that person's sex would be different.' " We hold that Johnson Controls' fetal-protection policy is sex discrimination forbidden under Title VII unless respondent can establish that sex is a "bona fide occupational qualification."

IV.

Under § 703(e)(1) of Title VII, an employer may discriminate on the basis of "religion, sex, or national origin in those certain instances where religion, sex, or national origin is a bona fide occupational qualification reasonably necessary to the normal operation of that particular business or enterprise." We therefore turn to the question whether Johnson Controls' fetal-protection policy is one of those "certain instances" that come within the BFOQ exception.

The BFOQ defense is written narrowly, and this Court has read it narrowly. Our emphasis on the restrictive scope of the BFOQ defense is grounded on both the language and the legislative history of § 703.

* * *

Johnson Controls argues that its fetal-protection policy falls within the so-called safety exception to the BFOQ. Our cases have stressed that discrimination on the basis of sex because of safety concerns is allowed only in narrow circumstances. In Dothard v. Rawlinson, 433 U.S. 321 (1977), this Court indicated that danger to a woman herself does not justify discrimination. We there allowed the employer to hire only male guards in contact areas of maximum-security male penitentiaries only because more was at stake than the "individual woman's decision to weigh and accept the risks of employment." We found sex to be a BFOQ inasmuch as the employment of a female guard would create real risks of safety to others if violence broke out because the guard was a woman. Sex discrimination was tolerated because sex was related to the guard's ability to do the job—maintaining prison security. We also required in *Dothard* a high correlation between sex and ability to perform job functions and refused to allow employers to use sex as a proxy for strength although it might be a fairly accurate one.

Similarly, some courts have approved airlines' layoffs of pregnant flight attendants at different points during the first five months of pregnancy on the ground that the employer's policy was necessary to ensure the safety of passengers. In two of these cases, the courts pointedly indicated that fetal, as opposed to passenger, safety was best left to the mother.

We considered safety to third parties in Western Airlines, Inc. v. Criswell, 472 U.S. 400 (1985), in the context of the ADEA. We focused upon "the nature of the flight engineer's tasks," and the "actual capabilities of persons over age 60" in relation to those tasks. Our safety concerns were not independent of the individual's ability to perform the assigned tasks, but rather involved the possibility that, because of age-connected debility, a flight engineer might not properly assist the pilot, and might thereby cause a safety emergency. Furthermore, although we considered the safety of third parties in *Dothard* and *Criswell*, those third parties were indispensable to the particular business at issue. In *Dothard*, the third parties were the inmates; in *Criswell*, the third parties were the passengers on the plane. We stressed that in order to qualify as a BFOQ, a job qualification must relate to the "essence," or to the "central mission of the employer's business."

The concurrence ignores the "essence of the business" test and so concludes that "the safety to fetuses in carrying out the duties of battery manufacturing is as much a legitimate concern as is safety to third parties in guarding prisons (*Dothard*) or flying airplanes (*Criswell*)." By limiting its discussion to cost and safety concerns and rejecting the "essence of the business" test that our case law has established, the concurrence seeks to expand what is now the narrow BFOQ defense. Third-party safety considerations properly entered into the BFOQ analysis in *Dothard* and *Criswell* because they went to the core of the employee's job performance. Moreover, that performance involved the central purpose of the enterprise. *Dothard* ("The essence of a correctional counselor's job is to maintain prison security"); *Criswell* (the central mission of the airline's business was the safe transportation of its passengers). The concurrence attempts to transform this case into one of customer safety. The unconceived fetuses of Johnson Controls' female employees, however, are neither customers nor third parties whose safety is essential to the business of battery manufacturing. No one can disregard the possibility of injury to future children; the BFOQ, however, is not so broad that it transforms this deep social concern into an essential aspect of batterymaking.

Our case law, therefore, makes clear that the safety exception is limited to instances in which sex or pregnancy actually interferes with the employee's ability to perform the job. This approach is consistent with the language of the BFOQ provision itself, for it suggests that permissible distinctions based on sex must relate to ability to perform the duties of the job. Johnson Controls suggests, however, that we expand the exception to allow fetal-protection policies that mandate particular standards for pregnant or fertile women. We decline to do so. Such an expansion contradicts not only the language of the BFOQ and the narrowness of its exception but the plain language and history of the Pregnancy Discrimination Act.

The PDA's amendment to Title VII contains a BFOQ standard of its own: unless pregnant employees differ from others "in their ability or inability to work," they must be "treated the same" as other employees "for all employment-related purposes." This language clearly sets forth

Congress' remedy for discrimination on the basis of pregnancy and potential pregnancy. Women who are either pregnant or potentially pregnant must be treated like others "similar in their ability * * * to work." In other words, women as capable of doing their jobs as their male counterparts may not be forced to choose between having a child and having a job.

* * *

V.

We have no difficulty concluding that Johnson Controls cannot establish a BFOQ. Fertile women, as far as appears in the record, participate in the manufacture of batteries as efficiently as anyone else. Johnson Controls' professed moral and ethical concerns about the welfare of the next generation do not suffice to establish a BFOQ of female sterility. Decisions about the welfare of future children must be left to the parents who conceive, bear, support, and raise them rather than to the employers who hire those parents. Congress has mandated this choice through Title VII, as amended by the Pregnancy Discrimination Act. Johnson Controls has attempted to exclude women because of their reproductive capacity. Title VII and the PDA simply do not allow a woman's dismissal because of her failure to submit to sterilization.

Nor can concerns about the welfare of the next generation be considered a part of the "essence" of Johnson Controls' business. Judge Easterbrook in this case pertinently observed: "It is word play to say that 'the job' at Johnson [Controls] is to make batteries without risk to fetuses in the same way 'the job' at Western Air Lines is to fly planes without crashing."

Johnson Controls argues that it must exclude all fertile women because it is impossible to tell which women will become pregnant while working with lead. This argument is somewhat academic in light of our conclusion that the company may not exclude fertile women at all; it perhaps is worth noting, however, that Johnson Controls has shown no "factual basis for believing that all or substantially all women would be unable to perform safely and efficiently the duties of the job involved." Even on this sparse record, it is apparent that Johnson Controls is concerned about only a small minority of women. Of the eight pregnancies reported among the female employees, it has not been shown that any of the babies have birth defects or other abnormalities. The record does not reveal the birth rate for Johnson Controls' female workers but national statistics show that approximately nine percent of all fertile women become pregnant each year. The birthrate drops to two percent for blue collar workers over age 30. Johnson Controls' fear of prenatal injury, no matter how sincere, does not begin to show that substantially all of its fertile women employees are incapable of doing their jobs.

VI.

A word about tort liability and the increased cost of fertile women in the workplace is perhaps necessary. One of the dissenting judges in this case expressed concern about an employer's tort liability and concluded that liability for a potential injury to a fetus is a social cost that Title VII does not require a company to ignore. It is correct to say that Title VII does not prevent the employer from having a conscience. The statute, however, does prevent sex-specific fetal-protection policies. These two aspects of Title VII do not conflict.

More than 40 States currently recognize a right to recover for a prenatal injury based either on negligence or on wrongful death. According to Johnson Controls, however, the company complies with the lead standard developed by OSHA and warns its female employees about the damaging effects of lead. It is worth noting that OSHA gave the problem of lead lengthy consideration and concluded that "there is no basis whatsoever for the claim that women of childbearing age should be excluded from the workplace in order to protect the fetus or the course of pregnancy." Instead, OSHA established a series of mandatory protections which, taken together, "should effectively minimize any risk to the fetus and newborn child." Without negligence, it would be difficult for a court to find liability on the part of the employer. If, under general tort principles, Title VII bans sex-specific fetal-protection policies, the employer fully informs the woman of the risk, and the employer has not acted negligently, the basis for holding an employer liable seems remote at best.

Although the issue is not before us, the concurrence observes that "it is far from clear that compliance with Title VII will preempt state tort liability."

* * *

If state tort law furthers discrimination in the workplace and prevents employers from hiring women who are capable of manufacturing the product as efficiently as men, then it will impede the accomplishment of Congress' goals in enacting Title VII. Because Johnson Controls has not argued that it faces any costs from tort liability, not to mention crippling ones, the pre-emption question is not before us. We therefore say no more than that the concurrence's speculation appears unfounded as well as premature.

The tort-liability argument reduces to two equally unpersuasive propositions. First, Johnson Controls attempts to solve the problem of reproductive health hazards by resorting to an exclusionary policy. Title VII plainly forbids illegal sex discrimination as a method of diverting attention from an employer's obligation to police the workplace. Second, the spectre of an award of damages reflects a fear that hiring fertile women will cost more. The extra cost of employing members of one sex, however, does not provide an affirmative Title VII defense for a discriminatory refusal to hire members of that gender. Indeed, in passing the PDA, Congress considered at length the considerable cost of providing equal treatment of pregnancy and related conditions, but made the "decision to forbid special treatment of pregnancy despite the social costs associated therewith."

We, of course, are not presented with, nor do we decide, a case in which costs would be so prohibitive as to threaten the survival of the employer's business. We merely reiterate our prior holdings that the incremental cost of hiring women cannot justify discriminating against them.

VII.

Our holding today that Title VII, as so amended, forbids sex-specific fetal-protection policies is neither remarkable nor unprecedented. Concern for a woman's existing or potential offspring historically has been the excuse for denying women equal employment opportunities. Congress in the PDA prohibited discrimination on the basis of a woman's ability to become pregnant. We do no more than hold that the Pregnancy Discrimination Act means what it says.

It is no more appropriate for the courts than it is for individual employers to decide whether a woman's reproductive role is more important to herself and her family than her economic role. Congress has left this choice to the woman as hers to make.

The judgment of the Court of Appeals is reversed and the case is remanded for further proceedings consistent with this opinion.

It is so ordered.

■ JUSTICE WHITE, with whom THE CHIEF JUSTICE and JUSTICE KENNEDY join, concurring in part and concurring in the judgment.

The Court properly holds that Johnson Controls' fetal protection policy overtly discriminates against women, and thus is prohibited by Title VII unless it falls within the bona fide occupational qualification (BFOQ) exception, set forth at 42 U.S.C. § 2000e–2(e). The Court erroneously holds, however, that the BFOQ defense is so narrow that it could never justify a sex-specific fetal protection policy. I nevertheless concur in the judgment of reversal because on the record before us summary judgment in favor of Johnson Controls was improperly entered by the District Court and affirmed by the Court of Appeals.

* * *

The Court dismisses the possibility of tort liability by no more than speculating that if "Title VII bans sex-specific fetal-protection policies, the employer fully informs the woman of the risk, and the employer has not acted negligently, the basis for holding an employer liable seems remote at best." Such speculation will be small comfort to employers. First, it is far from clear that compliance with Title VII will pre-empt state tort liability, and the Court offers no support for that proposition.

Second, although warnings may preclude claims by injured *employees,* they will not preclude claims by injured children because the general rule is that parents cannot waive causes of action on behalf of their children, and the parents' negligence will not be imputed to the children. Finally, although state tort liability for prenatal injuries generally requires negligence, it will be difficult for employers to determine in advance what will constitute negligence. Compliance with OSHA standards, for example, has been held not to be a defense to state tort or criminal liability. Moreover, it is possible that employers will be held strictly liable, if, for example, their manufacturing process is considered "abnormally dangerous."

* * *

■ JUSTICE SCALIA, concurring in the judgment.

I generally agree with the Court's analysis, but have some reservations, several of which bear mention.

First, I think it irrelevant that there was "evidence in the record about the debilitating effect of lead exposure on the male reproductive system." Even without such evidence, treating women differently "on the basis of pregnancy" constitutes discrimination "on the basis of sex," because Congress has unequivocally said so.

Second, the Court points out that "Johnson Controls has shown no factual basis for believing that all or substantially all women would be unable to perform safely * * * the duties of the job involved," (internal quotations omitted). In my view, this is not only "somewhat academic in light of our conclusion that the company may not exclude fertile women at all," ibid.; it is entirely irrelevant. By reason of the Pregnancy Discrimination Act, it would not matter if all pregnant women placed their children at risk in taking these jobs, just as it does not matter if no men do so. As Judge Easterbrook put it in his dissent below, "Title VII gives parents the power to make occupational decisions affecting their families. A legislative forum is available to those who believe that such decisions should be made elsewhere."

Third, I am willing to assume, as the Court intimates, that any action required by Title VII cannot give rise to liability under state tort law. That assumption, however, does not answer the question whether an action *is* required by Title VII (including the BFOQ provision) even if it is subject to liability under state tort law. It is perfectly reasonable to believe that Title VII has *accommodated* state tort law through the BFOQ exception. However, all that need be said in the present case is that Johnson has not demonstrated a substantial risk of tort liability—which is alone enough to defeat a tort-based assertion of the BFOQ exception.

NOTES AND QUESTIONS

1.   Based on the majority opinion, would it violate Title VII for a hospital to require that already-pregnant x-ray technicians be reassigned to other jobs in the hospital for the duration of their pregnancy?

2.   Justice Blackmun's opinion relies on the principle of autonomy. "The bias in Johnson Controls' policy is obvious. Fertile men, but not fertile women, are given a choice as to whether they wish to risk their reproductive health for a particular job." To what extent should decisions about risk acceptability be left to employees? Does the OSH Act rely on autonomy or paternalism? What about the Americans with Disabilities Act? For a further discussion see Chapter 4.

3.   In Young v. United Parcel Service, 135 S. Ct. 1338 (2015), a part-time delivery driver whose job included lifting parcels up to 70 pounds, became pregnant. Because she had a history of miscarriages her doctor told her she should not lift more than 20 pounds for the first 20 weeks of her pregnancy or more than 10 pounds thereafter. When she asked her employer for an accommodation she was told that she could not work with a lifting restriction. She then brought an action alleging discrimination under the Pregnancy Discrimination Act (PDA). The Supreme Court, in an opinion by Justice Breyer, held that there is no duty of reasonable accommodation (or what the Court termed "most favored employee status") under Title VII, as amended by the PDA. Nevertheless, an employee may allege disparate treatment sex discrimination if the employer accommodated other employees "similar in their ability or inability to work." Id. at 1341.

CHAPTER 9

DISABLING INJURY AND ILLNESS

The United States maintains a complicated and imperfectly coordinated system of income support for workers who become physically or mentally unable to continue working. Every state has a workers' compensation system. These systems require employers to obtain insurance (from private companies in some states and a state fund in others) or to self-insure against the economic consequences of certain workplace injuries and illnesses. If a worker becomes disabled, and the job was *not* the specific cause, he or she may or may not receive disability benefits from the employer depending on the coverage of the employer's private disability plan.

In 2015, the latest year for which data are available, the annual cost of all workers' compensation payments was $61.9 billion, about equally divided between compensation and medical and hospitalization. Social Security Administration, 2017 Annual Statistical Supplement to the Social Security Bulletin, Table 9.B1 (2017), available at http://www.ssa.gov/policy/docs/statcomps/supplement/2017/supplement17.pdf. The percentage of payments for medical and hospitalization has increased significantly in recent years and likely already now exceeds payments for compensation.

In 2015, state and federal workers' compensation laws covered about 135.6 million employees. Most, but not all, states cover agricultural workers, domestic service workers, small employers, and casual labor. Many states exempt employees of nonprofit, charitable, or religious institutions. The coverage of state and local employees also differs among the states.

Three groups of private employees excluded from state workers' compensation laws are railroad employees engaged in interstate commerce (covered by the Federal Employers' Liability Act, see infra p. 849), seamen (covered by the Jones Act, see infra p. 850), and longshore and harbor workers (covered by the Longshore and Harbor Workers' Compensation Act, see infra p. 850).

Workers' compensation coverage is compulsory for virtually all non-exempt employers. In Texas, coverage is elective. If an employer rejects coverage, however, it loses the customary defenses to suits by employees based on common law negligence. Tex. Lab. Code § 406.033.

Workers' compensation presents important and complicated legal issues, and also poses challenging questions about what an American worker should be able to expect upon illness or injury, as well as about how to run a fair and efficient benefit program in heavily legalized America.

A. INTRODUCTION TO WORKERS' COMPENSATION

Workers' compensation programs require employers to provide cash benefits, medical care, and rehabilitative services for workers who suffer injuries or illnesses arising out of and in the course of their employment. All laws provide benefits for workers with occupational diseases, but they do not all cover every form of occupational disease.

Approximately three-fourths of all workers' compensation cases involve only medical benefits. Cash wage replacement benefits, which compensate workers for lost income and earning capacity, are awarded based on the duration and severity of the disability, according to the following categories.

Temporary total disability. Most compensation cases involving cash payments are for temporary total disability. In these cases, the worker is temporarily prevented from performing the pre-injury job or another job with the employer that the worker could have performed before the injury. When the worker's lost time from work exceeds the statutory waiting period (3 to 7 days, depending on the state), the worker receives a percentage of his or her weekly wage (typically two-thirds) up to a statewide maximum.

Temporary partial disability. These benefits are paid during a period of reduced earnings caused by a job-related injury. The benefits cease when the worker returns to full wages or is found to be eligible for permanent total or permanent partial benefits.

Permanent total disability. After a worker reaches "maximum medical improvement" following an injury or illness, if a serious impairment remains that causes total disability for an indefinite period of time, the worker is eligible for benefits for permanent total disability. Relatively few compensation cases fall in this category.

Permanent partial disability. When the worker has permanent impairments that do not completely limit the ability to work, permanent partial disability benefits are paid. The method for determining these benefits varies among the states, which may consider the severity of the impairment, lost earning capacity, and vocational factors such as age, education, and job experience.

Death benefits. Compensation is awarded to survivors of workers who die from a work-related injury or illness. The amount of the award is based on the worker's earnings and number of dependents.

Medical benefits. All workers' compensation acts require medical aid to be furnished without delay, typically with no co-payment by the worker. Covered medical services include first aid, physician services, surgical and hospital care, nursing care, medications, medical supplies, appliances, and prosthetic devices. Most states also pay for vocational rehabilitation.

Employers meet their statutory obligation to compensate injured workers through various forms of insurance. Private insurance carriers pay approximately two-thirds of all workers' compensation benefits. State-run insurance funds pay about 23 percent of all claims. The remainder are covered by employers through self-insurance.

In cases in which an injured worker's right to recovery is undisputed, benefit payments may be initiated by either agreement or direct payment. The agreement system operates in a majority of states. Under that system, the employer does not begin payments until it and the injured worker have reached an agreement in writing regarding the benefits to be paid. Because of the delays and potential bargaining disadvantages occasioned by the agreement system, many workers retain lawyers, even though their claims are uncontested. If an agreement cannot be reached, the claim is referred to the workers' compensation commission. In direct payment states, the employer must, within a prescribed number of days, begin paying benefits to the injured worker or file a notice with the state administrative agency of its intent to contest the claim.

After an employer's liability has been established, the extent or duration of that liability may be limited through compromise and release settlements. Under these settlements, the employer pays benefits to the injured worker in a lump sum in exchange for a release from further liability.

NOTE

According to the U.S. Chamber of Commerce, six objectives underlie workers' compensation laws:

1.　Provide sure, prompt, and reasonable income and medical benefits to work-accident victims, or income benefits to their dependents, regardless of fault;

2.　Provide a single remedy and reduce court delays, costs, and workloads arising out of personal-injury litigation;

3.　Relieve public and private charities of financially draining incidents associated with uncompensated industrial accidents;

4.　Eliminate payment of fees to lawyers and witnesses as well as time-consuming trials and appeals;

5.　Encourage maximum employer interest in safety and rehabilitation through appropriate experience-rating mechanisms; and

6.　Promote frank study of causes of accidents (rather than concealment of fault) thereby reducing the number of preventable accidents and consequent human suffering.

U.S. Chamber of Commerce, 2019 Analysis of Workers' Compensation Laws 6 (2019).

As you read the rest of this chapter, consider whether these objectives are being met. Specifically, consider the viability of the basic workers' compensation "bargain": employees gave up the right to bring common law damage actions against their employer in exchange for a system of compensation that was to be prompt, certain, and reasonable in amount. Employers gave up the fault basis of liability and the common law defenses of contributory negligence, assumption of the risk, and the fellow servant rule in exchange for immunity from personal injury actions and relatively fixed costs that can be passed along to consumers.

In many ways, workers' compensation was a grand experiment—the first comprehensive no-fault system, an attempt to eliminate the all-or-nothing harshness of the tort system, and a recognition of the unacceptably high transaction costs of the courts. The following pages consider some of the many legal issues raised by this experiment.

B. WORKERS' COMPENSATION COVERAGE

1. "EMPLOYEE"

Eckis v. Sea World Corp.
134 Cal.Rptr. 183 (Cal. Ct. App. 1976).

■ AULT, PRESIDING JUSTICE.

Defendants Sea World and Kent Burgess have appealed from a judgment entered on a jury verdict awarding Anne E. Eckis $75,000 in compensatory damages. Plaintiff had sought both compensatory and punitive damages for personal injuries she sustained while riding "Shamu the Whale," framing her complaint on three theories: fraud, negligence, and liability for an animal with vicious or dangerous propensities. Before the case was submitted to the jury, the trial court denied Sea World's motion for a nonsuit on the fraud cause of action. Later its motions for judgment notwithstanding the verdict and for a new trial were also denied.

* * *

The major issue raised on appeal is the contention there was no substantial evidence to support the jury's finding that plaintiff's injuries did *not* occur in the course of her employment by Sea World. The facts which govern this issue are not in dispute.

When injured on April 19, 1971, plaintiff Anne E. Eckis, then 22 years old, was a full-time employee of Sea World. First hired by Sea World in 1967, she had worked variously as ticket sales girl, receptionist, in the accounting department, and in 1970 became the secretary for Kent Burgess, the director of Sea World's animal training department. From then on her job title was secretary, and that is what she considered herself to be, although from time to time she did other tasks at Burgess' request, such as taking the water temperature, doing research, and running errands. She worked five days a week, for which she was paid a salary of $450 per month. When first hired, plaintiff, like all other Sea World employees, had signed an authorization for reproduction of her physical likeness. Plaintiff was also an excellent swimmer, with some scuba diving experience, and had occasionally worked as a model, sometimes for pay.

Shamu and friend in happier times. © Allen Matheson/Photohome.com. Reprinted by permission.

In April 1971 Gail MacLaughlin, Sea World's public relations director, and Kent Burgess asked plaintiff if she would like to ride Shamu, the killer whale, in a bikini for some publicity pictures for Sea World. Although the ride was not made a condition of her keeping her job, plaintiff eagerly agreed, thinking it would be exciting. Although warned in general terms that the ride involved dangers and aware that she might fall off, plaintiff was confident of her swimming ability and anxious to do it. She had never heard of whales pushing riders around.

Burgess had been responsible for training Shamu ever since Sea World first acquired the animal. He knew Shamu was conditioned to being ridden only by persons wearing wetsuits, and that Shamu had in the past attacked persons who attempted to ride her in an ordinary bathing suit: first a Catalina swimsuit model and then Jim Richards, one of the trainers at Sea World. In addition, Burgess had read training records which showed Shamu had been behaving erratically since early March 1971. This information he did not disclose to plaintiff.

Plaintiff was trained for the ride by Sea World trainers in the tank at Sea World during normal office working hours. First she practiced riding Kilroy, a smaller, more docile whale, while wearing a bathing suit. During her one practice session on Shamu, she wore a wetsuit, fell off, but swam to the edge of the tank without incident.

On April 19 plaintiff became apprehensive for the first time when one of Sea World's trainers said he was not going to watch her ride Shamu because it was "really dangerous." Plaintiff then went to Burgess and told him of her concern. He told her not to worry, said there was nothing to be concerned about, and that the ride was "as safe as it could be." He still did not tell her about the problems they had been having with Shamu or about the earlier incidents involving Richards and the swimsuit model. Thus reassured, plaintiff, wearing a bikini Sea World had paid for, then took three rides on Shamu. During the second ride one of the trainers noticed Shamu's tail was fluttering, a sign the animal was upset. During the third ride plaintiff fell off when Shamu refused to obey a signal. Shamu then bit her on her legs and hips and held her in the tank until she could be rescued.

Plaintiff suffered 18 to 20 wounds which required from 100 to 200 stitches and left permanent scars. She was hospitalized five days and out of work several weeks. She also suffered some psychological disturbance. Sea World paid all her medical expenses and continued to pay her salary as usual during this period. On advice of her counsel, she filed this civil action and a workers' compensation claim.

When an employee's injuries are compensable under the Workers' Compensation Act, the right of the employee to recover the benefits provided by the Act is his exclusive remedy against the employer.

Where a reasonable doubt exists as to whether an act of an employee is contemplated by the employment, or as to whether an injury occurred in the course of the employment, section 3202 requires courts to resolve the doubt against the right of the employee to sue for civil damages and in favor of the applicability of the Compensation Act. The importance of adhering to the rule requiring a liberal construction of the Act in favor of its applicability in civil litigation was emphasized by the court in *Scott*:

"Though it may be more opportunistic for a particular plaintiff
to seek to circumscribe the purview of compensation coverage
because of his immediate interest and advantage, the courts

must be vigilant to preserve the spirit of the act and to prevent a distortion of its purposes. That the question before us in this case arises out of litigation prosecuted in the superior court is all the more reason for care lest rules of doubtful validity, out of harmony with the objectives of the Act, be formulated." * * *

Governed by these legal principles, we examine the evidence to determine whether it supports the finding plaintiff was not acting within the course and scope of her employment at Sea World when she sustained her injuries.

The undisputed evidence shows: at the time she was injured plaintiff was an employee of Sea World; she was injured on the employer's premises during what were her regular working hours; she was injured while engaging in an activity which her employer had requested her to perform and for which it had provided her with the training and the means to perform; in riding Shamu the Whale for publicity pictures, plaintiff was not engaged in an activity which was personal to her, but rather one which was related to, furthered, and benefited the business of her employer.

Despite this formidable array of factors which indicate her injuries did arise out of and occurred in the course and scope of her employment plaintiff maintains substantial evidence supports the special finding to the contrary. She premises her position on the claim she was hired to be a secretary, not to ride a whale. Since her injuries were unrelated to the secretarial duties she was originally hired to perform, she argues her employment "had nothing whatsoever to do with her injury" and that her case does not come within the purview of the Compensation Act. Because of the highly unusual circumstances under which she was injured, she maintains the rules and formulas traditionally used to determine whether injuries have arisen out of or occurred in the course of employment are neither applicable nor helpful.

These arguments are without merit. The right to compensation is not limited to those cases where the injury occurs while the employee is performing the classical duties for which he was originally hired. Far less than a direct request by the employer operates to bring an injury-causing activity within the provisions of the Compensation Act. For example, in Lizama v. Workmen's Comp. Appeals Bd., 40 Cal.App.3d 363, 115 Cal.Rptr. 267, the employee was injured on the employer's premises after he had clocked out from work while using a table saw to construct a bench to sit on at lunch time. Although his assigned duties did not include use of the saw and he had never used it before, the injury was held compensable because the employer had expressly or impliedly permitted such use of equipment. At page 370, 115 Cal.Rptr. at page 271, the court stated:

> "Textwriters have long proposed and California courts have applied a 'quantum theory of work-connection' that seems peculiarly appropriate for application here. The theory merges

the 'course of employment' and 'arising out of employment' tests, but does not dispense with a minimum 'quantum of work-connection.' There were at least these connections between petitioner's injury and his employment: the accident occurred on the employer's premises when petitioner was using the employer's equipment while constructing a bench for his personal comfort to be used on the employer's premises; and the employer expressly or impliedly permitted petitioner to use its equipment. * * * "

Where, as here, an employee is injured on the employer's premises during regular working hours, when the injury occurs while the employee is engaged in an activity which the employer has requested her to undertake, and when the injury-causing activity is of service to the employer and benefits the employer's business, the conditions imposing liability for compensation under Labor Code section 3600 are met as a matter of law, and it is immaterial that the activity causing the injury was not related to the employee's normal duties or that the circumstances surrounding the injury were unusual or unique.

It would be wholly incongruous and completely at variance with the long declared purposes and policies of the Workers' Compensation Law to say that an employee who sustained injuries under the circumstances of this case is not entitled to the benefits of the Workers' Compensation Act. Since her injuries fall within the scope of the Act, a proceeding under it constitutes plaintiff's exclusive remedy.

NOTES AND QUESTIONS

1.   What facts in this case are most damaging to the plaintiff's claim that she was not injured during the course of her employment? If she was not an employee, what was she?

2.   Why does the plaintiff want to be considered an independent contractor rather than an employee? As an independent contractor the plaintiff is not entitled to workers' compensation, but she is not precluded from bringing a tort action in negligence. Under workers' compensation, a claimant receives a percentage of lost income plus medical expenses. In a common law action the plaintiff may recover compensatory damages for pain and suffering and may even be awarded punitive damages. (The $75,000 the jury awarded the plaintiff in *Eckis* was undoubtedly much more than she would receive under workers' compensation.) As long as workers' compensation benefit levels are relatively low, injured workers will attempt to "get out" of the workers' compensation system. For a further discussion of this issue, see pp. 834–839, infra.

3.   Theoretically, independent contractors are excluded from coverage because they are not "employees." See, e.g., Ives Carmago's Case, 96 N.E.3d 673 (Mass. 2018) (newspaper delivery agent was independent contractor). Some classifications of employees statutorily excluded from coverage in one or more states include domestic servants, casual employees, real estate

licensees, farmworkers, newspaper vendors, employees of public charities, professional athletes, and clergy. Why exclude these employees? For a collection of the coverage provisions of state workers' compensation laws, see U.S. Chamber of Commerce, 2019 Analysis of Workers' Compensation Laws 15–24 (2019).

2. "COURSE OF EMPLOYMENT"

Perry v. State

134 P.3d 1242 (Wyo. 2006).

■ KITE, JUSTICE.

Eleanor L. Perry appeals from the district court's order affirming the Office of Administrative Hearings' (OAH) denial of her claim for worker's compensation benefits. The OAH hearing examiner denied her claim in accordance with the test enunciated in Smith v. Husky Terminal Restaurant, Inc., 762 P.2d 1193 (Wyo. 1988), because she was injured while violating a safety regulation. We conclude OAH properly applied the *Smith* test to Ms. Perry's claim and there was substantial evidence to support OAH's factual findings. Consequently, we affirm.

ISSUES

Ms. Perry articulates a single issue on appeal:

When an employee deviates from a prescribed safety rule resulting in injury, should worker['s] compensation benefits be denied?

The Division phrases the issue a little differently:

In limited situations, an employee can be found to have acted outside the scope of employment by violating a work restriction when the four elements in Smith v. Husky Terminal Restaurant, Inc., 762 P.2d 1193 (Wyo. 1988) are present. The issue presented in this appeal is whether the hearing examiner's application of *Smith* to Perry's case was in accordance with law[.]

FACTS

On October 7, 2003, Ms. Perry began work as a certified nurse assistant (CNA) for Mountain Towers Healthcare and Rehabilitation Center (Mountain Towers) in Cheyenne. Mountain Towers is a nursing home facility. When she began work, Ms. Perry had just finished her training as a CNA, which included education about proper lifting techniques. On her first day of work, Ms. Perry attended Mountain Towers' employment orientation. The orientation included instructions for lifting patients who required help. Ms. Perry was informed that certain patients were classified as "two-person lifts," meaning that two people were required in order to lift the patient. Mountain Towers had a written policy forbidding its employees from lifting a patient classified as a "two-person lift" alone, and Ms. Perry signed a document acknowledging the policy. The policy was intended to protect Mountain Towers' employees and patients. The policy stated that, if another employee was not available to help with a two-person lift, the employee was to make the patient comfortable and wait for assistance. Ms. Perry was informed that violating the two-person lift policy could result in termination from employment with Mountain Towers.

On October 26 through 27, 2003, Ms. Perry was working a night shift, from 10:00 p.m. through 6:00 a.m. During that shift, there were typically only three people on staff per floor—two CNAs and one licensed practical nurse (LPN). At approximately 2:30 a.m., Ms. Perry was making the rounds to check on patients, when one patient requested assistance in using the bathroom. The patient was classified as a "two-person lift" so Ms. Perry sought help. The other CNA was assisting another patient and could not immediately help Ms. Perry. The LPN refused to help her because lifting was not part of her job duties. Ms. Perry offered the patient a bed pan, but the patient refused and insisted upon getting up to use the bathroom.

Ms. Perry assisted the patient to the bathroom and, at some point in the process as she was lifting the patient, the wheelchair moved. In order to prevent the patient from falling, Ms. Perry twisted and strained her lower back. She felt the strain but did not experience pain until after she had finished her shift and returned home. She was scheduled to work the next night, but called in and said she was unable to work because she had injured her back.

Ms. Perry filed a report of injury in which she stated she injured her lower back when she was "transferring a 2 person transfer by [herself] and twisted and strained [her] back the wrong way while trying not to drop [the] resident as her wheelchair started to move even with [the] locks on." She sought medical treatment from various doctors for her back injury and requested worker's compensation benefits as a result of the injury. Mountain Towers objected to Ms. Perry's request for worker's compensation benefits, and the Division issued a final determination denying Ms. Perry's request for benefits on several bases.

The case was referred to OAH, and a hearing examiner held a contested case hearing on May 6, 2004. The Division argued there were several reasons to deny Ms. Perry's request for worker's compensation benefits, including: Ms. Perry failed to timely report her injury to her employer and to the Division, her back injury was preexisting, her back injury did not occur while she was at work, and she was injured while violating a safety regulation. The hearing examiner found Ms. Perry had reported her injury in a timely fashion, she was injured while at work, and she did not suffer from a preexisting condition which would prevent her from obtaining worker's compensation benefits. However, the hearing examiner found Ms. Perry had violated Mountain Towers' safety rule prohibiting unassisted two person lifts and concluded, under the holding in *Smith*, she was not entitled to worker's compensation benefits. Ms. Perry petitioned the district court for review of the OAH decision, and the district court affirmed. She, subsequently, filed a notice of appeal from the district court's order.

* * *

DISCUSSION

Ms. Perry claims the hearing examiner erred by ruling that she should be denied benefits for violating the two-person lift rule. The hearing examiner relied upon our decision in *Smith* in concluding Ms. Perry was not entitled to worker's compensation benefits. Smith was a cook at a truck stop restaurant and had previously suffered back pain, although it was not clear her prior back pain was job related. She sought medical treatment for her back condition, and her physician ordered her not to lift anything weighing more than fifteen pounds. Smith's employer received a letter from her doctor containing the lifting restriction and discussed the restriction with her. The doctor's letter was posted above the manager's desk, and Smith was instructed "to have someone else lift any heavy items for her if that became necessary." One night, Smith attempted to drain a bucket of marinated chickens and injured her back. She sought worker's compensation benefits for her injury, but her employer objected because her injury resulted from her violation of the lifting restriction. The district court denied benefits, and Smith appealed.

In reviewing the case, we looked to the definition of an "injury" which qualifies for compensation under the worker's compensation system. The statutory definition of a compensable injury requires that an injury "arise out of and in the course of employment." Wyo. Stat. Ann. § 27–14–102(a)(xi). The determination of whether an injury arose out of and in the course of employment is a question of fact. In considering the employer's defense that Smith violated a known safety rule, we stated: "[p]recedent concerning the type of misconduct that is a deviation from the scope of a particular employment focuses on whether the employee knowingly does certain work specifically prohibited, as opposed to an employee's doing authorized work in an unauthorized way."

* * *

In the case at bar, the hearing examiner found Ms. Perry had violated the rule prohibiting her from performing a two-person lift unassisted and, under *Smith*, she was not entitled to benefits. The factual record clearly supports the hearing examiner's conclusion. The first and second elements of the *Smith* test require the employer expressly and carefully inform the employee she must not perform a specific task while in its employ and the employee know and understand the restriction. At the contested case hearing, Lacrecia Patterson, Mountain Towers' executive director, testified all employees receive instruction on safety policies when they are hired. Mountain Towers had a written policy stating the two-person lift restriction, and Ms. Perry signed a document acknowledging the policy. Ms. Perry testified that, at her employment orientation, Mountain Towers instructed she was not to perform a two-person lift without assistance. She acknowledged performing a two-person lift alone was a serious violation of Mountain Towers' safety policies, which could result in disciplinary action, including termination. Obviously, there was ample evidence to support a fining that the first two elements were satisfied.

The third element of the *Smith* test is the employer did not knowingly accept the benefit of a violation of the restriction by the employee. This element was contested at the hearing. Ms. Perry testified she was instructed to honor the patients' rights to privacy and she believed, at the time she was injured, she was complying with the requirement by helping the patient use the restroom. She also testified the "graveyard shift" was habitually understaffed, causing her to have to choose between honoring the patient's rights and complying with the two-person lift restriction. In fact, she testified she had violated the two-person lift rule several times in her short tenure with Mountain Towers. Thus, she claimed Mountain Towers accepted the benefit of her violation of the two-person lift restriction.

The record contains no evidence to support Ms. Perry's claim the graveyard shift was understaffed in accordance with industry or legal standards. Furthermore, Ms. Perry did not testify she had notified Mountain Towers prior to her injury about the perceived staffing problem. Although evidence showing other employees routinely violated the two-person lift policy may have supported Ms. Perry's claim of understaffing, no such evidence exists in the record. To the contrary, Ms. Patterson denied knowledge of prior incidences of employees violating the two-person lift rule, and she testified violating the policy was a serious breach of Mountain Towers' employment regulations which could result in termination of employment. Ms. Patterson also testified Mountain Towers did not benefit from violation of the rule because it placed both the employee and the patient at risk.

With regard to this particular incident, Ms. Perry did not testify as to how long she and the patient would have had to wait for assistance from the other CNA. Instead, she simply asserted she was required to violate the safety regulation in order to make the patient comfortable and to comply with her obligation to respect the patient's right to privacy. In doing so, she injured herself and nearly dropped the patient, which were exactly the dangers the policy was designed to prevent. Substantial evidence supports the hearing examiner's conclusion that Mountain Towers did not knowingly accept the benefit of Ms. Perry's violation of the two-person lift restriction.

The record also supports the hearing examiner's finding the final element of the *Smith* test was satisfied. Ms. Perry admitted her back injury occurred because she performed a two-person lift by herself. She strained her back when she twisted to prevent the patient from falling.

In fact, Ms. Perry's own statement in her employee incident report acknowledged her violation of the policy caused her injury. One question on the report asked: "What were you doing at the time of the incident, and what could you have done to prevent this incident?" Her handwritten answer stated: "I could [have] had 2 people to help with the transfer if the other CNA would have helped. . . ."

* * *

When compared with the facts of *Smith*, Ms. Perry's actions were similarly outside the scope of her employment and constituted a prohibited "thing" not a "method". Ms. Perry was specifically directed not to perform a two-person lift alone. She was clearly aware of the rule and the fact the patient was classified as a two-person lift. Ms. Perry knew she was violating the rule, doing a prohibited thing and risking termination from her position when she did it. The dissent in Smith argued the evidence was unclear as to whether the bucket of chicken Ms. Smith lifted exceeded the fifteen-pound weight limitation. No similar uncertainty existed in this case.

Affirmed.

■ HILL, CHIEF JUSTICE, dissenting, with whom BURKE, JUSTICE, joins.

* * *

NOTES AND QUESTIONS

1. Do you agree with the majority that the claimant's actions in attempting to lift the patient were outside the scope of her employment? What relevance, if any, should the employer's alleged low staffing level have on the outcome of the case? Do you agree with the *Smith* factors cited by the majority?

2. The *Perry* decision seems to be at variance with the general rule that workers' compensation benefits are awarded if the employee's actions were a good faith effort to advance the interest of his or her employer. In Wyoming, workers' compensation benefits are not available if the employee was intoxicated at the time of the injury. Coleman v. State ex rel. Wyo. Workers' Comp. Div., 915 P.2d 595 (Wyo. 1996). What other types of conduct should operate to disqualify an employee from benefits?

3. In Layne v. Crist Elec. Contractor, Inc., 768 S.E.2d 261 (Va. App. 2015), an employee suffered severe injuries when a scissor lift he was operating was struck by a crane, and he plunged to the floor in a large warehouse. The Virginia Court of Appeals held that the claimant was not entitled to workers' compensation benefits because his violation of the "lock-out-tagout" safety rule was a willful violation. The employee knew of the rule and had followed it in the past. He was unable to explain his failure in the case because his severe brain injuries prevented him from testifying. What does it mean to "willfully" violate a safety standard?

4. Bates and McDaniel were employees at a sugar cooperative. While performing his work duties Bates encountered McDaniel and began attacking him with a brass hammer because Bates had discovered on the

Internet that McDaniel is a registered sex offender. Bates was immediately fired, and McDaniel filed for workers' compensation benefits. Is McDaniel entitled to recover for the injuries caused by his coworker? See McDaniel v. Western Sugar Coop., 867 N.W.2d 302 (Neb. Ct. App. 2015) (held: no; the injury did not "arise out of" employment because it was not caused by or exacerbated by the employment).

5.   The issue of "course of employment" frequently arises in the case of workers' compensation claims for recreational injuries. The claimants, who are often unable to assert a common law claim due to the lack of fault on the part of any party, seek to prove that the injury occurred in the course of employment. The courts have adopted several different approaches, including whether the employer benefited from the employee's participation (such as through publicity or improved morale) and whether employees were reasonably expected to participate in the recreational activity. See Ezzy v. Workers' Comp. Appeals Bd., 194 Cal.Rptr. 90 (Cal.Ct.App.1983) (law student injured in law firm's summer softball game entitled to compensation because firm's partners expected her to play); Calumet School District #132 v. Illinois Workers' Comp. Comm'n, 67 N.E.3d 966 (Ill. Ct. App. 2016) (teacher's injury in an after-school basketball game with students was compensable because he was pressured to play by the principal); Michalak v. Liberty N.W. Ins. Corp., 175 P.3d 893 (Mont. 2008) (employee injured riding wave runner at company picnic was within the course and scope of his employment). But see Combs v. Virginia Elec. & Power Co., 525 S.E.2d 278 (Va.2000) (employee's negligence action based on injury sustained during lunchtime aerobics class offered by employer was barred by workers' compensation).

6.   Injuries sustained while an employee is traveling to and from work are generally not compensable because they do not arise out of and in the course of employment. Exceptions are made for employer-supplied transportation, injuries occurring on the employer's property, and where the employee is engaged in some work-related duty. See Thayer v. State, 653 N.W.2d 595 (Iowa 2002) (employee injured while riding in van provided by employer was entitled to compensation); Straub v. City of Scottsbluff, 784 N.W.2d 886 (Neb. 2010) (off-duty police officer injured while driving to hospital to take employer-ordered MRI after work-related injury was within the course and scope of employment and therefore entitled to compensation for second injury). In Ex parte Shelby County Health Care Auth., 850 So.2d 332 (Ala.2002), a respiratory technician at a hospital worked 16 hours on Saturday and 16 hours on Sunday with an eight-hour break between shifts. She fell asleep while driving home and sustained serious injuries. Is she entitled to workers' compensation for her injuries? Held: no.

7.   Frantz Pierre, a lawfully admitted migrant farmworker from Haiti, fractured his ankle when he fell, during non-work time, on a wet sidewalk at the housing provided by the company. South Carolina's workers' compensation agency denied his claim because he was not injured while working and he was not required to live in the housing provided by the employer. The South Carolina Circuit Court affirmed, but the South Carolina Supreme Court reversed. It held that because the source of Mr.

Pierre's injury was a risk associated with the conditions under which the employees lived, the injury was covered by workers' compensation. South Carolina thus joined the majority of jurisdictions to adopt the "bunkhouse rule," holding compensable employee injuries sustained at employer-provided housing. Pierre v. Seaside Farms, 689 S.E.2d 615 (S.C. 2010).

8. Another "course of employment" issue involves horseplay or "skylarking." Angel Diaz was hosing down with water certain frames lying on the floor. He playfully squirted water on the legs of Frank Waters, a co-worker. Waters retaliated by throwing at Diaz a bucket of a clear liquid that he thought was water. Actually, the bucket contained lacquer, which was ignited by a nearby open flame, severely burning Diaz. Is Diaz entitled to compensation for his burns? See Diaz v. Newark Indus. Spraying, Inc., 174 A.2d 478 (N.J.1961) (held: yes). A factor often considered by the courts is whether the employer had prior knowledge or had previously condoned horseplay. See Bare v. Wayne Poultry Co., 318 S.E.2d 534 (N.C.Ct.App.1984) (chicken deboners were known to play with knives).

Estate of Sullwold v. The Salvation Army
108 A.3d 1265 (Me. 2015).

■ HJELM, J.

The Salvation Army appeals from an order of the Workers' Compensation Board Appellate Division affirming the decision of the Board to grant an award of compensation to the estate of Gregory Sullwold. The Salvation Army contends that the hearing officer improperly applied the rebuttable presumption in 39–A M.R.S. § 327 (2014) to conclude that Sullwold's death from a heart attack was a personal injury arising out of and in the course of employment. Because we find no error in the hearing officer's application of the presumption, we affirm the judgment.

I. Background

The hearing officer found the following facts. On February 23, 2010, Gregory Sullwold died of a heart attack while exercising on a treadmill in his home. At the time of his death, he was employed by the Salvation Army as a portfolio specialist and comptroller and was responsible for overseeing investor relations and the financial interests of the Salvation Army's Eastern Division, which were then valued at approximately $2.5 billion.

Sullwold had lived in Maine since 2009, when he moved from New York City, where the Eastern Division's office is located. The Salvation Army permitted him to work remotely from home, supplying him with a computer, BlackBerry, and other office materials. On the day of his death, Sullwold started working at 8:30 a.m. in his home office and continued working until about 3:30 p.m., when he took a break to walk on the treadmill, bringing his BlackBerry with him. About thirty minutes later, his wife found him unconscious on the floor with the treadmill still running and the BlackBerry next to him. Emergency medical professionals were called, but were unable to revive him.

Sullwold had previously suffered a heart attack in 1993. As a result, his doctors recommended that he make lifestyle changes by dieting and exercising regularly, which he did. He continued to be treated for coronary artery disease and atherosclerosis, and shortly before his death he reported to his doctor that he was experiencing chest pain while walking his dog. There is no evidence that Sullwold reported any concerns about his workload or work-related stress to any of his doctors, although shortly before his death he suffered a panic attack, which he attributed to "overload." His wife and coworkers also reported that he experienced stress from working long hours and traveling frequently, and that this stress was exacerbated by increased donor contributions after September 11, 2001, and the effect of the 2008 economic downturn on the Salvation Army's finances.

On January 28, 2011, Sullwold's widow filed a petition for award of compensation with the Workers' Compensation Board, alleging that Sullwold's "work resulted in a myocardial infarction and cardiac arrest." Following a hearing, the Board granted the petition. The Salvation Army filed a motion for findings of fact and conclusions of law pursuant to 39–A M.R.S. § 318 (2011), and the hearing officer issued a decision reaffirming the original order and making further findings of fact regarding her determination that work stress was a major causal factor in Sullwold's death.

The Salvation Army then filed appeals with the Workers' Compensation Board Appellate Division and with this Court. In March 2013, we dismissed the appeal to this Court, holding that the case was subject to initial review by the Appellate Division. In November 2013, the Appellate Division affirmed the Board's award of compensation, concluding that the hearing officer did not err in finding that the evidence triggered the presumption found in 39–A M.R.S. § 327 and that the Salvation Army failed to rebut the presumption. We granted the Salvation Army's petition for appellate review pursuant to 39–A M.R.S. § 322 (2014).

II. Discussion

The Salvation Army argues on this appeal that the hearing officer erroneously applied the presumption in 39–A M.R.S. § 327 and that she misconstrued the nature of the burden needed to rebut the presumption. In determining whether the hearing officer correctly applied the presumption, "[w]e accept the hearing officer's findings of fact," but review questions of law, including statutory interpretation, de novo, "When construing provisions of the Workers' Compensation Act, our purpose is to give effect to the Legislature's intent."

A.   Application of the Section 327 Presumption

Title 39–A M.R.S. § 201(1) (2014) provides that an employee covered by the Maine Workers' Compensation Act "must be paid compensation" if he or she "receives a personal injury arising out of and in the course of employment." Pursuant to 39–A M.R.S. § 327,

> In any claim for compensation, when the employee has been killed or is physically or mentally unable to testify, there is a rebuttable presumption that the employee received a personal injury arising out of and in the course of employment, that sufficient notice of the injury has been given and that the injury or death was not occasioned by the willful intention of the employee to injure or kill the employee or another.

The Salvation Army contends that the evidence was not sufficient to generate the statutory presumption that Sullwold's death arose out of and in the course of his employment and that the hearing officer erred in applying the presumption in this case.

In Toomey v. City of Portland, 391 A.2d 325, 330 (Me.1978), we interpreted the virtually identical precursor statute to section 327. There, we concluded that the statute contained an "implied requirement of preliminary linkage" between the employment and the incident underlying the claim. Because the Legislature intended to allow the presumption "only for the benefit of a compensation claimant whose filing of a claim is a rational act," there must be evidence that, were the employee available to testify, the incident at issue would have "some rational potential of eventuating in an award of compensation." Under this standard, "hopeless claims" do not receive the benefit of the presumption, but claims that have a rational possibility of success do. Whether the presumption arises is determined based on the evidence actually presented and "testimony which, within reasonable limits, may be conceived as potentially forthcoming from the employee were the employee available as a witness." Therefore, the presumption is properly invoked here if the evidence presented to the hearing officer, combined with any facts to which Sullwold may reasonably have testified if he were alive, could rationally result in an award of compensation.

In order for the estate's claim to be successful without the benefit of the presumption, the estate would have to establish affirmatively that the injury (1) occurred in the course of the employment and (2) arose out of the employment. The hearing officer did not err in determining, based on the evidence presented to her and Sullwold's inferred testimony, that there was a rational prospect that the estate could have proved both elements. Consequently, the hearing officer properly applied the presumption created by section 327.

As to the first element, the evidence in the record supported the hearing officer's conclusion that the estate could reasonably have proved that Sullwold's death occurred in the course of employment. Whether an injury arose in the course of employment depends on "the time, place, and circumstances under which an injury occurs, the place where the employee reasonably may be in performance of the employee's duties, and whether it occurred while fulfilling those duties or engaged in something incidental to those duties." Here, the hearing officer found that, although Sullwold was walking on the treadmill at the time of his death, his injury occurred during work hours, in a place that the Salvation Army sanctioned for his work, and while he was using the BlackBerry that the Salvation Army provided to him for his work. In fact, as the hearing officer observed, Sullwold's use of a treadmill to exercise allowed him to work while exercising. Even without anticipating how Sullwold would have testified if he had been available, the evidence presented to the hearing officer was sufficient to demonstrate that this part of the claim was not "hopeless" and that there was a "rational potential" for success.

The evidence before the hearing officer also supported the conclusion that the estate had a rational chance of proving the second element—that Sullwold's injury arose out of his employment. As a general matter, for an injury to arise out of employment, "there must be some causal connection between the conditions under which the employee worked and the injury, or that the injury, in some proximate way, had its origin, its source, or its cause in the employment." More specifically, pursuant to 39–A M.R.S. § 201(4) (2014), an injury, such as Sullwold's heart attack, resulting from a pre-existing physical condition "is compensable only if contributed to by the employment in a significant manner." The hearing officer found that "Ms. Sullwold testified convincingly about the stress her husband experienced," including the demands of frequent travel, long workdays, and the effects of the economic recession. In particular, Sullwold "typically began working early in the day and worked well into the evening," and "[s]ometimes at night he would check emails and news on world markets." Shortly before his death, he suffered a panic attack that he attributed to the demands of his job. Based on this testimony, the hearing officer found that Sullwold "was under extraordinary and relentless stress in performing his duties."

The hearing officer also found, based on the testimony of a medical expert, that Sullwold's "longstanding, chronic and relentless work stress significantly accelerated and combined with his underlying coronary [atherosclerotic] heart disease, which resulted in sudden cardiac death." Although there was competing evidence that factors unrelated to Sullwold's employment may have contributed to his death, the hearing officer did not err in concluding that the evidence of work-related stress could rationally result in a determination that the employment contributed "in a significant manner" to the fatal heart attack and that it therefore arose out of his employment.

In addition to the facts found by the hearing officer, it was also reasonably possible based on the evidence in the record that, had Sullwold been available, he would have augmented the record by testifying that he was under significant work-related stress and that he was engaged in work-related activities at the time of his death. Therefore, because the actual evidence, both with and without Sullwold's possible testimony, created the rational potential for an award of compensation, the hearing officer did not err in invoking the presumption created by section 327 that Sullwold's fatal injury arose out of and in the course of his employment.

* * *

Judgment affirmed.

NOTES AND QUESTIONS

1.   Many employers acquiesce in or encourage employees to perform work off-site, including at home, at times beyond normal business hours. Often, mobile devices help to maintain the link to business messages and documents. Based on *Sullwold*, does this mean that workers' compensation coverage extends to all of the injuries sustained by employees who are sending emails and text messages from the golf course or a child's school play? If so, is this a good thing that recognizes the realities of modern working arrangements, or is it a bad thing because it means a substantial increase in employers' workers' compensation liability?

2.   In Atkins v. Webcon, 419 P.3d 1 (Kan. 2018), a general laborer was working out of town on a roofing job. As he was walking from a bar to his hotel at 2:20 a.m., he was hit by a drunk driver and sustained catastrophic injuries. The Supreme Court of Kansas affirmed the denial of benefits, saying that if the employee had been injured in a hotel fire, then his injuries would have been compensable, but walking back to his hotel from a bar late at night was "too far removed" from his work duties. Suppose he was walking back to his hotel at 6:00 p.m. after dinner, where he and other workers reviewed plans for the next day's roofing work?

C. OCCUPATIONAL DISEASE

Guess v. Sharp Manufacturing of America
114 S.W.3d 480 (Tenn. 2003).

■ WILLIAM M. BARKER, JUSTICE.

The dispositive issue in this workers' compensation action is whether, under the Tennessee Workers' Compensation Law, the plaintiff suffered a compensable mental injury stemming from perceived exposure to the Human Immunodeficiency Virus (HIV). The appellee filed a workers' compensation claim seeking relief based upon a chronic mental disorder that arose after she came into contact with the blood of a co-worker, whom she believed to be HIV positive. The Chancery Court for Shelby County found that the appellee had suffered a vocational disability as a result of the psychological consequences of the event and awarded benefits. Prior to argument and consideration by the Special

Workers' Compensation Panel, an order was entered directing that the case be heard by the entire court. After conducting our own de novo review of the record, we hold that a plaintiff seeking workers' compensation benefits for a mental injury due to exposure to HIV must demonstrate actual exposure through a medically recognized channel of transmission. Accordingly, the Chancery Court erred in awarding benefits to the appellee based on a finding that the appellee suffered a 38% disability to her mental faculties. The judgment of the trial court is reversed.

FACTUAL BACKGROUND

The appellee, Mary Guess, began working for the appellant, Sharp Manufacturing Company of America ("Sharp"), in 1984 as an assembly line worker. At the time of the trial, she was a fifty-year-old individual with a high school education and no other additional formal education or vocational training. On November 6, 1998, one of Guess's co-workers lacerated his hand, which resulted in some of the co-worker's blood getting on Guess's hand. While there was no penetrating injury to Guess, she testified that she had open cuts on her hands as well as a fresh manicure.

Guess testified that as a result of getting this blood on her hands, she was "out of control," "nervous," "screaming for help," "upset," "shaking," and "hysterical." She explained that she believed the blood that she got on her hands to be HIV positive. Her subjective conclusion that her co-worker had AIDS was based on the following: the co-worker was sick all the time; he had been isolated in the work environment; he had friends at work who had died of AIDS; he appeared very frail; he was on the mailing list of a gay rights organization; and he "looked and acted gay."

Guess testified that she was hysterical from the time of the incident and began having panic attacks about a week or so thereafter. She sought medical treatment from her family practitioner who took her off work for six weeks beginning November 11, 1998, due to "agitated depression." Guess testified that she has significant limitations as a result of her injury and subsequent condition. She disinfects her bathroom every time she uses it; she has only been able to go to restaurants with her family on a few occasions; she has difficulty sleeping; she tries to distance herself from others; and on the occasions that she attends church, she sits between her daughters for security. She has attended a few family gatherings, but stays by herself in a room. She no longer has sexual relations with her husband.

Appellant Sharp referred Guess to psychiatrist Dr. Joel Reisman and his partner, psychologist Dr. Roland Lee. Both Drs. Reisman and Lee have treated Guess since January 4, 1999 and were continuing to treat her at the time of trial. At trial, the court admitted into evidence the deposition testimony of these two doctors, as well as the deposition testimony of Dr. Michael Gelfand, a specialist in the field of infectious disease.

Dr. Reisman diagnosed Guess with Post-Traumatic Stress Disorder (PTSD) caused by the "work related injury of November 1998." Dr. Reisman has prescribed various medications to combat Guess's symptoms and continued to prescribe these medications at the time of the trial. Dr. Reisman assigned Guess a permanent impairment rating under the 5th edition of the American Medical Association Guidelines of a Class III, moderate impairment. He stated that Guess was vocationally impaired because she should not engage in assembly line or production work where blood could be shed, work involving the public, or work that would require a great deal of concentration or focus.

Dr. Lee testified that Guess's psychological condition was caused by her fear of being exposed to HIV positive blood on November 6, 1998. He further testified that her fear is real and that her perception of the events that transpired is her reality. According to Dr. Lee, this fear interferes with Guess's cognitive functioning and social interaction.

Dr. Michael Gelfand, an infectious disease specialist, testified that Guess had been tested five times for HIV and all five tests were negative. Dr. Gelfand testified that Guess's chance of becoming infected was infinitely small by virtue of the unknown status of the source and the mechanism of claimed contact.

On February 7, 2002, the trial court entered its final order in which it concluded that Guess suffered a vocational disability as a result of the psychological consequences of her injury. Based on this finding, the trial court awarded Guess permanent partial disability of 38% to her mental faculties, a scheduled member injury. See Tenn. Code Ann. § 50–6–207(3)(A)(ii)(ff)(1999).

Appellant Sharp sought review of the judgment, arguing that the evidence preponderated against the finding that Guess suffered a compensable injury. The appellant also raised several evidentiary issues: whether the court erred in allowing into evidence certain documentation purportedly establishing the sexual orientation of the co-worker with whose blood Guess came into contact; whether the court committed reversible error by not allowing the testimony of the appellant's expert Dr. David Schraberg; and whether the court erred in not allowing the appellant's counsel to cross-examine Guess on the issue of the content of her treatment sessions. Appellee Guess submitted one additional argument on appeal—whether the trial court erred in awarding only 38% vocational disability.

Prior to oral arguments before the Special Workers' Compensation Panel, the case was transferred to the entire Supreme Court for review. As noted, the primary issue is what, if any, benefits the appellee is entitled to for alleged mental injuries arising from her exposure to the blood of a co-worker. Before this Court, Appellant argues that because

Guess offered no credible proof that she was actually exposed to HIV-contaminated blood, there was no basis for her fear and therefore she did not suffer a compensable injury. Guess argues that her vocational disability award should be increased to 75% or more because of the severity of her limitations resulting from the work-related injury.

We agree with the appellant that absent proof of actual exposure to HIV, the appellee has not suffered a compensable injury under the Workers' Compensation Law. Therefore, for the reasons contained herein, we reverse the judgment of the chancery court.

* * *

DISCUSSION

This case presents an issue of first impression in Tennessee: is an employee alleging mental injuries based on perceived exposure to HIV in the work environment entitled to workers' compensation benefits where there is no proof of *actual* exposure to the virus?

Under the statutory scheme governing Tennessee workers' compensation claims, injuries by accident "arising out of and in the scope of employment" are compensable. The statutory requirements that the injury "arise out of" and occur "in the course of" the employment are not synonymous. The phrase "in the course of" refers to time, place and circumstances, and "arising out of" refers to cause or origin. An accidental injury arises out of and is in the course and scope of employment if it has a rational connection to the work and occurs while the employee is engaged in the duties of employment.

We have previously determined that an injury that is purely mental in nature is compensable under the Workers' Compensation Law. See Ivey v. Trans Global Gas & Oil, 3 S.W.3d 441, 446 n.10 (Tenn. 1999). In *Ivey*, we interpreted Tennessee Code Annotated Section 50–6–207(3)(A)(ii)(ff) to cover two types of injuries to one's "mental faculties": (1) mental impairment resulting from physical trauma to the brain; and (2) mental or emotional injuries resulting from non-physical harm or trauma. In discussing the latter type of injury, we stated that the absence of physical harm or physical trauma does not lessen the possible effects that such injury can have on both cognitive and vocational abilities.

To be compensable, the mental injury must have resulted from an identifiable stressful, work-related event that produced a sudden mental stimulus such as fright, shock, or excessive unexpected anxiety. On the other hand, "worry, anxiety or emotional stress of a general nature" is not compensable, because the workers' compensation system "does not embrace every stress or strain of daily living or every undesirable experience encountered in carrying out the duties of a contract of employment."

Appellee Guess argues that *Ivey* is controlling because, like the claimant in *Ivey*, she suffered a mental injury as a result of an "identifiable stressful, work-related event," that led to fright, anxiety and shock. She alleges that her mental injury is exactly the type contemplated in *Ivey* and that no proof of actual exposure to HIV is necessary. We do not question the validity of the medical experts' diagnosis of Post Traumatic Stress Disorder stemming out of the incident during which Guess got blood of a co-worker on her hand. While PTSD can, in some circumstances, be a compensable workers' compensation injury, the facts of this case are such that Appellee's injury was not one "arising out of" her employment.

While this court has not previously visited the issue of whether a mental injury stemming from the fear of contracting HIV or AIDS is compensable in the context workers' compensation claims, we have addressed this issue in the context of a claim for negligent infliction of emotion distress. In Carroll v. Sisters of Saint Francis Health Servs., Inc., 868 S.W.2d 585 (Tenn. 1993), the plaintiff sued a hospital to recover damages stemming from her fear of contracting AIDS after pricking her fingers on discarded needles. There, we held that to recover damages for emotional distress based on the fear of contracting HIV or AIDS, "a plaintiff must prove, at a minimum, that he or she was actually exposed to HIV."

In Bain v. Wells, 936 S.W.2d 618 (Tenn. 1997), we again held that in order to maintain a claim for negligent infliction of emotional distress based on exposure to HIV or AIDS, there must be proof of actual exposure. Bain, a patient at a drug and alcohol rehabilitation center, was placed in the same room with a patient who was HIV positive without being given a warning or obtaining consent. During that time, the two shared a bathroom, and Bain had an open cut on his buttocks. Additionally, on one occasion, Bain mistakenly used his roommate's disposable razor. Id. We found that the defendant was entitled to summary judgment because Bain failed to offer proof that he had actually been exposed to HIV through one of the accepted means of transmission. In so doing, we explained that in Carroll, we implicitly held that emotional distress injuries are not reasonable, as a matter of law, in a fear-of-contracting-AIDS case unless the plaintiff actually had been exposed to HIV.

Bain basically stands for the proposition that without proof of actual exposure, the plaintiff failed to show the proximate cause element of negligent infliction of emotional distress. Applying a similar analysis in the context of this workers' compensation claim, we find that without proof of actual exposure, the appellee cannot show that her injury arises out of her employment.

As in *Bain*, Guess has offered no credible evidence that she was actually exposed to HIV. There is nothing in the record to establish whether the blood in question was even HIV positive. Guess's fears of contamination are based on speculation regarding her co-worker's sexual orientation and her subsequent assumption that he was HIV positive.

Aside from this speculation by the plaintiff, there was no evidence that the blood with which she came into contact was infected with the virus.

Appellee Guess asks us to rely solely on *Ivey* in finding her mental injuries to be compensable. However, *Ivey* is distinguishable from the case at hand. The plaintiff in *Ivey* was an employee in a convenience store who was robbed at gunpoint one night. The sudden, identifiable work-related event faced by Ivey was one that put her in real, undeniable danger. Unlike Ivey, the sudden stimulus facing Guess was not one in which she was exposed to any real danger. Because Guess had no proof that her co-worker was in fact HIV positive, there was no rational connection between her injury and employment. This is particularly true considering the fact that no less than five tests were administered and came back negative for the virus.

We are unwilling to accept the appellee's subjective impressions concerning the co-worker's sexual orientation or frail medical condition as proof that his blood was in fact contaminated. To do so would be to further the prejudices and stereotypes surrounding AIDS. In *Bain*, we specially cautioned against allowing damages based on an unfounded fear of contracting AIDS on public policy grounds.

* * *

If a plaintiff were allowed to recover under the facts of the present case, anybody suffering from a mental injury stemming from any perceived or imagined exposure to harmful substances or situations would be entitled to recovery. We find such a result contrary to the original purpose and continued viability of the Tennessee Workers' Compensation Law. As such, we are unwilling to award disability benefits to a claimant who suffers from an irrational fear of exposure to HIV when there is no proof of actual exposure via a medically recognized channel of transmission. Accordingly, we reverse the decision of the trial court in its assignment of 38% permanent partial disability to her mental faculties.

NOTES AND QUESTIONS

1.　Was the decision based on the irrationality of the plaintiff's fear or the prejudice and stereotyping underlying the irrationality? Should workers' compensation for mental distress be limited to rational fears? Suppose the plaintiff had been a nurse in the HIV clinic, and the exposure occurred while taking blood from a patient who was being tested for HIV (which test ultimately was negative). Is her emotional distress compensable?

2.　Workers' compensation mental distress cases generally fall into one of the following three categories: (1) physical-mental, where a work-related physical injury leads to mental distress; (2) mental-physical, where work-related mental distress leads to physical manifestations; and (3) mental-mental, where a work-related mental distress leads to mental illness. The third category of cases has proven to be the most difficult for claimants.

3. Other doctrines have been used to limit compensation for emotional distress. For example, in Adams v. Temple Inland, 858 So.2d 855 (La. Ct. App. 2003), writ denied, 867 So.2d 695 (La. 2004), an employee was subjected to sexual harassment, including threats of rape, over a period of time. The court affirmed denial of workers' compensation benefits on the grounds that there can be no award of benefits without proof that the mental injury was caused by a single, unexpected, and extraordinary event.

4. In Rivers v. Grimsley Oil Co., 842 So.2d 975 (Fla. Dist. Ct. App. 2003), writ denied, 853 So.2d 1070 (Fla. 2003), a gas station employee working alone at night was robbed at gunpoint and she sought workers' compensation for her severe emotional distress. The denial of her workers' compensation claim was affirmed on the ground that compensation is not available for mental or nervous injury resulting from stress, fright, or excitement. Her related claim for negligent infliction of emotional distress was rejected because Florida law follows the "impact rule" for emotional distress claims. But see Kelly v. State Dep't of Corrections, 218 P.3d 291 (Alaska 2009) (prison guard who suffered severe emotional distress after being threatened by convicted murderer demonstrated that his stress was "extraordinary and unusual" in comparison to co-workers as required by the statute); Family Dollar Stores, Inc. v. Edwards, 245 S.W.3d 181 (Ark. Ct. App. 2006) (cashier who suffered heart attack one day after being robbed at gunpoint entitled to compensation).

5. In Bertoch v. NBD Corp., 813 N.E.2d 1159 (Ind. 2004), a security guard with a pre-existing heart condition suffered a fatal heart attack while responding to a fire alarm. The Indiana Supreme Court held that his widow was entitled to full death benefits because the working conditions aggravated the employee's pre-existing condition. See also Carpenter's Case, 923 N.E.2d 1026 (Mass. 2010) (widow of employee who suffered sudden cardiac death while operating snow blower was entitled to compensation, notwithstanding the employee's preexisting coronary artery disease).

Kilburn v. Granite State Insurance Co.
522 S.W.3d 384 (Tenn. 2017).

■ ROGER A. PAGE, J.:

* * *

I. Facts and Procedural History

On November 6, 2008, Charles Kilburn, a trim carpenter, was severely injured in a motor vehicle accident during the course of his employment. His employer was Ryan Brown ("Employer"). As a result of the accident, Mr. Kilburn incurred fractures to the C3 and C4 vertebrae in his neck and disc herniations at the L4-5 and L5-S1 areas of his lower back. Dr. Jacob Schwarz, a neurosurgeon, performed an anterior cervical discectomy and surgical fusion of the C3 and C4 vertebrae on July 29, 2009, which improved Mr. Kilburn's neck pain. After physical therapy and an epidural steroid injection, Mr. Kilburn still complained of severe back pain when bending forward or backward, pain that was more severe on his left side than on the right, and lower extremity pain. Mr. Kilburn also felt heaviness in his legs after walking for a short period of time such that he would have to sit down, which Dr. Schwarz opined was a symptom of neurogenic claudication. As a result, Dr. Schwarz recommended surgery to the L4-5 and L5-S1 areas of Mr. Kilburn's lower back. However, Mr. Kilburn's insurance company denied coverage for the surgery due to a peer review by three physicians disagreeing with Dr. Schwarz's findings. The insurance company also denied Dr. Schwarz's recommendation for epidural steroid injections. Dr. Schwarz then referred Mr. Kilburn to a pain management clinic and wrote a letter to Mr. Kilburn's insurance adjustor asserting that Mr. Kilburn's pain was debilitating enough to prevent him from returning to work.

On January 4, 2010, Mr. Kilburn was evaluated by Dr. William Leone, a pain management specialist. Dr. Leone's notes reflect that he was concerned with Mr. Kilburn's consumption of alcohol while taking his medication. Mr. Kilburn also admitted that because he felt the medication was no longer effective, he was taking two opioid tablets at once even though he had only been prescribed one tablet at a time. The urinary drug screen conducted that day showed the presence of both alcohol and the opioid medication. As a result, Dr. Leone recommended weaning Mr. Kilburn off the opioid medication and trying other options. Dr. Leone prescribed 350 mg of Soma twice daily and 15 mg of oxycodone four times daily. As part of his treatment, Mr. Kilburn initialed and signed an agreement stating, "I will control my usage of narcotic medications as directed by the attending physician. There are no exceptions. If medication is inadequate for [my] pain level, [I] must call before adjusting dosage."

During the trial, Phillip Manning, Mr. Kilburn's brother-in-law, and Judy Kilburn, Mr. Kilburn's wife, explained that prior to the 2008 motor vehicle accident, Mr. Kilburn was friendly and outgoing and was very active. However, after the injury and neck surgery, Mr. Kilburn's lower back pain seemed to Mr. Manning to be "[p]retty bad" and uncomfortable, and Mr. Kilburn was "upset" about not being able to have the lower back surgery. Mr. Manning opined that Mr. Kilburn "had anxiety about not having medication and not having the surgery" but that Mr. Kilburn never appeared hopeless, just ready to be back to full capacity. Mr. Manning stated that Mr. Kilburn started skipping doses of his medication because he was scared that he was going to run out of the medication and would be unable to obtain more.

* * *

Ms. Kilburn found Mr. Kilburn unresponsive in bed on the morning of January 28, 2010. The medical examiner's report specifically stated that the cause of death was acute oxycodone toxicity with contributory causes of hypertension, tobacco use, and alcohol use. His death was deemed an accident. Mr. Kilburn was forty years old at the time of his death.

At trial, Dr. Alistair Finlayson and Dr. Jeffrey Hazlewood testified by deposition about their review of Mr. Kilburn's medical records. Dr. Finlayson was a psychiatrist with a subspecialty in addictions and a clinical associate professor in psychiatry at Vanderbilt University Medical Center. He was also the medical director of the Comprehensive Assessment Program at Vanderbilt, which evaluates professionals to determine if they are "fit for duty." He performed a records review at the request of Ms. Kilburn. Dr. Finlayson stated that it was "more likely than not" that Mr. Kilburn was suffering from severe pain or anxiety at the time of his death and that it was "certainly possible" that those conditions diminished Mr. Kilburn's faculties and contributed to his risk of overdose.

* * *

Dr. Finlayson stated that when a person is used to taking an opioid but then takes less or stops taking the medication, "the pain is intensified and anxiety is intensified as a . . . withdrawal." Dr. Finlayson stated that drugs like OxyContin, Soma, and Valium all contribute to feelings of depression and hopelessness, which could potentially influence a person's judgment. He further opined that he did not believe that Mr. Kilburn was addicted to his medication but rather that "it [was] possible that . . . he was so discouraged, depressed, anxious about what was going to happen and experiencing some withdrawal symptoms that he . . . took maybe more medication than he intended to, combined with more alcohol than he intended to."

* * *

Dr. Hazlewood was a board-certified physician in physical medicine, rehabilitation, and pain management and had been practicing in pain management for nineteen years. He conducted a records review at the request of the Employer. Dr. Hazlewood agreed with Dr. Leone's recommendation to slowly decrease Mr. Kilburn's intake of narcotics, rather than increasing the dosage, because of Mr. Kilburn's building tolerance to the medication and because of Mr. Kilburn's use of alcohol. He opined that taking 60 mg of oxycodone daily along with consuming alcohol was inadvisable. When discussing the effect of Mr. Kilburn's pain and anxiety on his judgment, Dr. Hazlewood stated that while acute pain such as breaking several bones at one time can cloud a person's judgment, he did not think that chronic pain such as Mr. Kilburn's could cloud a person's judgment. Dr. Hazlewood agreed that anxiety, depression, and suicidal ideations could cloud a person's judgment but stated that he was not qualified to state whether pain can cause an anxiety disorder.

* * *

Both doctors agreed that while tobacco use and hypertension were tangentially related to Mr. Kilburn's health and ability to withstand the acute oxycodone toxicity, Mr. Kilburn's use of alcohol was the primary contributing factor.

After hearing the evidence, the trial court issued its decision as a written memorandum. The trial court accredited the opinion of Dr. Finlayson over that of Dr. Hazlewood. The court found that Ms. Kilburn had sustained her burden of proof to show that Mr. Kilburn's death was a direct and natural consequence of his work injury. It awarded workers' compensation death benefits to Ms. Kilburn. Employer has timely appealed, asserting that the evidence preponderates against the trial court's finding of compensability and that Mr. Kilburn's conduct constituted an independent intervening cause of his death.

* * *

III. Analysis

* * *

"The basic rule is that a subsequent injury, whether an aggravation of the original injury or a new and distinct injury, is compensable if it is the direct and natural result of a compensable primary injury." Therefore, " 'all the medical consequences and sequelae that flow from the primary injury are compensable.' " Anderson v. Westfield Grp., 259 S.W.3d 690, 696 (Tenn. 2008) (quoting 1 Larson's Workers' Compensation Law § 10.01 (2004)). However, that rule has a limit that "hinges on whether the subsequent injury is the result of independent intervening causes, such as the employee's own conduct." Stated another way, " 'the progressive worsening or complication of a work-connected injury remains compensable so long as the worsening is not shown to have been produced by an intervening nonindustrial cause.' " The *Anderson* court provided several examples of cases in which the injured employee's conduct constituted an independent intervening cause that rendered the subsequent injury to be non-compensable: Simpson v. H.D. Lee Co., 793 S.W.2d 929, 931–32 (Tenn. 1990) (concluding that medication taken contrary to instructions constituted an intervening cause); Guill v. Aetna Life & Cas. Co., 660 S.W.2d 42, 43–44 (Tenn. 1983) (determining that injecting medication contrary to medical instructions was an intervening cause); and Jones v. Huey, 210 Tenn. 162, 357 S.W.2d 47, 49–50 (1962) (deciding that the negligent operation of a tractor after a work-related back injury was not compensable). The *Anderson* Court adopted the reasoning of Jones v. Huey and stated:

> [W]e reject the employee's argument that only reckless or intentional misconduct can constitute an intervening cause. Instead, we find, as we did in *Jones*, that negligence is the appropriate standard for determining whether an independent intervening cause relieves an employer of liability for a

subsequent injury purportedly flowing from a prior work-related injury.

Anderson, 259 S.W.3d at 698–99. Application of the intervening cause principle is not an affirmative defense but, rather, is a "way of assessing the scope of an employer's liability for injuries occurring after a compensable injury."

* * *

Based on the above analysis, we conclude that the evidence preponderates against the trial court's findings. We conclude that * * * Mr. Kilburn failed to take his pain medication in accordance with his physician's instructions, which ultimately caused his demise. Therefore, his death was no longer causally related to his work-related injury, and his overdose was an independent intervening cause.

Conclusion

In summary, we conclude that Mr. Kilburn's failure to consume his medication in accordance with his doctor's instructions was an independent intervening cause. As such, we reverse the judgment of the trial court. The costs of this appeal are taxed to the plaintiff, Judy Kilburn.

NOTES AND QUESTIONS

1. Most courts hold that claimants are entitled to additional compensation for the aggravation of an injury or illness attributable to medical malpractice. See, e.g., McCorkle v. McCorkle, 265 S.W.2d 779 (Ky. 1954); Gray v. Church's Fried Chicken, Inc., 504 So. 2d 979 (La. Ct. App. 1987); Mallete v. Mercury Outboard Supply Co., 321 S.W.2d 816 (1959); Combs v. Virginia Electric & Power Co. , 525 S.E.2d 278 (2000). Should the additional harm caused by the "negligence" of the claimant be compensable?

2. A woman slipped and fell while walking to work, incurring multiple injuries for which she received compensation. Years later, she requested, but was denied additional benefits to treat her lumbar spondylosis, a new condition she argued was a "flow-through" from her original injuries. Expert testimony, however, found that her failure to lose weight, combined with natural aging was the proximate cause of her current ailment, not her prior slip and fall. Accordingly, the court affirmed the denial of additional compensation. Leasure v. UVMC, 2017 WL 3446986 (Ohio Ct. App. 2017).

3. In light of the opioid crisis, would it violate public policy to award compensation for opioid misuse? In an unpublished opinion, the North Carolina Court of Appeals held that an employee's accidental overdose of opioids, among other drugs prescribed to treat a work injury, was compensable. The court held that the original work injury was a proximate cause of the overdose death. Brady v. Best Buy Co., 2017 N.C. App. LEXIS 844 (2017). By contrast, an Arkansas court held that an intentional opioid overdose constituted an independent and intervening cause of death (an employee overdosed on methadone while in recovery from addiction to the opioids that were prescribed to treat a compensable injury) and denied workers' compensation death benefits. Loar v. Cooper Tire & Rubber Co., 2014 Ark. App. 240 (Ark. Ct. App. 2014).

4.   Firefighters are exposed to various dusts, fumes, gases, and other hazardous exposures. If they develop cancer or another illness it is often impossible for them to prove that a specific occupational exposure was the cause. To prevent the unfairness of this burden of proof, most states have enacted special laws that presume that firefighters' (or in some states, also police or other public employees') diseases of the heart or lungs are occupationally related. See City of Philadelphia Fire Department v. Workers' Compensation Appeal Board, 195 A.3d 197 (Pa. 2018) (firefighter not required to prove that identified carcinogen actually caused his cancer).

5.   An employee had a non-work related medical emergency causing her heart to stop beating. Her employer had an automated external defibrillator (AED), but did not use it and merely called for the EMS. Although the EMS personnel were able to revive her, she suffered brain damage that she alleged was caused by the delay. She sought workers' compensation for her additional injuries. The Supreme Court of Tennessee held that an employer has a duty to supply *reasonable* medical assistance to an employee in an emergency, but it had no duty to use the AED, even though it was available. Therefore, the employee's claim did not arise out of her employment. Chaney v. Team Technologies, Inc., 568 S.W.3d 576 (Tenn. 2019).

D. DETERMINING BENEFIT LEVELS

1. IMPAIRMENT AND DISABILITY

It is important to define the terms impairment and disability. Impairment is a medical assessment of the degree of loss of an individual's body structure or function. Disability is a legal term representing the effects of impairment. According to the American Medical Association:

> The relationship between impairment and disability remains both complex and difficult, if not impossible, to predict. In some conditions there is a strong association between the level of injury and the degree of functional loss expected in one's personal sphere or activity (mobility or ADLs [activities of daily living]. The same level of injury is in no way predictive of an affected individual's ability to participate in major life functions (including work) when appropriate motivation, technology, and sufficient accommodations are available. Disability may be influenced by physical, psychological, and psychosocial factors that can change over time.

American Medical Association, Guides to the Evaluation of Permanent Impairment vii (6th ed. 2008).

The degree of impairment, its duration, and its effect on the claimant's ability to continue work are used to determine how the claimant's disability is classified and the level of benefits to which he or she is entitled.

Turner v. American Mutual Insurance Co.
390 So.2d 1330 (La. 1980).

■ DENNIS, JUSTICE.

The issue presented in this workers' compensation case is whether the plaintiff is unable "to engage in any gainful occupation for wages" and thus should be awarded compensation for permanent total disability. The court of appeal, affirming the trial court, held that the plaintiff, a mentally retarded woodcutter whose right foot had been crushed, was not permanently disabled because he could still perform "some type of gainful employment." We reverse and remand.

In Oster v. Wetzel Printing, Inc., 390 So.2d 1318 (La.1980) we held that the odd-lot doctrine should be used as the guiding concept in determining whether an injured employee is unable "to engage in any gainful occupation for wages" and is thus totally and permanently disabled. In the present case, the plaintiff's employment capabilities were severely restricted because of his mental and physical limitations, and the employer did not demonstrate the existence of an actual job in the employee's general locality at which he has a reasonable opportunity to be employed. Because the plaintiff established a prima facie showing of total and permanent disability, we reverse the holdings of the lower courts, but remand to allow the defendant a fuller opportunity to rebut by showing an actual job is available.

Silton Turner, a twenty year old black man, was employed as a sawhand for a logging contractor. His job required that he perform manual labor, including the operation of a power saw and, at times, a log skidder, in cutting and moving logs in the woods. On February 22, 1977, while riding on the front of a log skidder, plaintiff received serious injury to his right foot when the operator of the skidder raised the blade, pinning Turner's foot between the blade and the radiator of the skidder, breaking several bones. Turner was initially taken to Dr. LaCour in Oakdale and then transported to Rapides General Hospital where he was treated by Dr. Cedric Lowrey, an orthopedic specialist. After two operations conducted by Dr. Lowrey, plaintiff was ultimately released by the doctor with a residual disability of thirty to forty per cent in the right foot.

Turner was paid workers' compensation benefits until Dr. Lowrey notified the employer's insurer that he felt the plaintiff could resume work on a trial basis. Upon receiving this report, the insurer terminated compensation payments. Turner sued claiming that the payments were improperly discontinued because he was permanently disabled. * * *

Under the odd-lot test as announced in Oster v. Wetzel Printing, Inc., supra, an injured employee is entitled to total, permanent disability compensation if he can perform no services other than those which are so limited in quality, dependability, or quantity that a reasonably stable market for them does not exist. This determination is made after scrutiny of the evidence of the worker's physical impairment as well as his mental capacity, education, and training. If the worker establishes that he falls into the odd-lot category, he is entitled to total, permanent disability compensation unless the employer or his insurer is able to show that some form of suitable work is regularly and continuously available to the employee within reasonable proximity to the worker's residence.

In applying this analysis to the present case, we find that the concrete evidence is virtually undisputed. Turner sustained fractures of the second and third metatarsals of the right foot with a dislocation of all tarsometatarsal joints. He was required to undergo two surgical operations and wear a cast on his leg. His second metatarsal achieved questionable healing, resulting in a precarious union that makes him much more susceptible to injury than a normal person. Approximately one year after the accident, it was determined that he had lost virtually all motion of his great toe and 50% of the motion of his other toes. Atrophy of his right calf muscles had decreased the size of his limb by one inch in circumference. His doctors concluded that the 30 to 40% disability of his foot, and its added thickness, would require him to wear mismatched shoes.

Turner began working at the age of fifteen and labored primarily as a log cutter. He worked briefly in cannery and as a combination truck loader and driver for a pecan company. He attempted to go back to work as a log cutter as his doctor advised. He quit after three or four hours, however, when his foot became swollen and painful. He has attempted to exercise his foot by walking, but he experiences pain after standing or walking for long periods. Turner testified that he cannot perform any job that requires such use of his injured foot. He conceded that he could drive an automobile with an automatic transmission by applying the brake with his healthy left foot, but he testified that he could not operate a standard transmission truck or skidder, which would require manipulation of the brake with his injured foot.

Doctor Lowrey, the orthopedist who treated and performed surgery on Turner, testified the employee could eventually return full time to the job of log cutter. The doctor acknowledged that his patient had a 30–40% disability of the foot and a precarious union of one bone which could develop into a pseudo-arthrosis. He also acknowledged that Turner's foot could be reinjured easily if it was jerked up or down. The doctor did not doubt that Turner experiences pain and has a stiff forefoot, but the physician thought that the condition would improve if Turner forced himself to walk on it. The doctor was of the opinion that Turner could not do work that required him to put a great deal of weight or pressure on his toes. Although the doctor confessed he was not too familiar with logging, he said he did not think it involved standing or pushing up on one's toes.

On the other hand, Dr. Joffrion, an orthopedist who saw Turner on one occasion for purposes of evaluation, testified that in his opinion the patient cannot perform the duties of a logger because he can no longer stand or walk for extended periods. According to the doctor, Turner's disability results from a permanent stiffness of the midfoot which, together with the malunion of one bone, alters the mechanics of the foot, and causes excessive force at the ankle and toe area. Dr. Joffrion testified that he was familiar with the physical requirements of the job of logger and that Turner could not perform them because his condition made prolonged walking, standing, stopping or climbing impossible. Consequently, he recommended that the plaintiff be given rehabilitation and training for a sedentary occupation.

George Hearn, PhD, an industrial psychologist and vocational rehabilitationist, testified that he interviewed Turner and gave him a battery of intelligence, achievement, aptitude and psychological tests. According to the tests, Turner has an intelligence quotient of 64, and has attained education grade levels of 4.6 in reading, 4.0 in spelling, and 2.3 in arithmetic. He is mentally retarded, quite limited in academic skills, and his eye-hand motor coordination is consistent with his level of intellect, his achievement and his experience. In the psychologist's opinion, however, Turner's job skills in these areas had not been further impaired because of the accident.

* * *

The trial court and court of appeal, of course, did not attempt to decide the case in accordance with the odd-lot doctrine. Although we mean no criticism of their failure to do so, in the absence of an expression by this Court on the subject, the result reached below illustrates the dangers of a simplistic or mechanical application of statutory rules in the field of workers' compensation. Turner, a mentally retarded, unskilled laborer, who sustained a permanent 30–40% disability of his foot, was denied either permanent partial disability or permanent total disability benefits. Both lower courts seemed to reject the opinion of the one doctor who said Turner could return to the work in which he was engaged at the time of the accident. But they based their decisions largely on the testimony of the vocational psychologist, who, in essence, stated that there were jobs available at various places in the state which a person with Turner's disability could perform. Thus, the trial court and court of appeal never focused on the question of whether Silton Turner, considering both his physical and mental limitations, can successfully obtain and hold regular employment in actual jobs available to him within reasonable proximity to his residence.

* * *

Turner lives in the small town of Simmesport. It is unknown how many jobs there were available to the plaintiff before he was injured, considering his mental capabilities. There is also no indication of whether there are any opportunities within a reasonable area for a person who can drive a truck or operate a skidder, but who cannot do other work which often is combined with those activities. Ultimately, it has not been shown that there is an occupation available within a reasonable area in which Turner can work considering his physical disability, education, and mental deficiencies.

We believe that a remand in this case is appropriate. We only recently announced in *Oster* that the odd-lot doctrine would be used to determine the extent of a worker's disability. We did not remand in *Oster* because the evidence showed that the injured elderly bookbinder could not engage in gainful employment even if a suitable job existed. Since it is possible that an actual job in Turner's vicinity exists that might afford the plaintiff gainful employment, we feel that the defendant should be allowed an opportunity to make this showing. On remand the plaintiff also will be allowed to introduce further evidence to support his case under the doctrine.

If the employer is successful in rebutting Turner's prima facie showing of total disability, the trial judge should reconsider the appropriateness of compensation for partial disability under La.R.S. 23:1221(3). If it is found that Turner can return to gainful employment, though not to the same or similar-work, then he would be entitled to an award of partial disability rather than the schedule loss under La.R.S. 23:1221(4)(g) and (o).

REVERSED AND REMANDED TO THE DISTRICT COURT.

NOTES AND QUESTIONS

1.   Many employers are self-insured and others are experience-rated. This means that a workers' compensation claim for permanent disability may be quite costly. Would the *Turner* decision tend to discourage employers from hiring workers such as Silton Turner who, if they sustained ordinarily nondisabling injuries, are likely to be found totally disabled under the "odd lot" doctrine? If so, is there a solution to this problem?

2.   In *Turner*, the "aggravating" factor limiting the claimant's employment opportunities was his intellectual disability. Should a claimant's age (nearing retirement) be relevant? See Cargill Feed Div./Cargill Malt v. Labor & Indus. Rev. Comm'n, 789 N.W.2d 326 (Wis. Ct. App. 2010) (held: yes; under "odd-lot doctrine," courts consider age, education, and employment experience). In the era of an aging work force, what are the implications of considering age?

3.   The term "odd lot" was first used in the English case of Cardiff Corp. v. Hall, 1 K.B. 1009 (1911), where the court stated: "If I might be allowed to use such an undignified phrase, I should say that if the accident leaves the workman's labour in the position of an 'odd lot' in the labour market, the employer must shew that a customer can be found who will take it. * * * " Id. at 1021. The doctrine was first used in the United States by Judge Cardozo in Jordan v. Decorative Co., 130 N.E. 634 (N.Y.1921).

4. Should the burden of proof regarding employability rest with the claimant or the employer? Most jurisdictions hold that once the claimant proves inability to perform in the former job the burden shifts to the employer to show that there is other work available that the worker is capable of performing. See, e.g., Barrett v. Otis Elevator Co., 246 A.2d 668 (Pa.1968); Balczewski v. Department of Indus., Labor & Human Rels., 251 N.W.2d 794 (Wis.1977).

A NOTE ON BENEFIT LEVELS

Benefits for total disability are based upon a percentage (usually two-thirds) of the worker's prior wages up to the statewide average weekly wage. This precludes very highly paid individuals from receiving exorbitant awards. Statutory maximum provisions, however, may also preclude workers from receiving enough money to live on. For example, in 2019 the maximum award for a totally disabled worker in Mississippi was $494.48 per week. In some states a person receiving the maximum award is still below the poverty level. In several states, workers' compensation awards are offset by benefits received under Social Security or unemployment compensation. States also have minimum benefit levels. In 2019, in Arkansas the minimum benefit for a totally disabled worker was $20 per week. U.S. Chamber of Commerce, 2019 Analysis of Workers' Compensation Laws 51–59 (2019).

Scheduled benefits for permanent partial disability are artificial and do not consider the effect of the scheduled injury on the particular individual. (Benefits for unscheduled injuries and illnesses are determined on an individual basis.) The benefit levels are often illogical in the distinctions drawn among injuries and the benefit levels vary dramatically among jurisdictions for identical injuries.

2. REHABILITATION AND OTHER SERVICES

Stone Container Corp. v. Castle

657 N.W.2d 485 (Iowa 2003).

■ TERNUS, JUSTICE.

The issue presented in this case is whether the industrial commissioner correctly required an injured worker's employer to pay for a laptop computer pursuant to the employer's obligation to "furnish reasonable and necessary . . . appliances" under Iowa Code section 85.27 (1999). The district court affirmed the commissioner's award, but the court of appeals, in a split decision, reversed. In view of the unique circumstances presented by the case before us, we think the commissioner was right. Accordingly, we vacate the court of appeals decision and affirm the district court judgment.

* * *

II. *Background Facts and Proceedings.*

The appellee, Walker Castle, suffered catastrophic injuries in an industrial accident while working for the appellant, Stone Container Corporation. Castle, who was nineteen years old at the time, lost both his legs at the hip joint, as well as his buttocks, rectum and a testicle. He has undergone numerous surgeries, including skin grafts and colon resections. Castle suffers from chronic phantom limb pain, a "painful sensation of the presence of a limb that has been amputated."

In addition, Castle is very sensitive to temperature due to his extensive skin grafts and scaring. Normal room temperature causes his skin to break down. As a result, he is forced to spend most of his time in seclusion in his room at Opportunities Unlimited where the temperature can be kept cooler. Moreover, he is often unable to use his wheelchair because his skin problems prevent him from sitting. Therefore, he uses a "prone cart" that permits him to lie on his stomach and chest. Castle also suffers from post-traumatic stress disorder and other psychological injuries as a result of the accident. He has lived in a medically supervised environment from the time he was injured in April 1997.

Prior to the accident, Castle had no education or training beyond high school. He did not own a computer. At his request, however, Stone Container's worker's compensation carrier, appellant, National Union Fire Insurance Company, provided Castle with a laptop computer in October 1997. (In the remainder of this opinion, we will refer to the insurer and the employer jointly as the employer.) Following that acquisition, Castle completed ten hours of college course work.

Eventually Castle's computer ceased to work and could not be repaired, prompting him to file an application for alternate medical care pursuant to Iowa Code section 85.27, on August 30, 2000. Castle requested the employer be required to provide him with a laptop computer, including adaptations that would facilitate his use of it in his wheelchair and the prone cart.

At the hearing on Castle's application, his attorney asserted Castle needed a computer to assist him "in his educational pursuits, rehabilitation pursuits, and the computer . . . would serve . . . to replace function that he has lost . . . due to his injuries." Castle called two employees of Opportunities Unlimited who supported his claim: a computer teacher who was certified by Microsoft, and a licensed occupational therapist. The employer argued in response that a computer did not qualify as medical care under section 85.27 and therefore the employer had no obligation to provide Castle with one.

The deputy industrial commissioner, who had been delegated the authority to issue a final agency decision on Castle's request, concluded the computer and adaptive devices were appropriate expenses under section 85.27. Relying on the common meaning of the statutory terms as well as an administrative rule defining "appliance," see Iowa Admin.

Code r. 876–8.5, the deputy stated that "the computer is, in this case[,] an appliance because of the rehabilitative and therapeutic use it provides in an occupational therapy setting to increase [Castle's] vocational and personal independence, which were lost as a result of his injuries."

As previously noted, this ruling was affirmed by the district court on judicial review, but was reversed by the court of appeals. We granted Castle's application for further review.

* * *

V.   *Computer as an "Appliance."*

A.   *Applicable legal principles.* In pertinent part, Iowa Code section 85.27 provides:

> The employer, for all injuries compensable under this chapter or chapter 85A, *shall furnish reasonable* surgical, *medical,* dental, osteopathic, chiropractic, podiatric, physical rehabilitation, nursing, ambulance and hospital *services and supplies therefor* and shall allow reasonably necessary transportation expenses incurred for such services. The employer *shall also furnish reasonable and necessary* crutches, artificial members and appliances but shall not be required to furnish more than one set of permanent prosthetic devices.

* * *

> *For purposes of this section, the employer is obliged to furnish reasonable services and supplies to treat an injured employee,* and has the right to choose the care . . . If the employee has reason to be dissatisfied with the care offered, the employee should communicate the basis of such dissatisfaction to the employer, in writing if requested, following which the employer and the employee may agree to alternate care reasonably suited to treat the injury. If the employer and employee cannot agree on such alternate care, the commissioner may, upon application and reasonable proofs of the necessity therefor, allow and order other care.

Iowa Code § 85.27 (emphasis added). Reduced to its essentials, section 85.27 requires an insurer to furnish reasonable medical services and supplies and reasonable *and* necessary appliances to treat an injured employee.

The scope of the latter obligation is partially explained in Iowa Administrative Code rule 876–8.5. That rule contains the following definition of the word "appliance" as used in section 85.27:

> Appliances are defined as hearing aids, corrective lenses, orthodontic devices, dentures, orthopedic braces, or *any other artificial device used to provide function or for therapeutic purposes.*

> Appliances which are for the correction of a condition resulting from an injury . . . are compensable under Iowa Code section 85.27.

Iowa Admin. Code r. 876–8.5 (emphasis added). Thus, under the agency's interpretation of section 85.27, an employer must provide any device that furnishes an action or affords a function impaired or lost as a result of the employee's injury, or that treats or remedies a condition resulting from the injury.

B. *Employer's arguments*. We turn now to the employer's contentions on appeal. The employer does not challenge the agency's rule defining "appliance." Rather, it claims a computer does not fall within this definition, or within section 85.27 generally. More specifically, the employer argues that section 85.27 obligates it to provide only (1) reasonable and necessary medical or surgical care, or (2) devices that improve function. A computer, asserts the employer, is not medical care and does not supply function. The employer appears to take the position that because a computer would not restore *physical* mobility to Castle, it does not "provide function" lost by Castle as a result of his injuries. *See* Iowa Admin. Code r. 876–8.5.

C. *Analysis*. Because we think the peculiar facts of this case support the deputy's conclusion that a computer constitutes an appliance within the meaning of section 85.27, we confine our discussion to that issue. We begin our analysis with a brief review of two prior cases that have applied section 85.27 under unique, but somewhat similar, circumstances: Manpower Temporary Services v. Sioson, 529 N.W.2d 259 (Iowa 1995) and Quaker Oats Co. v. Ciha, 552 N.W.2d 143 (Iowa 1996).

In *Sioson*, work-related injuries rendered the employee, Sioson, a quadriplegic. 529 N.W.2d at 261. Due to her condition, Sioson was equipped with an electric "puff and sip" wheelchair. When she traveled long distances, however, she had to use a manual wheelchair because her electric wheelchair was too large and heavy to be loaded in and transported by a passenger vehicle. Because a manual wheelchair and the process of shifting her from one wheelchair to the other posed risks of injury and medical complications, Sioson requested that the employer provide her with a specially equipped van so she could use the electric wheelchair when she left her home.

In affirming the commissioner's award of this expense to the employee, the key question addressed by this court was whether the modified van was an "appliance" within the meaning of section 85.27. Id. at 264. We concluded that under the "extremely rare" factual situation presented in *Sioson* it was:

> We begin with the unusually strong medical evidence of necessity and of the record that [Sioson's] family status and past lifestyle reveal no other use of the van. That evidence refutes any contention that the van is a frill or luxury and reveals what can be described as an appliance, not greatly different from crutches or a wheelchair. The point is that a van is necessary in order to make [Sioson's] wheelchair fully useful.

We have agreed with the dictionary definition that describes the term "appliance" as "a means to an end." The "end" of the van is merely an extension of [Sioson's] 300-pound wheelchair. Without a van she is, more than need be, a prisoner of her severe paralysis. The commissioner could thus reasonably view the van as an appliance, a necessary part of [Sioson's] care.

Our *Ciha* case also involved an employee who suffered from quadriplegia as a result of a work-related accident. 552 N.W.2d at 147. In that case, the employer refused to pay the expense of modifying a van so as to allow the employee, Ciha, to drive to work. The commissioner allowed the expense, noting "an appliance has been held to be a device that serves to replace a physical function lost by the injury." We affirmed, relying on our discussion in *Sioson* that an "appliance" is "a means to an end." We concluded the van modifications were "merely an extension of Ciha's wheelchair," and therefore were properly allowed by the commissioner as an appliance, "a necessary part of Ciha's care."

These cases stand, in part, for the principle that an expense falls within the scope of section 85.27 if it covers the cost of a device that replaces a function lost by the employee as a result of the employee's work-related injury. We reject the employer's contention that an appliance must be necessary for *medical* care, which was one anticipated use of the van in *Sioson*—transportation of Sioson to doctor appointments. The determinative circumstance in *Sioson* and *Ciha* was the fact that the van and van modifications provided physical mobility lost by the employees due to their quadriplegia. We think a similar circumstance exists under the unique facts before us.

Castle, even more so than Sioson and Ciha, is a prisoner of his injuries. Like them, he has lost the ability to physically move about without the assistance of a mechanical device. But unlike them, a van cannot replace this lost function for long-distance movement because, for now, Castle must remain in the controlled environment of his room to avoid additional medical complications. A computer in this case is comparable to the van in *Sioson* and *Ciha*: it provides Castle with access to the outside world—access that has been denied to him by his devastating injuries, and access that can only be gained through this artificial device.

Granted, a computer does not provide physical mobility; but we do not think such precise substitution is required under the liberal interpretation we are required to give to our worker's compensation statute. As we implied in *Sioson* and *Ciha*, it is the end function that is important; an appliance, whatever its form, is simply a means to get there. Here, the end function is the ability to interact with the outside world, not simply physical mobility. Viewed in this manner, a computer is a viable and necessary means to this end.

In summary, we conclude the agency properly interpreted section 85.27 in ruling a computer is an appliance for which Castle's employer is responsible. This conclusion makes it unnecessary to consider Castle's alternative contention that the computer is an appliance because it is an "artificial device used . . . for therapeutic purposes" within the meaning of rule 876–8.5.

Having rejected the employer's contention that the deputy commissioner erred in his interpretation of the governing law, we also disagree with the employer's assertion there is not substantial evidence to support the deputy's findings. The employer argues "the evidence in this case was of inferior quality" because "no qualified medical provider expressed the opinion that Castle needed a computer." It does not take a "qualified medical provider" to make apparent the effect on Castle of his undeniable injuries. Nor is testimony from a "qualified medical provider" required to allow the deputy to conclude that a computer would replace, electronically, the function lost by Castle as a result of his injuries, the ability to physically move about in the world. We conclude, therefore, that the agency's decision does not lack the necessary factual support simply because Castle did not have medical testimony, in addition to that offered by his occupational therapist, to support his application.

Finding no error in the agency decision, we affirm the district court judgment reaching the same conclusion. We vacate the court of appeals' contrary decision.

NOTES AND QUESTIONS

1.   The compensation liability for an individual who is permanently and totally disabled is quite substantial compared with the cost of a laptop computer. Indeed, the cost of litigating the case was, no doubt, much more than the cost of the laptop. Why contest this claim?

2.   In essence, the employer is arguing that it has paid for Mr. Castle's medical expenses and a portion of his lost income, and that is the extent of its statutory obligation. Why should the employer have to pay for a computer? Should the employer have to pay for internet service? Should the employer have to pay for a television set?

3.   Workers' compensation laws usually provide for the rehabilitation of individuals suffering from a work-related injury or illness. Medical services, nursing care, prosthetic devices, physical therapy, and vocational rehabilitation are customarily available. The case law differs on whether claimants are entitled to more unusual services.

4.   Claimants have been awarded a wide range of "other" services. See Thornton v. American Interstate Insurance Co., 897 N.W.2d 445 (Iowa 2017) (handicap-accessible home modifications compensable); Simmons v. Precast Haulers, Inc., 849 N.W.2d 117 (Neb. 2014) (wheelchair-accessible van compensable); Hall v. United States Xpress, Inc., 808 S.E.2d 595 (N.C. Ct. App. 2017) (rent contribution to enable claimant to live in accessible apartment compensable). But see Hensley v. D.C. Department of Employment Services, 49 A.3d 1195 (D.C. 2012) (home attendant to provide personal services not compensable); Elmore v. Missouri State Treasurer, 345

S.W.3d 361 (Mo. Ct. App. 2011) (voice-activated computer or one-handed keyboard not compensable); Dennis v. Erin Truckways, Ltd., 188 S.W.3d 578 (Tenn. 2006) (wheelchair-accessible house not compensable).

5.   A laborer on a refuse-collecting truck suffered a work-related injury that left him able to be employed only in sedentary occupations. The claimant sought reimbursement for the costs of a four-year college education to study computer science and accounting. What result? See City of Salem v. Colegrove, 321 S.E.2d 654 (Va.1984) (held: not entitled). Accord, Beaver Valley Corp. v. Priola, 477 So.2d 408 (Ala.1985).

3.   A NOTE ON DISPUTED CLAIMS

When an injured worker files a claim for benefits, the employer or the employer's insurer can contest it on one of two grounds. First, the insurer can argue that the injury is not compensable. Second, the insurer can admit liability, but challenge the extent of disability caused by the injury.

Compensable Injuries. The most frequently litigated question in the workers' compensation system involves whether any particular injury is compensable. The requirement that an injury "arise out of and in the course of employment" can present difficult questions of causation. For example, how can a worker prove that an increased risk of heart attack or chronic nervousness arose out of employment? Similarly, is a worker acting in the course of employment when he or she is injured during an altercation in the firm lunch room? Occupational diseases, which originally were not covered by workers' compensation, pose special problems. Not only is it difficult to establish a causal link between a worker's job and disease, but the employer's insurer may use the long latency period to question whether the injury occurred while the worker was employed by its insured.

Extent of Disability. Even if the worker can prove that the injury is compensable, it is still possible to dispute the extent of disability. Controversies frequently arise over the injured worker's medical record, which may be incomplete, inconclusive, or incorrect. Where the record is sufficient, the employer or insurer may challenge the worker's interpretation of it. Some injuries, such as back pain, cannot be objectively determined and the medical record is of little help. Beyond the uncertainty inherent in the medical record, a determination of how debilitating the injury is or how long the worker will be impaired is affected by a host of personal factors, including the worker's age, weight, and lifestyle.

Medical Benefits

Successful workers' compensation claimants are entitled to payment of their medical expenses. The right to medical benefits is independent of the right to disability benefits. Therefore, individuals who sustain job-related injuries that necessitate medical care but do not prevent their continued employment are entitled to medical benefits even though they have suffered no wage loss.

There is some variation among the states about the choice of physician. Many states authorize claimants to use their own physicians with the approval of the workers' compensation administrators. In some jurisdictions, claimants are limited to choosing from a panel of physicians compiled by a state administrative agency or the employer.

Claimants are entitled only to "reasonable and necessary" medical treatment, and this is sometimes a disputed issue. Pennsylvania enacted a law permitting a self-insured employer or a commercial insurer that challenges a medical claim to withhold payment for the disputed item pending an independent utilization review under the auspices of the state workers' compensation bureau. In American Mfrs. Mut. Ins. Co. v. Sullivan, 526 U.S. 40 (1999), the Supreme Court upheld the statute against a due process challenge.

4. THE REALITY OF WORKERS' COMPENSATION

Emily A. Spieler & John F. Burton, Jr., The Lack of Correspondence between Work-Related Disability and Receipt of Workers' Compensation Benefits*
55 Am. J. Indus. Med. 487, 487–88, 496–98 (2012).

* * *

A basic tenet of workers' compensation programs since their inception is that workers are supposed to receive quick and sure, though limited, payments for work-induced injuries—irrespective of fault by the employer or the worker. In return for expanded financial responsibility for workplace injuries under a no-fault system, employers received immunity from tort litigation, and workers' compensation benefits specified by statute became the exclusive remedy for injured workers. But now, for many workers, the workers' compensation system is dizzying and frustrating in its complexity and apparent irrationality. While the rules may be understandable to repeat players—particularly insurers and third party administrators of claims—they are obscure to many workers who are caught up in the delays and denials. Some say it is no accident that Franz Kafka worked in a workers' compensation bureau: the term Kafkaesque is fitting for the experience of many injured workers.

* * *

As noted above, studies have consistently shown that a substantial number of workplace injuries and illnesses are not compensated. Many of these are not compensated because workers simply do not file claims:

---

they do not even initiate the process. There are, of course, also barriers to the payment of claims once they are filed. These are discussed in the next section.

Reasons that injured workers fail to file for benefits including the following:

Ignorance of workers' compensation and eligibility. This is likely to be true most often in small, private sector, or nonunionized workplaces.

Ignorance of the work-relatedness of the condition. Some workers know they are suffering from an impairment but do not know the health condition was caused by work.

Reimbursement for medical care or short-term disability benefits is available from an alternative system. This correlates with the fact that workers in smaller firms are more likely to file claims, as large firms are more likely to provide a full range of private insurance coverage.

Belief that the injury is lacking in sufficient severity. This belief need not, and often does not, fully correlate with whether the injury is severe enough to qualify for benefits. Nevertheless, the most consistent factor for a decision to file claims is the severity of the injury, including whether the worker is off work for more than 7 days or work restrictions are imposed.

Alternatively, workers may not want to report the condition as work-related. Concerns regarding job loss or other forms of retaliation by employers permeate the process of claims filing. Studies that have inquired about this issue have found it to be a factor in decisions not to file claims. Workers also do not want to be perceived as complainers or as careless. In a GAO study of OSHA reporting, occupational health providers and other stakeholders repeatedly pointed to workers' fear of retaliation as a reason for underreporting in general: 67% of occupational health providers in the survey "reported observing worker fear of disciplinary action for reporting an injury or illness". Fear of retaliation rises for more vulnerable workers, of course, including immigrants, and during times of high unemployment.

Consistent with this is the fact that unionized workers are more likely to file claims and, conversely, unorganized workers are less likely to file. Unionized workers have increased protections from retaliation under collective bargaining agreement provisions governing due process and grounds for discipline and dismissal.

Decisions based on negative experiences of co-workers or others. As others they know face long waits, repeat medical examinations by nontreating physicians, embarrassing questions from lawyers and insurance company representatives, and even video surveillance, workers may choose to avoid the entire system. This may be easiest for those with alternative sources of health and short or long-term disability benefits, but it is unlikely to be limited to this group.

Fear of the stigma associated with being a workers' compensation beneficiary. The focus on "fraud" and the tales of cheating workers may have had a pervasive effect, increasing levels of stigmatization and, as a result, probably decreasing the likelihood that an injured worker will file for benefits. Stigma has been widely studied in the context of other transfer payment programs, particularly welfare programs. Although less well studied in the workers' compensation arena, it is widely discussed by injured workers, labor organizations, and others.

Pressure from co-workers. Safety incentive programs in workplaces—sometimes referred to as safety bingo by worker advocates—create incentives not to report. Often, nonreporting will lead to rewards for a work group. Thus, if one worker reports his or her injury, the entire cohort may pay the price. Again, the 2009 GAO Report found this to be a troubling factor contributing to underreporting to OSHA.

Decisions to file are also influenced by the healthcare provider who sees the worker after an injury. Those workers who see company physicians are less likely to file claims. It is not clear whether this is the result of pressure from the physician, or failure to inform the worker of the work-relatedness of the condition, or another factor.

The willingness of workers to file claims varies by industry and occupation. This is likely to reflect the different cultures, rates of unionization, likelihood of retaliation and other factors. It does not, however, correlate with whether the work is physically demanding: As noted, agriculture/forestry/fishing and construction ranked higher in incidence of work-related injury or illness and lower in claim filing; the farming/forestry/fishing occupations ranked highest in incidence and second lowest in claims filing.

Corporate culture generally may have significant effects on whether a worker will file a claim for benefits. The reporting of occupational injuries and illnesses—and the related though not identical issues of claims filing by workers—involve a series of complex events that affect the likelihood a report or a claim will be made. All of these decisional points are influenced by factors that relate to the individuals, the work environment, and the larger economic, legal and social context.

NOTES AND QUESTIONS

1.   Workers' compensation sought to replace an inefficient tort system with a more efficient no-fault system. With more than 40 percent of payments going to administrative expenses, it has failed in its goal of efficient delivery of benefits.

2.   In reviewing the six objectives of workers' compensation, supra p. 807, how many of these are currently being met? For a further discussion, see Emily Spieler, (Re)Assessing the Grand Bargain: Compensation for Work Injuries in the United States, 1900–2017, 69 Rutgers L. Rev. 891 (2017).

E. COMPENSATION SYSTEMS FOR SPECIAL INDUSTRIES

In addition to the state workers' compensation laws already discussed, there are important federal compensation laws applicable to federal employees and private sector employees in certain industries.

Federal Employees' Compensation Act

The Federal Employees' Compensation Act (FECA), 5 U.S.C. §§ 8101–8193, provides compensation for the work-related injuries and illnesses of federal civilian employees. The FECA is similar in structure to state workers' compensation statutes.

FECA is a no-fault system. Compensation awards are based on loss of earning capacity. FECA awards, however, are much more generous than comparable awards under state workers' compensation laws. FECA is administered by the Office of Workers' Compensation Programs in the Department of Labor. Disputed claims are adjudicated by the Employees' Compensation Appeals Board.

Federal Employers' Liability Act

The Federal Employers' Liability Act (FELA), 45 U.S.C. §§ 51–60, provides the exclusive remedy for the injury, illness, or death of railroad employees caused by the negligence of the employer where the employee and the railroad are engaged in interstate or foreign commerce. The Act supersedes all state laws.

Liability must be based on the employer's negligence, which is determined by federal law and is broadly construed. FELA case law has held that the injured employee must only prove that employer negligence played "any part, even the slightest" in producing the injury or death.

The employer's defenses are limited. Contributory negligence is the only defense, and it will not bar recovery, but may be used to reduce the damages according to fault. Furthermore, where the injury or death was contributed to by the carrier's violation of a statute enacted for the safety of employees, contributory negligence does not apply at all.

The Act provides that the carrier is liable in damages to any employee suffering injury or death. It has been held that the employee may recover a sum that will compensate for pecuniary loss, both past and future, including loss of income, medical and other necessary expenses, as well as damages for pain and suffering. When death results, a claim also arises for the benefit of eligible dependents to recover their reasonable expectation of pecuniary benefits.

Actions may be brought in United States district court "in the district of the residence of the defendant, or in which the cause of action arose, or in which the defendant shall be doing business at the time of commencing such action" or in the state courts. Generally, once an action is initiated in state court it may not be removed.

Jones Act

The Jones Act, 46 U.S.C. § 688, extends to "seamen" the same rights against their employers as are extended to railroad employees under the FELA. The term "seaman" is defined as "a master or member of a crew of any vessel."

Longshore and Harbor Workers' Compensation Act

The Longshore and Harbor Workers' Compensation Act (LHWCA), 33 U.S.C. §§ 901–950, provides compensation to private employees working in maritime employment upon the navigable waters of the United States. The principal employments covered are stevedoring and ship service operations. The LHWCA is administered by the Office of Workers' Compensation Programs in the Department of Labor.

Benefits are provided to injured employees and, in case of death, to dependents. These benefits may not be waived, assigned, released, or commuted unless provided by the Act. Beyond compensation for injury, the employer must also furnish medical benefits for such period as the nature of the injury or the process of recovery requires. Death benefits are also available. If the injury is covered by the Act, the employer has no liability to the employees under other forms of legal action. All disputed LHWCA claims are resolved by the Benefits Review Board.

Black Lung

The federal black lung program "was intended to rectify the historical lack of adequate state compensation schemes for miners suffering from pneumoconiosis." Hall v. Harris, 487 F.Supp. 535, 538 (W.D.Va.1980). When enacted in 1969, it was estimated that compensation would be awarded to 100,000 retired miners. Aided by some liberalizing amendments in 1972 and 1978, by the end of 1981, some 542,000 living miners, their spouses and dependents, and survivors of deceased miners, had collected more than $10 billion in benefits paid from general appropriations. A 1978 Trust Fund, financed by a producer's tonnage tax and designed to pay claims of former miners who had left mining before 1970, had a $1.4 billion deficit by 1981. See John S. Lopatto, The Federal Black Lung Program: A 1983 Primer, 85 W.Va.L.Rev. 677 (1983).

The Black Lung Benefits Amendments of 1981, 26 U.S.C. § 4121, were an attempt to restore the black lung program to solvency. They doubled the producers' tax on each ton of coal mined. They also significantly tightened the eligibility requirements for claims filed after January 1, 1982. Among other things, they deleted the presumptions of entitlement to benefits based on duration of coal mine employment and placed the burden of proving disability upon the claimant. See Robert L. Ramsey & Robert S. Habermann, The Federal Black Lung Program— The View From the Top, 87 W.Va.L.Rev. 575 (1985).

The black lung program is often cited as an example of a benefits program run amok, in which deserving claimants wait years, yet thousands of meritless claims are awarded. The problem that the program sought to address, however, is a real one, complicated by problems of causation and identifying the responsible employer. The black lung laws opted for a system of cost-sharing between employers and the public, and attempted to relieve adjudicatory problems through the use of medical presumptions. Despite the criticism of the federal black lung program, industry-specific and disease-specific compensation systems have been proposed for workers disabled by asbestos and other substances. It is unlikely that any single model can be used for more than one industry. For example, the black lung system is supported by taxes on coal. Without an ongoing industry to tax, funds must be derived from other sources. The need for such specific programs, however, can be traced directly to inadequate preventive measures and inadequate existing workers' compensation laws.

Energy Employees

The Energy Employees Occupational Illness Compensation Program Act, Pub. L. No. 106–398 (2000)(42 U.S.C. § 7384 et seq.), approved as an amendment to the Defense Department authorization bill for fiscal 2001, is designed to compensate 4,000 to 6,000 nuclear weapons workers. Each worker who developed an occupational disease as a result of exposure while helping to build the nation's nuclear arsenal is entitled to a one-time payment of $150,000 and medical benefits. Most of these workers do not qualify for benefits under state workers' compensation laws due to the limited coverage for occupational disease.

F. TORT ACTIONS AND "EXCLUSIVITY"

Workers' compensation laws were intended to supplant common law actions. In the language of many of the state statutes, resort to the compensation system is the "exclusive remedy" of workers and their families. An increasing number of exceptions, however, have been carved out of the exclusivity rule. These exceptions are of two main classes: actions against the employer and actions against third parties.

It is not difficult to understand why ill and injured workers, their dependents, and their lawyers would attempt to find an exception to the exclusivity rule. Tort recoveries, where available, are usually much greater than workers' compensation awards for comparable occupational injury and illness.

From the workers' perspective, tort actions are often uncertain, unfair, and protracted, but they offer the only chance for recovery of a reasonable amount of money. From the employers' perspective, tort actions are often uncertain, expensive to defend (win or lose), and undermine the viability of the entire compensation system.

1. ACTIONS AGAINST THE EMPLOYER

a. DUAL CAPACITY

Weinstein v. St. Mary's Medical Center

68 Cal.Rptr.2d 461 (Cal. Ct. App. 1997).

■ WALKER, ASSOCIATE JUSTICE.

* * *

Factual and Procedural Background

On October 14, 1994, [Beth] Weinstein sustained injuries to her left foot while acting in the course and scope of her duties as an employee of the Hospital. Weinstein had to use crutches due to her injury. Although still employed, she stopped working at the Hospital on November 7, 1994, and filed a workers' compensation claim. As a result of the injuries she sustained on October 14, Weinstein began drawing temporary disability and ongoing medical payments from the Hospital's workers' compensation administrator.

On January 10, 1995, while still on crutches, Weinstein went to the Hospital to receive medical treatment for her injury. After undergoing an MRI (magnetic resonance imaging) procedure on her foot, Weinstein was escorted from the MRI building to the radiology department by a medical technician employed by the Hospital. As this was happening, Weinstein slipped and fell on a watery liquid substance in one of the Hospital's hallways. The fall aggravated the previous injury to Weinstein's left foot, resulting in a condition of chronic intense pain.

On January 25, 1995, Weinstein was laid off from her job at the Hospital due to downsizing. Through Applied Risk Management, its worker's compensation carrier, the Hospital continues to pay the cost of medical treatment related to Weinstein's injuries sustained in the January 10 accident.

On December 12, 1995, Weinstein filed her complaint in this personal injury action against the Hospital. The form pleading, labeled "premises liability," seeks compensatory damages according to proof based on the January 10, 1995, accident. The Hospital filed an answer alleging as an affirmative defense the exclusivity of Weinstein's workers' compensation remedy under sections 3600, 3601, 3602 and 5300.

On May 21, 1996, the Hospital filed a motion for summary judgment based on the sole ground that Weinstein's "exclusive remedy is her ongoing Workers' Compensation action and the instant civil action is statutorily barred under Labor Code sections 3600 and 3602." In support of the motion, the Hospital argued that Weinstein was its employee at the time of the January 10, 1995, accident, and was present at the Hospital on that date in order to receive medical treatment for a previous injury suffered in the course of her employment, for which she was receiving workers' compensation benefits. On this basis, the Hospital contended that undisputed facts established the "conditions of compensation" existed between Weinstein and the Hospital at the time of her injury, her exclusive remedy was under the workers' compensation law, and her complaint against the Hospital was therefore barred under section 3602, subdivision (a). The Hospital specifically argued that the "dual capacity" doctrine is inapplicable to a premises liability action against an employer as owner or occupier of real property.

Weinstein opposed the motion for summary judgment on the grounds of the dual capacity doctrine. She argued that at the time of the accident on January 10, 1995, the Hospital was acting in its capacity as a medical facility rendering care to her as a member of the public, and not as Weinstein's employer. Thus the "conditions of compensation" were not met, and Weinstein was not restricted to the remedy of workers' compensation. At the hearing on the motion, Weinstein argued the dual capacity exception applied because she was at the Hospital as a patient rather than as an employee, and the Hospital was acting as a medical provider and not as an employer. The Hospital countered that it owed Weinstein the same duty to maintain safe premises whether she was there as a patient or an employee. Because Weinstein's claim was based on premises liability rather than professional malpractice, the Hospital argued she could not rely on the dual capacity "exception" to the rule of workers' compensation exclusivity.

The trial court agreed with the Hospital. In its order granting the motion for summary judgment, the court stated: "[N]o triable issue of material fact exists as to the sole cause of action for premises liability against [the Hospital]. Specifically, [Weinstein] conceded that at the time of her alleged slip and fall accident on January 10, 1995, she was an employee of [the Hospital] and was receiving workers compensation benefits related to a prior industrial injury she sustained while employed by [the Hospital]. The doctrine of dual capacity is inapplicable under Labor Code section 3602[, subdivision] (a) since the [Hospital]'s duty to provide a safe premises pre-existed the injury." The trial court entered judgment for the Hospital. This appeal followed.

Discussion

* * *

Section 3852 is the origin of the "dual capacity" exception to the exclusive remedy of workers' compensation. Under the dual capacity doctrine, an employee may recover in tort for negligent aggravation of an initial industrial injury against an employer who assumes the capacity of medical care provider by undertaking to treat the employee's injury itself. (Duprey v. Shane (1952) 249 P.2d 8) The dual capacity doctrine is not necessarily limited to situations in which the employer's alternate second capacity toward the employer is that of medical care provider. "[T]he decisive test of dual capacity is whether the nonemployer aspect of the employer's activity generates a different set of obligations by the employer toward the employee."

Dual capacity is thus legal shorthand for describing a situation in which a party has a duty of care that arises independently of any employment relationship. It is based on the distinction between two entirely separate sets of duties: (1) the duties of an employer to an employee arising from the existence of an employment relationship under the workers' compensation law; and (2) the common law (or other statutory) duties of care arising from other, nonemployment relationships, such as those of a medical care provider to a patient, or of a business or property owner to an invitee. For example, an employer's duty to its employees requires it to provide, among other things, a safe place of employment. This duty is distinct from the obligation of a property owner or business to an invitee, based on the common law tort duty of care. The nature of an employer's duty in a given situation depends on the circumstances of the parties' relationship at the time of the incident. Just because a person *is* an employee clearly does not mean he or she is *acting* as an employee under all circumstances.

In order to bear its burden of establishing the complete affirmative defense of workers' compensation exclusivity in this case, the Hospital was required to show that, at the time of her injury on January 10, 1995, Weinstein was performing services growing out of and incidental to her employment, and was acting within the course of her employment. The fact Weinstein was an employee of the Hospital at the time of the accident is not controlling, since the nature of the Hospital's duty in this case depends not simply on whether Weinstein was an employee, but on the question whether she was acting within the course and scope of her employment at the time of her injury. Neither does the Hospital's duty to its employees to provide a safe work place have any relevance unless all the conditions of compensation were present at the time of the subject accident.

There is no dispute that Weinstein was performing employment-related services and acting within the course and scope of her employment with the Hospital at the time of her initial accidental injury on October 14, 1994. It is also undisputed Weinstein was still an employee of the Hospital at the time of her second injury on January 10, 1995. However, the Hospital had the burden on its motion for summary judgment of establishing that when Weinstein returned for treatment on January 10, 1995, she went *in her capacity as an employee.* It failed to do so. There was no evidence suggesting that any of Weinstein's actions during her visit to the Hospital on that date were within the course and scope of her employment with the Hospital, that she was performing any service growing out of or incidental to her employment, or that she was even working at all. In short, the Hospital did not bear its burden as the defendant moving for summary judgment of establishing that the "conditions of compensation" set out in section 3600, subdivision (a)(2) "concur[red]" in this case.

* * *

The key distinguishing element is the distinction between an employer's duty to its employees arising from its contractual obligation as employer, and the common law duty of care of a business or property owner to an invitee. As an employer, the Hospital had a duty to provide compensation for Weinstein's injuries, but was under no duty or obligation to treat her personally. It is only when an employer imposes a contractual duty on the employee to obtain treatment from it, or itself undertakes a duty to provide such treatment as one of the direct benefits of employment, that any medical treatment it provides to the employee become a part of the employer-employee relationship. Where, as in this case, the employer simply accepts the employee as a patient and provides medical treatment separate from any of the conditions, obligations or benefits of employment, it acts in a different capacity toward the employee than that of employer.

This duty logically encompasses not only a professional duty of care in the provision of medical treatment, but a general duty of care to provide safe premises independent of any duty arising from the employment relationship.

* * *

The judgment is reversed.

NOTES AND QUESTIONS

1. The court in *Weinstein* applied the dual capacity doctrine, which permits employees to recover from their employer if the employer "possesses a second persona so completely independent from and unrelated to his status as employer that by established standards the law recognizes 'that persona' as a separate legal person." 6 Lex K. Larson, Workers' Compensation Law § 113.01[1] (2010). The dual capacity doctrine remains the minority rule. Compare Guy v. Arthur H. Thomas Co., 378 N.E.2d 488 (Ohio 1978) (upholding rule) with Boyle v. Breme, 453 A.2d 1335 (N.J.Super.Ct.App.Div. 1982) and McAlister v. Methodist Hosp., 550 S.W.2d 240 (Tenn.1977) (rejecting rule).

2. Injured workers and their estates have asserted a wide range of dual capacity or dual persona claims. For example, Veronica Soriano and her daughter Michelle were killed, and Soriano's coworker Sara Singhas was injured in an automobile accident. Allegedly, the accident was caused by the state's negligence in failing to properly stripe and place signs along the highway. At the time of the accident, Soriano and her husband were both public defenders employed by the state. Is a wrongful death action barred by workers' compensation because the decedent was a state employee and the complaint alleged negligence on the part of the state, or can the plaintiff use the dual capacity doctrine to sue the state because the state's negligence was

in a capacity other than employer? See Singhas v. New Mexico State Highway Dep't, 946 P.2d 645 (N.M.1997) (held: action barred).

b.   WILLFUL AND INTENTIONAL TORTS

In every jurisdiction workers' compensation is the exclusive remedy only for "accidental" injury or illness. Thus, in cases where employees are punched, stabbed, or shot by employers, workers' compensation does not bar actions for assault and battery. The courts, however, traditionally have required a plaintiff to prove that the employer had a specific intent to injure.

Conceptually, willful, wanton, and reckless misconduct lies between intentional and negligent conduct. Should willful misconduct be considered an intentional act, for which workers' compensation is not a bar to recovery, or should it be considered a negligent act, for which workers' compensation is the exclusive remedy?

Lucenti v. Laviero
176 A.3d 1 (Conn. 2018).

■ ROBINSON, J.:

* * *

In this certified appeal, we consider the contours of the proof necessary * * * for an employee to establish an employer's subjective intent to create a dangerous situation with a "substantial certainty of injury" to the employee, for purposes of avoiding application of General Statutes § 31–284 (a), the exclusive remedy provision of the Workers' Compensation Act (act), General Statutes § 31–275 et seq. The plaintiff, Dominick Lucenti, appeals, upon our grant of his petition for certification, from the judgment of the Appellate Court affirming the trial court's grant of summary judgment in favor of the defendants, Greg Laviero and Martin Laviero Contractors, Inc. (Laviero Contractors). On appeal, the plaintiff claims that the Appellate Court improperly concluded that evidence regarding warnings to Laviero from the plaintiff and other employees about the dangers posed by the use of a particular excavator, which would operate only when "rigged" to run at full throttle, did not establish a genuine issue of material fact as to whether the defendants subjectively believed that the plaintiff's subsequent injuries from the use of that excavator were substantially certain to occur. We conclude that, in the absence of any evidence demonstrating the hallmarks typical of such employer misconduct, the plaintiff has failed to establish a genuine issue of material fact with respect to the defendants' subjective beliefs. Accordingly, we affirm the judgment of the Appellate Court.

* * *

By way of background, we observe that this court has consistently "interpreted the exclusivity provision of the [a]ct . . . as a total bar to common law actions brought by employees against employers for job related injuries with one narrow exception that exists when the employer has committed an intentional tort or where the employer has engaged in wilful or serious misconduct." This exclusivity represents a balancing of interests, insofar as the purpose of the act "is to compensate the worker for injuries arising out of and in the course of employment, without regard to fault, by imposing a form of strict liability on the employer. . . . The act is to be broadly construed to effectuate the purpose of providing compensation for an injury arising out of and in the course of the employment regardless of fault. . . . Under typical workers' compensation statutes, employers are barred from presenting certain defenses to the claim for compensation, the employee's burden of proof is relatively light, and recovery should be expeditious. In a word, these statutes compromise an employee's right to a common law tort action for work related injuries in return for relatively quick and certain compensation." Put differently, "[a] damage suit as an alternative or additional source of compensation, becomes permissible only by carving a judicial exception in an uncarved statute. . . . Neither moral aversion to the employer's act nor the shiny prospect of a large damage verdict justifies interference with what is essentially a policy choice of the [l]egislature." The "principle of exclusivity is not eroded . . . when the plaintiff alleges an intentional tort, in which case an employee is permitted to pursue remedies beyond those contemplated by the act."

This court first recognized this narrow intentional tort exception to workers' compensation exclusivity in Jett v. Dunlap, 425 A.2d 1263 (Conn. 1979). In *Jett*, this court exempted from workers' compensation exclusivity an employer's tortious act of intentionally directing or authorizing another employee to assault the injured party.

Moving beyond actual intent to injure, * * * this court declined to extend *Jett*'s intentional tort exception to the workers' compensation exclusivity provision to situations in which an injury resulted from the employer's intentional, wilful, or reckless violations of safety standards as established pursuant to federal or state laws. Instead, this court held: "To bypass the exclusivity of the act, the intentional or deliberate . . . conduct alleged must have been designed to cause the injury that resulted." This court noted that "the mere knowledge and appreciation of a risk, short of substantial certainty, is not the equivalent of intent." Accordingly, this court concluded that reckless misconduct differs from intentional misconduct, and that the employee must establish that the employer knew that injury was substantially certain to follow its deliberate course of action.

"The substantial certainty test differs from the true intentional tort test but still preserves the statutory scheme and the overall purposes of the act. The problem with the intentional tort test, i.e., whether the employer intended the specific injury, appears to be that it allows employers to injure and even kill employees and suffer only workers' compensation damages so long as the employer did not specifically intend to hurt the worker. . . . Prohibiting a civil action in such a case would allow a corporation to cost-out an investment decision to kill workers. . . . The substantial certainty test provides for the intent to injure exception to be strictly construed and still allows for [an employee] to maintain a cause of action against an employer where the evidence is sufficient to support an inference that the employer deliberately instructed an employee to injure himself."

* * *

Although Connecticut has an ample body of appellate case law rejecting employees' claims of entitlement to the substantial certainty exception in a variety of factual settings, this court has yet to describe the kind of evidence that would allow for an inference that an employer subjectively believed that employee injury was substantially certain to follow its actions.

In this regard, we note that the substantial certainty exception is a common feature in workers' compensation law in other jurisdictions. We find particularly instructive a series of decisions from New Jersey. Applying that state's leading decision articulating the substantial certainty test, Millison v. E.I. du Pont de Nemours & Co., A.2d 505 (N.J. 1985), New Jersey courts "engage in a [two step] analysis. First, a court considers the conduct prong, examining the employer's conduct in the setting of the particular case. . . . Second, a court analyzes the context prong, considering whether the resulting injury or disease, and the circumstances in which it is inflicted on the worker, [may] fairly be viewed as a fact of life of industrial employment, or whether it is plainly beyond anything the legislature could have contemplated as entitling the employee to recover only under the [New Jersey Workers' Compensation Act]." Van Dunk v. Reckson Associates Realty Corp., 45 A.3d 965 (N.J. 2012).

With respect to the conduct prong, which is closely akin to the factual inquiry that Connecticut courts undertake in determining whether the employer knew of a substantial certainty of employee harm, the New Jersey Supreme Court has emphasized that "[m]ere knowledge by an employer that a workplace is dangerous does not equate to an intentional wrong. . . . [T]he dividing line between negligent or reckless conduct on the one hand and intentional wrong on the other must be drawn with caution, so that the statutory framework . . . is not circumvented simply because a known risk later blossoms into reality. We must demand a virtual certainty.". In considering whether the totality of the circumstances indicates that the conduct prong is satisfied, New Jersey courts consider factors such as: (1) prior similar accidents related to the conduct at issue that have resulted in employee injury, death, or a near-miss, (2) "deliberate deceit" on the part of the employer with respect to the existence of the dangerous condition, (3) "intentional and persistent" violations of safety regulations over a lengthy period of time, and (4) affirmative disabling of safety devices. With respect to decisions made to cut corners as to safety in order to save time or money, the New Jersey Supreme Court considers a "profit motive" of only "limited relevance," applicable "only to critique an employer's long-term choice specifically to sacrifice employee safety for product-production efficiency."

* * *

Other sister state cases applying the substantial certainty doctrine are consistent with the factors applied in New Jersey.

* * *

Connecticut's appellate case law also is consistent with New Jersey's multifactor standard, including our decisions that stand for the proposition that, although warnings to the employer regarding the safety of workplace conditions are relevant evidence, they do not, without more, raise a genuine issue of material fact to defeat summary judgment with respect to whether an employer subjectively believes that its employee's injuries are substantially certain to result from its action.

* * *

For the following reasons, we conclude that the evidence in this record fails to establish the existence of a genuine issue of material fact with respect to whether the defendants believed there was a substantial certainty that the rigged excavator would injure the plaintiff or any other employee. First, there is no evidence of prior accidents involving the rigged excavator causing, or nearly causing, injury or death. Second, there is no evidence of an extensive or protracted history of workplace safety violations by Laviero with respect to his motor equipment or, in particular, this excavator. Third, there is no evidence of deception on the part of the defendants, particularly Laviero himself, with respect to any danger presented by the rigged excavator. In fact, the record established that Laviero knew that the plaintiff was aware of the purported danger. Thus, Laviero reasonably could presume that the plaintiff would try his best to avoid injuring himself if injury could be avoided with the exercise of due care.

* * *

Finally, notwithstanding the dissenting justices' characterization of our decision as a virtual nullification of the substantial certainty exception, we note that a holding to the contrary in this case would have the effect of elevating relatively routine workplace disagreements about safety to evidence that would defeat the high bar of workers' compensation exclusivity. This represents a drastic undermining of the purpose of the act, which this court—and many others throughout the United States—have understood "to limit common-law tort actions for injuries arising out of and in the course of employment and to satisfy as many claims as possible under the . . . act." It also would be inconsistent with this court's historic view of the substantial certainty exception, which we did "not believe [would] encourage significant additional litigation, for only in those rare instances when an employer's conduct allegedly falls within the very narrow exception to the act will such litigation result.". Accordingly, we conclude that the Appellate Court properly affirmed the judgment of the trial court, which granted the defendants' motion for summary judgment.

[Concurring and dissenting opinions omitted]

NOTES

1. Mandolidis v. Elkins Industries, Inc., 246 S.E.2d 907 (1978), was one of the first cases to hold that the intentional injury exception to a state workers' compensation "exclusive remedy" provision should be extended to an employer's willful, wanton, or reckless misconduct. *Mandolidis* was a controversial decision, and in 2005 the West Virginia Legislature amended the workers' compensation statute to narrow the "deliberate intent" language and make it more difficult for plaintiffs to recover. Ohio originally followed *Mandolidis*, but an Ohio law also enacted in 2005 now provides that injured employees must prove that their employer acted "with a deliberate intent to cause injury."

2. In *Lucenti*, the Supreme Court of Connecticut relied on New Jersey case law, and also cited to cases in Florida, Turner v. PCR, Inc., 754 So. 2d 683 (Fla. 2000), superseded in part by Fla. Stat. § 440.11 (2009), South Dakota, Fryer v. Kranz, 616 N.W.2d 102 (S.D. 2000), and Utah, Helf v. Chevron U.S.A., Inc., 203 P.3d 962 (Utah 2009), in adopting the "substantial certainty" standard for intentional injury. North Carolina, Woodson v. Rowland, 407 S.E.2d 222 (N.C. 1991), and Oklahoma, Jordan v. Western Farmers Electrical Co-op., 290 P.3d 9 (Okla. 2012), also have adopted the substantial certainty test, but the rest of the states still require an intent to injure. Under Texas law, if the gross negligence of an employer results in an employee's death, the worker's estate may recover punitive damages from the employer. Granite Construction Co. v, Mendoza, 816 S.W.2d 756 (Tex. Ct. App. 1994).

3. Other intentional tort causes of action have been alleged for false imprisonment, intentional infliction of emotional distress, defamation, and fraudulent concealment of hazards or employee health effects. These other actions are extremely difficult to prove.

2. ACTIONS AGAINST THIRD PARTIES

Even under such exceptions as dual capacity and intentional acts, tort actions against the employer of an injured or ill employee are difficult to maintain. Therefore, workers have frequently sued "third parties." There are three lines of cases.

First, actions may be brought against other employers that are not so closely connected with the primary employer as to be "co-employers."

Some examples: (1) an action may be brought against an affiliated company, such as where a parent company assumed the duty of providing safety and health information and services; (2) some states permit damage actions against general contractors by employees of subcontractors, although most states make general contractors liable for the workers' compensation of employees of subcontractors, thereby giving the general contractor immunity, (3) some states also permit employees of a general contractor or a subcontractor to sue other subcontractors; (4) an action may lie against an architect, engineer, or safety and health consultant; (5) an action may be brought against a property owner, especially in states with scaffolding or structural work acts which create a nondelegable duty on the part of the owner to provide safe scaffolds; and (6) in a minority of jurisdictions a negligence action may be brought against a co-employee. The key to these actions is proof that a duty was owed to the worker by the defendant.

Second, actions have been brought against insurance companies, labor unions, and government agencies alleging that the negligent performance of a safety and health inspection at the worker's place of employment was the proximate cause of an injury or illness. About half the states permit actions against insurers, but actions against unions are rarely successful because of preemption by the federal labor laws and other defenses, and actions against federal and state governments are clouded by sovereign immunity and other doctrines.

In United Steelworkers of Am. v. Rawson, 495 U.S. 362 (1990), following a tragic fire that killed 91 miners in Kellogg, Idaho, the plaintiffs sued the union in state court on two theories. First, plaintiffs alleged that the union was negligent in performing inspections of the mine to identify safety violations. Second, plaintiffs claimed that the union breached its duty of fair representation. The Supreme Court of Idaho held that the duty of fair representation claim was properly dismissed for failure to plead facts alleging more than mere negligence and the Supreme Court agreed. With regard to the common law negligence claim, the Supreme Court reversed the Supreme Court of Idaho and held that the common law negligence action was preempted by § 301 of the Labor Management Relations Act. The union's right to participate and its duties arising from that right came solely from the collective bargaining agreement.

Third, by far the most important third party actions are products liability suits brought against the manufacturers of defective products that caused an injury or illness in the workplace.

Kesner v. Superior Court

384 P.3d 283 (Cal. 2016).

■ LIU, J.:

These two cases ask whether employers or landowners owe a duty of care to prevent secondary exposure to asbestos. Such exposure, sometimes called domestic or take-home exposure, occurs when a worker who is directly exposed to a toxin carries it home on his or her person or clothing, and a household member is in turn exposed through physical proximity or contact with that worker or the worker's clothing. Plaintiffs in these actions for personal injury and wrongful death allege that take-home exposure to asbestos was a contributing cause to the deaths of Lynne Haver and Johnny Kesner, and that the employers of Lynne's former husband and Johnny's uncle had a duty to prevent this exposure. Defendants argue that users of asbestos have no duty, either as employers or as premises owners, to prevent nonemployees who have never visited their facilities from being exposed to asbestos used in defendants' business enterprises.

After the trial and appellate courts in these two cases reached varying conclusions as to the existence of this duty, we granted review and consolidated both cases for oral argument and decision to address the following questions: Does an employer that uses asbestos in the workplace have a duty of care to protect employees' household members from exposure to asbestos through off-site contact with employees who carry asbestos fibers on their work clothing, tools, vehicles, or persons? How, if at all, does this duty differ when the plaintiff states a claim for premises liability rather than general negligence? If an employer or premises owner has such a duty, is that duty limited to immediate family members or to members of the employee's household? Or does the duty extend to visitors, guests, or other persons with whom the employee may come into contact?

We hold that the duty of employers and premises owners to exercise ordinary care in their use of asbestos includes preventing exposure to asbestos carried by the bodies and clothing of on-site workers. Where it is reasonably foreseeable that workers, their clothing, or personal effects will act as vectors carrying asbestos from the premises to household members, employers have a duty to take reasonable care to prevent this means of transmission. This duty also applies to premises owners who use asbestos on their property, subject to any exceptions and affirmative defenses generally applicable to premises owners, such as the rules of contractor liability. Importantly, we hold that this duty extends only to members of a worker's household. Because the duty is premised on the foreseeability of both the regularity and intensity of contact that occurs in a worker's home, it does not extend beyond this circumscribed category of potential plaintiffs.

I.

* * *

II.

A plaintiff in any negligence suit must demonstrate " 'a legal duty to use due care, a breach of such legal duty, and [that] the breach [is] the proximate or legal cause of the resulting injury.' " Here we are tasked solely with deciding whether Abex or BNSF [the employers] had a legal duty to prevent the injuries alleged by Kesner and the Havers.

"Duty is a question of law for the court, to be reviewed de novo on appeal." "California law establishes the general duty of each person to exercise, in his or her activities, reasonable care for the safety of others. (Civ. Code, § 1714, subd. (a).)" Civil Code section 1714, subdivision (a) provides in relevant part: "Everyone is responsible, not only for the result of his or her willful acts, but also for an injury occasioned to another by his or her want of ordinary care or skill in the management of his or her property or person, except so far as the latter has, willfully or by want of ordinary care, brought the injury upon himself or herself." " 'Courts . . . invoke[ ] the concept of duty to limit generally "the otherwise potentially infinite liability which would follow from every negligent act. . . ." ' " The conclusion that a defendant did not have a duty constitutes a determination by the court that public policy concerns outweigh, for a particular category of cases, the broad principle enacted by the Legislature that one's failure to exercise ordinary care incurs liability for all the harms that result. "The history of the concept of duty in itself discloses that it is not an old and deep-rooted doctrine but a legal device of the latter half of the nineteenth century designed to curtail the feared propensities of juries toward liberal awards." As a result, "in the absence of a statutory provision establishing an exception to the general rule of Civil Code section 1714, courts should create one only where 'clearly supported by public policy.' "

In determining whether policy considerations weigh in favor of such an exception, we have said the most important factors are "the foreseeability of harm to the plaintiff, the degree of certainty that the plaintiff suffered injury, the closeness of the connection between the defendant's conduct and the injury suffered, the moral blame attached to the defendant's conduct, the policy of preventing future harm, the extent of the burden to the defendant and consequences to the community of imposing a duty to exercise care with resulting liability for breach, and the availability, cost, and prevalence of insurance for the risk involved." establishes a general duty to exercise ordinary care in one's activities, which includes the use of asbestos in one's business or on one's premises, we rely on these factors not to determine "whether a *new duty* should be created, but whether an *exception* to Civil Code section 1714 . . . should be created."

Because a judicial decision on the issue of duty entails line-drawing based on policy considerations, "the Rowland [v. Christian, 443 P.2d 561 (Cal. 1968)] factors are evaluated at a relatively broad level of factual generality. . . . In applying the . . . *Rowland* factors, . . . we have asked not whether they support an exception to the general duty of reasonable care on the facts of the particular case before us, but whether carving out an entire category of cases from that general duty rule is justified by clear considerations of policy. . . . By making exceptions to Civil Code section 1714's general duty of ordinary care only when foreseeability and policy considerations justify a categorical no-duty rule, we preserve the crucial distinction between a determination that the defendant owed the plaintiff no duty of ordinary care, which is for the *court* to make, and a determination that the defendant did not breach the duty of ordinary care, which in a jury trial is for the *jury* to make."

In this respect, duty differs from the other elements of a tort. Breach, injury, and causation must be demonstrated on the basis of facts adduced at trial, and a jury's determination of each must take into account the particular context in which any act or injury occurred. Analysis of duty occurs at a higher level of generality.

* * *

Here, because "the general duty to take ordinary care in the conduct of one's activities" applies to the use of asbestos on an owner's premises or in an employer's manufacturing processes, "the issue is also properly stated as whether a categorical exception to that general rule should be made" exempting property owners and employers from potential liability to individuals who were exposed to asbestos by way of employees carrying it on their clothes or person. In answering this question, our task is not to decide whether Kesner or the Havers have proven that asbestos from Abex or BNSF actually and foreseeably reached Johnny Kesner or Lynne Haver, or whether Abex's or BNSF's asbestos contributed to the disease that Johnny or Lynne suffered, or whether Abex or BNSF had adequate procedures in place to prevent take-home exposure. Our task is to determine whether household exposure is *categorically* unforeseeable and, if not, whether allowing the possibility of liability would result in such significant social burdens that the law should not recognize such claims. As noted, we will not "carv[e] out an entire category of cases from th[e] general duty rule" of section 1714, subdivision (a), unless doing so "is justified by clear considerations of policy."

III.

The *Rowland* factors fall into two categories. Three factors—foreseeability, certainty, and the connection between the plaintiff and the defendant—address the foreseeability of the relevant injury, while the other four—moral blame, preventing future harm, burden, and availability of insurance—take into account public policy concerns that might support excluding certain kinds of plaintiffs or injuries from relief.

As explained below, we conclude that the exposure of household members to take-home asbestos is generally foreseeable and that BNSF and Abex have not shown that categorically barring take-home claims is justified by clear considerations of policy. Accordingly, Abex and BNSF owed plaintiffs a duty of ordinary care to prevent take-home exposure.

A.

The most important factor to consider in determining whether to create an exception to the general duty to exercise ordinary care articulated by section 1714 is whether the injury in question was foreseeable. With respect to this factor, we conclude that it was foreseeable that people who work with or around asbestos may carry asbestos fibers home with them and expose members of their household. This factor weighs in favor of the existence of a duty.

"[A]s to foreseeability, . . . the court's task in determining duty 'is not to decide whether a particular plaintiff's injury was reasonably foreseeable in light of a particular defendant's conduct, but rather to evaluate more generally whether the category of negligent conduct at issue is sufficiently likely to result in the kind of harm experienced that liability may appropriately be imposed. . . .' " For purposes of duty analysis, " 'foreseeability is not to be measured by what is more probable than not, but includes whatever is likely enough in the setting of modern life that a reasonably thoughtful [person] would take account of it in guiding practical conduct.' . . . [I]t is settled that what is required to be foreseeable is the general character of the event or harm—e.g., being struck by a car while standing in a phone booth—not its precise nature or manner of occurrence."

A reasonably thoughtful person making industrial use of asbestos during the time periods at issue in this case (i.e., the mid-1970s) would take into account the possibility that asbestos fibers could become attached to an employee's clothing or person, travel to that employee's home, and thereby reach other persons who lived in the home. It is a matter of common experience and knowledge that dust or other substances may be carried from place to place on one's clothing or person, as anyone who has cleaned an attic or spent time in a smoky room can attest. Defendants would not need to know "the precise . . . manner" that exposure occurred (i.e., that Lynne laundered Mike's clothing or that George roughhoused with his nephew Johnny) in order to recognize the general risk posed by workers leaving an area with airborne dust-based toxins and then coming into contact with members of their households.

* * *

Defendants are correct that a finding of " "[n]o duty" ' " is in effect " 'a global determination that, for some overriding policy reason, courts should not entertain causes of action for cases that fall into certain categories,' " even if some defendants in such cases did actually cause the harm of which the plaintiffs complained. Even if recognizing a duty would enable some plaintiffs to obtain legitimate compensation for their injuries, the argument goes, this interest is outweighed by the costs—to the defendants, the judicial system, and society as a whole—of unremitting litigation by other plaintiffs whose claims are tenuous at best.

But recognizing a duty with respect to one set of potential plaintiffs does not imply that any plaintiff may make a similar claim. "If the actor's conduct creates such a recognizable risk of harm only to a particular class of persons, the fact that it in fact causes harm to a person of a different class, to whom the actor could not reasonably have anticipated injury, does not make the actor liable to the persons so injured." Although defendants raise legitimate concerns regarding the unmanageability of claims premised upon incidental exposure, as in a restaurant or city bus, these concerns do not clearly justify a categorical rule against liability for foreseeable take-home exposure. Instead, the concerns point to the need for a limitation on the scope of the duty here.

We hold that an employer's or property owner's duty to prevent take-home exposure extends only to members of a worker's household, i.e., persons who live with the worker and are thus foreseeably in close and sustained contact with the worker over a significant period of time. To be sure, there are other persons who may have reason to believe they were exposed to significant quantities of asbestos by repeatedly spending time in an enclosed space with an asbestos worker—for example, a regular carpool companion. But any duty rule will necessarily exclude some individuals who, as a causal matter, were harmed by the conduct of potential defendants. By drawing the line at members of a household, we limit potential plaintiffs to an identifiable category of persons who, as a class, are most likely to have suffered a legitimate, compensable harm.

This limitation comports with our duty analysis under *Rowland*. Our finding of foreseeability turned on the fact that a worker can be expected to return home each workday and to have close contact with household members on a regular basis over many years. Persons whose contact with the worker is more incidental, sporadic, or transitory do not, as a class, share the same characteristics as household members and are therefore not within the scope of the duty we identify here. This rule strikes a workable balance between ensuring that reasonably foreseeable injuries are compensated and protecting courts and defendants from the costs associated with litigation of disproportionately meritless claims.

* * *

NOTES AND QUESTIONS

1.   The court in *Kesner* recognized the potential liability to the member of a household, but it declined to permit other types of "stranger" exposure cases. Is this a reasonable way to extend, but limit, liability?

2. Most of the "take home" exposure cases involve asbestos, but plaintiffs also have brought actions based on exposure to other substances. See, e.g., Schwartz v. Accuratus Corp., 2016 WL 3947572 (3d Cir. 2016) (woman alleging exposure to beryllium from her boyfriend's work clothes could proceed with products liability claim).

3. A slight majority of the states to consider "take home" exposure cases have held that employers have a duty to the members of an employee's household. See Quisenberry v. Huntington Ingalls, Inc., 818 S.E.2d 805 (Va. 2018) (collecting cases).

4. See generally Mark A. Behrens, Asbestos Trust Transparency, 87 Fordham L. Rev. 107 (2018); Brendan Kelly, Comment, Take-Home Toxin: Following *Kesner's* Lead and Creating a Consistent Framework for Determining Duty Toward Victims of Secondary Asbestos Exposure, 77 Md. L. Rev. 1166 (2018); Symposium: The Evolution of Asbestos Litigation: Enduring Issues and the Administration of Trusts, 88 Tulane L. Rev. 1021 (2014).

PART IV

TERMINATING THE RELATIONSHIP

CHAPTER 10

DISCHARGE

Discharge has been called the "capital punishment" of the workplace, and anyone who has ever been fired knows how apt that description is: loss of employment means not only loss of income but in our culture is often equated with loss of character and identity as well. Being fired, as opposed to quitting or being laid off due to economic circumstances, labels one a failure, unfit for employment. Justifiable causes for discharge include theft, dishonesty, falsification of records, fighting on company premises, possession or use of alcohol or drugs while on duty, insubordination, use of profane or abusive language to a supervisor, dangerous horseplay, sleeping on the job, excessive absenteeism, refusal to accept a work assignment, and disloyalty. There is also a wide range of unjustifiable or questionable reasons for discharge. Discharges lacking in good cause are at issue in several of the cases in this chapter.

Historically, management was entitled under common law to hire and fire whomever it pleased, as part of its right to run its business. The employer's position was, as stated by one early case, "May I not refuse to trade with any one? May I not dismiss my domestic servant for dealing, or even visiting, where I forbid? And if my domestic, why not my farm-hand, or my mechanic, or teamster? And, if one of them, then why not all four? And, if all four, why not a hundred or a thousand of them?" Payne v. Western & Atl. Ry., 81 Tenn. 507, 518 (1884). To a great extent, this thinking still dominates employment law over a century later.

Theoretically, the at-will rule operates on a principle of mutuality: both the employer and the employee are free to terminate their relationship at any time, without reason and without notice. From its inception, however, the rule has been criticized as unduly harsh on employees, whose inferior bargaining power relative to employers renders the mutuality of the "at-will" principle illusory. Usually, the employer's threat of discharge is a serious one for employees, whereas the relative fungibility of workers in low level jobs means that the employee's threat of quitting places few constraints on the employer. In practice, it is usually easier for a company to replace employees than it is for an employee to find a new job. With the distinct exceptions of government workers protected by civil service systems, members of labor unions with collective bargaining agreements, employees at companies that have granted their workers procedural protections against unfair dismissal, and small subsets of workers such as tenured professors who enjoy substantial job security, the vast majority of workers in the U.S. economy are subject to at-will employment.

The basic question posed in this chapter is what rights employers and employees should have in employment. To what extent should an essentially private relationship be governmentally regulated, by legislation or judicial rule? Is it desirable to shift from a rule of employment at-will to some other presumption governing the duration and termination of the employment relationship? Should the law treat wrongs to this relationship as torts or breaches of contract? Which cause of action is a preferable means of protecting employees' interests while still giving employers sufficient latitude to run their businesses? Finally, what does the development of the wrongful discharge doctrine indicate about the concept of employment and the individual's "right" to a job?

A. STATUTORY AND CONSTITUTIONAL PROTECTIONS OF EMPLOYEES

1. WHISTLEBLOWER LAWS

At-will employment is limited by government's need to implement effectively its regulatory goals. For example, Title VII, discussed in Chapter 4, supra, prohibits discriminatory firings, firings in retaliation for asserting the rights guaranteed by the statute, and firings for reporting violations of Title VII prohibitions to the government, labor unions, or any other agencies or authorities.

Governments have also sought to curtail employer rights to dismiss an employee for reporting the employer's unlawful conduct. The Whistleblower Protection Act of 1989, 5 U.S.C. § 2301(b)(9), expanded protection for federal employees who expose violations of law, gross mismanagement or waste of funds, abuse of authority, or substantial and specific danger to public health or safety in government agencies. Nearly all the states have enacted some form of statutory protection for whistleblowers as well, although the scope of protected activity varies from jurisdiction to jurisdiction and sometimes from statute to statute.

Bard v. Bath Iron Works Corp.
590 A.2d 152 (Me. 1991).

■ BRODY, JUDGE:

Leon E. Bard, Jr., appeals from a final judgment on his complaint alleging retaliatory discharge in violation of the Whistleblowers' Protection Act, breach of employment contract, wrongful discharge, and breach of implied covenant of good faith and fair dealing. Bard contends that the [lower] court erred in granting a motion for judgment made by Bath Iron Works Corporation (BIW) after the close of his evidence on the whistleblower claim.

* * *

Bard was employed by BIW from 1979 to 1986. In 1983, he became an inspector in the quality assurance department with responsibility for inspecting shipping documents and test reports accompanying incoming steel purchased by BIW from various steel mills. In the course of his inspection job, Bard discovered what he believed to be flaws in BIW's quality assurance process. He feared that these practices were contrary to provisions in BIW's contracts with the United States Navy. Beginning in 1984, Bard on several occasions called the suspected problem to the attention of his supervisors as well as Navy inspectors on site at BIW.

Bard received his last salary increase in January of 1984. Evaluations of his job performance by his supervisors, although generally good at first, became increasingly critical of his attitude and ability to work with others as a result of numerous complaints that his supervisors received about his performance. Bard was counseled about his attitude and performance on more than one occasion and was given a written warning in January of 1986. Eventually, other BIW employees had to be assigned to help him get his work done. Finally, on September 12, 1986, BIW discharged Bard for deliberately restricting output and creating a nuisance.

In response to his termination, Bard filed a complaint against BIW alleging breach of employment contract and reprisal in violation of the Whistleblowers' Protection Act. The complaint was subsequently amended to add the additional counts of wrongful discharge and breach of implied covenant of good faith and fair dealing. On May 4, 1989, the court granted BIW's motion for summary judgment on all counts but the whistle blower count. Shortly afterward, the court granted BIW's motion to strike Bard's whistle blower claim from the jury trial list on the ground that the Legislature had amended the Whistleblowers' Protection Act to eliminate the statutory right to a jury trial. * * * The case was then tried without a jury on June 6–11, 1990. At the close of Bard's evidence, BIW successfully moved for judgment pursuant to M.R. Civ. P. 50(d).

On appeal, Bard first challenges the judgment in favor of BIW on his claim for retaliatory discharge in violation of the Whistleblowers' Protection Act. The statute prohibits an employer from, among other things, terminating an employee for reporting illegal activities. The relevant section of the Act provides in pertinent part:

1. *Discrimination prohibited.* No employer may discharge, threaten or otherwise discriminate against an employee regarding the employee's compensation, terms, conditions, location or privileges of employment because:

A. The employee, acting in good faith, or a person acting on behalf of the employee, reports orally or in writing to the employer or a public body what the employee has reasonable cause to believe is a violation of a law or rule adopted under the laws of this State, a political subdivision of this State or the United States. . . .

Bard challenges the court's conclusion of law that he presented no evidence showing that he had reasonable cause to believe that a law or rule had been violated. He contends that BIW's alleged violation of MIL–Q–9858, a standard clause in its contract with the Navy, was also a violation of a specific federal regulation dealing with government procurement contracts. He contends alternatively that, in order to come under the protection of the Act, he need only have had a good faith belief that BIW had violated some law or rule. We are not persuaded by either argument.

By ruling as it did, the trial court in effect concluded that the evidence presented in Bard's case in chief was insufficient to establish a prima facie case of retaliatory discharge in violation of the Act. In general, a prima facie case of reprisal for whistleblowing requires that the employee show that (1) he engaged in activity protected by the statute, (2) he was the subject of adverse employment action, and (3) there was a causal link between the protected activity and the adverse employment action. The court essentially concluded that the evidence was legally insufficient to show that Bard had engaged in activity protected by the Whistleblowers' Protection Act.

* * *

Bard presented no evidence to show a belief on his part, as required by the Whistleblowers' Protection Act, that BIW was in any way acting illegally. In fact, his testimony at trial established no more than that he believed that a violation of contract provisions might have occurred. "I was afraid that [BIW's practices] would be in nonconformance with Navy contracts and lose contracts with the Navy," he testified. "[BIW is] one of the largest employers in the state and it would be a shame to lose work." Bard never testified or presented any other evidence to show that he had "reasonable cause to believe" that BIW had violated any "law or rule adopted under the laws of this State, a political subdivision of this State or the United States."

* * *

In view of Bard's failure to establish a prima facie case of reprisal for whistleblowing by failing to show preliminarily that he had engaged in activity protected by the Whistleblowers' Protection Act, the court properly granted BIW's motion for judgment.

* * *

Judgment affirmed.

NOTES AND QUESTIONS

1. Courts often employ subjective standards to determine the reasonableness of a whistleblower's accusation. In order to qualify for protection under the Texas Whistleblower Act, a plaintiff must demonstrate

a belief that the conduct reported was a violation of law and that the belief was reasonable in light of the employee's training and experience.

Under Texas common law, the courts recognize "the Legislature's decision to enact a number of narrowly-tailored whistleblower statutes instead." D'Unger, an officer of a charitable foundation that owned a ranch used for wildlife research, became concerned that the ranch's foreman was harassing migrants. The Foundation's CEO said "drop it." D'Unger contacted a congressman, the IRS, and the Mexican Consulate. He was then fired. D'Unger said his dismissal was unlawful retaliation. He also said that his $80,000 annual salary created a promise of definite employment for a year. The Texas Supreme Court rejected both claims. "[E]mployment is presumed to be at-will in Texas absent an unequivocal agreement to be bound for that term." The court also held that Texas law protects employees "who are asked to *commit* a crime, not those who are asked not to *report* one." Ed Rachal Fdn. v. D'Unger, 207 S.W.3d 330 (Tex.2006).

2.   The degree of protection offered employees by whistleblowing legislation may also depend on the kind of information reported. The Sarbanes-Oxley Act, 15 U.S.C. § 7201–7266, enacted in 2002 in response to the Enron, Worldcom, and other accounting fraud scandals, protects whistleblowers at public companies who report financial wrongdoing. The whistleblower files a complaint with the U.S. Department of Labor and can receive reinstatement, back pay with interest, and compensatory damages. The act does not provide for either punitive damages or a jury trial. In addition, an executive who retaliates, "including interference with the lawful employment or livelihood of any person, for providing to a law enforcement officer any truthful information," can be prosecuted and can receive a sentence of up to ten years in prison. The Sarbanes-Oxley Act also requires that the whistleblower be a person who "provide[s] information * * * regarding any conduct which the employee reasonably believes constitutes a violation" of the pertinent laws listed in the act. The First and Fourth Circuits interpreted the term "reasonable belief" to have both a subjective and objective component. See Day v. Staples, Inc., 555 F.3d 42 (1st Cir. 2009); Welch v. Chao, 536 F.3d 269 (4th Cir. 2008). While the complaints must be made in subjective good faith and be based on objectively reasonable belief, the whistleblower need not reference a specific statute or prove actual harm. Finally, the employer's explanations given to the employee for the challenged practices are also relevant to the objective reasonableness of the belief. In Day v. Staples, the court held that "Day's beliefs were not initially reasonable as beliefs in shareholder fraud and they became less reasonable as he was given explanations."

Plaintiffs were employees of private companies that advise or manage mutual funds. They alleged that they blew the whistle on putative fraud relating to the mutual funds (which themselves had no employees) and then suffered retaliation from their employer. Defendant argued that Sarbanes-Oxley only protects employees of the public company about which they blow the whistle. A divided Supreme Court held that whistleblower protection includes employees of a public company's private contractors and subcontractors. Lawson v. FMR LLC, 134 S.Ct. 1158 (2014) (6–3). Justice

Sotomayor, dissenting, said: "The Court . . . holds that the law encompasses any household employee of the millions of people who work for a public company and any employee of the hundreds of thousands of private businesses that contract to perform work for a public company. . . . [This] authorizes a babysitter to bring a federal case against his employer—a parent who happens to work at the local Walmart . . .—if the parent stops employing the babysitter after he expresses concern that the parent's teenage son may have participated in an Internet purchase fraud."

The Dodd-Frank Act strengthened the whistleblower protection provisions of the Sarbanes-Oxley Act, allowed monetary awards for whistleblowers who provide original information to the Securities and Exchange Commission (SEC) or the Commodity Futures Trading Commission, and created additional whistleblower retaliation causes of action. 2010 HR 4173, §§ 748, 922–924. Under section 922, the SEC shall pay a reward to individuals who provide original information to the SEC which results in monetary sanctions exceeding $1 million. The SEC has the discretion to allow an award that ranges from 10 to 30 percent of the amount recouped. If the amount awarded is less than 10 percent or more than 30 percent of the amount recouped, a whistleblower may appeal the SEC's determination by filing an appeal in the appropriate federal court of appeals within 30 days of the determination.

The anti-retaliation provision of the Dodd-Frank Act cannot be enforced in U.S. courts by a Taiwan-based employee of a Chinese subsidiary of a parent European corporation. Liu Meng-Lin v. Siemens AG, 763 F.3d 175 (2014). Plaintiff said he was fired for reporting that Siemens employees were making improper payments to officials in North Korea and China in connection with the sale of medical equipment in those countries.

Dodd-Frank only protects an employee who reports securities-law violations to the SEC. There is no protection for an employee who reports a violation to management and then asserts that his or her dismissal was unlawful retaliation. Digital Realty Trust, Inc. v. Somers, 138 S.Ct. 767 (2018).

Menendez complained to Halliburton management about what he thought were questionable accounting practices. He also complained to the SEC. Halliburton let Menendez's colleagues know that he had been the whistleblower. The colleagues, whom he had essentially accused of fraud, ostracized him. Held: What Halliburton did was illegal retaliation under section 806 of the Sarbanes-Oxley Act. Halliburton, Inc. v. Admin. Rev. Bd., 771 F.3d 254 (5th Cir. 2014).

3.   Wiest sued Tyco pursuant to Sarbanes-Oxley's whistleblower protection provision, section 806. Held: the district court erred in requiring that Wiest's communications to his superiors "definitively and specifically relate to" a violation of an anti-fraud law as opposed to expressing "a reasonable belief the actions of managers could run afoul" of a law. One issue was whether a "Mermaid Greeters" and "Costumed Pirates/Wenching" party at a resort in the Bahamas held by Tyco (after Tyco and its then-CEO Dennis Kozlowski had been in trouble for various corporate scandals) was an appropriate

advertising event. Wiest alleged that his dismissal was unlawful retaliation for this and other disagreements with Tyco management about corporate expenditures. Wiest v. Lynch, 710 F.3d 121 (3d Cir. 2013). On remand, the U.S. District Court held that Wiest had "adequately pleaded [an] alternative, agency based relationship so as to bring the company and [a] fourth individual within the rule extending SOX Act protection to employees of agents of public held companies." Wiest v. Lynch, 15 F.Supp.3d 543 (2014).

4. Legislation eliminates any question about there being a state policy against firing employees for opposing employer practices or protesting company safety or health standards. Some courts refuse to recognize a cause of action for whistleblowing absent a statutorily conferred right. See, e.g., Nieman v. Nationwide Mut. Ins. Co., 706 F.Supp.2d 897 (C.D.Ill. 2010). In some states, however, courts have ruled that the existence of statutory whistleblower remedies will preempt common law claims, including the public policy exception to at-will employment, discussed infra. See, e.g., Dudewicz v. Norris-Schmid, Inc., 503 N.W.2d 645 (Mich. 1993); Higgins v. Pascack Valley Hosp., 730 A.2d 327 (N.J. 1999).

5. The 2009 economic stimulus law (the American Recovery and Reinvestment Act) protects employees of state and local government and of contractors who whistleblow. See section 1553. The provision protects employee whistleblowers alleging waste of stimulus funds. It covers disclosure of information reasonably believed to be evidence of gross mismanagement, gross waste, or abuse of authority. Most other federal whistleblower statutes protect only disclosure of illegal conduct or fraud.

6. The Homeland Security Act, enacted in 2002, requires the Transportation Security Administration to prohibit disclosure of information detrimental to transportation security. MacLean, a federal air marshal, believed that cancelling certain missions from Las Vegas was dangerous and illegal. He told a newspaper reporter about the TSA decision he didn't like. TSA fired him. MacLean sued, alleging that his disclosure was whistleblowing protected by a federal statute protecting employees who disclose "any violation of any law, rule, or regulation," or "a substantial . . . danger to public . . . safety." The Supreme Court ruled for MacLean, saying that the exception to whistleblowing protection for leaking information in violation of law did not create an exception for violations of the regulation TSA had issued concerning "sensitive security information." A regulation, said the Court majority, is not a "law." Dep't of Homeland Sec. v. MacLean, 135 S. Ct. 913 (2015) (7–2).

7. Henry Roop was fired by Southern Pharmaceuticals Corporation (SPC) one day after he told his boss on the telephone that another executive had offered to make payments to the wife of Patrick Gregory, clinical coordinator at Central Medical Health Services, if Gregory referred diabetic equipment purchases to SPC. The wife, Josephine, would not be expected to perform work for SPC. The Mississippi Supreme Court said the jury had enough evidence to conclude that Roop was fired for reporting conduct that violated the federal Medicare and Medicaid Anti-Kickback statute and that terminating him for that reason violated the "narrow public-policy exception to Mississippi's employment-at-will doctrine." Roop v. Southern Pharm. Corp., 188 So.3d 1179 (Miss. 2016).

8.   One of the most common statutes whistleblowers seek protection under is the False Claims Act (FCA). 31 U.S.C. §§ 3729, 3730(b-g). The FCA empowers private plaintiffs to bring suits on behalf of the government against persons who knowingly present false or fraudulent claims to the government for approval or payment. In Universal Health Services Inc. v. US ex rel Julio Escobar, 136 S.Ct. 1989 (2016), the Supreme Court expanded the basis upon which these claims can be made. Specifically, the Court held that false claims may be the basis for liability when two conditions are satisfied: (1) the claim does not merely request payment, but also makes specific representations about the goods or services provided; and (2) the defendant's failure to disclose noncompliance with material statutory, regulatory, or contractual requirements makes those representations misleading half-truths.

2.   CONSTITUTIONAL PROTECTIONS

In addition to the legislation enacted by federal and state governments, federal and state constitutions can also limit the ability of employers to discharge at-will employees. As discussed in Chapter 7, an employer may not be permitted to interfere with an employee's exercise of constitutional rights, including freedom of expression, freedom of religion, and the right to privacy. See, e.g., Pickering v. Board of Education, 391 U.S. 563 (1968), supra p. 711, on the reach of the free speech rights of public employees.

Private sector employees may not challenge their discharge as violating federal constitutional guarantees, such as due process, equal protection, and privacy. Novosel v. Nationwide Ins. Co., 721 F.2d 894 (3d Cir.1983), held that the First Amendment could establish a public policy from which a common law action for wrongful discharge would arise on behalf of a private sector employee. *Novosel*, however, has not been followed by any other court because it would seemingly abrogate the government action requirement for constitutional claims. See Lisa B. Bingham, Employee Free Speech in the Workplace: Using the First Amendment as Public Policy for Wrongful Discharge Actions, 55 Ohio St. L. 341 (1994).

In most states, government action is required before an individual may claim a violation of the state constitution. See, e.g., Luedtke v. Nabors Alaska Drilling, Inc., 768 P.2d 1123 (Alaska 1989). Seven state constitutions (Ariz., Cal., Haw., Ill., La., Mo., Wash.), however, expressly recognize a constitutional right of privacy that might be violated by private employers. It remains to be seen, however, whether this theory will be accepted by the courts in wrongful discharge cases.

Developments in discharge law in the public sector—which antedate those in the private sector—have indeed surrounded the status of employment "with the kind of safeguards once reserved for personality" in certain cases, because of limits placed on state action by the Fourteenth Amendment to the United States Constitution, which reads in part:

> No State shall abridge the privileges or immunities of citizens of the United States; nor shall any State deprive any person of life, liberty or property without due process of law; nor deny to any person within its jurisdiction the equal protection of the laws.

Adverse personnel action against an employee by government in its role as an employer is considered "state action" for purposes of invoking the protections of the fourteenth amendment. If an individual has a protected liberty or property interest, it cannot be taken away absent due process.

Goetz v. Windsor Central School District

698 F.2d 606 (2d Cir. 1983).

■ CARDAMONE, CIRCUIT JUDGE:

Alleging a deprivation of property and liberty interests without due process of law, Dennis Goetz commenced this action under 42 U.S.C. § 1983 against the Windsor Central School District [School District] and four of its officials. The United States District Court for the Northern District of New York granted defendants' motion for summary judgment. We affirm as to the claimed deprivation of a property interest and reverse and remand to permit discovery on the claimed deprivation of a liberty interest.

In October 1979 the School District appointed Dennis Goetz to the position of "cleaner." One year later School District officials became aware of a series of thefts which had been occurring at the district offices. The New York State Police were notified and a formal investigation commenced. Shortly thereafter plaintiff was arrested and charged with third degree burglary.

On January 10, 1981 Goetz was suspended by the School District because of his alleged participation in these break-ins. Two days later [Ellen Skoviera, the School Business Executive] sent Goetz a letter requesting a full written explanation of his involvement in the matter. Goetz's application for an extension of time to respond was granted by Skoviera, but the record indicates that he never responded to Skoviera's letter. On January 19, 1981 plaintiff, through the attorney representing him in the criminal proceedings, wrote Skoviera indicating that Goetz had been suspended without an opportunity to be heard, in violation of his constitutional rights, and requesting an opportunity to be heard. However, as a result of not receiving a written explanation from Goetz, the School District terminated his employment on January 22. No information regarding the reasons for Goetz's termination from employment was placed in his personnel file.

On January 12, the same day that Skoviera wrote Goetz, she also circulated a memo to Supervisors Decker and Mulcahy directing that they and their staffs maintain the strictest confidentiality regarding the recent events at the School. No direct mention of Goetz was contained in that memo.

In March 1981 the burglary charge against plaintiff was reduced to a misdemeanor and he was granted an adjournment in contemplation of dismissal pursuant to New York Criminal Procedure Law § 170.55 (McKinney 1982).

On October 6, 1981 plaintiff instituted the present action charging that defendants had deprived him of property and liberty interests without due process of law.

* * *

Before one may be deprived of property the Fourteenth Amendment mandates that the dictates of due process be satisfied. Some property interest must exist in favor of the person seeking shelter under the Amendment's broad umbrella. In deciding whether a person possesses a property interest a court must carefully sift through abstract needs and unilateral expectations until it locates a legitimate claim of entitlement. Board of Regents v. Roth, 408 U.S. 564, 577 (1972). The source of such interests are not to be found in the Constitution. Rather their existence and dimensions are defined by "existing rules or understandings that stem from an independent source such as state law—rules or understandings that secure certain benefits and that support claims of entitlement to those benefits." Thus, a property interest in employment can be created by local ordinance or by implied contract. In either case, the sufficiency of the claim of entitlement rests on state law.

Plaintiff concedes that he possesses no protectable property interest under New York State's Civil Service Law. His position of "cleaner" is classified in the regulations as an unskilled labor position covered by section 42 of the Civil Service Law (McKinney 1973). New York law provides that after five years of service such employees may only be removed for incompetency or misconduct and must be afforded a hearing before removal. As an unskilled laborer with less than five years of service plaintiff's position was one terminable at will.

Supreme Court cases make clear that at will employees possess no protectable property interest in continued employment. In *Roth*, the Court noted that a person may possess a protected property interest in public employment if contractual or statutory provisions guarantee continued employment absent "sufficient cause" for discharge. Even a *de facto* system of tenure, if proved, is sufficient to create a property interest. See Perry v. Sindermann, 408 U.S. 593. * * * Plaintiff urges that a property interest arises from Article 9 of his collective bargaining agreement which provides that:

> In the case of employee release, at least one-day notice of release and reasons for such action to incorporate evaluation reports will be given to the employee. The employee, if he/she feels such reasons for release are essentially inadequate or inaccurate, may request an immediate audience with the Chief School Administrator, or his designee, to explain his/her reasons for contradicting the release order.

Goetz argues that where reasons for discharge must be provided to the employee, as here, the employer must come forward and justify the termination. He claims that the collective bargaining agreement changed his status from an employee who served at will to one who could be discharged solely for cause. For this contention plaintiff relies upon In re King v. Sapier.

In our view neither *King* nor the collective bargaining agreement supports plaintiff's argument. *King* dealt with the requisite notice to be afforded a probationary state employee under New York's Civil Service regulatory scheme. The court found little justification for expanding the notice requirement of Section 4.5 of the Rules and Regulations of the Department of Civil Service to include notice of unsatisfactory performance "when, in the status which he then occupies, the probationer may not compel the appointing authority to justify the termination." As the court in *King* recognized, it is the employee's *status* which determines whether he has a legitimate expectation of future employment. The mere fact that an employer may be required to notify an employee of the reasons for discharge does not alter the employee's status. While a collective bargaining agreement may add to an employee's procedural rights, and even create a property interest in continued employment, nothing in the relevant agreement altered Goetz's status as an at-will employee. Because he possessed no property interest in his employment, plaintiff's claim that he was denied due process of law for lack of a hearing must fail.

Liberty as guaranteed by the Fourteenth Amendment denotes the right of the individual to engage in the common occupations of life and to enjoy privileges recognized as essential to the orderly pursuit of happiness. Under the Constitution its meaning must be "broad indeed." A liberty interest is therefore implicated and a name-clearing hearing required where an employer creates and disseminates a false and defamatory impression about an employee in connection with the employee's termination. In viewing this record there is no question but that the allegation that plaintiff is a thief is stigmatizing information which arose in connection with plaintiff's discharge. The factual issue as to whether this information is true or false cannot be resolved on a motion for summary judgment. Thus, plaintiff should be prevented from proceeding with his case at this stage of the litigation only if defendants have conclusively demonstrated that they did not disseminate the stigmatizing impression that plaintiff was fired because he is a thief.

In this connection defendants supplied affidavits attesting to their efforts to keep the defamatory information secret. Plaintiff, on the other hand, presented affidavits indicating that many of his fellow townspeople were fully aware of the allegation of thievery. Some of the information concerning thievery may have arisen from the public nature of plaintiff's arrest and handcuffing while on school premises. It may well turn out that the public in this small community came upon this stigmatizing impression from sources other than the defendants; but, alternatively, it may be established that school district employees or board members were in fact responsible for public awareness of the allegedly defamatory charge made against plaintiff. If so, notice and an opportunity to be heard are essential to protect his due process rights.

* * *

We hold, finally, that plaintiff's failure to take advantage of the opportunity to provide an explanation for his alleged involvement in this affair does not constitute a waiver of his right to assert a due process claim. If it is found that Goetz was deprived of a liberty interest, he may well be entitled to more due process than the procedure under the collective bargaining agreement afforded him. Failure to take advantage of that procedure may not, therefore, be interpreted as a waiver of the full due process to which he would be entitled.

The matter is remanded therefore for further proceedings consistent with this opinion.

NOTES AND QUESTIONS

1.   The Supreme Court first recognized a property interest in employment for government employees sufficient to invoke the due process clause of the fourteenth amendment in Board of Regents v. Roth, 408 U.S. 564 (1972), and Perry v. Sindermann, 408 U.S. 593 (1972). In *Roth,* an assistant professor sued the University of Wisconsin when his one-year appointment was not renewed at the end of the academic year; in *Perry,* Sindermann, a ten-year veteran of the Texas state college system was not offered a new one-year contract after he became embroiled in a disagreement with his Board of Regents after having been elected president of the Texas Junior College Teachers Association. The Supreme Court held that Roth was not entitled to any due process regarding the decision not to renew his contract because he had no property interest in his employment beyond the one-year contract, but that Sindermann was, because of the de facto tenure system in operation at his college. In *Roth,* the Court stated:

> To have a property interest in a benefit, a person clearly must have more than an abstract need or desire for it. He must have more than a unilateral expectation of it. He must, instead, have a legitimate claim of entitlement to it.

* * *

Property interests, of course, are not created by the Constitution. Rather, they are created and their dimensions are defined by existing rules or understandings that stem from an independent source such as state law—rules or understandings that secure certain benefits and that support claims of entitlement to those benefits.

408 U.S. at 577.

In *Perry*, the Court elaborated on its holding in *Roth:*

We have made clear in *Roth* * * * that "property" interests subject to procedural due process protection are not limited by a few rigid, technical forms. Rather, "property" denotes a broad range of interests that are secured by "existing rules or understandings." * * * A person's interest in a benefit is a "property" interest for due process purposes if there are such rules or mutually explicit understandings that support his claim of entitlement to the benefit and that he may invoke at a hearing.

A written contract with an explicit tenure provision clearly is evidence of a formal understanding that supports a teacher's claim of entitlement to continued employment unless sufficient "cause" is shown. Yet absence of such an explicit contractual provision may not always foreclose the possibility that a teacher has a "property" interest in re-employment. For example, the law of contract in most, if not all, jurisdictions long has employed a process by which agreements, though not formalized in writing, may be "implied." 3 Corbin on Contracts, §§ 561–672A. Explicit contractual provisions may be supplemented by other agreements implied from "the promisor's words and conduct in the light of the surrounding circumstances."

408 U.S. at 601.

Both federal and state courts have refused to find a protected property interest in cases where there was merely a unilateral expectation on the employee's part of continued employment. See Deen v. Darosa, 414 F.3d 731 (7th Cir. 2005) (police officer did not have a legitimate claim of entitlement to reinstatement to active duty, and thus no property interest in his restatement); Elmore v. Cleary, 399 F.3d 279 (3d Cir. 2005) (a personnel policy handbook stating that the township would not take disciplinary action against an employee without just cause did not create a property interest in continued employment); Romero v. Administrative Office of Courts, 157 S.W.3d 638 (Ky.2005) (freelance court interpreters had "at most a mere expectancy of future employment" which meant no property interest entitled to due process protection); Merrell v. Chartiers Valley Sch. Dist., 855 A.2d 713 (Pa.2004) ("It is axiomatic that there is no inherent property interest in prospective employment").

2. What is a "liberty," as opposed to a "property," interest? In *Goetz,* the court indicated that a liberty interest is implicated "where an employer creates and disseminates a false and defamatory impression about an employee in connection with the employee's termination." As interpreted by the courts, a liberty interest is generally recognized in an individual's good name and his freedom to work, but the courts have had more difficulty pinning down the concept of liberty than they have in identifying property interests, particularly following the Supreme Court's decision in Paul v. Davis, 424 U.S. 693 (1976), holding that stigma alone resulting from defamatory statements is insufficient to invoke the liberty interest protection of the due process clause unless it accompanies discharge. In Wells v. Doland, 711 F.2d 670 (5th Cir. 1983), the Fifth Circuit held that an employee's liberty interests are violated when: (1) he is stigmatized as a result of the discharge process, where charges made against the individual seriously damaged his standing and associations in his community or foreclosed his freedom to take advantage of other employment opportunities *and* were false; (2) the charges were made public; and (3) the individual was denied a meaningful name-clearing hearing. The charges typically include immorality, dishonesty, alcoholism or drug abuse, disloyalty, and subversion. Even where an individual's liberty interests have been violated, the remedy ordered is generally not reinstatement, but only an opportunity to refute the false charges.

The individual's interest in reputation alone, without a more tangible interest such as employment, has been found not to be a protected "liberty" interest within the meaning of the due process clause. See, e.g., Hill v. Borough of Kutztown, 455 F.3d 225 (3d. Cir. 2006) ("to make out a due process claim for deprivation of a liberty interest in reputation, a plaintiff must show a stigma to his reputation *plus* deprivation of some additional right or interest"). The Fifth Circuit has laid out its test for finding a deprivation of a "liberty" interest, stating that the employee must have been "terminated for a reason which was (i) false, (ii) publicized, and (iii) stigmatizing to his standing or reputation in his community or terminated for a reason that was (i) false and (ii) had a stigmatizing effect such that (iii) he was denied other employment opportunities as a result." Whiting v. University of So. Miss., 451 F.3d 339 (5th Cir. 2006).

3. What "process" is "due" before an employee with a protected property or liberty interest in a job can be terminated? In *Roth,* the Supreme Court indicated that the rudimentary elements of due process include a statement of reasons for the termination and a hearing prior to the decision to terminate. In Cleveland Bd. of Educ. v. Loudermill, 470 U.S. 532 (1985), the Court elaborated on what constitutes due process for employees with protectable interests in their jobs. Specifically, the Court held that employees are entitled to notice and an explanation of the charges, as well as an opportunity to respond and to be heard *before* being discharged, even if the employer has elaborate post-discharge hearing procedures and even if there is no dispute that the individual has committed the acts for which he or she is being discharged.

4. What actions by an employer can qualify as a stigma to a worker's reputation so as to deprive the worker of a liberty interest? As the Seventh Circuit noted, "[s]imple charges of professional incompetence do not impose the sort of stigma that actually infringes an employee's liberty to pursue an occupation." Head v. Chicago Sch. Reform Bd. of Trustees, 225 F.3d 794 (7th Cir. 2000).

5.   When are states and cities constitutionally permitted to reduce pensions or make budgetary decisions that alter public employees' expected benefits? After the financial crisis of 2007–08 forced many states to rework their pension plans, Illinois's unfunded pension debt continued to grow, leading to financial instability and downgraded credit status. In 2013, the Illinois legislature passed a bill intended to save $160 billion in pension payments over the next 30 years. The Illinois Supreme Court struck down the law as violating the state's Constitution ("Membership in any pension or retirement system of the State, any unit of local government or school district, or any agency or instrumentality thereof, shall be an enforceable contractual relationship, the benefits of which shall not be diminished or impaired." Ill. Const. art. VIII, § 5). In re Pension Reform Litigation, 2015 IL 118585. Only five other states include a form of pension protection in their Constitution. Most states allow protection of pension benefits under contract law; six states protect them as a property right; and two states use a "gratuity approach," providing little or no protection. (Tyler Bond, National Public Pension Coalition, *What are the Legal protections for Public Pensions?* (2018), *available at* https://protectpensions.org/2018/05/14/legal-protections-public-pensions/.

6.   Connecticut violated the First Amendment rights of employees to freedom of association by discriminatorily laying off only union members when reducing the state's work force. State Emp. Bargaining Agent Coalition v. Rowland, 718 F.3d 126 (2d Cir. 2013), cert. denied, 134 S.Ct. 1002 (2014). See also United Auto., Aerospace, AGR, v. Fortuño, 633 F.3d 37 (1st Cir. 2011) permitting Puerto Rico's governor to respond to a budget deficit with layoffs and suspension of worker constitutional protections.

7.   A superintendent of schools had a property interest in his employment contract. That interest was not violated when the school board voted to buy out the two years remaining on the contract, because that superintendent had no constitutionally protected liberty or property interest in the intangible benefits of serving in the position itself. Holloway v. Reeves, 277 F.3d 1035 (8th Cir. 2002).

When a property interest in employment exists, what room is left for employment-at-will? In County of Dallas v. Wiland, 216 S.W.3d 344 (Tex. 2007), deputy constables were de facto terminated when the newly elected constable failed to swear them into office again. The deputy constables brought an action claiming due process violations. The court looked to the Dallas County Administrative Policies and Procedures Manual to determine whether the county conveyed a property interest to its constables. While admitting that the manual was not clear, the court concluded that the manual created an expectation of continued employment despite the clauses explicitly disavowing creation of an employment contract. The court reasoned that a "fair import" of the manual as a whole is that covered employees are not to be discharged without being given a reason they can contest. "This expectation in continued employment except for just cause, while not a contract right, as the manual expressly disavows, is nevertheless a property interest of which employees may not be deprived without due process." Interestingly the court also stated that the "important procedures for hearing and deciding grievances" established by the manual do not alone "create a property interest"; moreover, the entitlement to such procedures, without more, does not alter an employee's at-will status, thereby creating a property interest in continued employment. Do you find the court's argument regarding the unaltered status of employment at-will satisfying? Doesn't an entitlement to a procedural hearing infer some sort of right to employment beyond employment at will?

8. Who is a government employer or employee for purposes of Due Process clause protection? This question is important as it applies to employees of government contractors, i.e., private employees doing government work. In Milo v. Cushing Mun. Hosp., 861 F.2d 1194 (10th Cir. 1988), the personnel actions of a private corporation hired by a municipal authority to operate a publicly funded hospital were held to constitute state action. If an individual is deprived of his employment in the private sector due to the actions of government officials, he or she is deemed protected by the Due Process clause to the extent that a public employee is (e.g., the individual must demonstrate a reasonable expectation in continued employment to establish a property interest). Merritt v. Mackey, 827 F.2d 1368 (9th Cir. 1987). For the status of government employment under the Equal Protection Clause, see Engquist v. Oregon Dep't of Agric., 553 U.S. 591 (2008).

9. Military retirees sued the United States, alleging that recruiters had promised free lifetime medical care for them and their dependents in exchange for 20 years of service and that the government did not honor this promise. Held: Congress did not delegate to the military the authority to make such promises. Also, a holding that recruitment promises bind future Congresses would violate the Appropriations Clause of the Constitution. Schism v. United States, 316 F.3d 1259 (Fed. Cir. 2002), cert. denied, 539 U.S. 910 (2003).

10. Linhoff had worked at University of Connecticut Health Center for 15 years as a "skilled maintainer . . . changing heating, ventilation and air conditioning filters on hospital roof" with no prior discipline. A police officer spotted him sitting with a coworker in a state van while smoking marijuana. He was fired. The arbitrator under a public employee union contract said Linhoff should be suspended from work for 6 months without pay and after that experience random drug testing for a year. Connecticut appealed and the trial court said Linhoff should be terminated. The Supreme Court reversed and approved the arbitrator's much lighter punishment, saying it did not violate public policy. State of Connecticut v. Connecticut Employees Union, 142 A.3d 1122 (Conn. 2016).

But see City of Richfield v. Law Enforcement Labor Services, Inc., 910 N.W.2d 465 (Minn. Ct. App. 2018). A police officer was terminated for failing to report his use of force in violation of the employer's policy. He had previously been disciplined, trained, and counseled for prior infractions. An arbitrator ruled that the officer should be reinstated. The appellate court overturned that decision based on the "clear public policy in favor of transparency . . . on the use of force."

11. When Indiana by state statute revoked tenure rights of public school teachers, it violated the Contracts Clause of the U.S. Constitution. Elliott v. Board of School Trustees, 876 F.3d 926 (7th Cir. 2017), cert. denied, 2018 WL 1243305.

3. STATUTORY CONTRACTS—THE MONTANA EXCEPTION

Montana is unique among the 50 states in its statutory requirement of just cause for termination. Mont. Code Ann. § 30–2–901 et seq. The statute, enacted in 1987, prohibits private employers from firing employees if the action was without "good cause" as defined in the statute or if the action was in violation of public policy or in violation of the express provisions of the employer's own written personnel policy. Wrongfully discharged employees may be awarded up to four years' lost wages and benefits, as well as punitive damages in limited cases.

Marcy v. Delta Airlines
166 F.3d 1279 (9th Cir. 1999).

■ BOOCHEVER, CIRCUIT JUDGE:

In this case, we must determine whether the Montana Wrongful Discharge from Employment Act ("WDEA"), Mont. Code Ann. §§ 39–2–901 et seq., provides a cause of action to an employee discharged by her employer for a reason based on mistaken facts, but where the employer exercised good faith in reaching its decision.

After a jury found that Delta Airlines wrongfully discharged Suzanne Marcy under the WDEA and the district court entered judgment for Marcy, Delta moved for judgment as a matter of law, or in the alternative, for a new trial, arguing that Marcy had failed to state a valid claim under the WDEA because she did not sufficiently prove that Delta had acted in bad faith in discharging her. The district court denied both motions, and Delta filed this timely appeal. We have jurisdiction pursuant to 28 U.S.C. § 1291. We affirm.

Suzanne Marcy became an employee of Delta Airlines in 1987 when Delta merged with Marcy's former employer. At the time of her discharge, Marcy worked as a Senior Customer Service Representative at Delta's Gallatin Airport facility in Bozeman, Montana. She was generally rated as an "outstanding Delta employee." Delta terminated Marcy after she submitted her payroll records with three incorrect entries which would have allowed her to collect about $250 in unearned wages. While Marcy acknowledges that there were mistakes on her payroll records, she has maintained all along that the mistakes were unintentional, and that such mistakes were common in Delta's payroll system. Delta, on the other hand, has been equally steadfast in its assertion that Marcy's mistakes were part of an intentional plan to defraud the company. Marcy's mistakes were contained in two Delta personnel documents—the "Daily Work Schedule" and the "Daily Attendance Record."

Delta's scheduling tool at the Bozeman facility, called the Daily Work Schedule ("DWS"), was basically a sheet listing which shift and in what position each employee had been assigned to work for that day. The DWS would also list, among other things, which employees had taken that day off using vacation or compensatory ("comp") time. The DWS was prepared by Delta supervisors weekly, and approximately seven to ten days in advance. Schedule changes due to employees calling in sick or swapping shifts, for example, were not uncommon, and because the DWS was not always updated to include these changes, the actual number of hours that an employee worked might not be accurately reflected in the DWS.

The Daily Attendance Record ("DAR") was the document used by Delta to track the hours its employees worked and to calculate payroll. For example, an employee who recorded that she worked from "6:00 to 12:00" in the DAR would be paid for six hours. Delta employees were responsible for recording their own hours in the DAR on a daily basis, and Delta relied on its employees to record their information accurately.

When an employee wanted to take time off using her accrued vacation or comp time, Delta required the employee to follow several procedures. First, she had to obtain approval from a Delta supervisor by having the supervisor sign a "Time-Off Request Form." The supervisor would then staple the signed Time-Off Request Form to the back of the DWS for the day that the employee was taking off. Second, the employee would have to make a special notation on her DAR so that she would be paid for her time off, but would also have her vacation or comp time account deducted. For example, an employee using a vacation day would record "6:00 to 12:00—VAC DAY 6.0" in her DAR. This would inform Delta that it should pay the employee for six hours that day, but that it also should deduct six hours from that employee's vacation account. An employee using comp time to take all or part of a day off was similarly required to make a notation on the DAR so that her comp time account could be deducted.

When Marcy submitted her DAR for the first two weeks of May, 1993, it contained three mistaken entries, each involving the failure to note on the DAR that she had used vacation or comp time to take time off. These mistakes, left unnoticed, would have resulted in Marcy being paid about $250 in unearned wages without having her vacation or comp time accounts deducted.

* * *

Marcy's supervisor, Pam Bracken discovered the mistakes on May 11, and informed the station manager, Jack Reese, on May 14. They both agreed that they would not ask Marcy about the mistakes, but would return the DAR to where it belonged and see if Marcy would correct the mistakes on her own. The DAR binder was available to Marcy on May 11, 12, and 17, but she did not correct the mistakes. Reese and Bracken confronted Marcy on the morning of May 18. Marcy stated that all of the false entries were the result of honest mistakes. Marcy explained that on May 17, she had tried to find the DAR to see if her DAR entries were correct, but she could not find it because it was not hanging where it was supposed to be. Marcy stated that because she had taken off seven days that pay period using vacation and comp time, and had also switched shifts with another employee to take an eighth day off, she wanted to check the DAR to make sure it was correctly updated.

Later, after she became busy handling a flight, she stated that she simply forgot to go back to look at the DAR. Marcy was not worried though, because she stated that mistakes were not uncommon in Delta's payroll system, and that it was Bracken's usual practice to call employees to clarify any discrepancies between the DWS and DAR. Marcy assumed that she could correct any mistakes when Bracken asked her.

Marcy could not explain why her Time-Off Request form was missing or why her name was erased as an employee on vacation on the May 10 DWS sheet. She stated that the entry, made in her handwriting, adding her to the May 10 work schedule was the result of a simple mistake— Marcy thought that she was writing on the DWS sheet for May 11, when she actually was scheduled to work. She also stated that she told Reese that a co-worker, Stephanie Dunagan, would verify her story, but he did not investigate.

Based on the false payroll entries, as well as a previous incident of alleged fraud involving personal long-distance phone calls of minimal value made by Marcy, Reese prepared a report recommending the termination of Marcy. Other than interviewing Marcy, Reese did not question any witnesses or investigate any further. On May 18, Marcy's case was forwarded to Delta headquarters in Atlanta for review by a four-person panel consisting of Delta managers. Reese indicated that he thought Marcy's actions were intentional, and recommended that Marcy be terminated. The panel decided to terminate Marcy. On May 27, Reese called Marcy into his office and offered Marcy the right to resign, but she refused. Marcy was then terminated.

In December 1993, Marcy sued Delta in Montana state court, alleging numerous claims relating to her discharge, including one for wrongful discharge under the Montana WDEA. Delta removed the case to the United States District Court for the District of Montana.

* * *

The parties disagree whether an employer may be held liable for wrongful discharge under the WDEA when the employer makes its decision to discharge in good faith, but where the reason given rests on a mistaken interpretation of the facts. Under Delta's proposed interpretation of the WDEA, so long as the employer acts in good faith, it cannot be held liable for wrongful discharge, even if the factual bases that it relies upon are mistaken. For example, if an employer in good faith discharges an employee for stealing, but when the facts are later brought before a jury, the jury determines that there was in fact no theft, Delta would nevertheless have the court conclude that the employee has no claim under the WDEA.

* * *

At the time of her discharge, Marcy was not a probationary employee, and the parties stipulated that Marcy was generally rated as an outstanding employee. Thus, this appeal involves only whether Delta terminated Marcy for "[a] legitimate business reason." The WDEA, unfortunately, does not further define what constitutes a "legitimate business reason." Recognizing the need to clarify this term, the Montana Supreme Court stated that "a legitimate business reason is a reason that is neither false, whimsical, arbitrary or capricious, and it must have some logical relationship to the needs of the business."

* * *

Although neither the plain language of the WDEA nor its legislative history supports Delta's pretext requirement, Delta relies on the Montana Supreme Court's decision in Mysse v. Martens, 279 Mont. 253, 926 P.2d 765 (1996), where the court stated:

> In order to defeat a motion for summary judgment on the issue of good cause, this court requires the employee to prove that the given reason for the discharge * * * is a pretext and not the honest reason for the discharge.

Delta argues that this language requires Marcy to prove that Delta's stated reason for her discharge was pretextual. We agree with the district court that Delta places too much significance on the Montana Supreme Court's use of the word "pretext."

A close review of the WDEA case law reveals that the Montana Supreme Court will find that the stated reason for an employee's discharge is not legitimate under the WDEA if the reason given for the employee's discharge: (1) is invalid as a matter of law under the WDEA; (2) rests on a mistaken interpretation of the facts; or (3) is not the honest reason for the discharge, but rather a pretext for some other illegitimate reason. A discharged employee need only prove that one of these three types is true in her case to demonstrate that the reason for her discharge was not legitimate.

Thus, contrary to Delta's argument, proof that the employer acted in bad faith by using a pretext to discharge its employee is only one possible way of demonstrating that the employer's stated reason was not a legitimate one. All the Montana Supreme Court cases that have interpreted the WDEA are consistent with this reading.

* * *

The Montana Supreme Court has repeatedly found that an employee discharged for a reason based on a mistaken interpretation of the facts has a valid claim under the WDEA, even if the employer acted in good faith.

* * *

Marcy claimed that Delta's reason for terminating her—intentional falsification of payroll records—rested on a mistaken interpretation of the facts. She did not allege that such a reason was invalid under the WDEA, or that Delta had acted in bad faith by using that reason as a pretext for some other illegitimate reason. Thus, once Marcy offered sufficient evidence to raise a genuine issue of material fact that her recording errors were unintentional, the case properly went before a jury to determine that factual issue. Marcy was not required to prove that Delta had acted in bad faith because that issue was irrelevant to whether Delta was mistaken.

Marcy raised a genuine issue of fact on whether she acted intentionally. Before her discharge, she was generally rated as an outstanding employee, and she offered evidence that mistakes were common in Delta's payroll system. Further, she offered evidence that Delta supervisors would consult employees about any discrepancies between the DAR and DWS. Whether Marcy intentionally entered mistaken payroll entries on her DAR squarely presented a factual issue for the jury, which found in favor of Marcy, and on appeal Delta does not challenge that verdict as against the weight of the evidence.

Because we hold that Marcy was not required to prove that Delta's stated reason for her discharge was pretextual, we conclude that the district court did not err in denying Delta's motion for judgment as a matter of law, or alternatively, for a new trial. Because we affirm the district court on these grounds, we decline to reach the district court's alternative bases for denying Delta's motions.

AFFIRMED.

■ GRABER, CIRCUIT JUDGE, dissenting:

I respectfully dissent, because the majority has departed from proper methods of statutory construction and has created an opportunity for forum-shopping in Montana wrongful termination cases.

* * *

The Montana Wrongful Discharge from Employment Act (WDEA) permits an employee to maintain a successful action for wrongful discharge "only if . . . the discharge was not for good cause." " 'Good cause' means reasonable job-related grounds for dismissal based on a failure to satisfactorily perform job duties, disruption of the employer's operation, or other legitimate business reason." The Montana Supreme Court has defined "legitimate business reason" to mean a reason that has "some logical relationship to the needs of the business" and is "neither false, whimsical, arbitrary or capricious." The question in this case is: When an employer conducts a proper investigation and, at the time it acts, fires an employee for a reason that bears a "logical relationship to the needs of the business" that is not "whimsical," that is not "arbitrary," that is not "capricious," and that is not then known to be "false," has the employer fired a person for "good cause," or is it open to the employee to demonstrate after the fact that the reason given was erroneous?

* * *

The facts of this case reveal the disquieting prospect of a court's second-guessing of employers' day-to-day personnel decisions, a prospect that is inherent in the majority's interpretation of the Montana statute. Here, defendant fired plaintiff for recording false time-sheet entries. Those entries claimed 14.5 hours of time that plaintiff had not worked; those hours, of course, would have translated into unearned wage payments. Plaintiff does not dispute that the entries were wrong. She does not claim that, in general, a firing for recording false time-sheet entries fails the "legitimate business reason" test established by the Montana statute. Plaintiff does not claim and did not prove that defendant fired her for some illegitimate reason or had any ulterior motive. Finally, and significantly, plaintiff did not prove that defendant failed to follow proper procedures in investigating or carrying out the termination. To the contrary, it is undisputed that defendant provided plaintiff with an opportunity to explain the false time-sheet entries. When she only said that she had made a "big mistake," defendant discharged her. Defendant's decision not to believe plaintiff's story was reasonable in the light of the fact that, on a prior occasion, plaintiff had admitted to falsifying company telephone logs. In these circumstances, I do not think that Montana law permits a jury to second-guess defendant's decision to fire plaintiff by deciding that it would have credited her "big mistake" explanation.

At best, the majority's interpretation of Montana law is plausible. Nonetheless, at a minimum, a different interpretation of "good cause," Mont.Code Ann. §§ 39–2–903(5), 39–2–904(2), is equally plausible. In the circumstances, I would decline to guess at the meaning of Montana law and would submit a certified question to the Montana Supreme Court.

NOTES AND QUESTIONS

1.   By a 4–3 vote, the Montana Supreme Court upheld the constitutional validity of the state's Wrongful Discharge From Employment Act. Meech v. Hillhaven West, Inc., 776 P.2d 488 (Mont.1989). The act was challenged under the Montana constitutional provision assuring an individual "full legal redress," and also as a violation of equal protection of the laws because it denies full tort damages to some plaintiffs (dismissed employees) but not others. The majority opinion said that the legislature may alter the common law, and specifically that it may prescribe remedies and procedures for particular wrongs. Justice Sheehy, dissenting, wrote: "This is the blackest

judicial day in the eleven years that I have sat on this Court. Indeed it may be the blackest judicial day in the history of the state. * * * The decision today cleans the scalpel for the legislature to cut away unrestrainedly at the whole field of tort redress. * * * The legislature, in effect, has converted the tort of wrongful discharge into a sort of contract action * * *."

2. How much evidence does a plaintiff need in order to prove a firing decision was not made for "good cause"? In Moe v. Butte-Silver Bow County, 371 P.3d 415 (Mont. 2016), the plaintiff, a human resources director, was fired for inappropriate conduct and job performance deficiencies articulated in a complaint by a subordinate. The court reversed the district court, finding that there was a genuine issue of material fact as to whether the plaintiff was fired for good cause because the plaintiff's response letter "presented exhaustive responses to the allegations against her." In Bird v. Cascade County, 386 P.3d. 602 (Mont. 2016), the plaintiff, also a human resources director, was terminated for, among other allegations, using public resources for political purposes and disclosing confidential information. Distinguishing *Moe,* the court upheld the decision for summary judgment largely because the majority of the plaintiff's response letter amounted to "conclusory statements, speculative assertions, and mere denials."

B. CONTRACTUAL EXCEPTIONS TO EMPLOYMENT AT WILL

1. BREACH OF CONTRACT

While Montana has statutorily adopted a just cause standard for termination, in other states, courts have generally maintained a presumption of at-will employment, albeit a rebuttable one. Indeed, employers and employees are free to contract around the at-will presumption. Consequently, claims for wrongful discharge based on breach of contract have raised many of the same issues as any other breach of contract case: mutuality of obligation and consideration. How could the employee be free to quit and the employer not be free to terminate? What consideration beyond services for which the employer paid directly did the employee provide in order to secure a promise that termination would only occur for just cause?

a. WRITTEN CONTRACTS

Gordon v. Matthew Bender & Co.

562 F.Supp. 1286 (N.D. Ill. 1983).

■ HART, DISTRICT JUDGE:

The plaintiff Joel Gordon ("Gordon"), a citizen of Illinois, has brought a twelve-count First Amended Complaint ("complaint") against Matthew Bender & Company, Inc. ("Matthew Bender"), a New York corporation with its principal place of business in New York.* * *

Gordon began working for Matthew Bender on November 5, 1973, as one of its law book sales representatives in a territory which included parts of Chicago and the surrounding areas. The employment agreement between Gordon and Matthew Bender stated no definite period during which the parties remained obligated to each other. Gordon developed into a commendable employee who reached or exceeded the goals set for him by his employer.

On July 24, 1980, Gordon was informed by his superior at Matthew Bender that his territory would be reduced on September 1, 1980. On October 7, 1980, he was told that he would be terminated if he failed to achieve in his new territory the same sales goals which had been set for the territory he worked in prior to the September 1 change. Thus though Gordon's territory had been diminished, his sales goals remained the same. He did not meet the goals and was fired on January 8, 1981.

* * *

Gordon alleges that it was "Matthew Bender's policy and practice * * * to condition its sales representatives' continued employment on 'acceptable sales performance.'" He refers to a letter from Matthew Bender to Gordon placing him on probationary status. This letter states that if Gordon meets his goals, he will be "restored to the same status of acceptable sales performance as other Matthew Bender sales representatives." Gordon alleges that this letter created a contract for continuous employment conditioned upon acceptable sales performance, which Matthew Bender breached by firing him even though he met or exceeded the requirement of acceptable sales performance.

Matthew Bender has moved to dismiss Count II on a variety of grounds, including: (1) this was a contract terminable at will, and therefore Gordon's discharge is not actionable; (2) the contract lacks mutuality and therefore is not actionable; (3) the oral contract is unenforceable under the statute of frauds since it is for an indefinite period. Since the Court finds that this was a contract terminable at will, the other arguments will not be addressed.

Gordon claims that though this was a contract for no definite period, it was not a contract without terms governing its duration. Gordon's length of employment would depend on his "satisfactory performance" or "acceptable sales performance." Therefore, the argument goes, so long as the condition of acceptable performance was being met—and this is a fact issue which precludes the granting of a motion to dismiss, since the Court must accept the plaintiff's allegations as true—the contract could not be terminated. Gordon relies heavily on Scaramuzzo v. Glenmore Distilleries Co., 501 F.Supp. 727 (N.D.Ill.1980).

In *Scaramuzzo,* the fired plaintiff alleged that the defendant-employer had promised that Scaramuzzo "would be discharged only for good cause, and [that] he would retain all corporate responsibilities assigned to him as long as he competently executed such responsibilities." Defendant moved for summary judgment on grounds that this was an employment agreement terminable at will. The court denied the motion, stating that "[a] contract that fails to specify the length of the term of employment, but that does set conditions upon which termination may be based, is not terminable at will—it is terminated upon the existence of those conditions." Since there existed a fact question as to whether such conditions existed—whether the plaintiff could be discharged only for good cause, and whether he would retain his responsibilities as long as he executed them competently—summary judgment could not be granted.

Gordon argues that there existed a condition to his employment contract with Matthew Bender—"acceptable sales performance"—so that, as in *Scaramuzzo,* a legal claim exists which at the very least precludes a dismissal of this count of the complaint. But Gordon cannot distinguish two other cases precisely on point. In Buian v. J.L. Jacobs and Company, 428 F.2d 531 (7th Cir. 1970), the court found that the following contract language did not raise any fact issue, and that a contract terminable at will existed: "It is scheduled that your assignment in Saudi Arabia will continue for a period of eighteen (18) months. * * * It is intended that all staff associates assigned to the Saudi Arabia projects will remain in Saudi Arabia * * * throughout the duration of the specified assignments. This of course presumes *satisfactory service* by each associate * * *."

In Payne v. AHFI/Netherlands, B.V., 522 F.Supp. 18 (N.D.Ill.1980), the court construed terms similar to those at issue in *Buian* and also found that a contract at will existed. The duration of the *Payne* contract was to depend on factors such as "individual performance."

Buian and *Payne* clearly stand for the proposition that satisfactory or acceptable performance language does not transform a contract with no definite period—one at will—into a contract which cannot be terminated by either party at any time for any reason. The Court finds that these cases control. Further, *Scaramuzzo* is not contrary authority. It is distinguishable on its facts—no discharge except "for good cause" (an objective criterion) has a different meaning, in this employment context, from an employment which lasts as long as performance is "acceptable" (a subjective decision).

Further, two Illinois cases hold that a "satisfactory performance" contract is terminable at will. See Kendall v. West, 196 Ill. 221, 63 N.E. 683 (1902) (employment contract lasting as long as employee performed "satisfactory services" may be terminated at any time for any reason); Vogel v. Pekoc, 157 Ill. 339, 42 N.E. 386 (1895) (employment agreement "to continue only so long as satisfactory" may be terminated at any time for any reason).

Gordon disparages *Kendall* and *Vogel* as "turn-of-the-century cases." However, it is clear that at least *Kendall* has continuing vitality as it formed the basis of a recent decision of the Illinois appellate court.

In addition, the Illinois courts have shown no disposition to abandon the at will doctrine except in carefully defined areas. * * *

A "condition" of satisfactory or acceptable performance theoretically could be implied in every employment contract. Such an end-run around the at will doctrine would eviscerate it altogether, and the Illinois courts do not seem inclined to do so. The motion to dismiss Count II is granted.

NOTES AND QUESTIONS

1. In *Gordon*, the court distinguished contracts that continue as long as performance is "acceptable" or "satisfactory" from contracts that limit discharge to "good cause." The court concluded that in the former, the employment remains at will because subjective criteria would be used in making a decision to discharge, whereas in the latter the employment is not at will because objective criteria would be used. Do you agree with this reasoning? In *Gordon*, how was "acceptable" performance to be determined?

2. The general rule regarding written contracts is that if the contract is for a definite term the employee may be discharged before the expiration date only for breach of a contractual provision or other "good cause." When the employee establishes that he or she was discharged in violation of an employment contract, the burden of proof shifts to the employer to prove the existence of good cause for the discharge. See Ross v. Garner Printing Co., 285 F.3d 1106 (8th Cir. 2002).

3. A sales representative has a written contract detailing the salary and commissions she is to receive as well as other terms and conditions of employment. The contract is not for any definite term. If the employer later reduces the amount of commission she is to receive, does the employee have a cause of action for breach of contract? See Green v. Edward J. Bettinger Co., 608 F.Supp. 35 (E.D.Pa.1984), affirmed, 791 F.2d 917 (3d Cir. 1986), cert. denied, 479 U.S. 1069 (1987) (holding that there was no breach of contract). Section 2.03(a) of the Restatement Third of Employment Law (tentative draft 2009) states that "an employer must have cause for termination of (1) an unexpired agreement for a definite term of employment or (2) an agreement for an indefinite term of employment requiring cause for termination."

4. When an employer notifies an at-will employee that the terms of employment are being changed, such as a reduction in salary, the employee has the option of accepting the new conditions or resigning. "[T]he employer can terminate the old contract and make an offer for a unilateral contract under new terms." DiGiacinto v. Ameriko-Omserv Corp., 69 Cal.Rptr.2d 300, 304 (Ct.App.1997). "If the employee continues working with knowledge of the changes, he has accepted the changes as a matter of law." Hathaway v. General Mills, Inc., 711 S.W.2d 227, 229 (Tex.1986).

Scribner v. Worldcom, Inc.

249 F.3d 902 (9th Cir. 2001).

■ TROTT, CIRCUIT JUDGE:

In this appeal, we must decide what the words "termination without cause" mean in the context of a stock option contract between an employer and employee. The question is whether the employer, who retains discretion to construe the contract, can define the word "cause" to mean something other than its ordinary meaning without informing the employee that the ordinary meaning is irrelevant. Under the circumstances of this case, we conclude that the answer is no.

The parties are Donald Scribner and WorldCom, Inc., Scribner's former employer. Scribner owned unvested options to purchase shares of WorldCom stock, which were to become immediately exercisable if WorldCom terminated him "without cause." WorldCom eventually terminated Scribner, not because of shortcomings in his performance, but to facilitate the sale of the division in which he worked. Scribner claimed that his termination was "without cause" and attempted to exercise his options. WorldCom, however, claimed that although Scribner had not been let go for deficient performance, his termination was nonetheless "with cause" for stock option purposes. Scribner sued. Both parties filed motions for summary judgment; the district court granted WorldCom's and denied Scribner's.

Scribner appeals, and this battle over the meaning of words is now before us. His lawyer has drawn our attention to an apt quote from Lewis Carroll, whose depictions of the reverse-logic of childhood fantasy worlds all too often resemble adult reality. Describing a confrontation between Alice and Humpty Dumpty as to the extent of language's elasticity, Carroll wrote:

> "I don't know what you mean by 'glory,' " Alice said.
>
> Humpty Dumpty smiled contemptuously. "Of course you don't-till I tell you. . . . When *I* use a word," Humpty Dumpty said in a rather scornful tone, "it means just what I choose it to mean—neither more nor less."
>
> "The question is," said Alice, "whether you *can* make words mean so many different things."

LEWIS CARROLL, *Through the Looking Glass, in* THE COMPLETE WORKS OF LEWIS CARROLL 154, 196 (1994).

Like Alice, we are of the opinion that language is not infinitely elastic. We conclude that, under the facts of this case, "termination with cause" could only mean termination for deficient performance. Summary judgment in favor of Scribner, not WorldCom, is appropriate, and, accordingly, we REVERSE.

The essential facts of this case are not in dispute. Donald Scribner served as the vice-president of WorldCom's Operator Services Division from 1994 until mid-1997. Scribner was by all accounts an exemplary employee. In 1995, in recognition of his value to the company, WorldCom granted him an option to purchase 9,000 shares of WorldCom stock. In 1996, it granted him an option to purchase an additional 2,000 shares. These options were to vest and become exercisable over a period of several years. Scribner exercised these options as they vested, but in mid-1997, when this dispute arose, the number of unvested options he held had grown to 10,000 due to stock splits.

WorldCom's Stock Option Plan ("The Plan") required generally that option holders be currently employed with WorldCom in order to exercise their options. The Plan provided that "subject to earlier termination as provided herein, any outstanding option and all unexercised rights thereunder shall expire and terminate automatically upon ... the cessation of the employment or engagement of the Optionee by the Company for any reason other than retirement, death, or disability." Scribner's contracts contained such an "early termination" exception, providing that his options would immediately vest if WorldCom terminated him "without cause." The pertinent language reads:

> the Option[s] shall vest and, subject and pursuant to the provisions of the Plan and this Agreement, shall be exercisable with respect to all of the Option Shares immediately upon ... any termination by the Company of the Employee's employment with the company by reason of the Employee's disability or *without cause.*

Scribner's contracts and the Stock Option Plan do not define the phrase "without cause," nor do they explain what would constitute termination "with cause." However, the Plan gives a Stock Option Committee appointed by WorldCom's Board of Directors ("the Committee") broad discretion to interpret the terms of the Plan and contracts made under it. Part of this discretion is the authority to determine whether or not terminations are "with cause" or "without cause." The Plan also provides that the Committee's determinations are "conclusive and binding on all Optionees." The Plan further instructs the Committee to exercise its authority in a manner consistent with the best interests of WorldCom. However, the Plan precludes the Committee from amending existing option contracts without the consent of the option holders.

Scribner was terminated from WorldCom in late 1996, when WorldCom negotiated the sale of the Operator Services division to another company, ILD Communications, Inc. To make the purchase viable, ILD needed Scribner and other essential employees who ran the division to come work for ILD. WorldCom therefore promised ILD that it would terminate Scribner and all other key Operator Service employees upon closing, and that it would not rehire any of those employees to fill other positions at WorldCom.

WorldCom management informed Scribner and other key employees of the upcoming sale in early 1997. It also told them that because ILD needed their expertise, they would be terminated from WorldCom and given an option to work for ILD. Thus, it was clear that Scribner's termination was not caused by any inadequacy of performance. Several months later, however, WorldCom told these employees that their terminations would be considered "with cause" for stock options purposes. The Committee also determined that Scribner and other terminated employees could purchase seven-twelfths of the shares that had been scheduled to vest on January 1, 1998, *if* they agreed to go to work for ILD. In order to exercise even this partial option, however, terminated employees had to release WorldCom from all liability arising from their termination and their option contracts. At this time, WorldCom informed the terminated employees that the Committee had treated unvested stock options in the same manner in two previous transactions in which WorldCom divisions had been sold.

Scribner, however, claimed that his termination was "without cause," and refused to sign the release. He also attempted to exercise all of his remaining options, which would have vested in 1998 and 1999. WorldCom refused his tender, claiming his termination was "with cause." The dispute in this case thus centers around the meaning of the word "cause," and the extent of the Committee's authority to define—or redefine—that word.

* * *

We must first decide what "with cause" and "without cause" mean under the Plan and Scribner's stock option contracts. The parties have not cited, and we have not found, any Washington case dealing specifically with stock option contracts. However, cases from other jurisdictions involving such contracts suggest that there is nothing unique about them, and that general rules of contract law should be used to interpret them. These cases also make clear that, as with any contract, determination of parties' rights under a stock option contract is a fact-specific inquiry. We therefore look to the specific language of the Plan and Scribner's contracts, the facts of this case, and general contract interpretation principles as set forth by Washington courts to guide our analysis as to what "cause" means. All of these factors indicate that a termination "with cause" means a termination due to some fault of the employee.

* * *

In light of Washington law, the language of the contract, the context in which it was drafted, and the subsequent dealings of the parties, we hold that "cause" is a performance-related concept. WorldCom concedes that Scribner's termination was not due to any deficiency on his part. Scribner was therefore terminated "without cause" as a matter of law, and summary judgment in his favor is appropriate.

To support its argument that it was entitled to summary judgment, WorldCom relies on the Plan's broad grant of discretion to the Committee to interpret contract terms. We do not dispute that the Committee had broad discretion to construe the Plan, but note that it nonetheless had a duty to exercise its interpretive authority in good faith.

* * *

We therefore conclude that the discretion retained by the Committee was the discretion to determine whether Scribner had in fact been terminated for deficient performance. The Committee did not retain the power to redefine the term "cause" in a way that would undermine Scribner's justified expectations as to what that word meant. Although the Committee had broad discretion to *interpret* the contract, it did not have the authority to *redefine* its terms. The contract and the context in which it was drafted indicate that "cause" can only mean termination for performance-related reasons. The discretion retained by the Committee allowed it to determine, as a factual matter, whether Scribner had been terminated for performance-related reasons, but did not authorize it to change the ordinary meaning of words after the fact and without notice.

NOTES AND QUESTIONS

1. The Restatement Third of Employment Law § 2.04 (2014) supplies reasons that can justify an employer in terminating a fixed-term contract: "if the employee has engaged in misconduct, other malfeasance, or other material breach of the agreement, such as persistent neglect of duties, gross negligence, or failure to perform the duties of the position due to a permanent disability." On the other hand an agreement for indefinite term can also be terminated "because of a significant change in the employer's economic circumstances, [such that] the employer no longer has a business need for the services that the employee is providing."

2. The offer letter said: "Your base salary will be at an annual rate of $125,000.00 paid semi-monthly." The Employment Agreement said: "I understand . . . my employment with the Company is 'at will.'" The Fifth Circuit said that under Texas law the offer of an annual salary would create a presumption of a one-year contract but that the presumption is overcome in this case by the reference to an at-will relationship in the Employment Agreement. Hamilton v. Segue Software, Inc., 232 F.3d 473 (5th Cir. 2000).

3. A written employment contract said: "This contract shall be non-terminable by Thompson [Printing Company]. In the event Thompson shall terminate the employment of Jerry [Fields], all of the benefits * * * shall continue in accordance with the terms and provisions of this Agreement." The employer fired Fields, president of the company, after three female employees made allegations that he had sexually harassed them. Held: Thompson must pay the benefits. Employers may separate an employee in violation of written contract terms, but cannot simply refuse contractually provided benefits. Fields v. Thompson Printing Co., Inc., 363 F.3d 259 (3d Cir. 2004).

4. A director of a university institute had a written contract saying he could be dismissed only for "just cause." Held: the employer prevails if it "genuinely believed that [plaintiff] was incompetent or willfully neglectful of his duties . . . ; whether [he] was *actually* incompetent . . . is irrelevant. . . ." Thus the proper question for judicial determination is whether the employer "acted in objective good faith. . . . The jury's inquiry should center on whether an employee's termination was based on any arbitrary, capricious, or illegal reason. . . . [T]he fact-finding prerogative remains with the employer." This result follows from "the strong judicial policy against interfering with the business judgment of private business entities." Dissenting, Chief Justice Bell said that "it seems clear to me that an employee's proof of the non-existence of the purported factual basis for his or her termination is quintessentially and a fortiori proof of bad faith and therefore, the lack of good faith." Towson Univ. v. Conte, 862 A.2d 941 (Md. 2004).

5. Former employees said the employer fraudulently induced them to accept employment with a wholly owned subsidiary by hiding its plan to sell off the subsidiary, resulting in their losing many of their job benefits. The Texas Supreme Court, repeating their strong commitment to at-will employment, said that since the employees had no right to their jobs, being tricked into leaving the job was not unlawful fraud. Sawyer v. E.I. Du Pont de Nemours, 430 S.W.3d 396 (2014) (Tex. 2014).

6. The University of Washington promised to give every faculty member "who is deemed to be meritorious in performance" at least a 2 percent salary increase in the following year. But the unilateral promise also had a "Funding Cautions" provision: "Without the influx of new money or in the event of decreased State support, a revaluation of this Faculty Salary Policy may prove necessary." In 2009, early in the financial crisis, the university suspended the 2 percent guarantee. Held: because of the "Cautions" provision, the university's action was not a breach of contract. Justice McCloud, dissenting, said the university's right to "reevaluate" does not justify "revocation." Storti v. University of Washington, 330 P.3d 159 (Wash. 2014) (5–4).

b. CONTRACTS IMPLIED FROM CONDUCT

Unlike Joel Gordon, most employees have no individual written contract which sets out specific terms of employment or the parties' understandings. In seeking a contract analysis solution to the problem of unfair terminations in these cases, the courts have had to look beyond the express terms of the contract to implied ones.

Pugh v. See's Candies, Inc.
171 Cal.Rptr. 917 (Cal. Ct. App. 1981).

■ GRODIN, J.:

After 32 years of employment with See's Candies, Inc., in which he worked his way up the corporate ladder from dishwasher to vice president in charge of production and member of the board of directors,

Wayne Pugh was fired. Asserting that he had been fired in breach of contract and for reasons which offend public policy he sued his former employer seeking compensatory and punitive damages for wrongful termination, and joined as a defendant a labor organization which, he alleged, had conspired in or induced the wrongful conduct. The case went to trial before a jury, and upon conclusion of the plaintiff's case-in-chief the trial court granted defendants' motions for nonsuit, and this appeal followed.

* * *

The defendant employer is in the business of manufacturing fresh candy at its plants in Los Angeles and South San Francisco and marketing the candy through its own retail outlets.

Pugh began working for See's at its Bay Area plant (then in San Francisco) in January 1941 washing pots and pans. From there he was promoted to candy maker, and held that position until the early part of 1942, when he entered the Air Corps. Upon his discharge in 1946 he returned to See's and his former position. After a year he was promoted to the position of production manager in charge of personnel, ordering raw materials, and supervising the production of candy. When, in 1950, See's moved into a larger plant in San Francisco, Pugh had responsibility for laying out the design of the plant, taking bids, and assisting in the construction. While working at this plant, Pugh sought to increase his value to the company by taking three years of night classes in plant layout, economics, and business law. When See's moved its San Francisco plant to its present location in South San Francisco in 1957, Pugh was given responsibilities for the new location similar to those which he undertook in 1950. By this time See's business and its number of production employees had increased substantially, and a new position of assistant production manager was created under Pugh's supervision.

In 1971 Pugh was again promoted, this time as vice president in charge of production and was placed upon the board of directors of See's northern California subsidiary, "in recognition of his accomplishments." In 1972 he received a gold watch from See's "in appreciation of 31 years of loyal service."

In May 1973 Pugh travelled with Charles Huggins, then president of See's, and their respective families to Europe on a business trip to visit candy manufacturers and to inspect new equipment. Mr. Huggins returned in early June to attend a board of director's meeting while Pugh and his family remained in Europe on a planned vacation.

Upon Pugh's return from Europe on Sunday, June 25, 1973, he received a message directing him to fly to Los Angeles the next day and meet with Mr. Huggins.

Pugh went to Los Angeles expecting to be told of another promotion. The preceding Christmas season had been the most successful in See's history, the Valentine's Day holiday of 1973 set a new sales record for

See's, and the March 1973 edition of See's Newsletter, containing two pictures of Pugh, carried congratulations on the increased production.

Instead, upon Pugh's arrival at Mr. Huggins' office, the latter said, "Wayne, come in and sit down. We might as well get right to the point. I have decided your services are no longer required by See's Candies. Read this and sign it." Huggins handed him a letter confirming his termination and directing him to remove that day "only personal papers and possessions from your office," but "absolutely no records, formulas or other material"; and to turn in and account for "all keys, credit cards, et cetera." The letter advised that Pugh would receive unpaid salary, bonuses and accrued vacation through that date, and the full amount of his profit sharing account, but "No severance pay will be granted." Finally, Pugh was directed "not to visit or contact Production Department employees while they are on the job."

The letter contained no reason for Pugh's termination. When Pugh asked Huggins for a reason, he was told only that he should "look deep within [him]self" to find the answer, that "Things were said by people in the trade that have come back to us." Pugh's termination was subsequently announced to the industry in a letter which, again, stated no reasons.

When Pugh first went to work for See's, Ed Peck, then president and general manager, frequently told him: "if you are loyal to [See's] and do a good job, your future is secure." Laurance See, who became president of the company in 1951 and served in that capacity until his death in 1969, had a practice of not terminating administrative personnel except for good cause, and this practice was carried on by his brother, Charles B. See, who succeeded Laurance as president.

During the entire period of his employment, there had been no formal or written criticism of Pugh's work. No complaints were ever raised at the annual meetings which preceded each holiday season, and he was never denied a raise or bonus. He received no notice that there was a problem which needed correction, nor any warning that any disciplinary action was being contemplated.

Pugh's theory as to why he was terminated relates to a contract which See's at that time had with the defendant union. * * * [Pugh had objected in 1968 negotiations to a provision which permitted See's to pay seasonal employees at a lower rate. When asked in 1971 to be part of the company's negotiating team, Pugh responded that he would like to, but he was bothered by the possibility that See's had a "sweetheart" contract with the union, by which Pugh meant one that permitted the employer to get a competitive advantage over other employers by paying lower wages to some employees, with the collusion of the union.]

The union's alleged participation in Pugh's termination was in the form of a statement attributed to Mr. Button (the individual who succeeded Pugh as production manager) at a negotiating meeting between the company and the union in June 1973. According to one witness, Mr. Button stated at the commencement of the meeting, "Now we've taken care of Mr. Pugh. What are you going to do for us."

* * *

In recent years, there have been established by statute a variety of limitations upon the employer's power of dismissal. Employers are precluded, for example, from terminating employees for a variety of reasons, including union membership or activities, race, sex, age or political affiliation. Legislatures in this country have so far refrained, however, from adopting statutes, such as those which exist in most other industrialized countries, which would provide more generalized protection to employees against unjust dismissal. And while public employees may enjoy job security through civil service rules and due process, the legal principles which give rise to these protections are not directly applicable to employees in private industry.

Even apart from statute or constitutional protection, however, the employer's right to terminate employees is not absolute. * * * Two relevant limiting principles have developed, one of them based upon public policy and the other upon traditional contract doctrine. The first limitation precludes dismissal "when an employer's discharge of an employee violates fundamental principles of public policy," the second when the discharge is contrary to the terms of the agreement, express or implied. * * *

The presumption that an employment contract is intended to be terminable at will is subject, like any presumption, to contrary evidence. This may take the form of an agreement, express or implied, that the relationship will continue for some fixed period of time. Or, and of greater relevance here, it may take the form of an agreement that the employment relationship will continue indefinitely, pending the occurrence of some event such as the employer's dissatisfaction with the employee's services or the existence of some "cause" for termination. Sometimes this latter type of agreement is characterized as a contract for "permanent" employment, but that characterization may be misleading. In one of the earliest California cases on this subject, the Supreme Court interpreted a contract for permanent employment as meaning "that plaintiffs' employment * * * was to continue indefinitely, and until one or the other of the parties wish, *for some good reason,* to sever the relation."

A contract which limits the power of the employer with respect to the reasons for termination is no less enforceable because it places no equivalent limits upon the power of the employee to quit his employment. "If the requirement of consideration is met, there is no additional requirement of * * * equivalence in the values exchanged, or 'mutuality of obligation.' " (Rest.2d Contracts, § 81 (Tent. Draft No. 2, 1965); 1A Corbin on Contracts (1963) § 152, pp. 13–17).

Moreover, while it has sometimes been said that a promise for continued employment subject to limitation upon the employer's power of termination must be supported by some "independent consideration," i.e., consideration other than the services to be rendered, such a rule is contrary to the general contract principle that courts should not inquire into the adequacy of consideration. "A single and undivided consideration may be bargained for and given as the agreed equivalent of one promise or of two promises or of many promises." (1 Corbin on Contracts (1963) § 125, pp. 535–536.) Thus there is no analytical reason why an employee's promise to render services, or his actual rendition of services over time, may not support an employer's promise both to pay a particular wage (for example) and to refrain from arbitrary dismissal.

* * *

In determining whether there exists an implied-in-fact promise for some form of continued employment courts have considered a variety of factors in addition to the existence of independent consideration. These have included, for example, the personnel policies or practices of the employer, the employee's longevity of service, actions or communications by the employer reflecting assurances of continued employment, and the practices of the industry in which the employee is engaged.

Here * * *, there were facts in evidence from which the jury could determine the existence of such an implied promise: the duration of appellant's employment, the commendations and promotions he received, the apparent lack of any direct criticism of his work, the assurances he was given, and the employer's acknowledged policies. While oblique language will not, standing alone, be sufficient to establish agreement, it is appropriate to consider the totality of the parties' relationship: Agreement may be " 'shown by the acts and conduct of the parties, interpreted in the light of the subject matter and of the surrounding circumstances.' " (Marvin v. Marvin (1976) 18 Cal.3d 660, 678, fn. 16). We therefore conclude that it was error to grant respondents' motions for nonsuit as to See's.

Since this litigation may proceed toward yet uncharted waters, we consider it appropriate to provide some guidance as to the questions which the trial court may confront on remand. We have held that appellant has demonstrated a prima facie case of wrongful termination in violation of his contract of employment. The burden of coming forward with evidence as to the reason for appellant's termination now shifts to the employer. Appellant may attack the employer's offered explanation, either on the ground that it is pretextual (and that the real reason is one prohibited by contract or public policy), or on the ground that it is insufficient to meet the employer's obligations under contract or applicable legal principles. Appellant bears, however, the ultimate burden of proving that he was terminated wrongfully.

By what standard that burden is to be measured will depend, in part, upon what conclusions the jury draws as to the nature of the contract between the parties. The terms "just cause" and "good cause," "as used in a variety of contexts * * * have been found to be difficult to define with precision and to be largely relative in their connotation, depending upon the particular circumstances of each case." Essentially, they connote "a fair and honest cause or reason, regulated by good faith on the part of the party exercising the power." Care must be taken, however, not to interfere with the legitimate exercise of managerial discretion. "Good cause" in this context is quite different from the standard applicable in determining the propriety of an employee's termination under a contract for a specified term. And where, as here, the employee occupies a sensitive managerial or confidential position, the employer must of necessity be allowed substantial scope for the exercise of subjective judgment.

Evidence as to what appellant's successor told union representatives after his termination ("Now we've taken care of Mr. Pugh. What are you going to do for us?"), while hardly in itself weighty, is nevertheless sufficient in context given principles applicable to nonsuits, to justify an inference that appellant was terminated in response to the union's insistence. A union is privileged to induce a breach of contract between employer and employee in the pursuit of a legitimate labor objective; alternatively, a union's efforts to cause termination of a supervisory employee for reasons bearing upon his relationship to the union may constitute an unfair labor practice subject to the exclusive jurisdiction of the National Labor Relations Board (29 U.S.C. § 158(b)(1)(B)). At this stage, however, the record is inadequate to support definitive application of either privilege or preemption. We therefore conclude that the judgment of nonsuit was erroneously granted with respect to the union as well.

Reversed.

NOTES AND QUESTIONS

1.   In concluding that Pugh's employment contract was not terminable at will, the court relied on statements made by See's former president Ed Peck that "If you are loyal to See's and do a good job, your future is secure." Were these statements sufficient to establish an implied contract? Would the result have been the same if Pugh had only worked for See's for two years, instead of 29? What factors does the court identify as determinants of employees' contract rights in employment? Which ones were used to establish Pugh's right to his job? What specific right does he have: a right to "permanent" employment, not to be discharged at will, not to be discharged except for cause, or something else?

2.   How does the court treat the issue of consideration? What consideration did Pugh offer in exchange for See's promise of future employment? How does mutuality of obligation fit into the court's analysis?

3. The union representing production employees at See's arguably had a role in Pugh's termination. Is there legal redress for such interference? How would you prove the union's culpability? What effective remedy could be ordered? Consider whether any state law claim in contract or tort would be preempted by an unfair labor practice claim under the National Labor Relations Act.

4. Pugh sued in both tort and contract to challenge his discharge. His tort claim was dismissed because the court concluded that the employer's actions, while morally reprehensible, did not fall within its narrow definition of the public policy exception. Should the employer be potentially liable in both tort and contract? See *Foley,* infra p. 929. Alternatively, can an employer be liable in both tort and contract *automatically*? Is not protecting the integrity of contracts an important "public policy" which the courts should want to include within the exception to the at-will rule? See Tameny v. Atlantic Richfield Co., 610 P.2d 1330, 1339 (Cal.1980) (Clark, J., dissenting).

5. In Calleon v. Miyagi, 876 P.2d 1278 (Haw.1994), the Supreme Court of Hawaii declined to adopt the *Pugh* rationale, expressing doubt about "subjecting each discharge to judicial incursions into the amorphous concept of bad faith." Does *Pugh* really subject every discharge to a bad faith standard?

6. In Miller v. Pepsi-Cola Bottling Co., 259 Cal.Rptr. 56 (Ct.App.1989), and Davis v. Consolidated Freightways, 34 Cal.Rptr.2d 438 (Ct.App.1994), summary judgment for employers was granted where the only evidence of an implied contract was the employee's longevity of service, regular salary increases, and promotions. The court in *Miller* stated that these factors "should not change the status of an at-will employee to one that is dischargeable only for cause." Does this help to define the scope of *Pugh?*

Restatement Third of Employment Law § 2.03 (2014) rejects "the skeptical view that some courts take of indefinite term employment contracts," especially those with no definite term. The Restatement points to Shebar v. Sanyo Bus. Sys. Corp., 544 A.2d 377 (N.J. 1988). In Shebar, the court held that although an oral agreement not to be terminated except for cause did not establish a contract for lifetime employment, the promise did establish an oral agreement providing for termination only for cause, however, including economic needs of the employer.

7. Should *Pugh* apply to situations other than discharge, or is it the thin end of the wedge regarding the enforceability of oral promises from employers to employees? The New Hampshire Supreme Court held that an employer's promise to continue salary, pension, and insurance benefits for three months after possible layoffs could constitute an enforceable unilateral contract, if there was an offer that was accepted by an employee by continuing to perform his regular duties. Panto v. Moore Bus. Forms, Inc., 547 A.2d 260 (N.H.1988). Similarly, the Eighth Circuit held that laid-off employees could sue their employer for compensatory damages over failing to keep its promise of at will re-employment following a corporate restructuring. Bower v. AT & T Techs., Inc., 852 F.2d 361 (8th Cir. 1988).

8. Kevin Rooney said that, pursuant to an oral contract in 1982 between himself and Cus D'Amato, legal guardian and manager of Mike Tyson (then a minor), he was to be Tyson's trainer "for as long as [Tyson] fought" and would be paid 10 percent of Tyson's boxing earnings. The New York Court of Appeals said that this contract provides a definite, legally cognizable duration. (The trial court jury had rendered a verdict for Rooney for $4.4 million.) Rooney v. Tyson, 697 N.E.2d 571 (N.Y.1998).

9. Wisconsin offers no cause of action for intentional misrepresentation to induce continued employment. A former at-will employee, a Grade 14 Sales Services and Development Manager, alleged that after a reorganization at Miller Brewing his supervisor misrepresented that his job would not be affected. In fact his job was reduced to Grade 13, without stock options, and he was soon after dismissed entirely for "bad judgment" after a female former subordinate complained that he had told her about a sexually suggestive episode of "Seinfeld" which made her uncomfortable. A jury awarded the plaintiff $24,703,000. The court said that if employers had to disclose information about future plans that employees might like to have, employees would be assigned a parallel duty. "There are many perfectly good reasons that an employee may wish to keep a personal fact from his or her employer * * *." Mackenzie v. Miller Brewing Co., 623 N.W.2d 739 (Wis.2001).

c. MODIFICATION OF CONTRACTS—EMPLOYEE HANDBOOKS

In addition to finding enforceable promises in oral statements made to employees during their term of employment, a number of courts have responded to employees' claims that unilaterally issued personnel manuals can create binding obligations on employers.

Woolley v. Hoffmann-La Roche, Inc.

491 A.2d 1257 (N.J. 1985), modified, 499 A.2d 515 (N.J. 1985).

■ WILENTZ, C.J.:

The issue before us is whether certain terms in a company's employment manual may contractually bind the company. We hold that absent a clear and prominent disclaimer, an implied promise contained in an employment manual that an employee will be fired only for cause may be enforceable against an employer even when the employment is for an indefinite term and would otherwise be terminable at will.

Plaintiff, Richard Woolley, was hired by defendant, Hoffmann-La Roche, Inc., in October 1969, as an Engineering Section Head in defendant's Central Engineering Department at Nutley. There was no written employment contract between plaintiff and defendant. Plaintiff began work in mid-November 1969. Some time in December, plaintiff received and read the personnel manual on which his claims are based.

In 1976, plaintiff was promoted, and in January 1977 he was promoted again, this latter time to Group Leader for the Civil Engineering, the Piping Design, the Plant Layout, and the Standards and Systems Sections. In March 1978, plaintiff was directed to write a report to his supervisors about piping problems in one of defendant's buildings in Nutley. This report was written and submitted to plaintiff's immediate supervisor on April 5, 1978. On May 3, 1978, stating that the General Manager of defendant's Corporate Engineering Department had lost confidence in him, plaintiff's supervisors requested his resignation. Following this, by letter dated May 22, 1978, plaintiff was formally asked for his resignation, to be effective July 15, 1978.

Plaintiff refused to resign. Two weeks later defendant again requested plaintiff's resignation, and told him he would be fired if he did not resign. Plaintiff again declined, and he was fired in July.

Plaintiff filed a complaint alleging breach of contract, intentional infliction of emotional distress, and defamation, but subsequently consented to the dismissal of the latter two claims. The gist of plaintiff's breach of contract claim is that the express and implied promises in defendant's employment manual created a contract under which he could not be fired at will, but rather only for cause, and then only after the procedures outlined in the manual were followed.[1] Plaintiff contends that he was not dismissed for good cause, and that his firing was a breach of contract.

Defendant's motion for summary judgment was granted by the trial court, which held that the employment manual was not contractually binding on defendant, thus allowing defendant to terminate plaintiff's employment at will.[2] The Appellate Division affirmed. We granted certification.[3]

Hoffmann-La Roche contends that the formation of the type of contract claimed by plaintiff to exist—Hoffmann-La Roche calls it a permanent employment contract for life—is subject to special contractual requirements: the intent of the parties to create such an undertaking

---

[1]   According to the provisions of the manual, defendant could, and over the years apparently did, unilaterally change these provisions.

[2]   It may be of some help to point out some of the manual's general provisions here. It is entitled "Hoffmann-La Roche, Inc. Personnel Policy Manual" and at the bottom of the face page is the notation "issued to: [and then in handwriting] Richard Woolley 12/1/69." The portions of the manual submitted to us consist of eight pages. It describes the employees "covered" by the manual ("all employees of Hoffmann-La Roche"), the manual's purpose ("a practical operating tool in the equitable and efficient administration of our employee relations program"); five of the eight pages are devoted to "termination." In addition to setting forth the purpose and policy of the termination section, it defines "the types of termination" as "layoff," "discharge due to performance," "discharge, disciplinary," "retirement" and "resignation." As one might expect, layoff is a termination caused by lack of work, retirement a termination caused by age, resignation a termination on the initiative of the employee, and discharge due to performance and discharge, disciplinary, are both terminations for cause. There is no category set forth for discharge without cause. The termination section includes "Guidelines for discharge due to performance," consisting of a fairly detailed procedure to be used before an employee may be fired for cause. Preceding these definitions of the five categories of termination is a section on "Policy," the first sentence of which provides: "It is the policy of Hoffmann-La Roche to retain to the extent consistent with company requirements, the services of all employees who perform their duties efficiently and effectively."

[3]   Mr. Woolley died prior to oral argument before this Court. The claim for damages, while diminished, survives.

must be clear and definite; in addition to an explicit provision setting forth its duration, the agreement must specifically cover the essential terms of employment—the duties, responsibilities, and compensation of the employee, and the proof of these terms must be clear and convincing; the undertaking must be supported by consideration in addition to the employee's continued work. Woolley claims that the requirements for the formation of such a contract have been met here and that they do not extend as far as Hoffmann-La Roche claims. Further, Woolley argues that this is not a "permanent contract for life," but rather an employment contract of indefinite duration that may be terminated only for good cause and in accordance with the procedure set forth in the personnel policy manual. Both parties agree that the employment contract is one of indefinite duration; Hoffmann-La Roche contends that in New Jersey, when an employment contract is of indefinite duration, the inescapable legal conclusion is that it is an employment at will; Woolley claims that even such a contract—of indefinite duration—may contain provisions requiring that termination be only for cause.

* * *

We are thus faced with the question of whether this is the kind of employment contract—a "long-range commitment"—that must be construed as one of indefinite duration and therefore at will * * *, or whether ordinary contractual doctrine applies. In either case, the question is whether Hoffmann-La Roche retained the right to fire with or without cause or whether, as Woolley claims, his employment could be terminated only for cause. We believe another question, not explicitly treated below, is involved: should the legal effect of the dissemination of a personnel policy manual by a company with a substantial number of employees be determined solely and strictly by traditional contract doctrine? Is that analysis adequate for the realities of such a workplace?

* * *

Given the facts before us and the common law of contracts interpreted in the light of sound policy applicable to this modern setting, we conclude that the termination clauses of this company's Personnel Policy Manual, including the procedure required before termination occurs, could be found to be contractually enforceable. Furthermore, we conclude that when an employer of a substantial number of employees circulates a manual that, when fairly read, provides that certain benefits are an incident of the employment (including, especially, job security provisions), the judiciary, instead of "grudgingly" conceding the enforceability of those provisions, should construe them in accordance with the reasonable expectations of the employees.

The employer's contention here is that the distribution of the manual was simply an expression of the company's "philosophy" and therefore free of any possible contractual consequences. The former employee claims it could reasonably be read as an explicit statement of company policies intended to be followed by the company in the same manner as if they were expressed in an agreement signed by both employer and employees. From the analysis that follows we conclude that a jury, properly instructed, could find, in strict contract terms, that the manual constituted an offer; put differently, it could find that this portion of the manual (concerning job security) set forth terms and conditions of employment.

In determining the manual's meaning and effect, we must consider the probable context in which it was disseminated and the environment surrounding its continued existence. The manual, though apparently not distributed to all employees ("in general, distribution will be provided to supervisory personnel * * * "), covers all of them. Its terms are of such importance to all employees that in the absence of contradicting evidence, it would seem clear that it was intended by Hoffmann-La Roche that all employees be advised of the benefits it confers.

We take judicial notice of the fact that Hoffmann-La Roche is a substantial company with many employees in New Jersey. The record permits the conclusion that the policy manual represents the most reliable statement of the terms of their employment. At oral argument counsel conceded that it is rare for any employee, except one on the medical staff, to have a special contract. Without minimizing the importance of its specific provisions, the context of the manual's preparation and distribution is, to us, the most persuasive proof that it would be almost inevitable for an employee to regard it as a binding commitment, legally enforceable, concerning the terms and conditions of his employment. Having been employed, like hundreds of his co-employees, without any individual employment contract, by an employer whose good reputation made it so attractive, the employee is given this one document that purports to set forth the terms and conditions of his employment, a document obviously carefully prepared by the company with all of the appearances of corporate legitimacy that one could imagine. If there were any doubt about it (and there would be none in the mind of most employees), the name of the manual dispels it, for it is nothing short of the official *policy* of the company, it is the Personnel *Policy* Manual. As every employee knows, when superiors tell you "it's company policy," they mean business.

The mere fact of the manual's distribution suggests its importance. Its changeability—the uncontroverted ability of management to change its terms—is argued as supporting its non-binding quality, but one might as easily conclude that, given its importance, the employer wanted to keep it up to date, especially to make certain, given this employer's good reputation in labor relations, that the benefits conferred were sufficiently competitive with those available from other employers, including benefits found in collective bargaining agreements. The record suggests that the changes actually made almost always favored the employees.

Given that background, then, unless the language contained in the manual were such that no one could reasonably have thought it was intended to create legally binding obligations, the termination provisions of the policy manual would have to be regarded as an obligation undertaken by the employer. It will not do now for the company to say it did not mean the things it said in its manual to be binding. Our courts will not allow an employer to offer attractive inducements and benefits to the workforce and then withdraw them when it chooses, no matter how sincere its belief that they are not enforceable.

* * *

Having concluded that a jury could find the Personnel Policy Manual to constitute an offer, we deal with what most cases deem the major obstacle to construction of the terms as constituting a binding agreement, namely, the requirement under contract law that consideration must be given in exchange for the employer's offer in order to convert that offer into a binding agreement. The cases on this subject deal with such issues as whether there was a promise in return for the employer's promise (the offer contained in the manual constituting, in effect, a promise), or whether there was some benefit or detriment bargained for and in fact conferred or suffered, sufficient to create a unilateral contract; whether the action or inaction, the benefit or the detriment, was done or not done in reliance on the employer's offer or promise; whether the alleged agreement was so lacking in "mutuality" as to be insufficient for contractual purposes—in other words, whether the fundamental requirements of a contract have been met.

We conclude that these job security provisions contained in a personnel policy manual widely distributed among a large workforce are supported by consideration and may therefore be enforced as a binding commitment of the employer.

In order for an offer in the form of a promise to become enforceable, it must be accepted. Acceptance will depend on what the promisor bargained for: he may have bargained for a return promise that, if given, would result in a bilateral contract, both promises becoming enforceable. Or he may have bargained for some action or nonaction that, if given or withheld, would render his promise enforceable as a unilateral contract. In most of the cases involving an employer's personnel policy manual, the document is prepared without any negotiations and is voluntarily distributed to the workforce by the employer. It seeks no return promise from the employees. It is reasonable to interpret it as seeking continued work from the employees, who, in most cases, are free to quit since they are almost always employees at will, not simply in the sense that the employer can fire them without cause, but in the sense that they can quit without breaching any obligation. Thus analyzed, the manual is an offer that seeks the formation of a unilateral contract—the employees' bargained-for action needed to make the offer binding being their continued work when they have no obligation to continue.

The lack of definiteness concerning the other terms of employment—its duration, wages, precise service to be rendered, hours of work, etc., does not prevent enforcement of a job security provision. The lack of terms (if the complete manual is similarly lacking) can cause problems of interpretation about these other aspects of employment, but not to the point of making the job security term unenforceable. Realistically, the objection has force only when the agreement is regarded as a special one between the employer and an individual employee. There it might be difficult to determine whether there was good cause for termination if one could not determine what it was that the employee was expected to do. That difficulty is one factor that suggests the employer did not intend a lifetime contract with one employee. Here the question of good cause is made considerably easier to deal with in view of the fact that the agreement applies to the entire workforce, and the workforce itself is rather large. Even-handedness and equality of treatment will make the issue in most cases far from complex; the fact that in some cases the "for cause" provision may be difficult to interpret and enforce should not deprive employees in other cases from taking advantage of it. If there is a problem arising from indefiniteness, in any event, it is one caused by the employer. It was the employer who chose to make the termination provisions explicit and clear. If indefiniteness as to other provisions is a problem, it is one of the employer's own making from which it should gain no advantage. * * *

We therefore reverse the Appellate Division's affirmance of the trial court's grant of summary judgment and remand this matter to the trial court for further proceedings consistent with this opinion. Those proceedings should have the benefit of the entire manual that was in force at the time Woolley was discharged. The provisions of the manual concerning job security shall be considered binding unless the manual elsewhere prominently and unmistakably indicates that those provisions shall not be binding or unless there is some other similar proof of the employer's intent not to be bound. * * * Woolley need not prove consideration—that shall be presumed. Furthermore, it shall not be open to defendant to prove that good cause in fact existed on the basis of which Woolley could have been terminated. If the court or jury concludes that the manual's job security provisions are binding, then, according to those provisions, even if good cause existed, an employee could not be fired unless the employer went through the various procedures set forth in the manual, steps designed to rehabilitate that employee in order to *avoid* termination. On the record before us the employer's failure to do so is undeniable. If that is the case, we believe it would be unfair to allow this employer to try now to recreate the facts as they might have existed had the employer given to Woolley that which the manual promised, namely, a set of detailed procedures, all for Woolley's benefit, designed to see if there was some way he could be retained by Hoffmann-La Roche. * * *

We are aware that problems that do not ordinarily exist when collective bargaining agreements are involved may arise from the enforcement of employment manuals. Policy manuals may not generally be as comprehensive or definite as typical collective bargaining agreements. Further problems may result from the employer's explicitly reserved right unilaterally to change the manual. We have no doubt that, generally, changes in such a manual, including changes in terms and conditions of employment, are permitted. We express no opinion, however, on whether or to what extent they are permitted when they adversely affect a binding job security provision.

Our opinion need not make employers reluctant to prepare and distribute company policy manuals. Such manuals can be very helpful tools in labor relations, helpful both to employer and employees, and we would regret it if the consequence of this decision were that the constructive aspects of these manuals were in any way diminished. We do not believe that they will, or at least we certainly do not believe that that constructive aspect *should* be diminished as a result of this opinion.

All that this opinion requires of an employer is that it be fair. It would be unfair to allow an employer to distribute a policy manual that makes the workforce believe that certain promises have been made and then to allow the employer to renege on those promises. What is sought here is basic honesty: if the employer, for whatever reason, does not want the manual to be capable of being construed by the court as a binding contract, there are simple ways to attain that goal. All that need be done is the inclusion in a very prominent position of an appropriate statement that there is no promise of any kind by the employer contained in the manual; that regardless of what the manual says or provides, the employer promises nothing and remains free to change wages and all other working conditions without having to consult anyone and without anyone's agreement; and that the employer continues to have the absolute power to fire anyone with or without good cause.

Reversed and remanded for trial.

NOTES AND QUESTIONS

1.   A number of jurisdictions have recognized employee rights grounded in employment handbooks or personnel manuals. See, e.g., Toussaint v. Blue Cross & Blue Shield of Mich., 292 N.W.2d 880 (Mich.1980); Pine River State Bank v. Mettille, 333 N.W.2d 622 (Minn.1983). Other courts have been reluctant to bind employers to the terms of an "agreement" which can hardly said to have been bargained for in any traditional sense, among them, Florida, Illinois, Indiana, and Texas. See also Note, Employee Handbooks and Employment-at-Will Contracts, 1985 Duke L.J. 196.

Courts have continued to divide on the question whether statements in a handbook or personnel manual give employees protection against at-will termination; not too surprisingly, the actual outcome in a number of cases depends on the exact nature of the statements in the handbook. See, e.g., St.

Peters v. Shell Oil Co., 77 F.3d 184 (7th Cir. 1996) (Under Illinois law, even assuming employee handbook imposed contractual obligation on employer to use progressive discipline prior to termination, employer satisfied such contractual obligations when it terminated employee for insubordination without first engaging in progressive discipline since the handbook provided that insubordination would result in immediate dismissal unless mitigating circumstances justified less drastic action, and record indicated that employer considered mitigating circumstances prior to terminating employee); Jones v. Lake Park Care Ctr., Inc., 569 N.W.2d 369 (Iowa 1997) (employer breached employment contract created by employee handbook when it summarily discharged employee rather than providing written warning as provided in the handbook).

2. In *Woolley,* what contract theory formed the legal basis for the court's finding a just cause right for Woolley: unilateral contract, bilateral contract, promissory estoppel, or something else? What would be the elements of each theory? The employer's defenses? Section 2.04, comment b of the Restatement Third of Employment Law (tentative draft 2009) discusses the efforts by some courts to fit the analysis of unilateral employer statements into the traditional offer/acceptance framework of contract law. The Restatement notes that this is awkward because "[e]mployees are rarely made aware, and even more rarely make themselves aware, of the content of these statements when they first accept employment." Thus, some courts as well as the Restatement base the enforceability of unilateral employer statements on general principles of estoppel. See, e.g., Toussaint v. Blue Cross & Blue Shield of Mich., 292 N.W.2d 880 (Mich.1980). There, the Michigan Supreme Court focused on the benefit that accrued to an employer when it established desirable personnel policies.

3. Employee handbooks are issued unilaterally by employers. May they be changed unilaterally as well, or do employee rights or benefits contained therein "vest" at some point? Would it make a difference whether the employer modified or eliminated a "right," such as job security, or a "benefit," such as severance pay? See Bankey v. Storer Broadcasting Co., 443 N.W.2d 112 (Mich.1989). Brodie v. Gen. Chem. Corp., 934 P.2d 1263 (Wyo.1997), held that an employer cannot reduce contractual rights employees already retain without new consideration and continued employment is insufficient consideration for such a change. Other courts have held that remaining with an employer after receipt of a personnel manual promising job security supplies the necessary consideration to make the promise legally enforceable. Sisco v. GSA Nat'l Capital Fed. Credit Union, 689 A.2d 52 (D.C.1997). See generally Stephen F. Befort, Employee Handbooks and the Legal Effect of Disclaimers, 13 Indus. Rel. L.J. 326 (1993).

4. If an employer may unilaterally change the terms of an employment handbook, how, if at all, must these changes be communicated to the employee? See Durtsche v. American Colloid Co., 958 F.2d 1007 (10th Cir. 1992) (inconspicuous changes in a handbook were ineffective to notify an employee of change in his status from permanent employee to at-will employee). Cf. Adams v. Square D. Co., 775 F.Supp. 869 (D.S.C.1991) (new handbook, issued after employee was hired and which made employment at-will, superseded implied promises in prior handbook).

5. The rights employees may have under the terms of a handbook are not limited to substantive reasons for discharge, but may extend to procedural protection as well. In Mobil Coal Producing, Inc. v. Parks, 704 P.2d 702 (Wyo.1985), the discharge was held unlawful because the employer failed to follow the progressive discipline system it had established in its employee manual. Cf. Fiscella v. General Accident Ins. Co., 114 L.R.R.M. 2611 (E.D.Pa.1983), affirmed, 735 F.2d 1348 (3d Cir. 1984).

6. The California Supreme Court ruled that employees can bring a breach-of-implied-contract action for wrongful demotion against their employer if they can show that the employer has violated its own employment policies. Because the employer intended to be bound by its policies, which were specific, detailed, and exhaustive, the policies created an implied contract not to demote except for just cause. Scott v. Pacific Gas & Elec. Co., 904 P.2d 834 (Cal.1995). For the opposite view, see Baragar v. State Farm Ins. Co., 860 F.Supp. 1257 (W.D.Mich.1994) (employee policy which gave rise to expectations of job security would not be extended to claims for wrongful demotion).

7. In order to minimize the risk of a breach of contract claim following a termination, employers have been advised to avoid overselling job security at the time of initial hire. One possible approach is for the employer to include a disclaimer in the application form or to require the successful job applicant to sign a waiver of job security as a condition of hire. See, e.g., Finch v. Farmers Co-op. Oil Co. of Sheridan, 109 P.3d 537 (Wyo. 2005) (an employment application with an at-will disclaimer forms "a written, at-will employment contract"). But see also Korslund v. Dyncorp Tri-Cities Servs., Inc., 125 P.3d 119 (Wash. 2005) (employee's signing an application stating that his employment was at will did not preclude his justifiable reliance on promises in employee policy manuals, and thus did not bar his claim of breach of promise of specific treatment in specific situations.)

Personnel manuals, application forms, letters of hire, and the like are not the only possible sources of trouble for employers. In Belknap, Inc. v. Hale, 463 U.S. 491 (1983), the employer had advertised in the newspaper for "permanent replacements" for striking workers. When the strike was settled and the original employees returned to their jobs, the replacements were laid off. The Supreme Court held that the replacements' suit against the employer in state court for breach of contract was not preempted by federal labor laws.

8. As the court noted at the end of its opinion in *Woolley*, the easiest way for employers to eliminate the ambiguity of any job security that could be read into its employee handbooks would be to include prominent disclaimers that absolved them of any obligations based on the handbooks' contents. In his detailed analysis of *Woolley* and the circumstances surrounding the case, Professor J.H. Verkerke discusses the ramifications of the court's ruling:

> By far the most important legacy of the Woolley decision, however, is the widespread use of handbook disclaimers and

confirmations of atwill status. The court's opinion begins and ends by inviting employers to contract expressly to maintain an at-will relationship. In between, the court relies heavily on what I have called the legal-information-forcing rationale for enforcement. The opinion repeatedly expresses concern that unsophisticated employees will misinterpret the terms of an employer's policy manual . . . The court thus demands that the legally sophisticated party bear the burden of clarifying the prevailing legal rules. As we saw, employers throughout the country have responded to this and similar decisions by including prominent disclaimers and requiring workers to acknowledge in writing that they have no contractual protection against termination. The question remains, however, whether these exculpatory terms function as the information-forcing argument supposes that they will. Although disclaimers ostensibly serve the purpose of clarifying the parties' legal relationship, it seems doubtful that boilerplate clauses genuinely inform the majority of employees about prevailing legal rules. Like many similar documents, employees frequently sign them without reading. If this practice is truly widespread, then perhaps we need a new justification for these legal-information-forcing doctrines . . .

J.H. Verkerke, " 'Woolley v. Hoffmann-La Roche': Finding a Way to Enforce Employee Handbook Promises," University of Virginia Legal Working Paper Series (June 2006).

Despite their increasing prevalence, disclaimers have not entirely eliminated the ambiguity that can result from statements made within employee handbooks.

Russell v. Board of County Commissioners
952 P.2d 492 (Okla. 1997).

■ OPALA, J.:

Ten deputy sheriffs of Carter County commenced a breach-of-employment-contract action against the Board of County Commissioners to recover overtime pay alleged to be due them under an at-will employment arrangement with the county. The deputies pressed for summary relief, arguing that the commissioners (a) established uniform personnel policies for county employees, (b) published the policies in a handbook which embodied the Board's practice of paying overtime to county employees, and (c) distributed the manual to county employees. They are entitled to the overtime benefits sought, the deputies argue, because (a) the handbook states that law enforcement (and other county) personnel are to be paid overtime compensation, (b) deputy sheriffs are law enforcement officers, and (c) under the terms of the manual, other sheriff employees receive overtime and holiday pay. The written policy, the deputies urge, became a part of their at-will employment contract, which the county has breached by its refusal to provide the overtime compensation pressed for payment.

The Board also sought victory by summary adjudication process, arguing that the handbook did not constitute a contract. Even if some language in the manual could create contractual obligations, the Board urges, material fact issues exist as to whether (a) the handbook rises to the level of a contract and (b) its overtime provisions apply to these deputy sheriffs.

The trial court gave summary judgment to the Board, and the deputies appealed. The Court of Civil Appeals [COCA] reversed . . . The Board seeks our review by certiorari.

* * *

The question pressed by the deputies regarding their alleged contract claim calls for an analysis of the principles that govern the legal efficacy of employee personnel handbooks (or manuals).

Oklahoma jurisprudence recognizes that an employee handbook may form the basis of an implied contract between an employer and its employees if four traditional contract requirements exist: (1) competent parties, (2) consent, (3) a legal object and (4) consideration. Two limitations on the scope of implied contracts via an employee handbook stand identified by extant caselaw: (1) the manual only alters the at-will relationship with respect to accrued benefits and (2) the promises in the employee manual must be in definite terms, not in the form of vague assurances. Although the existence of an implied contract generally presents an issue of fact, if the alleged promises are nothing more than vague assurances the issue can be decided as a matter of law. This is so because in order to create an implied contract the promises must be definite.

While an employer may deny (or disclaim) any intent to make the provisions of a personnel manual part of the employment relationship, the disclaimer must be clear. An employer's conduct—i.e., representations and practices—which is inconsistent with its disclaimer may negate the disclaimer's effect. *The efficacy of a disclaimer is generally a mixed question of law and of fact.*

We cannot, on this record, decide the contractual efficacy of the handbook as a matter of law. While the manual states that its purpose is "to provide a working guide" to county officials and that the personnel policies do not represent an "employment contract," conflicting inferences may be drawn from other statements made in the same handbook. The manual's "overtime" provisions state that county employees "who are not exempt, law enforcement personnel or emergency medical personnel, *shall be entitled* to overtime payment." Under the "general statement" section, the employer offers "paid holidays" for "full-time employees of the county." The deputies' evidentiary materials indicate that other personnel in the sheriff's office have received overtime pay in accordance with these written personnel policies. Because they are *law enforcement personnel* and county employees, the deputies urge, they should receive the same benefits and stand on the same footing with others. The deputies' evidentiary materials raise a material fact question whether the *effectiveness* of the Board's written disclaimer is negated by inconsistent employer conduct.

If the disclaimer is found to be ineffective, there remains a material fact issue whether deputy sheriffs (a) are included in the category of *law enforcement personnel* eligible for overtime pay or (b) fall within the exempt classification that is excluded from these benefits. The manual *fails* to identify the county employees that fall within these categories. The Board's explanation (by affidavits attached to its summary judgment response) that deputy sheriffs were not intended to be included within the manual's overtime pay classifications points out an ambiguity in the handbook that must be clarified by extrinsic evidence. It is not the function of summary adjudication process to afford a *trial by affidavit;* rather, it is to afford a method of summarily deciding some issues or terminating a case when there is nothing presented but a question of law.

Whether—either on application of an implied-contract or of promissory-estoppel theory—the personnel policy handbook creates a binding obligation on the county to pay the deputy sheriffs for overtime and holiday hours worked presents a question for an evaluative determination of the trier. The record reveals disputed material facts as well as undisputed material facts from which conflicting inferences may be drawn.

* * *

On certiorari granted upon the Board's petition, the Court of Civil Appeals' opinion is vacated, the trial court's summary judgment reversed and the cause remanded for further proceedings consistent with today's pronouncement.

NOTES AND QUESTIONS

1. In Geldreich v. American Cyanamid Co., 691 A.2d 423 (N.J.Super.Ct.App.Div.1997), the court upheld a verdict against an employer for violation of termination provisions in an employee handbook. The court held that where the handbook stated that the employer would attempt to find alternative employment for an employee who was downsized, it created an enforceable commitment necessitating more than a generalized disclaimer that the policy manual is not intended to create any contractual right.

2. In New Jersey, juries decide whether "an employee could reasonably expect that the [manual] provided for job security, thereby creating an implied contract of employment," and also whether the content of a disclaimer is effective. Witkowski v. Thomas J. Lipton, Inc., 643 A.2d 546 (N.J.1994); Nicosia v. Wakefern Food Corp., 643 A.2d 554 (N.J.1994). For a discussion of the employee handbook issue more sympathetic to employers, see Mitchell v. Zilog, Inc., 874 P.2d 520 (Idaho 1994); Gilmore v. Enogex, Inc., 878 P.2d 360 (Okl.1994).

3.   The New York Court of Appeals held that "the existence of a private employer's written policy does not, in and of itself, limit the right to discharge an at-will employee." Because the plaintiff, the administrative director of a counseling center, had been employed long before the policy in question came into effect, he could not prove detrimental reliance, and so his wrongful discharge claim that the employer did not follow certain handbook procedures was dismissed. In the matter of De Petris v. Union Settlement Ass'n, Inc., 657 N.E.2d 269 (N.Y.1995).

4.   Implied-in-fact contract remedies are available against public sector employers. However, such employment agreements may not bind a public employer where the condition of employment is generally subject to statutory control. However, if the manual had been adopted by an act of the legislature, such contractual rights will be binding. Cooper v. Mayor of Haddon Heights, 690 A.2d 1036 (N.J.Super.Ct.App.Div.1997).

5.   Disclaimer language in an acknowledgment form signed by the employee when he received the handbook prevents later oral statements of job security from attaining "promise" status. Plaintiff testified that the Director of Human Resources told him that his "need to take off work" to determine whether he had contagious tuberculosis was acceptable to the employer. The court said the handbook waiver trumped any such oral promise. Honorable v. American Wyott Corp., 11 P.3d 928 (Wyo.2000).

6.   A statement in a personnel manual that "[e]mployees may be dismissed for cause" does not declare that dismissal may be *only* for cause. Matagorda County Hosp. Dist. v. Burwell, 189 S.W.3d 738 (Tex. 2006).

2.   GOOD FAITH AND FAIR DEALING

One major approach used by courts to redress a wrongful discharge in the absence of express individual contractual rights is to find a covenant of good faith and fair dealing implicit in the employment contract. This covenant is well established in contract law, and can be found in the Restatement (Second) of Contracts, § 205 ("Every contract imposes upon each party a duty of good faith and fair dealing in its performance and its enforcement.") or in § 1–304 of the Uniform Commercial Code ("Every contract or duty within [the Uniform Commercial Code] imposes an obligation of good faith in its performance and enforcement."). Good faith and fair dealing obligates each party to a contract to refrain from injuring in any way the other's right to receive the benefits of the contract.

Traditionally, the covenant of good faith and fair dealing has been applied only to commercial transactions. If such an obligation is appropriate to impose on impersonal commercial dealings, however, is it not equally applicable to the employment relationship? In the absence of any apparent reason to except employment from the covenant, the good faith and fair dealing theory has considerable intuitive appeal in its insistence that employment relations be characterized by fairness and good faith. However, the problems associated with defining and limiting the covenant of good faith and fair dealing are numerous.

Fortune v. National Cash Register Co.
364 N.E.2d 1251 (Mass. 1977).

■ ABRAMS, JUSTICE.

Orville E. Fortune (Fortune), a former salesman of The National Cash Register Company (NCR), brought a suit to recover certain commissions allegedly due as a result of a sale of cash registers to First National Stores Inc. (First National) in 1968. Counts 1 and 2 of Fortune's amended declaration claimed bonus payments under the parties' written contract of employment. The third count sought recovery in quantum meruit for the reasonable value of Fortune's services relating to the same sales transaction. Judgment on a jury verdict for Fortune was reversed by the Appeals Court, and this court granted leave to obtain further appellate review. We affirm the judgment of the Superior Court. We hold, for the reasons stated herein, there was no error in submitting the issue of "bad faith" termination of an employment at will contract to the jury.

* * *

Fortune was employed by NCR under a written "salesman's contract" which was terminable at will, without cause, by either party on written notice. The contract provided that Fortune would receive a weekly salary in a fixed amount plus a bonus for sales made within the "territory" (i.e., customer accounts or stores) assigned to him for "coverage or supervision," whether the sale was made by him or someone else. The amount of the bonus was determined on the basis of "bonus credits," which were computed as a percentage of the price of products sold. Fortune would be paid a percentage of the applicable bonus credit as follows: (1) 75% if the territory was assigned to him at the date of the order, (2) 25% if the territory was assigned to him at the date of delivery and installation, or (3) 100% if the territory was assigned to him at both times. The contract further provided that the "bonus interest" would terminate if shipment of the order was not made within eighteen months from the date of the order unless (1) the territory was assigned to him for coverage at the date of delivery and installation, or (2) special engineering was required to fulfill the contract. In addition, NCR reserved the right to sell products in the salesman's territory without paying a bonus. However, this right could be exercised only on written notice.

In 1968, Fortune's territory included First National. This account had been part of his territory for the preceding six years; he had been successful in obtaining several orders from First National, including a million dollar order in 1963. Sometime in late 1967, or early 1968, NCR introduced a new model cash register, Class 5. Fortune corresponded with First National in an effort to sell the machine. He also helped to arrange for a demonstration of the Class 5 to executives of First National on October 4, 1968. NCR had a team of men also working on this sale.

* * * On November 29, 1968, First National signed an order for 2,008 Class 5 machines to be delivered over a four-year period at a purchase price of approximately $5,000,000. Although Fortune did not participate in the negotiation of the terms of the order, his name appeared on the order form in the space entitled "salesman credited." The amount of the bonus credit as shown on the order was $92,079.99.

On January 6, 1969, the first working day of the new year, Fortune found an envelope on his desk at work. It contained a termination notice addressed to his home dated December 2, 1968. Shortly after receiving the notice, Fortune spoke to the Boston branch manager with whom he was friendly. The manager told him, "You are through," but, after considering some of the details necessary for the smooth operation of the First National order, told him to "stay on," and to "[k]eep on doing what you are doing right now." Fortune remained with the company in a position entitled "sales support." In this capacity, he coordinated and expedited delivery of the machines to First National under the November 29 order as well as servicing other accounts.

Commencing in May or June, Fortune began to receive some bonus commissions on the First National order. Having received only 75% of the applicable bonus due on the machines which had been delivered and installed, Fortune spoke with his manager about receiving the full amount of the commission. Fortune was told "to forget about it." Sixty-one years old at that time, and with a son in college, Fortune concluded that it "was a good idea to forget it for the time being."

NCR did pay a systems and installations person the remaining 25% of the bonus commissions due from the First National order although contrary to its usual policy of paying *only* salesmen a bonus. * * *

Approximately eighteen months after receiving the termination notice, Fortune, who had worked for NCR for almost twenty-five years, was asked to retire. When he refused, he was fired in June of 1970. Fortune did not receive any bonus payments on machines which were delivered to First National after this date.

* * * By agreement of counsel, the case was sent to the jury for special verdicts on two questions:

"1. Did the Defendant act in bad faith * * * when it decided to terminate the Plaintiff's contract as a salesman by letter dated December 2, 1968, delivered on January 6, 1969?

"2. Did the Defendant act in bad faith * * * when the Defendant let the Plaintiff go on June 5, 1970?"

The jury answered both questions affirmatively, and judgment entered in the sum of $45,649.62.

The central issue on appeal is whether this "bad faith" termination constituted a breach of the employment at will contract. * * *

The contract at issue is a classic terminable at will employment contract. It is clear that the contract itself reserved to the parties an explicit power to terminate the contract without cause on written notice. It is also clear that under the express terms of the contract Fortune has received all the bonus commissions to which he is entitled. Thus, NCR claims that it did not breach the contract, and that it has no further liability to Fortune. According to a literal reading of the contract, NCR is correct.

However, Fortune argues that, in spite of the literal wording of the contract, he is entitled to a jury determination on NCR's motives in terminating his services under the contract and in finally discharging him. We agree. We hold that NCR's written contract contains an implied covenant of good faith and fair dealing, and a termination not made in good faith constitutes a breach of the contract.

We do not question the general principles that an employer is entitled to be motivated by and to serve its own legitimate business interests; that an employer must have wide latitude in deciding whom it will employ in the face of the uncertainties of the business world; and that an employer needs flexibility in the face of changing circumstances. We recognize the employer's need for a large amount of control over its work force. However, we believe that where, as here, commissions are to be paid for work performed by the employee, the employer's decision to terminate its at will employee should be made in good faith. NCR's right to make decisions in its own interest is not, in our view, unduly hampered by a requirement of adherence to this standard.

On occasion some courts have avoided the rigidity of the "at will" rule by fashioning a remedy in tort. We believe, however, that in this case there is remedy on the express contract. In so holding we are merely recognizing the general requirement in this Commonwealth that parties to contracts and commercial transactions must act in good faith toward one another. Good faith and fair dealing between parties are pervasive requirements in our law; it can be said fairly, that parties to contracts or commercial transactions are bound by this standard. See G.L. c. 106, § 1–203 (good faith in contracts under Uniform Commercial Code); G.L. c. 93B, § 4(3)(c) (good faith in motor vehicle franchise termination).

The requirement of good faith was reaffirmed in RLM Assocs. v. Carter Mfg. Corp., 356 Mass. 718, 248 N.E.2d 646 (1969). In that case the plaintiff (RLM), a manufacturer's representative of the defendant (Carter), was entitled to a commission on all of Carter's sales within a specified territory. Either party could terminate this arrangement on thirty days' notice. Carter cancelled the agreement shortly before being awarded a contract discovered and brought to Carter's attention by RLM. Because "[t]he evidence permitted the conclusion that Carter's termination of the arrangement was in part based upon a desire to avoid paying a commission to RLM", we held that the question of bad faith was properly placed before the jury. The present case differs from *RLM Assocs.*, in that Fortune was credited with the sale to First National but was fired immediately thereafter. NCR seeks to avoid the thrust of *RLM Assocs.* by arguing that bad faith is not an issue where it has been careful to protect a portion of Fortune's bonus commission under the contract. We disagree. The fact that the discharge was after a portion of the bonus vested still creates a question for the jury on the defendant's motive in terminating the employment.

Recent decisions in other jurisdictions lend support to the proposition that good faith is implied in contracts terminable at will. In a recent employment at will case, Monge v. Beebe Rubber Co., 114 N.H. 130, 133, 316 A.2d 549, 552 (1974), the plaintiff alleged that her oral contract of employment had been terminated because she refused to date her foreman. The New Hampshire Supreme Court held that "[i]n all employment contracts, whether at will or for a definite term, the employer's interest in running his business as he sees fit must be balanced against the interest of the employee in maintaining his employment, and the public's interest in maintaining a proper balance between the two. * * * We hold that a termination by the employer of a contract of employment at will which is motivated by bad faith or malice * * * constitutes a breach of the employment contract. * * * Such a rule affords the employee a certain stability of employment and does not interfere with the employer's normal exercise of his right to discharge, which is necessary to permit him to operate his business efficiently and profitably."

We believe that the holding in the *Monge* case merely extends to employment contracts the rule that " 'in *every* contract there is an implied covenant that neither party shall do anything which will have the effect of destroying or injuring the right of the other party to receive the fruits of the contract, which means that in *every* contract there exists an implied covenant of good faith and fair dealing' [emphasis supplied]."

In the instant case, we need not pronounce our adherence to so broad a policy nor need we speculate as to whether the good faith requirement is implicit in every contract for employment at will. It is clear, however, that, on the facts before us, a finding is warranted that a breach of the contract occurred. Where the principal seeks to deprive the agent of all compensation by terminating the contractual relationship when the agent is on the brink of successfully completing the sale, the principal has acted in bad faith and the ensuing transaction between the principal and the buyer is to be regarded as having been accomplished by the agent. Restatement (Second) of Agency § 454, and Comment a (1958). The same result obtains where the principal attempts to deprive the agent of any portion of a commission due the agent. Courts have often applied this rule to prevent overreaching by employers and the forfeiture by employees of benefits almost earned by the rendering of substantial services. In our view, the Appeals Court erroneously focused only on literal compliance with payment provisions of the contract and failed to consider the issue of bad faith termination.

NCR argues that there was no evidence of bad faith in this case; therefore, the trial judge was required to direct a verdict in any event. We think that the evidence and the reasonable inferences to be drawn there from support a jury verdict that the termination of Fortune's twenty-five years of employment as a salesman with NCR the next business day after NCR obtained a $5,000,000 order from First National was motivated by a desire to pay Fortune as little of the bonus credit as it could. The fact that Fortune was willing to work under these circumstances does not constitute a waiver or estoppel; it only shows that NCR had him "at their mercy."

NCR also contends that Fortune cannot complain of his firing in June, 1970, as his employment contract clearly indicated that bonus credits would be paid only for an eighteen-month period following the date of the order. As we have said, the jury could have found that Fortune was stripped of his "salesman" designation in order to disqualify him for the remaining 25% of the commissions due on cash registers delivered prior to the date of his first termination. Similarly, the jury could have found that Fortune was fired (or not assigned to the First National account) so that NCR could avoid paying him *any* commissions on cash registers delivered after June, 1970.

* * *

We think that NCR's conduct in June, 1970 permitted the jury to find bad faith.

* * *

Judgment of the Superior Court affirmed.

NOTES AND QUESTIONS

1. Why does the court recognize a new cause of action in the *Fortune* case? Would a simple suit in contract have sufficed to redress Fortune's loss? Although an implied covenant of good faith and fair dealing in employment contracts has not received as widespread acceptance as some other developments in wrongful discharge, it nonetheless has received support. See Savodnik v. Korvettes, Inc., 488 F.Supp. 822 (E.D.N.Y.1980); Reed v. Municipality of Anchorage, 782 P.2d 1155 (Alaska 1989); Cleary v. American Airlines, 168 Cal.Rptr. 722 (Cal.App.1980); Metcalf v. Intermountain Gas Co., 778 P.2d 744 (Idaho 1989); Prout v. Sears, Roebuck & Co., 772 P.2d 288 (Mont.1989); K Mart Corp. v. Ponsock, 732 P.2d 1364 (Nev.1987). Many jurisdictions have expressly rejected the doctrine, primarily on the theory that the doctrine of employment at will, under which an employer can discharge an employee for any reason, even a bad one, is inherently inconsistent with an implied covenant of good faith and fair dealing. See, e.g., McCormick v. Sears, Roebuck & Co., 712 F.Supp. 1284 (W.D.Mich.1989);

Scholtes v. Signal Delivery Serv., Inc., 548 F.Supp. 487 (W.D.Ark.1982); Jeffers v. Bishop Clarkson Mem. Hosp., 387 N.W.2d 692 (Neb.1986); Nelson v. Crimson Enter., Inc., 777 P.2d 73 (Wyo.1989).

2. Does a covenant of good faith and fair dealing exist in every contract and thus in every employment contract? See Restatement Second of Contracts § 231 (1979) and Uniform Commercial Code § 1–203 (1978). The Restatement Third of Employment Law § 2.07 (2014) says: "Each party to an employment contract, including at-will employment, owes a non-waivable duty of good faith and fair dealing to each other party . . . In at-will employment, the implied duty of good faith and fair dealing must be read consistently with the at-will nature of the relationship such that it cannot be used to require cause for termination in an employment agreement otherwise terminable at will. . . . [T]he employer's implied duty . . . includes the duty not to terminate . . . for the purpose of preventing the vesting or accrual of an employee right or benefit, or retaliating against the employee for performing the employee's obligations . . ."

3. Would the result in *Fortune* have been the same if NCR had terminated Fortune at a time when it did not owe him a commission? See McKinney v. National Dairy Council, 491 F.Supp. 1108 (D.Mass.1980) (extending *Fortune* to "voluntary" retirement taken under duress).

4. Does the covenant of good faith and fair dealing impose procedural as well as substantive obligations on employers prior to terminating employees?

5. Before suing their employers, both Fortune and Monge failed to follow grievance procedures which existed either internally (Fortune) or through a union (Monge). How should that affect their claims?

6. What other aspects of the employment relationship are affected by the covenant of good faith and fair dealing? To the extent that there exists such a covenant in employment contracts, presumably it applies to both parties to that agreement. What are *employees'* obligations under the covenant? See Note, The Implied Covenant of Good Faith and Fair Dealing: Examining Employees' Good Faith Duties, 39 Hastings L.J. 483 (1988).

7. Texas does not impose on an employer "a duty of good faith and fair dealing to its employees." The Supreme Court said that "the elements which make the relationship between an insurer and an insured a special one are absent in the relationship between an employer and its employees." City of Midland v. O'Bryant, 18 S.W.3d 209 (Tex.2000). Good faith claims do, however, reach the courts in Texas. When they do, should there be an affirmative requirement of good faith or just the lack of bad faith? Is there a difference? What if an employer erred in interpreting a clause in an employment compensation agreement, but that agreement granted broad interpretive rights to the employer as long as the employer did so absent bad faith? See, e.g., Kern v. Sitel Corp., 517 F.3d 306 (5th Cir. 2008). The court of appeals held that in interpreting an employment compensation agreement under Texas law, an employer's interpretive rights reserved by the agreement would be honored, absent a showing that the employer acted in bad faith. Although agreeing that the plaintiff's interpretation of an incentive compensation clause entitled the plaintiff to an extra $150,000 in bonus pay, the Fifth Circuit nevertheless affirmed the District Court's grant of summary judgment in favor of the employer. The Court affirmed that the employer retained final interpretive authority over the terms of the contract and did not act in bad faith. Should an employer be able to hold onto such broad interpretive rights over the terms of an employment contract?

C. TORT EXCEPTIONS TO EMPLOYMENT AT WILL

1. GOOD FAITH AND FAIR DEALING REVISITED

Although the covenant of good faith and fair dealing traditionally sounds in contract, some courts have expanded the availability of tort remedies in good faith and fair dealing claims. California was one of the first states to allow tort remedies, although as you will see, this expansion was relatively short-lived.

Cleary v. American Airlines
111 Cal.App.3d 443 (Cal. Ct. App. 1980).

■ JEFFERSON, ACTING P.J.:

[T]wo causes of action are set forth in the . . . complaint. The first cause is directed against plaintiff's former employer, defendant American Airlines, seeking compensatory damages for breach of contract. Plaintiff alleges that he entered into an oral contract with defendant employer on December 8, 1958, pursuant to which he became a permanent employee of the airline. The terms of employment, it is alleged, included defendant employer's regulation 135–4, which expressed the employer's policy and procedure with respect to employee grievances and discharge. Plaintiff further alleges, in the context of the contract cause of action, a breach of an implied-in-law covenant of good faith and fair dealing by the employer—a covenant contained in the contract which insures that neither contracting party will do anything which would injure the right of the other to receive the benefits of the contract. It is alleged that from 1958 to 1976, an 18-year period, plaintiff worked for defendant employer as a payroll clerk, a ramp agent, and, from 1961 forward, as an airport operations agent.

Plaintiff alleges that the contractual breach occurred on December 23, 1976, through American Airlines "wrongfully and without just cause suspending plaintiff" from his employment, and, "without fair, complete or honest investigation charging plaintiff falsely and without just cause, with theft, leaving his work area . . . without authorization and threatening a fellow employee with bodily harm, all in violation of [American Airline's] Regulations." Plaintiff further sets forth in his pleading that he was terminated by American Airlines "wrongfully and without just cause" on December 30, 1976, for "allegedly committing said violations of said Regulations but actually for plaintiff's union organizing activities"; and that "[thereafter] defendant American Airlines failed to afford plaintiff, as required by said Regulations, a fair, impartial and objective hearing of his protest of said suspension and discharge, a fair, impartial and objective determination of his appeal and a fair, impartial and objective review by a Review Board of the decision of the Hearing Officer on plaintiff's said protest of said suspension and discharge."

* * *

We have indicated herein the continuing trend toward recognition by the courts and the Legislature of certain implied contract rights to job security, necessary to ensure social stability in our society. As was concluded by a commentator, "[the] existence of separate consideration, the common law of the job, and rights accruing through longevity are all factors for courts to consider in evaluating whether an implied contractual right to job security exists. The conflict between an employee's right to job security and an employer's right to fire for cause or with economic justification should be resolved by judicial balancing of the competing equities."

Two factors are of paramount importance in reaching our result that plaintiff has pleaded a viable cause of action. One is the longevity of service by plaintiff—18 years of apparently satisfactory performance. Termination of employment without legal cause after such a period of time offends the implied-in-law covenant of good faith and fair dealing contained in all contracts, including employment contracts. As a result of this covenant, a duty arose on the part of the employer, American Airlines, to do nothing which would deprive plaintiff, the employee, of the benefits of the employment bargain—benefits described in the complaint as having accrued during plaintiff's 18 years of employment.

The second factor of considerable significance is the expressed policy of the employer (probably in response to the demands of employees who were union members), set forth in regulation 135–4. This policy involves the adoption of specific procedures for adjudicating employee disputes such as this one. While the contents of the regulation are not before us, its existence compels the conclusion that this employer had recognized its responsibility to engage in good faith and fair dealing rather than in arbitrary conduct with respect to *all* of its employees.

In the case at bench, we hold that the longevity of the employee's service, together with the expressed policy of the employer, operate as a form of estoppel, precluding any discharge of such an employee by the employer without good cause. We recognize, of course, that plaintiff has the burden of proving that he was terminated unjustly, and that the employer, American Airlines, will have its opportunity to demonstrate that it did in fact exercise good faith and fair dealing with respect to plaintiff. Should plaintiff sustain his burden of proof, he will have established a cause of action for wrongful discharge that sounds in both contract and in tort. He will then be entitled to an award of compensatory damages, and, in addition, punitive damages if his proof complies with the requirements for the latter type of damages.

* * *

The judgment is reversed.

Foley v. Interactive Data Corp.
765 P.2d 373 (Cal. 1988).

■ LUCAS, CHIEF JUSTICE:

After Interactive Data Corporation (defendant) fired plaintiff Daniel D. Foley, an executive employee, he filed this action seeking compensatory and punitive damages for wrongful discharge. In his second amended complaint, plaintiff asserted three distinct theories: (1) a tort cause of action alleging a discharge in violation of public policy, (2) a contract cause of action for breach of an implied-in-fact promise to discharge for good cause only, and (3) a cause of action alleging a tortious breach of the implied covenant of good faith and fair dealing. * * * entered judgment for defendant.

The Court of Appeal affirmed on the grounds (1) plaintiff alleged no statutorily based breach of public policy sufficient to state a cause of action; (2) plaintiff's claim for breach of the covenant to discharge only for good cause was barred by the statute of frauds; and (3) plaintiff's cause of action based on breach of the covenant of good faith and fair dealing failed because it did not allege necessary longevity of employment or express formal procedures for termination of employees. We granted review to consider each of the Court of Appeal's conclusions.

We will hold that the Court of Appeal properly found that * * * plaintiff failed to allege facts showing a violation of a fundamental public policy. We will also conclude, however, that plaintiff has sufficiently alleged a breach of an "oral" or "implied-in-fact" contract, and that the statute of frauds does not bar his claim so that he may pursue his action in this regard. Finally, we will hold that the covenant of good faith and fair dealing applies to employment contracts and that breach of the covenant may give rise to contract but not tort damages.

* * *

According to the complaint, plaintiff is a former employee of defendant, a wholly owned subsidiary of Chase Manhattan Bank that markets computer-based decision-support services. Defendant hired plaintiff in June 1976 as an assistant product manager at a starting salary of $18,500. As a condition of employment defendant required plaintiff to sign a "Confidential and Proprietary Information Agreement" whereby he promised not to engage in certain competition with defendant for one year after the termination of his employment for any reason. The agreement also contained a "Disclosure and Assignment of Information" provision that obliged plaintiff to disclose to defendant all computer-related information known to him, including any innovations, inventions or developments pertaining to the computer field for a period of one year following his termination. Finally, the agreement imposed on plaintiff a continuing obligation to assign to defendant all rights to his computer-related inventions or innovations for one year following termination. It did not state any limitation on the grounds for which plaintiff's employment could be terminated.

Over the next six years and nine months, plaintiff received a steady series of salary increases, promotions, bonuses, awards and superior performance evaluations. In 1979 defendant named him consultant manager of the year and in 1981 promoted him to branch manager of its Los Angeles office. His annual salary rose to $56,164 and he received an additional $6,762 merit bonus two days before his discharge in March 1983. He alleges defendant's officers made repeated oral assurances of job security so long as his performance remained adequate.

Plaintiff also alleged that during his employment, defendant maintained written "Termination Guidelines" that set forth express grounds for discharge and a mandatory seven-step pretermination procedure. Plaintiff understood that these guidelines applied not only to employees under plaintiff's supervision, but to him as well. On the basis of these representations, plaintiff alleged that he reasonably believed defendant would not discharge him except for good cause, and therefore he refrained from accepting or pursuing other job opportunities.

The event that led to plaintiff's discharge was a private conversation in January 1983 with his former supervisor, vice president Richard Earnest. During the previous year defendant had hired Robert Kuhne and subsequently named Kuhne to replace Earnest as plaintiff's immediate supervisor. Plaintiff learned that Kuhne was currently under investigation by the Federal Bureau of Investigation for embezzlement from his former employer, Bank of America.[1] Plaintiff reported what he knew about Kuhne to Earnest, because he was "worried about working for Kuhne and having him in a supervisory position * * *, in view of Kuhne's suspected criminal conduct." Plaintiff asserted he "made this disclosure in the interest and for the benefit of his employer," allegedly because he believed that because defendant and its parent do business with the financial community on a confidential basis, the company would have a legitimate interest in knowing about a high executive's alleged prior criminal conduct.

In response, Earnest allegedly told plaintiff not to discuss "rumors" and to "forget what he heard" about Kuhne's past. In early March, Kuhne informed plaintiff that defendant had decided to replace him for "performance reasons" and that he could transfer to a position in another division in Waltham, Massachusetts. Plaintiff was told that if he did not

---

[1] In September 1983, after plaintiff's discharge, Kuhne pleaded guilty in federal court to a felony count of embezzlement.

accept a transfer, he might be demoted but not fired. One week later, in Waltham, Earnest informed plaintiff he was not doing a good job, and six days later, he notified plaintiff he could continue as branch manager if he "agreed to go on a 'performance plan.' Plaintiff asserts he agreed to consider such an arrangement." The next day, when Kuhne met with plaintiff, purportedly to present him with a written "performance plan" proposal, Kuhne instead informed plaintiff he had the choice of resigning or being fired. Kuhne offered neither a performance plan nor an option to transfer to another position.

Defendant demurred to all three causes of action. After plaintiff filed two amended pleadings, the trial court sustained defendant's demurrer without leave to amend and dismissed all three causes of action. The Court of Appeal affirmed the dismissal as to all three counts. We will explore each claim in turn.

[The majority found that Foley had not alleged facts sufficient to establish that he had been discharged in violation of public policy. He alleged that he was discharged in violation of a "substantial public policy" imposing a legal duty on employees to report relevant business information to management. The court concluded that whether or not there was such a statutory duty, no *public* interest barred discharge of Foley for disclosing information of the sort he had: "When the duty of an employee to disclose information to his employer serves only the private interest of the employer, the rationale underlying the [public policy] cause of action is not implicated."

[With respect to Foley's breach of contract claim, the Court found that he had pleaded facts sufficient to establish, if proved, an implied-in-fact contract limiting the company's right to dismiss him arbitrarily.]

* * *

We turn now to plaintiff's cause of action for tortious breach of the implied covenant of good faith and fair dealing. * * * [P]laintiff asserts we should recognize tort remedies for such a breach in the context of employment termination.

The distinction between tort and contract is well grounded in common law, and divergent objectives underlie the remedies created in the two areas. Whereas contract actions are created to enforce the intentions of the parties to the agreement, tort law is primarily designed to vindicate "social policy." The covenant of good faith and fair dealing was developed in the contract arena and is aimed at making effective the agreement's promises. Plaintiff asks that we find that the breach of the implied covenant in employment contracts also gives rise to an action seeking an award of tort damages.

In this instance, where an extension of tort remedies is sought for a duty whose breach previously has been compensable by contractual remedies, it is helpful to consider certain principles relevant to contract law. First, predictability about the cost of contractual relationships plays an important role in our commercial system. Moreover, "Courts traditionally have awarded damages for breach of contract to compensate the aggrieved party rather than to punish the breaching party." With these concepts in mind, we turn to analyze the role of the implied covenant of good faith and fair dealing and the propriety of the extension of remedies urged by plaintiff.

"Every contract imposes upon each party a duty of good faith dealing in its performance and its enforcement." (Rest.2d Contracts, § 205.) This duty has been recognized in the majority of American jurisdictions, the Restatement, and the Uniform Commercial Code. Because the covenant is a contract term, however, compensation for its breach has almost always been limited to contract rather than tort remedies. As to the scope of the covenant, "[t]he precise nature and extent of the duty imposed by such an implied promise will depend on the contractual purposes." (Egan v. Mutual of Omaha Ins. Co. (1979) 24 Cal.3d 809, 818.) Initially, the concept of a duty of good faith developed in contract law as "a kind of 'safety valve' to which judges may turn to fill gaps and qualify or limit rights and duties otherwise arising under rules of law and specific contract language." As a contract concept, breach of the duty led to imposition of contract damages determined by the nature of the breach and standard contract principles.

An exception to this general rule has developed in the context of insurance contracts where, for a variety of policy reasons, courts have held that breach of the implied covenant will provide the basis for an action in tort. * * *

In Egan v. Mutual of Omaha Ins. Co., supra, 24 Cal.3d 809, we described some of the bases for permitting tort recovery for breach of the implied covenant in the insurance context. "The insured in a contract like the one before us does not seek to obtain a commercial advantage by purchasing the policy—rather, he seeks protection against calamity." Thus, "As one commentary has noted, 'The insurers' obligations are * * * rooted in their status as purveyors of a vital service labeled quasi-public in nature. Suppliers of services affected with a public interest must take the public's interest seriously, where necessary placing it before their interest in maximizing gains and limiting disbursements. * * * [A]s a supplier of a public service rather than a manufactured product, the obligations of insurers go beyond meeting reasonable expectations of coverage. The obligations of good faith and fair dealing encompass qualities of decency and humanity inherent in the responsibilities of a fiduciary.'"

In addition, the *Egan* court emphasized that "the relationship of insurer and insured is inherently unbalanced; the adhesive nature of insurance contracts places the insurer in a superior bargaining position." This emphasis on the "special relationship" of insurer and insured has been echoed in arguments and analysis in subsequent scholarly commentary and cases which urge the availability of tort remedies in the employment context.

The first California appellate case to permit tort recovery in the employment context was *Cleary,* 111 Cal.App.3d 443. To support its holding that tort as well as contract damages were appropriate to compensate for a breach of the implied covenant, the *Cleary* court relied on insurance cases without engaging in comparative analysis of insurance and employment relationships and without inquiring into whether the insurance cases' departure from established principles of contract law should generally be subject to expansion.

Similarly, *Cleary's* discussion of two previous California employment cases was insufficient. It found a "hint" in Coats v. General Motors Corp. (1934) 3 Cal.App.2d 340, to support the proposition that "on occasion, it may be incumbent upon an employer to demonstrate *good faith* in terminating an employee", but failed to acknowledge that in *Coats,* the employee sought recovery of only contract damages. Next, the *Cleary* court placed undue reliance on dictum in this court's *Tameny* decision, which suggested that tort remedies might be available when an employer breaches the implied covenant of good faith and fair dealing. The qualified *Tameny* dictum was based exclusively on precedent in insurance cases from this state, and two out-of-state employment cases. The out-of-state cases included Monge v. Beebe Rubber Company (N.H.1974) 316 A.2d 549, in which the court permitted an action for wrongful discharge but limited the plaintiff's recovery to contract damages, specifically excluding recovery for mental distress. Moreover, the New Hampshire Supreme Court thereafter confined *Monge* to cases in which the employer's actions contravene public policy. In the second case, Fortune v. National Cash Register Co. (Mass.1977) 364 N.E.2d 1251, the court created a right of action based on breach of the implied covenant, but limited recovery to benefits the employee had already earned under the contract. Subsequent Massachusetts cases have pursued the same limited course.

In fact, although Justice Broussard asserts that the weight of authority is in favor of granting a tort remedy, the clear majority of jurisdictions have either expressly rejected the notion of tort damages for breach of the implied covenant in employment cases or impliedly done so by rejecting any application of the covenant in such a context.

* * *

In our view, the underlying problem in the line of cases relied on by plaintiff lies in the decisions' uncritical incorporation of the insurance model into the employment context, without careful consideration of the fundamental policies underlying the development of tort and contract law in general or of significant differences between the insurer/insured and employer/employee relationships. When a court enforces the implied covenant it is in essence acting to protect "the interest in having promises performed"—the traditional realm of a contract action—rather than to protect some general duty to society which the law places on an employer without regard to the substance of its contractual obligations to its employee. Thus, in *Tameny*, as we have explained, the court was careful to draw a distinction between "ex delicto" and "ex contractu" obligations. An allegation of breach of the implied covenant of good faith and fair dealing is an allegation of breach of an "ex contractu" obligation, namely one arising out of the contract itself. The covenant of good faith is read into contracts in order to protect the express covenants or promises of the contract, not to protect some general public policy interest not directly tied to the contract's purposes. The insurance cases thus were a major departure from traditional principles of contract law. We must, therefore, consider with great care claims that extension of the exceptional approach taken in those cases is automatically appropriate if certain hallmarks and similarities can be adduced in another contract setting. With this emphasis on the historical purposes of the covenant of good faith and fair dealing in mind, we turn to consider the bases upon which extension of the insurance model to the employment sphere has been urged.

* * *

After review of the various commentators, and independent consideration of the similarities between the two areas, we are not convinced that a "special relationship" analogous to that between insurer and insured should be deemed to exist in the usual employment relationship which would warrant recognition of a tort action for breach of the implied covenant. Even if we were to assume that the special relationship model is an appropriate one to follow in determining whether to expand tort recovery, a breach in the employment context does not place the employee in the same economic dilemma that an insured faces when an insurer in bad faith refuses to pay a claim or to accept a settlement offer within policy limits. When an insurer takes such actions, the insured cannot turn to the marketplace to find another insurance company willing to pay for the loss already incurred. The wrongfully terminated employee, on the other hand, can (and must, in order to mitigate damages) make reasonable efforts to seek alternative employment. Moreover, the role of the employer differs from that of the "quasi-public" insurance company with whom individuals contract specifically in order to obtain protection from potential specified economic harm. The employer does not similarly "sell" protection to its employees; it is not providing a public service. Nor do we find convincing the idea that the employee is necessarily seeking a different kind of financial security than those entering a typical commercial contract. If a small dealer contracts for goods from a large supplier, and those goods are vital to the small dealer's business, a breach by the supplier may have financial significance for individuals employed by the dealer or to the dealer himself. Permitting only contract damages in such a situation has ramifications no different from a similar limitation in the direct employer-employee relationship.

Finally, there is a fundamental difference between insurance and employment relationships. In the insurance relationship, the insurer's and insured's interest are financially at odds. If the insurer pays a claim, it diminishes its fiscal resources. The insured of course has paid for protection and expects to have its losses recompensed. When a claim is paid, money shifts from insurer to insured, or, if appropriate, to a third party claimant.

Putting aside already specifically barred improper motives for termination which may be based on both economic and noneconomic considerations [such as statutorily prohibited discrimination and wrongful discharge in violation of public policy], as a general rule it is to the employer's economic benefit to retain good employees. The interest of employer and employee are most frequently in alignment. If there is a job to be done, the employer must still pay someone to do it. This is not to say that there may never be a "bad motive" for discharge not otherwise covered by law. Nevertheless, in terms of abstract employment relationships as contrasted with abstract insurance relationships, there is less inherent relevant tension between the interests of employers and employees than exists between that of insurers and insureds. Thus the need to place disincentives on an employer's conduct in addition to those already imposed by law simply does not rise to the same level as that created by the conflicting interests at stake in the insurance context. Nor is this to say that the Legislature would have no basis for affording employees additional protections. It is, however, to say that the need to extend the special relationship model in the form of judicially created relief of the kind sought here is less compelling.

We therefore conclude that the employment relationship is not sufficiently similar to that of insurer and insured to warrant judicial extension of the proposed additional tort remedies in view of the countervailing concerns about economic policy and stability, the traditional separation of tort and contract law, and finally, the numerous protections against improper terminations already afforded employees.

* * *

Plaintiff may proceed with his cause of action alleging a breach of an implied-in-fact contract promise to discharge him only for good cause. His cause of action for a breach of public policy pursuant to *Tameny* was properly dismissed because the facts alleged, even if proven, would not establish a discharge in violation of public policy. Finally, as to his cause of action for tortious breach of the implied covenant of good faith and fair dealing, we hold that tort remedies are not available for breach of the implied covenant in an employment contract to employees who allege they have been discharged in violation of the covenant.[42]

■ KAUFMAN, JUSTICE, concurring in part, dissenting in part:

* * *

Thirty years ago, in Comunale v. Traders & General Ins. Co. (1958) 50 Cal.2d 654, this court first recognized that breach of the implied duty of good faith and fair dealing may give rise to a cause of action sounding in tort. I would not have thought, after these many years, that it was still necessary to defend and explain this basic principle. In purporting to trace its origins, however, the majority fundamentally misstates the nature of the tort, and thereby subverts the powerful impetus for its extension to the area of employment termination. A brief summary of familiar principles, therefore, may be useful.

In attempting to emphasize its contractual origins, the majority characterize the covenant of good faith and fair dealing as "a contract term" "aimed at making effective the agreement's promises." That characterization is simply incorrect under the decisions of this court and the authorities on which they relied. It is true that the law implies in every *contract* a duty of good faith and fair dealing. The duty to deal fairly and in good faith with the other party to a contract, however, "is a *duty imposed by law, not one arising from the terms of the contract itself.* In other words, this duty of dealing fairly and in good faith is nonconsensual in origin rather than consensual." While the nature of the obligations imposed by this duty is dependent upon the nature and purpose of the contract and the expectations of the parties, these obligations are not consensual, not agreed to in the contract; they are *imposed by law* and thus reflect the normative values of society as a whole. The interest which the duty of good faith and fair dealing is designed to preserve and protect is essentially not the *parties'* interest in having their promises performed, but *society's* interest in protecting its members from harm on account of nonconsensual conduct.

Because tort actions enforce "duties of conduct * * * imposed by law, and are based primarily upon social policy, and not necessarily upon the will or intention of the parties * * *", it was quite natural that courts would eventually approve the extension of tort remedies, in appropriate circumstances, to violations of the duty of good faith and fair dealing. Indeed, this court was among the first to recognize that the nature of the obligations, the purposes of the contract and the expectations of the parties all combine to impose a heightened duty upon insurers. As we explained in Egan v. Mutual of Omaha Ins. Co., supra, 24 Cal.3d 809, "The insured in a contract like the one before us does not seek to obtain a commercial advantage by purchasing the policy—rather, he seeks protection against calamity * * *. [T]he major motivation for obtaining

---

[42] *Cleary,* 111 Cal.App.3d 443 and its progeny accordingly are disapproved to the extent that they permit a cause of action seeking tort remedies for breach of the implied covenant.

disability insurance is to provide funds during periods when the ordinary source of the insured's income—his earnings—has stopped. The purchase of such insurance provides peace of mind and security in the event the insured is unable to work." We also observed that "the relationship of insurer and insured is inherently unbalanced; the adhesive nature of insurance contracts places the insurer in a superior bargaining position."

In the classic tradition of the common law, which adapts functional principles from precedent as changing social and economic conditions require, a number of courts and commentators have distilled from our holdings in the insurance context a relatively narrow but serviceable "bad faith" doctrine for application in other areas: Breach of the duty of good faith and fair dealing may give rise to an action in tort where the contractual relation manifests elements similar to those which characterize the "special relationship" between insurer and insured, *i.e.* elements of public interest, adhesion, and financial dependency.

[R]ecent Court of Appeal decisions have unanimously recognized that willful and malicious discharge from employment may give rise to tort remedies.

The majority is not unmindful of these numerous authorities which have concluded that the criteria which make the relationship between insurer and insured suitable for tort remedies, apply with even greater force in the employment context. Indeed, the majority reviews the pertinent cases and authorities with considerable care. At the end of this lengthy prologue, however, the majority concludes that *all* of the arguments are deficient in comparative analysis, and proceeds to explain why it is "not convinced" that a relationship analogous to that between insurer and insured exists in the employment context. * * *

Such conclusions, in my view, expose an unrealistic if not mythical conception of the employment relationship. They also reveal a misplaced reluctance to define the minimal standards of decency required to govern that relationship. The delineation of such standards is not, as the majority strongly implies, judicial legislation, but rather constitutes this court's fundamental obligation.

It is, at best, naive to believe that the availability of the "marketplace," or that a supposed "alignment of interests," renders the employment relationship less special or less subject to abuse than the relationship between insurer and insured. Indeed, I can think of no relationship in which one party, the employee, places more reliance upon the other, is more dependent upon the other, or is more vulnerable to abuse by the other, than the relationship between employer and employee. And, ironically, the relative imbalance of economic power between employer and employee tends to increase rather than diminish the longer that relationship continues. Whatever bargaining strength and marketability the employee may have at the moment of hiring, diminishes rapidly thereafter. Marketplace? What market is there for the factory worker laid-off after 25 years of labor in the same plant, or for the middle-aged executive fired after 25 years with the same firm?

Financial security? Can anyone seriously dispute that employment is generally sought, at least in part, for financial security and all that that implies: food on the table, shelter, clothing, medical care, education for one's children. Clearly, no action for breach of the covenant of good faith and fair dealing will lie *unless* it has first been proved that, expressly or by implication, the employer has given the employee a reasonable expectation of continued employment so long as the employee performs satisfactorily. And that expectation constitutes a far greater and graver security interest than any which inheres in the insurance context. Most of us can live without insurance. Few of us could live without a job.

Peace of mind? One's work obviously involves more than just earning a living. It defines for many people their identity, their sense of self-worth, their sense of belonging. The wrongful and malicious destruction of one's employment is far more certain to result in serious emotional distress than any wrongful denial of an insurance claim.

If everything this court has written concerning the relation between insurer and insured has any deeper meaning; if we have created a living principle based upon justice, reason and common sense and not merely a fixed, narrow and idiosyncratic rule of law, then we must acknowledge the irresistible logic and equity of extending that principle to the employment relationship. We can reasonably do no less.

* * *

■ [The concurring and dissenting opinion of JUSTICE BROUSSARD and the dissenting opinion of JUSTICE MOSK have been omitted.]

NOTES AND QUESTIONS

1.   Although the majority in *Foley* did not eliminate the cause of action for a violation of the covenant of good faith and fair dealing, it undercut the vitality of litigation in the area by restricting remedies to contract damages. The kind of damages available in good faith and fair dealings cases is far from settled at the state level. Some state courts have prohibited tort damages, interpreting good faith and fair dealing as a contract law doctrine. See, e.g., ARCO Alaska, Inc. v. Akers, 753 P.2d 1150, 1153 (Alaska 1988); Decker v. Browning-Ferris Indus. of Colo., Inc., 931 P.2d 436 (Colo. 1997); Brockmeyer v. Dun & Bradstreet, 335 N.W.2d 834 (Wis.1983). Other jurisdictions have allowed tort damages, albeit with some limitations. See K Mart Corp. v. Ponsock, 732 P.2d 1364 (Nev.1987); Dubrowski v. State ex rel. Wyoming Liquor Comm'n, 1 P.3d 631, 633 (Wyo. 2000).

2.   The availability of tort remedies in good faith and fair dealing suits will play a significant role in the ongoing development of wrongful discharge law. In those states that allow punitive damages under tort law, plaintiffs find it easier to secure counsel, as lawyers working on contingency will be attracted

to their share of any award of punitive damages. States that limit good faith and fair dealing damages to those available under contract law, however, will encounter fewer suits, as plaintiffs and their attorneys lack the individual financial incentives to bring suit.

3.   In Wallis v. Superior Court, 207 Cal.Rptr. 123 (Cal.App.1984), a pre-*Foley* case, a senior employee entered into an agreement with his employer immediately prior to a permanent layoff in which the employer agreed to pay certain severance benefits until the employee reached age 65. When the employer breached the agreement and refused to pay, the employee sued for, among other things, breach of the covenant of good faith and fair dealing. Using the analogy to insurance cases, the court extended the reach of the covenant to the agreement between Wallis and his employer, to reverse the lower court's dismissal of Wallis' complaint. Following *Foley,* would *Wallis* be decided the same way?

4.   Is a legislature better able than a court to make a judgment regarding proper remedies in wrongful discharge cases, as the majority asserts? Why or why not?

5.   Why is the majority so concerned about the ability of lower courts to make decisions regarding good faith in determining whether tort damages are appropriate in individual cases? Isn't that a task routinely undertaken by courts? What is the importance of unpredictability regarding damages? If it is an undesirable trait in the judicial system, can it be eliminated or minimized? How?

6.   In a footnote, the majority stated: "Unlike collective bargaining agreements that contain 'screening mechanisms' whereby 'unions sift out grievances that are viewed as unmeritorious or less important,' the proposed tort action essentially has no entry-level limitation." Is that true? If it is, what does it suggest about the majority's practical concerns in permitting tort actions? What weight should those concerns have in deciding whether to permit tort damages?

7.   In comparing insurance and employment contracts, one common element that the majority discusses—and minimizes in the employment context—is disparity of bargaining power. But California Labor Code Section 923 states "the individual unorganized worker is helpless to exercise actual liberty of contract and to protect his freedom of labor, and thereby to obtain acceptable terms and conditions of employment." What role should such a statutory finding play in the court's decision-making process?

8.   The California Supreme Court ruled 4–3 that an employee may not sue an employer for fraud arising out of the employee's wrongful termination. Since employment is fundamentally contractual, tort actions arising from the termination may not be maintained in the same case. Tort actions may be brought if not connected with the termination itself, if not precluded by the Workers' Compensation Act. Hunter v. Up-Right, Inc., 864 P.2d 88 (Cal.1993). However, employer misrepresentations which induce a future employee's reliance do support a tort claim for fraud, although any wrongful termination claim would be limited to the contract claim. Lazar v. Superior Court, 909 P.2d 981 (Cal.1996).

Guz v. Bechtel National, Inc.

8 P.3d 1089 (Cal. 2000).

■ BAXTER, J.

This case presents questions about the law governing claims of wrongful discharge from employment, as it applies to an employer's motion for summary judgment. Plaintiff Guz, a longtime employee of Bechtel National, Inc. (BNI), was released at age 49 when his work unit was eliminated and its tasks were transferred to another Bechtel office. Guz sued BNI and its parent, Bechtel Corporation (hereinafter collectively Bechtel), alleging age discrimination, breach of an implied contract to be terminated only for good cause, and breach of the implied covenant of good faith and fair dealing. The trial court granted Bechtel's motion for summary judgment and dismissed the action. In a split decision, the Court of Appeal reversed. The majority found that Bechtel had demonstrated no grounds to foreclose a trial on any of the claims asserted in the complaint.

Having closely reviewed the Court of Appeal's decision, we reach the following conclusions:

First, the Court of Appeal used erroneous grounds to reverse summary judgment on Guz's implied contract cause of action. The Court of Appeal found triable evidence (1) that Guz had an actual agreement, implied in fact, to be discharged only for good cause and (2) that the elimination of Guz's work unit lacked good cause because Bechtel's stated reason—a "downturn in . . . workload"—was not justified by the facts, and was, in truth, a pretext to discharge the unit's workers for poor performance without following the company's "progressive discipline" policy. We acknowledge a triable issue that Guz, like other Bechtel workers, had implied contractual rights under specific provisions of Bechtel's written personnel policies. But neither the policies, nor other evidence, suggest any contractual restriction on Bechtel's right to eliminate a work unit as it saw fit, even where dissatisfaction with unit performance was a factor in the decision. The Court of Appeal's ruling on Guz's implied contract claim must therefore be reversed. The Court of Appeal did not reach the additional ground on which Guz claims a contractual breach—i.e., that Bechtel failed to follow its fair layoff policies when, during and after the reorganization, it made individual personnel decisions leading to Guz's release. Accordingly, we leave that issue to the Court of Appeal on remand.

Second, the Court of Appeal erred in restoring Guz's separate cause of action for breach of the implied covenant of good faith and fair dealing. Here Guz claims that even if his employment included no express or implied-in-fact agreement limiting Bechtel's right to discharge him, and was thus "at will" (Lab.Code, § 2922), the covenant of good faith and fair dealing, implied by law in every contract, precluded Bechtel from terminating him arbitrarily, as by failing to follow its own policies, or in bad faith. But while the implied covenant requires mutual fairness in applying a contract's actual terms, it cannot substantively *alter* those terms. If an employment is at will, and thus allows either party to terminate for *any or no reason,* the implied covenant cannot decree otherwise. Moreover, although any breach of the actual terms of an employment contract also violates the implied covenant, the measure of damages for such a breach remains solely contractual. Hence, where breach of an actual term is alleged, a separate implied covenant claim, based on the same breach, is superfluous. On the other hand, where an implied covenant claim alleges a breach of obligations beyond the agreement's actual terms, it is invalid.

Finally, we disagree with the Court of Appeal that Guz's claim of prohibited age discrimination has triable merit. Bechtel presented evidence, largely undisputed, that the reasons for its personnel decisions leading to Guz's release had nothing to do with his age. In the face of this showing, evidence cited by Guz that certain workers preferred over him were substantially younger is insufficient to permit a rational inference that age played any significant role in his termination.

For the reasons set forth above, we will reverse the judgment of the Court of Appeal, and will remand to that court for further proceedings consistent with this opinion.

* * *

In 1971, Bechtel hired Guz as an administrative assistant at a salary of $750 per month. Throughout his Bechtel career, Guz worked in "management information," performing, at various times, duties on both the "awarded" and "overhead" sides of this specialty. He received steady raises and promotions. His performance reviews were generally favorable, though his March 1992 evaluation indicated he needed to follow through on ideas and should become "fully computer literate in order to improve his long-term job success."

BNI, a division of Bechtel Corporation, is an engineering, construction, and environmental remediation company, which focuses on federal government programs, principally for the Departments of Energy and Defense. Prior to 1993, BNI had its own in-house management information unit, the BNI Management Information Group (BNI-MI). BNI-MI itself represented a 1986 consolidation of two Bechtel management information units, which resulted in the work of these groups being done by fewer people. Between 1986 and 1991, BNI-MI's size was further reduced from 13 to six persons, and its costs were reduced from $748,000 in 1986 to $400,000 in 1991.

Guz had worked for BNI-MI since 1986. In 1992, at age 49, he was employed as a financial reports supervisor, responsible for supervising BNI-MI's overhead section, which included himself and 44-year-old Dee Minoia. At salary grade 27, Guz earned $5,940 per month. BNI-MI's six-member staff also included its manager, Ron Goldstein (age 50),

Goldstein's secretary Pam Fung (age 45), Robert Wraith (age 41), and Christine Siu (age 34). Guz's immediate superior was his longtime friend and colleague Goldstein. Goldstein, in turn, reported to Edward Dewey, BNI's manager of government services.

During this time, Bechtel maintained Personnel Policy 1101, dated June 1991, on the subject of termination of employment (Policy 1101). Policy 1101 stated that "Bechtel employees have no employment agreements guaranteeing continuous service and may resign at their option or be terminated at the option of Bechtel."

Policy 1101 also described several "Categories of Termination," including "Layoff" and "Unsatisfactory Performance." With respect to Unsatisfactory Performance, the policy stated that "[e]mployees who fail to perform their jobs in a satisfactory manner may be terminated, provided the employees have been advised of the specific shortcomings and given an opportunity to improve their performance." A layoff was defined as "a Bechtel-initiated termination of employees caused by a reduction in workload, reorganizations, changes in job requirements, or other circumstances. . . ." Under the Layoff policy, employees subject to termination for this reason "may be placed on 'holding status' if there is a possible Bechtel assignment within the following 3-month period." Guz understood that Policy 1101 applied to him.

In January 1992, Robert Johnstone became president of BNI. While previously running another Bechtel entity, Johnstone had received management information services from the San Francisco Regional Office Management Information Group (SFRO-MI) headed by James Tevis. BNI-MI and SFRO-MI performed similar functions, and John Shaeffer, a veteran Bechtel employee who was several months older than Guz, had overhead reporting duties for SFRO-MI that were similar to Guz's job within BNI-MI.

Johnstone soon became unhappy with the size, cost, and performance of BNI-MI. In April 1992, he advised Dewey, Goldstein, and Guz that BNI-MI's work could be done by three people. A May 1992 memo from Dewey to Goldstein warned that Dewey and Johnstone had agreed BNI-MI's 1992 overhead budget of $365,000 was a "maximum *not* to be exceeded" and was "subject to further analysis and review, since the real guideline was far below this level."

Between April and October 1992, Guz and Goldstein discussed how to reduce BNI-MI's work force. In September 1992, Dee Minoia was told to look for another job. In October 1992, on Dewey's recommendation, Goldstein advised Guz to seek another Bechtel position, citing BNI-MI's reduced budget as the "biggest factor." By that time, as Guz knew, BNI-MI's overhead costs for 1992 had already run well over its strict budget.

* * *

On December 9, 1992, Goldstein informed Guz that BNI-MI was being disbanded, that its work would be done by SFRO-MI, and that Guz was being laid off. Goldstein told Guz the reason he had been selected for layoff was to reduce costs.

* * *

Labor Code section 2922 provides that "[a]n employment, having no specified term, may be terminated at the will of either party on notice to the other." An at-will employment may be ended by either party "at any time without cause," for any or no reason, and subject to no procedure except the statutory requirement of notice.

* * *

While the statutory presumption of at-will employment is strong, it is subject to several limitations. For instance, as we have observed, "the employment relationship is fundamentally contractual." Thus, though Labor Code section 2922 prevails where the employer and employee have reached no other understanding, it does not overcome their "fundamental . . . freedom of contract" to depart from at-will employment. The statute does not prevent the parties from *agreeing* to any limitation, otherwise lawful, on the employer's termination rights.

* * *

The contractual understanding need not be express, but may be *implied in fact,* arising from the parties' *conduct* evidencing their actual mutual intent to create such enforceable limitations. In *Foley,* we identified several factors, apart from express terms, that may bear upon "the existence *and content* of an . . . [implied-in-fact] agreement" placing limits on the employer's right to discharge an employee. These factors might include " 'the personnel policies or practices of the employer, the employee's longevity of service, actions or communications by the employer reflecting assurances of continued employment, and the practices of the industry in which the employee is engaged.' "

Foley asserted that "the totality of the circumstances" must be examined to determine whether the parties' conduct, considered in the context of surrounding circumstances, gave rise to an implied-in-fact contract limiting the employer's termination rights. We did not suggest, however, that every vague combination of *Foley* factors, shaken together in a bag, necessarily allows a finding that the employee had a right to be discharged only for good cause, as determined in court.

* * *

As we shall explain, we find triable evidence that Bechtel's *written personnel documents* set forth implied contractual limits on the circumstances under which Guz, and other Bechtel workers, would be terminated. On the other hand, we see *no* triable evidence of an implied agreement between Guz and Bechtel on *additional, different, or broader* terms of employment security. As Bechtel suggests, the personnel documents themselves did not restrict Bechtel's freedom to reorganize, reduce, and consolidate its work force for whatever reasons it wished.

Thus, contrary to the Court of Appeal's holding, Bechtel had the absolute right to eliminate Guz's work unit and to transfer the unit's responsibilities to another company entity, even if the decision was influenced by dissatisfaction with the eliminated unit's performance, and even if the personnel documents entitled an individual employee to progressive discipline procedures before being fired for poor performance.

* * *

A number of post-*Foley* California decisions have suggested that long duration of service, regular promotions, favorable performance reviews, praise from supervisors, and salary increases do not, without more, imply an employer's contractual intent to relinquish its at-will rights. These decisions reason that such events are but natural consequences of a well-functioning employment relationship, and thus have no special tendency to prove that the employer's at-will implied agreement, reasonably understood as such by the employee, has become one that limits the employer's future termination rights.

We agree that an employee's *mere* passage of time in the employer's service, even where marked with tangible indicia that the employer approves the employee's work, cannot *alone* form an implied-in-fact contract that the employee is no longer at will. Absent other evidence of the employer's intent, longevity, raises and promotions are their own rewards for the employee's continuing valued service; they do not, *in and of themselves,* additionally constitute a contractual guarantee of future employment security. A rule granting such contract rights on the basis of successful longevity alone would discourage the retention and promotion of employees.

* * *

The Court of Appeal did not address Guz's second theory, i.e., that Bechtel also breached its implied contract by failing, during and after the reorganization, to provide him personally with the fair layoff protections, including force ranking and reassignment help, which are set forth in its Policies and RIF Guidelines. This theory raises difficult questions, including what the proper remedy, if any, should be if Guz ultimately shows that Bechtel breached a contractual obligation to follow certain procedural policies in the termination process. However, we commonly decline to decide issues not addressed by the Court of Appeal. We will follow that practice here. On remand, the Court of Appeal should confront this issue and should determine whether Guz has raised a triable issue on this theory.

Bechtel next urges that the trial court properly dismissed Guz's separate claim for breach of the implied covenant of good faith and fair dealing because, on the facts and arguments presented, this theory of recovery is either inapplicable or superfluous. We agree.

The sole asserted basis for Guz's implied covenant claim is that Bechtel violated its established personnel policies when it terminated him without a prior opportunity to improve his "unsatisfactory" performance, used no force ranking or other objective criteria when selecting him for layoff, and omitted to consider him for other positions for which he was qualified. Guz urges that *even if his contract was for employment at will,* the implied covenant of good faith and fair dealing precluded Bechtel from "unfairly" denying him the contract's benefits by failing to follow its own termination policies.

Thus, Guz argues, in effect, that the implied covenant can impose substantive terms and conditions beyond those to which the contract parties actually agreed. However, as indicated above, such a theory directly contradicts our conclusions in *Foley.* The covenant of good faith and fair dealing, implied by law in every contract, exists merely to prevent one contracting party from unfairly frustrating the other party's right to receive the *benefits of the agreement actually made.* The covenant thus cannot "'be endowed with an existence independent of its contractual underpinnings.'" It cannot impose substantive duties or limits on the contracting parties beyond those incorporated in the specific terms of their agreement.

* * *

A breach of the contract may also constitute a breach of the implied covenant of good faith and fair dealing. But insofar as the employer's acts are directly actionable as a breach of an implied-in-fact contract term, a claim that merely realleges that breach as a violation of the covenant is superfluous. This is because, as we explained at length in *Foley,* the remedy for breach of an employment agreement, including the covenant of good faith and fair dealing implied by law therein, is *solely contractual.* In the employment context, an implied covenant theory affords no separate *measure of recovery,* such as tort damages. Allegations that the breach was wrongful, in bad faith, arbitrary, and unfair are unavailing; there is no tort of "bad faith breach" of an employment contract.

We adhere to these principles here. To the extent Guz's implied covenant cause of action seeks to impose limits on Bechtel's termination rights *beyond* those to which the parties actually agreed, the claim is invalid. To the extent the implied covenant claim seeks simply to invoke terms to which the parties *did* agree, it is superfluous. Guz's remedy, if any, for Bechtel's alleged violation of its personnel policies depends on proof that they were contract terms to which the parties actually agreed. The trial court thus properly dismissed the implied covenant cause of action.

NOTES AND QUESTIONS

1. Review the various contract law approaches to wrongful discharge. Which seems most effective? How can the tools of traditional contract analysis be used to prevent unfair or abusive discharges? The courts have not yet applied the doctrines of unconscionability, adhesion, standard forms,

or illegality of provisions to wrongful discharge cases brought in contract. Should violations of those doctrines give rise to tort damages? Is there something different about the employment relationship that makes it less amenable to standard contract analysis than, say, an agreement to buy a used car?

2. Answering a question from the Ninth Circuit, the California Supreme Court stated that an employer with a "unilaterally adopted policy of retaining employees so long as a specified condition does not occur" may thereafter unilaterally terminate the policy "if the condition is one of indefinite duration and the employer effects the change after a reasonable time, on reasonable notice, and without interfering with the employees' vested benefits." In 1986 Pacific Bell had issued a "Management Employment Security Policy" stating that the company would "offer all management employees who continue to meet our changing business expectations employment security through reassignment to and retraining for other management positions, even if their present jobs are eliminated." The policy was ended on April 1, 1992, the company saying that the purpose was "to achieve more flexibility in conducting its business and compete more successfully in the marketplace." Severance and pension benefits were improved.

The court said that once the promisor in a unilateral contract determines that it will terminate or modify the contract, additional consideration is not required. "Continuing to work after the policy termination constituted acceptance of the new employment terms." The dissent said that "the entire analysis of the majority opinion rests upon the single false premise that the contractual condition permitting Pacific Bell to terminate—the occurrence of a 'change that will materially affect Pacific Bell's business plan achievement'—does not describe 'an ascertainable event that could be measured in any reasonable manner.'" The dissent also said that the majority's result "condones and encourages manipulative, oppressive, and unfair treatment of employees." Asmus v. Pacific Bell, 999 P.2d 71 (Cal.2000) (4–3).

2. PUBLIC POLICY

Contract law, with its doctrines of mutuality of obligation and consideration, was not historically sympathetic to the individual who had made a "bad bargain," unless fraud, duress, or coercion could be shown, and none of those applied in the typical employment relationship. But the facts of some cases cried out for a legal remedy of some sort, and the judicial activism first encouraged by the employment discrimination laws ultimately spilled over into other aspects of employment. Discharges in violation of public policy soon became a recognized tort:

A principal justification for this public-policy cause of action is that . . . certain discharges that contravene established norms of public policy harm not only the specific employee but also the interests of the parties and society as a whole. Recognition of the public-policy cause of action compels employers to internalize the costs of the harm they cause, and thereby encourages behavior consistent with those norms. Restatement of Employment Law Third § 5.01 comment (a) (2014).One of the first wrongful discharge cases was Petermann v. Teamsters Local 396, 344 P.2d 25 (Cal.App.1959). The plaintiff, a business agent for the union, refused to perjure himself as instructed by his employer in testimony before a state legislative committee and was discharged the following day. In recognizing a cause of action for wrongful discharge, the court noted that the right to discharge an employee under an at-will contract could be limited by statute or public policy. It further stated:

> The commission of perjury is unlawful. It is also a crime to solicit the commission of perjury. * * * The threat of criminal prosecution would, in many cases, be a sufficient deterrent upon both the employer and employee, the former from soliciting and the latter from committing perjury. However, in order to more fully effectuate the state's declared policy against perjury, the civil law, too, must deny the employer his generally unlimited right to discharge an employee whose employment is for an unspecified duration, when the reason for the dismissal is the employee's refusal to commit perjury. * * * The public policy of this state as reflected in the Penal Code sections referred to above would be seriously impaired if it were to be held that one could be discharged by reason of his refusal to commit perjury. To hold that one's continued employment could be made contingent upon his commission of a felonious act at the instance of his employer would be to encourage criminal conduct upon the part of both the employee and employer and serve to contaminate the honest administration of public affairs.

344 P.2d at 27.

In *Petermann,* public policy was found in the state's penal code. Gradually, other states began to recognize limited public policy exceptions to the at-will rule. In Frampton v. Central Ind. Gas Co., 297 N.E.2d 425 (Ind.1973), the Indiana Supreme Court had no difficulty extending the reasoning of *Petermann* to an employee who had been discharged for filing a claim for an injury sustained on the job under the Indiana Workmen's Compensation Act: "We agree with the Court of Appeals that, under ordinary circumstances, an employee at-will may be discharged without cause. However, when an employee is discharged solely for exercising a statutorily conferred right an exception to the general rule must be recognized."

As the following cases illustrate, however, courts in general have found public policy a slippery concept to define satisfactorily, while several jurisdictions have refused to recognize the public policy exception to the at-will rule altogether.

a.   Legal Duties

Gantt v. Sentry Insurance
824 P.2d 680 (Cal. 1992).

■ Arabian, Justice:

We granted review in this case to consider whether an employee who was terminated in retaliation for supporting a coworker's claim of sexual harassment may state a cause of action for tortious discharge against public policy and, if so, whether the exclusive remedy provisions of the Workers' Compensation Act bar the action. We hold that the claim is actionable * * * and is not preempted by the workers' compensation law.

* * *

Viewing the record most strongly in favor of the judgment, as we must, the following pertinent chronology of facts appears: In September 1979, Sentry hired Gantt to serve as the sales manager of its Sacramento office. His mission was to develop the Sacramento sales force. How successfully he performed this task was the subject of conflicting evidence at trial. However, as explained below, the record amply supports the jury's specific finding that his demotion and constructive discharge were the product of his support for another employee's sexual harassment claim rather than the result of any legally valid business reason.

The specific circumstances which led to Gantt's estrangement from Sentry centered on Joyce Bruno, who was hired in January 1980 to be the liaison between trade associations and Sentry's Sacramento and Walnut Creek offices. In that capacity, Ms. Bruno reported to both Gantt and Gary Desser, the manager of the Walnut Creek office, as well as Brian Cullen, a technical supervisor at regional headquarters in Scottsdale, Arizona.

Shortly after she was hired, Ms. Bruno experienced sexual harassment at the hands of Desser. As the harassment continued, she complained to Gantt. He recommended she report it to Cullen in Scottsdale. Ultimately, Gantt himself contacted both Bonnie Caroline, who was responsible for receiving complaints of sexual discrimination, and Dave Berg, his immediate supervisor, about the problem. Despite these reports, the harassment continued. Accordingly, Gantt took it upon himself to speak a second time with both Berg and Ms. Caroline. Finally, in early 1981, Desser was demoted from sales manager to sales representative and replaced by Robert Warren. In March, Ms. Bruno was transferred to a sales representative position. A month later, however, she was fired.

Gantt stated that he was present at the April meeting in which Berg directed Warren to fire Bruno and ridiculed Gantt for supporting her. The following month, Berg himself resigned from Sentry following an investigation into claims that he had engaged in sexual harassment. Berg's replacement, Frank Singer, assumed the title "Director of Sales" and recruited John Tailby to assume Berg's old position supervising the various sales offices. According to one witness, Tailby said Singer told him that getting rid of Gantt was to be one of his first tasks. Tailby resisted, however, and in 1981 Gantt was ranked among Sentry's top district managers in premium growth.

Bruno, meanwhile, filed a complaint with the Department of Fair Employment and Housing (DFEH). She alleged harassment by Desser and failure by Sentry's higher management to act on her complaints. Caroline Fribance, Sentry's house counsel in charge of labor-related matters, undertook to investigate the matter. Gantt informed Fribance that he had reported Bruno's complaints to personnel in Scottsdale. However, Gantt gained the impression that he was being pressured by Fribance to retract his claim that he had informed Scottsdale of the complaints. Later, following the interview with Fribance, Tailby cautioned Gantt that Singer and others in the company did not care for Gantt. In a follow-up memorandum, Tailby cautioned Gantt that "it sometimes appears that you are involved in some kind of 'intrigue' and 'undercover' operation." In December 1982, Tailby rated Gantt's overall work performance for the year as "acceptable." Without directly informing Gantt, Singer changed the rating to "borderline acceptable/ unacceptable."

Shortly thereafter, John Thompson, a DFEH investigator, contacted Fribance to arrange interviews with certain employees, including Gantt. Because of his growing unease about Fribance, Gantt arranged to meet secretly with Thompson before the scheduled interview. Gantt told him the facts of which he was aware, including his reporting of Bruno's complaints to Scottsdale, and Thompson assured him that he would be protected under the law from any retaliation for his statements. Thompson gained the impression that Gantt felt he was being pressured and was extremely fearful of retaliation because of his unfavorable testimony.

* * *

Less than two months later, on March 3, 1983, Gantt attended an awards ceremony in Scottsdale to accept a life insurance sales award on behalf of his office. The following morning, Singer and Tailby informed him that he was being demoted to sales representative. Shortly thereafter, Gantt's new supervisor, Neil Whitman, warned him that he would be fired if he attempted to undermine Whitman's authority. Gantt was also informed that he would not be given a "book" of existing accounts to start his new job; according to Gantt, such a book was necessary to survive.

During the following month, Gantt was in the office only intermittently. He experienced a variety of illnesses and took vacation time and sick leave. In mid-April he was offered and accepted a position with another company. He left Sentry's payroll in early May. Two months later, he filed the instant lawsuit alleging that "as a result of the pressure applied by the defendants * * * he was forced to resign."

As noted earlier, the jury returned a special verdict in favor of Gantt, finding, inter alia, that Gantt had been constructively discharged; that Sentry lacked an "honest good faith belief the termination was warranted for legally valid business reasons"; that Gantt was discharged "in retaliation for his refusal to testify untruthfully or to withhold testimony"; that Gantt was further discharged in retaliation for his "actions or statements with respect to Joyce Bruno's sexual harassment allegations;" and that in committing these acts Sentry acted with malice, oppression or fraud.

* * * [F]ollowing the seminal California decision in Petermann v. International Brotherhood of Teamsters, the vast majority of states have recognized that an at-will employee possesses a tort action when he or she is discharged for performing an act that public policy would encourage, or for refusing to do something that public policy would condemn.

Yet despite its broad acceptance, the principle underlying the public policy exception is more easily stated than applied. The difficulty, of course, lies in determining where and how to draw the line between claims that genuinely involve matters of public policy, and those that concern merely ordinary disputes between employer and employee. This determination depends in large part on whether the public policy alleged is sufficiently clear to provide the basis for such a potent remedy. In Foley v. Interactive Data Corp., infra, we endeavored to provide some guidelines by noting that the policy in question must involve a matter that affects society at large rather than a purely personal or proprietary interest of the plaintiff or employer; in addition, the policy must be "fundamental," "substantial" and "well established" at the time of the discharge.

We declined in Foley to determine whether the violation of a statute or constitutional provision is invariably a prerequisite to the conclusion that a discharge violates public policy. A review of the pertinent case law in California and elsewhere, however, reveals that few courts have recognized a public policy claim absent a statute or constitutional provision evidencing the policy in question. Indeed, as courts and commentators alike have noted, the cases in which violations of public policy are found generally fall into four categories: (1) refusing to violate a statute; (2) performing a statutory obligation; (3) exercising a statutory right or privilege; and (4) reporting an alleged violation of a statute of public importance.

To be sure, those courts which have addressed the issue appear to be divided over the question whether nonlegislative sources may ever provide the basis of a public policy claim. Pierce v. Ortho Pharmaceutical

Corp. (1980) 84 N.J. 58, 417 A.2d 505 is the leading case for a broad interpretation. As the New Jersey Supreme Court explained: "The sources of public policy [which may limit the employer's right of discharge] include legislation; administrative rules, regulation, or decision; and judicial decisions. In certain instances, a professional code of ethics may contain an expression of public policy." Several other states have adopted similarly broad views of the public policy exception.

Other courts have applied a stricter definition to public policy claims. The leading case is Brockmeyer v. Dun & Bradstreet (1983) 113 Wis.2d 561, 335 N.W.2d 834. There, the Wisconsin Supreme Court, while recognizing a public policy exception to the employment at-will doctrine, nevertheless limited plaintiffs to contract damages and confined such claims to statutory or constitutional violations. "Given the vagueness of the concept of public policy," the court explained, "it is necessary that we be more precise about the contours of the public policy exception. A wrongful discharge is actionable when the termination clearly contravenes the public welfare and gravely violates paramount requirements of public interest. The public policy must be evidenced by a constitutional or statutory provision." Other courts have adopted similarly restrictive views of the contours of the public policy exception.

* * *

Although we have not taken a position on this precise issue, it is true, as plaintiff notes, that this court has not previously confined itself to legislative enactments when determining the public policy of the state. We have, for example, long declined to enforce contracts inimical to law or the public interest, and long ago declared racial discrimination to be contrary to public policy under the common law duty of innkeepers and common carriers to furnish accommodations to all persons.

* * *

Unfortunately, as we have also previously acknowledged, "[t]he term 'public policy' is inherently not subject to precise definition * * *. 'By "public" policy is intended that principle of law which holds that no citizen can lawfully do that which has a tendency to be injurious to the public or against the public good * * *.'" It was this rather open-ended definition on which the court relied in *Petermann,* the seminal decision articulating the public policy exception to the employment at-will doctrine.

* * *

[C]ourts in *wrongful discharge actions* may not declare public policy without a basis in either the constitution or statutory provisions. A public policy exception carefully tethered to fundamental policies that are delineated in constitutional or statutory provisions strikes the proper balance among the interests of employers, employees and the public. The employer is bound, at a minimum, to know the fundamental public policies of the state and nation as expressed in their constitutions and statutes; so limited, the public policy exception presents no impediment to employers that operate within the bounds of law. Employees are protected against employer actions that contravene fundamental state policy. And society's interests are served through a more stable job market, in which its most important policies are safeguarded.

* * *

Initially, the parties dispute whether the discharge of an employee in retaliation for reporting a coworker's claim of sexual harassment to higher management may rise to the level of a *Tameny* violation. Sentry argues that such reporting inures only to the benefit of the employee in question rather than to the public at large, and questions the constitutional or statutory basis of such a claim. Plaintiff responds that the same constitutional provision that prohibits sexual discrimination against employees and demands a workplace free from the pernicious influence of sexual harassment also protects the employee who courageously intervenes on behalf of a harassed colleague.

Although Sentry did not discriminate against Gantt on account of his sex within the meaning of the constitutional provision, there is nevertheless direct statutory support for the jury's express finding that Sentry violated a fundamental public policy when it constructively discharged plaintiff "in retaliation for his refusal to testify untruthfully or to withhold testimony" in the course of the DFEH investigation.

* * *

The FEHA specifically enjoins any obstruction of a DFEH investigation. Government Code section 12975 provides: "Any person who shall willfully resist, prevent, impede or interfere with any member of the department or the commission or any of its agents or employees in the performance of duties pursuant to the provisions of this part relating to employment discrimination, * * * is guilty of a misdemeanor" punishable by fine or imprisonment. Nowhere in our society is the need greater than in protecting well motivated employees who come forward to testify truthfully in an administrative investigation of charges of discrimination based on sexual harassment. It is self-evident that few employees would cooperate with such investigations if the price were retaliatory discharge from employment.

Thus, any attempt to induce or coerce an employee to lie to a DFEH investigator plainly contravenes the public policy of this State. Accordingly, we hold that plaintiff established a valid *Tameny* claim based on the theory of retaliation for refusal to withhold information or to provide false information to the DFEH.

* * *

In sum, we hold that the Workers' Compensation Act does not preempt plaintiff's *Tameny* action for tortious discharge in contravention of fundamental public policy.

The judgment of the Court of Appeal is affirmed.

NOTES AND QUESTIONS

1. *Gantt* illustrates the most widely accepted formulations of the public policy exception to the at-will rule, under which individuals may not be discharged for: (1) refusing to commit unlawful acts; (2) exercising statutory rights; (3) performing public functions; or (4) reporting an employer's unlawful conduct.

2. An employee's acquiescence in past illegal acts does not preclude a wrongful discharge claim as against public policy. In Jacobs v. Universal Dev. Corp., 62 Cal.Rptr.2d 446 (Ct.App.1997), an employee fearing a retaliatory discharge had initialed purchase orders including illegal rebates. The court noted that "an employee initially acquiescing in his employer's criminality should be encouraged to cease such activity and not left without recourse when he is consequently fired."

3. Christine McKennon worked for the Nashville Banner for 30 years and was discharged in a work force reduction. McKennon, 62, alleged that she had been a victim of unlawful age discrimination. When the Banner took her deposition in the lawsuit, McKennon testified that she had copied confidential documents about the company's financial condition, taken them home, and showed them to her husband. The company then terminated her again, this time for violating its rule against unauthorized copying. The Banner said that had the company known of the copying earlier, it would have terminated her for that reason. Should the grounds for dismissal that came to light during the deposition protect the employer from the age discrimination claim? See McKennon v. Nashville Banner Publishing Co., 513 U.S. 352 (1995).

4. A nurse employed by a spine center was the victim of extreme sexual harassment by a doctor, who demanded that she leave her husband to service him and, when she refused, terminated her employment. The Virginia Supreme Court said the nurse could sue not only the hospital, her employer, but also the doctor, "an individual . . . who participated in the wrongful firing of the plaintiff." The Court said Virginia was strict about at-will employment but made an exception for a requirement that a worker violate the law, in this case by committing adultery. VanBuren v. Grubb, 733 S.E.2d 919 (Va. 2012) (4–3).

Arres v. IMI Cornelius Remcor, Inc.
333 F.3d 812 (7th Cir. 2003).

■ EASTERBROOK, CIRCUIT JUDGE:

IMI Cornelius Remcor, Inc., a manufacturer of soft drink dispensing machines, hired Janice Arres as a human resources administrator in

1996 and fired her three years later. * * * On appeal Arres has abandoned her claims under federal law and contends only that Illinois law blocks an employer from firing someone who tries to remove from the payroll aliens not entitled to work in the United States.

In March 1999 the Social Security Administration informed Remcor that 10% of the W-2 forms filed by its employees showed names or numbers that did not agree with federal records. After cross-checking, Arres found that the fault lay with the workers rather than with Remcor. She believed that persons who would furnish bogus Social Security numbers must be aliens who lack visas that authorize work within the United States. Arres recommended to both her immediate supervisor, Dan Weinick, and Weinick's supervisor, Mike Long, that Remcor immediately fire these employees. According to Arres, Remcor's longstanding practice had been to discharge persons who furnished fraudulent information. At Long's direction, Weinick informed Arres that he would handle the situation. After consulting with the Social Security Administration and one of Remcor's attorneys, Weinick decided to send letters to the employees asking them to correct any errors. Arres believed that approach to be unlawful, and she refused to process the information employees submitted in response. Arres submits that Remcor fired her because of this refusal, a step that she says constitutes retaliatory discharge in violation of Illinois law.

* * *

Arres is wrong to suppose that either state or federal law gives her any right to follow an idiosyncratic view of the law's demands. Remcor did exactly what the Social Security Administration and its legal counsel suggested: before firing anyone, it tried to separate those who had made inadvertent errors from those who are not entitled to work in the United States. Doing this enabled Remcor to respect the rights of aliens who have work authorization while also following its duties under §§ 1324 and 1324a. A human resources manager is not free to impose a different approach unilaterally; that's nothing but insubordination. Imagine the disruption in workplaces everywhere if every person were legally privileged to act (or not act) based on her own view of what the law (federal or state) requires, and managers were helpless to do anything in response. Neither state nor federal law creates such an untenable system. * * * Remcor sought out and followed legal advice. It was entitled to insist that Arres, like its other employees, follow the advice received from counsel—which is not alleged to be erroneous, let alone so transparently wrong that even a lay person is bound to know better. (Even with the aid of discovery, Arres has not established that the employees in question were aliens, let alone that any aliens among them lacked green cards. For all this record shows, each had made a simple error in transcribing a Social Security number.)

* * *

Federal immigration power is not just superior to that of the states; it is exclusive of any state power over the subject. Illinois is not entitled to have a policy on the question what precautions should be taken to evaluate the credentials of aliens who may, or may not, hold visas authorizing them to work. Whether persons in Arres' position are entitled to implement private understandings of federal immigration policy, free from any risk to their status within the firm, is a question of federal law alone. Congress provided an antiretaliation provision in § 1324b and omitted one from § 1324a. Illinois is not free to obliterate this difference through state law—and we have no reason to suppose that the Supreme Court of Illinois would try. That leaves Arres without a legal footing for her claim of retaliatory discharge and makes it unnecessary for us to explore the question whether Arres has established causation.

NOTES AND QUESTIONS

1. Not all states have endorsed the public policy exception to the at-will rule. In Murphy v. American Home Prods. Corp., 448 N.E.2d 86 (N.Y. 1983). Joseph Murphy, the 59-year-old assistant treasurer for the defendant corporation, claimed he was discharged "because of his disclosure to top management of alleged accounting improprieties on the part of corporate personnel." The court refused to allow the claim:

> Those jurisdictions that have modified the traditional at-will rule appear to have been motivated by conclusions that the freedom of contract underpinnings of the rule have become outdated, that individual employees in the modern work force do not have the bargaining power to negotiate security for the jobs on which they have grown to rely, and that the rule yields harsh results for those employees who do not enjoy the benefits of express contractual limitations on the power of dismissal. Whether these conclusions are supportable or whether for other compelling reasons employers should, as a matter of policy, be held liable to at-will employees discharged in circumstances for which no liability has existed at common law, are issues better left to resolution at the hands of the Legislature. In addition to the fundamental question whether such liability should be recognized in New York, of no less practical importance is the definition of its configuration if it is to be recognized.

> Both of these aspects of the issue, involving perception and declaration of relevant public policy are best and more appropriately explored and resolved by the legislative branch of our government. The Legislature has infinitely greater resources and procedural means to discern the public will, to examine the variety of pertinent considerations, to elicit the views of the various segments of the community that would be directly affected and in any event critically interested, and to investigate and anticipate the impact of imposition of such liability. Standards should doubtless be established applicable to the multifarious types of

employment and the various circumstances of discharge. If the rule of nonliability for termination of at-will employment is to be tempered, it should be accomplished through a principled statutory scheme, adopted after opportunity for public ventilation, rather than in consequence of judicial resolution of the partisan arguments of individual adversarial litigants.

Additionally, if the rights and obligations under a relationship forged, perhaps some time ago, between employer and employee in reliance on existing legal principles are to be significantly altered, a fitting accommodation of the competing interests to be affected may well dictate that any change should be given prospective effect only, or at least so the Legislature might conclude.

448 N.E.2d at 89–90.

The New York Court of Appeals reaffirmed the position it stated in Murphy in Sullivan v. Harnisch, 969 N.E.2d 758 (N.Y. 2012)(5–2). Joseph Sullivan, compliance officer of a hedge fund, said he was fired by William Harnisch, the CEO and majority owner, for objecting that sales of stock by Harnisch for his personal account and the accounts of family members were "front-running" (sales in anticipation of sales by clients of the firm that were likely to lower stock prices). So it remains the case that New York's only affirmation of the public policy tort was Wieder v. Skala, 609 N.E.2d 105 (1992) (tort for law firm to fire lawyer for standing up for the ethical obligations of members of the bar).

2. "Public policy" can include the public policy of a foreign country. A New Jersey employee was permitted to allege that he was discharged in retaliation for objecting to excessive levels of benzene in gasoline produced and sold by the employer's subsidiary in Japan in violation of Japanese law. Mehlman v. Mobil Oil Corp., 707 A.2d 1000 (N.J.1998). Finding an articulated public policy is often difficult. In Lynn v. Wal-Mart Stores, Inc., 280 S.W.3d 574 (Ark. Ct. App. 2008), Lynn, an employee, asserted a claim of wrongful discharge in violation of public policy alleging that he was terminated for reporting inhumane workplace conditions in manufacturing facilities from which Wal-Mart buys goods. Lynn claimed his termination violated the public policy articulated in the Arkansas Deceptive Trade Practices Act, which protects the consumer from the deceptive practice of making false representation concerning the source or certification of goods. Lynn claimed Wal-Mart did just that in the company's annual report about its factory-certification process. The court affirmed a grant of summary judgment, holding that even if the court were to accept Lynn's factual allegation as true, "Lynn has simply shown no nexus between his reports of problems with the factory-certification process and any public policy of this state."

3. An at-will employee asserted that he was fired in retaliation for obeying a federal grand jury subpoena. The Supreme Court said that this states a claim for damages under the Civil Rights Act of 1871, 42 U.S.C.A. § 1985(2), which proscribes conspiracies to "deter, by force, intimidation, or threat, any

* * * witness * * * from attending such court * * *." Haddle v. Garrison, 525 U.S. 121 (1998).

4. In 2006, Debra Parks was fired by Alpharma, Inc. after having complained about Alpharma's policy of failing to inform doctors and the FDA that its drug Kadian could be harmful if taken in conjunction with other pain medications or with alcohol. Parks argued that a public policy exception should apply because the public has an interest in not being unknowingly poisoned. The Court of Appeals of Maryland, answering a certified question from the Fourth Circuit, declined to apply a public policy exception, noting that "Maryland has adopted a more conservative view of what is actionable, not wishing to involve the courts in borderline claims where the violation of public policy is not so clear." Parks v. Alpharma, Inc., 25 A.3d 200 (Md. 2011). The Fourth Circuit essentially accepted this position, holding that Parks failed to satisfy the notice prong of her retaliation claim. The court emphasized that the employer must be aware of an employee's conduct to be held to have unlawfully retaliated. U.S. ex rel. Parks v. Alpharma, Inc., 493 F. App'x 380 (4th Cir. 2012) (unpublished).

b.   STATUTORY AND CONSTITUTIONAL RIGHTS

Another public policy exception to at-will employment that the courts have enforced is the employee's right to be free from discharge for exercising statutory or constitutional rights, including the whistleblower protections discussed in Part A, supra, as well as other rights such as filing worker's compensation claims discussed in Chapter 10. But what happens when the employer's right to create workplace standards clashes with the constitutional rights of its employees?

Hansen v. America Online, Inc.
96 P.3d 950 (Utah 2004).

■ NEHRING, JUSTICE:

Messrs. Hansen, Melling and Carlson, whom for convenience we will refer to as "the employees," were employed by America Online ("AOL") at its call center in Ogden, Utah. The Ogden call center is located in a strip mall. AOL leased, and reserved for its exclusive use, up to 350 parking stalls from the strip mall's larger public parking lot.

AOL's company policy prohibited employees at the Ogden Call Center from carrying or possessing a firearm of any type at the call center or in its exclusive parking lot. Printed notice of the policy was displayed in the entrance lobby to the Ogden Call Center. The employees admitted that they each had seen this policy displayed and knew the terms of AOL's Workplace Violence Prevention Policy at the time they brought firearms onto the AOL parking lot.

On September 14, 2000, the three employees, all of whom were off-duty at the time, met in the lot where their cars were parked. Each had a firearm in his car, and they planned to go target shooting at a local gun range. An AOL security camera recorded Messrs. Melling and Carlson transferring their guns to Mr. Hansen's car in the parking lot. Four days later, AOL discharged the employees. Although each employee was an at-will employee and could be terminated without cause, AOL acknowledged that the men were discharged because they violated AOL's Workplace Violence Prevention Policy.

The employees then filed a lawsuit alleging wrongful termination. They alleged that, the AOL Workplace Violence Prevention Policy notwithstanding, AOL was liable for their wrongful discharge because their possession of firearms on the AOL parking lot was protected by a clear and substantial public, policy. Both the employees and AOL filed motions for summary judgment. The trial court issued a memorandum decision denying the employees' motion and granting AOL's motion. The employees appeal. We affirm.

* * *

Owing to the stability and predictability afforded employers and employees by the at-will rule, we have been justifiably wary of brushing broad public policy landscapes on the canvas of these cases, electing instead to limit the horizon of these cases by their facts. We have, however, outlined four categories of public policies eligible for consideration under the exception. These are:

(i) refusing to commit an illegal or wrongful act, such as refusing to violate the antitrust laws; (ii) performing a public obligation, such as accepting jury duty; (iii) exercising a legal right or privilege, such as filing a workers' compensation claim; or (iv) reporting to a public authority criminal activity of the employer.

The third category of conduct, exercising a legal right or privilege, poses analytical challenges different from, and generally greater than, the others. An employer owes a duty to an employee, independent of any duty imposed by the contract of employment, not to exploit the employment relationship by demanding that an employee choose between continued employment and violating a law or failing to perform a public obligation of clear and substantial public import. The employer's legal duty emanates from the recognition that the extortionate use of termination to coerce an employee to commit unlawful acts or avoid public obligations serves no legitimate economic objective and corrodes civil society.

By contrast, an employer's insistence that an employee relinquish a legal right or privilege, even a right or privilege which carries strong public policy credentials, will not expose the employee to possible criminal penalties or other legal sanctions. In most cases, such demands by an employer will not thrust the employee between conflicting imperatives of wage earning and responsible citizenship. The analysis of whether the public policy exception applies to a particular legal right or privilege will frequently require a balancing of competing legitimate interests: the interests of the employer to regulate the workplace environment to promote productivity, security, and similar lawful business objectives, and the interests of the employees to maximize access to their statutory and constitutional rights within the workplace. When an employee, like the employees here, seeks protection within the exercise of a legal right or privilege category of the public policy exception, both the employer and the employee may appeal to public policy in aid of their cause.

* * *

During its 2004 annual general session, the legislature enacted a chapter of the Utah Code known as the "Uniform Firearms Laws." [The bill regulates sale and possession of firearms]. * * * Debate of the bill in the House of Representatives echoed the Senate's sensitivity to the bill's private property implications. Representative Stephen Urquhart was a particularly vigorous advocate of the preeminence of private property rights, stating that it was the intention of the bill that private property rights govern * * *.

This debate amply captures the tension between two familiar antagonists: the right to regulate one's own private property and the right to keep and bear arms. Our task is to determine whether the right to keep and bear arms in Utah is a public policy which is so clear and substantial as to supersede an employer's attempt to restrict weapons in the workplace by contract. We hold that it does not. We read the language of [the statute] to indicate that the legislature has purposefully declined to give the right to keep and bear arms absolute preeminence over the right to regulate one's own private property.

The employees attempt to add heft to their argument that their right to possess firearms is sufficiently substantial to overcome the at-will doctrine with citations to anecdotal evidence that private and public security is better safeguarded by an armed citizenry. According to the employees, Utah's Constitution and statutes have so embraced this doctrine of peacekeeping that fundamental protections of private property must give way to it. The debates within our legislature suggest otherwise.

The legislative debates over [the statute] suggest that to the extent Utah has a "clear and substantial" public policy relating to the possession of firearms, public policy does not implicate an employer's right to restrict firearms in a parking lot leased by the employer and to terminate an at-will employee for violating that prohibition. Thus, in keeping with our view that the public policy exception may be invoked only sparingly in circumstances where the cause of an employee's discharge implicates a public policy of such clarity and substance to impose on the employer a legal duty independent of contract rights inherent in the at-will doctrine, we affirm the judgment of the trial court.

NOTES AND QUESTIONS

1. *Hansen* forces the court to balance two legitimate issues: the employee's legal right or privilege and the employer's interest in regulating the workplace environment. The *Hansen* court stressed the importance of the workplace being a private property and weighed that factor heavily in ultimately ruling in favor of the employer. Would the outcome be different if the property did not belong to the employer? In Plona v. UPS, 2007 WL 509747 (N.D. Ohio 2007), an employee of UPS was terminated when he was discovered with a disassembled gun locked in his car during work. The possession of the weapon was legal but not allowed under UPS policies. The employee challenged the termination as a violation of public policy. The district court, in dismissing UPS's motion for summary judgment, stated that the Ohio constitution which gives people a right to bear arms for their defense and security creates a clear public policy. Furthermore, the district court emphasized that the important question is where a right is being limited. The employee's car was found in a public parking accessible to both UPS employees and others. Therefore, "punishing employees for exercising constitutional rights while outside the workplace jeopardizes public policy to a much greater degree." For a further discussion of employee guns in the workplace, see p. 770, note 7.

2. In cases where statutory-constitutional conflicts like the one discussed in *Hansen* do not exist, many jurisdictions have upheld an employee's right to be free from discharge for exercising statutory rights. See, e.g., Perks v. Firestone Tire & Rubber Co., 611 F.2d 1363 (3d Cir. 1979) (discharge for refusal to take statutorily prohibited polygraph test); Smith v. Atlas Off-Shore Boat Serv., Inc., 653 F.2d 1057 (5th Cir. 1981) (discharge for filing injury suit under Jones Act); Savodnik v. Korvettes, Inc., 488 F.Supp. 822 (E.D.N.Y.1980) (discharge to prevent pension from vesting); Bowman v. State Bank, 331 S.E.2d 797 (Va.1985) (employee-stockholders discharged for refusing to vote in favor of merger to which they were opposed). But see Martin v. Tapley, 360 So.2d 708 (Ala.1978) (contract "at-will" means what it says; where employee compensated for work-related injuries, employer has satisfied whatever implied contractual duty it owed to employee at-will in regards to Workmen's Compensation Act).

3. A California court of appeals narrowed the scope of the public policy wrongful discharge tort in Sequoia Ins. Co. v. Superior Court, 16 Cal.Rptr.2d 888 (Cal.App.1993). Interpreting *Gantt,* the court held that a public policy must be based on policies delineated by a statutory or constitutional provision and must be described "in detail * * * with sharpness or vividness" to allow the employer to know the fundamental public policies expressed in that law. An administrative regulation issued by an agency to which the legislature has delegated authority can be the basis for a public policy tort. Plaintiff was employed by a child care facility. Her employer, seeking to earn higher profits, wanted to have a teacher-child ratio that plaintiff reasonably believed would violate a regulation issued by the state Department of Human Services. The Iowa Supreme Court affirmed a jury determination that plaintiff's discharge for contesting the employer's policies was tortious, though it reduced some of the emotional distress and punitive damages. Jasper v. H. Nizam, Inc., 764 N.W.2d 751 (Iowa 2009).

4. In Wagenseller v. Scottsdale Mem. Hosp., 710 P.2d 1025 (Ariz. 1985), Catherine Wagenseller went on a company rafting trip where she "refused to join in the group's staging of a parody of the song 'Moon River,' which allegedly concluded with members of the group 'mooning' the audience." Wagenseller claimed that she was discharged for her failure to participate, in violation public policy. The court agreed, citing the state's indecent exposure statute as a recognition of "bodily privacy as a 'citizen's social right.'" The Arizona legislature responded with the Arizona Employment Protection Act, Ariz. Rev. Stat. § 23–1501 et seq., in 1996. In its introduction, the statute states that "an employer may be held liable for civil damages in the event it discharges from employment an employee for a reason that is against the public policy of this state. However, public policy is expressly determined by the legislature in the form of statutory provisions."

5. Some states have attempted to prevent the unfair treatment of employees by expanding the classes of persons protected by statutory anti-discrimination provisions or otherwise granting employees additional statutory rights in employment. For example, more than half the states have laws providing that it is unlawful to discriminate against private sector employees who engage in political activity. See Nelson v. McClatchy Newspapers, Inc., supra p. 746. But Idaho public policy was not violated when a bank told a teller that if she ran for county treasurer she would have to resign her job two weeks before the primary. McKay v. Ireland Bank, 59 P.3d 990 (Idaho App.2002). Other states prohibit discrimination based on status as a recipient of public assistance (e.g., Minn.), for filing a complaint alleging domestic violence (e.g., R.I.), or marital status. In Minnesota v. Floyd Wild, Inc., 384 N.W.2d 185 (Minn.Ct.App.1986), the court held that the state's marital status discrimination law did not apply to the discharge of the former daughter-in-law of the employer following a contentious divorce.

6. Reporting an employer's unlawful conduct has been protected under the public policy exception to at-will employment. However, courts have distinguished cases where employees are discharged for reporting wrongdoing to law enforcement agencies or regulatory agencies, and those where the wrongdoing is reported internally, within the company. See, e.g., Fox v. MCI Commc'ns Corp., 931 P.2d 857 (Utah 1997) (retaliatory discharge for reporting employee's fraudulent sales practices to employer does not contravene public policy, but discharge resulting from informing the police or authorities will support an action for wrongful discharge).

7. In Pennsylvania, retaliatory termination in violation of the federal Occupational Safety and Health Act would not trigger the public policy exception to at-will employment because OSHA is not "a clear and substantial public policy in this Commonwealth." Pennsylvania looks to "our own Constitution, court decisions and statutes promulgated by the legislature." The dissenting justices said that the Pennsylvania Health and Safety Act provides "a sufficient basis for Appellant's allegation of a public policy violation." McLaughlin v. Gastrointestinal Specialists, Inc., 750 A.2d 283 (Pa. 2000).

In California, the Compassionate Use Act of 1996, approved by voter referendum, allows people who use marijuana for medical purposes a defense against state criminal charges of possession. Possession of marijuana, however, continues to be prohibited under federal law which lists marijuana as a highly addictive substance. United States v. Oakland Cannabis Buyers' Co-op., 532 U.S. 483 (2001). Does the Compassionate Use Act state a clear California public policy? If so, how do these conflicting state and federal policies apply in the employment context? In Ross v. RagingWire Telecomms., Inc., 174 P.3d 200 (Cal. 2008), a newly hired employee who suffered chronic pain from a past injury received while serving in the Air Force was required to take a drug test before starting work as a lead systems administrator. Despite showing his employer his physician's recommendation for the use of marijuana, the employee was terminated when he failed to pass a pre-employment drug test despite that drug use occurring during off-duty hours and not affecting the employee's job performance. The California Supreme Court affirmed a holding that the employee did not state an action for termination in violation of public policy, reasoning that the Compassionate Use Act was not intended to eliminate an employer's "legitimate interest in whether an employee uses the drug" and the measure was not intended to "address the respective rights and duties of employers and employees." Similarly, the Court held that the California Fair Employment and Housing Act (FEHA), which protects employees from disability-based discrimination, does not require an employer to accommodate an employee who uses marijuana for medicinal purposes. Judges Kennard and Moreno, dissenting, argued that the majority decision lacks compassion and thwarts the will of the people of California who voted for this law, also violating the employee's right not to be discriminated against under FEHA. The dissent agreed with the majority, however, that because federal law prohibits marijuana possession, the employee cannot support a claim of termination in violation of public policy.

8.   Wisconsin refused to grant public policy protection against discharge to an employee fired for giving racist comments to a newspaper. Graebel v. Am. Dynatec Corp., 604 N.W.2d 35 (Wis. Ct. App. 1999).

9.   Plaintiff said she was terminated for saying that she would consult an attorney before signing a written warning of inadequate performance. Held: public policy does not support a right to consult with an attorney. Porterfield v. Mascari II, Inc., 823 A.2d 590 (Md. 2003).

10.   An employee who alleged that he was terminated because he was a victim of domestic violence did not state a public policy exception to at-will employment. Plaintiff had been hospitalized when his wife shot him. "Domestic violence is * * * but one of many social problems * * *. Poverty, child abuse, juvenile delinquency, substance—all are examples of social ills our General Statutes seek to alleviate * * *. We do not interpret such statutes, however, as creating specialized and protected classes of persons entitled to employment and other status protection." Imes v. City of Asheville, 594 S.E.2d 397 (N.C. App. 2004), aff'd, 606 S.E.2d 117 (N.C. 2004).

11. Nathan Berry, employed by Liberty Holdings, was involved in an auto accident with Premier Concrete Pumping. Both Premier and Liberty were partially owned by the same person, Brent Voss. Berry successfully filed a personal injury lawsuit and nine months later was fired. Berry asserted that public policy protected him from being terminated for exercising his right to file lawsuits. The Iowa Supreme Court said that much like the right to consult with an attorney, the right to file lawsuits against an employer is not supported by public policy. The court said that the existence of a legal framework permitting an activity is insufficient to prove a state public policy in favor of the activity. More broadly, "legislative pronouncements that are limited in scope may not support a public policy beyond the specific scope of the statute." Berry v. Liberty Holdings, Inc., 803 N.W.2d 106 (Iowa 2011).

12. Joyce Martin had been working at Clinical Pathology Laboratories (CPL) for three years when she requested permission to leave work early to vote in the general election. CPL refused permission, but Martin nonetheless left work 15 minutes early to vote. Two days later, CPL terminated Martin's employment. Martin claimed public policy protection for her right to vote, citing the Texas Election Code, which prohibits employers from refusing to permit employees to be absent from work on election day for the purpose of attending the polls to vote. The Texas Court of Appeals, however, concluded that the criminal penalties of the Texas Election Code were sufficient and that the legislature did not intend to create a common-law exception to at-will employment: "Our general rule is that we, as an intermediate appellate court, will not adopt new common-law exceptions to the employment-at-will doctrine." Martin v. Clinical Pathology Laboratories, Inc., 343 S.W.3d 885 (Tex. Ct. App. 2011).

c.   PUBLIC HEALTH AND SAFETY

Some courts have upheld wrongful discharge claims on a public policy basis even without a statutory rationale. Public health and safety has been recognized by courts as an important non-statutory source for public policy exceptions.

Gardner v. Loomis Armored, Inc.

913 P.2d 377 (Wash. 1996).

■ DOLLIVER, J.:

Plaintiff, Kevin M. Gardner, worked for Defendant, Loomis Armored Inc. (Loomis), as a guard and driver of an armored car. On March 10, 1994, Gardner and his partner, Steffon Sobosky, made a scheduled stop at a Seafirst Bank branch in Spokane. Sobosky got out of the truck and entered the bank while Gardner stayed in the driver's compartment.

Gardner then saw a woman, whom he recognized as the bank manager, run out of the bank while pointing behind her and screaming. Gardner looked behind the manager and saw a man with a knife chasing her. The armed man (hereinafter referred to as the suspect) was approximately 15 feet behind the manager. While running past the front of the truck, the manager looked straight at Gardner and cried out, "Help me, help me." * * * Gardner looked around the parking lot and saw nobody coming to help the manager. After the manager and the suspect ran past the front of the truck, Gardner got out, locking the door behind him. As he got out of the truck, he temporarily lost sight of the manager and the suspect, who were both on the passenger side of the truck. While out of Gardner's view, the manager reached a drive-in teller booth across the parking lot, where she found refuge. It is unclear whether the manager was safe before Gardner left the truck, but by the time Gardner walked forward to a point where he could see the suspect, the suspect had already grabbed another woman who was walking into the bank. Gardner recognized the second woman as Kathy Martin, an employee of Plant World, who watered plants at the bank. The suspect put the knife to Ms. Martin's throat and dragged her back into the bank. Gardner followed them into the bank where he observed his partner, Sobosky, with his gun drawn and aimed at the suspect. When Sobosky distracted the suspect, Gardner and a bank customer tackled the suspect and disarmed him. The police arrived immediately thereafter and took custody of the suspect. Ms. Martin was unharmed.

Loomis has a "fundamental" company rule forbidding armored truck drivers from leaving the truck unattended. The employee handbook states, "[v]iolations of this rule will be grounds for termination." Drivers may not exit the compartment under any circumstance. This rule is for the safety of both the driver and the partner who enters the businesses to make pickups or deliveries. The rule is so absolute, the driver is not allowed to get out of the truck when pulled over by someone who appears to be a police officer. Instead, the driver must show the officer a card which explains the driver will follow the officer to the police station. When emergencies arise, the driver, although confined to the compartment, can summon help or take other action using the two-way radio, public address system, and sirens.

Gardner was fired for violating this work rule by exiting the truck during the March 10, 1994, incident. Gardner's partner was not disciplined in any way for his involvement with the hostage situation. Gardner sued Loomis * * * [claiming] wrongful discharge in violation of public policy.

* * *

We find that Gardner's discharge for leaving the truck and saving a woman from an imminent life threatening situation violates the public policy encouraging such heroic conduct. This holding does not create an affirmative legal duty requiring citizens to intervene in dangerous life threatening situations. We simply observe that society values and encourages voluntary rescuers when a life is in danger. Additionally, our adherence to this public policy does nothing to invalidate Loomis' work rule regarding drivers' leaving the trucks. The rule's importance cannot be understated, and drivers do subject themselves to a great risk of harm by leaving the driver's compartment. Our holding merely forbids Loomis from firing Gardner when he broke the rule because he saw a woman who faced imminent life-threatening harm, and he reasonably believed his intervention was necessary to save her life. Finally, by focusing on the narrow public policy encouraging citizens to save human lives from life threatening situations, we continue to protect employers from frivolous lawsuits.

■ GUY, J., concurring:

I concur in the result reached by the majority because I believe it was a violation of public policy when the employer applied this work rule *under the facts existing here* in order to fire Mr. Gardner. I would not find this work rule to be in violation of public policy in a general sense. However, in this case Mr. Gardner was faced with the decision whether to break what is normally a sensible and reasonable rule for his own and his partner's safety and save a woman's life *or* adhere to the rule and watch a woman he knew be murdered in front of him while he sat safely in his truck with a gun in hand. It defies what I believe is true about human nature that anyone would be willing to watch a person die in order to comply with a company safety rule. I believe our nature would cause any decent person, under these dire circumstances, to break the rule and save the life. Even normally good rules must have exceptions and yield to a higher good. When the company chose to enforce the rule under these facts, it failed to recognize that Mr. Gardner was acting for the higher good, as would any right-thinking person.

■ MADSEN, J., dissenting:

Relying on a dubious formulation of public policy, the majority today invalidates a company work rule designed to protect the lives of men and women employed as drivers in the unique and highly dangerous occupation of operating armored cars. I dissent.

* * *

Instead of leaving the armored car when emergencies arise, the driver can summon help by using the truck's two-way radio, public address system, and sirens. Indeed, it is likely that in most instances these measures would be more effective in saving lives than would be the driver's actions in leaving an armored car. The majority's earlier criticism of people engaging in law enforcement is equally pertinent to a situation where a driver leaves the safety of an armored vehicle to confront an uncertain and dangerous situation: "Public policy is not furthered by encouraging citizens to jump into the midst of every criminal situation. Citizens have not had law enforcement training, and their involvement in many situations can create additional risks of harm to those involved."

Loomis argues persuasively that its work rule promotes rather than conflicts with a policy of saving lives:

The armored car business operates in a very dangerous world, where the goal of those few citizens who necessitate the very use of armored cars is to get the people inside the car to open it up to the people outside the car. It is not hyperbole to state that, in such situations, the armored car, with its bulletproof glass, sirens and two-way radios, is as much a lifeline for the driver/guards and their custodian/partners who are out of the armored truck as it is a secure depository for valuable commodities.

* * * [The majority] takes no notice of the fact that armored car companies and their drivers are relatively few in number, or that their rule forbidding a driver from leaving a truck is actually intended to save lives. I agree with Loomis that "[w]hen one looks past the limited and emotionally charged facts of the instant case, it becomes clear that Loomis' maligned work rule actually serves the interests of society, is consistent with public policy and therefore cannot be the basis of a claim for wrongful termination in violation of public policy."

* * *

Moreover, the majority takes no notice of the new role that its opinion will thrust upon the courts of this state. Under the guise of a claim that the public policy exception to the terminable-at-will doctrine should apply, courts will now be forced to analyze an employer's work rules to determine whether they provide proper cause for termination. This type of micromanagement of business is a complete misapplication of the public policy exception, and can hardly be the result intended by the court's [earlier] acceptance of a narrow exception to the at-will rule.

There is no question that the Loomis rule forbidding Gardner from leaving the truck is based on the substantiated conclusion that a driver's departure endangers his own and/or another's life. I therefore cannot conclude that the Loomis rule violates a public policy in favor of saving lives and would uphold the enforcement of that rule in this case. Mr. Gardner's termination does not fit within the narrow parameters of a wrongful discharge in violation of public policy.

NOTES AND QUESTIONS

1.   Employee grabbed and subdued a robber at 4 a.m. in violation of the employer's policy. Held: the right of self-defense is a substantial public policy of the state of West Virginia. The court quoted a 1923 West Virginia case: "In defending himself, his family or his property from the assault of an intruder, one is not limited to his immediate home or castle; his right to stand his ground in defense thereof without retreating extends to his place of business also and where it is necessary he may take the life of his assailant or intruder." But the employer may rebut the employee's prima facie case of wrongful discharge in violation of public policy by demonstrating a plausible and legitimate business reason, such as protection of customers or other

workers, for terminating the employee. Feliciano v. 7-Eleven, Inc., 559 S.E.2d 713 (W.Va.2001).

2. An aircraft parts inspector was discharged for objecting to the shipping of defective airline parts to airline manufacturers, although there was no express statutory provision dealing with such a situation. The employee brought an action for wrongful discharge in violation of public policy. The Supreme Court of California found that "the federal safety regulations promulgated to address important public safety concerns may serve as a source of fundamental public policy. The regulations satisfy our requirement that the action be tethered to fundamental policies delineated in a statutory or constitutional provision." Green v. Ralee Eng'g Co., 960 P.2d 1046, 1050 (Cal. 1998).

Furthermore, in Franklin v. Monadnock Co., 59 Cal.Rptr.3d 692 (Cal. Ct. App. 2007), the court held that public policy requires employers to provide safe and secure workplaces. The court reversed a grant of summary judgment in favor of the employer based on this holding. The plaintiff claimed that he warned his employer that a colleague was threatening to kill the plaintiff and others in the workplace. When the employer did nothing to address the situation, plaintiff reported it to authorities and was subsequently terminated. The court reasoned that plaintiff stated a claim because public policy supports encouraging employees to report credible threats of violence in the workplace.

3. In the absence of a direct nexus to the workplace, assertions of a general public policy in favor of safety and health have been rejected. For example, in Upton v. JWP Businessland, 682 N.E.2d 1357 (Mass.1997), a single mother was discharged for refusing to work newly-imposed long hours (8:15 A.M. to 10 P.M. six days a week), because it would prevent her from being with her young child. The court upheld the discharge, rejecting the argument that a purported public policy favoring care and protection of children supported a common law action for wrongful discharge.

4. Plaintiff, a hospital employee, was terminated for violating a patient's confidentiality by revealing to a school teacher that a student in the teacher's class might pose a public health risk. The hospital terminated the employee for violating patient confidentiality. The appellate court agreed with the plaintiff, reversing the trial court's grant of summary judgment in favor of the hospital. The court cited numerous New Jersey statutes dealing with the protection of children as sufficient evidence of a public policy mandate. Do you agree? What about the competing public policy of patient confidentiality? Does healthcare require special public policy protection due to the special nature of the consequences? Serrano v. Christ Hosp., 945 A.2d 1288 (N.J. 2008). Compare Turner v. Memorial Med. Ctr., 911 N.E.2d 369 (Ill. 2009), where the plaintiff, a licensed respiratory therapist working for the defendant hospital, was asked to speak with a surveyor from the Joint Commission on Accreditation of Healthcare Organizations during an accreditation inspection. The plaintiff truthfully advised the surveyor that the hospital's policy on charting patient care differed from the accreditation standards, thereby endangering patient safety. After being discharged, the plaintiff sued claiming a violation of the public policy of promoting patient safety. The Supreme Court of Illinois held that "patient safety" was not a clearly mandated public policy of the state and therefore would not support a claim for retaliatory discharge.

5.   Phyllis Delaney said she was dismissed for seeking four weeks off from work to donate a kidney to her brother. The Missouri Court of Appeals held that the state's public policy encourages organ donation and reversed a trial court decision dismissing Ms. Delaney's lawsuit. Delaney v. Signature Health Care Foundation, 376 S.W.3d 55 (Mo. Ct. App. 2012). California law requires 30 days of paid leave for an employee who is an organ donor. Cal. Lab. Code §§ 1508–1513.

d.   STANDARDS OF PROFESSIONAL CONDUCT

In *Gantt,* the court refused to find a public policy basis for wrongful discharge that was not grounded in a constitutional or statutory provision. However, a number of jurisdictions have recognized non-legislative sources of public policy. For example, in Rocky Mtn. Hosp. & Med. Serv. v. Mariani, 916 P.2d 519 (Colo.1996), Diana Mariana refused to violate the Colorado State Board of Accountancy Rules of Professional Conduct and was discharged as a result. The court ruled that rules of professional conduct for accountants have an important public purpose, and thus the discharge of an accountant for refusing to violate such rules was void as against public policy. See also Boyle v. Vista Eyewear, Inc., 700 S.W.2d 859 (Mo.Ct.App.1985) (regulatory provisions, judicial decisions, and professional codes of ethics are acceptable).

Similarly, New York cut back on at-will employment in Wieder v. Skala, 609 N.E.2d 105 (N.Y.1992), by limiting a law firm's unfettered right to discharge an associate. The dismissed attorney alleged that he was fired for insisting that the firm report the professional misconduct of another associate to the Bar disciplinary committee. Subsequently, however, Horn v. New York Times, 790 N.E.2d 753 (N.Y. 2003), rejected the argument that an implied contract term precluded an employer from dismissing a physician because she refused to share patients' medical records with individuals not authorized to have them. Dr. Horn was associate medical director of the New York Times' medical department.

PROBLEMS

In which of the following circumstances should the employee have an action for wrongful discharge in violation of public policy? Why? What is the public policy at issue?

a.   A doctor was discharged for refusing to violate the Hippocratic oath by performing experimental human research using a controversial drug she believed to be harmful. See Pierce v. Ortho Pharmaceutical Corp., 417 A.2d 505 (N.J.1980) (holding that because the employee contended that the drug was controversial, rather than harmful, she had no claim). Consider also the experienced nurse who was discharged for opposing her employer's proposed staffing cuts, which in her professional opinion would have left the hospital grossly understaffed. See Lampe v. Presbyterian Med. Ctr., 590 P.2d 513 (Colo.App.1978) (holding that the broad, general statement of policy contained in statutes creating State Board of Nursing and giving Board authority to discipline nurses permitted discharge). Cf. Dabbs v. Cardiopulmonary Mgmt. Servs., 234 Cal.Rptr. 129 (Cal.App.1987).

b.   The wife and two year-old daughter of a supermarket employee were shopping in the supermarket when a glass container exploded, causing a piece of glass to enter the child's eye. After rejecting a $200 settlement offer from the store's insurance company, the employee sued, on his daughter's behalf, the supermarket and the container manufacturer. He was discharged when he refused to withdraw the suit. See DeMarco v. Publix Super Mkts., Inc., 384 So.2d 1253 (Fla.1980) (Supreme Court held that employee could not maintain his action for wrongful termination of employment, in light of fact that there was no civil cause of action for interference with exercise of right to access to courts).

c.   An employee got into a fight in the company parking lot with another employee who was drunk: the sober employee had refused to return the drunk employee's car keys to him, to keep him from driving while drunk, and a fight broke out. The company discharged both employees. Is the sober employee's discharge a violation of the public policy against drunk driving? See Stilphen v. Northrop Corp., 515 N.E.2d 154 (Ill.App.1987) (holding that the employee was discharged because the means which he employed in the furtherance of those goals, regardless of the merit of his alleged goals, led to his fighting with a fellow employee in his employer's parking lot, which was itself a legitimate reason for discharge).

3. OVERLAPPING AND CONFLICTING REMEDIES

In one sense, the various causes of action that have lately been recognized by the judiciary as providing potential remedies for employees who have been wrongly discharged break new legal ground, in that individuals who had no legal redress in the past may now seek objective judicial evaluation of their right to employment. In another sense, however, these common law actions are not so much harbingers of a more pro-employee legal system as they are the newest arrivals to a legal landscape already populated with federal and state statutes that attempt to protect employees from unfair employer practices. In many instances, a wrongfully discharged individual may have several alternative courses of action, not all of which are necessarily consistent. For instance, a victim of sexual harassment could sue under Title VII of the Civil Rights Act of 1964 or for intentional infliction of emotional distress. To the extent that the trend toward increased recognition of individual rights continues, there will be more cases where statutory and common law rights and remedies overlap—and sometimes conflict.

Should an aggrieved employee be permitted to pursue several possible remedies simultaneously, should he or she have to make an election among them, or should the existence of one preclude access to the others? Prior developments in other employment cases establish two quite distinct—indeed, contradictory—lines of precedent, one arising under the National Labor Relations Act and the other under Title VII.

In San Diego Bldg. Trades Council v. Garmon, 359 U.S. 236 (1959), the Supreme Court held that the primary jurisdiction of the National Labor Relations Board preempted state regulation of behavior which was either "arguably protected" or "arguably prohibited" under §§ 7 and 8 of the NLRA, unless the challenged activity was of only peripheral concern to the Act or the regulated conduct "touched interests so deeply rooted in local feeling and responsibility that, in the absence of compelling congressional direction, we could not infer that Congress had deprived the states of the power to act." In later cases, the Court elucidated its holding in *Garmon:* the federal statute would preempt state jurisdiction only if the controversy presented in state court was identical to the one which was or could have been presented to the NLRB.

In sharp contrast, the Supreme Court held in Alexander v. Gardner-Denver Co., 415 U.S. 36 (1974), that arbitration of a discrimination claim under a collective bargaining agreement did not foreclose subsequent administrative and judicial proceedings under Title VII. The Court concluded that the legislative history of Title VII manifested a congressional intent to permit independent claims under Title VII and parallel federal or state laws, as well as private contracts (e.g., a collective bargaining agreement): "Title VII was designed to supplement, rather than supplant, existing laws and institutions relating to employment discrimination." Individuals may file independent claims under Title VII and the grievance-arbitration provisions of a collective bargaining agreement; filing in one forum has no preclusive effect, substantively or procedurally, on the other action. For example, filing a grievance does not toll the statute of limitations for a Title VII complaint. The Supreme Court has extended this parallel remedies approach beyond Title VII to the Fair Labor Standards Act, Barrentine v. Arkansas-Best Freight Sys., Inc., 450 U.S. 728 (1981), and actions under the Civil Rights Act of 1871, McDonald v. City of West Branch, 466 U.S. 284 (1984).

Matters were further complicated with the Supreme Court's holdings in Belknap, Inc. v. Hale, 463 U.S. 491 (1983), and Allis-Chalmers Corp. v. Lueck, 471 U.S. 202 (1985). In *Belknap,* the Court held that state actions for misrepresentation and breach of contract filed by "permanent replacements" who had been terminated by the employer following settlement of a strike were not preempted by the NLRA. According to the Court, the issues which would be litigated in the state action would not have "anything in common" with issues before the Board on unfair labor practice charges, so no preemption was necessary in order to protect federal labor policy. In contrast, in *Allis-Chalmers,* an employee's state law tort claim for bad faith handling of an insurance claim under a disability plan included in a collective bargaining agreement was preempted by section 301 of the LMRA.

Not surprisingly, these different approaches to parallel remedies raise a number of problems which have resulted in confusion, conflicting judicial interpretations, and considerable debate over the appropriate accommodation between common law and statute in regulating the employment relationship. The debate focuses on the extent to which permitting parallel remedies undermines the statutory policies established by legislative action and on how to determine and strike the appropriate balance between competing causes of action.

Lingle v. Norge Division of Magic Chef, Inc.
486 U.S. 399 (1988).

■ JUSTICE STEVENS delivered the opinion of the Court.

In Illinois an employee who is discharged for filing a worker's compensation claim may recover compensatory and punitive damages from her employer. The question presented in this case is whether an employee covered by a collective-bargaining agreement that provides her with a contractual remedy for discharge without just cause may enforce her state law remedy for retaliatory discharge. The Court of Appeals held that the application of the state tort remedy was preempted by § 301 of the Labor Management Relations Act of 1947, 61 Stat. 156, 29 U.S.C. § 185. We disagree.

Petitioner was employed in respondent's manufacturing plant in Herrin, Illinois. On December 5, 1984, she notified respondent that she had been injured in the course of her employment and requested compensation for her medical expenses pursuant to the Illinois Workers' Compensation Act. On December 11, 1984, respondent discharged her for filing a "false worker's compensation claim."

The union representing petitioner promptly filed a grievance pursuant to the collective-bargaining agreement that covered all production and maintenance employees in the Herrin plant. The agreement protected those employees, including petitioner, from discharge except for "proper" or "just" cause, and established a procedure for the arbitration of grievances. The term grievance was broadly defined to encompass "any dispute between * * * the Employer and any employee, concerning the effect, interpretation, application, claim of breach or violation of this Agreement." Ultimately, an arbitrator ruled in petitioner's favor and ordered respondent to reinstate her with full back pay.

Meanwhile, on July 9, 1985, petitioner commenced this action against respondent by filing a complaint in the Illinois Circuit Court for Williamson County, alleging that she had been discharged for exercising her rights under the Illinois worker's compensation laws. Respondent removed the case to the Federal District Court on the basis of diversity of citizenship, and then filed a motion praying that the Court either dismiss the case on pre-emption grounds or stay further proceedings pending the completion of the arbitration. Relying on our decision in Allis-Chalmers Corp. v. Lueck, 471 U.S. 202 (1985), the District Court dismissed the complaint. It concluded that the "claim for retaliatory discharge is 'inextricably intertwined' with the collective bargaining provision prohibiting wrongful discharge or discharge without just cause" and that allowing the state-law action to proceed would undermine the arbitration procedures set forth in the parties' contract.

The Court of Appeals agreed that the state-law claim was preempted by § 301. In an en banc opinion, over the dissent of two judges, it rejected petitioner's argument that the tort action was not "inextricably intertwined" with the collective-bargaining agreement because the disposition of a retaliatory discharge claim in Illinois does not depend upon an interpretation of the agreement; on the contrary, the Court concluded that "the same analysis of the facts" was implicated under both procedures.

Section 301(a) of the Labor Management Relations Act of 1947, 61 Stat. 156, 29 U.S.C. § 185(a), provides:

> "Suits for violation of contracts between an employer and a labor organization representing employees in an industry affecting commerce as defined in this Act, or between any such labor organizations, may be brought in any district court of the United States having jurisdiction of the parties, without respect to the amount in controversy or without regard to the citizenship of the parties."

In Textile Workers v. Lincoln Mills, 353 U.S. 448 (1957), we held that § 301 not only provides federal-court jurisdiction over controversies involving collective-bargaining agreements, but also "authorizes federal courts to fashion a body of federal law for the enforcement of these collective bargaining agreements." Id., at 451.

In Teamsters v. Lucas Flour Co., 369 U.S. 95 (1962), we were confronted with a straightforward question of contract interpretation: whether a collective-bargaining agreement implicitly prohibited a strike that had been called by the union. The Washington Supreme Court had answered that question by applying state-law rules of contract interpretation. We rejected that approach, and held that § 301 mandated resort to federal rules of law in order to ensure uniform interpretation of collective-bargaining agreements, and thus to promote the peaceable, consistent resolution of labor-management disputes.[3]

---

[3]   Our discussion of the pre-emptive scope of § 301 bears repeating:

* * * The dimensions of § 301 require the conclusion that substantive principles of federal labor law must be paramount in the area covered by the statute. Comprehensiveness is inherent in the process by which the law is to be formulated under the mandate of *Lincoln Mills*, requiring issues raised in suits of a kind covered by § 301 to be decided according to the precepts of federal labor policy.

"More important, the subject matter of § 301(a) 'is peculiarly one that calls for uniform law.' * * * The possibility that individual contract terms might have different meanings under state and federal law would inevitably exert a disruptive influence

In Allis-Chalmers Corp. v. Lueck, 471 U.S. 202 (1985), we considered whether the Wisconsin tort remedy for bad-faith handling of an insurance claim could be applied to the handling of a claim for disability benefits that were authorized by a collective-bargaining agreement. We began by examining the collective-bargaining agreement, and determined that it provided the basis not only for the benefits, but also for the right to have payments made in a timely manner. We then analyzed the Wisconsin tort remedy, explaining that it "exists for breach of a 'duty devolv[ed] upon the insurer by reasonable implication from the express terms of the contract,' the scope of which, crucially, is 'ascertained from a consideration of the contract itself.' " Since the "parties' agreement as to the manner in which a benefit claim would be handled [would] necessarily [have been] relevant to any allegation that the claim was handled in a dilatory manner," we concluded that § 301 pre-empted the application of the Wisconsin tort remedy in this setting.

Thus, *Lueck* faithfully applied the principle of § 301 pre-emption developed in *Lucas Flour:* if the resolution of a state-law claim depends upon the meaning of a collective-bargaining agreement, the application of state law (which might lead to inconsistent results since there could be as many state-law principles as there are States) is pre-empted and federal labor-law principles—necessarily uniform throughout the nation—must be employed to resolve the dispute.

Illinois courts have recognized the tort of retaliatory discharge for filing a worker's compensation claim, Kelsay v. Motorola, Inc., 74 Ill.2d 172, 384 N.E.2d 353 (1978), and have held that it is applicable to employees covered by union contracts, Midgett v. Sackett-Chicago, Inc., 105 Ill.2d 143, 473 N.E.2d 1280 (1984), cert. denied, 474 U.S. 909 (1985). "[T]o show retaliatory discharge, the plaintiff must set forth sufficient facts from which it can be inferred that (1) he was discharged or threatened with discharge and (2) the employer's motive in discharging or threatening to discharge him was to deter him from exercising his

---

upon both the negotiation and administration of collective agreements. Because neither party could be certain of the rights which it had obtained or conceded, the process of negotiating an agreement would be made immeasurably more difficult by the necessity of trying to formulate contract provisions in such a way as to contain the same meaning under two or more systems of law which might someday be invoked in enforcing the contract. Once the collective bargain was made, the possibility of conflicting substantive interpretation under competing legal systems would tend to stimulate and prolong disputes as to its interpretation. Indeed, the existence of possibly conflicting legal concepts might substantially impede the parties' willingness to agree to contract terms providing for final arbitral or judicial resolution of disputes.

"The importance of the area which would be affected by separate systems of substantive law makes the need for a single body of federal law particularly compelling. The ordering and adjusting of competing interests through a process of free and voluntary collective bargaining is the keystone of the federal scheme to promote industrial peace. State law which frustrates the effort of Congress to stimulate the smooth functioning of that process thus strikes at the very core of federal labor policy. With due regard to the many factors which bear upon competing state and federal interests in this area, * * * we cannot but conclude that in enacting § 301 Congress intended doctrines of federal labor law uniformly to prevail over inconsistent local rules." 369 U.S., at 103–104 (citations omitted, footnote omitted).

rights under the Act or to interfere with his exercise of those rights." Horton v. Miller Chemical Co., 776 F.2d 1351, 1356 (C.A.7 1985), cert. denied, 475 U.S. 1122 (1986). Each of these purely factual questions pertains to the conduct of the employee and the conduct and motivation of the employer. Neither of the elements requires a court to interpret any term of a collective-bargaining agreement. To defend against a retaliatory discharge claim, an employer must show that it had a nonretaliatory reason for the discharge; this purely factual inquiry likewise does not turn on the meaning of any provision of a collective-bargaining agreement. Thus, the state-law remedy in this case is "independent" of the collective-bargaining agreement in the sense of "independent" that matters for § 301 pre-emption purposes: resolution of the state-law claim does not require construing the collective-bargaining agreement.

The Court of Appeals seems to have relied upon a different way in which a state-law claim may be considered "independent" of a collective-bargaining agreement. The court wrote that "the just cause provision in the collective-bargaining agreement may well prohibit such retaliatory discharge," and went on to say that if the state law cause of action could go forward, "a state court would be deciding precisely the *same issue* as would an arbitrator: whether there was 'just cause' to discharge the worker." The Court concluded, "the state tort of retaliatory discharge is inextricably intertwined with the collective-bargaining agreements here, because it implicates the *same analysis of the facts* as would an inquiry under the just cause provisions of the agreements." We agree with the Court's explanation that the state-law analysis might well involve attention to the same factual considerations as the contractual determination of whether Lingle was fired for just cause. But we disagree with the Court's conclusion that such parallelism renders the state-law analysis dependent upon the contractual analysis. For while there may be instances in which the National Labor Relations Act pre-empts state law on the basis of the subject matter of the law in question, § 301 pre-emption merely ensures that federal law will be the basis for interpreting collective-bargaining agreements, and says nothing about the substantive rights a State may provide to workers when adjudication of those rights does not depend upon the interpretation of such agreements.[9] In other words, even if dispute resolution pursuant to a collective-bargaining agreement, on the one hand, and state law, on the other, would require addressing precisely the same set of facts, as long

---

[9]   Whether a union may *waive* its members' individual, nonpre-empted state-law rights, is, likewise, a question distinct from that of whether a claim is pre-empted under § 301, and is another issue we need not resolve today. We note that under Illinois law, the parties to a collective-bargaining agreement may not waive the prohibition against retaliatory discharge nor may they alter a worker's rights under the state worker's compensation scheme. Before deciding whether such a state law bar to waiver could be pre-empted under federal law by the parties to a collective-bargaining agreement, we would require "clear and unmistakable" evidence in order to conclude that such a waiver had been intended. No such evidence is available in this case.

as the state-law claim can be resolved without interpreting the agreement itself, the claim is "independent" of the agreement for § 301 pre-emption purposes.[10]

The result we reach today is consistent both with the policy of fostering uniform, certain adjudication of disputes over the meaning of collective-bargaining agreements and with cases that have permitted separate fonts of substantive rights to remain unpre-empted by other federal labor-law statutes.

First, as we explained in *Lueck,* "[t]he need to preserve the effectiveness of arbitration was one of the central reasons that underlay the Court's holding in *Lucas Flour.* * * * A rule that permitted an individual to sidestep available grievance procedures would cause arbitration to lose most of its effectiveness, * * * as well as eviscerate a central tenet of federal labor contract law under § 301 that it is the arbitrator, not the court, who has the responsibility to interpret the labor contract in the first instance." Today's decision should make clear that interpretation of collective-bargaining agreements remains firmly in the arbitral realm; judges can determine questions of state law involving labor-management relations only if such questions do not require construing collective-bargaining agreements.

Second, there is nothing novel about recognizing that substantive rights in the labor relations context can exist without interpreting collective-bargaining agreements.

> This Court has, on numerous occasions, declined to hold that individual employees are, because of the availability of arbitration, barred from bringing claims under federal statutes. See, e.g., McDonald v. West Branch, 466 U.S. 284 (1984); Barrentine v. Arkansas-Best Freight System, Inc., 450 U.S. 728 (1981); Alexander v. Gardner-Denver Co., 415 U.S. 36 (1974).

---

[10] Thus, what we said in Caterpillar Inc. v. Williams, 482 U.S. 386, 394–395 (1987) (emphasis in original), is relevant here:

"Caterpillar asserts that respondents' state-law contract claims are in reality completely pre-empted § 301 claims, which therefore arise under federal law. We disagree. Section 301 governs claims founded directly on rights created by collective-bargaining agreements, and also claims 'substantially dependent on analysis of a collective-bargaining agreement.' Electrical Workers v. Hechler, 481 U.S. 851, 863, n. 5 (1987); see also Allis-Chalmers Corp. v. Lueck, 471 U.S., at 220. Respondents allege that Caterpillar has entered into and breached *individual* employment contracts with them. Section 301 says nothing about the content or validity of individual employment contracts. It is true that respondents, bargaining unit members at the time of the plant closing, possessed substantial rights under the collective agreement, and could have brought suit under § 301. As masters of the complaint, however, they chose not to do so.

"Moreover, contrary to Caterpillar's assertion, * * * respondents' complaint is not substantially dependent upon interpretation of the collective-bargaining agreement. It does not rely upon the collective agreement indirectly, nor does it address the relationship between the individual contracts and the collective agreement. As the Court has stated, 'it would be inconsistent with congressional intent under [§ 301] to pre-empt state rules that proscribe conduct, or establish rights and obligations, independent of a labor contract.' Allis-Chalmers Corp., supra, at 212."

> Although the analysis of the question under each statute is quite distinct, the theory running through these cases is that notwithstanding the strong policies encouraging arbitration, "different considerations apply *where the employee's claim is based on rights arising out of a statute designed to provide minimum substantive guarantees to individual workers.*" Barrentine, supra, 450 U.S., at 737.

Atchison, T. & S.F.R. Co. v. Buell, 480 U.S. 557, 564–565 (1987) (emphasis added).

Although our comments in *Buell,* construing the scope of Railway Labor Act pre-emption, referred to independent *federal* statutory rights, we subsequently rejected a claim that federal labor law pre-empted a *state* statute providing a one-time severance benefit to employees in the event of a plant closing. In Fort Halifax Packing Co. v. Coyne, 482 U.S. 1, 21 (1987), we emphasized that "pre-emption should not be lightly inferred in this area, since the establishment of labor standards falls within the traditional police power of the State." We specifically held that the Maine law in question was not pre-empted by the NLRA, "since its establishment of a minimum labor standard does not impermissibly intrude upon the collective-bargaining process." Id., at 23.

The Court of Appeals "recognize[d] that § 301 does not pre-empt state anti-discrimination laws, even though a suit under these laws, like a suit alleging retaliatory discharge, requires a state court to determine whether just cause existed to justify the discharge." The court distinguished those laws because Congress has affirmatively endorsed state anti-discrimination remedies in Title VII of the Civil Rights Act of 1964, 78 Stat. 241, see 42 U.S.C. §§ 2000e–5(c) and 2000e–7, whereas there is no such explicit endorsement of state worker's compensation laws. As should be plain from our discussion in Part III, this distinction is unnecessary for determining whether § 301 pre-empts the state law in question. The operation of the anti-discrimination laws does, however, illustrate the relevant point for § 301 pre-emption analysis that the mere fact that a broad contractual protection against discriminatory—or retaliatory—discharge may provide a remedy for conduct that coincidentally violates state law does not make the existence or the contours of the state law violation dependent upon the terms of the private contract. For even if an arbitrator should conclude that the contract does not prohibit a particular discriminatory or retaliatory discharge, that conclusion might or might not be consistent with a proper interpretation of state law. In the typical case a state tribunal could resolve either a discriminatory or retaliatory discharge claim without interpreting the "just cause" language of a collective-bargaining agreement.

In sum, we hold that an application of state law is pre-empted by § 301 of the Labor Management Relations Act of 1947 only if such application requires the interpretation of a collective-bargaining agreement.[12]

The judgment of the Court of Appeals is reversed.

NOTES AND QUESTIONS

1. In *Lingle,* the Supreme Court held that Lingle's tort claim was not preempted, even though her employment was covered by a collective bargaining agreement. A few years earlier, the Court had preempted a state law tort claim in Allis-Chalmers v. Lueck, mentioned in the majority opinion. In upholding the employee's right to file a separate state law claim in *Allis-Chalmers,* the Wisconsin Supreme Court had held:

> [T]he tort of bad faith is not a tortious breach of contract. It is a separate intentional wrong, which results from a breach of duty imposed as a consequence of the relationship established by contract. * * * Lueck's claim is not for a breach of contract; rather, it is a separate and independent claim arising out of the manner in which his disability claim was handled. For purposes of pursuing this claim, Lueck need only first establish that the defendants owed him a duty by virtue of the insurance contract. Even though that duty arose initially because of the insurance provided through the labor agreement, that fact alone does not persuade us that Lueck's claim is in essence a contractual claim.

Lueck v. Aetna Life Ins. Co., 342 N.W.2d 699, 702 (Wis.1984), reversed, 471 U.S. 202 (1985).

Why is Lueck's claim preempted but not Lingle's? Why was the Supreme Court not persuaded by the Wisconsin Supreme Court's interpretation of the nature of the rights involved in *Allis-Chalmers?* Did the Supreme Court broaden or narrow the standard for section 301 preemption in *Lingle?* What is the new standard? To what extent should the characterization of a claim as tort or contract determine the preemptive effect of federal law in wrongful discharge actions?

2. Preemption problems arise in several different ways: there is the section 301 preemption addressed in *Lingle,* in which rights under a collective bargaining agreement and under state common law may overlap. Preemption may also be an issue when other federal statutes overlap state common law remedies, or when state statutory and common law causes of action overlap. One reason why Lingle's wrongful discharge claim was not

---

[12] A collective-bargaining agreement may, of course, contain information such as rate of pay and other economic benefits that might be helpful in determining the damages to which a worker prevailing in a state law suit is entitled. Although federal law would govern the interpretation of the agreement to determine the proper damages, the underlying state law claim, not otherwise pre-empted, would stand. Thus, as a general proposition, a state law claim may depend for its resolution upon both the interpretation of a collective-bargaining agreement and a separate state law analysis that does not turn on the agreement. In such a case, federal law would govern the interpretation of the agreement, but the separate state law analysis would not be thereby pre-empted. As we said in Allis-Chalmers Corp. v. Lueck, 471 U.S., at 211, "not every dispute * * * tangentially involving a provision of a collective-bargaining agreement is pre-empted by § 301 * * *."

preempted was because of the importance the Supreme Court attached to the process of collective bargaining and its concern that if Lingle's claim were preempted, unionized employees would have fewer rights than unorganized employees and collective bargaining under the National Labor Relations Act would be undermined. What the Court left open in *Lingle* is the extent to which that same, or analogous, reasoning would apply to other preemption problems.

In Screen Extras Guild, Inc. v. Superior Court, 800 P.2d 873 (Cal.1990), the Supreme Court of California held that the Labor-Management Reporting and Disclosure Act (LMRDA) preempted state causes of action for wrongful discharge and related torts when brought against a union-employer by a former management or policymaking employee. The court cited to the strong federal policy favoring union democracy, which would be furthered by not interfering with the ability of elected union leaders to carry out the will of the members they represent.

3.   Compare Hagan v. Feld Enter., Inc., 365 F.Supp. 2d 700 (E.D. Va.2005). The plaintiff was a lion tamer hired by Feld to work for Ringling Bros. and Barnum & Bailey Circus as a lion handler. One summer, as the circus train traveled through the Mojave Desert en route to Fresno, temperatures began to climb, and the lions began to overheat. The Train Master refused to stop the train to let Hagan cool the lions off, and after one of the lions died, Hagan was instructed not to discuss the lion's death with anyone, which Hagan understood to mean no conversations with the U.S.D.A. inspectors. When he continued to talk about the lion's death, he was terminated, and Hagan and his daughter were left in California with no way to get home. Hagan brought suit. The court held that while Hagan's claim of wrongful discharge was not preempted by the Labor Management Relations Act, his claim of intentional infliction of emotional distress was precluded by California's workers' compensation law.

4.   Title VII of the Civil Rights Act of 1964 applies to unionized and nonunionized individuals. It expressly provides, in section 708, "Nothing in this subchapter shall be deemed to exempt or relieve any person from any liability, duty, penalty or punishment provided by any present or future law of any State or political subdivision of a State * * *." What does this section mean with respect to preemption of state tort actions arising out of violations of federal law (regardless of the existence of a collective bargaining agreement)? For example, is emotional distress arising out of unlawful sexual harassment actionable under Title VII? See Blum v. Witco Chem. Corp., 829 F.2d 367 (3d Cir. 1987), reversed in part on other grounds, 888 F.2d 975 (3d Cir. 1989); Lapinad v. Pac. Oldsmobile-GMC, Inc., 679 F.Supp. 991 (D.Hawai'i 1988); Ford v. Revlon, Inc., 734 P.2d 580 (Ariz.1987).

5.   In comparison to section 708 of Title VII, most workers' compensation statutes provide that workers' compensation will be the employee's exclusive remedy for injuries arising in the course of employment. How should the existence and availability of a workers' compensation statute affect an individual's ability to sue in state court for wrongful discharge? See Beard v. Flying J, Inc., 266 F.3d 792 (8th Cir. 2001) (the common law claims of a female employee who was subjected to several acts of unwanted sexual contact were not preempted by the workers' compensation system).

6.   Federal law is not the only limit on common law causes of action. In a number of cases, state statutes also have been held to preempt common law remedies, on the theory that the enactment of a comprehensive legislative scheme formally establishing the state's policy provides the exclusive remedy and preempts common law actions. But parallel common law claims such as breach of contract or intentional infliction of emotional distress may not be preempted, depending on the state. See, e.g., Monaco v. American Gen. Assur. Co., 359 F.3d 296 (3d. Cir. 2004) (New Jersey law does not provide a separate breach of contract cause of action on the basis of generalized anti-discrimination language in an employee handbook where the alleged discrimination would be in violation of the New Jersey Law Against Discrimination); Pavon v. Swift Trans. Co., Inc., 192 F.3d 902 (9th Cir. 1999) (under Oregon law, a plaintiff may bring a common law wrongful discharge claim when terminated as a result of his or her pursuit of a job-related right only where there is an absence of an adequate statutory remedy which protects the interests of society); Flenker v. Willamette Indus., Inc., 162 F.3d 1083 (10th Cir. 1998) (OSHA does not preclude Kansas common law wrongful discharge claim).

7.   An employee who brings a claim under New Jersey's whistleblower statute, the Conscientious Employee Protection Act, is not precluded by CEPA's waiver provision from asserting independent common law claims as well. Young had objected to his employer's testing of a veterinary drug without reporting it to several government agencies and was terminated. The court held that the retaliatory discharge claim did not preclude independent claims for owed but unpaid severance and defamation. Young v. Schering Corp., 660 A.2d 1153 (N.J.1995).

8.   Employees brought state-court actions arising from employer's alleged secret videotaping of restrooms through two-way mirrors. The court of appeals concluded that both the employees' invasion of privacy claim and their emotional distress claim were independent of the collective bargaining agreement and therefore not preempted by Labor Management Relations Act. Cramer v. Consolidated Freightways Inc., 255 F.3d 683 (9th Cir. 2001), cert. denied, 534 U.S. 1078 (2002).

PROBLEMS

Should the following claims be preempted? On what basis?

a.   After the employer announced proposed layoffs pursuant to a collective bargaining agreement, it offered a one-time lump sum payment to employees who voluntarily opted to cease working. By accepting the severance payment, employees would forfeit their seniority and any rehire rights; a company spokesman allegedly told employees that they could be rehired if new jobs were created, but they would have to apply like anyone else. A number of employees accepted the company's offer. Two years later, new positions opened up, and when former employees applied, they were informed by management that they were ineligible for consideration. The employees sued in state court for fraud and misrepresentation. The employer moved for removal to federal court under § 301. How should the court rule? See Wells v. General Motors Corp., 881 F.2d 166 (5th Cir. 1989), cert. denied, 495 U.S. 923 (1990) (held: not preempted).

b.   An employee was induced by a rival company to leave his prior employment and move to a different city. According to the employee, the new employer stated that he would be guaranteed employment for the reasonably foreseeable future and that any job offered would be permanent. Five months after he started the new job, the employee was laid off as part of a company-wide reduction in force, pursuant to the terms of a collective bargaining agreement applicable to him. He sued in state court for breach of contract, and the employer sought removal. What result? Berda v. CBS, Inc., 881 F.2d 20 (3d Cir. 1989), cert. denied, 493 U.S. 1062 (1990) (held: not preempted). Cf. Terwilliger v. Greyhound Lines, Inc., 882 F.2d 1033 (6th Cir. 1989), cert. denied, 495 U.S. 946 (1990).

c.   Two airline employees were discharged for union organizing activities, and they filed suit in state court for wrongful discharge. Should their suit be preempted under the Railway Labor Act (which applies to airline employees)? See Price v. PSA, Inc., 829 F.2d 871 (9th Cir. 1987), cert. denied, 486 U.S. 1006 (1988) (held: not completely preempted).

d.   An at-will employee was fired for refusing to drive vehicles that did not conform to state mandatory safety equipment requirements. He filed a complaint with the Secretary of Labor alleging that his discharge violated the federal Surface Transportation Assistance Act and also sued in state court for wrongful discharge (breach of public policy). The employer moved to dismiss the state claim on the basis of lack of subject matter jurisdiction. How should the court rule? See Todd v. Frank's Tong Serv., Inc., 784 P.2d 47 (Okla.1989) (held: not preempted).

4.   COMMON LAW CLAIMS

In contrast to the relatively recent development of the wrongful discharge cause of action, there are a number of torts for which employees have traditionally been able to sue employers, other employees, or any individuals who interfere with the employment relationship. These actions include intentional infliction of emotional distress; invasion of privacy; fraud and misrepresentation; slander, defamation and libel; negligence; and tortious interference with contractual relations. Although circumstances giving rise to such actions occurred relatively infrequently in the past, developments in wrongful discharge law have resulted in an increase in the number of these cases being filed as well.

Wilson v. Monarch Paper Co.

939 F.2d 1138 (5th Cir. 1991).

■ E. GRADY JOLLY, CIRCUIT JUDGE:

In this employment discrimination case, Monarch Paper Company, et al., appeals a $3,400,000 jury verdict finding it liable for age discrimination and retaliation under the Age Discrimination in Employment Act (ADEA), 29 U.S.C. § 621, and for intentional infliction of emotional distress under Texas state law. Monarch challenges the sufficiency of the evidence. It also challenges the district court's denial of their motions for directed verdict, for judgment non obstante veredicto (JNOV), for new trial, and for remittitur. Upon review of the entire record, we affirm.

Because Monarch is challenging the sufficiency of the evidence, the facts are recited in the light most favorable to the jury's verdict. In 1970, at age 48, Richard E. Wilson was hired by Monarch Paper Company. Monarch is an incorporated division of Unisource Corporation, and Unisource is an incorporated group of Alco Standard Corporation. Wilson served as manager of the Corpus Christi division until November 1, 1977, when he was moved to the corporate staff in Houston to serve as "Corporate Director of Physical Distribution." During that time, he routinely received merit raises and performance bonuses. In 1980, Wilson received the additional title of "Vice President." In 1981, Wilson was given the additional title of "Assistant to John Blankenship," Monarch's President at the time.

While he was Director of Physical Distribution, Wilson received most of his assignments from Blankenship. Blankenship always seemed pleased with Wilson's performance and Wilson was never reprimanded or counseled about his performance. Blankenship provided Wilson with objective performance criteria at the beginning of each year, and Wilson's bonuses at the end of the year were based on his good performance under that objective criteria. In 1981, Wilson was placed in charge of the completion of an office warehouse building in Dallas, the largest construction project Monarch had ever undertaken. Wilson successfully completed that project within budget.

In 1981, Wilson saw a portion of Monarch's long-range plans that indicated that Monarch was presently advancing younger persons in all levels of Monarch management. Tom Davis, who was hired as Employee Relations Manager of Monarch in 1979, testified that from the time he started to work at Monarch, he heard repeated references by the division managers (including Larry Clark, who later became the Executive Vice President of Monarch) to the age of employees on the corporate staff, including Wilson.

In October 1981, Blankenship became Chairman of Monarch and Unisource brought in a new, 42-year-old president from outside the company, Hamilton Bisbee. An announcement was made that Larry

Clark would be assuming expanded responsibilities in physical distribution. According to the defendants, one of Blankenship's final acts as President was to direct Clark (who was in his mid-forties at the time) to assume expanded responsibility for both the operational and physical distribution aspects of Monarch.

When Bisbee arrived at Monarch in November 1981, Wilson was still deeply involved in the Dallas construction project. Richard Gozon, who was 43 years old and the President of Unisource, outlined Blankenship's new responsibilities as Chairman of the company and requested that Blankenship, Bisbee, Wilson, and John Hartley of Unisource "continue to work very closely together on the completion of the Dallas project." Bisbee, however, refused to speak to Wilson or to "interface" with him. This "silent treatment" was apparently tactical; Bisbee later told another Monarch employee, Bill Shehan, "if I ever stop talking to you, you're dead." Shehan also testified that at a meeting in Philadelphia at about the time Bisbee became President of Monarch, Gozon told Bisbee, "I'm not telling you that you have to fire Dick Wilson. I'm telling you that he cannot make any more money."

* * *

Blankenship was diagnosed with cancer in February 1982. In March 1982, Wilson was hospitalized for orthopedic surgery. Immediately after Blankenship's death in June 1982, Bisbee and Snelgrove gave Wilson three options: (1) he could take a sales job in Corpus Christi at half his pay; (2) he could be terminated with three months' severance pay; or (3) he could accept a job as warehouse supervisor in the Houston warehouse at the same salary but with a reduction in benefits. The benefits included participation in the management bonus plan, and the loss of the use of a company car, a company club membership, and a company expense account.

Wilson accepted the warehouse position. Wilson believed that he was being offered the position of Warehouse Manager, the only vacant position in the Houston warehouse at the time. When Wilson reported for duty at the warehouse on August 16, 1982, however, he was placed instead in the position of an entry level supervisor, a position that required no more than one year's experience in the paper business. Wilson, with his thirty years of experience in the paper business and a college degree, was vastly overqualified and overpaid for that position.

Soon after he went to the warehouse, Wilson was subjected to harassment and verbal abuse by his supervisor, Operations Manager and Acting Warehouse Manager Paul Bradley (who had previously been subordinate to Wilson). Bradley referred to Wilson as "old man" and admitted posting a sign in the warehouse that said "Wilson is old." In Bradley's absence, Wilson was placed under the supervision of a man in his twenties. Finally, Wilson was further demeaned when he was placed in charge of housekeeping but was not given any employees to assist him in the housekeeping duties. Wilson, the former vice-president and assistant to the president, was thus reduced finally to sweeping the floors and cleaning up the employees' cafeteria, duties which occupied 75 percent of his working time.

In the late fall of 1982, Wilson began suffering from respiratory problems caused by the dusty conditions in the warehouse and stress from the unrelenting harassment by his employer. On January 6, 1983, Wilson left work to see a doctor about his respiratory problems. He was advised to stay out of a dusty environment and was later advised that he had a clinically significant allergy to dust. Shortly after January 6, 1983, Wilson consulted a psychiatrist who diagnosed him as suffering from reactive depression, possibly suicidal, because of on-the-job stress. The psychiatrist also advised that Wilson should stay away from work indefinitely.

Wilson filed an age discrimination charge with the EEOC in January 1983. Although he continued being treated by a psychiatrist, his condition deteriorated to the point that in March 1983, he was involuntarily hospitalized with a psychotic manic episode. Prior to the difficulties with his employer, Wilson had no history of emotional illness.

Wilson's emotional illness was severe and long-lasting. He was diagnosed with manic-depressive illness or bipolar disorder. After his first hospitalization for a manic episode, in which he was locked in a padded cell and heavily sedated, he fell into a deep depression. The depression was unremitting for over two years and necessitated an additional hospital stay in which he was given electroconvulsive therapy (shock treatments). It was not until 1987 that Wilson's illness began remission, thus allowing him to carry on a semblance of a normal life.

On February 27, 1984, Wilson filed suit against the defendants, alleging age discrimination and various state law tort and contract claims. The defendants filed a counterclaim, seeking damages in excess of $10,000 for libel and slander, but later dismissed it. Before trial, the district court dismissed one of Wilson's claims on the basis of factual or legal insufficiency. The court also dismissed his emotional distress claim to the extent that "the alleged conduct occurred in the administration of [defendants'] disability plan" on grounds of ERISA preemption. On November 30 and December 28, 1988, the case was tried before a jury on Wilson's remaining claims that the defendants (1) reassigned him because of his age; (2) intentionally inflicted emotional distress; and (3) terminated his long-term disability benefits in retaliation for filing charges of age discrimination under the Age Discrimination in Employment Act (ADEA).

The district court denied the defendants' motions for directed verdict. The jury returned a special verdict in favor of Wilson on his age discrimination claim, awarding him $156,000 in damages, plus an equal amount in liquidated damages. The jury also found in favor of Wilson on his claim for intentional infliction of emotional distress, awarding him past damages of $622,359.15, future damages of $225,000, and punitive damages of $2,250,000. The jury found in favor of the defendants on Wilson's retaliation claim. The district court entered judgment for $3,409,359.15 plus prejudgment interest. The district court denied the defendants' motions for judgment NOV, new trial, or, alternatively, a remittitur. The defendants appeal.

* * *

Wilson's claim for intentional infliction of emotional distress is a pendent state law claim. As such, we are bound to apply the law of Texas in determining whether the defendant's motions should have been granted. The Texas Supreme Court has not expressly recognized the tort of intentional infliction of emotional distress. We, however, have nonetheless recognized on at least two prior occasions, see, e.g., Blankenship v. Kerr County, 878 F.2d 893, 898 (5th Cir. 1989) and Dean v. Ford Motor Credit Co., 885 F.2d 300 (5th Cir. 1989), that such a cause of action exists in Texas, based on the Texas Court of Appeals' decision in Tidelands Auto. Club v. Walters, 699 S.W.2d 939 (Tex.App.—Beaumont 1985, writ ref'd n.r.e.). To prevail on a claim for intentional infliction of emotional distress, Texas law requires that the following four elements be established:

(1) that the defendant acted intentionally or recklessly;

(2) that the conduct was "extreme and outrageous";

(3) that the actions of the defendant caused the plaintiff emotional distress; and

(4) that the emotional distress suffered by the plaintiff was severe.

The sole issue before us is whether Monarch's conduct was "extreme and outrageous."

"Extreme and outrageous conduct" is an amorphous phrase that escapes precise definition. In *Dean* however, we stated that

[l]iability [for outrageous conduct] has been found only where the conduct has been so outrageous in character, and so extreme in degree, as to go beyond all possible bounds of decency, and to be regarded as atrocious, and utterly intolerable in a civilized community * * *. Generally, the case is one in which a recitation of the facts to an average member of the community would lead him to exclaim, "Outrageous."

885 F.2d at 306 (citing Restatement (Second) of Torts § 46, Comment d (1965)). The Restatement also provides for some limits on jury verdicts by stating that liability "does not extend to mere insults, indignities, threats, annoyances, petty oppressions, or other trivialities * * *. There is no occasion for the law to intervene in every case where someone's feelings are hurt."

The facts of a given claim of outrageous conduct must be analyzed in context, and ours is the employment setting. We are cognizant that "the work culture in some situations may contemplate a degree of teasing and taunting that in other circumstances might be considered cruel and outrageous." We further recognize that properly to manage its business, every employer must on occasion review, criticize, demote, transfer, and discipline employees. We also acknowledge that it is not unusual for an employer, instead of directly discharging an employee, to create unpleasant and onerous work conditions designed to force an employee to quit, i.e., "constructively" to discharge the employee. In short, although this sort of conduct often rises to the level of illegality, except in the *most* unusual cases it is not the sort of conduct, as deplorable as it may sometimes be, that constitutes "extreme and outrageous" conduct.

Our recent decision in *Dean* is instructive in determining what types of conduct in the employment setting will constitute sufficiently outrageous conduct so as to legally support a jury's verdict. In *Dean,* the plaintiff presented evidence that (1) when she expressed interest in transferring to a higher paying position in the collection department, she was told that "women don't usually go into that department"; (2) she was denied a transfer to the collection department, and a lesser qualified man was selected; (3) the defendant's attitude toward the plaintiff changed after she complained about alleged discriminatory treatment; (4) management began to transfer her from desk to desk within the administrative department; (5) a coworker testified she believed management was trying to "set * * * [the plaintiff] up"; (6) she was called upon to do more work than the other clerks "and subjected to unfair harassment"; and (7) management used "special" annual reviews (that only the plaintiff received) to downgrade her performance. Far more significant to the claim for intentional infliction of emotional distress, however, (8) the plaintiff proved that a supervisor, who had access to the employer's checks, intentionally placed checks in the plaintiff's purse in order to make it appear that she was a thief, or to put her in fear of criminal charges for theft. We expressly held that the "check incidents" were "precisely what [took] this case beyond the realm of an ordinary employment dispute and into the realm of an outrageous one." We concluded that without the "check incidents" the employer's conduct "would not have been outrageous."

Wilson argues that Monarch's conduct is sufficiently outrageous to meet the *Dean* standard; in the alternative, he argues that Monarch's actions are certainly more outrageous than the conduct in Bushell v. Dean, 781 S.W.2d 652 (Tex.App. 1989), writ denied in part, rev'd in part on other grounds, 803 S.W.2d 711 (Tex.1991), which is a recent pronouncement by the Texas courts on the subject. Monarch contends that Wilson's evidence of outrageous conduct, that is, his reassignment to a job he did not like, his strained relationship with the company president, and isolated references to his age, is the same evidence that he used to prove his age discrimination claim. According to Monarch, unless all federal court discrimination lawsuits are to be accompanied by pendent state law claims for emotional distress, this court must make it clear that ordinary employment disputes cannot support an emotional distress claim. We agree with Monarch that more is required to prove intentional infliction of emotional distress than the usual ADEA claim.

In *Dean,* we found that the "check incidents" took the case beyond an ordinary discrimination case and supported the claim of infliction of emotional distress. Wilson contends that Monarch's conduct was equally outrageous as the "check incidents" in *Dean.* Generally, Wilson argues that an average member of the community would exclaim "Outrageous!" upon hearing that a 60-year-old man, with 30 years of experience in his industry, was subjected to a year-long campaign of harassment and abuse because his company wanted to force him out of his job as part of its expressed written goal of getting rid of older employees and moving younger people into management. More precisely, Wilson argues that substantial evidence of outrageous conduct supports the jury's verdict, including: (1) his duties in physical distribution were assigned to a younger person; (2) Bisbee deliberately refused to speak to him in the hallways of Monarch in order to harass him; (3) certain portions of Monarch's long-range plans expressed a desire to move younger persons into sales and management positions; (4) Bisbee wanted to replace Wilson with a younger person; (5) other managers within Monarch would not work with Wilson, and he did not receive his work directly from Bisbee; (6) he was not offered a fully guaranteed salary to transfer to Corpus Christi; (7) he was assigned to Monarch's Houston warehouse as a supervisor, which was "demeaning"; (8) Paul Bradley, the Warehouse Manager, and other Monarch managers, referred to Wilson as old; (9) Bradley prepared a sign stating "Wilson is old" and, subsequently, "Wilson is a Goldbrick"; and (10) Monarch filed a counterclaim against Wilson in this action. We are not in full agreement.

Most of Monarch's conduct is similar in degree to conduct in *Dean* that failed to reach the level of outrageousness. We hold that all of this conduct, except as explicated below, is within the "realm of an ordinary employment dispute," and, in the context of the employment milieu, is not so extreme and outrageous as to be properly addressed outside of Wilson's ADEA claim.

Wilson argues, however, that what takes this case out of the realm of an ordinary employment dispute is the degrading and humiliating way that he was stripped of his duties and demoted from an executive manager to an entry level warehouse supervisor with menial and demeaning duties. We agree. Wilson, a college graduate with thirty years experience in the paper field, had been a long-time executive at Monarch. His title was Corporate Director of Physical Distribution, with the added title of Vice-President and Assistant to the President. He had been responsible for the largest project in the company's history, and had completed the project on time and under budget. Yet, when transferred to the warehouse, Wilson's primary duty became housekeeping chores around the warehouse's shipping and receiving area. Because Monarch did not give Wilson any employees to supervise or assist him, Wilson was frequently required to sweep the warehouse. In addition, Wilson also was reduced to cleaning up after the employees in the warehouse cafeteria after their lunch hour. Wilson spent 75 percent of his time performing these menial, janitorial duties.

Monarch argues that assigning an executive with a college education and thirty years experience to janitorial duties is not extreme and outrageous conduct. The jury did not agree and neither do we. We find it difficult to conceive a workplace scenario more painful and embarrassing than an executive, indeed a vice-president and the assistant to the president, being subjected before his fellow employees to the most menial janitorial services and duties of cleaning up after entry level employees: the steep downhill push to total humiliation was complete. The evidence, considered as a whole, will fully support the view, which the jury apparently held, that Monarch, unwilling to fire Wilson outright, *intentionally and systematically* set out to humiliate him in the hopes that he would quit.[5] A reasonable jury could have found that this employer conduct was intentional and mean spirited, so severe that it resulted in institutional confinement and treatment for someone with no history of mental problems. Finally, the evidence supports the conclusion that this conduct was, indeed, so outrageous that civilized society should not tolerate it. *Dean*, 885 F.2d at 307.[6] Accordingly, the judgment of the district court in denying Monarch's motions for directed verdict, JNOV and a new trial on this claim is affirmed.

* * *

In conclusion, we express real concern about the consequences of applying the cause of action of intentional infliction of emotional distress to the workplace. This concern is, however, primarily a concern for the State of Texas, its courts and its legislature. Although the award in this case is astonishingly high, neither the quantum of damages, nor the applicability of punitive damages has been appealed.

For the reasons set forth above, the district court's denial of the motions for direct verdict, new trial and JNOV with respect to the intentional infliction of emotional distress verdict is AFFIRMED. The

---

[5]   Nevertheless, we are not unaware of the irony in this case: if Monarch had chosen only to fire Wilson outright, leaving him without a salary, a job, insurance, etc., it would not be liable for intentional infliction of emotional distress. There is some suggestion in the record, however, that Monarch was unwilling to fire Wilson outright because it had no grounds and perhaps feared a lawsuit. Although Monarch was willing to accept Wilson's resignation, Wilson was unwilling to resign. Once he was unwilling to resign, the evidence supports the inference that Monarch's efforts intensified to force his resignation.

[6]   We suppose that the threat of an emotional distress claim also provides the irony of "civilizing" discrimination; or stated differently, employers will have to behave like ladies and gentlemen when discriminating.

denial of Monarch's motions with respect to the age discrimination and back pay is also AFFIRMED.

NOTES AND QUESTIONS

1. Wilson was an at-will employee. Therefore, it would have been lawful for Monarch to tell him he was not needed in his former capacity and that the only available job was a menial job in the warehouse. What was it in the case, beyond this, that results in liability?

2. To what extent was the finding of liability affected by the magnitude of the psychological harm suffered by the plaintiff? Who should have the burden of proving that Wilson would not have had the same health problems if he were simply discharged?

3. In footnotes 5 and 6, the court points out the "irony" that the holding in *Wilson* could lead to more "civilized" firings of employees. Is this ironical or the essence of the case?

4. In a subsequent Fifth Circuit case, McCann v. Litton Sys., Inc., 986 F.2d 946 (5th Cir. 1993), the court reversed a jury award for an employee in an age discrimination case. The court held that an employee was not constructively discharged when he was asked to accept a 12 percent pay cut and to work for a supervisor half his age. Unlike *Wilson,* in *McCann* the employee was not personally humiliated by the demotion.

5. In Wallis v. Superior Court, 207 Cal.Rptr. 123 (Cal. Ct. App.1984), the plaintiff sued for intentional infliction of emotional distress as well as breach of the covenant of good faith and fair dealing. Quoting an earlier decision, the *Wallis* court stated:

> The modern rule [defining outrageous conduct] is that there is liability for conduct exceeding all bounds usually tolerated by a decent society, of a nature which is especially calculated to cause, and does cause, mental distress. * * * Behavior may be considered outrageous if a defendant (1) abuses a relation or position which gives him power to damage the plaintiff's interest; (2) knows the plaintiff is susceptible to injuries through mental distress; or (3) acts intentionally or unreasonably with the recognition that the acts are likely to result in illness through mental distress.

6. In Harris v. Arkansas Book Co., 700 S.W.2d 41 (Ark.1985), the company discharged without severance pay or a pension an employee who had worked there for 49 years. The Arkansas Supreme Court rejected not only the employee's wrongful discharge claim but also his claim for intentional infliction of emotional distress, on the ground that since the employer has the right to discharge an at-will employee, it cannot be held liable for emotional distress based on the discharge itself. The employer could only be found liable if the *manner* in which the discharge was accomplished met the "extreme and outrageous" test, which was not the case here. See also Newberry v. Allied Stores, Inc., 773 P.2d 1231 (N.M.1989) (supervisor's yelling at employee on sales floor that he did not trust employee did not constitute extreme and outrageous conduct). But "outrageous conduct" was found where a supervisor intentionally placed company-endorsed checks in an employee's possession to make it appear that she was stealing from the company. Dean v. Ford Motor Credit Co., 885 F.2d 300 (5th Cir. 1989).

7.   Intentional infliction of emotional distress is also used as a doctrinal remedy for sexual harassment. However, the harassment must rise to the level of "extreme and outrageous" conduct. Courts have been reluctant to allow for the use of this tort, finding that the conduct is outrageous only if it "is atrocious and surpasses all possible bounds of decency such that it is utterly intolerable in a civilized community." In Gearhart v. Eye Care Ctrs. of Am., 888 F.Supp. 814 (S.D.Tex.1995), a female employee was told that she could get promoted only by sleeping with the boss and that she had to wear a specific type of pantyhose. Although her superior also touched her breasts, kicked her in the buttocks, and made numerous sexual comments, this did not constitute "extreme and outrageous conduct." Compare Bustamento v. Tucker, 607 So.2d 532 (La.1992), where sexual harassment rose to the level of "extreme and outrageous conduct" when over a two-year period, a male employee made numerous sexual comments to a female co-worker and threatened to run her over with a forklift, rape her, and run her out of the plant. Physically, the co-worker terrorized her by driving his forklift at her and pinning her against the wall. In one instance, he slapped her on the buttocks. Is there a problem in using the "civilized community standard" for cases of sexual harassment? Are the courts acknowledging that less severe sexual harassment is tolerable in a civilized community?

8.   A terminated employee sued the employer in tort, saying it negligently failed to supervise its supervisors, who "dishonestly reported Garcia's job performance." The court said that Texas law imposes no such duty on employers, and that permitting this cause of action would "run the risk of abrogating the traditional at-will employment relationship, which is the norm in Texas." Garcia v. Allen, 28 S.W.3d 587 (Tex.App.2000).

9.   Plaintiff accepted a job and moved to Michigan from New Jersey. One year later he was laid off for economic reasons. He said that the company financial documents he was shown before he accepted the job, while accurate, were from a previous year and the employer already knew that economic performance was declining. He also said that the employer committed "silent fraud" by not sharing information about its negative performance during the employee's period at work. The Michigan Supreme Court found that these allegations did not state a cause of action, reversing a jury verdict for $175,000. Hord v. Environmental Research Inst., 617 N.W.2d 543 (Mich.2000) (5–2).

10. Cha, a pastor, was discharged and asserted state common law theories of wrongful discharge and tortious interference with contract. The court said that the free exercise clause of the First Amendment barred civil courts from review of ecclesiastical disputes. Cha v. Korean Presbyterian Church of Wash., 553 S.E.2d 511 (Va.2001), cert. denied, 535 U.S. 1035 (2002).

D. RETHINKING EMPLOYMENT AT WILL

Has the employment at will doctrine outlived its usefulness? Judicial recognition of wrongful discharge as an actionable wrong has naturally resulted in a dramatic increase in litigation of these cases. Virtually all of the states have permitted former employees to sue for wrongful discharge, although there is no uniformity in the legal basis on which such suits are allowed. Some states recognize only a narrow exception to the public policy rule; others permit plaintiffs to sue only in contract. In other jurisdictions, plaintiffs may sue under either theory. The proliferation of different legal standards on a case-by-case basis and wide variations in the amount of recovery in jury cases have caused many advocates on both sides to argue that the time has come to consider modification of the common law by legislative action rather than judicial fiat. Others maintain that the flexibility of judicial decisionmaking is desirable in this transitional area of the law in order to promote full, balanced, and nonpoliticized consideration of the nature of an employee's right to continued employment. Yet a third group argues that the employment at will rule has survived as long as it has because it serves the purposes of the parties in the majority of cases and that modification—judicial or legislative—would be ill-advised, if not actually counterproductive.

Ultimately, the question in actions for wrongful discharge is: should the presumption in favor of employment at will be modified or eliminated? If so, what theoretical structure should apply to the changed contours of the law? Compare the contract and tort approaches adopted in the cases above. Which form of action would do a better job of eliminating abusive discharges while at the same time permitting employers' productive activity to proceed in an efficient fashion? Should wronged employees be permitted to sue in both tort and contract? Or should these common law actions be replaced by a statutory scheme which imposes uniformity of treatment on all wrongful discharge cases?

1. DEFENDING AT-WILL EMPLOYMENT

Richard A. Epstein, In Defense of the Contract At-Will
51 U.Chi.L.Rev. 947 (1984).

There is thus today a widely held view that the contract at will has outlived its usefulness. But this view is mistaken. The contract at will is not ideal for every employment relation. No court or legislature should ever command its use. Nonetheless, there are two ways in which the contract at will should be respected: one deals with entitlements against regulation and the other with presumptions in the event of contractual silence.

First, the parties should be permitted as of right to adopt this form of contract if they so desire. The principle behind this conclusion is that freedom of contract tends both to advance individual autonomy and to promote the efficient operation of labor markets.

Second, the contract at will should be respected as a rule of construction in response to the perennial question of gaps in contract language: what term should be implied in the absence of explicit agreement on the question of duration or grounds for termination? The applicable standard asks two familiar questions: what rule tends to lend predictability to litigation and to advance the joint interests of the parties? On both these points I hope to show that the contract at will represents in most contexts the efficient solution to the employment relation.

* * *

The recent efforts to undermine or abolish the contract at will should be evaluated not in terms of what they *hope* to achieve, whether stated in terms of worker participation, industrial harmony, fundamental fairness, or enlightened employment relations. Instead they should be evaluated for the generally harsh results that they actually produce. They introduce an enormous amount of undesirable complexity into the law of employment relations; they increase the frequency of civil litigation; and over the broad run of cases they work to the disadvantage of both the employers and the employees whose conduct they govern.

* * *

The strong fairness argument in favor of freedom of contract makes short work of the various for-cause and good-faith restrictions upon private contracts. Yet the argument is incomplete in several respects. In particular, it does not explain why the presumption in the case of silence should be in favor of the contract at will. Nor does it give a descriptive account of *why* the contract at will is so commonly found in all trades and professions. Nor does the argument meet on their own terms the concerns voiced most frequently by the critics of the contract at will. Thus, the commonplace belief today (at least outside the actual world of business) is that the contract at will is so unfair and one-sided that it cannot be the outcome of a rational set of bargaining processes any more than, to take the extreme case, a contract for total slavery. * * *

In order to rebut this charge, it is necessary to do more than insist that individuals as a general matter know how to govern their own lives. It is also necessary to display the structural strengths of the contract at will that explain why rational people would enter into such a contract, if not all the time, then at least most of it. The implicit assumption in this argument is that contracts are typically for the mutual benefit of both parties. Yet it is hard to see what other assumption makes any sense in analyzing institutional arrangements (arguably in contradistinction to idiosyncratic, nonrepetitive transactions). To be sure, there are occasional cases of regret after the fact, especially after an infrequent, but costly, contingency comes to pass. There will be cases in which parties are naive, befuddled, or worse. Yet in framing either a rule of policy or a rule of construction, the focus cannot be on that biased set of cases in which the contract aborts and litigation ensues. Instead, attention must be directed to standard repetitive transactions, where the centralizing tendency powerfully promotes expected mutual gain. It is simply incredible to postulate that either employers or employees, motivated as they are by self-interest, would enter routinely into a transaction that leaves them worse off than they were before, or even worse off than their next best alternative.

From this perspective, then, the task is to explain how and why the at-will contracting arrangement (in sharp contrast to slavery) typically works to the mutual advantage of the parties.

* * *

The reason why these contracts at will are effective is precisely that the employer must always pay an implicit price when he exercises his right to fire. He no longer has the right to compel the employee's service, as the employee can enter the market to find another job. The costs of the employer's decision therefore are borne in large measure by the employer himself, creating an implicit system of coinsurance between employer and employee against employer abuse. Nor, it must be stressed, are the costs to the employer light. It is true that employees who work within a firm acquire specific knowledge about its operation and upon dismissal can transfer only a portion of that knowledge to the new job. Nonetheless, the problem is roughly symmetrical, as the employer must find, select, and train a replacement worker who may not turn out to be better than the first employee. Workers are not fungible, and sorting them out may be difficult: resumes can be misleading, if not fraudulent; references may be only too eager to unload an unsuitable employee; training is expensive; and the new worker may not like the job or may be forced to move out of town. In any case, firms must bear the costs of voluntary turnover by workers who quit, which gives them a frequent reminder of the need to avoid self-inflicted losses. The institutional stability of employment contracts at will can now be explained in part by their legal fragility. The right to fire is exercised only infrequently because the threat of firing is effective.

* * *

The proposed reforms in the at-will doctrine cannot hope to transfer wealth systematically from rich to poor on the model of comprehensive systems of taxation or welfare benefits. Indeed it is very difficult to identify in advance any deserving group of recipients that stands to gain unambiguously from the universal abrogation of the at-will contract. The proposed rules cover the whole range from senior executives to manual labor. At every wage level, there is presumably some differential in workers' output. Those who tend to slack off seem on balance to be most vulnerable to dismissal under the at-will rule; yet it is very hard to imagine why some special concession should be made in their favor at the expense of their more diligent fellow workers.

NOTES AND QUESTIONS

1.   Are you convinced by Professor Epstein's defense of the employment at will doctrine? His argument is premised on a number of assumptions about the nature of the labor market. What are they? Do you agree with them?

2.   Epstein admits that the doctrine of employment at will is not appropriate for all types of employment relationships. What types would he except from the rule's general application?

3.   Elsewhere in the article, Epstein specifically addresses long term relationships similar to those which existed in many of the previous cases in this chapter. He asserts that both the employer and the employee have incentives to preserve such relationships because of the "capital" which they have built up over time: the employee is entitled to greater vacation, sick leave, pension and other benefits because of job tenure, and the long-term employee is more valuable to the employer because of his or her intimate knowledge of the business. Furthermore, it is costly for the employer to seek and train replacements. What forces operate to counteract these incentives?

4.   In one response to Epstein, the author wrote:

> When we come down to cases, an employment contract is a very curious creature, since the nature of the exchange is not made very explicit in most instances. On one hand, employment is an authoritarian relationship in which the employee undertakes an obligation to follow certain orders and commands of the employer. On the other hand, it contains important elements of delegation in which the employee is given latitude within broad limits to behave in the interests of the firm. Some elements of the contract are express or clearly implied and are actionable for breach (e.g., nonpayment for work done or misappropriation of firm property). But most terms of the contract (not merely its duration), are left unspecified, precisely because it is too costly to write them down and to verify that they have been performed. These therefore represent an *implicit understanding* about which there may be significant scope for disagreements through asymmetrical information.
>
> At-will contracts protect both parties against actions by the other that are beyond the terms of this mutual implicit understanding. * * * But some of the cases discussed by Epstein left me uneasy. I kept asking myself what the mutual understanding might have been and whether the actions taken were conformable with it. If some monitoring is necessary to achieve efficiency in contracting, precisely why is it that these implicit terms should not be actionable, as they are, for example, in commercial law? (Emphasis in original.)

Sherwin Rosen, Commentary: In Defense of the Contract at Will, 51 U.Chi.L.Rev. 983 (1984).

The at-will model of employment allows an employer to discharge an employee for any reason or for no reason at all. What happens when actions required of an employee during the course of employment violate his or her beliefs? Should an employee be allowed to refuse to do a required job function but still be allowed to keep the job if that belief is a matter of conscience for her? For example, a pharmacist at your local drug store does not believe in contraception. Should he or she be excused from dispensing birth control? If the pharmacist refuses, does an employer have a right to fire the employee? States have taken various positions on this issue. Some states, like South Dakota and Mississippi, passed "conscience clause" legislation protecting pharmacists who refuse to dispense birth control. Conscience clause legislation has extended beyond its original scope of abortion and is increasingly applied to broader issues in healthcare. How do you reconcile this with the employment at-will model and an employer's right to choose its employees? There are many constitutional issues latent in this debate, including freedom of religion. See James A. Sonne, Firing Thoreau: Conscience and At-Will Employment, 9 U. Pa. J. Lab. & Emp. L 235 (2007) ("contend[ing] that no protection of employee conscience is proper without a due consideration of the countervailing employer interest in at-will authority.")

5. Epstein questions whether employees as a class benefit from the erosion of the employment at will rule. When one employee is dismissed, another is typically hired to take his or her place, so that the net employment (or unemployment) effect is zero. In fact, Epstein argues, eliminating the rule is harmful to employees, in that under the at will rule, the employer is more willing to give marginal or risky employees a chance, since they can easily be terminated if their performance is unsatisfactory. What benefits, if any, do employees as a class gain from modifications of the at will doctrine?

Consider the situation presented in Campbell v. PMI Food Equip. Group, Inc., 509 F.3d 776 (6th Cir. 2007). PMI decided to downsize a plant in Piqua, Ohio, after the expiration of its favorable tax-abatement agreement with the city. In the process, PMI terminated all 66 of the plant's hourly employees. PMI replaced the hourly workers with individuals from a temporary employment agency. The workers claimed that of the 66 hourly employees terminated 51 were over the age of 40 while the average age of the temporary workers used to replace the hourly workers was 34. The Sixth Circuit found this was not a violation of the ADEA as it was a workforce reduction that terminated 100 percent of its hourly employees regardless of whether they were over or under 40 years old. Furthermore, the hourly workers were never "replaced" as PMI did not employ the temporary workers but relied on a temp agency, an independent contractor. Do you believe the employment at-will model has worked adequately in this situation? Do you believe the hourly workers, who did have a collective bargaining agreement, should have done a better job in negotiating their rights, or has the employer been given the opportunity to side-step the law by using temporary workers?

6. Resistance to efforts to reform the at will doctrine come from pro-employee advocates as well as from the management community. See Catler, The Case Against Proposals to Eliminate the Employment at Will Rule, 5 Indus.Rel.L.J. 471 (1983), arguing that modification of the at will rule should be limited to breaches of public policy. The author contends that employee rights in the workplace are best secured through collective bargaining with the employer; in the long run, any legislated just cause provision will significantly undermine employees' incentive to unionize. The solution, according to Catler, is not for the government to provide job security for those who are not now protected by a just cause clause, but to eliminate barriers to their obtaining such security themselves, through such actions as extending coverage of the National Labor Relations Act to permit unionization by more employees, consolidating all legal actions relating to employment in one forum, and adopting broader protection against discrimination in employment than the narrow bases protected in Title VII and other statutes.

7. Although organized labor now supports efforts to reform the at-will rule, this was not always the case. Many union leaders were concerned that limiting an employer's ability to terminate employees at will would eliminate the most attractive feature that unions have to offer. See Nancy R. Hauserman & Cheryl L. Maranto, The Union Substitution Hypothesis Revisited: Do Judicially Created Exceptions to the Termination-at-Will Doctrine Hurt Unions?, 72 Marquette L.Rev. 317 (1989).

2. WORKER PERCEPTIONS

Professor Epstein asserts in his article that the parties in the employment relationship should be free to contract as they wish. But what if one of the parties is mistaken as to what, exactly, the at-will employment relationship entails? Professor Pauline Kim surveyed over 330 unemployed workers in the St. Louis metropolitan area to see how much job protection they believed the law afforded them.

Pauline Kim, Bargaining With Imperfect Information: A Study of Worker Perceptions of Legal Protection in an At-Will World
83 Cornell L. Rev. 105 (1997).

* * *

The survey data reveal a striking level of misunderstanding among respondents of the most basic legal rules governing the employment relationship. In Part I, which asked whether certain specified reasons for discharging an at-will employee are lawful, the average score was 51%; in other words, respondents gave correct responses barely half the time. Because each question had only two possible answers—lawful or unlawful—it appears at first glance that respondents' ability to apply the at-will rule to specific factual situations was no better than if they were guessing randomly.

A closer look at the data, however, reveals more systematic errors in the respondents' beliefs about the relevant legal rules. Table 1 reports separately the responses given to each of the eight questions in Part I. Examining the results for individual questions makes clear that the errors are not randomly distributed, but result from respondents' systematic overestimation of legal protection in certain circumstances. For example, overwhelming majorities of the respondents erroneously believed that an employer cannot legally fire an employee in order to hire someone else at a lower wage (82.2%), for reporting internal wrongdoing by another employee (79.2%), based on a mistaken belief of the employee's own wrongdoing (87.2%), or out of personal dislike of the employee (89%). Comparison of error rates confirms this systematic bias. When the discharge described is in fact unlawful, the average error rate is 9.6%; in contrast, the average error rate in identifying lawful discharges is 60.7%. 154 Thus, in assessing their legal rights, the respondents overwhelmingly erred in the same direction, tending to believe discharges are unlawful when they are in fact lawful.

TABLE 1
RESPONSES TO PART I OF SURVEY
(N=337)

Reason for Discharge	% of Total Responses			Legal Rule in Missouri: Discharge Is	Error Rate
	Lawful	Unlawful	No Response		
1. Employer plans to hire another person to do same job at a lower wage	17.8	82.2	0	Lawful	82.2
2. Unsatisfactory job performance	92.0	7.7	.3	Lawful	7.7
3. Retaliation for reporting theft by another employee to supervisor	20.8	79.2	0	Lawful	79.2
4. Mistaken belief that employee stole money (employee can prove mistake)	10.4	87.2	2.4	Lawful	87.2
5. Retaliation for reporting violation of fire regulations to government agency	8.9	88.7	2.4	Unlawful	8.9
6. Lack of work	78.6	18.7	2.7	Lawful	18.7
7. Personal dislike of employee	8.0	89.0	3.0	Lawful	89.0
8. Retaliation for refusing to participate in illegal billing practice	10.4	87.2	2.4	Unlawful	10.4

* * *

Looking only at these six questions [omitting questions 2 and 6]—in which the employer fires a worker for a reason unlikely to be sufficient under a just-cause standard—respondents, on average, answered only 40% of the questions correctly. As noted above, the errors are not randomly distributed. Rather, for all six questions, respondents overwhelmingly believed that discharges under the circumstances described are unlawful. The only two questions that large majorities answered correctly (Part I, Questions 5 and 8) were those in which the discharges described are in fact unlawful. For the remaining four questions, similar majorities persisted in believing—erroneously in those situations—that the discharge is prohibited. Thus, respondents consistently assumed that an employee cannot be discharged without a good reason, apparently believing that workers have something akin to just-cause protection by law.

* * *

By contradicting a key assumption of the traditional economic defense of the at-will rule, this study undermines the faith that observed market outcomes reflect an efficient solution. But though its findings are more consistent with assumptions commonly made by critics of the at-will rule, these data offer no certainty that a mandatory just-cause requirement would prove more efficient. At most, the results of this study suggest the appropriateness of a just-cause default rule.

3. REASONS FOR ADOPTING A JUST-CAUSE REGIME

Cynthia L. Estlund, Wrongful Discharge Protections in an At-Will World
74 Tex. L. Rev. 1655 (1996).

The fundamental problem with the existing "bad motive" exceptions to employment at will is the inherent difficulty of proving that bad motive. The burden invariably lies with the employee (or an agency on the employee's behalf) to prove a particular prohibited motive on the part of an employer who is almost certainly better advised than the employee and who creates and controls virtually all of the relevant documents and employs most of the potential witnesses.

This burden is all the greater for imperfect employees who have made mistakes, fallen short of the employer's standards on occasion, or sometimes been absent or late or irritating. Although the law protects imperfect as well as perfect employees from discrimination and retaliation, the burden of proving the bad motive may be overwhelming for the former. The problems of proof are further magnified to the extent that employers and their supervisors are reasonably well-educated about the employment laws, reasonably cautious in avoiding statements evidencing bad motives, and reasonably diligent in documenting employee shortcomings. The cautious, liability-conscious employer has means, motive, and opportunity to create a plausible record in support of what may in fact be an illegally motivated discharge.

But in fact the employer need not document any legitimate motive; that is what the at-will rule means in the context of a wrongful discharge action. This point was driven home in the context of Title VII by the Supreme Court's recent decision in St. Mary's Honor Center v. Hicks [discussed in Chapter 4, p. 240, supra]. The plaintiff in *Hicks* had made out a prima facie case of race discrimination: he was black, he was fired, and he was replaced by a white employee. This showing shifted to the employer the burden of coming forward with a nondiscriminatory explanation for the decision. The employer did so, but Hicks refuted this explanation to the satisfaction of the lower court, leaving his prima facie case unanswered. The Supreme Court held that this was not enough to establish Title VII liability; the plaintiff must still prove the presence of a discriminatory motive. Whether that interpretation of Title VII is right or wrong (and it is not obviously wrong), it vividly illustrates the gravitational pull of the at-will presumption even within the most entrenched province of wrongful discharge law. When liability depends on proof of a particular bad reason for discharge, "no reason" or even a demonstrably false or fabricated reason is good enough for the employer to escape liability.

The at-will rule continues to rear its head even after proof of an unlawful motive. For once an employee has shown that her discharge was motivated in part by an unlawful consideration such as race, sex, or protected activity, the employer still has an opportunity to prove that it would have made the same decision anyway for permissible reasons. These are the "mixed motive" cases. As a justification for giving the unlawfully motivated employer this opportunity to escape liability, the Supreme Court has cited "employer prerogatives," which are epitomized by employment at will. Employment at will also makes this employer defense an especially potent weapon against plaintiffs, for employment at will means that "permissible reasons" need not be fair or just or reasonable, but simply not unlawful. Employment at will means that the entire universe of foolish, petty, unfounded, or arbitrary reasons for discharge—as long as they are not unlawfully discriminatory or retaliatory—are [sic] available to the employer to excuse a discharge that has already been proven to be motivated in part by unlawful reasons * * *.

The at-will doctrine also has some consequences that are peculiar to either the antidiscrimination or the antiretaliation field. Let me begin with the antiretaliation doctrines, which generally protect some voluntary activity on the part of the employee that society wishes to encourage, such as discussions of unionization or the disclosure of unsafe conditions or unlawful activity. Most of these protected employee activities threaten the interests of the employer, or are thought to do so; otherwise it would not be necessary to prohibit employer retaliation. Moreover, most of these employee activities chiefly benefit others—other employees, customers, the public at large. They are, in short, public goods that are likely to be "underproduced" even without the threat of retaliation.

To the extent that the law does not effectively remedy or deter retaliation—and I believe that is the net effect of the various hurdles to relief described above—then employees are likely to be deterred from engaging in the socially valued activity that the law purports to protect. In this way, I believe the powerful and often overpowering pull of at-will undermines each of the policies underlying the antiretaliation laws.

Let me suggest an analogy to freedom of speech as against the government. The analogy is in fact quite apt, because many of the antiretaliation laws do protect employee expression of some kind against retaliation by the employer, or the "government" of the workplace. Suppose the government were prohibited from retaliating against its citizens because of their criticism of public officials, but were otherwise free to punish them for "good reason, bad reason, or no reason at all," without notice or a hearing. The citizen who was thrown in jail, and who believed it was based on her political dissent, could bring a lawsuit; if she proved that the government's motive was to censure protected speech, she would be released from jail and awarded damages. Would the cautious citizen feel free to speak against the government? The answer seems clear: without basic due process protections, free speech rights would be extremely vulnerable. It seems equally clear to me that the existing wrongful discharge doctrines, and the rights of freedom of speech and action that they purport to secure, are undermined by the absence of a basic regime of substantive and procedural fairness in the workplace * * *.

This proposition profoundly unsettles the foundations of the economic defense of at-will. For example, the defenders argue that the number of unjustified discharges is actually quite low, and that the adoption of a just cause requirement would impose significant costs on employers with very little payoff in avoidance of arbitrary discharges. But suppose that part of the explanation for the relatively small number of arbitrary discharges is that employees are choosing not to engage in socially valued conduct that might get them fired? That employees' vulnerability to discharge leads them to comply with unjustified employer demands? If that is true, then the prevalence of unjustified discharges may be only a small part of the picture that is relevant to the assessment of at-will employment and its costs * * *.

Let us look at the present legal environment through the eyes of a prospective complainant. In the at-will workplace, simple negligence, lack of notice or of warnings, personal favoritism, pique, or sloppiness in evaluation or investigation gives no basis for relief. The at-will employee must make a plausible claim of unlawful discrimination (or retaliation) in order to secure any impartial review of her otherwise unappealable termination. Those who fit into one of the classes protected by antidiscrimination law—mainly women, minorities, older, or handicapped workers—may consequently see and claim discrimination when there is simple garden-variety unfairness. Certainly if they consult an attorney about their legal options, they will be encouraged to look for signs of discrimination. So the gap between the protections of the antidiscrimination laws and the non-protections of at-will may push employees to claim discrimination in response to perceived unfairness of any kind * * *.

Let us now look at this landscape from the standpoint of employees who are not members of a protected class. The problems of proof that an alleged victim faces may not be enough to dispel the perception among some of her white coworkers that she is getting something they are not—that the employer is especially cautious when dealing with minority employees (and women), and considers and reviews adverse decisions affecting those groups more carefully, while white men in particular remain subject to the unalloyed and merciless at-will regime. However ineffectual existing remedies for discrimination may be for most employees, their availability to some may foster resentment by others. Employees who are not "protected" by those laws may perceive fairness itself as a special privilege from which they are excluded. The claim of "reverse discrimination" is a tempting response that mirrors the victim-orientation of wrongful discharge law and aggravates the dynamic of fragmentation and polarization * * *.

Fair treatment should not be or appear to be a special privilege. The time may have come to move from the old rule of unfettered employer discretion, riddled as it now is with exceptions, to a new rule of fair treatment. A requirement of just cause for discharge and a fair process for enforcing it would help to realize the policies underlying each of the existing exceptions to employment at will while responding to the concerns—both the valid concerns and those that are understandable but exaggerated—of those who do not normally qualify for any of those exceptions.

4. SYNTHESIZING JUST-CAUSE AND EMPLOYMENT AT-WILL

Stewart J. Schwab, Life-Cycle Justice: Accommodating Just Cause and Employment At-Will
92 Mich. L. Rev. 8 (1993).

* * *

If we recall the life cycle of the career employee, we can identify a more systematic pattern of legal intervention. Over the life cycle of a career employee, a sequence of possibilities for opportunism exists. A career employee is particularly vulnerable to opportunism at the beginning and end of his career. By contrast, employers are especially vulnerable to opportunism at the employee's midcareer. The cases suggest that courts are sensitive to this life cycle. Courts are most likely to scrutinize firings at the beginning and end of the life cycle. Courts do not get involved during midcareer unless they see an obvious case of particular opportunism, such as a firing before a pension vests or a sales commission is due

* * *

[C]ourts sometimes allow claims by beginning-career employees who are arbitrarily fired after moving or quitting a prior job. Some courts use a promissory estoppel or reliance theory, some find an implied contract for a reasonable time to allow the employee to recoup his expenses, and some simply use the decision to move or to quit as evidence of an actual definite-term agreement. Regardless of the theory for recovery, one can explain these cases as attempts to regulate opportunistic firings early in the life cycle. Employers have not yet invested in the relationship and thus are not hurt if they arbitrarily dismiss the new employee. This means that the relationship is not self-enforcing, as it is when both parties have incurred sunk costs.

Nevertheless, protection for beginning-career employees is far from universal. Many or even most courts refuse to find that reliance on an at-will job offer is reasonable. In these cases, an employee quits another job or moves to a new job at his own risk.

The ambivalence of courts in this area is understandable. For at least three reasons, the opportunistic termination rationale for protecting employees is weaker in these beginning-career cases than it is later in the life cycle. First, very often the employer also makes substantial investments early in the relationship. Recruiting and training new employees can be a major cost to many firms. As Paul Weiler describes recruiting costs:

> The recruiting process itself imposes significant costs on the firm; not merely on the personnel department, which must do the initial advertising and screening, but also on the operating divisions, which must interview and judge the suitability of candidates. The magnitude of these costs can vary widely, depending on the nature of the job, the skills required, the number of applicants, and so on, but on occasion they can be substantial indeed.

One study estimated that a typical firm spends 160 hours in hiring and training a new worker in the first three months on the job, and that these costs are nearly thirty percent of the value of an experienced coworker during the three-month period. If the employer as well as the employee sustain heavy early costs, the risk of opportunistic termination is smaller. An employer that arbitrarily or unjustifiably fires an employee hurts itself as well, for it wastes the expenses of recruiting.

Second, even if recruiting costs are insignificant—as they will be in many cases—so that arbitrarily firing the employee does not penalize the employer, the employer gains nothing from firing a person early in his career. Thus, while employees often suffer no penalty from an arbitrary beginning-career firing, they gain no benefit from them either. This fact distinguishes beginning-career from late-career firings, in which the employer can gain from firing employees whom it pays more than their current output.

A final problem with job protection for new employees is that employers often need a probationary period to sort out hiring mistakes, wherein they can fire employees without explanation or extensive documentation of their reasons. Relevant here is the fact that competitive firms, largely responding to the entry and exit of early-career employees, virtually always contract for at-will dismissal. Even the Model Employment Termination Act, which calls for general good-cause protection for employees, refuses to protect employees with less than a year of service.

In sum, in many situations employer opportunism against beginning employees is either a trivial threat or outweighed by legitimate needs to maintain employer flexibility. In these situations, courts do not scrutinize the sudden termination. Still, the potential for opportunistic employer offers is real. An employer engages in opportunistic behavior when it hires a better person before training anyone but after the first job applicant has relied on the offer. Courts protect beginning employees from such opportunism.

Late-career employees face the greatest danger of opportunistic firings. At the end of their life cycle, they often earn more than their current productivity. If they do, the employer has a financial incentive to terminate them, even if it violates an implicit promise to allow the employee to reap the rewards of hard work earlier in his career.

* * *

Late in an employee's career, the usual checks against opportunistic firings unravel. Courts enter to monitor the bargain. The bargain does not give late-career employees complete job security. They can be dismissed for cause, because otherwise the shirking problems would be immense, but the employer does not prove cause simply by proving that salary exceeds current productivity. That is the typical life-cycle pattern that both sides to career employment anticipate and, ex ante, it is in the interests of both sides.

Once the employer has begun to make substantial, asset-specific investments in an employee, the risk of arbitrary firing diminishes. The greater danger of opportunistic behavior—at least, behavior that an appropriate dismissal standard could limit—comes from the employee's side. Because the employer does not want to repeat recruiting and training costs with another employee, the incumbent employee has an opportunity to shirk without fear of dismissal. Shirking at midcareer can occur even if the employer has the right to dismiss at will, but the shirking problem can be exacerbated if the employer must also surmount the hurdle of proving just cause.

This is not to say that the employer cannot exploit the midcareer employee. Indeed, as I emphasized above, being trapped by investments in firm-specific capital and in community roots can make a midcareer employee ripe for exploitation. But the exploitation will not take the form of firing because the employer is making money from the relationship. Rather than fire a midcareer employee, an employer may pay him less than would be called for under a fair division of the gains from the long-term relationship or make his workload or working conditions more onerous. Just cause cannot protect the midcareer employee from these abuses. Better, then, for the law to focus on something it can handle, which is deterrence of shirking by midcareer employees. The courts seem to have intuited this fact by refusing, in general, to create contract protections against arbitrary terminations for midcareer workers. Midcareer employees have made the fewest contributions to the doctrinal erosion of at-will employment.

In summary, my argument is that the general pattern of good-faith and implied-contract cases reflects an intuitive understanding by the courts that employees are subject to opportunistic discharge at the end, and less consistently at the beginning, of the life cycle. Courts are reluctant, however, to give general protection against arbitrary dismissal to midcareer employees. The economic self-interest of employers should keep such dismissals in check. The greater concern is with employee shirking.

To clarify the distinction I draw between scrutinizing opportunistic late-career terminations and scrutinizing all employment decisions under a just-cause standard, let me return to the facts of Murphy v. American Home Products [discussed supra, p. 955]. Murphy, like the California Foley, was an internal whistleblower who reported to upper management wrongdoing by immediate supervisors. While bucking the corporate hierarchy often gets employees into trouble, courts are hesitant to referee the resulting turf fights. Internal whistleblowing resembles too closely legitimate, but practically unverifiable, concerns that an employee is not a team player or that an employee creates difficulty in the office. Legal limning of these situations is probably not worth the costs.

Thus, I would have greater sympathy for Murphy if he claimed that he was fired after twenty-three years of service because he was no longer pulling his weight or earning his salary. Unless the parties have clearly agreed to at-will dismissals throughout the life cycle, such a firing smacks of an employer opportunistically firing an employee who has committed the best years of his life and should reap, based on the norms of seniority, the benefits of a career commitment to the employer. In fact, Murphy did claim age discrimination—a claim that was still being litigated a decade after his discharge. But a legitimate defense might be that opportunism had nothing to do with the termination; he was fired because he attempted to buck the corporate system. Of course, when an employer fires an older worker allegedly for such a reason, the proof problems in sorting out the real reason for discharge are enormous. This dilemma quite likely will make employers wary of firing older workers. My point, in short, is that just-cause protection should be limited to an inquiry into whether the employee was fired in breach of the life-cycle commitment to pay seniority-based wages and benefits or for other opportunistic reasons.

* * *

The life-cycle framework that courts have developed provides the parties in a career employment relationship a legal structure that checks opportunistic behavior. Its fundamental premise is that both employer and employees can act opportunistically. Consequently, a life-cycle analysis does not categorically condemn or celebrate employment at will. It supports, in broad outline, the contract law inroads that have been made on the at-will doctrine, particularly at the beginning and the end of an employee's career, and it explains the continued vitality of the at-will rule for midcareer employees. The current position of the courts is superior to a dogmatic insistence on the old at-will regime, which creates an excessive risk of opportunistic terminations for long-term, and sometimes beginning-career workers. Moreover, the current hesitant, intermediate position may also be superior to a general just-cause standard, which would lead to excessive shirking by midcareer workers.

The life-cycle framework therefore makes coherent the seemingly schizophrenic behavior by courts in employment termination cases. Within the framework, courts will protect employees when the danger of employer opportunism is high, but they will retain the at-will presumption when the employer is more vulnerable. One can thus argue that the courts are reacting appropriately to the employment-termination cases they encounter. This coherence in the common law is internal to the system. In particular, it assumes that common law litigation is the chosen method of resolving these disputes, and that the courts largely do not consider the systemic costs of litigation. It may be preferable, all things considered, to opt for an administrative or arbitration system that requires just cause for all employment terminations. But it is unfair, in arguing for such a change, to portray the current common law as hopeless chaos. Far from being chaotic, the current common law provides optimal rules for regulating employment terminations.

CHAPTER 11

EMPLOYEES' DUTIES TO THE EMPLOYER

Just as the at-will doctrine allows an employer to fire an employee for any reason or for no reason, so long as the reason is not illegal, theoretically the at-will doctrine also allows an employee to quit for any reason or for no reason. In practice, this freedom to end the employment relationship tends to be less useful to employees than to employers. It is usually more difficult and disruptive for an employee to find a new job than it is for an employer to find a new employee, so quitting to resolve employment disputes is often a recourse of last resort for employees, particularly those who are unskilled or who possess skills that are widely held. Furthermore, like the employer's right to fire at-will, the employee's right to quit is also limited in various ways. Because these limitations tend to increase with the employee's skills and responsibilities, they effectively constrain the post-employment choices of those employees in better bargaining positions who would be better able to exercise the option to quit and to find suitable alternative employment. This chapter will cover limitations on an employee's right to quit that allow an employer to safeguard its investment in its employees.

A. BREACH OF CONTRACT BY AN EMPLOYEE

1. BREACH OF EXPRESS TERMS

Handicapped Children's Education Board v. Lukaszewski
332 N.W.2d 774 (Wis. 1983).

■ CALLOW, JUSTICE.

This review arises out of an unpublished decision of the court of appeals which affirmed in part and reversed in part a judgment of the Ozaukee county circuit court, Judge Warren A. Grady.

In January of 1978 the Handicapped Children's Education Board (the Board) hired Elaine Lukaszewski to serve as a speech and language therapist for the spring term. Lukaszewski was assigned to the Lightfoot School in Sheboygan Falls which was approximately 45 miles from her home in Mequon. Rather than move, she commuted to work each day. During the 1978 spring term, the Board offered Lukaszewski a contract to continue in her present position at Lightfoot School for the 1978–79 school year. The contract called for an annual salary of $10,760. Lukaszewski accepted.

In August of 1978, prior to the beginning of the school year, Lukaszewski was offered a position by the Wee Care Day Care Center which was located not far from her home in Mequon. The job paid an annual salary of $13,000. After deciding to accept this offer, Lukaszewski notified Thomas Morrelle, the Board's director of special education, that she intended to resign from her position at the Lightfoot School. Morrelle told her to submit a letter of resignation for consideration by the Board. She did so, and the matter was discussed at a meeting of the Board on August 21, 1978. The Board refused to release Lukaszewski from her contract. On August 24, 1978, the Board's attorney sent a letter to Lukaszewski directing her to return to work. The attorney sent a second letter to the Wee Care Day Care Center stating that the Board would take legal action if the Center interfered with Lukaszewski's performance of her contractual obligations at the Lightfoot School. A copy of this letter was sent to the Department of Public Instruction.

Lukaszewski left the Wee Care Day Care Center and returned to Lightfoot School for the 1978 fall term. She resented the actions of the Board, however, and retained misgivings about her job. On September 8, 1978, she discussed her feelings with Morrelle. After this meeting Lukaszewski felt quite upset about the situation. She called her doctor to make an appointment for that afternoon and subsequently left the school.

Dr. Ashok Chatterjee examined Lukaszewski and found her blood pressure to be high. Lukaszewski asked Dr. Chatterjee to write a letter explaining his medical findings and the advice he had given her. In a letter dated September 11, 1978, Dr. Chatterjee indicated that Lukaszewski had a hypertension problem dating back to 1976. He reported that on the day he examined Lukaszewski she appeared agitated, nervous, and had blood pressure readings up to 180/100. It was his opinion that, although she took hypotensive drugs, her medical condition would not improve unless the situation which caused the problem was removed. He further opined that it would be dangerous for her to drive long distances in her agitated state.

Lukaszewski did not return to work after leaving on September 8, 1978. She submitted a letter of resignation dated September 13, 1978, in which she wrote:

"I enclose a copy of the doctor's statement concerning my health. On the basis of it, I must resign. I am unwilling to jeopardize my health and I am also unwilling to become involved in an accident. For these reasons, I tender my resignation."

A short time later Lukaszewski reapplied for and obtained employment at the Wee Care Day Care Center.

After Lukaszewski left, the Board immediately began looking for a replacement. Only one qualified person applied for the position. Although this applicant had less of an educational background than Lukaszewski, she had more teaching experience. Under the salary schedule agreed upon by the Board and the teachers' union, this applicant would have to be paid $1,026.64 more per year than Lukaszewski. Having no alternative, the Board hired the applicant at the higher salary.

In December of 1978 the Board initiated an action against Lukaszewski for breach of contract. The Board alleged that, as a result of the breach, it suffered damage in the amount of the additional compensation it was required to pay Lukaszewski's replacement for the 1978–79 school year ($1,026.64). A trial was held before the court. The trial court ruled that Lukaszewski had breached her contract and awarded the Board $1,249.14 in damages ($1,026.64 for breach of contract and $222.50 for costs).

* * *

There are two issues presented on this review: (1) whether Lukaszewski breached her employment contract with the Board; and (2) if she did breach her contract, whether the Board suffered recoverable damages therefrom.

It is undisputed that Lukaszewski resigned before her contract with the Board expired. The only question is whether her resignation was somehow justified. Lukaszewski argues that, because she resigned for health reasons, the trial court erred in finding a breach of contract. According to Lukaszewski, the uncontroverted evidence at trial established that her employment with the Board endangered her health. Therefore, her failure to fulfill her obligation under the employment contract was excused.

We recognize that under certain conditions illness or health dangers may excuse nonperformance of a contract. This court held long ago that "where the act to be performed is one which the promisor alone is competent to do, the obligation is discharged if he is prevented by sickness or death from performing it." Jennings v. Lyons, 39 Wis. 553, 557 (1876). Even assuming this rule applies to Lukaszewski's failure to perform, we are not convinced that the trial court erred in finding a breach of contract.

A health danger will not excuse nonperformance of a contractual obligation when the danger is caused by the nonperforming party. Nor will a health condition or danger which was foreseeable when the contract was entered into justify its breach. It would be fundamentally unfair to allow a breaching party to escape liability because of a health danger which by his or her own fault has precluded performance.

In the instant case the trial court expressly found that the danger to Lukaszewski's health was self-induced. Lukaszewski testified that it was stressful for her to return to the Lightfoot School in the fall of 1978 because she did not want to work there and because she resented the Board's actions to compel her to do so. Citing this testimony, the court concluded: "The Court finds that the defendant's medical excuse was a result of the stress condition she had created by an attempted repudiation of her contract, and was not the product of any unsubstantiated, so-called, harrassment [sic] by the plaintiff's board." Lukaszewski further complained about the hazard of driving 45 miles to and from Sheboygan Falls each day. She alone, however, caused this commute by choosing to live in Mequon. The trial court pointed out in its decision from the bench that she could have eliminated this problem by simply moving to Sheboygan Falls. Thus the court clearly found that any health danger associated with performance of the employment contract was the fault of Lukaszewski, not the Board. This factual finding alone is enough to invalidate the medical excuse for Lukaszewski's breach.

The medical excuse is defective for a second reason. In order to excuse Lukaszewski's nonperformance, the trial court would have to have made a factual finding that she resigned for health reasons. The oral decision and supplemental written decision of the trial court indicate that it found otherwise. In its written decision the court stated:

> "[Lukaszewski's] reasons for resignation were succinctly stated in her testimony, upon cross-examination * * * as follows: '* * * I had found a job that was closer in proximity to my home and it offered a different type of challenge, * * * also that the pay was, was more, and I asked them if I could be released from my contract.'"

The trial court did not include the health danger. Indeed, the court appeared to doubt that Lukaszewski resigned for health reasons. The trial judge observed that Lukaszewski had a history of hypertension dating back at least five or six years. Her blood pressure would fluctuate at the slightest provocation. He further noted that she was able to commute between Sheboygan Falls and Mequon from January, 1978, through the middle of the following summer. In short, the decisions indicate that the court believed Lukaszewski resigned for reasons other than her health.

These factual findings by the trial court invalidate Lukaszewski's medical excuse and thereby establish a breach.

* * *

We conclude that the trial court's findings of fact are not against the great weight and clear preponderance of the evidence and, therefore, must be upheld. Accordingly, we affirm that portion of the court of appeals' decision which affirmed the circuit court's determination that Lukaszewski breached her employment contract.

This court has long held that an employer may recover damages from an employee who has failed to perform an employment contract. Damages in breach of contract cases are ordinarily measured by the expectations of the parties. The nonbreaching party is entitled to full compensation for the loss of his or her bargain—that is, losses necessarily flowing from the breach which are proven to a reasonable certainty and were within contemplation of the parties when the contract was made.

Thus damages for breach of an employment contract include the cost of obtaining other services equivalent to that promised but not performed, plus any foreseeable consequential damages.

In the instant case it is undisputed that, as a result of the breach, the Board hired a replacement at a salary exceeding what it had agreed to pay Lukaszewski. There is no question that this additional cost ($1,026.64) necessarily flowed from the breach and was within the contemplation of the parties when the contract was made. Lukaszewski argues and the court of appeals held, however, that the Board was not damaged by this expense. The amount a teacher is paid is determined by a salary schedule agreed upon by the teachers' union and the Board. The more education and experience a teacher has the greater her salary will be. Presumably, then, the amount of compensation a teacher receives reflects her value to the Board. Lukaszewski argues that the Board suffered no net loss because, while it had to pay more for the replacement, it received the services of a proportionately more valuable teacher. Accordingly, she maintains that the Board is not entitled to damages because an award would place it in a better position than if the contract had been performed.

We disagree. Lukaszewski and the court of appeals improperly focus on the objective value of the services the Board received rather than that for which it had bargained. Damages for breach of contract are measured by the expectations of the parties. The Board expected to receive the services of a speech therapist with Lukaszewski's education and experience at the salary agreed upon. It neither expected nor wanted a more experienced therapist who had to be paid an additional $1,026.64 per year. Lukaszewski's breach forced the Board to hire the replacement and, in turn, to pay a higher salary. Therefore, the Board lost the benefit of its bargain. Any additional value the Board may have received from the replacement's greater experience was imposed upon it and thus cannot be characterized as a benefit. We conclude that the Board suffered damages for the loss of its bargain in the amount of additional compensation it was required to pay Lukaszewski's replacement.

This is not to say that an employer who is injured by an employee's breach of contract is free to hire the most qualified and expensive replacement and then recover the difference between the salary paid and the contract salary. An injured party must take all reasonable steps to mitigate damages. Therefore, the employer must attempt to obtain equivalent services at the lowest possible cost. In the instant case the Board acted reasonably in hiring Lukaszewski's replacement even though she commanded a higher salary. Upon Lukaszewski's breach, the Board immediately took steps to locate a replacement. Only one qualified person applied for the position. Having no alternative, the Board hired this applicant. Thus the Board properly mitigated its damages by hiring the least expensive, qualified replacement available.

We hold that the Board is entitled to have the benefit of its bargain restored. Therefore, we reverse that portion of the court of appeals' decision which reversed the trial court's damage award.

The decision of the court of appeals is affirmed in part and reversed in part.

■ DAY, JUSTICE (dissenting).

I dissent. The majority opinion correctly states, "The only question is whether her resignation is somehow justified." I would hold that it was.

Elaine Lukaszewski left her employment with the school board. She suffered from high blood pressure and had been treated for several years by her physician for the condition. She claimed her hypertension increased due to stress caused when the Board refused to cancel her teaching contract. Stress can cause a precipitous rise in blood pressure. High blood pressure can bring on damage to other organs of the body.

She was upset over what she perceived was the unreasonable attitude of her employer in refusing to cancel her contract. Following an unpleasant exchange with the Board's Director of Special Education, Mr. Morrelle, she went to her physician. He found her blood pressure to be 180 over 100 which he testified was very high. He advised her to rest and to get out of the situation that was causing her symptoms which she properly interpreted to mean "quit the job." He also told her that her elevated blood pressure made it dangerous for her to drive the ninety miles round-trip each day, that commuting from her home in Mequon to Sheboygan Falls entailed.

The trial court and the majority of this court conclude she could have obviated the danger of driving by moving to Sheboygan Falls. But the fact is that would not have eliminated her illness nor the hazards to her health that her condition posed. There is not a shred of medical evidence that her blood pressure problems would be cured or appreciably alleviated if she moved from her home to Sheboygan Falls.

Once the dangerous hypertension is established, and here the only medical testimony did just that, it should follow that one should be relieved of a contractual obligation for services unless malingering is shown. In this case no one denies she has the condition. But, the trial court says, the condition was one "she had created," which the majority on this court refer to as "self induced." The majority here seized on the rationale that illness that is "self induced" is somehow less worthy of judicial consideration than illness caused by others, or by outside forces over which the patient has no control.

It seems clear from the trial judge's comments that if he had found her physical condition had been caused by the Board's "harassment," he would have let her out of the contract. This is the only logical conclusion from the statement by the trial judge that, "The Court finds that the defendant's medical excuse was a result of the stress condition she had created by an attempted repudiation of her contract, and was not the product of any unsubstantiated, so-called, harrassment [sic] by the plaintiff's board."

In either instance, whether "caused" by the Board or "self induced" because of her gnawing feeling of being unfairly treated, the objective symptoms would be the same.

Either, in my opinion, should justify termination of the contract where the physical symptoms are medically certifiable as they admittedly are here.

The majority makes the following assertion, "It would be fundamentally unfair to allow a breaching party to escape liability because of a health danger which by his or her own fault has precluded performance."

Happily no authority is cited for this sweeping statement which means that it will be easier to ignore it, gloss over it, "distinguish" it or overrule it in the future. Under this new found axiom, could a concert violinist under contract be sued to cover any added costs of his replacement if he lost an arm in an accident where he was found 100 percent negligent? Or could another party to a personal service contract be held liable if he was unable to perform because of a debilitating illness clearly caused by negligent health habits?

Jennings is cited by the majority to bolster its position. The case is not really in point. * * *

This court said that since the husband must have known his wife was four months pregnant when they took the job and that she would be unable to complete the year of work, therefore no recovery was allowed. This court said "For when performance becomes impossible by reason of contingencies which should have been foreseen and provided against in the contract, the promisor is held answerable." * * *

The precedential value of *Jennings* is doubtful but to the extent the rules stated may still be valid it provides no support for the majority. Here there is an illness, "an act of God," there is nothing in the record to show that the severe increase in Elaine Lukaszewski's hypertension was foreseeable when she signed the contract. Thus, even under *Jennings,* the teacher should be excused from performance.

Hypertension is a health problem that when caused by stress, however induced, may require a job change. That is what occurred here.

* * *

What the trial court said was that the desire to take the better job brought on the physical symptoms when release from her contract by the Board was refused.

If the trial court had found that she quit merely for the better job and *not* because of her health problems brought on by the high blood pressure, this would be an entirely different case. However, that is *not* what the trial court found in my opinion. The trial court found her medical problems were self induced and concluded they were therefore unworthy of consideration.

I would reverse the court of appeals decision that held she breached her contract.

Because I would hold that on this record there was no breach, I would not reach the damage question.

NOTES AND QUESTIONS

1. The majority and dissenting opinions construe somewhat differently the trial court's ambiguous statements about whether Lukaszewski's hypertension was the real reason for her resignation. Should the court have remanded the case to the trial court for a clearer finding on this issue?

2. The majority opinion in *Lukaszewski* recognizes that ill health on the part of the employee would excuse nonperformance, but that health problems brought on by the employee herself would not be a valid excuse. Is this a meaningful distinction? Suppose the health problems were self-induced through cigarette smoking, overeating, or skiing? Perhaps what the court means to hold as inexcusable were health problems resulting from the attempt to repudiate the contract. Is this distinction better?

3. Other legal grounds for avoiding employment contracts include incapacity, undue influence, duress, fraud, act of God, illegality, intoxication, and misrepresentation. Can you think of examples of how these defenses could arise? When and how might these defenses be utilized by an employee seeking to avoid contractual obligations?

4. Employers often spend substantial sums of money in training new employees. Are these sums recoverable in the event the employee breaches the employment contract? A truck driver signed a three-year contract which included a provision stating that if the employee terminated the agreement the employee would have to pay $1500 to reimburse the employer for training expenses. Colorado law allows employers to recoup training expenses for any employee who works less than two years with the employer. Such an arrangement, however, must be specified in the employment agreement. Dresser Indus. v. Sandvick, 732 F.2d 783 (10th Cir. 1984). New York State United Teachers v. Thompson, 459 F.Supp. 677 (N.D.N.Y.1978), upheld a cause of action in a lawsuit alleging that an employee should reimburse his employer for tuition paid by the employer when the employee refused to meet his contractual obligation to return to the job after an educational leave of absence.

5. With regard to damages, the court follows the general rule that damages for breach of an employment contract include the cost of obtaining equivalent services plus foreseeable consequential damages. Should the plaintiff or defendant have the burden of proving the reasonableness of the damages? Lukaszewski argued that even though the board hired a replacement at a higher salary, it obtained a more experienced teacher, and was therefore not damaged. The court rejected this line of reasoning. It awarded the board "the benefit of its bargain," which amounted primarily to the difference between the replacement's salary and Lukaszewski's salary. Is this an adequate measure of the damages suffered by the school board? In thinking about this, consider whether a higher salaried employee always confers a greater benefit on the employer. How would the calculus change if the only available replacement had a Ph.D. and 20 years experience and was paid twice as much as Lukaszewski?

2.   BREACH OF IMPLIED TERMS

Employees owe some duties to their employers in all jurisdictions. In general, an employee is required to refrain from (1) competing with the employer during the period of employment, (2) appropriating the employer's trade secrets or other confidential information, and (3) otherwise using the employer's resources in such a way as to further potentially competing ends. See, e.g., Restatement (Third) of Employment Law § 8.01 (2014); Restatement (Third) of Agency § 8.04 (2006). Importantly, employees' duties govern conduct that would not normally fall within the scope of non-compete agreements or trade-secret protections. The Eighth Circuit held in Vigoro Indus., Inc. v. Crisp, 82 F.3d 785 (8th Cir. 1996), that an employee who leaves for a competing company may not solicit other employees to join that competitor. The California Court of Appeal has held that an employer may terminate employees who take steps to start a competing business. Stokes v. Dole Nut Co., 41 Cal.App.4th 285 (Cal. Ct. App. 1995). The *Stokes* court found that an employer has the right to expect the "undivided loyalty" of its employees. In all, while the specific obligations of employees depend on the jurisdiction, most courts will prohibit employees from advancing their own interests at the employer's expense.

Depending on his or her position, an employee may be held to various standards of performance that are not mentioned in a contract but are implied under the law of agency. Some employees owe their employers fiduciary duties, duties of care, and duties of loyalty which insure that the employee is acting in the best interests of the employer.

Lamorte Burns & Co. v. Walters
770 A.2d 1158 (N.J. 2001).

■ LaVecchia, J.:

In this case, we consider whether an employee has incurred liability for activities undertaken to plan and prepare for future employment in a newly created business entity established by the employee to compete directly with his current employer. Plaintiff, Lamorte Burns & Co. (Lamorte), filed suit against two of its former employees, Michael Walters and Nancy Nixon, in connection with their conduct in establishing a competing business. Plaintiff's complaint charged that Walters breached the restrictive covenant clauses of his employment agreement, and that both Walters and Nixon breached their duty of loyalty, tortiously interfered with Lamorte's economic advantage, misappropriated its confidential and proprietary information, and competed unfairly.

The trial court granted plaintiff's motion for summary judgment as to liability only. After a hearing, the trial court awarded $232,684 in compensatory damages and an additional $62,816.23 in punitive damages covering counsel fees and costs. In an unpublished opinion, the Appellate Division agreed that Walters had breached his employment contract, but reversed that part of the decision that granted plaintiff summary judgment on its tort claims. The court reasoned that there were disputed facts concerning the confidential and proprietary nature of the information defendants had taken from plaintiff, as well as issues concerning whether defendants' conduct was acceptable competitive behavior or malicious and in violation of the "rules of the game" of the parties' business. We granted certification and now reverse, in part, and reinstate the trial court's judgment sustaining plaintiff's tort claims.

We regard the facts as not significantly in dispute. Where they are, we accord all inferences in favor of defendant as this matter is before us on an appeal from a motion for summary judgment. Lamorte has been in the business of investigating and adjusting claims for both marine and nonmarine liability insurers, their associations, and owners, in the United States and abroad since 1938. Incorporated in Delaware, Lamorte has its principal place of business in Wilton, Connecticut, and maintains a New Jersey office in Clark. The Clark office opened in 1986 chiefly to handle two types of marine insurance claims: protection and indemnity claims (P & I claims) consisting essentially of personal injury claims and federal longshore and harbor workers' compensation claims.

Walters met Nixon in the Clark office, where they both worked on P & I claims. When Walters arrived at Lamorte in 1990, Nixon had already established herself at the company. Walters, on the other hand, was recruited from out of state by Lamorte's President, Harold J. Halpin, to manage the Clark office, handle P & I claims, and supervise other employees, including Nixon. Walters, an attorney, had experience in the field. He previously had been employed in the P & I division of St. Paul Fire & Marine Insurance Company in Ohio, and before that, in the admiralty department of a Florida law firm.

Lamorte entrusted Walters with substantial responsibility. Lamorte introduced Walters to many of its existing clients, but expected him to locate, establish, and maintain new clients. Because of his prior work, Walters knew many insurance carriers and P & I associations that offered P & I coverage. As it turned out, Walters proved successful at soliciting and establishing new business; he claims to have brought in thirty new clients to Lamorte.

Approximately one month after Walters's arrival at Lamorte, Halpin asked him to sign an employment agreement. The relevant paragraphs of that agreement stated as follows:

2.   You agree to devote your full time and best efforts to the performance of your duties for the Company and not to engage in any other business activities without the prior written consent of the Company.

4.   You agree to maintain in confidence all proprietary data and other confidential information (whether concerning the Company, or any of its affiliated companies, or any of their respective clients or cases being handled for clients) obtained or developed by you in the course of your employment with the Company. Such information and data shall include, but not be limited to, all information covering clients and cases being handled for clients. All such information and data is and shall remain the exclusive property of the Company and/or affiliated companies. In addition you assign to the Company all right, title, and interest in and to any and all ideas, inventions, discoveries, trademarks, trade names, copyrights, patents and all other information and data of any kind developed by you during the entire period of your employment with the Company and related to the work performed by you for the Company.

* * *

Your obligation under this paragraph shall survive any termination of your employment.

Employee agrees that so long as you are an employee of the Company, and for a period of twelve (12) month after your termination, whether voluntary or involuntary, you will not solicit or accept any claim, case or dispute which is being handled or directed by the Company or any of its affiliated companies during the term of your employment with the Company

* * *

Walters signed the contract, but he never believed it was enforceable against him. He reasoned that because he was an at-will employee, the employment contract lacked consideration for its restrictive covenant clauses. Also, the agreement was never signed by Lamorte. A Florida attorney privately corroborated his view. Walters never expressed his beliefs to anyone at Lamorte, however, out of fear that he would be fired.

In the Spring of 1996, Walters quietly began entertaining the idea of resigning and starting a competing business. By that time, Halpin had informed defendants that Lamorte would be de-emphasizing P & I work and increasing the workers' compensation area of the practice. For Walters, that constituted the impetus for his decision to start a competing business. Also about that time, two other employees departed the P & I department because there was not enough work to support the staff.

Walters spoke only with co-employees Nixon and John Treubig about his idea of starting a competing business. Walters showed Nixon some financial estimates he had developed, suggesting that she would improve her position if she were to join in his enterprise. Eventually, Walters lost interest in Treubig. Soon after, Halpin directed Walters to fire Treubig based on allegations that Treubig had tried to solicit a Lamorte client for his private benefit.

On July 17, 1996, Walters incorporated the new business, "The Walters Nixon Group" (WNG). Thereafter, even while Walters and Nixon attended to their duties at Lamorte, they secretly worked on the commencement of their new business venture. Each time they worked on a Lamorte P & I claim file, they added to a target solicitation list they were compiling using information from their employer's client files. That information included client names, addresses, phone and fax numbers, file numbers, claim incident dates, claim contact information, and names of the injured persons. In total, the list included approximately thirty of Lamorte's clients, all but one or two of the company's P & I clients. As that information was gathered, it was transferred to Walters's home computer.

Walters testified that he did not believe the names of Lamorte's clients and information concerning pending claims was Lamorte's proprietary and confidential information. He reasoned that the information, although not generally available to the public, was not secret. He asserted that the discrete information could be obtained by calling directly and inquiring of insurance companies and vessel owners. Further, other than the reference to "confidential and proprietary information" in his employment agreement that Walters believed was unenforceable, he never had been told by Lamorte that any of the specific information he was gathering in connection with his P & I work was confidential and proprietary. Halpin, himself, never discussed the confidentiality of the information. During Walters's deposition, however, he answered "No" to the following question:

> Would you have given that information to a competitor if he walked in the door and said, I want to go after your customers[?] Give me a complete listing of their files, reference numbers, adjusters and fax numbers and I will use that to solicit them. You would have given that information to them?

In September 1996, Halpin confronted defendants concerning rumors that they were thinking of leaving to start a competing business. They reassured Halpin the rumors were untrue. Walters testified that he feared he would be fired if Halpin knew the truth. The truth was that Walters and Nixon were well on their way to establishing a competing business.

* * *

On Thursday and Friday, December 18 and 19, 1997, Walters called in sick. In fact, Walters was at WNG's office installing computers, setting up furniture, and preparing to activate the business solicitation plan over the coming weekend. Telephone records showed that on December 19, 1997, calls were placed to several of Lamorte's clients from WNG's office. Walters, however, denies that during those conversations he informed Lamorte's clients that he was about to resign and denies that he attempted to solicit any of them.

At 9 a.m. on Saturday, December 20, Walters and Nixon telephoned Lamorte's Clark office and received no answer. They then drove to that empty office and spent two or three hours "putting away files and removing their personal belongings." At 2:56 p.m., Walters and Nixon faxed their respective resignation letters to Halpin's private office in Wilton, Connecticut.

* * *

On Sunday morning, December 21, Walters and Nixon began to fax solicitation letters and transfer authorization forms to all but one of Lamorte's P & I clients, thirty-three in all. On that first day, defendants exclusively targeted Lamorte's clients from whose files they had taken the client information noted earlier. A typical letter notified the client that defendants, who had been handling that client's claim file, had resigned from Lamorte and started a new business. It stated "Our fee structure will be *less* than Lamorte Burns' fee structure for 1998." The client was told that it had absolute discretion in deciding whether to continue with Lamorte or to have its claim files in progress transferred to WNG or to any other firm. The letter was accompanied by a transfer request form. The form included "a list of open files *we* have been handling for you." (emphasis added). In addition to the client's file number, the transfer form included the client's name, the name of the injured person, and the accident date. The client was instructed simply to mark an "X" next to each listed file that it wished to have transferred from Lamorte to WNG.

By Monday, December 22, 1997, ten of Lamorte's clients returned to WNG signed transfer authorization forms instructing Lamorte to transfer their active P & I claims to WNG. By January 7, 1998, all forms were returned and all thirty-three of Lamorte's P & I clients requested transfer of their active claim files to WNG, totaling a transfer of 116 individual Lamorte P & I claims. By the time the summary judgment motion was heard, 153 of Lamorte's 350 active P & I claim files had been transferred to WNG. According to Walters, the clients that had requested a transfer included clients he had brought into Lamorte, as well as clients that had been existing Lamorte clients when he arrived at the company. Walters conceded that "[he] had people faxing from up and down the Eastern Seaboard and from overseas within an hour or less of getting his sudden announcement." Customers were sending their congratulations.

Upon consideration of the summary judgment record, the trial court concluded that defendants had breached their duty of loyalty, tortiously interfered with an economic advantage, misappropriated confidential and proprietary information, and competed unfairly.

* * *

In New Jersey, customer lists of service businesses have been afforded protection as trade secrets

* * *

Importantly, however, information need not rise to the level of a trade secret to be protected.

* * *

Other jurisdictions also have held that information not technically meeting the strict requirements of trade secrets may be protected as "confidential information" and may serve as the basis for a tort action.

* * *

Those cases follow the philosophy expressed in the Restatement (Second) on Agency, which states that "[u]nless otherwise agreed, an agent is subject to a duty to the principal not to use or to communicate information confidentially given him by the principal or acquired by him during the course of or on account of his agency or in violation of his duties as agent, in competition with or to the injury of the principal."

* * *

We disagree with the Appellate Division's conclusion that a trial is needed to determine whether the information secretly gathered by defendants was legally protected. Although we are persuaded that the facts show that plaintiff's information should be entitled to trade secret protection, certainty in that regard is not essential to our decision. The specific information provided to defendants by their employer, in the course of employment, and for the sole purpose of servicing plaintiff's customers, is legally protectable as confidential and proprietary information.

The information surreptitiously gathered by defendants from plaintiff was not generally available to the public, but was shared between plaintiff and its clients. Defendants would not have been aware of that information but for their employment. The information went beyond the mere names of plaintiff's clients. It included specific information concerning the clients' claims, such as the name of the injured party, and the type and date of injury. Defendants admitted that that information gave them an advantage in soliciting plaintiff's clients once they resigned. But, the information was available to defendants for their use in servicing clients on behalf of Lamorte only.

* * *

Having concluded that plaintiff's client claim file information is legally protectable, resolution of plaintiff's breach of the duty of loyalty claim is relatively straightforward. Loyalty from an employee to an employer consists of certain very basic and common sense obligations. An employee must not while employed act contrary to the employer's interest . . . Consistent with our approach to this common-law duty, the Restatement (Second) Agency provides that "[u]nless otherwise agreed, an agent is subject to a duty not to compete with the principal concerning the subject matter of his agency." Restatement (Second) of Agency, § 393 (1958). Comment e to that section further states:

> [B]efore the end of his employment, [the employee] can properly purchase a rival business and upon termination of employment immediately compete. He is not, however, entitled to solicit customers for such rival business before the

transmitted their resignations to plaintiff.

* * *

But, although an employee has end of his employment nor can he properly do other similar acts in direct competition with the employer's business.

* * *

Defendants maintain that they did not compete with Lamorte while employed essentially because no solicitations of Lamorte clients occurred until the day after they the right to make preparations to start a competing business, the employee may not breach the undivided duty of loyalty he or she owes to his or her employer while still employed by soliciting the employer's customers or engaging in other acts of secret competition.

* * *

An employee's duty of loyalty to his or her employer goes beyond refraining from privately soliciting the employer's customers while still employed. The duty of loyalty prohibits the employee from taking affirmative steps to injure the employer's business. Defendants purloined protected information from plaintiff's P & I claim files while still employed, for the sole purpose of effecting an advantage in competing with plaintiff immediately upon their resignation and the commencement of their new competitive business. Defendants here intentionally began a process of subverting their employer's business while still employed. That process included gathering by stealth plaintiff's legally protected information admittedly to seek an advantage in competing with plaintiff once they resigned. Obviously those actions were contrary to plaintiff's interest, and in the case of Walters, directly conflicted with the terms of his employment agreement as well, as the courts below held.

* * *

NOTES

1. *Lamorte Burns* relied on the Restatement (Second) of Agency in concluding that the defendants should not have started the competing business. See Restatement (Second) of Agency §§ 393–94 (1958). The relevant sections state that an agent generally has a duty "not to compete with the principal concerning the subject matter of his agency" and "not to act . . . during the period of his agency for persons whose interests conflict with those of the principal." The Restatement (Third) of Agency has replaced this language with a single provision stating that "an agent has a duty to refrain from taking action on behalf of or otherwise assisting the principal's competitors." Restatement (Third) of Agency § 8.04 (2006).

2. Rehab Solutions alleged that its in-house accountant, Mignon Willis, failed to fulfill many duties of her employment which eventually resulted in tax liens levied against Rehab's building. The Supreme Court of Mississippi held that theories of unjust enrichment and negligence do not support lawsuits by Rehab against Willis for nonfeasance of Willis's duties. Willis v. Rehab Solutions, PLLC, 82 So.3d 583 (Miss. 2012). The court cited the facts that Willis did not engage in illegal activity and that Rehab failed to properly oversee Willis.

Mercer Management Consulting, Inc. v. Wilde
920 F.Supp. 219 (D.D.C. 1996).

■ JOYCE HENS GREEN, DISTRICT JUDGE.

After defendants Dean L. Wilde, II and Dean R. Silverman established a competing business, Dean & Co. Strategy Consultants, Inc., and, along with defendant Moray P. Dewhurst, left the employ of plaintiff Mercer Management Consulting, Inc., Mercer brought a ten-count complaint alleging, inter alia, breach of fiduciary duty, breach of contract, and tortious interference with contractual relationships. Defendants Wilde and Silverman counterclaimed for breach of contract, stemming from Mercer's alleged failure to honor an agreement to make certain payments to Wilde and Silverman.

Following denial of defendants' second motion for summary judgment (except as to one claim relating to defendant Dewhurst), this case was tried to the Court. After the trial, counsel submitted extensive proposed findings of fact and conclusions of law. Upon consideration of the record and evidence introduced at trial, including the testimony of witnesses whose credibility, demeanor, and behavior the Court has had an opportunity to observe and fully evaluate, for the reasons set forth below judgment shall be entered in favor of plaintiff on its claims relating to breach of the 1982 Agreement by defendants Dean Wilde and Dean Silverman, and in favor of defendants on all of Mercer's other claims. Judgment shall be entered in Mercer's favor on Wilde's and Silverman's counterclaim.

Mercer is a management consulting and strategic planning company incorporated under the laws of Delaware. Mercer is an indirect subsidiary of Marsh & McLennan Companies, Inc. In 1987, MMC acquired, through a subsidiary, a management consulting and strategic planning company known as Temple Barker Sloane, Inc. On February 14, 1990, MMC acquired Strategic Planning Associates, Inc., by merging it with TBS. The resulting company became known as Mercer Management Consulting, Inc., the plaintiff company in this case.

Defendants Wilde, Silverman, and Dewhurst were employed by SPA, and subsequently by Mercer, as management consultants. Each defendant quickly rose through the ranks. Wilde joined SPA in 1980 after his graduation from the Massachusetts Institute of Technology's Sloane School of Management. He became a vice president of SPA in 1984 and an executive vice-president and member of SPA's Policy Committee in 1988. Moreover, he served on Mercer's Board of Directors and Mercer's "inside board" from approximately October 1991 until his resignation on April 2, 1993.

Silverman, a graduate of Columbia Law School, joined SPA in 1979 after three years in a law firm and another management consulting business. Like Wilde, Silverman became a vice president in approximately 1984, and became an executive vice president and Policy Committee member in 1988. He too served on Mercer's Board of Directors and the "inside board" from approximately October 1991 until his resignation on April 2, 1993.

Dewhurst joined SPA in 1980 after his graduation from MIT's Sloane School of Management. He became a vice president of SPA in 1984 and served in that position until his resignation on March 15, 1993. In 1982, Wilde, Silverman, and Dewhurst each executed an employment agreement with SPA. The 1982 Agreement provides, inter alia, that each defendant will refrain from "render[ing] competitive services" to any client or active prospect of SPA, or from hiring or assisting in hiring any SPA employee, for a period of one year following the termination of employment with SPA. Such agreements are typical in the management consulting industry. Thomas Waylett, Chairman of Mercer Management, testified that the agreements served as Mercer's "protection that people wouldn't just walk out the door, set up in business, and take clients and employees." As part of its "due diligence" investigation prior to the TBS/SPA merger, Mercer sought to ascertain whether SPA's employees had previously signed non-solicitation agreements, and it learned of the 1982 Agreements in the course of that investigation.

In 1989, as a condition of the merger between TBS and SPA, Mercer required five senior employee-stockholders of SPA, including Wilde and Silverman, to enter into employment agreements. Wilde and Silverman each executed the 1990 Agreement in December 1989. The agreements became effective as of the merger date—February 14, 1990.

Among its key provisions, the 1990 Agreement assured continued employment at a guaranteed level of compensation for a period of three years from the date of the merger. The agreement obligated Wilde and Silverman to "perform and discharge well and faithfully the[ir] duties". For a three-year period commencing on the date of the merger, the agreement prohibited Wilde and Silverman from offering competitive services within a 50-mile radius, soliciting or accepting business from any Mercer client or active prospect, or soliciting any management consulting professional to terminate employment with Mercer.

Pivotal to the instant dispute is paragraph 14 of the 1990 Agreement, which concerns the relationship between the 1990 Agreement and prior employment agreements. Paragraph 14 states, in pertinent part:

> 14. Entire Agreement. This instrument contains the entire agreement of the parties with respect to employment following the Merger Date and supersedes all prior oral or written agreements and understandings between and among the Employee [and] the Company * * * with respect to employment following the Merger Date, except for any agreements or understandings restricting or prohibiting the competition or solicitation activities of the Employee or the use of confidential information of the Company or its clients which shall remain in full force and effect, provided that in the event of a conflict between the provisions of this Agreement and those of any other agreement which survive hereunder, the provisions of this Agreement shall control.

The meaning of paragraph 14 and its effect on the survival of the 1982 Agreements is paramount to Mercer's breach of contract claims.

* * *

The Court previously denied defendants' motion for summary judgment on Mercer's claims relating to breach of fiduciary duty, stating that "resolution of the question of whether defendants' actions constituted a breach of fiduciary duty * * * requires 'a thoroughgoing examination of the facts and circumstances' presented in this case." Having heard and evaluated the testimony elicited at trial, the Court has concluded that defendants' actions, while perhaps questionable on moral or ethical grounds, do not rise to the level of a breach of fiduciary duty. The claims of breach of the "well and faithfully" clause in the 1990 Agreements, the facts and analysis of which parallel the fiduciary duty claim, similarly fail.

Corporate officers and directors owe "an undivided and unselfish loyalty to the corporation" such that "there shall be no conflict between duty and self-interest." Similarly, "an agent is subject to a duty not to compete with the principal concerning the subject matter of his agency." At the same time, however, the law is clear that "an agent can make arrangements or plans to go into competition with his principal before terminating his agency, provided no unfair acts are committed or injury done his principal."

Still, as the Court stated in Science Accessories, "[t]he right to make arrangements to compete is by no means absolute and the exercise of the privilege may, in appropriate circumstances, rise to the level of a breach of an employee's fiduciary duty of loyalty." The limitations of an officer's preparatory activities have been described as follows:

Prior to termination of employment, an officer may not solicit for himself or herself business which the position requires the employee to obtain for the employer. The officer must refrain from actively and directly competing with the employer for customers and employees, and must continue to exert his or her best efforts on behalf of the employer.

In preparing to compete, an employee may not commit fraudulent, unfair, or wrongful acts, such as misuse of confidential information, solicitation of the firm's customers, or solicitation leading to a mass resignation of the firm's employees. At the same time, failure to disclose plans to enter into competition is not itself necessarily a breach of fiduciary duty. Thus, "the ultimate determination of whether an employee has breached his fiduciary duties to his employer by preparing to engage in a competing enterprise must be grounded upon a thoroughgoing examination of the facts and circumstances of the particular case." The evidence at trial established that while still employed by Mercer, Wilde and Silverman in particular, and to a lesser extent Dewhurst, took numerous actions to establish what was to become Dean & Co., a competing business. Not only did they incorporate Dean & Co., but they made arrangements for office space, inquired about benefit packages, investigated computer systems, and met with an accountant.

It is evident to the Court that by at least late February 1993, Wilde and Silverman were intent upon forming their own company. The precise contours of the business might not have been fully developed, but Wilde and Silverman were plainly moving quickly down the road toward starting their own competing consulting business. Indeed, Dean & Co. was incorporated on February 25, 1993.

At no time prior to their departure did Wilde, Silverman, or Dewhurst disclose their actions or intentions to their colleagues at Mercer. They continued to perform work for Mercer, including meetings with clients they would later solicit on behalf of Dean & Co. Wilde and Silverman continued to attend with clients they would later solicit on behalf of Dean & Co. Wilde and Silverman continued to attend meetings of the Board of Directors and inside board, at which information of the most confidential sort was discussed.

At the same time, the record is clear that at no time prior to their departure from Mercer did Wilde, Silverman, or Dewhurst solicit Mercer's clients on behalf of what was to become Dean & Co., or perform any competing consulting work under the auspices of Dean & Co. Mercer urges the Court to find that defendants breached their fiduciary duty by performing work for Mercer until their departures, because, in Mercer's view, these efforts were plainly aimed at solidifying relationships to inure to the benefit of Dean & Co. While the Court does not doubt the sincerity of plaintiff's view, the Court is not persuaded that an employee breaches his fiduciary duty by performing work for his employer at a time when he is planning to leave his employment. The Court recognizes that personal relationships with clients are paramount in the management consulting business, and that defendants' contacts with Mercer's clients, if positive, could potentially work to the benefit of defendants' competing business. However, the Court finds unreasonable and unrealistic the proposition that any client contact prior to leaving one's employment and starting a competing business constitutes a breach of one's fiduciary duty. In the absence of evidence that any overt solicitation was made or other improper actions taken in the course of defendants' client contacts, the Court does not find the Bell Canada meeting or other client contacts to constitute a breach of fiduciary duty.

In the final analysis, upon full consideration and evaluation of all of the facts and circumstances presented in this case, the Court has determined that while defendants' covert actions in establishing Dean & Co. were not particularly admirable, they did not constitute a breach of their legal fiduciary duties of loyalty to Mercer. As previously noted, the Court finds that Wilde and Silverman did not solicit Dewhurst to leave Mercer and join Dean & Co. Moreover, while the record is clear that Wilde and Silverman extended invitations to a dinner to solicit Mercer employees while they were still employed by Mercer, it is equally clear that the dinner did not take place until after the conclusion of Wilde's and Silverman's last day of employment at Mercer, albeit later that same day. Moreover, it appears that none of the individuals solicited by Wilde and Silverman at the dinner ultimately joined Dean & Co. Consequently, Mercer's damages resulting from the dinner are not evident.

Similarly, during the time they were establishing Dean & Co. and preparing to compete, all three defendants continued to perform fully their duties for Mercer. Indeed, Mercer's Chairman testified at trial that time was not the issue with respect to defendants' alleged disloyalty; rather, the issue was defendants' preparations to compete with Mercer while still on Mercer's payroll.

Apart from the stealth with which defendants established their competing business, the most troublesome aspect of Wilde's and Silverman's actions concerned their compilation and mailing to two major clients (AT & T and Sara Lee) tape diskettes containing the history of Mercer's work for those clients. The timing and unprecedented nature of these actions leaves no doubt that Wilde and Silverman intended for the diskettes to increase AT & T and Sara Lee's comfort level with switching their business from Mercer to Dean & Co. Arguably this action constituted misuse of confidential information in violation of Wilde's and Silverman's fiduciary duties. However, in view of the uncontroverted testimony of Wilde and Silverman that they have not had access to the information on the tape at any time, and the utter lack of testimony from relevant officials at AT & T or Sara Lee concerning the effect, if any, of the tapes on their decision to switch their business to Dean & Co., the Court finds that the compilation and mailing of the tapes, while certainly inappropriate, did not rise to the level of a breach of defendants' fiduciary duty.

For the foregoing reasons, judgment shall be entered for Wilde, Silverman, and Dewhurst on Mercer's claims relating to breach of fiduciary duty. Because Mercer's allegations concerning breach of the "well and faithfully" clause of the 1990 Agreements are based on the same facts and circumstances as the fiduciary duty claim, judgment shall similarly be entered in defendants' favor on this breach of contract claim.

A threshold question to be resolved in connection with Mercer's breach of contract claims relating to Wilde's and Silverman's 1982 Agreements concerns whether the Agreements survived the 1990 Agreement. As previously discussed, paragraph 14 of the 1990 Agreements states that the 1990 Agreement contains the full agreement of the parties, except for non-compete or non-solicit agreements or agreements relating to confidential information, which shall remain in full force and effect, unless a conflict existed between those provisions and the 1990 Agreement, in which case the 1990 Agreement controls.

"The basic rule of contract construction gives priority to the intentions of the parties." In ascertaining the meaning and intent of contract language, the starting point is obviously the language itself. A contract is construed as a whole, giving effect to all of the contract's provisions and avoiding a construction which would render one of those provisions meaningless. While extrinsic evidence may be considered when a contract is subject to a number of different interpretations, the greatest weight should be given to the express language of the contract itself. Finally, in determining intent, the overt acts and statements of the parties are examined through the eyes of an objective observer.

Because the Court previously determined that the language in paragraph 14 was subject to a number of different interpretations, the Court allowed extrinsic evidence on paragraph 14's meaning and intent. That evidence failed to elucidate a definitive explanation of the parties' expressed intentions at the time of contract formation. Thus, the Court must ascertain the reasonable meaning and effect of paragraph 14 primarily from the language itself, with the extrinsic evidence of the parties' negotiations as a backdrop.

Upon careful evaluation of the language of the contract and the evidence presented at trial, the Court is persuaded that paragraph 14's proviso clause did not eviscerate the exceptions clause. Moreover, the Court is persuaded that no conflict existed between the 1982 Agreement and the 1990 Agreement. Accordingly, the restrictions contained in the 1982 Agreements survived the 1990 Agreement.

* * *

No inherent conflict existed between the two contracts. Each provided Mercer a certain type of protection against competition and solicitation of its clients and employees. The 1990 Agreement assured Mercer that Wilde and Silverman would not compete with Mercer or solicit its clients or employees. However, those protections expired three years from the date of the merger. The 1982 Agreement provided Mercer protection against interference with its clients and employees for one year from the termination of Wilde's and Silverman's employment, whenever that termination occurred. If the termination happened to occur within two years of the merger, then the 1982 Agreement's restrictions would yield to the 1990 Agreement's restrictions, due to the stricter restrictions contained in the 1990 Agreement. In any other instance, the 1982 Agreement's one-year restriction would be triggered.

In any case, because the 1990 Agreement expired in February 1993, no conflict existed between its provisions and the restrictions contained in the 1982 Agreements. Even though the 1990 Agreement was no longer in effect at the time Wilde and Silverman left Mercer's employ, the 1982 Agreement was still viable.

Defendants contend that the 1982 Agreements are void as violative of the public policy against restrictive covenants. In order to be valid, covenants not to compete must protect some legitimate interest of the employer and must be reasonable in their scope. Restrictions are unreasonable if "the restraint is greater than is needed to protect the promisee's legitimate interest, or * * * the promisee's need is outweighed by the hardship to the promisor and the likely injury to the public." Significantly, a "restraint is easier to justify * * * if the restraint is limited to the taking of his former employer's customers as contrasted with competition in general."

Here, the Court finds that Mercer has demonstrated a legitimate purpose in requiring its employees to sign the 1982 Agreement—namely that Mercer wished to protect the investment it made in its employees, preserve the confidentiality of information gleaned in the course of employment at Mercer, and protect itself from its employees leaving and capitalizing on Mercer's client base. The Court finds unpersuasive defendants' argument that because Mercer's post-merger policy concerning restrictive covenants was inconsistent, Mercer necessarily cannot demonstrate a legitimate interest in the agreements. In the years prior to the merger, SPA required all consultants to sign such agreements. TBS required similar agreements of its senior employees. Mercer presently requires all senior officials to sign such agreements. The fact that for a period of time following the merger not all employees of the former TBS were required to sign such agreements does not eradicate Mercer's legitimate interests, particularly in view of the disarray and multitude of issues facing the merged company immediately following the merger.

Significantly, the 1982 Agreements do not broadly prohibit competition with Mercer generally, but rather are limited to restricting the rendering of services to Mercer's clients or hiring Mercer's employees. The restrictions are limited to a one-year period of time. In view of the substantial investment Mercer made in its employees, the vital importance of its client base to its business, and the close contacts established between its consultants and its client base, the Court finds that the modest restrictions contained in the 1982 Agreements are reasonable and enforceable.

The evidence at trial failed to establish that Dewhurst breached the 1982 Agreement. Dewhurst attended two meetings with AT & T-DCS immediately after joining Dean & Co., and he assisted in the preparation of a proposal for AT & T-DCS, but both Dewhurst and Wilde presented uncontroverted testimony that the proposal was rejected and Dean & Co. obtained no work and no pay as a result of the proposal. Thus, the Court finds that Dewhurst did not "render competitive services" to a Mercer client within one year of the termination of his employment.

Similarly, while Dewhurst was knowledgeable of Wilde's and Silverman's plan to solicit and hire Mercer employees, there is no evidence that Dewhurst assisted in hiring either Adams or Lowell, who are the only Mercer employees identified by Mercer as being hired by Dean & Co. within one year of defendant's departure. Accordingly, judgment in Dewhurst's favor on the breach of contract claim is appropriate.

The situation differs with respect to Wilde and Silverman. The evidence at trial established that Wilde and Silverman both "render[ed] competitive services" and hired Mercer employees, namely Lowell and Adams, within one year of their termination of employment with Mercer. These actions constituted material breaches of the 1982 Agreements for which Wilde and Silverman are liable.

* * *

As previously noted, the 1982 Agreement does not expressly prohibit solicitation of SPA's (now Mercer's) clients, but states that the consultant shall not "render competitive services . . . to any person or firm" to which SPA (now Mercer) had rendered services or solicited business. The agreement is clear that the prohibition on rendering services applies to the "firm," not a "client" or "division" or "department" within the firm. This language is understandable in light of the intense efforts consulting companies make to develop business relationships with their clients, and is reasonable in light of the one-year limit on the restrictions. Thus, Wilde and Silverman breached their agreements by rendering services not only to AT & T-DCS, but also to AT & T-FTS2000 and AT & T Trans Tech.

At the same time, the 1982 Agreement is clear that only "render[ing] competitive services," and not mere solicitation, is prohibited. Mercer argues that it should be permitted to recover damages for work performed by Wilde and Silverman in the year following the expiration of the 1982 Agreement, insofar as the work was solicited or begun prior to the expiration of the agreement. In detailing Dean & Co.'s revenues, Mercer did not differentiate between work begun prior to the expiration of the 1982 Agreement and work solicited but not begun prior to that time. Because the 1982 Agreement does not prohibit solicitation, Wilde and Silverman cannot be held liable for those activities. And because Mercer did not isolate those revenues resulting from work begun prior to the expiration of the 1982 Agreements, the Court has no reasonable basis upon which to award damages for that work.

With respect to "services rendered" in the year following Wilde's and Silverman's departure from Mercer, the Court has determined that the appropriate measure of damages is the profits Mercer would have received had the work been performed by Mercer instead of Dean & Co. It is evident that Wilde and Silverman would not have been in the position to solicit and perform the work for AT & T and Sara Lee had they not developed close ties and vast experience with these companies during their tenure at Mercer. Moreover, in estimating damages in the context of the management consulting business, the Court must be mindful of the paramount importance of a firm's client-consultant relationships. It is reasonable to presume, given Mercer's close relationship and long experience with those companies, that Mercer would have been in a position to acquire and perform the work had Wilde and Silverman not left Mercer's employ and solicited the work on behalf of their new company.

According to the unrebutted testimony of Mercer's witnesses, Mercer's return on revenues from communications consulting was 20 percent in 1993, and 13.5 percent in other practice areas. Thus, Mercer is entitled to 20 percent of the $1,664,597 in revenues received by Dean & Co. for its work for AT & T prior to April 2, 1994, or $332,919.40. Mercer is also entitled to 13.5 percent of the $2,500 Dean & Co. received from Sara Lee, or $337.50, for total damages of $333,256.90.

In addition, Wilde and Silverman breached the 1982 Agreements by hiring Ware Adams and Gregory Lowell within one year of Wilde's and Silverman's departures from Mercer. According to Michael Muldowney, Mercer's replacement cost for hiring new consultant is $22,338 per consultant, and Mercer shall be awarded these costs as damages. In the absence of testimony demonstrating that work did not get performed due to Adams' and Lowell's departures, Mercer shall not be allowed to recover lost profits.

Counts VIII and IX allege that Wilde, Silverman, Dewhurst, and Dean & Co. interfered with Mercer's client and business relationships by soliciting business from Mercer clients. To sustain a claim of intentional interference with business relationships, Mercer must establish 1) the existence of a business relationship; 2) defendants' knowledge of the business relationship; 3) intentional interference with the relationship by defendants; and 4) resulting damages. Moreover, the defendants' interference must be improper. "Competitive activity does not by itself constitute intentional interference with prospective business advantage" unless accomplished by wrongful or improper means, such as fraud, violence, or civil suits.

Essentially, the facts underlying this claim are the same as Mercer's claims relating to defendants' breaches of their 1982 Agreements. The Court has determined that Dewhurst did not render competitive services to Mercer's clients; accordingly, Dewhurst's actions do not constitute intentional interference with Mercer's business relationships. Even if they did, Mercer has shown no damages stemming from Dewhurst's activities.

With respect to defendants Wilde and Silverman, unquestionably their actions in soliciting and rendering services to former Mercer clients interfered with Mercer's business relationships with these clients. Moreover, their actions were improper in the sense of being violative of the 1982 Agreements. However, during the time of their interference with Mercer's clients, Wilde and Silverman apparently did not believe they were under any restrictions against competitive activities. As such, the Court cannot find that they acted with the level of wrongful intent to constitute tortious interference. Nor has Mercer demonstrated that defendants wrongfully utilized confidential information in soliciting the work at issue. Accordingly, judgment shall be entered for defendants on this count. For the same reasons, judgment shall be entered for defendant Dean & Co. on the intentional interference count against it.

NOTES AND QUESTIONS

1.   An employee with sufficient authority must exercise the duty of care that a reasonable person in similar circumstances would use. In determining whether the duty of care was breached, courts generally use a business judgment rule. They do not question the wisdom of the judgment so long as the director or officer (1) had no conflict of interest when he or she made the decision, (2) gathered a reasonable amount of information before deciding, and (3) did not act wholly irrationally. There is more scrutiny of the procedure than of the content of the decision. A director in violation of the duty of care is personally liable for money damages to the corporation, whether or not the director derived personal benefit from the transaction.

2.   Consider the outcome of Cameco, Inc. v. Gedicke, 724 A.2d 783 (N.J. 1999), in which the Supreme Court of New Jersey held that "employees should inform employers of their plans before establishing an independent business that might conflict with that of the employer." As a manager overseeing the shipment of Cameco's food products, Gedicke was responsible for negotiating shipment rates. While still employed by Cameco, Gedicke and

two coworkers formed Newton Transportation Services, which provided the same sort of shipping services to other companies, including two of Cameco's competitors. Evidence showed that Gedicke had performed some Newton-related work at his Cameco office. The court ultimately remanded the case for resolution of a factual dispute as to whether Gedicke had breached a "duty of loyalty" to Cameco. On the one hand, the court held that "slight assistance to a direct competitor could constitute a breach of the employee's duty of loyalty." On the other hand, the court noted that "Cameco . . . [did] not contend that Newton was a direct competitor" since Newton's business consisted of transporting goods rather than producing food. To what extent does this ruling simply give an employer the power to forbid any conduct it deems "competitive"?

3. Bildman was CEO of Astra USA, a subsidiary of the Swedish pharmaceutical giant AstraZeneca. In his last five years he was paid about $1 million per year. Business Week magazine found that Bildman had committed numerous acts of sexual harassment and had used company funds to pay some of the employees he had harassed. Astra had adopted clear anti-harassment policies. Business Week published a cover story under the title "Abuse of Power: The Astonishing Tale of Sexual Harassment at Astra USA." When Astra employed a law firm to investigate, the firm found that in addition to the sexual harassment matters, Bildman had charged Astra for $2 million in repairs to his primary residence and his Vermont vacation home, had billed the company when he hired female "escorts" for himself and others, and had directed Astra to pay $16,000 in legal costs he incurred contesting a speeding ticket fining him $66. Held: Bildman must forfeit all compensation paid to him during his period of disloyalty. Astra USA, Inc. v. Bildman, 914 N.E.2d 36 (Mass. 2009, cert. denied, 560 U.S. 904 2010). This decision reversed the trial judge's determination that Astra was not entitled to recover Bildman's past pay because the compensation had been "commensurate with his value to the company." Reversing, the Massachusetts Supreme Judicial Court held that New York law applied because that was the state of incorporation for Astra and that New York's "faithless servant" doctrine required equitable forfeiture of all of his pay during the period of his disloyalty. Regarding the New York doctrine, see also Phansalkar v. Andersen Weinroth & Co., 344 F.3d 184 (2d Cir. 2003).

B. POST-EMPLOYMENT RESTRICTIONS

Employers often spend a great deal of time and money training their employees, and often provide access to protected trade secrets developed at great expense. To safeguard these investments when employees leave their jobs, employers may try to place restrictions on future employment. Such post-employment restrictions impose another important practical limitation on the employee's freedom to quit.

1. FUTURE EMPLOYMENT

Estee Lauder Cos., Inc. v. Batra

430 F.Supp. 2d 158 (S.D. N.Y. 2006).

■ SWEET, DISTRICT JUDGE.

Plaintiff Estee Lauder Companies, Inc. has moved by order to show cause for a temporary restraining order and preliminary injunction pursuant to Rule 65, Fed. R. Civ. P., to restrain defendant Shashi Batra from breaching the terms of his Confidentiality, Non-solicitation, and Non-competition Agreement with Estee Lauder and from engaging in employment with N.V. Perricone M.D. Ltd.

Estee Lauder employs approximately 6,700 employees in New York and approximately 1,800 employees in California. Senior Management of Estee Lauder is located in New York, including the chief executive officer, chief operating officer, chief financial officer, head of operations, manufacturing, head of information systems, senior counsel, head of worldwide Human Resources, and group presidents. Of the 14 General Brand Managers, 11 are located in New York. The Darphin general manager is located in Paris, the R+F General Brand Manager is located in San Francisco, and the Aveda General Brand Manager is located in Minneapolis.

In 2003, Estee Lauder acquired R+F, a dermatologist-founded skin care brand, and Darphin, a Paris-based pharmacy skin care and make-up company. Both the R+F and Darphin brands market and sell their products in the cosmetic dermatology market.

* * *

Batra was hired as Global General Brand Manager of R+F as of January 5, 2004. Effective July 1, 2005, Batra also assumed the role as General Manager for Darphin, North America. In his role for R+F, Batra was the senior executive in charge of the brand and was responsible for overseeing all aspects of R+F's business, including, research and development, marketing and distribution, pricing, packaging development, corporate finance, regulatory affairs, internet development, and public relations. In his role for Darphin, Batra was responsible for marketing and distribution, pricing and overall accounts management strategies for the Darphin brands in North America.

Batra had worldwide responsibility for R+F * * * At the commencement of his employment, Batra signed an employment agreement with Estee Lauder, which contained confidentiality, non-solicitation, non-competition provisions. In return for signing the agreement (which all Estee Lauder executive employees are required to sign) Batra received a $100,000 signing bonus. In addition, Batra was provided with a compensation package of $300,000 per year, benefits, an automobile allowance, stock options, and bonus eligibility. On July 1,

2004, Batra's base salary was increased to $325,000. In July, 2005, in conjunction with his new responsibilities for Darphin, Estee Lauder increased Batra's base salary to $375,000.

The non-competition clause, contained in Paragraph 4 of the employment agreement that Batra signed in January 2004, provides as follows:

> You recognize that the Company's business is very competitive and that to protect its Confidential Information the Company expects you not to compete with it for a period of time. You therefore agree that during your employment with the Company, and for a period of twelve months after termination of you employment with the Company, regardless of the reason for the termination, you will not work for or otherwise actively participate in any business on behalf of any Competitor in which you could benefit the Competitor's business or harm the Company's business by using or disclosing Confidential Information. This restriction shall apply only in the geographic areas for which you had work-related responsibility during the last twelve months of your employment by the Company and in any other geographic area in which you could benefit the Competitor's business through the use or disclosure of Confidential Information.

In addition, the agreement contained a non-solicitation provision, contained in Paragraph 5, pursuant to which Batra agreed that he would:

> not, directly or indirectly, solicit, induce, recruit, or encourage any of the Company's employees to terminate their employment with the Company or to perform services for any other business.

Paragraph 7 of the agreement provides that:

> During the period in which you are subject to the non-competition restrictions of paragraph 4, the Company will continue to pay you your last regular salary at the Company. If at any time during this period the Company gives you a written release from the restriction, the Company will no long be obligated to make the payments provided for in this Paragraph.

Batra's employment agreement with Estee Lauder also contains a confidentiality provision * * *.

Finally, the Non-compete Agreement contained a choice of law provision, which states:

> This agreement shall be governed by, and construed and interpreted in accordance with, the laws of the State of New York without regard to the conflict of law rules thereof * * *.

In fall of 2006, Batra began discussing an opportunity at Perricone with Nick Perricone. Throughout the fall, Batra met with Perricone and individuals from an investment company called, TSG Consumer

Products. At that time, TSG was interested in purchasing Perricone, and Batra was asked to give his opinion on how good the Perricone brand was, so that TSG could determine whether or not it would be a profitable investment.

While Batra initially intended to leave Estee Lauder in November 2005, his discussions with TSG and Perricone continued into the winter of 2005 and 2006. Throughout this time, Batra routinely worked on Perricone matters during his day at Estee Lauder in breach of his duty of loyalty to Estee Lauder, preparing for upcoming meetings with TSG and Perricone and even drafting the press release for his new position with Perricone on an Estee Lauder computer.

Additionally, during this time, Batra solicited advice and assistance on his work with Perricone from another R+F senior executive, the executive director of marketing, Annie Jackson. There were several emails exchanged establishing that throughout this time, Batra regularly solicited Jackson to breach her duty of loyalty to Estee Lauder by assisting him on preparing for meetings with TSG and Perricone. Both Jackson and Batra completed at least some of this work for Perricone during time that should have been devoted to Estee Lauder projects, using their Estee Lauder computers and email. On one occasion, Batra admits that he invited and brought Jackson to such a meeting. At this meeting on February 7, 2006, Batra and Jackson worked to persuade TSG that Perricone was a good brand and a good acquisition.

The evidence in these emails also establishes that even though he never made an explicit offer of employment, Batra was actively soliciting Jackson to leave her position with R+F to come to Perricone with him.

Following the February 7, 2006 meeting, Batra began creating a strategy for Perricone to begin to grow its business, which he drafted on his Estee Lauder computer.

On or about March 7, 2006, Batra telephoned Bousquet-Chavanne and informed him that he was resigning from Estee Lauder to become the Worldwide General Manager of Perricone. During this telephone call, Bousquet-Chavanne reminded Batra of his obligations under the Non-compete Agreement. Batra acknowledged these obligations and responded that he did not believe that Estee Lauder would be able to enforce the Non-compete Agreement because he understood that California law does not recognize such agreements.

Later that day, Batra sent an email to Bousquet-Chavanne at 2:40 P.M. suggesting that he would attend a meeting the following Wednesday, March 15, 2006, despite having already discussed with TSG and Perricone that same day the possibility of filing a lawsuit in California in the near future. In order to ensure obtaining jurisdiction in California, Batra misled Bousquet-Chavanne into thinking that he would seriously consider staying on at Estee Lauder for a transitional period, even though he admits he was ninety-five percent certain he would not return there. Batra admitted that it was in his interest to persuade Estee Lauder that he was continuing to negotiate in good faith so that Estee Lauder would not sue him to enforce the Non-compete Agreement in New York before he had an opportunity to file his suit against Estee Lauder in California.

Contrary to his word, Batra did not come to the office on March 13, 2006. Rather, on Monday, March 13, 2006, Batra telephoned Bousquet-Chavanne and informed him that he was confirming his resignation, effective the prior Tuesday, March 7, 2006. On that same day, Batra and Perricone commenced a lawsuit in California state court seeking a declaratory judgment that the Non-compete Agreement is unenforceable under California law.

Batra began employment as President of Perricone on Tuesday, March 14, 2006. In the course of the proceedings, he agreed to refrain from taking up his Perricone position until the resolution of the instant motions.

* * *

As a threshold matter, the Court first must determine which state's law controls—New York's or California's. As a court is to apply the choice-of-law rules prevailing in the state in which the court sits, New York law governs the choice of law determination.

Although New York recognizes the "choice of law principle that parties to a contract have a right to choose the law to be applied to their contract, this freedom of choice on the part of the parties is not absolute." To determine the appropriateness of the parties' choice of law, New York follows the "substantial relationship" approach, as stated in Restatement (Second) of Conflicts of Law § 187.

* * *

[W]hile Batra's employment relationship does not overwhelmingly point to New York, the management and control of Estee Lauder is entirely in New York, and a significant portion of Batra's responsibilities were centered in New York.

* * *

With respect to whether the application of New York law is contrary to a fundamental policy of California, Section 16600 of the California Business and Professions Code provides that "every contract by which anyone is restrained from engaging in a lawful profession, trade, or business of any kind is to that extent void".

* * *

Because, pursuant to California's fundamental policy against the enforcement of restrictive covenants, non-compete agreements, such as the one at issue in this case, are declared null and void under California law, the enforcement of Batra's agreement by this Court would be contrary to a fundamental policy of California, notwithstanding Estee Lauder's contention that there is no conflict between California's policy and the application of New York law. Although restrictive covenants are enforceable under California law where there has been a misappropriation of trade secrets, Estee Lauder has not demonstrated that to date there has been such a misappropriation. Absent such a showing, the Non-compete Agreement would not be enforceable under California law. However, in spite of the fact that the application of New York law would run contrary to the fundamental policy of California, it is concluded that California's interest in this dispute is not materially greater than that of New York and that therefore, New York law shall apply.

Accordingly, based upon New York's policy of enforcing restrictive covenants that are reasonable in time and scope and given New York's interest in having a predictable body of law that companies can rely on when employing individuals who will have close contact with trade secrets and confidential information, it is concluded that California's interest is not "materially greater" than New York's.

* * *

It is concluded that Estee Lauder has carried its burden of demonstrating irreparable injury for the following reasons. First, if Batra does misappropriate Estee Lauder's trade secrets, it would be "very difficult to calculate the monetary damages that would successfully redress the loss," given the difficulty in ascertaining empirically how much of a competitive advantage such information gives Perricone and/or how much detriment it might cause to the future profitability of R+F and/or Darphin products. Additionally, the employment agreement between Batra and Estee Lauder "concedes that in the event of breach of the post-employment competition provision, shall be entitled to injunctive relief, because it would cause irreparable injury."

* * *

Estee Lauder has established that Batra possesses trade secrets. The fact that Batra was not the scientist behind the formulas and the development of new products bears not on whether or not Estee Lauder has carried its burden of demonstrating irreparable injury. Even if, as he contends, Batra knew no more about the components or technologies of Estee Lauder products than "the average consumer who can read the product ingredient label," it is conceded that he was responsible for developing the R+F brand strategies for the 2007 and 2008 fiscal years and was intimately involved in developing the Darphin brand strategies for the same time period. Moreover, his deposition testimony also indicates that Batra was knowledgeable more than just marketing plans. He was knowledgeable about confidential products currently under development and product innovations scheduled for the coming years. Additionally, Batra has confidential information about the stage of development of products in the pipeline, wholly apart from specific secrets concerning its process, which is entitled to protection.

Finally, Batra seeks employment with a direct competitor of Estee Lauder. * * *

Accordingly, it is concluded that Estee Lauder has demonstrated that the measure of the damage caused by the misappropriation of its trade secrets is unquantifiable and that, therefore, Estee Lauder will suffer irreparable injury absent an injunction.

* * *

It is concluded that the geographical limitation of the covenant is reasonable under the circumstances. While under some circumstances, such a widespread restriction would be patently unreasonable, on the facts presented, it is not so here, given the scope of Batra's responsibilities for R+F and Darphin and the international scope of Estee Lauder's business and the cosmetic industry in general. Such broad geographic limitations have been deemed reasonable where warranted by the nature and scope of the employer's business.

Given that Estee Lauder contracted to pay Batra his salary for the duration of the twelve months, the fact that the geographic scope is all-encompassing will not render it overbroad and therefore void. In other words, although, under the contract, Batra essentially is prohibited from working for a competitor of R+F or Darphin anywhere in the world, the concern that the breadth of such a prohibition would make it impossible for him to earn a living is assuaged by the fact that he will continue to earn his salary from Estee Lauder, as he contracted to do so.

With respect to the durational restriction imposed upon Batra by the Non-compete Agreement, it is concluded that twelve months is not warranted in order to adequately protect Estee Lauder's interests.

* * *

Therefore, in accordance with the authority to grant partial enforcement, a five-month period of enforcement is deemed reasonable.

* * *

NOTES AND QUESTIONS

1. In Estee Lauder v. Batra, the court put a great deal of weight on the likelihood that Batra would eventually use the trade secrets he had learned during his employment at Estee Lauder. Were there other reasonable options the court had for protecting Estee Lauder's trade secrets?

2. Most states test restraints by a rule of reason. That is the view of the Restatement of Contracts 2d § 188 (1981):

(1) A promise to refrain from competition that imposes a restraint that is ancillary to an otherwise valid transaction or relationship is unreasonably in restraint of trade if

(a) the restraint is greater than is needed to protect the promisee's legitimate interest, or

(b) the promisee's need is outweighed by the hardship to the promisor and the likely injury to the public.

(2) Promises imposing restraints that are ancillary * * * include * * *:

* * *

(b) a promise by an employee or other agent not to compete with his employer or other principal; * * *

3. Compare the duty not to compete with the "fiduciary" duty. The fiduciary duty requires the employee not only to refrain from competing against the employer but also to act affirmatively in furtherance of the employer's interests. Most courts have declined to find any fiduciary duty for ordinary employees. In general, the fiduciary duty exists only for individuals who exercise broad managerial discretion in operating a business. See, e.g., Arrowood v. Lyon, 279 S.W.2d 801 (Ky. 1955). This is also the position of the Restatement (Third) of Employment Law, approved by the American Law Institute in 2014. Section 8.01 provides that only employees "in a position of trust and confidence" owe a fiduciary duty to their employers. The Comments explain that "Employees occupy such a position when they exercise managerial responsibilities for the employer or have substantial discretion and little direct oversight in carrying out their tasks, and especially when they have been entrusted with the employer's trade secrets."

4. Can the duty of loyalty be shared with the right to engage in collective labor activity? Workers seeking a better contract pressured Jimmy John's restaurants by distributing posters suggesting that the company's sandwiches posed a health risk to consumers. The workers wanted paid sick days. The ads showed one sandwich "made by a healthy Jimmy John's Worker" and an unattractive sandwich "made by a sick Jimmy John's worker." The Washington Supreme Court held this was "so disloyal as to exceed [the workers'] right to engage in concerted activities protected by the National Labor Relations Act." The court also said that the employer "complied with Minnesota Department of Health regulations by requiring employees to call in sick if they had experienced flu-like symptoms in the last 24 hours." Thus the ads made false statements and therefore the employer did not violate the workers' rights when it discharged them. See MikLin Enterprises, Inc. v. Nat'l Labor Relations Bd., 861 F.3d 812 (8th Cir. 2017).

5. Who should bear the burden of proof when the reasonableness of a promise not to compete is at issue? In some states, presumably due to the general policy against restraints of trade, the party seeking enforcement has the burden of demonstrating the reasonableness of the non-competition clause. See, e.g., Curtis 1000, Inc. v. Youngblade, 878 F.Supp. 1224 (N.D.Iowa 1995). Is it fair that in these states the employer has the burden of proof in all cases, including those where an employee freely and knowingly consents to such a clause and later seeks to avoid it? Florida law does not place a burden on an employer to show that its non-competition agreement was reasonably necessary. See DeSantis v. Wackenhut Corp., 732 S.W.2d 29

(Tex.Ct.App.1987), modified, 793 S.W.2d 670 (Tex.1990) (construing Florida law). What are the problems with this rule? Florida court decisions on this subject were overturned by the Florida Legislature. According to the current Florida statute, Fla. Stat. § 542.335(1)(c), the party seeking enforcement has to show that the covenant was necessary to protect its legitimate interests.

6. In recent years, reforms have tended towards curbing non-compete pacts. Two bills were introduced in Congress in 2016: the Limiting the Ability to Demand Detrimental Employment Restrictions Act (LADDER Act) and the Mobility and Opportunity for Vulnerable Employees Act (MOVE Act). Each bill would prohibit employers from entering into non-compete pacts with low-wage employees. On November 14, 2019, the Senate Committee on Small Business and Entrepreneurship reviewed a new noncompete bill, the Workforce Mobility Act of 2019 (Mobility Act), introduced by senators to develop a uniform nationwide noncompete law. The Mobility Act proposes a disassociation from a partnership; or (2) the sale of a business. Noncompetes that fall under one of the two exceptions may only prevent the restricted parties from "carrying on a like business" in the same geographic region in which the partnership or business operated prior to the respective dissolution, disassociation or sale. The noncompete restrictions in those contexts cannot be longer than one year in duration. The Mobility Act would give the Federal Trade Commission and the Department of Labor the ability to enforce the prohibition on noncompetes by (1) issuing civil penalties, including fines in an amount not to exceed $5,000 per each week the employer is in violation of the law; and (2) pursuing judicial action on behalf of aggrieved employees. Further, the Mobility Act would create a private right of action for aggrieved employees. New state laws restrict non-compete covenants, employing a variety of approaches. Hawaii passed a law in 2015 prohibiting non-competes in the technology industry. Oregon and Utah have limited the duration of non-compete arrangements: in Oregon, a non-compete agreement is only enforceable for 18 months while in Utah a non-compete is only enforceable for 1 year. New Mexico has exempted medical professionals from non-compete agreements. After almost a decade of negotiation, Massachusetts passed a non-compete reform bill in 2018 that limits the duration of non-compete agreements to 12 months post-employment and requires "mutually-agreed upon consideration" for employees to enter into non-compete agreements with their employers. Idaho bucked the trend in 2016 by passing legislation that was friendlier to employers, but in 2018 repealed the two-year-old act after pressure from the technology industry. For up-to-date discussion of various statutory and judicial developments concerning non-competes, see Orly Lobel, Noncompetes, Human Capital Policy & Regional Competition, University of San Diego research paper No. 19–417 (2019).

7. A few states reject enforcement of such agreements altogether. See, e.g., Cal. Bus. & Prof. Code § 16600: "[E]very contract by which anyone is restrained from engaging in a lawful profession, trade, or business of any kind is to that extent void." California enacted this law in 1941. Professor Ronald J. Gilson has suggested that one of the primary reasons Silicon Valley became the center of technological innovation, rather than Boston (home to many pioneering computer firms), was because of California's complete prohibition of non-compete agreements. How would this prohibition spur innovation in the industry and make California more attractive to technology start-ups? For more on how California's refusal to enforce restrictive covenants may have contributed to the development of technology companies by facilitating "knowledge spillovers" between firms, see Ronald J. Gilson, The Legal Infrastructure of High Technology Industrial Districts: Silicon Valley, Route 128, and Covenants Not to Compete, 74 N.Y.U. L. Rev. 575 (1999).

8. It is not only "key" employees in high-skill industries that are required to sign non-compete agreements by their employers; low-wage workers have increasingly been subject to signing non-compete agreements. A spin on the non-compete agreement is the "no poach" deal, a clause buried in some fast-food franchise agreements that prevents one franchise from hiring employees away from another one. This often locks low-wage workers into their positions. What effect does a non-poach clause have on workers' economic mobility? If the primary justification for non-compete agreements is the protection of a company's trade secrets, why would low-wage workers be subject to these non-competes?

9. The question of whether non-compete agreements and similar restrictions violate the Thirteenth Amendment has arisen in various contexts. In Pollock v. Williams, 322 U.S. 4 (1944), the Supreme Court struck down a Florida criminal statute making failure to perform services after receiving an advance payment prima facie evidence of misdemeanor fraud. Justice Jackson wrote for the Court: "The undoubted aim of the Thirteenth Amendment as implemented by the Antipeonage Act was not merely to end slavery but to maintain a system of completely free and voluntary labor throughout the United States. * * * When the master can compel and the laborer cannot escape the obligation to go on, there is no power below to redress [oppressive working conditions] and no incentive above to relieve a harsh overlordship or unwholesome conditions of work." See also Lorch, Inc. v. Bessemer Mall Shopping Ctr., Inc., 310 So.2d 872 (Ala.1975).

Similarly, specific performance is a remedy that is not available in employment or personal service contracts because ordering the performance of work can be considered involuntary servitude in violation of the Thirteenth Amendment. Specific performance as a remedy is also considered undesirable to compel the continuance of a personal association after disputes have arisen and confidence and loyalty are gone. Restatement (Second) of Contracts § 367 (1981); Beverly Glen Music, Inc. v. Warner Communications, Inc., 224 Cal.Rptr. 260 (Cal.App.1986) (Thirteenth Amendment forbids injunction against performance by singer in violation of her contract).

A question also arises as to whether the extension of non-compete agreements to low-wage workers performing unskilled work violates the workers' right to contract. It has been argued that employees' lack of bargaining power and employers' ability to legally coerce former employees not to obtain similar employment makes non-compete agreements for low-wage workers a violation of the Thirteenth Amendment. For a more in-depth discussion, see Ayesha Bell Hardaway's The Paradox of the Right to Contract.

10. What constitutes "competition" for the purposes of a non-compete agreement? Consider the dispute that arose in Wenzell v. Ingrim, 228 P.3d 103 (Alaska 2010). Ingrim sold his dental practice to Wenzell. The terms of the sale specified that Ingrim was not allowed to engage in the " 'practice of dentistry' within fifteen miles of his old clinic for two years and within ten miles for an additional three years." Wenzell sued for breach of the non-compete agreement after Ingrim took up employment with the Alaska Native Medical Center (ANMC), a federally funded non-profit clinic located two miles away. In response, Ingrim argued that the ANMC was sufficiently different from a private practice that it did not compete with the old clinic. The Supreme Court of Alaska held that whether the ANMC actually posed a competitive threat was a factual question to be determined by the trial court on remand.

11. In many jurisdictions, a court may modify an overly broad non-compete agreement by striking the overreaching provisions and upholding the remainder of the agreement. Consider the extent to which this rule creates an incentive for employers to draft the broadest possible restrictions. In jurisdictions that allow such "blue-penciling," employers might try to create a maximally restrictive agreement by purposely including questionable provisions and leaving the court with the burden of striking those parts that are judicially unacceptable. By contrast, employers would tend to be more cautious in jurisdictions that take an "all or none" view of the validity of non-compete agreements. In such jurisdictions, a single overreaching provision can invalidate the entire agreement. In New York, both considerations—the risk that employers will be overly broad or overly cautious—are taken into account. Courts will allow for partial enforcement of overly broad restrictive covenants, but only if the employer demonstrates "an absence of overreaching, coercive use of dominant bargaining power, or other anti-competitive misconduct." BDO Seidman v. Hirshberg, 712 N.E. 2d 1220 (N.Y. 1999). This is essentially the position of the Restatement as well, see the Restatement (Third) of Employment Law, approved by the American Law Institute in 2014:

> § 8.06 Enforcement of Restrictive Covenants: [A] covenant * * * restricting a former employee's working activities is enforceable only if it is reasonably tailored in scope, geography, and time to further a protectable interest of the employer * * *

> § 8:08 Modification of Unreasonable Restrictive Covenant: A court may delete or modify provisions in an overbroad restrictive covenant * * * and then enforce the covenant as modified unless * * * the employer lacked a reasonable and good-faith basis for believing the covenant was enforceable. Lack of a reasonable and good-faith basis for believing a covenant was enforceable may be manifested by its overbreadth alone, or by overbreadth coupled with other evidence that the employer sought to do more than protect its legitimate interests.

12. The rule of Lumley v. Wagner came to the American courts from the English Court of Equity. *Lumley* held that although opera singer Johanna Wagner could not be ordered to perform her contract, she would be enjoined from singing at any competing music hall for the duration of the remaining time on her contract. After initial rejection in the United States, the *Lumley* doctrine of enjoining other employment became accepted. Lea VanderVelde, The Gendered Origins of the *Lumley* Doctrine: Binding Men's Consciences and Women's Fidelity, 101 Yale L.J. 775 (1992), asks why *Lumley*, rather than other rulings by eminent American judges, became the canon:

> The answer appears to be related to the gendered context in which the rule was examined at the time that American courts constructed the canon. Suits involving the services of women constituted the core of cases and provided the central contextual focus in which the rule was examined. Many more actresses than actors were sued under this cause of action. Indeed, in the nineteenth century, all of the prominent cases in this line involved the services of women, and only women performers were subjected to permanent injunctions against performing elsewhere for the duration of the contract. In the corpus of reported cases, no male performer was ever permanently enjoined from quitting and performing elsewhere during the entire nineteenth century * * *.

> [U]nlike male actors, nineteenth-century women performers were less likely to be viewed as free and independent employees. Nineteenth-century women were generally perceived as relationally bound to men. In this line of cases, that perception of women manifested itself in the need to bind actresses to their male theater managers. Moreover, in the view of the dominant culture, women performers were more likely to be perceived as subordinate than were their male counterparts. The decision in this line of cases reflect larger "belief system out of which knowledge is constructed, [belief systems that] place constraints on thought [and] that have real consequences for the behavior of individuals who live within them." This conceptualization of women in the nineteenth century paved the way for the adoption of the *Lumley* rule in America.

The *Lumley* rule is now applied to many kinds of performers and other employees with unique talents. Can you think of a better way to balance the rights of employer and employee than the *Lumley* rule? If not, do you nevertheless reject the *Lumley* rule because of its gendered origins?

13. When is injunctive relief an appropriate remedy for an employee's breach of a promise not to compete? The New York Court of Appeals in Reed, Roberts Assoc., Inc. v. Strauman, 353 N.E.2d 590 (N.Y.1976), stated that the services of the employee must be "unique or extraordinary." Contrast this with the Supreme Court of Pennsylvania's decision to grant an injunction in John G. Bryant Co., Inc. v. Sling Testing & Repair, Inc., 369 A.2d 1164 (Pa. 1977):

> It is not the initial breach of a covenant which necessarily established the existence of irreparable harm but rather the threat

of the unbridled continuation of the violation and the resultant incalculable damage to the former employer's business that constitutes the justification for equitable intervention. * * * The covenant seeks to prevent more than just the sales that might result by the prohibited contract but also the covenant is designed to prevent a disturbance in the relationship that has been established between appellees and their accounts through prior dealings. It is the possible consequences of this unwarranted interference with customer relationships that is unascertainable and not capable of being fully compensated by money damages. It is for this reason we noted * * * that where a covenant of this type meets the test of reasonableness, it is prima facie enforceable in equity.

14. Many courts have held that non-compete agreements are completely unenforceable in regards to attorneys. The same blanket unenforceability has not been extended to other professions. Promises by physicians not to compete receive heightened scrutiny because of public policy concerns, though they are not as completely unenforceable. Valley Med. Specialists v. Farber, 982 P.2d 1277 (Ariz.1999). Some courts have gone as far as holding that all physician non-compete agreements are void unless prescribed by statute. Murfreesboro Med. Clinic, P.A. v. Udom, 166 S.W.3d 674 (Tenn. 2005).

15. Is it relevant whether an employee subject to a non-compete agreement quits or is fired? If the employee is dismissed, does it matter whether the employer had good cause? Robert S. Weiss & Assoc., Inc. v. Wiederlight, 546 A.2d 216 (Conn. 1988), held that "the reasonableness of a restrictive covenant of employment does not turn on whether the employee subject to the covenant left his position voluntarily or was dismissed by the employer." In contrast, Iowa's highest court implied that termination can invalidate the covenant and is certainly a factor opposing the grant of an injunction against the employee. Ma & Pa, Inc. v. Kelly, 342 N.W.2d 500 (Iowa 1984).

16. Subsequent to the commencement of an at-will employment relationship, should an employer's promise of continued employment constitute sufficient consideration for the employee's promise not to compete? This remains an unsettled issue. See 51 A.L.R.3d 825. Many courts have held that a promise of continued employment is illusory because the employer maintains the right to discharge at will. See George W. Kistler, Inc. v. O'Brien, 347 A.2d 311 (Pa.1975). Some jurisdictions, however, have upheld continued employment as adequate consideration. Many of these courts recognize that the employer would merely discharge the employee and reestablish the employment relationship in order to circumvent a decision to the contrary. Other courts have held that an employer's promise to further train an employee for a management position or inform them of trade secrets, although illusory, constitutes consideration once the employer's end if fulfilled. See, e.g., Alex Sheshunoff Mgmt. Servs. v. Johnson, 209 S.W.3d 644 (Tex. 2006).

17. An insurance firm's vice president, whose wife was employed by the same company, had a provision in his contract prohibiting him from competing "directly or indirectly." If his wife opens a competing business, has her husband violated his contract? See Rash v. Hilb, Rogal & Hamilton Co., 467 S.E.2d 791 (Va. 1996) (held: yes).

18. Does a right against wrongful discharge protect an employee who is dismissed for refusing to sign a non-disclosure and non-compete agreement? The Wisconsin Supreme Court held no. Wisconsin has "a strong public policy against enforcement of trade restraints which are determined to be unreasonable * * * [but no] public policy contrary to an employer's requirement that its employees sign a non-disclosure/non-compete agreement which that employee considers to be unreasonable * * * " Chief Justice Abrahamson, dissenting, said: "What the majority opinion fails to see * * * is that when an employer terminates an at-will employee for refusing to sign an illegal nondisclosure agreement, the employer is enforcing the illegal agreement." Tatge v. Chambers & Owen, Inc., 579 N.W.2d 217 (Wis.1998).

2. TRADE SECRETS

NOTES AND QUESTIONS

1. Employers usually draft restrictive covenants to prevent former employees from using proprietary information, such as client lists and trade secrets, to establish competing businesses. Query, however, the extent to which courts will enforce such restrictions when the conduct in question falls short of outright competition. The Supreme Court of Texas held in Johnson v. Brewer & Pritchard, P.C., 73 S.W.3d 193 (Tex. 2002), that an associate at a law firm generally has no obligation to refer potential clients to that firm. The court emphasized its concern that the existence of such a duty might restrain lawyers from giving honest advice as to whether a particular firm is suited to the potential client's needs. At the same time, the court cautioned that it did not intend to "set forth a broad rule governing all employees who might divert a business opportunity from their employer without receiving any compensation or benefit in return." The court reaffirmed in particular that an employee "may not act for his future interests at the expense of his employer by using the employer's funds or employees for personal gain or by a course of conduct designed to hurt the employer." In all, *Johnson* suggests that the incidental redirection of business away from one's employer does not amount to a cognizable "competitive" act.

2. What type and how much damage must an employer show before invoking trade secret protection against former employees? Teradyne, Inc. v. Clear Communications Corp., 707 F.Supp. 353 (N.D.Ill.1989), held that a complaint invoking Illinois trade secret protection must do more than allege "a high degree of probability of inevitable and immediate * * * use * * * of trade secrets." The complaint was dismissed:

> Here there is no allegation that defendants have in fact threatened to use Teradyne's secrets or that they will inevitably do so. An allegation that the defendants said they would use secrets or disavowed their confidentiality agreements would serve this

purpose. An allegation that Clear could not operate without Teradyne's secrets because Teradyne's secret technology is the only one that will work would suffice though more technical facts may be necessarily included in such a pleading. The defendants' claimed acts, working for Teradyne, leaving its business, hiring employees from Teradyne and entering the same field (though in a market not yet serviced by Teradyne) do not state a claim of threatened misappropriation.

3.   In SI Handling Sys., Inc. v. Heisley, 753 F.2d 1244 (3d Cir. 1985), a court held that the employees would not have breached SI Handling's rights if they had made use of their knowledge of General Motors' "needs" and its "key decisionmakers." Why should former employees of SI Handling be able to take away and use such valuable information, which they only obtained as employees on the former job? In a case similar to *SI Handling,* a court said that the result should be heavily influenced by how much information the employee brought to the prior job when he or she was hired there. The court distinguished the facts before it, in which the employee had worked for ten years for the Air Force and four years for the Draper Laboratory at MIT before joining plaintiff, a military contractor, from situations where an employee obtains all his knowledge on a job and then tries to use it elsewhere. How well does this distinction capture the reality that individuals are constantly learning and developing, that they bring ability and knowledge even to their first job, and that later attempts to tell them what they can and cannot use will be difficult to enforce? Dynamics Research Corp. v. Analytic Sciences Corp., 400 N.E.2d 1274 (Mass. App. Ct. 1980).

4.   Should it make a difference if the former employee sets out on her own or if she joins a different company? In Fox v. Millman, 45 A.3d 332 (N.J. 2012), the defendant had worked for Target Industries, a plastic bag manufacturer, as a sales representative. When her employment was terminated, she took her former employer's customer list with her, despite the confidentiality agreement that she had signed. When she was hired by a new employer, Polymer Plastics, shortly thereafter, she gave them the customer list, which she presented as her own. When questioned by Polymer, she denied that she was under any confidentiality agreement with Target. Polymer made no further inquiries into the matter, such as contacting Target, and subsequently used the list to generate substantial profits. Polymer Plastics admitted that they knew that Millman had previously worked at Target, and at no other plastic manufacturing company, and that Polymer themselves required all of their employees to sign confidentiality agreements. Nonetheless, the New Jersey Supreme Court held that an employer does not have a duty to inquire as to whether materials received from a new employee are bound by a prior confidentiality agreement.

5.   What is the appropriate relief when a former employee has violated a valid restriction against using trade secrets? In Lamb-Weston, Inc. v. McCain Foods, Ltd., 941 F.2d 970 (9th Cir. 1991), the Ninth Circuit upheld the district court's eight-month injunction against McCain Foods for stealing Lamb-Weston's processing system that made curlicue french fries. The order banned McCain Foods from selling any curlicue french fries world-wide for the enjoined period. "An injunction in a trade secret case seeks to protect the secrecy of misappropriated information and to eliminate any unfair head start the defendant may have gained. A worldwide injunction here is consistent with those goals because it 'place[s the defendant] in the position it would have occupied if the breach of confidence had not occurred prior to the public disclosure, * * *' " The court also ruled that eight months was not overbroad in time. "[T]he appropriate duration for the injunction should be the period of time it would have taken [the defendant], either by reverse engineering or by independent development, to develop [the product] legitimately without use of [plaintiff's] trade secrets." (citing K-2 Ski Co. v. Head Ski Co., 506 F.2d 471, 474 (9th Cir. 1974)). Was that a fair basis for deciding how long defendant should be barred?

6.   Usually trade secret cases contain a lengthy discussion of the technology in dispute. Trade secret cases, like patent cases, are fact-specific, and a reader is sometimes uncertain whether a busy judge has in fact mastered the scientific or engineering issues.

7.   Sometimes, disclosure of information obtained as an employee is a crime. See, e.g., Mass.Gen.Laws ch. 266 § 30(4): "Whoever steals, or * * * copies with intent to convert any trade secret of another, regardless of value, * * * shall be guilty of larceny * * *."

See Edmund W. Kitch, The Law and Economics of Rights in Valuable Information, 9 J. Legal Stud. 683 (1980):

> The difficulties of detection and enforcement make this a logical area for the use of strong criminal penalties. Since the number of detectable thefts is small, the activity can only be effectively deterred if heavy penalties are imposed on thieves who are caught. Trade secrecy skillfully executed is not a crime under the traditional criminal statutes. Entry only to copy is not entry with felonious intent and hence not burglary. Information is not the kind of property that falls within the scope of traditional theft statutes. Bribery of an employee to provide information, but not property of the employer, is not a crime. When property is taken, a crime has been committed. In the late 1960s and early 1970s, twenty-six states passed statutes to make trade-secrecy theft a crime. There have, however, been very few prosecutions under these statutes. The statutes came about as the result of a ring organized to steal systematically process secrets and materials from an American drug company and sell them to Italian manufacturers who at that time operated under an umbrella created by the lack of drug patents under Italian law. The ring proved very difficult for the company to break, and the problem highlighted a gap in the criminal laws that many legislatures were willing to fill.
>
> The new statutes require the theft of a trade secret. Therefore, in the criminal prosecution determining whether what was taken was a trade secret is a central issue. The defense must prove that what was taken was not kept secret by the company nor known to other concerns in the industry. To defend on that issue, the defense must

ask for large amounts of material relevant to the technology in issue. Procedures for protecting the confidentiality of this material exist, but its assembly and dissemination during the litigation process obviously increase the risk of further loss. In a California case, a convicted thief of trade secrets from IBM argued that his conviction should be set aside because he was the only one who had ever been prosecuted under the statute.

8.   (a) In some jurisdictions customer lists have been held to be trade secrets. Under California trade secret law as long as a customer list is not generally known or readily accessible to others and is protected by efforts that are "reasonable under the circumstances" it is entitled to protection. Surgidev Corp. v. Eye Tech., Inc., 828 F.2d 452 (8th Cir. 1987), employed this standard, holding that a list of physicians who were "high volume implanters" of intraocular lenses was a trade secret and was protected under California law. The court upheld the enjoining of a former employee who attempted to utilize the information in setting up a competing medical supply business.

Contrast the California standard with that utilized by a federal district court in applying New York law:

> As a general rule "where the customers are readily ascertainable outside the employer's business as prospective users or consumers of the employer's services or products, trade secret protection will not attach and courts will not enjoin an employee from soliciting his employer's customers." Where customers are discoverable only through extraordinary efforts and the employer's clientele has been secured by many years expenditure of time and money then a court may confer trade secret status upon a customer list.

Consolidated Brands, Inc. v. Mondi, 638 F.Supp. 152 (E.D.N.Y.1986), quoting Leo Silfen, Inc. v. Cream, 278 N.E.2d 636 (N.Y. 1972).

A former employee cannot use memorized information about the former employer's customers any more than he or she could use a written list. Ed Nowogroski Ins., Inc. v. Rucker, 971 P.2d 936 (Wash.1999).

(b) What about the names and addresses of a firm's clients? The California Court of Appeal held such information is a trade secret. Morlife, Inc. v. Perry, 66 Cal.Rptr.2d 731 (Cal.Ct.App. 1997). Morlife, a roofing company, had accumulated a collection of customers' business cards. Prior to resigning from Morlife, Perry used the business cards to solicit customers for his own roofing company. Invoking the Uniform Trade Secrets Act, the court found that Perry had misappropriated Morlife's trade secret. The customer list contained information "not generally known to the roofing industry," and Morlife had taken steps to "maintain the secrecy of [the customer list] by limiting the circulation [of the list]." In all, "Morlife's customers were not readily ascertainable, but only discoverable with great effort" and that development of the list required "considerable time and money." Perry could not use the hard-earned information to advance his own competing business.

(c) Pepsi obtained an injunction enjoining William Redmond, a former PepsiCo employee, from divulging Pepsi trade secrets and confidential information in his new job with Quaker, makers of Snapple and Gatorade, and from assuming any duties relating to beverage pricing, marketing, and distribution. Redmond had signed a confidentiality agreement. Pepsi successfully argued that Redmond knew about Pepsi's "Strategic Plan," its "Annual Operating Plan," and its policies regarding shelf space and merchandising. "Redmond cannot help but rely on [Pepsi] trade secrets as he helps plot Gatorade and Snapple's new course, and * * * these secrets will enable Quaker to achieve a substantial advantage by knowing exactly how [Pepsi] will price, distribute, and market its sports drinks and new age drinks * * * " PepsiCo, Inc. v. Redmond, 54 F.3d 1262 (7th Cir. 1995).

9.   In order to promote the utilization of inventions arising from federally supported research, the Bayh-Dole Act sets forth a three-tier system for patent rights ownership of "subject inventions." 35 U.S.C. §§ 200, 202–203 (2012). For "subject inventions," which include "any invention of the contractor conceived or first actually reduced to practice in the performance of work under a funding agreement," the Act awards patent rights first to the federal contractor, second to the federal government, and third to the inventor.

The National Institutes of Health provided Stanford with funding for research related to HIV measurement techniques. As part of his employment with Stanford, Dr. Mark Holodniy signed an agreement stating that he agreed to assign his interest in any invention to the university. Holodniy then began conducting research at Cetus, a California-based company, as part of his employment with Stanford. Holodniy signed an agreement stating that he was assigning his interest in any invention to Cetus. Later, Roche Molecular Systems, Inc. acquired Cetus and commercialized the HIV measurement technique developed by Holodniy and patented by Stanford.

Stanford sued Roche for patent infringement. The Supreme Court held that Roche had acquired an ownership interest in the patents from Holodniy's assignment of rights to Cetus and that this interest was not extinguished by the Bayh-Dole Act. The Court reasoned that when Congress had previously divested inventors of their rights in inventions, it had done so unambiguously. Here, the Act applied only to an "invention of the contractor"—for example, an invention which had been properly assigned to the contractor—and did not automatically divest an inventor of rights in an invention. Board of Trustees of the Leland Stanford Junior University v. Roche Molecular Systems, 563 U.S. 776 (2011).

Note that the Court did not say that patent rights cannot be automatically assigned to the employer, only that the BDA should not be construed to have done so. In Alzheimer's Institute of America, Inc. v. Avid Radiopharmaceuticals, 952 F.Supp.2d 740 (E.D. Pa. 2011), a federal district court made note of this, holding that a University of South Florida employee automatically assigned the patent rights to his discovery of the Swedish Mutation, linked to Alzheimer's disease, to the university. That court noted that the Florida statute—as opposed to the BDA—unambiguously assigned ownership of patents earned by Florida universities' employees' to the universities.

10. Many states have blacklisting statutes aimed at preventing employers from exchanging information about past employees with the intent of preventing those employees from obtaining future employment within the industry. Do employer suits to enforce non-compete agreements and to protect trade secrets fall within the scope of a state's blacklisting statute? Indiana's blacklisting statute prohibits any company from permitting its agents to blacklist a discharged employee or "attempt[ing] by . . . any means whatever, to prevent such discharged employee, or any employee who may have voluntarily left said company's service, from obtaining employment with any other person, or company . . . " Ind. Code § 22–5–3–2 (2012). The Supreme Court of Indiana ruled that a suit to protect alleged trade secrets does not fall within the scope of the state's blacklisting statute because the language of the statute did not support such a construction and an employee's interests in being free from frivolous litigation were better served by other remedies and defenses including the common law torts of malicious prosecution and abuse of process, motions to dismiss under federal and state rules of civil procedure, and anti-trust laws. Loparex, LLC v. MPI Release Technologies, LLC, 964 N.E.2d 806 (Ind. 2012).

CHAPTER 12

BANKRUPTCY AND UNEMPLOYMENT

As Chapter 10 shows, judicial decisions interpreting the common law and (as to government employees) the Fourteenth Amendment have reduced the vulnerability of workers to arbitrary dismissal. To some unquantifiable extent, a job has become "property." To that extent, workers have obtained a set of legally protected expectations in the continuation of the employment relationship.

Nevertheless, the U.S. remains committed to an economy in which there is risk, adaptation, and flexibility, and so to a labor market in which there is extensive mobility. The legal structure of our employment relationships must therefore balance legitimate worker expectations and entitlements with employer authority to hire, contract out, revise production methods, transfer operations elsewhere in the U.S. or abroad, diminish the scale of operations, and ultimately shut down. As in so many areas of employment relations, law restrains employer discretion. Regarding layoffs, there has been extensive litigation about whether Title VII of the 1964 Civil Rights Act prevents dismissals on the basis of seniority if the consequence is retention of most white workers and layoff of many nonwhites. That topic was considered in Chapter 4. This chapter begins with discussion of the bankruptcy system which gives workers certain limited rights: to wages they earned before bankruptcy, to compensation for work done after bankruptcy, and to a degree of protection for contractual expectations. The chapter then considers federal and state plant-closing legislation; those laws require notice to workers of impending shut-downs in certain situations. Next, the chapter examines in depth the major national program dealing with dismissed workers—the federally mandated unemployment insurance system. That program offers broad coverage for the first 26 weeks of unemployment (and has recently been extended to 99 weeks for many workers). One set of questions is relevant to all the material in this chapter: Should long-term unemployment (for example, unemployment extending beyond the time that unemployment insurance benefits usually last) be the target of a systematic national program? If so, what shape should that effort take?

A. BANKRUPTCY

In recent years, large and small American companies have become bankrupt—either as a means of terminating business, or as a way of reorganizing and continuing to operate. Worker expectations for continued employment can be rudely interrupted by bankruptcy. They may be owed wages on the day bankruptcy occurs. They may believe they have a contractual right to benefits: health care, disability protection, life insurance, pension. They may have a written contract assuring continued employment or, more likely, implied contract rights to the job, or against arbitrary dismissal.

In the important case of NLRB v. Bildisco & Bildisco, 465 U.S. 513 (1984), the Supreme Court held unanimously that a collective bargaining agreement is only an "executory contract," and thus can be rejected by the employer after bankruptcy if the agreement "burdens the estate, and * * * after careful scrutiny, the equities balance in favor of rejecting the labor contract." The Supreme Court also held, by five to four vote, that an employer commits no unfair labor practice if it unilaterally alters the terms of an existing collective bargaining agreement after a bankruptcy petition has been filed but before review by a bankruptcy court of the arguments for altering the contract.

Congress reacted speedily to prescribe the procedures that should be followed by a bankrupt company seeking relief from its collectively bargained obligations. 11 U.S.C. § 1113.

1. PROCEDURAL PROTECTION FOR EXECUTORY CONTRACTS

11 U.S.C. § 1113.

* * *

(b)(1) Subsequent to filing a petition and prior to filing an application seeking rejection of a collective bargaining agreement, the debtor in possession or trustee * * *, shall—

(A) make a proposal to the authorized representative of the employees covered by such agreement, based on the most complete and reliable information available at the time of such proposal, which provides for those necessary modifications in the employees' benefits and protections that are necessary to permit the reorganization of the debtor and assures that all creditors, the debtor and all of the affected parties are treated fairly and equitably; and

(B) provide, subject to subsection (d)(3), the representative of the employees with such relevant information as is necessary to evaluate the proposal.

(2) During the period beginning on the date of the making of a proposal provided for in paragraph (1) and ending on the date of the hearing provided for in subsection (d)(1), the trustee shall meet, at reasonable times, with the authorized representative to confer in good faith in attempting to reach mutually satisfactory modifications of such agreement.

(c) The court shall approve an application for rejection of a collective bargaining agreement only if the court finds that—

(1) the trustee has, prior to the hearing, made a proposal that fulfills the requirements of subsection (b)(1);

(2) the authorized representative of the employees has refused to accept such proposal without good cause; and

(3) the balance of the equities clearly favors rejection of such agreement.

* * *

(e) If during a period when the collective bargaining agreement continues in effect, and if essential to the continuation of the debtor's business, or in order to avoid irreparable damage to the estate, the court, after notice and a hearing, may authorize the trustee to implement interim changes in the terms, conditions, wages, benefits, or work rules provided by a collective bargaining agreement.

NOTE

Nonunion employees in many states have rights against arbitrary dismissal. Those rights can be considered a form of contract, implied or otherwise. See Chapter 10. If the employer of such employees seeks bankruptcy protection, those workers are likely to lose much of the value of their contractual rights. Looking at 11 U.S.C. section 1113, what statutory provision would you support for nonunion workers who have rights in their job but get no benefits from 11 U.S.C. § 1113 because they have no collective bargaining agreement? Could a court reason from 11 U.S.C. § 1113 and create such rights without new congressional action?

2. PRIORITIES IN BANKRUPTCY

Two statutory "preferences" provide a degree of advantage for employees of a bankrupt firm. First, section 507(a)(4) of the federal bankruptcy law gives workers preference over certain general creditors as to wages earned but uncollected before bankruptcy. This preference is limited to $10,000 per employee.

Second, and far more important, once the bankruptcy filing occurs, those who supply goods and services to the bankrupt firm have a right to be paid. Under the statutory scheme, these are "administrative expenses" of the bankruptcy, and must be paid before prebankruptcy creditors receive money. Under section 503(b)(1)(A) of the Bankruptcy Code, these goods and services are considered administrative expenses, which include "the actual, necessary costs and expenses of preserving the estate, including wages, salaries, or commissions for services rendered after the commencement of the case," and which, pursuant to the priority scheme set forth in section 507, must be paid before most prebankruptcy creditors receive money. The reason for this policy is that the law seeks to encourage continued operation of the enterprise, and such operation requires assurance that new obligations will have priority over those still unpaid from the past. Clearly, therefore, wage claims for post-bankruptcy work are administrative expenses. The law is less clear about, and is currently wrestling with, how to handle claims against employers such as severance pay and accrued pension obligations, that are at the intersection between new obligations and leftover duties contracted before bankruptcy.

Howard Delivery Services, Inc. v. Zurich American Insurance Co.

547 U.S. 651 (2006).

■ JUSTICE GINSBURG delivered the opinion of the Court.

The Bankruptcy Code accords a priority, among unsecured creditors' claims, for unpaid "wages, salaries, or commissions," 11 U.S.C.A. § 507(a)(4)(A) (Supp. 2006), and for unpaid contributions to "an employee benefit plan," § 507(a)(5). It is uncontested here that § 507(a)(5) covers fringe benefits that complete a pay package—typically pension plans, and group health, life, and disability insurance—whether unilaterally provided by an employer or the result of collective bargaining. This case presents the question whether the § 507(a)(5) priority also encompasses claims for unpaid premiums on a policy purchased by an employer to cover its workers' compensation liability. We hold that premiums owed by an employer to a workers' compensation carrier do not fit within § 507(a)(5).

* * *

Petitioner Howard Delivery Service, Inc. (Howard), for many years owned and operated a freight trucking business. Howard employed as many as 480 workers and operated in about a dozen States. Each of those States required Howard to maintain workers' compensation coverage to secure its employees' receipt of health, disability, and death benefits in the event of on-the-job accidents. Howard contracted with Zurich to provide this insurance for Howard's operations in ten States.

On January 30, 2002, Howard filed a Chapter 11 bankruptcy petition. Zurich filed an unsecured creditor's claim in that proceeding, seeking priority status for some $400,000 in unpaid workers' compensation premiums. In an amended proof of claim, Zurich asserted that these unpaid premiums qualified as "[c]ontributions to an employee benefit plan" entitled to priority under § 507(a)(5).

* * *

We granted certiorari to resolve a split among the Circuits concerning the priority status of premiums owed by a bankrupt employer to a workers' compensation carrier.

* * *

Adjoining subsections of the Bankruptcy Code, § 507(a)(4) and (a)(5), are centrally involved in this case. Subsections 507(a)(4) and (5) currently provide: "(a) The following expenses and claims have priority in the following order:" (4) Fourth, allowed unsecured claims * * * for—"(A) wages, salaries, or commissions, including vacation, severance, and sick leave pay earned by an individual. . . . * * * " (5) Fifth, allowed unsecured claims for contributions to an employee benefit plan—"(A) arising from services rendered within 180 days before the date of the filing of the [bankruptcy] petition or the date of the cessation of the debtor's business, whichever occurs first. . . ." * * *

The provision, currently contained in § 507(a)(5), allows the provider of an employee benefit plan to recover unpaid premiums—albeit only after the employees' claims for "wages, salaries, or commissions" have been paid. § 507(a)(4).

Beyond genuine debate, the main office of § 507(a)(5) is to capture portions of employee compensation for services rendered not covered by § 507(a)(4). * * * The current Code's juxtaposition of the wages and employee benefit plan priorities manifests Congress' comprehension that fringe benefits generally complement, or "substitute" for, hourly pay.

Congress tightened the linkage of (a)(4) and (a)(5) by imposing a combined cap on the two priorities, currently set at $10,000 per employee. Because (a)(4) has a higher priority status, all claims for wages are paid first, up to the $10,000 limit; claims under (a)(5) for contributions to employee benefit plans can be recovered next up to the remainder of the $10,000 ceiling. No other subsections of § 507 are joined together by a common cap in this way.

* * *

[W]e recognize that Congress left undefined the § 507(a)(5) terms: "contributions to an employee benefit plan * * * arising from services rendered within 180 days before the date of the filing of the [bankruptcy] petition." * * * Zurich urges the Court to borrow the encompassing definition of employee benefit plan contained in the Employee Retirement Income Security Act of 1974 (ERISA).

* * *

Federal courts have questioned whether ERISA is appropriately used to fill in blanks in a Bankruptcy Code provision, and the panel below parted ways on this issue.

* * *

ERISA's omnibus definition does show, at least, that the term "employee welfare benefit plan" is susceptible of a construction that would include workers' compensation plans. That Act's signals are mixed, however, for 29 U.S.C. § 1003(b)(3) specifically exempts from ERISA's coverage the genre of plan here at issue, i.e., one "maintained solely for the purpose of complying with applicable work[ers'] compensation laws." The § 1003(b)(3) exemption strengthens our resistance to Zurich's argument.

* * *

This case turns, we hold, not on a definition borrowed from a statute designed without bankruptcy in mind, but on the essential character of workers' compensation regimes. Unlike pension provisions or group life, health, and disability insurance plans—negotiated or granted as pay supplements or substitutes—workers' compensation prescriptions have a dominant employer-oriented thrust: They modify, or substitute for, the common-law tort liability to which employers were exposed for work-related accidents.

Workers' compensation regimes provide something for employees—they assure limited fixed payments for on-the-job injuries—and something for employers—they remove the risk of large judgments and heavy costs generated by tort litigation. * * * No such tradeoff is involved in fringe benefit plans that augment each covered worker's hourly pay.

Employer-sponsored pension plans, and group health or life insurance plans, characteristically insure the employee (or his survivor) only. In contrast, workers' compensation insurance, in common with other liability insurance in this regard, e.g., fire, theft, and motor vehicle insurance, shield the insured enterprise: Workers' compensation policies both protect the employer-policyholder from liability in tort, and cover its obligation to pay workers' compensation benefits. * * * When an employer fails to secure workers' compensation coverage, or loses coverage for nonpayment of premiums, an affected employee's remedy would not lie in a suit for premiums that should have been paid to a compensation carrier. Instead, employees who sustain work-related injuries would commonly have recourse to a state-maintained fund. * * * Or, in lieu of the limited benefits obtainable from a state fund under workers' compensation schedules, the injured employee might be authorized to pursue the larger recoveries successful tort litigation ordinarily yields.

Further distancing workers' compensation arrangements from bargained-for or voluntarily accorded fringe benefits, nearly all States, with limited exceptions, require employers to participate in their workers' compensation systems. * * * We do not suggest * * * that a compensation carrier would gain § 507(a)(5) priority for unpaid premiums in States where workers' compensation coverage is elective. Nor do we suggest that wage surrogates or supplements, e.g., pension and health benefits plans, would lose protection under § 507(a)(5) if a State were to mandate them. We simply count it a factor relevant to our assessment that States overwhelmingly prescribe and regulate insurance coverage for on-the-job accidents, while commonly leaving pension, health, and life insurance plans to private ordering.

* * *

Zurich argues that according its claim an (a)(5) priority will give workers' compensation carriers an incentive to continue coverage of a failing enterprise, thus promoting rehabilitation of the business. It may be doubted whether the projected incentive would outweigh competing financial pressure to pull the plug swiftly on an insolvent policyholder, and thereby contain potential losses. An insurer undertakes to pay the scheduled benefits to workers injured on the job while the policy is in effect. In the case of serious injuries, however, benefits may remain payable years after termination of coverage. While cancellation relieves the insurer from responsibility for future injuries, the insurer cannot escape the obligation to continue paying benefits for enduring maladies or disabilities, even though no premiums are paid by the former policyholder. An insurer would likely weigh in the balance the risk of incurring fresh obligations of long duration were it to continue insuring employers unable to pay currently for coverage.

* * *

Rather than speculating on how workers' compensation insurers might react were they to be granted an (a)(5) priority, we are guided in reaching our decision by the equal distribution objective underlying the Bankruptcy Code, and the corollary principle that provisions allowing preferences must be tightly construed.

* * *

Every claim granted priority status reduces the funds available to general unsecured creditors and may diminish the recovery of other claimants qualifying for equal or lesser priorities. * * * "To give priority to a claimant not clearly entitled thereto is not only inconsistent with the policy of equality of distribution; it dilutes the value of the priority for those creditors Congress intended to prefer." * * * Opening the (a)(5) priority to workers' compensation carriers could shrink the amount available to cover unpaid contributions to plans paradigmatically qualifying as wage surrogates, prime among them, pension and health benefit plans.

In sum, we find it far from clear that an employer's liability to provide workers' compensation coverage fits the § 507(a)(5) category "contributions to an employee benefit plan . . . arising from services rendered." Weighing against such categorization, workers' compensation does not compensate employees for work performed, but instead, for on-the-job injuries incurred; workers' compensation regimes substitute not for wage payments, but for tort liability. Any doubt concerning the appropriate characterization, we conclude, is best resolved in accord with the Bankruptcy Code's equal distribution aim. We therefore reject the expanded interpretation Zurich invites. Unless and until Congress otherwise directs, we hold that carriers' claims for unpaid workers' compensation premiums remain outside the priority allowed by § 507(a)(5).

For the reasons stated, the judgment of the United States Court of Appeals for the Fourth Circuit is reversed, and the case is remanded for further proceedings consistent with this opinion.

Law v. Law Trucking Co.

488 A.2d 1225 (R.I. 1985).

■ BEVILACQUA, CHIEF JUSTICE.

This is an appeal from a petition by the permanent receiver of Law Trucking Company seeking instructions whether or not to pay claims filed with the receiver by * * * five employees. * * * [F]ive former Law Trucking employees claim back wages and seek priority to the extent permitted by the United States Bankruptcy Code, 11 U.S.C.A. § 507(a)(3) and (4) (1979) [now 11 U.S.C.A. § (a)(4) and (5)].

* * *

The company evidently had fallen upon hard times, and in hopes of surmounting the financial difficulty, Robert Law, president of Law Trucking, approached the drivers and asked for certain wage concessions that he would plow back into the company with the aim of keeping it afloat. In return, he promised that if the company made a profit at the end of the year, the employees would be entitled to reimbursement for their "loan."

At the time of this agreement, the drivers were working under a union contract that paid them $12.71 for straight time and $19.06 for overtime, based upon a forty-hour week. Law asked that they accept $10 an hour for straight time and $15 an hour for overtime. Only five of the twelve drivers agreed to accept the wage-cut proposal. The acceptors then signed an agreement to this effect.[5]

The employees contend that the terms of a collective-bargaining agreement cannot be altered individually to conflict with the terms of the contract originally entered into by the employer and the union representatives. This issue, however, was not raised below and we will not entertain it now for the first time.

In addition, employees contend that because there was no mutuality of obligation in the alleged agreement, it should fail. The trial justice found that testimony elicited at the hearing provides ample evidence of mutual obligation. Such evidence consisted of the following: Law promised to keep the company open for a year in exchange for the loans; the bookkeeper testified that the company was in serious debt at that time; and because employees were aware of the financial difficulty that

---

[5] The text of the agreement signed by the employees:

"I will loan to Law Trucking Company without interest, my earnings over $10.00 per hour straight time, over $15.00 per hour of overtime, and the 5 personal holidays due in 1981.

"This money is refundable to me at the end of the year in the event of a company profit."

the company was facing, the trial justice could have easily inferred that the employees understood the risk involved. We find no error in the trial justice's conclusion that mutuality of obligation sufficient to support an enforceable contract was present.

Finally, we examine the employees' claim for priority status under the Bankruptcy Code * * * Priority status operates upon the premise that the moneys withheld constitutes wages. If the moneys withheld did not constitute wages, we need not proceed to the issues of statutory application and construction.

The trial justice found that the moneys withheld were loans and not wages. There is ample evidence in the record to support this finding, which is further buttressed by reference to the written agreement signed by the employees. The language in the agreement refers to a loan to the company. Moreover, the moneys withheld were not treated as wages by the bookkeeper; no taxes, and no social security or disability deductions were withheld from sums earned above the wage-rate ceiling set forth in the new agreement.

In our review of these findings we detect neither error nor misconstruction of evidence; therefore, we will not disturb the findings of the trial justice.

NOTES AND QUESTIONS

1.　Congress amended 11 U.S.C. §§ 503 and 507 as part of the Bankruptcy Abuse Prevention and Consumer Protection Act of 2005. The changes apply to cases filed after October 17, 2005. The amendments increased the amount of unsecured claims for wages given priority under section 507(a)(4)(A) to $10,000.00 ($12,475 as of 2014) and lengthened the "reachback" period for pre-petition wage claims from 90 days to 180 days. The amendments also shifted section 507 priority of administrative expenses of wages, salaries and commissions from first to second priority. First priority status under section 507 is now reserved for unsecured claims for domestic support obligations "owed to or recoverable by [among others] a spouse, former spouse, or child of the debtor. . . ." The amendments also added new subsection 503(b)(1)(A)(ii), granting "administrative status" to certain back pay awards pursuant to a judicial or NLRB proceeding.

2.　Having read Law v. Law Trucking Co., how would you have structured this transaction to protect the employees' right to their wages?

3.　In re Growers Seed Ass'n, 49 B.R. 17 (Bkrtcy.Tex.1985), refused to allow a priority claim for moving expenses on the ground that the statute gives priority only to employee claims for wages, salaries, commissions, vacation pay, sick pay, and severance pay.

4.　By statute in most states, a discharged or laid off employee must be paid back wages immediately. See, e.g., Cal.Lab.Code § 201.

5.　Under 11 U.S.C. § 362(a), the commencement of a case under the Bankruptcy Code stays all judicial proceedings against a debtor or property of the estate which could have been brought before the commencement of the case, except in those cases specifically enumerated in section 362(b). 11 U.S.C.A. § 362(a). Courts have held that under the police or regulatory power exception of section 362(b)(4), the EEOC, as a governmental unit, may pursue actions under Title VII against a debtor despite the automatic stay provision. See EEOC v. Hall's Motor Transit Co., 789 F.2d 1011, 1013–14 (3d Cir. 1986). Likewise, the National Labor Relations Board's unfair labor practice and enforcement proceedings are exempt from the automatic stay provision. See NLRB v. 15th Ave. Iron Works, Inc., 964 F.2d 1336, 1137 (2d Cir. 1992) (per curiam). The EEOC and NLRB may obtain only a liability determination, however, and may not collect on any monetary judgment without petitioning the bankruptcy court for relief from the automatic stay.

6. Other countries around the world treat priorities for wages and benefits in bankruptcy differently than in the United States. Some of them also have wage guarantee schemes. For a review of the 32 countries that make up the Organization of Economic Cooperation and Development (OECD) and how they treat employee wages and benefits in bankruptcy, see Paul M. Secunda, An Analysis of the Treatment of Employee Pension and Wage Claims in Insolvency and Under Guarantee Schemes in OECD Countries: Comparative Law Lessons for Detroit and the United States, 41 Fordham Urb. L.J. 867 (2014).

a. VACATION PAY

In re American Housing Foundation, Debtor
2010 WL 2371072 (Bkrtcy. N.D. Tex. 2010).

■ ROBERT L. JONES, BANKRUPTCY JUDGE.

Jack Traeger seeks approval of an administrative claim in the amount of $7,539.38, which amount consists of unpaid expenses of $1,898.35 and accrued vacation benefits of $5,641.03. The debtor, American Housing Foundation ("AHF"), objects to allowance of the accrued vacation pay but admits that Traeger was not paid his expense reimbursement. The Official Unsecured Creditors Committee objects to the entire amount. The Creditors Committee contends Traeger was not an employee of AHF but, rather, of a separate entity, "Administaff"; they also contend that Traeger is not entitled, upon separation, to payment for accrued vacation pay and, as to the expenses, that he had not provided proof of the expenses. Certain creditors . . . assert the same objections as does the Creditors Committee.

This bankruptcy case started with an involuntary petition filed against AHF on April 21, 2009. * * *

Traeger served as the "Portfolio Manager" for AHF's operations for approximately four years prior to the filing of the bankruptcy case. He testified that he was handling all financial matters for AHF at the time the involuntary bankruptcy petition was filed. As of that time, Traeger was paid $160,000.00 per year; he testified that he accrued three weeks of vacation pay per year. Traeger continued in his position after both the involuntary filing and the consolidation of the voluntary petition with the involuntary petition, but was terminated by AHF on December 11, 2009.

As a chapter 11 debtor, AHF is somewhat unusual. It purports to be a nonprofit corporation that was created for the purpose of providing affordable housing for moderate income families. The housing units, over 13,000, are generally owned by limited liability companies and limited partnerships; AHF is affiliated with these entities as a member, with respect to the limited liability companies, or general partner, with respect to the limited partnerships. In some instances, affiliation as a member or general partner may be indirect with an intermediate entity between AHF and the entity that owns the housing facility. Traeger, as with all AHF "employees", was actually an employee of Administaff, from whom AHF leases all its employees. Traeger was paid by Administaff but he contends that Administaff merely serves an "HR" function. Administaff has a stated vacation policy. It states that employees are entitled to vacation benefits and sets forth how vacation time accrues. The policy does not state that employees are paid accrued vacation pay in the event of termination, however ... Traeger testified that certain other employees received payment for accrued vacation time when they voluntarily left AHF (or Administaff). There is no real dispute among the parties concerning the manner in which vacation pay accrues or the way in which the claimed amount is calculated by Traeger.

To qualify as an administrative expense priority claim under section 507(a)(2), a claim must represent the "actual, necessary costs and expenses of preserving the estate" under section 503(b). Section 503(b)(1) specifically includes "wages, salaries, and commissions for services rendered after the commencement of the case," but does not specifically identify vacation, severance, or sick pay as an administrative expense claim. Section 507(a)(4), in contrast, specifically includes "vacation, severance, and sick pay" as an administrative priority if earned within 180 days before the filing of the petition. 11 U.S.C.A. § 507(a)(4). Despite the specific inclusion of vacation and sick pay in section 507 and the omission of such benefits in section 503, courts have generally held that payments for unused benefits such as vacation or sick leave are considered a part of an employee's wages, and thus may qualify as an administrative priority claim under section 503 for the amount accrued for post-petition services.

While vacation pay may constitute an administrative claim, the Court must determine whether Traeger is in fact entitled to payment for accrued vacation time. In this regard, Traeger relies upon the vacation policy of Administaff and his own testimony to support his contention that he is entitled to be paid. An employer is only obligated to pay for unused vacation time if the right to payment for such benefits is specifically expressed in an employment contract. Employee handbooks or policy manuals merely constitute guidelines for the employment relationship and do not create an employment contract unless language contained therein specifically expresses an intention to be bound by the terms of the policy.

Here, there is no employment contract between Traeger and Administaff; Administaff's policy does not constitute an employment contract. Even if the policy expressed an intent to contractually bind Administaff (or AHF), the policy itself fails to expressly state that, upon termination or separation, payment will be made for unused vacation time accrued by an employee. Thus, no right exists for Traeger to recover payments for unused vacation time. * * *

While a claim of payment for unused vacation time may qualify as an administrative priority claim under section 503 of the Bankruptcy Code, Traeger failed to establish any right to such payment. No employment contract evidencing such a right exists, and the policy relied upon does not expressly include the right to payment for vacation pay. It is unclear, based upon the evidence presented, which party, AHF or Administaff, ultimately has the responsibility for payment of wages under the leasing arrangement between AHF and Administaff. Traeger did not provide evidence of any agreement by which AHF was obligated to pay Traeger (as opposed to Administaff). It appears that Traeger's claim, even if allowable under Texas state law, would lie against Administaff. Regardless, Traeger failed to establish a right to payment for accrued vacation time.

Traeger did establish that he is owed $1,898.35 for expenses incurred for travel and other matters. AHF admitted that he had not been paid for such expenses. The expense report is an AHF expense report. The Court will allow Traeger's reimbursement claim for such expenses as an administrative claim.

NOTES

1.   In Peters v. Pikes Peak Musicians Ass'n, 462 F.3d 1265 (10th Cir. 2006), the court granted priority administrative status to the wages and benefits of musicians who played for the bankrupt Colorado Springs Symphony Orchestra. Adopting the majority position, the court held that claims under a collective bargaining agreement are not entitled to a "superpriority" because of section 1113 and that section 1113 does not trump the priority scheme prescribed in sections 503 and 507. The court, however, allowed administrative status because the musicians sought wages and benefits pertaining to post-petition services and those services were necessary to the preservation of the estate.

2.   In a Chapter 11 bankruptcy, a trustee or debtor in possession may request the court to approve rejection of a collective bargaining agreement only after seeking modifications of the agreement "that are necessary to permit the reorganization of the debtor and assures that all creditors, the debtor, and all of the affected parties are treated fairly and equitably." 11 U.S.C. § 1113(b)(1)(A). The union must be provided with relevant materials

to evaluate the agreement and the debtor in possession must meet with the union at reasonable times and in good faith. The requirements of section 1113 were transformed into a nine-part test in In re Am. Provision Co., 44 B.R. 907 (Bankr.D.Minn.1984), which has been restated in numerous later decisions. This test may be phrased simply as:

1. The debtor in possession must propose modification of the agreement;

2. The proposal must be based on the most complete and reliable information available;

3. The modification proposed must be necessary to reorganization;

4. The modification proposed must treat creditors and affected parties equitably;

5. The debtor in possession must provide the labor union with relevant information to review the proposal;

6. The debtor in possession must meet at reasonable times with the labor union;

7. The debtor in possession must negotiate in good faith with the labor union;

8. The labor union must have refused the proposed modification without good cause; and

9. The balance of the equities must clearly favor rejection of the agreement.

A split has developed among the circuits as to the interpretation of part three of the test, the requirement that the modification proposed must be necessary to reorganization. The Third Circuit has held that "necessary" must be strictly construed and that any modifications proposed must be the minimum necessary to allow the Chapter 11 trustee or debtor in possession to avoid short-term liquidation. Wheeling-Pittsburgh Steel Corp. v. United Steelworkers of Am., 791 F.2d 1074 (3d Cir. 1986). The Second Circuit has held that the debtor in possession or trustee satisfies the necessary requirement when the proposal contains necessary although not absolutely minimal changes which will enable it to reorganize successfully. Truck Drivers Local 807 v. Carey Transp., Inc., 816 F.2d 82 (2d Cir. 1987). What arguments could be made to support the strict construction of the Third Circuit? What arguments support the Second Circuit's conclusion?

3. For a case involving severance pay in lieu of notice of dismissal, see In re Tucson Yellow Cab Co., 789 F.2d 701 (9th Cir. 1986). On September 1, 1978, Mary Ingrum lost the lower part of one leg in a collision between a taxicab and a motorcycle on which she was a passenger. She sued the Tucson Yellow Cab Company for negligence and received a judgment of $437,016. However, because the company had the bare minimum of insurance, Ingrum received only $100,000 and the company filed for bankruptcy under Chapter 11 on January 27, 1981. In March 1982, the company was sold. In accordance with the wishes of the purchaser of the company, on April 5, 1982 the bankruptcy court approved rejection of the collective bargaining agreement

which included a provision for two weeks' notice of firing or two weeks' severance pay in lieu of notice. On April 16, 1982 the employees were fired. Despite the obvious equitable considerations against allowing the employees to recover from the estate at the expense of Ingrum, the court held that this severance pay was a form of wages that has administrative expense priority. The court reasoned that the fair value of the work under the collective bargaining agreement had been the take-home wages and the severance pay provision, and that there was no reason to value the work less in the eleven days between the rejection of the collective bargaining agreement and the firing of the employees.

Was this form of "severance pay" earned by post-bankruptcy work? Prebankruptcy, it was already an entitlement of the workers. Why is it considered an "administrative expense" of the bankruptcy? Why should it receive priority over Mary Ingrum's tort claim? Certainly, her claim has far more significance to her than any of the severance pay claims could have had to any of the fired employees.

4.   Bachman v. Commercial Fin. Servs., Inc., 246 F.3d 1291 (10th Cir.2001), refused priority administrative treatment to substantial lump-sum termination payments paid to employees who remained on the job for three weeks after the bankruptcy.

b.   UNFUNDED PENSION OBLIGATIONS

In re A.C.E. Elevator Co., Inc.
347 B.R. 473 (Bkrtcy. S.D. N.Y. 2006).

■ ROBERT D. DRAIN, UNITED STATES BANKRUPTCY JUDGE.

The trustees of the National Elevator Industry Benefit Plans (the "Plans," consisting of the Pension Plan, the Welfare Plan and the Educational Plan) seek an order directing the debtor, A.C.E. Elevator Co., Inc. to pay delinquent Plan contributions, interest, liquidated damages, and attorney's fees and costs as expenses entitled to administrative priority. * * *

ACE concedes that it has not paid certain Plan contributions but contends that its obligation to do so arose before December 21, 2004, the date that it filed its chapter 11 petition and, therefore, that the Trustees' claim is not entitled to administrative priority. ACE also argues that because the Trustees induced ACE's covered employees to walk off their jobs shortly after the start of the chapter 11 case in an attempt to coerce ACE to pay the Delinquent Contributions in violation of both the automatic stay under 11 U.S.C. § 362(a) and the collective bargaining agreement under which ACE's Plan funding obligations arise, the Trustees' claim should be disallowed or subordinated. The Trustees contest these allegations, which also are the subject of a pending adversary proceeding. * * *

ACE's business was, and, to the extent that it still has a business, is, the construction, modernization, maintenance and repair of elevators in the New York City area. ACE built the elevator systems in the World Trade Center and until September 11, 2001 had been their sole servicer, from which it derived 90 percent of its revenue. Unable to make up enough of that income from other sources, ACE filed under chapter 11 on December 21, 2004. * * *

As noted, ACE concedes that it has not paid the Delinquent Contributions to the Plans, excusing such default, however, on the basis that the Delinquent Contributions are on account of prepetition hours worked by its employees and, therefore, prepetition obligations that ACE is precluded from paying ahead of other prepetition unsecured claims. The parties agree that ACE has paid its Plan contributions attributable to all postpetition hours worked. * * *

The Trustees argue that the Delinquent Contribution claim is entitled to administrative priority because the Plans accepted and processed ACE's reports, and determined the amounts owing, postpetition. ACE argues, to the contrary, that because its Delinquent contributions to the Plans are based on its Union employees' hours worked prepetition, the Delinquent Contributions are prepetition claims not entitled to administrative priority.

In the light of Bankruptcy Code section 503(b)(1)(A)'s plain meaning, relevant case law, and the underlying nature of the Delinquent Contribution claim, ACE's position is correct; the Delinquent Contribution claim is not entitled to priority. * * *

Here, the right to administrative expense priority for the Delinquent Contributions is [unsupportable] * * * because the parties' agreements . . . clearly provide that ACE's funding obligation is "for each hour of work performed" by the covered employees and the Delinquent Contributions concededly are in respect of prepetition hours worked. Moreover, * * * employer contributions to pension and welfare plans, like those at issue here, together with wages, remunerate employees for services rendered. If the contributions at issue are in respect of employees' services that were rendered prepetition, as here, * * * the claim for such contributions cannot be accorded priority status. * * *

Moreover, even if it were legally relevant that ACE sent its Plan contribution reports to the Trustees postpetition, it is clear under the Plan Agreements that ACE's liability stems from the CBA (with its "for hours worked" formulation), not the administrative processes by which the Trustees calculate contributions amounts after-the-fact. * * *

Lastly, the Trustees contend that the Welfare Plan is entitled to be paid the Delinquent Contributions due it, as "retiree benefits."

Section 1114(e) of the Bankruptcy Code states in pertinent part:

(e)(1) Notwithstanding any other provision of this title, the debtor in possession . . . shall timely pay and shall not modify any retiree benefits. . . .

(2) Any payment for retiree benefits required to be made before a plan confirmed under section 1129 of this title is effective has the status of an allowed administrative expense as provided in section 503 of this title.

Therefore, the Bankruptcy Code apparently provides for the timely payment of any retiree benefits before confirmation of a chapter 11 plan and accords such obligation administrative expense priority, regardless of when earned. That is, by its plain terms Bankruptcy Code section 1114(e) does not appear to make any distinction between retiree benefit obligations on account of prepetition consideration and those arising postpetition; each would be payable as an administrative expense. * * *

Having determined that Congress in Bankruptcy Code section 1114(e) overrode the pre/postpetition distinction, three issues remain, although the first, whether the Delinquent Contributions to the Welfare Plan are "retiree payments" under Bankruptcy Code section 1114(a), is easily resolved. As a health plan, the Welfare Plan fits within the section.

The second issue is whether the Delinquent Contributions to the Welfare Plan are nevertheless excluded from section 1114(a) because that Plan is a multiemployer plan and nothing in the record suggests that any beneficiaries of the Welfare Plan are ACE retirees, their spouses or dependents.

It appears clear, however, that a debtor's contributions to a multiemployer health plan are entitled to administrative priority under even though the debtor may not have any retired employees receiving benefits under the plan. * * *

The final issue is whether all of the Delinquent Contributions owing to the Welfare Plan are entitled to priority or, instead, only ACE's contributions in respect of the Welfare Plan's health benefits attributable to retirees and their spouses and dependents. . . . If a material portion of the Delinquent Contributions to the Welfare Plan were used to fund benefits for current employees and their families, arguably the statute would not apply to such payments, particularly given that priorities in bankruptcy must be construed narrowly. * * *

Given the importance of this question and the fact that the parties have not addressed it, either in the factual record or their briefing, the Court will require further submissions on the issue. * * *

NOTES

1. Employees have a priority for wages paid after the bankruptcy filing so that they will continue working and the bankrupt employer can attempt to stay in business. They have a priority for unpaid wages earned before the filing only to a limited dollar amount. Do you agree that pension

contributions earned with pre-bankruptcy work should not have post-filing priority even though they will produce retirement payments in the future and will encourage committed post-filing work? Do you also agree that retirees should have a priority for their health benefits that the bankrupt company should pay before it pays other and more conventional pre-bankruptcy creditors? And if there is to be such a priority for retiree health benefits, should it extend to a multi-employer insurance plan even if few of that particular company's former employees are current beneficiaries?

2.   The court in Bayly Corp. v. PBGC, 163 F.3d 1205 (10th Cir. 1998) refused priority administrative treatment to a PBGC claim for the amount of the debtor's underfunded liability resulting from a terminated pension plan. According to the court, "all liabilities under the Plan stem from . . . benefits accrued by employees as a result of pre-petition labor." PBGC's claim, therefore, was a contingent claim that became liquidated post-petition. To attain administrative status, a claim must accrue and not merely become payable post-petition. The Court also held that while ERISA may determine whether PBGC has a claim at all, the Bankruptcy Code determines the priority status of that claim.

3.   The opposite case from the dismissed employee struggling for severance pay is the executive whose board of directors awards a "golden parachute," an extremely generous cash or stock payment usually triggered by the takeover of the firm by hostile interests. Critics say that golden parachutes waste stockholder assets by giving executives more compensation than they deserve. The allegation is that boards award such contracts in an effort to deter raids by outsiders seeking control of the company. In the bankruptcy context, hefty executive golden parachutes have taken on new significance as companies go under as a result of executive corruption. The Sarbanes-Oxley Act (SOX) was passed in response to public outrage over corrupt business practices that resulted in wealthy businessmen making fortunes and regular Americans losing their hard earned savings. (The Enron scandal is a well-known example of this.) Like many people, Congresswoman Barbara Lee believed that "CEOs and high-ranking executives should forego their golden parachutes and multimillion-dollar-year bonuses while their companies are going bankrupt, and instead give workers and investors first rights to these funds." Section 308(a) of SOX, "The Fair Funds For Investors Provision," was enacted to deal with this problem. This section allows the Securities and Exchange Commission to take civil penalties that corrupt companies were forced to pay and give them to injured investors. This conflicts with section 510(b) of the Bankruptcy Code. Section 510(b) says that civil damages claims have the same priority as the claim of other creditors. How will this conflict be resolved? *See* Zach Christensen, The Fair Funds for Investors Provision of Sarbanes-Oxley: Is it Unfair to the Creditors of a Bankrupt Debtor? 2005 U. Ill. L. Rev. 339 (2005). For information about how widespread golden parachutes have become, and analysis of the legal questions they raise, see Note, Golden Parachutes: Executive Employment Contracts, 40 Wash. & Lee L.Rev. 1117 (1983).

B. PLANT CLOSINGS

Local 1330, United Steel Workers of America v. United States Steel Corp.

631 F.2d 1264 (6th Cir. 1980).

■ EDWARDS, CHIEF JUDGE.

This appeal represents a cry for help from steelworkers and townspeople in the City of Youngstown, Ohio who are distressed by the prospective impact upon their lives and their city of the closing of two large steel mills. These two mills were built and have been operated by the United States Steel Corporation since the turn of the century. The Ohio Works began producing in 1901; the McDonald Works in 1918. The District Court which heard this cause of action found that as of the notice of closing, the two plants employed 3,500 employees.

The leading plaintiffs are two labor organizations, Locals 1330 and 1307 of the United Steel Workers of America. This union has had a collective bargaining contract with the United States Steel Corporation for many years. These local unions represent production and maintenance employees at the Ohio and McDonald Works, respectively.

In the background of this litigation is the obsolescence of the two plants concerned, occasioned both by the age of the facilities and machinery involved and by the changes in technology and marketing in steelmaking in the years intervening since the early nineteen hundreds.

For all of the years United States Steel has been operating in Youngstown, it has been a dominant factor in the lives of its thousands of employees and their families, and in the life of the city itself. The contemplated abrupt departure of United States Steel from Youngstown will, of course, have direct impact on 3,500 workers and their families. It will doubtless mean a devastating blow to them, to the business community and to the City of Youngstown itself. While we cannot read the future of Youngstown from this record, what the record does indicate clearly is that we deal with an economic tragedy of major proportion to Youngstown and Ohio's Mahoning Valley. As the District Judge who heard this case put the matter:

> Everything that has happened in the Mahoning Valley has been happening for many years because of steel. Schools have been built, roads have been built. Expansion that has taken place is because of steel. And to accommodate that industry, lives and destinies of the inhabitants of that community were based and planned on the basis of that institution: Steel.

In the face of this tragedy, the steel worker local unions, the Congressman from this district, and the Attorney General of Ohio have sued United States Steel Corporation, asking the federal courts to order the United States Steel Corporation to keep the two plants at issue in operation. Alternatively, if they could not legally prevail on that issue, they have sought intervention of the courts by injunction to require the United States Steel Corporation to sell the two plants to the plaintiffs under an as yet tentative plan of purchase and operation by a community corporation and to restrain the piecemeal sale or dismantling of the plants until such a proposal could be brought to fruition.

Defendant United States Steel Corporation answered plaintiffs' complaints, claiming that the plants were unprofitable and could not be made otherwise due to obsolescence and change in technology, markets, and transportation. The company also asserts an absolute right to make a business decision to discharge its former employees and abandon Youngstown. It states that there is no law in either the State of Ohio or the United States of America which provides either legal or equitable remedy for plaintiffs.

The District Judge, after originally restraining the corporation from ceasing operations as it had announced it would, and after advancing the case for prompt hearing, entered a formal opinion holding that the plants had become unprofitable and denying all relief. We believe the dispositive paragraphs of a lengthy opinion entered by the District Judge are the following:

> This Court has spent many hours searching for a way to cut to the heart of the economic reality—that obsolescence and market forces demand the close of the Mahoning Valley plants, and yet the lives of 3500 workers and their families and the supporting Youngstown community cannot be dismissed as inconsequential. United States Steel should not be permitted to leave the Youngstown area devastated after drawing from the lifeblood of the community for so many years.

> Unfortunately, the mechanism to reach this ideal settlement, to recognize this new property right, is not now in existence in the code of laws of our nation.

* * *

> This Court is mindful of the efforts taken by the workers to increase productivity, and has applauded these efforts in the preceding paragraphs. In view of the fact, however, that this Court has found that no contract or enforceable promise was entered into by the company and that, additionally, there is clear evidence to support the company's decision that the plants were not profitable, the various acts of forebearance taken by the plaintiffs do not give them the basis for relief against defendant.

Plaintiffs-appellants claim that certain of the District Judge's findings of fact are clearly erroneous, that he has misconstrued federal and state contract law, and that he failed to grant a hearing on their antitrust claims.

With this introduction, we turn to the legal issues presented by this appeal.

Plaintiffs assert jurisdiction in the federal courts, pursuant to Section 301 of the National Labor Relations Act, as amended, 29 U.S.C. § 185 (1976). They also assert diversity jurisdiction, pursuant to 28 U.S.C. § 1332 (1976). By so doing they claim that this action is brought under the fundamental labor law of the country and under the laws of Ohio which federal courts follow when a cause of action between citizens of one state is brought against citizens of another state.

The primary issue in this case is a claim on the part of the steel worker plaintiffs that United States Steel made proposals to the plaintiffs and/or the membership of the plaintiffs to the general effect that if the workers at the two steel plants concerned put forth their best efforts in terms of productivity and thereby rendered the two plants "profitable," the plants would then not be closed. It is clear that this claimed contract does not rest upon any formal written document, either authorized or signed by the parties to this lawsuit.

Plaintiffs themselves recognize that they cannot rely upon any formal contract law. Nonetheless, in this section we shall discuss relationships between the parties which plaintiffs have not raised in order to place their issues in proper context.

As noted above, the steelworkers have a formal collective bargaining contract with the U.S. Steel Corporation. In this record there is no indication that there ever was any formal negotiation or amendment of that contract in relation to the issues of this case.

* * *

The collective bargaining agreement applicable in this period also contains three sections which management asserts bear directly upon its claim of unilateral right to close any plant. These provisions are two rather general paragraphs on page 15 of the contract entitled "Management" which recite as follows:

SECTION 3—MANAGEMENT

The Company retains the exclusive rights to manage the business and plants and to direct the working forces. The Company, in the exercise of its rights, shall observe the provisions of this Agreement.

The rights to manage the business and plants and to direct the working forces include the right to hire, suspend or discharge for proper cause, or transfer and the right to relieve employees from duty because of lack of work or for other legitimate reasons.

More directly applicable to the present case is Section 16 entitled "Severance Allowance." This section provides in detail for severance allowances in terms of weeks of pay of employees with more than three years seniority, and concludes with the sentence which says, "Acceptance of severance allowance shall terminate employment and continuous service for all purposes under this Agreement."

* * *

We are unable to construe any claims set forth in the instant litigation as being based upon any language contained in this collective bargaining agreement. Indeed, plaintiffs make no claim in this case that the United States Steel Corporation has violated the provisions of this section (or any section) of the collective bargaining agreement.

* * *

Appellants' principal argument in this appeal is, however, that the District Court should have found a contract based upon the equitable doctrine of promissory estoppel, which contract is enforceable in the federal courts under § 301 of the National Labor Relations Act. The doctrine of promissory estoppel recognizes the possibility of the formation of a contract by action or forbearance on the part of a second party, based upon a promise made by the first party under circumstances where the actions or forbearance of the second party should reasonably have been expected to produce the detrimental results to the second party which they did produce.

* * *

Thus, appellants' contract claim depends essentially upon oral statements and newspaper releases concerning the efforts of the company to secure increased productivity by enlisting the help of the workers of the plant and upon the employee responses thereto. The representations as set forth in the steelworkers' complaint include many oral statements made over the "hotline" employed by management in the plants to advise U.S. Steel employees of company policy.

* * *

[The court quoted at length from statements by U.S. Steel executives. It then described examples of individual worker reliance on the company's statements.]

As we read this lengthy record, and as the District Judge read it, it does not contain any factual dispute over the allegations as to company statements or the responsive actions of steelworkers in relation thereto. It is beyond argument that the local management of U.S. Steel's Youngstown plants engaged in a major campaign to enlist employee participation in an all-out effort to make these two plants profitable in order to prevent their being closed. It is equally obvious that the employees responded wholeheartedly.

The District Judge, however, rejected the promissory estoppel contract theory on three grounds. The first ground was that none of the statements made by officers and employees of the company constituted a definite promise to continue operation of the plants if they did become profitable. The second ground was that the statements relied upon by plaintiffs were made by employees and public relations officers of the company and not by company officers. The third ground was a finding of fact that "The condition precedent of the alleged contract and promise—profitability of the Youngstown facilities—was never fulfilled, and the actions in contract and for detrimental reliance cannot be found for plaintiffs."

The District Judge's fundamental disposition of plaintiffs-appellants' contract claims is stated in this finding of fact:

> [T]here is clear evidence to support the company's decision that the plants were not profitable, the various acts of forebearance taken by the plaintiffs do not give them the basis for relief against defendant.

Our examination of this record offers no ground for our holding that this finding of fact is "clearly erroneous."

* * *

We believe that this record demonstrates without significant dispute that the profitability issue in the case depends in large part upon definition. The plaintiffs wish to employ the direct costs of operating the two plants, compared to the total selling price of their products. The difference, they contend, is "profit." This formula would eliminate such charges as corporate purchasing and sales expense allocable to the Youngstown plants, and allocable corporate management expenses including, but not limited to marketing, engineering, auditing, accounting, advertising. Obviously, any multiplant corporation could quickly go bankrupt if such a definition of profit was employed generally and over any period of time.

Plaintiffs-appellants point out, however, that this version of Youngstown profitability was employed by the Youngstown management in setting a goal for its employees and in statements which described achieving that goal. The standard of Restatement (Second) of Contracts § 90, upon which plaintiffs-appellants rely, however, is one of reasonable expectability of the "promise" detrimentally relied upon. The District Judge did not find, nor can we, that reliance upon a promise to keep these plants open on the basis of coverage of plant fixed costs was within reasonable expectability. We cannot hold that the District Judge erred legally or was "clearly erroneous" in his fact finding when he held that the "promise" to keep the plants open had to be read in the context of normal corporate profit accounting and that profitability had not been achieved.

Complete analysis of plaintiffs-appellants' promissory estoppel claims against the background of the collective bargaining agreement and Section 301 of the National Labor Relations Act would be a formidable task. We decline to undertake it, however, since even if we decided those issues favorably to plaintiffs, we would nonetheless be forced to decide the contract claim adversely to them because of failure to prove profitability.

THE COMMUNITY PROPERTY CLAIM

At a pretrial hearing of this case on February 28, 1980, the District Judge made a statement at some length about the relationship between the parties to this case and the public interest involved therein. He said:

> Everything that has happened in the Mahoning Valley has been happening for many years because of steel. Schools have been built, roads have been built. Expansion that has taken place is because of steel. And to accommodate that industry, lives and destinies of the inhabitants of that community were based and planned on the basis of that institution: Steel.
>
> * * *
>
> We are talking about an institution, a large corporate institution that is virtually the reason for the existence of that segment of this nation [Youngstown]. Without it, that segment of this nation perhaps suffers, instantly and severely. Whether it becomes a ghost town or not, I don't know. I am not aware of its capability for adapting.
>
> * * *
>
> But what has happened over the years between U.S. Steel, Youngstown and the inhabitants? Hasn't something come out of that relationship, something that out of which—not reaching for a case on property law or a series of cases but looking at the law as a whole, the Constitution, the whole body of law, not only contract law, but tort, corporations, agency, negotiable instruments—taking a look at the whole body of American law and then sitting back and reflecting on what it seeks to do, and that is to adjust human relationships in keeping with the whole spirit and foundation of the American system of law, to preserve property rights.
>
> * * *
>
> It would seem to me that when we take a look at the whole body of American law and the principles we attempt to come out with—and although a legislature has not pronounced any laws with respect to such a property right, that is not to suggest that there will not be a need for such a law in the future dealing with similar situations—it seems to me that a property right has arisen from this lengthy, long-established relationship between United States Steel, the steel industry as an institution, the community in Youngstown, the people in Mahoning County and the Mahoning Valley in having given and devoted their lives to this industry. Perhaps not a property right to the extent that can be remedied by compelling U.S. Steel to remain in

Youngstown. But I think the law can recognize the property right to the extent that U.S. Steel cannot leave that Mahoning Valley and the Youngstown area in a state of waste, that it cannot completely abandon its obligation to that community, because certain vested rights have arisen out of this long relationship and institution.

Subsequently thereto, steelworkers' complaint was amended, realleging the first cause of action, paragraphs 1–49, claiming pendent jurisdiction over claims arising out of the laws of the State of Ohio and asserting as follows:

52. A property right has arisen from the long-established relation between the community of the 19th Congressional District and Plaintiffs, on the one hand, and Defendant on the other hand, which this Court can enforce.

53. This right, in the nature of an easement, requires that Defendant:

a.   Assist in the preservation of the institution of steel in that community;

b.   Figure into its cost of withdrawing and closing the Ohio and McDonald Works the cost of rehabilitating the community and the workers;

c.   Be restrained from leaving the Mahoning Valley in a state of waste and from abandoning its obligation to that community.

This court has examined these allegations with care and with great sympathy for the community interest reflected therein. Our problem in dealing with plaintiffs' fourth cause of action is one of authority. Neither in brief nor oral argument have plaintiffs pointed to any constitutional provision contained in either the Constitution of the United States or the Constitution of the State of Ohio, nor any law enacted by the United States Congress or the Legislature of Ohio, nor any case decided by the courts of either of these jurisdictions which would convey authority to this court to require the United States Steel Corporation to continue operations in Youngstown which its officers and Board of Directors had decided to discontinue on the basis of unprofitability.

This court has in fact dealt with this specific issue in Charland v. Norge Division, Borg-Warner Corp., 407 F.2d 1062 (6th Cir.), cert. denied, 395 U.S. 927.

* * *

This court's response to Charland's claims bears repetition here:

* * *

The claim presented by this appellant brings sharply into focus such problems as unemployment crises, the mobility of capital, technological change and the right of an industrial owner to go out of business. Thus far federal law has sought to protect the human values to which appellant calls our attention by means of such legislation as unemployment compensation. These statutes afford limited financial protection to the individual worker, but they assume his loss of employment.

Whatever the future may bring, neither by statute nor by court decision has appellant's claimed property right been recognized to date in this country.

* * *

In the view of this court, formulation of public policy on the great issues involved in plant closings and removals is clearly the responsibility of the legislatures of the states or of the Congress of the United States.

NOTES

1. The court found insufficient evidence that U.S. Steel's statements encouraged justifiable reliance by workers. Do you know other cases, from Chapter 10 or from your Contracts course, that you could cite in opposition to this conclusion? The tone of the court's opinion suggests a view that "something should be done" but Congress or the state legislature should do it. What legislation would you support? How much help would these workers have gotten if the Worker Adjustment and Retraining Notification Act, infra, had been law? Would worker ownership be a desirable alternative to the plant closing?

2. In Charter Twp. of Ypsilanti v. General Motors Corp., 8 Indiv.Empl.Rts. Cases (BNA) 385 (Mich.Cir.Ct.1993), a Michigan Circuit Court judge enjoined General Motors from transferring production of cars from a plant in Ypsilanti to a plant in Arlington, Texas. The judge distinguished Local 1330 and another federal case because of the specific representations made by General Motors when it sought a tax abatement, and because General Motors stipulated that economic necessity was not a defense.

The judge concluded:

[T]his Court, perhaps unlike the judges there, simply finds that the failure to act in this case would result in a terrible injustice and that the doctrine of promissory estoppel should be applied. Each judge who dons this robe assumes the awesome, and lonely responsibility to make decisions about justice, and injustice, which will dramatically affect the way people are forced to live their lives. Every such decision must be the judge's own and it must be made honestly and in good conscience * * *. Perhaps another judge in another court would not feel moved by that injustice and would labor to find a legal rationalization to allow such conduct. But in this Court it is my responsibility to make that decision. My conscience will not allow this injustice to happen.

The decision was later reversed because the trial court's finding of a promise to maintain production in Ypsilanti was found to be clearly erroneous.

Charter Township of Ypsilanti v. General Motors, 506 N.W.2d 556 (Mich.App.1993), remanded, 509 N.W.2d 152 (Mich.1993).

3.   See Daniel A. Farber & John H. Matheson, Beyond Promissory Estoppel: Contract Law and the "Invisible Handshake," 52 U.Chi.L.Rev. 903, 929 (1985):

> A revised rule of promissory obligation should accept the fundamental fact that commitments are often made to promote economic activity and obtain economic benefits without any specific bargained-for exchange. Promisors expect various benefits to flow from their promise-making. A rule that gives force to this expectation simply reinforces the traditional free-will basis of promissory liability, albeit in an expanded context of relational and institutional interdependence.

> Our proposed rule is simply that commitments made in furtherance of economic activity should be enforced. * * * The proposed rule is a major departure from traditional contract law in that it requires neither satisfaction of traditional notions of consideration nor the specific showing of detriment associated with promissory estoppel. * * *

> According to the approach set forth by our proposed rule, Local 1330 was wrongly decided. The employees and the company had, over the years, developed the kind of interdependent relationship that promotes action on the basis of an "invisible handshake." U.S. Steel must be understood to have sought economic benefits by leading employees to increase their efforts. A traumatic time such as that surrounding a possible plant closing creates both a need to cooperate to salvage the operations and an atmosphere of distrust. In such a setting, the need to reinforce trust with legal sanctions is especially strong. * * *

> The representations of profitability were unequivocal and were calculated to invoke the workers' trust. Nonetheless, both the district and appellate courts found that the employees should not have relied on these representations. * * *

> We find this result unconscionable. Whatever the prevailing definition of "profit" in corporate accounting, a continuous and consistent pattern of declaring the plants profitable, commending the employees for their achievements, and urging them forward should have tipped the scales against defendant U.S. Steel on this issue. There can be little doubt from the steady stream of communications about the achievement of profitability that employees did as they were expected to do when they relied on the representations of profitability.

> The fact that the Local 1330 courts placed such emphasis on the meaning of one term, "profitability," may well underscore the need for a rule which * * * examines the full context in which promises are made with a view to their social effects. * * * The company had a strong community base and a stable work force that was willing

to engage in the kind of long-term planning and commitment which is economically beneficial and perhaps even essential to a major industry. * * *

In the long run, allowing breach of the employer's promise in this situation injures society as a whole. Employees will be less likely to put forth the extra effort to save a plant if employers can violate their promises by semantic quibbles. In breaching its understanding with its employees, U.S. Steel polluted the pool of trust from which it had drawn. The pool is large and individual breaches of trust may be small, but the effect of pollution is cumulative. Not only justice to the employees, but also society's interest in preserving the integrity of a vital social resource, require enforcement of the employer's promise in this situation.

Do you agree? What are the problems with the proposed rule? Does it act as an incentive for the company to say nothing to induce greater worker productivity? Does this expansive notion of reliance devalue the importance of positive reinforcement? Will the company say "If you don't work harder, we'll close," rather than "If you work harder we'll stay open"? Is this an accurate statement of the company's options?

What about the proprietary interests of workers? Do the authors imply that inviolable rights accrue with each promise made? Are these rights contractual or proprietary? Does it make a difference in terms of the courts' likely willingness to grant relief?

4. Sidney Degan sued Ford Motor Company and the UAW, alleging breach of an oral agreement to pay special early-retirement benefits. The court of appeals held that common-law contract claims concerning pensions are preempted by ERISA, and that under ERISA only the written plan documents have legal force. "Oral agreements would undermine Congress's goal of fashioning a comprehensive system of federal law designed to strengthen and protect the interests of employers in their expected retirement benefits." Thus, there is no legal forum for Degan's "sympathetic, estoppel-based argument." Degan v. Ford Motor Co., 869 F.2d 889 (5th Cir. 1989).

5. Singer Company took millions in union "give-backs" and agreed in return to spend $2 million to restructure its Elizabeth, N.J., sewing machine factory. Eight months later, Singer announced plans to shut the plant. The court found no promise by Singer to "surrender * * * the prerogative of any company to go out of business when it so desires." Therefore, it refused to enter an injunction preventing closure of the plant. But it found that Singer breached "a clearcut obligation both to spend $2 million to restructure the plant and to use its best efforts to * * * maintain the facility * * *." It said money damages would be the greater of the value of the "give-backs" or the promised $2 million. Singer had argued that it owed no damages because decreased demand for sewing machines would have forced closing of the plant even if the company had spent the $2 million, so the failure to spend it had no effect on the workers' welfare. The court did not reach (but expressed "serious doubts" about) claims made by residents of the Elizabeth community as "third-party beneficiaries of the collective bargaining agreement." Local 461, IUERM v. Singer Co., 540 F.Supp. 442 (D.N.J.1982).

6. Former workers and their spouses alleged fraudulent misrepresentation and intentional infliction of emotional distress, saying that the company knew it planned to close a factory when it recruited new workers. The Ninth Circuit held that the claim established a cause of action under Oregon law, including a cause of action for a spouse whose life was altered because the family was misled into moving to Eugene, Oregon. Judge Kozinski, concurring, said: "if the question were presented to the Oregon Supreme Court, I believe it would hold that an employer who makes false representations to a prospective employee who is married must expect that the employee will share the information with the spouse, who may rely on it in consenting to the move." Meade v. Cedarapids, Inc., 164 F.3d 1218 (9th Cir. 1999).

7. The unions and other plaintiffs petitioned the court for an injunction to allow them to buy the two plants with what the court called a "tentative plan of purchase and operation by a community corporation. . . ." Had the plaintiffs had more than a "tentative plan" and been able to purchase the company, would it have saved the plants? Do you think the plaintiffs would have owned the plants for as long as United States Steel Corporation owned them? Consider Alan Hyde, In Defense of Employee Ownership, 67 Chi.-Kent L.Rev. 159 (1991):

> The model that suggests that employee ownership is just about always good for just about everybody does so because it sees employee ownership as the solution to more or less universal problems experienced by employees of modern industrial or service firms: loss of control of work, alienation, an experience of passively following orders.
>
> Across the Library, perhaps, in the economics section, lies a competing body of theoretical literature that suggests that employee ownership cannot possibly ever work for anybody. In this version, employee owners would (like other neoclassical economic actors) maximize their current income, so that every dollar that comes in would be paid out in wages; the firm would never plan or invest; it would never expand, since each new employee would just divide this static income stream into a smaller rivulet; the firm could generate no internal funds for investment, while no sane outside investor would ever finance such a firm; which would go to a speedy grave unless imposed on the unwilling through force of law.
>
> * * *
>
> Employee-owned firms often begin during economic recessions, when employees buy out failed or failing conventional firms. (Note how damaging is this simple fact to the "never" school; there are many examples of successful employee-owned firms where the identical firm, when conventionally owned, was failing or actually failed). Such recession births succeed because workers

will make concessions to themselves—lower wages, reduced staffing levels, other productivity gains—that they would not make to a management that might use them opportunistically. When the general economic climate improves, the employees sell the firm to private investors. (Obviously damaging to the "always" school. Yet employee-owned firms do indeed frequently sell out to private investors.)

It seems to me that the empirical literature on employee ownership is difficult if not impossible to interpret within the frameworks of the existing conceptual literature. The answer to the riddle of employee ownership simply cannot be, in our economy, either "never" or "always." This points out the need for newer models of the employee owned firm, that will better explain its pattern of successes. The answer to [the] question, "When Does Worker Ownership Work?", will have to start with the word "sometimes."

8. For examples of state legislation encouraging employee ownership and analysis of their content, see Virginia L. Duquet, Note, Advantages and Limitations of Current Employee Ownership Assistance Acts to Workers Facing a Plant Closure, 36 Hastings L.J. 93 (1984).

9. For a discussion of worker participation in business management and Employee Stock Ownership Plans, see generally Jeffery N. Gordon, Employee Stock Ownership as a Transitional Device: The Case of the Airline Industry, in The Handbook of Airline Economics (1996); Joseph R. Blasi, Employee Ownership: Revolution or Ripoff (1988); Henry Hansmann, When Does Worker Ownership Work? ESOPs, Law Firms, Codetermination and Economic Democracy, 99 Yale L.J. 1749 (1990); Charles S. Mishkind & David E. Khorey, Employee Stock Ownership Plans: Fables and Facts, 11 Employee Rel. L.J. 89 (1985); Robert B. Moberly, New Directions in Worker Participation, 87 W.Va.L.Rev. 765 (1987); Corey Rosen & Alan Cohen, Employees to the Rescue: The Record of Worker Buyouts, 6 J. Law & Commerce 213 (1986).

NOTE ON FEDERAL PLANT-CLOSING AND MASS-LAYOFF LAW

In 1988, Congress enacted the first federal statute restricting employer authority to shut factories. The Worker Adjustment and Retraining Notification Act (WARN), 29 U.S.C. §§ 2101–2109, applies to businesses that employ at least 100 workers. A "plant closing" is defined as a shutdown at a single site resulting in loss of work for at least 50 employees. A mass layoff is defined as a reduction in force that is not the result of a plant closing and that results in employment loss at a single employment site during a 30-day period for (1) at least 33 percent of employees and at least 50 employees or (2) at least 500 employees, excluding in either case part-time employees. Employers cannot engage in such a plant closing or mass layoffs without giving 60 days' notice to a union (if there is one), to each worker (if there is no union), and to state and local government officials. The notice provides affected workers time to adjust to a job loss, find new employment, or obtain retraining. Workers laid off without appropriate notice are entitled to back pay and any fringe benefits they may have lost.

Gross v. Hale-Halsell Co.
554 F.3d 870 (10th Cir. 2009).

■ KELLY, CIRCUIT JUDGE.

Plaintiffs-Appellants, all former employees of Hale-Halsell Company, appeal the grant of summary judgment in favor of Defendant-Appellee HHC on their claim that HHC violated the Worker Adjustment and Retraining Notification Act (WARN Act). * * *

The WARN Act imposes a federal mandate on employers requiring 60 days advance notice to employees of a plant closing or a mass layoff. The Act applies to any business that employs 100 or more employees, and the parties do not dispute that HHC is subject to its provisions. Congress acknowledged through specific exceptions to the WARN Act's notice requirements that notice is not always practicable or possible. Notwithstanding, "an employer 'shall give as much notice as is practicable and at that time shall give a brief statement of the basis for reducing the notification period.'"

Plaintiffs were employed by HHC, a wholesale grocery warehouse and distribution center in Tulsa, Oklahoma. HHC owned fifty percent of United Supermarkets, which also happened to be HHC's largest customer. HHC and United had a satisfactory thirty-one-year business relationship with United Supermarkets providing forty percent of HHC's orders. At times, HHC fell short on United's submitted orders, i.e., experiencing "stockouts," or "outs." For example, during the week of December 14, 2002, recorded stockouts hit 6%; in the week of December 28, 2002, stockouts hit 6.3%; and by the end of November 2003, stockouts had reached as high as 18.9%. A United official testified that, as of the end of November 2003, despite HHC's failure to fulfill United's orders, United was not "sure what was going to happen," but that United was not considering terminating its relationship with HHC at that time. By January 7, 2004, stockouts had reached an "all time high" of 53.8%, but United still had not decided to end the relationship. During this same period, HHC was awaiting approval of a working capital loan from LaSalle Bank. In November 2003, LaSalle felt "positive" about the loan being approved, and as late as December 8, 2003, LaSalle was still considering a $15 million loan to HHC. However, at some point after United's announcement in January 2004, it appears that LaSalle declined to approve the funding.

HHC and United communicated on various occasions about HHC's failure to satisfy United's orders. In November and December 2003, "there was a lot of conversation back and forth" about the issue. On December 17, 2003, United began asking HHC to inform United of available stock, so United could advertise for those items instead of for the "out" items. By then, HHC's ware-house operations were struggling, but LaSalle auditors were on the premises collecting information. On January 8, 2004, United wrote to let HHC know that United would have to "place orders with alternative suppliers," but also reiterated its willingness to continue doing business with HHC despite the stockouts. In essence, United was "not saying that [it] want[ed] to discontinue ordering from [HHC] or that United [was] terminating its supply relationship with [HHC]," but rather warning HHC that its orders would be declining. Aplt. App. 100. On January 9, 2004, HHC replied, informing United of various business developments and assuring United that it expected to hear from LaSalle shortly regarding the loan. Then, on Thursday, January 15, 2004, United wrote to HHC, informing HHC of the difficult decision it had made to "use Affiliated Foods as its primary supplier, with [HHC] as a secondary supplier. That decision is going to affect the volume of orders that United places with [HHC]." On Friday, January 16, 2004, HHC replied to United, indicating that its decision would "put [HHC] in a bad situation," but still expressing hope that HHC would "solve [its] difficulties."

Events after the January 16 letter unfolded as follows. In 2004, Martin Luther King Jr. Day fell on Monday, January 19, and banks were closed, so HHC met with F & M Bank, its primary accounts holder, as well as consultants Alvarez & Marsal, on Tuesday, January 20. It was after those meetings that HHC "decided that [it] was not going to be able to survive." Id. The next day, Wednesday, January 21, 2004, HHC met with office personnel and later warehouse staff, informing them of the impending layoffs. The approximately 200 individuals to be laid off would be informed by notice included in their paychecks the following day. That same day, the Associated Press issued a news release indicating that HHC had announced that it would "lay off about 200 Tulsa warehouse workers after losing a key customer." HHC President Rob Hawk was quoted in the news release as stating, "[United's] unexpected action has had a dramatic impact not only on [HHC], but on the lives of so many of our long-term, valued employees and [the] Tulsa community." Finally, on Thursday, January 22, 2004, HHC informed employees by letter that they would be laid off, citing as the reason the loss of United as its primary customer. HHC later filed for bankruptcy.

Thereafter, Plaintiffs brought this action and HHC moved for summary judgment on the basis that it was excused from the WARN Act requirements based upon the unforeseeable business circumstance exception, and the faltering company exception. The district court granted summary judgment based upon the former exception, holding that United's termination of HHC was unforeseeable and caused the mass layoffs, and that HHC had provided notice "as soon as practicable." Plaintiffs appeal, arguing the district court did not view the facts in the light most favorable to the non-moving party when it held that (1) the unforeseeable business circumstance exception applied to HHC, and (2) HHC gave notice of the layoffs "as soon as practicable." * * *

The WARN Act requires employers to give at least sixty days notice in advance of a mass layoff, calculated from a fourteen-day window during which the layoff is expected to occur. Under 29 U.S.C. § 2102(b)(2)(A), "[a]n employer may order a plant closing or mass layoff before the conclusion of the 60-day period if the closing or mass layoff is caused by business circumstances that were not reasonably foreseeable as of the time that notice would have been required." The "employer bears the burden of proof that conditions for the exceptions have been met." To satisfy these conditions, the defending party must establish that (1) the circumstance was unforeseeable, and (2) the layoffs were caused by that circumstance. * * *

Plaintiffs argue that the grant of summary judgment was improper because they presented a genuine issue of material fact as to whether the unforeseeable business circumstance exception applied to HHC. They argue that the facts relied upon by the district court were legally insufficient and not conclusively established. The disputed facts are as follows: (1) that HHC and United had suffered through similar business difficulties before and their relationship had survived, (2) that HHC had reason to believe its financial position would improve over time, and (3) that HHC had reason to believe its relationship with United would continue because of a long-standing relationship between the parties. * * *

At the end of 2003, HHC was experiencing "financial difficulties that affected its relationship with its largest customer, United." These difficulties culminated in United's January 8, 2004, letter, indicating that it would be placing orders with other suppliers and that HHC should not be "surprised that the orders from United [would] declin[e]." As noted above, the stockouts at the close of 2003 had increased from the same time the year before, and United's orders had decreased in the same fashion. However, even with these facts known to it, United simply did not decide until its January 15, 2004 letter to terminate its primary supplier relationship with HHC.

While HHC was aware of United's dissatisfaction, that knowledge alone does not bar the application of the unforeseeable business circumstance exception. Rather, an objective focus is required—whether a "similarly situated employer in the exercise of commercially reasonable business judgment would have foreseen" United's withdrawal. In this evaluation, "we consider the facts and circumstances that led to the [layoffs] in light of the history of the business and of the industry in which that business operated." While the situation leading up to United's eventual termination of the primary supplier relationship "would undoubtedly raise the eyebrows of any prudent businessperson," the evidence does not suggest that United's decision was reasonably foreseeable prior to HHC's receipt of the January 15 letter. For thirty-one years, United's relationship with HHC had flourished, and even when stockouts reached a new high in early 2004, United still confirmed its interest in doing business with HHC. In fact, United, in its January 8 letter, indicated that it valued its longstanding relationship with HHC a great deal, reiterated that the relationship had provided mutual benefit over the years, and acknowledged its hope that the LaSalle loan negotiations would close successfully. More-over, even though HHC's warehouse operations had been disrupted, LaSalle continued to gather information concerning HHC to determine whether it would approve a sizeable loan and remained "positive" about the financing even in December 2003. In addition, HHC's own attorneys indicated that the company should focus on "turnaround efforts," and stated that the "avoidance of bankruptcy filings" was one of its primary goals, in addition to "planning for the possibility, however remote, of bankruptcy filings."

Free enterprise always involves risk, yet most businesses operate as going concerns, notwithstanding those risks. Business downturns in a cyclical economy are not unusual, and we should not burden employers with the "task of notifying employees of possible contract cancellation and concomitant lay-offs every time there is a cost overrun" or similar difficulty. Such an indiscriminate practice could undermine morale, let alone exacerbate the problem. Such difficulties are invariable, and "most often do not lead to contract cancellation." Here, HHC experienced the loss of a major customer in a very short period of time on top of all of its other difficulties; HHC met its summary judgment burden of establishing that United's January 15, 2004, withdrawal, while always a possibility, was unforeseeable. * * *

The unforeseeable business circumstance exception also requires an employer to "give as much notice [of the layoff] as is practicable" upon knowledge of the causal event. Plaintiffs argue that a jury could have found in their favor that the written notice given to employees in their paychecks on January 22, 2004, was not delivered as soon as practicable. Other than pointing out that HHC knew of United's withdrawal on January 16, and that news of the layoffs were reported in the media on January 21, 2004, Plaintiffs offer no other evidence that HHC unduly delayed in advising employees of the layoffs. As discussed, HHC behaved in a commercially reasonable way when it failed to foresee United's withdrawal in the sixty days leading up to the January 15 letter. HHC then took three business days to discuss the matter with its financial advisers and lawyers, and acted quickly in light of the devastating news. We do not think HHC violated the WARN Act's notice requirements, nor did it act unreasonably, in taking just three business days to determine whether "it could survive the carnage."

AFFIRMED.

NOTE

Does the "unforeseeable business circumstances" exception to the WARN Act defeat its main purpose of giving sufficient notice to workers? Or is this exception a necessary compromise with the realities of ever-changing business plans and workplaces? If the latter, does unemployment insurance provide enough of a safety net for workers fired with little warning and should unemployment insurance be used as a substitute for notice?

Administaff v. New York Joint Board
337 F.3d 454 (5th Cir. 2003).

■ EDITH H. JONES, CIRCUIT JUDGE.

The district court granted Administaff Companies, Inc. summary judgment, concluding that it was not liable for violations of the Worker Adjustment *456 and Retraining Notification Act (WARN Act). We affirm.

Administaff provides personnel management, payroll, and administrative services for other businesses, essentially operating as an off-site human resources department. TheCustomShop.com, the former owner of a men's clothing production plant in New Jersey, contracted for the services of Administaff. In late 2000, TCS began to encounter financial difficulties. When attempts to raise capital and to sell the business failed, TCS closed its New Jersey facility without providing the sixty days notice required by 29 U.S.C. § 2102(a). Administaff did not participate in TCS's decision to close its New Jersey plant and was not aware of the closing until after it occurred.

In April 2001, the Joint Board, the union representing the employees of the New Jersey facility, demanded that Administaff, as an employer under the WARN Act, compensate each member of the bargaining unit for sixty days of pay plus benefits because the employees did not receive proper WARN Act notice.

* * *

First, based on the plain language of the statute, Administaff is not liable for failure to give WARN Act notice because it did not order the closing of the New Jersey facility. * * * The WARN Act provides that [a]ny employer who orders a plant closing or mass layoff in violation of section 3 of this Act [(the 60-day notice provision)] shall be liable to each aggrieved employee who suffers an employment loss as a result of such closing or layoff for [back pay and benefits].

Under a plain reading of 29 U.S.C. § 2104(a)(1), Administaff cannot be liable for the lack of WARN Act notice because it did not order the closing of TCS's New Jersey facility. * * * TCS ordered the closing of its New Jersey facility and informed Administaff of its decision after the fact.

We also affirm summary judgment for the reasons stated by the district court. The Joint Board argued that Administaff should be held liable for WARN act violations as a "joint employer" with TCS, but the district court determined that under the five-factor test set forth in 20 C.F.R. § 639.3(a)(2) (the DOL factors),[2] Administaff's relationship with TCS did not make it an employer for WARN Act purposes.

The WARN Act and DOL regulations define an employer as any business enterprise that employs 100 or more employees. Employers who violate the WARN Act are liable for back pay and benefits. Administaff did not employ those who worked at TCS's New Jersey facility in the normal business sense; although Administaff "co-employed" TCS employees so that they could receive group medical benefits and workmen's compensation through Administaff policies, TCS employees did not perform any work or services for Administaff.[3] For Administaff to be liable as an employer under the WARN Act to those who lost their jobs at TCS's New Jersey plant, Administaff must therefore be considered a single business enterprise with TCS, responsible for TCS's WARN Act obligations.

The first two factors are not at issue in this case. The third factor, de facto exercise of control, "allows the factfinder to consider whether the [business in question] has specifically directed the allegedly illegal employment practice that forms the basis for the litigation." It is undisputed that Administaff had no role in, or even advance knowledge of, TCS's decision to close its New Jersey plant.

With respect to the fourth factor, Administaff and TCS did not have a unity of personnel policies emanating from a common source; they had separate responsibilities regarding personnel issues. Under the Client Service Agreement between Administaff and TCS, Administaff was responsible for the payment of salaries and wages and the provision of employee benefits. It also reserved the right to hire and terminate employees, maintain employee records, and resolve disputes not subject to the collective bargaining agreement. The Client Service Agreement placed responsibility for the payment of commissions, bonuses, paid leaves of absence, severance payments, nonqualified deferred compensation, and equity based compensation on TCS. TCS alone was responsible for the operation of its business and the decision to close its New Jersey plant.

---

[2] The regulation states:

Under existing legal rules, independent contractors and subsidiaries which are wholly or partially owned by a parent company are treated as separate employers or as a part of the parent or contracting company depending upon the degree of their independence from the parent. Some of the factors to be considered in making this determination are (i) common ownership, (ii) common directors and/or officers, (iii) de facto exercise of control, (iv) unity of personnel policies emanating from a common source, and (v) the dependency of operations.

[3] Administaff may satisfy the statutory definition of "employer" by employing more than 100 employees of its own, but Administaff's status as a WARN Act employer with respect to its own employees is not relevant to its relationship with TCS's employees.

Regarding the fifth factor, dependency of operations, "courts generally consider the existence of arrangements such as the sharing of administrative or purchasing services, interchanges of employees or equipment, and commingled finances." While Administaff provided administrative services to TCS, the companies did not share administrative services; there was no interchange of equipment or commingled finances. Administaff "co-employed" TCS's employees so that they could receive group medical benefits and workmen's compensation through Administaff policies, but TCS's employees did not perform any work or services for Administaff.

* * *

Finally, that TCS agreed to indemnify Administaff in the event of a WARN Act violation does not alter our analysis. Administaff most likely bargained for indemnification to protect itself in the event it was held liable for its client's WARN Act violations. But the indemnification provision in no way suggests Administaff's liability. For the foregoing reasons, we affirm the district court judgment.

NOTES AND QUESTIONS

1.   In February 1993, the General Accounting Office released a report on the operation of the WARN Act in 11 states during the first three years that it was in force. The report found that 70% of covered employers failed to give advance notice to employees before a mass layoff or plant closing and 54% failed to file advance notice with state officials as required by the Act.

The GAO Report found that the Act's numerous exceptions limited its effectiveness. In many cases, employers were able to avoid coverage by spreading layoffs across various work sites, by firing employees gradually over a period of months, or by firing 49 employees (one short of the statutory minimum).

The Report also found that enforcement under the Act was inadequate. In its current form, the Act is enforced through private actions by employees and public actions by local governments. However, available remedies are so limited that costly and time consuming federal cases are impractical for most employees. Moreover, local governments are reluctant to bring cases for fear of appearing anti-business. The GAO concluded that better enforcement would improve compliance with the Act and suggested that the Department of Labor should be given enforcement authority. See also Ethan Lipsig & Keith R. Fentonmiller, A WARN Act Road Map, 11 Lab. Law 273 (1996); Richard W. McHugh, Fair Warning or Foul? An Analysis of the Worker Adjustment Retraining and Notification (WARN) Act in Practice, 14 Berkeley J. Emp. & Lab. L. 1 (1993).

2.   In Cruz v. Robert Abbey, Inc., 1990 WL 84349 (E.D.N.Y.1990), a lamp manufacturer employing mostly Hispanic immigrants, laid off more than 50 employees without notice and for an indefinite period of time. The employer then recalled several employees for weekly or bi-weekly periods before laying them off again. The employees filed an action for violation of the WARN Act's

notice provisions. In court, the employer argued that "of the * * * employees enough were recalled to work at Abbey during the two 90 day periods so that 50 or more employees were not laid off for a full 90 days." The court apparently perceived the employer's actions as an attempt to evade the requirements of the WARN Act. Those actions were covered under section 2102(d), "an attempt by employer to evade numerical predicates to WARN notice requirement of section 2102[a][3] [mass layoff] negates separate and distinct layoff defense." The court found an issue of material fact whether the layoffs constituted a "mass layoff" or "plant closing" under the Act.

3. In Rifkin v. McDonnell Douglas Corp., 78 F.3d 1277 (8th Cir. 1996), the defendant laid off 609 employees in a two-month period, none of whom received the WARN Act's required 60 days notice. The court ruled that in discounting for part-time employees, rehired employees, employees electing for early retirement, and the "single site" requirement, only 481 employees actually suffered employment loss. Thus, the WARN Act did not apply to this series of lay-offs. How does this compare with the ruling in Cruz v. Robert Abbey, Inc., supra?

4. In Deveraturda v. Globe Aviation Sec. Servs., 454 F.3d 1043 (9th Cir. 2006), a putative class of airport screeners sued their former employer, a security services company, after being laid off when the government federalized airport security and took over operations post 9/11. The workers complained that Globe failed to provide the requisite 60 days' notice required by the WARN Act prior to the layoff. Affirming judgment on the pleadings in favor of Globe, the Court held the WARN Act was inapplicable because Globe did not "order a plant closing or mass layoff." Rather, the layoffs resulted from the federal government replacing plaintiffs with federal employees. The government and not Globe, therefore, ordered plaintiffs out of work.

5. In Pena v. American Meat Packing Corp., 362 F.3d 418 (7th Cir. 2004), the court reversed the district court, which had granted summary judgment in favor of the employer, a slaughter house. For well over a year, the employer had received multiple warnings and notices from the USDA that its operations were unsanitary and not compliant with the USDA regulations. The employer attempted on several occasions to correct the deficiencies but to no avail. The USDA ultimately ordered the employer to destroy millions of dollars of meat and to close shop. The employer did so without providing the 60-day notice to its 350 employees as required by the WARN Act. The employer argued that it was relieved from the duty of having to provide prior notice under the WARN Act because it was forced to close as a result of an unforeseen business circumstance. The district court agreed. The Seventh Circuit, however, held that there was "a genuine issue of material fact as to whether the business conditions that caused [the facility] to close were unforeseeable." Moreover, assuming the conditions were unforeseeable, the court held that it was unclear whether it would have qualified the employer for a reduction in its required notice period or to a complete elimination of it.

The Seventh Circuit again addressed the unforeseen business exception in Roquet v. Arthur Andersen, LLP, 398 F.3d 585 (7th Cir. 2005). There, the court held that former accounting giant Arthur Andersen's failure to provide its employees a full 60 days notice prior to a mass layoff was justified as an unforeseeable business circumstance. The court conceded that Andersen could have provided notice sooner than it did (even if not a full 60 days notice), but thought that under the facts of the case, a "company, faced with this unprecedented cataclysmic event, reasonably needed a little time to assess how things would shake out * * * [before] it ran up the white flag of surrender and gave the bad news to its employees." A dissenting judge agreed that 60 days notice was likely not possible but would have remanded the case to determine when Andersen could reasonably have provided notice to its employees. He explained that the court in Pena v. American Meat Packing Corp., "left open the question whether a sufficient unforeseen circumstance occurring within the 60-day window excused an employer from providing any notice at all, or if instead it merely reduced the amount of notice required." He would have held that the 60-day period is reduced but not eliminated when the need for a mass layoff or plant closing becomes apparent within that timeframe.

6.   Prior to enactment of the federal law, more than half the states had enacted "plant closing" laws. In Fort Halifax Packing Co. v. Coyne, 482 U.S. 1 (1987), the Supreme Court decided by 5 to 4 vote that these laws were not preempted by ERISA. Section 2105 of the new federal law explicitly permits state regulation of this subject. One such state "mass-layoff law," the California WARN Act, provides, unlike the Federal WARN Act, that it applies to temporary layoffs that are as brief as five weeks long. Because such a stoppage is a "layoff" under California law, it triggers the requirement of 60 days' notice to affected employees. See Int'l Brotherhood of Boilermakers v. Nassco Holdings, 17 Cal. App. 5th 1105 (Cal. Ct. App. 2017).

7.   Massachusetts has enacted special protection for employees laid off after a "takeover" of the employer. See Mass.Gen.Laws Ch. 149, § 183(b) (1989): "Any employee * * * whose employment is terminated within twenty-four calendar months after the transfer of control of his employer is entitled to a one time lump sum payment * * * equal to the product of twice his weekly compensation multiplied by each completed year of service."

8.   A 1985 Connecticut law requires an employer relocating or closing a plant to continue group health insurance for 120 days. Conn.Stat. § 31–51o(a).

9.   Atari, Inc. v. Carson, 212 Cal.Rptr. 773 (Cal.App. 1985), was a class action brought by nonunion employees seeking damages for the harm caused to them when the employer did not notify them of a decision to relocate a plant. The workers claimed breach of an implied contract and breach of an implied covenant of good faith and fair dealing. There is a close connection between this cause of action and the right of the worker to protection against arbitrary dismissal considered in Chapter 10. The case was eventually settled, with the employees receiving an amount equal to four weeks' wages. Barbara Rhine, Business Closings and Their Effects on Employees—Adaptations of the Tort of Wrongful Discharge, 8 Indus.Rel.L.J. 362, 371–72 n. 50 (1986).

10. If employees are denied their 60 days notice of a plant closing, the remedy is pay for the 60 days. Held: workers can collect only for what would have been work days within the 60 day period. Burns v. Stone Forest Indus., Inc., 147 F.3d 1182 (9th Cir. 1998), cert. denied, 525 U.S. 1040 (1998).

11. The Wisconsin Business Closing and Mass Layoff Law requires 60 days notice of a "business closing," defined as a "permanent or temporary shutdown of an employment site." This does not include the sale of business assets where there is no interruption in operations. The new employer hired all but 47 of the 396 former employees (out of a total of 459) who applied. State v. T.J. Int'l, Inc., 628 N.W.2d 774 (Wis.2001).

12. The Ninth Circuit held in Collins v. Gee West Seattle LLC that an employee who leaves his or her job because the business is closing has not "voluntarily departed" and may be eligible for WARN Act relief just like an employee who suffers an "employment loss": departure because of a business closing, therefore, is "generally not voluntary, but a consequence of the shutdown and must be considered a loss of employment . . ." Collins v. Gee West Seattle LLC, 631 F.3d 1001, 1006 (9th Cir. 2011). The court added that employees who would have retired, would have been discharged for cause, or voluntarily departed independent of a business closure are not considered to have suffered an employment loss.

13. Kohler Company hired temporary workers in the middle of a strike and then dismissed them at the strike's conclusion without providing WARN Act notice. The Eighth Circuit held that only workers fired and not replaced count for determining whether there was a mass layoff. Here 123 temporary workers were laid off and 103 striking workers were rehired to their jobs so the layoff was of only twenty, not enough to satisfy the WARN Act numerosity requirement. Sanders v. Kohler Co., 641 F.3d 290 (8th Cir. 2011).

14. The United Steelworkers sued U.S. Steel for failing to provide WARN Act notice prior to a mass layoff in a Keewatin, Minnesota, plant in December 2008, at the height of the financial crisis. Held: the statute's exception for unforeseeable business circumstances prevents this from being a statutory violation. (Nearly all the workers were rehired by December 2009.) The court wrote: "U.S. Steel thought it could survive the economic downturn until the unprecedented effects on the steel industry manifested themselves in late November 2008, thus requiring immediate action . . ." United Steelworkers of America Local 2670 v. United States Steel Corp., 683 F.3d 882 (8th Cir. 2012).

C. DISPLACED WORKERS

Who Are Displaced Workers?

Empirical literature on job displacement shows that it is widespread and countercyclical: It tends to peak during economic downturns. Since 1984, the Employment and Training Administration of the U.S. Department of Labor has sponsored surveys collecting data on displaced workers. The following information is largely taken from these surveys for the two-year period 2007–2009.

The official government definition of displaced worker is persons at least 20 years old, with at least three years on the job, (excluding temporary or seasonal jobs), who lost jobs because their plant or company closed or moved (31%), there was insufficient work for them to do (43%), or their position or shift was abolished (27%).

From January 2007 through December 2009, 6.9 million workers (up from 3.8 million workers from January 2003 through December 2005) in the United States qualified as displaced, according to the Bureau of Labor Statistics, U.S. Department of Labor. That number climbed to 15.4 million if counting individuals who held jobs less than three years.

As of January 2010, 49% of displaced workers were reemployed. Men were more likely to be still displaced than women (39% versus 31%), but women were more likely to have left the workforce (20% of women versus 12% of men). Reemployment rates during this period for African Americans, whites and Latinos were slightly higher than for Asians. Some studies, however, suggest that the women and minorities historically have a harder time becoming reemployed than white men.

Displaced workers were disproportionately represented in manufacturing sectors. During the 2007–2009 period, 1.6 million factory workers were displaced. About half that number were displaced in wholesale and trade sectors. While there was displacement among "white collar" workers (e.g., management, professional workers), it was relatively short-term.

What Policies and Programs Exist to Assist Displaced Workers?

The WARN Act, discussed in the prior section of this chapter, and state unemployment insurance, discussed subsequently, are two policies intended to assist workers who may become or who are displaced. However, as we have seen, WARN, which requires employers to provide advance notice to workers at least 60 days before a plant closing or mass layoff, contains numerous exceptions and many believe, is not particularly helpful to workers on the brink of losing their jobs.

Federal law grants assistance to workers displaced as a result of the North American Free Trade Agreement ("NAFTA"). The NAFTA Transitional Adjustment Assistance program ("NAFTA-TAA") provides a specific program for workers displaced due to increased imports from or shifts of production to Canada and Mexico. The TAA program was initially established in the 1960s in an effort to aid workers who lost jobs due to increased import competition. Congress created a separate NAFTA-TAA program in 1993. The TAA Reform Act of 2002 consolidated the TAA and NAFTA-TAA programs into a single program. "[T]oday's TAA program entitles eligible workers to receive benefits which may include employment services (such as career counseling, resume-writing and interview skills workshops, and job referral programs), vocational training, job search and relocation allowances, income support payments" and tax credit for health insurance coverage. Former Employees of BMC Software, Inc. v. U.S. Sec'y of Labor, 454 F.Supp.2d 1306 (C.I.T. 2006).

In January of 2020, President Trump signed into law a new version of NAFTA called the USMCA (or U.S.-Mexico-Canada Agreement). Commentators have noted that the USMCA has better language about labor and environmental protections than NAFTA, but there still are no real enforcement provisions, as discussed in the following excerpts. Importantly, major labor groups called the USMCA reforms as far as TAA and other labor provisions "wholly inadequate."

Displaced workers seeking benefits under TAA must apply with the Department of Labor. Some contend the process is ineffective and damaging to those the law was designed to help: displaced workers. Consider the following:

> That flaws exist in the Labor Department's process for certification of workers for the TAA program is not news. More than a decade ago, the General Accounting Office (GAO) issued a report estimating that the Labor Department committed errors in at least 63% of its investigations of TAA petitions. But what is news is the dramatically increased attention being paid to the issue of jobs lost to foreign workers, whether through full-scale plant transfers or departmental/functional outsourcing. A particularly bright spotlight shined on the issue of outsourced jobs and assistance programs throughout the 2004 campaign; in the aftermath of the elections, The New York Times called on both the President and Congress to "aggressively finance and, more important, manage, America's neglected Trade Adjustment Assistance program."

* * *

> Obviously, TAA cannot address all of the job losses or other economic problems created by foreign competition and outsourcing. Nor should we expect it to. However, as long as the TAA program remains on the books, and funded at any level, it should nevertheless be administered in a fair and effective manner. * * * In my opinion, the overarching problem in TAA certification is the lack of clear guidelines for DOL, both in undertaking its investigation and identifying/evaluating the information it receives, especially with respect to the definition of "production" in a given case. * * * At present, TAA does not allow a worker to be certified for benefits until that worker shows she was engaged in "production" of an import-impacted good. But defining "production" is not simple, particularly in the ever-changing world of manufacturing. For this reason, DOL's process for investigating the activities of both the petitioning workers and their former company must be sufficiently

competent to answer this critical, starting question. At present, it is not.

With a petition form that requires little more than basic information and summary conclusions, investigations that are seemingly incapable of eliciting or collecting useful information, and a lack of established standards through which DOL can analyze the information that is collected, DOL's certification process for TAA is, quite simply, certifiably broken. And although the courts reviewing DOL's work have identified problems with DOL's process, the judiciary has failed to agree on the fixes. As a result, not only are workers who are petitioning for TAA being denied, in effect, a form of procedural due process, the result is something akin to a lack of substantive due process in the disposition of their claims. Possibly worse, these failings may lead to an effective absence of due process altogether, as thousands of eligible workers may not even bother applying.

Brad Brooks-Rubin, The Certification Process for Trade Adjustment Assistance: Certifiably Broken, 7 U. Pa. J. Lab. & Empl. L. 797 (2005).

For further reading on displaced workers and the policies intended to assist them, see Munford Page Hall, II, Remands in Trade Adjustment Assistance Cases, 39 J. Marshall L. Rev. 9 (2005); Bruce C. Fallick, A Review of the Recent Empirical Literature on Displaced Workers, 50 Indus. & Lab. Rel. Rev. 5 (1996).

Considering the ineffectiveness of WARN and obstacles surrounding such programs as the TAA, what policies or programs might you implement to assist displaced workers? Would your answer depend on the reason for displacement, e.g., whether workers are displaced as a result of technological advances at home or jobs lost to workers in other countries?

NOTE

College-educated workers are less likely to be displaced than workers with only a high school diploma or the equivalent. Moreover, men typically are displaced at higher rates than women. Do you think that gap will widen due to the fact that more women than men are going to college now? Today only about 42% of the college population is male. Men at college are less likely than women to get their bachelor's degree in four or five years. They also tend to get lower grades. See Tamar Lewin, At Colleges, Women are Leaving Men in the Dust, N.Y. Times, July 9, 2006. Do you think job training and re-training programs will change because of this phenomenon? Does your answer change based on the fact that many men who are currently getting laid-off are choosing not to re-enter the workforce? See Louis Uchitelle & David Leonhardt, Men Not Working, and Not Wanting Just Any Job, N.Y. Times, July 31, 2006. What, if anything, should be done about this trend?

D. UNEMPLOYMENT INSURANCE

Fifty states, the District of Columbia, and Puerto Rico have individual unemployment insurance (UI) programs determining the length of unemployment insurance benefits, their amounts for qualifying recipients, and the employer taxes that finance the benefits. In most states, the standard program length over many years has been 26 weeks, though the period has been lengthened in economic downturns, and during the recession that began in 2008 it sometimes reached 99 weeks. As of 2014, however, states were reducing the length of their benefits, some to 20 weeks. Only about 40% of those unemployed were collecting benefits, the average amount being about half what those individuals had earned while working. The total amount paid had reached about $138 billion in 2010 and was about $62 billion in 2013.

1. HISTORY

John A. Garraty, Unemployment in History: Economic Thought and Public Policy*
6–7, 134–136, 213–214 (1978).

Genesis tells us that work is punishment for sin and the fate of humankind, that idleness is the normal condition of the blameless soul (it was the Lord, not Adam, who planted the Garden of Eden), and that even the Lord, despite his omnipotence, felt the need to take a day off. Historically, the tension between the wish to work and the wish to be idle has been a source of confusion to statesmen, employers, social workers, and others concerned with the problem of unemployment. Aside from persons physically unable to work, there appear to be in any society numbers of individuals who for emotional, cultural, or perhaps even philosophical reasons are simply unwilling to work. Separating these "unemployables" from the rest of the jobless has always been difficult, in large measure because every person is in a sense "unwilling" to work. Because of this human ambivalence toward labor, policy makers have for centuries debated the relative merits of the carrot and stick approaches to the unemployed. To the extent that the work ethic predominates, it pays to encourage and sustain them; if it does not, then leaving them to their own devices or even punishing the idle may appear reasonable.

* * *

The [British] unemployment-insurance system was the world's first; the much-admired German social-welfare legislation of the 1880s had not dealt with unemployment. The person most responsible for the measure was Winston Churchill, president of the Board of Trade and then Home

---

* Excerpt from pages 6–7, 213–214 in UNEMPLOYMENT IN HISTORY: Economic Thought and Public Policy by John A. Garraty. Copyright 8 1978 by John A. Garraty. Reprinted by permission of Harper & Row, Publishers, Inc.

Secretary in the cabinet of Prime Minister Herbert Asquith. Churchill knew relatively little about the technicalities of either insurance or the unemployment problem, but he recognized unemployment (the "Achilles heel" of British labor) as an important political and social issue. He quickly availed himself of the most advanced thinking on the subject— his mentors were Sidney and Beatrice Webb, who recognized Churchill's "capacity for the quick appreciation and rapid execution of ideas," and William H. Beveridge, an authority on labor exchanges, whom he met through the Webbs. Like many other English social reformers of the period, Churchill was also impressed by German welfare programs; before entering the cabinet he wrote an important article proposing "a sort of Germanized network of state intervention and regulation" for the protection of the jobless.

Churchill did not, however, merely assimilate the ideas of others. The Webbs in particular, being ardent preventionists, were wary of compulsory unemployment insurance, which might seem "an easy alternative to complicated measures of prevention," but which they believed would encourage malingering and be extremely expensive. Under a compulsory system, Beatrice Webb wrote in 1909, "the state gets nothing for its money in the way of conduct." The Webbs favored instead a voluntary insurance program of the Ghent type, which, they argued, would encourage workers to develop thrift, foresight, independence, and "the willingness to subordinate the present to the future," and also free the government from the need to administer a complex system. Insurance was, in any case, only a palliative; the true task was to get rid of unemployment.

* * *

For various reasons, Churchill did not follow the Webbs's advice. Preventing unemployment might, as they said, be possible, but it would take longer than the politician in Churchill could afford to wait. Moreover, he rejected the argument of the Webbs and so many other social workers and reformers that programs of relief ought to aim at improving the character and morals of recipients. Getting something from the unemployed "in the way of conduct" did not appeal to him. "I do not like mixing up moralities and mathematics," he wrote in 1909. "Our concern is with the evil, not with the causes. With the fact of unemployment, not with the character of the unemployed." Even a worker discharged because of drunkenness should be entitled to unemployment benefits if he had paid insurance premiums. Conversely, where the Webbs favored compulsory labor exchanges, seeing them as a way to organize the labor market and prevent the malingering they believed an inherent danger in any insurance system, Churchill considered such a restriction on individuals unjust. Compulsory insurance, on the other hand, did not restrict anyone's freedom. Furthermore—in this he was following Beveridge—it would create "a motive for the voluntary support of Labour Exchanges," a point which the Webbs eventually conceded. Churchill and the Asquith government went ahead with compulsory insurance and, after linking it with a health-insurance measure devised by Lloyd George, pushed it through Parliament in December 1911. The scheme covered about two and a quarter million workers and provided modest benefits, roughly equivalent to a third of the wage of a low-paid worker, for up to fifteen weeks of joblessness.

* * *

The most important result of the high unemployment of the depression in the United States was the passage in 1935 of a national unemployment-insurance law. The measure did not come earlier because of the same popular prejudice against expanding federal authority and also because of disagreements among the advocates of insurance. The idea that an unemployment-insurance system could *prevent* unemployment, which had been advanced before the Great War by John R. Commons and others, was put to the test in Commons's own state of Wisconsin in 1932. The Wisconsin law required each company employing ten or more workers to build up an unemployment reserve fund, financed by the employer but administered by the government, from which that employer's workers would draw benefits when unemployed. The law provided that once the fund had reached a sum equal to $75 for each worker, the employer would not have to add to it except to make up for what was paid out to workers that had been laid off—presumably, therefore, employers would use every means possible to spread out work to avoid having to discharge anyone.

Other supporters of insurance preferred some variant of the British system, with workers as well as employers contributing to a single national fund. The issue was complicated by the opposition, until 1932, of many important labor leaders to any compulsory insurance system and their resistance thereafter to employee contributions, and by fears that no system could remain actuarily sound in the face of political pressures. There were also genuine constitutional concerns—it seemed likely that the Supreme Court would throw out any law setting up a nationally administered system. To get around the constitutional problem, Senator Robert F. Wagner of New York introduced a bill calling for a national payroll tax against which employer payments into any state insurance fund could be offset—thus federal law would force all states to enact unemployment insurance laws, yet not interfere with the Wisconsin system or for that matter prevent other states from devising whatever forms of insurance they wished.

President Roosevelt's position on unemployment insurance was not unlike Winston Churchill's in 1910, although he played a much smaller role in planning and pushing through the necessary legislation. Like Churchill, he did not allow the lack of detailed knowledge to keep him from espousing the principle whole-heartedly. He actually told Secretary of Labor Frances Perkins that he favored "cradle to the grave" insurance for all Americans against illness, unemployment, and old age, "operated through the post offices," but aside from insisting that workers should contribute to the insurance fund so as to have an irrefutable claim to benefits, he did not commit himself to any particular system. He accepted the idea of separate state insurance embodied in Wagner's bill, and when experts who wanted a centralized system objected, he pointed out the political and constitutional problems and put them off with the bromide "We cannot eat the whole cake at one meal." The Social Security Act of 1935 insured against both old age and unemployment. By leaving the particulars to the individual states it created a confused and inequitable unemployment-insurance system. But, under the impetus of the tax offset provision, all the states swiftly established systems. Despite its limitations, the act was, as the historian Arthur M. Schlesinger, Jr. wrote, "a tremendous break with the inhibitions of the past" and in the American context a "prodigious achievement."

NOTES

1. Alice Kessler-Harris, a leading historian of women's labor, more recently analyzed the history of the Social Security Act, arguing that the Unemployment Insurance system was originally intended to benefit primarily the white male breadwinner:

> Because the level of the [unemployment insurance] benefits received was expected to be potentially higher if fewer and more consistent workers drew on them, workers had every incentive to help their employers limit the pool of eligible workers. Industry and employed workers thus colluded in the belief that including casual laborers, inefficient workers, part-timers, and so on would incur additional expenses. That these were among the poorest and least secure members of the labor force could not have escaped notice. They were also disproportionately black, female and married. Married women, it was thought, could potentially be costly to employers by dropping in and out of work.

Alice Kessler-Harris, In Pursuit of Equity: Women, Men and the Quest for Economic Citizenship in 20th-Century America 97–98 (2001).

2. As of 2014, three states and New York City had made it illegal to refuse a job to an individual because that individual is unemployed. Many other states had considered similar legislation. In California, Governor Jerry Brown vetoed such legislation when presented to him by the legislature. The EEOC and President Obama unsuccessfully sought to make such discrimination unlawful as a matter of federal law.

2. THE UNEMPLOYMENT INSURANCE SYSTEM

Walter Nicholson & Karen Needels, Unemployment Insurance: Strengthening the Relationship Between Theory and Policy

20 J. Econ. Persp. 47 (Summer 2006).

Ever since the U.S. federal-state system of unemployment insurance was founded in the 1930s, it has provided partial, temporary replacement of wages to eligible workers who lose jobs "through no fault of their own" (as determined by state-level regulations). Unemployment insurance is one of the largest social insurance programs in the United States, with benefits paid totaling about $34 billion in 2004. This figure is considerably smaller than for Social Security, Medicare or Medicaid, but it exceeds spending on such major programs as Workers' Compensation, Temporary Assistance to Needy Families (TANF) or Food Stamps.

* * * [T]he main goals of the program * * * include: 1) sustaining consumption for workers and their families; 2) helping recipients to make efficient job choices during a period of financial stress; and 3) minimizing the adverse incentives that may accompany partial wage replacement. Of course, these goals can come into conflict—for example, if replacing wages for an unemployed worker also discourages that worker from aggressively searching for or accepting a new job[.] * * *

Some would also add a fourth goal for unemployment compensation: helping to stabilize the overall economy. * * * In principle, such stabilization could occur through a build-up of trust fund accounts during strong economic times and the net payouts during weak economic times. * * *

The Federal-State Unemployment Insurance System

Unemployment insurance reflects the structure of American government. There are 53 separate unemployment insurance jurisdictions—50 states, the District of Columbia, Puerto Rico and the Virgin Islands—each with unique laws and operating procedures. * * * The system is formally financed through a federal tax on payrolls, but this tax includes a credit for taxes paid to state programs that meet federal guidelines, which is all of them, so the majority of the benefits paid by the system are actually collected by state-level taxes. Additional federal involvement in the unemployment insurance system occurs during recessions, when both "permanent" extended and temporary "emergency" programs for additional benefits are often enacted.

Table 1 provides a snapshot of the unemployment insurance program in 2004, during which $34 billion was paid to 8.4 million recipients. On average, recipients collected weekly benefits of $262 for about 16 weeks, and 42 percent of those who started receiving benefits eventually collected all the benefits to which they were entitled—a process referred to as "exhausting" those benefits. Individuals who exhaust their benefits cannot collect additional regular benefits until they reestablish eligibility after returning to employment. During 2004, only about 36 percent of all unemployed workers collected unemployment insurance benefits. Here are some of the principal reasons for nonreceipt: 1) many unemployed workers were not covered for unemployment insurance benefits because they were recent entrants to the labor market or because they voluntarily quit their previous job; 2) some unemployed workers were not eligible for unemployment insurance benefits because they had had not earned enough in their recent previous jobs to make them eligible; 3) some otherwise eligible workers opted not to file for benefits; and 4) some unemployed workers had exhausted all of the benefits to which they were entitled.

Because the federal government establishes guidelines and provides most of the funds to administer the unemployment insurance program, federal policymakers might seem to have considerable leverage to establish consistency across the states. For historical reasons, however, states vary considerably along practically all dimensions of the program. With respect to taxation that funds unemployment benefits, for example, there is considerable variation in the amount of wages taxed (states' wage bases for taxation vary between $7,000 and $30,000 in annual earnings) and in the tax rate charged on this base (between 1 and 4 percent). Rates of taxation on total wages range between about 0.3 percent and 1.2 percent. Similarly, although all states are required to use "experience-rating" that results in lower tax rates for firms with few layoffs, the effectiveness of these tax schedules varies widely across states. The primary reason for such variation is the existence of binding floors and ceilings in the tax rates that the states apply to specific firms.

* * * [A] complete review of state-specific variation in unemployment insurance regulations and benefit schedules would fill volumes. These figures illustrate some of the ways in which program differences are manifest in the experience of the typical worker. * * *

[In 2004] average weekly benefits ranged from below $230 (Florida) to more than $330 (New Jersey). Average weeks of benefits that were collected range from 12 weeks (Georgia) to nearly 19 weeks (Illinois). The rates of benefit collection among unemployed workers generally also varied significantly, from below 20 percent (Texas) to over 50 percent (New Jersey). * * *

These variations in average recipient's program experience stem both from differences in state labor markets and from programmatic choices that the states have made in four general areas: 1) rules about eligibility for benefits of workers in covered jobs; 2) decisions about what jobs are covered by unemployment insurance; 3) variations in weekly benefit amounts available to eligible workers; and 4) variations in the number of weeks for which a worker can collect benefits before his or her initial entitlement is exhausted. * * *

Eligibility

To be eligible for unemployment insurance benefits, covered workers who lose their jobs must meet three sets of conditions: 1) a "monetary standard" that determines whether a worker had sufficient employment during some defined base period; 2) a "nonmonetary standard" that determines whether the worker had an acceptable reason for his or her job separation; and 3) "continuing eligibility standards" that determine whether the worker continues to be unemployed and thus eligible for benefits.

All states require a minimum level of prior employment as a condition for unemployment insurance eligibility, but their methods for doing so vary in ways that can affect who is eligible. The most typical rule is to require that workers become eligible for unemployment insurance if they have quarterly earnings of at least $2,500–$3,500. Such rules can affect collection rates; for example, econometric analysis suggests that the tightening of monetary eligibility requirements in the early 1980s, which made it harder to qualify for benefits, may have caused as much as 10 percent of the decline in unemployment insurance claims during that decade. * * *

Using a monetary standard for determining prior employment raises some concerns. For example, low-wage workers may be ineligible for benefits if they do not work full time. Temporary employees, an important and growing segment of the labor force, may also be ineligible. * * * A similar issue is that workers who lose a job they only recently obtained may not qualify for benefits, because many states' accounting systems for determining earnings operate with three-to six-month lags. * * * In some cases, states also may use monetary eligibility formulas to bar workers in seasonal jobs from eligibility. * * *

The main purpose of state nonmonetary eligibility provisions is to ensure that workers cannot voluntarily quit their jobs or be fired for cause and collect unemployment insurance; instead, workers must have lost their jobs "through no fault of their own." Three types of issues dominate these regulations: 1) differentiating between voluntary separations and layoffs; 2) clarifying the meaning of dismissals for "cause"; and 3) determining eligibility for unemployment insurance of workers in a labor dispute. * * *

The proper definition of "quits" has been a contentious issue, and states vary widely in how they define acceptable reasons for quitting a job. For example, some states consider following a spouse who relocates to be an acceptable reason for leaving a job, while other states do not. The prevalence of part-time work and other nonstandard employment arrangements has also increased the complexity of determining whether a worker's separation was voluntary. * * *

States use "continuing eligibility standards" to ensure that unemployment insurance recipients remain able and available for work while collecting unemployment benefits. These standards are usually grouped under three headings: 1) availability for work; 2) active job search; and 3) refusal of suitable employment. Precise distinctions among the categories are not always possible, however. All states require that recipients be "able and available for work" to continue receiving benefits, but interpretations of this requirement vary widely. Some states require availability for "any work," whereas others require availability for "suitable" work or work in the claimant's "usual occupation." Other issues include geographic definitions of availability, availability during pregnancy, and availability if the claimant has a disability. Many states treat active job search as one indication of availability for work, and all states require registration at local employment offices as one indication of such activity. In some cases, people must provide evidence of contact with potential employers to show they have been looking for work. States also vary in whether they require workers in training or education programs to seek work actively. Under federal law, states cannot deny benefits to someone enrolled in an "approved" training course, but state-level rules often distinguish between "training" and "education" courses. As a consequence, many students cannot collect benefits, although their courses may be job-related. Similarly, some states require that workers who are pursuing self-employment opportunities search for jobs, even though doing so might impair their success at self-employment. Workers seeking part-time work do not necessarily meet states' availability tests. Some states consider the refusal of a full-time job as disqualifying in all cases; others allow a refusal if the worker had usually worked part-time.

* * *

Unemployment Insurance Job Coverage

Nearly all wage and salary workers are covered by the unemployment insurance system. Two areas in which coverage is less than complete are seasonal employment and self-employment. The most prominent example of seasonal employment is agriculture, but other industries with a substantial seasonal component include construction, transportation and retailing. * * *

Two issues have dominated the debate over covering self-employed workers. First, granting unemployment insurance coverage to the self-employed poses significant conceptual and administrative problems in determining when a job is "lost." Taxing each self-employed worker to cover his or her own unemployment is also problematic. A second policy issue concerns "independent contractors." Legal questions about this employment relationship are complex, but many firms have incentives to classify workers as independent contractors rather than employees. In such cases, those workers are often ineligible for benefits. * * *

The Weekly Benefit Allowance and Wage Replacement

Unemployment insurance seeks to sustain the consumption of workers during periods of job loss. Traditionally, success in achieving this goal has been judged by comparing the unemployment insurance weekly benefit with weekly consumption spending. Gruber (1999) and Hamermesh and Slesnick (1995) find that unemployment insurance benefits do an adequate job, on average, of preventing major declines in consumption spending in response to layoffs. However, these studies do not examine variations in experience across workers. In addition, their conclusion applies only to unemployed workers who actually collect benefits. The unemployment insurance system (even with the federal extensions that may be enacted) replaces only 8 to 15 percent of economy-wide earnings lost during recessions.

Studies of the degree to which weekly unemployment insurance benefits replace previous weekly wages find substantial variation among workers, primarily as a result of variation in the maximum benefit amounts that states provide. Procedures for establishing these maximums vary significantly across the states. Thirty-four states use a formula that ties the maximum to the state's average weekly wage; the maximum is usually between 50 and 70 percent of the average weekly wage. Other states set their maxima by statute, which typically yields lower maxima relative to average wages. This variation means that high-wage workers experience very different wage replacement rates based on the state in which they file.

* * *

Duration of Unemployment Insurance Benefits

The number of weeks for which an unemployed worker can collect benefits is determined by both state and federal law. State laws determine potential duration under the regular unemployment insurance program, whereas federal laws determine the availability of additional weeks of "extended" benefits during recessions.

In the regular state-level program, nine states provide a "uniform" maximum potential duration—usually 26 weeks—to all recipients. In the other states, a worker's maximum potential duration is determined by earnings history. The formulas vary widely across states; most provide 26 weeks to workers with substantial work experience, but potential durations may be as short as ten to twelve weeks. Several researchers have shown that when duration is short, the proportion of workers who exhaust their benefits rises significantly. The national average potential duration of benefits in the regular unemployment insurance program has remained remarkably constant at about 24 weeks over the past 50 years. Because the average duration of unemployment has risen in recent years, the proportion of workers' unemployment spells during which benefits are received has been shrinking.

In contrast to the stability in state regulations about the duration of regular unemployment insurance benefits, the history of programs that extend the duration of benefits during recessionary periods has been quite eventful. A program of extended benefits that would be triggered automatically by worsening labor market conditions became a permanent feature of unemployment insurance law in the early 1970s and led to large additional benefit payments during recessions in the 1970s and early 1980s. The significance of this automatic program was greatly reduced after 1985 because of changes in the criteria for which these benefits become available. However, the federal government also has implemented additional, "emergency" benefits programs for every recession since 1971. Each emergency program had its own special duration provisions and other unique features. Depending on the emergency program, potential benefit collection was extended by between 13 and 39 weeks.

* * *

NOTES

1. In response to the September 11, 2001 terrorist attacks, the federal government enacted the Temporary Extended Unemployment Compensation Act of 2002, (26 U.S.C. § 3304 (Supp. 2003)), an emergency benefits program designed to extend the maximum length of unemployment benefits for workers in the airline and related industries who lost their jobs as a direct result of the attacks. See also In re Dzinovic, 803 N.Y.S.2d 321 (App.Div.2005).

2. The fact that the unemployment compensation insurance regime is primarily one of state (as opposed to federal) law is illustrated by the problem of telecommuters. David L. Gregory, 19th Century Local Unemployment Compensation Insurance Law in the 21st Century Global Economy, 44 Santa Clara L. Rev. 1113 (2004). A claimant who telecommuted via telephone and the Internet from Florida, where she was physically present, to New York, where her employer was located, was deemed ineligible for New York state unemployment benefits. In re Allen, 794 N.E.2d 18 (N.Y.2003).

Lori G. Kletzer & Howard Rosen, Reforming Unemployment Insurance for the Twenty-First Century Workforce

The Brookings Institution (Sept. 2006), https://www.brookings.edu/research/reforming-unemployment-insurance-for-the-twenty-first-century-workforce/,
1–15 (Sept. 2006).

Introduction

The unemployment insurance (UI) system is the foundation of the U.S. government's response to the hardships associated with economic downturns and related job loss. In response to the Great Depression, the Social Security Act of 1935 established the UI and Social Security systems.[4] There have been no major changes in the basic structure of the

---

[4] Widespread economic hardship experienced in the 1930s had a huge impact on the nation's conscience and contributed to a sea change in the view of the role of the government in the United States. People in need began looking to the government, as opposed to families and

UI system since then, despite significant changes in U.S. labor market conditions. Currently, just over one-third of unemployed workers actually receive assistance under the program, and that assistance is modest, at best. The 50 states, the District of Columbia, Puerto Rico, and the Virgin Islands each administers and finances its own UI program, resulting in vast differences in benefit levels and tax rates, which do not appear to reflect local labor market conditions. The goals of UI are to provide income support during the period of unemployment * * * and to provide insurance against the risk of job loss. The failure to provide extended assistance in an orderly and timely fashion has seriously hindered the program's ability to achieve one of its other objectives: to provide countercyclical stimulus during periods of economic downturns.

While the basics of UI have remained unchanged, the U.S. labor market and workforce have experienced significant changes over the past half-century. The agricultural-manufacturing economy of the 1940s and 1950s has been transformed into the service economy of the late twentieth and early twenty-first centuries. The entry of women into the labor force, the decline of traditional employer-based full-time employment, and the rise of contingent and part-time employment are just some of the sweeping changes that have taken place over the past 70 years. In addition, UI has never served the self-employed, who now total more than 10 million workers.[5] Our starting point is that the current UI system is seriously out of date, given the needs of a twenty-first century workforce. Although the basic structure is sound, important aspects of the system are in desperate need of reform.

* * *

I.　Changes in the U.S. Labor Market

* * * A significant rise in population, fueled in large part by the postwar Baby Boom, and the increasing participation of women in the labor force resulted in its tripling in size—from slightly more than 50 million people in 1939 to almost 150 million people in 2004. The most significant change over the past 40 years has been the entry of women into the labor force. Since 1960, the female labor force participation rate has increased by 20 percentage points, while the male labor force participation rate has declined slightly.

The composition of employment has also changed significantly. Agricultural employment, in decline for the better part of a century, * * * is currently just below 2 percent of total employment. Manufacturing employment, as a share of total employment, has fallen by half * * * to

---

other social institutions, as the primary provider of assistance. Social Security and UI constitute the most comprehensive social welfare programs in the history of the United States.

　[5]　Based on Current Population Survey data, 10.3 million workers were self-employed in 2003, accounting for 7.5 percent of total employment. Self-employment as a share of employment has fallen, however, over the more than 70 years since the establishment of UI. Much of that decline is explained by the declining importance of agriculture in employment. * * *

17.5 percent currently. Services have dominated employment since the 1960s * * *.

In addition to changes in the demographics and the composition of employment, there have been changes in the nature of unemployment. After rising between the 1960s and the 1980s, the average unemployment rate began falling in the 1990s, reaching a low of 4 percent in 2000 and remaining moderate over the past six years.

Despite overall declines in the unemployment rate, the average and median duration of unemployment has increased. These two conflicting trends suggest a change in the source of joblessness—from temporary layoff to permanent displacement * * *. Overall, new entrants account for a smaller share of the unemployed, and job losers account for a larger share of the unemployed. * * *

For most of the past century, employment and unemployment were highly correlated with the business cycle. This relationship appears to have changed in recent years. First, with the exception of the early 1980s, there has been a decline in the official length of recessions. Second, there has also been a decline in the magnitude of job losses occurring during economic slowdowns. Third, employment declines have continued for at least one year after the end of the last two recessions and employment recovery has taken longer. Taken together, these three developments suggest that something has changed in the underlying structure of the U.S. labor market in recent years.

* * * [T]here has been a significant decline in variation across state unemployment rates over the past 30 years. During the late 1970s, states in the Northeast and Midwest—regions with high concentrations of traditional industries such as automobile manufacturing, textiles and apparel, and steel—experienced significantly higher unemployment rates than states in other regions. Beginning in the 1980s, state unemployment rates began converging toward the national average, reflecting a slow decline in overall unemployment and more similarity in state unemployment rates. * * *

To summarize, we have identified the following five major developments in the U.S. labor market:

1.   There has been an increase in labor market participation by various demographic groups. The typical worker of 1935 was not the typical worker of 2006.

2.   The shift of employment from agriculture to manufacturing has been joined by a shift from manufacturing to services.

3.   Despite a moderate aggregate unemployment rate, the duration of unemployment has increased, with a greater incidence of permanent job loss than of temporary layoffs.

4.   State unemployment rates are converging, reflecting a reduction in their variation.

5.   Changes in employment and unemployment seem to be due more to structural rather than to cyclical factors.

* * *

The original UI program was designed to offset income losses during cyclical periods of temporary involuntary unemployment. By contrast, current workers face short-term transitional unemployment as they move from job to job, and they face long-term structural unemployment. The existing UI system is inadequate in responding to these labor market conditions. The system also does not assist workers who seek part-time employment, workers who voluntarily leave one job in order to take another, or workers who experience long-term unemployment. New entrants and reentrants into the labor market are not currently eligible for UI, since these two groups of unemployed do not fit well with one of the program's original objectives, i.e., insuring against the risk of involuntary job loss. * * *

Underlining these macroeconomic changes to the U.S. labor market is a shift from traditional employer-based full-time employment to an increased reliance on contingent and part-time employment. The shift to these nontraditional forms of employment reflects additional shortfalls in the current UI program. A system designed to provide income support during temporary layoffs for workers who were permanently attached to a single employer is not well designed for a labor market with considerable self-employment and contingent, part-time, and low-wage employment.

II.   The Current UI Program

Federal law established the UI program in 1935 in order to provide temporary and partial wage replacement to workers involuntary separated from their jobs. It was believed that UI would serve as a countercyclical mechanism to help stabilize the economy during economic slowdowns * * *.

The UI program was modest at first. Coverage was limited to employers with more than eight employees working at least 20 weeks a year. The program did not originally cover workers employed in agriculture, nonprofits, or the government.[6] * * * Approximately 500 million unemployed workers have received more than $600 billion in assistance since the establishment of the program.

As established in 1935, the UI program is a federal-state system. The federal government establishes rules and standards, primarily on minimum coverage and eligibility criteria, and sets a minor tax to finance the overall administration of the program. Individual states set their own benefit amounts, duration of assistance, and means of financing that assistance.

---

[6]   As a result of various extensions, workers in these sectors are currently covered.

Like Social Security and Medicare, UI, which buffers income losses associated with involuntary job loss, is a social insurance program * * *. The universality of UI means that receipt of benefits is conditional only on job loss, and is not based on an individual's income or wealth. * * *

Some important insurance principles are built into the UI system. Premiums are paid in advance through employer taxes on wages earned.[7] Individual eligibility requires earnings and employment experience above a state-specified minimum, and entry into unemployment must be through involuntary job loss resulting from a list of acceptable causes. The covered earnings requirement means that eligible workers are those with some labor force attachment. Continued receipt of benefits requires being able, available for, and actively seeking full-time work * * *.

Coverage and Eligibility

The most significant changes in UI since 1935 are related to coverage. Over the years, various changes have widened the net of covered employment to include almost all wage and salary workers, with the exception of agricultural and household workers. Self-employed workers are still not covered under the program.

Eligibility criteria for receiving assistance, listed below, are based on monetary and nonmonetary determinations; the application of these criteria varies by state:

- record of recent earnings, over a base year
- length of job tenure (calendar quarters employed)
- cause of job loss
- ability and willingness to seek and accept suitable employment

Monetary eligibility is essentially a sufficient work history prior to job loss * * *. Nonmonetary criteria pose more significant hurdles for many workers. Most state programs assist only those workers who lose their jobs through no fault of their own, as determined by state law. In more detail, reasons for ineligibility of UI include the following:

- voluntary separation from work without good cause
- inability or unwillingness to accept full-time work
- discharge for misconduct connected with work
- refusal of suitable work without good cause
- unemployment resulting from a labor dispute

There is enormous variation across states in the definition of *good cause* for voluntary separation, i.e., leaving to accept other work, compulsory retirement, sexual or other harassment, domestic violence, and relocation to be with a spouse. Forty-three programs restrict good

---

[7]   Taxes are levied on employers, but the incidence is likely passed on to employees.

cause to reasons connected to work.[8] Program discretion in setting these standards results in numerous inconsistencies. For example, workers who quit to move with a spouse and meet the monetary eligibility criteria are eligible to receive UI benefits in some programs—including California, Kansas, and New York—but not in others—including Connecticut, Delaware, the District of Columbia, and Massachusetts. Workers who quit because they have been victims of sexual or other harassment are potentially eligible for UI benefits in all programs except six: Alabama, Georgia, Hawaii, Missouri, New Hampshire, and Vermont * * *. In a highly mobile society, with integrated labor markets, it is difficult to imagine a plausible argument in support of these differences in state programs.

The base period monetary criteria are used as an imperfect proxy for labor market attachment. One unfortunate consequence is that some workers have insufficient work experience to meet the base period requirement, i.e., reentrants into the labor market who are actively seeking employment are not eligible for UI. As a result, women who decide to postpone returning to work after childbirth and workers who return to school or who take up training following a job loss can be ruled ineligible for UI. * * *

The percent of total unemployed workers receiving assistance, the *recipiency rate*, has declined over the past two decades. The recipiency rate peaked in 1975 when half of all unemployed workers received UI. * * * [I]n recent years only a little more than one-third of unemployed workers actually have received assistance under the UI program.

Benefit Levels

One of the initial goals of UI was to replace half of lost wages. Because of the federal-state nature of the program, each state sets its own minimum and maximum weekly benefit amounts. Although several states have set their maximum weekly benefit at approximately two-thirds the state weekly wage, currently only one state—Hawaii—has achieved the initial goal of actually replacing, on average, half of lost wages. Almost all states set their maximum weekly benefits somewhere between $200 and $500 * * *. Puerto Rico has the lowest maximum weekly benefit ($133). States with the highest maximum weekly benefits include Massachusetts ($551 to $826), Minnesota ($350 to $515), New Jersey ($521), and Rhode Island ($492 to $615). The average weekly benefit in 2004 ranged from $106.50 in Puerto Rico to $351.35 in Massachusetts. The average weekly benefit for the entire country was $262.50. This average is almost 10 percent less than the weekly equivalent of the poverty level for a family of three that was set by the U.S. Census Bureau.

* * *

---

[8]　California, New York and eight other jurisdictions allow for good personal cause.

Financing UI

* * * Currently, federal taxes finance 17 percent of the UI program. The remaining 83 percent is financed by state taxes * * *.

The federal tax established by the Federal Unemployment Tax Act (FUTA) is currently 6.2 percent on the first $7,000 of annual salary by covered employers on behalf of covered employees. Employers must pay the tax on behalf of employees who earn at least $1,500 during a calendar quarter.

* * *

Federal guidelines dictate that states have in place UI payroll tax systems that are experience rated. With experience rating, firms that lay off fewer workers face a lower tax rate on their payroll. States have the discretion to structure their own experience rating system, and those systems, as with the tax rates, vary considerably among the states.

* * *

Some aspects of the current UI system work well and deserve to be highlighted. Examples are the contribution of the UI program to income smoothing and consumption smoothing and insuring workers against the risk of job loss. UI constitutes an important source of income for unemployed workers and their families, particularly for the long-term unemployed. The Congressional Budget Office (2004) reports that UI benefits played a significant role in maintaining the family income of recipients who experienced long-term spells of unemployment in 2001 and early 2002, particularly for those families that had only one wage earner. Before becoming unemployed, recipients' average family income was about $4,800 per month. When recipients lost their job, that income—excluding UI benefits—dropped by almost 60 percent. Including UI benefits reduced the income loss to about 40 percent.

NOTE

As of 2014, Unemployment Insurance benefits in California, New Jersey, and Rhode Island cover absence from work after childbirth or adoption. Those states and some others have laws requiring employers to provide unpaid leave. See Gillian Lester, A Defense of Paid Family Leave, 28 Harv. J.L. & Gender 1 (2005).

3.　LEGAL ISSUES IN UNEMPLOYMENT INSURANCE

a.　YEAR-ROUND JOBS

Zambrano v. Reinert

291 F.3d 964 (7th Cir. 2002).

■ KANNE, CIRCUIT JUDGE.

After being denied unemployment compensation benefits in accordance with Wis. Stat. § 108.02(15)(k)(14) (the "Cannery Rule"), Rene Zambrano filed suit pursuant to 42 U.S.C. § 1983, alleging that the Cannery Rule was in conflict with two federal statutes and violated the Equal Protection Clause of the Fourteenth Amendment. The district court upheld the validity of the Cannery Rule, and we affirm.

Under Wisconsin's unemployment compensation scheme, "base period" wages count towards unemployment compensation eligibility. Base period wages include, inter alia, wages earned during employment, and "employment" is defined as "any service . . . performed by an individual for pay." However, in applying the Cannery Rule, the definition of employment does not include services

> by an individual for an employer which is engaged in the processing of fresh perishable fruits or vegetables within a given calendar year if the individual has been employed by the employer solely within the active-processing season or seasons * * * and the individual's base period wages with the employer are less than the wages required to start a benefit year under § 108.04(4)(a), unless the individual was paid wages of $200 or more for services performed in employment * * * other than work performed for the processing employer, during the 4 most recently completed quarters preceding the individual's first week of employment by the processing employer within that year.

In other words, for a seasonal fruit or vegetable processing worker to meet the definition of "employment," and thus be eligible to receive unemployment compensation benefits, he must have 1) been employed with the processor outside the "active processing season"; 2) been separately eligible under Wis. Stat. § 108.04(4)(a); or 3) earned over $200 in another job during the time period outlined in the statute.

Zambrano, a Texas resident, provided seasonal labor for vegetable processor Seneca Foods, Inc. in Mayville, Wisconsin from June 11 to October 7, 1999, earning $10,290.98. On April 4, 2000, Zambrano filed for unemployment compensation in Wisconsin. Because Zambrano was employed by Seneca, a processor of vegetables, the Department for Workforce Development (the "DWD") noted that his claim for unemployment compensation fell under the purview of the Cannery Rule and thus found that Zambrano was ineligible to receive unemployment compensation benefits.

To be eligible for benefits, Zambrano had to meet one of three conditions listed in the Cannery Rule: First, Zambrano would have had to have worked for Seneca outside the active processing season. Zambrano concedes that he did not, and therefore this provision is irrelevant to our present review.

Second, he would have been eligible if his "base period wages" with Seneca were equal to or greater than the wages described in Wis. Stat. § 108.04(4)(a). To start a benefit year under that section, an applicant's base period wages must, among other things, be equal to at least four times his weekly benefit rate "in one or more quarters outside of the quarter within the claimant's base period in which the claimant has the highest base period wages." In this case, as Zambrano concedes, the amount of wages that he earned during this time period was $1,159.81, and this amount was less than four times his weekly benefit rate of $305 (i.e., 4 × $305 = $1,200). Thus, the DWD concluded that Zambrano did not meet the second condition to be eligible for unemployment compensation benefits under the Cannery Rule.

Finally, Zambrano would have been entitled to receive benefits had he earned more than $200 from an employer other than Seneca during the four most recently completed quarters preceding his first week of work at Seneca (the "Other Employment" provision). Zambrano's only income from Wisconsin employers other than Seneca that year was $1,250 that he earned for work performed for Lifestyle Staffing during May and June 1999. However, because these wages were earned in the same quarter as the start of his employment with Seneca, and not in the preceding quarter, the DWD concluded that Zambrano was not eligible to receive benefits because he did not meet the requirements of the Other Employment provision of the Cannery Rule.

As a result of this ruling, Zambrano brought suit against Jennifer Reinert in her official capacity as Secretary of the DWD, alleging that the Cannery Rule ran afoul of two federal statutes and that it violated principles of equal protection. The district court granted summary judgment in favor of the Secretary, upholding the Cannery Rule in the face of Zambrano's challenges.

* * *

Initially, Zambrano contends that the Cannery Rule conflicts with section 503(a)(1) (the "When Due Clause") of the Social Security Act (the "SSA"). Under the SSA, federal funds are made available to states in order to encourage them to enact unemployment insurance laws. However, before the federal government will provide funds to a state to administer its unemployment insurance laws, the Secretary of Labor must certify that the recipient state's unemployment program meets certain statutory requirements. * * * The basic thrust of the When Due

Clause is timeliness—the state should determine who is eligible to receive unemployment compensation and make payments to such individuals at the earliest stage that is administratively feasible.

The first step in deciding whether a state statute violates the When Due Clause is to determine whether the state provision is an administrative provision or an eligibility requirement. An administrative provision governs when eligibility is determined or when unemployment benefits are paid, while an eligibility requirement governs who is eligible to receive unemployment compensation benefits. Drawing this distinction is important because eligibility requirements do not fall under the purview of the When Due Clause, whereas administrative provisions do.

* * * [T]he Other Employment provision [of the Cannery Rule] sets forth a method of determining whether work performed by an applicant is "employment" and thus whether the applicant is eligible to receive benefits. Therefore, because it determines who is eligible to receive benefits, as opposed to when the eligibility determination is made or when an eligible person receives benefits, the Cannery Rule is an eligibility requirement that is "beyond the reach of the 'when due' clause."

* * *

The Federal Unemployment Tax Act ("FUTA") taxes employers on the wages they pay to their employees and provides a tax credit for employers' contributions to federally-approved state unemployment compensation laws. For the Secretary of Labor to approve a state's unemployment compensation law (as the Secretary of Labor did in this case), he must find, among other things, that the state law does not operate to cancel "wage credits" or reduce "benefit rights" for reasons other than fraud or misconduct.

Zambrano asserts that the Cannery Rule cancels wage credits or benefit rights for reasons other than fraud or misconduct and thus violates 26 U.S.C. § 3304(a)(10). In order for the Cannery Rule to have cancelled Zambrano's wage credits or reduced his benefit rights, he must have had such wage credits or benefits in the first place. Thus, the initial issue is whether Zambrano earned wage credits or benefit rights—a matter of state law. We have previously noted that states have "free rein" to design eligibility requirements for receiving unemployment compensation. In the present case, eligibility is calculated from wages earned during employment—employment being a statutorily defined term. The Cannery Rule qualifies that statutory definition of employment, excluding wages earned by fruit and vegetable processors unless those workers meet one of the three aforementioned conditions. As discussed above, the Cannery Rule merely sets forth requirements for being eligible to receive unemployment compensation, and Zambrano concedes that he did not meet those requirements. Therefore, he never had any wage credits or benefit rights to cancel or reduce in the first place, and accordingly, the application of the Cannery Rule in this case does not violate FUTA.

Zambrano argues that seasonal fruit and vegetable workers are denied equal protection because they are subject to different eligibility requirements under Wisconsin's unemployment compensation laws than are other workers. Seasonal fruit and vegetable workers are not a suspect classification, nor does Zambrano's claim implicate fundamental rights. Therefore, we will address Zambrano's equal protection claim under the familiar rational basis test, and uphold the Cannery Rule if "there is any reasonably conceivable state of facts that could provide a rational basis for the classification."

The Secretary asserts that Wisconsin's interest in treating seasonal fruit and vegetable processing workers differently is to ensure that workers receiving unemployment compensation benefits are firmly committed to the Wisconsin labor market. Because fruit and vegetable processing occurs during only three to four months a year, employment availability and duration in this line of work is necessarily limited. Nevertheless, under the Cannery Rule, individuals working in seasonal fruit and vegetable processing can show a commitment to the Wisconsin labor market, and consequently gain unemployment compensation eligibility, by meeting the requirements of the Other Employment provision. Under this provision, seasonal fruit and vegetable processors are eligible to receive benefits if they earned a mere $200 in unrelated employment in the year prior to the quarter in which they began working for seasonal processors. Thus, the Other Employment provision of the Cannery Rule has a rational basis for its classification, which is sufficiently linked to the government purpose of ensuring commitment to the Wisconsin labor market.

For the foregoing reasons, we AFFIRM the district court's grant of summary judgment in favor of the Secretary.

NOTES AND QUESTIONS

1.   Due to the transient nature of seasonal agricultural work, does the Cannery Rule impose an undue burden on such workers to "show a commitment to the Wisconsin labor market"? For treatment of the year-round jobs issue in a different context, see Toledo Area Private Industry Council v. Steinbacher, 534 N.E.2d 363 (Ohio App.1987) (declaring a summer youth program to be a "seasonal industry") and Denver Symphony Ass'n v. Industrial Comm'n, 526 P.2d 685 (Colo.App.1974) (permitting musicians to collect unemployment insurance during weeks when the orchestra had no work for them).

2.   Sometimes teachers who do not have "reasonable assurance" of employment following the summer break may collect unemployment insurance benefits during that period. This rule usually applies to substitute or part-time teachers. See, e.g., Pechman v. Employment Sec. Dep't., 893 P.2d 677 (Wash.Ct.App. 1995) (granting UI benefits to full-time teacher

taking substitute position for following school year); Cervisi v. Unemployment Ins. Appeals Bd., 256 Cal.Rptr. 142 (Ct.App.1989) (holding that part-time faculty at community college did not have "reasonable assurance" of employment and were thus eligible for UI benefits).

3. The seasonal employment issue pinpoints a central feature of the U.S. unemployment insurance system. An employer pays a tax that bears a relationship to the claims made by that employer's former workers. But the relationship of tax to claims is imperfect. There is a maximum tax rate and a minimum. Also, small employers are in a "pool." Thus for some employers, arranging their work in a seasonal way transfers wage costs to the general unemployment insurance fund.

b. SEPARATIONS

An unemployed person seeking benefits files a claim in the appropriate state office. The state notifies the former employer and offers the employer an opportunity to contest the claimant's eligibility. The employer has an incentive to challenge claimants believed ineligible, because the employer's annual unemployment insurance tax is substantially based on claims paid to that employer's former workers. If there is a challenge, the dispute will be heard and decided by the state agency.

Most disputes about initial eligibility concern whether the claimant left the former job "voluntarily and with 'good cause'," or whether he or she was fired "for just cause." Because the law generally favors the continuation of an employment relationship, it punishes the party that is responsible for the termination of the relationship. Thus, when an employee quits for good cause or is fired without just cause, the employer is viewed as responsible for terminating the relationship; the employee receives unemployment insurance benefits and the employer pays a higher unemployment tax rate. On the other hand, an employee who is fired for just cause or who quits without good cause is viewed as responsible for the end of the employment and loses some or all entitlement to benefits.

(i) Good Cause Quit

Jaime v. Director, Department of Employment Security

704 N.E.2d 721 (Ill. Ct. App. 1998).

■ McNAMARA, JUSTICE.

* * *

[Plaintiff Maria] Jaime worked for Miniat for approximately 10 years, and for the duration of her employment there, she resided at 2307 South Marshall Boulevard in Chicago. In December 1995, Miniat moved its place of business from 38th Street and Halsted Street in Chicago to

16250 South Dakin in South Holland, a distance of 16 miles. Following Miniat's move, Jaime continued to work for the company for about six weeks. * * * On February 11, 1996, Jaime applied for unemployment compensation benefits, and on February 13, 1996, she resigned from Miniat.

Miniat filed a protest of Jaime's claim * * * stating that Jaime was not entitled to benefits because she had left work voluntarily. * * * [T]he claims adjudicator denied her claim for benefits, finding that Jaime had "voluntarily left work without good cause attributable to [her] employer." Jaime requested reconsideration of the claims adjudicator's determination, stating that she had left her job due to a lack of transportation after her employer moved close to Indiana.

On April 25, 1996, a hearing was held before a referee regarding Jaime's eligibility for benefits. At that hearing, Jaime appeared pro se and was accompanied by a Spanish translator. * * * Jaime stated that following Miniat's move, she continued to work for the company, obtaining a ride with a coworker. She asserts that she resigned from Miniat on February 13, however, because the coworker with whom she had been getting a ride had stopped working for the company and Jaime therefore had no means of getting to work. * * *

The referee * * * affirm[ed] the decision of the claims adjudicator and den[ied] Jaime unemployment insurance benefits. The referee found that Jaime "voluntarily left her job because she lost her means of transportation to get to work."

Thereafter, Jaime retained counsel [and] requested review of the referee's decision by the Board of Review. [The Board] affirm[ed] the referee's decision and conclud[ed] that Jaime had properly been denied unemployment insurance benefits, because she had left work due to transportation problems, which were not attributable to her employer. * * *

On August 23, 1996, Jaime filed her complaint for administrative review of the Board of Review's decision * * *. * * * [T]he circuit court issued an order, reversing the Board of Review's decision, finding it contrary to law. The court * * * declared that it would have been too great a burden on Jaime to have required her to take public transportation to Miniat's new location. The court concluded that it found the Board of Review's decision "contrary to law in this particular case only" and that it reached this decision because it was aware that Jaime did not drive.

The main purpose of the [Illinois] Unemployment Insurance Act (Act) is to alleviate the economic insecurity and burden caused by involuntary unemployment. "The Act is intended to benefit only those persons who become unemployed through no fault of their own." Section 601(A) of the Act therefore provides that "an individual shall be ineligible for benefits [because] he has left work voluntarily without good cause attributable to the employing unit."

* * *

"While unemployment insurance benefits are a conditional right and the burden of establishing eligibility rests with the claimant, the Act must be liberally construed to favor the awarding of benefits."

* * *

Defendants assert that the Board of Review's decision to deny Jaime unemployment insurance benefits, because she voluntarily left work without good cause attributable to her employer, was not against the manifest weight of the evidence. * * * Defendants point out that Jaime did not present evidence regarding her salary or the increased distance she would be required to travel, which would have allowed the Board of Review to weigh the increased transportation expenses she would incur in traveling to Miniat's new location, against the compensation that she was receiving.

Defendants further claim that while Jaime asserted that she quit work due to transportation problems, she failed to demonstrate that she made reasonable efforts to resolve those problems which arose as the result of Miniat's move, such as finding alternative means of transportation. Defendants assert that the record is devoid of any evidence that she made any effort to employ public transportation, that she spoke to her employer in an effort to resolve any transportation problems, that she spoke to other employees regarding the possibility of riding with them after the coworker with whom she was getting a ride to work resigned or that she could not purchase a car. * * *

Alternatively, defendants argue that Jaime's decision to continue working for two months following her employer's move precludes her from claiming that her subsequent decision to resign was due to good cause attributable to her employer. They assert that Jaime presented no evidence that during this time period, she spoke to her employer in an effort to resolve the problems confronting her. Rather, defendants argue that because Jaime remained where the working conditions had changed, she is therefore not entitled to claim that change as good cause for leaving.

* * *

Because the critical issue with which we are presented concerns whether Jaime's leaving her employment was for "good cause attributable to the employing unit," it is imperative that we define the phrases "good cause" and "attributable to the employing unit." " 'Good cause' connotes a reason for rejecting work that would be deemed by reasonable men and women as valid and not indicative of an unwillingness to work." "Good cause" for voluntarily leaving employment has also been defined as that which results from circumstances producing real and substantial pressure to terminate employment and which under the circumstances would compel a reasonable person to act in the same manner. "A cause 'attributable to the employer' is one which is produced, caused, created or [is the] result of actions by the employer and also includes inaction by the employer." The salient question is whether the conduct of the employer caused the termination of employment to occur. A "substantial, unilateral change in employment which renders the job unsuitable" may prevent disqualification based on voluntarily leaving one's employment.

In the present case, the Board of Review stated the following in its decision:

> The company moved to the suburbs and the claimant then got a ride from another employee for about one and a half months. After that employee left, the claimant had no means to get to work, and was forced to quit. Nevertheless her leaving [her job] was because of transportation, which was not attributable to the employer.

* * *

* * * [W]e find that Miniat's moving of its plant from the south side of Chicago to South Holland, a distance of about 16 miles, constituted "good cause attributable to the employer" with regard to Jaime's leaving her job.

Jaime's testimony at the hearing demonstrates that she made reasonable efforts to maintain her employment. Miniat, her employer of 10 years, moved its plant from a site near her home in Chicago to a suburban location approximately 16 miles away. Jaime continued to work for Miniat for six weeks following the move, obtaining a ride with a coworker. Jaime resigned only after said coworker quit her job, as Jaime no longer had a means of getting to work.

The findings of the Board of Review clearly demonstrate that Jaime desired and attempted to continue to work for Miniat after its move and that the relocation of the company was an act of Miniat, done for its benefit, over which Jaime had no control. A reasonable person would view Jaime's reason for leaving her employment as a valid one and not indicative of an unwillingness to work on her part. Notably, the Board of Review did not find her unwilling to work either. While an employee's transportation to and from work is generally not the responsibility of the employer, Jaime's inability to maintain her employment is the direct result of Miniat's moving its location, thereby significantly changing the circumstances of her employment. Therefore, we find that the credible evidence Jaime presented was sufficient to meet her burden of proving her entitlement to benefits, as it showed that her leaving was for "good cause attributable to her employer." We find this to be particularly true under the circumstances, where Jaime, accompanied by a Spanish translator because she does not speak English fluently, appeared pro se at the hearing, during which her work record of 10 years was never criticized. Jaime showed a causal connection between Miniat's change of location and her inability to get to work, despite her reasonable attempts to do so. Indeed, the circuit court noted that "the public transportation to get to that particular location in South Holland would really create an undue burden on [Jaime]." Our findings are in sync with our legislature's policy that a person who becomes unemployed through no fault of his own should be entitled to unemployment compensation benefits.

Furthermore, we find no merit in defendants' alternative, if not disingenuous, contention that Jaime's decision to continue working for a period of time following Miniat's move to South Holland precludes her from claiming that her subsequent decision to resign was due to "good cause attributable to her employer." Jaime should not be penalized for her attempt to continue working after Miniat chose to move its location to another city. Rather, Jaime's efforts should be commended; they comport with state policy that unemployment benefits should go only to those who are not at fault in their unemployment. It is important to note that courts of other jurisdictions have also upheld the award of unemployment benefits where a person has left his employment due to workplace relocation, even in the instance where the person had attempted to work at the new location, as Jaime did here.

* * *

Accordingly, we hold that the trial court did not err, when it reversed the Board of Review's decision finding Jaime ineligible for unemployment benefits.

* * *

NOTES AND QUESTIONS

1.   Here Miniat was happy to keep employing Maria Jaime, but she stopped coming to work. Yet surely the court was right that her resignation was reasonable, involuntary, and not her fault. Should the country, and the economy, provide up to 99 weeks of benefits to someone in Jaime's situation? Do you think that the fact that Jaime appeared pro se at her hearing and testified through a Spanish translator had any bearing on the referee's decision to deny her unemployment benefits? How did the appeals court view the circumstances of Jaime's hearing?

2.   A Pennsylvania court granted unemployment benefits to a claimant who quit her job as a nurse's aide after realizing that her arthritis did not permit her to do the lifting that the job required. "Because Claimant had a necessitous and compelling reason to terminate her employment, and because Employer did not adequately and accurately inform Claimant of the requirements of the job, thereby necessitating Claimant's informing Employer of her back condition, we conclude that Claimant was unemployed through no fault of her own." Schnee v. Unemployment Comp. Bd. of Rev., 701 A.2d 994 (Pa.Cmwlth.1997).

3.   Paul Platt worked as a locker room attendant at a private golf and tennis club for 70 to 80 hours a week, including 64 consecutive days without

a full day off. Both Platt and his fellow attendant quit when no additional help was hired. A claims adjudicator and appeals referee both ruled that Platt quit his work without good cause. The appeals court reversed, holding that the reasons for quitting are good cause when the "average, able-bodied, qualified worker" would quit and noted that Platt's fellow attendant also quit. Platt v. Unemployment Appeals Comm'n, 618 So.2d 340 (Fla.Dist.Ct. App.1993).

4.   Marilyn Davis, hired to set up pre-schooling for three to five year-olds, was told to work with emotionally disturbed children when funding for the other program ran out. Feeling unqualified for the new work, she developed headaches and became upset. When she resigned, an Illinois appellate court said she had not left the job "without good cause attributable to the employing unit" and therefore should be eligible for unemployment insurance benefits. "A substantial, unilateral change in the employment may render the job unsuitable and entitle the worker to benefits even if he leaves voluntarily." Davis v. Board of Rev., 465 N.E.2d 576 (Ill. Ct. App. 1984).

5.   Francisco Olmeda could not get to work because his driver's license was suspended for traffic violations. Eligibility for unemployment insurance was denied because "he brought his unemployment on himself." Olmeda v. Director of the Div. of Emp. Sec., 475 N.E.2d 1216 (Mass.1985).

6.   In re Claim of Knoblauch, 657 N.Y.S.2d 250 (App.Div.1997), a graphic artist resigned following her employer's decision to reduce her hours and eliminate her health insurance benefits. The court upheld her eligibility for unemployment benefits, stating that "good cause may be found where the circumstances surrounding the employment would have justified the claimant in refusing the employment in the first instance, such as where the wages, hours and benefits are substantially less favorable than those of similar positions in the locality."

7.   Tashika Sykes was denied unemployment benefits under the Minnesota "quit for a better job" exception to good cause quit when a court found that although Tashika's new job paid $10,000 more per year, its lesser benefits package (notably its lack of health care coverage) made it not substantially better than the job Tashika left. Tashika quit her job with Northwest when she was offered an "early out" that enabled her to retain her health insurance benefits through Northwest so long as she did not have employment that provided health insurance. Sykes v. Northwest Airlines, Inc., 789 N.W.2d 253 (Minn.App.2010). Is the Minnesota court's distinction in the law of good cause quit between departing for a better job and switching to one substantially the same appropriate? Note that this issue only arises when the claimant loses his or her second job.

8.   In Arizona, the disqualification for unemployment eligibility is termination for "*work-related misconduct*," not "just cause." "Just cause" tends to be broader. This same type of distinction is present in many jurisdictions. On the other hand, *quitting* for "good cause" will entitle the person to benefits—that is the standard for a qualifying resignation.

Quik 'N Tasty Foods, Inc. v. Division of Employment Security

17 S.W.3d 620 (Mo. Ct. App. 2000).

■ HOLLIGER, JUDGE.

* * *

Wendy Foley was employed by Quik 'N Tasty as a machine operator for more than three years. At the end of the work day on March 24, 1999, Ms. Foley was called to the office of her employer. She had previously been told by a co-worker that her attendance record was being reviewed. She believed she was being called to the office that day to be reprimanded for excessive absenteeism. She testified that she did not go to the office voluntarily and that she had not planned to resign from her job that day. At the conclusion of the meeting, however, Ms. Foley resigned.

On March 29, 1999, Ms. Foley applied for unemployment benefits with the Division of Employment Security. * * * [A] deputy with the Division issued a determination that Ms. Foley was disqualified for benefits because she left her work voluntarily without good cause attributable to her work or employer. Foley filed her appeal and a hearing was held before an Appeals Referee[, who] concluded that Ms. Foley left her work voluntarily because she felt she would be discharged and she did not want a discharge on her employment record; that there was no specific evidence from which it could be reasonably inferred that the claimant was told she would be discharged if absent on March 29; that the evidence only showed that the claimant was told she needed to find someone else to take her children to the dentist that day; and that the employer only suggested that perhaps it would look better for her if she resigned. The Tribunal concluded that the employer did not advise Ms. Foley she had to leave work voluntarily or be discharged, and further concluded that Ms. Foley's decision to leave her work voluntarily was unreasonable, not in good faith, and without good cause attributable to the work or to the employer. The Appeals Referee, therefore, held Ms. Foley to be disqualified for unemployment benefits until she earned wages equal to ten times her weekly benefit. Ms. Foley then appealed the Tribunal's decision to the Labor and Industrial Commission, which reversed the decision of the Tribunal and found that Ms. Foley's actions were reasonable, her resignation was in good faith, and that she was, therefore, not disqualified from benefits.

Quik 'N Tasty now appeals the decision of the Commission.

Ms. Foley testified before the Appeals Referee that she had recently been under stress due to personal problems and that she had been absent from work for personal reasons, including illnesses and bad weather. Present in the office on March 24, 1999, when Ms. Foley arrived, were her immediate supervisor (her team leader, Tina James), two other team leaders, and in an office nearby was the manufacturing plant manager.

The office door was closed. Ms. James testified that Ms. Foley was called to the meeting to be issued a "redirect" regarding her attendance problems. A "redirect" is a verbal warning, the first step in progressive discipline. Ms. Foley testified that she did not recall that occurring. There is no evidence that Ms. Foley was aware of the progressive discipline procedures Quik 'N Tasty had in place. During the meeting, Ms. Foley's supervisor informed her that she had heard rumors that Ms. Foley was looking for another job and that it would be easier on both of them if she were honest about it. Ms. Foley became upset and began to cry. She advised Ms. James that she was under a lot of stress and was worried about being fired, and that she required time off the following Monday, March 29, 1999, to take her children to the dentist. Ms. Foley was told that her absence on Monday would be unacceptable, and that she needed to find someone else to take her children to the dentist. Ms. Foley did not feel anyone else could go in her stead because her son was expected to require a root canal, and her daughter was afraid of doctors.

It was also suggested by her supervisor in the meeting that Ms. Foley consider resigning, because a resignation would look better on her employment record than would a discharge. Ms. James suggested she and Ms. Foley go together to see the personnel manager to determine what severance benefits would be available. The personnel manager provided Ms. Foley with a resignation form, which she completed and signed. It indicated that her last day of work would be two days later, on March 26, 1999. In the section requesting the employee's reason for quitting, Ms. Foley wrote "personal," as suggested by the personnel manager. She returned later that day and changed it to read "distance & transportation & day care duress."

Ms. Foley admits she was not told she would be discharged if she did not resign, nor was she told she would be discharged if she failed to report to work the following Monday. Nonetheless, she claimed she was placed under duress and coerced into resigning by her employer during the meeting because she was being advised that her absence on March 29 would be unacceptable and she was in fear of being discharged if she did not report to work that day.

* * *

The Commission's determination of whether an employee voluntarily left her employment or was discharged is a factual determination, and we will defer to the Commission as to its finding that the claimant left her employment voluntarily. However, the question of whether the claimant had good cause to leave her employment is a legal issue and thus we do not defer to the Commission's determination on the matter.

The Commission argues that Ms. Foley quit in lieu of certain discharge; that she had no choice. The Commission says it could be argued that Ms. Foley's action in resigning was not a freewill, volitional act on her part because of the threat of imminent discharge. The Commission says this is a case of first impression; that there is no decision on whether the threat of imminent discharge constitutes good cause to voluntarily leave work. Quik 'N Tasty counters that the decision, if upheld, would constitute the extension of unemployment benefits to those who were "constructively discharged."

Neither the commission nor Quik 'N Tasty is entirely correct. In Missouri Division of Employment Security v. Labor and Industrial Relations Comm'n, 739 S.W.2d 747 (Mo.App.W.D.1987), this court held that an employee who quit his employment in anticipation of a plant layoff had not left involuntarily and was therefore disqualified from benefits. The court did conceptually acknowledge that under some circumstances a quit or resignation from employment might not be voluntary. There is other authority for the principle that a resignation may, in fact, be considered involuntary and therefore a discharge. In Davis v. Labor and Industrial Relations Comm'n, 554 S.W.2d 541 (Mo.App.E.D. 1977), the court acknowledged the principle that under a "pressure of the circumstances" test a resignation could be found nevertheless to be a "discharge" for purposes of unemployment compensation; the court rejected the employee's argument for application of the rule in that case because there was substantial evidence to support the commission's finding that he had not been "discharged."

* * *

* * * [T]here was no factual finding by the Commission that Ms. Foley was constructively discharged or that she was acting under such duress that her resignation was not voluntary. To the contrary, the Appeals Referee and Commission both found that she voluntarily quit.

A claimant is not entitled to unemployment benefits if she voluntarily quits her job absent good cause attributable to her work or to her employer. It is the claimant who bears the burden of proving that her voluntary termination resulted from good cause attributable to her work or employer. * * *

"Good cause" for purposes of determining eligibility for unemployment benefits has no fixed or precise meaning, and is judged by the facts of each case. "Good cause" has been interpreted to mean "cause that would motivate the average able-bodied and qualified worker in a similar situation to terminate his or her employment." Conditions which motivate the employee to voluntarily leave "must be real, not imaginary, substantial, not trifling, and reasonable, not whimsical, and good faith is an essential element." The determination of good cause is a question of law, and there are two elements of good cause—reasonableness and good faith.

Ordinarily, our inquiry would focus on whether the employee's action in voluntarily terminating her employment was reasonable and whether the employee acted in good faith. Although the Commission argues that Ms. Foley acted reasonably and in good faith, we need not reach those issues and it would confuse the analysis to do so. We do not disagree that Ms. Foley's actions, subjectively measured, were reasonable from her point of view.

The good cause necessary to support an award of unemployment benefits where an employee voluntarily quits must be cause attributable to her work or her employment. * * * Whether the cause is so attributable involves the application of the law to the facts; that, therefore, is a question of law which we review independently of the Commission's determination. * * * [T]he phrase "attributable to his work or to his employer" means "that it must be the work or employer himself that creates the condition making it unreasonable to expect this employee to continue work."

The Commission makes no argument that any condition created by the employer, other than the suggestion to resign rather than be discharged, may itself wholly constitute "good cause" sufficient for the exception from benefit disqualification; nor do we believe that the prospective denial of a day off alone constitutes good cause. We do not consider whether such employer actions, if coupled with an already existing employer-created condition, might constitute good cause or a non-disqualifying voluntary termination because there is no such condition present here. The Commission award, therefore, erroneously applied the law.

We, therefore, reverse the Commission's decision that Wendy Foley left her job voluntarily with good cause attributable to her work or to her employer. We remand to the Commission to enter an order consistent with this opinion.

NOTES

1. A Louisiana appellate court found "good cause" when an employee volunteered to resign in the face of company layoffs in lieu of allowing a less senior colleague to be dismissed. South Cent. Bell Tel. Co. v. Department of Labor, 527 So.2d 1113 (La. Ct. App. 1988), cert. denied 532 So.2d 153 (La. 1988).

2. *Quik 'N Tasty* highlights the challenges faced by female employees who are trying to juggle childcare with the demands of work. In an Indiana case, Tenner Jones worked as a cook for three months from 9 a.m. to 3 p.m. Told that if she could not work to 6 p.m. someone else would be hired, she accepted a change to a 9–6 day. One day later she said she could not work those hours because she had four children at home. Because Ms. Jones accepted the change in hours, she did not have good cause for her quit and was disqualified from eligibility for UI. Jones v. Review Bd., 399 N.E.2d 844 (Ind. Ct. App. 1980).

3. Pregnancy itself may also lead female workers to voluntarily terminate their employment. A New York social worker in the midst of a high-risk pregnancy resigned for fear that the stress from her work environment would jeopardize the health of her baby. The court decided that she was ineligible for unemployment benefits because she failed to inform her employer of her pregnancy and resigned rather than sought a leave of absence. In re Claim of Kohen, 793 N.Y.S.2d 640 (App.Div.2005).

However, in Michigan, a nurse's aide left her employment on the advice of her doctor during the last few weeks of her pregnancy. Here, the court did not even decide the issue of good cause quit, as her leave was due to "factors beyond her control." Since she left "involuntarily, the inquiry ends and she is entitled to unemployment compensation." Warren v. Caro Commun. Hosp., 579 N.W.2d 343 (Mich.1998).

4.   Tina Moore was employed in the marketing department of Melaleuca, Inc., developing a high-end skin-care line for the company. When she told her supervisor of her pregnancy, he said that she should stay home to care for her child, as her husband made enough money so that she did not have to work. When Moore resumed her position following her maternity leave, her supervisor reduced her raise from a recommended 4% to 2.5%. Believing that the decrease in raise was due to her decision to work after the birth of her child, she quit. The court found that Moore was discriminated against due to her pregnancy coupled with her decision not to stay home with her child. Thus, the court concluded, she had good cause to terminate her employment. Moore v. Melaleuca, Inc., 43 P.3d 782 (Idaho 2002).

5.   In Norman v. Unemployment Ins. Appeals Bd., 663 P.2d 904 (Cal.1983), the court determined that a California woman who terminated her employment in order to follow her fiancé to Washington did not establish "good cause" for her voluntary departure and was thus properly denied unemployment compensation benefits. "She did not . . . represent that her marriage was imminent, that her presence in Washington was required to prepare for the wedding, or, indeed, that she had any definite or fixed marital plans." The court added: "In the absence of legislation which grants to members of a nonmarital relationship the same benefits as those granted to spouses, no basis exists in this context for extending to nonmarital relations the preferential status afforded to marital relations."

However, in Reep v. Commissioner of Dep't of Emplt. & Training, 593 N.E.2d 1297 (Mass.1992), a Massachusetts woman who quit her job to move with her male domestic partner of 13 years received unemployment insurance benefits. The court found that the "urgent, compelling, and necessitous nature" clause treating separations as involuntary should be read liberally and that a "legally cognizable relationship" was not necessary for statutory protection.

In another case, Patricia MacGregor quit her job as a waitress to move with her fiancé and their child to live with and take care of the fiancé's ailing father. The Supreme Court of California granted benefits, recognizing that, despite the lack of a formal marriage, there was a family unit that needed to stay together. The court reaffirmed California's view that "the importance of preserving the marital or familial relationship may provide good cause for the other spouse's decision to follow." MacGregor v. Unemployment Ins. Appeals Bd., 689 P.2d 453 (Cal.1984).

Tri-County Youth Programs, Inc. v. Acting Deputy Director of Division of Employment & Training

765 N.E.2d 810 (Mass. App. Ct. 2002).

■ GELINAS, J.

* * * Lawrie was hired in 1996 as a shift manager in a residence for emotionally troubled adolescents operated by Tri-County in Northampton. On November 22, 1997, in connection with her duties, Lawrie took two Tri-County clients on a shopping trip. While driving the company van, Lawrie was sexually assaulted by one of the clients, a fourteen year old male. Lawrie promptly reported the assault to her superiors. Without objection, but with no assistance from Tri-County, Lawrie reported the assault to police and pressed charges. Lawrie's assailant was arrested and placed into the custody of the Department of Youth Services (DYS). On December 4, 1997, Lawrie's supervisor informed her that her assailant would probably be returned to Lawrie's work site, with a "stay-away" order in place.

On December 10, 1997, Lawrie's assailant admitted delinquency to sexual assault, was adjudicated delinquent, and was placed on two years' probation. The court also ordered the juvenile to stay away from Lawrie and to have no contact with her. Later that day, with the assent of Tri-County, DYS returned the juvenile to the same residential facility where Lawrie worked. After discussion with her superiors, Lawrie resigned her position, effective January 7, 1998, giving as the reason her dissatisfaction with her employer's handling of the sexual assault incident. On December 15, 1997, at a meeting with her supervisor, Lawrie was informed that Tri-County had decided to make her resignation effective immediately. Lawrie made application for unemployment benefits, which were granted. Tri-County appealed, and a review examiner denied the benefits; Lawrie applied to the board for a review of the examiner's decision. The board, concluding that the examiner's decision was based on an error of law, modified the examiner's decision and awarded Lawrie benefits for the week ending December 27, 1997, and for subsequent weeks. Tri-County then petitioned the District Court to vacate the board's decision. From a judgment affirming the board's decision, Tri-County appeals to this court.

* * *

* * * [W]e conclude that the board's findings were neither inconsistent with the board's conclusion that Lawrie had been subject to sexual harassment, creating a hostile, humiliating, or sexually offensive work environment, nor unsupported by substantial evidence.

More specifically, the conclusion that Lawrie left due to sexual harassment, and the examiner's (and the board's) finding that she "left her job because of dissatisfaction with the employer's handling of [the] sexual assault incident," are not inconsistent. The board specifically found that Lawrie had been sexually assaulted by her employer's client, and that this client had been criminally prosecuted and ordered to stay away from Lawrie. From these specific material subsidiary findings, the board could draw the reasonable inference that Lawrie was subject to an "intimidating, hostile, humiliating and sexually offensive work environment" when her assailant returned to the same facility where she worked and that Tri-County made "no . . . effort" to stop the creation of such an environment. * * * This conclusion accords with the finding that Lawrie left her employment because she was dissatisfied with the way her employer handled the sexual assault, and it supports the further determination that her resignation was involuntary, with good cause attributable to Tri-County.

The board's conclusion in this regard was also consistent with the finding that Lawrie would not have had "any problems in performing her job duties" even if her assailant was returned to the facility wherein she worked. It is not inconsistent for an employee to be able to perform job duties but still be working within a hostile, humiliating, and sexually offensive environment. Further, Tri-County's argument, that Lawrie failed to raise the sexual harassment issue with the initial examiner, or with the board, is contradicted by the record. Lawrie's application for further review and her counsel's oral argument to the examiner, that Tri-County's stance in taking back the offending client without "anything in the works" for a transfer for Lawrie, were sufficient, in our view, to raise the issue that Tri-County had created a work environment that was sexually hostile.

* * * We reject Tri-County's argument that Lawrie failed to sustain her burden of proof. Generally, it is the employee's burden to show that the employee left work involuntarily with good cause attributable to the employer, and that "he or she took reasonable steps to preserve his or her employment . . . unless the circumstances indicate that such efforts would be futile or result in retaliation." In cases involving allegations of sexual harassment, however, the claimant need not show that she took all or even "reasonable steps" to preserve her employment. * * * Hence, while the board explained that "the findings suggest [Lawrie] may not have taken all necessary measures to preserve her employment prior to resigning," under the statute and regulation Lawrie was not required to show that she had taken such measures.

It appears Lawrie would have sustained her burden even under the more stringent requirement. As noted, in its decision, the board concluded that Tri-County was aware of the existence of the harassment, and that, given the seriousness of the offense, it should have taken affirmative steps to transfer Lawrie permanently to another job site, but no such effort was made. The board further concluded that, given the extent of its "control over the non-employee's [client's] conduct," Tri-County was unreasonable in expecting Lawrie to work in the same residential facility that housed the person who assaulted her. Implicit here is the board's determination that nothing in the facts found by the examiner required that Tri-County accept the return of the client, or that he be housed in the same unit where Lawrie worked. To the extent that it could have refused the client's return, or have housed him in a different facility, Tri-County had control over the client's conduct.

Tri-County further contends in this context that the board erred because it did not consider the fact that, when the client returned, he was subject to a court order to stay away from Lawrie. This argument is unavailing; in coming to its decision the board adopted the examiner's findings of fact, which contained several references to the client's return subject to a stay away order. * * * While recognizing that the factual findings reflected some possible effort on Tri-County's part to offer Lawrie a transfer to a location where clients were female, we could not conclude that, on the record before it, the board's determination—that Tri-County's efforts in this regard were insufficient—was arbitrary or capricious.

* * * We address Tri-County's further argument that we are under obligation to consider "the absolute fact that [Lawrie] was hired to work with youths at risk, kids [who] were emotionally disturbed, victims of severe physical and sexual abuse and adolescent sex offenders," and that the conduct she experienced was not only a foreseeable risk of the job, but "clearly a reasonable probability given the client population served." Tri-County's argument suggests that Lawrie's assuming the risk of sexual assault mitigated the effect of 430 Code Mass. Regs. § 4.04(5)(c)(1)(b) and § 4.04(5)(d), diminishing the board's ability to apply these regulations to her situation. * * *

Tri-County's argument must fail, as it leads to the untenable conclusion that possible criminal sexual assault is the price that an employee must pay to maintain employment, and that, if the employee is unprepared to accept the "reasonable probability" of such occurrences on the job, then leaving after such an incident means leaving without good cause. The section of the employment security law dealing with sexual harassment, G. L. c. 151A, § 25(e), suggests no such limitation on an employee's eligibility for benefits, when the employee leaves for reasons of sexual harassment. Further, 430 Code Mass. Regs. § 4.04(5)(a)(2)(a), by explicit language, defines sexual harassment in part as being subject to sexual conduct as "a term or condition of employment." While an employee may accept employment knowing of the possibility of the risk of sexual assault, leaving employment because of sexual assault cannot be made a basis for denial of benefits under the employment security act, if the employer does not take appropriate measures to ameliorate the situation. As the board determined, the possibility of sexual assault in the workplace places a heavy burden on the employer to take steps to create a situation favorable to the employee, and in the absence of such effort benefits will be payable. In the face of the statutory language and the thrust of the regulations, we cannot say that the board's determination in this regard was arbitrary, capricious, or unreasonable.

* * *

From the record, Tri-County's argument in this regard faces an additional acclivity. Tri-County has in place a detailed protocol for the "Risk Management and Treatment of Adolescent Sex Offenders," precisely to exert appropriate control over the behavior of clients like the assailant. This protocol states, "We believe the specialized assessment and treatment performed by those who are trained in working with adolescent sex offenders is [sic] the first step to be taken if sexual assault and its consequences are to be addressed properly. We assume a responsibility to protect the safety and well-being of other clients, many of whom are victims, and Tri-County staff from the possibility of victimization of those who have been identified as sexual offenders." The existence of this protocol suggests that Tri-County has acknowledged the responsibility of shielding its employees from risk. The protocol's existence further supports the board's determination that Tri-County failed in its duty to make suitable arrangements for Lawrie's protection and continued employment.

The District Court judge did not err in affirming the decision of the board.

* * *

NOTES AND QUESTIONS

1.   In Hoerner Boxes v. Mississippi Employment Sec. Comm'n, 693 So.2d 1343 (Miss.1997), a female employee suffered ongoing harassment from a co-worker, behavior which included sexually explicit remarks and nonconsensual touching. On at least seven occasions, she reported the behavior to her immediate supervisor, who responded that the co-worker was only "kidding around." The supervisor also threatened to punish her if she complained to upper management. The court found that the employee quit for good cause, concluding that "if an employee is sexually harassed to such a degree that an ordinary prudent employee would leave the ranks of the employed for the unemployed, then the employee should not be denied unemployment compensation benefits." Does Lawrie in *Tri-County Youth* meet this "ordinary prudent employee" standard?

2.   Compare *Tri-County Youth* and *Hoerner* with Esselman v. Job Serv. N.D., 548 N.W.2d 400 (N.D.1996), where an addiction counselor was verbally attacked, intimidated, and scapegoated by her colleagues and superiors. She claimed that the stressful conditions of her work environment caused her to suffer medical symptoms, including migraine headaches, leading to her resignation. The court held that Esselman had voluntarily quit her job without good cause, as her employer had made a "good faith attempt" to resolve the situation by arranging a retreat and using an employee assistance program. "An employee does not have good cause attributable to an employer to quit a job merely because the employee experiences

irreconcilable differences with coworkers or is frustrated or dissatisfied with working conditions."

3. Racial, as well as sexual, harassment may constitute good cause for voluntary termination of employment. See Curry v. Gatson, 376 S.E.2d 166 (W.Va. 1988).

(ii) Discharge for Misconduct

Pesce v. Board of Review
515 N.E.2d 849 (Ill. Ct. App. 1987).

■ PRESIDING JUSTICE SCARIANO delivered the opinion of the court:

Plaintiff, Barry Pesce, brought an administrative review action in the circuit court of Cook County, seeking review of a decision of the Illinois Department of Employment Security, Board of Review. The Board found, pursuant to section 602(A) of the Unemployment Insurance Act, that plaintiff was ineligible for unemployment insurance benefits because he was discharged from his job for misconduct. The circuit court reversed the Board's decision, and the Board has appealed, contending that its decision was supported by the manifest weight of the evidence and was in accordance with the law.

Plaintiff was employed as a driver of a medicar, used to transport patients to and from hospitals and nursing homes, for A.C.S. Medicar (employer) for approximately three and one-half months. During that time, he was involved in four accidents with the employer's vehicle. Each of these accidents occurred while plaintiff was backing up and resulted in plaintiff striking a stationary object with the vehicle. There were no patients in the medicar at the times of these accidents and none of the accidents caused severe damage. Plaintiff was suspended from work for three days after the first accident, paid the employer for the damage to the medicar after the second accident, and was again suspended after the third accident. After the fourth accident, the plaintiff was discharged because his involvement in the accidents violated a company rule.

Plaintiff's application for unemployment insurance benefits was denied by a claims adjudicator and plaintiff filed an appeal of that determination. An administrative hearing was conducted at which plaintiff appeared pro se. The employer was represented by Steve Rabin, vice president of operations. Rabin testified that the employer felt that there was no choice but to terminate the plaintiff because he had some type of problem when he was backing up the medicar. Rabin also stated that plaintiff was a member of a union while working for the employer and that a union rule provided for discharge after two accidents. When asked by the hearing referee whether the employee is allowed leeway for accidents that are not his fault, Rabin answered affirmatively and indicated that was why plaintiff was discharged after four accidents rather than after two. The hearing referee issued a decision denying benefits, finding plaintiff ineligible because his actions constituted misconduct within the meaning of the Act.

Plaintiff thereafter retained counsel and appealed the referee's decision to the Board. The Board affirmed the denial of benefits pursuant to section 602 A of the Act. Plaintiff subsequently filed a complaint in the circuit court for administrative review of the Board's determination. The circuit court reversed the Board's decision finding it to be incorrect as a matter of law. On appeal the Board contends that the circuit court erred. * * *

Every justifiable discharge does not disqualify the discharged employee from receiving unemployment benefits. An employee's conduct may be such that the employer may properly discharge him. Such conduct may not, however, constitute "misconduct connected with the work" which disqualifies him from receiving unemployment benefits. Misconduct has been defined as conduct evincing such wilful or wanton disregard of an employer's interests as is found in deliberate violations or disregard of standards of behavior which the employer had the right to expect of his employee, or in carelessness or negligence of such degree or recurrence as to manifest equal culpability, wrongful intent or evil design, or to show an intentional and substantial disregard of the employer's interests or of the employee's duties and obligations to his employer.

Every violation of a company rule will not constitute misconduct. The rule must be a reasonable rule governing the conduct or performance of an employee. In addition to the existence of such a rule, it must be shown that the breach of the rule is deliberate or its equivalent, as indicated in the above definition.

In this case, the record shows that the plaintiff had four accidents with stationary objects while backing up in the employer's vehicle. There is no evidence of deliberate conduct or a wilful or wanton disregard of the employer's interests. Similarly, we do not find that the plaintiff's conduct can be characterized as carelessness or negligence of such a degree or recurrence as to manifest equal culpability, wrongful intent or evil design, or to show an intentional and substantial disregard of the employer's interests or of the plaintiff's duties and obligations to his employer. We hold that a finding of misconduct is improper where there was no showing of an unreasonable and improper course of conduct from which could be imputed a lack of proper regard for the employer's interests.

The Board states in its reply brief that plaintiff was discharged due to his inability to back up the employer's vehicle. The Board then goes on to equate the plaintiff's inability to back up the vehicle with gross indifference to the interests of his employer, thereby disqualifying him from receiving unemployment insurance benefits. We do not agree with this conclusion. The Board argues that a finding of misconduct is necessary to avoid the potential of his injuring or aggravating an existing injury of one of the patients who relied on him for transportation. This is, however, an erroneous construction of section 602 A of the Act. As previously stated, although the employer's discharge of the plaintiff may have been proper, there is insufficient evidence in the record to establish that plaintiff's conduct constituted misconduct under the statute.

For the foregoing reasons, we hold that the circuit court's reversal of the Board's decision finding it to be incorrect as a matter of law was proper. The judgment of the circuit court of Cook County is affirmed.

Notes and Questions

1.　The common cases about discharge for misconduct concern breach of employer rules. The unemployment insurance administrators evaluate the validity of the rule and the reasonableness of its application. The unemployment insurance system thus gives us a body of law on the subject of whether a discharge was "for misconduct." That body of law would become relevant if discharges themselves ever became administratively or judicially reviewable. Wrongful discharge is the subject of Chapter 10.

An example of a "run-of-the-mill" discharge-for-misconduct case is MacLeod v. Commissioner of Div. of Emp. & Training, 742 N.E.2d 96 (Mass. App.Ct. 2001), where the court affirmed the denial of unemployment insurance benefits to a former Filene's department store "beauty advisor" who was fired for seeking and receiving credit on merchandise that she had received "gratis." She had previously signed a copy of the employee handbook, which stated that gratis merchandise was for employee use only and could not be returned to the store for credit. The handbook also stated that "any deviations from [this policy] will result in disciplinary action up to and including termination." This evidence, coupled with her lack of credibility at the hearing, where she testified that she had purchased the merchandise herself, was sufficient to conclude that she had the requisite intent to violate employer rules.

Another "run-of-the-mill" discharge-for-misconduct case concerns failure of an employee to meet the employer's absenteeism written policy. In Wisconsin Dept. of Workforce Develop. v. Wisconsin Lab. & Indus. Rev. Comm. & Beres, 914 N.W. 2d 625 (Wis. 2018), the Wisconsin Supreme Court held that if an employee violates an employer's written absenteeism policy, that employee engages in "misconduct" and is not eligible for unemployment compensation benefits. More specifically, a written absenteeism policy stated that an employee can be terminated for incurring a single absence during his/her probationary period if he/she does not provide prior notice of the absence. Beres (the former employee) incurred a single absence due to "flu-like" symptoms, did not provide prior notice that she would be absent, and was fired. Even though the Wisconsin statute was more lenient in defining what constitutes misconduct for unemployment compensation purposes, the Court concluded that the pertinent Wisconsin statute (Wis. Stat. § 104.05(e)) allows employers to create and enforce their own written absenteeism policy more strict than the statute, and that if an employee acknowledges receipt of that policy and violates that written policy, the violation constitutes "misconduct."

A Pennsylvania court found no violation of the free exercise clause of the First Amendment when a parochial school teacher, dismissed for violating church doctrine, was denied unemployment benefits because of her misconduct in marrying a non-Catholic man previously divorced from a Catholic woman. Bishop Leonard Regional Catholic Sch. v. Unemployment Comp. Bd. of Rev., 593 A.2d 28 (Pa.Cmwlth.1991), appeal denied, 600 A.2d 540 (Pa.1991), cert. denied, 503 U.S. 985 (1992).

2. Cases interpreting statutes using the "willful misconduct" standard sometimes yield different results from "just cause" cases. See, e.g., Wedgewood v. Director of Div. of Emp. Sec., 514 N.E.2d 680 (Mass.App.Ct. 1987) (repeatedly sleeping on the job is not "willful misconduct"). Which standard better serves the policy goals of unemployment insurance?

Under the willful misconduct standard, the Supreme Court of Montana held that an employee must show "intentional disregard of the employer's expectation." Negligence will not suffice to cut off unemployment benefits. LaVe v. Montana State Dep't of Lab. & Indus., 780 P.2d 189 (Mont.1989).

3. In Western Dairymen Co-op., Inc. v. Board of Rev., 684 P.2d 647 (Utah 1984), a cheese processing plant instituted a new rule requiring all workers to be clean shaven, after a state health inspector complained of employees' misuse and disuse of beard nets. Five days after the new policy announcement, thirty-five employees reported to work unshaven and were subsequently discharged. The court upheld the denial of UI benefits, holding that when an employee is fired for violating a company rule as to dress, grooming, or hygiene, the "most important factor in determining wrongful discharge is whether the rule has a reasonable business purpose, i.e., whether it advances the employer's interests, or is simply a [rule which] . . . operates only as a condition of employment and is unrelated to actual job needs or performance." Here, the court decided that, in view of the employer's need to maintain high standards of sanitation, and in the absence of full employee cooperation in the past, the grooming rule was reasonable. Compare *Western Dairymen* to the grooming issues discussed in Chapter 7. Is the right rule that the employee should have no right to prevent discharge for this reason but a right to collect unemployment insurance benefits?

4. Rudy Castaneda, employed as a social worker at a boys ranch, did his supervisor a favor by accompanying a resident juvenile to a hearing. While at the hearing, Castaneda received a call from his fiancée who believed she was miscarrying and who was without transportation. After informing the juvenile's attorney and his case worker of a personal emergency and determining that the juvenile's presence was not necessary at the hearing, Castaneda returned the juvenile to the ranch and went to his fiancée. When Castaneda appeared at the ranch the next morning, he declined to discuss the details of the emergency with his supervisor, preferring to discuss it instead with his former supervisor or with the assistant director of the ranch. The assistant director fired him less than a week later. The state court of appeals found that Castaneda's absence was due to urgent domestic responsibility and rejected the argument that he did not have a "legally sufficient relationship" with his fiancée for the miscarriage to qualify as a "domestic" matter. Castaneda v. Arizona Dep't of Econ. Sec., 815 P.2d 418 (Ariz.Ct.App.1991).

5. A nursing assistant was discharged because he refused to work with AIDS patients for fear of acquiring the virus. The court affirmed the denial of unemployment benefits, stating that the claimant, "despite his training, harbored unnecessary fears and misconceptions concerning AIDS. * * * A subjective belief alone does not constitute good cause for actions that would otherwise disqualify a claimant from benefits." The court added: "Because an employer has the right to make reasonable changes in an employee's duties, only when an employee's refusal to employ such directive directly threatens that person's health or safety will we refuse to hold that the employee's actions were willful misconduct." Dougherty v. Unemployment Comp. Bd. of Rev., 686 A.2d 53 (Pa. Cmwlth. 1996).

6. After several warnings, an assistant professor of geography was dismissed because he had made insufficient efforts to complete his Ph.D. work. The college opposed award of unemployment insurance benefits, saying the termination was for misconduct. A Pennsylvania court agreed with the college. Millersville State Coll. v. Commonwealth, 335 A.2d 857 (Pa.Cmwlth.1975). Do you agree? Is unsatisfactory performance the same thing as misconduct?

7. Opara v. Carnegie Textile Co., 498 N.E.2d 485 (Ohio Ct.App.1985), held that an employee fired for using anti-Semitic epithets against a co-worker who was Jewish had no claim to benefits under an unemployment insurance scheme denying benefits to those terminated for just cause:

> [S]ome language can be so disruptive and provocative that the employer's ability to maintain a productive environment is severely compromised. * * * [The employee's] extreme anti-Semitic remarks were presumably intended to provoke a bitter response. They successfully disrupted employment that day and were likely to impair his working relationship for an extended interval with the subjects of his attack. The employer was justified in discharging him to alleviate the problem he created.

Opara concerned a private company. Would the result have been different if the employer had been a government agency?

8. Fred Weller was fired for violating the company drug use policy after failing a test for marijuana in which his urine sample was determined to contain cannabinoids at a concentration of 60 ng/ml. The court held that the termination was not for work-related misconduct and should not disqualify Weller from unemployment benefits. The court found that the employer could not demonstrate that Weller was ever impaired while on the job, and that it "introduced no evidence whatever to show that its 50 ng/ml value for a positive test result was anything more than its own arbitrarily established figure" or that the 60 ng/ml level of Weller's sample was a result of direct intentional inhalation rather than passive inhalation of second-hand smoke. As a result, the court found that where the only evidence of misconduct was a "positive" urinalysis which did not indicate impairment of the employee's abilities at work, the employee was not terminated for misconduct which would disqualify him from unemployment benefits, although he was unlikely to have a wrongful discharge claim. Weller v. Arizona Dep't of Econ. Sec., 860 P.2d 487 (Ariz.Ct.App.1993).

However, in Desilet v. Glass Dr., 132 P.3d 412 (Idaho 2006), the court affirmed the denial of unemployment benefits for a glazier who was discharged for failing a marijuana drug test, finding that he was "discharged for misconduct in connection with his employment." In response to Desilet's claim that he used drugs only during non-working hours, the court stated that off-duty conduct can be considered work-related if it is "so closely connected with the business interests of the employer as to warrant disqualification for unemployment benefits." The court concluded that Glass Doctor's "interest in keeping its employees who work with glass and drive company vehicles not only unimpaired, but free from illegal drugs is the type of closely connected legitimate business interest" warranting the disqualification of UI benefits.

9. Is failing or refusing to take a drug test "misconduct"? Compare Glide Lumber Products Co. v. Employment Division, 741 P.2d 907 (Or.Ct.App. 1987) (no; minority rule) with Johnson v. Department of Emp. Sec., 782 P.2d 965 (Utah Ct.App.1989) (yes; majority rule).

10. Hafner was hired by DuBray Land Services as a right-of-way agent to purchase easement rights. While employed by DuBray, Hafner applied for a job with Conoco, obtained the job, took a physical examination, was terminated because of the results of the physical, and filed a discrimination claim against Conoco. DuBray assigned Hafner to work on the Conoco account. Hafner did not tell DuBray that he was in litigation against Conoco. The court held that DuBray, when it discovered the conflict of interest, discharged Hafner for misconduct, so Hafner was ineligible for unemployment insurance benefits. Hafner v. Montana Dep't of Labor & Indus., 929 P.2d 233 (Mont.1996). For the disability discrimination litigation that followed, see Hafner v. Conoco, Inc., 977 P.2d 330 (Mont.1999).

11. Claimant was fired for pleading no contest to a domestic violence felony. The dismissal was not for "misconduct in connection with work," and thus should not disqualify the claimant from Unemployment Insurance benefits. "There was no proof that [the employee] intentionally or knowingly acted to harm [the employer's] interests or that he, in fact, harmed his employer's interests." Baldor Elec. Co. v. Arkansas Emp. Sec. Dep't, 27 S.W.3d 771 (Ark.Ct.App.2000).

12. Going to work with a hockey stick and behaving in a violent and threatening manner as a result of a bipolar disorder is misconduct, disqualifying the dismissed employee from receiving unemployment compensation. Johns Hopkins Univ. v. Board of Labor, Lic. & Regs., 761 A.2d 350 (Md.App.2000).

13. AnMed Health fired Pamela Crowe because she refused to comply with its policy requiring her to get a flu shot. Crowe's daughter had died at age 25, possibly from a disease triggered by a flu shot. Held: Crowe was not

discharged for cause so is eligible for unemployment benefits. AnMed Health v. South Carolina Dep't of Employment & Workforce, 743 S.E.2d 854 (S.C. Ct. App. 2013).

Amador v. Unemployment Insurance Appeals Board

677 P.2d 224 (Cal. 1984).

■ BIRD, CHIEF JUSTICE.

Is a worker disqualified from collecting unemployment insurance benefits when she has been discharged for wilfully refusing to perform work which she reasonably and in good faith believed would jeopardize the health of others?

Nelly Amador appeals from a judgment of the superior court rejecting her petition for a writ of mandate. She sought to compel the Unemployment Insurance Appeals Board (board) to vacate its ruling that she was ineligible for unemployment insurance benefits because she had been discharged for "misconduct."

The San Mateo County (Chope) Community Hospital hired Nelly Amador as a histotechnician in May of 1976. Histotechnicians prepare tissue samples for microscopic analysis by pathologists, physicians who specialize in the interpretation and diagnosis of changes in tissues caused by disease. During Amador's tenure at Chope, she was one of two histotechnicians on the staff.

Amador completed her training in histology at Stanford University. She was licensed as a histotechnician by the American Society of Clinical Pathologists. Prior to her employment at Chope, she worked as a histotechnician for about four years at hospitals operated by Stanford University and by Oxford University.

Beginning about six months after Amador started work at Chope, two doctors asked her on several occasions to perform a procedure known as "grosscutting." Grosscutting consists of the selection and removal of small tissue samples of approximately one centimeter in breadth from organs or other large (gross) specimens removed by a doctor from a patient. On the basis of a microscopic examination of these samples, a pathologist diagnoses the patient's condition.

Amador declined to perform grosscutting on tissue removed from live patients. She explained that in her view grosscutting exceeded her capabilities as a histotechnician. She believed that the accuracy of a pathologist's diagnosis depends in large part on the selection and cutting of the small samples. And, in turn, a patient's life and health could hinge on the quality of the diagnosis. In her view, such life-and-death matters should be handled by physicians or by specially trained technicians. This view accorded with her experience at Stanford and Oxford, where histotechnicians had not been permitted to perform grosscutting.

Amador did not object to grosscutting on organs taken from cadavers. Nor did she decline to process small-size specimens selected and removed from live patients by doctors.

Until September of 1978, Chope respected Amador's objection. Her supervisors rated her performance "standard" in a May 1978 evaluation.

Eventually, however, the other histotechnician complained about having to do all of the grosscutting work. On September 29, Amador was again asked to perform the work. She refused. A Chope official warned her that she could be subject to discipline. She maintained her position and was suspended from work for two days in October. After a full adversary hearing, the county civil service commission (commission) upheld the suspension on February 2, 1979.

Sometime before the hearing, Amador contacted three outside pathologists. One, a professor of pathology at Stanford, had been a teacher of hers. Another had worked with her at the Stanford University Medical Center. The third was an official of the American Society of Clinical Pathologists, from which Amador held her license as a histotechnician. These three physicians supported her refusal to perform grosscutting.

In the week following the decision of the commission, Amador was repeatedly ordered to perform grosscutting or face discharge. Standing on her past experience and on the opinions of the outside pathologists, she continued to refuse. On February 26, Chope discharged her for incompetence and insubordination.

Shortly after her discharge, Amador applied for unemployment benefits. Chope objected, arguing that Amador was ineligible under section 1256 of the code, which provides that employees discharged for "misconduct" are disqualified for benefits. The claims interviewer rejected Chope's argument and awarded benefits.

Chope pursued an administrative appeal. At the hearing, it relied primarily on the fact-finding report of the commission, which had found that Chope's orders were "reasonable" and that Amador had committed "insubordination" in disobeying them. In addition, Amador's supervisor and another Chope official testified regarding her repeated refusals to perform the work in spite of warnings of possible disciplinary action.

Amador gave uncontroverted testimony as to the reasons for her refusal. She presented signed statements by two of the outside pathologists, and testified that the third was available to testify by phone. The statements set forth the doctors' opinions that histotechnicians should not perform grosscutting, and indicated that Amador had consulted with them regarding those opinions.

The administrative law judge (ALJ) ruled that Amador had committed misconduct by repeatedly and wilfully violating her employer's orders. He gave collateral estoppel effect to the commission's findings on the reasonableness of Chope's orders and on Amador's "insubordination." He concluded that her deliberate violation of a reasonable order constituted misconduct within the meaning of section 1256.

Amador appealed to the board, which held that the evidence was sufficient to support the ruling on misconduct. She then petitioned the superior court for a writ of mandate. After an independent review of the record, the court denied the petition.

"An individual is disqualified for unemployment compensation benefits if the director finds that he or she left his or her most recent work voluntarily without good cause or that he or she has been discharged for misconduct connected with his or her most recent work." (§ 1256.)

The term "misconduct," as used in the code, is limited to "conduct evincing such wilful or wanton disregard of an employer's interests as is found in deliberate violations or disregard of standards of behavior which the employer has the right to expect of his employee, or in carelessness or negligence of such degree or recurrence as to manifest equal culpability, wrongful intent or evil design, or to show an intentional and substantial disregard of the employer's interests or of the employee's duties and obligations to his employer. On the other hand mere inefficiency, unsatisfactory conduct, failure in good performance as the result of inability or incapacity, inadvertencies or ordinary negligence in isolated instances, or good faith errors in judgment or discretion are not to be deemed 'misconduct' within the meaning of the statute."

The policy of the code is to provide benefits to "persons unemployed through no fault of their own." (§ 100.) "Accordingly, fault is the basic element to be considered in interpreting and applying the code sections on unemployment compensation." The determination of fault is not concluded by a finding that the discharge was justified. The claimant's conduct must evince culpability or bad faith. "The conduct may be harmful to the employer's interests and justify the employee's discharge; nevertheless, it evokes the disqualification for unemployment insurance benefits only if it is wilful, wanton or equally culpable."

* * *

A claimant may not be denied benefits solely on the basis of a "good faith error in judgment."

Although this case involves a discharge for "misconduct," the law concerning voluntary terminations for "good cause" is also relevant. If a claimant's reasons for refusing work constitute "good cause" sufficient to justify resignation, it follows that they should also justify the less drastic step of refusing a work assignment.

In view of the statutory objective of "reducing the hardship of unemployment" "the concept of 'good cause' cannot be arbitrarily limited; the board must take account of 'real circumstances, substantial reasons, objective conditions, palpable forces that operate to produce correlative results, adequate excuses that will bear the test of reason, just grounds for action, and always the element of good faith.' "

* * *

Applying the substantial evidence test, this court concludes that the record lacks sufficient evidence to support the denial of benefits.

* * *

This court's duty "[t]o construe the code liberally to benefit the unemployed" precludes the adoption of a draconian rule that would require an employee who reasonably and in good faith fears harm to herself or others to sacrifice her right to unemployment benefits because she has acted on that concern. Accordingly, this court holds that a worker who has been discharged for wilfully refusing to perform work which she reasonably and in good faith believed would jeopardize the health of others has not committed "misconduct" within the meaning of section 1256. * * *

The judgment is reversed. The trial court is directed to issue its writ of mandate ordering respondent to pay to appellant the unemployment insurance benefits withheld.

■ MOSK, JUSTICE, dissenting.

I dissent. Apparently everyone in the administrative and judicial hierarchy is out of step but my colleagues.

* * *

In view of the * * * record, reviewed over and over by five successive layers of administrative and judicial authority, I cannot allow sympathy for one who is denied unemployment benefits to outweigh the well established principle that misconduct and insubordination should not be rewarded. This employee was ordered to perform tasks that, as the trial court found, were within her job description. She received numerous warnings, not the least of which was from the civil service commission, that in refusing to follow reasonable orders of her employer she was being insubordinate. Nevertheless she persisted in prescribing her own rules of conduct.

* * *

There are occasions when stubbornness in devotion to even misguided principle is to be respected. That is euphemistically called "good faith error in judgment."

Under these circumstances, however, the law does not permit a recalcitrant employee to dictate employment conditions in conflict with the job description pursuant to which she was hired.

The judgment should be affirmed.

NOTES AND QUESTIONS

1. In Cargal v. Review Bd., 428 N.E.2d 85 (Ind. Ct. App. 1981), the court denied UI benefits to a former claims deputy for the State Employment Security Division who refused for religious reasons to be Employment Service Interviewer for liquor, movie, and dancing establishments. The court was influenced by the fact that Mr. Cargal had known the requirements of the job when he obtained it (although he had worked successfully for five months interviewing for "sales, domestics, and laundry" before being given the new assignment).

In Employment Div. v. Smith, 494 U.S. 872 (1990), the Supreme Court vacated an Oregon Supreme Court decision in favor of UI eligibility for drug and alcohol abuse rehabilitation counselors who were discharged after ingesting peyote during a religious ceremony of the Native American Church. The Supreme Court noted that possession of peyote is a felony in Oregon. *Smith* was legislatively overruled by the Religious Freedom Restoration Act (RFRA) of 1993, 42 U.S.C. §§ 2000bb et seq. The Act declares that *Smith* "virtually eliminated the requirement that the government justify burdens on religious exercise imposed by laws neutral toward religion." It provides that the "compelling interest test" should apply to all cases where the free exercise of religion is substantially burdened. The Act was declared partially unconstitutional in City of Boerne v. Flores, 521 U.S. 507 (1997); the RFRA still applies to federal acts, as confirmed by Gonzales v. O Centro Espirita Beneficente Uniao Do Vegetal, 546 U.S. 418 (2006).

2. A referee determined that a fired public schoolteacher was ineligible for unemployment benefits because her wearing of a religious head wrap was insubordination and thus misconduct. The teacher was a member of "the original African Hebrew Israelites out of Ethiopia." The Supreme Court of Mississippi held that wearing the religious head wrap was constitutionally protected religious and cultural expression, and so she should receive UI benefits. Mississippi Emp. Sec. Comm'n v. McGlothin, 556 So.2d 324 (Miss.1990) (5–4), cert. denied, 498 U.S. 879 (1990).

3. After nine weeks on the job, Victoria Genier was dismissed as a secretary-receptionist by Oral Surgery Associates. The employer contested her claim for unemployment insurance benefits on the ground that she misrepresented her qualifications when she obtained the job. At her interview (there was no written application form), she had named previous jobs but had not said she had held them only on a temporary basis. Also, she had not volunteered the information that she had recently been terminated by another employer. The Employment Security Board said Genier's "misrepresentations" had evidenced "substantial disregard for the employer's business interests." The Vermont Supreme Court reversed, saying a job applicant is "under no duty to disclose more than she was asked. The information she gave was accurate." Thus unemployment insurance benefits could not be denied. Genier v. Department of Emp. Sec., 438 A.2d 1116 (Vt.1981). But see Wilson v. Mortgage Resource Center, Inc., 888 N.W. 2d 452 (Minn. 2016) (finding that false statements when applying for job is misconduct under exclusive definition provided under state unemployment insurance statute, and therefore employee is not eligible for unemployment insurance when she lost her job on that basis).

4.   An HIV-positive salesperson lied to his supervisor about the reason he needed to miss work one day a month. He said that he was working a job on the side, but the real reason for his absences was to receive treatment for his medical condition. A Florida court ruled the employee's actions did not amount to misconduct, holding he did not act "willfully, wantonly or with such a substantial disregard of his employer's interests so as to warrant the denial of benefits." Hummer v. Unemployment Appeals Comm'n, 573 So.2d 135 (Fla.Dist.Ct.App.1991).

5.   In Colorado, alcoholism is not "misconduct" if the condition has progressed to a point where drinking has become non-volitional. See City & County of Denver v. Industrial Comm'n, 756 P.2d 373 (Colo.1988).

6.   Often, the determination of initial eligibility for unemployment benefits reaches an official conclusion about the circumstances of the former employee's departure from work: whether the employee committed the misconduct; whether the employer enforced its rules fairly; what the employer's motivation was. For the argument that that determination should carry significant weight in a later proceeding by the employee for reinstatement or back pay under a collective bargaining agreement, see Stephen A. Mazurak, Effects of Unemployment Compensation Proceedings on Related Labor Litigation, 64 Marq. L. Rev. 133 (1980). See also Note, Issue Preclusion: Unemployment Compensation Determinations and Section 301 Suits, 31 Case W. Res. L. Rev. 862 (1981). If state law actions for wrongful discharge proliferate, see Chapter 10, questions will arise about the relevance and admissibility of unemployment insurance eligibility decisions in those proceedings. Currently, many companies do not contest unemployment insurance claims. Also in some states it is relatively easy for former workers to establish eligibility, since the consequence is "only" 26 weeks of benefits. If UI eligibility becomes the first step toward proving wrongful discharge (with the possibility of large money damage awards or even reinstatement), will employers invest more resources in contesting UI claims? Will more workers then need legal representation to establish their claim?

Sauerland v. Florida Unemployment Appeals Commission

923 So.2d 1240 (Fla. Dist. Ct. App. 2006).

■ LEWIS, J.

Claimant, Jason Sauerland, appeals a final order of the Unemployment Appeals Commission, which affirmed the appeals referee's ruling that claimant was disqualified from receiving unemployment compensation benefits. * * * Claimant contends that the Commission erred in ruling that he was discharged for misconduct connected with work. Concluding that the referee's findings are supported by competent, substantial evidence and that the Commission properly interpreted the law, we affirm.

Claimant, who worked as a juvenile detention officer for the employer, was required to perform ten-minute visual checks or rounds of each room he was assigned to monitor and to record those checks in a log book. On September 28, 2004, claimant made log entries at 3:00 a.m., 3:30 a.m., 3:40 a.m., and 3:50 a.m. However, a videotape of claimant's shift showed that claimant did not do rounds at 3:00 a.m., 3:40 a.m., or 3:50 a.m. As the appeals referee found, "Comparison of the content of the tapes and the claimant's log entries revealed at least two logged rounds that did not occur." Claimant admitted to making entries in the log book for rounds that did not occur and did not contest the accuracy of the employer's records. Claimant's supervisor informed claimant that falsification of official records constituted a critical offense that would result in termination. Claimant testified that he was aware of the employer's policy concerning the necessity to conduct rounds every ten minutes, that he attended an employee orientation, and that he received an employee handbook containing his job requirements.

The appeals referee concluded that claimant was discharged for misconduct connected with work and was, thus, disqualified from receiving unemployment compensation benefits. The Commission affirmed the referee's ruling. This appeal followed.

"Misconduct" for purposes of unemployment compensation benefits is defined in section 443.036(29), Florida Statutes (2004), which provides:

> Misconduct includes, but is not limited to, the following, which may not be construed in pari materia with each other:
>
> (a) Conduct demonstrating willful or wanton disregard of an employer's interests and found to be a deliberate violation or disregard of the standards of behavior which the employer has a right to expect of his or her employee; or
>
> (b) Carelessness or negligence to a degree or recurrence that manifests culpability, wrongful intent, or evil design or shows an intentional and substantial disregard of the employer's interests or of the employee's duties and obligations to his or her employer.
>
> Whether a claimant commits misconduct connected with work is a question of law. An appeals referee's findings of fact must be accepted if supported by competent, substantial evidence.
>
> [D]ishonesty is and should be grounds for dismissal and denial of benefits. . . . * * *

* * *

Here, * * * competent, substantial evidence supports the appeals referee's findings. The referee specifically found that claimant was observed making his rounds at intervals in excess of ten minutes and that claimant's log entries revealed at least two rounds that did not occur. Claimant admitted to making entries in the log book for rounds that did not occur. Claimant also testified that he was aware of the employer's policy concerning the necessity to conduct rounds every ten minutes, that he attended an employee orientation, and that he received an employee handbook containing his job requirements.

While the dissent relies upon the rule of law that misconduct sufficient to constitute disqualification from receipt of benefits usually involves repeated violations of explicit policies after several warnings, the cases it cites in support of that proposition are distinguishable from the instant case in that none of them involved dishonesty. See Saunders v. Unemployment Appeals Comm'n, 888 So. 2d 69 (Fla. 4th DCA 2004) (holding that the claimant's conduct in leaving children at a child care center unsupervised in order to receive emergency medical treatment did not constitute misconduct connected with work); Riveras v. Unemployment Appeals Comm'n, 884 So. 2d 1143 (Fla. 2d DCA 2004) (holding that the claimant's act in allowing a customer to draw funds from checking and savings accounts opened the previous day in violation of the employer's policy constituted a single act of poor judgment, not misconduct connected with work); Ash v. Fla. Unemployment Appeals Comm'n, 872 So. 2d 400 (Fla. 1st DCA 2004) (holding that the claimant's failure to correct her timecard constituted an isolated instance of poor judgment); Thomas v. United Parcel Serv., Inc., 864 So. 2d 567, 570 (Fla. 2d DCA 2004) (holding that the claimant's refusal to submit to a search of his bag at work may have been poor judgment but was not misconduct connected with work).

The dissent also relies upon the fact that claimant performed some rounds at seven-minute intervals. However, while claimant made log entries at 3:00 a.m., 3:30 a.m., 3:40 a.m., and 3:50 a.m., the tapes revealed that claimant did not do rounds at 3:00 a.m., 3:40 a.m., or 3:50 a.m. Whether claimant made rounds close to those times does not serve to mitigate claimant's knowing misrepresentation in the log book. Claimant was aware that the ten-minute rounds were a critical part of his job. Claimant's supervisor also informed him that falsification of official records constituted a critical offense that would result in termination. Although the dissent equates claimant's action in falsifying the log book to an act of poor judgment, we cannot agree that claimant's wilful disregard of the employer's interests was anything other than misconduct connected with work.

Accordingly, because the referee's findings are supported by competent, substantial evidence and because the Commission properly interpreted the law in ruling that claimant engaged in misconduct connected with work, the Commission's order is AFFIRMED.

■ ERVIN, J. dissenting.

I respectfully dissent. In my judgment, the employee's conduct which resulted in his discharge was an instance of poor judgment rather than the "willful or wanton disregard of an employer's interests . . . found to be a deliberate violation or disregard of the standards of behavior which the employer has a right to expect of his or her employee," nor was it "[c]arelessness or negligence to a degree or recurrence that manifests culpability, wrongful intent, or evil design" that "shows an intentional and substantial disregard of the employer's interests or of the employee's duties and obligations to his or her employer," which is the required showing under * * * Florida Statutes (2004), to render an employee ineligible for unemployment compensation benefits based on misconduct.

* * *

At the telephone hearing before the appeals referee, the employee's supervisor admitted there had been no prior incidents involving the employee, nor had he been the subject of any warnings or disciplinary actions during his employment. The appeals referee ascertained that during orientation, staff are provided a copy of the handbook which they review with the human-resources staff at the facility. The ten-minute checks are stressed as a critical part of the job, and failure to meet the policy has severe consequences, including discharge. The supervisor explained there are thirteen rooms, each with windows, on the module assigned to the employee. The employee was required to look in each room every ten minutes, and note each check in a log book.

The employee acknowledged he had been informed that he could be discharged for failing to meet the employer's requirements, which he understood were mandated by the Florida Department of Juvenile Justice. The employee pointed out that he was discharged for a first offense, while on other occasions employees at the facility had received oral and written reprimands before termination of employment. The employer's representative stated the employee handbook lists offenses as minor, major, and critical; falsification of the log book is considered a critical offense which can result in immediate termination, because it is a state record. The representative further stated that such conduct "is considered a felony offense."

* * *

Whether a claimant commits misconduct connected with work is a question of law. When the alleged misconduct involves company policy, misconduct sufficient to constitute disqualification from receipt of unemployment benefits " 'usually involves repeated violations of explicit policies after several warnings.' "

To meet its burden of proving the employee was terminated for misconduct connected with work, "the employer must show more than an employee's inefficiency, unsatisfactory conduct, or failure to perform in the work-place." Actions which warrant an employee's discharge are not necessarily "sufficiently egregious, willful, or wanton to support a denial of unemployment benefits." * * *

Although the employer in this case may have had sufficient grounds to discharge the employee, I cannot agree that the employee was guilty of misconduct as would disqualify him from receipt of unemployment benefits within the meaning of section 443.036(29). The room checks at issue constituted a single instance of the employee's violation of the employer's policy, and, indeed, the evidence the appeals referee relied upon shows the employee performed some checks at seven-minute intervals, thus closer in time than the prescribed ten-minute intervals. One check exceeded the prescribed ten-minute interval, and that by only three minutes. Contrary to the view expressed in the majority's opinion, my review of the record does not establish that the employee failed to perform required checks. Rather, it appears the employee admitted making log entries for rounds that did not occur at precisely the time initialed in the logbook. The employee had no history of violating the policy, and had never before received a warning or reprimand. Under the circumstances, I am of the opinion the employee's conduct did not rise to such degree of egregious behavior that justifies his disqualification from receipt of unemployment compensation benefits.

Therefore, I conclude the Commission erred as a matter of law, and I would reverse the Commission's order and remand the case for a determination that the employee was not discharged for misconduct connected with work, thereby qualifying him to receive unemployment benefits.

NOTES AND QUESTIONS

1.   If the claimant in *Sauerland* had not falsified the log book (but still failed to make the visits at the required ten-minute intervals), do you think that the court would have still concluded that he was discharged for misconduct connected with work?

2.   Susan Medeiros was working as a restaurant hostess at a resort hotel, where she had been employed for over twenty years, when she placed her hands around a coworker's neck and shook her lightly for five seconds, blaming her for a change in the work schedule. Medeiros and the coworker had a good working relationship and a history of joking around with each other. Nevertheless, because of the employer's "zero tolerance for violence in the workplace" policy, Medeiros was fired. The court upheld a denial of unemployment benefits, stating that her conduct demonstrated a willful or wanton disregard for the standards of behavior that the employer had a right to expect and thus constituted misconduct connected with work. Medeiros v. Hawaii Dep't of Lab. & Indus. Rels., 118 P.3d 1201 (Hawaii 2005).

3.   In In re Claim of Guibert, 679 N.Y.S.2d 452 (App.Div.1998), an AIDS program coordinator at a community center was discharged for violating the employer's confidentiality policy by divulging information about a prospective client. The court held that the employee engaged in disqualifying

misconduct, as her actions were contrary to the employer's known policy and potentially detrimental to the employer's best interests.

4. An employee's acts may constitute misconduct even if there is no written policy explicitly barring such behavior. See, e.g., Brown v. National Am. Univ., 686 N.W.2d 329 (Minn.Ct.App.2004), where an administrative assistant at a university was fired for borrowing money from students after repeated warnings.

However, in Nelson v. Department of Emp. Sec., 655 P.2d 242 (Wash. 1982), the claimant, a cashier, pleaded guilty to shoplifting and was discharged. The Washington Supreme Court said that since the off-the-job misconduct violated no rule of the employer, the discharge was not for "misconduct connected with his or her work," and therefore she could receive unemployment insurance benefits.

5. A claimant may be eligible for UI benefits even if her conduct causes the employer to suffer significant losses. Sarita Riveras, a teller supervisor who had been employed by Atlantic State Bank for almost three years, was discharged after she allowed a customer to withdraw funds from accounts opened the previous day, resulting in a $6000 loss for her employer. Because the accounts had been opened with counter checks, bank policy required a ten-day hold on the accounts before any withdrawals to assure that the checks had cleared. The court ruled that even though Ms. Riveras's mistake cost her employer a significant amount of money, that fact alone does not transform her isolated lapse of judgment into "wanton disregard" of her employer's interests or "negligence to a degree * * * that manifests culpability, wrongful intent, or evil design or shows an intentional and substantial disregard of the employer's interests or of the employee's duties and obligations" to the employer. The court added that "[i]nefficiency, unsatisfactory conduct, inability, inadvertence, and ordinary negligence do not constitute misconduct connected with work." Riveras v. Unemployment Appeals Comm'n, 884 So.2d 1143 (Fla.Dist.Ct.App.2004).

c. CONTINUING ELIGIBILITY

As well as deciding who is initially eligible, the state must supervise "continuing eligibility." Statutes require benefit recipients to be "available" and not to refuse "suitable work." Usually claimants are required to report weekly to the state unemployment insurance office, but it is difficult to make sure that they are trying sufficiently hard to find work. Also, whereas the former employer is at least sometimes the adversary in the initial eligibility proceeding, no private adversary is available to contest continuing eligibility. Administrative and judicial decision-makers are responsible for verifying eligibility and either awarding benefits or disqualifying claimants for voluntary quit, discharge for misconduct, unavailability for work, or refusing suitable work.

(i) Availability

Petty v. University of Delaware

450 A.2d 392 (Del. 1982).

■ HORSEY, JUSTICE.

This appeal concerns whether an administrative board correctly determined that claimant-appellant was ineligible for unemployment compensation benefits because she was not "able to work" and "available for work" within the meaning of the Delaware Unemployment Compensation Law * * *.

Mercedes Petty, in her second month of pregnancy and while in the employ of the University of Delaware, experienced bleeding problems associated with her pregnancy. This resulted in her physician's advising her not to "lift, climb or stand for prolonged periods." Her doctor confirmed these restrictions on her activities in a letter to the University in which the doctor stated, "if the above conditions are involved in her job, I would recommend that she be moved to another department."

Ms. Petty's employment with the University consisted of custodial work. Her job classification required her to perform "heavy cleaning tasks" ranging from sweeping, vacuuming and window washing to moving furniture and handling bulk trash. Ms. Petty had been so employed for six years.

The University determined that Ms. Petty could not continue in her custodial work and that determination is not questioned. Ms. Petty asked if there were not some other work available for her at the University; but the University also determined that, given her medical restrictions, there was no other position available for which she was qualified. The University then placed Ms. Petty on a maternity leave of absence for the duration of her doctor's medical restrictions. Her leave was without pay (although certain of her employment benefits were continued) and, upon termination of her medical restrictions, Ms. Petty could return to work. She then applied for State unemployment compensation benefits.

Ms. Petty's application was initially denied by a claims officer, later approved by a referee, and finally denied by the Delaware Unemployment Insurance Appeal Board. The Board ruled that Ms. Petty was "not able to perform any job for which she was qualified and [thus] is ineligible for benefits until her medical restrictions are lifted." The Board's ruling was based on its construction of 19 Del. C. § 3314(3), which provides in pertinent part:

> An unemployed individual shall be eligible to receive benefits with respect to any week only if the Commission finds that he:
>
> . . .
>
> (3) Is able to work, and is available for work, and is actively seeking work. . . .

On appeal by Ms. Petty, Superior Court affirmed. The Court found the Board's ruling to be supported by substantial evidence and not erroneous as a matter of law.

* * *

The central issue, of course, is whether claimant, concededly unable to work as a custodian, was otherwise "able to work" and "available to work" during her remaining six months of pregnancy so as to be eligible for unemployment benefits under § 3314(3). We conclude that there was substantial evidence to support the Board's ultimate finding: that due to Ms. Petty's medical condition, she was "not able to perform any job for which she was qualified" by her training and experience.

The two quoted statutory terms, "able to work" and "available to work", though complementary, are not synonymous. Each has a separate meaning and must be satisfied for the award of benefits. Moreover, "the burden is on the claimant to establish his [or her] right to unemployment compensation."

An individual seeking unemployment benefits is "available" for work within the meaning of § 3314(3) only to the extent that she is willing, able and ready to accept employment which she has no good cause to refuse, that is, she is genuinely attached to the labor market. Superior Court correctly stated:

> The determination of 'availability' for unemployment compensation purposes is a subjective one [in the sense that] the ability of a particular employee to secure work must be measured by the skill of that employee in an identifiable labor market. In the case of pregnancy, an employee is available for work only to the extent that the conditions of her pregnancy do not present a medical barrier to the discharge of those duties for which she is trained and suited.

As so defined, the term "availability" for employment incorporates both the requirement of ability to work and qualification through skill, training or experience for a particular occupation, commonly expressed in terms of "an identifiable labor market."

From the evidence before it, the Board found claimant to be an employee who "due to physical condition, was unable to perform her normal job functions [because she was] prohibited from doing her normal job by her doctor." The Board also found that claimant lacked "training to do any type of secretarial work." Further, the Board, implicitly relying on its experience and expertise in cases of this nature, reasoned, "we can think of no job for which claimant was qualified which would eliminate standing for a prolonged period." From this, the Board concluded that "claimant, due to her physical condition, was simply not able, within the meaning of [19 Del. C. § 3314(3)] to perform any job function."

The Board's decision reflects understanding as well as proper application of the statutory requirements of § 3314(3) * * *. The Board properly focused on claimant's physical limitations due to her pregnancy illness, her education, training and experience and the labor market that was available for a person possessing her attributes. Clearly there was substantial evidence to support the Board's finding that claimant's lack of training or job experience with typing or shorthand effectively foreclosed her from "any type of secretarial work." Claimant's only testimony of experience in clerical-type work was that she had spent six months some time in the past as a bookstore clerk; and she acknowledged that such work required lifting and standing for lengthy periods of time. Hence, the Board's findings of fact outlined above being clearly supported by substantial evidence, must be deemed "conclusive" and be affirmed.

* * *

We find no merit to claimant's contention that the Board committed reversible error by unduly narrowing the job market for which claimant should have been considered to the University rather than the general labor market. We base this conclusion not only upon a fair reading of the Board's findings but also upon an examination of the transcript.

Finally, claimant makes a related argument that Superior Court committed legal error in too narrowly defining claimant's available labor market by stating that Ms. Petty had "become identified with a portion of the labor market which requires significant physical exertion." What the Court stated concerning claimant's availability for work in terms of the labor market was as follows:

> But, again, the claimant's medical limitations may be considered to the extent her occupational experience indicates that she has become identified with a portion of the labor market which requires significant physical exertion. With the exception of a limited typing ability, all of claimant's experience and aptitude has been in jobs requiring lifting, bending and prolonged standing.

The Court's statement in context was clearly appropriate and not legal error. Since claimant presented no evidence of other job skills beyond that recounted by the Court, the Court's conclusions are both factually and legally correct.

Affirmed.

NOTES AND QUESTIONS

1. In Glick v. Unemployment Ins. Appeals Bd., 591 P.2d 24 (Cal.1979), a California court held that Enid Ballantyne, a single mother of three and full-time law student at the University of California at Los Angeles, was "available for work." The "evidence shows that claimant could indeed balance full-time law school attendance—which allowed her to leave school as early as 2 p.m. two days a week and arrive as late as 11 a.m. two other days—with

a *substantial* array of suitable employment," including work at a movie theater. The court added:

> Given the "indispensable role which education plays in the modern industrial state" we cannot impose upon Ballantyne the Hobson's choice of the neglect of her professional education or the sacrifice of entitlement to benefits. Indeed, Ballantyne's full-time attendance at school comports ideally with the purposes of the Unemployment Insurance Code to provide benefits to persons unemployed through no fault of their own, and to reduce involuntary unemployment to a minimum. Ballantyne's training in law school will enable her most effectively to alleviate the hardships of involuntary unemployment, which she has suffered in the past, as well as to avoid the recurrence of such hardships in the future.

The dissent argued that accepting substantial employment in light of her school and family obligations would be a "herculean undertaking." Do you agree with the dissent that the majority opinion in effect "reduce[s] to a nullity the 'availability for work' requirement"?

In spite of *Glick*, full-time students have usually been deemed unavailable for work. See, e.g., McCoy v. Board of Rev., 885 A.2d 453 (N.J.Super.Ct.App.Div.2005). The claimant, a home health aide, decided to attend school full-time. She consequently sought to change her full-time work schedule so that it would accommodate her hours in school. Although work was available to the claimant, she was unable to accept it because of her class schedule. The court ruled that she was "not 'attached to the labor market' at crucial times, and therefore fail[ed] the availability test." "[T]o be available for work," the court reasoned, "the potential employee must demonstrate an ability and willingness to conform to a reasonable work schedule offered by the employer." However, a Nebraska student who attended classes only on Saturdays from 8 a.m. to 12 p.m. was deemed available for work. Lecuona v. Cramer, 714 N.W.2d 786 (Neb.Ct.App.2006).

2. A schoolteacher moved from Anchorage to an Alaskan village of approximately 100 people to be with her husband, a fisherman. She could not obtain work as a teacher in her town, as all teachers were hired only as married couples. The Supreme Court of Alaska found that although the claimant was willing to accept all suitable work, she was not "available for work" because she had moved from an area in which her services were in demand to a place "where work [was] nearly non-existent in her profession." Lind v. Employment Sec. Div., Dep't of Labor, 608 P.2d 6 (Alaska 1980).

3. A Mexican citizen who was no longer eligible to work in the United States sought benefits for work performed while she was legally qualified to work in California. However, a California appellate court found that she could not receive benefits because her lack of work authorization from the Immigration and Naturalization Service rendered her no longer available for work. Gutierrez v. Employment Dev. Dep't, 18 Cal.Rptr.2d 705 (Cal.App. 1993). Should today's involuntary inability to work preclude an alien from collecting benefits earned through work legally performed in the past?

4. Lawsuits have challenged state presumptions that mothers of newborns are not "available" for work and are therefore ineligible for unemployment insurance benefits. According to Elizabeth F. Thompson, Unemployment Compensation: Women and Children—The Denials, 46 U. Miami L. Rev. 751, 765–66 (1992):

> [An] obstacle for unemployment compensation claimants is meeting the three-prong definition of "availability"—the claimant must be "willing, able, and ready" to accept suitable employment.— "Willing" means that an employee must exercise due diligence to find a job. * * * "Able" generally means physically capable of handling the work. "Ready" means willing at once.—Of the three prongs, the "readiness" requirement poses the greatest obstacle to working mothers. This is because many working mothers with child-care responsibilities are not immediately ready to accept a job opportunity. Many cases interpreting the readiness requirement disqualify working mothers because they have restricted their hours and locations.

One such case is Azimi v. Virginia Emp. Comm'n, 57 Va. Cir. 1 (Va.Cir.Ct. 2001), where the claimant, due to childcare obligations, was able to work only from 3 p.m. to 12 a.m. The court held that she was unavailable for work, as the restrictions on her availability were "not usual or customary in the occupation[s]" (retail cashier positions) she sought. Should the definition of "availability" be expanded to accommodate the challenges of working parents?

5. An Ohio claimant with sleep apnea, upon directions of his physician, was not available to work from 9 p.m. to 5 a.m. The claimant's entire work history was in the factory or trucking business, industries that normally require evening or nighttime work. The court reversed a determination that he was unavailable for suitable work, stating the "degree of risk to the claimant's health" must be considered when deciding availability. Johnson v. Unemployment Comp. Rev. Comm'n, 742 N.E.2d 1231 (Ohio Com.Pl. 2000).

6. Is an individual "unemployed" while taking unpaid leave under the Family and Medical Leave Act (FMLA)? The Supreme Court of Texas, in Texas Workforce Commission v. Wichita County, 548 S.W. 3d 489 (Tex. 2018), found that the employee did not qualify as "unemployed" under the Texas Unemployment Compensation law while she was taking unpaid leave from her job. More specifically, the court found that she was "unemployed" because she clearly met the Act's definition of "totally unemployed"; that is, she was not "perform[ing] services for wages." Tex. Lab. Code § 201.091(a). On the other hand, in response to claims that its holding in the case led to an absurd result, the court pointed out that because eligibility for benefits requires more than unemployed status, it was expressing no opinion on whether an individual on FMLA leave is entitled to unemployment benefits (but at least hinted that most employees on unpaid FMLA leave will not be able to simultaneously obtain unemployment benefits).

(ii) Suitable Work

Lester v. Department of Employment Security
819 N.E.2d 1143 (Ill. App. Ct. 2004).

■ JUSTICE SOUTH delivered the opinion of the court.

Plaintiff Susan Lester filed a claim for unemployment benefits with the Illinois Department of Employment Security (IDES). After her claim was denied by an adjudicator and a referee, plaintiff appealed to the Board of Review (Board), which affirmed these decisions, stating that plaintiff was ineligible for benefits because she failed, without good cause, to accept suitable work offered by her former employer under section 603 of the Illinois Unemployment Insurance Act (Act). On administrative review, the circuit court affirmed the Board's decision. On appeal, plaintiff contends that the circuit court erred in affirming the Board's decision, as the Board's decision was based on manifestly erroneous factual findings and errors of law.

The following facts are undisputed. Plaintiff worked as a diverting coordinator for Purity Supermarketing, Inc. (Purity), for 7 1/2 years. She worked out of a regional office located in a Kmart store 1.3 miles from her home. On May 23, 2001, her position was eliminated for financial reasons. Prior to her termination, she had taken maternity leave, but she had returned to work in April 2001 and was working 35 hours per week at a salary of $70,200 per year. Between April and May 23, 2001, there was not enough work for plaintiff due to changes within the Kmart structure and her hours gradually diminished until she was only working three days per week at a lower salary. Upon plaintiff's termination, Purity gave her severance pay from May 23, 2001, through September 23, 2001, totaling $25,800. On July 18, 2001, Daniel Davis, director of partnership programs for Purity, offered plaintiff a position at Purity's other headquarters working out of a Dominick's supermarket, which was located 30 miles from her home. The offer included an annual salary of $70,200, plus benefits. Plaintiff refused the position.

On November 6, 2001, plaintiff filed for unemployment insurance. In her application for benefits, plaintiff stated that, although she felt she was competent to fill the job offered to her, she refused it because the salary was insufficient, as her workload would have increased two to three times, required farther travel to and from work, required her to supervise a staff, and did not include guaranteed quarterly bonuses. Karen McGrath, Purity's human resource representative, filed a response that the job offered to plaintiff was not substantially different from her former position, e.g., it was within 30 minutes of her old office, required 40 hours of work per week, paid $70,200 per year, plus two quarterly bonuses, and included insurance and all other benefits. In addition, McGrath stated that $50,000 to $60,000 per year was the standard salary for similar employment.

* * *

Section 603 of the Act provides, in relevant part:

An individual shall be ineligible for benefits if he has failed, without good cause, * * * to accept suitable work when offered him by the employment office or an employing unit * * *.

In determining whether or not any work is suitable for an individual, consideration shall be given to the degree of risk involved to his health, safety, and morals, his physical fitness and prior training, his experience and prior earnings, his length of unemployment and prospects for securing local work in his customary occupation, and the distance of the available work from his residence.

The Act must be construed liberally for the unemployed worker's benefit. The burden of proving eligibility for unemployment insurance rests with the claimant. To be eligible for unemployment compensation, a claimant must show that he is ready and willing to accept suitable work. A claimant who refuses a job offer with suitable wages and conditions is not deemed involuntarily unemployed, but unemployed by his own choosing, thereby making him ineligible for unemployment compensation. Perkins v. Board of Review, 485 N.E.2d 575 (Ill.App.Ct.1985) (plaintiff's refusal of work on the condition that it must include 50% administrative functions, as it did her previous job, was unreasonable, as it was within her field of professional training and had a higher rate of pay).

A claimant must manifest good-faith behavior consistent with a general desire to be employed. Behling v. Department of Labor, 525 N.E.2d 1021 (Ill.App.Ct.1988) (claimant not required to accept offer of employment where he was never told what his pay, benefits or job duties would be). A refusal to work must be supported by real, substantial, and reasonable circumstances and cannot be predicated on mere inconvenience. "Good cause" to refuse work may be found in reasons connected with the employer, the claimant's personal circumstances, or the claimant's unsuitability for a particular job, and should be judged by the reasonableness of the claimant's actions in light of the circumstances of his individual case. "Good cause" to refuse work may be found in reasons connected with the employer, the claimant's personal circumstances, or the claimant's unsuitability for a particular job, and should be judged by the reasonableness of the claimant's actions in light of the circumstances of his individual case.

Here, the evidence showed that Purity offered plaintiff $70,200 per year, benefits and guaranteed bonuses, which was more than a typical lead coordinator at Purity, who earned a maximum of $54,000 per year, would earn. Plaintiff had experience in the field and she and Davis agreed that she was competent to fill the position. The additional travel time, working 40, instead of 35, hours per week, and the added liaison responsibility did not make the offered position unsuitable. This evidence supports the Board's determination that the work offered to plaintiff was suitable and that her refusal of work was without good cause.

The cases cited by plaintiff are distinguishable, in that they involve circumstances where the jobs offered to the claimants were not commensurate with the skill levels and pay rates of their previous jobs. See, e.g., Eddings v. Department of Labor, 496 N.E.2d 1167 (1986) (plaintiffs, who previously had full-time employment, were entitled to unemployment insurance where they were offered day-to-day substitute teaching positions at a 40% reduction in pay); Komarec v. Illinois Department of Labor, 494 N.E.2d 1257 (1986) (offer of employment unsuitable where the claimant was to receive no benefits and earn 72% less than he previously made); Mangan v. Bernardi, 477 N.E.2d 13 (1985) (claimant had good cause to refuse part-time offer of employment where her income would be substantially reduced, she would not receive medical insurance, and she was actively seeking other employment options); Crocker v. Department of Labor, 459 N.E.2d 332 (1984) (offer of unskilled position to skilled claimant was unsuitable where it paid him 30% less an hour than he previously earned and he had been unemployed for only 12 weeks). In this case, the skill level and pay rate of plaintiff's previous position and the new position offered to her were not disparate. The position offered to plaintiff did not require her to perform tasks beyond her skill or competency level and her rate of pay actually increased, as she was offered the same salary, plus two guaranteed quarterly bonuses, and benefits. Therefore, we, find no reason to disturb the Board's decision, as it was not against the manifest weight of the evidence.

Accordingly, the judgment of the circuit court is affirmed.

NOTES AND QUESTIONS

1.   James Graves worked for 19 years as a mattress tape edger at Eclipse Sleep Products of New England. He was paid on a piecework basis, his earnings ranging from $100 to $300 per week. After a layoff, Graves was recalled to work, but at a much lower rate of pay. "An employer cannot defeat the payment of unemployment benefits by offering to reemploy claimants at sharply reduced wages." Graves v. Director of Div. of Employment Sec., 429 N.E.2d 705 (Mass.1981).

However, a claimant who had been employed as an administrative assistant earning $23 per hour was offered a similar position at the rate of $14 per hour, a rate within the prevailing range of salaries paid for such positions in that area. The claimant refused the offer. A New York court affirmed the denial of UI benefits, reasoning that the "the mere fact that the salary offered * * * was less than that previously earned by claimant does not constitute good cause for refusing employment." In re Claim of Heller, 658 N.Y.S.2d 518 (App.Div.1997).

Pennsylvania has applied a different approach to determining the suitability of an offer when it involves compensation that is significantly lower than that of the claimant's previous job. In Department of Educ. v. Unemployment Comp. Bd. of Rev., 890 A.2d 1232 (Pa.Cmwlth.2006), two weeks after being discharged, a clerk-typist was offered a temporary position, which she refused, from her former employer at a significantly reduced wage and with no benefits. In analyzing the claimant's eligibility for unemployment benefits, the court used a balancing test, "considering the reduction in pay on one hand against the duration of unemployment on the other, with the weight of the former decreasing as the latter increases." The court concluded that refusal of the offered position in this case did not constitute a failure to accept suitable work.

2. A claimant who had worked as a paralegal was offered a legal secretary position by her former employer. The court reversed the Board's decision disqualifying the claimant from receiving benefits because she refused offer of suitable employment without good cause. "While both the paralegal position and the legal secretary position were characterized as legal support staff, the paralegal duties are more extensive and required different skills than that of a legal secretary." In the Matter of the Claim of Marina Feldman, 785 N.Y.S.2d 600 (App.Div.2004).

3. The suitable work requirement can pose a special challenge to working mothers. According to Elizabeth F. Thompson, Unemployment Compensation: Women and Children—The Denials, 46 U. Miami L. Rev. 751, 766 (1992):

> * * * Unfortunately, * * * courts still interpret suitability as fitting in skill, experience, and salary, rather than taking into account other circumstances of the employee that may render previously suitable employment unsuitable. The lack of recognition of child-care responsibilities shows how a restrictive view of suitability hinders women seeking unemployment. Under this rigid definition of suitability, a woman who had previously held a factory job, was laid off, and then was offered new factory employment at the same pay and time is classified as being offered suitable work, irrespective of whether her babysitter left or her husband died or abandoned her in the interim, leaving her with new and pressing child-care problems. Under most state systems, such a woman would be denied benefits if she refuses to accept the job offered to her. As long as the suitability [and] availability * * * requirements remain formal and unyielding, the seriousness of domestic responsibility situations poses great barriers to women receiving benefits.

More recent decisions, however, e.g. Gilbert v. Director Ohio Dep't of Job & Family Servs., 2004 Ohio 4663 (Ct.App.2004), may indicate a willingness by courts to be more flexible when applying the suitability requirement to workers with special family obligations. In *Gilbert*, the claimant's position was changed by her employer from part-time to full-time. She declined the position because of her responsibilities of caring for a special-needs child. The court held that Gilbert did not reject an offer of suitable work: "[Her] work history had been to work part-time, not to maintain some more desirable lifestyle or to avoid permanent work, but for the laudable purpose of providing care for a four-year-old child with special needs. * * * In this extraordinary situation, suitable work for Gilbert was part-time work."

4. THE POLICY DEBATE

Martin Feldstein, Rethinking Social Insurance*
95 Am. Econ. Rev. 1, 13–15 (Mar. 2005).

* * *

Although unemployment insurance is a relatively small program with total federal and state outlays in 2003 of $39 billion, it is particularly important because of its impact on macroeconomic performance. It is also significant as an illustration of how reforms have been able to reduce distortion while retaining protection for those who need it. Moreover, it is a form of social insurance where further reforms through investment-based accounts could achieve substantial economic gains.

The unemployment insurance program in the United States was created in 1935 in the depth of the depression. The program is administered by the individual states but under federal rules that substantially restrict the scope of state governments' actions. Benefits of a typical recipient are 50 percent of previous earnings and can be collected for up to six months. The European unemployment benefit programs are substantially more generous in both the relative level and the duration of benefits, with clearly adverse effects on European unemployment rates.

Thirty years ago, when I began doing research on unemployment insurance, there was a general perception that unemployment benefits were relatively low and that they had little or no effect on economic behavior. People were assumed to be unemployed solely because there was inadequate aggregate demand. Reformers focused on seeking increases in the level and duration of benefits to help those who were unemployed for what were assumed to be reasons beyond their own control.

We now know that perception was wrong. Unemployment insurance benefits raise the unemployment rate in a variety of ways that economists have now analyzed and measured. But back in the 1960s and 1970s, the higher unemployment rates that were actually induced by unemployment insurance were instead incorrectly perceived as due to inadequate demand. When the government tried to reduce this high structural unemployment with expansionary monetary and fiscal policies, the result was rising inflation. Fortunately, this is now better

---

*   Reprinted by permission of the author.

understood. Monetary policy no longer tries to reduce structural unemployment. But although unemployment insurance is therefore no longer a source of increased inflation, it continues to raise the rate of unemployment. This is a particularly serious problem in Europe where unemployment rates remain close to 10 percent.

The old notion that unemployment benefits were too low to affect the economy was the result of a misleading comparison of the average weekly unemployment benefit and the average weekly wage. Although the average benefit was only about 30 percent of the average wage of all workers, the unemployed had substantially lower pre-unemployment wages than the labor force as a whole. Unemployment insurance benefits actually averaged about 50 percent of the pre-unemployment income of those who received benefits, with even higher replacement rates in states that supplemented the basic benefit with payments for spouses and children. But even this substantially understated the relevant replacement rate because benefits were not subject to the income and payroll taxes that were levied on wages. Since the combined marginal rate of income and payroll tax for the spouse of a high-earning individual could then easily exceed 50 percent, the ratio of untaxed UI benefits to the individual's net-of-tax potential earnings could exceed 100 percent. For such a person, it was possible to have a higher net income by remaining unemployed than by returning to work.

Even significantly lower benefit replacement rates could have substantial adverse incentive effects, as a number of studies eventually showed. Although macroeconomists came to recognize that much unemployment was not of an involuntary Keynesian type but was a productive search for good job matches, the accumulating evidence showed that UI benefits were inducing excessively long periods of searching in which the gain from the marginal search was less than the value of the foregone output. For example, Larry Katz and Bruce Meyer (1990) showed that the probability that an unemployed person takes a job rises dramatically in the few weeks just before their benefits would expire. Jim Poterba and I (1984) found that the median value of the reported reservation wage of new UI recipients was actually higher than the wage on their previous job, that it was an increasing function of the UI replacement rate, and that it came down only very slowly during their spell of unemployment.

Longer durations of unemployment are not the only adverse effect of UI benefits. The practice of temporary layoffs in which unemployed individuals have a spell of unemployment but return to their original employer is substantially encouraged by high UI replacement rates. High benefits also encourage individuals to accept work in firms with high seasonal or cyclical layoffs. That reduces the wage that such firms have to pay and thus subsidizes the expansion of those high unemployment industries.

As all of this became clear, the most obvious first reform was to include unemployment benefits in taxable income. Although there was initially strong opposition to this idea, it was hard to argue with the position that cash income is cash income and should be taxed. The notion that taxing unemployment insurance would inappropriately burden the poor was clearly contrary to the fact that the income tax allows a substantial exclusion of income before any tax is levied. A poor UI recipient would pay no tax.

The initial legislative compromise was to include only half of UI benefits in taxable income and to do so only for relatively high-income taxpayers. This provided a natural experiment that Gary Solon (1985) used to show that the relative duration of unemployment fell for those whose benefits were taxed. Later, in the Tax Reform Act of 1986, the UI benefits were fully subject to the income tax like all other forms of labor income.

Taxing UI benefits eliminated the possibility that an individual could have a higher net income from UI benefits than by working. It is hard to know what the aggregate effect on unemployment has been, but my personal estimate is that the unemployment rate probably fell by about one-half percentage point after benefits were taxed, an effect equal to more than 500,000 jobs at any time.

The evidence that UI benefits cause substantial distortion led to analytic studies of the level of benefits that optimally balances distortion and protection. Martin Bailey (1978) presented an analytic model in which the optimal level of benefits depends on the individual's coefficient of relative risk aversion and on the elasticity of the duration of unemployment with respect to the UI benefit replacement ratio. John Gruber (1997) used this framework to derive an explicit optimal UI benefit based on data on the effect of unemployment on household food consumption, concluding that the optimal replacement rate should be much less than the 50 percent in current law. More recently, however, Raj Chetty (2003) showed that the measure of risk aversion that is relevant to designing the optimal UI benefit may be substantially greater than the risk aversion that is relevant to financial investments, because many types of household spending cannot be adjusted in the short-run, which is relevant to unemployment spells. Chetty's analysis points to optimal UI replacement rates that are close to the levels that we observe in the United States.

These calculations of optimal UI benefits assume that individuals have no financial assets. In contrast, if individuals save optimally, the optimal value of UI benefits—especially for short and moderate spells would be very much less. Although there is evidence that individuals who face greater income uncertainty have somewhat higher saving rates, it would be wrong to assume that in the absence of unemployment insurance everyone would save enough to finance consumption optimally during spells of unemployment. Some individuals would be too short-sighted to save for potential unemployment.

What is the optimal response to this problem? One possibility would be to continue the current system of paying UI benefits but with the level and time path of benefits selected to balance the gain from protection and the loss from distortion. Another possibility would be to shift to a means[-]tested program, although that would induce some individuals to game the system, saving nothing so that they could qualify for means-tested benefits when they became unemployed. The same problem of asymmetric information would prevail, as in the case of Social Security retirement benefits * * *: the government could not distinguish individuals who were too short-sighted to save from those who were gaming the system. On efficiency grounds, the choice between the current system and government means-tested benefits would depend on the response of unemployment to the benefit level and on the relative number of those who would save optimally, those too shortsighted to save, and those who would choose not to save in order to qualify for the means-tested benefits.

A third possibility is to require everyone to have an unemployment insurance savings account earmarked to pay benefits if unemployment occurs. * * * In a typical plan, each individual would be required to accumulate funds in an unemployment insurance savings account until the balance was enough to pay benefits for two spells of six months at 50 percent of the individual's current wage. These funds would be invested and would earn a market rate of return. After a transition period to accumulate account balances, anyone who would be eligible for unemployment benefits under today's UI rules would instead be able to withdraw the same amount from his unemployment insurance savings account [(UISA)]. If a balance remains in the account when the individual reaches retirement age, the funds would be available for the individual to take and spend. An individual who dies before retirement bequeaths the account balance. In short, individuals would regard the funds in the UISA as their own money. For someone who expects to have a positive balance in his account until retirement, the UISA plan would provide the same income protection as the current UI system, but without any distortion.

What about individuals who experience so much unemployment that they use up the funds in their UISA? Such individuals would be able to borrow from a government UI fund to receive the same benefits that they would withdraw if they had a positive account balance. After they return to work, they would again save to repay the loan with interest and to rebuild their UISA balance. If they expect their account to accumulate a positive balance in the future, the dollars that they borrow would be a very real obligation and the incentives to return to work would not be distorted by the government loan. They would have full protection and no distortion while unemployed and would accumulate personal wealth after they returned to work.

It is only those who expect that they will have a negative balance in their account when they retire for whom this plan would represent no improvement over current law. For them, the protection and distortion would be the same as it is with the current UI rules.

The extent of the gain from introducing unemployment insurance savings accounts therefore depends on the proportion of the unemployed who expect to retire with negative balances and on the sensitivity of unemployment to the change in incentives. Dan Altman and I did some preliminary empirical analysis of this approach using a sample of men in the National Longitudinal Survey. We found that, even with no favorable behavioral response of unemployment to the improved incentives, less than 10 percent of benefits would be paid to those who eventually retire with negative balances (or who had negative balances when our data sample ended).

Our analysis thus implied that the UI program could be redesigned around individual unemployment insurance savings accounts in a way that substantially reduces the current distorting effect while not reducing either the availability of funds when unemployment occurs or the protection against relatively large cumulative amounts of lifetime unemployment. More research on this potential form of unemployment insurance would certainly be valuable.

Andrew Stettner & Maurice Emsellem, Unemployment Insurance Is Vital to Workers, Employers and the Struggling Economy

National Employment Law Project (Dec. 2002),
https://www.nelp.org/wp-content/uploads/2015/03/UI-Benefits-Workers-Employers-and-the-Struggling-Economy.pdf.

* * *

In the "Report of the Committee on Economic Security," transmitted to Congress by President Franklin D. Roosevelt in 1935, the creation of the UI system was proposed to establish the "first line of defense" against economic hardship. The most authoritative recent statement of the intent of the UI program was drafted by the federal Advisory Council on Unemployment Compensation (ACUC) a bipartisan body created by Congress in 1993 to evaluate the adequacy of the nation's UI system. According to the ACUC (1996):

> The related goals of the UI program are providing involuntarily unemployed workers with adequate, temporary income replacement as well as automatically stabilizing the economy by using accumulated trust funds to maintain consumer spending during an economic downturn. Secondary

goals include supporting the job search of unemployed individuals by permitting them to find work that matches their prior experience and skills, as well as enabling employers to retain experienced workers during layoffs.

This statement of the multiple goals of the UI program is consistent with other formulations expressed over the years since the program was enacted as part of the Social Security Act of 1935. Below, these specific goals are explored in more detail.

UI Alleviates Worker Hardship

"The unemployed worker does not have to wait until savings and resources are exhausted to be eligible for it. Instead, unemployment insurance is designed to prevent poverty by immediately providing a cash payment to help the worker sustain some of the financial objectives normally supported by the lost wage income." (W.E. Upjohn Institute, 1993).

UI substantially reduces poverty. During the last recession, UI prevented tens of thousands of workers from falling into poverty * * *. [W]ithout regular and extended UI benefits, over 70% of UI recipients would have fallen into poverty, compared to the 40% who experienced poverty after exhausting their regular UI benefits. Only one in ten of these workers were living in poverty before they started collecting UI. According to the same study, average weekly earnings were $676 when the workers first became unemployed. Without federal extended benefits, their average earnings would have amounted to just $183 a week.

Keeping food on the table. Rigorous economic research has demonstrated that UI plays a substantial role in preventing workers from being forced to cut back on meals. M.I.T. economist Jonathan Gruber (1997) concludes that without UI, unemployed workers would consume 22% less food compared to when they were working. Tracking UI recipients over time, Gruber finds that food consumption returns to normal levels after re-employment thus illustrating how the program effectively tides workers over when the help is needed most.

Maintaining the family's housing. By providing workers the income they need to keep their homes while they find a new job, UI offers workers, their families, and communities important stability. The presence of UI reduces the chances that a worker will be forced to sell the family home by almost one-half. It also prevents a potential 23% drop in spending on rental or mortgage payments.

Preserving hard-earned savings. UI also enables some workers to hold on to their hard-earned savings through periods of unemployment. UI benefits, by themselves, prevent workers from losing about 36% of their wealth. Moreover, [research] indicates that the average worker only had sufficient financial assets to cover 5.4 weeks of unemployment.

Workers on UI have few other sources of support. In a recent Washington State survey, two-thirds of UI recipients indicated that UI provided their household's main source of income, and one-third said it was their only source of income. Other research confirms that workers on UI have few other means to support themselves. * * * [L]ess than one in ten unemployed workers accessed other forms of income support (food stamps, welfare, retirement savings, or social security) while collecting UI.

Workers spend UI on their basic family needs. In Washington State (2002), families receiving UI spend 104% of their income (meaning, on average, families go into debt) while comparable households spend only 88.5% of their income. Washington families on UI spend 41% of their household budget on housing and 13% on food, thus spending more on these basic necessities than other consumers in the Western U.S.

UI Stabilizes the Economy

"By maintaining essential consumer purchasing power, on which production plans are based, the program provides a brake on down-turns in business activity, helps to stabilize employment, and lessens the momentum of deflation during periods of recession." (U.S. Dep't. of Labor, 1950).

In recessions, UI saves jobs and fuels local economies. An extensive study by the prominent economist Lawrence Chimerine (1999) demonstrates that UI has greatly reduced the negative impact of the last five recessions. Chimerine finds that UI saved an average of 131,000 jobs in each downturn, and quelled the drop in production (as measured by Gross Domestic Product) by 15%. Moreover, when workers spend UI dollars on basic goods, the money ripples through the economy and creates additional business. Chimerine estimates that each $1 of UI leads to $2.15 of economic growth. Moreover, Chimerine's research asserts that UI has become an even more substantial economic stabilizer over time, thus increasing its impact during the last recession compared with the recession of the 1980s.

During this recession, UI has already contributed billions of dollars to struggling local economies. * * * In March, Congress enacted the Temporary Extended Unemployment Compensation program (TEUC), which is paid for entirely out of the federal unemployment trust fund. Since the program began in March, the program has pumped an estimated $10.7 billion into local economies throughout the nation. Thus far, the TEUC program has contributed $3.7 billion to the economies of the ten states with the highest unemployment, not counting the ripple effect documented in the Chimerine study. The stronger the state's UI program, the greater the boost to the state's economy. * * * This TEUC investment is in addition to the automatic upsurge in regular state UI benefits which has contributed billions of dollars more to those economies hit hardest by unemployment. * * *

UI Makes the Labor Market Function Better for Workers

"Unemployment insurance is of value to the worker, not only as a partial replacement of his lost earnings, but as an aid in preserving his skills for a reasonable period of time until he can find suitable work. The unemployment insurance claimant can refuse unsuitable work and still receive his benefits. He thus can avoid having to take jobs far below his skill and abilities which may downgrade his status and make it more difficult for him to 'land' a suitable job when it becomes available." (Haber & Murray, 1966).

UI maintains worker's earnings after unemployment. UI enables workers to find jobs that match their previous skills and earnings. Kiefer and Neumann (1979) estimate that the reemployment wage was $240/higher per month than it would have been without average UI benefits (economists refer to this concept as the reservation wage). This result is quite substantial given that average monthly wages were just $600/month in their sample of Pennsylvania workers. Looking at experienced older male workers alone, Ehrenberg and Oaxaca (1976) similarly find that UI benefits lead to a 30% higher re-employment wage. Fishe (1982) estimates a smaller but significant effect for Florida workers (a state with an especially restrictive UI program), finding that UI benefits lead to a 12–14% increase in the re-employment wage.

UI helps preserve jobs skills. UI enables laid off workers to return to their previous jobs during temporary economic downturns. Getting rehired by a prior employer is among the best outcomes for unemployed workers, who can earn extra wages for the firm specific skills they have developed.

"Partial" UI keep workers attached to the labor market. Workers can collect UI when they are "partially" unemployed, which most often includes those workers who hours were reduced from full to part-time employment. With UI, these workers remain firmly attached to the labor market as they seek permanent opportunities that match their previous earnings and skills or they are able to return to full-time employment with the current employer. These claims account for 9% of all weeks of UI benefits that are compensated in the United States.

UI provides a strong incentive for workers to stay in the labor market. The safety net provided by UI helps "makes work pay" for many families. This is especially true for people who are less attached to the labor market, including many women coming off of welfare. A carefully specified econometric model developed by Hamermesh (1980) indicates that UI benefits draw significant numbers of married women into the labor force.

UI Provides a More Stable Labor Force to Employers

"[T]he payment of unemployment compensation to his former employees is of advantage to an employer during short layoffs, since it tends to preserve his labor force intact until he can re-employ it. Workers are not forced to scatter in search of jobs, at least during short layoffs. While this restricts the mobility of labor, it is of value to the employer, as well as the worker and community." (Haber & Murray, 1966).

With UI, employers are able to preserve their existing workforce. UI policies have evolved in many states to make special allowances for employers to maintain their workforce with the help of UI benefits. For example, 18 states operate "short-time compensation" programs, allowing companies to retain their workers while cutting back their hours. The reduced hours are then compensated for in part by the UI system. In another seven states, employers file UI claims on behalf of groups of workers who remain employed during regularly scheduled production slowdowns. During these temporary layoffs (often coinciding with holiday schedules), workers are exempted from having to look for other work so that they will return promptly once they are recalled.

Lori G. Kletzer & Howard Rosen, Reforming Unemployment Insurance for the Twenty-First Century Workforce

The Brookings Institution (Sept. 2006),
https://www.brookings.edu/research/reforming-unemployment-insurance-for-the-twenty-first-century-workforce/.

* * *

In recent years, the U.S. labor market has come under increased pressures from intensified domestic and international competition. These pressures have changed the nature of job turnover in the United States. Unlike the cyclical job losses that characterized the labor market and economy from 1945 to the 1980s, job losses are now related more to structural factors, with workers simultaneously changing jobs, industries, and occupations.

* * *

* * * After seven decades of experience, there is widespread agreement that the government should play an important role in providing insurance against job loss and income support to smooth consumption. The basic structure of UI serves that function well, even though changes are necessary to update the precise details of the program * * *.

For individual workers, the most prominent distortion is the reduced incentive to save for unemployment spells and the reduced incentive to begin a search for a new job immediately after separation. A sizeable literature has established a link between receipt of UI and longer unemployment duration. The magnitude of the effect, however, is not overwhelming, and longer job searches may lead to more productive job matches, although the evidence is admittedly mixed on this latter point. Furthermore, it is important to note that these disincentives are a result of specific program designs, and are not inherent in the program itself. * * * The broader point is that it is important to balance any costs of the distortions against the benefits of the program.

* * *

The federal-state structure of UI is a relic of its 1935 establishment * * *. The very basic structure of UI must be reformed, broadening from the single-employer, full-time worker, temporary layoff model to an approach that accommodates permanent job loss, part-time or contingent work, self-employment, and the incidence of job loss and national, rather than local or regional, unemployment. American workers are currently facing considerable pressure due to continued technological change and intensified competition resulting from globalization. Despite significant changes in U.S. labor market conditions, there have been no major changes in the basic structure of UI since it was established 70 years ago. Reforming the nation's UI program is necessary in order to make it relevant to the labor market of the twenty-first century.

CHAPTER 13

RETIREMENT

Employment law remains relevant during a worker's retirement years; retirees and their former employers face many of the same legal issues that preoccupy working employees and their employers. What promises can an employer make to its retirees? What duties do these promises create? How may an employer differentiate among employees in the creation, implementation, and modification of its promises? These issues recur and are complicated by the Employee Retirement Income Security Act (ERISA), the intricate 1974 federal law that regulates employee benefit plans.

Chapter 4 examines ADEA's age discrimination provisions, but age discrimination with regards to retirement and retired employees is a complex issue. Federal law prohibits mandatory retirement based on age, but employers may offer early retirement "deals" to encourage their eldest employees to retire early. The first section of this chapter discusses these issues, as well as the application of the age discrimination rules of ADEA and ERISA to retiree benefit plans.

The second section of this chapter discusses employer-provided pensions. Pensions are an important source of income for retirees; in 2017, individuals received $2.0 trillion from retirement income benefits, including $737.4 billion from private pension and profit sharing plans, $450.2 billion from public employer retirement plans (federal civilian employee, state and local government, military, and railroad), and $812.4 billion from Social Security Old Age, Survivors, and Disability Insurance. Governing rules regarding private pensions stem from ERISA, which creates tax incentives for employers that create pension plans meeting ERISA's complex requirements. ERISA also imposes a set of fiduciary duties on administrators and managers of ERISA-qualified plans; these duties have become a fertile source of litigation. The second section discusses these issues, as well as sex discrimination in pension plans and certain legal issues raised by government pension plans.

The third section discusses Social Security, which continues to be the primary source of income for most elderly. The elderly poor receive additional support from Supplemental Security Income (SSI). Among Social Security beneficiaries (85 out of 100 people over 65 are beneficiaries), 50% of married couples and 71% of unmarried persons receive more than 50% of their income from Social Security. This is so because roughly 51% of the workforce has no pension coverage and 34% of workers have no savings set aside for retirement. This section outlines the method by which Social Security benefits are calculated, the interplay between Social Security and gender, and the debate over whether Social Security beneficiaries have a constitutionally-recognized property interest in their Social Security benefits.

Finally, the fourth section examines retiree health care benefits. Given the rising cost of health care, employers have been trying to trim retiree health care costs. Such efforts raise important legal issues regarding the interplay of retiree health care and bankruptcy law and the enforceability of retiree health care promises.

One recurring theme examined by this chapter is the extent to which these institutions are and will be strained by the aging of the American population. The Census Bureau estimates that Americans over 65 constituted 15.6% of the population in 2019, up from 9.2% in 1960 and 11.3% in 1980. This figure is expected to rise to 19% in 2030. These demographic changes are partly a result of longer life expectancy. Also, they reflect the retirement of the "baby boomers"—the generation born during the late forties, fifties, and early sixties, when the end of World War II and newfound prosperity caused birth rates to skyrocket. The aging of America means that an ever-increasing number of retirees must be supported by a proportionally smaller workforce. Accordingly, Social Security, pensions, and other retirement programs will become more costly. These cost increases will in turn prompt employers (and the government) to attempt to modify, trim, or eliminate retirement benefits, paving the way for an even larger number of legal battles over the issues discussed in this chapter.

A. MANDATORY RETIREMENT AND AGE DISCRIMINATION IN RETIREE BENEFIT PLANS

1. MANDATORY RETIREMENT

The Age Discrimination in Employment Act (ADEA), considered supra at pp. 430–440 makes it illegal for an employer to set a mandatory retirement age for covered employees. 29 U.S.C. § 623(a), 623(f)(2). When the ADEA was first enacted in 1967, its anti-discrimination provisions only applied to individuals aged 40–65. This age cap was raised to 70 in 1978 and repealed entirely in 1986. Thus, employers cannot normally mandate retirement based on age.

Employers can, however, impose mandatory retirement based on age when "age is a bona fide occupational qualification reasonably necessary to the normal operation of the particular business." 29 U.S.C. § 623(f)(1). The Supreme Court elaborated on this exception in Western Air Lines v. Criswell, 472 U.S. 400 (1985), where it invalidated an airline's attempt to require flight engineers (who monitor an instrument panel on the side of an airplane's cockpit and only fly planes if both the pilot and first officer are incapacitated) to retire at 60. The court emphasized that the ADEA focuses on an individualized determination of "the process of physiological and psychological degeneration caused by aging." It then endorsed the two-part test first enunciated in *Usery v. Tamiami Trail Tours, Inc.*, 531 F.2d 224 (5th Cir. 1976), under which an employer can mandate retirement based on age if it can show (1) that the age-related job qualification is "reasonably necessary to the essence of [the employer's] business" and (2) either that all or substantially all of the persons over a certain age cannot perform the duties of the job safely and efficiently or alternatively that it would be "impossible or highly impractical to deal with older employees on an individualized basis." Though *Criswell* struck down a mandatory retirement age for flight engineers, courts have repeatedly upheld, under the BFOQ exception, an F.A.A. regulation that requires pilots to retire at 60. See, e.g., *Coupe v. Federal Express Corp.*, 121 F.3d 1022 (6th Cir. 1997).

NOTES AND QUESTIONS

1.   By its own force (without a congressional statute), the equal protection clause does not bar mandatory retirement on account of age. *Massachusetts Bd. of Ret. v. Murgia*, 427 U.S. 307 (1976). Colonel Murgia was a state police official forced to retire at age 50 by a state law. The Court's per curiam opinion stated that strict scrutiny was inappropriate because the aged have not suffered purposeful unequal treatment on the basis of stereotyped characteristics. Justice Marshall dissented, arguing that discrimination based on age should be subject to intermediate scrutiny. The ADEA did not help Murgia because that law was not amended to cover public sector workers until 1974.

2.   There are several sets of employees who are not covered by the ADEA's ban on mandatory retirement. First, a mandatory retirement age for police officers and firefighters is permissible if it is implemented according to a state or local law that was in effect on March 3, 1983 or one enacted after September 30, 1996. If the law was enacted after September 30, 1996, the mandatory retirement age must not be lower than 55. 29 U.S.C. § 623(j).

Second, an employer may institute a mandatory retirement program for "bona fide executive[s]" or employees in "a high policymaking position" if the employee is entitled to a nonforfeitable annual retirement benefit worth at least $44,000. 29 U.S.C. § 631(c). The EEOC, in its implementing regulation, has interpreted this exception narrowly to only include employers' "very few top level executives" and "top level employees [who] play a significant role in the development of corporate policy." 29 C.F.R. § 1625.12. Courts have approved of this narrow view. See *Passer v. American Chem. Soc'y*, 935 F.2d 322 (D.C.Cir. 1991) (holding that the head of a division with a $4M budget and 25 employees qualifies as a bona fide executive); *Whittlesey v. Union Carbide Corp.*, 742 F.2d 724 (2d Cir. 1984) (upholding lower court's decision that a chief labor counsel with limited supervision duties is not a high policymaking employee or bona fide executive); *Wendt v. New York Life Ins. Co.*, 1998 WL 118168 (S.D.N.Y. 1998) (holding that senior vice president qualifies as "bona fide executive").

Courts have also found that individuals who can better be classified as "employers" rather than "employees" are not covered by the mandatory retirement ban (or the ADEA's other prohibitions). Courts thus find that some partners are considered to be "employers" and therefore exempt from the mandatory retirement ban. Whether a particular partner will be considered to be an "employer" or "employee" for ADEA purposes depends on their ability to set their own compensation and that of others and their input into the decision-making process of the partnership. See EEOC v. Sidley Austin Brown & Wood, 315 F.3d 696 (7th Cir. 2002) (remanding for consideration of whether 32 law firm partners who did not participate in the 36-member committee that set compensation and made most decisions were "employers" for the purposes of the ADEA). The EEOC filed suit on behalf of the partners in 2005 and Sidley Austin agreed to pay $27.5 million in 2007 pursuant to a consent decree.

Individuals elected to state office, their personal staff, and appointees "on the policymaking level" are also exempt from the ADEA, including its ban on mandatory retirement. 29 U.S.C. § 630(f).

3. Most other countries continue to permit age-based mandatory retirement and in some countries mandatory retirement from many jobs occurs at 60 or earlier. Is the United States wrong to ban age-based retirement (1) because younger persons need and deserve the jobs; (2) because retirement based on age is a humane alternative to telling people that their skills have declined and they are no longer adequate workers; or (3) because, without mandatory retirement, a significant number of workers will work past the age at which their efforts become inefficient due to loss of skills?

For criticism of the ADEA's ban on mandatory retirement, see Samuel Issacharoff & Erica Worth Harris, Is Age Discrimination Really Age Discrimination? The ADEA's Unnatural Solution, 72 N.Y.U. L. Rev. 780 (1997). Professors Issacharoff and Harris argued that employees are overpaid during the final years of their careers to make up for being underpaid in earlier years and so that employers can raise employees' wages throughout their careers. Mandatory retirement based on age facilitates this system, they argue, by creating a predetermined end point for employees' overpaid years. They then criticize the ban on mandatory retirement as a form of rent-seeking:

> The elderly lack the critical features of disadvantaged group status that give some elementary coherence to an antidiscrimination model. Far from being discrete and insular, the elderly represent the normal unfolding of life's processes for all persons. As a group, older Americans do not suffer from poverty or face the disabling social stigmas characteristically borne by black Americans at the start of the civil rights era.

> * * * [P]articularly after the emergence of the American Association of Retired Persons (AARP) as a powerful lobbying presence, advocates of expansive ADEA remedies essentially abandoned the issue of job acquisition that had been at the heart of the initial passage of the Act. * * * Through a carefully orchestrated assault on mandatory retirement and targeted employee

retirement incentive programs, the AARP-inspired amendments of the ADEA provoked a significant one-time transfer of resources to the generation whose members are currently drawing to the close of their working careers. * * * [T]he dramatic shift in wealth toward older Americans and the diminished job prospects of the young provoke grave concerns that a misguided antidiscrimination model has allowed a concerted and politically powerful group of Americans to engage in a textbook example of what economists would term "rent seeking."

2. AGE DISCRIMINATION IN EMPLOYEE BENEFITS PLANS

Solon v. Gary Community School Corp.

180 F.3d 844 (7th Cir. 1999).

■ ROVNER, CIRCUIT JUDGE.

Since 1984, the Gary Community School Corporation ("Gary Schools") has offered early retirement incentives to teachers aged 58 to 61. Eligible teachers who elect to retire early receive monthly payments until they turn 62. Teachers who retire on their 58th birthday receive the maximum forty-eight months of benefits available under this plan; teachers who retire later receive the same monthly payments but fewer of them, as the payments terminate at age 62. A similar plan is in place for school administrators. The plaintiffs in this case are teachers and administrators who were eligible for the early retirement incentives but chose not to retire at age 58. They contend that the incentive plan is inconsistent with the Age Discrimination in Employment Act, because the plan doles out unequal benefits based on age. * * *

Between 1970 and 1984, the student enrollment within the Gary public school system dropped by one-third, precipitating lay-offs among teachers and administrators. In 1982, the Gary Teacher's Union proposed that the school system adopt an early retirement incentive plan. The aim of the plan was to induce teachers at the top of the pay scale to retire sooner than they would otherwise, thereby enabling the school system to retain more teachers who were lower in seniority and earned smaller salaries.

After study and negotiations, an early retirement incentive plan ("ERIP") was included in the collective bargaining agreement ("CBA") that the union and the school system adopted in 1983 for the 1984 calendar year. The ERIP specified the following eligibility criteria for teachers wishing to participate: (1) a minimum of fifteen years of creditable service, with at least ten of those years earned in the Gary Community School Corporation; (2) a Bachelor's Degree; and (3) a minimum age of 58 and a maximum age of 61. Teachers who met these criteria could receive early retirement incentive pay for up to forty-eight months, ending at age 62. These payments were calculated with reference to the starting salary paid to a teacher with a Bachelor's Degree during the year that the early retiree became eligible to participate in the ERIP. [A second, similar ERIP was later adopted for administrators.] * * *

The thirty-four plaintiffs in this case were all employees of Gary Schools when the ERIPs for teachers and administrators were first implemented in 1984. Each was below the age of 58 when the plans were adopted and subsequently remained employed through at least June 1995, shortly before this suit was filed. During that time period, each of the plaintiffs became eligible to participate in the ERIPs upon turning 58 years old and thus had the option to retire at that age and receive the maximum benefits available. Each chose instead to continue working beyond age 58, foregoing some or all of the incentives provided for in the ERIPs. At the time this case was tried, twelve of the plaintiffs had retired, most after they had reached the age of 62 (meaning they received no early retirement benefits at all). One had died before trial while still in the school district's employ. The remaining twenty-one plaintiffs were still working for Gary Schools when the trial commenced.

Asserting that the age-based nature of the Gary Schools ERIPs was discriminatory, the plaintiffs filed suit under the ADEA. * * *

The ADEA bars an employer from discriminating against any individual in the "compensation, terms, conditions, or privileges of employment, because of such individual's age[.]" That bar, Congress has now made clear, extends to "virtually all employee benefits and benefit plans," including early retirement plans. Thus, although an employer of course has no duty to offer early retirement incentives, once the employer elects to do so it must make those benefits available on nondiscriminatory terms, just as it must with any other fringe benefit. * * *

[The court first concluded that plaintiffs had standing to bring their ADEA claims, despite the fact that each earned more money by working than they would have through the ERIP.]

The principal issue we must consider is whether the plaintiffs successfully established a prima facie case of age discrimination. As we noted earlier, the district court concluded that Gary Schools had waived the affirmative defenses set out in 29 U.S.C. § 623(f). Gary Schools does not challenge that ruling and therefore cannot resort to the statutory defenses in the effort to avoid liability. Instead, it insists that the plaintiffs have not even made out a prima facie case of discrimination, obviating any need to mount a defense. However, our opinion in Karlen v. City Colleges of Chicago [837 F.2d 314 (7th Cir.), cert. denied, 486 U.S. 1044 (1988)] makes short work of that argument.

The early retirement plan at issue in Karlen was in significant respects similar to the Gary Schools ERIPs. The plan was designed in part to encourage more senior teachers, who were of course employed at higher salaries, to retire early and enable the municipal college system to hire new teachers at lower salaries. The plan was open to any faculty member between the ages of 55 and 69 who had been employed on a full-time basis for at least ten continuous years. An individual who retired under the plan would receive a pension based on his highest four years of salary and the length of his service. That component of the plan, which was not keyed to the employee's age, was not challenged. Two other aspects were. First, upon retirement, the employee would also receive a lump sum equal to a certain percentage of his accumulated sick pay. Those retiring at ages 55 to 58 would receive fifty percent, those retiring at 59 would receive sixty percent, and those retiring at 60 to 64 would be paid eighty percent. Those who retired at 65 to 70, however, would receive only forty-five percent of their accumulated sick pay. In addition, faculty members who retired between the ages of 55 and 64 continued to be covered by the colleges' comprehensive group insurance plan until they reached the age of 70, while those who retired at age 65 or later would lose that coverage unless they elected to shoulder the premiums themselves. Thus, employees who retired at age 64 or earlier received significantly greater benefits than those who waited until age 65.

We found the terms of this plan sufficient to establish a prima facie case of age discrimination. We emphasized that this was not a case like Henn, in which the retirement incentives were offered to everyone over a given age on the same terms: [In Henn v. National Geographic Soc'y, 819 F.2d 824 (7th Cir.), cert. denied, 484 U.S. 964 (1987), the court upheld against an ADEA challenge a plan that made a one-time offer of benefits to all employees then over 55].

> In the present case, there is discrimination against the older worker. Everyone between 55 and 69 is eligible for early retirement, but those between 64 and 69—an older age group— are disfavored relative to the younger employees in the eligible group. If the City Colleges said to their faculty, at age 65 you lose your free parking space (or dental insurance, or any other fringe benefit), they would be guilty, prima facie, of age discrimination. Early-retirement benefits are another fringe benefit—and they plummet at age 65.

We proceeded to consider the City Colleges' arguments in defense of the plan disparities, and in the course of that discussion firmly rejected the notion that establishing a presumptive age of "early" retirement is permissible under the ADEA.

A feature common to both the sick-pay and insurance components of the Early Retirement Plan is the sharp drop in benefits at age 65. The Colleges cannot and do not argue that the drop in benefits at age 65 is justified by the higher cost of benefits to a 65-year-old retiree as compared to a 64-year-old one (because of more accumulated sick leave, valued at a higher base pay, and because of higher insurance costs). They argue that in order to induce early retirement of faculty members in the 65–69 year bracket they have to make 65 a breaking point. They say that if the decline in benefits with age were gradual, as it would have to be to reflect accurately the changing cost of the retirement package, no one would retire before 70. The small annual decline in sick-pay distribution and in insurance coverage would be more than offset by the growth in the pension component of the retirement package as a result of salary raises and additional years of service. So the purpose of the Early Retirement Program—to induce early retirement—would be defeated.

This strikes us as a damaging admission rather than a powerful defense. To withhold benefits from older persons in order to induce them to retire seems precisely the form of discrimination at which the Age Discrimination in Employment Act is aimed. Rather than offering a carrot to all workers 55 years and older, as in the *Henn* case, the City Colleges are offering the whole carrot to workers 55 to 64 and taking back half for workers 65 to 69. The reason is that the Colleges want to induce workers to retire by 65. In effect they have two early retirement programs; a munificent one for workers 55 to 64 and a chintzy one for workers 65 to 69.

In this case, there is an equally obvious difference in the benefits that retirees will receive under the ERIPs depending upon their age. Those retiring at age 58 will receive four years of incentive payments, those retiring at age 60 only two years, and those retiring at age 62 or later, nothing. Those employees who elect to retire at 62 or later are put at a disadvantage for not retiring when they were 58 to 61, no matter how "early" their later separation may be in terms of their length of service or previous retirement plans. And even for those within the 58 to 61 age group, we have exactly the situation that we did in *Karlen*—a full "carrot" for those aged 58, and an increasingly smaller piece of that carrot (25 percent less per year) for those closer to age 62. The amount of the benefits varies depending upon the retiree's age, nothing else. Just as in *Karlen*, the terms of the ERIPs establish a prima facie case of age discrimination. * * *

That the disadvantage employees over the age of 58 experience is the withdrawal of a "carrot" rather than the sting of a "stick" makes no difference to the analysis. * * *

Nor does it matter that each of the plaintiffs could have retired within the framework of the ERIPs and received the maximum available benefits. The point of the plaintiffs' case is not that they were never eligible for the incentives, but that the terms of the plans put them to an unlawful choice. Employees are offered incentives to retire sooner than they otherwise plan, but "early" retirement is defined exclusively in terms of age. Yet one's ability to retire is typically dependent on a host of factors other than age: one's years of service with the employer (which will typically affect pension benefits), savings, dependents, health, and so on. Consequently, not all 58-year-olds will be equally situated to retire. * * *

Of course, the disparity of which the plaintiffs complain results from the maximum age (62) that the ERIPs impose on the receipt of early retirement benefits, and Gary Schools reminds us that we found such a maximum lawful in Dorsch v. L.B. Foster Co., 782 F.2d 1421, 1428 (7th Cir. 1986). The plan under scrutiny there offered employees whose age plus years of service totaled 75 or more incentive payments of $600 per month until they reached the age of 62. By virtue of the age cap, qualified younger retirees would receive the monthly payments for a greater number of years and would therefore earn greater total benefits than older workers. Nonetheless, we found nothing in that arrangement inconsistent with the ADEA. * * *

It was several years after we decided *Dorsch*, however, that Congress enacted the Older Workers Benefit Protection Act, which made substantial revisions to the ADEA, including changes to the provisions concerning early retirement plans. Among the new provisions is one stating that it is not a prima facie violation of the Act for a "defined benefit plan" to offer "Social Security supplements for plan participants that commence before the age and terminate at the age (specified by the plan) when participants are eligible to receive reduced or unreduced old-age insurance benefits under title II of the Social Security Act . . . and that do not exceed such old-age insurance benefits."* The ADEA thus sanctions "bridge" payments which span the gap between an employee's age upon early retirement and the age at which she first becomes eligible for reduced or unreduced Social Security benefits. Those payments might look something like the $600 monthly payments we examined in *Dorsch*, which terminated when an employee reached age 62—the minimum eligibility age for reduced Social Security benefits. In fact, the legislative history of the OWBPA explicitly addresses *Dorsch*, and limits its rationale to these types of bridge payments. Thus, as amended by the OWBPA, the ADEA does permit an employer to offer, as an early retirement incentive, monthly payments which terminate at a specified age, even though younger workers will stand to receive greater benefits under that arrangement than older workers. However, those payments must satisfy the criteria specified in the statute, key among them being the requirement that the payments not exceed the payments that the retiree is likely to receive once she is eligible for Social Security benefits. Here, the record reveals no connection between the ERIP payments and the Social Security benefits that early retirees could be expected to receive at age 62, when the incentive payments cease. On the contrary, the assistant superintendent for fiscal integrity conceded that Gary Schools never undertook any type of analysis as to the age at which early retirees actually opt to begin receiving Social Security payments or the

---

* Note: A defined benefit plan is one that pays out a promised level of benefits, rather than a plan such as a 401(k) in which an employer makes a set level of contributions to an employee's account, and the employee receives the amount of money accumulated in the account upon retirement. For more on the differences between the two types of plans, see the next section of this chapter.

specific dollar amounts of the Social Security payments that teachers and administrators would receive. Consequently, neither *Dorsch* (as limited by the OWBPA) nor the narrow provision of the statute permitting Social Security bridge payments is of any help to Gary Schools. * * *

Finally, Gary Schools suggests that the plaintiffs have been given a windfall by having been awarded the benefits (or the right to receive the benefits) offered by the ERIPs without having to retire at the age specified by the plans. In effect, the plaintiffs' victory has transformed the early retirement incentives into severance payments made to all employees upon retirement. That argument has some intuitive appeal. None of the plaintiffs who testified, for example, indicated that she retired sooner than she otherwise planned or was prepared to do. There is no way to know on this record, then, whether any of the plaintiffs "earned" the incentives by retiring "early." That may simply be the price Gary Schools has to pay, however, for establishing an early retirement plan which turns on the employee's age. * * *

NOTES AND QUESTIONS

1. The ADEA provides a statutory exception to its anti-discrimination rules for "voluntary early retirement incentive plan[s] consistent with the relevant purpose or purposes of this chapter." 29 U.S.C. § 623(f)(2)(B)(ii). Plans are not considered voluntary if there is evidence of fraud, a threat of termination, or other forms of coercion; also, plans are not considered voluntary if "under the circumstances, a reasonable person would have concluded that there was no choice but to accept the offer." Auerbach v. Board of Educ., 136 F.3d 104, 113 (2d Cir. 1998).

A plan is not considered consistent with the purposes of the ADEA if it only provides benefits to employees under a certain age. See, e.g., Jankovitz v. Des Moines Indep. Cmty. Sch. Dist., 421 F.3d 649 (8th Cir. 2005) (holding that an early retirement plan that was only available to employees aged 55 to 65 violated the ADEA). Also, a plan is not considered consistent with the purposes of the ADEA if it relies on age stereotypes. See EEOC v. Crown Point Cmty. Sch. Corp., 72 FEP Cases 1803 (N.D.Ind.1997) (holding that an early retirement plan that was only available to employees under age 65 violated the ADEA, rejecting defendant's contention that most employees would retire at 65 anyway). As the court notes in *Solon*, Gary Schools did not try to fit its plan within this exception, probably because it did not think that a court would find it consistent with the purposes of the ADEA.

2. The second exception to the ADEA's anti-discrimination provisions that applies to employee benefits plans is the so-called 4(f)(2) safe harbor. Under this provision, "it is not unlawful for an employer, employment agency, labor organization to observe the terms of * * * any bona fide employee benefit plan such as retirement, pension, or insurance plan, which is not a subterfuge to evade the purposes of this Act, except that no such employee benefit plan shall excuse the failure to hire any individual, and no such * * * employee benefit plan shall require or permit the involuntary retirement of any

individual specified by section 12(a) of this Act because of the age of such individuals."

3. Also, recall that the ADEA provides that it "shall not be unlawful for an employer * * * to take any action otherwise prohibited [by 623(a)] * * * where the differentiation is based on reasonable factors other than age."

4. Can an employer reduce retiree health benefits for its retirees who are eligible for state-run health insurance (such as Medicare)? In Erie County Retirees Ass'n v. County of Erie, 220 F.3d 193 (3d Cir. 2000), the Third Circuit considered an ADEA suit filed against an employer that provided its Medicare-eligible retirees with a different plan than the one that it provided for its non-Medicare-eligible retirees The Third Circuit held that the county's provision of two separate plans could only be consistent with the ADEA if it met section 4(f)(2)'s equal cost or benefit standard (on remand, the lower court found for the plaintiffs, concluding that the two plans were not equal in cost or benefit).

In reaching this conclusion, the Third Circuit first held that section 623(a) of the ADEA prohibited discrimination in retiree benefits plans. The county had argued that section 623(a) did not apply to retiree benefit plans. Section 623(a) states that "It shall be unlawful for an employer to * * * discriminate against any individual with respect to his compensation, terms, conditions, or privileges of employment." Section 630(*l*) provides that the phrase "compensation, terms, conditions, or privileges of employment" includes "all employee benefits." The county argued that since retirees are no longer its employees, retiree health care plans are not "employee benefit" plans. The court rejected this argument, noting that the words "employer" and "employee" are inherently ambiguous and can include former employees and their employers. The court next held that Medicare-eligibility was used as a proxy for age and thus was not a "reasonable factor other than age." The court also held that section 628, which gives the Secretary of Labor the authority to create "reasonable exemptions" to the ADEA's provisions, did not give the EEOC authority to create an applicable exemption.

At first, the EEOC implemented a regulation that was consistent with *Erie*. But, the increased cost that this imposed on retiree health care plans (which were becoming increasingly expensive anyway due to factors examined later in this chapter) was causing many employers to stop offering retiree health care. The EEOC then changed its position, adopting a regulation that allowed employers to provide less health care benefits to retirees after they became eligible for Medicare without regard to the equal cost/equal benefit standard.

The AARP filed suit in the Eastern District of Pennsylvania (where *Erie*, as a Third Circuit precedent, would be binding), challenging the new regulation. Interestingly, representatives from labor unions, employers, and the health industry mostly supported the EEOC's new position. Initially, the court invalidated the EEOC regulation. AARP v. EEOC, 383 F.Supp.2d 705 (E.D.Pa.2005).

Yet, National Cable & Telecomms. Ass'n v. Brand X Internet Servs., 545 U.S. 967 (2005), forced the court to reconsider its position. *Brand X* built on the framework created by Chevron, U.S.A., Inc. v. NRDC, 467 U.S. 837 (1984), in which the Supreme Court announced a two-step procedure for judicial review of some agency interpretations of statutes. The *Chevron* analysis is only applicable if there is evidence that Congress intended the agency's interpretation of a statute to have the force of law; otherwise, agency interpretations have only persuasive power in Art. III courts. Under *Chevron*, a court should first determine whether Congress has "spoken to the precise question at issue"—in other words, whether the plain language of a statute compels a specific interpretation or it leaves room for more than one interpretation regarding an issue. If a court finds that the statute leaves room for interpretation, then, under the second step of the *Chevron* test, it should ask whether the agency's decision is a reasonable interpretation of the statute. If the interpretation is unreasonable, the court should strike down the agency regulation and interpret the statute itself. In *Brand X*, the Supreme Court took this approach a step further, holding that a judicial ruling on the second step of the *Chevron* test does not preclude an agency from issuing a different, but reasonable ruling.

After *Brand X*, the EEOC filed a motion to set aside the judgment in AARP v. EEOC. On reconsideration, the court found that *Erie's* interpretation of the ADEA was a *Chevron* step-two analysis, and thus that it did not preclude conflicting but reasonable agency regulations. Therefore, the court concluded, the EEOC regulation was valid. AARP v. EEOC, 390 F. Supp. 2d 437, 446 (E.D. Pa. 2005). In concluding that *Erie* was a step-two decision, the court reasoned that:

> *Erie County* does not explicitly state that its holding is the "only permissible reading of the statute." Indeed, in its discussion of whether defendants could satisfy the "reasonable factors other than age" safe harbor, the *Erie County* court seems to acknowledge that its decision is not the only possible interpretation: "While it is possible that Congress intended Medicare eligibility to be a 'reasonable factor other than age,' we believe it is more likely that Congress would have drafted a specific provision addressing the issue. . . ." * * * I cannot conclude that the court, on the basis of admittedly ambiguous statutory language, admittedly contradictory legislative history, and an admittedly "difficult task of statutory interpretation," could have reached the only possible interpretation of the statute. Because that is what *Brand X* demands of *Erie County's* holding in order for it to foreclose a later, conflicting interpretation of section 4(a)(1) by the EEOC, in light of *Brand X*, *Erie County* no longer forecloses a contrary EEOC interpretation.

Id. at 25–26, 32.

The court reasoned that the statute was ambiguous as to whether Medicare-eligibility was a reasonable factor other than age. The court also found that the ADEA was ambiguous on the issue of whether section 623(a) applied to retiree benefits. The court noted that it would probably uphold an EEOC regulation that stated that section 623(a) did not apply to all retiree benefits. Given this ambiguity, the court reasoned, the EEOC could use the power to make exemptions given to it by section 628 to conclude that, while section 623(a) applies to retirement benefits generally, it does not apply to retiree health benefits.

If the EEOC issued a regulation stating that discrimination against the young is in fact age discrimination (overturning Gen. Dynamics v. Cline, infra note 6), would the court be required to uphold it? What if the EEOC ruled that affirmative action violates Title VII (overturning United Steelworkers v. Weber, supra p. 399)?

5. ERISA also prohibits ceasing reducing benefit accrual rates based on age. 29 U.S.C. §§ 1054(b)(1)(H)(i), 623(i)(1). Plans that exclude employees on the basis of age also do not qualify for ERISA tax treatment. 29 U.S.C. § 1052(a)(2).

6. General Dynamics v. Cline, 540 U.S. 581 (2004), concluded that the ADEA did not prohibit discrimination against the young. Also recall that ERISA section 510 prohibits discriminating against beneficiaries with the purpose of interfering with the attainment of ERISA benefits.

B. THE PRIVATE PENSION SYSTEM

1. BACKGROUND

Alicia Haydock Munnell, The Economics of Private Pensions
7–12 (1982).

The development of the social security program and private pension system, in the wake of the Great Depression, reflected a shift in the nation's preference away from individual saving for retirement and toward organized savings plans. The two systems developed simultaneously, since neither program provided adequate retirement income. Yet they clearly are alternative ways to accomplish the same goal—namely, providing an adequate retirement income. In fact, many private plans are explicitly integrated with social security and so reduce private pension benefits as social security benefits are increased. Because of the substitutability of the two programs, as the gap between desired and actual retirement assets narrows, an expansion in either social security or private pensions will lead to a decline in the relative role of the other.

In the 1970s social security benefits grew particularly fast as a result of ad hoc increases and automatic cost-of-living adjustments. Despite this growth, a substantial gap still exists—especially for workers with above-average earnings—between retirees' income needs and social security benefits.

The Growth of Private Plans

Although private pension plans date officially from 1875, the early plans were financially vulnerable and most were bankrupted by the

Great Depression. Contemporary U.S. pension plans, both public and private, are rooted in the desire for financial security that became part of the national psychology after the onset of the Depression. The expansion of private plans was stimulated by the inflation, tax changes, and wage controls of World War II.

The introduction of a few private plans by large industrial employers during the last quarter of the nineteenth century reflected the United States' transition from a rural agricultural society to an urban industrial economy.

* * *

While large industrial employers were establishing pension plans, a small number of trade unions were instituting their own schemes for retirement benefits. Mutual benefit societies, predating modern insurance schemes, for survivors, sickness, and disability were traditional among unions; the first union old-age plan, established by the Granite Cutters' International Association of America, did not appear until 1905.

* * *

The Great Depression had a disastrous effect on both the industrial and trade union plans. Many railroads had become unprofitable during the late 1920s, and by the early 1930s they were operating in the red. Despite emergency measures to cut costs through reduction of wages and pension benefits, the railroads' financial situation continued to deteriorate. Approximately 25 percent of railway workers were approaching retirement, but the railroads, with virtually no reserves, were incapable of fulfilling benefit promises. Because so many people were involved, strong pressure developed for legislative action to bail out the railroads. Thus the Railroad Retirement Act of 1935 was enacted, which rescued the failing pension plans by establishing a quasi-public retirement system for railway employees.

Employees covered by other industry plans were not so fortunate as the railroad workers. Beginning in 1929, as business activity declined, many companies were unable to meet both operating expenses and rising pension payments. In response, they made substantial cutbacks in pension benefits, ranging from tightening eligibility requirements and suspending pension credit accumulation to abolishing pension plans and terminating benefit payments even for retired employees. The trade union plans also floundered; with high unemployment and competing demands on the union treasuries, it was impossible to increase dues enough to support the growing number of union retirees. Within a few years after the Depression began, almost all union welfare plans had collapsed.

The Depression not only bankrupted most trade union and industrial pension plans but also undermined American confidence in the historic tradition of self-reliance and in the virtue of individual thrift as a way to provide for old age. By 1933 nearly 13 million people were unemployed and the lifetime savings of many were erased. The nation was therefore sympathetic to the need for the Social Security Act of 1935 and the subsequent development of negotiated funded private pension plans.

Although World War II initially consumed much of the nation's resources that might have been directed toward improved provisions for old age, two wartime factors—wage control policies and tax changes—greatly stimulated the expansion of private plans. The wage stabilization program instituted during the war impeded employers' ability to attract and hold employees in the tight civilian labor market. The War Labor Board attempted to relieve the pressure on management and labor from the legal limitations on cash wages by permitting employers to bid for workers by offering attractive fringe benefits. The cost to the firms of establishing pension plans to attract workers was minimal in light of the tax deductibility of contributions and the wartime excess profits tax on corporate income.

The rate of growth of new pension plans fell off markedly during the immediate postwar period as employees focused on cash wage increases in an attempt to recover the ground lost during the period of wage stabilization. By 1949, however, pension benefits again became a major issue of labor negotiation because of the increased resistance to further wage increases and a weak economy. The importance of pensions was highlighted by a presidential fact-finding board, which concluded that while a cash wage increase in the steel industry was not justified, the industry did have a social obligation to provide workers with pensions. This decision was based in part on the obvious inadequacy of social security benefits, which averaged $26 a month at the time. Labor's drive for pension benefits was aided further when the Supreme Court confirmed a 1948 ruling of the National Labor Relations Board that employers had a legal obligation to negotiate the terms of pension plans. Both the United Steelworkers of America and the United Automobile Workers then launched successful drives for pension benefits under the influence of the 1949 recession.

The main expansion of today's private pension system, then, actually began during the 1950s. Private pension coverage grew rapidly during this period, not only in union plans but also among nonunionized industries. The economic impact of the Korean War further stimulated the pension movement as employers once again competed for workers in the face of wage and salary controls and excess profits taxes. The mid-1950s marked the beginning of substantial collective bargaining gains in multiemployer pension plans. These plans were established in industries containing many small companies and involving frequent job changes that prevented employees from remaining with a single employer long enough to qualify for pensions. The multiemployer pension movement, encouraged by the success of the United Mine Workers of America, spread to such industries as construction, food, apparel, and transportation.

The growth of private pensions continued into the 1960s. But much of the increase in coverage during that decade was due to an expansion of employment in firms that already had pension plans, in contrast to the growth during the 1950s, which resulted primarily from the introduction of new plans. Coverage under multiemployer plans grew more than twice as fast as single-employer plans during the 1960s, owing in part to the merging of single-employer plans into multiemployer ones.

NOTE

The number of working Americans in 2018 was about 160 million, of whom 22.4 million had government jobs. In 1980, after 1978 legislation that authorized 401(k) type plans that allow employees to contribute to their own retirement plan on a pre-tax basis, there were about 30 million private sector job participants in defined benefit (DB) plans and about 19 million in defined contribution (DC) plans. By 2017, there were about three times as many workers in DC plans as in DB plans. DC plan assets were about $6.55 trillion and DB plan assets about $3.21 trillion. DC plans distributed about $494 billion and DB plans about $243 billion. U.S. Department of Labor, Private Pension Plan Bulletin: Abstract of 2017 Form 5500 Annual Reports, Employee Benefits Security Administration, extracted July 19, 2019, Table A1, September 2019.

2. ERISA

a. THE ERISA SCHEME

For many years there was an effort in Congress to offer statutory protection for private sector pensioners.* Some national employers sought federal regulations to ease the burdens of complying with varying state laws. That goal was supported by "Wall Street" institutions: big banks and insurance companies that managed the billions of dollars in pension fund assets. A key stimulus for more comprehensive federal legislation came from Ralph Nader's efforts to expose defects in the existing localized system. In 1973, Nader and Kate Blackwell published *You and Your Pension,* a book sharply critical of the private pension system in which the authors documented numerous instances of workers who experienced benefit denials despite holding their jobs for at least 20 years.

In one example, a factory worker with 24 years' experience at a Colorado manufacturer was denied his pension benefit after the company shut the factory where he worked. Believing he could soon collect his pension, the man declined a job in one of the company's other facilities and, when he reached age 65 and applied for his pension, he was

---

* Prior to the passage of ERISA in 1974, pensions were governed by state trust laws (for this reason, state trust law is often a relevant source for courts facing difficult ERISA questions).

ineligible due to his decision to leave the company before its designated retirement age.

In another case, a coal mining company laid off a worker with 23 years of service, forcing him to find another job. After doing so outside the coal industry, the man eventually applied for his pension but was also ineligible. He applied 13 years after leaving the company, meaning his required 20+ years of service were not within the 30 years preceding his application for benefits, and were therefore outside the company's pension benefit policy guidelines.

In a third example, a woman who had been with a company for 17 years left for five years because of paralysis of her arm and fingers resulting from an industrial accident. During that time she worked at another job. After recovering, she returned to her former employer and worked an additional nine years. Despite a total of 26 years with the same company, she was denied her pension because she had not spent 20 consecutive years at her job. In a similar case, a man with 32 years' service was forced by a stroke to quit work at age 48, only to find that he had no pension because he had stopped working before age 50.

When the Studebaker company closed its plants in 1964, it left more than 8500 employees with reduced or eliminated pension benefits. Because the company's pension plan had been severely underfunded, only employees who were 60 or older with at least ten years of service received full benefits. Workers between 40 and 59 with ten years of service received only 15 percent of their promised benefits, and the remaining employees received nothing.

Congress responded to the calls of reformers such as Nader by passing the Employee Retirement Income Security Act of 1974 (ERISA). ERISA does not require employers to provide pensions. Rather, it says that persons and firms conforming to its provisions receive income tax advantages—essentially the opportunity for employers to deduct pension costs when funds are set aside. Beneficiaries do not declare income until decades later when they receive both the employers' contribution, interest, and dividends, the latter two compounded alongside capital contributions. This gave firms an overwhelming incentive to comply with ERISA's rules.

Three retirement plan structures have emerged in the wake of ERISA's enactment: defined benefit (DB) plans, cash balance (CB) plans and defined contribution (DC) plans. Defined benefit plans, common at the time of ERISA's passage, promised specific payouts to retirees upon retirement, typically recurring until death. CB plans similarly represent an employer's promise to pay an employee's retirement benefit, but that promise is in the form of a lump sum or recurring annuity rather than a series of guaranteed lifetime payouts. DC plans, which have experienced the most rapid growth in recent decades, relieve employers of any monetary promise at retirement. Instead, participants are allowed to make tax-deferred payments to an employer-sponsored retirement plan, with most employers offering a "matching" contribution at the time of a participant's deferral of salary. DC plans, and to a lesser extent CB plans, offer employees the time value of the employer's contribution (coupled with more aggressive investments by the participant) in exchange for zero liability for the participant's retirement funding afterward. CB plans and DC plans are discussed in greater depth later in this chapter.

ERISA's participation and vesting standards enable workers to establish a legal claim to benefits. By requiring all employees who have reached age 21 and who have completed one year of service (at least 1000 hours of work) to be covered by their company's pension plan, the Act broadens the number of people eligible to participate in private pension plans. Once workers begin to participate, their benefits become vested after they have completed a minimum period of service designated by the employer. The law gives companies two minimum vesting options: (1) 100 percent vesting after five years of service (with no vesting prior to five years); (2) graduated vesting over seven years (20 percent vesting after three years followed by 20 percent vesting per year for the fourth, fifth, sixth, and seventh years). These vesting requirements do not apply to multi-employer benefit plans; participants in those plans need not be 100 percent vested until after ten years of service. Once they are fully vested, employees cannot lose their pension benefits even if they leave their jobs before retirement. Thus, ERISA encourages worker mobility by permitting an employee to accumulate pension rights while working different jobs.

ERISA also contains a complicated set of anti-backloading rules that seek to prevent employers from providing a retirement plan that only grows substantially in the last few years of an individual's employment. There are several different ways for retirement plans to satisfy these rules. To give one example, a defined benefit plan will meet the anti-backloading rules if the employee, upon leaving the job after his or her benefits have vested, would receive 3% of the sum to which he or she would be entitled had he or she retired at 65 multiplied by the number of years (not exceeding 33 1/3) that the employee worked (i.e., if an employee worked for 5 years, the employee would be entitled to 15% of the retirement benefits that he or she would have received if he or she had retired at 65).

In addition to its participation, vesting, and anti-backloading provisions, ERISA imposes minimum funding standards for defined benefit plans (but not for defined contribution plans, like 401k's). The Pension Protection Act of 2006 tightened those minimums. Previously, defined benefit plan sponsors were required to fund 90% of the present value of their commitments. The 2006 Act created a 100% funding requirement phased in between 2007 and 2011. While the increased funding requirements are both reasonable and desirable under normal economic circumstances, many businesses could not meet their new funding obligations during the financial crisis. On December 23, 2008, the President signed into law the Worker, Retiree, and Employer Act, P.L. 110–458 (H.R. 7327), which made technical corrections related to the 2006 Act. The new law allowed temporary extension of the funding improvement and rehabilitation periods for multiemployer pension plans in critical and endangered status for 2008 and 2009 and temporary waiver of required minimum distribution rules for certain retirement plans and accounts. The rules were eased to help businesses temporarily allocate more of their financial resources to other business operating needs.

To guard against abuse of pension plan assets, ERISA imposes various fiduciary requirements. Individuals identified as fiduciaries by ERISA include persons who exercise discretionary control over pension plan assets or who, for a fee, offer investment advice relating to the management of pension plan assets. Fiduciaries must, among other things, exercise the investment skill and care of a "prudent man," diversify the pension portfolio (without investing more than 10% percent of the plan's assets in the employer's securities), and refrain from using their access to plan assets to benefit themselves or other "parties-in-interest."

In addition to imposing fiduciary requirements, ERISA created the Pension Benefit Guarantee Corporation (PBGC), a nonprofit corporation within the Department of Labor, to insure against loss of pension benefits when plans are terminated. The Act requires that employers providing defined benefit plans purchase termination insurance through annual premiums. The premium rates are based on the number of participants in the pension plan and the plan's status as either a single-employer plan (covering the employees of one employer) or a multi-employer plan (maintained under a collective bargaining agreement to which more than one employer contributes). In 2014, the flat-rate premium was set at $49 per participant in a single-employer plan and $12 per participant in a multi-employer plan. The PBGC insures benefits only after a plan has been in effect for five years. Whereas retired employees are insured in full, employees who are still working are insured only for the benefits that have vested at the time the pension plan terminates. For both groups, ERISA insures pension benefits only up to a dollar limit (in 2014, the maximum insurance benefit insured for an employee retiring at 65 was $59,318.16 per year).

Under ERISA's reporting and disclosure provisions, plan administrators must provide employees summaries of their benefit plans, updates of major alterations, and synopses of annual reports on the financing and operation of the plans. Although employees may request a report on the status of their accrued pension benefits at any time, these reports must automatically be given to employees who leave their jobs temporarily or permanently. Plan administrators must also report certain detailed financial and actuarial data annually to the IRS.

The Department of Labor and the Internal Revenue Service of the Department of the Treasury administer (i.e., promulgate regulations pertaining to), monitor, and enforce compliance with ERISA's provisions. To promote ERISA's federalizing policy goals, specific provisions state explicitly that the law preempts state and local laws on pension plan participation and vesting, funding, fiduciary responsibilities, termination insurance, as well as disclosure and reporting procedures. The IRS is responsible for enforcing ERISA's participation, vesting, and funding standards. It enforces the participation and vesting requirements by disqualifying offending plans from tax-exempt status. It achieves compliance with the minimum funding standards through an excise tax on accumulated funding deficiencies. The Labor Department has general responsibility for investigating possible violations of all of ERISA's provisions and specific responsibility for handling breaches of the Act's fiduciary standards and reporting and disclosure requirements. It enforces ERISA's fiduciary standards by relieving fiduciaries of their duties, suing fiduciaries to recover losses they cause, and assessing civil penalties against parties-in-interest who engage in prohibited transactions. It administers the Act's reporting and disclosure requirements by suing plan administrators to force compliance or by retaining accountants and actuaries to gather information plan administrators should have provided. ERISA supplements these means of enforcement by granting a private right of action to plan participants and beneficiaries who are harmed by violations of the Act's provisions. As far as the statute of limitations, ERISA § 413 provides either a six-year limitation after the date of the last action which constitutes part of the breach or the date on which the fiduciary could have cured or the breach, or alternatively, three years after the earliest date on which the plaintiff had actual knowledge of the breach. The U.S. Supreme Court in Intel Corp. Inv. Pol'y Comm. v. Sulyma, 140 S.Ct. 768 (2020), decided in February of 2020 the meaning of the term "actual knowledge" in the 3-year limitation provision. More specifically, the Court decided that such language did not apply in a plan mismanagement case where the employer simply posted plan information online and sent disclosures in the mail and there was no evidence he actually knew about the employer's employee benefit plan actions.

ERISA does not apply to government employees—federal, state, or local. Many state and local government pension plans are severely underfunded, and will present a social problem when obligations come due that can only be met by tax increases.

b.   DEFINED CONTRIBUTION PLANS

During the past two decades, defined contribution pension plans have grown significantly in importance. Defined benefit plans provide a formula, related to final years' salary, for computing benefits that extend from retirement to death. Thus the employer sets aside and invests funds while accepting the risks associated with investment performance. Defined contribution plans, on the other hand, do not specify the amount of benefits to be paid at retirement. Instead, the employer—typically at the employee's option—sets aside pre-tax money during the employee's working years; the employee may add those contributions, and may choose investment vehicles from the options—various stock and bond funds—offered by the employer. Thus, the retiree's financial resources depend on the amount that was invested and the performance of the investments. The private sector version of these plans is often referred to as a 401(k) plan. ERISA compliance costs are substantially lower than the heavily regulated defined benefit plans.

Recent growth of defined contribution plans is in part a reflection of mounting corporate frustration with defined benefit plans, which can create large liabilities on balance sheets if they are underfunded or if pension investments perform poorly. Some employees, too, seem to favor defined contribution plans. Portability, control over investment assets, and a perception that the assets in defined contribution accounts are the "employee's money" are reasons for employees' preference for 401(k) plans. In addition, as large companies increasingly seek to cut the cost of expensive defined benefit plans, employees might view defined contribution plans as less susceptible to employer modification. Finally, since ERISA's provisions regulating defined contribution plans are less complex, regulatory compliance costs for defined contribution plans are much less than they are for defined benefit plans—this benefit can be passed down to employees in the form of lower fees for account maintenance and investment management.

ERISA regulates defined contribution plans differently and (for the most part) more lightly than defined benefit plans. Most defined contribution plans, for example, are exempt from the diversification requirement. Moreover, a fiduciary's duties with regards to a defined contribution plan can be significantly lessened if the defined contribution plan meets certain criteria. Section 404(c) of ERISA relieves fiduciaries of significant responsibilities if the participant exercises control over their retirement account. Also, note that the Pension Benefit Guaranty Corporation does not insure defined contribution plans.

(i)   Changes in the Law Governing Defined Contribution Plans

In 2006, Congress passed and President Bush signed the Pension Protection Act (PPA). In addition to tightening the funding requirements of defined benefit plans, the law also contained a number of significant changes to the ERISA provisions covering 401(k) plans. Companies had previously been reluctant to enroll newly hired workers automatically— in other words, setting an "opt out" default—in a 401(k) account and, when they did, placed employees in the most conservative investments to avoid liability in a private lawsuit. As a result of the liability concerns prior to the PPA, an overwhelming amount of "defaulted" savings was placed and held in assets such as guaranteed insurance contracts and money market funds. The Pension Protection Act created safe harbors from employer liability for investment losses associated with defaulted funds. The law left primary responsibility for determining what investments qualified as defaults to the Department of Labor, which promulgated a regulation designating three types of diversified investment strategies as Qualified Default Investment Alternatives (QDIAs). Those investments use either a risk or age-based strategy with the latter adjusting its investment mix gradually as an investor nears retirement. The age-based or "target-date" strategies have proved the most popular default setting among employers. According to Morningstar, target-date mutual fund assets reached more than $650 billion as of March 31, 2014. See pages 1–3 of Morningstar 2014 Target-Date Series Research Paper (http://corporate.morningstar.com/us/documents/MethodologyDocuments/MethodologyPapers/2014-Target-Date-Series-Research-Paper.pdf).

DOL's default investment regulations require companies to follow a "prudent" process in selecting a default fund, and specify that investment strategies be based on three considerations: age, life expectancy, or retirement date. If the employer meets these criteria, however, the participants are deemed to have exercised control over their investments despite their never having elected the default investment. Under ERISA's 404(c) provision, mentioned above, this relieves the employer of liability for investment losses even in a default investment.

Controversy erupted over the default investments, in particular target-date funds, during the 2008 market crisis when the downturn revealed that some target-date funds were invested aggressively in equities despite being managed for participants only a few years away from retirement. As a result, the DOL has proposed changes to the regulatory guidance, but not the formal rule, governing the default investments to increase disclosure to plan participants at the time of investment. Given that the automatic enrollment and default provisions are designed to take advantage of investor apathy and inaction, is increased disclosure alone a viable solution?

Despite the recent criticism, much evidence has shown that the PPA's automatic enrollment and default investment provisions have been a success in increasing retirement savings. The Employee Benefit Research Institute recently found that automatic enrollment had decreased the number of employees at risk of falling short of savings in retirement by more than ten percentage points across several generational categories.

(ii) Employer Liability for Managing DC Plans

While Section 404(c) and the new qualified default investment rule significantly scale back any possible employer liability for investment losses in 401(k) accounts, employers are still fiduciaries under ERISA and their selection and administration of 401(k) plans creates other sources of liabilities and exposure to claims by participants. In late 2006, a St. Louis law firm filed suit against seven major U.S. employers—including Lockheed Martin, General Dynamics, International Paper and United Technologies—alleging that the employers had allowed 401(k) service providers to charge excessive fees to participants in the plans. Those suits have since expanded as other plaintiffs' firms have taken notice, and while some cases have settled, courts have also made clear that a prudent process, even more than a particular level of fees, is the essential ingredient to employers meeting their fiduciary responsibilities of selecting and overseeing the 401(k) service provider.

A second ripe source of 401(k) litigation is the inclusion of company stock in plans. Particularly as a result of court decisions stemming from the Enron implosion and subsequent corporate scandals, employers have significantly scaled back the use of company stock in 401(k) plans, as executives are faced with the dual roles of fiduciary to shareholders, and fiduciary to 401(k) participants in providing the investment in the employer's DC plan.

LaRue v. DeWolff, Boberg & Associates, Inc.
552 U.S. 248 (2008).

■ JUSTICE STEVENS delivered the opinion of the Court.

In Massachusetts Mut. Life Ins. Co. v. Russell, 473 U.S. 134 (1985), we held that a participant in a disability plan that paid a fixed level of benefits could not bring suit under § 502(a)(2) of the Employee Retirement Income Security Act of 1974 (ERISA) to recover consequential damages arising from delay in the processing of her claim. In this case we consider whether that statutory provision authorizes a participant in a defined contribution pension plan to sue a fiduciary whose alleged misconduct impaired the value of plan assets in the participant's individual account. Relying on our decision in Russell, the Court of Appeals for the Fourth Circuit held that § 502(a)(2) "provides remedies only for entire plans, not for individuals. . . . Recovery under this subsection must 'inure[ ] to the benefit of the plan as a whole,' not to particular persons with rights under the plan." While language in our Russell opinion is consistent with that conclusion, the rationale for Russell's holding supports the opposite result in this case.

Petitioner filed this action in 2004 against his former employer, DeWolff, Boberg & Associates, and the ERISA-regulated 401(k) retirement savings plan administered by DeWolff. The Plan permits participants to direct the investment of their contributions in accordance with specified procedures and requirements. Petitioner alleged that in 2001 and 2002 he directed DeWolff to make certain changes to the investments in his individual account, but DeWolff never carried out these directions. Petitioner claimed that this omission "depleted" his interest in the Plan by approximately $150,000, and amounted to a breach of fiduciary duty under ERISA. The complaint sought " 'make-whole' or other equitable relief as allowed by [§ 502(a)(3)]," as well as "such other and further relief as the court deems just and proper."

Respondents filed a motion for judgment on the pleadings, arguing that the complaint was essentially a claim for monetary relief that is not recoverable under § 502(a)(3). Petitioner countered that he "d[id] not wish for the court to award him any money, but . . . simply want[ed] the plan to properly reflect that which would be his interest in the plan, but for the breach of fiduciary duty." The District Court concluded, however, that since respondents did not possess any disputed funds that rightly belonged to petitioner, he was seeking damages rather than equitable relief available under § 502(a)(3). Assuming, arguendo, that respondents had breached a fiduciary duty, the District Court nonetheless granted their motion. . .

Section 502(a)(2) provides for suits to enforce the liability-creating provisions of § 409, concerning breaches of fiduciary duties that harm plans. . .

As the case comes to us we must assume that respondents breached fiduciary obligations defined in § 409(a), and that those breaches had an adverse impact on the value of the plan assets in petitioner's individual account. Whether petitioner can prove those allegations and whether respondents may have valid defenses to the claim are matters not before us. Although the record does not reveal the relative size of petitioner's account, the legal issue under § 502(a)(2) is the same whether his account includes 1% or 99% of the total assets in the plan.

As we explained in *Russell*, and in more detail in our later opinion in Varity Corp. v. Howe, 516 U.S. 489 (1996), § 502(a) of ERISA identifies six types of civil actions that may be brought by various parties. The second, which is at issue in this case, authorizes the Secretary of Labor as well as plan participants, beneficiaries, and fiduciaries, to bring actions on behalf of a plan to recover for violations of the obligations defined in § 409(a). The principal statutory duties imposed on fiduciaries by that section "relate to the proper management, administration, and investment of fund assets," with an eye toward ensuring that "the benefits authorized by the plan" are ultimately paid to participants and beneficiaries. . . The misconduct alleged by the petitioner in this case falls squarely within that category.

The misconduct alleged in *Russell*, by contrast, fell outside this category. The plaintiff in Russell received all of the benefits to which she was contractually entitled, but sought consequential damages arising from a delay in the processing of her claim. In holding that § 502(a)(2) does not provide a remedy for this type of injury, we stressed that the text of § 409(a) characterizes the relevant fiduciary relationship as one "with respect to a plan," and repeatedly identifies the "plan" as the victim of any fiduciary breach and the recipient of any relief. The legislative history likewise revealed that "the crucible of congressional concern was misuse and mismanagement of plan assets by plan administrators." Finally, our review of ERISA as a whole confirmed that §§ 502(a)(2) and 409 protect "the financial integrity of the plan," whereas other provisions specifically address claims for benefits. . .

Russell's emphasis on protecting the "entire plan" from fiduciary misconduct reflects the former landscape of employee benefit plans. That landscape has changed.

Defined contribution plans dominate the retirement plan scene today. In contrast, when ERISA was enacted, and when Russell was decided, "the [defined benefit] plan was the norm of American pension practice." Unlike the defined contribution plan in this case, the disability plan at issue in Russell did not have individual accounts; it paid a fixed benefit based on a percentage of the employee's salary.

The "entire plan" language in Russell speaks to the impact of § 409 on plans that pay defined benefits. Misconduct by the administrators of a defined benefit plan will not affect an individual's entitlement to a defined benefit unless it creates or enhances the risk of default by the entire plan. It was that default risk that prompted Congress to require defined benefit plans (but not defined contribution plans) to satisfy complex minimum funding requirements, and to make premium payments to the Pension Benefit Guaranty Corporation for plan termination insurance.

For defined contribution plans, however, fiduciary misconduct need not threaten the solvency of the entire plan to reduce benefits below the amount that participants would otherwise receive. Whether a fiduciary breach diminishes plan assets payable to all participants and beneficiaries, or only to persons tied to particular individual accounts, it creates the kind of harms that concerned the draftsmen of § 409. Consequently, our references to the "entire plan" in Russell, which accurately reflect the operation of § 409 in the defined benefit context, are beside the point in the defined contribution context. . .

We therefore hold that although § 502(a)(2) does not provide a remedy for individual injuries distinct from plan injuries, that provision does authorize recovery for fiduciary breaches that impair the value of plan assets in a participant's individual account. Accordingly, the judgment of the Court of Appeals is vacated, and the case is remanded for further proceedings consistent with this opinion.

NOTE ON CASH BALANCE PLANS

Many employers also offer so-called cash balance pension plans, which are a hybrid between defined benefit and defined contribution plans. Under most cash balance plans, employees are given a hypothetical cash account that is credited with a defined sum of hypothetical dollars each year that they work. In addition to the yearly credits of "cash," an employees' cash balance account is also increased by "interest credits," which pay hypothetical interest, at a set rate (often the t-bills rate plus one percentage point) on the accumulated value of the employees' "cash." Upon retirement, an employee can receive the value of his cash balance account in real money.

Though cash balance plans combine features of defined benefit and defined contribution plans, for the purposes of ERISA they are considered to be defined benefit plans. Despite this, the use of cash balance plans has increased even as companies shed traditional defined benefit plans. Typically, cash balance plans are used by companies that wish to transition away from defined benefit plans.

Prior to the Pension Protection Act of 2006, one court found that cash balance plans violated ERISA's requirement that rates of benefit accrual must not decrease according to age. See Richards v. FleetBoston Fin. Corp., 427 F.Supp.2d 150 (D. Conn. 2006), superseded by statute, Pension Protection Act of 2006, 120 Stat. 780 (2006). *Richards* reasoned that older employees receive less money from "interest credits" than younger employees do, since older employees will retire sooner and thus will receive the interest credits for fewer years. Other courts rejected this conclusion. See, e.g., Cooper v. IBM, 457 F.3d 636 (7th Cir. 2006). The Pension Protection Act effectively overturned *Richards* by providing that interest credits do not violate ERISA if they are not greater than the "market rate of return," as defined by the Secretary of the Treasury.

NOTES AND QUESTIONS

1.   ERISA also bars plan amendments that decrease accrued or vested benefits. In Shaw v. International Workers Pension Plan, 750 F.2d 1458 (9th Cir.), cert. denied, 471 U.S. 1137 (1985), plaintiff retired with a union pension plan that had a cost-of-living feature indexing benefits to salary increases in his former position. When the pension plan looked underfunded, delegates to the union convention voted to phase out the cost of living increase provision. The court held that the formula for benefit increases was an "accrued benefit" and could not be reduced.

In Central Laborer's Pension Fund v. Heinz, 541 U.S. 739 (2004), a multi-employer plan toughened the rules covering when alternative post-retirement employment (double-dipping) triggers suspension of benefits. The Supreme Court held that this action cut back accrued benefits and thus violated ERISA.

In Osberg v. Foot Locker, 862 F.3d. 198 (2d Cir. 2017), cert. denied, 138 S. Ct. 981 (2018), the company was found by the district court to have violated ERISA by converting to a cash balance pension plan that cut back employee benefits without explaining the changes properly to its employees. On appeal, the parties disputed the proper nature of equitable relief under ERISA section 502(a)(3). The court sided with the employees in reforming the plan to what they should have received before the conversion to the cash balance plan that breached the employer's fiduciary duties, even though this reformation resulted in a windfall to certain plan participants.

2. Even if a plan says benefits are limited to the amount in the fund, ERISA declares "nonforfeitable" the participant's right to the full set of promises made in the plan. Thus, solvent employers are liable to the full extent of plan commitments. Nachman Corp. v. Pension Benefit Guaranty Corp., 446 U.S. 359 (1980).

3. Is ERISA too paternalistic? ERISA's coverage rules require that all eligible employees be included for ERISA plans, whether they wish to be or not. 29 U.S.C. § 1052. ERISA also requires that each qualifying plan provide a survivor's annuity. 29 U.S.C. § 1055. It also has strict anti-alienation provisions. 29 U.S.C. § 1056(d). More fundamentally, is ERISA's core purpose—strongly encouraging employees and employers to save for retirement—misguided? Should employees and employers be allowed to make their own retirement planning decisions?

Some argue that chronic under-saving is evidence that ERISA should be more, not less, paternalistic. See Paul M. Secunda, The Behavioral Economic Case for Paternalistic Workplace Pensions, 91 Ind. L. J. 505 (2016) (maintaining that auto-enrollment and auto-enrollment should be used to default employee into 401(k) plans); Susan J. Stabile, Paternalism Isn't Always a Dirty Word. Can the Law Better Protect Defined Contribution Plan Participants?, 5 Emp. Rts. Emp. Pol'y J. 491 (2001) (arguing that, in order to increase retirement savings, participant direction in 401(k) investments should be eliminated and employees should not be given the option to cash out their 401(k) plans when they switch jobs). By contrast, others argue that ERISA should be modified to allow employees greater access to their defined contribution plans. See Edward J. Gac & Wayne M. Gazur, Tapping "Rainy Day" Funds for the Reluctant Entrepreneur: Downsizing, Paternalism, and the Internal Revenue Code, 86 Ky. L.J. 127 (1998) (arguing that employees should be able to tap their defined contribution accounts in order to fund the creation of new businesses).

4. Not all commentators are particularly enamored of the growth of defined contribution plans:

> The private pension system is only incidentally about retirement income. To be sure, private pension plans do and will deliver retirement income to many participants, but in its larger dimension the system is best understood as part of a group of tax shelters that are designed to abate the progressivity of the income tax for the affluent * * *

> More and more of the wealth that is channeled through private pension accounts is being accumulated not for the purpose of providing retirement income but for discretionary savings and for intergenerational wealth transfer to children and grandchildren. The use of pension accounts as tax-favored savings, investment, and wealth transmission devices is possible only in a defined contribution system, in which the participant builds an individual account whose unexpected proceeds can be accessed for non-retirement purposes or left to transferees. In a 401(k) * * *, the participant can cash out in whole or in part at any time (free of

penalty after age fifty-nine and a half). If the participant or spouse leaves unexpended proceeds at death, the minimum distribution rules allow heirs or other transferees to perpetuate the tax shelter for many years as they draw down the account. These attributes of individual account plans have been a major attraction in the notable shift from defined benefit to defined contribution plans * * * Defined benefit plans typically pay retirement income only, and only for the participant and spouse. If they die early, the shortening of the payment obligation benefits the plan sponsor, not the heirs.

John H. Langbein, *Social Security and the Pension System*, In Search of Retirement Security (Theresa Ghilarduccia et al., eds., 2004).

Is Professor Langbein's criticism persuasive? The answer to this question likely depends on one's view of the proper objectives of pension plans. Are pension plans a type of employer-provided safety net, designed to ensure a minimum standard of living for the elderly? Or are they a form of deferred compensation? If pension plans are a form of compensation, shouldn't pension plan beneficiaries be able to bequeath their pension plan savings to their heirs? Does this argument justify allowing heirs to benefit from ERISA's tax advantages? The Setting Every Community Up for Retirement Enhancement Act (Secure) Act, enacted on December 20, 2019, no longer permits so-called "stretch" Individual Retirement Accounts (IRAs) so that such retirement accounts cannot be held by heirs of deceased account holders for more than ten years (though this does not apply to defined benefit pension plans). Historically, most of these inherited IRAs were bequeathed from wealthy relatives at death and were being utilized as tax-shelters by their younger descendants until they themselves became the minimum age for penalty-free distribution at age 59 1/2. This provisions applies to death of IRA holders that occur after 2019.

5.   Pension funds hold a staggering amount of assets. Has the dramatic increase in the amount of assets controlled by pension plans effected a fundamental change in the American economy?

> If "socialism is defined as 'ownership of the means of production by the workers' "—and this is the orthodox definition—then the United States it the most "socialist" country in the world * * *
>
> [The] large employee pension funds * * * own a controlling interest in * * * the 1000 largest industrial corporations [and] the 50 largest companies in each of the "non-industrial" groups—that is, banking, insurance, retail, communications, and transportation. Indeed, a larger sector of the American economy (outside of farming) today is owned by the American workers—through his investment agent, the pension fund—then Allende in Chile proposed to bring under government ownership to make Chile a "socialist country," [or] than Castro's Cuba has actually nationalized * * *

The United States, without even consciously trying, has "socialized" the economy without "nationalizing it." * * *

Altogether, America's "pension fund 'socialism'" teaches that the 19th-century ideologies of the "system"—the juxtaposition, especially, of "capitalism" and "socialism"—have become obsolete, if not meaningless. "Pension fund 'socialism'" is genuine "socialism"; if anybody, 100 years ago, could have foreseen this outcome, he would surely have predicted it to have profound impact on the "system." Power relationships would change radically; the role and function of management, if not our institutions themselves, would be changed drastically * * * None of these things has happened. In fact, the coming of "socialism" to American has not had the slightest discernable impact on American institutions.

Peter Drucker, Pension Fund "Socialism," The Public Interest, 3–6, 44–46 (1976).

6. About 55 million American workers have no access to an employer-created retirement savings plan. As a solution, several states passed or were considering legislation that would require certain employers or permit certain cities or counties to enroll workers in a state plan. The Obama Department of Labor issued a rule encouraging states to do this. But the Republican Congress and President Trump have now most recently "disapproved" the rule so that "such rule shall have no force or effect." The Senate vote was 50–49. Public Law 115–35, 115th Congress.

c.   FIDUCIARY DUTIES UNDER ERISA

As noted above, ERISA imposes fiduciary duties on various persons responsible for management of ERISA plans and their assets. Although in some cases it is relatively clear which individuals or entities are ERISA fiduciaries, often this issue is quite complex. The relevant provision of ERISA states: "a person is a fiduciary with respect to a plan to the extent (i) he exercises any discretionary authority or discretionary control respecting management of such plan or exercises any authority or control respecting management or disposition of its assets, (ii) he renders investment advice for a fee or other compensation, direct or indirect, with respect to any moneys or other property of such plan, or has any authority or responsibility to do so, or (iii) he has any discretionary authority or discretionary responsibility in the administration of such plan." 29 U.S.C. § 1002(21)(A). Also, "the definition [of fiduciaries] includes persons who have authority and responsibility with respect to the matter in question, regardless of their formal title." H.R. Rep.No. 1280, 93d Cong., 2d Sess., reprinted in 1974 U.S. Code Cong. & Admin. News 4639, 5038, 5103.

Varity Corp. v. Howe
516 U.S. 489 (1996).

■ JUSTICE BREYER delivered the opinion of the Court.

The key facts, as found by the District Court after trial, include the following: Charles Howe, and the other respondents, used to work for Massey-Ferguson, Inc., a farm equipment manufacturer, and a wholly owned subsidiary of the petitioner, Varity Corporation. (Since the lower courts found that Varity and Massey-Ferguson were "alter egos," we shall refer to them interchangeably.) These employees all were participants in, and beneficiaries of, Massey-Ferguson's self-funded employee welfare benefit plan—an ERISA-protected plan that Massey-Ferguson itself administered. In the mid-1980's, Varity became concerned that some of Massey-Ferguson's divisions were losing too much money and developed a business plan to deal with the problem.

The business plan—which Varity called "Project Sunshine"—amounted to placing many of Varity's money-losing eggs in one financially rickety basket. It called for a transfer of Massey-Ferguson's money-losing divisions, along with various other debts, to a newly created, separately incorporated subsidiary called Massey Combines. The plan foresaw the possibility that Massey Combines would fail. But it viewed such a failure, from Varity's business perspective, as closer to a victory than to a defeat. That is because Massey Combine's failure would not only eliminate several of Varity's poorly performing divisions, but it would also eradicate various debts that Varity would transfer to Massey Combines, and which, in the absence of the reorganization, Varity's more profitable subsidiaries or divisions might have to pay.

Among the obligations that Varity hoped the reorganization would eliminate were those arising from the Massey-Ferguson benefit plan's promises to pay medical and other nonpension benefits to employees of Massey-Ferguson's money-losing divisions. Rather than terminate those benefits directly (as it had retained the right to do), Varity attempted to avoid the undesirable fallout that could have accompanied cancellation by inducing the failing divisions' employees to switch employers and thereby voluntarily release Massey-Ferguson from its obligation to provide them benefits (effectively substituting the new, self-funded Massey Combines benefit plan for the former Massey-Ferguson plan). Insofar as Massey-Ferguson's employees did so, a subsequent Massey Combines failure would eliminate—simply and automatically, without distressing the remaining Massey-Ferguson employees—what would otherwise have been Massey-Ferguson's obligation to pay those employees their benefits.

To persuade the employees of the failing divisions to accept the change of employer and benefit plan, Varity called them together at a special meeting and talked to them about Massey Combines' future business outlook, its likely financial viability, and the security of their employee benefits. The thrust of Varity's remarks was that the employees' benefits would remain secure if they voluntarily transferred to Massey Combines. As Varity knew, however, the reality was very different. Indeed, the District Court found that Massey Combines was insolvent from the day of its creation and that it hid a $46 million negative net worth by overvaluing its assets and underestimating its liabilities.

After the presentation, about 1,500 Massey-Ferguson employees accepted Varity's assurances and voluntarily agreed to the transfer. * * * Unfortunately for these employees, Massey Combines ended its first year with a loss of $88 million, and ended its second year in a receivership, under which its employees lost their nonpension benefits. Many of those employees * * * brought this lawsuit, seeking the benefits they would have been owed under their old, Massey-Ferguson plan, had they not transferred to Massey Combines. * * *

Varity has raised two additional issues. First, Varity points out that the relevant ERISA section imposes liability only upon plan *fiduciaries*; and it argues that it was acting only as an *employer* and not as a plan *fiduciary* when it deceived its employees. Second, it argues that, in any event, its conduct did not violate the fiduciary standard that ERISA imposes. * * *

We begin with the question of Varity's fiduciary status. In relevant part, the statute says that a "person is a fiduciary with respect to a plan," and therefore subject to ERISA fiduciary duties, "to the extent" that he or she "exercises any discretionary authority or discretionary control respecting management" of the plan, or "has any discretionary authority or discretionary responsibility in the administration" of the plan. ERISA § 3(21)(A).

Varity was *both* an employer *and* the benefit plan's administrator, as ERISA permits. But, obviously, not all of Varity's business activities involved plan management or administration. Varity argues that when it communicated with its Massey-Ferguson workers about transferring to Massey Combines, it was not administering or managing the plan; rather, it was acting only in its capacity as an *employer* and not as a plan *administrator*. * * *

The relevant factual circumstances include the following: In the spring of 1986, Varity summoned the employees of Massey-Ferguson's money-losing divisions to a meeting at Massey-Ferguson's corporate headquarters for a 30-minute presentation. The employees saw a 90-second videotaped message from Mr. Ivan Porter, a Varity vice president and Massey Combines' newly appointed president. They also received four documents: (a) a several-page, detailed comparison between the employee benefits offered by Massey-Ferguson and those offered by Massey Combines; (b) a question-and-answer sheet; (c) a transcript of the Porter videotape; and (d) a cover letter with an acceptance form. Each of these documents discussed employee benefits and benefit plans, some briefly in general terms, and others at length and in detail * * *

[The documents and videotape stated that the new entity would be responsible for transferred employees benefits and contained assurances that transferred employees' benefits, including their pension benefits, would remain the same. The videotape also stated that "employment conditions in the future will depend on the success of the Massey Combines Corporation and should changes be deemed appropriate or necessary, they will be made. Finally, despite the depression which persists in the North American economy, I am excited about the future of Massey Combines Corporation."]

To decide whether Varity's actions fall within the statutory definition of "fiduciary" acts, we must interpret the statutory terms which limit the scope of fiduciary activity to discretionary acts of plan "management" and "administration." These words are not self-defining, and the activity at issue here neither falls clearly within nor outside of the common understanding of these words. * * * [it is] important here to look to the common law, which, over the years, has given to terms such as "fiduciary" and trust "administration" a legal meaning to which, we normally presume, Congress meant to refer. The ordinary trust law understanding of fiduciary "administration" of a trust is that to act as an administrator is to perform the duties imposed, or exercise the powers conferred, by the trust documents. The law of trusts also understands a trust document to implicitly confer "such powers as are necessary or appropriate for the carrying out of the purposes" of the trust. Conveying information about the likely future of plan benefits, thereby permitting beneficiaries to make an informed choice about continued participation, would seem to be an exercise of a power "appropriate" to carrying out an important plan purpose. After all, ERISA itself specifically requires administrators to give beneficiaries certain information about the plan. And administrators, as part of their administrative responsibilities, frequently offer beneficiaries more than the minimum information that the statute requires—for example, answering beneficiaries' questions about the meaning of the terms of a plan so that those beneficiaries can more easily obtain the plan's benefits. To offer beneficiaries detailed plan information in order to help them decide whether to remain with the plan is essentially the same kind of plan-related activity.

Moreover, as far as the record reveals, Mr. Porter's letter, videotape, and the other documents came from those within the firm who had authority to communicate as fiduciaries with plan beneficiaries. Varity does not claim that it authorized only special individuals, not connected with the meeting documents, to speak as plan administrators.

Finally, reasonable employees, in the circumstances found by the District Court, could have thought that Varity was communicating with them *both* in its capacity as employer *and* in its capacity as plan administrator. Reasonable employees might not have distinguished consciously between the two roles. But they would have known that the employer was their plan's administrator and had expert knowledge about how their plan worked. The central conclusion ("your benefits are secure") could well have drawn strength from their awareness of that expertise, and one could reasonably believe that the employer, aware of the importance of the matter, so intended.

We conclude, therefore, that the factual context in which the statements were made, combined with the plan-related nature of the activity, engaged in by those who had plan-related authority to do so, together provide sufficient support for the District Court's legal conclusion that Varity was acting as a fiduciary. * * *

Varity says that when it made the statements that most worried the District Court—the statements about Massey Combines' "bright future"—it must have been speaking only as employer (and not as fiduciary), for statements about a new subsidiary's financial future have virtually nothing to do with administering benefit plans. But this argument parses the meeting's communications too finely. The ultimate message Varity intended to convey—"your benefits are secure"—depended in part upon its repeated assurances that benefits would remain "unchanged," in part upon the detailed comparison of benefits, and in part upon assurances about Massey Combines' "bright" financial future. Varity's workers would not necessarily have focused upon each underlying supporting statement separately, because what primarily interested them, and what primarily interested the District Court, was the truthfulness of the ultimate conclusion that transferring to Massey Combines would not adversely affect the security of their benefits. And, in the present context, Varity's statements about the security of benefits amounted to an act of plan administration. That Varity intentionally communicated its conclusion through a closely linked set of statements * * * does not change this conclusion.

We do not hold * * * that Varity acted as a fiduciary simply because it made statements about its expected financial condition or because "an ordinary business decision turned out to have an adverse impact on the plan." Instead, we accept the undisputed facts found, and factual inferences drawn, by the District Court, namely, that Varity *intentionally* connected its statements about Massey Combines' financial health to statements it made about the future of benefits, so that its intended communication about the security of benefits was rendered materially misleading. And we hold that making intentional representations about the future of plan benefits in that context is an act of plan administration.

Third, Varity says that an employer's decision to amend or terminate a plan (as Varity had the right to do) is not an act of plan administration. How then, it asks, could conveying information about the likelihood of termination be an act of plan administration? While it may be true that amending or terminating a plan (or a common-law trust) is beyond the power of a plan administrator (or trustee)—and, therefore, cannot be an act of plan "management" or "administration"—it does not follow that making statements about the likely future of the plan is also beyond the scope of plan administration. As we explained above, plan administrators often have, and commonly exercise, discretionary authority to communicate with beneficiaries about the future of plan benefits.

NOTES AND QUESTIONS

1. Generally, employers are not fiduciaries with respect to plans that they create. Usually, as *Varity* notes, when employers create, change, or terminate a plan, they are not acting as fiduciaries; instead they are acting in a capacity that is somewhat analogous to the settlor of a trust. See Lockheed v. Spink, 517 U.S. 882, 890–901 (1996). Yet, employers become a fiduciary when they are named administrator of a plan. Also, if the plan does not name an administrator, the employer becomes the administrator by default, in which case it is an ERISA fiduciary. Finally, employers can become fiduciaries even if they appoint a separate administrator if they actually exercise the types of authority (or render investment advice for a fee) outlined by 29 U.S.C. § 1002(21)(A). The Secure Act of 2019 added a new safe harbor for fiduciaries who follow appropriate steps when selecting life-time income options for defined contribution plans, like annuities. Under these provisions, (1) fiduciaries must make a prudent selection but may rely on written representations from insurers regarding their financial standing under state insurance law; (2) a fiduciary is not required to select the lowest cost contract and may consider other features and benefits and attributes of the insurer; (3) fiduciaries are not required to monitor the continued appropriateness of a selection after the purchase of a contract; and (4) fiduciaries are deemed to conduct a periodic review if they obtain written representations from the insurer on an annual basis.

2. When a corporation is named as a fiduciary, its officers and directors can also become fiduciaries, although courts apply different approaches to this issue. In Confer v. Custom Eng'g Co., 952 F.2d 34 (3d Cir. 1991), the Third Circuit held that a corporation's officers do not become fiduciaries unless they are officially given some individual discretionary role in plan administration (as would happen, for example, if the corporation designates an officer as plan administrator). Officers who exercise discretionary control over a plan without such an official delegation of authority are not fiduciaries. Other courts disagree, finding that officers who actually exercise discretionary authority in managing plans can become fiduciaries, even without an official designation of authority. See, e.g., Kayes v. Pacific Lumber Co., 51 F.3d 1449, 1459–61 (9th Cir. 1995). Which approach is more faithful to the statutory language?

3. Is it sensible to expect a high-ranking business executive to change hats and make decisions as a pension plan fiduciary? The leading case is Donovan v. Bierwirth, 680 F.2d 263 (2d Cir. 1982), cert. denied, 459 U.S. 1069 (1982). John Bierwirth was Chairman of the Board of Grumman Corporation, an aircraft manufacturer on Long Island. LTV sought to buy Grumman, which would have moved many jobs to southern California. Bierwirth and colleagues used Grumman pension money to buy Grumman stock so they could vote it (and the substantial amount of Grumman stock the pension plan already held) against the takeover. (ERISA permits 10 percent of the funds in a company pension plan to be invested in that company's stock.) Judge Henry Friendly found this in violation of their ERISA duty to act "solely in the interests of the participants and beneficiaries" since it seemed likely that rejecting the merger would cause Grumman stock to decline in price. In a footnote he noted that "Bierwirth was a law school graduate and had practiced for 3 years." For criticism of the Bierwirth decision see Daniel Fischel & John Langbein, ERISA's Fundamental Contradiction: The Exclusive Benefit Rule, 55 U. Chi. L. Rev. 1105 (1986).

Increasingly, companies (and their officers and directors) that are the targets of large securities and corporate fraud lawsuits also find themselves under attack by ERISA beneficiaries claiming a breach of ERISA fiduciary duties. Many of these ERISA suits raise complex issues regarding plan document interpretation and the imposition of fiduciary duties. For example, in In re WorldCom, Inc. ERISA Litigation, 263 F.Supp.2d 745 (S.D.N.Y. 2003), the court considered WorldCom's plan, which authorized "any" WorldCom officer to perform tasks as "investment fiduciary" if WorldCom did not appoint such a person. The court dismissed ERISA claims against three WorldCom officers, holding that such a provision does not make an officer who does not actually manage or administer the plan a fiduciary. The court reasoned that to hold otherwise would substitute the word "all" for "any."

The WorldCom plaintiffs also argued that WorldCom's directors became ERISA fiduciaries by reserving the right to appoint and remove individuals who exercised fiduciary functions. The WorldCom court rejected this argument, reasoning that it "would make any supervisor of an ERISA fiduciary also an ERISA fiduciary." Id. at 760. By contrast, in Tittle v. Enron Corp., 284 F.Supp.2d 511 (S.D.Tex.2003), the court held that Enron chairman Kenneth Lay was a fiduciary because he had appointed individuals to fiduciary positions for Enron's ERISA plans. The court found that Lay had a duty to monitor his appointees. The court distinguished WorldCom by noting that the WorldCom directors had not actually appointed individuals to their fiduciary positions. Do you find anything wrong with such a distinction?

4.   Attorneys, accountants, actuaries, and other professional service providers generally are not held to be ERISA fiduciaries if their only connection with the plan is the ordinary provision of professional services. Yet, when professional service firms go beyond their traditional advisory function and in effect assert discretionary authority over plan management, they may be held liable as fiduciaries. See Tittle v. Enron Corp., 284 F.Supp.2d 511 (S.D.Tex.2003) (denying motion to dismiss ERISA breach of fiduciary duty claims against Arthur Andersen, the accounting firm that allegedly assisted Enron's fraudulent practices, and some of its individual accountants).

5.   If a professional services firm is not a fiduciary, it will usually qualify as a "party-in-interest." ERISA prohibits parties-in-interest from making certain transactions with the plan, including the sale, exchange, or leasing

1198 TERMINATING THE RELATIONSHIP PART IV

of property or other assets (an oft-used exception allows some loans to plan beneficiaries). 29 U.S.C. §§ 1106, 1008. The 2006 Pension Protection Act relaxed these requirements somewhat to allow defined contribution plans to contract with investment advisors to provide advice (which must meet certain requirements) to participants. Parties-in-interest also may not knowingly assist fiduciaries in breaching their fiduciary duties. While ERISA fiduciaries can be personally liable for plan losses, parties-in-interest are only subjected to equitable relief.

In a case to be decided in 2020 by the United States Supreme Court, Thole v. U.S. Bank, the question presented is whether defined benefit plan fiduciaries breached their fiduciary duties and engaged in prohibited transactions under ERISA by investing the Plan's entire investment portfolio in equities, including over 40 percent of the Plan's assets in parent company U.S. Bancorp's own mutual funds and lost a billion dollars. While the lawsuit was pending, defendants made $311 million in voluntary excess contributions to the Plan, thereby causing the plan to once again become overfunded and then moved to dismiss the case because the plaintiffs allegedly had no standing. The Eighth Circuit agreed that no injury exists where the plan is overfunded and is now in conflict with the Second, Third and Sixth Circuits, which have held that no individual financial loss is necessary to seek injunctive relief under ERISA § 502(a)(3).

6. The full text of the section defining ERISA fiduciaries' duties states:

    a fiduciary shall discharge his duties with respect to a plan solely in the interest of the participants and beneficiaries and—

    (A) for the exclusive purpose of:

    (i) providing benefits to participants and their beneficiaries; and

    (ii) defraying reasonable expenses of administering the plan;

    (B) with the care, skill, prudence, and diligence under the circumstances then prevailing that a prudent man acting in a like capacity and familiar with such matters would use in the conduct of an enterprise of a like character and with like aims;

    (C) by diversifying the investments of the plan so as to minimize the risk of large losses, unless under the circumstances it is clearly prudent not to do so; and

    (D) in accordance with the documents and instruments governing the plan insofar as such documents and instruments are consistent with the provisions of this subchapter and subchapter III of this chapter.

29 U.S.C. § 1104(1).

The "exclusive benefit" rule, described by *Bierwirth* as requiring that decisions be made "with an eye single to the interest of participants," is often referred to as ERISA fiduciaries' "duty of loyalty." Similarly, § 1104(1)(B) is often referred to as the "duty of prudence," while § 1104(1)(C) is often referred to as the "duty of diversification."

7.   What if union officials serving as trustees of a pension plan refuse to invest in stock of nonunion or antiunion companies? What if some workers urge the trustees to sell stock in tobacco companies (or companies with poor environmental records, defense contractors, manufacturers of "morning after" pills, etc.)? Which investment policy is "solely in the interest" of plan beneficiaries, as ERISA requires?

The Department of Labor, in an interpretive bulletin, states that "investments selected for the economic benefits they create apart from their investment return to the employee benefit plan * * * [would violate the duty of prudence if] it would be expected to provide a plan with a lower rate of return than available alternative investments with commensurate degrees of risk or is riskier than alternative available investments with commensurate rates of return." 29 C.F.R. § 2509–94.1. Such a position would appear to prohibit ERISA fiduciaries from making some politically-motivated investment decisions (also known as "socially responsible investing"). Would it prevent the actions taken by Lewis or Grumman?

8.   In Leigh v. Engle, 727 F.2d 113 (7th Cir. 1984), cert. denied, 489 U.S. 1078 (1989), administrators of an employee pension plan used pension funds to participate in corporate control contests in which they had an interest. The administrators won the takeover battles and the plan reaped enormous benefit. Nevertheless, the Seventh Circuit held the administrators liable for their breach of fiduciary duty:

> The [Trust's investments] * * * produced in the aggregate the extraordinary return on investment of 72%, exclusive of dividends. It is clear that the trust lost no money in the challenged transactions. The district court held that ERISA creates no cause of action where a breach of fiduciary duty does not cause financial harm to the benefit plan, * * * but the district court erred in this statement of the law. ERISA clearly contemplates actions against fiduciaries who profit by using trust assets, even where the plan beneficiaries do not suffer direct financial loss. A fiduciary who breaches his duties "shall be personally liable * * * to restore to such plan any profits of such fiduciary which have been made through use of assets of the plan by the fiduciary." 29 U.S.C. § 1109(a).

> The nature of the breach of fiduciary duty alleged here is not the *loss* of plan assets but instead the *risking* of the trust's assets at least in part to aid the defendants in their acquisition program. ERISA expressly prohibits the use of assets for purposes other than the best interests of the beneficiaries, and the language of section 1109(a) providing for disgorgement of profits from improper use of trust assets is the appropriate remedy. On the record before us, we are unable to determine the extent of the defendants' total profits, and we certainly cannot measure the extent, if any, to which any profits resulted from the defendants' use of the trust assets. However, those questions are relevant only in measuring damages. * * * At this point in the analysis, we need only say that plaintiffs are not required to show that the trust lost money as a result of the

alleged breaches of fiduciary duties. If ERISA fiduciaries breach their duties by risking trust assets for their own purposes, beneficiaries may recover the fiduciaries' profits made by misuse of the plan's assets.

727 F.2d at 121–122.

9. Fiduciary liability for misrepresentation and failure to disclose information is complicated. In the second section of his opinion in *Varity*, Justice Breyer found that Varity had violated its fiduciary duties:

> The second question—whether Varity's deception violated ERISA-imposed fiduciary obligations—calls for a brief, affirmative answer. ERISA requires a "fiduciary" to "discharge his duties with respect to a plan solely in the interest of the participants and beneficiaries." To participate knowingly and significantly in deceiving a plan's beneficiaries in order to save the employer money at the beneficiaries' expense is not to act "solely in the interest of the participants and beneficiaries." As other courts have held, "lying is inconsistent with the duty of loyalty owed by all fiduciaries." Because the breach of this duty is sufficient to uphold the decision below, we need not reach the question whether ERISA fiduciaries have any fiduciary duty to disclose truthful information on their own initiative, or in response to employee inquiries.

516 U.S. at 506.

In cases where there is no evidence that a fiduciary intentionally misled plan participants, some circuits distinguish *Varity* and hold that such a "negligent" (as opposed to "intentional") misrepresentation is not a breach of fiduciary duty. See, e.g., Frahm v. Equitable Life Assur. Soc'y of the United States, 137 F.3d 955 (7th Cir. 1998). In *Frahm*, an employer changed its retiree health care plan so that retirees would shoulder more of its cost. Plaintiffs alleged that the employer had breached its fiduciary duty by causing them to think that their benefits could not be altered. The court found that the employer correctly trained its benefits staff to give accurate advice and thus that the employer did not undertake a systematic campaign of disinformation. In the absence of such a campaign, the court held, this case was distinguishable from *Varity*: "slipups in managing any complex enterprise are inevitable, and negligence * * * is not actionable." By contrast, other circuits find that "negligent misrepresentation" can be a breach of fiduciary duty. See, e.g., Krohn v. Huron Mem. Hosp., 173 F.3d 542 (6th Cir. 1999) (personnel assistant erroneously told an employee who was injured in an accident that long-term benefits would not be available; as a result, the employee missed a filing deadline and did not receive long-term benefits. The court held that the plan administrator was liable for a breach of fiduciary duty regardless of whether the personnel assistant's misrepresentation was intentional or negligent).

The more contentious issue is whether fiduciaries have an affirmative duty to disclose information necessary to protect a participant. A few courts, analogizing to the common law of trusts, have found that such a duty exists. See Glaziers & Glassworkers Union Local No. 252 Annuity Fund v.

Newbridge Secs., Inc., 93 F.3d 1171, 1181 (3d Cir. 1996) (holding that a financial services firm might have breached its fiduciary duty by not disclosing an internal investigation into unethical practices by a vice president who advised plaintiff union retirement funds, even though plaintiff had not requested any such information); Tittle v. Enron, supra p. 1197. (denying a motion to dismiss breach of fiduciary duty claims against Enron directors and officers who failed to disclose material information regarding employees' ERISA plan investments in Enron stock and continued to encourage employees to purchase and hold Enron stock in their defined contribution plans after the directors and officers obtained non-public information suggesting that Enron stock was not a safe investment). Most courts do not recognize so sweeping of a duty to disclose.

10. Fiduciaries who breach their fiduciary duties are "personally liable to make good to [the ERISA plan] any losses to the plan resulting from each such breach, and to restore to such plan any profits of such fiduciary which have been made through use of assets of the plan by the fiduciary, and shall be subject to such other equitable or remedial relief as the court may deem appropriate, including removal of such fiduciary." 29 U.S.C. § 1109(a).

11. ERISA benefit plan assets are ordinarily held in trust. A trustee is appointed by a named fiduciary and is normally given the authority to manage the assets. Accordingly, trustees are normally fiduciaries. However, ERISA plans can also require that trustees adhere to the investment decisions of the fiduciaries, in which case the trustees are called "directed trustees." Directed trustees are subject to a lesser degree of liability for claims of breach of fiduciary duty. Ordinarily, directed trustees will not be held liable for breach of fiduciary duty when they follow the directions of fiduciaries, as long as the decision does not contradict the provisions of ERISA or the plan's documents. See DiFelice v. U.S. Airways, Inc., 397 F.Supp.2d 735 (E.D.Va.2005) (Fidelity trust management was named as the trustee of US Air's 401(k) plan and was given broad managerial and administrative powers over the trust, but was not given the authority to determine which investment options would be available to employees. That authority was retained by U.S. Air. U.S. Air included among its investment options one that focused primarily on company stock. This option remained available to employees over a period during which the price of U.S. Air stock fell dramatically. The court held that, with respect to the decision to offer the U.S. Air stock investment option, Fidelity was acting as a directed trustee, and thus would not have a duty to investigate whether the stock remained a prudent investment decision. Since the investment in US Air stock did not contradict ERISA or the terms of the plan, Fidelity was held not to have incurred liability.)

12. A fiduciary can become liable for a breach of fiduciary duty by co-fiduciaries if she (1) knowingly participates in or conceals the breach, (2) enables the co-fiduciary's breach by her own breach, or (3) has knowledge of the co-fiduciary's breach and does not make a reasonable effort to remedy it. 29 U.S.C. § 1105(a).

13. Concerning the equitable relief available when the fiduciary duty is violated, see Great-West Life & Annuity Ins. Co. v. Knudson, p. 630. See also

CIGNA Corp. v. Amara, 131 S.Ct. 1866 (2011), holding that the Summary Plan Description is not an enforceable part of the ERISA plan; that ERISA does not give a federal court the authority to reform the terms of the plan as remedy; but that a court can grant "other appropriate equitable relief," including the benefits to which the plan says employees and prior employees are entitled. Equitable remedies recognized in *Amara* include surcharge, reformation, and estoppel.

14. Plaintiffs failed to establish that Morgan Stanley Investment Management knew or should have known that certain mortgage-backed securities were pension investments that failed to meet their fiduciary responsibilities. A decline in market price (stemming from the real-estate bubble and subsequent financial crisis) of a type of security does not, by itself, give rise to a reasonable inference that it was imprudent to purchase or hold that type of security." The court applied "the duty of prudence . . . 'measured according to the objective prudent person standard developed in the common law of trusts.' " Pension Benefit Guaranty Corp. on behalf of Saint Vincent Catholic Medical Centers Retirement Plan v. Morgan Stanley Investment Management Inc., 712 F.3d 705 (2d Cir. 2013) (2–1).

15. In Fifth Third Bancorp v. Dudenhoeffer, 573 U.S. 409 (2014), the Supreme Court held that fiduciaries' investments in company stock were not entitled to a "presumption of prudence," and instead held that "[t]o state a claim for breach of the duty of prudence on the basis of inside information, a plaintiff must plausibly allege an alternative action that the defendant could have taken that would have been consistent with the securities laws and that a prudent fiduciary in the same circumstances would not have viewed as more likely to harm the fund than to help it." In Amgen Inc. v. Harris, 136 S. Ct. 758 (2016), the Court clarified that the plaintiff bears a significant burden of proposing an alternative course of action so clearly beneficial that a prudent fiduciary could *not* conclude that it would be more likely to harm the fund than to help it. Mostly recently, in Retirement Plans Committee of IBM v. Jander, there were general allegations that disclosure of fraud is always inevitable and that disclosure sooner rather than later is always more prudent to satisfy the pleading standard articulated in Fifth Third Bancorp v. Dudenhoeffer. After hearing oral argument in the case, the Supreme Court in a per curiam opinion vacated and remanded the case on January 14, 2020, to have the lower courts consider securities law arguments, including whether the Supreme Court should adopt a bright-line rule under which ERISA never could obligate fiduciaries to use insider information whether ERISA should not be interpreted to impose any separate duty of disclosure on plan fiduciaries because securities laws already provide a comprehensive framework for requiring the disclosure of material information about public companies.

    In Whitley v. BP, P.L.C., 838 F.3d 523 (5th Cir. 2016), former investors of the BP Stock Fund, an employee stock ownership plan (ESOP) comprised primarily of the company's stock, sued the company for breaching their fiduciary duties under ERISA. The Fifth Circuit reversed and remanded the district court's judgment in granting the stockholders' motion to amend the complaint because it found that the amended complaint failed to state a plausible claim under the new pleading standards. Similarly, in Rinehart v. Lehman Bros. Holdings Inc., 817 F.3d 56 (2d Cir. 2016), cert. denied, 137 S.Ct. 1067 (2017) former participants in an employee stock ownership plan (ESOP) who invested exclusively in Lehman's common stock filed suit against the company for breaching their fiduciary duties under ERISA by continuing to permit investment in Lehman stock in circumstances arguably foreshadowing its bankruptcy in 2008. The Second Circuit affirmed the district court's judgment in granting the defendant fiduciaries' motion to dismiss because plaintiffs failed to plead plausibly that defendants breached their ERISA duties. Under *Amgen* standards, the Court found here that a prudent fiduciary could have concluded divesting Lehman stock, or simply holding it without purchasing more, "would do more harm than good."

16. In June 2017, the Supreme Court ruled unanimously that religiously affiliated hospitals can run their pension plans as church plans, which are exempt from ERISA requirements. The ruling reverses the decisions of three federal appeals courts, which had held that a church plan exempt from ERISA requirements must be established by a church. The Supreme Court disagreed, holding that a church plan may include pension plans that are established by an organization that is not a church but is affiliated with a church. The decision permits religious affiliated hospitals to avoid compliance with ERISA and its rules designed to protect the beneficiaries of pension plans. Advocate Health Care Network v. Stapleton, 137 S.Ct. 1652 (2017).

17. Difficult issues arise with multi-employer plans, which are usually managed by relevant labor unions. See Treasury Department (decision by famous mediator Ken Feinberg) blocking Teamsters' Central States Pension Fund from cutting benefits to retirees to attempt to keep fund solvent. Decades ago, the plan had four active workers contributing for each retiree collecting. Now there are more retirees than active workers. It has about $17 billion in assets and $35 billion in liabilities. The highest compensated retirees get about $2,400 per month. See Wall St. J., May 7, 2016, page B1.

18. Another pension arrangement is a multiple employer pension (MEP). On July 31, 2019, the Department of Labor issued rules that made it easier for unaffiliated employers, outside of a collective bargaining contract, to provide 401(k) plan to small business employees, the self-employed, and workers in the gig economy. The Secure Act of 2019 allows for the first time so-called Open MEPs, which allow *unaffiliated* employers to pool their resources and offer retirement plans to their employees under the statutory protections of ERISA. This model allows both employers and employees to pool their retirement contributions, and get the best investment options at the lowest prices. The advantages for employers is the tax deduction that comes with such retirement contributions, the competitive advantage in obtaining better workers by offering a better benefit package, and the ability to off-load most of their fiduciary liability in co-sponsoring such a plan with Professional Employee Organizations (PEOs). For employees, the hope would be that because of their significant purchasing power and economies of scale, these Open MEPs would have access to the lowest-price wholesale mutual funds and other investments so that workers would automatically default into a highly-diversified, low-fee retirement plan. For more on these recent developments, see Paul M. Secunda, The Emerging Law of Portable Retirement Plan Benefits, 95 Chi. Kent L. Rev. (forthcoming 2020).

19. Early in 2016, the Obama Department of Labor issued new fiduciary standards for those who provide retirement investment advice. The regulations were meant to protect retirement savers from conflicts of interest faced by brokers and advisers who charge for investment recommendations. With their new fiduciary status, investment managers would have to recommend products that best suit their clients' interests as opposed to those that maximize their own profits.

In Chamber of Commerce of the United States of America v. United States Department of Labor, 885 F.3d 360 (5th Cir. 2018), a divided Fifth Circuit vacated the Fiduciary Rule. The Fiduciary Rule sought to expand the definition of fiduciary under ERISA section 3(21)(A) to include individuals and entities that provide investment advice for a fee to ERISA-covered plans and their participants and beneficiaries, individual retirement account (IRA) owners, and health savings account (HSA) holders. Reversing an earlier decision by the District Court for the Northern District of Texas, the Fifth Circuit found that DOL exceeded its statutory authority under ERISA in promulgating the Fiduciary rule. The majority decision focused on the DOL's five factor test for determining whether a service provider is an ERISA fiduciary and specifically noted that "[f]or the past forty years, the DOL has considered the hallmarks of an 'investment advice' fiduciary's business to be his 'regular' work on behalf of a client and the client's reliance on that advice as the 'primary basis' for her investment decisions." The majority held the Fiduciary rule was a vast expansion of this historical interpretation that was not authorized by ERISA and in violation of the *Chevron* doctrine—providing for judicial deference to administrative interpretations—and the Administrative Procedure Act (APA). The case vacated the Fiduciary Rule in its entirety and issued a nationwide injunction against its enforcement.

20. In Tibble v. Edison Int'l, 575 U.S. 523 (2015), beneficiaries of a defined-contribution 401(k) retirement savings plan filed a class action suit against the plan fiduciaries, alleging that the employer breached its fiduciary duties by offering higher-priced retail-class mutual funds as plan investments when materially-identical lower-price institutional-class mutual funds were available. After the Supreme Court vacated the Ninth Circuit's decision that ERISA's six-year statute of limitation barred the plaintiffs' claim, the en banc court on remand vacated the district court's judgment in favor of the plan fiduciaries and held that the duty of prudence required defendants to reevaluate investments periodically and to take into account their power to obtain favorable investment products, particularly when those products were substantially identical—other than their lower cost—to products they had already selected. Tibble v. Edison Int'l, 843 F.3d 1187 (9th Cir. 2016).

d. ARBITRARY AND CAPRICIOUS DECISIONS BY PENSION FUND
    TRUSTEES

ERISA states that an ERISA plan participant can bring a civil action "to recover benefits due to him under the terms of his plan, to enforce his rights under the terms of the plan, or to clarify his rights to future benefits under the terms of the plan." 29 U.S.C. § 1132(a)(1)(B). Yet ERISA does not tell courts the standard of review they should employ in reviewing the decisions of a plan administrator. Enforcing a similar provision for union-managed pension funds in the Taft-Hartley Act, federal courts had borrowed from state trust law and established a federal common law of fiduciary duties to plan beneficiaries. The Supreme Court then borrowed this standard for ERISA, stating that the Act "essentially codified the strict fiduciary standards" that a trustee of a Taft-Hartley trust fund must meet. See NLRB v. Amax Coal Co., 453 U.S. 322 (1981). Under this standard, ERISA administrators' decisions can be overturned if they are "arbitrary and capricious." To give one illustration of the operation of this standard, courts have ruled that it is arbitrary and capricious to treat similarly situated participants differently. See, e.g., Frary v. Shorr Paper Prods., 494 F.Supp. 565 (N.D.Ill.1980).

The Supreme Court then altered this framework in Firestone Tire & Rubber Co. v. Bruch, 489 U.S. 101 (1989). Firestone sold five plants to another company, which rehired most of the employees, providing them with the same pay and benefits that they had received from Firestone, including pension and severance plans governed by ERISA. Firestone's severance plan provided that termination pay would be given to an employee "released because of a reduction in work force." Firestone denied applications for severance plan benefits on the grounds that the sale of the plants to the new company did not constitute a "reduction in work force." In an opinion by Justice O'Connor, the Court then held that courts should review the decisions of administrators de novo when the plan documents do not explicitly give the administrator discretionary authority to determine eligibility for benefits or to construe the terms of a plan. By contrast, Justice O'Connor wrote, courts should employ an "abuse of discretion" standard of review (most courts assume this to be interchangeable with "arbitrary and capricious") over decisions of administrators who are explicitly given such authority. Justice O'Connor then found that Firestone's plan did not explicitly give the administrator the requisite authority and employed the de novo standard to strike down Firestone's decision. As a result of this opinion, nearly all ERISA plans contain "magic words" that explicitly confer on the administrator the authority to construe the terms of plans and determine eligibility for benefits; thus, most decisions by ERISA plan administrators continue to be reviewed under the "arbitrary and capricious" standard.

NOTES AND QUESTIONS

1. Professors Langbein and Wolk have cast a quizzical eye at the *Firestone* Court's borrowing from the law of trusts to support its "de novo" standard for judicial review of trustee decisions. The Court cites the Restatement of Trusts (Second) § 187 (1957). That section states: "Where discretion is conferred upon the trustee with respect to the exercise of a power, its exercise is not subject to control by the court except to prevent an abuse by the trustee of his discretion." This section of the Restatement seems to call for a standard of review very much like—if not identical to—the arbitrary and capricious standard rejected by the court in *Firestone.* The Court manages this judicial sleight of hand by quoting a passage from Nichols v. Eaton, 91 U.S. 716 (1875). *Nichols* called for a deferential standard when discretion is vested in trustees "by the instrument under which they act." From this premise, the *Firestone* Court draws the conclusion that a deferential standard is proper *only* when discretionary power is specifically delegated by a trust instrument.

This analysis raises two troubling issues. First, while *Nichols* holds that a deferential standard is proper when called for by the terms of the instrument, the case does not say that such a standard should be employed only when set forth by the instrument. Second, the Court's conclusion that the instrument must confer discretionary powers contradicts Restatement of Trusts § 187, the source from which its analysis originated. Comment (a) to that section states: "The exercise of a power is discretionary except to the extent to which its exercise is required by the terms of the trust or by the principles of law applicable to the duties of the trustees."

In any event, company pension plan documents are regularly revised by company lawyers. After *Firestone,* wouldn't most plans be revised to grant discretion to trustees? If so, what will be the significance of the *Firestone* decision? See John H. Langbein & Bruce A. Wolk, Pension and Employee Benefit Law 610–14 (1990).

2. *Firestone* does not determine the standard of review courts should employ when reviewing decisions by plan administrators who have been given the "magic words" authority but also have an interest adverse to that of plan participants. Most circuits have concluded that evidence of an administrator's conflict of interest can be used in two ways: (1) as evidence that the administrator's decision was the result of an abuse of discretion and (2) to reduce the level of judicial deference (i.e., apply a stricter standard of review) accorded to administrators' decisions. See, e.g., Pitman v. Blue Cross & Blue Shield of Okla., 217 F.3d 1291 (10th Cir. 2000). A few circuits find that evidence of a conflict of interest does not trigger a stricter standard of review unless a plaintiff also has evidence that the conflict of interest in fact influenced the administrator's decision. See, e.g., Pulvers v. First UNUM Life Ins. Co., 210 F.3d 89 (2d Cir. 2000). The Ninth Circuit held that it would not apply a different standard of review in conflict of interest cases, finding that *Firestone* requires abuse of discretion review in all conflict of interest cases. However, the Ninth Circuit stated that it would apply de novo review to an administrative decision that flagrantly violated ERISA's procedural requirements (such as its notice, reporting, and claims processing procedural requirements). Abatie v. Alta Health & Life Ins. Co., 458 F.3d 955 (9th Cir. 2006).

For the argument that courts should apply a less deferential standard of review in cases where there is a possibility of a conflict of interest, see John H. Langbein, Trust Law as Regulatory Law: The Unum/Provident Scandal and Judicial Review of Benefit Denials under ERISA, 101 Northwestern University Law Review 1315 (2007). Professor Langbein argues that scandals have suggested that plan administrators might be led astray in situations where there is a conflict of interest. One disability insurance company, he notes, engaged in a systematic campaign to deny valid claims; the company even awarded a "hungry vulture" award to employees who were especially apt at denying claims. Also, Professor Langbein argues, employing a less deferential standard of review in these circumstances is inconsistent with several ERISA provisions and is not justified by an analogy to trust law.

3. The issue in *Firestone* was whether workers qualified for severance benefits when a factory was sold. What is the right answer? Since pension plans last for a long time and over time issues frequently arise that were not expected when the plan was written, who should—in effect—create the terms not decided at the onset? If this is a task for the courts, isn't it likely to be an onerous undertaking, prompting a large volume of disputes?

4. Consider Judge Posner's defense of the arbitrary and capricious standard in Van Boxel v. Journal Co. Employees' Pension Trust, 836 F.2d 1048 (7th Cir. 1987).

> [In the] ERISA setting, the arbitrary and capricious standard may be inapt, a historical mistake, or a mechanical extrapolation from different settings, at once too lax and too stringent, but even if it is any or all of these things it is saved from doing serious harm by its vagueness and elasticity. There are more verbal distinctions among the standards of judicial review than there are real differences. It is easier to multiply standards than actually to differentiate among them—to keep them from overlapping—in the setting of a particular case. The fundamental difference in the depth or penetration or exactingness of judicial review is between deferential and nondeferential review, that is, between reversing a tribunal's decision because it is unreasonable and reversing it merely because it is wrong. Sometimes even this difference blurs. When the members of the tribunal—for example, the trustees of a pension plan—have a serious conflict of interest, the proper deference to give their decisions may be slight, even zero; the decision if wrong may be unreasonable. The less likely it is that the trustees' judgment was impaired by their having a stake, however indirect, in the outcome, the less inclined a reviewing court will be to override their judgment unless strongly convinced that they erred.

As this example shows, flexibility in the scope of judicial review need not require a proliferation of different standards of review; the arbitrary and capricious standard may be a range, not a point. There may be in effect a sliding scale of judicial review of trustees' decisions—more penetrating the greater is the suspicion of partiality, less penetrating the smaller that suspicion is. * * *

Flexibly interpreted, the arbitrary and capricious standard, though infelicitously—perhaps even misleadingly—worded, allows the reviewing court to make the necessary adjustments for possible bias in the trustees' decision. So there is no urgent need to throw it overboard and cast about for an alternative verbalization. Where the claimant does not argue or is unable to show that the trustees had a significant conflict of interest, we reverse the denial of benefits only if the denial is completely unreasonable. The greater the conflict of interest of a majority of the trustees, the less we defer to a denial of benefits that appears to be wrong.

Van Boxel was decided while *Firestone*'s appeal to the Supreme Court was pending. Does Judge Posner's analysis adequately address the concerns expressed in *Firestone?*

5. A benefit plan made payments to employees and dependents who entered an extended care facility before age 70 but not to those who entered after. The age 70 rule was not included in the plan handbook. Suing under ERISA § 102(b), plaintiff survived a motion to dismiss with her plea that her costs should be paid because she would not have entered the Northside Convalescent Center had she known the rule. Zittrouer v. Uarco Inc. Grp. Benefit Plan, 582 F.Supp. 1471 (N.D.Ga.1984).

6. ERISA bars amendments that decrease "accrued benefits." Plaintiff worked for the Machinists Union. At the time he retired, the union's pension plan had a cost-of-living feature indexing benefits to salary increases in the position held before retirement. When the pension plan looked underfunded, delegates to the union convention voted to phase out this provision of the plan. Shaw v. International Ass'n of Machinists & Aerospace Workers Pension Plan, 750 F.2d 1458 (9th Cir.), cert. denied, 471 U.S. 1137 (1985), held that the formula for benefit increases was an "accrued benefit" and could not be reduced.

7. Even if a plan says benefits are limited to the amount in the fund, ERISA declares "nonforfeitable" the participant's right to the full set of promises made in the plan. Thus solvent employers are liable to the full extent of plan commitments. Nachman Corp. v. Pension Benefit Guaranty Corp., 446 U.S. 359 (1980). Four justices dissented because *Nachman* imposed this obligation on a company that sought to limit its obligations by terminating its plan before ERISA took effect.

8. If an ERISA plan grants interpretive discretion to the plan administrator, is that discretion revoked if the administrator makes a wrong decision? The Supreme Court said no, rejecting the "one strike and you're out" approach that some lower federal courts had applied. Chief Justice Roberts wrote: "People make mistakes. Even administrators of ERISA plans.

That should come as no surprise, given that [ERISA] is an 'enormously complex and detailed statute'..." Justice Breyer, dissenting, said the administrator had made three mistakes, but he did not make the point that "three strikes and you're out." Conkright v. Frommert, 559 U.S. 506 (2010) (5–3).

e.   FEDERAL PREEMPTION OF STATE LAW

As discussed in Chapter 6, supra p. 638, ERISA preempts state laws that "relate to" ERISA plans. 29 U.S.C. § 1144(a). Courts employ two tests to determine whether a state law "relates to" an ERISA plan. The first, the "connection with" test, is examined in Chapter 6. Under the second test, courts find that ERISA preempts state laws that "refer to" ERISA plans.

In Mackey v. Lanier Collection Agency & Serv., 486 U.S. 825 (1988), the Court held that ERISA preempted Ga. Code Ann. § 18–4–22.1 (1982), which provided that "[f]unds or benefits of a pension, retirement, or employee benefit plan or program subject to the provisions of [ERISA] shall not be subject to the process of garnishment * * * unless such garnishment is based upon a judgment for alimony or for child support * * *" The court noted that the "statute at issue here expressly refers to—indeed, solely applies to—ERISA employee benefit plans." It also held that the fact that the Georgia law was meant to effectuate ERISA's provisions did not save it from preemption; legislative "good intentions" did not protect the law from ERISA preemption. By contrast, the Court held that Georgia's general garnishment law was not preempted by ERISA, because it did not "single out" ERISA plans and garnishment of plans did not seem inconsistent with the Act. The fact that the garnishment of ERISA assets might impose administrative costs on ERISA plans was not sufficient to require the preemption of the general garnishment statute.

In Ingersoll-Rand Co. v. McClendon, 498 U.S. 133 (1990), the Court considered a Texas common law cause of action that allowed an employee to bring a suit for wrongful discharge when an employer terminated an employee in order to prevent his pension benefits from vesting. The Court held that ERISA preempted this cause of action, reasoning that the "existence of a pension plan is a critical factor in establishing liability under the State's wrongful discharge law. As a result, this cause of action relates not merely to pension benefits, but to the essence of the pension plan itself." Ingersoll-Rand Co. v. McClendon, 498 U.S. 133, 140 (1990).

NOTES

1.   Recall from Chapter 6, supra at p. 647 that ERISA does not preempt qualified domestic relations orders; criminal laws; and laws regulating insurance, banking, and securities. Also, recall that courts have been more reluctant, at times, to find that ERISA preempts state laws that regulate subjects traditionally regulated by the states, such as health care, although

this reluctance has not stopped the court from finding that ERISA preempts some such state laws, including testamentary transfer regulations. See MacLean v. Ford Motor Co., 831 F.2d 723 (7th Cir.1987).

2. A U.S. statute applying to federal employees allows an employee to name a beneficiary for life insurance proceeds. A Virginia statute revokes a beneficiary designation from a former spouse where there was a change in the decedent's marital status. Virginia, home of many federal employees, established a cause of action rendering the former spouse liable to give an insurance benefit back to the party (often presumably a latter spouse or offspring) who would have received the money had not the federal law preempted Virginia's attempt to regulate the payments. The Supreme Court held that Virginia cannot interfere in this way with rules laid down by the national government. Hillman v. Maretta, 133 S.Ct. 1943 (2013).

3. The ex-wife of a military retiree filed a motion to enforce a divorce decree that granted her 50% of her ex-husband's military retirement pay (MRP). After he waived a portion of MRP in order to collect service-related disability benefits, the former wife's share was reduced. The MRP reduction reduced the MRP amount by about $250 per month, thus $125 each for husband and former wife. (The veteran made that decision because retirement benefits are taxable and disability benefits are not.) The Arizona Supreme Court ruled that the divorce award from family court should survive the reduction in the husband's MRP. The U.S. Supreme Court reversed, deciding unanimously that the federal statute allowing states to treat as community property and divide at divorce a veteran's MRP payments exempts from this grant of permission any amount that the federal government deducts as a result of a waiver that the veteran must make in order to receive disability benefits. Howell v. Howell, 136 S. Ct. 1704 (2017).

4. Although private pension benefits under ERISA are nonforfeitable in *most* cases, murder under so-called state slayer statues is one where pension rights can be lost. See Pension Fund v. Miscevic, 880 F.3d 927 (7th Cir. 2018) (holding that ERISA does not preempt Illinois state slayer statute which barred participant's wife from recovering participant's pension benefits after she was found not guilty of murdering him by reason of insanity).

f. PENSION PLAN TERMINATION

Pension plans can become overfunded for several reasons. One major cause of overfunded pensions has been the existence of a strong stock market. In the past, companies looked at their pension plan assets when stock prices were high and decided they had better uses for the money. They also feared that a surplus would make the company a takeover target. As a result, companies would terminate their pension plans and start new plans with the proper amount of cash reserves, keeping the excess funds.

Employees have argued that the pension plan is "their money," and the company should not be able to withdraw it. Employers have replied that they are responsible for increasing contributions if plans turn out to be underfunded, so if their estimates are conservative and excess funds accumulate, those funds belong to the company.

Where terminations did not comply with contractual provisions in the plan, courts have invalidated them. See, e.g., Delgrosso v. Spang & Co., 769 F.2d 928 (3d Cir. 1985), cert. denied, 476 U.S. 1140 (1986). But any legal doubts about the basic legitimacy of excess fund recovery were put to rest by Title XI of the Consolidated Omnibus Budget Reconciliation Act of 1985, P.L. No. 99–272, which imposes procedural requirements on plan termination. The company must buy a fully-funded annuity for plan beneficiaries who are already retired, and must create an adequately funded new plan for current workers. See also ERISA § 4044(d)(1), permitting (in limited circumstances) excess earnings to be withdrawn without termination of the plan.

Certain other requirements must also be met before a defined benefit plan may be cancelled if it is not fully funded. If the plan's assets are sufficient to cover all liabilities for benefits earned to date, then the plan sponsor may terminate it as long as certain notice requirements are satisfied. 29 U.S.C. § 1341(b). If a plan's assets are not sufficient to cover liabilities for benefits earned to date, the plan may only be terminated if each employer contributing to the plan is "distressed." An employer is distressed if (1) a petition for liquidation of the employer has been filed under bankruptcy laws; (2) the employer is in the process of reorganizing under bankruptcy laws, the bankruptcy court finds that the employer will be unable to both pay its plan debts and to continue business outside of reorganization without the plan termination, and the bankruptcy court approves the termination; (3) the employer demonstrates to the PBGC that it will be unable to both pay its debts when they are due and continue in business unless the distress termination occurs; or (4) the employer demonstrates to the PBGC that its pension plans have become unreasonably burdensome solely as a result of a decline in the employer's workforce. 29 U.S.C. § 1341(c)(2)(B). These requirements were enacted in 1986. Before their passage, plan sponsors could terminate a plan at any time; this created an incentive to underfund plans, since plan sponsors could always terminate their plans and pass on unfunded liabilities to the PBGC.

Pension Benefit Guaranty Corp. v. LTV Corp.

496 U.S. 633 (1990).

■ JUSTICE BLACKMUN delivered the opinion of the Court.

In this case we must determine whether the decision of the Pension Benefit Guaranty Corporation (PBGC) to restore certain pension plans under § 4047 of the Employee Retirement Income Security Act of 1974 (ERISA) was, as the Court of Appeals concluded, arbitrary and capricious or contrary to law, within the meaning of § 706 of the Administrative Procedure Act.

Petitioner PBGC is a wholly owned United States Government corporation, * * *. The Board of Directors of the PBGC consists of the Secretaries of the Treasury, Labor, and Commerce. The PBGC administers and enforces Title IV of ERISA. Title IV includes a mandatory Government insurance program that protects the pension benefits of over 30 million private-sector American workers who participate in plans covered by the Title.[1] In enacting Title IV, Congress sought to ensure that employees and their beneficiaries would not be completely "deprived of anticipated retirement benefits by the termination of pension plans before sufficient funds have been accumulated in the plans."

When a plan covered under Title IV terminates with insufficient assets to satisfy its pension obligations to the employees, the PBGC becomes trustee of the plan, taking over the plan's assets and liabilities. The PBGC then uses the plan's assets to cover what it can of the benefit obligations. The PBGC then must add its own funds to ensure payment of most of the remaining "nonforfeitable" benefits, i.e., those benefits to which participants have earned entitlement under the plan terms as of the date of termination. * * *

The cost of the PBGC insurance is borne primarily by employers that maintain ongoing pension plans. Sections 4006 and 4007 of ERISA require these employers to pay annual premiums. The insurance program is also financed by statutory liability imposed on employers who terminate under-funded pension plans. Upon termination, the employer becomes liable to the PBGC for the benefits that the PBGC will pay out. Because the PBGC historically has recovered only a small portion of that liability, Congress repeatedly has been forced to increase the annual premiums. Even with these increases, the PBGC in its most recent Annual Report noted liabilities of $4 billion and assets of only $2.4 billion, leaving a deficit of over $1.5 billion.

As noted above, plan termination is the insurable event under Title IV. Plans may be terminated "voluntarily" by an employer or "involuntarily" by the PBGC. An Employer may terminate a plan voluntarily in one of two ways. It may proceed with a "standard termination" only if it has sufficient assets to pay all benefit commitments. A standard termination thus does not implicate PBGC insurance responsibilities. If an employer wishes to terminate a plan whose assets are insufficient to pay all benefits, the employer must demonstrate that it is in financial "distress" as defined in 29 U.S.C. § 1341(c). Neither a standard nor a distress termination by the employer, however, is permitted if termination would violate the terms of an existing collective-bargaining agreement.

---

[1] Title IV covers virtually all "defined benefit" pension plans sponsored by private employers. A defined benefit plan is one that promises to pay employees, upon retirement, a fixed benefit under a formula that takes into account factors such as final salary and years of service with the employer. . . .

The PBGC, though, may terminate a plan "involuntarily," notwithstanding the existence of a collective-bargaining agreement. Section 4042 of ERISA provides that the PBGC may terminate a plan whenever it determines that:

"(1) the plan has not met the minimum funding standard * * *

"(2) the plan will be unable to pay benefits when due,

"(3) the reportable event described in section 1343(b)(7) of this title has occurred, or

"(4) the possible long-run loss of the [PBGC] with respect to the plan may reasonably be expected to increase unreasonably if the plan is not terminated."

Termination can be undone by PBGC. Section 4047 of ERISA provides:

"In the case of a plan which has been terminated under section 1341 or 1342 of this title the [PBGC] is authorized in any such case in which [it] determines such action to be appropriate and consistent with its duties under this subchapter, to take such action as may be necessary to restore the plan to its pretermination status, including, but not limited to, the transfer to the employer or a plan administrator of control of part or all of the remaining assets and liabilities of the plan."

When a plan is restored, full benefits are reinstated, and the employer, rather than the PBGC, again is responsible for the plan's unfunded liabilities.

This case arose after respondent The LTV Corporation and many of its subsidiaries, including LTV Steel Company Inc., in July 1986 filed petitions for reorganization under Chapter 11 of the Bankruptcy Code. At that time, LTV Steel was the sponsor of three defined benefit pension plans (the Plans) covered by Title IV of ERISA. Two of the Plans were the products of collective-bargaining negotiations with the United Steelworkers of America. The third was for non-union salaried employees. Chronically underfunded, the Plans, by late 1986, had unfunded liabilities for promised benefits of almost $2.3 billion. Approximately $2.1 billion of this amount was covered by PBGC insurance.

It is undisputed that one of LTV Corp.'s principal goals in filing the Chapter 11 petitions was the restructuring of LTV Steel's pension obligations, a goal which could be accomplished if the Plans were terminated and responsibility for the unfunded liabilities was placed on the PBGC. LTV Steel then could negotiate with its employees for new pension arrangements. LTV, however, could not voluntarily terminate the Plans because two of them had been negotiated in collective bargaining. LTV therefore sought to have the PBGC terminate the Plans.

To that end, LTV advised the PBGC in 1986 that it could not continue to provide complete funding for the Plans. PBGC estimated that, without continued funding, the Plans' $2.1 billion underfunding could increase by as much as $65 million by December 1987 and by another $63 million by December 1988, unless the Plans were terminated. Moreover, extensive plant shutdowns were anticipated. These shutdowns, if they occurred before the Plans were terminated, would have required the payment of significant "shutdown benefits." The PBGC estimated that such benefits could increase the Plans' liabilities by as much as $300 million to $700 million, of which up to $500 million was covered by PBGC insurance. Confronted with this information, the PBGC, invoking § 4042(a)(4) of ERISA, determined that the Plans should be terminated in order to protect the insurance program from the unreasonable risk of large losses, and commenced termination proceedings in the District Court. With LTV's consent, the Plans were terminated effective January 13, 1987. . . .

The PBGC objected to these new pension agreements, characterizing them as "follow-on" plans. It defines a follow-on plan as a new benefit arrangement designed to wrap around the insurance benefits provided by the PBGC in such a way as to provide both retirees and active participants substantially the same benefits as they would have received had no termination occurred. The PBGC's policy against follow-on plans stems from the agency's belief that such plans are "abusive" of the insurance program and result in the PBGC's subsidizing an employer's ongoing pension program in a way not contemplated by Title IV. The PBGC consistently has made clear its policy of using its restoration powers under § 4047 if an employer institutes an abusive follow-on plan. * * *

In early August 1987, the PBGC determined that the financial factors on which it had relied in terminating the Plans had changed significantly. Of particular significance to the PBGC was its belief that the steel industry, including LTV Steel, was experiencing a dramatic turnaround. As a result, the PBGC concluded it no longer faced the imminent risk, central to its original termination decision, of large unfunded liabilities stemming from plant shutdowns. * * *

The Director issued a Notice of Restoration on September 22, 1987, indicating the PBGC's intent to restore the terminated Plans. * * *

The Court of Appeals first held that the restoration decision was arbitrary and capricious under § 706(2)(A) because the PBGC did not take account of all the areas of law the court deemed relevant to the restoration decision. The court expressed the view that "[b]ecause ERISA, bankruptcy and labor law are all involved in the case at hand, there must be a showing on the administrative record that PBGC, before reaching its decision, considered all of these areas of law, and to the extent possible, honored the policies underlying them." * * *

The PBGC contends that the Court of Appeals misapplied the general rule that an agency must take into consideration all relevant factors by requiring the agency explicitly to consider and discuss labor and bankruptcy law. We agree.

First, and most important, we do not think that the requirement imposed by the Court of Appeals upon the PBGC can be reconciled with the plain language of § 4047, under which the PBGC is operating in this case. This section gives the PBGC the power to restore terminated plans in any case in which the PBGC determines such action to be "appropriate and consistent with its duties *under this title.*" The statute does not direct the PBGC to make restoration decisions that further the "public interest" generally, but rather empowers the agency to restore when restoration would further the interests that Title IV of ERISA is designed to protect. Given this specific and unambiguous statutory mandate, we do not think that the PBGC did or could focus "inordinately" on ERISA in making its restoration decision.

Even if Congress' directive to the PBGC had not been so clear, we are not entirely sure that the Court of Appeals' holding makes good sense as a general principle of administrative law. The PBGC points up problems that would arise if federal courts routinely were to require each agency to take explicit account of public policies that derive from federal statutes other than the agency's enabling act. To begin with, there are numerous federal statutes that could be said to embody countless policies. If agency action may be disturbed whenever a reviewing court is able to point to an arguably relevant statutory policy that was not explicitly considered, then a very large number of agency decisions might be open to judicial invalidation.

The Court of Appeals' directive that the PBGC give effect to the "policies and goals" of other statutes, apart from what those statutes actually provide, is questionable for another reason as well. Because the PBGC can claim no expertise in the labor and bankruptcy areas, it may be ill-equipped to undertake the difficult task of discerning and applying the "policies and goals" of those fields. * * *

The Court of Appeals also rejected the grounds for restoration that the PBGC *did* assert and discuss. The court found that the first ground the PBGC proffered to support the restoration—its policy against follow-on plans—was contrary to law because there was no indication in the text of the restoration provision, § 4047, or its legislative history that Congress intended the PBGC to use successive benefit plans as a basis for restoration. The PBGC argues that in reaching this conclusion the Court of Appeals departed from traditional principles of statutory interpretation and judicial review of agency construction of statutes. Again, we must agree. * * *

[F]ollow-on plans may tend to frustrate one of the objectives of ERISA that the PBGC is supposed to accomplish—the "continuation and maintenance of voluntary private pension plans." In addition, follow-on plans have a tendency to increase the PBGC's deficit and increase the insurance premiums all employers must pay, thereby frustrating another related statutory objective—the maintenance of low premiums. In short, the PBGC's construction based upon its conclusion that the existence of follow-on plans will lead to more plan terminations and increased PBGC liabilities is "assuredly a permissible one." Indeed, the judgments about the way the real world works that have gone into the PBGC's anti-follow-on policy are precisely the kind that agencies are better equipped to make than are courts. * * *

We conclude that the PBGC's failure to consider all potentially relevant areas of law did not render its restoration decision arbitrary and capricious. We also conclude that the PBGC's anti-follow-on policy, an asserted basis for the restoration decision, is not contrary to clear congressional intent and is based on a permissible construction of § 4047. Finally, we find the procedures employed by the PBGC to be consistent with the APA. Accordingly, the judgment of the Court of Appeals is reversed and the case is remanded for further proceedings consistent with this opinion.

NOTES AND QUESTIONS

1.   As noted in the section on fiduciary duties, supra p. 1191, when an employer terminates a plan, it is not acting as an ERISA fiduciary, so it cannot be liable for breach of fiduciary duty.

2.   Why does the PBGC object to "follow-on" plans? Is the situation worse for the government-guaranteed pension insurance program if companies *and* unions have an incentive to transfer pension obligations to the insurance fund? If workers must lose 20% of their benefits upon termination of the plan, will the company be deterred from following that course?

3.   Is it appropriate to separate ERISA law from bankruptcy law as the PBGC did and the Supreme Court approved? If LTV is in fact in economic trouble and the bankruptcy process will find that the company cannot meet its pension obligations, what will be the practical significance of the *LTV* decision?

4.   In general, a bankrupt debtor must relinquish all assets to a bankruptcy trustee. However, bankruptcy law provides an exception: "A restriction on the transfer of a beneficial interest of the debtor in a trust that is enforceable under applicable nonbankruptcy law is enforceable in a case under this title." 11 U.S.C. § 541(c)(2). In Patterson v. Shumate, 504 U.S. 753 (1992), the Supreme Court held that this provision is an enforceable "applicable nonbankruptcy law" and thus that ERISA-protected pensions are excluded from a bankruptcy estate and protected against attempts by bankruptcy trustees to seize them for the benefit of creditors. However, it appears that, due to complexities in ERISA, certain pension plans maintained by non-profit employers are not protected by § 541(c)(2). See Rhiel v. Adams, 302 B.R. 535 (6th Cir. BAP 2003).

5. The Retiree Benefits Bankruptcy Protection Act of 1988 was enacted as a result of the bankruptcy by LTV. The legislation codified the requirement that Chapter 11 debtors continue to pay retiree benefits. 11 U.S.C. § 1114(b)(2). The Act has had a profound impact on the way courts look at the priority that all benefits, including pension plans, must receive if a company goes bankrupt. Often, when the retiree committee of a corporation in Chapter 11 petitions the court for priority against other creditors, the trustees file cross motions claiming economic hardship. Frequently, the result is delays or decreases in retiree payments.

g. DISCRIMINATION IN PRIVATE PENSIONS

City of Los Angeles v. Manhart
435 U.S. 702 (1978).

■ MR. JUSTICE STEVENS delivered the opinion of the Court.

As a class, women live longer than men. For this reason, the Los Angeles Department of Water and Power required its female employees to make larger contributions to its pension fund than its male employees. We granted certiorari to decide whether this practice discriminated against individual female employees because of their sex in violation of § 703(a)(1) of the Civil Rights Act of 1964, as amended.

For many years the Department has administered retirement, disability, and death-benefit programs for its employees. Upon retirement each employee is eligible for a monthly retirement benefit computed as a fraction of his or her salary multiplied by years of service.[3] The monthly benefits for men and women of the same age, seniority, and salary are equal. Benefits are funded entirely by contributions from the employees and the Department, augmented by the income earned on those contributions. No private insurance company is involved in the administration or payment of benefits.

Based on a study of mortality tables and its own experience, the Department determined that its 2,000 female employees, on the average, will live a few years longer than its 10,000 male employees. The cost of a pension for the average retired female is greater than for the average male retiree because more monthly payments must be made to the average woman. The Department therefore required female employees to make monthly contributions to the fund which were 14.84% higher than the contributions required of comparable male employees. Because employee contributions were withheld from paychecks a female employee took home less pay than a male employee earning the same salary.

---

[3] The plan itself is not in the record. In its brief the Department states that the plan provides for several kinds of pension benefits at the employee's option, and that the most common is a formula pension equal to 2% of the average monthly salary paid during the last year of employment times the number of years of employment. The benefit is guaranteed for life.

Since the effective date of the Equal Employment Opportunity Act of 1972, the Department has been an employer within the meaning of Title VII of the Civil Rights Act of 1964. In 1973, respondents brought this suit in the United States District Court for the Central District of California on behalf of a class of women employed or formerly employed by the Department. They prayed for an injunction and restitution of excess contributions.

* * *

There are both real and fictional differences between women and men. It is true that the average man is taller than the average woman; it is not true that the average woman driver is more accident prone than the average man. Before the Civil Rights Act of 1964 was enacted, an employer could fashion his personnel policies on the basis of assumptions about the differences between men and women, whether or not the assumptions were valid.

It is now well recognized that employment decisions cannot be predicated on mere "stereotyped" impressions about the characteristics of males or females. Myths and purely habitual assumptions about a woman's inability to perform certain kinds of work are no longer acceptable reasons for refusing to employ qualified individuals, or for paying them less. This case does not, however, involve a fictional difference between men and women. It involves a generalization that the parties accept as unquestionably true: Women, as a class, do live longer than men. The Department treated its women employees differently from its men employees because the two classes are in fact different. It is equally true, however, that all individuals in the respective classes do not share the characteristic that differentiates the average class representatives. Many women do not live as long as the average man and many men outlive the average woman. The question, therefore, is whether the existence or nonexistence of "discrimination" is to be determined by comparison of class characteristics or individual characteristics. A "stereotyped" answer to that question may not be the same as the answer that the language and purpose of the statute command.

The statute makes it unlawful "to discriminate against any *individual* with respect to his compensation, terms, conditions, or privileges of employment, because of such *individual's* race, color, religion, sex, or national origin." The statute's focus on the individual is unambiguous. It precludes treatment of individuals as simply components of a racial, religious, sexual, or national class. If height is required for a job, a tall woman may not be refused employment merely because, on the average, women are too short. Even a true generalization about the class is an insufficient reason for disqualifying an individual to whom the generalization does not apply.

That proposition is of critical importance in this case because there is no assurance that any individual woman working for the Department will actually fit the generalization on which the Department's policy is based. Many of those individuals will not live as long as the average man. While they were working, those individuals received smaller paychecks because of their sex, but they will receive no compensating advantage when they retire.

It is true, of course, that while contributions are being collected from the employees, the Department cannot know which individuals will predecease the average woman. Therefore, unless women as a class are assessed an extra charge, they will be subsidized, to some extent, by the class of male employees.[14] It follows, according to the Department, that fairness to its class of male employees justifies the extra assessment against all of its female employees.

But the question of fairness to various classes affected by the statute is essentially a matter of policy for the legislature to address. Congress has decided that classifications based on sex, like those based on national origin or race, are unlawful. Actuarial studies could unquestionably identify differences in life expectancy based on race or national origin, as well as sex.[15] But a statute that was designed to make race irrelevant in the employment market, see Griggs v. Duke Power Co., [supra p. 318], could not reasonably be construed to permit a take-home-pay differential based on a racial classification.

Even if the statutory language were less clear, the basic policy of the statute requires that we focus on fairness to individuals rather than fairness to classes. Practices that classify employees in terms of religion, race, or sex tend to preserve traditional assumptions about groups rather than thoughtful scrutiny of individuals. The generalization involved in this case illustrates the point. Separate mortality tables are easily interpreted as reflecting innate differences between the sexes, but a significant part of the longevity differential may be explained by the social fact that men are heavier smokers than women.

Finally, there is no reason to believe that Congress intended a special definition of discrimination in the context of employee group insurance coverage. It is true that insurance is concerned with events that are individually unpredictable, but that is characteristic of many employment decisions. Individual risks, like individual performance, may not be predicted by resort to classifications proscribed by Title VII. Indeed, the fact that this case involves a group insurance program highlights a basic flaw in the Department's fairness argument. For when

---

[14] The size of the subsidy involved in this case is open to doubt, because the Department's plan provides for survivors' benefits. Since female spouses of male employees are likely to have greater life expectancies than the male spouses of female employees, whatever benefits men lose in "primary" coverage for themselves, they may regain in "secondary" coverage for their wives.

[15] For example, the life expectancy of a white baby in 1973 was 72.2 years; a nonwhite baby could expect to live 65.9 years, a difference of 6.3 years. See Public Health Service, IIA Vital Statistics of the United States, 1973, Table 5–3.

insurance risks are grouped, the better risks always subsidize the poorer risks. Healthy persons subsidize medical benefits for the less healthy; unmarried workers subsidize the pensions of married workers;[18] persons who eat, drink, or smoke to excess may subsidize pension benefits for persons whose habits are more temperate. Treating different classes of risks as though they were the same for purposes of group insurance is a common practice that has never been considered inherently unfair. To insure the flabby and the fit as though they were equivalent risks may be more common than treating men and women alike;[19] but nothing more than habit makes one "subsidy" seem less fair than the other.[20]

An employment practice that requires 2,000 individuals to contribute more money into a fund than 10,000 other employees simply because each of them is a woman, rather than a man, is in direct conflict with both the language and the policy of the Act. Such a practice does not pass the simple test of whether the evidence shows "treatment of a person in a manner which but for that person's sex would be different." It constitutes discrimination and is unlawful unless exempted by the Equal Pay Act of 1963 or some other affirmative justification.

[The Court considered and rejected the argument that the Bennett Amendment authorized the Los Angeles practice.]

Notes and Questions

1.   The Supreme Court opinion in *Manhart* held that the new policy should not apply retroactively. Justice Marshall dissented from that part of the holding. Chief Justice Burger and Justice Rehnquist agreed only with that part.

2.   In Arizona Governing Committee for Tax Deferred Annuity & Deferred Comp. Plans v. Norris, 463 U.S. 1073 (1983), the Supreme Court held that Title VII prohibits an employer from offering its employees the option of receiving retirement benefits from one of several companies, all of which pay women lower monthly benefits than men because women as a group live longer than men. Citing *Manhart*, the Court majority said the "classification of employees on the basis of sex is no more permissible at the pay-out stage

---

[18] A study of life expectancy in the United States for 1949–1951 showed that 20-year-old men could expect to live to 60.6 years of age if they were divorced. If married, they could expect to reach 70.9 years of age, a difference of more than 10 years.

[19] The record indicates, however, that the Department has funded its death-benefit plan by equal contributions from male and female employees. A death benefit—unlike a pension benefit—has less value for persons with longer life expectancies. Under the Department's concept of fairness, then, this neutral funding of death benefits is unfair to women as a class.

[20] A variation on the Department's fairness theme is the suggestion that a gender-neutral pension plan would itself violate Title VII because of its disproportionately heavy impact on male employees. This suggestion has no force in the sex discrimination context because each retiree's total pension benefits are ultimately determined by his *actual life span*; any differential in benefits paid to men and women in the aggregate is thus "based on [a] factor other than sex," and consequently immune from challenge under the Equal Pay Act. Even under Title VII itself—assuming disparate-impact analysis applies to fringe benefits,—the male employees would not prevail. Even a completely neutral practice will inevitably have *some* disproportionate impact on one group or another. *Griggs* does not imply, and this Court has never held, that discrimination must always be inferred from such consequences.

of a retirement plan than at the pay-in stage." The decision was by five to four vote. A different five to four decision (with Justice O'Connor as the "swing vote") said that the holding of *Norris* should apply only prospectively, as to pension plan benefits derived from contributions collected after the effective date of the judgment. The consequence of the nonretroactivity of *Manhart* and *Norris* is that workers will be receiving sex-determined pension benefits for several decades into the twenty-first century. For the argument that this wrongly "compromised Title VII's goal of full relief in favor of third-party contractual rights and employer solvency," see Wendy A. Wolf, Sex-Discrimination in Pension Plans: The Problem of Incomplete Relief, 9 Harv. Women's L.J. 83 (1986).

3. Formerly, many employers permitted women to retire at age 62 with full pension benefits, but men were not permitted to draw full benefits until age 65. Is this practice unlawful under *Manhart*?

4. As a class, blacks do not live as long as whites. The insurance industry has not used race-segregated actuarial tables similar to the sex-segregated tables at issue in *Manhart* because most states have had for many years statutes which prohibit discrimination in insurance on the basis of race. Should employers be permitted to charge gay men more for life or health insurance because of the risk of AIDS?

5. Where an employer's practice adversely affects a member of a group protected under Title VII, the employer is required to seek less discriminatory alternatives. What factors other than race or sex could the insurance industry use to separate individuals into appropriate risk groups for insurance purposes?

6. The insurance industry contended in *Manhart* that forcing it to combine male and female mortality tables would result in male retirees subsidizing female retirees. Many annuity plans offered to retirees include a survivors' benefits option for spouses of the annuitant; as a result, males have been subsidizing females (the widows of other retirees who died earlier) for years.

7. Does the use of unisex mortality tables make it more expensive for an employer to hire a female, and so discourage female hiring? How should the cost of female longevity be spread? Would reducing retirement benefits for men in order to pay men and women the same benefits violate the Equal Pay Act, which states that no one's wages may be reduced in order to bring an employer into compliance with the law?

8. Life insurance presents the reverse side of the annuity problem: because women live longer than men, the use of unisex mortality tables for life insurance will result in women "subsidizing" men. Does a switch to unisex mortality tables result in a net financial gain or loss for women, when one combines life and retirement insurance benefits?

9. The Retirement Equity Act of 1984, 29 U.S.C. § 1052(b)(5)(A), allows men and women to take parental leave for up to five years and not lose their pension rights.

10. Recall that ERISA § 510 also prevents discrimination against a participant or beneficiary for the exercise of rights given by ERISA or with the purpose of interfering with the attainment of rights given by ERISA. 29

U.S.C. § 1140. See Chapter 6, supra, p. 632. Alternatively, ERISA § 702, technically part of HIPAA, prohibits discrimination against individuals based on health status factors, including claims experience, medical costs or disability. Can one see how providing retirement incentives to active employees in the form of transition benefits, but not to current retirees, based on higher claims experience associated with retirees might violate ERISA § 702?

11. Plans that qualify for ERISA tax treatment must also satisfy ERISA's provisions against discrimination in favor of "highly compensated employees." For the purposes of these provisions, an employee is "highly compensated" if he or she (1) owns more than 5% of the employer or (2) receives compensation more than a minimum amount ($80K in 1996, indexed for inflation) and is one of the employer's 20% highest-paid employees. 26 U.S.C. § 414(q).

ERISA's anti-discrimination provisions require that pension plans be both nondiscriminatory in coverage and nondiscriminatory in contributions or benefits. A plan is nondiscriminatory in coverage if it satisfies the "ratio percentage test" (the ratio of covered non-highly compensated to highly compensated employees must be at least 7:10) or the more complicated "average benefits percentage test." To be nondiscriminatory in contributions or benefits, highly-compensated employees must not receive too much of the pension pot or contribute too little to it. A plan will not be considered discriminatory in contributions if it allocates contributions according to a fixed percentage of each employee's salary (i.e., making everyone contribute 3% of their salary) or if it satisfies other more complex formulae. Similarly, the provision of benefits must not be discriminatory. See IRC section 401(a)(4), 410(b).

In order to avoid violating these provisions, employers often provide one or more separate pension plans for their executives, which generally do not qualify for ERISA tax treatment, in addition to the ERISA plans that they provide for their other employers.

3. GOVERNMENT PENSIONS AS CONTRACT

After the recession that began in 2008, many state and local governments attempted to reduce their employee pension obligations. Long-term unfunded public pension obligations total more than $1 trillion. Public pensions are exempt from ERISA regulation, so government employees and retirees challenged the attempts to reduce their entitlements as violations of state and federal constitutional provisions covering Contracts, Due Process and Takings.

Public employees asserting Due Process and Takings violations have not succeeded. Federal and state constitutional contract clause challenges have fared better. Case law varies among jurisdictions but often includes a four-pronged analysis: (A) does a contract exist? and if so (B) when is the contract formed? (C) is the alteration a substantial impairment of the contract? and (D) is the alteration reasonable and necessary to serve an important public purpose?

a.   DOES A CONTRACT EXIST?

Under the traditional approach, as was true of private pensions before ERISA, pensions are not contracts but mere gratuities that employers may modify at will. It has been difficult for public employees to prevail in federal court unless legislative language states that public pension obligations are contractual. For courts to find a contract to which the government is party, legislation must state that the government intends a contract to exist "in terms too plain to be mistaken." The purpose of this so-called "unmistakability doctrine" is preserving the state's sovereign power.

A court will find legislative intent where statutory language states clearly that a contract exists. For example, New York's constitution states: "membership in any pension or retirement system of the state or of a civil division thereof shall be a contractual relationship, the benefits of which shall not be diminished or impaired." Michigan's and Illinois's constitutions contain similar provisions.

Where state constitutions and statutes are silent, some courts have found legislative intent under implied contract and promissory estoppel theories. Only Indiana and Texas state courts consider public pensions mere gratuities.

b.   WHEN IS A CONTRACT FORMED?

Decisions holding that pension plans constitute contracts vary as to when the contract starts. The date of contract existence determines the level of legal protection. For example, in California, contracts are formed upon employment, so the law prohibits the state from modifying its obligations upon the employee's first day on the job. On the other side of the spectrum, Kentucky finds contract formation only after an employee retires. Until then, the state government is free to alter pension obligations.

c.   CONTRACT CLAUSE ANALYSIS

(i)   U.S. Trust Co. Analysis

For an employee to prevail under traditional Contract Clause analysis, established in U.S. Trust Co. of New York v. New Jersey, 431 U.S. 1, 25 (1977), the state pension modification must be a substantial impairment of the contract that is unreasonable and unnecessary to serve an important public purpose.

The first prong of the analysis, a substantial impairment of the contract, is easy for pension plaintiffs to show. The necessity factor is difficult for states to prove. They must show that there was no other possible way to achieve their desired public policy. Further, they must show a reason for the modifications other than refinancing untenable debt obligations.

(ii) Comparable Benefit Analysis

California courts have upheld public pension modifications that offset employee disadvantages with "comparable new advantages." It is unclear whether the "comparable new advantage" test is an elaboration on or an alternative to traditional Contract Clause analysis.

(iii) Critique

In "Statutes as Contracts? The California Rule and Its Impact on Public Pension Reform," Professor Amy Monahan criticizes the California approach for unduly restricting state governments.[*] The California legislature may not amend accrued or future pension obligations.

> Hard policy choices need to be made with respect to the funding of many public pension plans in the coming years. Financial projections suggest that many state pension plans are significantly underfunded and will require sizable contributions from the state or its employees to maintain the plans at their current benefit levels. It may therefore be both necessary and advisable in some states to make changes to benefit structures. It is clear that earned benefits are entitled to a very high standard of legal protection. Such benefits can be changed only under a legitimate exercise of a state's police power—a difficult hurdle to clear. It is less clear, however, that future pension accruals should be entitled to the same level of protection. In some states, notably California, courts have ruled not only that retroactive reductions in pension benefits are impermissible but also that the state is prohibited from prospectively changing accrual rates for any current employees. This California Rule, adopted by many other states, improperly infringes on legislative power by holding that a legislative contract exists without ever evaluating whether there is clear and unambiguous evidence of legislative intent to form a contract. [binding the state to pay future pension accruals at a set rate]. Even in the absence of a legislative contract, long-standing precedent protects earned pension benefits under the theory that earned compensation is protected by an implied contract, but there is no such basis for protecting future accruals absent an explicit agreement. Protecting such future accruals absent an explicit agreement to do so is inconsistent with contract theory, economically inefficient, and simply forces the state to make other changes to the terms and conditions of public employment that may be less desirable to employees, less effective at stabilizing public pension funds, and potentially

---

[*] Amy B. Monahan, Statutes As Contracts? The "California Rule" and Its Impact on Public Pension Reform, 97 Iowa L. Rev. 1029, 1070 (2012).

more damaging to the state and its citizens. To the extent that courts continue to protect future accruals, they owe it to their states' citizens to clearly set out the legal basis on which such accruals are entitled to protection.

Professor Jack Beerman takes issue with Monahan's critique, defending California's bold protection of public employees:

> Monahan may be correct that California law is contrary to general legal principles and more protective of employees than federal Contract Clause jurisprudence, but I do not find California law "surprising . . ." There are good reasons to treat statutory promises to government employees different from promises contained in other regulatory statutes. Most people have multiple employment options at the outset and at various stages of their careers. Retirement promises form part of the inducement for individuals to choose and remain in government employment. While businesses may be in a similar situation and may suffer . . . when the regulatory rug is pulled out from under them, individuals have much less ability to diversify regulatory risk than businesses. Employees cannot be expected to save two or three times for retirement or change jobs every so often so their retirement promises come from multiple employers. This recognition helps explain why federal law protects private pensions through ERISA and the programs administered by the Pension Benefit Guaranty Corporation. That the federal Contracts Clause may be less protective than state law is no reason for state law to change. Under familiar understandings of federalism, in many situations, federal law should be lenient with regard to state law, especially when the state's own operations are involved, stepping in only in extreme cases.
>
> As to Monahan's claim that protecting pension promises is inefficient because the optimal result may be reduced pension promises rather than layoffs that might be necessary to fund remaining employees' pensions, this is a dilemma that is familiar to anyone studying labor economics. As wages and benefits increase, employers may hire fewer employees, may fire existing employees, and may replace employees with technology or workers in jurisdictions with lower salaries. Some unions have dealt with this problem by agreeing to lower wages and benefits for new employees while protecting the wages and benefits of incumbents. More fundamentally, although Monahan clearly understands that pension promises are a form of deferred compensation, her argument in favor of greater flexibility virtually ignores the ex ante perspective of the parties. At the time the contract was made, had the employees known that their pension promises were subject to significant revision, they may not have accepted government employment

or they may have demanded significantly higher current compensation. Normally, the security of contract enforcement is thought to increase efficiency, and Monahan does not refute that general tendency.

Monahan's strongest point is that protecting future accrual levels significantly reduces pension flexibility. If she is correct that public employees are "generally at-will employees, with no guaranteed period of employment," then it would make legal and practical sense to allow prospective changes to the terms of a contract that both parties could simply terminate at any time. At-will employees' reliance on future benefits may be viewed as unworthy of protection. However, there are reasons to doubt her premise. Government employees are highly unionized and are much more likely than private employees to have job security in the form of contractual or civil service protections. Further, advocates of prospective change should recognize that, for example, a twenty-year government employee suddenly faced with significantly lower future accrual of retirement benefits may be seriously damaged economically by the change and may not be in a position to seek alternate employment or take some other action to ameliorate the effects of the change.*

NOTES AND QUESTIONS

1.   Are agreements between governments and their citizens different from ordinary contracts? Do conflicts arise when the government wears two hats as employer and representative? How might these conflicts undermine efficient contract formation?

2.   Connecticut required male state employees to work until age 60 (with 10 years' service; 55 with 25 years' service) to earn pension benefits, while females could collect the same benefits at 55 (with 10 years' service; 50 with 25 years). This was held to be unlawful sex discrimination in Fitzpatrick v. Bitzer, 390 F.Supp. 278 (D.Conn.1974), affirmed in part and reversed in part on other grounds, 519 F.2d 559 (2d Cir. 1975), affirmed in part, reversed in part, 427 U.S. 445 (1976) (eleventh amendment does not bar award against the state of back pay of attorneys' fees because Title VII is authorized by section 5 of the fourteenth amendment). The legislature changed the law to put females in the situation of males. Thus, in the name of equality, women were required to work until a later age before being entitled to their pensions. Some of the women sued, arguing that the change was an unconstitutional impairment of express and implied contract rights. The Connecticut Supreme Court held that female employees had no contractual right to the lower retirement ages, stating that "[a]lthough there is a seductive appeal in the contract-oriented approaches [to construing rights to government pensions] adopted by other jurisdictions, we decline to depart

---

*   Jack M. Beerman, "The Public Pension Crisis." 70 Wash. & Lee L. Rev. 3, 58–60, 42 (2013).

from the well established rules of statutory construction discussed earlier, namely that a statute does not create vested contractual rights absent a clear statement of legislative intent to contract." Pineman v. Oechslin, 488 A.2d 803, 808 (Conn.1985).

In re Pension Reform Litigation
(Heaton v. Quinn)
32 N.E.3d 1 (Ill. 2015).

■ JUSTICE KARMEIER delivered the judgment of the court, with opinion.

At issue on this appeal is the constitutionality of Public Act 98–599 (eff. June 1, 2014), which amends the Illinois Pension Code by reducing retirement annuity benefits for individuals who first became members of four of Illinois' five State-funded pension systems prior to January 1, 2011. Members of the retirement systems affected by Public Act 98–599 and groups representing those members brought five separate actions challenging the validity of the new law on the grounds that it violated numerous provisions of the Illinois Constitution of 1970, including article XIII, section 5 (Ill. Const. 1970, art. XIII, § 5), popularly known as the pension protection clause.

* * *

Illinois has established five State-funded retirement systems for public employees. * * * These systems provide traditional defined benefit plans under which members earn specific benefits based on their years of service, income and age. All are subject to the pension protection clause of our state constitution, which provides: "Membership in any pension or retirement system of the State, any unit of local government or school district, or any agency or instrumentality thereof, shall be an enforceable contractual relationship, the benefits of which shall not be diminished or impaired." Ill. Const. 1970, art. XIII, § 5.

Among the benefits which members of the five State-funded retirement systems are entitled to receive are retirement annuities. The amount of a member's retirement annuity and how soon a member is eligible to begin receiving annuity payments depends on when the member first began making contributions into one of the retirement systems. Members who first contributed prior to January 1, 2011, receive what arc known as "Tier 1" annuity benefits. Members first contributing on or after January 1, 2011, receive a lower level of benefits designated as "Tier 2." Public Act 98–599, the legislation challenged in this case, is directed primarily at Tier 1 annuities and is limited in its application to benefits earned under the [four of the pension plans]. Annuities paid to judges under the JRS system were intentionally excluded from the law and are not affected by it.

Tier 1 retirement annuity benefits and eligibility requirements differ somewhat between the various systems. Because they all operate in approximately the same way, however, we will choose just one, SERS, to illustrate their basic features.

Members of [one plan] are eligible to retire at age 60 if they have at least eight years of credited service. They may retire with full benefits at any age if their age plus years of service credit equal 85. They are also eligible to retire if they are between the ages of 55 and 60 and have at least 25 years of credited service, but their benefit will be reduced by half of 1% for each month they are under the age of 60.

The amount of the retirement annuity benefit under SERS is calculated based on (1) the member's final average compensation, which is the average monthly compensation they received during their highest-paid 48 consecutive months of service over the previous ten years, (2) their total credited service, and (3) a multiplier, which changes depending on (a) whether or not the member is also covered by Social Security or (b) qualifies for an "alternative retirement annuity" (applicable to, *e.g.*, pilots and state policemen). For members who do have Social Security and are not subject to the alternative retirement annuity rules, the multiplier is 1.67% per year of credited service. Accordingly, a member of SERS who is eligible to retire, who has also paid into Social Security, and who has final average compensation of $1800 per month and 30 years of credited service will receive a retirement annuity of $901.80 per month (30 x .0167 x $1800).

SERS members may earn a retirement annuity of up to 75% of their final average compensation, although for members covered by Social Security, it would take nearly 45 years of State service to do so. These annuity payments are subject to 3% automatic annual increases beginning after the member's first full year of retirement, except that some members who retire before 60 and do not meet the rule of 85 will not receive the increases until they turn 60 and have been retired at least one full year. The annual annuity adjustments are built-in to the pension benefit and are not tied to the cost of living. As a result, the real value of annuities may either increase or erode depending on economic conditions, notwithstanding the adjustments.

Funding to pay benefits under each of Illinois' five State-funded systems is derived from three basic sources: contributions by the State through appropriation by the General Assembly; contributions by or on behalf of members based on their salaries; and income, interest and dividends derived from retirement fund deposits and investments. The contributions to the systems by or on behalf of members of the systems have not been problematic. There is no dispute that employees have paid their full share as required by law at all times relevant to this litigation. That has not been the case with respect to the contributions owed by the General Assembly.

For as long as there have been public pension systems in Illinois, there has been tension between the government's responsibility for funding those systems, on the one hand, and the costs of supporting governmental programs and providing governmental services, on the other. In the resulting political give and take, public pensions have chronically suffered. As long ago as 1917, a report commissioned by the General Assembly characterized the condition of State and municipal pension systems as "one of insolvency" and "moving toward a crisis" because of financial provisions which were "entirely inadequate for paying the stipulated pensions when due."

* * *

Concern over ongoing funding deficiencies and the attendant threat to the security of retirees in public pension systems eventually led directly to adoption of article XIII, section 5, the pension protection clause, when the new constitution was adopted in 1970.

* * *

Despite the consistent warnings from the Pension Laws Commission, the current budgeting of pension costs necessary to ensure the financial stability of these funds, the General Assembly has failed to meet its commitments to finance the pension obligations on a sound basis.

* * *

The solution proposed by the drafters and ultimately approved by the people of Illinois was to protect the benefits of membership in public pension systems not by dictating specific funding levels, but by safeguarding the benefits themselves. Delegate Green explained that the pension protection clause does this in two ways: "[i]t first mandates a contractual relationship between the employer and the employee; and secondly, it mandates the General Assembly not to impair or diminish these rights." Subsequent comments by other delegates reaffirmed that the provision was designed to confer contractual protection on the benefits of membership in public retirement systems and afford beneficiaries, pensioners or their dependents " 'a basic protection against abolishing their rights completely or changing the terms of their rights after they have embarked upon the employment— to lessen them."

* * *

By the end of June, 2013, the five State-funded retirement systems contained a total of only 41.1% of the funding necessary to meet their accrued liabilities based on the market value of fund assets. The funding rate was thus nearly unchanged from the 41.8% funding rate prior to ratification of the 1970 Constitution and its pension protection clause.

* * *

Following downgrades in the State's credit rating and facing the prospect that its credit rating would be reduced even further, the

General Assembly engaged in heated and protracted debate over possible legislative strategies for dealing with the State's fiscal problems through further changes to its pension obligations. After numerous failed attempts to reach consensus, the General Assembly ultimately enacted what became Public Act 98–599, the legislation challenged in this case.

Introduced as Senate Bill 1 and passed during the legislature's fall, 2013, "veto session," Public Act 98–599 was described as an attempt to address the State's large debts and deficits, plummeting credit ratings, and imperiled discretionary spending programs "that are essential to the people of Illinois" and to help shore up the long-term fiscal stability of both the State and its retirement systems. The mechanism chosen under the Act to accomplish those purposes was restructuring State-funded retirement systems. The law does not pertain to all five of the State-funded retirement systems, however. As noted earlier, JRS, the Judges Retirement System, was deliberately excluded.

* * *

The Act provides a limited number of Tier 1 plan participants with the opportunity, at a future date, to participate in a defined contribution plan. It affords a nominal reduction in the percentage of their salaries Tier 1 plan participants are required to contribute toward the employee share of annuity costs. Going forward, it bars persons hired by certain nongovernmental organizations from participating in the public pension system and prohibits new hires from using accumulated sick or vacation time to boost their pension benefits. Public Act 98–599 also eliminates the duty of employers to engage in collective bargaining or interest arbitration "over matters affected by the changes, the impact of changes, and the implementation of changes" made to the [pension] systems by the new law.

The centerpiece of Public Act 98–599, however, is a comprehensive set of provisions designed to reduce annuity benefits for members entitled to Tier 1 benefits, i.e., members who belonged to those systems prior to January 1, 2011. The new law utilizes five different mechanisms for achieving this goal. First, it delays, by up to five years, when members under the age of 46 are eligible to begin receiving their retirement annuities. Second, with certain exceptions and qualifications, it caps the maximum salary that may be considered when calculating the amount of a member's retirement annuity. Third, it jettisons the current provisions under which retirees receive flat 3% annual increases to their annuities and replaces them with a system under which annual annuity increases are determined according to a variable formula and are limited. Fourth, it completely eliminates at least one and up to five annual annuity increases depending on the age of the pension system member at the time of the Act's effective date. Finally, with respect to the TRS and SURS systems, the Act also alters how the base annuity amount is determined for purposes of what is known as the "money purchase" formula, something available to members of those two systems who began employment prior to July 1, 2005, as an alternative to the standard formula for calculating pensions. Because of this change, which involves use of a different interest rate, affected members will have smaller base pensions.

* * *

The first issue, whether Public Act 98–599's reduction of retirement annuity benefits violates this State's pension protection clause, is easily resolved. The pension protection clause clearly states: "[m]embership in any pension or retirement system of the State * * * shall be an enforceable contractual relationship, *the benefits of which shall not be diminished or impaired*." This clause has been construed by our court on numerous occasions, most recently in *Kanerva v. Weems*, 2014 IL 115811. We held in that case that the clause means precisely what it says: "if something qualifies as a benefit of the enforceable contractual relationship resulting from membership in one of the State's pension or retirement systems, it cannot be diminished or impaired."

This construction of article XIII, section 5, was not a break from prior law. To the contrary, it was a reaffirmation of principles articulated by this court and the appellate court on numerous occasions since the 1970 Constitution took effect. Under article XIII, section 5, members of pension plans subject to its provisions have a legally enforceable right to receive the benefits they have been promised. The protections afforded to such benefits by article XIII, section 5 attach once an individual first embarks upon employment in a position covered by a public retirement system, not when the employee ultimately retires. Accordingly, once an individual begins work and becomes a member of a public retirement system, any subsequent changes to the Pension Code that would diminish the benefits conferred by membership in the retirement system cannot be applied to that individual.

* * *

That the annuity reduction provisions of Public Act 98–599 violate the pension protection clause's prohibition against the diminishment of the benefits of membership in a State-funded retirement system is one the State has now all but conceded. After this court reaffirmed in *Kanerva v. Weems* that the pension protection clause means precisely what it says, the State shifted its focus to an argument it did not raise and we did not consider in *Kanerva*. The State's position now rests on its affirmative defense that funding for the pension systems and State finances in general have become so dire that the General Assembly is authorized, even compelled, to invoke the State's "reserved sovereign powers," i.e., its police powers, to override the rights and protections afforded by article XIII, section 5, of the Illinois Constitution in the interests of the greater public good. This argument must also fail.

The circumstances presented by this case are not unique. Economic conditions are cyclical and expected, and fiscal difficulties have confronted the State before. In the midst of previous downturns, the State or political subdivisions of the State have attempted to reduce or eliminate expenditures protected by the Illinois Constitution, as the General Assembly is attempting to do with Public Act 98–599. Whenever those efforts have been challenged in court, we have clearly and consistently found them to be improper.

* * *

The State seeks to avoid this conclusion by arguing that because membership in public retirement systems is an enforceable contractual relationship under article XIII, section 5, it should be subject to the same limitations as all other contractual rights; that under "a century and a half of federal and state law defining contractual relationships," these rights remain subject to modification—even invalidation—by the General Assembly through the exercise of the State's police power; and that the reduction in retirement annuity benefits under Public Act 98–599 is a valid exercise of police power because it is necessary and reasonable to secure the State's fiscal health and the well being of its citizens.

This argument was rejected by the circuit court. We reject it as well. As a preliminary matter, the precedent on which the State relies does not involve the pension protection clause under article XIII, section 5. It arises, instead, under article I, section 16, and that provision's counterpart in the United States Constitution. Those provisions, which are popularly referred to as the "contracts clause," provide that the State shall not pass any "law impairing the obligation of contracts."

* * *

This is not surprising. While impairment of a contract may survive scrutiny under the contracts clause if reasonable and necessary to serve an important public purpose, " '[t]he severity of the impairment measures the height of the hurdle the state legislation must clear.' " Changes in the factors used to compute public pension benefits constitute an impairment which is "obviously substantial."

The United States Supreme Court has made clear that the United States Constitution "bar[s] Government from forcing some people alone to bear public burdens which, in all fairness and justice, should be borne by the public as a whole." Through Public Act 98–599, however, the General Assembly addressed the financial challenges facing our State by doing just that. It made no effort to distribute the burdens evenly among Illinoisans. It did not even attempt to distribute the burdens evenly among those with whom it has contractual relationships. Although it is undisputed that many vendors face delays in payment, the terms of their contracts are unchanged, and under the State Prompt Payment Act, vendors are actually entitled to additional compensation in the form of statutory interest if their bills are not paid within specified periods. In no sense is this comparable to the situation confronted by members of public retirement systems under Public Act 98–599, which, if allowed to take effect, would actually negate substantive terms of their contractual relationships and reduce the benefits due and payable to them in a real and absolute way. Under all of these circumstances, it is clear that the State could prove no set of circumstances that would satisfy the contracts clause. Its resort to the contracts clause to support its police powers argument must therefore be rejected as a matter of law.

* * *

Given the history of article XIII, section 5, and the language that was ultimately adopted, we therefore have no possible basis for interpreting the provision to mean that its protections can be overridden if the General Assembly deems it appropriate, as it sometimes can be under the contracts clause. To confer such authority on the legislature through judicial fiat would require that we ignore the plain language of the constitution and rewrite it to include "restrictions and limitations that the drafters did not express and the citizens of Illinois did not approve." Indeed, accepting the State's position that reducing retirement benefits is justified by economic circumstances would require that we allow the legislature to do the very thing the pension protection clause was designed to prevent it from doing. Article XIII, section 5, would be rendered a nullity.

The State protests that this conclusion is tantamount to holding that the State has surrendered its sovereign authority, something it may not do. The State is incorrect. Article XIII, section 5, is in no sense a surrender of any attribute of sovereignty. Rather, it is a statement by the people of Illinois, made in the clearest possible terms, that the authority of the legislature does not include the power to diminish or impair the benefits of membership in a public retirement system. This is a restriction the people of Illinois had every right to impose.

* * *

The financial challenges facing state and local governments in Illinois are well known and significant. In ruling as we have today, we do not mean to minimize the gravity of the State's problems or the magnitude of the difficulty facing our elected representatives. It is our obligation, however, just as it is theirs, to ensure that the law is followed. That is true at all times. It is especially important in times of crisis when, as this case demonstrates, even clear principles and long-standing precedent are threatened. Crisis is not an excuse to abandon the rule of law. It is a summons to defend it. How we respond is the measure of our commitment to the principles of justice we are sworn to uphold.

More than two centuries ago, as adoption of the Constitution of the United States was being considered by the citizens of our new nation, James Madison wrote:

> "If men were angels, no government would be necessary. * * * In framing a government which is to be administered by men over men, the great difficulty lies in this: you must first enable the government to control the governed; and in the next place oblige it to control itself." James Madison, Federalist No. 51 (1788).

Obliging the government to control itself is what we are called upon to do today. The Constitution of Illinois and the precedent of our court admit of only one conclusion: the annuity reduction provisions of Public Act 98–599 enacted by the legislature and signed into law by the Governor violate article XIII, section 5's express prohibition against the diminishment of the benefits of membership in public retirement systems. The circuit court was therefore entirely correct when it declared those provisions void and unenforceable.

NOTES

1. This decision was followed in 2016 by a case reaching the same conclusion regarding Chicago's obligation to keep its pension promises. Jones v. Municipal Employees' Annuity & Benefit Fund, 50 N.E.3d 596 (2016). On the same day, the same Supreme Court refused to enforce an arbitration decision directing the state to pay a 2% wage increase to state employees covered by a multiyear collective bargaining agreement in State v. AFSCME, 51 N.E.3d 738 (Ill. 2016). It vacated the award and held that because the state's constitution and statutes provide a well-defined and dominant public policy in which collective bargaining agreements are subject to the appropriation power of the State (i.e., the State has the ability to appropriate and expend public funds), the arbitration award violated this public policy.

Further, the Illinois state court of appeals distinguished *Jones* in Pisani v. City of Springfield, 73 N.E.3d 129 (Ill. Ct. App. 2017), where it held that the city's elimination of a pension-spiking opportunity did not violate the state constitution's pension protection clause.

2. Michigan imposed substantial employee contribution charges in the pension plan and made changes in the retiree benefit plan for public school employees. The Michigan Supreme Court found no contract clause or other constitutional violation. AFT Michigan v. State, 866 N.W.2d 782 (Mich. 2015). The Oregon Supreme Court overturned changes in public pensions as they affected benefits earned before particular dates in 2013, but found constitutional the reduction of retiree COLA payments prospectively from 2013. Moro v. State, 351 P.3d 1 (Or. 2015). The New Hampshire Supreme Court held that the state did not violate state and federal constitutional clauses when it raised contribution levels for pensions. Prof'l Fire Fighters of N.H. v. State, 107 A.3d 1229 (N.H. 2014).

In Berg v. Christie, 137 A.3d 1143 (N.J. 2016), retired government employees filed suit against various New Jersey state defendants for suspending state pension cost-of-living adjustments (COLAs) in 2011, alleging that plaintiffs had contractual, statutory, and constitutional rights to pension COLAs. The Supreme Court of New Jersey held that although the state legislature enacted a non-forfeitable-right statute in 1997, the proof of unequivocal intent to create a non-forfeitable right to yet-unreceived COLAs is lacking, and the state legislature retained its inherent sovereign right to act in the best judgment of the public interest and to enact legislation suspending further COLAs.

3. Since 1996, retired employees of the City and County of San Francisco ("City") have been eligible to receive a supplemental COLA as part of their pension benefits when the retirement fund's earnings from the previous year exceeded projected earnings. Protect Our Benefits, a political action committee representing the interests of retired City employees, sought to invalidate a 2011 amendment to the city's Charter to condition the payment of the supplemental COLA on the retirement fund being "fully funded" based on the market value of the assets for the previous year as an impairment of a vested contractual pension right under the contract clauses of the federal and state constitutions. The California Court of Appeals held that the 2011 amendment may be constitutionally applied to employees who retired before the 1996 initiative establishing the supplemental COLA, but not to current employees or those who retired after the 1996 initiative. It found that employees who retired before 1996 do not have the same vested rights based on the contract in effect during their employment because they did not have a contractual expectation while in service that they would receive a supplement COLA. Protect Our Benefits v. City & Cnty. of San Francisco, 185 Cal. Rptr. 3d 410 (Cal. Ct. App. 2015).

Current county employees brought suit to halt a legislative amendment that would implement a revised formula for calculating retirement income to respond to the concerns of "pension spiking," by which some public employees attempt to inflate their income and retirement benefits. The California Court of Appeals upheld the lower court's finding that the state legislature did not act impermissibly because although a public employee has a vested right to a pension, that right is only to a "reasonable" pension, not an immutable entitlement to the most optimal formula of calculating the pension. As long as the legislature's modifications do not deprive the employee of a "reasonable" pension, there is no constitutional violation of the employee's contractual rights. Marin Ass'n of Public Employees v. Marin Cnty. Employees' Retirement Ass'n, 206 Cal. Rptr. 3d 365 (Cal. Ct. App. 2016).

4. In a non-pension case involving a life insurance policy beneficiary designation, the United States Supreme Court found that Minnesota's automatic-revocation-on-divorce statute that permits divorce alone to annul a life insurance policy in favor of the former spouse did not violate the Contracts Clause. This is because the Court found that the Minnesota did not substantially impair pre-existing contractual arrangements. Only Justice Gorsuch dissented. Sveen v. Melin, 138 S. Ct. 1815 (2018).

C. SOCIAL SECURITY RETIREMENT BENEFITS

1. BACKGROUND

Originally enacted in 1935, Social Security today refers to a number of different programs, including disability benefits, benefits for the spouse and children of a deceased worker, and Supplemental Security Income, which provides additional support for low-income retirees and disabled people. Social Security's core, however, is a government-managed pension program for retirees.

Eligibility for Social Security's retirement benefit is governed by a "credits" system. As individuals work and pay taxes, they earn Social Security "credits." Most workers need 40 credits in order to be eligible for Social Security pension benefits (netting more than 40 credits does not increase an individual's Social Security payments or benefit the individual in any other way). In 2010, a worker gained one credit for each $1,120 of earnings (this amount increases each year); one can earn a maximum of 4 credits per year. Thus, most people become eligible for Social Security after 10 years of work.[*]

Once an individual earns enough credits, he or she can collect Social Security benefits if he or she has reached a certain age regardless of whether he or she is still working. Originally, individuals could receive the full amount of their Social Security benefits at age 65. Now, the age at which an individual is eligible for their full retirement benefits (also known as the "full retirement age") varies according to an individual's year of birth. The full retirement age for individuals born in 1937 or earlier is 65; it rises incrementally until, for those born in 1960 or later, it becomes 67.

All individuals can retire as early as 62. Workers who retire early, however, only receive a percentage of the retirement benefits that they would have been entitled to had they waited until the normal retirement age. This percentage varies based on the number of months between the individual's retirement date and the date at which he or she would have obtained full benefits. Also, workers' benefits are incrementally increased for every month that they wait to retire after their full retirement age (although benefits stop increasing once the individual reaches age 70).

Full retirement benefits are calculated using a formula based on the wages that an individual receives during his or her best-paid 35 years of work. In order to compute an individual's full retirement benefit, one must first compute his or her Average Indexed Monthly earnings (AIME). To calculate the AIME, one must first adjust each year of income that the individual received to reflect the changes in average American wages. Next, one must compute the individual's Primary Insurance Amount (PIA). The PIA is calculated by a formula that reduces the AIME to take

---

[*] Note: benefits and eligibility formulae change often. This information describes the formulae used to calculate eligibility and benefits for individuals who retired in 2010.

account of the fact that Social Security replaces less of an individual's wages as the individual's income rises. Full retirement benefits are capped at a certain amount; for an individual retiring in 2014 at 66 years old, the maximum allowable benefit was $2,642/month.

The Social Security system is financed by a tax on wages. In 2014 the tax paid by workers was 6.2% on the first $117,000 of wages. Employers pay an equal amount. Self-employed individuals must pay 12.4%. Revenue from Social Security taxes exceeds outlays for benefits, as it has since the program's inception. The surplus is invested in long-term, low-risk U.S. government bonds. That surplus, however, is expected to turn to a deficit by 2021, until reserves are depleted in 2033. The OASI Trust Fund is expected to be depleted by 2035 and the DI Trust Fund by 2016.

2. CONSTITUTIONAL STATUS AS PROPERTY

Flemming v. Nestor
363 U.S. 603 (1960).

■ MR. JUSTICE HARLAN delivered the opinion of the Court. From a decision of the District Court for the District of Columbia holding § 202(n) of the Social Security Act unconstitutional, the Secretary of Health, Education, and Welfare takes this direct appeal. The challenged section provides for the termination of old age, survivor, and disability insurance benefits payable to, or in certain cases in respect of, an alien individual who after September 1, 1954 is deported under the Immigration and Nationality Act on any one of certain grounds specified in § 202(n).

Appellee, an alien, immigrated to this country from Bulgaria in 1913, and became eligible for old-age benefits in November 1955. In July 1956 he was deported for having been a member of the Communist Party from 1933 to 1939. This being one of the benefit-termination deportation grounds specified in § 202(n), appellee's benefits were terminated soon thereafter, and notice of the termination was given to his wife, who had remained in this country. * * *

We think that the District Court erred in holding that § 202(n) deprived appellee of an "accrued property right." Appellee's right to Social Security benefits cannot properly be considered to have been of that order. * * *

The Social Security system may be accurately described as a form of social insurance, enacted pursuant to Congress' power to "spend money in aid of the 'general welfare,' "whereby persons gainfully employed, and those who employ them, are taxed to permit the payment of benefits to the retired and disabled, and their dependents. Plainly the expectation is that many members of the present productive work force will in turn become beneficiaries rather than supporters of the program. But each worker's benefits, though flowing from the contributions he made to the national economy while actively employed, are not dependent on the degree to which he was called upon to support the system by taxation. It is apparent that the noncontractual interest of an employee covered by the Act cannot be soundly analogized to that of the holder of an annuity, whose right to benefits is bottomed on his contractual premium payments. * * *

To engraft upon the Social Security system a concept of "accrued property rights" would deprive it of the flexibility and boldness in adjustment to ever-changing conditions which it demands. It was doubtless out of an awareness of the need for such flexibility that Congress included in the original Act, and has since retained, a clause expressly reserving to it "[t]he right to alter, amend, or repeal any provision" of the Act. 42 U.S.C. § 1304. * * *

We must conclude that a person covered by the Act has not such a right in benefit payments as would make every defeasance of "accrued" interests violative of the Due Process Clause of the Fifth Amendment.

This is not to say, however, that Congress may exercise its power to modify the statutory scheme free of all constitutional restraint. The interest of a covered employee under the Act is of sufficient substance to fall within the protection from arbitrary governmental action afforded by the Due Process Clause. In judging the permissibility of the cut-off provisions of § 202(n) from this standpoint, it is not within our authority to determine whether the congressional judgment expressed in that section is sound or equitable, or whether it comports well or ill with the purposes of the Act. * * * Particularly when we deal with a withholding of a noncontractual benefit under a social welfare program such as this, we must recognize that the Due Process Clause can be thought to interpose a bar only if the statute manifests a patently arbitrary classification, utterly lacking in rational justification.

Such is not the case here. The fact of a beneficiary's residence abroad—in the case of a deportee, a presumably permanent residence—can be of obvious relevance to the question of eligibility. One benefit which may be thought to accrue to the economy from the Social Security system is the increased over-all national purchasing power resulting from taxation of productive elements of the economy to provide payments to the retired and disabled, who might otherwise be destitute or nearly so, and who would generally spend a comparatively large percentage of their benefit payments. This advantage would be lost as to payments made to one residing abroad. For these purposes, it is, of course, constitutionally irrelevant whether this reasoning in fact underlay the legislative decision, as it is irrelevant that the section does not extend to all to whom the postulated rationale might in logic apply. * * *

We need go no further to find support for our conclusion that this provision of the Act cannot be condemned as so lacking in rational justification as to offend due process. * * * It is said that the termination of appellee's benefits amounts to punishing him without a judicial trial, that the termination of benefits constitutes the imposition of punishment by legislative act, rendering § 202(n) a bill of attainder; and that the punishment exacted is imposed for past conduct not unlawful when engaged in, thereby violating the constitutional prohibition on ex post facto laws. Essential to the success of each of these contentions is the validity of characterizing as "punishment" in the constitutional sense the termination of benefits under § 202(n). * * *

Turning, then, to the particular statutory provision before us, appellee cannot successfully contend that the language and structure of § 202(n), or the nature of the deprivation, requires us to recognize a punitive design. Here the sanction is the mere denial of a noncontractual governmental benefit. No affirmative disability or restraint is imposed, and certainly nothing approaching the "infamous punishment" of imprisonment, as in Wong Wing v. United States, 163 U.S. 228, on which great reliance is mistakenly placed. * * *

■ MR. JUSTICE BLACK, dissenting. * * * I agree with the District Court that the United States is depriving appellee, Ephram Nestor, of his statutory right to old-age benefits in violation of the United States Constitution.

Nestor came to this country from Bulgaria in 1913 and lived here continuously for 43 years, until July 1956. He was then deported from this country for having been a Communist from 1933 to 1939. At that time membership in the Communist Party as such was not illegal and was not even a statutory ground for deportation. From December 1936 to January 1955 Nestor and his employers made regular payments to the Government under the Federal Insurance Contributions Act, 26 U.S.C. §§ 3101–3125. These funds went to a special federal old-age and survivors insurance trust fund under 42 U.S.C. § 401, in return for which Nestor, like millions of others, expected to receive payments when he reached the statutory age. In 1954, 15 years after Nestor had last been a Communist, and 18 years after he began to make payments into the old-age security fund, Congress passed a law providing, among other things, that any person who had been deported from this country because of past communist membership under 66 Stat. 205, 8 U.S.C. § 1251(a)(6)(C) should be wholly cut off from any benefits of the fund to which he had contributed under the law. 68 Stat. 1083, 42 U.S.C. § 402(n). After the Government deported Nestor in 1956 it notified his wife, who had remained in this country, that he was cut off and no further payments would be made to him. This action, it seems to me, takes Nestor's insurance without just compensation and in violation of the Due Process Clause of the Fifth Amendment. Moreover, it imposes an ex post facto law and bill of attainder by stamping him, without a court trial, as unworthy to receive that for which he has paid and which the Government promised to pay him. The fact that the Court is sustaining this action indicates the extent to which people are willing to go these days to overlook violation of the Constitution perpetrated against anyone who has ever even innocently belonged to the Communist Party.

In Lynch v. United States, 292 U.S. 571, this court unanimously held that Congress was without power to repudiate and abrogate in whole or in part its promises to pay amounts claimed by soldiers under the War Risk Insurance Act of 1917, §§ 400–405, 40 Stat. 409. This Court held that such a repudiation was inconsistent with the provision of the Fifth Amendment that "No person shall be * * * deprived of life, liberty, or property, without due process of law; nor shall private property be taken for public use, without just compensation." The Court today puts the *Lynch* case aside on the ground that "It is hardly profitable to engage in conceptualizations regarding 'earned rights' and 'gratuities.' " From this sound premise the Court goes on to say that while "The 'right' to Social Security benefits is in one sense 'earned,' " yet the Government's insurance scheme now before us rests not on the idea of the contributors to the fund earning something, but simply provides that they may "justly call" upon the Government "in their later years, for protection from 'the rigors of the poor house as well as from the haunting fear that such a lot awaits them when journey's end is near.' " These are nice words but they cannot conceal the fact that they simply tell the contributors to this insurance fund that despite their own and their employers' payments the Government, in paying the beneficiaries out of the fund, is merely giving them something for nothing and can stop doing so when it pleases. This, in my judgment, reveals a complete misunderstanding of the purpose Congress and the country had in passing that law. It was then generally agreed, as it is today, that it is not desirable that aged people think of the Government as giving them something for nothing. * * * The people covered by this Act are now able to rely with complete assurance on the fact that they will be compelled to contribute regularly to this fund whenever each contribution falls due. I believe they are entitled to rely with the same assurance on getting the benefits they have paid for and have been promised, when their disability or age makes their insurance payable under the terms of the law. The Court did not permit the Government to break its plighted faith with the soldiers in the *Lynch* case; it said the Constitution forbade such governmental conduct. I would say precisely the same thing here.

The Court consoles those whose insurance is taken away today, and others who may suffer the same fate in the future, by saying that a decision requiring the Social Security system to keep faith "would deprive it of the flexibility and boldness in adjustment to ever-changing conditions which it demands." People who pay premiums for insurance usually think they are paying for insurance, not for "flexibility and boldness." I cannot believe that any private insurance company in America would be permitted to repudiate its matured contracts with its policyholders who have regularly paid all their premiums in reliance upon the good faith of the company. It is true, as the Court says, that the original Act contained a clause, still in force, that expressly reserves to Congress "[t]he right to alter, amend, or repeal any provision" of the Act. Congress, of course, properly retained that power. It could repeal the Act so as to cease to operate its old-age insurance activities for the future. This means that it could stop covering new people, and even stop increasing its obligations to its old contributors. But that is quite different from disappointing the just expectations of the contributors to the fund which the Government has compelled them and their employers to pay its Treasury. There is nothing "conceptualistic" about saying, as this court did in *Lynch,* that such a taking as this the Constitution forbids. * * *

Charles A. Reich, The New Property*
73 Yale L.J. 733 (1964).

THE NEW FEUDALISM

The characteristics of the public interest state are varied, but there is an underlying philosophy that unites them. This is the doctrine that the wealth that flows from government is held by its recipients conditionally, subject to confiscation in the interest of the paramount state. This philosophy is epitomized in the most important of all judicial decisions concerning government largess, the case of Flemming v. Nestor. * * *

The implications of Flemming v. Nestor are profound. No form of government largess is more personal or individual than an old age pension. No form is more clearly earned by the recipient, who, together with his employer, contributes to the Social Security fund during the years of his employment. No form is more obviously a compulsory substitute for private property; the tax on wage earner and employer might readily have gone to higher pay and higher private savings instead. No form is more relied on, and more often thought of as property. No form is more vital to the independence and dignity of the individual. Yet under the philosophy of Congress and the Court, a man or woman, after a lifetime of work, has no rights which may not be taken away to serve some public policy. The Court makes no effort to balance the interests at stake. The public policy that justifies cutting off benefits need not even be an important one or a wise one—so long as it is not utterly irrational, the Court will not interfere. In any clash between individual rights and public policy, the latter is automatically held to be superior.

The philosophy of Flemming v. Nestor resembles the philosophy of feudal tenure. Wealth is not "owned," or "vested" in the holders. Instead, it is held conditionally, the conditions being ones which seek to ensure the fulfillment of obligations imposed by the state. Just as the feudal system linked lord and vassal through a system of mutual dependence,

* Reprinted by permission of The Yale Law Journal Company and Fred B. Rothman & Company from *The Yale Law Journal,* Vol. 73, pp. 768–74, 787.

obligation, and loyalty, so government largess binds man to the state. And, it may be added, loyalty or fealty to the state is often one of the essential conditions of modern tenure. In the many decisions taking away government largess for refusal to sign loyalty oaths, belonging to "subversive" organizations, or other similar grounds, there is more than a suggestion of the condition of fealty demanded in older times.

* * *

The public interest state is not with us yet. But we are left with large questions. If the day comes when most private ownership is supplanted by government largess, how then will governmental power over individuals be contained? What will dependence do to the American character? What will happen to the Constitution, and particularly the Bill of Rights, if their limits may be bypassed by purchase, and if people lack an independent base from which to assert their individuality and claim their rights? Without the security of the person which individual wealth provides and which largess fails to provide, what, indeed, will we become? * * *

The public interest state, as visualized above, represents in one sense the triumph of society over private property. This triumph is the end point of a great and necessary movement for reform. But somehow the result is different from what the reformers wanted. Somehow the idealistic concept of the public interest has summoned up a doctrine monstrous and oppressive. It is time to take another look at private property, and at the "public interest" philosophy that dominates its modern substitute, the largess of government.

* * *

During the industrial revolution, when property was liberated from feudal restraints, philosophers hailed property as the basis of liberty, and argued that it must be free from the demands of government or society. But as private property grew, so did abuses resulting from its use. In a crowded world, a man's use of his property increasingly affected his neighbor, and one man's exercise of a right might seriously impair the rights of others. Property became power over others; the farm landowner, the city landlord, and the working man's boss were able to oppress their tenants or employees. Great aggregations of property resulted in private control of entire industries and basic services capable of affecting a whole area or even a nation. At the same time much private property lost its individuality and in effect became socialized. Multiple ownership of corporations helped to separate personality from property, and property from power. When the corporations began to stop competing, to merge, agree, and make mutual plans, they became private governments. Finally, they sought the aid and partnership of the state, and thus by their own volition became part of public government.

These changes led to a movement for reform, which sought to limit arbitrary private power and protect the common man. Property rights were considered more the enemy than the friend of liberty. The reformers argued that property must be separated from personality. * * *

The struggle between abuse and reform made it easy to forget the basic importance of individual private property. The defense of private property was almost entirely a defense of its abuses—an attempt to defend not individual property but arbitrary private power over other human beings. Since this defense was cloaked in a defense of private property, it was natural for the reformers to attack too broadly. Walter Lippmann saw this in 1934:

> But the issue between the giant corporation and the public should not be allowed to obscure the truth that the only dependable foundation of personal liberty is the economic security of private property. * * * For we must not expect to find in ordinary men the stuff of martyrs, and we must, therefore, secure their freedom by their normal motives. There is no surer way to give men the courage to be free than to insure them a competence upon which they can rely. [Lippmann, The Method of Freedom 101 (1934).]

The reform took away some of the power of the corporations and transferred it to government. In this transfer there was much good, for the power was made responsive to the majority rather than to the arbitrary and selfish few. But the reform did not restore the individual to his domain. What the corporation had taken from him, the reform simply handed on to government. And government carried further the powers formerly exercised by the corporation. Government as an employer, or as a dispenser of wealth, has used the theory that it was handing out gratuities to claim a managerial power as great as that which the capitalists claimed. Moreover, the corporations allied themselves with, or actually took over, part of government's system of power. Today it is the combined power of government and the corporations that presses against the individual.

From the individual's point of view, it is not any particular kind of power, but all kinds of power, that are to be feared.

* * *

If the individual is to survive in a collective society, he must have protection against its ruthless pressures. There must be sanctuaries or enclaves where no majority can reach. To shelter the solitary human spirit does not merely make possible the fulfillment of individuals; it also gives society the power to change, to grow, and to regenerate, and hence to endure. These were the objects which property sought to achieve, and can no longer achieve. The challenge of the future will be to construct, for the society that is coming, institutions and laws to carry on this work. Just as the Homestead Act was a deliberate effort to foster individual values at an earlier time, so we must try to build an economic basis for liberty today—a Homestead Act for rootless twentieth century man. We must create a new property.

NOTE AND QUESTIONS

1. Ten years after Flemming v. Nestor, the Supreme Court signaled that it might reconsider its position that government benefits are gratuities. In Goldberg v. Kelly, 397 U.S. 254 (1970), Justice Brennan's majority opinion (which cited Professor Reich's work heavily) stated that it "may be realistic today to regard welfare entitlements as more like 'property' than a 'gratuity.'" However, the opinion's holding—that the due process clause requires a hearing before termination of welfare benefits—was limited by Mathews v. Eldridge, 424 U.S. 319 (1976) (holding that the due process clause does not require a hearing before the termination of Social Security disability payments) and arguably superseded by the changes made to welfare in 1996 (the 1996 welfare reform act provided in part: "No individual entitlement: This part shall not be interpreted to entitle any individual or family to assistance under any State program funded under this part." 42 U.S.C. § 601(b).). See State ex rel. K.M. v. West Va. Dep't of Health & Human Res., 575 S.E.2d 393 (W. Va. 2002) (holding that, under post-1996 welfare law, the federal due process clause does not require a pre-termination hearing).

Reich later described the approach to alleviating poverty taken by *Goldberg* as a "modest, moderate decision giving procedural protection to welfare recipients" but argued that "the moderate, due process, cost-benefit approach to individual security must surely be deemed a failure * * * I believe that * * * the due process clause gives every person in America a constitutional right to minimum subsistence and housing, to child care, education, employment, health insurance, retirement, and to a clean and healthy natural environment." Charles A. Reich, Symposium: the Legacy of Goldberg v. Kelly: A Twenty Year Perspective: Beyond the New Property: an Ecological View of Due Process, 56 Brook. L. Rev. 731–733 (1990).

2. In the 1930s, Congress passed unemployment benefit legislation for railroad employees, who often traveled across state lines and were thereby ineligible for local benefits. Initially, railroad employees received more generous packages than state UI-eligible workers. Today, a separate federal agency, the Railroad Retirement Board, manages the railroad benefit program, but payouts have been reduced to mirror the social security system.

Employees who worked in both the railroad and non-railroad industries sometimes qualified for a "windfall" from both programs. In 1974, Congress, attempting to cut costs, limited the number of dual benefit recipients according to retirement date and employment length. In United States Railroad Retirement Board v. Fritz, 449 U.S. 166 (1980), employees challenged the reductions under the Takings and Equal Protection clauses.

Justice Rehnquist, delivering the majority opinion, held that "railroad benefits, like social security benefits, are not contractual and may be altered or can be eliminated at any time." The Equal Protection claim also failed, as the Court applied a deferential standard of review and did not find the classification "patently arbitrary or irrational."

Is it wrong for employers to reduce expected benefits? What would be the gains and costs from giving such expectations constitutional protection? Does it matter if the employer is public or private?

3.   GENDER DISCRIMINATION IN SOCIAL SECURITY

Califano v. Goldfarb
430 U.S. 199 (1977).

■ MR. JUSTICE BRENNAN announced the judgment of the Court and delivered an opinion in which MR. JUSTICE WHITE, MR. JUSTICE MARSHALL, and MR. JUSTICE POWELL joined.

Under the Federal Old-Age, Survivors, and Disability Insurance Benefits (OASDI) program, 42 U.S.C. §§ 401–431 (1970 ed. and Supp. V), survivors' benefits based on the earnings of a deceased husband covered by the Act are payable to his widow. Such benefits on the basis of the earnings of a deceased wife covered by the Act are payable to the widower, however, only if he "was receiving at least one-half of his support" from his deceased wife. The question in this case is whether this gender-based distinction violates the Due Process Clause of the Fifth Amendment.

* * *

Mrs. Hannah Goldfarb worked as a secretary in the New York City public school system for almost 25 years until her death in 1968. During that entire time she paid in full all social security taxes required by the Federal Insurance Contributions Act. She was survived by her husband, Leon Goldfarb, now aged 72, a retired federal employee. Leon duly applied for widower's benefits. The application was denied with the explanation that

> "You do not qualify for a widower's benefit because you do not meet one of the requirements for such entitlement. This requirement is that you must have been receiving at least one-half support from your wife when she died."

* * *

Weinberger v. Wiesenfeld, 420 U.S. 636 (1975), like the instant case, presented the question in the context of the OASDI program. There the Court held unconstitutional a provision that denied father's insurance benefits to surviving widowers with children in their care, while authorizing similar mother's benefits to similarly situated widows. Paula Wiesenfeld, the principal source of her family's support, and covered by the Act, died in childbirth, survived by the baby and her husband Stephen. Stephen applied for survivors' benefits for himself and his infant son. Benefits were allowed the baby but denied the father on the ground that "mother's benefits" under § 402(g) were available only to women. The Court reversed, holding that the gender-based distinction made by § 402(g) was "indistinguishable from that invalidated in [Frontiero v. Richardson, 411 U.S. 677 (1973)]" and therefore:

> "[While] the notion that men are more likely than women to be the primary supporters of their spouses and children is not entirely without empirical support, * * * such a gender-based generalization cannot suffice to justify the denigration of the efforts of women who do work and whose earnings contribute significantly to their families' support.

> "Section 402(g) clearly operates, as did the statutes invalidated by our judgment in *Frontiero*, to deprive women of protection for their families which men receive as a result of their employment. Indeed, the classification here is in some ways more pernicious. * * * [I]n this case social security taxes were deducted from Paula's salary during the years in which she worked. Thus, she not only failed to receive for her family the same protection which a similarly situated male worker would have received, but she also was deprived of a portion of her own earnings in order to contribute to the fund out of which benefits would be paid to others."

Precisely the same reasoning condemns the gender-based distinction made by § 402(f)(1)(D) in this case. For that distinction, too, operates "to deprive women of protection for their families which men receive as a result of their employment": social security taxes were deducted from Hannah Goldfarb's salary during the quarter century she worked as a secretary, yet, in consequence of § 402(f)(1)(D), she also "not only failed to receive for her [spouse] the same protection which a similarly situated male worker would have received [for his spouse] but she also was deprived of a portion of her own earnings in order to contribute to the fund out of which benefits would be paid to others." *Wiesenfeld* thus inescapably compels the conclusion reached by the District Court that the gender-based differentiation created by § 402(f)(1)(D)—that results in the efforts of female workers required to pay social security taxes producing less protection for their spouses than is produced by the efforts of men—is forbidden by the Constitution, at least when supported by no more substantial justification than "archaic and overbroad" generalizations, or "'old notions,'" such as "assumptions as to dependency," that are more consistent with "the role-typing society has long imposed," than with contemporary reality. Thus § 402(f)(1)(D) "'[b]y providing dissimilar treatment for men and women who are * * * similarly situated * * * violates the [Fifth Amendment].' * * * "

Appellant, however, would focus equal protection analysis, not upon the discrimination against the covered wage earning female, but rather upon whether her surviving widower was unconstitutionally discriminated against by burdening him but not a surviving widow with proof of dependency. The gist of the argument is that, analyzed from the perspective of the widower, "the denial of benefits reflected the congressional judgment that aged widowers as a class were sufficiently likely not to be dependent upon their wives that it was appropriate to deny them benefits unless they were in fact dependent."

* * *

From its inception, the social security system has been a program of social insurance. Covered employees and their employers pay taxes into a fund administered distinct from the general federal revenues to purchase protection against the economic consequences of old age, disability, and death. But under § 402(f)(1)(D) female insureds received less protection for their spouses solely because of their sex. Mrs. Goldfarb worked and paid social security taxes for 25 years at the same rate as her male colleagues, but because of § 402(f)(1)(D) the insurance protection received by the males was broader than hers. Plainly then § 402(f)(1)(D) disadvantages women contributors to the social security system as compared to similarly situated men. The section then "impermissibly discriminates against a female wage earner because it provides her family less protection than it provides that of a male wage earner, even though the family needs may be identical." In a sense, of course, both the female wage earner and her surviving spouse are disadvantaged by operation of the statute, but this is because "Social Security is designed * * * for the protection of the *family*," and the section discriminates against one particular category of family—that in which the female spouse is a wage earner covered by social security. Therefore decision of the equal protection challenge in this case cannot focus solely on the distinction drawn between widowers and widows but, as *Wiesenfeld* held, upon the gender-based discrimination against covered female wage earners as well.

* * *

We conclude, therefore, that the differential treatment of nondependent widows and widowers results not, as appellant asserts, from a deliberate congressional intention to remedy the arguably greater needs of the former, but rather from an intention to aid the dependent spouses of deceased wage earners, coupled with a presumption that wives are usually dependent. This presents precisely the situation faced in *Wiesenfeld.* The only conceivable justification for writing the presumption of wives' dependency into the statute is the assumption * * * that it would save the Government time, money, and effort simply to pay benefits to all widows, rather than to require proof of dependency of both sexes. We held in *Wiesenfeld,* and therefore hold again here, that such assumptions do not suffice to justify a gender-based discrimination in the distribution of employment-related benefits.

Affirmed.

[Justice Stevens concurred, focusing on the husband's claim for benefits rather than on the wife's tax obligation, but concluding that "this discrimination against a group of males is merely the accidental byproduct of a traditional way of thinking about females."

[Justice Rehnquist, for four dissenters, would have upheld the provision's constitutionality.]

NOTES AND QUESTIONS

1.   Congress responded to Califano v. Goldfarb by repealing the dependency requirement for widowers and husbands but (to avoid an unacceptable fiscal problem for the Social Security trust fund) mandating that retired federal and state workers offset their government pensions against what they would receive as the spouse of a Social Security participant. Social Security Amendments of 1977, codified at 42 U.S.C. § 402(b)(4)(A), (c)(1), (c)(2), (f)(1). But, to protect the reliance interests of those counting on benefits under the old rules, the new law exempted those eligible for special benefits for the five-year period 1977–82. The effect was to continue for five years the discrimination in favor of independent widows and wives that had been held unconstitutional in *Goldfarb*. The Supreme Court unanimously upheld this phase-in of the end of gender-based discrimination. Heckler v. Mathews, 465 U.S. 728 (1984).

2.   *Goldfarb* was followed with respect to Missouri's Workers' Compensation law in Wengler v. Druggists Mut. Ins. Co., 446 U.S. 142 (1980) (striking down provision that widower collects only if incapacitated or dependent, but widow collects without such showing).

3.   The Social Security Act provided that illegitimate children ineligible to inherit under state law could receive benefits based on their father's disability only if he had acknowledged paternity by paying for their support prior to the onset of the disability. The Supreme Court held that the rule denied plaintiff "the equal protection of the law guaranteed by the due process provisions of the Fifth Amendment." The Court found the statutory distinctions both overinclusive (compensating some, for example some legitimate children, who had not been dependent on their disabled father) and under-inclusive (denying certain illegitimates the opportunity to show dependence). Justice Rehnquist, dissenting, called the Court's opinion "a rather impressionistic determination that Congress' efforts to cope with spurious claims of entitlement * * * are simply not satisfactory to the members of this Court." Jimenez v. Weinberger, 417 U.S. 628 (1974).

But in Califano v. Boles, 443 U.S. 282 (1979), the Court upheld denial of "mother's insurance benefits" (a misnomer: they are also paid to fathers) to the mother or father of the decedent's illegitimate children. The Court split five to four, the opinions differing over whether the benefit was mainly cash for the spouse or a way to permit the surviving parent to stay home and care for the children. If the latter, a categorization that refuses the advantage to illegitimate children is hard to distinguish from *Jimenez*.

In 2012, the Supreme Court decided that whether or not posthumously conceived children qualify for Social Security survivor benefits depends on state intestacy law. Although one court of appeals had held that children conceived in vitro after the father's death are "children" within the definition of Social Security Act, Gillett-Netting v. Barnhart, 371 F.3d 593 (9th Cir. 2004), the Supreme Court held that "it was nonetheless Congress' prerogative to legislate for the generality of cases. It did so here by employing eligibility to inherit under state intestacy law as a workable substitute for burdensome case-by-case determinations whether the child was, in fact, dependent on her father's earnings." The Court then applied Florida law and found that a posthumously conceived offspring was not eligible for survivor benefits. Astrue v. Capato ex rel. B.N.C., 132 S.Ct. 2021 (2012). Accord MacNeil v. Berryhill, 869 F.3d 109 (2d Cir. 2017) (under New York state intestacy law, finding that child conceived from frozen sperm of father who died 11 years earlier not entitled to Social Security survivor benefits).

4.   The Social Security Act provides for widow's benefits only to women who were married to the deceased for at least nine months before his death. The purpose is to prevent marriages arranged solely to obtain the benefits. A three-judge district court found this an unacceptable irrebuttable presumption. The Supreme Court, per Justice Rehnquist, reversed. "The question is whether Congress, its concern having been reasonably aroused by the possibility of an abuse which it legitimately desired to avoid, could rationally have concluded both that a particular limitation or qualification would protect against its occurrence, and that the expense and other difficulties of individual determination justified the inherent imprecision of a prophylactic rule. We conclude that the duration-of-relationship test meets this constitutional standard." Among Justice Rehnquist's distinctions from earlier irrebuttable presumption decisions was the statement that "unlike the claims involved in *Stanley* [parental fitness] and *LaFleur* [job], a noncontractual claim to receive funds from the public treasury enjoys no constitutionally protected status * * * Unlike the statutory scheme in *Vlandis* [in-state tuition at state university], the Social Security Act does not purport to speak in terms of the bona fides of the parties to a marriage, but then make plainly relevant evidence of such bona fides inadmissible." Justices Douglas, Brennan, and Marshall found the result "flatly contrary to several recent decisions, specifically * * * Jimenez v. Weinberger." Weinberger v. Salfi, 422 U.S. 749 (1975).

5.   An applicant for widow's benefits whose purported marriage to a deceased worker was not valid under state law can nonetheless recover widow's benefits if (1) the applicant married the wage earner in good faith, without knowing of the legal impediment to the validity of the marriage, (2) the applicant was living with the wage earner at the time of his death, and (3) no other widow "is or has been entitled to a benefit" under the state's marital status test. 42 U.S.C. § 416(h)(1)(B). See Davis v. Califano, 603 F.2d 618 (7th Cir. 1979) (The first wife and the second wife of a deceased worker sued to recover widow's benefits. The court awarded the widow's benefits to the first wife, finding that the deceased worker's marriage to his second wife was never valid because he had not obtained a legal divorce from his first wife, and thus the second wife did not satisfy the requirements of 42 U.S.C. § 416(h)(1)(B).)

6. Bowen v. Owens, 476 U.S. 340 (1986), upheld against a "rationality" challenge Social Security's policy of paying more to widowed spouses than to divorced spouses upon remarriage. Justices Brennan, Marshall, and Blackmun dissented, saying the discrimination is unconstitutional.

4. SOCIAL SECURITY POLICY

Current political debates about Social Security focus on two issues: fixing Social Security's long-term financial deficit and Social Security "privatization."

In their 2013 report, the trustees of Social Security reported that the system can pay full benefits until 2035, when it will be able to pay about three-fourths of promised benefits. The average current monthly benefit is about $1,250, thus about $15,000 per annum. Most people age 65 and older get two-thirds or more of their income from Social Security. As of 2004, Social Security replaced 42 percent of the typical retiree's pre-retirement earnings. Statutory changes since then will reduce that number to about 31 percent by 2030. In order to fix this financial problem, taxes must be raised, benefits must be cut, or both (of course, the problem could also be "fixed" by borrowing, but this would only postpone the necessary benefit cuts or tax increases). One oft-discussed proposal would be to index increases in future benefits to inflation rather than to wage growth. The current formula for Social Security benefits ensures that benefits increase to keep pace with the increase in average wages. Since wages normally increase faster than inflation, changing the Social Security formula so that benefits increase according to inflation would essentially cut the level of promised future benefits. Some proposals recommend inflation-indexing only for higher-income beneficiaries. Others propose that the retirement age be raised, indexed to reflect future longevity increases, or both. On the revenue side, proposals include raising tax rates and eliminating the cap on taxable earnings (i.e., taxing all earnings instead of only the first $117,000).

As mentioned earlier, the other key flashpoint in the Social Security debate is "privatization." Free-market thinkers have long argued that individuals should be allowed to invest the money set aside for them by Social Security, much as individuals are allowed to invest the funds in their 401(k) or IRA. Privatization proponents argue that individuals would be able to get a higher rate of return on these assets than the government can by investing them in treasury bills. Such scholars also argue that privatization would give workers a positive sense of ownership over their accounts (these arguments often cite Flemming v. Nestor and Reich's criticism of it, supra p. 1241). Critics respond that investments that receive a higher return (like stocks) are riskier, and that allowing individuals to risk their Social Security funds would undermine Social Security's ability to provide a dependable safety net for retirees and near-retirees.

NOTES AND QUESTIONS

1. Social Security's formula for the computation of benefits is progressive, in that lower-income workers' receive a greater percentage of their average wages from Social Security than higher-income workers do. For example, a 65 year-old who retired in 2013 with a lifetime of "medium" earnings (about $44,000 in 2012) would receive about $18,000 per year, which would replace about 42 percent of past earnings. A "low" earner who made about $20,000 in 2012 would receive about $11,000, which would replace about 56 percent. A worker who always earned the "maximum" ($117,000 in 2014) would get benefits that replace about 26 percent of prior earnings. Annual Trustees' Report, Social Security Administration (2013). Note, however, that the progressive nature of Social Security benefits is somewhat offset by Social Security's regressive tax system. Social Security also transfers income from people with low life expectancies to people with high life expectancies. Some critics argue that this treats minorities with lower life expectancies unfairly. Additionally, Social Security transfers money between generations; past generations' retirement is subsidized by transfers from current and future generations. Which of these types of income redistribution are justifiable?

2. Social Security Numbers (SSNs) were originally created to facilitate the administration of the Social Security system, but they are now used for a wide variety of purposes by both public and private entities, functioning almost like a national identifier. Their importance has caused them to be the target of a number of widespread identity theft schemes.

The use and disclosure of SSNs is not regulated by a comprehensive legal scheme but rather by a hodgepodge of federal and state laws. The Identify Theft Act of 1998 makes it a crime to "knowingly transfer, possess, or use without lawful authority," another person's means of identification (including SSNs) "with the intent to commit, or to aid or abet, or in connection with, any unlawful activity that constitutes a violation of Federal law, or that constitutes a felony under any applicable state or local law." Several other federal laws regulate the use of SSNs and other personal information by specific employers or industries. California state law prohibits certain uses of SSNs and requires that businesses and state agencies notify individuals when their SSN is known or reasonably believed to have been acquired by an unauthorized person. Several states have enacted similar prohibitions on the use of SSNs and a few have also adopted notification provisions. These notification provisions have prompted several large organizations to inform individuals of massive incidents of unauthorized access to their personal information. The lack of a comprehensive regulatory scheme protecting SSNs has drawn criticism, as many argue that the current piecemeal approach leaves several regulatory gaps and that compliance with some of the existing laws is under-enforced. See generally Government Accountability Office, Social Security Numbers: More Could be Done to Protect SSNs, Government Accountability Office (2006).

D. RETIREE HEALTH CARE

One of the most important benefits that retirees can receive from their former employers is health care cost subsidization. But employers are trimming retiree health care plans for several reasons. Unions have become less influential. Retiring baby boomers increase the cost of all retirement benefit plans. Economic downturns prompt employers to try to cut costs. Also, FASB–106, passed in 1993, required companies to record retiree health care commitments as a current liability on balance sheets. See Eduardo Porter & Mary Williams Walsh, Benefits Go the Way of Pensions, N.Y. Times, Feb. 9, 2006, at C6.

The main reason, however, that employers are seeking to trim their retiree health care plans is the skyrocketing cost of retiree health care. Chapter 6, supra p. 607 explains the increased cost of health care in general. Retiree health care plans bear the additional burden of high prescription drug costs. Spending on prescription drugs has risen dramatically over the past several years, becoming one of the most expensive components of retiree health care plans.

Adding to the woes of retirees expecting reimbursement for health care costs, many retiree health care plans appear severely underfunded. ERISA does not impose funding requirements on retiree health care plans, because they are "welfare" plans, which are exempted from ERISA's funding provisions. But companies must show retiree health obligations on their balance sheets.

Given that retiree health care plans are both underfunded and on the corporate cost-cutting chopping block, the legal issue of when retiree health care plans can be cut or terminated is becoming very important. As noted, retiree health care plans are "welfare" plans, 29 U.S.C. § 1051(1), and benefits under a welfare plan vest only if and when the plan provides that they vest. When retiree health care plans are ambiguous as to if or when these benefits vest, courts engage in something akin to contractual analysis of the retiree health care plan's key documents.

Vallone v. CNA Financial Corp.

375 F.3d 623 (7th Cir. 2004).

■ CUDAHY, CIRCUIT JUDGE:

This case involves another episode in the widespread efforts of corporations to reduce their liabilities by cutting back on retiree benefits. The law in this circuit is well-established, but this does nothing to cushion the hardship of pensioners faced with a new drain on their limited resources. * * *

In November 1991, Continental offered a Voluntary Special Retirement Program (VSRP) to its employees who had 85 years of combined age and service (with minima of 55 years of age and 10 years of service). The VSRP included a monthly Health Care Allowance (HCA), a welfare benefit that was offered to all retirees. However, the HCA benefit offered as part of the VSRP differed from the HCA benefit available to regular retirees. It is the nature of this difference that is at issue here. Accompanying the VSRP were explanatory materials, some of which the plaintiffs claim expressed Continental's intent to vest the HCA benefit, and others which CNA claims did just the opposite. The potential early retirees were also told, both orally and in writing, that the HCA benefit would be a "lifetime benefit." The plaintiffs are three of the 347 Continental employees who accepted early retirement under the VSRP in early 1992. Continental was acquired by CNA in 1995.

All went smoothly until August 1998, when CNA notified the early retirees that their HCA benefit would be eliminated as of January 1, 1999. * * *

Continental is also alleged to have made oral representations to the potential early retirees regarding the nature of the HCA benefit. During group and individual meetings that took place in late 1991 between Continental's human resources representatives and eligible employees in various locations around the country, the HCA was consistently described as a "lifetime" benefit. Heidemann, who was an assistant vice president of human resources for the Great Lakes region and an officer of the company at the time of her retirement, testified at deposition that she had been told by her superiors in human resources that the HCA benefit was a "lifetime" benefit. She could not recall anyone ever telling her that the VSRP benefits were irrevocable. She strongly believed the VSRP was separate and distinct from the general retirement plan, and since no one in human resources ever told her the benefits *could* be revoked, and none of the documents specifically discussing the VSRP contained a disclaimer, she assumed that the "lifetime" benefits were irrevocable. When Heidemann presented the VSRP to the eligible employees in her region (including Vallone), she represented the benefits as being for "your lifetime" but did not say anything about their irrevocability. * * *

On December 28, 2000, the district court granted CNA's motion for summary judgment on the plaintiffs' claims of wrongful denial of benefits under ERISA (Count II), breach of ERISA and common law contract (Count IV) and equitable estoppel (Count V). On March 28, 2003, the district court granted CNA's motion for summary judgment on the plaintiffs' one remaining count, their breach of fiduciary duty claim (Count III). * * *

A.   ERISA Violation for Failure to Pay Benefits (Count II)

[The court first concluded that the relevant plan documents gave the plan administrator discretionary authority to determine eligibility for benefits and construe the terms of the plan and thus, under *Firestone*, supra p. 1205, that its decisions would be reviewed under an arbitrary and capricious standard.]

As they argued in the district court, the plaintiffs maintain that under the VSRP, which they believe was separate and distinct from the general retirement plan, they received a vested "lifetime" HCA benefit, and the Plan Administrator therefore violated ERISA when he terminated their HCA benefit. * * * The VSRP was a modification of the general retirement plan (and the 1992 Retirement Guide was specifically incorporated into the VSRP). Hence, the reservation of rights clauses in the general retirement plan documents became part of the VSRP. * * *

We start from the premise that "employers . . . are generally free under ERISA, for any reason at any time, to adopt, modify, or terminate welfare plans." For this reason, if ERISA welfare benefits "vest at all, they do so under the terms of a particular contract." Given our presumption against the vesting of welfare benefits, silence indicates that welfare benefits are not vested ("Our presumption against vesting, it is important to emphasize, kicks in only if all the court has to go on is silence."). Moreover, although ERISA itself "left open * * * the possibility that a written plan may be combined with an oral promise, such as an undertaking to give a worker twice the benefits so established," wholly oral promises cannot be used to require the employer to provide irrevocable benefits. If there is some ambiguity in the language of the written agreement that is not disambiguated elsewhere in the document, only then may we consider evidence of the parties' intent that is "extrinsic" to the written documents, such as oral representations. * * *

The plaintiffs argue that the VSRP documents indicate that the HCA is a "lifetime" benefit, and that this had been confirmed in oral representations made to them. Specifically, they assert that the personalized calculation worksheet, which states that eligible employees will receive an HCA allowance of $465 per month to age 65 and $180 per month thereafter, indicates that this benefit is "for life." The payment election form, which prescribes the same HCA allowance amounts as appear on the personalized calculation worksheet and which allows eligible employees to choose to have their surviving spouses receive the HCA benefit after their death, is also offered for the implication that the benefits were for life (and even beyond).

That the HCA benefit was a "lifetime" benefit—both for regular retirees and for retirees who accepted the VSRP package—is actually conceded by CNA. The problem for the plaintiffs is that "lifetime" may be construed as "good for life unless revoked or modified." This construction is particularly plausible if the contract documents include a reservation of rights clause (which, as will be shown, is the case here). See UAW v. Rockford Powertrain, Inc., 350 F.3d 698, 704 (7th Cir. 2003) ("We must resolve the tension between the lifetime benefits clause, and the plan termination and reservation of rights clauses, by giving meaning to all of them. Reading the document in its entirety, the clauses explain that although the plan in its current iteration entitles retirees to health coverage for the duration of their lives and the lives of their eligible surviving spouses, the terms of the plan—including the plan's continued existence—are subject to change at the will of [the employer]. The health insurance section of the plan description unambiguously does not provide the plaintiffs with vested lifetime health insurance benefits.") (internal citations omitted); see also In re Unisys Corp. Retiree Med. Benefit "ERISA" Litig., 58 F.3d 896, 904 (3d Cir. 1995) ("An employer who promises lifetime medical benefits, while at the same time reserving the right to amend the plan under which those benefits were provided, has informed plan participants of the time period during which they will be eligible to receive benefits provided the plan continues to exist."). As laypersons, the plaintiffs' confusion on this issue is understandable; it is also very unfortunate, if it was a basis for their accepting the VSRP package. But in the perhaps beady eyes of the law, the "lifetime" nature of a welfare benefit does not operate to vest that benefit if the employer reserved the right to amend or terminate the benefit, given "what it takes to overcome the presumption that welfare benefits do not vest, combined with [our] reluctance to interpret a contract as being at war with itself."

It is true that some of our decisions have indicated that the use of "lifetime" to denote the duration of benefits may create an ambiguity and is not tantamount to silence (with its presumption against vesting). See id. at 306 (finding that separate agreement containing entitlement to lifetime benefits modified reservation of rights clause incorporated from another agreement and entitled retirees to welfare benefits for their lifetime); Bidlack, 993 F.2d at 608 ("But the agreements are not silent on the issue; they are merely vague. They say that once retired employees reach the age of 65 the company will pick up the full tab for their health insurance and that when they die their spouses will continue to receive supplemental health benefits, again at the company's cost. This could be thought a promise to retired employees that they and their spouses will be covered for the rest of their lives."). However, none of those decisions involve situations where a reservation of rights clause is an integral part of the contract that provides the "lifetime" benefits. In Diehl, we found that the contract providing "lifetime" benefits "was an independent contract, supported by separate consideration and capable of modifying or supplanting prior contractual arrangements," such as the one that contained the reservation of rights clause. Here, the nature of the HCA as a "lifetime" benefit is not one of the enhancements created by the VSRP because the HCA is also a "lifetime" benefit for regular retirees according to the general retirement plan documents. Thus, unlike Diehl, the "lifetime" nature of the HCA benefit could not abrogate the reservation of rights clause included in the 1992 Retirement Guide and other general retirement plan documents because both were offered by the same contract.

The plaintiffs next argue that, as a separate and distinct program, the benefits in the VSRP were not subject to the reservations of rights clauses in the various general retirement plan documents, and that the documents specifically mentioning the VSRP did not contain reservation of rights clauses. However, regardless of how the plaintiffs believe the VSRP was marketed to the early retirees, their initial premise that the VSRP was separate and distinct from the general retirement plan is incorrect. This is evident from a review of the Brief Description Newsletter, which repeatedly refers to the general retirement plan in discussing the VSRP's enhanced benefits, making clear that the general retirement plan is the baseline program to which the VSRP's enhancements would be made. The plaintiffs themselves admit that the VSRP was a modification of the regular retirement plan. We also note that if the plaintiffs were correct that the VSRP was comprised only of those documents that specifically mentioned the VSRP, it would lack such fundamental prerequisites as administrative procedures and descriptions of the very benefits being offered.

Moreover, the Covering Memo [to the VSRP] specifically incorporated the 1992 Retirement Guide and its reservation of rights clause. The Covering Memo stated that "retirement means a major change in lifestyle for most people, and you'll need to weigh the pros and cons carefully. The enclosed materials are intended to help you arrive at the right decision for you." One of the enclosed documents was the 1992 Retirement Guide, which eligible employees were told "provides information about the benefits available to you during retirement and highlights the decisions you need to make regarding those benefits." Continental thus unambiguously stated in writing that the 1992 Retirement Guide, which included a reservation of rights clause, was part of the VSRP program and contained information about retirement benefits under the VSRP, including Continental's reserved right to alter or terminate those benefits. The reservation of rights clause appears in a box near the bottom of the last page of the 15-page document: "The coverages described in this Guide may be amended, revoked or suspended at the Company's discretion at any time, even after your retirement. No management representative has the authority to change, alter or amend these coverages." [citation omitted] * * *

C.   Estoppel (Count V)

In order to prevail on an estoppel claim under ERISA, we ordinarily require that plaintiffs show (1) a knowing misrepresentation; (2) that was made in writing; (3) with reasonable reliance on that misrepresentation by them; (4) to their detriment. However, we have found an exception when plan documents are ambiguous or misleading, in which case oral representations as to the meaning of the documents may be relevant. The district court found that exception inapplicable here—a finding that is not contested by the plaintiffs—and decided the issue on the basis that the plaintiffs unreasonably relied on the representation that the HCA benefit was a "lifetime" benefit as meaning that it was also a vested benefit. Their reliance was unreasonable given that the general retirement plan documents, to which the plaintiffs were referred, contained "numerous, unambiguous provisions reserving CNA's right to amend, suspend, or terminate the health care subsidy." As a guideline for the boundaries of ERISA estoppel, we have emphasized the "narrow scope" of estoppel claims and have noted that "only extreme circumstances" justify such claims.

In their brief on appeal, the plaintiffs argue that there is a material question of fact whether a promise made to them in writing that their HCA benefit would not be terminated, referring specifically to the heading in the Brief Description Newsletter stating that there would be no reduction in the HCA benefit. But this estoppel claim fails for two reasons. First, the plaintiffs have not shown a knowing misrepresentation of fact. Although "representations about plans and intentions could be false if, at the time the statements were made, the speaker actually had a different intention," the district court found that, at the time the VSRP was offered, Continental had no intention of terminating the "lifetime" HCA benefit. Moreover, the plaintiffs have pointed to no false statements about whether the HCA benefit could be terminated, and the district court's uncontested finding that the early retirees were not told explicitly that the "lifetime" benefits were irrevocable is therefore dispositive. The fact that the benefits were "lifetime" was not a misrepresentation; as we have discussed, the plaintiffs' confusion stems from their erroneous (though understandable) equation of "lifetime" with "vested."

Second, the plaintiffs cannot show reasonable reliance. We agree with the district court that, even if there were material written misrepresentations as to the nature of the HCA benefit, the plaintiffs unreasonably ignored the reservations of rights clauses in the general retirement plan documents that put them on notice that the HCA benefit could be terminated or modified. * * *

D.   Breach of ERISA Fiduciary Duty (Count III)

ERISA requires a trustee or other fiduciary to "discharge his duties with respect to a plan solely in the interest of the participants and beneficiaries." In interpreting this statute, the Supreme Court has held that an employer breaches its fiduciary obligation by lying to employees in order to induce them to surrender their benefits. *Varity Corp. v. Howe*, 516 U.S. 489 (1996). The plaintiffs point us to decisions from the Second, Third and Sixth Circuits which have supported claims for breach of fiduciary duty on similar facts. The Second Circuit, which has given the broadest scope to ERISA fiduciary duty claims, has held that representing to plan participants that a plan's benefits are "lifetime" when they are not vested can create a genuine issue of material fact as to whether misrepresentations were made or whether there was a failure to provide complete and accurate information. The Third Circuit has held that a fiduciary duty claim could proceed, despite the employer's reservation of the right to terminate retirement benefits, when oral and written representations were made to employees that the benefits would continue for life and the employer was aware that retirement decisions were being based on the mistaken assumption that the benefits were also vested. And the Sixth Circuit has held that a breach of fiduciary duty claim was made out where a company—both of its own accord and in response to specific employee inquiries—misrepresented to employees that a reservation of rights clause in the plan did not allow retirement benefits to be changed when the legal effect of the clause was precisely the opposite.

In this circuit, a breach of fiduciary duty exists if fiduciaries "mislead plan participants or misrepresent the terms or administration of a plan." "Although not every error in communicating information regarding a plan will be found to violate a fiduciary's duty under ERISA, we have made clear that fiduciaries must communicate material facts affecting the interests of plan participants or beneficiaries and that this duty to communicate exists when a participant or beneficiary 'asks fiduciaries for information, and even when he or she does not.' " However, in *Frahm*, we found that advice to employees stressing the availability of "lifetime" benefits without any qualifiers indicating that the employer reserved the right to change or terminate the benefits was not a breach of fiduciary duty. As we noted in *Frahm*:

> Some readers must have mentally added the word "unreduced" after a word such as "lifetime." Yet unless § 1104(a)(1) is a guarantor of accurate information at all times and for the indefinite future—unless it creates not only a duty of care, but also a duty of prevision—then claims that one or another bit of advice was misleading do not violate this statute.

We also found in *Frahm* that "the district court's finding that [the employer] did not set out to deceive or disadvantage plan participants therefore forecloses plaintiffs' claim under § 1104(a)(1)." * * *

The plaintiffs also assert that, contrary to the district court's finding, there *was* a "campaign of disinformation" here as in *Varity*. If this were correct, that would indeed serve to distinguish *Frahm*, but there is no evidence of any intent to purposefully mislead employees. Rather, our conclusion that Continental fulfilled its duty of loyalty with respect to the potential early retirees is supported by the district court's finding that at the time the VSRP was offered, Continental had no intention of eliminating the "lifetime" HCA benefit in the future. The plaintiffs characterize Continental's failure to explain, expressly and clearly, that the HCA benefit could be altered or terminated—just like the other welfare benefits offered to all retiring Continental employees—as "an intentional failure to warn VSRP participants" that Continental or a future merger partner could terminate the HCA at any time, and, even more egregiously, as "a concerted effort by CNA to remain silent about the HCA termination potential, in order to achieve its goals of maximizing retirements." But just because Continental wanted as many of its eligible employees as possible to accept the VSRP does not mean that it purposefully violated its duty of loyalty by failing to provide an explicit warning when the necessary information was already in the early retirees' hands. If anything, the failure to provide an explicit warning is just as easily explainable by non-actionable negligence as by a disloyal intent, and in that sense, *Frahm* is on all fours. *See Frahm*, 137 F.3d at 959 ("Slipups in managing any complex enterprise are inevitable, and negligence—a violation of the duty of care—is not actionable."). In this respect, it is significant that the reduction of retiree welfare benefits in the face of rising health care costs is generally a relatively recent development, and warning of that possibility only recently became important. * * *

Thus, the plaintiffs' fiduciary duty claim fails.

NOTES AND QUESTIONS

1. As noted in *Vallone*, the Seventh Circuit employs a presumption against vesting if the plan is silent on that issue; this presumption disappears if the plan is ambiguous as to if or when retiree health care benefits vest. See Rossetto v. Pabst Brewing Co., 217 F.3d 539 (7th Cir. 2000). The Sixth Circuit, too, effectively employs a presumption against vesting; in that circuit, retiree benefits only vest if there is "clear and express" language to that effect. Sengpiel v. B. F. Goodrich Co., 156 F.3d 660, 667 (6th Cir. 1998).

This doctrine is not universally followed. Some circuits do not employ a presumption against or for vesting. Deboard v. Sunshine Mining & Ref. Co., 208 F.3d 1228, 1240 (10th Cir. 2000); Barker v. Ceridian Corp., 122 F.3d 628, 634 (8th Cir. 1997). Courts do not appear to use a general presumption in favor of vesting, although some circuits use such a presumption only in the collective bargaining context. See, e.g., Maurer v. Joy Techs., Inc., 212 F.3d 907 (6th Cir. 2000). Does it make sense to employ a presumption in favor of vesting in the collective bargaining context but not in the non-union context? Aren't unionized employees more likely to be able to bargain for an explicit guarantee of vested benefits than non-unionized employees?

The circuits that employ a presumption against vesting reason that vesting should not be inferred lightly because it creates an unalterable, expensive commitment. Yet one of the main goals of ERISA was to ensure that retirees could depend on the benefits that were promised them. Does a presumption against vesting of retiree health benefits conflict with that goal? Or does the fact that Congress created a complicated vesting structure for pension plans, but declined to do so for welfare plans, support a presumption against vesting?

2. As the *Vallone* opinion notes, most courts do conclude that retiree health care plans may be terminated or trimmed when plan documents contain both a proper reservation of rights clause and language describing retiree health care benefits as "lifetime." See, e.g., In re Unisys Corp. Retiree Med. Benefit "ERISA" Litig., 58 F.3d 896 (3d Cir. 1995).

But even though plans can be terminated unless they clearly say the contrary, when human resources personnel were not truthful with employees deciding whether to take a retirement deal, the company was obligated to reinstate those employees' retirement health benefits. In re Unisys Corp. Retiree Medical Benefits ERISA Litigation, 579 F.3d 220 (3d Cir. 2009).

3. Constitutional issues have recently arisen similar to those arising when public employers modify employees' pension plans (see Section Three of this chapter ('Government Pensions as Contract') as state and local governments have sought to reduce expensive retiree health benefits. The Michigan Court of Appeals found unconstitutional under the Takings, Due Process and Contracts clauses a 2010 statute requiring public school districts to withhold three percent of each employee's wages and remit the money as an "employer contribution" to fund retiree health care benefits. AFT Michigan v. State of Michigan, 825 N.W.2d 595 (Mich. Ct. App. 2012), review denied, 822 N.W.2d 226 (Mich. 2012).

Cincinnati reduced retiree healthcare benefits in 2009, adding a deductible of $200 and an out-of-pocket cap of $2,000. Held: these changes were not unconstitutional. Gamel v. City of Cincinnati, 983 N.E.2d 375 (Ohio Ct. App. 2012). But see Savela v. City of Duluth, Minnesota, 806 N.W.2d 793 (Minn. 2011), holding that the collective bargaining agreements between Duluth and its employees guaranteed retirees the same health insurance benefits that the city provides to current employees See also Kanerva v. Weems, 2014 IL 115811, protecting retiree health benefits under a state constitutional provision deeming "membership in any . . . retirement system of the state" an "enforceable contractual relationship."

4. Should courts afford pension plans and healthcare benefit plans different levels of protections? The Sixth Circuit in Reese v. CNH America LLC, 694 F.3d 681, 683–684 (6th Cir. 2012), permitted greater leeway for healthcare benefit modifications:

Unlike pension obligations [ ], healthcare benefits cannot readily be monetized at retirement or for that matter practically fixed. Doctors and medical-insurance providers come and go. Medical plans change from year to year. And fixed, unalterable medical benefits at all events are not what retirees want. Nothing, indeed, would make employers happier than to know that vesting in the healthcare-benefits context meant the *same thing* as vesting in the pension context. For then, a company faced with the obligation could account for what it had spent on each employee for healthcare benefits on the day of retirement, then commit to spend no less through the end of the retiree's (and spouse's) life. Nor would most employers be troubled if this commitment, like most defined-benefit pension plans, increased based on inflation as measured by the consumer-price index. The reality is that, even though we have relied on language tying healthcare benefits to pension benefits as a basis for determining that healthcare benefits have vested, vesting in the context of healthcare benefits provides an evolving, not a fixed, benefit.

The rub for retirees and employers alike is that healthcare benefits—what is provided and what it costs—have not been remotely static in modern memory. The reason has little to do with traditional causes of inflation and more to do with the expansion of the benefit: the remarkable growth in modern life-saving and comfort-improving medical procedures, devices and drugs. New and better medical procedures arise while others become obsolete. And it is the rare medical innovation that costs *less* than the one it replaces. Retirees, quite understandably, do not want lifetime eligibility for the medical-insurance plan in place on the day of retirement, even if that means they would pay no premiums for it. They want eligibility for up-to-date medical-insurance plans, all with access to up-to-date medical procedures and drugs. Whatever else vesting in the healthcare context means, all appear to agree that it does not mean that beneficiaries receive a bundle of services fixed once and for all. Companies want the freedom to change health-insurance plans. And beneficiaries want something more than a fixed, unalterable bundle of services; they want coverage to account for new and better, yet likely more expensive, procedures and medications than the ones in existence at retirement.

5.   Should non-union retirees have a voice when their health benefits are being changed? And can unions fairly represent retirees when the interests of the retirees and of the current workers are so different? Should companies stop offering retiree health benefits and put former employees in Medicare with most Americans over age 65?

M & G Polymers USA v. Tackett

574 U.S. 427 (2015).

■ JUSTICE THOMAS delivered the opinion of the Court.

This case arises out of a disagreement between a group of retired employees and their former employer about the meaning of certain expired collective-bargaining agreements. The retirees (and their former union) claim that these agreements created a right to lifetime contribution-free health care benefits for retirees, their surviving spouses, and their dependents. The employer, for its part, claims that those provisions terminated when the agreements expired. The United States Court of Appeals for the Sixth Circuit sided with the retirees, relying on its conclusion * * * that retiree health care benefits are unlikely to be left up to future negotiations. We granted certiorari and now conclude that such reasoning is incompatible with ordinary principles of contract law. We therefore vacate the judgment of the Court of Appeals and remand for it to apply ordinary principles of contract law in the first instance.

Respondents * * * worked at (and retired from) the Point Pleasant Polyester Plant in Apple Grove, West Virginia. During their employment, respondent United Steel, Paper and Forestry, Rubber, Manufacturing, Energy, Allied Industrial and Service Workers International Union,

AFL-CIO-CLC, or its predecessor unions, represented them in collective bargaining. Tackett and Pyles retired in 1996, and Conley retired in 1998. They represent a class of retired employees from the Plant, along with their surviving spouses and other dependents. Petitioner M&G Polymers USA, LLC, is the current owner of the Plant.

When M&G purchased the Plant in 2000, it entered a master collective-bargaining agreement and a Pension, Insurance, and Service Award Agreement (P & I agreement) with the Union, generally similar to agreements the Union had negotiated with M&G's predecessor. The P & I agreement provided for retiree health care benefits as follows:

"Employees who retire on or after January 1, 1996 and who are eligible for and receiving a monthly pension under the 1993 Pension Plan . . . whose full years of attained age and full years of attained continuous service . . . at the time of retirement equals 95 or more points will receive a full Company contribution towards the cost of [health care] benefits described in this Exhibit B-1. . . . Employees who have less than 95 points at the time of retirement will receive a reduced Company contribution. The Company contribution will be reduced by 2% for every point less than 95. Employees will be required to pay the balance of the health care contribution, as estimated by the Company annually in advance, for the [health care] benefits described in this Exhibit B-1. Failure to pay the required medical contribution will result in cancellation of coverage."

Exhibit B-1, which described the health care benefits at issue, opened with the following durational clause: "Effective January 1, 1998, and for the duration of this Agreement thereafter, the Employer will provide the following program of hospital benefits, hospital-medical benefits, surgical benefits and prescription drug benefits for eligible employees and their dependents. . . ." The P & I agreement provided for renegotiation of its terms in three years.

In December 2006, M&G announced that it would begin requiring retirees to contribute to the cost of their health care benefits. Respondent retirees, on behalf of themselves and others similarly situated, sued M&G and related entities, alleging that the decision to require these contributions breached both the collective-bargaining agreement and the P & I agreement, in violation of § 301 of the Labor Management Relations Act, 1947 (LMRA) and [ERISA]. Specifically, the retirees alleged that M&G had promised to provide lifetime contribution-free health care benefits for them, their surviving spouses, and their dependents. They pointed to the language in the 2000 P & I agreement providing that employees with a certain level of seniority "will receive a full Company contribution towards the cost of [health care] benefits described in . . . Exhibit B-1." The retirees alleged that, with this promise, M&G had created a vested right to such benefits that continued beyond the expiration of the 2000 P & I agreement.

* * *

This case is about the interpretation of collective-bargaining agreements that define rights to welfare benefits plans.

* * *

ERISA treats [pension plans and welfare benefit plans] differently. Although ERISA imposes elaborate minimum funding and vesting standards for pension plans, it explicitly exempts welfare benefits plans from those rules. Welfare benefits plans must be "established and maintained pursuant to a written instrument," § 1102(a)(1), but "[e]mployers or other plan sponsors are generally free under ERISA, for any reason at any time, to adopt, modify, or terminate welfare plans." As we have previously recognized, "[E]mployers have large leeway to design disability and other welfare plans as they see fit." And, we have observed, the rule that contractual "provisions ordinarily should be enforced as written is especially appropriate when enforcing an ERISA [welfare benefits] plan." That is because the "focus on the written terms of the plan is the linchpin of a system that is not so complex that administrative costs, or litigation expenses, unduly discourage employers from offering [welfare benefits] plans in the first place."

We interpret collective-bargaining agreements, including those establishing ERISA plans, according to ordinary principles of contract law, at least when those principles are not inconsistent with federal labor policy. "In this endeavor, as with any other contract, the parties' intentions control." "Where the words of a contract in writing are clear and unambiguous, its meaning is to be ascertained in accordance with its plainly expressed intent."

In this case, the Court of Appeals applied the *Yard-Man* inferences to conclude that, in the absence of extrinsic evidence to the contrary, the provisions of the contract indicated an intent to vest retirees with lifetime benefits. As we now explain, those inferences conflict with ordinary principles of contract law.

The Court of Appeals has long insisted that its *Yard-Man* inferences are drawn from ordinary contract law. In *Yard-Man* itself, the court purported to apply "traditional rules for contractual interpretation." The court first concluded that the provision governing retiree insurance benefits—which stated only that the employer "will provide" such benefits—was ambiguous as to the duration of those benefits. To resolve that ambiguity, it looked to other provisions of the agreement. The agreement included provisions for terminating active employees' insurance benefits in the case of layoffs and for terminating benefits for a retiree's spouse and dependents in case of the retiree's death before the expiration of the collective-bargaining agreement, but no provision specifically addressed the duration of retiree health care benefits. From the existence of these termination provisions and the absence of a termination provision specifically addressing retiree benefits, the court inferred an intent to vest those retiree benefits for life.

* * *

We disagree with the Court of Appeals' assessment that the inferences applied in *Yard-Man* and its progeny represent ordinary principles of contract law.

As an initial matter, *Yard-Man* violates ordinary contract principles by placing a thumb on the scale in favor of vested retiree benefits in all collective-bargaining agreements. That rule has no basis in ordinary principles of contract law. And it distorts the attempt "to ascertain the intention of *the parties.*" *Yard-Man*'s assessment of likely behavior in collective bargaining is too speculative and too far removed from the context of any particular contract to be useful in discerning the parties' intention.

* * *

The Court of Appeals also failed even to consider the traditional principle that courts should not construe ambiguous writings to create lifetime promises. The court recognized that "traditional rules of contractual interpretation require a clear manifestation of intent before conferring a benefit or obligation," but asserted that "the duration of the benefit once clearly conferred is [not] subject to this stricture." In stark contrast to this assertion, however, the court later applied that very stricture to noncollectively bargained contracts offering retiree benefits. The different treatment of these two types of employment contracts only underscores *Yard-Man*'s deviation from ordinary principles of contract law.

Similarly, the Court of Appeals failed to consider the traditional principle that "contractual obligations will cease, in the ordinary course, upon termination of the bargaining agreement." That principle does not preclude the conclusion that the parties intended to vest lifetime benefits for retirees. Indeed, we have already recognized that "a collective-bargaining agreement [may] provid[e] in explicit terms that certain benefits continue after the agreement's expiration." But when a contract is silent as to the duration of retiree benefits, a court may not infer that the parties intended those benefits to vest for life.

There is no doubt that *Yard-Man* and its progeny affected the outcome here. As in its previous decisions, the Court of Appeals here cited the "context of . . . labor-management negotiations" and reasoned that the Union likely would not have agreed to language ensuring its members a "full Company contribution" if the company could change the level of that contribution. It similarly concluded that the tying of eligibility for health care benefits to receipt of pension benefits suggested an intent to vest health care benefits. And it framed its analysis from beginning to end in light of the principles it announced in *Yard-Man* and its progeny.

We reject the *Yard-Man* inferences as inconsistent with ordinary principles of contract law. But because "[t]his Court is one of final review, not of first view," the Court of Appeals should be the first to review the agreements at issue under the correct legal principles. We vacate the judgment of the Court of Appeals and remand the case for that court to apply ordinary principles of contract law in the first instance.

JUSTICE GINSBURG, with whom JUSTICE BREYER, JUSTICE SOTOMAYOR, and JUSTICE KAGAN join, concurring.

Today's decision rightly holds that courts must apply ordinary contract principles, shorn of presumptions, to determine whether retiree health-care benefits survive the expiration of a collective-bargaining agreement. Under the "cardinal principle" of contract interpretation, "the intention of the parties, to be gathered from the whole instrument, must prevail." To determine what the contracting parties intended, a court must examine the entire agreement in light of relevant industry-specific "customs, practices, usages, and terminology." When the intent of the parties is unambiguously expressed in the contract, that expression controls, and the court's inquiry should proceed no further. But when the contract is ambiguous, a court may consider extrinsic evidence to determine the intentions of the parties.

Contrary to M&G's assertion, no rule requires "clear and express" language in order to show that parties intended health-care benefits to vest. "[C]onstraints upon the employer after the expiration date of a collective-bargaining agreement," we have observed, may be derived from the agreement's "explicit terms," but they "may arise as well from . . . implied terms of the expired agreement."

On remand, the Court of Appeals should examine the entire agreement to determine whether the parties intended retiree health-care benefits to vest. Because the retirees have a vested, lifetime right to a monthly pension, a provision stating that retirees "will receive" health-care benefits if they are "receiving a monthly pension" is relevant to this examination. So is a "survivor benefits" clause instructing that if a retiree dies, her surviving spouse will "continue to receive [the retiree's health-care] benefits . . . until death or remarriage." If, after considering all relevant contractual language in light of industry practices, the Court of Appeals concludes that the contract is ambiguous, it may turn to extrinsic evidence—for example, the parties' bargaining history. The Court of Appeals, however, must conduct the foregoing inspection without *Yard-Man*'s "thumb on the scale in favor of vested retiree benefits."

Because I understand the Court's opinion to be consistent with these basic rules of contract interpretation, I join it.

NOTES

1.   The Supreme Court provided some guidance concerning the meaning of "ordinary principles of contract law" in CNH Industrial N.V. v. Reese, 138 S.

Ct. 761 (2018) (per curiam). In *CNH Industrial*, the Court thought the contract straightforward that no lifetime retiree health benefits vested.

> Shorn of *Yard-Man* inferences, this case is straightforward. The 1998 agreement contained a general durational clause that applied to all benefits, unless the agreement specified otherwise. No provision specified that the health care benefits were subject to a different durational clause. The agreement stated that the health benefits plan "r[an] concurrently" with the collective-bargaining agreement, tying the health care benefits to the duration of the rest of the agreement. If the parties meant to vest health care benefits for life, they easily could have said so in the text. But they did not. And they specified that their agreement "dispose[d] of any and all bargaining issues" between them. Thus, the only reasonable interpretation of the 1998 agreement is that the health care benefits expired when the collective-bargaining agreement expired in May 2004. "When the intent of the parties is unambiguously expressed in the contract, that expression controls, and the court's inquiry should proceed no further."

See also International Union, United Automobile Workers v. Kelsey-Hayes Co., 854 F.3d 862 (6th Cir. 2017) (2–1 that union contract meant to promise retiree medical benefits for life), cert. granted, judgment vacated in light of CNH Industrial N.V. v. Reese, 138 S. Ct. 761 (2018); Cole v. Meritor, Inc., 855 F.3d 695 (6th Cir. 2017) (contract did not create lifetime health benefits).

2. The Michigan Supreme Court found no constitutional violations in changes made to the retiree benefits plan for public school employees. The court also upheld changes to the pension plan. AFT Michigan v. State, 866 N.W.2d 782 (Mich. 2015).

3. In Gallo v. Moen Inc., 813 F.3d 265 (6th Cir. 2016), retirees and union filed suit against employer, seeking declaration that collective bargaining agreements (CBAs) entitled retirees to vested healthcare benefits for life. The Sixth Circuit reversed the district court's ruling in order to rule consistently with *M&G Polymers USA* and held that under the "ordinary rules of contract law" without an inference in favor of vesting healthcare benefits for life, a series of CBAs cannot be interpreted as a lifetime guarantee of unalterable healthcare benefits to retirees and their dependents.

4. Because retiree health benefits do not vest like pension benefits under ERISA, the Sixth Circuit found that although Honeywell had promised retiree health benefits previously in the last collective bargaining contract, once Honeywell sold the plant and that contract expired, ERISA permitted the company to stop paying for its former employees' retiree healthcare. Watkins v. Honeywell, 875 F.3d 321 (6th Cir. 2017). What incentives do you see this ruling providing to covered employers looking to unload large retiree health care obligations associated with previous union contracts?

INDEX

References are to Pages